D1457682

Table of Contents

Page

IMMIGRATION AND NATIONALITY ACT SECTION CLASSIFICATION TO U.S.C.A. ---- V

I. IMMIGRATION AND NATIONALITY ACT

Title I. General Provisions ---- 17
Title II. Immigration ---- 47
Title III. Nationality and Naturalization ---- 367
Title IV. Miscellaneous and Refugee Assistance ---- 419
Title V. Alien Terrorist Removal Procedures ---- 436

II. ADDITIONAL STATUTES

Title 5, U.S. Code, Government Organization and Employees ---- 452
Designation and Adjustment of Soviet and Indochinese Refugees ---- 459
Personal Responsibility and Work Opportunity Reconciliation Act of 1996 ---- 463
Illegal Immigration Reform and Immigrant Responsibility Act of 1996 ---- 491
Nicaraguan Adjustment and Central American Relief Act ---- 501
Haitian Refugee Immigration Fairness Act of 1998 ---- 512
Admiral James W. Nance and Meg Donovan Foreign Relations Authorization Act ---- 516
Foreign Affairs Reform and Restructuring Act ---- 517

III. EXCERPTS FROM CODE OF FEDERAL REGULATIONS

Title 8, Aliens and Nationality ---- 519
Title 20, Employees' Benefits ---- 638

IV. OTHER FEDERAL MATERIALS [671]

V. SELECTED STATE PROVISIONS

Proposition 187 (California) ---- 673

VI. INTERNATIONAL REFUGEE CONVENTIONS

Convention Relating to the Status of Refugees ---- 679
Protocol Relating to the Status of Refugees ---- 699

VII. U.S. CONSTITUTION [703]

VIII. SELECTED IMMIGRATION FORMS [717]

Basic documents ---- 717
- I-94, Arrival-departure record ---- 718
- Sample nonimmigrant visa ---- 719
- I-551, Alien registration card ---- 720
- I-797B, Notice of action ---- 721

TABLE OF CONTENTS

Basic documents—Continued | Page

Border crossing card 723

G-28, Notice of entry of appearance as attorney or representative 724

Petitions and applications 726

I-129, Petition for nonimmigrant worker 726

I-130, Petition for alien relative 746

I-751, Petition to remove the conditions on residence 751

I-140, Immigrant petition for alien worker 755

ETA 750, Application for alien employment certification 761

I-485, Application to register permanent residence or adjust status 765

I-589, Application for asylum and withholding of removal 772

Visa application 795

OF-156, Nonimmigrant visa application 795

OF-230, Application for immigrant visa and alien registration 799

Affidavits of support 803

I-864, Affidavit of support under section 213A of the Act 803

I-864A Contract between sponsor and household member 814

Employment 817

I-9, Employment eligibility verification 817

M-274, Handbook for employers, instructions for completing form I-9 820

I-765, Application for employment authorization 831

Administrative removal 838

I-851, Notice of intent to issue final administrative removal order 838

I-851A, Final administrative removal order 840

Expedited removal 841

I-867AB Record of sworn statement in proceedings under section 235(b)(1) of the Act 841

M-444, Information about credible fear interview 843

I-869, Record of negative credible fear finding and request for review by immigration judge 845

I-863, Notice of referral to immigration judge 846

I-860, Notice and order of expedited removal 848

Immigration court 849

I-862, Notice to appear 849

EOIR-42A, Application for cancellation of removal for certain permanent residents 851

EOIR-42B, Application for cancellation of removal and adjustment of status for certain nonpermanent residents 862

Naturalization 874

N-400, Application for naturalization 874

INDEX 881

TABLE
IMMIGRATION AND NATIONALITY ACT SECTION CLASSIFICATION TO U.S.C.A.

Date	Pub.L	Ch.	Sec.	66 Stat. Page	U.S.C.A. Title	U.S.C.A. Section
1952–June 27	414	477	101	166	8	1101
			102	173	8	1102
			103	173	8	1103
			104	174	8	1104
			105	175	8	1105
			201	175	8	1151
			202	176	8	1152
			203	178	8	1153
			204	179	8	1154
			205	180	8	1155
			206	181	8	1156
			207	—	8	1157
			208	—	8	1158
			209	—	8	1159
			210	—	8	1160
			211	181	8	1181
			212	181	8	1182
			213	188	8	1183
			213A	—	8	1183a
			214	189	8	1184
			215	190	8	1185
			216	—	8	1186a
			216A	—	8	1186b
			217	—	8	1187
			218	—	8	1188
			219	—	8	1189
			221	191	8	1201
			222	193	8	1202
			223	194	8	1203
			224	195	8	1204
			231	195	8	1221
			232	196	8	1222
			233	—	8	1223
			234	198	8	1224
			235	198	8	1225
			235A	—	8	1225a
			236	200	8	1226
			237	201	8	1227
			238	202	8	1228
			239	203	8	1229
			240	204	8	1229a
			240A	—	8	1229b
			240B	—	8	1229c
			240C	—	8	1230
			241	204	8	1231
			242	208	8	1252
			243	212	8	1253
			244	—	8	1254
			245	217	8	1255
			245A	—	8	1255a
			246	217	8	1256

TABLE

Date	Pub.L	Ch.	Sec.	66 Stat. Page	U.S.C.A. Title	Section
1952–June 27	414	477	247	218	8	1257
			248	218	8	1258
			249	219	8	1259
			250	219	8	1260
			251	219	8	1281
			252	220	8	1282
			253	221	8	1283
			254	221	8	1284
			255	222	8	1285
			256	223	8	1286
			257	223	8	1287
			258	—	8	1288
			261	223	8	1301
			262	224	8	1302
			263	224	8	1303
			264	224	8	1304
			265	225	8	1305
			266	225	8	1306
			271	226	8	1321
			272	226	8	1322
			273	227	8	1323
			274	228	8	1324
			274A	—	8	1324a
			274B	—	8	1324b
			274C	—	8	1324c
			274D	—	8	1324d
			275	229	8	1325
			276	229	8	1326
			277	229	8	1327
			278	230	8	1328
			279	230	8	1329
			280	230	8	1330
			281	230	8	1351
			282	231	8	1352
			283	231	8	1353
			284	232	8	1354
			285	232	8	1355
			286	232	8	1356
			287	233	8	1357
			288	234	8	1358
			289	234	8	1359
			290	234	8	1360
			291	234	8	1361
			292	235	8	1362
			293	—	8	1363
			294	—	8	1363a
			301	235	8	1401
			302	236	8	1402
			303	236	8	1403
			304	237	8	1404
			305	237	8	1405
			306	237	8	1406
			307	237	8	1407
			308	238	8	1408
			309	238	8	1409
			310	239	8	1421
			311	239	8	1422
			312	239	8	1423

TABLE

Date	Pub.L	Ch.	Sec.	66 Stat. Page	U.S.C.A. Title	U.S.C.A. Section
1952–June 27	414	477	313	240	8	1424
			314	241	8	1425
			315	242	8	1426
			316	242	8	1427
			317	243	8	1428
			318	244	8	1429
			319	244	8	1430
			320	245	8	1431
			321	245	8	1432
			322	246	8	1433
			324	246	8	1435
			325	248	8	1436
			326	248	8	1437
			327	248	8	1438
			328	249	8	1439
			329	250	8	1440
			329A	—	8	1440-1
			330	251	8	1441
			331	252	8	1442
			332	252	8	1443
			333	253	8	1444
			334	254	8	1445
			335	255	8	1446
			336	257	8	1447
			337	258	8	1448
			338	259	8	1449
			339	259	8	1450
			340	260	8	1451
			341	263	8	1452
			342	263	8	1453
			343	263	8	1454
			344	264	8	1455
			346	266	8	1457
			347	266	8	1458
			349	267	8	1481
			351	269	8	1483
			356	272	8	1488
			357	272	8	1489
			358	272	8	1501
			359	273	8	1502
			360	273	8	1503
			361	—	8	1504
			404	274	8	1101nt
			405	274	8	1101nt
			406	275	8	1101nt
			411	—	8	1521
			412	—	8	1522
			413	—	8	1523
			414	—	8	1524
			501	—	8	1531
			502	—	8	1532
			503	—	8	1533
			504	—	8	1534
			505	—	8	1535
			506	—	8	1536
			507	—	8	1537

*

IMMIGRATION AND NATIONALITY LAWS OF THE UNITED STATES

SELECTED STATUTES, REGULATIONS AND FORMS

*

I. IMMIGRATION AND NATIONALITY ACT [INA § ___]

TITLE I—GENERAL PROVISIONS

Sec.

101. Definitions [8 U.S.C.A. § 1101].
102. Diplomatic and semidiplomatic immunities [8 U.S.C.A. § 1102].
103. Powers and duties [8 U.S.C.A. § 1103].
  (a) Attorney General.
  (b) Land acquisition authority.
  (c) Commissioner; appointment.
  (d) Statistical information system.
  (e) Annual report.
  (f) Minimum number of agents in states.
104. Powers and duties of Secretary of State; Bureau of Consular Affairs [8 U.S.C.A. § 1104].
  (a) Powers and duties.
  (b) Designation and duties of Administrator.
  (c) Passport Office, Visa Office, and other offices; directors.
  (d) Transfer of duties.
  (e) General Counsel of Visa Office; appointment and duties.
105. Liaison with internal security officers [8 U.S.C.A. § 1105].
106. Repealed [8 U.S.C.A. § 1105a].

TITLE II—IMMIGRATION

CHAPTER I—SELECTION SYSTEM

201. Worldwide level of immigration [8 U.S.C.A. § 1151].
  (a) In general.
  (b) Aliens not subject to direct numerical limitations.
  (c) Worldwide level of family-sponsored immigrants.
  (d) Worldwide level of employment-based immigrants.
  (e) Worldwide level of diversity immigrants.
202. Numerical limitations on individual foreign states [8 U.S.C.A. § 1152].
  (a) Per country level.
  (b) Rules for chargeability.
  (c) Chargeability for dependent areas.
  (d) Changes in territory.
  (e) Special rules for countries at ceiling.
203. Allocation of immigrant visas [8 U.S.C.A. § 1153].
  (a) Preference allocation for family-sponsored immigrants.
  (b) Preference allocation for employment-based immigrants.
  (c) Diversity immigrants.
  (d) Treatment of family members.
  (e) Order of consideration.
  (f) Authorization for issuance.
  (g) Lists.
204. Procedure for granting immigrant status [8 U.S.C.A. § 1154].
  (a) Petitioning procedure.

Sec.
(b) Investigation; consultation; approval; authorization to grant preference status.
(c) Limitation on orphan petitions approved for a single petitioner; prohibition against approval in cases of marriages entered into in order to evade immigration laws; restriction on future entry of aliens involved with marriage fraud.
(d) Recommendation of valid home-study.
(e) Subsequent finding of non-entitlement to preference classification.
(f) Preferential treatment for children fathered by United States citizens and born in Korea, Vietnam, Laos, Kampuchea, or Thailand after 1950 and before October 22, 1982.
(g) Restrictions on petitions based on marriages entered while in exclusion or deportation proceedings.
(h) Survival of rights to petition.
(i) Professional athletes.
205. Revocation of approval of petitions; notice of revocation; effective date [8 U.S.C.A. § 1155].
206. Unused immigrant visas [8 U.S.C.A. § 1156].
207. Annual admission of refugees and admission of emergency situation refugees [8 U.S.C.A. § 1157].
(a) Maximum number of admissions; increases for humanitarian concerns; allocations.
(b) Determinations by President respecting number of admissions for humanitarian concerns.
(c) Admission by Attorney General of refugees; criteria; admission status of spouse or child; applicability of other statutory requirements; termination of refugee status of alien, spouse or child.
(d) Oversight reporting and consultation requirements.
(e) "Appropriate consultation" defined.
(f) Training United States officials adjudicating refugee cases.
208. Asylum procedure [8 U.S.C.A. § 1158].
(a) Authority to apply for asylum.
(b) Conditions for granting asylum.
(c) Asylum status.
(d) Asylum procedure.
209. Adjustment of status of refugees [8 U.S.C.A. § 1159].
(a) Criteria and procedures applicable for admission as immigrant; effect of adjustment.
(b) Maximum number of adjustments; recordkeeping.
(c) Applicability of other Federal statutory requirements.
210. Special agricultural workers [8 U.S.C.A. § 1160].
(a) Lawful residence.
(b) Applications for adjustment of status.
(c) Waiver of numerical limitations and certain grounds for exclusion.
(d) Temporary stay of exclusion or deportation and work authorization for certain applicants.
(e) Administrative and judicial review.
(f) Temporary disqualification of newly legalized aliens from receiving aid to families with dependent children.
(g) Treatment of special agricultural workers.
(h) Seasonal agricultural services defined.

Sec.

CHAPTER II—ADMISSION QUALIFICATIONS FOR ALIENS; TRAVEL CONTROL OF CITIZENS AND ALIENS

211. Admission of immigrants into the United States [8 U.S.C.A. § 1181].
(a) Documents required; admission under quotas before June 30, 1968.
(b) Readmission without required documents; Attorney General's discretion.
(c) Nonapplicability to aliens admitted as refugees.
212. Excludable aliens [8 U.S.C.A. § 1182].
(a) Classes of aliens ineligible for visas or admission.
(b) Notices of denials.
(c) Repealed.
(d) Temporary admission of nonimmigrants.
(e) Educational visitor status; foreign residence requirement; waiver.
(f) Suspension of entry or imposition of restrictions by President.
(g) Bond and conditions for admission of aliens excludable on health-related grounds.
(h) Waiver of subsection (a)(2)(A)(i)(I), (II), (B), (D), and (E).
(i) Admission of immigrant excludable for fraud or willful misrepresentation of material fact.
(j) Limitation on immigration of foreign medical graduates.
(k) Attorney General's discretion to admit otherwise excludable aliens who possess immigrant visas.
(*l*) Guam; waiver of requirements for nonimmigrant visitors; conditions of waiver; acceptance of funds from Guam.
(m) Requirements for admission of nonimmigrant nurses during five-year period.
(n) Labor condition application.
(*o*) Repealed.
(p) Computation of prevailing wage level.
(q) [untitled].
(r) Certification for certain alien nurses.
213. Admission of aliens on giving bond or undertaking; return upon permanent departure [8 U.S.C.A. § 1183].
213A. Requirements for sponsor's affidavit of support [8 U.S.C.A. § 1183a].
(a) Enforceability.
(b) Reimbursement of government expenses.
(c) Remedies.
(d) Notification of change of address.
(e) Jurisdiction.
(f) "Sponsor" defined.
(h) [sic] Federal poverty line defined.
(i) Sponsor's social security account number required to be provided.
214. Admission of nonimmigrants [8 U.S.C.A. § 1184].
(a) Regulations.
(b) Presumption of status; written waiver.
(c) Petition of importing employer; involvement of Departments of Labor and Agriculture.
(d) Issuance of visa to fiancée or fiancé of citizen.
(e) Nonimmigrant professionals and annual numerical limit.
(f) Denial of crewmember status in case of certain labor disputes.
(g) Temporary workers and trainees; limitation on numbers.
(h) Intention to abandon foreign residence.
(i) "Specialty occupation" defined.

Sec.

(j) Labor disputes.
(k) Numerical limitations; period of admission; conditions for admission and stay; annual report.
(*l*) [sic] Restrictions on waiver.
(*l*) [sic] Foreign students.
215. Travel control of citizens and aliens [8 U.S.C.A. § 1185].
(a) Restrictions and prohibitions.
(b) Citizens.
(c) Definitions.
(d) Nonadmission of certain aliens.
(e) Revocation of proclamation as affecting penalties.
(f) Permits to enter.
216. Conditional permanent resident status for certain alien spouses and sons and daughters [8 U.S.C.A. § 1186a].
(a) In general.
(b) Termination of status if finding that qualifying marriage improper.
(c) Requirements of timely petition and interview for removal of condition.
(d) Details of petition and interview.
(e) Treatment of period for purposes of naturalization.
(f) Treatment of certain waivers.
(g) Definitions.
216A. Conditional permanent resident status for certain alien entrepreneurs, spouses, and children [8 U.S.C.A. § 1186b].
(a) In general.
(b) Termination of status if finding that qualifying entrepreneurship improper.
(c) Requirements of timely petition and interview for removal of condition.
(d) Details of petition and interview.
(e) Treatment of period for purposes of naturalization.
(f) Definitions.
217. Visa waiver pilot program for certain visitors [8 U.S.C.A. § 1187].
(a) Establishment of pilot program.
(b) Waiver of rights.
(c) Designation of pilot program countries.
(d) Authority.
(e) Carrier agreements.
(f) Definition of pilot program period.
(g) Pilot program country with probationary status.
218. Admission of temporary H_2A workers [8 U.S.C.A. § 1188].
(a) Conditions for approval of H_2A petitions.
(b) Conditions for denial of labor certification.
(c) Special rules for consideration of applications.
(d) Roles of agricultural associations.
(e) Expedited administrative appeals of certain determinations.
(f) Violators disqualified for 5 years.
(g) Authorizations of appropriations.
(h) Miscellaneous provisions.
(i) Definitions.
219. Designation of foreign terrorist organizations [8 U.S.C.A. § 1189].
(a) Designation.
(b) Judicial review of designation.
(c) Definitions.

Sec.

CHAPTER III—ISSUANCE OF ENTRY DOCUMENTS

221. Issuance of visas [8 U.S.C.A. § 1201].
(a) Immigrants; nonimmigrants.
(b) Registration; photographs; waiver of requirement.
(c) Period of validity; requirement of visa.
(d) Physical examination.
(e) Surrender of visa.
(f) Surrender of documents.
(g) Nonissuance of visas or other documents.
(h) Nonadmission upon arrival.
(i) Revocation of visas or documents.
222. Application for visas [8 U.S.C.A. § 1202].
(a) Immigrant visas.
(b) Other documentary evidence for immigrant visas.
(c) Nonimmigrant visas; immigrant registration; form, manner and contents of application.
(d) Other documentary evidence for nonimmigrant visas.
(e) Signing and verification of application.
(f) Confidential nature of records.
(g) Voidness of nonimmigrant visa for stay beyond authorized period.
223. Re-entry permit [8 U.S.C.A. § 1203].
(a) Application; contents.
(b) Issuance of permit; nonrenewability.
(c) Multiple reentries.
(d) Presented and surrendered.
(e) Permit in lieu of visa.
224. Immediate relative and special immigrant visas [8 U.S.C.A. § 1204].

CHAPTER IV—INSPECTION, APPREHENSION, EXAMINATION, EXCLUSION, AND REMOVAL

231. Lists of alien and citizen passengers arriving and departing [8 U.S.C.A. § 1221].
(a) Shipment or aircraft manifest; arrival; form and contents; exclusions.
(b) Departure; shipment or aircraft manifest; form and contents; exclusions.
(c) Record of citizens and resident aliens leaving permanently for foreign countries.
(d) Penalties against noncomplying shipments or aircraft.
(e) Waiver of requirements.
232. Detention of aliens for physical and mental examination [8 U.S.C.A. § 1222].
(a) Detention of aliens.
(b) Physical and mental examination.
(c) Certification of certain helpless aliens.
233. Entry through or from foreign territory and adjacent islands [8 U.S.C.A. § 1223].
(a) Necessity of transportation contract.
(b) Landing stations.
(c) Landing agreements.
(d) Definitions.
(e) Redesignated (d).
234. Designation of ports of entry for aliens arriving by aircraft [8 U.S.C.A. § 1224].

Sec.
235. Inspection by immigration officers; expedited removal of inadmissible arriving aliens; referral for hearing [8 U.S.C.A. § 1225].
(a) Inspection.
(b) Inspection of applicants for admission.
(c) Removal of aliens inadmissible on security and related grounds.
(d) Authority relating to inspections.
235A. Preinspection at foreign airports [8 U.S.C.A. § 1225a].
(a) Establishment of preinspection stations.
(b) Establishment of carrier consultant program.
236. Apprehension and detention of aliens [8 U.S.C.A. § 1226].
(a) Arrest, detention, and release.
(b) Revocation of bond or parole.
(c) Detention of criminal aliens.
(d) Identification of criminal aliens.
(e) Judicial review.
237. Deportable aliens [8 U.S.C.A. § 1227].
(a) Classes of deportable aliens.
(b) Deportation of certain nonimmigrants.
(c) Waiver of grounds for deportation.
(d) Repealed.
(e) Redesignated (b).
(f) and (g) Repealed.
(h) Redesignated (c).
238. Expedited removal of aliens convicted of committing aggravated felonies [8 U.S.C.A. § 1228].
(a) Removal of criminal aliens.
(b) Removal of aliens who are not permanent residents.
(c) [sic] Presumption of deportability.
(c) [sic] Judicial removal.
(d) Redesignated (c).
239. Initiation of removal proceedings [8 U.S.C.A. § 1229].
(a) Notice to appear.
(b) Securing of counsel.
(c) Service by mail.
(d) Prompt initiation of removal.
240. Removal proceedings [8 U.S.C.A. § 1229a].
(a) Proceeding.
(b) Conduct of proceeding.
(c) Decision and burden of proof.
(d) Stipulated removal.
(e) Definitions.
240A. Cancellation of removal; adjustment of status [8 U.S.C.A. § 1229b].
(a) Cancellation of removal for certain permanent residents.
(b) Cancellation of removal and adjustment of status for certain nonpermanent residents.
(c) Aliens ineligible for relief.
(d) Special rules relating to continuous residence or physical presence.
(e) Annual limitation.
240B. Voluntary departure [8 U.S.C.A. § 1229c].
(a) Certain conditions.
(b) At conclusion of proceedings.
(c) Aliens not eligible.
(d) Civil penalty for failure to depart.

Sec.
(e) Additional conditions.
(f) Judicial review.
240C. Records of admission [8 U.S.C.A. § 1230].
241. Detention and removal of aliens ordered removed [8 U.S.C.A. § 1231].
(a) Detention, release, and removal of aliens ordered removed.
(b) Countries to which aliens may be removed.
(c) Removal of aliens arriving at port of entry.
(d) Requirements of persons providing transportation.
(e) Payment of expenses of removal.
(f) Aliens requiring personal care during removal.
(g) Places of detention.
(h) Statutory construction.
(i) Incarceration.
242. Judicial review of orders of removal [8 U.S.C.A. § 1252].
(a) Applicable provisions.
(b) Requirements for review of orders of removal.
(c) Requirements for petition.
(d) Review of final orders.
(e) Judicial review of orders under section 235(b)(1).
(f) Limit on injunctive relief.
(g) Exclusive jurisdiction.
243. Penalties related to removal [8 U.S.C.A. § 1253].
(a) Penalty for failure to depart.
(b) Willful failure to comply with terms of release under supervision.
(c) Penalties relating to vessels and aircraft.
(d) Discontinuing granting visas to nationals of country denying or delaying accepting alien.
244. Temporary protected status [8 U.S.C.A. § 1254].
(a) Granting of status.
(b) Designations.
(c) Aliens eligible for temporary protected status.
(d) Documentation.
(e) Relation of period of temporary protected status to cancellation of removal.
(f) Benefits and status during period of temporary protected status.
(g) Exclusive remedy.
(h) Limitations on consideration in the Senate of legislation adjusting status.
(i) Annual report and review.

CHAPTER V—ADJUSTMENT AND CHANGE OF STATUS

245. Adjustment of status of nonimmigrant to that of person admitted for permanent residence [8 U.S.C.A. § 1255].
(a) Status as person admitted for permanent residence upon application and eligibility for immigrant visa.
(b) Record of lawful admission for permanent residence; reduction of preference visas.
(c) Alien crewmen, aliens continuing or accepting unauthorized employment, and aliens admitted in transit without visa.
(d) Alien admitted for permanent residence on conditional basis; fiancée or fiancé of citizen.
(e) Restrictions on adjustment of status based on marriages entered while in exclusion or deportation proceedings; bona fide marriage exception.

Sec.
(f) Limitation on adjustment of status.
(g) Special immigrants.
(h) Application with respect to special immigrants.
(i) Adjustment of status of certain aliens physically present in the United States.
(j) Adjustment to permanent resident status.
(k) Inapplicability of certain provisions for certain employment-based immigrants
245A. Adjustment of status of certain entrants before January 1, 1982, to that of person admitted for lawful residence [8 U.S.C.A. § 1255a].
(a) Temporary resident status.
(b) Subsequent adjustment to permanent residence and nature of temporary resident status.
(c) Applications for adjustment of status.
(d) Waiver of numerical limitations and certain grounds for exclusion.
(e) Temporary stay of deportation and work authorization for certain applicants.
(f) Administrative and judicial review.
(g) Implementation of section.
(h) Temporary disqualification of newly legalized aliens from receiving certain public welfare assistance.
(i) Dissemination of information on legalization program.
246. Rescission of adjustment of status; effect upon naturalized citizen [8 U.S.C.A. § 1256].
247. Adjustment of status of certain resident aliens to nonimmigrant status; exceptions [8 U.S.C.A. § 1257].
248. Change of nonimmigrant classification [8 U.S.C.A. § 1258].
249. Record of admission for permanent residence in the case of certain aliens who entered the United States prior to January 1, 1972 [8 U.S.C.A. § 1259].
250. Removal of aliens falling into distress [8 U.S.C.A. § 1260].

CHAPTER VI—SPECIAL PROVISIONS RELATING TO ALIEN CREWMEN

251. Alien crewmen [8 U.S.C.A. § 1281].
(a) Arrival; submission of list; exceptions.
(b) Reports of illegal landings.
(c) Departure; submission of list; exceptions.
(d) Violations.
(e) Regulations.
252. Conditional permits to land temporarily [8 U.S.C.A. § 1282].
(a) Period of time.
(b) Revocation; expenses of detention.
(c) Penalties.
253. Hospital treatment of alien crewmen afflicted with certain diseases [8 U.S.C.A. § 1283].
254. Control of alien crewmen [8 U.S.C.A. § 1284].
(a) Penalties for failure.
(b) Prima facie evidence against transportation line.
(c) Deportation on other than arriving vessel or aircraft; expenses.
255. Employment on passenger vessels of aliens afflicted with certain disabilities [8 U.S.C.A. § 1285].
256. Discharge of alien crewmen; penalties [8 U.S.C.A. § 1286].

Sec.
257. Alien crewmen brought into the United States with intent to evade immigration laws; penalties [8 U.S.C.A. § 1287].
258. Limitations on performance of longshore work by alien crewmen [8 U.S.C.A. § 1288].
(a) In general.
(b) Longshore work defined.
(c) Prevailing practice exception.
(d) State of Alaska exception.
(e) Reciprocity exception.

CHAPTER VII—REGISTRATION OF ALIENS

261. Alien seeking entry; contents [8 U.S.C.A. § 1301].
262. Registration of aliens [8 U.S.C.A. § 1302].
(a) In general.
(b) Aliens less than fourteen years of age.
(c) Waiver of fingerprinting requirement.
263. Registration of special groups [8 U.S.C.A. § 1303].
264. Forms for registration and fingerprinting [8 U.S.C.A. § 1304].
(a) Preparation; contents.
(b) Confidential nature.
(c) Information under oath.
(d) Certificate of alien registration or alien receipt card.
(e) Personal possession of registration or receipt card; penalties.
(f) Social security account number.
265. Notices of change of address [8 U.S.C.A. § 1305].
(a) Notification of change.
(b) Current address of natives of any one or more foreign states.
(c) Notice to parent or legal guardian.
266. Penalties [8 U.S.C.A. § 1306].
(a) Willful failure to register.
(b) Failure to notify change of address.
(c) Fraudulent statements.
(d) Counterfeiting.

CHAPTER VIII—GENERAL PENALTY PROVISIONS

271. Prevention of unauthorized landing of aliens [8 U.S.C.A. § 1321].
(a) Failure to report; penalties.
(b) Prima facie evidence.
(c) Liability of owners and operators of international bridges and toll roads.
272. Bringing in aliens subject to denial of admission on a health-related ground; persons liable; clearance papers; exceptions; "person" defined [8 U.S.C.A. § 1322].
273. Unlawful bringing of aliens into United States [8 U.S.C.A. § 1323].
(a) Persons liable.
(b) Evidence.
(c) Remission or refund.
(d) Repealed.
(e) Reduction, refund or waiver.
274. Bringing in and harboring certain aliens [8 U.S.C.A. § 1324].
(a) Criminal penalties.
(b) Seizure and forfeiture.
(c) Authority to arrest.
(d) Admissibility of videotaped witness testimony.

Sec.
274A. Unlawful employment of aliens [8 U.S.C.A. § 1324a].
(a) Making employment of unauthorized aliens unlawful.
(b) Employment verification system.
(c) No authorization of national identification cards.
(d) Evaluation and changes in employment verification system.
(e) Compliance.
(f) Criminal penalties and injunctions for pattern or practice violations.
(g) Prohibition of indemnity bonds.
(h) Miscellaneous provisions.
(i) Repealed.
(j) Repealed.
(k) Repealed.
(*l*) Repealed.
(m) Repealed.
(n) Repealed.
274B. Unfair immigration-related employment practices [8 U.S.C.A. § 1324b].
(a) Prohibition of discrimination based on national origin or citizenship status.
(b) Charges of violations.
(c) Special Counsel.
(d) Investigation of charges.
(e) Hearings.
(f) Testimony and authority of hearing officers.
(g) Determinations.
(h) Awarding of attorneys' fees.
(i) Review of final orders.
(j) Court enforcement of administrative orders.
(k) Termination dates.
(*l*) Dissemination of information concerning anti-discrimination provisions.
274C. Penalties for document fraud [8 U.S.C.A. § 1324c].
(a) Activities prohibited.
(b) Exception.
(c) Construction.
(d) Enforcement.
(e) Criminal penalties for failure to disclose role as document preparer.
(f) Falsely make.
274D. Civil penalties for failure to depart [8 U.S.C.A. § 1324d].
(a) In general.
(b) Construction.
275. Improper entry by alien [8 U.S.C.A. § 1325].
(a) Improper time or place; avoidance of examination or inspection; misrepresentation and concealment of facts.
(b) Civil penalty for illegal entry.
(c) Marriage fraud.
(d) Immigration-related entrepreneurship fraud.
276. Reentry of removed alien; criminal penalties for reentry of certain removed aliens [8 U.S.C.A. § 1326].
277. Aiding or assisting certain aliens to enter [8 U.S.C.A. § 1327].
278. Importation of alien for immoral purpose [8 U.S.C.A. § 1328].
279. Jurisdiction of district courts [8 U.S.C.A. § 1329].
280. Collection of penalties and expenses [8 U.S.C.A. § 1330].

Sec.

CHAPTER IX—MISCELLANEOUS

281. Nonimmigrant visa fees [8 U.S.C.A. § 1351].
282. Printing of reentry permits and blank forms of manifest and crew lists; sale to public [8 U.S.C.A. § 1352].
283. Travel expenses and expense of transporting remains of officers and employees dying outside of United States [8 U.S.C.A. § 1353].
284. Applicability to members of the armed forces [8 U.S.C.A. § 1354].
285. Disposal of privileges at immigrant stations; rentals; retail sale; disposition of receipts [8 U.S.C.A. § 1355].
286. Disposition of monies collected under the provisions of this subchapter [8 U.S.C.A. § 1356].
(a) Detention, transportation, hospitalization, and all other expenses of detained aliens; expenses of landing stations.
(b) Purchase of evidence.
(c) Fees and administrative fines and penalties; exception.
(d) Schedule of fees.
(e) Limitations on fees.
(f) Collection.
(g) Provision of immigration inspection and preinspection services.
(h) Disposition of receipts.
(i) Reimbursement.
(j) Regulations.
(k) Advisory committee.
(*l*) Report to Congress.
(m) Immigration Examinations Fee Account.
(n) Reimbursement of administrative expenses; transfer of deposits to General Fund of United States Treasury.
(*o*) Annual financial reports to Congress.
(p) Additional effective dates.
(q) Land border inspection fee account.
(r) Breached Bond/Detention Fund.
287. Powers of immigration officers and employees [8 U.S.C.A. § 1357].
(a) Powers without warrant.
(b) Administration of oath; taking of evidence.
(c) Search without warrant.
(d) Detainer of aliens for violation of controlled substances laws.
(e) Restricting warrantless entry in case of outdoor agricultural operations.
(f) Fingerprinting and photographing of certain aliens.
(g) Acceptance of State services to carry out immigration enforcement.
288. Local jurisdiction over immigrant stations [8 U.S.C.A. § 1358].
289. Application to American Indians born in Canada [8 U.S.C.A. § 1359].
290. Establishment of central file; information from other departments and agencies [8 U.S.C.A. § 1360].
291. Burden of proof upon alien [8 U.S.C.A. § 1361].
292. Right to counsel [8 U.S.C.A. § 1362].
293. Deposit of and interest on cash received to secure immigration bonds [8 U.S.C.A. § 1363].
294. Undercover investigation authority [8 U.S.C.A. § 1363a].
(a) In general.
(b) Disposition of proceeds no longer required.
(c) Disposition of certain corporations and business entities.
(d) Financial audits.

Sec.

TITLE III—NATIONALITY AND NATURALIZATION

CHAPTER I—NATIONALITY AT BIRTH AND COLLECTIVE NATURALIZATION

301. Nationals and citizens of United States at birth [8 U.S.C.A. § 1401].
302. Persons born in Puerto Rico on or after April 11, 1899 [8 U.S.C.A. § 1402].
303. Persons born in the Canal Zone or Republic of Panama on or after February 26, 1904 [8 U.S.C.A. § 1403].
304. Persons born in Alaska on or after March 30, 1867 [8 U.S.C.A. § 1404].
305. Persons born in Hawaii [8 U.S.C.A. § 1405].
306. Persons living in and born in the Virgin Islands [8 U.S.C.A. § 1406].
307. Persons living in and born in Guam [8 U.S.C.A. § 1407].
308. Nationals but not citizens of the United States at birth [8 U.S.C.A. § 1408].
309. Children born out of wedlock [8 U.S.C.A. § 1409].

CHAPTER II—NATIONALITY THROUGH NATURALIZATION

310. Naturalization authority [8 U.S.C.A. § 1421].
   (a) Authority in Attorney General.
   (b) Court authority to administer oaths.
   (c) Judicial review.
   (d) Sole procedure.
311. Eligibility for naturalization [8 U.S.C.A. § 1422].
312. Requirements as to understanding the English language, history, principles and form of government of the United States [8 U.S.C.A. § 1423].
313. Prohibition upon the naturalization of persons opposed to government or law, or who favor totalitarian forms of government [8 U.S.C.A. § 1424].
314. Ineligibility to naturalization of deserters from the armed forces [8 U.S.C.A. § 1425].
315. Citizenship denied alien relieved of service in armed forces because of alienage [8 U.S.C.A. § 1426].
316. Requirements of naturalization [8 U.S.C.A. § 1427].
   (a) Residence.
   (b) Absences.
   (c) Physical presence.
   (d) Moral character.
   (e) Determination.
   (f) Persons making extraordinary contributions to national security.
317. Temporary absence of persons performing religious duties [8 U.S.C.A. § 1428].
318. Prerequisite to naturalization; burden of proof [8 U.S.C.A. § 1429].
319. Married persons and employees of certain nonprofit organizations [8 U.S.C.A. § 1430].
320. Children born outside United States of one alien and one citizen parent; conditions for automatic citizenship [8 U.S.C.A. § 1431].
321. Children born outside of United States of alien parents; conditions for automatic citizenship [8 U.S.C.A. § 1432].
322. Children born outside United States; application for certificate of citizenship requirements [8 U.S.C.A. § 1433].
   (a) Naturalization on application of citizen parents; requirements.
   (b) Adopted children.

Sec.
(c) Specified period of residence for adopted children; waiver of proof; requirements.
323. Repealed [8 U.S.C.A. § 1434].
324. Former citizens regaining citizenship [8 U.S.C.A. § 1435].
(a) Requirements.
(b) Additional requirements.
(c) Oath of allegiance.
(d) Persons losing citizenship for failure to meet physical presence retention requirement.
325. Nationals but not citizens; residence within outlying possessions [8 U.S.C.A. § 1436].
326. Resident Philippine citizens excepted from certain requirements [8 U.S.C.A. § 1437].
327. Former citizens losing citizenship by entering armed forces of foreign countries during World War II [8 U.S.C.A. § 1438].
(a) Requirements; oath; certified copies of oath.
(b) Exceptions.
(c) Status.
(d) Span of World War II.
(e) Inapplicability to certain persons.
328. Naturalization through service in the armed forces [8 U.S.C.A. § 1439].
(a) Requirements.
(b) Exceptions.
(c) When service not continuous.
(d) Residence requirements.
(e) Moral character.
329. Naturalization through active-duty service in the armed forces during World War I, World War II, Korean hostilities, Vietnam hostilities, or other periods of military hostilities [8 U.S.C.A. § 1440].
(a) Requirements.
(b) Exceptions.
(c) Revocation.
(d) Repealed.
329A. Posthumous citizenship through death while on active-duty service in the armed forces during World War I, World War II, the Korean hostilities, the Vietnam hostilities, or in other periods of military hostilities [8 U.S.C.A. § 1440–1].
(a) Permitting granting of posthumous citizenship.
(b) Noncitizens eligible for posthumous citizenship.
(c) Requests for posthumous citizenship.
(d) Documentation of posthumous citizenship.
(e) No benefits to survivors.
330. Constructive residence through service on certain United States vessels [8 U.S.C.A. § 1441].
331. Alien enemies [8 U.S.C.A. § 1442].
(a) Naturalization under specified conditions.
(b) Procedure.
(c) Exceptions from classification.
(d) Effect of cessation of hostilities.
(e) Apprehension and removal.
332. Administration [8 U.S.C.A. § 1443].
(a) Rules and regulations governing examination of petitioners.
(b) Instruction in citizenship.

Sec.
(c) Prescription of forms.
(d) Administration of oaths and depositions.
(e) Issuance of certificate of naturalization or citizenship.
(f) Copies of records.
(g) Furnished quarters for photographic studios.
(h) Public education regarding naturalization benefits.
333. Photographs; number [8 U.S.C.A. § 1444].
334. Application for naturalization; declaration of intention [8 U.S.C.A. § 1445].
(a) Evidence and form.
(b) Who may file.
(c) Hearings.
(d) Filing of application.
(e) Substitute filing place and administering oath other than before Attorney General.
(f) Declaration of intention.
335. Investigation of applicants; examination of applications [8 U.S.C.A. § 1446].
(a) Waiver.
(b) Conduct of examinations; authority of designees; record.
(c) Transmittal of record of examination.
(d) Determination to grant or deny application.
(e) Withdrawal of application.
(f) Transfer of application.
(g) Repealed.
(h) Repealed.
336. Hearings on denials of application for naturalization [8 U.S.C.A. § 1447].
(a) Request for hearing before immigration officer.
(b) Request for hearing before district court.
(c) Appearance of Attorney General.
(d) Subpena of witness.
(e) Change of name of petitioner.
337. Oath of renunciation and allegiance [8 U.S.C.A. § 1448].
(a) Public ceremony.
(b) Hereditary titles or orders of nobility.
(c) Expedited administration of oath.
(d) Rules and regulations.
338. Certificate of naturalization; contents [8 U.S.C.A. § 1449].
339. Functions and duties of clerks and records of declarations of intention and applicants for naturalization [8 U.S.C.A. § 1450].
340. Revocation of naturalization [8 U.S.C.A. § 1451].
(a) Concealment of material evidence; refusal to testify.
(b) Notice to party.
(c) Membership in certain organizations; prima facie evidence.
(d) Applicability to citizenship through naturalization of parents or spouse.
(e) Citizenship unlawfully procured.
(f) Cancellation of certificate of naturalization.
(g) Applicability of certificates of naturalization and citizenship.
(h) Power to correct, reopen, alter, modify, or vacate order.
341. Certificates of citizenship or U.S. non-citizen national status; procedure [8 U.S.C.A. § 1452].

Sec.
342. Cancellation of certificates issued by Attorney General, the Commissioner or a Deputy Commissioner; action not to affect citizenship status [8 U.S.C.A. § 1453].
343. Documents and copies issued by Attorney General [8 U.S.C.A. § 1454].
344. Fiscal provisions [8 U.S.C.A. § 1455].
345. Repealed [8 U.S.C.A. § 1456].
346. Publication and distribution of citizenship textbooks; use of naturalization fees [8 U.S.C.A. § 1457].
347. Compilation of naturalization statistics and payment for equipment [8 U.S.C.A. § 1458].
348. Repealed [8 U.S.C.A. § 1459].

CHAPTER III—LOSS OF NATIONALITY

349. Loss of nationality by native-born or naturalized citizen; voluntary action; burden of proof; presumptions [8 U.S.C.A. § 1481].
350. Repealed [8 U.S.C.A. § 1482].
351. Restrictions on loss of nationality [8 U.S.C.A. § 1483].
352–355. Repealed [8 U.S.C.A. §§ 1484–1487].
356. Nationality lost solely from performance of acts or fulfillment of conditions [8 U.S.C.A. § 1488].
357. Application of treaties; exceptions [8 U.S.C.A. § 1489].

CHAPTER IV—MISCELLANEOUS

358. Certificate of diplomatic or consular officer of United States as to loss of American nationality [8 U.S.C.A. § 1501].
359. Certificate of nationality issued by Secretary of State for person not a naturalized citizen of United States for use in proceedings of a foreign state [8 U.S.C.A. § 1502].
360. Denial of rights and privileges as national [8 U.S.C.A. § 1503].
(a) Proceedings for declaration of United States nationality.
(b) Application for certificate of identity; appeal.
(c) Application for admission to United States under certificate of identity; revision of determination.
361. Cancellation of United States passports and Consular Reports of Birth. [8 U.S.C.A. § 1504]

TITLE IV—MISCELLANEOUS AND REFUGEE ASSISTANCE

404. Authorization of appropriations [8 U.S.C.A. § 1101, note].
405. Savings Clause [8 U.S.C.A. § 1101, note]
406. Separability Clause [8 U.S.C.A. § 1101, note]
411. Office of Refugee Resettlement; establishment; appointment of Director; functions [8 U.S.C.A. § 1521].
412. Authorization for programs for domestic resettlement of and assistance to refugees [8 U.S.C.A. § 1522].
(a) Conditions and considerations.
(b) Program of initial resettlement.
(c) Project grants and contracts for services for refugees.
(d) Assistance for refugee children.
(e) Cash assistance and medical assistance for refugees.
(f) Assistance to States and counties for incarceration of certain Cuban nationals; priority for removal and return to Cuba.
413. Congressional reports [8 U.S.C.A. § 1523].
414. Authorization of appropriations [8 U.S.C.A. § 1524].

Sec.

TITLE V—ALIEN TERRORIST REMOVAL PROCEDURES

501. Definitions [8 U.S.C.A. § 1531].
502. Establishment of removal court [8 U.S.C.A. § 1532].
    (a) Designation of judges.
    (b) Terms.
    (c) Chief judge.
    (d) Expeditious and confidential nature of proceedings.
    (e) Establishment of panel of special attorneys.
503. Removal court procedure [8 U.S.C.A. § 1533].
    (a) Application.
    (b) Right to dismiss.
    (c) Consideration of application.
    (d) Exclusive provisions.
504. Removal hearing [8 U.S.C.A. § 1534].
    (a) In general.
    (b) Notice.
    (c) Rights in hearing.
    (d) Subpoenas.
    (e) Discovery.
    (f) Arguments.
    (g) Burden of proof.
    (h) Rules of evidence.
    (i) Determination of deportation.
    (j) Written order.
    (k) No right to ancillary relief.
505. Appeals [8 U.S.C.A. § 1535].
    (a) Appeal of denial of application for removal proceedings.
    (b) Appeal of determination regarding summary of classified information.
    (c) Appeal of decision in hearing.
    (d) Certiorari.
    (e) Appeal of detention order.
506. Custody and release pending removal hearing [8 U.S.C.A. § 1536].
    (a) Upon filing application.
    (b) Conditional release if order denied and review sought.
507. Custody and release after removal hearing [8 U.S.C.A. § 1537].
    (a) Release.
    (b) Custody and removal.
    (c) Continued detention pending trial.
    (d) Application of certain provisions relating to escape of prisoners.
    (e) Rights of aliens in custody.

TITLE I

GENERAL PROVISIONS

§ 101. Definitions [8 U.S.C.A. § 1101]

(a) As used in this Act—

(1) The term "administrator" means the official designated by the Secretary of State pursuant to section 104(b) of this Act [8 U.S.C.A. § 1104(b)].

(2) The term "advocates" includes, but is not limited to, advises, recommends, furthers by overt act, and admits belief in.

(3) The term "alien" means any person not a citizen or national of the United States.

(4) The term "application for admission" has reference to the application for admission into the United States and not to the application for the issuance of an immigrant or nonimmigrant visa.

(5) The term "Attorney General" means the Attorney General of the United States.

(6) The term "border crossing identification card" means a document of identity bearing that designation issued to an alien who is lawfully admitted for permanent residence, or to an alien who is a resident in foreign contiguous territory, by a consular officer or an immigration officer for the purpose of crossing over the borders between the United States and foreign contiguous territory in accordance with such conditions for its issuance and use as may be prescribed by regulations. Such regulations shall provide that **(A)** each such document include a biometric identifier (such as the fingerprint or handprint of the alien) that is machine readable and **(B)** an alien presenting a border crossing identification card is not permitted to cross over the border into the United States unless the biometric identifier contained on the card matches the appropriate biometric characteristic of the alien.

(7) The term "clerk of court" means a clerk of a naturalization court.

(8) The terms "Commissioner" and "Deputy Commissioner" mean the Commissioner of Immigration and Naturalization and a Deputy Commissioner of Immigration and Naturalization, respectively.

(9) The term "consular officer" means any consular, diplomatic, or other officer or employee of the United States designated under regulations prescribed under authority contained in this chapter, for the purpose of issuing immigrant or nonimmigrant visas or, when used in title III [8 U.S.C.A. § 1401 et seq.], for the purpose of adjudicating nationality.

(10) The term "crewman" means a person serving in any capacity on board a vessel or aircraft.

(11) The term "diplomatic visa" means a nonimmigrant visa bearing that title and issued to a nonimmigrant in accordance with such regulations as the Secretary of State may prescribe.

(12) The term "doctrine" includes, but is not limited to, policies, practices, purposes, aims, or procedures.

(13)(A) The terms "admission" and "admitted" mean, with respect to an alien, the lawful entry of the alien into the United States after inspection and authorization by an immigration officer.

(B) An alien who is paroled under section 212(d)(5) [8 U.S.C.A. § 1182(d)(5)] or permitted to land temporarily as an alien crewman shall not be considered to have been admitted.

(C) An alien lawfully admitted for permanent residence in the United States shall not be regarded as seeking an admission into the United States for purposes of the immigration laws unless the alien—

(i) has abandoned or relinquished that status,

(ii) has been absent from the United States for a continuous period in excess of 180 days,

(iii) has engaged in illegal activity after having departed the United States,

(iv) has departed from the United States while under legal process seeking removal of the alien from the United States, including removal proceedings under this Act and extradition proceedings,

(v) has committed an offense identified in section 212(a)(2) [8 U.S.C.A. § 1182(a)(2)], unless since such offense the alien has been granted relief under section 212(h) [8 U.S.C.A. § 1182(h)] or 240A(a) [8 U.S.C.A. § 1229b(a)], or

(vi) is attempting to enter at a time or place other than as designated by immigration officers or has not been admitted to the United States after inspection and authorization by an immigration officer.

(14) The term "foreign state" includes outlying possessions of a foreign state, but self-governing dominions or territories under mandate or trusteeship shall be regarded as separate foreign states.

(15) The term "immigrant" means every alien except an alien who is within one of the following classes of nonimmigrant aliens—

(A)(i) an ambassador, public minister, or career diplomatic or consular officer who has been accredited by a foreign government recognized de jure by the United States and who is accepted by the President or by the Secretary of State, and the members of the alien's immediate family;

(ii) upon a basis of reciprocity, other officials and employees who have been accredited by a foreign government recognized de jure by the United States, who are accepted by the Secretary of State, and the members of their immediate families; and

(iii) upon a basis of reciprocity, attendants, servants, personal employees, and members of their immediate families, of the officials and employees who have a nonimmigrant status under (i) and (ii) above;

(B) an alien (other than one coming for the purpose of study or of performing skilled or unskilled labor or as a representative of foreign press, radio, film, or other foreign information media coming to engage in such vocation) having a residence in a foreign country which he has no intention of abandoning and who is visiting the United States temporarily for business or temporarily for pleasure;

(C) an alien in immediate and continuous transit through the United States, or an alien who qualifies as a person entitled to pass in transit to and from the United Nations Headquarters District and foreign countries, under the provisions of paragraphs (3), (4), and (5) of section 11 of the Headquarters Agreement with the United Nations (61 Stat. 758);

(D)(i) an alien crewman serving in good faith as such in a capacity required for normal operation and service on board a vessel, as defined in section 258(a) [8 U.S.C.A. § 1288(a)] (other than a fishing vessel having its home port or an operating base in the United States), or aircraft, who intends to land temporarily and solely in pursuit of his calling as a crewman and to depart from the United States with the vessel or aircraft on which he arrived or some other vessel or aircraft;

(ii) an alien crewman serving in good faith as such in any capacity required for normal operations and service aboard a fishing vessel having its home port or an operating base in the United States who intends to land temporarily in Guam and solely in pursuit of his calling as a crewman and to depart from Guam with the vessel on which he arrived;

(E) an alien entitled to enter the United States under and in pursuance of the provisions of a treaty of commerce and navigation between the United States and the foreign state of which he is a national, and the spouse and children of any such alien if accompanying or following to join him: (i) solely to carry on substantial trade, including trade in services or trade in technology, principally between the United States and the foreign state of which he is a national; or (ii) solely to develop and direct the operations of an enterprise in which he has invested, or of an enterprise in which he is actively in the process of investing, a substantial amount of capital;

students— **(F)(i)** an alien having a residence in a foreign country which he has no intention of abandoning, who is a bona fide student qualified to pursue a full course of study and who seeks to enter the United States temporarily and solely for the purpose of pursuing such a course of study consistent with section 214(*l*) [8 U.S.C.A. § 1184(*l*)] at an established college, university, seminary, conservatory, academic high school, elementary school, or other academic institution or in a language training program in the United States, particularly designated by him and approved by the Attorney General after consultation with the Secretary of Education, which institution or place of study shall have agreed to report to the Attorney General the termination of attendance of each nonimmigrant student, and if any such institution of learning or place of study fails to make reports promptly the approval shall be withdrawn, and **(ii)** the alien spouse and minor children of any such alien if accompanying him or following to join him;

(G)(i) a designated principal resident representative of a foreign government recognized de jure by the United States, which foreign government is a member of an international organization entitled to enjoy privileges, exemptions, and immunities as an international organization under the International Organizations Immunities Act (59 Stat. 669), accredited resident members of the staff of such representatives, and members of his or their immediate family;

(ii) other accredited representatives of such a foreign government to such international organizations, and the members of their immediate families;

(iii) an alien able to qualify under (i) or (ii) above except for the fact that the government of which such alien is an accredited representative is not recognized de jure by the United States, or that the government of which he is an accredited representative is not a member of such international organization; and the members of his immediate family;

(iv) officers, or employees of such international organizations, and the members of their immediate families;

(v) attendants, servants, and personal employees of any such representative, officer, or employee, and the members of the immediate families of such attendants, servants, and personal employees;

(H) an alien

(i)(a) Repealed. Pub.L. 106–95, § 2(c), Nov. 12, 1999, 113 Stat. 1316.

(b) subject to section 212(j)(2) [8 U.S.C.A. § 1182(j)(2)], who is coming temporarily to the United States to perform services (other than services described in subclause (a) during the period in which such subclause applies and other than services described in subclause (ii)(a) or in subparagraph (O) or (P)) in a specialty occupation described in section 214(i)(1) [8 U.S.C.A. § 1184(i)(1)] or as a fashion model, who meets the requirements for the occupation specified in section 214(i)(2) [8 U.S.C.A. § 1184(i)(2)] or, in the case of a fashion model, is of distinguished merit and ability, and with respect to whom the Secretary of Labor determines and certifies to the Attorney General that the intending employer has filed with the Secretary an application under section 212(n)(1) [8 U.S.C.A. § 1182(n)(1)], or **(c)** who is coming temporarily to the United States to perform services as a registered nurse, who meets the qualifications described in section 212(m)(1) [8 U.S.C.A. § 1182(m)(1)], and with respect to whom the Secretary of Labor determines and certifies to the Attorney General that an unexpired attestation is on file and in effect under section 212(m)(2) [8 U.S.C.A. § 1182(m)(2)] for the facility (as defined in section 212(m)(6) [8 U.S.C.A. § 1182(m)(6)]) for which the alien will perform the services; or

(ii)(a) having a residence in a foreign country which he has no intention of abandoning who is coming temporarily to the United States to perform agricultural labor or services, as defined by the Secretary of Labor in regulations and including agricultural labor defined in section 3121(g) of Title 26 and agriculture as defined in section 203(f) of Title 29, of a temporary or seasonal nature, or **(b)** having a residence in a foreign country which he has no intention of abandoning who is coming temporarily to the United States to perform other temporary service or labor if unemployed persons capable of performing such service or labor cannot be found in this country, but this clause shall not apply to graduates of medical schools coming to the United States to perform services as members of the medical profession; or

(iii) having a residence in a foreign country which he has no intention of abandoning who is coming temporarily to the United States as a trainee, other than to receive graduate medical education or training, in a training program that is not designed primarily to provide productive employment; and the alien spouse and minor children of any such alien specified in this paragraph if accompanying him or following to join him;

(I) upon a basis of reciprocity, an alien who is a bona fide representative of foreign press, radio, film, or other foreign information media, who seeks to enter the United States solely to engage in such vocation, and the spouse and children of such a representative, if accompanying or following to join him;

(J) an alien having a residence in a foreign country which he has no intention of abandoning who is a bona fide student, scholar, trainee, teacher, professor, research assistant, specialist, or leader in a field of specialized knowledge or skill, or other person of similar description, who is coming temporarily to the United States as a participant in a program designated by the Director of the United States Information Agency, for the purpose of teaching, instructing or lecturing, studying, observing, conducting research, consulting, demonstrating special skills, or receiving training and who, if he is coming to the United States to participate in a program under which he will receive graduate medical education or training, also meets the requirements of section 212(j) [8 U.S.C.A. § 1182(j)], and the alien spouse and minor children of any such alien if accompanying him or following to join him;

(K) an alien who is the fiancee or fiance of a citizen of the United States and who seeks to enter the United States solely to conclude a valid marriage with the petitioner within ninety days after admission, and the minor children of such fiancee or fiance accompanying him or following to join him;

(L) an alien who, within 3 years preceding the time of his application for admission into the United States, has been employed continuously for one year by a firm or corporation or other legal entity or an affiliate or subsidiary thereof and who seeks to enter the United States temporarily in order to continue to render his services to the same employer or a subsidiary or affiliate thereof in a capacity that is managerial, executive, or involves specialized knowledge, and the alien spouse and minor children of any such alien if accompanying him or following to join him;

(M)(i) an alien having a residence in a foreign country which he has no intention of abandoning who seeks to enter the United States temporarily and solely for the purpose of pursuing a full course of study at an established vocational or other recognized nonacademic institution (other than in a language training program) in the United States particularly designated by him and approved by the Attorney General, after consultation with the Secretary of Education, which institution shall have agreed to report to the Attorney General the termination of attendance of each nonimmigrant nonacademic student and if any such institution fails to make reports promptly the approval shall be withdrawn, and **(ii)** the alien spouse and minor children of any such alien if accompanying him or following to join him;

(N)(i) the parent of an alien accorded the status of special immigrant under paragraph (27)(I)(i) (or under analogous authority under paragraph (27)(L)), but only if and while the alien is a child, or

(ii) a child of such parent or of an alien accorded the status of a special immigrant under clause (ii), (iii), or (iv) of paragraph (27)(I) (or under analogous authority under paragraph (27)(L));

(O) an alien who—

(i) has extraordinary ability in the sciences, arts, education, business, or athletics which has been demonstrated by sustained national or international acclaim or, with regard to motion picture and television productions a demonstrated record of extraordinary achievement, and whose achievements have been recognized in the field through extensive documentation, and seeks to enter the United States to continue work in the area of extraordinary ability; or

(ii)(I) seeks to enter the United States temporarily and solely for the purpose of accompanying and assisting in the artistic or athletic performance by an alien who is admitted under clause (i) for a specific event or events, Support staff

(II) is an integral part of such actual performance,

(III)(a) has critical skills and experience with such alien which are not of a general nature and which cannot be performed by other individuals, or **(b)** in the case of a motion picture or television production, has skills and experience with such alien which are not of a general nature and which are critical either based on a pre-existing longstanding working relationship or, with respect to the specific production, because significant production (including pre- and post-production work) will take place both inside and outside the United States and the continuing participation of the alien is essential to the successful completion of the production, and

(IV) has a foreign residence which the alien has no intention of abandoning; or

(iii) is the alien spouse or child of an alien described in clause (i) or (ii) and is accompanying, or following to join, the alien;

(P) an alien having a foreign residence which the alien has no intention of abandoning who—

(i)(a) is described in section 214(c)(4)(A) [8 U.S.C.A. § 1184(c)(4)(A)] (relating to athletes, or, **(b)** is described in section 214(c)(4)(B) [8 U.S.C.A. § 1184(c)(4)(B)] (relating to entertainment groups));

(ii)(I) performs as an artist or entertainer, individually or as part of a group, or is an integral part of the performance of such a group, and

(II) seeks to enter the United States temporarily and solely for the purpose of performing as such an artist or entertainer or with such a group under a reciprocal exchange program which is between an organization or organizations in the United States and an organization or organizations in one or more foreign states and which provides for the temporary exchange of artists and entertainers, or groups of artists and entertainers;

(iii)(I) performs as an artist or entertainer, individually or as part of a group, or is an integral part of the performance of such a group, and

(II) seeks to enter the United States temporarily and solely to perform, teach, or coach as such an artist or entertainer or with such a group under a commercial or noncommercial program that is culturally unique; or

(iv) is the spouse or child of an alien described in clause (i), (ii), or (iii) and is accompanying, or following to join, the alien;

(Q)(i) an alien having a residence in a foreign country which he has no intention of abandoning who is coming temporarily (for a period not to exceed 15 months) to the United States as a participant in an international cultural exchange program approved by the Attorney General for the purpose of providing practical training, employment, and the sharing of the history, culture, and traditions of the country of the alien's nationality and who will be employed under the same wages and working conditions as domestic workers; or (ii)(I) an alien 35 years of age or younger having a residence in Northern Ireland, or the counties of Louth, Monaghan, Cavan, Leitrim, Sligo, and Donegal within the Republic of Ireland, which the alien has no intention of abandoning who is coming temporarily (for a period not to exceed 36 months) to the United States as a participant in a cultural and training program approved by the Secretary of State and the Attorney General under section 2(a) of the Irish Peace Process Cultural and Training Program Act of 1998 for the purpose of providing practical training, employment, and the experience of coexistence and conflict resolution in a diverse society, and **(II)** the alien spouse and minor children of any such alien if accompanying the alien or following to join the alien;

(R) an alien, and the spouse and children of the alien if accompanying or following to join the alien, who—

(i) for the 2 years immediately preceding the time of application for admission, has been a member of a religious denomination having a bona fide nonprofit, religious organization in the United States; and

(ii) seeks to enter the United States for a period not to exceed 5 years to perform the work described in subclause (I), (II), or (III) of paragraph (27)(C)(ii); or

(S) subject to section 214(k) [8 U.S.C.A. § 1184(k)], an alien—

(i) who the Attorney General determines—

(I) is in possession of critical reliable information concerning a criminal organization or enterprise;

(II) is willing to supply or has supplied such information to Federal or State law enforcement authorities or a Federal or State court; and

(III) whose presence in the United States the Attorney General determines is essential to the success of an authorized criminal investigation or the successful prosecution of an individual involved in the criminal organization or enterprise; or

(ii) who the Secretary of State and the Attorney General jointly determine—

(I) is in possession of critical reliable information concerning a terrorist organization, enterprise, or operation;

(II) is willing to supply or has supplied such information to Federal law enforcement authorities or a Federal court;

(III) will be or has been placed in danger as a result of providing such information; and

(IV) is eligible to receive a reward under section 2708(a) of Title 22,

and, if the Attorney General (or with respect to clause (ii), the Secretary of State and the Attorney General jointly) considers it to be appropriate, the spouse, married and unmarried sons and daughters, and parents of an alien described in clause (i) or (ii) if accompanying, or following to join, the alien.

(16) The term "immigrant visa" means an immigrant visa required by this Act and properly issued by a consular officer at his office outside of the United States to an eligible immigrant under the provisions of this Act.

(17) The term "immigration laws" includes this Act and all laws, conventions, and treaties of the United States relating to the immigration, exclusion, deportation, expulsion, or removal of aliens.

(18) The term "immigration officer" means any employee or class of employees of the Service or of the United States designated by the Attorney General, individually or by regulation, to perform the functions of an immigration officer specified by this Act or any section thereof.

(19) The term "ineligible to citizenship," when used in reference to any individual, means, notwithstanding the provisions of any treaty relating to military service, an individual who is, or was at any time, permanently debarred from becoming a citizen of the United States under section 3(a) of the Selective Training and Service Act of 1940, as amended (54 Stat. 885; 55 Stat. 844), or under section 454(a) of Appendix to Title 50, or under any section of this title, or any other Act, or under any law amendatory of, supplementary to, or in substitution for, any of such sections or Acts.

(20) The term "lawfully admitted for permanent residence" means the status of having been lawfully accorded the privilege of residing permanently in the United States as an immigrant in accordance with the immigration laws, such status not having changed.

(21) The term "national" means a person owing permanent allegiance to a state.

(22) The term "national of the United States" means **(A)** a citizen of the United States, or **(B)** a person who, though not a citizen of the United States, owes permanent allegiance to the United States.

(23) The term "naturalization" means the conferring of nationality of a state upon a person after birth, by any means whatsoever.

(24) Repealed. Pub.L. 102–232, Title III, § 305(m)(1), Dec. 12, 1991, 105 Stat. 1750.

(25) The term "noncombatant service" shall not include service in which the individual is not subject to military discipline, court martial, or does not wear the uniform of any branch of the armed forces.

(26) The term "nonimmigrant visa" means a visa properly issued to an alien as an eligible nonimmigrant by a competent officer as provided in this Act.

(27) The term "special immigrant" means—

(A) an immigrant, lawfully admitted for permanent residence, who is returning from a temporary visit abroad;

(B) an immigrant who was a citizen of the United States and may, under section 324(a) [8 U.S.C.A. § 1435(a)] or 327 [8 U.S.C.A. § 1438], apply for reacquisition of citizenship;

(C) an immigrant and the immigrant's spouse and children if accompanying or following to join the immigrant, who—

(i) for at least 2 years immediately preceding the time of application for admission, has been a member of a religious denomination having a bona fide nonprofit, religious organization in the United States;

(ii) seeks to enter the United States—

(I) solely for the purpose of carrying on the vocation of a minister of that religious denomination,

(II) before October 1, 2000, in order to work for the organization at the request of the organization in a professional capacity in a religious vocation or occupation, or

(III) before October 1, 2000, in order to work for the organization (or for a bona fide organization which is affiliated with the religious denomination and is exempt from taxation as an organization described in section 501(c)(3) of Title 26) at the request of the organization in a religious vocation or occupation; and

(iii) has been carrying on such vocation, professional work, or other work continuously for at least the 2-year period described in clause (i);

(D) an immigrant who is an employee, or an honorably retired former employee, of the United States Government abroad, or of the American Institute in Taiwan, and who has performed faithful service for a total of fifteen years, or more, and his accompanying spouse and children: Provided, That the principal officer of a Foreign Service establishment (or, in the case of the American Institute in Taiwan, the Director thereof), in his discretion, shall have recommended the granting of special immigrant status to such alien in exceptional circumstances and the Secretary of State approves such recommendation and finds that it is in the national interest to grant such status;

(E) an immigrant, and his accompanying spouse and children, who is or has been an employee of the Panama Canal Company or Canal Zone Government before the date on which the Panama Canal Treaty of 1977 (as described in section 3602(a)(1) of Title 22) enters into force [October 1, 1979], who was resident in the Canal Zone on the effective date of the exchange of instruments of ratification of such Treaty [April 1,

1979], and who has performed faithful service as such an employee for one year or more;

(F) an immigrant, and his accompanying spouse and children, who is a Panamanian national and (i) who, before the date on which such Panama Canal Treaty of 1977 enters into force [October 1, 1979], has been honorably retired from United States Government employment in the Canal Zone with a total of 15 years or more of faithful service, or (ii) who, on the date on which such Treaty enters into force, has been employed by the United States Government in the Canal Zone with a total of 15 years or more of faithful service and who subsequently is honorably retired from such employment or continues to be employed by the United States Government in an area of the former Canal Zone;

(G) an immigrant, and his accompanying spouse and children, who was an employee of the Panama Canal Company or Canal Zone Government on the effective date of the exchange of instruments of ratification of such Panama Canal Treaty of 1977 [April 1, 1979], who has performed faithful service for five years or more as such an employee, and whose personal safety, or the personal safety of whose spouse or children, as a direct result of such Treaty, is reasonably placed in danger because of the special nature of any of that employment;

(H) an immigrant, and his accompanying spouse and children, who—

(i) has graduated from a medical school or has qualified to practice medicine in a foreign state,

(ii) was fully and permanently licensed to practice medicine in a State on January 9, 1978, and was practicing medicine in a State on that date,

(iii) entered the United States as a nonimmigrant under subsection (a)(15)(H) or (a)(15)(J) before January 10, 1978, and

(iv) has been continuously present in the United States in the practice or study of medicine since the date of such entry;

(I)(i) an immigrant who is the unmarried son or daughter of an officer or employee, or of a former officer or employee, of an international organization described in paragraph (15)(G)(i), and who **(I)** while maintaining the status of a nonimmigrant under paragraph (15)(G)(iv) or paragraph (15)(N), has resided and been physically present in the United States for periods totaling at least one-half of the seven years before the date of application for a visa or for adjustment of status to a status under this subparagraph and for a period or periods aggregating at least seven years between the ages of five and 21 years, and

(II) applies for a visa or adjustment of status under this subparagraph no later than his twenty-fifth birthday or six months after October 24, 1988, whichever is later;

(ii) an immigrant who is the surviving spouse of a deceased officer or employee of such an international organization, and who **(I)** while maintaining the status of a nonimmigrant under paragraph (15)(G)(iv) or paragraph (15)(N), has resided and been physically present in the United States for periods totaling at least one-half of the seven years before the date of application for a visa or for adjustment of status to a status under this subparagraph and for a period or periods aggregating at least 15 years before the date of the death of such officer or employee, and **(II)** files a petition for status under this subparagraph no later than six months after the date of such death or six months after October 24, 1988, whichever is later;

(iii) an immigrant who is a retired officer or employee of such an international organization, and who **(I)** while maintaining the status of a nonimmigrant under paragraph (15)(G)(iv), has resided and been physically present in the United States for periods totaling at least one-half of the seven years before the date of application for a visa or for adjustment of status to a status under this subparagraph and for a period or periods aggregating at least 15 years before the date of the officer or employee's retirement from any such international organization, and **(II)** files a petition for status under this subparagraph no later than six months after the date of such retirement or six months after October 25, 1994, whichever is later; or

(iv) an immigrant who is the spouse of a retired officer or employee accorded the status of special immigrant under clause (iii), accompanying or following to join such retired officer or employee as a member of his immediate family;

(J) an immigrant who is present in the United States—

(i) who has been declared dependent on a juvenile court located in the United States or whom such a court has legally committed to, or placed under the custody of, an agency or department of a State and who has been deemed eligible by that court for long-term foster care due to abuse, neglect, or abandonment;

(ii) for whom it has been determined in administrative or judicial proceedings that it would not be in the alien's best interest to be returned to the alien's or parent's previous country of nationality or country of last habitual residence; and

(iii) in whose case the Attorney General expressly consents to the dependency order serving as a precondition to the grant of special immigrant juvenile status; except that—

(I) no juvenile court has jurisdiction to determine the custody status or placement of an alien in the actual or constructive custody of the Attorney General unless the Attorney General specifically consents to such jurisdiction; and

(II) no natural parent or prior adoptive parent of any alien provided special immigrant status under this subparagraph shall thereafter, by virtue of such parentage, be accorded any right, privilege, or status under this chapter; or

(K) an immigrant who has served honorably on active duty in the Armed Forces of the United States after October 15, 1978, and after original lawful enlistment outside the United States (under a treaty or agreement in effect on October 1, 1991) for a period or periods aggregating—

(i) 12 years and who, if separated from such service, was never separated except under honorable conditions, or

(ii) 6 years, in the case of an immigrant who is on active duty at the time of seeking special immigrant status under this subparagraph and who has reenlisted to incur a total active duty service obligation of at least 12 years,

and the spouse or child of any such immigrant if accompanying or following to join the immigrant, but only if the executive department under which the immigrant serves or served recommends the granting of special immigrant status to the immigrant or

(L) an immigrant who would be described in clause (i), (ii), (iii), or (iv) of subparagraph (I) if any reference in such a clause—

(i) to an international organization described in paragraph (15)(G)(i) were treated as a reference to the North Atlantic Treaty Organization (NATO);

(ii) to a nonimmigrant under paragraph (15)(G)(iv) were treated as a reference to a nonimmigrant classifiable under NATO–6 (as a member of a civilian component accompanying a force entering in accordance with the provisions of the NATO Status-of-Forces Agreement, a member of a civilian component attached to or employed by an Allied Headquarters under the "Protocol on the Status of International Military Headquarters" set up pursuant to the North Atlantic Treaty, or as a dependent); and

(iii) to the Immigration Technical Corrections Act of 1988 or to the Immigration and Nationality Technical Corrections Act of 1994 were a reference to the American Competitiveness and Workforce Improvement Act of 1998.

(28) The term "organization" means, but is not limited to, an organization, corporation, company, partnership, association, trust, foundation or fund; and includes a group of persons, whether or not incorporated, permanently or temporarily associated together with joint action on any subject or subjects.

(29) The term "outlying possessions of the United States" means American Samoa and Swains Island.

(30) The term "passport" means any travel document issued by competent authority showing the bearer's origin, identity, and nationality if any, which is valid for the admission of the bearer into a foreign country.

(31) The term "permanent" means a relationship of continuing or lasting nature, as distinguished from temporary, but a relationship may be permanent even though it is one that may be dissolved eventually at the instance either of the United States or of the individual, in accordance with law.

(32) The term "profession" shall include but not be limited to architects, engineers, lawyers, physicians, surgeons, and teachers in elementary or secondary schools, colleges, academies, or seminaries.

(33) The term "residence" means the place of general abode; the place of general abode of a person means his principal, actual dwelling place in fact, without regard to intent.

(34) The term "Service" means the Immigration and Naturalization Service of the Department of Justice.

(35) The term "spouse", "wife", or "husband" do not include a spouse, wife, or husband by reason of any marriage ceremony where the contracting parties thereto are not physically present in the presence of each other, unless the marriage shall have been consummated.

(36) The term "State" includes the District of Columbia, Puerto Rico, Guam, and the Virgin Islands of the United States.

(37) The term "totalitarian party" means an organization which advocates the establishment in the United States of a totalitarian dictatorship or totalitarianism. The terms "totalitarian dictatorship" and "totalitarianism" mean and refer to systems of government not representative in fact, characterized by (A) the existence of a single political party, organized on a dictatorial basis, with so close an identity between such party and its policies and the governmental policies of the country in which it exists, that the party and the government constitute an indistinguishable unit, and (B) the forcible suppression of opposition to such party.

(38) The term "United States", except as otherwise specifically herein provided, when used in a geographical sense, means the continental United States, Alaska, Hawaii, Puerto Rico, Guam, and the Virgin Islands of the United States.

(39) The term "unmarried", when used in reference to any individual as of any time, means an individual who at such time is not married, whether or not previously married.

(40) The term "world communism" means a revolutionary movement, the purpose of which is to establish eventually a Communist totalitarian dictatorship in any or all the countries of the world through the medium of an internationally coordinated Communist political movement.

(41) The term "graduates of a medical school" means aliens who have graduated from a medical school or who have qualified to practice medicine in a foreign state, other than such aliens who are of national or international renown in the field of medicine.

(42) The term "refugee" means **(A)** any person who is outside any country of such person's nationality or, in the case of a person having no nationality, is outside any country in which such person last habitually resided, and who is unable or unwilling to return to, and is unable or unwilling to avail himself or herself of the protection of, that country because of persecution or a well-founded fear of persecution on account of race, religion, nationality, membership in a particular social group, or political opinion, or **(B)** in such special circumstances as the President after appropriate consultation (as defined in section 207(e) of this Act [8 U.S.C.A. § 1157(e)]) may specify, any person who is within the country of such person's nationality or, in the case of a person having no nationality, within the country in which such person is habitually residing, and who is persecuted or who has a well-founded fear of persecution on account of race, religion, nationality, membership in a particular social group, or political opinion. The term "refugee" does not include any person who ordered, incited, assisted, or otherwise participated in the persecution of any person on account of race, religion, nationality, membership in a particular social group, or political opinion. For purposes of determinations under this Act, a person who has been forced to abort a pregnancy or to undergo involuntary sterilization, or who has been persecuted for failure or refusal to undergo such a procedure or for other resistance to a coercive population control program, shall be deemed to have been persecuted on account of political opinion, and a person who has a well founded fear that he or she will be forced to undergo such a procedure or subject to persecution for such failure, refusal, or resistance shall be deemed to have a well founded fear of persecution on account of political opinion.

(43) The term "aggravated felony" means—

(A) murder, rape, or sexual abuse of a minor;

(B) illicit trafficking in a controlled substance (as defined in section 802 of Title 21), including a drug trafficking crime (as defined in section 924(c) of Title 18);

(C) illicit trafficking in firearms or destructive devices (as defined in section 921 of Title 18) or in explosive materials (as defined in section 841(c) of that title);

(D) an offense described in section 1956 of Title 18 (relating to laundering of monetary instruments) or section 1957 of that title (relating to engaging in monetary transactions in property derived from specific unlawful activity) if the amount of the funds exceeded $10,000;

(E) an offense described in—

(i) section 842(h) or (i) of Title 18, or section 844(d), (e), (f), (g), (h), or (i) of that title (relating to explosive materials offenses);

(ii) section 922(g)(1), (2), (3), (4), or (5), (j), (n), (*o*), (p), or (r) or 924(b) or (h) of Title 18 (relating to firearms offenses); or

(iii) section 5861 of Title 26 (relating to firearms offenses);

(F) a crime of violence (as defined in section 16 of Title 18, but not including a purely political offense) for which the term of imprisonment at least one year [sic];

(G) a theft offense (including receipt of stolen property) or burglary offense for which the term of imprisonment at least one year [sic];

(H) an offense described in section 875, 876, 877, or 1202 of Title 18 (relating to the demand for or receipt of ransom);

(I) an offense described in section 2251, 2251A, or 2252 of Title 18 (relating to child pornography);

(J) an offense described in section 1962 of Title 18 (relating to racketeer influenced corrupt organizations), or an offense described in section 1084 (if it is a second or subsequent offense) or 1955 of that title (relating to gambling offenses), for which a sentence of one year imprisonment or more may be imposed;

(K) an offense that—

(i) relates to the owning, controlling, managing, or supervising of a prostitution business;

(ii) is described in section 2421, 2422, or 2423 of Title 18 (relating to transportation for the purpose of prostitution) if committed for commercial advantage; or

(iii) is described in section 1581, 1582, 1583, 1584, 1585, or 1588 of Title 18 (relating to peonage, slavery, and involuntary servitude);

(L) an offense described in—

(i) section 793 (relating to gathering or transmitting national defense information), 798 (relating to disclosure of classified information), 2153 (relating to sabotage) or 2381 or 2382 (relating to treason) of Title 18;

(ii) section 421 of Title 50 (relating to protecting the identity of undercover intelligence agents); or

(iii) section 421 of Title 50 (relating to protecting the identity of undercover agents);

(M) an offense that—

(i) involves fraud or deceit in which the loss to the victim or victims exceeds $10,000; or

(ii) is described in section 7201 of Title 26 (relating to tax evasion) in which the revenue loss to the Government exceeds $10,000;

(N) an offense described in paragraph (1)(A) or (2) of section 274(a) [8 U.S.C.A. § 1324(a)] (relating to alien smuggling), except in the case of a first offense for which the alien has affirmatively shown that the alien committed the offense for the purpose of assisting, abetting, or aiding only the alien's spouse, child, or parent (and no other individual) to violate a provision of this Act;

(O) an offense described in section 275(a) [8 U.S.C.A. § 1325(a)] or 276 [8 U.S.C.A. § 1326] committed by an alien who was previously deported on the basis of a conviction for an offense described in another subparagraph of this paragraph;

(P) an offense **(i)** which either is falsely making, forging, counterfeiting, mutilating, or altering a passport or instrument in violation of section 1543 of Title 18, or is described in section 1546(a) of such title (relating to document fraud) and **(ii)** for which the term of imprisonment is at least 12 months, except in the case of a first offense for which the alien has affirmatively shown that the alien committed the offense for the purpose of assisting, abetting, or aiding only the alien's spouse, child, or parent (and no other individual) to violate a provision of this Act;

(Q) an offense relating to a failure to appear by a defendant for service of sentence if the underlying offense is punishable by imprisonment for a term of 5 years or more;

(R) an offense relating to commercial bribery, counterfeiting, forgery, or trafficking in vehicles the identification numbers of which have been altered for which the term of imprisonment is at least one year;

(S) an offense relating to obstruction of justice, perjury or subornation of perjury, or bribery of a witness, for which the term of imprisonment is at least one year;

(T) an offense relating to a failure to appear before a court pursuant to a court order to answer to or dispose of a charge of a felony for which a sentence of 2 years' imprisonment or more may be imposed; and

(U) an attempt or conspiracy to commit an offense described in this paragraph.

The term applies to an offense described in this paragraph whether in violation of Federal or State law and applies to such an offense in violation of the law of a foreign country for which the term of imprisonment was completed within the previous 15 years. Notwithstanding any other provision of law (including any effective date), the term applies regardless of whether the conviction was entered before, on, or after September 30, 1996.

(44)(A) The term "managerial capacity" means an assignment within an organization in which the employee primarily—

(i) manages the organization, or a department, subdivision, function, or component of the organization;

(ii) supervises and controls the work of other supervisory, professional, or managerial employees, or manages an essential function within the organization, or a department or subdivision of the organization;

(iii) if another employee or other employees are directly supervised, has the authority to hire and fire or recommend those as well as other personnel actions (such as promotion and leave authorization) or, if no other employee is directly supervised, functions at a senior level within the organizational hierarchy or with respect to the function managed; and

(iv) exercises discretion over the day-to-day operations of the activity or function for which the employee has authority.

A first-line supervisor is not considered to be acting in a managerial capacity merely by virtue of the supervisor's supervisory duties unless the employees supervised are professional.

(B) The term "executive capacity" means an assignment within an organization in which the employee primarily—

(i) directs the management of the organization or a major component or function of the organization;

(ii) establishes the goals and policies of the organization, component, or function;

(iii) exercises wide latitude in discretionary decision-making; and

(iv) receives only general supervision or direction from higher level executives, the board of directors, or stockholders of the organization.

(C) If staffing levels are used as a factor in determining whether an individual is acting in a managerial or executive capacity, the Attorney General shall take into account the reasonable needs of the organization, component, or function in light of the overall purpose and stage of development of the organization, component, or function. An individual shall not be considered to be acting in a managerial or executive capacity (as previously defined) merely on the basis of the number of employees that the individual supervises or has supervised or directs or has directed.

(45) The term "substantial" means, for purposes of paragraph (15)(E) with reference to trade or capital, such an amount of trade or capital as is established by the Secretary of State, after consultation with appropriate agencies of Government.

(46) The term "extraordinary ability" means, for purposes of § 101(a)(15)(O)(i), in the case of the arts, distinction.

(47)(A) The term "order of deportation" means the order of the special inquiry officer, or other such administrative officer to whom the Attorney General has delegated the responsibility for determining whether an alien is deportable, concluding that the alien is deportable or ordering deportation.

(B) The order described under subparagraph (A) shall become final upon the earlier of—

(i) a determination by the Board of Immigration Appeals affirming such order; or

(ii) the expiration of the period in which the alien is permitted to seek review of such order by the Board of Immigration Appeals.

(48)(A) The term "conviction" means, with respect to an alien, a formal judgment of guilt of the alien entered by a court or, if adjudication of guilt has been withheld, where—

(i) a judge or jury has found the alien guilty or the alien has entered a plea of guilty or nolo contendere or has admitted sufficient facts to warrant a finding of guilt, and

(ii) the judge has ordered some form of punishment, penalty, or restraint on the alien's liberty to be imposed.

(B) Any reference to a term of imprisonment or a sentence with respect to an offense is deemed to include the period of incarceration or confinement ordered by a court of law regardless of any suspension of the imposition or execution of that imprisonment or sentence in whole or in part.

(49) The term "stowaway" means any alien who obtains transportation without the consent of the owner, charterer, master or person in command of any vessel or aircraft through concealment aboard such vessel or aircraft. A passenger who boards with a valid ticket is not to be considered a stowaway.

(b) As used in titles I and II—

(1) The term "child" means an unmarried person under twenty-one years of age who is—

(A) a child born in wedlock;

(B) a stepchild, whether or not born out of wedlock, provided the child had not reached the age of eighteen years at the time the marriage creating the status of stepchild occurred;

(C) a child legitimated under the law of the child's residence or domicile, or under the law of the father's residence or domicile, whether in or outside the United States, if such legitimation takes place before the child reaches the age of eighteen years and the child is in the legal custody of the legitimating parent or parents at the time of such legitimation;

(D) a child born out of wedlock, by, through whom, or on whose behalf a status, privilege, or benefit is sought by virtue of the relationship of the child to its natural mother or to its natural father if the father has or had a bona fide parent-child relationship with the person;

(E)(i) a child adopted while under the age of sixteen years if the child has been in the legal custody of, and has resided with, the adopting parent or parents for at least two years: Provided, That no natural parent of any such adopted child shall thereafter, by virtue of such parentage, be accorded any right, privilege, or status under this Act; or

(ii) subject to the same proviso as in clause (i), a child who: **(I)** is a natural sibling of a child described in clause (i) or subparagraph (F)(i); **(II)** was adopted by the adoptive parent or parents of the sibling described in such clause or subparagraph; and **(III)** is otherwise described in clause (i), except that the child was adopted while under the age of 18 years; or

(F)(i) a child, under the age of sixteen at the time a petition is filed in his behalf to accord a classification as an immediate relative under section 201(b) [8 U.S.C.A. § 1151(b)], who is an orphan because of the death or disappearance of, abandonment or desertion by, or separation or loss from, both parents, or for whom the sole or surviving parent is incapable of providing the proper care and has in writing irrevocably released the child for emigration and adoption; who has been adopted abroad by a United States citizen and spouse jointly, or by an unmarried United States citizen at least twenty-five years of age, who personally saw and observed the child prior to or during the adoption proceedings; or who is coming to the United States for adoption by a United States citizen and spouse jointly, or by an unmarried United States citizen at least twenty-five years of age, who have or has complied with the preadoption requirements, if any, of the child's proposed residence: Provided, That the Attorney General is satisfied that proper care will be furnished the child if admitted to the United States: Provided further, That no natural parent or prior adoptive parent of any such child shall thereafter, by virtue of such parentage, be accorded any right, privilege, or status under this Act; or

(ii) subject to the same provisos as in clause (i), a child who: **(I)** is a natural sibling of a child described in clause (i) or subparagraph (E)(i); **(II)** has been adopted abroad, or is coming to the United States for adoption, by the adoptive parent (or prospective adoptive parent) or parents of the sibling described in such clause or subparagraph; and **(III)** is otherwise described in clause (i), except that the child is under the age of 18 at the time a petition is filed in his or her behalf to accord a classification as an immediate relative under section 201(b) [8 U.S.C.A. § 1151(b)].

(2) The terms "parent", "father", or "mother" mean a parent, father, or mother only where the relationship exists by reason of any of the circumstances set forth in subdivision (1) of this subsection, except that, for purposes of paragraph (1)(F) (other than the second proviso therein) in the case of a child born out of wedlock described in paragraph (1)(D) (and not described in paragraph (1)(C)), the term "parent" does not include the natural father of the child if the father has disappeared or abandoned or deserted the child or if the father has in writing irrevocably released the child for emigration and adoption.

(3) The term "person" means an individual or an organization.

(4) The term "immigration judge" means an attorney whom the Attorney General appoints as an administrative judge within the Executive Office for Immigration Review, qualified to conduct specified classes of proceedings, including a hearing under section 240 [8 U.S.C.A. § 1229a]. An immigration judge shall be subject to such supervision and shall perform such duties as the Attorney General shall prescribe, but shall not be employed by the Immigration and Naturalization Service.

(5) The term "adjacent islands" includes Saint Pierre, Miquelon, Cuba, the Dominican Republic, Haiti, Bermuda, the Bahamas, Barbados, Jamaica, the Windward and Leeward Islands, Trinidad,

Martinique, and other British, French, and Netherlands territory or possessions in or bordering on the Caribbean Sea.

(c) As used in title III—

(1) The term "child" means an unmarried person under twenty-one years of age and includes a child legitimated under the law of the child's residence or domicile, or under the law of the father's residence or domicile, whether in the United States or elsewhere, and, except as otherwise provided in sections 320 [8 U.S.C.A. § 1431] and 321 [8 U.S.C.A. § 1432], a child adopted in the United States, if such legitimation or adoption takes place before the child reaches the age of 16 years (except to the extent that the child is described in subparagraph (E)(ii) or (F)(ii) of subsection (b)(1)), and the child is in the legal custody of the legitimating or adopting parent or parents at the time of such legitimation or adoption.

(2) The terms "parent", "father", and "mother" include in the case of a posthumous child a deceased parent, father, and mother.

(d) Repealed. Pub.L. 100–525, § 9(a)(3), Oct. 24, 1988, 102 Stat. 2619.

(e) For the purposes of this Act—

(1) The giving, loaning, or promising of support or of money or any other thing of value to be used for advocating any doctrine shall constitute the advocating of such doctrine; but nothing in this paragraph shall be construed as an exclusive definition of advocating.

(2) The giving, loaning, or promising of support or of money or any other thing of value for any purpose to any organization shall be presumed to constitute affiliation therewith; but nothing in this paragraph shall be construed as an exclusive definition of affiliation.

(3) Advocating the economic, international, and governmental doctrines of world communism means advocating the establishment of a totalitarian Communist dictatorship in any or all of the countries of the world through the medium of an internationally coordinated Communist movement.

(f) For the purposes of this Act—

No person shall be regarded as, or found to be, a person of good moral character who, during the period for which good moral character is required to be established, is, or was—

(1) a habitual drunkard;

(2) Repealed. Pub.L. 97–116, § 2(c)(1), Dec. 29, 1981, 95 Stat. 1611

(3) a member of one or more of the classes of persons, whether inadmissible or not, described in paragraphs (2)(D), (6)(E), and (9)(A) of section 212(a) [8 U.S.C.A. § 1182(a)]; or subparagraphs (A) and (B) of section 212(a)(2) [8 U.S.C.A. § 1182(a)(2)] and subparagraph (C) thereof (except as such paragraph relates to a single offense of simple possession of 30 grams or less of marihuana), if the offense described therein, for which such person was convicted or of which he admits the commission, was committed during such period;

(4) one whose income is derived principally from illegal gambling activities;

(5) one who has been convicted of two or more gambling offenses committed during such period;

(6) one who has given false testimony for the purpose of obtaining any benefits under this Act;

(7) one who during such period has been confined, as a result of conviction, to a penal institution for an aggregate period of one hundred and eighty days or more, regardless of whether the offense, or offenses, for which he has been confined were committed within or without such period;

(8) one who at any time has been convicted of an aggravated felony (as defined in subsection (a)(43)).

The fact that any person is not within any of the foregoing classes shall not preclude a finding that for other reasons such person is or was not of good moral character.

(g) For the purposes of this Act any alien ordered deported or removed (whether before or after the enactment of this Act) who has left the United States, shall be considered to have been deported or removed in pursuance of law, irrespective of the source from which the expenses of his transportation were defrayed or of the place to which he departed.

(h) For purposes of section 212(a)(2)(E) [8 U.S.C.A. § 1182(a)(2)(E)], the term "serious criminal offense" means—

(1) any felony;

(2) any crime of violence, as defined in section 16 of Title 18; or

(3) any crime of reckless driving or of driving while intoxicated or under the influence of alcohol or of prohibited substances if such crime involves personal injury to another.

(June 27, 1952, c. 477, Title I, § 101, 66 Stat. 166; Sept. 11, 1957, Pub.L. 85–316, §§ 1, 2, 71 Stat. 639; July 7, 1958, Pub.L. 85–508, § 22, 72 Stat. 351; Mar. 18, 1959, Pub.L. 86–3, § 20(a), 73 Stat. 13; Sept. 21, 1961, Pub.L. 87–256, § 109(a), (b), 75 Stat. 534; Sept. 26, 1961, Pub.L. 87–301, §§ 1, 2, 7, 75 Stat. 650, 653; Oct. 3, 1965, Pub.L. 89–236, §§ 8, 24, 79 Stat. 916, 922; Nov. 2, 1966, Pub.L. 89–710, 80 Stat. 1104; Apr. 7, 1970, Pub.L. 91–225, § 1, 84 Stat. 116; Dec. 16, 1975, Pub.L. 94–155, 89 Stat. 824; Oct. 12, 1976, Pub.L. 94–484, Title VI, § 601(b), (e), 90 Stat. 2301, 2302; Oct. 20, 1976, Pub.L. 94–571, § 7(a), 90 Stat. 2706; Oct. 12, 1976, Pub.L. 94–484, Title VI, § 602(c), as added Aug. 1, 1977, Pub.L. 95–83, Title III, § 307(q)(3), 91 Stat. 395; Aug. 17, 1977, Pub.L. 95–105, Title I, § 109(b)(3), 91 Stat. 847; 1977 Reorg. Plan No. 2, § 7(a)(8), 42 F.R. 62461, 91 Stat. 1637; Sept. 27, 1979, Pub.L. 96–70, Title III, § 3201(a), 93 Stat. 496; Mar. 17, 1980, Pub.L. 96–212, Title II, § 201(a), 94 Stat. 102; Dec. 29, 1981, Pub.L. 97–116, §§ 2, 5(d)(1), 18(a), 95 Stat. 1611, 1614, 1619; Oct. 30, 1984,

Priv.Law 98–47, § 3, 98 Stat. 3435; Oct. 21,1986, Pub.L. 99–505, § 1, 100 Stat. 1806; Nov. 6, 1986, Pub.L. 99–603, Title III, §§ 301(a), 312, 315(a), 100 Stat. 3411, 3434, 3439; Nov. 14, 1986, Pub.L. 99–653, §§ 2, 3, 100 Stat. 3655; Oct. 1, 1988, Pub.L. 100–459, Title II, § 210(a), 102 Stat. 2203; Oct. 24, 1988, Pub.L. 100–525, §§ 2(O)(1), 8(b), 9(a), 102 Stat. 2613, 2617, 2619; Nov. 18, 1988, Pub.L. 100–690, Title VII, § 7342, 102 Stat. 4469; Nov. 21, 1989, Pub.L. 101–162, Title VI, § 611(a), 103 Stat. 1038; Dec. 18, 1989, Pub.L. 101–238, § 3(a), 103 Stat. 2100; Feb. 16, 1990, Pub.L. 101–246, Title 1, § 131(b), 104 Stat. 31; Nov. 29, 1990, Pub.L. 101–649, Title I, §§ 123, 151(a), 153(a), 162(f)(2)(A), Title II, §§ 203(c), 204(a), (c), 205(c)(1), (d), (e), 206(c), 207(a), 208, 209(a), Title IV, § 407(a)(2), Title V, §§ 501(a), 509(a), Title VI, § 603(a)(1), 104 Stat. 4995, 5004, 5005, 5012, 5018, 5019, 5020, 5022, 5023, 5024, 5026, 5027, 5040, 5048, 5051, 5082; Oct. 1, 1991, Pub.L. 102–110, § 2(a), 105 Stat. 555; Dec. 12, 1991, Pub.L. 102–232, Title II, §§ 203(a), 205(a) to (c), 206(b), (c)(1), (d), 207(b), Title III, §§ 302(e)(8)(A), 303(a)(5)(A), (7)(A), (14), 305(m)(1), 306(a)(1), 309(b)(1), (4), 105 Stat. 1737, 1740, 1741, 1746 to 1748, 1750, 1751, 1758; Apr. 30, 1994, Pub.L. 103–236, Title I, § 162(h)(1), 108 Stat. 407; Sept. 13, 1994, Pub.L. 103–322, Title XIII, § 130003(a), 108 Stat. 2024; Oct. 5, 1994, Pub.L. 103–337, Div. C, Title XXXVI, § 3605, 108 Stat. 3113; Oct. 25, 1994, Pub.L. 103–416, Title II, §§ 201, 202, 214, 219(a), 222(a), 108 Stat. 4310, 4311, 4314, 4316, 4320; Nov. 15, 1995, Pub.L. 104–51, § 1, 109 Stat. 467; Apr. 24, 1996, Pub.L. 104–132, Title IV, § 440(b), (e), 110 Stat. 1277; Sept. 30, 1996, Pub.L. 104–208, Div. C, Title I, § 104(a), Title III, §§ 301(a), 308(d)(3)(A), (4)(A), (e)(3), (f)(1)(A), (B), 321(a), (b), 322(a)(1), (2)(A), 361(a), 371(a), Title VI, §§ 601(a)(1), 625(a)(2), 671(a)(3)(B), (b)(5), (e)(2), 110 Stat. 3009–555, 3009–575, 3009–617, 3009–620, 3009–621, 3009–627, 3009–628, 3009–629, 3009–644, 3009–645, 3009–689, 3009–700, 3009–721 to 3009–723; Oct. 6, 1997, Pub.L. 105–54, § 1(a), 111 Stat. 1175; Nov. 26, 1997, Pub.L. 105–119, Title I, § 113, 111 Stat. 2460; Oct. 21, 1998, Pub.L. 105–277, Div. C, Title IV, § 421, Div. G, Title XXII, § 2222(e), 112 Stat. 2681–657, 2681–819; Oct. 30, 1998, Pub.L. 105–319, § 2(b)(1), (d)(2), 112 Stat. 3014, 3015; Nov. 12, 1999, Pub.L. 106–95, § 2(a), (c), 113 Stat. 1312; Dec. 7, 1999, Pub.L. 106–139, § (1)(a), (b)(1), 113 Stat. 1696.)

§ 102. Diplomatic and semidiplomatic immunities [8 U.S.C.A. § 1102]

Except as otherwise provided in this Act, for so long as they continue in the nonimmigrant classes enumerated in this section, the provisions of this Act relating to ineligibility to receive visas and the removal of aliens shall not be construed to apply to nonimmigrants—

(1) within the class described in paragraph (15)(A)(i) of section 101(a) [8 U.S.C.A. § 1101(a)], except those provisions relating to reasonable requirements of passports and visas as a means of identification and documentation necessary to establish their qualifications under such paragraph (15)(A)(i), and, under such rules and regulations as the President may deem to be necessary, the provisions of subparagraphs (A) through (C) of section 212(a)(3) [8 U.S.C.A. § 1182(a)(3)];

(2) within the class described in paragraph (15)(G)(i) of section 101(a) [8 U.S.C.A. § 1101(a)], except those provisions relating to reasonable requirements of passports and visas as a means of identification and documentation necessary to establish their qualifications under such paragraph (15)(G)(i), and the provisions of subparagraphs (A) through (C) of section 212(a)(3) [8 U.S.C.A. § 1182(a)(3)]; and

(3) within the classes described in paragraphs (15)(A)(ii), (15)(G)(ii), (15)(G)(iii), or (15)(G)(iv) of section 101(a) [8 U.S.C.A. § 1101(a)], except those provisions relating to reasonable requirements of passports and visas as a means of identification and documentation necessary to establish their qualifications under such paragraphs, and the provisions of subparagraphs (A) through (C) of section 212(a)(3) [8 U.S.C.A. § 1182(a)(3)].

(June 27, 1952, c. 477, Title I, § 102, 66 Stat. 173; Oct. 24, 1988, Pub.L. 100–525, § 9(b), 102 Stat. 2619; Nov. 29, 1990, Pub.L. 101–649, Title VI, § 603(a)(2), 104 Stat. 5082; Dec. 12, 1991, Pub.L. 102–232, Title III, § 307(i), 105 Stat. 1756; Sept. 30, 1996, Pub.L. 104–208, Div. C, Title III, § 308(d)(4)(B), 110 Stat. 3009–617.)

§ 103. Powers and duties [8 U.S.C.A. § 1103]

(a) Attorney General

(1) The Attorney General shall be charged with the administration and enforcement of this Act and all other laws relating to the immigration and naturalization of aliens, except insofar as this Act or such laws relate to the powers, functions, and duties conferred upon the President, the Secretary of State, the officers of the Department of State, or diplomatic or consular officers: Provided, however, That determination and ruling by the Attorney General with respect to all questions of law shall be controlling.

(2) He shall have control, direction, and supervision of all employees and of all the files and records of the Service.

(3) He shall establish such regulations; prescribe such forms of bond, reports, entries, and other papers; issue such instructions; and perform such other acts as he deems necessary for carrying out his authority under the provisions of this Act.

(4) He may require or authorize any employee of the Service or the Department of Justice to perform or exercise any of the powers, privileges, or duties conferred or imposed by this Act or regulations issued thereunder upon any other employee of the Service.

(5) He shall have the power and duty to control and guard the boundaries and borders of the United States against the illegal entry of aliens and shall, in his discretion, appoint for that purpose such number of employees of the Service as to him shall appear necessary and proper.

(6) He is authorized to confer or impose upon any employee of the United States, with the consent of the head of the Department or other independent establishment under whose jurisdiction the employee is serving, any of the powers, privileges, or duties conferred or imposed by this Act or regulations issued thereunder upon officers or employees of the Service.

(7) He may, with the concurrence of the Secretary of State, establish offices of the Service in foreign countries; and, after consultation with the Secretary of State, he may, whenever in his judgment such action may be necessary to accomplish the purposes of this Act, detail employees of the Service for duty in foreign countries. After consultation with the Secretary of State, the Attorney General may authorize officers of a foreign country to be stationed at preclearance facilities in the United States for the purpose of ensuring that persons traveling from or through the United States to that foreign country comply with that country's immigration and related laws. Those officers may exercise such authority and perform such duties as United States immigration officers are authorized to exercise and perform in that foreign country under reciprocal agreement, and they shall enjoy such reasonable privileges and immunities necessary for the performance of their duties as the government of their country extends to United States immigration officers.

(8) In the event the Attorney General determines that an actual or imminent mass influx of aliens arriving off the coast of the United States, or near a land border, presents urgent circumstances requiring an immediate Federal response, the Attorney General may authorize any State or local law enforcement officer, with the consent of the head of the department, agency, or establishment under whose jurisdiction the individual is serving, to perform or exercise any of the powers, privileges, or duties conferred or imposed by this Act or regulations issued thereunder upon officers or employees of the Service.

(9) The Attorney General, in support of persons in administrative detention in non-Federal institutions, is authorized—

(A) to make payments from funds appropriated for the administration and enforcement of the laws relating to immigration, naturalization, and alien registration for necessary clothing, medical care, necessary guard hire, and the housing, care, and security of persons detained by the Service pursuant to Federal law under an agreement with a State or political subdivision of a State; and

(B) to enter into a cooperative agreement with any State, territory, or political subdivision thereof, for the necessary construction, physical renovation, acquisition of equipment, supplies or materials required to establish acceptable conditions of confinement and detention services in any State or unit of local government which agrees to provide guaranteed bed space for persons detained by the Service.

(b) Land acquisition authority

(1) The Attorney General may contract for or buy any interest in land, including temporary use rights, adjacent to or in the vicinity of an international land border when the Attorney General deems the land essential to control and guard the boundaries and borders of the United States against any violation of this Act.

(2) The Attorney General may contract for or buy any interest in land identified pursuant to paragraph (1) as soon as the lawful owner of that interest fixes a price for it and the Attorney General considers that price to be reasonable.

(3) When the Attorney General and the lawful owner of an interest identified pursuant to paragraph (1) are unable to agree upon a reasonable price, the Attorney General may commence condemnation proceedings pursuant to the Act of August 1, 1888 (Chapter 728; 25 Stat. 357).

(4) The Attorney General may accept for the United States a gift of any interest in land identified pursuant to paragraph (1).

(c) Commissioner; appointment

The Commissioner shall be a citizen of the United States and shall be appointed by the President, by and with the advice and consent of the Senate. He shall be charged with any and all responsibilities and authority in the administration of the Service and of this Act which are conferred upon the Attorney General as may be delegated to him by the Attorney General or which may be prescribed by the Attorney General. The Commissioner may enter into cooperative agreements with State and local law enforcement agencies for the purpose of assisting in the enforcement of the immigration laws.

(d) Statistical information system

(1) The Commissioner, in consultation with interested academicians, government agencies, and other parties, shall provide for a system for collection and dissemination, to Congress and the public, of information (not in individually identifiable form) useful in evaluating the social, economic, environmental, and demographic impact of immigration laws.

(2) Such information shall include information on the alien population in the United States, on the rates of naturalization and emigration of resident aliens, on aliens who have been admitted, paroled, or granted asylum, on nonimmigrants in the United States (by occupation, basis for admission, and duration of stay), on aliens who have not been admitted or have been removed from the United States, on the number of applications filed and granted for cancellation of removal, and on the number of aliens estimated to be present unlawfully in the United States in each fiscal year.

(3) Such system shall provide for the collection and dissemination of such information not less often than annually.

(e) Annual report

(1) The Commissioner shall submit to Congress annually a report which contains a summary of the information collected under subsection (d) and an analysis of trends in immigration and naturalization.

(2) Each annual report shall include information on the number, and rate of denial administratively, of applications for naturalization, for each district office of the Service and by national origin group.

(f) Minimum number of agents in States

The Attorney General shall allocate to each State not fewer than 10 full-time active duty agents of the Immigration and Naturalization Service to carry out the functions of the Service, in order to ensure the effective enforcement of this Act.

(June 27, 1952, c. 477, Title I, § 103, 66 Stat. 173; Oct. 24, 1988, Pub.L. 100–525, § 9(c), 102 Stat. 2619, 2620; Nov. 29, 1990, Pub.L. 101–649, Title I, § 142, 104 Stat. 5004; Sept. 30, 1996, Pub.L 104–208, Div. C, Title I, §§ 102(d), 125, 134(a), Title III, §§ 308(d)(4)(C), (e)(4), 372, 373, 110 Stat. 3009–555, 3009–562, 3009–564, 3009–618, 3009–620, 3009–646, 3009–647.)

§ 104. Powers and duties of Secretary of State; Bureau of Consular Affairs [8 U.S.C.A. § 1104]

(a) Powers and duties

The Secretary of State shall be charged with the administration and the enforcement of the provisions of this Act and all other immigration and nationality laws relating to **(1)** the powers, duties, and functions of diplomatic and consular officers of the United States, except those powers, duties, and functions conferred upon the consular officers relating to the granting or refusal of visas; **(2)** the powers, duties, and functions of the Administrator; and **(3)** the determination of nationality of a person not in the United States. He shall establish such regulations; prescribe such forms of reports, entries and other papers; issue such instructions; and perform such other acts as he deems necessary for carrying out such provisions. He is authorized to confer or impose upon any employee of the United States, with the consent of the head of the department or independent establishment under whose jurisdiction the employee is serving, any of the powers, functions, or duties conferred or imposed by this Act or regulations issued thereunder upon officers or employees of the Department of State or of the American Foreign Service.

(b) Designation and duties of Administrator

The Secretary of State shall designate an Administrator who shall be a citizen of the United States, qualified by experience. The Administrator shall maintain close liaison with the appropriate committees of Congress in order that they may be advised regarding the administration of this Act by consular officers. The Administrator shall be charged with any and all responsibility and authority in the administration of this Act which are conferred on the Secretary of State as may be delegated to the Administrator by the Secretary of State or which may be prescribed by the Secretary of State, and shall perform such other duties as the Secretary of State may prescribe.

(c) Passport Office, Visa Office, and other offices; Directors

Within the Department of State there shall be a Passport Office, a Visa Office, and such other offices as the Secretary of State may deem to be appropriate, each office to be headed by a director. The Directors of the Passport Office and the Visa Office shall be experienced in the administration of the nationality and immigration laws.

(d) Transfer of duties

The functions heretofore performed by the Passport Division and the Visa Division of the Department of State shall hereafter be performed by the Passport Office and the Visa Office, respectively.

(e) General Counsel of Visa Office; appointment and duties

There shall be a General Counsel of the Visa Office, who shall be appointed by the Secretary of State and who shall serve under the general direction of the Legal Advisor of the Department of State. The General Counsel shall have authority to maintain liaison with the appropriate officers of the Service with a view to securing uniform interpretations of the provisions of this Act.

(June 27, 1952, c. 477, Title I, § 104, 66 Stat. 174; June 28, 1962, Pub.L. 87–510, § 4(a)(2), 76 Stat. 123; Aug. 14, 1964, Pub.L. 88–426, Title III, § 305(43), 78 Stat. 428; Aug. 17, 1977, Pub.L. 95–105, Title I, § 109(b)(1), 91 Stat. 847; Oct. 24, 1988, Pub.L. 100–525, § 9(d), 102 Stat. 2620; Apr. 30, 1994, Pub.L. 103–236, Title I, § 162(h)(2), 108 Stat. 407.)

§ 105. Liaison with internal security officers [8 U.S.C.A. § 1105]

The Commissioner and the Administrator shall have authority to maintain direct and continuous liaison with the Directors of the Federal Bureau of Investigation and the Central Intelligence Agency and with other internal security officers of the Government for the purpose of obtaining and exchanging information for use in enforcing the provisions of this Act in the interest of the internal security of the United States. The Commissioner and the Administrator shall maintain direct and continuous liaison with each other with a view to a coordinated, uniform, and efficient administration of this Act, and all other immigration and nationality laws.

(June 27, 1952, c. 477, Title I, § 105, 66 Stat. 175; Aug. 17, 1977, Pub.L. 95–105, Title I, § 109(b)(2), 91 Stat. 847; Apr. 30, 1994, Pub.L. 103–236, Title I, § 162(h)(3), 108 Stat. 408.)

§ 106. Repealed. Pub. L. 104–208, Div. C, Title III, § 306(b), Sept. 30, 1996, 110 Stat. 3009–612. [8 U.S.C.A. § 1105a]

TITLE II

IMMIGRATION

CHAPTER I—SELECTION SYSTEM

§ 201. Worldwide level of immigration [8 U.S.C.A. § 1151]

(a) In general

Exclusive of aliens described in subsection (b), aliens born in a foreign state or dependent area who may be issued immigrant visas or who may otherwise acquire the status of an alien lawfully admitted to the United States for permanent residence are limited to—

(1) family-sponsored immigrants described in section 203(a) [8 U.S.C.A. § 1153(a)] (or who are admitted under section 211(a) [8 U.S.C.A. § 1181(a)] on the basis of a prior issuance of a visa to their accompanying parent under section 203(a) [8 U.S.C.A. § 1153(a)]) in a number not to exceed in any fiscal year the number specified in subsection (c) for that year, and not to exceed in any of the first 3 quarters of any fiscal year 27 percent of the worldwide level under such subsection for all of such fiscal year;

(2) employment-based immigrants described in section 203(b) [8 U.S.C.A. § 1153(b)] (or who are admitted under section 211(a) [8 U.S.C.A. § 1181(a)] on the basis of a prior issuance of a visa to their accompanying parent under section 203(b) [8 U.S.C.A. § 1153(b)]), in a number not to exceed in any fiscal year the number specified in subsection (d) for that year, and not to exceed in any of the first 3 quarters of any fiscal year 27 percent of the worldwide level under such subsection for all of such fiscal year; and

(3) for fiscal years beginning with fiscal year 1995, diversity immigrants described in section 203(c) [8 U.S.C.A. § 1153(c)] (or who are admitted under section 211(a) [8 U.S.C.A. § 1181(a)] on the basis of a prior issuance of a visa to their accompanying parent under section 203(c) [8 U.S.C.A. § 1153(c)]) in a number not to exceed in any fiscal year the number specified in subsection (e) for that year, and not to exceed in any of the first 3 quarters of any fiscal year 27 percent of the worldwide level under such subsection for all of such fiscal year.

(b) Aliens not subject to direct numerical limitations

Aliens described in this subsection, who are not subject to the worldwide levels or numerical limitations of subsection (a), are as follows:

(1)(A) Special immigrants described in subparagraph (A) or (B) of section 101(a)(27) [8 U.S.C.A. § 1101(a)(27)].

(B) Aliens who are admitted under section 207 [8 U.S.C.A. § 1157] or whose status is adjusted under section 209 [8 U.S.C.A. § 1159].

(C) Aliens whose status is adjusted to permanent residence under section 210 [8 U.S.C.A. § 1160] or 245A [8 U.S.C.A. § 1255a].

(D) Aliens whose removal is cancelled under section 240A(a) [8 U.S.C.A. § 1229b(a)].

(E) Aliens provided permanent resident status under section 249 [8 U.S.C.A. § 1259].

(2)(A)(i) Immediate relatives.

For purposes of this subsection, the term "immediate relatives" means the children, spouses, and parents of a citizen of the United States, except that, in the case of parents, such citizens shall be at least 21 years of age. In the case of an alien who was the spouse of a citizen of the United States for at least 2 years at the time of the citizen's death and was not legally separated from the citizen at the time of the citizen's death, the alien (and each child of the alien) shall be considered, for purposes of this subsection, to remain an immediate relative after the date of the citizen's death but only if the spouse files a petition under section 204(a)(1)(A)(ii) [8 U.S.C.A. § 1154(a)(1)(A)(ii)] within 2 years after such date and only until the date the spouse remarries.

(ii) Aliens admitted under section 211(a) [8 U.S.C.A. § 1181(a)] on the basis of a prior issuance of a visa to their accompanying parent who is such an immediate relative.

(B) Aliens born to an alien lawfully admitted for permanent residence during a temporary visit abroad.

(c) Worldwide level of family-sponsored immigrants

(1)(A) The worldwide level of family-sponsored immigrants under this subsection for a fiscal year is, subject to subparagraph (B), equal to—

(i) 480,000, minus

(ii) the sum of the number computed under paragraph (2) and the number computed under paragraph (4), plus

(iii) the number (if any) computed under paragraph (3).

(B)(i) For each of fiscal years 1992, 1993, and 1994, 465,000 shall be substituted for 480,000 in subparagraph (A)(i).

(ii) In no case shall the number computed under subparagraph (A) be less than 226,000.

(2) The number computed under this paragraph for a fiscal year is the sum of the number of aliens described in subparagraphs (A) and (B) of subsection (b)(2) who were issued immigrant visas or who otherwise acquired the status of aliens lawfully admitted to the United States for permanent residence in the previous fiscal year.

(3)(A) The number computed under this paragraph for fiscal year 1992 is zero.

(B) The number computed under this paragraph for fiscal year 1993 is the difference (if any) between the worldwide level established under paragraph (1) for the previous fiscal year and the number of visas issued under section 203(a) [8 U.S.C.A. § 1153(a)] during that fiscal year.

(C) The number computed under this paragraph for a subsequent fiscal year is the difference (if any) between the maximum number of visas which may be issued under section 203(b) [8 U.S.C.A. § 1153(b)] (relating to employment-based immigrants) during the previous fiscal year and the number of visas issued under that section during that year.

(4) The number computed under this paragraph for a fiscal year (beginning with fiscal year 1999) is the number of aliens who were paroled into the United States under section 212(d)(5) [8 U.S.C.A. § 1182(d)(5)] in the second preceding fiscal year—

(A) who did not depart from the United States (without advance parole) within 365 days; and

(B) who (i) did not acquire the status of aliens lawfully admitted to the United States for permanent residence in the two preceding fiscal years, or (ii) acquired such status in such years under a provision of law (other than § 201(b)) which exempts such adjustment from the numerical limitation on the worldwide level of immigration under this section.

(5) If any alien described in paragraph (4) (other than an alien described in paragraph (4)(B)(ii)) is subsequently admitted as an alien lawfully admitted for permanent residence, such alien shall not again be considered for purposes of paragraph (1).

(d) Worldwide level of employment-based immigrants

(1) The worldwide level of employment-based immigrants under this subsection for a fiscal year is equal to—

(A) 140,000, plus

(B) the number computed under paragraph (2).

(2)(A) The number computed under this paragraph for fiscal year 1992 is zero.

(B) The number computed under this paragraph for fiscal year 1993 is the difference (if any) between the worldwide level established under paragraph (1) for the previous fiscal year and the number of visas issued under section 203(b) [8 U.S.C.A. § 1153(b)] during that fiscal year.

(C) The number computed under this paragraph for a subsequent fiscal year is the difference (if any) between the maximum number of visas which may be issued under section 203(a) [8 U.S.C.A. § 1153(a)] (relating to family-sponsored immigrants) during the previous fiscal year and the number of visas issued under that section during that year.

(e) Worldwide level of diversity immigrants

The worldwide level of diversity immigrants is equal to 55,000 for each fiscal year.

(June 27, 1952, c. 477, Title II, ch. 1, § 201, 66 Stat. 175; Oct. 3, 1965, Pub.L. 89–236, § 1, 79 Stat. 911; Oct. 20, 1976, Pub.L. 94–571, § 2, 90 Stat. 2703; Oct. 5, 1978, Pub.L. 95–412, § 1, 92 Stat. 907; Mar. 17, 1980, Pub.L. 96–212, Title II, § 203(a), 94 Stat. 106; Dec. 29, 1981, Pub.L. 97–116, § 20[(a)], 95 Stat. 1621; Nov. 29, 1990, Pub.L. 101–649, Title I, § 101(a), 104 Stat. 4980; Dec. 12, 1991, Pub.L. 102–232, Title III, § 302(a)(1), 105 Stat. 1742; Sept. 13, 1994, Pub.L. 103–322, Title IV, § 40701(b)(2), 108 Stat. 1954; Oct. 25, 1994, Pub.L. 103–416, Title II, § 219(b)(1), 108 Stat. 4316; Sept. 30, 1996, Pub.L. 104–208, Div. C, Title III, § 308(e)(5), (g)(8)(A)(i), Title VI, §§ 603, 671(d)(1)(A), 110 Stat. 3009–620, 3009–624, 3009–690, 3009–723.)

§ 202. Numerical limitations on individual foreign states [8 U.S.C.A. § 1152]

(a) Per country level

(1) Nondiscrimination

(A) Except as specifically provided in paragraph (2) and in sections 101(a)(27) [8 U.S.C.A. § 1101(a)(27)], 201(b)(2)(A)(i) [8 U.S.C.A. § 1151(b)(2)(A)(i)], and 203 [8 U.S.C.A. § 1153], no person shall receive any preference or priority or be discriminated against in the issuance of an immigrant visa because of the person's race, sex, nationality, place of birth, or place of residence.

(B) Nothing in this paragraph shall be construed to limit the authority of the Secretary of State to determine the procedures for the processing of immigrant visa applications or the locations where such applications will be processed.

(2) Per country levels for family-sponsored and employment-based immigrants

Subject to paragraphs (3) and (4), the total number of immigrant visas made available to natives of any single foreign state or dependent area under subsections (a) and (b) of section 203 [8 U.S.C.A. § 1153] in any fiscal year may not exceed 7 percent (in the case of a single foreign state) or 2 percent (in the case of a dependent area) of the total number of such visas made available under such subsections in that fiscal year.

(3) Exception if additional visas available

If because of the application of paragraph (2) with respect to one or more foreign states or dependent areas, the total number of visas available under both subsections (a) and (b) of section 203 [8 U.S.C.A. § 1153] for a calendar quarter exceeds the number of qualified immigrants who otherwise may be issued such a visa, paragraph (2) shall not apply to visas made available to such states or areas during the remainder of such calendar quarter.

(4) Special rules for spouses and children of lawful permanent resident aliens

(A) 75 percent of 2nd preference set-aside for spouses and children not subject to per country limitation

(i) In general

Of the visa numbers made available under section 203(a) [8 U.S.C.A. § 1153(a)] to immigrants described in section 203(a)(2)(A) [8 U.S.C.A. § 1153(a)(2)(A)] in any fiscal year, 75 percent of the 2–A floor (as defined in clause (ii)) shall be issued without regard to the numerical limitation under paragraph (2).

(ii) 2–A floor defined

In this paragraph, the term "2–A floor" means, for a fiscal year, 77 percent of the total number of visas made available under section 203(a) [8 U.S.C.A. § 1153(a)] to immigrants described in section 203(a)(2) [8 U.S.C.A. § 1153(a)(2)] in the fiscal year.

(B) Treatment of remaining 25 percent for countries subject to subsection (e)

(i) In general

Of the visa numbers made available under section 203(a) [8 U.S.C.A. § 1153(a)] to immigrants described in section 203(a)(2)(A) [8 U.S.C.A. § 1153(a)(2)(A)] in any fiscal year, the remaining 25 percent of the 2–A floor shall be available in the case of a state or area that is subject to subsection (e) only to the extent that the total number of visas issued in accordance with subparagraph (A) to natives of the foreign state or area is less than the subsection (e) ceiling (as defined in clause (ii)).

(ii) Subsection (e) ceiling defined

In clause (i), the term "subsection (e) ceiling" means, for a foreign state or dependent area, 77 percent of the maximum number of visas that may be made available under section 203(a) [8 U.S.C.A. § 1153(a)] to immigrants who are natives of the state or area under section 203(a)(2) [8 U.S.C.A. § 1153(a)(2)] consistent with subsection (e).

(C) Treatment of unmarried sons and daughters in countries subject to subsection (e)

In the case of a foreign state or dependent area to which subsection (e) applies, the number of immigrant visas that may be made available to natives of the state or area under section 203(a)(2)(B) [8 U.S.C.A. § 1153(a)(2)(B)] may not exceed—

(i) 23 percent of the maximum number of visas that may be made available under section 203(a) [8 U.S.C.A. § 1153(a)] to immigrants of the state or area described in section 203(a)(2) [8 U.S.C.A. § 1153(a)(2)] consistent with subsection (e), or

(ii) the number (if any) by which the maximum number of visas that may be made available under section 203(a) [8 U.S.C.A. § 1153(a)] to immigrants of the state or area described in section 203(a)(2) [8 U.S.C.A. § 1153(a)(2)] consistent with subsection (e) exceeds the number of visas issued under section 203(a)(2)(A) [8 U.S.C.A. § 1153(a)(2)(A)],

whichever is greater.

(D) Limiting pass down for certain countries subject to subsection (e)

In the case of a foreign state or dependent area to which subsection (e) applies, if the total number of visas issued under section 203(a)(2) [8 U.S.C.A. § 1153(a)(2)] exceeds the maximum number of visas that may be made available to immigrants of the state or area under section 203(a)(2) [8 U.S.C.A. § 1153(a)(2)] consistent with subsection (e) (determined without regard to this paragraph), in applying paragraphs (3) and (4) of section 203(a) [8 U.S.C.A. § 1153(a)] under subsection (e)(2) all visas shall be deemed to have been required for the classes specified in paragraphs (1) and (2) of such section.

(b) Rules for chargeability

Each independent country, self-governing dominion, mandated territory, and territory under the international trusteeship system of the United Nations, other than the United States and its outlying possessions, shall be treated as a separate foreign state for the purposes of a numerical level established under subsection (a)(2) when approved by the Secretary of State. All other inhabited lands shall be attributed to a foreign state specified by the Secretary of State. For the purposes of this Act the foreign state to which an immigrant is chargeable shall be determined by birth within such foreign state except that **(1)** an alien child, when accompanied by or following to join his alien parent or parents, may be charged to the foreign state of either parent if such parent has received or would be qualified for an immigrant visa, if necessary to prevent the separation of the child from the parent or parents, and if immigration charged to the foreign state to which such parent has been or would be chargeable has not reached a numerical level established under subsection (a)(2) for that fiscal year; **(2)** if an alien is chargeable to a different foreign state from that of his spouse, the foreign state to which such alien is chargeable may, if necessary to prevent the separation of husband and wife, be determined by the foreign state of the spouse he is accompanying or following to join, if such spouse has received or would be qualified for an immigrant visa and if immigration charged to the foreign state to which such spouse has been or would be chargeable has not reached a numerical level established under subsection (a)(2) for that fiscal year; **(3)** an alien born in the United States shall be considered as having been born in the country of which he is a citizen or subject, or, if he is not a citizen or subject of any country, in the last foreign country in which he had his residence as determined by the consular officer; and **(4)** an alien born within any foreign state in which neither of his parents was born and in which neither of his parents had a residence at the time of such alien's birth may be charged to the foreign state of either parent.

(c) Chargeability for dependent areas

Any immigrant born in a colony or other component or dependent area of a foreign state overseas from the foreign state, other than an alien described in section 201(b) [8 U.S.C.A. § 1151(b)], shall be chargeable for the purpose of the limitation set forth in subsection (a), to the foreign state.

(d) Changes in territory

In the case of any change in the territorial limits of foreign states, the Secretary of State shall, upon recognition of such change, issue appropriate instructions to all diplomatic and consular offices.

(e) Special rules for countries at ceiling

If it is determined that the total number of immigrant visas made available under subsections (a) and (b) of section 203 [8 U.S.C.A. § 1153] to natives of any single foreign state or dependent area will exceed the numerical limitation specified in subsection (a)(2) in any fiscal year, in determining the allotment of immigrant visa numbers to natives under subsections (a) and (b) of section 203 [8 U.S.C.A. § 1153], visa numbers with respect to natives of that state or area shall be allocated (to the extent practicable and otherwise consistent with this section and section 203 [8 U.S.C.A. § 1153]) in a manner so that—

(1) the ratio of the visa numbers made available under section 203(a) [8 U.S.C.A. § 1153(a)] to the visa numbers made available under section 203(b) [8 U.S.C.A. § 1153(b)] is equal to the ratio of the worldwide level of immigration under section 201(c) [8 U.S.C.A. § 1151(c)] to such level under section 201(d) [8 U.S.C.A. § 1151(d)];

(2) except as provided in subsection (a)(4), the proportion of the visa numbers made available under each of paragraphs (1) through (4) of section 203(a) [8 U.S.C.A. § 1153(a)] is equal to the ratio of the total number of visas made available under the respective paragraph to the total number of visas made available under section 203(a) [8 U.S.C.A. § 1153(a)], and

(3) the proportion of the visa numbers made available under each of paragraphs (1) through (5) of section 203(b) [8 U.S.C.A. § 1153(b)] is equal to the ratio of the total number of visas made available under the respective paragraph to the total number of visas made available under section 203(b) [8 U.S.C.A. § 1153(b)].

Nothing in this subsection shall be construed as limiting the number of visas that may be issued to natives of a foreign state or dependent area under section 203(a) [8 U.S.C.A. § 1153(a)] or 203(b) [8 U.S.C.A. § 1153(b)] if there is insufficient demand for visas for such natives under section 203(b) [8 U.S.C.A. § 1153(b)],or 203(a) [8 U.S.C.A. § 1153(a)], respectively, or as limiting the number of visas that may be issued under section 203(a)(2)(A) [8 U.S.C.A. § 1153(a)(2)(A)] pursuant to subsection (a)(4)(A).

(June 27, 1952, c. 477, Title II, ch. 1, § 202, 66 Stat. 176; Sept. 26, 1961, Pub.L. 87–301, § 9, 75 Stat. 654; Oct. 3, 1965, Pub.L. 89–236, § 2, 79 Stat. 911; Oct. 20, 1976, Pub.L. 94–571, § 3, 90 Stat. 2703; Oct. 5, 1978, Pub.L. 95–412, § 2, 92 Stat. 907; Mar. 17, 1980, Pub.L. 96–212, Title II, § 203(b), 94 Stat. 107; Dec. 29, 1981, Pub.L. 97–116, §§ 18(c), 20(b), 95 Stat. 1620, 1622; Nov. 6, 1986, Pub.L. 99–603, Title III, § 311(a), 100 Stat. 3434; Nov. 14, 1986, Pub.L. 99–653, § 4, 100 Stat. 3655; Oct. 24, 1988, Pub. L. 100–525, §§ 8(c), 9(f), 102 Stat. 2617, 2620; Nov. 29, 1990, Pub.L. 101–649, Title I, § 102, 104 Stat. 4982; Dec. 12, 1991, Pub.L. 102–232, Title III, § 302(a)(3), 105 Stat. 1742; Sept. 30, 1996, Pub.L. 104–208, Div. C, Title VI, § 633, 110 Stat. 3009–701.)

§ 203. Allocation of immigrant visas [8 U.S.C.A. § 1153]

(a) Preference allocation for family-sponsored immigrants

Aliens subject to the worldwide level specified in section 201(c) [8 U.S.C.A. § 1151(c)] for family-sponsored immigrants shall be allotted visas as follows:

(1) Unmarried sons and daughters of citizens

Qualified immigrants who are the unmarried sons or daughters of citizens of the United States shall be allocated visas in a number not to exceed 23,400, plus any visas not required for the class specified in paragraph (4).

(2) Spouses and unmarried sons and unmarried daughters of permanent resident aliens

Qualified immigrants—

(A) who are the spouses or children of an alien lawfully admitted for permanent residence, or

(B) who are the unmarried sons or unmarried daughters (but are not the children) of an alien lawfully admitted for permanent residence, shall be allocated visas in a number not to exceed 114,200, plus the number (if any) by which such worldwide level exceeds 226,000, plus any visas not required for the class specified in paragraph (1); except that not less than 77 percent of such visa numbers shall be allocated to aliens described in subparagraph (A).

(3) Married sons and married daughters of citizens

Qualified immigrants who are the married sons or married daughters of citizens of the United States shall be allocated visas in a number not to exceed 23,400, plus any visas not required for the classes specified in paragraphs (1) and (2).

(4) Brothers and sisters of citizens

Qualified immigrants who are the brothers or sisters of citizens of the United States, if such citizens are at least 21 years of age, shall be allocated visas in a number not to exceed 65,000, plus any visas not required for the classes specified in paragraphs (1) through (3).

(b) Preference allocation for employment-based immigrants

Aliens subject to the worldwide level specified in section 201(d) [8 U.S.C.A. § 1151(d)] for employment-based immigrants in a fiscal year shall be allotted visas as follows:

(1) Priority workers

Visas shall first be made available in a number not to exceed 28.6 percent of such worldwide level, plus any visas not required for the classes specified in paragraphs (4) and (5), to qualified immigrants who are aliens described in any of the following subparagraphs (A) through (C):

(A) Aliens with extraordinary ability

An alien is described in this subparagraph if—

(i) the alien has extraordinary ability in the sciences, arts, education, business, or athletics which has been demonstrated by sustained national or international acclaim and whose achievements have been recognized in the field through extensive documentation,

(ii) the alien seeks to enter the United States to continue work in the area of extraordinary ability, and

(iii) the alien's entry into the United States will substantially benefit prospectively the United States.

(B) Outstanding professors and researchers

An alien is described in this subparagraph if—

(i) the alien is recognized internationally as outstanding in a specific academic area,

(ii) the alien has at least 3 years of experience in teaching or research in the academic area, and

(iii) the alien seeks to enter the United States—

(I) for a tenured position (or tenure-track position) within a university or institution of higher education to teach in the academic area,

(II) for a comparable position with a university or institution of higher education to conduct research in the area, or

(III) for a comparable position to conduct research in the area with a department, division, or institute of a private employer, if the department, division, or institute employs at least 3 persons full-time in research activities and has achieved documented accomplishments in an academic field.

(C) Certain multinational executives and managers

An alien is described in this subparagraph if the alien, in the 3 years preceding the time of the alien's application for classification and admission into the United States under this subparagraph, has been employed for at least 1 year by a firm or corporation or other legal entity or an affiliate or subsidiary thereof and the alien seeks to enter the United States in order to continue to render services to the same employer or to a subsidiary or affiliate thereof in a capacity that is managerial or executive.

(2) Aliens who are members of the professions holding advanced degrees or aliens of exceptional ability

(A) In general

Visas shall be made available, in a number not to exceed 28.6 percent of such worldwide level, plus any visas not required for the classes specified in paragraph (1), to qualified immigrants who are members of the professions holding advanced degrees or their equivalent or who because of their exceptional ability in the sciences, arts, or business, will substantially benefit prospectively the national economy, cultural or educational interests, or welfare of the United States, and whose services in the sciences, arts, professions, or business are sought by an employer in the United States.

Job offer needed

(B) Waiver of job offer

(i) National interest waiver

Subject to clause (ii), the Attorney General may, when the Attorney General deems it to be in the national interest, waive the requirements of subparagraph (A) that an alien's services in the sciences, arts, professions, or business be sought by an employer in the United States.

(ii) Physicians working in shortage areas or veterans facilities

(I) In general

The Attorney General shall grant a national interest waiver pursuant to clause (i) on behalf of any alien physician with respect to whom a petition for preference classification has been filed under subparagraph (A) if—

(aa) the alien physician agrees to work full time as a physician in an area or areas designated by the Secretary of Health and Human Services as having a shortage of health care professionals or at a health care facility under the jurisdiction of the Secretary of Veterans Affairs; and

(bb) a Federal agency or a department of public health in any State has previously determined that the alien physician's work in such an area or at such facility was in the public interest.

(II) Prohibition

No permanent resident visa may be issued to an alien physician described in subclause (I) by the Secretary of State under section 204(b) [8 U.S.C.A. § 1154(b)], and the Attorney General may not adjust the status of such an alien physician from that of a nonimmigrant alien to that of a permanent resident alien under section 245 [8 U.S.C.A. § 1255], until such time as the alien has worked full time as a physician for an aggregate of 5 years (not including the time served in the status of an alien described in section 101(a)(15)(J) [8 U.S.C.A. § 1101(a)(15)(J)]), in an area or areas designated by the Secretary of Health and Human Services as having a shortage of health care professionals or at a health care facility under the jurisdiction of the Secretary of Veterans Affairs.

(III) Statutory construction

Nothing in this subparagraph may be construed to prevent the filing of a petition with the Attorney General for classification under section 204(a) [8 U.S.C.A. § 1154(a)], or the filing of an application for adjustment of status under section 245 [8 U.S.C.A. § 1255], by an alien physician described in subclause (I) prior to the date by which such alien physician has completed the service described in subclause (II).

(IV) Effective date

The requirements of this subsection do not affect waivers on behalf of alien physicians approved under subsection (b)(2)(B) of this section before the enactment date of this subsection. In the case of a physician for whom an application for a waiver was filed under subsection (b)(2)(B) of this section prior to November 1, 1998, the Attorney General shall grant a national interest waiver pursuant to subsection (b)(2)(B) of this section except that the alien is required to have worked full time as a physician for an aggregate of 3 years (not including time served in the status of an alien described in section 101(a)(15)(J) [8 U.S.C.A. § 1101(a)(15)(J)]) before a visa can be issued to the alien under section 204(b) [8 U.S.C.A. § 1154(b)] or the status of the alien is adjusted to permanent resident under section 245 [8 U.S.C.A. § 1255].

(C) Determination of exceptional ability

In determining under subparagraph (A) whether an immigrant has exceptional ability, the possession of a degree, diploma, certificate, or similar award from a college, university, school, or other institution of learning or a license to practice or certification for a particular profession or occupation shall not by itself be considered sufficient evidence of such exceptional ability.

(3) Skilled workers, professionals, and other workers

(A) In general

Visas shall be made available, in a number not to exceed 28.6 percent of such worldwide level, plus any visas not required for the classes specified in paragraphs (1) and (2), to the following classes of aliens who are not described in paragraph (2):

(i) Skilled workers

Qualified immigrants who are capable, at the time of petitioning for classification under this paragraph, of performing skilled labor (requiring at least 2 years training or experience), not of a temporary or seasonal nature, for which qualified workers are not available in the United States.

(ii) Professionals

Qualified immigrants who hold baccalaureate degrees and who are members of the professions.

(iii) Other workers

Other qualified immigrants who are capable, at the time of petitioning for classification under this paragraph, of performing unskilled labor, not of a temporary or seasonal nature, for which qualified workers are not available in the United States.

(B) Limitation on other workers

Not more than 10,000 of the visas made available under this paragraph in any fiscal year may be available for qualified immigrants described in subparagraph (A)(iii).

(C) Labor certification required

An immigrant visa may not be issued to an immigrant under subparagraph (A) until the consular officer is in receipt of a determination made by the Secretary of Labor pursuant to the provisions of section 212(a)(5)(A) [8 U.S.C.A. § 1182(a)(5)(A)].

(4) Certain special immigrants

Visas shall be made available, in a number not to exceed 7.1 percent of such worldwide level, to qualified special immigrants described in section 101(a)(27) [8 U.S.C.A. § 1101(a)(27)] (other than those described in subparagraph (A) or (B) thereof), of which not more than 5,000 may be made available in any fiscal year to special immigrants described in subclause (II) or (III) of section 101(a)(27)(C)(ii) [8 U.S.C.A. § 1101(a)(27)(C)(ii)].

(5) Employment creation

(A) In general

Visas shall be made available, in a number not to exceed 7.1 percent of such worldwide level, to qualified immigrants seeking to enter the United States for the purpose of engaging in a new commercial enterprise—

(i) which the alien has established,

(ii) in which such alien has invested (after November 29, 1990) or, is actively in the process of investing, capital in an amount not less than the amount specified in subparagraph (C), and

(iii) which will benefit the United States economy and create full-time employment for not fewer than 10 United States citizens or aliens lawfully admitted for permanent residence or other immigrants lawfully authorized to be employed in the United States (other than the immigrant and the immigrant's spouse, sons, or daughters).

(B) Set-aside for targeted employment areas

(i) In general

Not less than 3,000 of the visas made available under this paragraph in each fiscal year shall be reserved for qualified immigrants who establish a new commercial enterprise described in subparagraph (A) which will create employment in a targeted employment area.

(ii) Targeted employment area defined

In this paragraph, the term "targeted employment area" means, at the time of the investment, a rural area or an area which has experienced high unemployment (of at least 150 percent of the national average rate).

(iii) Rural area defined

In this paragraph, the term "rural area" means any area other than an area within a metropolitan statistical area or within the outer boundary of any city or town having a population of 20,000 or more (based on the most recent decennial census of the United States).

(C) Amount of capital required

(i) In general

Except as otherwise provided in this subparagraph, the amount of capital required under subparagraph (A) shall be $1,000,000. The Attorney General, in consultation with the Secretary of Labor and the Secretary of State, may from time to time prescribe regulations increasing the dollar amount specified under the previous sentence.

(ii) Adjustment for targeted employment areas

The Attorney General may, in the case of investment made in a targeted employment area, specify an amount of capital required under subparagraph (A) that is less than (but not less than ½ of) the amount specified in clause (i).

(iii) Adjustment for high employment areas

In the case of an investment made in a part of a metropolitan statistical area that at the time of the investment—

(I) is not a targeted employment area, and

(II) is an area with an unemployment rate significantly below the national average unemployment rate,

the Attorney General may specify an amount of capital required under subparagraph (A) that is greater than (but not greater than 3 times) the amount specified in clause (i).

(6) Special rules for "K" special immigrants

(A) Not counted against numerical limitation in year involved

Subject to subparagraph (B), the number of immigrant visas made available to special immigrants under section 101(a)(27)(K) [8 U.S.C.A. § 1101(a)(27)(K)] in a fiscal year shall not be subject to the numerical limitations of this subsection or of section 202(a) [8 U.S.C.A. § 1152(a)].

(B) Counted against numerical limitations in following year

(i) Reduction in employment-based immigrant classifications

The number of visas made available in any fiscal year under paragraphs (1), (2), and (3) shall each be reduced by ⅓ of the number of visas made available in the previous fiscal year to special immigrants described in section 101(a)(27)(K) [8 U.S.C.A. § 1101(a)(27)(K)].

(ii) Reduction in per country level

The number of visas made available in each fiscal year to natives of a foreign state under section 202(a) [8 U.S.C.A. § 1152(a)] shall be reduced by the number of visas made available in the previous fiscal year to special immigrants described in section 101(a)(27)(K) [8 U.S.C.A. § 1101(a)(27)(K)] who are natives of the foreign state.

(iii) Reduction in employment-based immigrant classifications within per country ceiling

In the case of a foreign state subject to section 202(e) [8 U.S.C.A. § 1152(e)] in a fiscal year (and in the previous fiscal year), the number of visas made available and allocated to each of paragraphs (1) through (3) of this subsection in the fiscal year shall be reduced by ⅓ of the number of visas made available in the previous fiscal year to special immigrants described in section 101(a)(27)(K) [8 U.S.C.A. § 1101(a)(27)(K)] who are natives of the foreign state.

(c) Diversity immigrants

(1) In general

Except as provided in paragraph (2), aliens subject to the worldwide level specified in section 201(e) [8 U.S.C.A. § 1151(e)] for diversity immigrants shall be allotted visas each fiscal year as follows:

(A) Determination of preference immigration

The Attorney General shall determine for the most recent previous 5–fiscal-year period for which data are available, the total number of aliens who are natives of each foreign state and who (i) were admitted or otherwise provided lawful permanent resident status (other than under this subsection) and (ii) were subject to the numerical limitations of section 201(a) [8 U.S.C.A. § 1151(a)] (other than paragraph (3) thereof) or who were admitted or otherwise provided lawful permanent resident status as an immediate relative or other alien described in section 201(b)(2) [8 U.S.C.A. § 1151(b)(2)].

(B) Identification of high-admission and low-admission regions and high-admission and low-admission states

The Attorney General—

(i) shall identify—

(I) each region (each in this paragraph referred to as a "high-admission region") for which the total of the numbers determined under subparagraph (A) for states in the region is greater than ⅙ of the total of all such numbers, and

(II) each other region (each in this paragraph referred to as a "low-admission region"); and

(ii) shall identify—

(I) each foreign state for which the number determined under subparagraph (A) is greater than 50,000 (each such state in this paragraph referred to as a "high-admission state"), and

(II) each other foreign state (each such state in this paragraph referred to as a "low-admission state").

(C) Determination of percentage of worldwide immigration attributable to high-admission regions

The Attorney General shall determine the percentage of the total of the numbers determined under subparagraph (A) that are numbers for foreign states in high-admission regions.

(D) Determination of regional populations excluding high-admission states and ratios of populations of regions within low-admission regions and high-admission regions

The Attorney General shall determine—

(i) based on available estimates for each region, the total population of each region not including the population of any high-admission state;

(ii) for each low-admission region, the ratio of the population of the region determined under clause (i) to the total of the populations determined under such clause for all the low-admission regions; and

(iii) for each high-admission region, the ratio of the population of the region determined under clause (i) to the total of the populations determined under such clause for all the high-admission regions.

(E) Distribution of visas

(i) No visas for natives of high-admission states

The percentage of visas made available under this paragraph to natives of a high-admission state is 0.

(ii) For low-admission states in low-admission regions

Subject to clauses (iv) and (v), the percentage of visas made available under this paragraph to natives (other than natives of a high-admission state) in a low-admission region is the product of—

(I) the percentage determined under subparagraph (C), and

(II) the population ratio for that region determined under subparagraph (D)(ii).

(iii) For low-admission states in high-admission regions

Subject to clauses (iv) and (v), the percentage of visas made available under this paragraph to natives (other than natives of a high-admission state) in a high-admission region is the product of—

(I) 100 percent minus the percentage determined under subparagraph (C), and

(II) the population ratio for that region determined under subparagraph (D)(iii).

(iv) Redistribution of unused visa numbers

If the Secretary of State estimates that the number of immigrant visas to be issued to natives in any region for a fiscal year under this paragraph is less than the number of immigrant visas made available to such natives under this paragraph for the fiscal year, subject to clause (v), the excess visa numbers shall be made available to natives (other than natives of a high-admission state) of the other regions in proportion to the percentages otherwise specified in clauses (ii) and (iii).

(v) Limitation on visas for natives of a single foreign state

The percentage of visas made available under this paragraph to natives of any single foreign state for any fiscal year shall not exceed 7 percent.

(F) Region defined

Only for purposes of administering the diversity program under this subsection, Northern Ireland shall be treated as a separate foreign state, each colony or other component or dependent area of a foreign state overseas from the foreign state shall be treated as part of the foreign state, and the areas described in each of the following clauses shall be considered to be a separate region:

(i) Africa.

(ii) Asia.

(iii) Europe.

(iv) North America (other than Mexico).

(v) Oceania.

(vi) South America, Mexico, Central America, and the Caribbean.

(2) Requirement of education or work experience

An alien is not eligible for a visa under this subsection unless the alien—

(A) has at least a high school education or its equivalent, or

(B) has, within 5 years of the date of application for a visa under this subsection, at least 2 years of work experience in an occupation which requires at least 2 years of training or experience.

(3) Maintenance of information

The Secretary of State shall maintain information on the age, occupation, education level, and other relevant characteristics of immigrants issued visas under this subsection.

(d) Treatment of family members

A spouse or child as defined in subparagraph (A), (B), (C), (D), or (E) of section 101(b)(1) [8 U.S.C.A. § 1101(b)(1)] shall, if not otherwise entitled to an immigrant status and the immediate issuance of a visa under subsection (a), (b), or (c), be entitled to the same status, and the same order of consideration provided in the respective subsection, if accompanying or following to join, the spouse or parent.

(e) Order of consideration

(1) Immigrant visas made available under subsection (a) or (b) shall be issued to eligible immigrants in the order in which a petition in behalf of each such immigrant is filed with the Attorney General (or in the case of special immigrants under section 101(a)(27)(D) [8 U.S.C.A. § 1101(a)(27)(D)], with the Secretary of State) as provided in section 204(a) [8 U.S.C.A. § 1154(a)].

(2) Immigrant visa numbers made available under subsection (c) (relating to diversity immigrants) shall be issued to eligible qualified immigrants strictly in a random order established by the Secretary of State for the fiscal year involved.

(3) Waiting lists of applicants for visas under this section shall be maintained in accordance with regulations prescribed by the Secretary of State.

(f) Authorization for issuance

In the case of any alien claiming in his application for an immigrant visa to be described in section 201(b)(2) [8 U.S.C.A. § 1151(b)(2)] or in subsection (a), (b), or (c) of this section, the consular officer shall not grant such status until he has been authorized to do so as provided by section 204 [8 U.S.C.A. § 1154].

(g) Lists

For purposes of carrying out the Secretary's responsibilities in the orderly administration of this section, the Secretary of State may make reasonable estimates of the anticipated numbers of visas to be issued during any quarter of any fiscal year within each of the categories under subsections (a), (b), and (c) and to rely upon such estimates in authorizing the issuance of visas. The Secretary of State shall terminate the registration of any alien who fails to apply for an immigrant visa within one year following notification to the alien of the availability of such visa, but the Secretary shall reinstate the registration of any such alien who establishes within 2 years following the date of notification of the availability of such visa that such failure to apply was due to circumstances beyond the alien's control.

(June 27, 1952, c. 477, Title II, ch. 1, § 203, 66 Stat. 178; Sept. 11, 1957, Pub.L. 85–316, § 3, 71 Stat. 639; Sept. 22, 1959, Pub.L. 86–363, §§ 1–3, 73 Stat. 644; Oct. 3, 1965, Pub.L. 89–236, § 3, 79 Stat. 912; Oct. 20, 1976, Pub.L. 94–571, § 4, 90 Stat. 2705; Oct. 5, 1978, Pub.L. 95–412, § 3, 92 Stat. 907; Oct. 5, 1978, Pub.L. 95–417, § 1, 92 Stat. 917; Mar. 17, 1980, Pub.L. 96–212, Title II, § 203(c), (i), 94 Stat. 107, 108; Nov. 29, 1990, Pub.L. 101–649, Title I, §§ 111, 121(a), 131, 162(a)(1), Title VI, § 603(a)(3), 104 Stat. 4986, 4987, 4997, 5009, 5082; Oct. 1, 1991, Pub.L. 102–110, § 2(b), 105 Stat. 555; Dec. 12, 1991, Pub.L. 102–232, Title III, § 302(b)(2), (e)(3), 105 Stat. 1743, 1745; Oct. 25, 1994, Pub.L. 103–416, Title II, §§ 212(b), 219(c), 108 Stat. 4314, 4316; Nov. 12, 1999, Pub.L. 106–95, § 5, 113 Stat. 1318; Nov. 29, 1999, Pub.L. 106–113, Div. B, § 1000(a)(1) [H.R. 3421, Title I, § 117], 113 Stat. 1535, 1537.)

§ 204. Procedure for granting immigrant status [8 U.S.C.A. § 1154]

(a) Petitioning procedure

(1)(A)(i) Any citizen of the United States claiming that an alien is entitled to classification by reason of a relationship described in paragraph (1), (3), or (4) of section 203(a) [8 U.S.C.A. § 1153(a)] or to an immediate relative status under section 201(b)(2)(A)(i) [8 U.S.C.A. § 1151(b)(2)(A)(i)] may file a petition with the Attorney General for such classification.

(ii) An alien spouse described in the second sentence of section 201(b)(2)(A)(i) [8 U.S.C.A. § 1151(b)(2)(A)(i)] also may file a petition with the Attorney General under this subparagraph for classification of the alien (and the alien's children) under such section.

(iii) An alien who is the spouse of a citizen of the United States, who is a person of good moral character, who is eligible to be classified as an immediate relative under section 201(b)(2)(A)(i) [8 U.S.C.A. § 1151(b)(2)(A)(i)], and who has resided in the United States with the alien's spouse may file a petition with the Attorney General under this subparagraph for classification of the alien (and any child of the alien if such a child has not been classified under clause (iv)) under such section if the alien demonstrates to the Attorney General that—

(I) the alien is residing in the United States, the marriage between the alien and the spouse was entered into in good faith by the alien, and during the marriage the alien or a child of the alien has been battered by or has been the subject of extreme cruelty perpetrated by the alien's spouse; and

(II) the alien is a person whose removal, in the opinion of the Attorney General, would result in extreme hardship to the alien or a child of the alien.

(iv) An alien who is the child of a citizen of the United States, who is a person of good moral character, who is eligible to be classified as an immediate relative under section 201(b)(2)(A)(i) [8 U.S.C.A. § 1151(b)(2)(A)(i)], and who has resided in the United States with the citizen parent may file a petition with the Attorney General under this subparagraph for classification of the alien under such section if the alien demonstrates to the Attorney General that—

(I) the alien is residing in the United States and during the period of residence with the citizen parent the alien has been battered by or has been the subject of extreme cruelty perpetrated by the alien's citizen parent; and

(II) the alien is a person whose removal, in the opinion of the Attorney General, would result in extreme hardship to the alien.

(B)(i) Any alien lawfully admitted for permanent residence claiming that an alien is entitled to a classification by reason of the relationship described in section 203(a)(2) [8 U.S.C.A. § 1153(a)(2)] may file a petition with the Attorney General for such classification.

(ii) An alien who is the spouse of an alien lawfully admitted for permanent residence, who is a person of good moral character, who is eligible for classification under section 203(a)(2)(A) [8 U.S.C.A. § 1153(a)(2)(A)], and who has resided in the United States with the alien's legal permanent resident spouse may file a petition with the Attorney General under this subparagraph for classification of the alien (and any child of the alien if such a child has not been classified under clause (iii)) under such section if the alien demonstrates to the Attorney General that the conditions described in subclauses (I) and (II) of subparagraph (A)(iii) are met with respect to the alien.

(iii) An alien who is the child of an alien lawfully admitted for permanent residence, who is a person of good moral character, who is eligible for classification under section 203(a)(2)(A) [8 U.S.C.A. § 1153(a)(2)(A)], and who has resided in the United States with the alien's permanent resident alien parent may file a petition with the Attorney General under this subparagraph for classification of the alien under such section if the alien demonstrates to the Attorney General that—

(I) the alien is residing in the United States and during the period of residence with the permanent resident parent the alien has been battered by or has been the subject of extreme cruelty perpetrated by the alien's permanent resident parent; and

(II) the alien is a person whose removal, in the opinion of the Attorney General, would result in extreme hardship to the alien.

(C) Any alien desiring to be classified under section 203(b)(1)(A) [8 U.S.C.A. § 1153(b)(1)(A)], or any person on behalf of such an alien, may file a petition with the Attorney General for such classification.

(D) Any employer desiring and intending to employ within the United States an alien entitled to classification under section 203(b)(1)(B) [8 U.S.C.A. § 1153(b)(1)(B)], 203(b)(1)(C) [8 U.S.C.A. § 1153(b)(1)(C)], 203(b)(2) [8 U.S.C.A. § 1153(b)(2)], or 203(b)(3) [8 U.S.C.A. § 1153(b)(3)] may file a petition with the Attorney General for such classification.

visa petition

(E)(i) Any alien (other than a special immigrant under section 101(a)(27)(D) [8 U.S.C.A. § 1101(a)(27)(D)]) desiring to be classified under section 203(b)(4) [8 U.S.C.A. § 1153(b)(4)], or any person on behalf of such an alien, may file a petition with the Attorney General for such classification.

(ii) Aliens claiming status as a special immigrant under section 101(a)(27)(D) [8 U.S.C.A. § 1101(a)(27)(D)] may file a petition only with the Secretary of State and only after notification by the Secretary that such status has been recommended and approved pursuant to such section.

(F) Any alien desiring to be classified under section 203(b)(5) [8 U.S.C.A. § 1153(b)(5)] may file a petition with the Attorney General for such classification.

(G)(i) Any alien desiring to be provided an immigrant visa under section 203(c) [8 U.S.C.A. § 1153(c)] may file a petition at the place and time determined by the Secretary of State by regulation.

Only one such petition may be filed by an alien with respect to any petitioning period established. If more than one petition is submitted all such petitions submitted for such period by the alien shall be voided.

(ii)(I) The Secretary of State shall designate a period for the filing of petitions with respect to visas which may be issued under section 203(c) [8 U.S.C.A. § 1153(c)] for the fiscal year beginning after the end of the period.

(II) Aliens who qualify, through random selection, for a visa under section 203(c) [8 U.S.C.A. § 1153(c)] shall remain eligible to receive such visa only through the end of the specific fiscal year for which they were selected.

(III) The Secretary of State shall prescribe such regulations as may be necessary to carry out this clause.

(iii) A petition under this subparagraph shall be in such form as the Secretary of State may by regulation prescribe and shall contain such information and be supported by such documentary evidence as the Secretary of State may require.

(H) In acting on petitions filed under clause (iii) or (iv) of subparagraph (A) or clause (ii) or (iii) of subparagraph (B), the Attorney General shall consider any credible evidence relevant to the petition. The determination of what evidence is credible and the weight to be given that evidence shall be within the sole discretion of the Attorney General.

(2)(A) The Attorney General may not approve a spousal second preference petition for the classification of the spouse of an alien if the alien, by virtue of a prior marriage, has been accorded the status of an alien lawfully admitted for permanent residence as the spouse of a citizen of the United States or as the spouse of an alien lawfully admitted for permanent residence, unless—

(i) a period of 5 years has elapsed after the date the alien acquired the status of an alien lawfully admitted for permanent residence, or

(ii) the alien establishes to the satisfaction of the Attorney General by clear and convincing evidence that the prior marriage (on the basis of which the alien obtained the status of an alien lawfully admitted for permanent residence) was not entered into for the purpose of evading any provision of the immigration laws.

In this subparagraph, the term "spousal second preference petition" refers to a petition, seeking preference status under section 203(a)(2) [8 U.S.C.A. § 1153(a)(2)], for an alien as a spouse of an alien lawfully admitted for permanent residence.

(B) Subparagraph (A) shall not apply to a petition filed for the classification of the spouse of an alien if the prior marriage of the alien was terminated by the death of his or her spouse.

(b) Investigation; consultation; approval; authorization to grant preference status

After an investigation of the facts in each case, and after consultation with the Secretary of Labor with respect to petitions to accord a status under section 203(b)(2) [8 U.S.C.A. § 1153(b)(2)] or 203(b)(3) [8 U.S.C.A. § 1153(b)(3)], the Attorney General shall, if he determines that the facts stated in the petition are true and that the alien in behalf of whom the petition is made is an immediate relative specified in section 201(b) [8 U.S.C.A. § 1151(b)] or is eligible for preference under subsection (a) or (b) of section 203 [8 U.S.C.A. § 1153], approve the petition and forward one copy thereof to the Department of State. The Secretary of State shall then authorize the consular officer concerned to grant the preference status.

(c) Prohibition against approval in cases of marriages entered into in order to evade immigration laws

Notwithstanding the provisions of subsection (b) no petition shall be approved if **(1)** the alien has previously been accorded, or has sought to be accorded, an immediate relative or preference status as the spouse of a citizen of the United States or the spouse of an alien lawfully admitted for permanent residence, by reason of a marriage determined by the Attorney General to have been entered into for the purpose of evading the immigration laws, or **(2)** the Attorney General has determined that the alien has attempted or conspired to enter into a marriage for the purpose of evading the immigration laws.

(d) Recommendation of valid home-study

Notwithstanding the provisions of subsections (a) and (b) no petition may be approved on behalf of a child defined in section 101(b)(1)(F) [8 U.S.C.A. § 1101(b)(1)(F)] unless a valid home-study has been favorably recommended by an agency of the State of the child's proposed residence, or by an agency authorized by that State to conduct such a study, or, in the case of a child adopted abroad, by an appropriate public or private adoption agency which is licensed in the United States.

(e) Subsequent finding of non-entitlement to preference classification

Nothing in this section shall be construed to entitle an immigrant, in behalf of whom a petition under this section is approved, to be admitted [sic] the United States as an immigrant under subsection (a), (b), or (c) of section 203 [8 U.S.C.A. § 1153] or as an immediate relative under section 201(b) [8 U.S.C.A. § 1151(b)] if upon his arrival at a port of entry in the United States he is found not to be entitled to such classification.

(f) Preferential treatment for children fathered by United States citizens and born in Korea, Vietnam, Laos, Kampuchea, or Thailand after 1950 and before October 22, 1982

(1) Any alien claiming to be an alien described in paragraph (2)(A) of this subsection (or any person on behalf of such an alien) may file a petition with the Attorney General for classification under section 201(b) [8 U.S.C.A. § 1151(b)], 203(a)(1) [8 U.S.C.A. § 1153(a)(1)], or 203(a)(3) [8 U.S.C.A. § 1153(a)(3)], as appropriate. After an investigation of the facts of each case the Attorney General shall, if the conditions described in paragraph (2) are met, approve the petition and forward one copy to the Secretary of State.

(2) The Attorney General may approve a petition for an alien under paragraph (1) if—

(A) he has reason to believe that the alien (i) was born in Korea, Vietnam, Laos, Kampuchea, or Thailand after 1950 and before October 22, 1982, and (ii) was fathered by a United States citizen;

(B) he has received an acceptable guarantee of legal custody and financial responsibility described in paragraph (4); and

(C) in the case of an alien under eighteen years of age, (i) the alien's placement with a sponsor in the United States has been arranged by an appropriate public, private, or State child welfare agency licensed in the United States and actively involved in the intercountry placement of children and (ii) the alien's mother or guardian has in writing irrevocably released the alien for emigration.

(3) In considering petitions filed under paragraph (1), the Attorney General shall—

(A) consult with appropriate governmental officials and officials of private voluntary organizations in the country of the alien's birth in order to make the determinations described in subparagraphs (A) and (C)(ii) of paragraph 2; and

(B) consider the physical appearance of the alien and any evidence provided by the petitioner, including birth and baptismal certificates, local civil records, photographs of, and letters or proof of financial support from, a putative father who is a citizen of the United States, and the testimony of witnesses, to the extent it is relevant or probative.

(4)(A) A guarantee of legal custody and financial responsibility for an alien described in paragraph (2) must—

(i) be signed in the presence of an immigration officer or consular officer by an individual (hereinafter in this paragraph referred to as the "sponsor") who is twenty-one years of age or older, is of good moral character, and is a citizen of the United States or alien lawfully admitted for permanent residence, and

(ii) provide that the sponsor agrees **(I)** in the case of an alien under eighteen years of age, to assume legal custody for the alien after the alien's departure to the United States and until the alien becomes eighteen years of age, in accordance with the laws of the State where the alien and the sponsor will reside, and **(II)** to furnish, during the five-year period beginning on the date of the alien's acquiring the status of an alien lawfully admitted for permanent residence, or during the period beginning on the date of the alien's acquiring the status of an alien lawfully admitted for permanent residence and ending on the date on which the alien becomes twenty-one years of age, whichever period is longer, such financial support as is necessary to maintain the family in the United States of which the alien is a member at a level equal to at least 125 per centum of the current official poverty line (as established by the Director of the Office of Management and Budget, under section 9902(2) of Title 42 and as revised by the Secretary of Health and Human Services under the second and third sentences of such section) for a family of the same size as the size of the alien's family.

(B) A guarantee of legal custody and financial responsibility described in subparagraph (A) may be enforced with respect to an alien against his sponsor in a civil suit brought by the Attorney General in the United States district court for the district in which the sponsor resides, except that a sponsor or his estate shall not be liable under such a guarantee if the sponsor dies or is adjudicated a bankrupt under Title 11.

(g) Restrictions on petitions based on marriages entered while in exclusion or deportation proceedings

Notwithstanding subsection (a), except as provided in section 245(e)(3) [8 U.S.C.A. § 1255(e)(3)], a petition may not be approved to grant an alien immediate relative status or preference status by reason of a marriage which was entered into during the period described in section 245(e)(2) [8 U.S.C.A. § 1255(e)(2)], until the alien has resided outside the United States for a 2–year period beginning after the date of the marriage.

(h) Survival of rights to petition

The legal termination of a marriage may not be the sole basis for revocation under section 205 [8 U.S.C.A. § 1155] of a petition filed under subsection (a)(1)(A)(iii) or a petition filed under subsection (a)(1)(B)(ii) pursuant to conditions described in subsection (a)(1)(A)(iii)(I).

(i) Professional athletes

(1) In general

A petition under subsection (a)(4)(D) for classification of a professional athlete shall remain valid for the athlete after the athlete changes employers, if the new employer is a team in the same sport as the team which was the employer who filed the petition.

(2) Definition

For purposes of paragraph (1), the term "professional athlete" means an individual who is employed as an athlete by—

(A) a team that is a member of an association of 6 or more professional sports teams whose total combined revenues exceed $10,000,000 per year, if the association governs the conduct of its members and regulates the contests and exhibitions in which its member teams regularly engage; or

(B) any minor league team that is affiliated with such an association.

(June 27, 1952, c. 477, Title II, ch. 1, § 204, 66 Stat. 179; Oct. 24, 1962, Pub.L. 87–885, § 3, 76 Stat. 1247; Oct. 3, 1965, Pub.L. 89–236, § 4, 79 Stat. 915; Oct. 20, 1976, Pub.L. 94–571, § 7(b), 90 Stat. 2706; Oct. 5, 1978, Pub.L. 95–417, §§ 2, 3, 92 Stat. 917; Oct. 19, 1980, Pub.L. 96–470, Title II, § 207, 94 Stat. 2245; Dec. 29, 1981, Pub.L. 97–116, §§ 3, 18(d), 95 Stat. 1611, 1620; Oct. 22, 1982, Pub.L. 97–359, 96 Stat. 1716; Nov. 10, 1986, Pub.L. 99–639, §§ 2(c), 4(a), 5(b), 100 Stat. 3541, 3543; Oct. 24, 1988, Pub. L. 100–525, § 9(g), 102 Stat. 2620; Nov. 29, 1990, Pub.L. 101–649, Title I, § 162(b), Title VII, § 702(b), 104 Stat. 5010, 5086; Dec. 12, 1991, Pub.L. 102–232, Title III, §§ 302(e)(4),(5), 308(b), 309(b)(5), 105 Stat. 1745, 1746, 1757, 1758; Sept. 13, 1994, Pub.L. 103–322, Title IV, § 40701(a), (b)(1), (c), 108 Stat. 1953, 1954; Oct. 25, 1994, Pub.L. 103–416, Title II, § 219(b)(2), 108 Stat. 4316; Sept. 30, 1996, Pub.L. 104–208, Div. C, Title III, § 308(e)(1)(A), (f)(2)(A), Title VI, § 624(b), 110 Stat. 3009–619, 3009–621, 3009–699.)

§ 205. Revocation of approval of petitions; notice of revocation; effective date [8 U.S.C.A. § 1155]

The Attorney General may, at any time, for what he deems to be good and sufficient cause, revoke the approval of any petition approved by him under section 204 [8 U.S.C.A. § 1154]. Such revocation shall be effective as of the date of approval of any such petition. In no case, however, shall such revocation have effect unless there is mailed to the petitioner's last known address a notice of the revocation and unless notice of the revocation is communicated through the Secretary of State to the beneficiary of the petition before such beneficiary commences his journey to the United States. If notice of revocation is not so given, and the beneficiary applies for admission to the United States, his admissibility shall be determined in the manner provided for by sections 235 [8 U.S.C.A. § 1225] and 240 [8 U.S.C.A. § 1229a].

(June 27, 1952, c. 477, Title II, ch. 1, § 205, 66 Stat. 180; Sept. 22, 1959, Pub.L. 86–363, § 5(a), (b), 73 Stat. 644; Sept. 26, 1961, Pub.L. 87–301, §§ 3, 10, 75 Stat. 650, 654; Oct. 3, 1965, Pub.L. 89–236, § 5, 79 Stat. 916; Sept. 30, 1996, Pub.L. 104–208, Div. C, Title III, § 308(g)(3)(A), 110 Stat. 3009–622.)

§ 206. Unused immigrant visas [8 U.S.C.A. § 1156]

If an immigrant having an immigrant visa is denied admission to the United States and removed, or does not apply for admission before the expiration of the validity of his visa, or if an alien having an immigrant visa issued to him as a preference immigrant is found not to be a preference immigrant, an immigrant visa or a preference immigrant visa, as the case may be, may be issued in lieu thereof to another qualified alien.

(June 27, 1952, c. 477, Title II, ch. 1, § 206, 66 Stat. 181; Oct. 3, 1965, Pub.L. 89–236, § 6, 79 Stat. 916; Sept. 30, 1996, Pub.L. 104–208, Div. C, Title III, § 308(d)(4)(D), 110 Stat. 3009–618.)

§ 207. Annual admission of refugees and admission of emergency situation refugees [8 U.S.C.A. § 1157]

(a) Maximum number of admissions; increases for humanitarian concerns; allocations

(1) Except as provided in subsection (b), the number of refugees who may be admitted under this section in fiscal year 1980, 1981, or 1982, may not exceed fifty thousand unless the President determines, before the beginning of the fiscal year and after appropriate consultation (as defined in subsection (e)), that admission of a specific number of refugees in excess of such number is justified by humanitarian concerns or is otherwise in the national interest.

(2) Except as provided in subsection (b), the number of refugees who may be admitted under this section in any fiscal year after fiscal year 1982 shall be such number as the President determines, before the beginning of the fiscal year and after appropriate consultation, is justified by humanitarian concerns or is otherwise in the national interest.

(3) Admissions under this subsection shall be allocated among refugees of special humanitarian concern to the United States in accordance with a determination made by the President after appropriate consultation.

(4) In the determination made under this subsection for each fiscal year (beginning with fiscal year 1992), the President shall enumerate, with the respective number of refugees so determined, the number of aliens who were granted asylum in the previous year.

(5) For any fiscal year, not more than a total of 1,000 refugees may be admitted under this subsection or granted asylum under section 208 [8 U.S.C.A. § 1158] pursuant to a determination under the third sentence of section 101(a)(42) [8 U.S.C.A. § 1101(a)(42)] (relating to persecution for resistance to coercive population control methods).

(b) Determinations by President respecting number of admissions for humanitarian concerns

If the President determines, after appropriate consultation, that (1) an unforeseen emergency refugee situation exists, (2) the admission of certain refugees in response to the emergency refugee situation is justified by grave humanitarian concerns or is otherwise in the national interest, and (3) the admission to the United States of these refugees cannot be accomplished under subsection (a), the President may fix a number of refugees to be admitted to the United States during the succeeding period (not to exceed twelve months) in response to the emergency refugee situation and such admissions shall be allocated among refugees of special humanitarian concern to the United States in accordance with a determination made by the President after the appropriate consultation provided under this subsection.

(c) Admission by Attorney General of refugees; criteria; admission status of spouse or child; applicability of other statutory requirements; termination of refugee status of alien, spouse or child

(1) Subject to the numerical limitations established pursuant to subsections (a) and (b), the Attorney General may, in the Attorney General's discretion and pursuant to such regulations as the Attorney General may prescribe, admit any refugee who is not firmly resettled in any foreign country, is determined to be of special humanitarian concern to the United States, and is admissible except as otherwise provided under paragraph (3) as an immigrant under this Act.

(2) A spouse or child (as defined in section 101(b)(1)(A), (B), (C), (D), or (E) [8 U.S.C.A. § 1101(b)(1)(A), (B), (C), (D), or (E)]) of any refugee who qualifies for admission under paragraph (1) shall, if not otherwise entitled to admission under paragraph (1) and if not a person described in the second sentence of section 101(a)(42) [8 U.S.C.A. § 1101(a)(42)], be entitled to the same admission status as such refugee if accompanying, or following to join, such refugee and if the spouse or child is admissible (except as otherwise provided under paragraph (3)) as an immigrant under this Act. Upon the spouse's or child's admission to the United States, such admission shall be charged against the numerical limitation established in accordance with the appropriate subsection under which the refugee's admission is charged.

(3) The provisions of paragraphs (4), (5), and (7)(A) of section 212(a) [8 U.S.C.A. § 1182(a)] shall not be applicable to any alien seeking admission to the United States under this subsection, and the Attorney General may waive any other provision of such section (other than paragraph (2)(C) or subparagraph (A), (B), (C), or (E) of paragraph (3)) with respect to such an alien for humanitarian purposes, to assure family unity, or when it is otherwise in the public interest. Any such waiver by the Attorney General shall be in writing and shall be granted only on an individual basis following an investigation. The Attorney General shall provide for the annual reporting to Congress of the number of waivers granted under this paragraph in the previous fiscal year and a summary of the reasons for granting such waivers.

(4) The refugee status of any alien (and of the spouse or child of the alien) may be terminated by the Attorney General pursuant to such regulations as the Attorney General may prescribe if the Attorney General determines that the alien was not in fact a refugee within the meaning of section 101(a)(42) [8 U.S.C.A. § 1101(a)(42)] at the time of the alien's admission.

(d) Oversight reporting and consultation requirements

(1) Before the start of each fiscal year the President shall report to the Committees on the Judiciary of the House of Representatives and of the Senate regarding the foreseeable number of refugees who will be in need of resettlement during the fiscal year and the anticipated allocation of refugee admissions during the fiscal year. The President shall provide for periodic discussions between designated representatives of the President and members of such committees regarding changes in the worldwide refugee situation, the progress of refugee admissions, and the possible need for adjustments in the allocation of admissions among refugees.

(2) As soon as possible after representatives of the President initiate appropriate consultation with respect to the number of refugee admissions under subsection (a) or with respect to the admission of refugees in response to an emergency refugee situation under subsection (b), the Committees on the Judiciary of the House of Representatives and of the Senate shall cause to have printed in the Congressional Record the substance of such consultation.

(3)(A) After the President initiates appropriate consultation prior to making a determination under subsection (a), a hearing to review the proposed determination shall be held unless public disclosure of the details of the proposal would jeopardize the lives or safety of individuals.

(B) After the President initiates appropriate consultation prior to making a determination, under subsection (b), that the number of refugee admissions should be increased because of an unforeseen emergency refugee situation, to the extent that time and the nature of the emergency refugee situation permit, a hearing to review the proposal to increase refugee admissions shall be held unless public disclosure of the details of the proposal would jeopardize the lives or safety of individuals.

(e) "Appropriate consultation" defined

For purposes of this section, the term "appropriate consultation" means, with respect to the admission of refugees and allocation of refugee admissions, discussions in person by designated Cabinet-level representatives of the President with members of the Committees on the Judiciary of the Senate and of the House of Representatives to review the refugee situation or emergency refugee situation, to project the extent of possible participation of the United States therein, to discuss the reasons for believing that the proposed admission of refugees is justified by humanitarian concerns or grave humanitarian concerns or is otherwise in the national interest, and to provide such members with the following information:

(1) A description of the nature of the refugee situation.

(2) A description of the number and allocation of the refugees to be admitted and an analysis of conditions within the countries from which they came.

(3) A description of the proposed plans for their movement and resettlement and the estimated cost of their movement and resettlement.

(4) An analysis of the anticipated social, economic, and demographic impact of their admission to the United States.

(5) A description of the extent to which other countries will admit and assist in the resettlement of such refugees.

(6) An analysis of the impact of the participation of the United States in the resettlement of such refugees on the foreign policy interests of the United States.

(7) Such additional information as may be appropriate or requested by such members.

To the extent possible, information described in this subsection shall be provided at least two weeks in advance of discussions in person by designated representatives of the President with such members.

(f) Training United States officials adjudicating refugee cases

(1) The Attorney General, in consultation with the Secretary of State, shall provide all United States officials adjudicating refugee cases under this section with the same training as that provided to officers adjudicating asylum cases under section 208 [8 U.S.C.A. § 1158].

(2) Such training shall include country-specific conditions, instruction on the internationally recognized right to freedom of religion, instruction on methods of religious persecution practiced in foreign countries, and applicable distinctions within a country between the nature of and treatment of various religious practices and believers.

(June 27, 1952, c. 477, Title II, ch. 1, § 207, as added Mar. 17, 1980, Pub.L. 96–212, Title II, § 201(b), 94 Stat. 103, and amended Oct. 24, 1988, Pub.L. 100–525, § 9(h), 102 Stat. 2620; Nov. 29, 1990, Pub.L. 101–649, Title I, § 104(b), Title VI, § 603(a)(4), 104 Stat. 4985, 5082; Dec. 12, 1991, Pub.L. 102–232, Title III, § 307(*l*)(1), 105 Stat. 1756; Sept. 30, 1996, Pub.L. 104–208, Div. C, Title VI,

§ 601(b), 110 Stat. 3009–689; Oct. 27, 1998, Pub.L. 105–292, Title VI, § 602(a), 112 Stat. 2812.)

§ 208. Asylum procedure [8 U.S.C.A. § 1158]

(a) Authority to apply for asylum

(1) In general

Any alien who is physically present in the United States or who arrives in the United States (whether or not at a designated port of arrival and including an alien who is brought to the United States after having been interdicted in international or United States waters), irrespective of such alien's status, may apply for asylum in accordance with this section or, where applicable, section 235(b) [8 U.S.C.A. § 1225(b)].

(2) Exceptions

(A) Safe third country

Paragraph (1) shall not apply to an alien if the Attorney General determines that the alien may be removed, pursuant to a bilateral or multilateral agreement, to a country (other than the country of the alien's nationality or, in the case of an alien having no nationality, the country of the alien's last habitual residence) in which the alien's life or freedom would not be threatened on account of race, religion, nationality, membership in a particular social group, or political opinion, and where the alien would have access to a full and fair procedure for determining a claim to asylum or equivalent temporary protection, unless the Attorney General finds that it is in the public interest for the alien to receive asylum in the United States.

(B) Time limit

Subject to subparagraph (D), paragraph (1) shall not apply to an alien unless the alien demonstrates by clear and convincing evidence that the application has been filed within 1 year after the date of the alien's arrival in the United States.

(C) Previous asylum applications

Subject to subparagraph (D), paragraph (1) shall not apply to an alien if the alien has previously applied for asylum and had such application denied.

(D) Changed circumstances

An application for asylum of an alien may be considered, notwithstanding subparagraphs (B) and (C), if the alien demonstrates to the satisfaction of the Attorney General either the existence of changed circumstances which materially affect the applicant's eligibility for asylum or extraordinary circumstances relating to the delay in filing an application within the period specified in subparagraph (B).

(3) Limitation on judicial review

No court shall have jurisdiction to review any determination of the Attorney General under paragraph (2).

(b) Conditions for granting asylum

(1) In general

The Attorney General may grant asylum to an alien who has applied for asylum in accordance with the requirements and procedures established by the Attorney General under this section if the Attorney General determines that such alien is a refugee within the meaning of section 101(a)(42)(A) [8 U.S.C.A. § 1101(a)(42)(A)].

(2) Exceptions

(A) In general

Paragraph (1) shall not apply to an alien if the Attorney General determines that—

(i) the alien ordered, incited, assisted, or otherwise participated in the persecution of any person on account of race, religion, nationality, membership in a particular social group, or political opinion;

(ii) the alien, having been convicted by a final judgment of a particularly serious crime, constitutes a danger to the community of the United States;

(iii) there are serious reasons for believing that the alien has committed a serious nonpolitical crime outside the United States prior to the arrival of the alien in the United States;

(iv) there are reasonable grounds for regarding the alien as a danger to the security of the United States;

(v) the alien is inadmissible under subclause (I), (II), (III), or (IV) of section 212(a)(3)(B)(i) [8 U.S.C.A. § 1182(a)(3)(B)(i)] or removable under section 237(a)(4)(B) [8 U.S.C.A. § 1227(a)(4)(B)] (relating to terrorist activity), unless, in the case only of an alien inadmissible under subclause (IV) of section 212(a)(3)(B)(i) [8 U.S.C.A. § 1182(a)(3)(B)(i)], the Attorney General determines, in the Attorney General's discretion, that there are not reasonable grounds for regarding the alien as a danger to the security of the United States; or

(vi) the alien was firmly resettled in another country prior to arriving in the United States.

(B) Special rules

(i) Conviction of aggravated felony

For purposes of clause (ii) of subparagraph (A), an alien who has been convicted of an aggravated felony shall be considered to have been convicted of a particularly serious crime.

(ii) Offenses

The Attorney General may designate by regulation offenses that will be considered to be a crime described in clause (ii) or (iii) of subparagraph (A).

(C) Additional limitations

The Attorney General may by regulation establish additional limitations and conditions, consistent with this section, under which an alien shall be ineligible for asylum under paragraph (1).

(D) No judicial review

There shall be no judicial review of a determination of the Attorney General under subparagraph (A)(v).

(3) Treatment of spouse and children

A spouse or child (as defined in section 101(b)(1)(A), (B), (C), (D), or (E) [8 U.S.C.A. § 1101(b)(1)(A), (B), (C), (D), or (E)]) of an alien who is granted asylum under this subsection may, if not otherwise eligible for asylum under this section, be granted the same status as the alien if accompanying, or following to join, such alien.

(c) Asylum status

(1) In general

In the case of an alien granted asylum under subsection (b), the Attorney General—

(A) shall not remove or return the alien to the alien's country of nationality or, in the case of a person having no nationality, the country of the alien's last habitual residence;

(B) shall authorize the alien to engage in employment in the United States and provide the alien with appropriate endorsement of that authorization; and

(C) may allow the alien to travel abroad with the prior consent of the Attorney General.

(2) Termination of asylum

Asylum granted under subsection (b) does not convey a right to remain permanently in the United States, and may be terminated if the Attorney General determines that—

(A) the alien no longer meets the conditions described in subsection (b)(1) owing to a fundamental change in circumstances;

(B) the alien meets a condition described in subsection (b)(2);

(C) the alien may be removed, pursuant to a bilateral or multilateral agreement, to a country (other than the country of the alien's nationality or, in the case of an alien having no nationality, the country of the alien's last habitual residence) in which the alien's life or freedom would not be threatened on account of race, religion, nationality, membership in a particular social group, or political opinion, and where the alien is eligible to receive asylum or equivalent temporary protection;

(D) the alien has voluntarily availed himself or herself of the protection of the alien's country of nationality or, in the case of an alien having no nationality, the alien's country of last habitual residence, by returning to such country with permanent resident status or the reasonable possibility of obtaining such status with the same rights and obligations pertaining to other permanent residents of that country; or

(E) the alien has acquired a new nationality and enjoys the protection of the country of his or her new nationality.

(3) Removal when asylum is terminated

An alien described in paragraph (2) is subject to any applicable grounds of inadmissibility or deportability under section [sic] 212(a) [8 U.S.C.A. § 1182(a)] and 237(a) [8 U.S.C.A. § 1227(a)], and the alien's removal or return shall be directed by the Attorney General in accordance with sections 240 [8 U.S.C.A. § 1229a] and 241 [8 U.S.C.A. § 1231].

(d) Asylum procedure

(1) Applications

The Attorney General shall establish a procedure for the consideration of asylum applications filed under subsection (a). The Attorney General may require applicants to submit fingerprints and a photograph at such time and in such manner to be determined by regulation by the Attorney General.

(2) Employment

An applicant for asylum is not entitled to employment authorization, but such authorization may be provided under regulation by the Attorney General. An applicant who is not otherwise eligible for employment authorization shall not be granted such authorization prior to 180 days after the date of filing of the application for asylum.

(3) Fees

The Attorney General may impose fees for the consideration of an application for asylum, for employment authorization under this section, and for adjustment of status under section 209(b) [8 U.S.C.A. § 1159(b)]. Such fees shall not exceed the Attorney General's costs in adjudicating the applications. The Attorney General may provide for the assessment and payment of such fees over a period of time or by installments. Nothing in this paragraph shall be construed to require the Attorney General to charge fees for adjudication services provided to asylum applicants, or to limit the authority of the Attorney General to set adjudication and naturalization fees in accordance with section 286(m) [8 U.S.C.A. § 1356(m)].

(4) Notice of privilege of counsel and consequences of frivolous application

At the time of filing an application for asylum, the Attorney General shall—

(A) advise the alien of the privilege of being represented by counsel and of the consequences, under paragraph (6), of knowingly filing a frivolous application for asylum; and

(B) provide the alien a list of persons (updated not less often than quarterly) who have indicated their availability to represent aliens in asylum proceedings on a pro bono basis.

(5) Consideration of asylum applications

(A) Procedures

The procedure established under paragraph (1) shall provide that—

(i) asylum cannot be granted until the identity of the applicant has been checked against all appropriate records or databases maintained by the Attorney General and by the Secretary of State, including the Automated Visa Lookout System, to determine any grounds on which the alien may be inadmissible to or deportable from the United States, or ineligible to apply for or be granted asylum;

(ii) in the absence of exceptional circumstances, the initial interview or hearing on the asylum application shall commence not later than 45 days after the date an application is filed;

(iii) in the absence of exceptional circumstances, final administrative adjudication of the asylum application, not including administrative appeal, shall be completed within 180 days after the date an application is filed;

(iv) any administrative appeal shall be filed within 30 days of a decision granting or denying asylum, or within 30 days of the completion of removal proceedings before an immigration judge under section 240 [8 U.S.C.A. § 1229a], whichever is later; and

(v) in the case of an applicant for asylum who fails without prior authorization or in the absence of exceptional circumstances to appear for an interview or hearing, including a hearing under section 240 [8 U.S.C.A. § 1229a], the application may be dismissed or the applicant may be otherwise sanctioned for such failure.

(B) Additional regulatory conditions

The Attorney General may provide by regulation for any other conditions or limitations on the consideration of an application for asylum not inconsistent with this Act.

(6) Frivolous applications

If the Attorney General determines that an alien has knowingly made a frivolous application for asylum and the alien has received the notice under paragraph (4)(A), the alien shall be permanently ineligible for any benefits under this Act, effective as of the date of a final determination on such application.

(7) No private right of action

Nothing in this subsection shall be construed to create any substantive or procedural right or benefit that is legally enforceable by any party against the United States or its agencies or officers or any other person.

(June 27, 1952, c. 477, Title II, ch. 1, § 208, as added Mar. 17, 1980, Pub.L. 96–212, Title II, § 201(b), 94 Stat. 105, and amended Nov. 29, 1990, Pub.L. 101–649, Title V, § 515(a)(1), 104 Stat. 5053; Sept. 13, 1994, Pub.L. 103–322, Title XIII, § 130005(b), 108 Stat. 2028; Apr. 24, 1996, Pub.L. 104–132, Title IV, § 421(a), 110 Stat. 1270; Sept. 30, 1996, Pub.L. 104–208, Div. C, Title VI, § 604(a), 110 Stat. 3009–690.)

§ 209. Adjustment of status of refugees [8 U.S.C.A. § 1159]

(a) Criteria and procedures applicable for admission as immigrant; effect of adjustment

(1) Any alien who has been admitted to the United States under section 207 [8 U.S.C.A. § 1157]—

(A) whose admission has not been terminated by the Attorney General pursuant to such regulations as the Attorney General may prescribe,

(B) who has been physically present in the United States for at least one year, and

(C) who has not acquired permanent resident status,

shall, at the end of such year period, return or be returned to the custody of the Service for inspection and examination for admission to the United States as an immigrant in accordance with the provisions of sections 235 [8 U.S.C.A. § 1225], 240 [8 U.S.C.A. § 1229a], and 241 [8 U.S.C.A. § 1231].

(2) Any alien who is found upon inspection and examination by an immigration officer pursuant to paragraph (1) or after a hearing before an immigration judge to be admissible (except as otherwise provided under subsection (c)) as an immigrant under this Act at the time of the alien's inspection and examination shall, notwithstanding any numerical limitation specified in this Act, be regarded as lawfully admitted to the United States for permanent residence as of the date of such alien's arrival into the United States.

(b) Maximum number of adjustments; recordkeeping

Not more than 10,000 of the refugee admissions authorized under section 207(a) [8 U.S.C.A. § 1157(a)] in any fiscal year may be made available by the Attorney General, in the Attorney General's discretion and under such regulations as the Attorney General may prescribe, to adjust to the status of an alien lawfully admitted for permanent residence the status of any alien granted asylum who—

(1) applies for such adjustment,

(2) has been physically present in the United States for at least one year after being granted asylum,

(3) continues to be a refugee within the meaning of section 101(a)(42)(A) [8 U.S.C.A. § 1101(a)(42)(A)] or a spouse or child of such a refugee,

(4) is not firmly resettled in any foreign country, and

(5) is admissible (except as otherwise provided under subsection (c)) as an immigrant under this Act at the time of examination for adjustment of such alien.

Upon approval of an application under this subsection, the Attorney General shall establish a record of the alien's admission for lawful permanent residence as of the date one year before the date of the approval of the application.

(c) Applicability of other Federal statutory requirements

The provisions of paragraphs (4), (5), and (7)(A) of section 212(a) [8 U.S.C.A. § 1182(a)] shall not be applicable to any alien seeking adjustment of status under this section, and the Attorney General may waive any other provision of such section (other than paragraph (2)(C) or subparagraph (A), (B), (C), or (E) of paragraph (3)) with respect to such an alien for humanitarian purposes, to assure family unity, or when it is otherwise in the public interest.

(June 27, 1952, c. 477, Title II, ch. 1, § 209, as added Mar. 17, 1980, Pub.L. 96–212, Title II, § 201(b), 94 Stat. 105, and amended Nov. 29, 1990, Pub.L. 101–649, Title I, § 104(a)(1), Title VI, § 603(a)(4), 104 Stat. 4985, 5082; Dec. 12, 1991, Pub.L. 102–232, Title III, § 307(*l*)(1), 105 Stat. 1756; Sept. 30, 1996, Pub.L. 104–208, Div. C, Title III, §§ 308(g)(3)(A), (4)(A), 371(b)(2), 110 Stat. 3009–622, 3009–645.)

§ 210. Special agricultural workers [8 U.S.C.A. § 1160]

(a) Lawful residence

(1) In general

The Attorney General shall adjust the status of an alien to that of an alien lawfully admitted for temporary residence if the Attorney General determines that the alien meets the following requirements:

(A) Application period

The alien must apply for such adjustment during the 18–month period beginning on the first day of the seventh month that begins after November 6, 1986.

(B) Performance of Seasonal Agricultural Services and residence in the United States

The alien must establish that he has—

(i) resided in the United States, and

(ii) performed seasonal agricultural services in the United States for at least 90 man-days,

during the 12–month period ending on May 1, 1986. For purposes of the previous sentence, performance of seasonal agricultural services in the United States for more than one employer on any one day shall be counted as performance of services for only 1 man-day.

(C) Admissible as immigrant

The alien must establish that he is admissible to the United States as an immigrant, except as otherwise provided under subsection (c)(2).

(2) Adjustment to permanent residence

The Attorney General shall adjust the status of any alien provided lawful temporary resident status under paragraph (1) to that of an alien lawfully admitted for permanent residence on the following date:

(A) Group 1

Subject to the numerical limitation established under subparagraph (C), in the case of an alien who has established, at the time of application for temporary residence under paragraph (1), that the alien performed seasonal agricultural services in the United States for at least 90 man-days during each of the 12–month periods ending on May 1, 1984, 1985, and 1986, the adjustment shall occur on the first day after the end of the one-year period that begins on the later of **(I)** the date the alien was granted such temporary resident status, or **(II)** the day after the last day of the application period described in paragraph (1)(A).

(B) Group 2

In the case of aliens to which subparagraph (A) does not apply, the adjustment shall occur on the day after the last day of the two-year period that begins on the later of **(I)** the date the alien was granted such temporary resident status, or **(II)** the day after the last day of the application period described in paragraph (1)(A).

(C) Numerical limitation

Subparagraph (A) shall not apply to more than 350,000 aliens. If more than 350,000 aliens meet the requirements of such subparagraph, such subparagraph shall apply to the 350,000 aliens whose applications for adjustment were first filed under paragraph (1) and subparagraph (B) shall apply to the remaining aliens.

(3) Termination of temporary residence

(A) During the period of temporary resident status granted an alien under paragraph (1), the Attorney General may terminate such status only upon a determination under this Act that the alien is deportable.

(B) Before any alien becomes eligible for adjustment of status under paragraph (2), the Attorney General may deny adjustment to permanent status and provide for termination of the temporary resident status granted such alien under paragraph (1) if—

(i) the Attorney General finds by a preponderance of the evidence that the adjustment to temporary resident status was the result of fraud or willful misrepresentation as set out in section 212(a)(6)(C)(i) [8 U.S.C.A. § 1182(a)(6)(C)(i)], or

(ii) the alien commits an act that (I) makes the alien inadmissible to the United States as an immigrant, except as provided under subsection (c)(2), or (II) is convicted of a felony or 3 or more misdemeanors committed in the United States.

(4) Authorized travel and employment during temporary residence

During the period an alien is in lawful temporary resident status granted under this subsection, the alien has the right to travel abroad (including commutation from a residence abroad) and shall be granted authorization to engage in employment in the United States and shall be provided an "employment authorized" endorsement or other appropriate work permit, in the same manner as for aliens lawfully admitted for permanent residence.

(5) In general

Except as otherwise provided in this subsection, an alien who acquires the status of an alien lawfully admitted for temporary residence under paragraph (1), such status not having changed, is considered to be an alien lawfully admitted for permanent residence (as described in section 101(a)(20) [8 U.S.C.A. § 1101(a)(20)]), other than under any provision of the immigration laws.

(b) Applications for adjustment of status

(1) To whom may be made

(A) Within the United States

The Attorney General shall provide that applications for adjustment of status under subsection (a) may be filed—

(i) with the Attorney General, or

(ii) with a designated entity (designated under paragraph (2)), but only if the applicant consents to the forwarding of the application to the Attorney General.

(B) Outside the United States

The Attorney General, in cooperation with the Secretary of State, shall provide a procedure whereby an alien may apply for adjustment of status under subsection (a)(1) at an appropriate consular office outside the United States. If the alien otherwise qualifies for such adjustment, the Attorney General shall provide such documentation of authorization to enter the United States and to have the alien's status adjusted upon entry as may be necessary to carry out the provisions of this section.

(2) Designation of entities to receive applications

For purposes of receiving applications under this section, the Attorney General—

(A) shall designate qualified voluntary organizations and other qualified State, local community, farm labor organizations, and associations of agricultural employers, and

(B) may designate such other persons as the Attorney General determines are qualified and have substantial experience, demonstrated competence, and traditional long-term involvement in the preparation and submittal of applications for adjustment of status under section 209 [8 U.S.C.A. § 1159]or 245 [8 U.S.C.A. § 1255], Public Law 89–732 [8 U.S.C.A. § 1255 note], or Public Law 95–145.

(3) Proof of eligibility

(A) In general

An alien may establish that he meets the requirement of subsection (a)(1)(B)(ii) through government employment records, records supplied by employers or collective bargaining organizations, and such other reliable documentation as the alien may provide. The Attorney General shall establish special procedures to credit properly work in cases in which an alien was employed under an assumed name.

(B) Documentation of work history

(i) An alien applying for adjustment of status under subsection (a)(1) has the burden of proving by a preponderance of the evidence that the alien has worked the requisite number of man-days (as required under subsection (a)(1)(B)(ii)).

(ii) If an employer or farm labor contractor employing such an alien has kept proper and adequate records respecting such employment, the alien's burden of proof under clause (i) may be met by securing timely production of those records under regulations to be promulgated by the Attorney General.

(iii) An alien can meet such burden of proof if the alien establishes that the alien has in fact performed the work described in subsection (a)(1)(B)(ii) by producing sufficient evidence to show the extent of that employment as a matter of just and reasonable inference. In such a case, the burden then shifts to the Attorney General to disprove the alien's evidence with a showing which negates the reasonableness of the inference to be drawn from the evidence.

(4) Treatment of applications by designated entities

Each designated entity must agree to forward to the Attorney General applications filed with it in accordance with paragraph (1)(A)(ii) but not to forward to the Attorney General applications filed with it unless the applicant has consented to such forwarding. No such entity may make a determination required by this section to be made by the Attorney General.

(5) Limitation on access to information

Files and records prepared for purposes of this section by designated entities operating under this section are confidential and the Attorney General and the Service shall not have access to such files or records relating to an alien without the consent of the alien, except as allowed by a court order issued pursuant to paragraph (6) of this subsection.

(6) Confidentiality of information

(A) In general

Except as provided in this paragraph, neither the Attorney General, nor any other official or employee of the Department of Justice, or bureau or agency thereof, may—

(i) use the information furnished by the applicant pursuant to an application filed under this section for any purpose other than to make a determination on the application, including a determination under subsection (a)(3)(B), or for enforcement of paragraph (7);

(ii) make any publication whereby the information furnished by any particular individual can be identified; or

(iii) permit anyone other than the sworn officers and employees of the Department or bureau or agency or, with respect to applications filed with a designated entity, that designated entity, to examine individual applications.

(B) Required disclosures

The Attorney General shall provide information furnished under this section, and any other information derived from such furnished information, to a duly recognized law enforcement entity in connection with a criminal investigation or prosecution, when such information is requested in writing by such entity, or to an official coroner for purposes of affirmatively identifying a deceased individual (whether or not such individual is deceased as a result of a crime).

(C) Construction

(i) In general

Nothing in this paragraph shall be construed to limit the use, or release, for immigration enforcement purposes or law enforcement purposes of information contained in files or records of the Service pertaining to an application filed under this section, other than information furnished by an applicant pursuant to the application, or any other information derived from the application, that is not available from any other source.

(ii) Criminal convictions

Information concerning whether the applicant has at any time been convicted of a crime may be used or released for immigration enforcement or law enforcement purposes.

(D) Crime

Whoever knowingly uses, publishes, or permits information to be examined in violation of this paragraph shall be fined not more than $10,000.

(7) Penalties for false statements in applications

(A) Criminal penalty

Whoever—

(i) files an application for adjustment of status under this section and knowingly and willfully falsifies, conceals, or covers up a material fact or makes any false, fictitious, or fraudulent statements or representations, or makes or uses any false writing or document knowing the same to contain any false, fictitious, or fraudulent statement or entry, or

(ii) creates or supplies a false writing or document for use in making such an application, shall be fined in accordance with Title 18, or imprisoned not more than five years, or both.

(B) Exclusion

An alien who is convicted of a crime under subparagraph (A) shall be considered to be inadmissible to the United States on the ground described in section 212(a)(6)(C)(i) [8 U.S.C.A. § 1182(a)(6)(C)(i)].

(c) Waiver of numerical limitations and certain grounds for exclusion

(1) Numerical limitations do not apply

The numerical limitations of sections 201 [8 U.S.C.A. § 1151] and 202 [8 U.S.C.A. § 1152] shall not apply to the adjustment of aliens to lawful permanent resident status under this section.

(2) Waiver of grounds for exclusion

In the determination of an alien's admissibility under subsection (a)(1)(C)—

(A) Grounds of exclusion not applicable

The provisions of paragraphs (5) and (7)(A) of section 212(a) [8 U.S.C.A. § 1182(a)] shall not apply.

(B) Waiver of other grounds

(i) In general

Except as provided in clause (ii), the Attorney General may waive any other provision of section 212(a) [8 U.S.C.A. § 1182(a)] in the case of individual aliens for humanitarian purposes, to assure family unity, or when it is otherwise in the public interest.

(ii) Grounds that may not be waived

The following provisions of section 212(a) [8 U.S.C.A. § 1182(a)] may not be waived by the Attorney General under clause (i):

(I) Paragraphs (2)(A) and (2)(B) (relating to criminals).

(II) Paragraph (4) (relating to aliens likely to become public charges).

(III) Paragraph (2)(C) (relating to drug offenses), except for so much of such paragraph as relates to a single offense of simple possession of 30 grams or less of marihuana.

(IV) Paragraph (3) (relating to security and related grounds), other than subparagraph (E) thereof.

(V) Omitted

(C) Special rule for determination of public charge

An alien is not ineligible for adjustment of status under this section due to being inadmissible under section 212(a)(4) [8 U.S.C.A. § 1182(a)(4)] if the alien demonstrates a history of employment in the United States evidencing self-support without reliance on public cash assistance.

(d) Temporary stay of exclusion or deportation and work authorization for certain applicants

(1) Before application period

The Attorney General shall provide that in the case of an alien who is apprehended before the beginning of the application period described in subsection (a)(1) and who can establish a nonfrivolous case of eligibility to have his status adjusted under subsection (a) (but for the fact that he may not apply for such adjustment until the beginning of such period), until the alien has had the opportunity during the first 30 days of the application period to complete the filing of an application for adjustment, the alien—

(A) may not be excluded or deported, and

(B) shall be granted authorization to engage in employment in the United States and be provided an "employment authorized" endorsement or other appropriate work permit.

(2) During application period

The Attorney General shall provide that in the case of an alien who presents a nonfrivolous application for adjustment of status under subsection (a) during the application period, and until a final determination on the application has been made in accordance with this section, the alien—

(A) may not be excluded or deported, and

(B) shall be granted authorization to engage in employment in the United States and be provided an "employment authorized" endorsement or other appropriate work permit.

(3) Use of application fees to offset program costs

No application fees collected by the Service pursuant to this subsection may be used by the Service to offset the costs of the special agricultural worker legalization program until the Service implements the program consistent with the statutory mandate as follows:

(A) During the application period described in subsection (a)(1)(A) the Service may grant temporary admission to the United States, work authorization, and provide an "employment authorized" endorsement or other appropriate work permit to any alien who presents a preliminary application for adjustment of status under subsection (a) at a designated port of entry on the southern land border. An alien who does not enter through a port of entry is subject to deportation and removal as otherwise provided in this Act.

(B) During the application period described in subsection (a)(1)(A) any alien who has filed an application for adjustment of status within the United States as provided in subsection (b)(1)(A) pursuant to the provision of 8 CFR section 210.1(j) is subject to paragraph (2) of this subsection.

(C) A preliminary application is defined as a fully completed and signed application with fee and photographs which contains specific information concerning the performance of qualifying employment in the United States and the documentary evidence which the applicant intends to submit as proof of such employment. The applicant must be otherwise admissible to the United States and must establish to the satisfaction of the examining officer during an interview that his or her claim to eligibility for special agriculture worker status is credible.

(e) Administrative and judicial review

(1) Administrative and judicial review

There shall be no administrative or judicial review of a determination respecting an application for adjustment of status under this section except in accordance with this subsection.

(2) Administrative review

(A) Single level of administrative appellate review

The Attorney General shall establish an appellate authority to provide for a single level of administrative appellate review of such a determination.

(B) Standard for review

Such administrative appellate review shall be based solely upon the administrative record established at the time of the determination on the application and upon such additional or newly discovered evidence as may not have been available at the time of the determination.

(3) Judicial review

(A) Limitation to review of exclusion or deportation

There shall be judicial review of such a denial only in the judicial review of an order of exclusion or deportation under section 106 [8 U.S.C.A. § 1105a] (as in effect before October 1, 1996).

(B) Standard for judicial review

Such judicial review shall be based solely upon the administrative record established at the time of the review by the appellate authority and the findings of fact and determinations contained in such record shall be conclusive unless the applicant can establish abuse of discretion or that the findings are directly contrary to clear and convincing facts contained in the record considered as a whole.

(f) Temporary disqualification of newly legalized aliens from receiving aid to families with dependent children

During the five-year period beginning on the date an alien was granted lawful temporary resident status under subsection (a), and notwithstanding any other provision of law, the alien is not eligible for aid under a State plan approved under part A of title IV of the Social Security Act [42 U.S.C.A. § 601 et seq.]. Notwithstanding the previous sentence, in the case of an alien who would be eligible for aid under a State plan approved under part A of title IV of the Social Security Act but for the previous sentence, the provisions of paragraph (3) of section 245A(h) [8 U.S.C.A. § 1255a(h)] shall apply in the same manner as they apply with respect to paragraph (1) of such section and, for this purpose, any reference in section 245A(h) [8 U.S.C.A. § 1255a(h)] to paragraph (1) is deemed a reference to the previous sentence.

(g) Treatment of special agricultural workers

For all purposes (subject to subsections (a)(5) and (f)) an alien whose status is adjusted under this section to that of an alien lawfully admitted for permanent residence, such status not having changed, shall be considered to be an alien lawfully admitted for permanent residence (within the meaning of section 101(a)(20) [8 U.S.C.A. § 1101(a)(20)]).

(h) "Seasonal agricultural services" defined

In this section, the term "seasonal agricultural services" means the performance of field work related to planting, cultural practices, cultivating, growing and harvesting of fruits and vegetables of every kind and other perishable commodities, as defined in regulations by the Secretary of Agriculture.

(June 27, 1952, c. 477, Title II, ch. 1, § 210, as added Nov. 6, 1986, Pub.L. 99–603, Title III, § 302(a)(1), 100 Stat. 3417, and amended Dec. 22, 1987, Pub.L. 100–202, § 101(a) [Title II, § 211], 101 Stat. 1329–18; Oct. 24, 1988, Pub. L. 100–525, § 2(m), 102 Stat. 2613; Dec. 18, 1989, Pub.L. 101–238, § 4, 103 Stat. 2103; Nov. 29, 1990, Pub.L. 101–649, Title VI, § 603(a)(5), 104 Stat. 5082; Dec. 12, 1991, Pub.L. 102–232, Title III, §§ 307(j), 309(b)(6), 105 Stat. 1756, 1758; Oct. 25, 1994, Pub.L. 103–416, Title II, § 219(d), (z)(7), 108 Stat. 4316, 4318; Apr. 24, 1996, Pub.L. 104–132, Title IV, § 431(b), 110 Stat. 1273; Aug. 22, 1996, Pub.L. 104–193, Title I, § 110(s)(1), 110 Stat. 2175; Sept. 30, 1996, Pub.L. 104–208, Div. C, Title III, §§ 308(g)(2)(B), 384(d)(1), Title VI, § 623(b), 110 Stat. 3009–622, 3009–653, 3009–697.)

CHAPTER II—ADMISSION QUALIFICATIONS FOR ALIENS; TRAVEL CONTROL OF CITIZENS AND ALIENS

§ 211. Admission of immigrants into the United States [8 U.S.C.A. § 1181]

(a) Documents required; admission under quotas before June 30, 1968

Except as provided in subsection (b) and subsection (c) no immigrant shall be admitted into the United States unless at the time of application for admission he **(1)** has a valid unexpired immigrant visa or was born subsequent to the issuance of such visa of the accompanying parent, and **(2)** presents a valid unexpired passport or other suitable travel document, or document of identity and nationality, if such document is required under the regulations issued by the Attorney General. With respect to immigrants to be admitted under quotas of quota areas prior to June 30, 1968, no immigrant visa shall be deemed valid unless the immigrant is properly chargeable to the quota area under the quota of which the visa is issued.

(b) Readmission without required documents; Attorney General's discretion

Notwithstanding the provisions of section 212(a)(7)(A) [8 U.S.C.A. § 1182(a)(7)(A)] in such cases or in such classes of cases and under such conditions as may be by regulations prescribed, returning resident immigrants, defined in section 101(a)(27)(A) [8 U.S.C.A. § 1101(a)(27)(A)], who are otherwise admissible may be readmitted to the United States by the Attorney General in his discretion without being required to obtain a passport, immigrant visa, reentry permit or other documentation.

(c) Nonapplicability to aliens admitted as refugees

The provisions of subsection (a) shall not apply to an alien whom the Attorney General admits to the United States under section 207 [8 U.S.C.A. § 1157].

(June 27, 1952, c. 477, Title II, ch. 2, § 211, 66 Stat. 181; Pub. L. 89–236, § 9, Oct. 3, 1965, 79 Stat. 917; Pub. L. 94–571, § 7(c), Oct. 20, 1976, 90 Stat. 2706; Pub. L. 96–212, Title II, § 202, Mar. 17, 1980, 94 Stat. 106; Pub.L. 101–649, Title VI, § 603(a)(7), Nov. 29, 1990, 104 Stat. 5083.)

§ 212. Excludable aliens [8 U.S.C.A. § 1182]

(a) Classes of aliens ineligible for visas or admission

Except as otherwise provided in this Act, aliens who are inadmissible under the following paragraphs are ineligible to receive visas and ineligible to be admitted to the United States:

(1) Health-related grounds

(A) In general

Any alien—

(i) who is determined (in accordance with regulations prescribed by the Secretary of Health and Human Services) to have a communicable disease of public health significance, which shall include infection with the etiologic agent for acquired immune deficiency syndrome,

(ii) except as provided in subparagraph (C), who seeks admission as an immigrant, or who seeks adjustment of status to the status of an alien lawfully admitted for permanent residence, and who has failed to present documentation of having received vaccination against vaccine-preventable diseases, which shall include at least the following diseases: mumps, measles, rubella, polio, tetanus and diphtheria toxoids, pertussis, influenza type B and hepatitis B, and any other vaccinations against vaccine-preventable diseases recommended by the Advisory Committee for Immunization Practices,

(iii) who is determined (in accordance with regulations prescribed by the Secretary of Health and Human Services in consultation with the Attorney General)—

pose threat to

(I) to have a physical or mental disorder and behavior associated with the disorder that may pose, or has posed, a threat to the property, safety, or welfare of the alien or others, or

(II) to have had a physical or mental disorder and a history of behavior associated with the disorder, which behavior has posed a threat to the property, safety, or welfare of the alien or others and which behavior is likely to recur or to lead to other harmful behavior, or

(iv) who is determined (in accordance with regulations prescribed by the Secretary of Health and Human Services) to be a drug abuser or addict,

is inadmissible.

(B) Waiver authorized

For provision authorizing waiver of certain clauses of subparagraph (A), see subsection (g).

(C) Exception from immunization requirement for adopted children 10 years of age or younger

Clause (ii) of subparagraph (A) shall not apply to a child who—

(i) is 10 years of age or younger,

(ii) is described in section 101(b)(1)(F) [8 U.S.C.A. § 1101(b)(1)(F)], and

(iii) is seeking an immigrant visa as an immediate relative under section 201(b) [8 U.S.C.A. § 1151(b)],

if, prior to the admission of the child, an adoptive parent or prospective adoptive parent of the child, who has sponsored the child for admission as an immediate relative, has executed an affidavit stating that the parent is aware of the provisions of subparagraph (A)(ii) and will ensure that, within 30 days of the child's admission, or at the earliest time that is medically appropriate, the child will receive the vaccinations identified in such subparagraph.

(2) Criminal and related grounds

(A) Conviction of certain crimes

(i) In general

Except as provided in clause (ii), any alien convicted of, or who admits having committed, or who admits committing acts which constitute the essential elements of—

(I) a crime involving moral turpitude (other than a purely political offense) or an attempt or conspiracy to commit such a crime, or

(II) a violation of (or a conspiracy or attempt to violate) any law or regulation of a State, the United States, or a foreign country relating to a controlled substance (as defined in section 802 of Title 21),

is inadmissible.

(ii) Exception

Clause (i)(I) shall not apply to an alien who committed only one crime if—

(I) the crime was committed when the alien was under 18 years of age, and the crime was committed (and the alien released from any confinement to a prison or correctional institution imposed for the crime) more than 5 years before the date of application for a visa or other documentation and the date of application for admission to the United States, or

(II) the maximum penalty possible for the crime of which the alien was convicted (or which the alien admits having committed or of which the acts that the alien admits having committed constituted the essential elements) did not exceed imprisonment for one year and, if the alien was convicted of such crime, the alien was not sentenced to a term of imprisonment in excess of 6 months (regardless of the extent to which the sentence was ultimately executed).

(B) Multiple criminal convictions

Any alien convicted of 2 or more offenses (other than purely political offenses), regardless of whether the conviction was in a single trial or whether the offenses arose from a single scheme of misconduct and regardless of whether the offenses involved moral turpitude, for which the aggregate sentences to confinement were 5 years or more is inadmissible.

(C) Controlled substance traffickers

Any alien who the consular officer or the Attorney General knows or has reason to believe—

(i) is or has been an illicit trafficker in any controlled substance or in any listed chemical (as defined in section 102 of the Controlled Substances Act (21 U.S.C. 802)), or is or has been a knowing aider, abettor, assister, conspirator, or colluder with others in the illicit trafficking in any such controlled or listed substance or chemical, or endeavored to do so; or

(ii) is the spouse, son, or daughter of an alien inadmissible under clause (i), has, within the previous 5 years, obtained any financial or other benefit from the illicit activity of that alien, and knew or reasonably should have known that the financial or other benefit was the product of such illicit activity,

is inadmissible.

(D) Prostitution and commercialized vice

Any alien who—

(i) is coming to the United States solely, principally, or incidentally to engage in prostitution, or has engaged in prostitution within 10 years of the date of application for a visa, admission, or adjustment of status,

(ii) directly or indirectly procures or attempts to procure, or (within 10 years of the date of application for a visa, admission, or adjustment of status) procured or attempted to procure or to import, prostitutes or persons for the purpose of prostitution, or receives or (within such 10–year period) received, in whole or in part, the proceeds of prostitution, or

(iii) is coming to the United States to engage in any other unlawful commercialized vice, whether or not related to prostitution,

is inadmissible.

(E) Certain aliens involved in serious criminal activity who have asserted immunity from prosecution

Any alien—

(i) who has committed in the United States at any time a serious criminal offense (as defined in section 101(h) [8 U.S.C.A. § 1101(h)]),

·committed crime

(ii) for whom immunity from criminal jurisdiction was exercised with respect to that offense,

·immune from crim. jurisd.

(iii) who as a consequence of the offense and exercise of immunity has departed from the United States, and

·left U.S. as consequence

(iv) who has not subsequently submitted fully to the jurisdiction of the court in the United States having jurisdiction with respect to that offense,

·not later submitted to jurisd. of the ct. in U.S. having jurisd.

is inadmissible.

(F) Waiver authorized

For provision authorizing waiver of certain subparagraphs of this paragraph, see subsection (h).

(G) Foreign government officials who have engaged in particularly severe violations of religious freedom

Any alien who, while serving as a foreign government official, was responsible for or directly carried out, at any time during the preceding 24–month period, particularly severe violations of religious freedom, as defined in section 6402 of Title 22, and the spouse and children, if any, are inadmissible.

(3) Security and related grounds

(A) In general

Any alien who a consular officer or the Attorney General knows, or has reasonable ground to believe, seeks to enter the United States to engage solely, principally, or incidentally in—

(i) any activity (I) to violate any law of the United States relating to espionage or sabotage or (II) to violate or evade any law prohibiting the export from the United States of goods, technology, or sensitive information,

(ii) any other unlawful activity, or

(iii) any activity a purpose of which is the opposition to, or the control or overthrow of, the Government of the United States by force, violence, or other unlawful means,

is inadmissible.

(B) Terrorist activities

(i) In general

Any alien who—

(I) has engaged in a terrorist activity,

(II) a consular officer or the Attorney General knows, or has reasonable ground to believe, is engaged in or is likely to engage after entry in any terrorist activity (as defined in clause (iii)),

(III) has, under circumstances indicating an intention to cause death or serious bodily harm, incited terrorist activity,

(IV) is a representative (as defined in clause (iv)) of a foreign terrorist organization, as designated by the Secretary under section 219 [8 U.S.C.A. § 1189], or

(V) is a member of a foreign terrorist organization, as designated by the Secretary under section 219 [8 U.S.C.A. § 1189], which the alien knows or should have known is a terrorist organization

is inadmissible. An alien who is an officer, official, representative, or spokesman of the Palestine Liberation Organization is considered, for purposes of this Act, to be engaged in a terrorist activity.

(ii) Terrorist activity defined

As used in this Act, the term "terrorist activity" means any activity which is unlawful under the laws of the place where it is committed (or which, if committed in the United States, would be unlawful under the laws of the United States or any State) and which involves any of the following:

(I) The hijacking or sabotage of any conveyance (including an aircraft, vessel, or vehicle).

(II) The seizing or detaining, and threatening to kill, injure, or continue to detain, another individual in order to compel a third person (including a governmental organization) to do or abstain from doing any act as an explicit or implicit condition for the release of the individual seized or detained.

(III) A violent attack upon an internationally protected person (as defined in section 1116(b)(4) of Title 18) or upon the liberty of such a person.

(IV) An assassination.

(V) The use of any—

(a) biological agent, chemical agent, or nuclear weapon or device, or

(b) explosive or firearm (other than for mere personal monetary gain),

with intent to endanger, directly or indirectly, the safety of one or more individuals or to cause substantial damage to property.

(VI) A threat, attempt, or conspiracy to do any of the foregoing.

(iii) Engage in terrorist activity defined

As used in this Act, the term "engage in terrorist activity" means to commit, in an individual capacity or as a member of an organization, an act of terrorist activity or an act which the actor knows, or reasonably should know, affords material support to any individual, organization, or government in conducting a terrorist activity at any time, including any of the following acts:

(I) The preparation or planning of a terrorist activity.

(II) The gathering of information on potential targets for terrorist activity.

(III) The providing of any type of material support, including a safe house, transportation, communications, funds, false documentation or identification, weapons, explosives, or training, to any individual the actor knows or has reason to believe has committed or plans to commit a terrorist activity.

(IV) The soliciting of funds or other things of value for terrorist activity or for any terrorist organization.

(V) The solicitation of any individual for membership in a terrorist organization, terrorist government, or to engage in a terrorist activity.

(iv) Representative defined

As used in this paragraph, the term "representative" includes an officer, official, or spokesman of an organization, and any person who directs, counsels, commands, or induces an organization or its members to engage in terrorist activity.

(C) Foreign policy

(i) In general

An alien whose entry or proposed activities in the United States the Secretary of State has reasonable ground to believe would have potentially serious adverse foreign policy consequences for the United States is inadmissible.

(ii) Exception for officials

An alien who is an official of a foreign government or a purported government, or who is a candidate for election to a foreign government office during the period immediately preceding the election for that office, shall not be excludable or subject to restrictions or conditions on entry into the

United States under clause (i) solely because of the alien's past, current, or expected beliefs, statements, or associations, if such beliefs, statements, or associations would be lawful within the United States.

(iii) Exception for other aliens

An alien, not described in clause (ii), shall not be excludable or subject to restrictions or conditions on entry into the United States under clause (i) because of the alien's past, current, or expected beliefs, statements, or associations, if such beliefs, statements, or associations would be lawful within the United States, unless the Secretary of State personally determines that the alien's admission would compromise a compelling United States foreign policy interest.

(iv) Notification of determinations

If a determination is made under clause (iii) with respect to an alien, the Secretary of State must notify on a timely basis the chairmen of the Committees on the Judiciary and Foreign Affairs of the House of Representatives and of the Committees on the Judiciary and Foreign Relations of the Senate of the identity of the alien and the reasons for the determination.

(D) Immigrant membership in totalitarian party

(i) In general

Any immigrant who is or has been a member of or affiliated with the Communist or any other totalitarian party (or subdivision or affiliate thereof), domestic or foreign, is inadmissible.

(ii) Exception for involuntary membership

Clause (i) shall not apply to an alien because of membership or affiliation if the alien establishes to the satisfaction of the consular officer when applying for a visa (or to the satisfaction of the Attorney General when applying for admission) that the membership or affiliation is or was involuntary, or is or was solely when under 16 years of age, by operation of law, or for purposes of obtaining employment, food rations, or other essentials of living and whether necessary for such purposes.

(iii) Exception for past membership

Clause (i) shall not apply to an alien because of membership or affiliation if the alien establishes to the satisfaction of the consular officer when applying for a visa (or to the satisfaction of the Attorney General when applying for admission) that—

(I) the membership or affiliation terminated at least—

(a) 2 years before the date of such application, or

(b) 5 years before the date of such application, in the case of an alien whose membership or affiliation was with the party controlling the government of a foreign state that is a totalitarian dictatorship as of such date, and

(II) the alien is not a threat to the security of the United States.

(iv) Exception for close family members

The Attorney General may, in the Attorney General's discretion, waive the application of clause (i) in the case of an immigrant who is the parent, spouse, son, daughter, brother, or sister of a citizen of the United States or a spouse, son, or daughter of an alien lawfully admitted for permanent residence for humanitarian purposes, to assure family unity, or when it is otherwise in the public interest if the immigrant is not a threat to the security of the United States.

(E) Participants in Nazi persecutions or genocide

(i) Participation in Nazi persecutions

Any alien who, during the period beginning on March 23, 1933, and ending on May 8, 1945, under the direction of, or in association with—

(I) the Nazi government of Germany,

(II) any government in any area occupied by the military forces of the Nazi government of Germany,

(III) any government established with the assistance or cooperation of the Nazi government of Germany, or

(IV) any government which was an ally of the Nazi government of Germany,

ordered, incited, assisted, or otherwise participated in the persecution of any person because of race, religion, national origin, or political opinion is inadmissible.

(ii) Participation in genocide

Any alien who has engaged in conduct that is defined as genocide for purposes of the International Convention on the Prevention and Punishment of Genocide is inadmissible.

Public charge

(4) Public charge

(A) In general

Any alien who, in the opinion of the consular officer at the time of application for a visa, or in the opinion of the Attorney General at the time of application for admission or adjustment of status, is likely at any time to become a public charge is inadmissible.

(B) Factors to be taken into account

(i) In determining whether an alien is inadmissible under this paragraph, the consular officer or the Attorney General shall at a minimum consider the alien's—

(I) age;

(II) health;

(III) family status;

(IV) assets, resources, and financial status; and

(V) education and skills.

(ii) In addition to the factors under clause (i), the consular officer or the Attorney General may also consider any affidavit of support under section 213A [8 U.S.C.A. § 1183a] for purposes of exclusion under this paragraph.

(C) Family-sponsored immigrants

Any alien who seeks admission or adjustment of status under a visa number issued under section 201(b)(2) [8 U.S.C.A. § 1151(b)(2)]or 203(a) [8 U.S.C.A. § 1153(a)] is inadmissible under this paragraph unless—

(i) the alien has obtained—

(I) status as a spouse or a child of a United States citizen pursuant to clause (ii), (iii), or (iv) of section 204(a)(1)(A) [8 U.S.C.A. § 1154(a)(1)(A)] or

(II) classification pursuant to clause (ii) or (iii) of section 204(a)(1)(B) [8 U.S.C.A. § 1154(a)(1)(B)]; or

(ii) the person petitioning for the alien's admission (including any additional sponsor required under section 213A(f) [8 U.S.C.A. § 1183a(f)] has executed an affidavit of support described in section 213A [8 U.S.C.A. § 1183a] with respect to such alien).

(D) Certain employment-based immigrants

Any alien who seeks admission or adjustment of status under a visa number issued under section 203(b) [8 U.S.C.A. § 1153(b)] by virtue of a classification petition filed by a relative of the alien (or by an entity in which such relative has a significant ownership interest) is inadmissible under this paragraph unless such relative has executed an affidavit of support described in section 213A [8 U.S.C.A. § 1183a] with respect to such alien.

(5) Labor certification and qualifications for certain immigrants

(A) Labor certification

(i) In general

Any alien who seeks to enter the United States for the purpose of performing skilled or unskilled labor is inadmissible, unless the Secretary of Labor has determined and certified to the Secretary of State and the Attorney General that—

(I) there are not sufficient workers who are able, willing, qualified (or equally qualified in the case of an alien described in clause (ii)) and available at the time of application for a visa and admission to the United States and at the place where the alien is to perform such skilled or unskilled labor, and

(II) the employment of such alien will not adversely affect the wages and working conditions of workers in the United States similarly employed.

(ii) Certain aliens subject to special rule

For purposes of clause (i)(I), an alien described in this clause is an alien who—

(I) is a member of the teaching profession, or

(II) has exceptional ability in the sciences or the arts.

(iii) Professional athletes

(I) In general

A certification made under clause (i) with respect to a professional athlete shall remain valid with respect to the athlete after the athlete changes employer, if the new employer is a team in the same sport as the team which employed the athlete when the athlete first applied for the certification.

(II) Definition

For purposes of subclause (I), the term "professional athlete" means an individual who is employed as an athlete by—

(aa) a team that is a member of an association of 6 or more professional sports teams whose total combined revenues exceed $10,000,000 per year, if the association governs the conduct of its members and regulates the contests and exhibitions in which its member teams regularly engage; or

(bb) any minor league team that is affiliated with such an association.

(B) Unqualified physicians

An alien who is a graduate of a medical school not accredited by a body or bodies approved for the purpose by the Secretary of Education (regardless of whether such school of medicine is in the United States) and who is coming to the United States principally to perform services as a member of the medical profession is inadmissible, unless the alien (i) has passed parts I and II of the National Board of Medical Examiners Examination (or an equivalent examination as determined by the Secretary of Health and Human Services) and (ii) is competent in oral and written English. For purposes of the previous sentence, an alien who is a graduate of a medical school shall be considered to have passed parts I and II of the National Board of Medical Examiners if the alien was fully and permanently licensed to practice medicine in a State on January 9, 1978, and was practicing medicine in a State on that date.

(C) Uncertified foreign health-care workers

Subject to subsection (r), any alien who seeks to enter the United States for the purpose of performing labor as a health-care worker, other than a physician, is inadmissible unless the alien presents to the consular officer, or, in the case of an adjustment of status, the Attorney General, a certificate from the Commission on Graduates of Foreign Nursing Schools, or a certificate from an equivalent independent credentialing organization approved by the Attorney General in consultation with the Secretary of Health and Human Services, verifying that—

(i) the alien's education, training, license, and experience—

(I) meet all applicable statutory and regulatory requirements for entry into the United States under the classification specified in the application;

(II) are comparable with that required for an American health-care worker of the same type; and

(III) are authentic and, in the case of a license, unencumbered;

(ii) the alien has the level of competence in oral and written English considered by the Secretary of Health and Human Services, in consultation with the Secretary of Education, to be appropriate for health care work of the kind in which the alien will be engaged, as shown by an appropriate score on one or more nationally recognized, commercially available, standardized assessments of the applicant's ability to speak and write; and

(iii) if a majority of States licensing the profession in which the alien intends to work recognize a test predicting the success on the profession's licensing or certification examination, the alien has passed such a test or has passed such an examination.

For purposes of clause (ii), determination of the standardized tests required and of the minimum scores that are appropriate are within the sole discretion of the Secretary of Health and Human Services and are not subject to further administrative or judicial review.

(D) Application of grounds

The grounds for inadmissibility of aliens under subparagraphs (A) and (B) shall apply to immigrants seeking admission or adjustment of status under paragraph (2) or (3) of section 203(b) [8 U.S.C.A. § 1153(b)].

(6) Illegal entrants and immigration violators

(A) Aliens present without admission or parole

(i) In general

An alien present in the United States without being admitted or paroled, or who arrives in the United States at any time or place other than as designated by the Attorney General, is inadmissible.

(ii) Exception for certain battered women and children

Clause (i) shall not apply to an alien who demonstrates that—

(I) the alien qualifies for immigrant status under subparagraph (A)(iii), (A)(iv), (B)(ii), or (B)(iii) of section 204(a)(1) [8 U.S.C.A. § 1154(a)(1)],

(II) **(a)** the alien has been battered or subjected to extreme cruelty by a spouse or parent, or by a member of the spouse's or parent's family residing in the same household as the alien and the spouse or parent consented or acquiesced to such battery or cruelty, or **(b)** the alien's child has been battered or subjected to extreme cruelty by a spouse or parent of the alien (without the active participation of the alien in the battery or cruelty) or by a member of the spouse's or parent's family residing in the same household as the alien when the spouse or parent consented to or acquiesced in such battery or cruelty and the alien did not actively participate in such battery or cruelty, and

(III) there was a substantial connection between the battery or cruelty described in subclause (I) or (II) and the alien's unlawful entry into the United States.

(B) Failure to attend removal proceeding

Any alien who without reasonable cause fails or refuses to attend or remain in attendance at a proceeding to determine the alien's inadmissibility or deportability and who seeks admission to the United States within 5 years of such alien's subsequent departure or removal is inadmissible.

(C) Misrepresentation

(i) In general

Any alien who, by fraud or willfully misrepresenting a material fact, seeks to procure (or has sought to procure or has procured) a visa, other documentation, or admission into the United States or other benefit provided under this Act is inadmissible.

(ii) Falsely claiming citizenship

Any alien who falsely represents, or has falsely represented, himself or herself to be a citizen of the United States for any purpose or benefit under this Act (including section 274A [8 U.S.C.A. § 1324a]) or any other Federal or State law is inadmissible.

(iii) Waiver authorized

For provision authorizing waiver of clause (i), see subsection (i).

(D) Stowaways

Any alien who is a stowaway is inadmissible.

(E) Smugglers

(i) In general

Any alien who at any time knowingly has encouraged, induced, assisted, abetted, or aided any other alien to enter or to try to enter the United States in violation of law is inadmissible.

(ii) Special rule in the case of family reunification

Clause (i) shall not apply in the case of alien who is an eligible immigrant (as defined in section 301(b)(1) of the Immigration Act of 1990), was physically present in the United States on May 5, 1988, and is seeking admission as an immediate relative or under section 203(a)(2) [8 U.S.C.A. § 1153(a)(2)] (including under section 112 of the Immigration Act of 1990) or benefits under section 301(a) of the Immigration Act of 1990 if the alien, before May 5, 1988, has encouraged, induced, assisted, abetted, or aided only the alien's spouse, parent, son, or daughter (and no other individual) to enter the United States in violation of law.

(iii) Waiver authorized

For provision authorizing waiver of clause (i), see subsection (d)(11).

(F) Subject of civil penalty

(i) In general

An alien who is the subject of a final order for violation of section 274C [8 U.S.C.A. § 1324c] is inadmissible.

(ii) Waiver authorized

For provision authorizing waiver of clause (i), see subsection (d)(12).

(G) Student visa abusers

An alien who obtains the status of a nonimmigrant under section 101(a)(15)(F)(i) [8 U.S.C.A. § 1101(a)(15)(F)(i)] and who violates a term or condition of such status under section 214(*l*) [8 U.S.C.A. § 1184(*l*)] is inadmissible until the alien has been outside the United States for a continuous period of 5 years after the date of the violation.

(7) Documentation requirements

(A) Immigrants

(i) In general

Except as otherwise specifically provided in this Act, any immigrant at the time of application for admission—

(I) who is not in possession of a valid unexpired immigrant visa, reentry permit, border crossing identification card, or other valid entry document required by this Act, and a valid unexpired passport, or other suitable travel document, or document of identity and nationality if such document is required under the regulations issued by the Attorney General under section 211(a) [8 U.S.C.A. § 1181(a)], or

(II) whose visa has been issued without compliance with the provisions of section 203 [8 U.S.C.A. § 1153],

is inadmissible.

(ii) Waiver authorized

For provision authorizing waiver of clause (i), see subsection (k).

(B) Nonimmigrants

(i) In general

Any nonimmigrant who—

(I) is not in possession of a passport valid for a minimum of six months from the date of the expiration of the initial period of the alien's admission or contemplated initial period of stay authorizing the alien to return to the country from which the alien came or to proceed to and enter some other country during such period, or

(II) is not in possession of a valid nonimmigrant visa or border crossing identification card at the time of application for admission,

is inadmissible.

(ii) General waiver authorized

For provision authorizing waiver of clause (i), see subsection (d)(4).

(iii) Guam visa waiver

For provision authorizing waiver of clause (i) in the case of visitors to Guam, see subsection (*l*).

(iv) Visa waiver pilot program

For authority to waive the requirement of clause (i) under a pilot program, see section 217 [8 U.S.C.A. § 1187].

(8) Ineligible for citizenship

(A) In general

Any immigrant who is permanently ineligible to citizenship is inadmissible.

(B) Draft evaders

Any person who has departed from or who has remained outside the United States to avoid or evade training or service in the armed forces in time of war or a period declared by the President to be a national emergency is inadmissible, except that this subparagraph shall not apply to an alien who at the time of such departure was a nonimmigrant and who is seeking to reenter the United States as a nonimmigrant.

(9) Aliens previously removed

(A) Certain aliens previously removed

(i) Arriving aliens

Insp. of aliens arriving

Any alien who has been ordered removed under section 235(b)(1) [8 U.S.C.A. § 1225(b)(1)] or at the end of proceedings under section 240 [8 U.S.C.A. § 1229a] initiated upon the alien's arrival in the United States and who again seeks admission within 5 years of the date of such removal (or within 20 years in the case of a second or subsequent removal or at any time in the case of an alien convicted of an aggravated felony) is inadmissible.

(ii) Other aliens

Any alien not described in clause (i) who—

(I) has been ordered removed under section 240 or any other provision of law, or

(II) departed the United States while an order of removal was outstanding,

and who seeks admission within 10 years of the date of such alien's departure or removal (or within 20 years of such date in the case of a second or subsequent removal or at any time in the case of an alien convicted of an aggravated felony) is inadmissible.

(iii) Exception

Clauses (i) and (ii) shall not apply to an alien seeking admission within a period if, prior to the date of the alien's reembarkation at a place outside the United States or attempt to be admitted from foreign contiguous territory, the Attorney General has consented to the alien's reapplying for admission.

(B) Aliens unlawfully present

(i) In general

Any alien (other than an alien lawfully admitted for permanent residence) who—

(I) was unlawfully present in the United States for a period of more than 180 days but less than 1 year, voluntarily departed the United States (whether or not pursuant to section 244(e) [8 U.S.C.A. § 1254(e)]) prior to the commencement of proceedings under section 235(b)(1) [8 U.S.C.A. § 1225(b)(1)]or section 239(a) [8 U.S.C.A. § 1229(a)], and again seeks admission within 3 years of the date of such alien's departure or removal, or

(II) has been unlawfully present in the United States for one year or more, and who again seeks admission within 10 years of the date of such alien's departure or removal from the United States,

is inadmissible.

(ii) Construction of unlawful presence

For purposes of this paragraph, an alien is deemed to be unlawfully present in the United States if the alien is present in the United States after the expiration of the period of stay authorized by the Attorney General or is present in the United States without being admitted or paroled.

(iii) Exceptions

(I) Minors

No period of time in which an alien is under 18 years of age shall be taken into account in determining the period of unlawful presence in the United States under clause (i).

(II) Asylees

No period of time in which an alien has a bona fide application for asylum pending under section 208 [8 U.S.C.A. § 1158] shall be taken into account in determining the period of unlawful presence in the United States under clause (i) unless the alien during such period was employed without authorization in the United States.

(III) Family unity

No period of time in which the alien is a beneficiary of family unity protection pursuant to section 301 of the Immigration Act of 1990 shall be taken into account in determining the period of unlawful presence in the United States under clause (i).

(IV) Battered women and children

Clause (i) shall not apply to an alien who would be described in paragraph (6)(A)(ii) if "violation of the terms of the alien's nonimmigrant visa" were substituted for "unlawful entry into the United States" in subclause (III) of that paragraph.

(iv) Tolling for good cause

In the case of an alien who—

(I) has been lawfully admitted or paroled into the United States,

(II) has filed a nonfrivolous application for a change or extension of status before the date of expiration of the period of stay authorized by the Attorney General, and

(III) has not been employed without authorization in the United States before or during the pendency of such application,

the calculation of the period of time specified in clause (i)(I) shall be tolled during the pendency of such application, but not to exceed 120 days.

(v) Waiver

The Attorney General has sole discretion to waive clause (i) in the case of an immigrant who is the spouse or son or daughter of a United States citizen or of an alien lawfully admitted for permanent residence, if it is established to the satisfaction of the Attorney General that the refusal of admission to such immigrant alien would result in extreme hardship to the citizen or lawfully resident spouse or parent of such alien. No court shall have jurisdiction to review a decision or action by the Attorney General regarding a waiver under this clause.

(C) Aliens unlawfully present after previous immigration violations

(i) In general

Any alien who—

(I) has been unlawfully present in the United States for an aggregate period of more than 1 year, or

(II) has been ordered removed under section 235(b)(1) [8 U.S.C.A. § 1225(b)(1)], section 240 [8 U.S.C.A. § 1229a], or any other provision of law,

and who enters or attempts to reenter the United States without being admitted is inadmissible.

(ii) Exception

Clause (i) shall not apply to an alien seeking admission more than 10 years after the date of the alien's last departure from the United States if, prior to the alien's reembarkation at a place outside the United States or attempt to be readmitted from a foreign contiguous territory, the Attorney General has consented to the alien's reapplying for admission.

(10) Miscellaneous

(A) Practicing polygamists

Any immigrant who is coming to the United States to practice polygamy is inadmissible.

(B) Guardian required to accompany helpless alien

Any alien—

(i) who is accompanying another alien who is inadmissible and who is certified to be helpless from sickness, mental or physical disability, or infancy pursuant to section 232(c) [8 U.S.C.A. § 1222(c)], and

(ii) whose protection or guardianship is determined to be required by the alien described in clause (i),

is inadmissible.

(C) International child abduction

(i) In general

Except as provided in clause (ii), any alien who, after entry of an order by a court in the United States granting custody to a person of a United States citizen child who detains or retains the child, or withholds custody of the child, outside the United States from the person granted custody by that order, is inadmissible until the child is surrendered to the person granted custody by that order.

(ii) Aliens supporting abductors and relatives of abductors

Any alien who—

(I) is known by the Secretary of State to have intentionally assisted an alien in the conduct described in clause (i),

(II) is known by the Secretary of State to be intentionally providing material support or safe haven to an alien described in clause (i), or

(III) is a spouse (other than the spouse who is the parent of the abducted child), child (other than the abducted child), parent, sibling, or agent of an alien described in clause (i), if such person has been designated by the Secretary of State at the Secretary's sole and unreviewable discretion, is inadmissible until the child described in clause (i) is surrendered to the person granted custody by the order described in that clause, and such person and child are permitted to return to the United States or such person's place of residence.

(iii) Exceptions

Clauses (i) and (ii) shall not apply—

(I) to a government official of the United States who is acting within the scope of his or her official duties;

(II) to a government official of any foreign government if the official has been designated by the Secretary of State at the Secretary's sole and unreviewable discretion; or

(III) so long as the child is located in a foreign state that is a party to the Convention on the Civil Aspects of International Child Abduction, done at The Hague on October 25, 1980.

(D) Unlawful voters

Any alien who has voted in violation of any Federal, State, or local constitutional provision, statute, ordinance, or regulation is inadmissible.

(E) Former citizens who renounced citizenship to avoid taxation

Any alien who is a former citizen of the United States who officially renounces United States citizenship and who is determined by the Attorney General to have renounced United States citizenship for the purpose of avoiding taxation by the United States is inadmissible.

(b) Notices of denials

(1) Subject to paragraphs (2) and (3), if an alien's application for a visa, for admission to the United States, or for adjustment of status is denied by an immigration or consular officer because the officer determines the alien to be inadmissible under subsection (a), the officer shall provide the alien with a timely written notice that—

(A) states the determination, and

(B) lists the specific provision or provisions of law under which the alien is inadmissible or ineligible for entry or adjustment of status.

(2) The Secretary of State may waive the requirements of paragraph (1) with respect to a particular alien or any class or classes of inadmissible aliens.

(3) Paragraph (1) does not apply to any alien inadmissible under paragraph (2) or (3) of subsection (a).

(c) Repealed. Pub.L. 104–208, Div. C, Title III, § 304(b), Sept. 30, 1996, 110 Stat. 3009–597.

(d) Temporary admission of nonimmigrants

(1) The Attorney General shall determine whether a ground for inadmissibility exists with respect to a nonimmigrant described in section 101(a)(15)(S) [8 U.S.C.A. § 1101(a)(15)(S)]. The Attorney General, in the Attorney General's discretion, may waive the application of subsection (a) (other than paragraph (3)(E)) in the case of a nonimmigrant described in section 101(a)(15)(S) [8 U.S.C.A. § 1101(a)(15)(S)], if the Attorney General considers it to be in the national interest to do so. Nothing in this section shall be regarded as prohibiting the Immigration and Naturalization Service from instituting removal proceedings against an alien admitted as a nonimmigrant under section 101(a)(15)(S) [8 U.S.C.A. § 1101(a)(15)(S)] for conduct committed after the alien's admission into the United States, or for conduct or a condition that was not disclosed to the Attorney General prior to the alien's admission as a nonimmigrant under section 101(a)(15)(S) [8 U.S.C.A. § 1101(a)(15)(S)].

(2) Repealed. Pub.L. 101–649, Title VI, § 601(d)(2)(A), Nov. 29, 1990, 104 Stat. 5076.

(3) Except as provided in this subsection, an alien (A) who is applying for a nonimmigrant visa and is known or believed by the consular officer to be ineligible for such visa under subsection (a) (other than paragraphs (3)(A)(i)(I), (3)(A)(ii), (3)(A)(iii), (3)(C), and (3)(E) of such subsection), may, after approval by the Attorney General of a recommendation by the Secretary of State or by the consular officer that the alien be admitted temporarily despite his inadmissibility, be granted such a visa and may be admitted into the United States temporarily as a nonimmigrant in the discretion of the Attorney General, or (B) who is inadmissible under subsection (a) (other than paragraphs (3)(A)(i)(I), (3)(A)(ii), (3)(A)(iii), (3)(C), and (3)(E) of such subsection), but who is in possession of appropriate documents or is granted a waiver thereof and is seeking admission, may be admitted into the United States temporarily as a nonimmigrant in the discretion of the Attorney General. The Attorney General shall prescribe conditions, including exaction of such bonds as may be necessary, to control and regulate the admission and return of inadmissible aliens applying for temporary admission under this paragraph.

(4) Either or both of the requirements of paragraph (7)(B)(i) of subsection (a) may be waived by the Attorney General and the Secretary of State acting jointly **(A)** on the basis of unforeseen emergency in individual cases, or **(B)** on the basis of reciprocity with respect to nationals of foreign contiguous territory or of adjacent islands and residents thereof having a common nationality with such nationals, or **(C)** in the case of aliens proceeding in immediate and continuous transit through the United States under contracts authorized in section 233(c) [8 U.S.C.A. § 1223(c)].

(5)(A) The Attorney General may, except as provided in subparagraph (B) or in section 214(f) [8 U.S.C.A. § 1184(f)], in his discretion parole into the United States temporarily under such conditions as he may prescribe only on a case-by-case basis for urgent humanitarian reasons or significant public benefit any alien applying for admission to the United States, but such parole of such alien shall not be regarded as an admission of the alien and when the purposes of such parole shall, in the opinion of the Attorney General, have been served the alien shall forthwith return or be returned to the custody from which he was paroled and thereafter his case shall continue to be dealt with in the same manner as that of any other applicant for admission to the United States.

(B) The Attorney General may not parole into the United States an alien who is a refugee unless the Attorney General determines that compelling reasons in the public interest with respect to that particular alien require that the alien be paroled into the United States rather than be admitted as a refugee under section 207 [8 U.S.C.A. § 1157].

(6) Repealed. Pub.L. 101–649, Title VI, § 601(d)(2)(A), Nov. 29, 1990, 104 Stat. 5076.

(7) The provisions of subsection (a) (other than paragraph (7)) shall be applicable to any alien who shall leave Guam, Puerto Rico, or the Virgin Islands of the United States, and who seeks to enter the continental United States or any other place under the jurisdiction of the United States. The Attorney General shall by regulations provide a method and procedure for the temporary admission to the United States of the aliens described in this proviso. Any alien described in this paragraph, who is denied admission to the United States, shall be immediately removed in the manner provided by section 241(c) [8 U.S.C.A. § 1231(c)].

(8) Upon a basis of reciprocity accredited officials of foreign governments, their immediate families, attendants, servants, and personal employees may be admitted in immediate and continuous transit through the United States without regard to the provisions of this section except paragraphs (3)(A), (3)(B), (3)(C), and (7)(B) of subsection (a) of this section.

(9), (10) Repealed. Pub.L. 101–649, Title VI, § 601(d)(2)(A), Nov. 29, 1990, 104 Stat. 5076.

(11) The Attorney General may, in his discretion for humanitarian purposes, to assure family unity, or when it is otherwise in the public interest, waive application of clause (i) of subsection (a)(6)(E) in the case of any alien lawfully admitted for permanent residence who temporarily proceeded abroad voluntarily and not under an order of removal, and who is otherwise admissible to the United States as a returning resident under section 211(b) [8 U.S.C.A. § 1181(b)] and in the case of an alien seeking admission or adjustment of status as an immediate relative or immigrant under section 203(a) [8 U.S.C.A. § 1153(a)] (other than paragraph (4) thereof), if the alien has encouraged, induced, assisted, abetted, or aided only an individual who at the time of such action was the alien's spouse, parent, son, or daughter (and no other individual) to enter the United States in violation of law.

(12) The Attorney General may, in the discretion of the Attorney General for humanitarian purposes or to assure family unity, waive application of clause (i) of subsection (a)(6)(F)—

(A) in the case of an alien lawfully admitted for permanent residence who temporarily proceeded abroad voluntarily and not under an order of deportation or removal and who is otherwise admissible to the United States as a returning resident under section 211(b) [8 U.S.C.A. § 1181(b)], and

(B) in the case of an alien seeking admission or adjustment of status under section 201(b)(2)(A) [8 U.S.C.A. § 1151(b)(2)(A)] or under section 203(a) [8 U.S.C.A. § 1153(a)],

if no previous civil money penalty was imposed against the alien under section 274C [8 U.S.C.A. § 1324c] and the offense was committed solely to assist, aid, or support the alien's spouse or child (and not another individual). No court shall have jurisdiction to review a decision of the Attorney General to grant or deny a waiver under this paragraph.

(e) Educational visitor status; foreign residence requirement; waiver

No person admitted under section 101(a)(15)(J) [8 U.S.C.A. § 1101(a)(15)(J)] or acquiring such status after admission (i) whose participation in the program for which he came to the United States was financed in whole or in part, directly or indirectly, by an agency of the Government of the United States or by the government of the country of his nationality or his last residence, (ii) who at the time of admission or acquisition of status under section 101(a)(15)(J) [8 U.S.C.A. § 1101(a)(15)(J)] was a national or resident of a country which the Director of the United States Information Agency, pursuant to regulations prescribed by him, had designated as clearly requiring the services of persons engaged in the field of specialized knowledge or skill in which the alien was engaged, or (iii) who came to the United States or acquired such status in order to receive graduate medical education or training, shall be eligible to apply for an immigrant visa, or for permanent residence, or for a nonimmigrant visa under section 101(a)(15)(H) [8 U.S.C.A. § 1101(a)(15)(H)] or section 101(a)(15)(L) [8 U.S.C.A. § 1101(a)(15)(L)] until it is established that such person has resided and been physically present in the country of his nationality or his last residence for an aggregate of at least two years following departure from the United States: *Provided*, That upon the favorable recommendation of the Director of the United States Information Agency, pursuant to the request of an interested United States Government agency, (or, in the case of an alien described in clause (iii), pursuant to the request of a State Department of Public Health, or its equivalent) or of the Commissioner of Immigration and Naturalization after he has determined that departure from the United States would impose exceptional hardship upon the alien's spouse or child (if such spouse or child is a citizen of the United States or a lawfully resident alien), or that the alien cannot return to the country of his nationality or last residence because he would be subject to persecution on account of race, religion, or political opinion, the Attorney General may waive the requirement of such two-year foreign residence abroad in the case of any alien whose admission to the United States is found by the Attorney General to be in the public interest except that in the case of a waiver requested by a State Department of Public Health, or its equivalent, or in the case of a waiver requested by an interested United States Government agency on behalf of an alien described in clause (iii), the waiver shall be subject to the requirements of section 214(k) [8 U.S.C.A. § 1184(k)]: And provided further, That, except in the case of an alien described in clause (iii), the Attorney General may, upon the favorable recommendation of the Director, waive such two-year foreign residence requirement in any case in which the foreign country of the alien's nationality or last residence has furnished the Director a statement in writing that it has no objection to such waiver in the case of such alien.

(f) Suspension of entry or imposition of restrictions by President

Whenever the President finds that the entry of any aliens or of any class of aliens into the United States would be detrimental to the interests of the United States, he may by proclamation, and for such period as he shall deem necessary, suspend the entry of all aliens or any class of aliens as immigrants or nonimmigrants, or impose on the entry of aliens any restrictions he may deem to be appropriate. Whenever the Attorney General finds that a commercial airline has failed to comply with regulations of the Attorney General relating to requirements of airlines for the detection of fraudulent documents used by passengers traveling to the United States (including the training of personnel in such detection), the Attorney General may suspend the entry of some or all aliens transported to the United States by such airline.

(g) Bond and conditions for admission of alien excludable on health-related grounds

The Attorney General may waive the application of—

(1) subsection (a)(1)(A)(i) in the case of any alien who—

(A) is the spouse or the unmarried son or daughter, or the minor unmarried lawfully adopted child, of a United States citizen, or of an alien lawfully admitted for permanent residence, or of an alien who has been issued an immigrant visa, or

(B) has a son or daughter who is a United States citizen, or an alien lawfully admitted for permanent residence, or an alien who has been issued an immigrant visa;

in accordance with such terms, conditions, and controls, if any, including the giving of bond, as the Attorney General, in the discretion of the Attorney General after consultation with the Secretary of Health and Human Services, may by regulation prescribe;

(2) subsection (a)(1)(A)(ii) in the case of any alien—

(A) who receives vaccination against the vaccine-preventable disease or diseases for which the alien has failed to present documentation of previous vaccination,

(B) for whom a civil surgeon, medical officer, or panel physician (as those terms are defined by section 34.2 of title 42 of the Code of Federal Regulations) certifies, according to such regulations as the Secretary of Health and Human Services may prescribe, that such vaccination would not be medically appropriate, or

(C) under such circumstances as the Attorney General provides by regulation, with respect to whom the requirement of such a vaccination would be contrary to the alien's religious beliefs or moral convictions; or

(3) subsection (a)(1)(A)(iii) in the case of any alien, in accordance with such terms, conditions, and controls, if any, including the giving of bond, as the Attorney General, in the discretion of the Attorney General after consultation with the Secretary of Health and Human Services, may by regulation prescribe.

(h) Waiver of subsection (a)(2)(A)(i)(I), (II), (B), (D), and (E)

The Attorney General may, in his discretion, waive the application of subparagraphs (A)(i)(I), (B), (D), and (E) of subsection (a)(2) and subparagraph (A)(i)(II) of such subsection insofar as it relates to a single offense of simple possession of 30 grams or less of marijuana if—

(1)(A) in the case of any immigrant it is established to the satisfaction of the Attorney General that—

(i) the alien is inadmissible only under subparagraph (D)(i) or (D)(ii) of such subsection or the activities for which the alien is inadmissible occurred more than 15 years before the date of the alien's application for a visa, admission, or adjustment of status,

(ii) the admission to the United States of such alien would not be contrary to the national welfare, safety, or security of the United States, and

(iii) the alien has been rehabilitated; or

(B) in the case of an immigrant who is the spouse, parent, son, or daughter of a citizen of the United States or an alien lawfully admitted for permanent residence if it is established to the satisfaction of the Attorney General that the alien's denial of admission would result in extreme hardship to the United States citizen or lawfully resident spouse, parent, son, or daughter of such alien; and

(2) the Attorney General, in his discretion, and pursuant to such terms, conditions and procedures as he may by regulations prescribe, has consented to the alien's applying or reapplying for a visa, for admission to the United States, or adjustment of status.

No waiver shall be provided under this subsection in the case of an alien who has been convicted of (or who has admitted committing acts that constitute) murder or criminal acts involving torture, or an attempt or conspiracy to commit murder or a criminal act involving torture. No waiver shall be granted under this subsection in the case of an alien who has previously been admitted to the United States as an alien lawfully admitted for permanent residence if either since the date of such admission the alien has been convicted of an aggravated felony or the alien has not lawfully resided continuously in the United States for a period of not less than 7 years immediately preceding the date of initiation of proceedings to remove the alien from the United States. No court shall have jurisdiction to review a decision of the Attorney General to grant or deny a waiver under this subsection.

(i) Admission of immigrant excludable for fraud or willful misrepresentation of material fact

(1) The Attorney General may, in the discretion of the Attorney General, waive the application of clause (i) of subsection (a)(6)(C) in the case of an immigrant who is the spouse, son, or daughter of a United States citizen or of an alien lawfully admitted for permanent residence if it is established to the satisfaction of the Attorney General that the refusal of admission to the United States of such immigrant alien would result in extreme hardship to the citizen or lawfully resident spouse or parent of such an alien.

(2) No court shall have jurisdiction to review a decision or action of the Attorney General regarding a waiver under paragraph (1).

(j) Limitation on immigration of foreign medical graduates

(1) The additional requirements referred to in section 101(a)(15)(J) [8 U.S.C.A. § 1101(a)(15)(J)] for an alien who is coming to the United States under a program under which he will receive graduate medical education or training are as follows:

(A) A school of medicine or of one of the other health professions, which is accredited by a body or bodies approved for the purpose by the Secretary of Education, has agreed in writing to provide the graduate medical education or training under the program for which the alien is coming to the United States or to assume responsibility for arranging for the provision thereof by an appropriate public or nonprofit private institution or agency, except that, in the case of such an agreement by a school of medicine, any one or more of its affiliated hospitals which are to participate in the provision of the graduate medical education or training must join in the agreement.

(B) Before making such agreement, the accredited school has been satisfied that the alien **(i)** is a graduate of a school of medicine which is accredited by a body or bodies approved for the purpose by the Secretary of Education (regardless of whether such school of medicine is in the United States); or **(ii)(I)** has passed parts I and II of the National Board of Medical Examiners Examination (or an equivalent examination as determined by the Secretary of Health and Human Services), **(II)** has competency in oral and written English, **(III)** will be able to adapt to the educational and cultural environment in which he will be receiving his education or training, and **(IV)** has adequate prior education and training to participate satisfactorily in the program for which he is coming to the United States. For the purposes of this subparagraph, an alien who is a graduate of a medical school shall be considered to have passed parts I and II of the National Board of Medical Examiners Examination if the alien was fully and permanently licensed to practice medicine in a State on January 9, 1978, and was practicing medicine in a State on that date.

(C) The alien has made a commitment to return to the country of his nationality or last residence upon completion of the education or training for which he is coming to the United States, and the government of the country of his nationality or last residence has provided a written assurance, satisfactory to the Secretary of Health and Human Services, that there is a need in that country for persons with the skills the alien will acquire in such education or training.

(D) The duration of the alien's participation in the program of graduate medical education or training for which the alien is coming to the United States is limited to the time typically required to complete such program, as determined by the Director of the United States Information Agency at the time of the alien's admission into the United States, based on criteria which are established in coordination with the Secretary of Health and Human Services and which take into consideration the published requirements of the medical specialty board which administers such education or training program; except that—

(i) such duration is further limited to seven years unless the alien has demonstrated to the satisfaction of the Director that the country to which the alien will return at the end of such specialty education or training has an exceptional need for an individual trained in such specialty, and

(ii) the alien may, once and not later than two years after the date the alien is admitted to the United States as an exchange visitor or acquires exchange visitor status, change the alien's designated program of graduate medical education or training if the Director approves the change and if a commitment and written assurance with respect to the alien's new program have been provided in accordance with subparagraph (C).

(E) The alien furnishes the Attorney General each year with an affidavit (in such form as the Attorney General shall prescribe) that attests that the alien **(i)** is in good standing in the program of graduate medical education or training in which the alien is participating, and **(ii)** will return to the country of his nationality or last residence upon completion of the education or training for which he came to the United States.

(2) An alien who is a graduate of a medical school and who is coming to the United States to perform services as a member of the medical profession may not be admitted as a nonimmigrant under section 101(a)(15)(H)(i)(b) [8 U.S.C.A. § 1101(a)(15)(H)(i)(b)] unless—

(A) the alien is coming pursuant to an invitation from a public or nonprofit private educational or research institution or agency in the United States to teach or conduct research, or both, at or for such institution or agency, or

(B)(i) the alien has passed the Federation licensing examination (administered by the Federation of State Medical Boards of the United States) or an equivalent examination as determined by the Secretary of Health and Human Services, and

(ii) (I) has competency in oral and written English or **(II)** is a graduate of a school of medicine which is accredited by a body or bodies approved for the purpose by the Secretary of Education (regardless of whether such school of medicine is in the United States).

(3) The Director of the United States Information Agency annually shall transmit to the Congress a report on aliens who have submitted affidavits described in paragraph (1)(E), and shall include in such report the name and address of each such alien, the medical education or training program in which such alien is participating, and the status of such alien in that program.

(k) Attorney General's discretion to admit otherwise inadmissible aliens who possess immigrant visas

Any alien, inadmissible from the United States under paragraph (5)(A) or (7)(A)(i) of subsection (a), who is in possession of an immigrant visa may, if otherwise admissible, be admitted in the discretion of the Attorney General if the Attorney General is satisfied that inadmissibility was not known to, and could not have been ascertained by the exercise of reasonable diligence by, the immigrant before the time of departure of the vessel or aircraft from the last port outside the United States and outside foreign contiguous territory or, in the case of an immigrant coming from foreign contiguous territory, before the time of the immigrant's application for admission.

***(l)* Guam; waiver of requirements for nonimmigrant visitors; conditions of waiver; acceptance of funds from Guam**

(1) The requirement of paragraph (7)(B)(i) of subsection (a) may be waived by the Attorney General, the Secretary of State, and the Secretary of the Interior, acting jointly, in the case of an alien applying for admission as a nonimmigrant visitor for business or pleasure and solely for entry into and stay on Guam for a period not to exceed fifteen days, if the Attorney General, the Secretary of State, and the Secretary of the Interior, after consultation with the Governor of Guam, jointly determine that—

(A) an adequate arrival and departure control system has been developed on Guam, and

(B) such a waiver does not represent a threat to the welfare, safety, or security of the United States or its territories and commonwealths.

(2) An alien may not be provided a waiver under this subsection unless the alien has waived any right—

(A) to review or appeal under this Act of an immigration officer's determination as to the admissibility of the alien at the port of entry into Guam, or

(B) to contest, other than on the basis of an application for asylum, any action for removal of the alien.

(3) If adequate appropriated funds to carry out this subsection are not otherwise available, the Attorney General is authorized to accept from the Government of Guam such funds as may be tendered to cover all or any part of the cost of administration and enforcement of this subsection.

(m) Requirements for admission of nonimmigrant nurses during five-year period

(1) The qualifications referred to in section 101(a)(15)(H)(i)(c) [8 U.S.C.A. § 1101(a)(15)(H)(i)(c)], with respect to an alien who is coming to the United States to perform nursing services for a facility, are that the alien—

(A) has obtained a full and unrestricted license to practice professional nursing in the country where the alien obtained nursing education or has received nursing education in the United States;

(B) has passed an appropriate examination (recognized in regulations promulgated in consultation with the Secretary of Health and Human Services) or has a full and unrestricted license under State law to practice professional nursing in the State of intended employment; and

(C) is fully qualified and eligible under the laws (including such temporary or interim licensing requirements which authorize the nurse to be employed) governing the place of intended employment to engage in the practice of professional nursing as a registered nurse immediately upon admission to the United States and is authorized under such laws to be employed by the facility.

(2)(A) The attestation referred to in section 101(a)(15)(H)(i)(c) [8 U.S.C.A. § 1101(a)(15)(H)(i)(c)], with respect to a facility for which an alien will perform services, is an attestation as to the following:

(i) The facility meets all the requirements of paragraph (6).

(ii) The employment of the alien will not adversely affect the wages and working conditions of registered nurses similarly employed.

(iii) The alien employed by the facility will be paid the wage rate for registered nurses similarly employed by the facility.

(iv) The facility has taken and is taking timely and significant steps designed to recruit and retain sufficient registered nurses who are United States citizens or immigrants who are authorized to perform nursing services, in order to remove as quickly as reasonably possible the dependence of the facility on nonimmigrant registered nurses.

(v) There is not a strike or lockout in the course of a labor dispute, the facility did not lay off and will not lay off a registered nurse employed by the facility within the period beginning 90 days before and ending 90 days after the date of filing of any visa petition, and the employment of such an alien is not intended or designed to influence an election for a bargaining representative for registered nurses of the facility.

(vi) At the time of the filing of the petition for registered nurses under section 101(a)(15)(H)(i)(c) [8 U.S.C.A. § 1101(a)(15)(H)(i)(c)], notice of the filing has been provided by the facility to the bargaining representative of the registered nurses at the facility or, where there is no such bargaining representative, notice of the filing has been provided to the registered nurses employed at the facility through posting in conspicuous locations.

(vii) The facility will not, at any time, employ a number of aliens issued visas or otherwise provided nonimmigrant status under section 101(a)(15)(H)(i)(c) [8 U.S.C.A. § 1101(a)(15)(H)(i)(c)] that exceeds 33 percent of the total number of registered nurses employed by the facility.

(viii) The facility will not, with respect to any alien issued a visa or otherwise provided nonimmigrant status under section 101(a)(15)(H)(i)(c) [8 U.S.C.A. § 1101(a)(15)(H)(i)(c)]—

(I) authorize the alien to perform nursing services at any worksite other than a worksite controlled by the facility; or

(II) transfer the place of employment of the alien from one worksite to another.

Nothing in clause (iv) shall be construed as requiring a facility to have taken significant steps described in such clause before the date of the enactment of the Nursing Relief for Disadvantaged Areas Act of 1999. A copy of the attestation shall be provided, within 30 days of the date of filing, to registered nurses employed at the facility on the date of filing.

(B) For purposes of subparagraph (A)(iv), each of the following shall be considered a significant step reasonably designed to recruit and retain registered nurses:

(i) Operating a training program for registered nurses at the facility or financing (or providing participation in) a training program for registered nurses elsewhere.

(ii) Providing career development programs and other methods of facilitating health care workers to become registered nurses.

(iii) Paying registered nurses wages at a rate higher than currently being paid to registered nurses similarly employed in the geographic area.

(iv) Providing reasonable opportunities for meaningful salary advancement by registered nurses.

The steps described in this subparagraph shall not be considered to be an exclusive list of the significant steps that may be taken to meet the conditions of subparagraph (A)(iv). Nothing in this subparagraph shall require a facility to take more than one step if the facility can demonstrate that taking a second step is not reasonable.

(C) Subject to subparagraph (E), an attestation under subparagraph (A)—

(i) shall expire on the date that is the later of—

(I) the end of the one-year period beginning on the date of its filing with the Secretary of Labor; or

(II) the end of the period of admission under section 101(a)(15)(H)(i)(c) [8 U.S.C.A. § 1101(a)(15)(H)(i)(c)] of the last alien with respect to whose admission it was applied (in accordance with clause (ii)); and

(ii) shall apply to petitions filed during the one-year period beginning on the date of its filing with the Secretary of Labor if the facility states in each such petition that it continues to comply with the conditions in the attestation.

(D) A facility may meet the requirements under this paragraph with respect to more than one registered nurse in a single petition.

(E)(i) The Secretary of Labor shall compile and make available for public examination in a timely manner in Washington, D.C., a list identifying facilities which have filed petitions for nonimmigrants under section 101(a)(15)(H)(i)(c) [8 U.S.C.A. § 1101(a)(15)(H)(i)(c)] and, for each such facility, a copy of the facility's attestation under subparagraph (A) (and accompanying documentation) and each such petition filed by the facility.

(ii) The Secretary of Labor shall establish a process, including reasonable time limits, for the receipt, investigation, and disposition of complaints respecting a facility's failure to meet conditions attested to or a facility's misrepresentation of a material fact in an attestation. Complaints may be filed by any aggrieved person or organization (including bargaining representatives, associations deemed appropriate by the Secretary, and other aggrieved parties as determined under regulations of the Secretary). The Secretary shall conduct an investigation under this clause if there is reasonable cause to believe that a facility fails to meet conditions attested to. Subject to the time limits established under this clause, this subparagraph shall apply regardless of whether an attestation is expired or unexpired at the time a complaint is filed.

(iii) Under such process, the Secretary shall provide, within 180 days after the date such a complaint is filed, for a determination as to whether or not a basis exists to make a finding described in clause (iv). If the Secretary determines that such a basis exists, the Secretary shall provide for notice of such determination to the interested parties and an opportunity for a hearing on the complaint within 60 days of the date of the determination.

(iv) If the Secretary of Labor finds, after notice and opportunity for a hearing, that a facility (for which an attestation is made) has failed to meet a condition attested to or that there was a misrepresentation of material fact in the attestation, the Secretary shall notify the Attorney General of such finding and may, in addition, impose such other administrative remedies (including civil monetary penalties in an amount not to exceed $1,000 per nurse per violation, with the total penalty not to exceed $10,000 per violation) as the Secretary determines to be appropriate. Upon receipt of such notice, the Attorney General shall not approve petitions filed with respect to a facility during a period of at least one year for nurses to be employed by the facility.

(v) In addition to the sanctions provided for under clause (iv), if the Secretary of Labor finds, after notice and an opportunity for a hearing, that a facility has violated the condition attested to under subparagraph (A)(iii) (relating to payment of registered nurses at the prevailing wage rate), the Secretary shall order the facility to provide for payment of such amounts of back pay as may be required to comply with such condition.

(F)(i) The Secretary of Labor shall impose on a facility filing an attestation under subparagraph (A) a filing fee, in an amount prescribed by the Secretary based on the costs of carrying out the Secretary's duties under this subsection, but not exceeding $250.

(ii) Fees collected under this subparagraph shall be deposited in a fund established for this purpose in the Treasury of the United States.

(iii) The collected fees in the fund shall be available to the Secretary of Labor, to the extent and in such amounts as may be provided in appropriations Acts, to cover the costs described in clause (i), in addition to any other funds that are available to the Secretary to cover such costs.

(3) The period of admission of an alien under section 101(a)(15)(H)(i)(c) [8 U.S.C.A. § 1101(a)(15)(H)(i)(c)] shall be 3 years.

(4) The total number of nonimmigrant visas issued pursuant to petitions granted under section 101(a)(15)(H)(i)(c) [8 U.S.C.A. § 1101(a)(15)(H)(i)(c)] in each fiscal year shall not exceed 500. The number of such visas issued for employment in each State in each fiscal year shall not exceed the following:

(A) For States with populations of less than 9,000,000, based upon the 1990 decennial census of population, 25 visas.

(B) For States with populations of 9,000,000 or more, based upon the 1990 decennial census of population, 50 visas.

(C) If the total number of visas available under this paragraph for a fiscal year quarter exceeds the number of qualified nonimmigrants who may be issued such visas during those quarters, the visas made available under this paragraph shall be issued without regard to the numerical limitation under subparagraph (A) or (B) of this paragraph during the last fiscal year quarter.

(5) A facility that has filed a petition under section 101(a)(15)(H)(i)(c) [8 U.S.C.A. § 1101(a)(15)(H)(i)(c)] to employ a nonimmigrant to perform nursing services for the facility—

(A) shall provide the nonimmigrant a wage rate and working conditions commensurate with those of nurses similarly employed by the facility;

(B) shall require the nonimmigrant to work hours commensurate with those of nurses similarly employed by the facility; and

(C) shall not interfere with the right of the nonimmigrant to join or organize a union.

(6) For purposes of this subsection and section 101(a)(15)(H)(i)(c) [8 U.S.C.A. § 1101(a)(15)(H)(i)(c)], the term 'facility' means a subsection (d) hospital (as defined in section 1886(d)(1)(B) of the Social Security Act (42 U.S.C. 1395ww (d)(1)(B))) that meets the following requirements:

(A) As of March 31, 1997, the hospital was located in a health professional shortage area (as defined in section 332 of the Public Health Service Act (42 U.S.C. 254e)).

(B) Based on its settled cost report filed under title XVIII of the Social Security Act for its cost reporting period beginning during fiscal year 1994—

(i) the hospital has not less than 190 licensed acute care beds;

(ii) the number of the hospital's inpatient days for such period which were made up of patients who (for such days) were entitled to benefits under part A of such title is not less than 35 percent of the total number of such hospital's acute care inpatient days for such period; and

(iii) the number of the hospital's inpatient days for such period which were made up of patients who (for such days) were eligible for medical assistance under a State plan approved under title XIX of the Social Security Act, is not less than 28 percent of the total number of such hospital's acute care inpatient days for such period.

(7) For purposes of paragraph (2)(A)(v), the term 'lay off', with respect to a worker—

(A) means to cause the worker's loss of employment, other than through a discharge for inadequate performance, violation of workplace rules, cause, voluntary departure, voluntary retirement, or the expiration of a grant or contract; but

(B) does not include any situation in which the worker is offered, as an alternative to such loss of employment, a similar employment opportunity with the same employer at equivalent or higher compensation and benefits than the position from which the employee was discharged, regardless of whether or not the employee accepts the offer.

Nothing in this paragraph is intended to limit an employee's or an employer's rights under a collective bargaining agreement or other employment contract.

(n) Labor condition application

(1) No alien may be admitted or provided status as an H–1B nonimmigrant in an occupational classification unless the employer has filed with the Secretary of Labor an application stating the following:

(A) The employer—

(i) is offering and will offer during the period of authorized employment to aliens admitted or provided status as a nonimmigrant described in section 101(a)(15)(H)(i)(b) [8 U.S.C.A. § 1101(a)(15)(H)(i)(b)] wages that are at least—

(I) the actual wage level paid by the employer to all other individuals with similar experience and qualifications for the specific employment in question, or

(II) the prevailing wage level for the occupational classification in the area of employment,

whichever is greater, based on the best information available as of the time of filing the application, and

(ii) will provide working conditions for such a nonimmigrant that will not adversely affect the working conditions of workers similarly employed.

(B) There is not a strike or lockout in the course of a labor dispute in the occupational classification at the place of employment.

(C) The employer, at the time of filing the application—

(i) has provided notice of the filing under this paragraph to the bargaining representative (if any) of the employer's employees in the occupational classification and area for which aliens are sought, or

(ii) if there is no such bargaining representative, has provided notice of filing in the occupational classification through such methods as physical posting in conspicuous locations at the place of employment or electronic notification to employees in the occupational classification for which H–1B nonimmigrants are sought.

(D) The application shall contain a specification of the number of workers sought, the occupational classification in which the workers will be employed, and wage rate and conditions under which they will be employed.

(E)(i) In the case of an application described in clause (ii), the employer did not displace and will not displace a United States worker (as defined in paragraph (4)) employed by the employer within the period beginning 90 days before and ending 90 days after the date of filing of any visa petition supported by the application.

(ii) An application described in this clause is an application filed on or after the date final regulations are first promulgated to carry out this subparagraph, and before October 1, 2001, by an H–1B-dependent employer (as defined in paragraph (3)) or by an employer that has been found, on or after October 21, 1998, under paragraph (2)(C) or (5) to have committed a willful failure or misrepresentation during the 5–year period preceding the filing of the application. An application is not described in this clause if the only H–1B nonimmigrants sought in the application are exempt H–1B nonimmigrants.

(F) In the case of an application described in subparagraph (E)(ii), the employer will not place the nonimmigrant with another employer (regardless of whether or not such other employer is an H–1B-dependent employer) where—

(i) the nonimmigrant performs duties in whole or in part at one or more worksites owned, operated, or controlled by such other employer; and

(ii) there are indicia of an employment relationship between the nonimmigrant and such other employer;

unless the employer has inquired of the other employer as to whether, and has no knowledge that, within the period beginning 90 days before and ending 90 days after the date of the placement of the nonimmigrant with the other employer, the other employer has displaced or intends to displace a United States worker employed by the other employer.

(G)(i) In the case of an application described in subparagraph (E)(ii), subject to clause (ii), the employer, prior to filing the application—

(I) has taken good faith steps to recruit, in the United States using procedures that meet industry wide standards and offering compensation that is at least as great as that required to be offered to H–1B nonimmigrants under subparagraph (A), United States workers for the job for which the nonimmigrant or nonimmigrants is or are sought; and

(II) has offered the job to any United States worker who applies and is equally or better qualified for the job for which the nonimmigrant or nonimmigrants is or are sought.

(ii) The conditions described in clause (i) shall not apply to an application filed with respect to the employment of an H–1B nonimmigrant who is described in subparagraph (A), (B), or (C) of section 203(b)(1).

The employer shall make available for public examination, within one working day after the date on which an application under this paragraph is filed, at the employer's principal place of business or worksite, a copy of each such application (and such accompanying documents as are necessary). The Secretary shall compile, on a current basis, a list (by employer and by occupational classification) of the applications filed under this subsection. Such list shall include the wage rate, number of aliens sought, period of intended employment, and date of need. The Secretary shall make such list available for public examination in Washington, D.C. The Secretary of Labor shall review such an application only for completeness and obvious inaccuracies. Unless the Secretary finds that the application is incomplete or obviously inaccurate, the Secretary shall provide the certification described in section 101(a)(15)(H)(i)(b) [8 U.S.C.A. § 1101(a)(15)(H)(i)(b)] within 7 days of the date of the filing of the application. The application form shall include a clear statement explaining the liability under subparagraph (F) of a place employer if the other employer described in such subparagraph displaces a United States worker as described in such subparagraph. Nothing in subparagraph (G) shall be construed to prohibit an employer from using legitimate selection criteria relevant to the job that are normal or customary to the type of job involved, so long as such criteria are not applied in a discriminatory manner.

(2)(A) Subject to paragraph (5)(A), the Secretary shall establish a process for the receipt, investigation, and disposition of complaints respecting a petitioner's failure to meet a condition specified in an application submitted under paragraph (1) or a petitioner's misrepresentation of material facts in such an application. Complaints may be filed by any aggrieved person or organization (including bargaining representatives). No investigation or hearing shall be conducted on a complaint concerning such a failure or misrepresentation unless the complaint was filed not later than 12 months after the date of the failure or misrepresentation, respectively. The Secretary shall conduct an investigation under this paragraph if there is reasonable cause to believe that such a failure or misrepresentation has occurred.

(B) Under such process, the Secretary shall provide, within 30 days after the date such a complaint is filed, for a determination as to whether or not a reasonable basis exists to make a finding described in subparagraph (C). If the Secretary determines that such a reasonable basis exists, the Secretary shall provide for notice of such determination to the interested parties and an opportunity for a hearing on the complaint, in accordance with section 556 of Title 5, within 60 days after the date of the determination. If such a hearing is requested, the Secretary shall make a finding concerning the matter by not later than 60 days after the date of the hearing. In the case of similar complaints respecting the same applicant, the Secretary may consolidate the hearings under this subparagraph on such complaints.

(C)(i) If the Secretary finds, after notice and opportunity for a hearing, a failure to meet a condition of paragraph (1)(b), (1)(e), or (1)(f), a substantial failure to meet a condition of paragraph (1)(c), (1)(d), or (1)(g)(i)(i), or a misrepresentation of material fact in an application—

(I) the Secretary shall notify the Attorney General of such finding and may, in addition, impose such other administrative remedies (including civil monetary penalties in an amount not to exceed $1,000 per violation) as the Secretary determines to be appropriate; and

(II) the Attorney General shall not approve petitions filed with respect to that employer under section 204 [8 U.S.C.A. § 1154] or 214(c) [8 U.S.C.A. § 1184(c)] during a period of at least 1 year for aliens to be employed by the employer.

(ii) If the Secretary finds, after notice and opportunity for a hearing, a willful failure to meet a condition of paragraph (1), a willful misrepresentation of material fact in an application, or a violation of clause (iv)—

(I) the Secretary shall notify the Attorney General of such finding and may, in addition, impose such other administrative remedies (including civil monetary penalties in an amount not to exceed $5,000 per violation) as the Secretary determines to be appropriate; and

(II) the Attorney General shall not approve petitions filed with respect to that employer under section 204 [8 U.S.C.A. § 1154] or 214(c) [8 U.S.C.A. § 1184(c)] during a period of at least 2 years for aliens to be employed by the employer.

(iii) If the Secretary finds, after notice and opportunity for a hearing, a willful failure to meet a condition of paragraph (1) or a willful misrepresentation of material fact in an application, in the course of which failure or misrepresentation the employer displaced a United States worker employed by the employer within the period beginning 90 days before and ending 90 days after the date of filing of any visa petition supported by the application—

(I) the Secretary shall notify the Attorney General of such finding and may, in addition, impose such other administrative remedies (including civil monetary penalties in an amount not to exceed $35,000 per violation) as the Secretary determines to be appropriate; and

(II) the Attorney General shall not approve petitions filed with respect to that employer under section 204 [8 U.S.C.A. § 1154] or 214(c) [8 U.S.C.A. § 1184(c)] during a period of at least 3 years for aliens to be employed by the employer.

(iv) It is a violation of this clause for an employer who has filed an application under this subsection to intimidate, threaten, restrain, coerce, blacklist, discharge, or in any other manner discriminate against an employee (which term, for purposes of this clause, includes a former employee and an applicant for employment) because the employee has disclosed information to the employer, or to any other person, that the employee reasonably believes evidences a violation of this subsection, or any rule or regulation pertaining to this subsection, or because the employee cooperates or seeks to cooperate in an investigation or other proceeding concerning the employer's compliance with the requirements of this subsection or any rule or regulation pertaining to this subsection.

(v) The Secretary of Labor and the Attorney General shall devise a process under which an H–1B nonimmigrant who files a complaint regarding a violation of clause (iv) and is otherwise eligible to remain and work in the United States may be allowed to seek other appropriate employment in the United States for a period not to exceed the maximum period of stay authorized for such nonimmigrant classification.

(vi)(I) It is a violation of this clause for an employer who has filed an application under this subsection to require an H–1B nonimmigrant to pay a penalty for ceasing employment with the employer prior to a date agreed to by the nonimmigrant and the employer. The Secretary shall determine whether a required payment is a penalty (and not liquidated damages) pursuant to relevant State law.

(II) It is a violation of this clause for an employer who has filed an application under this subsection to require an alien who is the subject of a petition filed under section 214(c)(1) [8 U.S.C.A. § 1184(c)(1)], for which a fee is imposed under section 214(c)(9) [8 U.S.C.A. § 1184(c)(9)], to reimburse, or otherwise compensate, the employer for part or all of the cost of such fee. It is a violation of this clause for such an employer otherwise to accept such reimbursement or compensation from such an alien.

(III) If the Secretary finds, after notice and opportunity for a hearing, that an employer has committed a violation of this clause, the Secretary may impose a civil monetary penalty of $1,000 for each such violation and issue an administrative order requiring the return to the nonimmigrant of any amount paid in violation of this clause, or, if the nonimmigrant cannot be located, requiring payment of any such amount to the general fund of the Treasury.

(vii)(I) It is a failure to meet a condition of paragraph (1)(A) for an employer, who has filed an application under this subsection and who places an H–1B nonimmigrant designated as a full-time employee on the petition filed under section 214(c)(1) [8 U.S.C.A. § 1184(c)(1)] by the employer with respect to the nonimmigrant, after the nonimmigrant has entered into employment with the employer, in nonproductive status due to a decision by the employer (based on factors such as lack of work), or due to the nonimmigrant's lack of a permit or license, to fail to pay the nonimmigrant full-time wages in accordance with paragraph (1)(A) for all such nonproductive time.

(II) It is a failure to meet a condition of paragraph (1)(A) for an employer, who has filed an application under this subsection and who places an H–1B nonimmigrant designated as a part-time employee on the petition filed under section 214(c)(1) [8 U.S.C.A. § 1184(c)(1)] by the employer with respect to the nonimmigrant, after the nonimmigrant has entered into employment with the employer, in nonproductive status under circumstances described in subclause (I), to fail to pay such a nonimmigrant for such hours as are designated on such petition consistent with the rate of pay identified on such petition.

(III) In the case of an H–1B nonimmigrant who has not yet entered into employment with an employer who has had approved an application under this subsection, and a petition under section 214(c)(1) [8 U.S.C.A. § 1184(c)(1)], with respect to the nonimmigrant, the provisions of subclauses (I) and (II) shall apply to the employer beginning 30 days after the date the nonimmigrant first is admitted into the United States pursuant to the petition, or 60 days after the date the nonimmigrant becomes eligible to work for the employer (in the case of a nonimmigrant who is present in the United States on the date of the approval of the petition).

(IV) This clause does not apply to a failure to pay wages to an H–1B nonimmigrant for nonproductive time due to non-work-related factors, such as the voluntary request of the nonimmigrant for an absence or circumstances rendering the nonimmigrant unable to work.

(V) This clause shall not be construed as prohibiting an employer that is a school or other educational institution from applying to an H–1B nonimmigrant an established salary practice of the employer, under which the employer pays to H–1B nonimmigrants and United States workers in the same occupational classification an annual salary in disbursements over fewer than 12 months, if—

(aa) the nonimmigrant agrees to the compressed annual salary payments prior to the commencement of the employment; and

(bb) the application of the salary practice to the nonimmigrant does not otherwise cause the nonimmigrant to violate any condition of the nonimmigrant's authorization under this Act to remain in the United States.

(VI) This clause shall not be construed as superseding clause (viii).

(viii) It is a failure to meet a condition of paragraph (1)(A) for an employer who has filed an application under this subsection to fail to offer to an H–1B nonimmigrant, during the nonimmigrant's period of authorized employment, benefits and eligibility for benefits (including the opportunity to participate in health, life, disability, and other insurance plans; the opportunity to participate in retirement and savings plans; and cash bonuses and non-cash compensation, such as stock options (whether or not based on performance)) on the same basis, and in accordance with the same criteria, as the employer offers to United States workers.

(D) If the Secretary finds, after notice and opportunity for a hearing, that an employer has not paid wages at the wage level specified under the application and required under paragraph (1), the Secretary shall order the employer to provide for payment of such amounts of back pay as may be required to comply with the requirements of paragraph (1), whether or not a penalty under subparagraph (C) has been imposed.

(E) If an H–1B-dependent employer places a nonexempt H–1B nonimmigrant with another employer as provided under paragraph (1)(f) and the other employer has displaced or displaces a United States worker employed by such other employer during the period described in such paragraph, such displacement shall be considered for purposes of this paragraph a failure, by the placing employer, to meet a condition specified in an application submitted under paragraph (1); except that the attorney general may impose a sanction described in subclause (ii) of subparagraph (C)(i), (C)(ii), or (C)(iii) only if the Secretary of labor found that such placing employer

(i) knew or had reason to know of such displacement at the time of the placement of the nonimmigrant with the other employer; or

(ii) has been subject to a sanction under this subparagraph based upon a previous placement of an H–1B nonimmigrant with the same other employer.

(F) The Secretary may, on a case-by-case basis, subject an employer to random investigations for a period of up to 5 years, beginning on the date (on or after October 21, 1998) on which the employer is found by the Secretary to have committed a willful failure to meet a condition of paragraph (1) (or has been found under paragraph (5) to have committed a willful failure to meet the condition of paragraph (1)(G)(i)(II)) or to have made a willful misrepresentation of material fact in an application. The preceding sentence shall apply to an employer regardless of whether or not the employer is an H–1B-dependent employer. The authority of the Secretary under this subparagraph shall not be construed to be subject to, or limited by, the requirements of subparagraph (A).

(G)(i) If the Secretary receives specific credible information from a source, who is likely to have knowledge of an employer's practices or employment conditions, or an employer's compliance with the employer's labor condition application under paragraph (1), and whose identity is known to the Secretary, and such information provides reasonable cause to believe that the employer has committed a willful failure to meet a condition of paragraph (1)(A), (1)(B), (1)(E), (1)(F), or (1)(G)(i)(I), has engaged in a pattern or practice of failures to meet such a condition, or has committed a substantial failure to meet such a condition that affects multiple employees, the Secretary may conduct a 30–day investigation into the alleged failure or failures. The Secretary (or the Acting Secretary in the case of the Secretary's absence or disability) shall personally certify that the requirements for conducting such an investigation have been met and shall approve commencement of the investigation. The Secretary may withhold the identity of the source from the employer, and the source's identity shall not be subject to disclosure under section 552 of Title 5.

(ii) The Secretary shall establish a procedure for any person, desiring to provide to the Secretary information described in clause (i) that may be used, in whole or in part, as the basis for commencement of an investigation described in such clause, to provide the information in writing on a form developed and provided by the Secretary and completed by or on behalf of the person. The person may not be an officer or employee of the Department of Labor, unless the information satisfies the requirement of clause (iii)(II) (although an officer or employee of the Department of Labor may complete the form on behalf of the person).

(iii) Any investigation initiated or approved by the Secretary under clause (i) shall be based on information that satisfies the requirements of such clause and that (I) originates from a source other than an officer or employee of the Department of Labor, or (II) was lawfully obtained by the Secretary of Labor in the course of lawfully conducting another Department of Labor investigation under this chapter or any other Act.

(iv) The receipt by the Secretary of information submitted by an employer to the Attorney General or the Secretary for purposes of securing the employment of an H–1B nonimmigrant shall not be considered a receipt of information for purposes of clause (i).

(v) No investigation described in clause (i) (or hearing described in clause (vii)) may be conducted with respect to information about a failure to meet a condition described in clause (i), unless the Secretary receives the information not later than 12 months after the date of the alleged failure.

(vi) The Secretary shall provide notice to an employer with respect to whom the Secretary has received information described in clause (i), prior to the commencement of an investigation under such clause, of the receipt of the information and of the potential for an investigation. The notice shall be provided in such a manner, and shall contain sufficient detail, to permit the employer to respond to the allegations before an investigation is commenced. The Secretary is not required to comply with this clause if the Secretary determines that to do so would interfere with an effort by the Secretary to secure compliance by the employer with the requirements of this subsection. There shall be no judicial review of a determination by the Secretary under this clause.

(vii) If the Secretary determines under this subparagraph that a reasonable basis exists to make a finding that a failure described in clause (i) has occurred, the Secretary shall provide for notice of such determination to the interested parties and an opportunity for a hearing, in accordance with section 556 of Title 5, within 60 days after the date of the determination. If such a hearing is requested, the Secretary shall make a finding concerning the matter by not later than 60 days after the date of the hearing.

(H) Nothing in this subsection shall be construed as superseding or preempting any other enforcement-related authority under this chapter (such as the authorities under section 274B [8 U.S.C.A. § 1324b]), or any other Act.

(3)(A) For purposes of this subsection, the term "H–1B-dependent employer" means an employer that

(i)(I) has 25 or fewer full-time equivalent employees who are employed in the United States; and **(II)** employs more than 7 H–1B nonimmigrants;

(ii)(I) has at least 26 but not more than 50 full-time equivalent employees who are employed in the United States; and **(II)** employs more than 12 H–1B nonimmigrants; or

(iii)(I) has at least 51 full-time equivalent employees who are employed in the United States; and **(II)** employs H–1B nonimmigrants in a number that is equal to at least 15 percent of the number of such full-time equivalent employees.

(B) For purposes of this subsection

(i) the term "exempt H–1B nonimmigrant" means an H–1B nonimmigrant who—

(I) receives wages (including cash bonuses and similar compensation) at an annual rate equal to at least $60,000; or

(II) has attained a master's or higher degree (or its equivalent) in a specialty related to the intended employment; and

(ii) the term "nonexempt H–1B nonimmigrant" means an H–1B nonimmigrant who is not an exempt H–1B nonimmigrant.

(C) For purposes of subparagraph (A)

(i) in computing the number of full-time equivalent employees and the number of H–1B nonimmigrants, exempt H–1B nonimmigrants shall not be taken into account during the longer of—

(I) the 6–month period beginning on October 21, 1998; or

(II) the period beginning on October 21, 1998 and ending on the date final regulations are issued to carry out this paragraph; and

(ii) any group treated as a single employer under subsection (b), (c), (m), or (*o*) of section 414 of the Internal Revenue Code of 1986 shall be treated as a single employer.

(4) For purposes of this subsection:

(A) The term "area of employment" means the area within normal commuting distance of the worksite or physical location where the work of the H–1B nonimmigrant is or will be performed. If such worksite or location is within a Metropolitan Statistical Area, any place within such area is deemed to be within the area of employment.

(B) In the case of an application with respect to one or more H–1B nonimmigrants by an employer, the employer is considered to "displace" a United States worker from a job if the employer lays off the worker from a job that is essentially the equivalent of the job for which the nonimmigrant or nonimmigrants is or are sought. A job shall not be considered to be essentially equivalent of another job unless it involves essentially the same responsibilities, was held by a United States worker with substantially equivalent qualifications and experience, and is located in the same area of employment as the other job.

(C) The term "H–1B nonimmigrant" means an alien admitted or provided status as a nonimmigrant described in section 101(a)(15)(H)(i)(b) [8 U.S.C.A. § 1101(a)(15)(H)(i)(b)].

(D)(i) The term "lays off", with respect to a worker—

(I) means to cause the worker's loss of employment, other than through a discharge for inadequate performance, violation of workplace rules, cause, voluntary departure, voluntary retirement, or the expiration of a grant or contract (other than a temporary employment contract entered into in order to evade a condition described in subparagraph (E) or (F) of paragraph (1)); but

(II) does not include any situation in which the worker is offered, as an alternative to such loss of employment, a similar employment opportunity with the same employer (or, in the case of a placement of a worker with another employer under paragraph (1)(F), with either employer described in such paragraph) at equivalent or higher compensation and benefits than the position from which the employee was discharged, regardless of whether or not the employee accepts the offer.

(ii) Nothing in this subparagraph is intended to limit an employee's rights under a collective bargaining agreement or other employment contract.

(E) The term "United States worker" means an employee who—

(i) is a citizen or national of the United States; or

(ii) is an alien who is lawfully admitted for permanent residence, is admitted as a refugee under section 207 [8 U.S.C.A. § 1157], is granted asylum under section 208 [8

U.S.C.A. § 1158], or is an immigrant otherwise authorized, by this chapter or by the Attorney General, to be employed.

(5)(A) This paragraph shall apply instead of subparagraphs (A) through (E) of paragraph (2) in the case of a violation described in subparagraph (B), but shall not be construed to limit or affect the authority of the Secretary or the Attorney General with respect to any other violation.

(B) The Attorney General shall establish a process for the receipt, initial review, and disposition in accordance with this paragraph of complaints respecting an employer's failure to meet the condition of paragraph (1)(G)(i)(II) or a petitioner's misrepresentation of material facts with respect to such condition. Complaints may be filed by an aggrieved individual who has submitted a resume or otherwise applied in a reasonable manner for the job that is the subject of the condition. No proceeding shall be conducted under this paragraph on a complaint concerning such a failure or misrepresentation unless the Attorney General determines that the complaint was filed not later than 12 months after the date of the failure or misrepresentation, respectively.

(C) If the Attorney General finds that a complaint has been filed in accordance with subparagraph (B) and there is reasonable cause to believe that such a failure or misrepresentation described in such complaint has occurred, the Attorney General shall initiate binding arbitration proceedings by requesting the Federal Mediation and Conciliation Service to appoint an arbitrator from the roster of arbitrators maintained by such Service. The procedure and rules of such Service shall be applicable to the selection of such arbitrator and to such arbitration proceedings. The Attorney General shall pay the fee and expenses of the arbitrator.

(D)(i) The arbitrator shall make findings respecting whether a failure or misrepresentation described in subparagraph (B) occurred. If the arbitrator concludes that failure or misrepresentation was willful, the arbitrator shall make a finding to that effect. The arbitrator may not find such a failure or misrepresentation (or that such a failure or misrepresentation was willful) unless the complainant demonstrates such a failure or misrepresentation (or its willful character) by clear and convincing evidence. The arbitrator shall transmit the findings in the form of a written opinion to the parties to the arbitration and the Attorney General. Such findings shall be final and conclusive, and, except as provided in this subparagraph, no official or court of the United States shall have power or jurisdiction to review any such findings.

(ii) The Attorney General may review and reverse or modify the findings of an arbitrator only on the same bases as an award of an arbitrator may be vacated or modified under section 10 or 11 of Title 9.

(iii) With respect to the findings of an arbitrator, a court may review only the actions of the Attorney General under clause (ii) and may set aside such actions only on the grounds described in subparagraph (A), (B), or (C) of section 706(a)(2) of Title 5. Notwithstanding any other provision of law, such judicial review may only be brought in an appropriate United States court of appeals.

(E) If the attorney general receives a finding of an arbitrator under this paragraph that an employer has failed to meet the condition of paragraph (1)(g)(i)(ii) or has misrepresented a material fact with respect to such condition, unless the attorney general reverses or modifies the finding under subparagraph (d)(ii)

(i) the Attorney General may impose administrative remedies (including civil monetary penalties in an amount not to exceed $1,000 per violation or $5,000 per violation in the case of a willful failure or misrepresentation) as the Attorney General determines to be appropriate; and

(ii) the Attorney General is authorized to not approve petitions filed, with respect to that employer and for aliens to be employed by the employer, under section 204 [8 U.S.C.A. § 1154] or 214(c) [8 U.S.C.A. § 1184(c)]—

(I) during a period of not more than 1 year; or

(II) in the case of a willful failure or willful misrepresentation, during a period of not more than 2 years.

(F) The Attorney General shall not delegate, to any other employee or official of the Department of Justice, any function of the Attorney General under this paragraph, until 60 days after the Attorney General has submitted a plan for such delegation to the Committees on the Judiciary of the United States House of Representatives and the Senate.

(*o*) Repealed.

(p) Computation of prevailing wage level

(1) In computing the prevailing wage level for an occupational classification in an area of employment for purposes of subsections (n)(1)(a)(i)(ii) and (a)(5)(a) in the case of an employee of

(A) an institution of higher education (as defined in section 1001(a) of Title 20), or a related or affiliated nonprofit entity; or

(B) a nonprofit research organization or a Governmental research organization,

the prevailing wage level shall only take into account employees at such institutions and organizations in the area of employment.

(2) With respect to a professional athlete (as defined in subsection (a)(5)(A)(iii)(II)) when the job opportunity is covered by professional sports league rules or regulations, the wage set forth in those rules or regulations shall be considered as not adversely affecting the wages of United States workers similarly employed and be considered the prevailing wage.

(q) Any alien admitted under section 101(a)(15)(B) [8 U.S.C.A. § 1101(a)(15)(B)] may accept an honorarium payment and associated incidental expenses for a usual academic activity or activities (lasting not longer than 9 days at any single institution), as defined by the Attorney General in consultation with the Secretary of Education, if such payment is offered by an institution or organization described in subsection (p)(1) and is made for services conducted for the benefit of that institution or entity and if the alien has not accepted such payment or expenses from more than 5 institutions or organizations in the previous 6–month period.

(r) Certification for certain alien nurses

Subsection (a)(5)(C) shall not apply to an alien who seeks to enter the United States for the purpose of performing labor as a nurse who presents to the consular officer (or in the case of an adjustment of status, the Attorney General) a certified statement from the Commission on Graduates of Foreign Nursing Schools (or an equivalent independent credentialing organization approved for the certification of nurses under subsection (a)(5)(C) by the Attorney General in consultation with the Secretary of Health and Human Services) that—

(1) the alien has a valid and unrestricted license as a nurse in a State where the alien intends to be employed and such State verifies that the foreign licenses of alien nurses are authentic and unencumbered;

(2) the alien has passed the National Council Licensure Examination (NCLEX);

(3) the alien is a graduate of a nursing program—

(A) in which the language of instruction was English;

(B) located in a country—

(i) designated by such commission not later than 30 days after the date of the enactment of the Nursing Relief for Disadvantaged Areas Act of 1999, based on such commission's assessment that the quality of nursing education in that country, and the English language proficiency of those who complete such programs in that country, justify the country's designation; or

(ii) designated on the basis of such an assessment by unanimous agreement of such commission and any equivalent credentialing organizations which have been approved under subsection (a)(5)(C) for the certification of nurses under this subsection; and

(C)(i) which was in operation on or before the date of the enactment of the Nursing Relief for Disadvantaged Areas Act of 1999; or

(ii) has been approved by unanimous agreement of such commission and any equivalent credentialing organizations which have been approved under subsection (a)(5)(C) for the certification of nurses under this subsection.

(June 27, 1952, c. 477, Title II, ch. 2, § 212, 66 Stat. 182; July 18, 1956, c. 629, Title III, § 301(a), 70 Stat. 575; July 7, 1958, Pub.L. 85–508, § 23, 72 Stat. 351; Mar. 18, 1959, Pub.L. 86–3, § 20(b), 73 Stat. 13; July 14, 1960, Pub.L. 86–648, § 8, 74 Stat. 505; Sept. 21, 1961, Pub.L. 87–256, § 109(c), 75 Stat. 535; Sept. 26, 1961, Pub.L. 87–301, §§ 11–15, 75 Stat. 654, 655; Oct. 3, 1965, Pub.L. 89–236, §§ 10, 15, 79 Stat. 917, 919; Apr. 7, 1970, Pub.L. 91–225, § 2, 84 Stat. 116; Oct. 12, 1976, Pub.L. 94–484, Title VI, § 601(a), (c), (d), 90 Stat. 2300, 2301; Oct. 20, 1976, Pub.L. 94–571, §§ 5, 7(d), 90 Stat. 2705, 2706; 1966 Reorg. Plan No. 3, §§ 1, 3, 31 F.R. 8855, 80 Stat. 1610; Aug. 1, 1977, Pub.L. 95–83, Title III, § 307(q)(1), (2), 91 Stat. 394; 1977 Reorg. Plan No. 2, § 7(a)(8), 42 F.R. 62461, 91 Stat. 1637; Oct. 30, 1978, Pub.L. 95–549, Title I, §§ 101, 102, 92 Stat. 2065; Sept. 27, 1979, Pub.L. 96–70, Title III, § 3201(b), 93 Stat. 497; Oct. 17, 1979, Pub.L. 96–88, Title III, § 301(a)(1), Title I, §§ 503, 509(b), 93 Stat. 677, 690, 695; Mar. 17, 1980, Pub.L. 96–212, Title II, § 203(d), (f), 94 Stat. 107; Dec. 17, 1980, Pub.L. 96–538, Title IV, § 404, 94 Stat. 3192; Dec. 29, 1981, Pub.L. 97–116, §§ 4, 5(a)(1), (2), (b), 18(e), 95 Stat. 1611, 1612, 1620; Oct. 5, 1984, Pub.L. 98–454, Title VI, § 602(a), 98 Stat. 1737; Oct. 12, 1984, Pub.L. 98–473, Title II, § 220(a), 98 Stat. 2028; Oct. 27, 1986, Pub.L. 99–396, § 14(a), 100 Stat. 842; Oct. 27, 1986, Pub.L. 99–570, Title I, § 1751(a), 100 Stat. 3207–47; Nov. 10, 1986, Pub.L. 99–639, § 6(a), 100 Stat. 3544; Oct. 24, 1988, Pub.L. 100–525, § 7(c)(1), 102 Stat. 2616; Nov. 10, 1986, Pub.L. 99–639, § 6(b), as added Oct. 24, 1988, Pub.L. 100–525, § 7(c)(3), 102 Stat. 2617; Nov. 14, 1986, Pub.L. 99–653, § 7(a), 100 Stat. 3657; Nov. 14, 1986, Pub. L. 99–653, § 7(d)(2), as added Oct. 24, 1988, Pub.L. 100–525, § 8(f), 102 Stat. 2617; Dec. 22, 1987, Pub.L. 100–204, § 806(c), 101 Stat. 1399; Oct. 24, 1988, Pub.L. 100–525, §§ 3(1)(A), 9(i), 102 Stat. 2614, 2620; Nov. 18, 1988, Pub.L. 100–690, Title VII, § 7349(a), 102 Stat. 4473; Dec. 18, 1989, Pub.L. 101–238, § 3(b), 103 Stat. 2100; Feb. 16, 1990, Pub.L. 101–246, Title I, § 131(a), (c), 104 Stat. 31; Nov. 29, 1990, Pub.L. 101–649, Title I, § 162(e)(1), (f)(2)(B), Title II, §§ 202(b), 205(c)(3), Title V, §§ 511(a), 514(a), Title VI, § 601(a), (b), (d), 104 Stat. 5011, 5012, 5014, 5020, 5052, 5053, 5067, 5075 to 5077; Dec. 12, 1991, Pub.L. 102–232, Title III, §§ 302(e)(6), (9), 303(a)(5)(B), (6), (7)(B), 306(a)(10), (12), 307(a) to (g), 309(b)(7), 105 Stat. 1746 to 1748, 1751, 1753 to 1755, 1759; June 10, 1993, Pub.L. 103–43, Title XX, § 2007(a), 107 Stat. 210; Aug. 26, 1994, Pub.L. 103–317, Title V, § 506(a), 108 Stat. 1765; Sept. 13, 1994, Pub.L. 103–322, Title XIII, § 130003(b)(1), 108 Stat. 2024; Oct. 25, 1994, Pub.L. 103–416, Title II, §§ 203(a), 219(e), (z)(1), (5), 220(a), 108 Stat. 4311, 4316, 4318, 4319; Apr. 24, 1996, Pub.L. 104–132, Title IV, §§ 411, 412, 440(d), 110 Stat. 1268, 1269, 1277; Sept. 30, 1996, Pub.L. 104–208, Div. C, Title I, § 124(b)(1), Title III, §§ 301(b)(1), (c)(1), 304(b), 305(c), 306(d), 308(c)(2)(B), (d)(1), (e)(1)(B), (C), (2)(A), (6), (f)(1)(C) to (F), (3)(A), (g)(1), (4)(B), (10)(A), (H), 322(a)(2)(B), 341(a), (b), 342(a), 343, 344(a), 345(a), 346(a), 347(a), 348(a), 349, 351(a), 352(a), 355, Title V, § 531(a), Title VI, §§ 602(a), 622(b), 624(a), 671(e)(3), 110 Stat. 3009–562, 3009–576, 3009–578, 3009–597, 3009–607, 3009–612, 3009–616, 3009–619, 3009–620, 3009–621, 3009–622, 3009–625, 3009–

629, 3009–635 to 3009–641, 3009–644, 3009–674, 3009–689, 3009–695, 3009–698, 3009–723; Nov. 12, 1997, Pub.L. 105–73, § 1, 111 Stat. 1459; Oct. 21, 1998, Pub.L. 105–277, Div. C, Title IV, §§ 412, 413, 415(a), 431(a), Div. G, Title XXII, § 2226, 112 Stat. 2681–642, 2681–643, 2681–645, 2681–648, 2681–649, 2681–650, 2681–651, 2681–654, 2681–658, 2681–820; Oct. 27, 1998, Pub.L. 105–292, Title VI, § 604(a), 112 Stat. 2814; Nov. 12, 1999, Pub.L. 106–95, §§ 2(b), 4(a), 113 Stat. 1312, 1317; Dec. 3, 1999, Pub.L. 106–120, Title VIII, § 809, 113 Stat. 1632.)

§ 213. Admission of aliens on giving bond or undertaking; return upon permanent departure [8 U.S.C.A. § 1183]

An alien inadmissible under paragraph (4) of section 212(a) [8 U.S.C.A. § 1182(a)] may, if otherwise admissible, be admitted in the discretion of the Attorney General (subject to the affidavit of support requirement and attribution of sponsor's income and resources under section 213A [8 U.S.C.A. § 1183a]) upon the giving of a suitable and proper bond or undertaking approved by the Attorney General, in such amount and containing such conditions as he may prescribe, to the United States, and to all States, territories, counties, towns, municipalities, and districts thereof holding the United States and all States, territories, counties, towns, municipalities, and districts thereof harmless against such alien becoming a public charge. Such bond or undertaking shall terminate upon the permanent departure from the United States, the naturalization, or the death of such alien, and any sums or other security held to secure performance thereof, except to the extent forfeited for violation of the terms thereof, shall be returned to the person by whom furnished, or to his legal representatives. Suit may be brought thereon in the name and by the proper law officers of the United States for the use of the United States, or of any State, territory, district, county, town or municipality in which such alien becomes a public charge, irrespective of whether a demand for payment of public expenses has been made.

(June 27, 1952, c. 477, Title II, ch. 2, § 213, 66 Stat. 188; July 10, 1970, Pub.L. 91–313, § 1, 84 Stat. 413; Nov. 29, 1990, Pub.L. 101–649, Title VI, § 603(a)(8), 104 Stat. 5083; Sept. 30, 1996, Pub.L. 104–208, Div. C, Title III, § 308(d)(3)(A), Title V, § 564(f), 110 Stat. 3009–617, 3009–684.)

§ 213A. Requirements for sponsor's affidavit of support [8 U.S.C.A. § 1183a]

(a) Enforceability

(1) Terms of affidavit

No affidavit of support may be accepted by the Attorney General or by any consular officer to establish that an alien is not excludable as a public charge under section 212(a)(4) [8 U.S.C.A. § 1182(a)(4)] unless such affidavit is executed by a sponsor of the alien as a contract—

(A) in which the sponsor agrees to provide support to maintain the sponsored alien at an annual income that is not less than 125 percent of the Federal poverty line during the period in which the affidavit is enforceable;

not < 125% of Fed. poverty during time affid.

(B) that is legally enforceable against the sponsor by the sponsored alien, the Federal Government, any State (or any political subdivision of such State), or by any other entity that provides any means-tested public benefit (as defined in subsection (e)), consistent with the provisions of this section; and

Legally enforced.

(C) in which the sponsor agrees to submit to the jurisdiction of any Federal or State court for the purpose of actions brought under subsection (b)(2).

(2) Period of enforceability

An affidavit of support shall be enforceable with respect to benefits provided for an alien before the date the alien is naturalized as a citizen of the United States, or, if earlier, the termination date provided under paragraph (3).

(3) Termination of period of enforceability upon completion of required period of employment, etc.

(A) In general

An affidavit of support is not enforceable after such time as the alien (i) has worked 40 qualifying quarters of coverage as defined under title II of the Social Security Act [42 U.S.C.A § 401 et seq.] or can be credited with such qualifying quarters as provided under subparagraph (B), and (ii) in the case of any such qualifying quarter creditable for any period beginning after December 31, 1996, did not receive any Federal means-tested public benefit (as provided under section 403 of the Personal Responsibility and Work Opportunity Reconciliation Act of 1996 [8 U.S.C.A. § 1613]) during any such period.

(B) Qualifying quarters

For purposes of this section, in determining the number of qualifying quarters of coverage under title II of the Social Security Act [42 U.S.C.A. § 401 et seq.] an alien shall be credited with—

(i) all of the qualifying quarters of coverage as defined under title II of the Social Security Act worked by a parent of such alien while the alien was under age 18, and

(ii) all of the qualifying quarters worked by a spouse of such alien during their marriage and the alien remains married to such spouse or such spouse is deceased.

No such qualifying quarter of coverage that is creditable under title II of the Social Security Act [42 U.S.C.A. § 401 et seq.] for any period beginning after December 31, 1996, may be credited to an alien under clause (i) or (ii) if the parent or spouse (as the case may be) of such alien received any Federal means-tested public benefit (as provided under section 403 of the Personal Responsibility and Work Opportunity Reconciliation Act of 1996 [8 U.S.C.A. § 1613]) during the period for which such qualifying quarter of coverage is so credited.

(C) Provision of information to SAVE system

The Attorney General shall ensure that appropriate information regarding the application of this paragraph is provided to the system for alien verification of eligibility (SAVE) described in section 1137(d)(3) of the Social Security Act [42 U.S.C.A. § 1320b–7(d)(3)].

(b) Reimbursement of government expenses

(1) Request for reimbursement

(A) Requirement

Upon notification that a sponsored alien has received any means-tested public benefit, the appropriate nongovernmental entity which provided such benefit or the appropriate entity of the Federal Government, a State, or any political subdivision of a State shall request reimbursement by the sponsor in an amount which is equal to the unreimbursed costs of such benefit.

(B) Regulations

The Attorney General, in consultation with the heads of other appropriate Federal agencies, shall prescribe such regulations as may be necessary to carry out subparagraph (A).

(2) Actions to compel reimbursement

(A) In case of nonresponse

If within 45 days after a request for reimbursement under paragraph (1)(A), the appropriate entity has not received a response from the sponsor indicating a willingness to commence payment an action may be brought against the sponsor pursuant to the affidavit of support.

(B) In case of failure to pay

If the sponsor fails to abide by the repayment terms established by the appropriate entity, the entity may bring an action against the sponsor pursuant to the affidavit of support.

(C) Limitation on actions

No cause of action may be brought under this paragraph later than 10 years after the date on which the sponsored alien last received any means-tested public benefit to which the affidavit of support applies.

(3) Use of collection agencies

If the appropriate entity under paragraph (1)(A) requests reimbursement from the sponsor or brings an action against the sponsor pursuant to the affidavit of support, the appropriate entity may appoint or hire an individual or other person to act on behalf of such entity acting under the authority of law for purposes of collecting any amounts owed.

(c) Remedies

Remedies available to enforce an affidavit of support under this section include any or all of the remedies described in section 3201, 3203, 3204, or 3205 of Title 28, as well as an order for specific performance and payment of legal fees and other costs of collection, and include corresponding remedies available under State law. A Federal agency may seek to collect amounts owed under this section in accordance with the provisions of subchapter II of chapter 37 of Title 31.

(d) Notification of change of address

(1) General requirement

The sponsor shall notify the Attorney General and the State in which the sponsored alien is currently a resident within 30 days of any change of address of the sponsor during the period in which an affidavit of support is enforceable.

(2) Penalty

Any person subject to the requirement of paragraph (1) who fails to satisfy such requirement shall, after notice and opportunity to be heard, be subject to a civil penalty of—

(A) not less than $250 or more than $2,000, or

(B) if such failure occurs with knowledge that the sponsored alien has received any means-tested public benefits (other than benefits described in section 401(b), 403(c)(2), or 411(b) of the Personal Responsibility and Work Opportunity Reconciliation Act of 1996 [8 U.S.C.A. § 1611(b), 1613(c)(2), or 1621(b)]) not less than $2,000 or more than $5,000.

The Attorney General shall enforce this paragraph under appropriate regulations.

(e) Jurisdiction

An action to enforce an affidavit of support executed under subsection (a) may be brought against the sponsor in any appropriate court—

(1) by a sponsored alien, with respect to financial support; or

(2) by the appropriate entity of the Federal Government, a State or any political subdivision of a State, or by any other nongovernmental entity under subsection (b)(2), with respect to reimbursement.

(f) "Sponsor" defined

(1) In general

For purposes of this section the term "sponsor" in relation to a sponsored alien means an individual who executes an affidavit of support with respect to the sponsored alien and who—

(A) is a citizen or national of the United States or an alien who is lawfully admitted to the United States for permanent residence;

(B) is at least 18 years of age;

(C) is domiciled in any of the several States of the United States, the District of Columbia, or any territory or possession of the United States;

(D) is petitioning for the admission of the alien under section 204 [8 U.S.C.A. § 1154]; and

(E) demonstrates (as provided in paragraph (6)) the means to maintain an annual income equal to at least 125 percent of the Federal poverty line.

(2) Income requirement case

Such term also includes an individual who does not meet the requirement of paragraph (1)(E) but accepts joint and several liability together with an individual under paragraph (5).

(3) Active duty armed services case

Such term also includes an individual who does not meet the requirement of paragraph (1)(E) but is on active duty (other than active duty for training) in the Armed Forces of the United States, is petitioning for the admission of the alien under section 204 [8 U.S.C.A. § 1154] as the spouse or child of the individual, and demonstrates (as provided in paragraph (6)) the means to maintain an annual income equal to at least 100 percent of the Federal poverty line.

(4) Certain employment-based immigrants case

Such term also includes an individual—

(A) who does not meet the requirement of paragraph (1)(D), but is the relative of the sponsored alien who filed a classification petition for the sponsored alien as an employment-based immigrant under section 203(b) [8 U.S.C.A. § 1153(b)] or who has a significant ownership interest in the entity that filed such a petition; and

(B)(i) who demonstrates (as provided under paragraph (6)) the means to maintain an annual income equal to at least 125 percent of the Federal poverty line, or

(ii) does not meet the requirement of paragraph (1)(E) but accepts joint and several liability together with an individual under paragraph (5).

(5) Non-petitioning case

Such term also includes an individual who does not meet the requirement of paragraph (1)(D) but who accepts joint and several liability with a petitioning sponsor under paragraph (2) or relative of an employment-based immigrant under paragraph (4) and who demonstrates (as provided under paragraph (6)) the means to maintain an annual income equal to at least 125 percent of the Federal poverty line.

(6) Demonstration of means to maintain income

(A) In general

(i) Method of demonstration

For purposes of this section, a demonstration of the means to maintain income shall include provision of a certified copy of the individual's Federal income tax return for the individual's 3 most recent taxable years and a written statement, executed under oath or as permitted under penalty of perjury under section 1746 of Title 28, that the copies are certified copies of such returns.

(ii) Flexibility

For purposes of this section, aliens may demonstrate the means to maintain income through demonstration of significant assets of the sponsored alien or of the sponsor, if such assets are available for the support of the sponsored alien.

(iii) Percent of poverty

For purposes of this section, a reference to an annual income equal to at least a particular percentage of the Federal poverty line means an annual income equal to at least such percentage of the Federal poverty line for a family unit of a size equal to the number of members of the sponsor's household (including family and non-family dependents) plus the total number of other dependents and aliens sponsored by that sponsor.

(B) Limitation

The Secretary of State, or the Attorney General in the case of adjustment of status, may provide that the demonstration under subparagraph (A) applies only to the most recent taxable year.

(h) [sic] Federal poverty line defined

For purposes of this section, the term "Federal poverty line" means the level of income equal to the official poverty line (as defined by the Director of the Office of Management and Budget, as revised annually by the Secretary of Health and Human Services, in accordance with section 9902(2) of Title 42) that is applicable to a family of the size involved.

(i) Sponsor's social security account number required to be provided

(1) An affidavit of support shall include the social security account number of each sponsor.

(2) The Attorney General shall develop an automated system to maintain the social security account number data provided under paragraph (1).

(3) The Attorney General shall submit an annual report to the Committees on the Judiciary of the House of Representatives and the Senate setting forth—

(A) for the most recent fiscal year for which data are available the number of sponsors under this section and the number of sponsors in compliance with the financial obligations of this section; and

(B) a comparison of such numbers with the numbers of such sponsors for the preceding fiscal year.

(June 27, 1952, c. 477, Title II, ch. 2, § 213A, as added Aug. 22, 1996, Pub.L. 104–193, Title IV, § 423(a), 110 Stat. 2271, and amended Sept. 30, 1996, Pub.L. 104–208, Div. C, Title V, § 551(a), 110 Stat. 3009–675.)

§ 214. Admission of nonimmigrants [8 U.S.C.A. § 1184]

(a) Regulations

(1) The admission to the United States of any alien as a nonimmigrant shall be for such time and under such conditions as the Attorney General may by regulations prescribe, including when he deems necessary the giving of a bond with sufficient surety in such sum and containing such conditions as the Attorney General shall prescribe, to insure that at the expiration of such time or upon failure to maintain the status under which he was admitted, or to maintain any status subsequently acquired under section 248 [8 U.S.C.A. § 1258], such alien will depart from the United States. No alien admitted to Guam without a visa pursuant to section 212(*l*) [8 U.S.C.A. § 1182(*l*)] may be authorized to enter or stay in the United States other than in Guam or to remain in Guam for a period exceeding fifteen days from date of admission to Guam. No alien admitted to the United States without a visa pursuant to section 217 [8 U.S.C.A. § 1187] may be authorized to remain in the United States as a nonimmigrant visitor for a period exceeding 90 days from the date of admission.

(2)(A) The period of authorized status as a nonimmigrant described in section 101(a)(15)(O) [8 U.S.C.A. § 1101(a)(15)(O)] shall be for such period as the Attorney General may specify in order to provide for the event (or events) for which the nonimmigrant is admitted.

(B) The period of authorized status as a nonimmigrant described in section 101(a)(15)(P) [8 U.S.C.A. § 1101(a)(15)(P)] shall be for such period as the Attorney General may specify in order to provide for the competition, event, or performance for which the nonimmigrant is admitted. In the case of nonimmigrants admitted as individual athletes under section 101(a)(15)(P) [8 U.S.C.A. § 1101(a)(15)(P)], the period of authorized status may be for an initial period (not to exceed 5 years) during which the nonimmigrant will perform as an athlete and such period may be extended by the Attorney General for an additional period of up to 5 years.

(b) Presumption of status; written waiver

Every alien (other than a nonimmigrant described in subparagraph (H)(i) or (L) of section 101(a)(15) [8 U.S.C.A. § 1101(a)(15)]) shall be presumed to be an immigrant until he establishes to the satisfaction of the consular officer, at the time of application for a visa, and the immigration officers, at the time of application for admission, that he is entitled to a nonimmigrant status under section 101(a)(15) [8 U.S.C.A. § 1101(a)(15)]. An alien who is an officer or employee of any foreign government or of any international organization entitled to enjoy privileges, exemptions, and immunities under the International Organizations Immunities Act [22 U.S.C.A. § 288 et seq.], or an alien who is the attendant, servant, employee, or member of the immediate family of any such alien shall not be entitled to apply for or receive an immigrant visa, or to enter the United States as an immigrant unless he executes a written waiver in the same form and substance as is prescribed by section 247(b) [8 U.S.C.A. § 1257(b)].

(c) Petition of importing employer; involvement of Departments of Labor and Agriculture

(1) The question of importing any alien as a nonimmigrant under section 101(a)(15)(H), (L), (O), or (P)(i) [8 U.S.C.A. § 1101(a)(15)(H), (L), (O), or (P)(i)] in any specific case or specific cases shall be determined by the Attorney General, after consultation with appropriate agencies of the Government, upon petition of the importing employer. Such petition, shall be made and approved before the visa is granted. The petition shall be in such form and contain such information as the Attorney General shall prescribe. The approval of such a petition shall not, of itself, be construed as establishing that the alien is a nonimmigrant. For purposes of this subsection with respect to nonimmigrants described in section 101(a)(15)(H)(ii)(a) [8 U.S.C.A. § 1101(a)(15)(H)(ii)(a)], the term "appropriate agencies of Government" means the Department of Labor and includes the Department of Agriculture. The provisions of section 218 [8 U.S.C.A. § 1188] shall apply to the question of importing any alien as a nonimmigrant under section 101(a)(15)(H)(ii)(a) [8 U.S.C.A. § 1101(a)(15)(H)(ii)(a)].

(2)(A) The Attorney General shall provide for a procedure under which an importing employer which meets requirements established by the Attorney General may file a blanket petition to import aliens as nonimmigrants described in section 101(a)(15)(L) [8 U.S.C.A. § 1101(a)(15)(L)] instead of filing individual petitions under paragraph (1) to import such aliens. Such procedure shall permit the expedited processing of visas for admission of aliens covered under such a petition.

(B) For purposes of section 101(a)(15)(L) [8 U.S.C.A. § 1101(a)(15)(L)], an alien is considered to be serving in a capacity involving specialized knowledge with respect to a company if the alien has a special knowledge of the company product and its application in international markets or has an advanced level of knowledge of processes and procedures of the company.

(C) The Attorney General shall provide a process for reviewing and acting upon petitions under this subsection with respect to nonimmigrants described in section 101(a)(15)(L) [8 U.S.C.A. § 1101(a)(15)(L)] within 30 days after the date a completed petition has been filed.

(D) The period of authorized admission for—

(i) a nonimmigrant admitted to render services in a managerial or executive capacity under section 101(a)(15)(L) [8 U.S.C.A. § 1101(a)(15)(L)] shall not exceed 7 years, or

(ii) a nonimmigrant admitted to render services in a capacity that involves specialized knowledge under section 101(a)(15)(L) [8 U.S.C.A. § 1101(a)(15)(L)] shall not exceed 5 years.

(3) The Attorney General shall approve a petition—

(A) with respect to a nonimmigrant described in section 101(a)(15)(O)(i) [8 U.S.C.A. § 1101(a)(15)(O)(i)] only after consultation in accordance with paragraph (6) or, with respect to aliens seeking entry for a motion picture or television production, after consultation with the appropriate union representing the alien's occupational peers and a management organization in the area of the alien's ability, or

(B) with respect to a nonimmigrant described in section 101(a)(15)(O)(ii) [8 U.S.C.A. § 1101(a)(15)(O)(ii)] after consultation in accordance with paragraph (6) or, in the case of such an alien seeking entry for a motion picture or television production, after consultation with such a labor organization and a management organization in the area of the alien's ability.

In the case of an alien seeking entry for a motion picture or television production, **(i)** any opinion under the previous sentence shall only be advisory, **(ii)** any such opinion that recommends denial must be in writing, **(iii)** in making the decision the Attorney General shall consider the exigencies and scheduling of the production, and (iv) the Attorney General shall append to the decision any such opinion. The Attorney General shall provide by regulation for the waiver of the consultation requirement under subparagraph (A) in the case of aliens who have been admitted as nonimmigrants under section 101(a)(15)(O)(i) [8 U.S.C.A. § 1101(a)(15)(O)(i)] because of extraordinary ability in the arts and who seek readmission to perform similar services within 2 years after the date of a consultation under such subparagraph. Not later than 5 days after the date such a waiver is provided, the Attorney General shall forward a copy of the petition and all supporting documentation to the national office of an appropriate labor organization.

(4)(A) For purposes of section 101(a)(15)(P)(i)(a) [8 U.S.C.A. § 1101(a)(15)(P)(i)(a)], an alien is described in this subparagraph if the alien—

(i) performs as an athlete, individually or as part of a group or team, at an internationally recognized level of performance, and

(ii) seeks to enter the United States temporarily and solely for the purpose of performing as such an athlete with respect to a specific athletic competition.

(B)(i) For purposes of section 101(a)(15)(P)(i)(b) [8 U.S.C.A. § 1101(a)(15)(P)(i)(b)], an alien is described in this subparagraph if the alien—

(I) performs with or is an integral and essential part of the performance of an entertainment group that has (except as provided in clause (ii)) been recognized internationally as being outstanding in the discipline for a sustained and substantial period of time,

(II) in the case of a performer or entertainer, except as provided in clause (iii), has had a sustained and substantial relationship with that group (ordinarily for at least one year) and provides functions integral to the performance of the group, and

(III) seeks to enter the United States temporarily and solely for the purpose of performing as such a performer or entertainer or as an integral and essential part of a performance.

(ii) In the case of an entertainment group that is recognized nationally as being outstanding in its discipline for a sustained and substantial period of time, the Attorney General may, in consideration of special circumstances, waive the international recognition requirement of clause (i)(I).

(iii)(I) The one-year relationship requirement of clause (i)(II) shall not apply to 25 percent of the performers and entertainers in a group.

(II) The Attorney General may waive such one-year relationship requirement for an alien who because of illness or unanticipated and exigent circumstances replaces an essential member of the group and for an alien who augments the group by performing a critical role.

(iv) The requirements of subclauses (I) and (II) of clause (i) shall not apply to alien circus personnel who perform as part of a circus or circus group or who constitute an integral and essential part of the performance of such circus or circus group, but only if such personnel are entering the United States to join a circus that has been recognized nationally as outstanding for a sustained and substantial period of time or as part of such a circus.

(C) A person may petition the Attorney General for classification of an alien as a nonimmigrant under section 101(a)(15)(P) [8 U.S.C.A. § 1101(a)(15)(P)].

(D) The Attorney General shall approve petitions under this subsection with respect to nonimmigrants described in clause (i) or (iii) of section 101(a)(15)(P) [8 U.S.C.A. § 1101(a)(15)(P)] only after consultation in accordance with paragraph (6).

(E) The Attorney General shall approve petitions under this subsection for nonimmigrants described in section 101(a)(15)(P)(ii) [8 U.S.C.A. § 1101(a)(15)(P)(ii)] only after consultation with labor organizations representing artists and entertainers in the United States.

(5)(A) In the case of an alien who is provided nonimmigrant status under section 101(a)(15)(H)(i)(b) [8 U.S.C.A. § 1101(a)(15)(H)(i)(b)] or 101(a)(15)(H)(ii)(b) [8 U.S.C.A. § 1101(a)(15)(H)(ii)(b)] and who is dismissed from employment by the employer before the end of the period of authorized admission, the employer shall be liable for the reasonable costs of return transportation of the alien abroad.

(B) In the case of an alien who is admitted to the United States in nonimmigrant status under section 101(a)(15)(O) [8 U.S.C.A. § 1101(a)(15)(O)] or 101(a)(15)(P) [8 U.S.C.A. § 1101(a)(15)(P)] and whose employment terminates for reasons other than voluntary resignation, the employer whose offer of employment formed the basis of such nonimmigrant status and the petitioner are jointly and severally liable for the reasonable cost of return transportation of the alien abroad. The petitioner shall provide assurance satisfactory to the Attorney General that the reasonable cost of that transportation will be provided.

(6)(A)(i) To meet the consultation requirement of paragraph (3)(A) in the case of a petition for a nonimmigrant described in section 101(a)(15)(O)(i) [8 U.S.C.A. § 1101(a)(15)(O)(i)] (other than with respect to aliens seeking entry for a motion picture or television production), the petitioner shall submit with the petition an advisory opinion from a peer group (or other person or persons of its choosing, which may include a labor organization) with expertise in the specific field involved.

(ii) To meet the consultation requirement of paragraph (3)(B) in the case of a petition for a nonimmigrant described in section 101(a)(15)(O)(ii) [8 U.S.C.A. § 1101(a)(15)(O)(ii)] (other than with respect to aliens seeking entry for a motion picture or television production), the petitioner shall submit with the petition an advisory opinion from a labor organization with expertise in the skill area involved.

(iii) To meet the consultation requirement of paragraph (4)(D) in the case of a petition for a nonimmigrant described in section 101(a)(15)(P)(i) [8 U.S.C.A. § 1101(a)(15)(P)(i)] or 101(a)(15)(P)(iii) [8 U.S.C.A. § 1101(a)(15)(P)(iii)], the petitioner shall submit with the petition an advisory opinion from a labor organization with expertise in the specific field of athletics or entertainment involved.

(B) To meet the consultation requirements of subparagraph (A), unless the petitioner submits with the petition an advisory opinion from an appropriate labor organization, the Attorney General shall forward a copy of the petition and all supporting documentation to the national office of an appropriate labor organization within 5 days of the date of receipt of the petition. If there is a collective bargaining representative of an employer's employees in the occupational classification for which the alien is being sought, that representative shall be the appropriate labor organization.

(C) In those cases in which a petitioner described in subparagraph (A) establishes that an appropriate peer group (including a labor organization) does not exist, the Attorney General shall adjudicate the petition without requiring an advisory opinion.

(D) Any person or organization receiving a copy of a petition described in subparagraph (A) and supporting documents shall have no more than 15 days following the date of receipt of such documents within which to submit a written advisory opinion or comment or to provide a letter of no objection. Once the 15–day period has expired and the petitioner has had an opportunity, where appropriate, to supply rebuttal evidence, the Attorney General shall adjudicate such petition in no more than 14 days. The Attorney General may shorten any specified time period for emergency reasons if no unreasonable burden would be thus imposed on any participant in the process.

(E)(i) The Attorney General shall establish by regulation expedited consultation procedures in the case of nonimmigrant artists or entertainers described in section 101(a)(15)(O) [8 U.S.C.A. § 1101(a)(15)(O)] or 101(a)(15)(P) [8 U.S.C.A. § 1101(a)(15)(P)] to accommodate the exigencies and scheduling of a given production or event.

(ii) The Attorney General shall establish by regulation expedited consultation procedures in the case of nonimmigrant athletes described in section 101(a)(15)(O)(i) [8 U.S.C.A. § 1101(a)(15)(O)(i)] or 101(a)(15)(P)(i) [8 U.S.C.A. § 1101(a)(15)(P)(i)] in the case of emergency circumstances (including trades during a season).

(F) No consultation required under this subsection by the Attorney General with a nongovernmental entity shall be construed as permitting the Attorney General to delegate any authority under this subsection to such an entity. The Attorney General shall give such weight to advisory opinions provided under this section as the Attorney General determines, in his sole discretion, to be appropriate.

(7) If a petition is filed and denied under this subsection, the Attorney General shall notify the petitioner of the determination and the reasons for the denial and of the process by which the petitioner may appeal the determination.

(8) The Attorney General shall submit annually to the Committees on the Judiciary of the House of Representatives and of the Senate a report describing, with respect to petitions under each subcategory of subparagraphs (H), (O), (P), and (Q) of section 101(a)(15) [8 U.S.C.A. § 1101(a)(15)] the following:

(A) The number of such petitions which have been filed.

(B) The number of such petitions which have been approved and the number of workers (by occupation) included in such approved petitions.

(C) The number of such petitions which have been denied and the number of workers (by occupation) requested in such denied petitions.

(D) The number of such petitions which have been withdrawn.

(E) The number of such petitions which are awaiting final action.

(9)(A) The attorney general shall impose a fee on an employer (excluding an employer described in subparagraph (A) or (B) of section 212(p)(1) [8 U.S.C.A. § 1182(p)(1)]) filing (on or after December 1, 1998, and before October 1, 2001) a petition under paragraph (1)

(i) initially to grant an alien nonimmigrant status described in section 101(a)(15)(H)(i)(b) [8 U.S.C.A. § 1101(a)(15)(H)(i)(b)];

(ii) to extend the stay of an alien having such status (unless the employer previously has obtained an extension for such alien); or

(iii) to obtain authorization for an alien having such status to change employers.

(B) The amount of the fee shall be $500 for each such petition.

(C) Fees collected under this paragraph shall be deposited in the Treasury in accordance with section 286(s) [8 U.S.C.A. § 1356(s)].

(d) Issuance of visa to fiancee or fiance of citizen

A visa shall not be issued under the provisions of section 101(a)(15)(K) [8 U.S.C.A. § 1101(a)(15)(K)] until the consular officer has received a petition filed in the United States by the fiancee or fiance of the applying alien and approved by the Attorney General. The petition shall be in such form and contain such information as the Attorney General shall, by regulation, prescribe. It shall be approved only after satisfactory evidence is submitted by the petitioner to establish that the parties have previously met in person within 2 years before the date of filing the petition, have a bona fide intention to marry and are legally able and actually willing to conclude a valid marriage in the United States within a period of ninety days after the alien's arrival. In the event the marriage with the petitioner does not occur within three months after the admission of the said alien and minor children, they shall be required to depart from the United States and upon failure to do so shall be removed in accordance with sections 240 [8 U.S.C.A. § 1229a] and 241 [8 U.S.C.A. § 1231], except that the Attorney General in his discretion may waive the requirement that the parties have previously met in person.

(e) Nonimmigrant professionals and annual numerical limit

(1) Notwithstanding any other provision of this Act, an alien who is a citizen of Canada and seeks to enter the United States under and pursuant to the provisions of Annex 1502.1 (United States of America), Part C—Professionals, of the United States–Canada Free–Trade Agreement to engage in business activities at a professional level as provided for therein may be admitted for such purpose under regulations of the Attorney General promulgated after consultation with the Secretaries of State and Labor.

(2) An alien who is a citizen of Canada or Mexico, and the spouse and children of any such alien if accompanying or following to join such alien, who seeks to enter the United States under and pursuant to the provisions of Section D of Annex 1603 of the North American Free Trade Agreement (in this subsection referred to as "NAFTA") to engage in business activities at a professional level as provided for in such Annex, may be admitted for such purpose under regulations of the Attorney General promulgated after consultation with the Secretaries of State and Labor. For purposes of this Act, including the issuance of entry documents and the application of subsection (b), such alien shall be treated as if seeking classification, or classifiable, as a nonimmigrant under section 101(a)(15) [8

U.S.C.A. § 1101(a)(15)]. The admission of an alien who is a citizen of Mexico shall be subject to paragraphs (3), (4), and (5). For purposes of this paragraph and paragraphs (3), (4), and (5), the term "citizen of Mexico" means "citizen" as defined in Annex 1608 of NAFTA.

(3) The Attorney General shall establish an annual numerical limit on admissions under paragraph (2) of aliens who are citizens of Mexico, as set forth in Appendix 1603.D.4 of Annex 1603 of the NAFTA. Subject to paragraph (4), the annual numerical limit—

(A) beginning with the second year that NAFTA is in force, may be increased in accordance with the provisions of paragraph 5(a) of Section D of such Annex, and

(B) shall cease to apply as provided for in paragraph 3 of such Appendix.

(4) The annual numerical limit referred to in paragraph (3) may be increased or shall cease to apply (other than by operation of paragraph 3 of such Appendix) only if—

(A) the President has obtained advice regarding the proposed action from the appropriate advisory committees established under section 2155 of Title 19.

(B) the President has submitted a report to the Committee on the Judiciary of the Senate and the Committee on the Judiciary of the House of Representatives that sets forth—

(i) the action proposed to be taken and the reasons therefor, and

(ii) the advice obtained under subparagraph (A);

(C) a period of at least 60 calendar days that begins on the first day on which the President has met the requirements of subparagraphs (A) and (B) with respect to such action has expired; and

(D) the President has consulted with such committees regarding the proposed action during the period referred to in subparagraph (C).

(5) During the period that the provisions of Appendix 1603.D.4 of Annex 1603 of the NAFTA apply, the entry of an alien who is a citizen of Mexico under and pursuant to the provisions of Section D of Annex 1603 of NAFTA shall be subject to the attestation requirement of section 212(m) [8 U.S.C.A. § 1182(m)], in the case of a registered nurse, or the application requirement of section 212(n) [8 U.S.C.A. § 1182(n)], in the case of all other professions set out in Appendix 1603.D.1 of Annex 1603 of NAFTA, and the petition requirement of subsection (c), to the extent and in the manner prescribed in regulations promulgated by the Secretary of Labor, with respect to sections 212(m) [8 U.S.C.A. § 1182(m)] and 212(n) [8

U.S.C.A. § 1182(n)], and the Attorney General, with respect to subsection (c).

(f) Denial of crewmember status in case of certain labor disputes

(1) Except as provided in paragraph (3), no alien shall be entitled to nonimmigrant status described in section 101(a)(15)(D) [8 U.S.C.A. § 1101(a)(15)(D)] if the alien intends to land for the purpose of performing service on board a vessel of the United States (as defined in section 2101(46) of Title 46) or on an aircraft of an air carrier (as defined in section 40102(a)(2) of Title 49) during a labor dispute where there is a strike or lockout in the bargaining unit of the employer in which the alien intends to perform such service.

(2) An alien described in paragraph (1)—

(A) may not be paroled into the United States pursuant to section 212(d)(5) [8 U.S.C.A. § 1182(d)(5)] unless the Attorney General determines that the parole of such alien is necessary to protect the national security of the United States; and

(B) shall be considered not to be a bona fide crewman for purposes of section 252(b) [8 U.S.C.A. § 1282(b)].

(3) Paragraph (1) shall not apply to an alien if the air carrier or owner or operator of such vessel that employs the alien provides documentation that satisfies the Attorney General that the alien—

(A) has been an employee of such employer for a period of not less than 1 year preceding the date that a strike or lawful lockout commenced;

(B) has served as a qualified crewman for such employer at least once in each of 3 months during the 12–month period preceding such date; and

(C) shall continue to provide the same services that such alien provided as such a crewman.

(g) Temporary workers and trainees; limitation on numbers

(1) The total number of aliens who may be issued visas or otherwise provided nonimmigrant status during any fiscal year (beginning with fiscal year 1992)—

(A) under section 101(a)(15)(H)(i)(b) [8 U.S.C.A. § 1101(a)(15)(H)(i)(b)], may not exceed—

(i) 65,000 in each fiscal year before fiscal year 1999;

(ii) 115,000 in fiscal year 1999;

(iii) 115,000 in fiscal year 2000;

(iv) 107,500 in fiscal year 2001; and

(v) 65,000 in each succeeding fiscal year;

(B) under section 101(a)(15)(H)(ii)(b) [8 U.S.C.A. § 1101(a)(15)(H)(ii)(b)] may not exceed 66,000.

(2) The numerical limitations of paragraph (1) shall only apply to principal aliens and not to be spouses or children of such aliens.

(3) Aliens who are subject to the numerical limitations of paragraph (1) shall be issued visas (or otherwise provided nonimmigrant status) in the order in which petitions are filed for such visas or status.

(4) In the case of a nonimmigrant described in section 101(a)(15)(H)(i)(b) [8 U.S.C.A. § 1101(a)(15)(H)(i)(b)], the period of authorized admission as such a nonimmigrant may not exceed 6 years.

(h) Intention to abandon foreign residence

The fact that an alien is the beneficiary of an application for a preference status filed under section 204 [8 U.S.C.A. § 1154] or has otherwise sought permanent residence in the United States shall not constitute evidence of an intention to abandon a foreign residence for purposes of obtaining a visa as a nonimmigrant described in subparagraph (H)(i) or (L) of section 101(a)(15) [8 U.S.C.A. § 1101(a)(15)] or otherwise obtaining or maintaining the status of a nonimmigrant described in such subparagraph, if the alien had obtained a change of status under section 248 [8 U.S.C.A. § 1258] to a classification as such a nonimmigrant before the alien's most recent departure from the United States.

(i) "Specialty occupation" defined

(1) For purposes of section 101(a)(15)(H)(i)(b) [8 U.S.C.A. § 1101(a)(15)(H)(i)(b)] and paragraph (2), the term "specialty occupation" means an occupation that requires—

(A) theoretical and practical application of a body of highly specialized knowledge, and

(B) attainment of a bachelor's or higher degree in the specific specialty (or its equivalent) as a minimum for entry into the occupation in the United States.

(2) For purposes of section 101(a)(15)(H)(i)(b) [8 U.S.C.A. § 1101(a)(15)(H)(i)(b)], the requirements of this paragraph, with respect to a specialty occupation, are—

(A) full state licensure to practice in the occupation, if such licensure is required to practice in the occupation,

(B) completion of the degree described in paragraph (1)(B) for the occupation, or

(C) **(i)** experience in the specialty equivalent to the completion of such degree, and **(ii)** recognition of expertise in the specialty through progressively responsible positions relating to the specialty.

(j) Labor disputes

Notwithstanding any other provision of this Act, an alien who is a citizen of Canada or Mexico who seeks to enter the United States under and pursuant to the provisions of Section B, Section C, or Section D of Annex 1603 of the North American Free Trade Agreement, shall not be classified as a nonimmigrant under such provisions if there is in progress a strike or lockout in the course of a labor dispute in the occupational classification at the place or intended place of employment, unless such alien establishes, pursuant to regulations promulgated by the Attorney General, that the alien's entry will not affect adversely the settlement of the strike or lockout or the employment of any person who is involved in the strike or lockout. Notice of a determination under this subsection shall be given as may be required by paragraph 3 of article 1603 of such Agreement. For purposes of this subsection, the term "citizen of Mexico" means "citizen" as defined in Annex 1608 of such Agreement.

(k) Numerical limitations; period of admission; conditions for admission and stay; annual report

(1) The number of aliens who may be provided a visa as nonimmigrants under section 101(a)(15)(S)(i) [8 U.S.C.A. § 1101(a)(15)(S)(i)] in any fiscal year may not exceed 200. The number of aliens who may be provided a visa as nonimmigrants under section 101(a)(15)(S)(ii) [8 U.S.C.A. § 1101(a)(15)(S)(ii)] in any fiscal year may not exceed 50.

(2) No alien may be admitted into the United States as such a nonimmigrant more than 7 years after the date of the enactment of this subsection [September 13, 1994].

(3) The period of admission of an alien as such a nonimmigrant may not exceed 3 years. Such period may not be extended by the Attorney General.

(4) As a condition for the admission, and continued stay in lawful status, of such a nonimmigrant, the nonimmigrant—

(A) shall report not less often than quarterly to the Attorney General such information concerning the alien's whereabouts and activities as the Attorney General may require;

(B) may not be convicted of any criminal offense punishable by a term of imprisonment of 1 year or more after the date of such admission;

(C) must have executed a form that waives the nonimmigrant's right to contest, other than on the basis of an application for withholding of removal, any action for removal of the alien instituted before the alien obtains lawful permanent resident status; and

(D) shall abide by any other condition, limitation, or restriction imposed by the Attorney General.

(5) The Attorney General shall submit a report annually to the Committee on the Judiciary of the House of Representatives and the Committee on the Judiciary of the Senate concerning—

(A) the number of such nonimmigrants admitted;

(B) the number of successful criminal prosecutions or investigations resulting from cooperation of such aliens;

(C) the number of terrorist acts prevented or frustrated resulting from cooperation of such aliens;

(D) the number of such nonimmigrants whose admission or cooperation has not resulted in successful criminal prosecution or investigation or the prevention or frustration of a terrorist act; and

(E) the number of such nonimmigrants who have failed to report quarterly (as required under paragraph (4)) or who have been convicted of crimes in the United States after the date of their admission as such a nonimmigrant.

(*l*) [sic] Restrictions on waiver

(1) In the case of a request by an interested State agency, or by an interested Federal agency, for a waiver of the 2–year foreign residence requirement under section 212(e) [8 U.S.C.A. § 1182(e)] on behalf of an alien described in clause (iii) of such section, the Attorney General shall not grant such waiver unless—

(A) in the case of an alien who is otherwise contractually obligated to return to a foreign country, the government of such country furnishes the Director of the United States Information Agency with a statement in writing that it has no objection to such waiver;

(B) in the case of a request by an interested State agency, the grant of such waiver would not cause the number of waivers allotted for that State for that fiscal year to exceed 20;

(C) in the case of a request by an interested Federal agency or by an interested State agency—

(i) the alien demonstrates a bona fide offer of full-time employment at a health facility or health care organization, which employment has been determined by the Attorney General to be in the public interest; and

(ii) the alien agrees to begin employment with the health facility or health care organization within 90 days of receiving such waiver, and agrees to continue to work for a total of not less than 3 years (unless the Attorney General determines that extenuating circumstances exist, such as closure of the facility or hardship to the alien, which would justify a lesser period of employment at such health facility or health care organization, in which case the alien must demonstrate another bona fide offer of employment at a health facility or health care organization for the remainder of such 3-year period); and

(D) in the case of a request by an interested Federal agency (other than a request by an interested Federal agency to employ the alien full-time in medical research or training) or by an interested State agency, the alien agrees to practice medicine in accordance with paragraph (2) for a total of not less than 3 years only in the geographic area or areas which are designated by the Secretary of Health and Human Services as having a shortage of health care professionals, except that, in the case of a request by the Department of Veterans Affairs, the alien shall not be required to practice medicine in a geographic area designated by the Secretary.

(2)(A) Notwithstanding section 248(2) [8 U.S.C.A. § 1258(2)], the Attorney General may change the status of an alien who qualifies under this subsection and section 212(e) [8 U.S.C.A. § 1182(e)] to that of an alien described in section 101(a)(15)(H)(i)(b) [8 U.S.C.A. § 1101(a)(15)(H)(i)(b)].

(B) No person who has obtained a change of status under subparagraph (A) and who has failed to fulfill the terms of the contract with the health facility or health care organization named in the waiver application shall be eligible to apply for an immigrant visa, for permanent residence, or for any other change of nonimmigrant status, until it is established that such person has resided and been physically present in the country of his nationality or his last residence for an aggregate of at least 2 years following departure from the United States.

(3) Notwithstanding any other provision of this subsection, the 2-year foreign residence requirement under section 212(e) [8 U.S.C.A. § 1182(e)] shall apply with respect to an alien described in clause (iii) of such section, who has not otherwise been accorded status under section 101(a)(27)(H) [8 U.S.C.A. § 1101(a)(27)(H)], if—

(A) at any time the alien ceases to comply with any agreement entered into under subparagraph (C) or (D) of paragraph (1); or

(B) the alien's employment ceases to benefit the public interest at any time during the 3-year period described in paragraph (1)(C).

(*l*) [sic] Foreign students

(1) An alien may not be accorded status as a nonimmigrant under section 101(a)(15)(F)(i) [8 U.S.C.A. § 1101(a)(15)(F)(i)] in order to pursue a course of study—

(A) at a public elementary school or in a publicly funded adult education program; or

(B) at a public secondary school unless—

(i) the aggregate period of such status at such a school does not exceed 12 months with respect to any alien, and (ii) the alien demonstrates that the alien has reimbursed the local educational agency that administers the school for the full, unsubsidized per capita cost of providing education at such school for the period of the alien's attendance.

(2) An alien who obtains the status of a nonimmigrant under section 101(a)(15)(F)(i) [8 U.S.C.A. § 1101(a)(15)(F)(i)] in order to pursue a course of study at a private elementary or secondary school or in a language training program that is not publicly funded shall be considered to have violated such status, and the alien's visa under section 101(a)(15)(F) [8 U.S.C.A. § 1101(a)(15)(F)] shall be void, if the alien terminates or abandons such course of study at such a school and undertakes a course of study at a public elementary school, in a publicly funded adult education program, in a publicly funded adult education language training program, or at a public secondary school (unless the requirements of paragraph (1)(B) are met).

(June 27, 1952, c. 477, Title II, ch. 2, § 214, 66 Stat. 189; Apr. 7, 1970, Pub.L. 91–225, § 3, 84 Stat. 117; Oct. 5, 1984, Pub.L. 98–454, Title VI, § 602(b), 98 Stat. 1737; Nov. 6, 1986, Pub.L. 99–603, Title III, §§ 301(b), 313(b), 100 Stat. 3411, 3438; Nov. 10, 1986, Pub.L. 99–639, § 3(a), (c), 100 Stat. 3542; Sept. 28, 1988, Pub.L. 100–449, Title III, § 307(b), 102 Stat. 1877; Nov. 6, 1986, Pub.L. 99–603, § 301(b); Oct. 24, 1988, Pub.L. 100–525, § 2(*l*)(1), 102 Stat. 2612; Nov. 29, 1990, Pub.L. 101–649, Title II, §§ 202(a), 205(a), (b), (c)(2), 206(b), 207(b), 104 Stat. 5014, 5019, 5020, 5023, 5025; Dec. 12, 1991, Pub.L. 102–232, Title II, §§ 202(a), 203(b), 204, 205(d), (e), 206(a), (c)(2), 207(a), (c)(1), Title III, § 303(a)(10), (11), (12), 105 Stat. 1737, 1738, 1740, 1741, 1748; Dec. 8, 1993, Pub.L. 103–182, Title III, § 341(b), (c), 107 Stat. 2116, 2117; Sept. 13, 1994, Pub.L. 103–322, Title XIII, § 130003(b)(2), 108 Stat. 2025; Oct. 25, 1994, Pub.L. 103–416, Title II, § 220(b), 108 Stat. 4319; Sept. 30, 1996, Pub.L. 104–208, Div. C, Title III, § 308(e)(1)(D), (2)(B), (f)(1)(G), (H), (3)(B), (g)(5)(A)(i), (g)(7)(A), Title VI, §§ 621, 622(c), 625(a)(1), 671(a)(3)(A), (e)(4)(A), 110 Stat. 3009–619, 3009–620, 3009–621, 3009–623, 3009–695, 3009–699, 3009–721, 3009–723; Oct. 27, 1997, Pub.L. 105–65, Title I, § 108, 111 Stat. 1350; Oct. 21, 1998, Pub.L. 105–277, Div. C, Title IV, §§ 411(a), 414(a), 112 Stat. 2681–642, 2681–651; Nov. 13, 1999, Pub.L. 106–104, § 2, 113 Stat. 1483.)

§ 215. Travel control of citizens and aliens [8 U.S.C.A. § 1185]

(a) Restrictions and prohibitions

Unless otherwise ordered by the President, it shall be unlawful—

(1) for any alien to depart from or enter or attempt to depart from or enter the United States except under such reasonable rules,

regulations, and orders, and subject to such limitations and exceptions as the President may prescribe;

(2) for any person to transport or attempt to transport from or into the United States another person with knowledge or reasonable cause to believe that the departure or entry of such other person is forbidden by this section;

(3) for any person knowingly to make any false statement in an application for permission to depart from or enter the United States with intent to induce or secure the granting of such permission either for himself or for another;

(4) for any person knowingly to furnish or attempt to furnish or assist in furnishing to another a permit or evidence of permission to depart or enter not issued and designed for such other person's use;

(5) for any person knowingly to use or attempt to use any permit or evidence of permission to depart or enter not issued and designed for his use;

(6) for any person to forge, counterfeit, mutilate, or alter, or cause or procure to be forged, counterfeited, mutilated, or altered, any permit or evidence of permission to depart from or enter the United States;

(7) for any person knowingly to use or attempt to use or furnish to another for use any false, forged, counterfeited, mutilated, or altered permit, or evidence of permission, or any permit or evidence of permission which, though originally valid, has become or been made void or invalid.

(b) Citizens

Except as otherwise provided by the President and subject to such limitations and exceptions as the President may authorize and prescribe, it shall be unlawful for any citizen of the United States to depart from or enter, or attempt to depart from or enter, the United States unless he bears a valid United States passport.

(c) Definitions

The term "United States" as used in this section includes the Canal Zone, and all territory and waters, continental or insular, subject to the jurisdiction of the United States. The term "person" as used in this section shall be deemed to mean any individual, partnership, association, company, or other incorporated body of individuals, or corporation, or body politic.

(d) Nonadmission of certain aliens

Nothing in this section shall be construed to entitle an alien to whom a permit to enter the United States has been issued to enter the United States, if, upon arrival in the United States, he is found to be inadmissible under any of the provisions of this Act, or any other law, relative to the entry of aliens into the United States.

(e) Revocation of proclamation as affecting penalties

The revocation of any rule, regulation, or order issued in pursuance of this section shall not prevent prosecution for any offense committed, or the imposition of any penalties or forfeitures, liability for which was incurred under this section prior to the revocation of such rule, regulation, or order.

(f) Permits to enter

Passports, visas, reentry permits, and other documents required for entry under this Act may be considered as permits to enter for the purposes of this section.

(June 27, 1952, c. 477, Title II, ch. 2, § 215, 66 Stat. 190; Oct. 7, 1978, Pub.L. 95–426, Title VII, § 707(a)-(d), 92 Stat. 992, 993; Oct. 25, 1994, Pub.L. 103–416, Title II, § 204(a), 108 Stat. 4311.)

§ 216. Conditional permanent resident status for certain alien spouses and sons and daughters [8 U.S.C.A. § 1186a]

(a) In general

(1) Conditional basis for status

Notwithstanding any other provision of this Act, an alien spouse (as defined in subsection (g)(1)) and an alien son or daughter (as defined in subsection (g)(2)) shall be considered, at the time of obtaining the status of an alien lawfully admitted for permanent residence, to have obtained such status on a conditional basis subject to the provisions of this section.

(2) Notice of requirements

(A) At time of obtaining permanent residence

At the time an alien spouse or alien son or daughter obtains permanent resident status on a conditional basis under paragraph (1), the Attorney General shall provide for notice to such a spouse, son, or daughter respecting the provisions of this section and the requirements of subsection (c)(1) to have the conditional basis of such status removed.

(B) At time of required petition

In addition, the Attorney General shall attempt to provide notice to such a spouse, son, or daughter, at or about the beginning of the 90–day period described in subsection (d)(2)(A), of the requirements of subsections (c)(1).

(C) Effect of failure to provide notice

The failure of the Attorney General to provide a notice under this paragraph shall not affect the enforcement of the provisions of this section with respect to such a spouse, son, or daughter.

(b) Termination of status if finding that qualifying marriage improper

(1) In general

In the case of an alien with permanent resident status on a conditional basis under subsection (a), if the Attorney General determines, before the second anniversary of the alien's obtaining the status of lawful admission for permanent residence, that—

(A) the qualifying marriage—

(i) was entered into for the purpose of procuring an alien's admission as an immigrant, or

(ii) has been judicially annulled or terminated, other than through the death of a spouse; or

(B) a fee or other consideration was given (other than a fee or other consideration to an attorney for assistance in preparation of a lawful petition) for the filing of a petition under section 214(a) [8 U.S.C.A. § 1154(a)] or 214(d) [8 U.S.C.A. § 1184(d)] with respect to the alien;

the Attorney General shall so notify the parties involved and, subject to paragraph (2), shall terminate the permanent resident status of the alien (or aliens) involved as of the date of the determination.

(2) Hearing in removal proceeding

Any alien whose permanent resident status is terminated under paragraph (1) may request a review of such determination in a proceeding to remove the alien. In such proceeding, the burden of proof shall be on the Attorney General to establish, by a preponderance of the evidence, that a condition described in paragraph (1) is met.

(c) Requirements of timely petition and interview for removal of condition

(1) In general

In order for the conditional basis established under subsection (a) for an alien spouse or an alien son or daughter to be removed—

(A) the alien spouse and the petitioning spouse (if not deceased) jointly must submit to the Attorney General, during the period described in subsection (d)(2), a petition which requests the removal of such conditional basis and which states, under penalty of perjury, the facts and information described in subsection (d)(1), and

(B) in accordance with subsection (d)(3), the alien spouse and the petitioning spouse (if not deceased) must appear for a personal interview before an officer or employee of the Service respecting the facts and information described in subsection (d)(1).

(2) Termination of permanent resident status for failure to file petition or have personal interview

(A) In general

In the case of an alien with permanent resident status on a conditional basis under subsection (a), if—

(i) no petition is filed with respect to the alien in accordance with the provisions of paragraph (1)(A), or

(ii) unless there is good cause shown, the alien spouse and petitioning spouse fail to appear at the interview described in paragraph (1)(B),

the Attorney General shall terminate the permanent resident status of the alien as of the second anniversary of the alien's lawful admission for permanent residence.

(B) Hearing in removal proceeding

In any removal proceeding with respect to an alien whose permanent resident status is terminated under subparagraph (A), the burden of proof shall be on the alien to establish compliance with the conditions of paragraphs (1)(A) and (1)(B).

(3) Determination after petition and interview

(A) In general

If—

(i) a petition is filed in accordance with the provisions of paragraph (1)(A), and

(ii) the alien spouse and petitioning spouse appear at the interview described in paragraph (1)(B),

the Attorney General shall make a determination, within 90 days of the date of the interview, as to whether the facts and information described in subsection (d)(1) and alleged in the petition are true with respect to the qualifying marriage.

(B) Removal of conditional basis if favorable determination

If the Attorney General determines that such facts and information are true, the Attorney General shall so notify the parties involved and shall remove the conditional basis of the parties effective as of the second anniversary of the alien's obtaining the status of lawful admission for permanent residence.

(C) Termination if adverse determination

If the Attorney General determines that such facts and information are not true, the Attorney General shall so notify the parties involved and, subject to subparagraph (D), shall terminate the permanent resident status of an alien spouse or an alien son or daughter as of the date of the determination.

(D) Hearing in removal proceeding

Any alien whose permanent resident status is terminated under subparagraph (C) may request a review of such determination in a proceeding to remove the alien. In such proceeding, the burden of proof shall be on the Attorney General to establish, by a preponderance of the evidence, that the facts and information described in subsection (d)(1) and alleged in the petition are not true with respect to the qualifying marriage.

(4) Hardship waiver

The Attorney General, in the Attorney General's discretion, may remove the conditional basis of the permanent resident status for an alien who fails to meet the requirements of paragraph (1) if the alien demonstrates that—

(A) extreme hardship would result if such alien is removed,

(B) the qualifying marriage was entered into in good faith by the alien spouse, but the qualifying marriage has been terminated (other than through the death of the spouse) and the alien was not at fault in failing to meet the requirements of paragraph (1), or

(C) the qualifying marriage was entered into in good faith by the alien spouse and during the marriage the alien spouse or child was battered by or was the subject of extreme cruelty perpetrated by his or her spouse or citizen or permanent resident parent and the alien was not at fault in failing to meet the requirements of paragraph (1).

In determining extreme hardship, the Attorney General shall consider circumstances occurring only during the period that the alien was admitted for permanent residence on a conditional basis. In acting on applications under this paragraph, the Attorney General shall consider any credible evidence relevant to the application. The determination of what evidence is credible and the weight to be given that evidence shall be within the sole discretion of the Attorney General. The Attorney General shall, by regulation, establish measures to protect the confidentiality of information concerning any abused alien spouse or child, including information regarding the whereabouts of such spouse or child.

(d) Details of petition and interview

(1) Contents of petition

Each petition under subsection (c)(1)(A) shall contain the following facts and information:

(A) Statement of proper marriage and petitioning process

The facts are that—

(i) the qualifying marriage—

(I) was entered into in accordance with the laws of the place where the marriage took place,

(II) has not been judicially annulled or terminated, other than through the death of a spouse, and

(III) was not entered into for the purpose of procuring an alien's admission as an immigrant; and

(ii) no fee or other consideration was given (other than a fee or other consideration to an attorney for assistance in preparation of a lawful petition) for the filing of a petition under section 204(a) [8 U.S.C.A. § 1154(a)] or 214(d) [8 U.S.C.A. § 1184(d)] with respect to the alien spouse or alien son or daughter.

(B) Statement of additional information

The information is a statement of—

(i) the actual residence of each party to the qualifying marriage since the date the alien spouse obtained permanent resident status on a conditional basis under subsection (a), and

(ii) the place of employment (if any) of each such party since such date, and the name of the employer of such party.

(2) Period for filing petition

(A) 90-day period before second anniversary

Except as provided in subparagraph (B), the petition under subsection (c)(1)(A) must be filed during the 90-day period before the second anniversary of the alien's obtaining the status of lawful admission for permanent residence.

(B) Date of petitions for good cause

Such a petition may be considered if filed after such date, but only if the alien establishes to the satisfaction of the Attorney General good cause and extenuating circumstances for failure to file the petition during the period described in subparagraph (A).

(C) Filing of petitions during removal

In the case of an alien who is the subject of removal hearings as a result of failure to file a petition on a timely basis in accordance with subparagraph (A), the Attorney General may stay such removal proceedings against an alien pending the filing of the petition under subparagraph (B).

(3) Personal interview

The interview under subsection (c)(1)(B) shall be conducted within 90 days after the date of submitting a petition under subsection (c)(1)(A) and at a local office of the Service, designated by the Attorney General, which is convenient to the parties involved. The Attorney General, in the Attorney General's discretion, may waive the deadline for such an interview or the requirement for such an interview in such cases as may be appropriate.

(e) Treatment of period for purposes of naturalization

For purposes of title III, in the case of an alien who is in the United States as a lawful permanent resident on a conditional basis under this section, the alien shall be considered to have been admitted as an alien lawfully admitted for permanent residence and to be in the United States as an alien lawfully admitted to the United States for permanent residence.

(f) Treatment of certain waivers

In the case of an alien who has permanent residence status on a conditional basis under this section, if, in order to obtain such status, the alien obtained a waiver under subsection (h) or (i) of section 212 [8 U.S.C.A. § 1182] of certain grounds of inadmissibility, such waiver terminates upon the termination of such permanent residence status under this section.

(g) Definitions

In this section:

(1) The term "alien spouse" means an alien who obtains the status of an alien lawfully admitted for permanent residence (whether on a conditional basis or otherwise)—

(A) as an immediate relative (described in section 201(b) [8 U.S.C.A. § 1151(b)]) as the spouse of a citizen of the United States,

(B) under section 214(d) [8 U.S.C.A. § 1184(d)] as the fiancee or fiance of a citizen of the United States, or

(C) under section 203(a)(2) [8 U.S.C.A. § 1153(a)(2)] as the spouse of an alien lawfully admitted for permanent residence,

by virtue of a marriage which was entered into less than 24 months before the date the alien obtains such status by virtue of such marriage, but does not include such an alien who only obtains such status as a result of section 203(d) [8 U.S.C.A. § 1153(d)].

(2) The term "alien son or daughter" means an alien who obtains the status of an alien lawfully admitted for permanent residence (whether on a conditional basis or otherwise) by virtue of being the son or daughter of an individual through a qualifying marriage.

(3) The term "qualifying marriage" means the marriage described to in paragraph (1).

(4) The term "petitioning spouse" means the spouse of a qualifying marriage, other than the alien.

(June 27, 1952, c. 477, Title II, ch. 2, § 216, as added Nov. 6, 1986, Pub.L. 99–639, § 2(a), 100 Stat. 3537, and amended Oct. 24, 1988, Pub.L. 100–525, § 7(a)(1), 102 Stat. 2616; Oct. 24, 1988, Pub.L. 100–525, § 7(a)(2), 102 Stat. 2616; Nov. 29, 1990, Pub.L. 101–649, Title VII, § 701(a), 104 Stat. 5085; Dec.12, 1991, Pub.L. 102–232, Title III, § 302(e) (8) (B), 105 Stat. 1746; Sept. 13, 1994, Pub.L. 103–322, Title IV, § 40702(a), 108 Stat. 1955; Sept. 30, 1996, Pub.L. 104–208, Div. C, Title III, § 308(d)(4)(E), (e)(7), (f)(1)(I), (J), 110 Stat. 3009–618, 3009–620, 3009–621.)

§ 216A. Conditional permanent resident status for certain alien entrepreneurs, spouses, and children [8 U.S.C.A. § 1186b]

(a) In general

(1) Conditional basis for status

Notwithstanding any other provision of this Act, an alien entrepreneur (as defined in subsection (f)(1)), alien spouse, and alien child (as defined in subsection (f)(2)) shall be considered, at the time of obtaining the status of an alien lawfully admitted for permanent residence, to have obtained such status on a conditional basis subject to the provisions of this section.

(2) Notice of requirements

(A) At time of obtaining permanent residence

At the time an alien entrepreneur, alien spouse, or alien child obtains permanent resident status on a conditional basis under paragraph (1), the Attorney General shall provide for notice to such an entrepreneur, spouse, or child respecting the provisions of this section and the requirements of subsection (c)(1) to have the conditional basis of such status removed.

(B) At time of required petition

In addition, the Attorney General shall attempt to provide notice to such an entrepreneur, spouse, or child, at or about the beginning of the 90–day period described in subsection (d)(2)(A), of the requirements of subsection (c)(1).

(C) Effect of failure to provide notice

The failure of the Attorney General to provide a notice under this paragraph shall not affect the enforcement of the provisions of this section with respect to such an entrepreneur, spouse, or child.

(b) Termination of status if finding that qualifying entrepreneurship improper

(1) In general

In the case of an alien entrepreneur with permanent resident status on a conditional basis under subsection (a), if the Attorney General determines, before the second anniversary of the alien's obtaining the status of lawful admission for permanent residence, that—

(A) the establishment of the commercial enterprise was intended solely as a means of evading the immigration laws of the United States,

(B)(i) a commercial enterprise was not established by the alien,

(ii) the alien did not invest or was not actively in the process of investing the requisite capital; or

(iii) the alien was not sustaining the actions described in clause (i) or (ii) throughout the period of the alien's residence in the United States, or

(C) the alien was otherwise not conforming to the requirements of section 203(b)(5) [8 U.S.C.A. § 1153(b)(5)],

then the Attorney General shall so notify the alien involved and, subject to paragraph (2), shall terminate the permanent resident status of the alien (and the alien spouse and alien child) involved as of the date of the determination.

(2) Hearing in removal proceeding

Any alien whose permanent resident status is terminated under paragraph (1) may request a review of such determination in a proceeding to remove the alien. In such proceeding, the burden of proof shall be on the Attorney General to establish, by a preponderance of the evidence, that a condition described in paragraph (1) is met.

(c) Requirements of timely petition and interview for removal of condition

(1) In general

In order for the conditional basis established under subsection (a) for an alien entrepreneur, alien spouse, or alien child to be removed—

(A) the alien entrepreneur must submit to the Attorney General, during the period described in subsection (d)(2), a petition which requests the removal of such conditional basis and which states, under penalty of perjury, the facts and information described in subsection (d)(1), and

(B) in accordance with subsection (d)(3), the alien entrepreneur must appear for a personal interview before an officer or employee of the Service respecting the facts and information described in subsection (d)(1).

(2) Termination of permanent resident status for failure to file petition or have personal interview

(A) In general

In the case of an alien with permanent resident status on a conditional basis under subsection (a), if—

(i) no petition is filed with respect to the alien in accordance with the provisions of paragraph (1)(A), or

(ii) unless there is good cause shown, the alien entrepreneur fails to appear at the interview described in paragraph (1)(B) (if required under subsection (d)(3)),

the Attorney General shall terminate the permanent resident status of the alien (and the alien's spouse and children if it was obtained on a conditional basis under this section or section 216 [8 U.S.C.A. § 1186a]) as of the second anniversary of the alien's lawful admission for permanent residence.

(B) Hearing in removal proceeding

In any removal proceeding with respect to an alien whose permanent resident status is terminated under subparagraph (A), the burden of proof shall be on the alien to establish compliance with the conditions of paragraphs (1)(A) and (1)(B).

(3) Determination after petition and interview

(A) In general

If—

(i) a petition is filed in accordance with the provisions of paragraph (1)(A), and

(ii) the alien entrepreneur appears at any interview described in paragraph (1)(B),

the Attorney General shall make a determination, within 90 days of the date of the such filing or interview (whichever is later), as to whether the facts and information described in subsection (d)(1) and alleged in the petition are true with respect to the qualifying commercial enterprise.

(B) Removal of conditional basis if favorable determination

If the Attorney General determines that such facts and information are true, the Attorney General shall so notify the alien involved and shall remove the conditional basis of the alien's status effective as of the second anniversary of the alien's lawful admission for permanent residence.

(C) Termination if adverse determination

If the Attorney General determines that such facts and information are not true, the Attorney General shall so notify the alien involved and, subject to subparagraph (D), shall terminate the permanent resident status of an alien entrepreneur, alien spouse, or alien child as of the date of the determination.

(D) Hearing in removal proceeding

Any alien whose permanent resident status is terminated under subparagraph (C) may request a review of such determination in a proceeding to remove the alien. In such proceeding, the burden of proof shall be on the Attorney General to establish, by a preponderance of the evidence, that the facts and information described in subsection (d)(1) and alleged in the petition are not true with respect to the qualifying commercial enterprise.

(d) Details of petition and interview

(1) Contents of petition

Each petition under subsection (c)(1)(A) shall contain facts and information demonstrating that—

(A) a commercial enterprise was established by the alien;

(B) the alien invested or was actively in the process of investing the requisite capital; and

(C) the alien sustained the actions described in subparagraphs (A) and (B) throughout the period of the alien's residence in the United States.

(2) Period for filing petition

(A) 90–day period before second anniversary

Except as provided in subparagraph (B), the petition under subsection (c)(1)(A) must be filed during the 90–day period before the second anniversary of the alien's lawful admission for permanent residence.

(B) Date petitions for good cause

Such a petition may be considered if filed after such date, but only if the alien establishes to the satisfaction of the Attorney General good cause and extenuating circumstances for failure to file the petition during the period described in subparagraph (A).

(C) Filing of petitions during removal

In the case of an alien who is the subject of removal hearings as a result of failure to file a petition on a timely basis in accordance with subparagraph (A), the Attorney General may stay such removal proceedings against an alien pending the filing of the petition under subparagraph (B).

(3) Personal interview

The interview under subsection (c)(1)(B) shall be conducted within 90 days after the date of submitting a petition under subsection (c)(1)(A) and at a local office of the Service, designated by the

Attorney General, which is convenient to the parties involved. The Attorney General, in the Attorney General's discretion, may waive the deadline for such an interview or the requirement for such an interview in such cases as may be appropriate.

(e) Treatment of period for purposes of naturalization

For purposes of title III, in the case of an alien who is in the United States as a lawful permanent resident on a conditional basis under this section, the alien shall be considered to have been admitted as an alien lawfully admitted for permanent residence and to be in the United States as an alien lawfully admitted to the United States for permanent residence.

(f) Definitions

In this section:

(1) The term "alien entrepreneur" means an alien who obtains the status of an alien lawfully admitted for permanent residence (whether on a conditional basis or otherwise) under section 203(b)(5) [8 U.S.C.A. § 1153(b)(5)].

(2) The term "alien spouse" and the term "alien child" mean an alien who obtains the status of an alien lawfully admitted for permanent residence (whether on a conditional basis or otherwise) by virtue of being the spouse or child, respectively, of an alien entrepreneur.

(June 27, 1952, c. 477, Title II, ch. 2, § 216A, as added Nov. 29, 1990, Pub.L. 101–649, Title I, § 121(b)(1), 104 Stat. 4990, and amended Dec. 12, 1991, Pub.L. 102–232, Title III, § 302(b)(3), 105 Stat. 1743; Sept. 30, 1996, Pub.L. 104–208, Div. C, Title III, § 308(e)(8), 110 Stat. 3009–620.)

§ 217. Visa waiver pilot program for certain visitors [8 U.S.C.A. § 1187]

(a) Establishment of pilot program

The Attorney General and the Secretary of State are authorized to establish a pilot program (hereinafter in this section referred to as the "pilot program") under which the requirement of paragraph (7)(B)(i)(II) of section 212(a) [8 U.S.C.A. § 1182(a)] may be waived by the Attorney General, in consultation with the Secretary of State and in accordance with this section, in the case of an alien who meets the following requirements:

(1) Seeking entry as tourist for 90 days or less

The alien is applying for admission during the pilot program period (as defined in subsection (e)) as a nonimmigrant visitor (described in section 101(a)(15)(B) [8 U.S.C.A. § 1101(a)(15)(B)]) for a period not exceeding 90 days.

(2) National of pilot program country

The alien is a national of, and presents a passport issued by, a country which—

(A) extends (or agrees to extend) reciprocal privileges to citizens and nationals of the United States, and

(B) is designated as a pilot program country under subsection (c).

(3) Executes immigration forms

The alien before the time of such admission completes such immigration forms as the Attorney General shall establish.

(4) Entry into the United States

If arriving by sea or air, the alien arrives at the port of entry into the United States on a carrier which has entered into an agreement with the Service to guarantee transport of the alien out of the United States if the alien is found inadmissible or deportable by an immigration officer.

(5) Not a safety threat

The alien has been determined not to represent a threat to the welfare, health, safety, or security of the United States.

(6) No previous violation

If the alien previously was admitted without a visa under this section, the alien must not have failed to comply with the conditions of any previous admission as such a nonimmigrant.

(7) Round-trip ticket

The alien is in possession of a round-trip transportation ticket (unless this requirement is waived by the Attorney General under regulations).

(b) Waiver of rights

An alien may not be provided a waiver under the pilot program unless the alien has waived any right—

(1) to review or appeal under this Act of an immigration officer's determination as to the admissibility of the alien at the port of entry into the United States, or

(2) to contest, other than on the basis of an application for asylum, any action for removal of the alien.

(c) Designation of pilot program countries

(1) In general

The Attorney General, in consultation with the Secretary of State, may designate any country as a pilot program country if it meets the requirements of paragraph (2).

(2) Qualifications

Except as provided in subsection (g) of this section, a country may not be designated as a pilot program country unless the following requirements are met:

(A) Low nonimmigrant visa refusal rate—Either—

(i) the average number of refusals of nonimmigrant visitor visas for nationals of that country during—

(I) the two previous full fiscal years was less than 2.0 percent of the total number of nonimmigrant visitor visas for nationals of that country which were granted or refused during those years; and

(II) either of such two previous full fiscal years was less than 2.5 percent of the total number of nonimmigrant visitor visas for nationals of that country which were granted or refused during that year; or

(ii) such refusal rate for nationals of that country during the previous full fiscal year was less than 3.0 percent.

(B) Machine readable passport program

The government of the country certifies that it has or is in the process of developing a program to issue machine-readable passports to its citizens.

(C) Law enforcement interests

The Attorney General determines that the United States law enforcement interests would not be compromised by the designation of the country.

(3) Continuing and subsequent qualifications

For each fiscal year (within the pilot program period) after the initial period—

(A) Continuing qualification

In the case of a country which was a pilot program country in the previous fiscal year, a country may not be designated as a pilot program country unless the sum of—

(i) the total of the number of nationals of that country who were denied admission at the time of arrival or withdrew their application for admission during such previous fiscal year as a nonimmigrant visitor, and

(ii) the total number of nationals of that country who were admitted as nonimmigrant visitors during such previous fiscal year and who violated the terms of such admission,

was less than 2 percent of the total number of nationals of that country who applied for admission as nonimmigrant visitors during such previous fiscal year.

(B) New countries

In the case of another country, the country may not be designated as a pilot program country unless the following requirements are met:

(i) Low nonimmigrant visa refusal rate in previous 2-year period

The average number of refusals of nonimmigrant visitor visas for nationals of that country during the two previous full fiscal years was less than 2 percent of the total number of nonimmigrant visitor visas for nationals of that country which were granted or refused during those years.

(ii) Low nonimmigrant visa refusal rate in each of the 2 previous years

The average number of refusals of nonimmigrant visitor visas for nationals of that country during either of such two previous full fiscal years was less than 2.5 percent of the total number of nonimmigrant visitor visas for nationals of that country which were granted or refused during that year.

(4) Initial period

For purposes of paragraphs (2) and (3), the term "initial period" means the period beginning at the end of the 30–day period described in subsection (b)(1) and ending on the last day of the first fiscal year which begins after such 30–day period.

(d) Authority

Notwithstanding any other provision of this section, the Attorney General, in consultation with the Secretary of State, may for any reason (including national security) refrain from waiving the visa requirement in respect to nationals of any country which may otherwise qualify for designation or may, at any time, rescind any waiver or designation previously granted under this section.

(e) Carrier agreements

(1) In general

The agreement referred to in subsection (a)(4) is an agreement between a carrier and the Attorney General under which the carrier agrees, in consideration of the waiver of the visa requirement with respect to a nonimmigrant visitor under the pilot program—

(A) to indemnify the United States against any costs for the transportation of the alien from the United States if the visitor is refused admission to the United States or remains in the United States unlawfully after the 90–day period described in subsection (a)(1)(A),

(B) to submit daily to immigration officers any immigration forms received with respect to nonimmigrant visitors provided a waiver under the pilot program, and

(C) to be subject to the imposition of fines resulting from the transporting into the United States of a national of a designated country without a passport pursuant to regulations promulgated by the Attorney General.

(2) Termination of agreements

The Attorney General may terminate an agreement under paragraph (1) with five days' notice to the carrier for the carrier's failure to meet the terms of such agreement.

(f) Definition of pilot program period

For purposes of this section, the term "pilot program period" means the period beginning on October 1, 1988, and ending on April 30, 2000.

(g) Duration and termination of designation

(1) In general

(A) Determination and notification of disqualification rate

Upon determination by the Attorney General that a pilot program country's disqualification rate is 2 percent or more, the Attorney General shall notify the Secretary of State.

(B) Probationary status

If the program country's disqualification rate is greater than 2 percent but less than 3.5 percent, the Attorney General shall place the program country in probationary status for a period not to exceed 2 full fiscal years following the year in which the determination under subparagraph (A) is made.

(C) Termination of designation

Subject to paragraph (3), if the program country's disqualification rate is 3.5 percent or more, the Attorney General shall terminate the country's designation as a pilot program country effective at the beginning of the second fiscal year following the fiscal year in which the determination under subparagraph (A) is made.

(2) Termination of probationary status

(A) In general

If the Attorney General determines at the end of the probationary period described in paragraph (1)(B) that the program country placed in probationary status under such paragraph has failed to develop a machine-readable passport program as required by section [sic] (c)(2)(C), or has a disqualification rate of 2 percent or more, the Attorney General shall terminate the designation of the country as a pilot program country. If the Attorney General determines that the program country has developed a machine-readable passport program and has a disqualification rate of less than 2 percent, the Attorney General shall redesignate the country as a pilot program country.

(B) Effective date

A termination of the designation of a country under subparagraph (A) shall take effect on the first day of the first fiscal year following the fiscal year in which the determination under such subparagraph is made. Until such date, nationals of the country shall remain eligible for a waiver under subsection (a).

(3) Nonapplicability of certain provisions

Paragraph (1)(C) shall not apply unless the total number of nationals of a pilot program country described in paragraph (4)(A) exceeds 100.

(4) Definition

For purposes of this subsection, the term "disqualification rate" means the percentage which—

(A) the total number of nationals of the pilot program country who were—

(i) denied admission at the time of arrival or withdrew their application for admission during the most recent fiscal year for which data are available; and

(ii) admitted as nonimmigrant visitors during such fiscal year and who violated the terms of such admission; bears to

(B) the total number of nationals of such country who applied for admission as nonimmigrant visitors during such fiscal year.

(June 27, 1952, c. 477, Title II, ch. 2, § 217, as added Nov. 6, 1986, Pub.L. 99–603, Title III, § 313(a), 100 Stat. 3435, and amended Oct. 24, 1988, Pub.L. 100–525, § 2(p)(1), 102 Stat. 2613; Oct. 24, 1988, Pub.L. 100–525, § 2(p)(2), 102 Stat. 2613; Nov. 29, 1990, Pub.L. 101–649, Title II, § 201(a), 104 Stat. 5012; Dec. 12, 1991, Pub.L. 102–232, Title III, §§ 303(a)(1),(2), 307(*l*)(3), 105 Stat. 1746, 1756; Oct. 25, 1994, Pub.L. 103–415, § 1(m), 108 Stat. 4301; Oct. 25, 1994, Pub.L. 103–416, Title II, §§ 210, 211, 108 Stat. 4312, 4313; Sept. 30, 1996, Pub.L. 104–208, Div. C, Title III, § 308(d)(4)(F), (e)(9), Title VI, § 635(a) to (c)(1), (3), 110 Stat. 3009-618, 3009-620, 3009-702, 3009-703; Nov. 26, 1997, Pub.L. 105–119, Title I, § 125, 111 Stat. 2471; Apr. 27, 1998, Pub.L. 105–173, §§ 1, 3, 112 Stat. 56.)

§ 218. Admission of temporary H–2A workers [8 U.S.C.A. § 1188]

(a) Conditions for approval of H–2A petitions

(1) A petition to import an alien as an H–2A worker (as defined in subsection (i)(2)) may not be approved by the Attorney General unless the petitioner has applied to the Secretary of Labor for a certification that—

(A) there are not sufficient workers who are able, willing, and qualified, and who will be available at the time and place needed, to perform the labor or services involved in the petition, and

(B) the employment of the alien in such labor or services will not adversely affect the wages and working conditions of workers in the United States similarly employed.

(2) The Secretary of Labor may require by regulation, as a condition of issuing the certification, the payment of a fee to recover the reasonable costs of processing applications for certification.

(b) Conditions for denial of labor certification

The Secretary of Labor may not issue a certification under subsection (a) with respect to an employer if the conditions described in that subsection are not met or if any of the following conditions are met:

(1) There is a strike or lockout in the course of a labor dispute which, under the regulations, precludes such certification.

(2)(A) The employer during the previous two-year period employed H–2A workers and the Secretary of Labor has determined, after notice and opportunity for a hearing, that the employer at any time during that period substantially violated a material term or condition of the labor certification with respect to the employment of domestic or nonimmigrant workers.

(B) No employer may be denied certification under subparagraph (A) for more than three years for any violation described in such subparagraph.

(3) The employer has not provided the Secretary with satisfactory assurances that if the employment for which the certification is sought is not covered by State workers' compensation law, the employer will provide, at no cost to the worker, insurance covering injury and disease arising out of and in the course of the worker's employment which will provide benefits at least equal to those provided under the State workers' compensation law for comparable employment.

(4) The Secretary determines that the employer has not made positive recruitment efforts within a multi-state region of traditional or expected labor supply where the Secretary finds that there are a significant number of qualified United States workers who, if recruited, would be willing to make themselves available for work at the time and place needed. Positive recruitment under this paragraph is in addition to, and shall be conducted within the same time period as, the circulation through the interstate employment service system of the employer's job offer. The obligation to engage in positive recruitment under this paragraph shall terminate on the date the H–2A workers depart for the employer's place of employment.

(c) Special rules for consideration of applications

The following rules shall apply in the case of the filing and consideration of an application for a labor certification under this section:

(1) Deadline for filing applications

The Secretary of Labor may not require that the application be filed more than 45 days before the first date the employer requires the labor or services of the H–2A worker.

(2) Notice within seven days of deficiencies

(A) The employer shall be notified in writing within seven days of the date of filing if the application does not meet the standards (other than that described in subsection (a)(1)(A)) for approval.

(B) If the application does not meet such standards, the notice shall include the reasons therefor and the Secretary shall provide an opportunity for the prompt resubmission of a modified application.

(3) Issuance of certification

(A) The Secretary of Labor shall make, not later than 30 days before the date such labor or services are first required to be performed, the certification described in subsection (a)(1) of this section if—

(i) the employer has complied with the criteria for certification (including criteria for the recruitment of eligible individuals as prescribed by the Secretary), and

(ii) the employer does not actually have, or has not been provided with referrals of, qualified eligible individuals who have indicated their availability to perform such labor or services on the terms and conditions of a job offer which meets the requirements of the Secretary.

In considering the question of whether a specific qualification is appropriate in a job offer, the Secretary shall apply the normal and accepted qualifications required by non-H–2A-employers in the same or comparable occupations and crops.

(B)(i) For a period of 3 years subsequent to the effective date of this section, labor certifications shall remain effective only if, from the time the foreign worker departs for the employer's place of employment, the employer will provide employment to any qualified United States worker who applies to the employer until 50 percent of the period of the work contract, under which the foreign worker who is in the job was hired, has elapsed. In addition, the employer will offer to provide benefits, wages and working conditions required pursuant to this section and regulations.

(ii) The requirement of clause (i) shall not apply to any employer who—

(I) did not, during any calendar quarter during the preceding calendar year, use more than 500 man-days of agricultural labor, as defined in section 203(u) of Title 29,

(II) is not a member of an association which has petitioned for certification under this section for its members, and

(III) has not otherwise associated with other employers who are petitioning for temporary foreign workers under this section.

(iii) Six months before the end of the 3–year period described in clause (i), the Secretary of Labor shall consider the findings of the report mandated by section 403(a)(4)(D) of the Immigration Reform and Control Act of 1986 [8 U.S.C.A. § 1188 note] as well as other relevant materials, including evidence of benefits to United States workers and costs to employers, addressing the advisability of continuing a policy which requires an employer, as a condition for certification under this section, to continue to accept qualified, eligible United States workers for employment after the date the H–2A workers depart for work with the employer. The Secretary's review of such findings and materials shall lead to the issuance of findings in furtherance of the Congressional policy that aliens not be admitted under this section unless there are not sufficient workers in the United States who are able, willing, and qualified to perform the labor or service needed and that the employment of the aliens in such labor or services will not adversely affect the wages and working conditions of workers in the United States similarly employed. In the absence of the enactment of Federal legislation prior to three months before the end of the 3–year period described in clause (i) which addresses the subject matter of this subparagraph, the Secretary shall immediately publish the findings required by this clause, and shall promulgate, on an interim or final basis, regulations based on his findings which shall be effective no later than three years from the effective date of this section.

(iv) In complying with clause (i) of this subparagraph, an association shall be allowed to refer or transfer workers among its members: Provided, That for purposes of this section an association acting as an agent for its members shall not be considered a joint employer merely because of such referral or transfer.

(v) United States workers referred or transferred pursuant to clause (iv) of this subparagraph shall not be treated disparately.

(vi) An employer shall not be liable for payments under section 655.202(b)(6) of title 20, Code of Federal Regulations (or any successor regulation) with respect to an H–2A worker who is displaced due to compliance with the requirement of this subparagraph, if the Secretary of Labor certifies that the H–2A worker was displaced because of the employer's compliance with clause (i) of this subparagraph.

(vii)(I) No person or entity shall willfully and knowingly withhold domestic workers prior to the arrival of H–2A workers in order to force the hiring of domestic workers under clause (i).

(II) Upon the receipt of a complaint by an employer that a violation of subclause (I) has occurred the Secretary shall immediately investigate. He shall within 36 hours of the receipt of the complaint issue findings concerning the alleged violation. Where the Secretary finds that a violation has occurred, he shall immediately suspend the application of clause (i) of this subparagraph with respect to that certification for that date of need.

(4) Housing

Employers shall furnish housing in accordance with regulations. The employer shall be permitted at the employer's option to provide housing meeting applicable Federal standards for temporary labor camps or to secure housing which meets the local standards for rental and/or public accommodations or other substantially similar class of habitation: Provided, That in the absence of applicable local standards, State standards for rental and/or public accommodations or other substantially similar class of habitation shall be met: Provided further, That in the absence of applicable local or State standards, Federal temporary labor camp standards shall apply: Provided further, That the Secretary of Labor shall issue regulations which address the specific requirements of housing for employees principally engaged in the range production of livestock: Provided further, That when it is the prevailing practice in the area and occupation of intended employment to provide family housing, family housing shall be provided to workers with families who request it: And provided further, That nothing in this paragraph shall require an employer to provide or secure housing for workers who are not entitled to it under the temporary labor certification regulations in effect on June 1, 1986.

(d) Roles of agricultural associations

(1) Permitting filing by agricultural associations

A petition to import an alien as a temporary agricultural worker, and an application for a labor certification with respect to such a worker, may be filed by an association of agricultural producers which use agricultural services.

(2) Treatment of associations acting as employers

If an association is a joint or sole employer of temporary agricultural workers, the certifications granted under this section to the association may be used for the certified job opportunities of any of its producer members and such workers may be transferred among its producer members to perform agricultural services of a temporary or seasonal nature for which the certifications were granted.

(3) Treatment of violations

(A) Member's violation does not necessarily disqualify association or other members

If an individual producer member of a joint employer association is determined to have committed an act that under subsection (b)(2) results in the denial of certification with respect to the member, the denial shall apply only to that member of the association unless the Secretary determines that the association or other member participated in, had knowledge of, or reason to know of, the violation.

(B) Association's violation does not necessarily disqualify members

(i) If an association representing agricultural producers as a joint employer is determined to have committed an act that under subsection (b)(2) results in the denial of certification with respect to the association, the denial shall apply only to the association and does not apply to any individual producer member of the association unless the Secretary determines that the member participated in, had knowledge of, or reason to know of, the violation.

(ii) If an association of agricultural producers certified as a sole employer is determined to have committed an act that under subsection (b)(2) results in the denial of certification with respect to the association, no individual producer member of such association may be the beneficiary of the services of temporary alien agricultural workers admitted under this section in the commodity and occupation in which such aliens were employed by the association which was denied certification during the period such denial is in force, unless such producer member employs such aliens in the commodity and occupation in question directly or through an association which is a joint employer of such workers with the producer member.

(e) Expedited administrative appeals of certain determinations

(1) Regulations shall provide for an expedited procedure for the review of a denial of certification under subsection (a)(1) of this section or a revocation of such a certification or, at the applicant's request, for a de novo administrative hearing respecting the denial or revocation.

(2) The Secretary of Labor shall expeditiously, but in no case later than 72 hours after the time a new determination is requested, make a new determination on the request for certification in the case of an H–2A worker if able, willing, and qualified eligible individuals are not actually available at the time such labor or services are required and a certification was denied in whole or in part because of the availability of qualified workers. If the employer asserts that any eligible individual who has been referred is not able, willing, or qualified, the burden of proof is on the employer to establish that the individual referred is not able, willing, or qualified because of employment-related reasons.

(f) Violators disqualified for 5 years

An alien may not be admitted to the United States as a temporary agricultural worker if the alien was admitted to the United States as such a worker within the previous five-year period and the alien during that period violated a term or condition of such previous admission.

(g) Authorizations of appropriations

(1) There are authorized to be appropriated for each fiscal year, beginning with fiscal year 1987, $10,000,000 for the purposes—

> **(A)** of recruiting domestic workers for temporary labor and services which might otherwise be performed by nonimmigrants described in section 101(a)(15)(H)(ii)(a) [8 U.S.C.A. § 1101(a)(15)(H)(ii)(a)], and
>
> **(B)** of monitoring terms and conditions under which such nonimmigrants (and domestic workers employed by the same employers) are employed in the United States.

(2) The Secretary of Labor is authorized to take such actions, including imposing appropriate penalties and seeking appropriate injunctive relief and specific performance of contractual obligations, as may be necessary to assure employer compliance with terms and conditions of employment under this section.

(3) There are authorized to be appropriated for each fiscal year, beginning with fiscal year 1987, such sums as may be necessary for the purpose of enabling the Secretary of Labor to make determinations and certifications under this section and under section 212(a)(5)(A)(i) [8 U.S.C.A. § 1182(a)(5)(A)(i)].

(4) There are authorized to be appropriated for each fiscal year, beginning with fiscal year 1987, such sums as may be necessary for the purposes of enabling the Secretary of Agriculture to carry out the Secretary's duties and responsibilities under this section.

(h) Miscellaneous provisions

(1) The Attorney General shall provide for such endorsement of entry and exit documents of nonimmigrants described in section 101(a)(15)(H)(ii) [8 U.S.C.A. § 1101(a)(15)(H)(ii)] as may be necessary to carry out this section and to provide notice for purposes of section 274A [8 U.S.C.A. § 1324a].

(2) The provisions of subsections (a) and (c) of section 214 [8 U.S.C.A. § 1184] and the provisions of this section preempt any State or local law regulating admissibility of nonimmigrant workers.

(i) Definitions

For purposes of this section:

(1) The term "eligible individual" means, with respect to employment, an individual who is not an unauthorized alien (as defined in section 274A(h)(3) [8 U.S.C.A. § 1324a(h)(3)]) with respect to that employment.

(2) The term "H–2A worker" means a nonimmigrant described in section 101(a)(15)(H)(ii)(a) [8 U.S.C.A. § 1101(a)(15)(H)(ii)(a)].

(June 27, 1952, c. 477, Title II, ch. 2, § 218, formerly § 216, as added Nov. 6, 1986, Pub.L. 99–603, Title III, § 301(c), 100 Stat. 3411, renumbered and amended Oct. 24, 1988, Pub.L. 100–525, § 2(*l*)(2), (3), 102 Stat. 2612; Dec. 12, 1991, Pub.L. 102–232, Title III, §§ 307(*l*)(4), 309(b)(8), 105 Stat. 1756, 1759; Oct. 25, 1994, Pub.L. 103–416, Title II, § 219(z)(8), 108 Stat. 4318; Oct. 22, 1999, Pub.L. 106–78, Title VII, § 748, 113 Stat. 1167.)

§ 219. Designation of foreign terrorist organizations [8 U.S.C.A. § 1189]

(a) Designation

(1) In general

The Secretary is authorized to designate an organization as a foreign terrorist organization in accordance with this subsection if the Secretary finds that—

(A) the organization is a foreign organization;

(B) the organization engages in terrorist activity (as defined in section 212(a)(3)(B) [8 U.S.C.A. § 1182(a)(3)(B)]); and

(C) the terrorist activity of the organization threatens the security of United States nationals or the national security of the United States.

(2) Procedure

(A) Notice

Seven days before making a designation under this subsection, the Secretary shall, by classified communication—

(i) notify the Speaker and Minority Leader of the House of Representatives, the President pro tempore, Majority Leader, and Minority Leader of the Senate, and the members of the relevant committees, in writing, of the intent to designate a foreign organization under this subsection, together with the findings made under paragraph (1) with respect to that organization, and the factual basis therefor; and

(ii) seven days after such notification, publish the designation in the Federal Register.

(B) Effect of designation

(i) For purposes of section 2339B of Title 18, a designation under this subsection shall take effect upon publication under subparagraph (A).

(ii) Any designation under this subsection shall cease to have effect upon an Act of Congress disapproving such designation.

(C) Freezing of assets

Upon notification under paragraph (2), the Secretary of the Treasury may require United States financial institutions possessing or controlling any assets of any foreign organization included in the notification to block all financial transactions involving those assets until further directive from either the Secretary of the Treasury, Act of Congress, or order of court.

(3) Record

(A) In general

In making a designation under this subsection, the Secretary shall create an administrative record.

(B) Classified information

The Secretary may consider classified information in making a designation under this subsection. Classified information shall not be subject to disclosure for such time as it remains classified, except that such information may be disclosed to a court ex parte and in camera for purposes of judicial review under subsection (c).

(4) Period of designation

(A) In general

Subject to paragraphs (5) and (6), a designation under this subsection shall be effective for all purposes for a period of 2 years beginning on the effective date of the designation under paragraph (2)(B).

(B) Redesignation

The Secretary may redesignate a foreign organization as a foreign terrorist organization for an additional 2–year period at the end of the 2–year period referred to in subparagraph (A) (but not sooner than 60 days prior to the termination of such period) upon a finding that the relevant circumstances described in paragraph (1) still exist. The procedural requirements of paragraphs (2) and (3) shall apply to a redesignation under this subparagraph.

(5) Revocation by Act of Congress

The Congress, by an Act of Congress, may block or revoke a designation made under paragraph (1).

(6) Revocation based on change in circumstances

(A) In general

The Secretary may revoke a designation made under paragraph (1) if the Secretary finds that—

(i) the circumstances that were the basis for the designation have changed in such a manner as to warrant revocation of the designation; or

(ii) the national security of the United States warrants a revocation of the designation.

(B) Procedure

The procedural requirements of paragraphs (2) through (4) shall apply to a revocation under this paragraph.

(7) Effect of revocation

The revocation of a designation under paragraph (5) or (6) shall not affect any action or proceeding based on conduct committed prior to the effective date of such revocation.

(8) Use of designation in trial or hearing

If a designation under this subsection has become effective under paragraph (1)(B), a defendant in a criminal action shall not be permitted to raise any question concerning the validity of the issuance of such designation as a defense or an objection at any trial or hearing.

(b) Judicial review of designation

(1) In general

Not later than 30 days after publication of the designation in the Federal Register, an organization designated as a foreign terrorist organization may seek judicial review of the designation in the United States Court of Appeals for the District of Columbia Circuit.

(2) Basis of review

Review under this subsection shall be based solely upon the administrative record, except that the Government may submit, for ex parte and in camera review, classified information used in making the designation.

(3) Scope of review

The Court shall hold unlawful and set aside a designation the court finds to be—

(A) arbitrary, capricious, an abuse of discretion, or otherwise not in accordance with law;

(B) contrary to constitutional right, power, privilege, or immunity;

(C) in excess of statutory jurisdiction, authority, or limitation, or short of statutory right;

(D) lacking substantial support in the administrative record taken as a whole or in classified information submitted to the court under paragraph (2), or

(E) not in accord with the procedures required by law.

(4) Judicial review invoked

The pendency of an action for judicial review of a designation shall not affect the application of this section, unless the court issues a final order setting aside the designation.

(c) Definitions

As used in this section—

(1) the term "classified information" has the meaning given that term in section 1(a) of the Classified Information Procedures Act (18 U.S.C. App.);

(2) the term "national security" means the national defense, foreign relations, or economic interests of the United States;

(3) the term "relevant committees" means the Committees on the Judiciary, Intelligence, and Foreign Relations of the Senate and the Committees on the Judiciary, Intelligence, and International Relations of the House of Representatives; and

(4) the term "Secretary" means the Secretary of State, in consultation with the Secretary of the Treasury and the Attorney General.

(June 27, 1952, c. 477, Title II, ch. 2, § 219, as added Apr. 24, 1996, Pub.L. 104–132, Title III, § 302(a), 110 Stat. 1248, and amended Sept. 30, 1996, Pub.L. 104–208, Div. C, Title III, § 356, Title VI, § 671(c)(1), 110 Stat. 3009–644, 3009–722.)

CHAPTER III—ISSUANCE OF ENTRY DOCUMENTS

§ 221. Issuance of visas [8 U.S.C.A. § 1201]

(a) Immigrants; nonimmigrants

Under the conditions hereinafter prescribed and subject to the limitations prescribed in this Act or regulations issued thereunder, a consular officer may issue (1) to an immigrant who has made proper application therefor, an immigrant visa which shall consist of the application provided for in section 222 [8 U.S.C.A. § 1202], visaed by such consular officer, and shall specify the foreign state, if any, to which the immigrant is charged, the immigrant's particular status under such foreign state, the preference, immediate relative, or special immigrant classification to which the alien is charged, the date on which the validity of the visa shall expire, and such additional information as may be required; and (2) to a nonimmigrant who has made proper application therefor, a nonimmigrant visa, which shall specify the classification under section 101(a)(15) [8 U.S.C.A. § 1101(a)(15)] of the nonimmigrant, the period during which the nonimmigrant visa shall be valid, and such additional information as may be required.

(b) Registration; photographs; waiver of requirement

Each alien who applies for a visa shall be registered in connection with his application, and shall furnish copies of his photograph signed by him for such use as may be by regulations required. The requirements of this subsection may be waived in the discretion of the Secretary of State in the case of any alien who is within that class of nonimmigrants enumerated in sections 101(a)(15)(A) [8 U.S.C.A. § 1101(a)(15)(A)], and 101(a)(15)(G) [8 U.S.C.A. § 1101(a)(15)(G)], or in the case of any alien who is granted a diplomatic visa on a diplomatic passport or on the equivalent thereof.

(c) Period of validity; requirement of visa

An immigrant visa shall be valid for such period, not exceeding six months, as shall be by regulations prescribed, except that any visa issued to a child lawfully adopted by a United States citizen and spouse while such citizen is serving abroad in the United States Armed Forces, or is employed abroad by the United States Government, or is temporarily abroad on business, shall be valid until such time, for a period not to exceed three years, as the adoptive citizen parent returns to the United States in due course of his service, employment, or business. A nonimmigrant visa shall be valid for such periods as shall be by regulations prescribed. In prescribing the period of validity of a nonimmigrant visa in the case of nationals of any foreign country who are eligible for such visas, the Secretary of State shall, insofar as practicable, accord to such nationals the same treatment upon a reciprocal basis as such foreign country accords to nationals of the United States who are within a similar class; except that in the case of aliens who are nationals of a foreign country and who either are granted refugee status and firmly resettled in an other foreign country, or are granted permanent residence and residing in another foreign country, the Secretary of State may prescribe the period of validity of such a visa based upon the treatment granted by that other foreign country to alien refugees and permanent residents, respectively, in the United States. An immigrant visa may be replaced under the original number during the fiscal year in which the original visa was issued for an immigrant who establishes to the satisfaction of the consular officer that he was unable to use the original immigrant visa during the period of its validity because of reasons beyond his control and for which he was not responsible: Provided, That the immigrant is found by the consular officer to be eligible for an immigrant visa and the immigrant pays again the statutory fees for an application and an immigrant visa.

(d) Physical examination

Prior to the issuance of an immigrant visa to any alien, the consular officer shall require such alien to submit to a physical and mental examination in accordance with such regulations as may be prescribed. Prior to the issuance of a nonimmigrant visa to any alien, the consular officer may require such alien to submit to a physical or mental examination, or both, if in his opinion such examination is necessary to ascertain whether such alien is eligible to receive a visa.

(e) Surrender of visa

Each immigrant shall surrender his immigrant visa to the immigration officer at the port of entry, who shall endorse on the visa the date and the port of arrival, the identity of the vessel or other means of transportation by which the immigrant arrived, and such other endorsements as may be by regulations required.

(f) Surrender of documents

Each nonimmigrant shall present or surrender to the immigration officer at the port of entry such documents as may be by regulation required. In the case of an alien crewman not in possession of any individual documents other than a passport and until such time as it becomes practicable to issue individual documents, such alien crewman may be admitted, subject to the provisions of this title, if his name appears in the crew list of the vessel or aircraft on which he arrives and the crew list is visaed by a consular officer, but the consular officer shall have the right to deny admission to any alien crewman from the crew list visa.

(g) Non-issuance of visas or other documents

No visa or other documentation shall be issued to an alien if **(1)** it appears to the consular officer, from statements in the application, or in the papers submitted therewith, that such alien is ineligible to receive a visa or such other documentation under section 212 [8 U.S.C.A. § 1182], or any other provision of law, **(2)** the application fails to comply with the provisions of this Act, or the regulations issued thereunder, or **(3)** the consular officer knows or has reason to believe that such alien is ineligible to receive a visa or such other documentation under section 212 [8 U.S.C.A. § 1182], or any other provision of law: Provided, That a visa or other documentation may be issued to an alien who is within the purview of section 212(a)(4) [8 U.S.C.A. § 1182(a)(4)], if such alien is otherwise entitled to receive a visa or other documentation, upon receipt of notice by the consular officer from the Attorney General of the giving of a bond or undertaking providing indemnity as in the case of aliens admitted under section 213 [8 U.S.C.A. § 1183]: Provided further, That a visa may be issued to an alien defined in section 101(a)(15)(B) or (F) [8

U.S.C.A. § 1101(a)(15)(B) or (F)], if such alien is otherwise entitled to receive a visa, upon receipt of a notice by the consular officer from the Attorney General of the giving of a bond with sufficient surety in such sum and containing such conditions as the consular officer shall prescribe, to insure that at the expiration of the time for which such alien has been admitted by the Attorney General, as provided in section 214(a) [8 U.S.C.A. § 1184(a)], or upon failure to maintain the status under which he was admitted, or to maintain any status subsequently acquired under section 248 [8 U.S.C.A. § 1258], such alien will depart from the United States.

(h) Nonadmission upon arrival

Nothing in this Act shall be construed to entitle any alien, to whom a visa or other documentation has been issued, to be admitted [sic] the United States, if, upon arrival at a port of entry in the United States, he is found to be inadmissible under this Act, or any other provision of law. The substance of this subsection shall appear upon every visa application.

(i) Revocation of visas or documents

After the issuance of a visa or other documentation to any alien, the consular officer or the Secretary of State may at any time, in his discretion, revoke such visa or other documentation. Notice of such revocation shall be communicated to the Attorney General, and such revocation shall invalidate the visa or other documentation from the date of issuance: Provided, That carriers or transportation companies, and masters, commanding officers, agents, owners, charterers, or consignees, shall not be penalized under section 273(b) [8 U.S.C.A. § 1323(b)] for action taken in reliance on such visas or other documentation, unless they received due notice of such revocation prior to the alien's embarkation.

(June 27, 1952, c. 477, Title II, ch. 3, § 221, 66 Stat. 191; Sept. 26, 1961, Pub.L. 87–301, § 4, 75 Stat. 651; Oct. 3, 1965, Pub.L. 89–236, §§ 11(a), (b), 17, 79 Stat. 918, 919; Dec. 29, 1981, Pub.L. 97–116, § 18(f), 95 Stat. 1620; Nov. 14, 1986, Pub.L. 99–653, § 5(a)(1) to (3), formerly § 5(a) to (c), 100 Stat. 3656; renumbered Oct. 24, 1988, Pub.L. 100–525, § 8 (d)(1), 102 Stat. 2617, and amended Nov. 29, 1990, Pub.L. 101–649, Title VI, § 603(a)(9), 104 Stat. 5083; Dec. 12, 1991, Pub.L. 102–232, Title III, § 302(e)(8)(C), 105 Stat. 1746; Sept. 30, 1996, Pub.L. 104–208, Div. C, Title III, § 308(d)(4)(G), (f)(2)(B), Title VI, § 631, 110 Stat. 3009–618, 3009–621, 3009–700.)

§ 222. Application for visas [8 U.S.C.A. § 1202]

(a) Immigrant visas

Every alien applying for an immigrant visa and for alien registration shall make application therefor in such form and manner and at such place as shall be by regulations prescribed. In the application the alien shall state his full and true name, and any other name which he has used or by which he has been known; age and sex; the date and place of his birth; and such additional information necessary to the identification of the applicant and the enforcement of the immigration and nationality laws as may be by regulations prescribed.

(b) Other documentary evidence for immigrant visa

Every alien applying for an immigrant visa shall present a valid unexpired passport or other suitable travel document, or document of identity and nationality, if such document is required under the regulations issued by the Secretary of State. The immigrant shall furnish to the consular officer with his application a copy of a certification by the appropriate police authorities stating what their records show concerning the immigrant; a certified copy of any existing prison record, military record, and record of his birth; and a certified copy of all other records or documents concerning him or his case which may be required by the consular officer. The copy of each document so furnished shall be permanently attached to the application and become a part thereof. In the event that the immigrant establishes to the satisfaction of the consular officer that any document or record required by this subsection is unobtainable, the consular officer may permit the immigrant to submit in lieu of such document or record other satisfactory evidence of the fact to which such document or record would, if obtainable, pertain.

(c) Nonimmigrant visas; nonimmigrant registration; form, manner and contents of application

Every alien applying for a nonimmigrant visa and for alien registration shall make application therefor in such form and manner as shall be by regulations prescribed. In the application the alien shall state his full and true name, the date and place of birth, his nationality, the purpose and length of his intended stay in the United States; his marital status; and such additional information necessary to the identification of the applicant, the determination of his eligibility for a nonimmigrant visa, and the enforcement of the immigration and nationality laws as may be by regulations prescribed. At the discretion of the Secretary of State, application forms for the various classes of nonimmigrant admissions described in section 101(a)(15) [8 U.S.C.A. § 1101(a)(15)] may vary according to the class of visa being requested.

(d) Other documentary evidence for nonimmigrant visa

Every alien applying for a nonimmigrant visa and alien registration shall furnish to the consular officer, with his application, a certified copy of such documents pertaining to him as may be by regulations required.

(e) Signing and verification of application

Except as may be otherwise prescribed by regulations, each application for an immigrant visa shall be signed by the applicant in the presence of the consular officer, and verified by the oath of the applicant administered by the consular officer. The application for an immigrant visa, when visaed by the consular officer, shall become the immigrant visa. The application for a nonimmigrant visa or other documentation as a nonimmigrant shall be disposed of as may be by regulations prescribed. The issuance of a nonimmigrant visa shall, except as may be otherwise by regulations prescribed, be evidenced by a stamp, or other [sic] placed in the alien's passport.

(f) Confidential nature of records

The records of the Department of State and of diplomatic and consular offices of the United States pertaining to the issuance or refusal of visas or permits to enter the United States shall be considered confidential and shall be used only for the formulation, amendment, administration, or enforcement of the immigration, nationality, and other laws of the United States, except that in the discretion of the Secretary of State certified copies of such records may be made available to a court which certifies that the information contained in such records is needed by the court in the interest of the ends of justice in a case pending before the court.

(g) Voidness of nonimmigrant visa for stay beyond authorized period

(1) In the case of an alien who has been admitted on the basis of a nonimmigrant visa and remained in the United States beyond the period of stay authorized by the Attorney General, such visa shall be void beginning after the conclusion of such period of stay.

(2) An alien described in paragraph (1) shall be ineligible to be readmitted to the United States as a nonimmigrant, except—

(A) on the basis of a visa (other than the visa described in paragraph (1)) issued in a consular office located in the country of the alien's nationality (or, if there is no office in such country, in such other consular office as the Secretary of State shall specify); or

(B) where extraordinary circumstances are found by the Secretary of State to exist.

(June 27, 1952, c. 477, Title II, ch. 3, § 222, 66 Stat. 193; Sept. 26, 1961, Pub.L. 87–301, § 6, 75 Stat. 653; Oct. 3, 1965, Pub.L. 89–236 § 11(c), 79 Stat. 918; Nov. 14, 1986, Pub.L. 99–653, § 6, 100 Stat. 3656; Oct. 24, 1988, Pub.L. 100–525, §§ 8(e), 9(j), 102 Stat. 2617, 2620; Oct. 25, 1994, Pub.L. 103–416, Title II, § 205(a), 108 Stat. 4311; Sept. 30, 1996, Pub.L. 104–208, Div. C, Title VI, §§ 632(a), 634, 110 Stat. 3009–701.)

§ 223. Re-entry permit [8 U.S.C.A. § 1203]

(a) Application; contents

(1) Any alien lawfully admitted for permanent residence, or **(2)** any alien lawfully admitted to the United States pursuant to clause 6 of section 3 of the Immigration Act of 1924, between July 1, 1924, and July 5, 1932, both dates inclusive, who intends to depart temporarily from the United States may make application to the Attorney General for a permit to reenter the United States, stating the length of his intended absence or absences, and the reasons therefor. Such applications shall be made under oath, and shall be in such form, contain such information, and be accompanied by such photographs of the applicant as may be by regulations prescribed.

(b) Issuance of permit; nonrenewability

If the Attorney General finds **(1)** that the applicant under subsection (a)(1) has been lawfully admitted to the United States for permanent residence, or that the applicant under subsection (a)(2) has since admission maintained the status required of him at the time of his admission and such applicant desires to visit abroad and to return to the United States to resume the status existing at the time of his departure for such visit, **(2)** that the application is made in good faith, and **(3)** that the alien's proposed departure from the United States would not be contrary to the interests of the United States, the Attorney General may, in his discretion, issue the permit, which shall be valid for not more than two years from the date of issuance and shall not be renewable. The permit shall be in such form as shall be by regulations prescribed for the complete identification of the alien.

(c) Multiple reentries

During the period of validity, such permit may be used by the alien in making one or more applications for reentry into the United States.

(d) Presented and surrendered

Upon the return of the alien to the United States the permit shall be presented to the immigration officer at the port of entry, and upon the expiration of its validity, the permit shall be surrendered to the Service.

(e) Permit in lieu of visa

A permit issued under this section in the possession of the person to whom issued, shall be accepted in lieu of any visa which otherwise would be required from such person under this Act. Otherwise a permit issued under this section shall have no effect under the immigration laws except to show that the alien to whom it was issued is returning from a temporary visit abroad; but nothing in this section shall be construed as making such permit the exclusive means of establishing that the alien is so returning.

(June 27, 1952, c. 477, Title II, ch. 3, § 223, 66 Stat. 194; Pub. L. 97–116, § 6, Dec. 29, 1981, 95 Stat. 1615.)

§ 224. Immediate relative and special immigrant visas [8 U.S.C.A. § 1204]

A consular officer may, subject to the limitations provided in section 221 [8 U.S.C.A. § 1201], issue an immigrant visa to a special immigrant or immediate relative as such upon satisfactory proof, under regulations prescribed under this Act, that the applicant is entitled to special immigrant or immediate relative status.

(June 27, 1952, c. 477, Title II, ch. 3, § 224, 66 Stat. 195; Pub. L. 89–236, § 11(d), Oct. 3, 1965, 79 Stat. 918.)

Chapter IV—Inspection, Apprehension, Examination, Exclusion, and Removal

§ 231. Lists of alien and citizen passengers arriving and departing [8 U.S.C.A. § 1221]

(a) Shipment or aircraft manifest; arrival; form and contents; exclusions

Upon the arrival of any person by water or by air at any port within the United States from any place outside the United States, it shall be the duty of the master or commanding officer, or authorized agent, owner, or consignee of the vessel or aircraft, having any such person on board to deliver to the immigration officers at the port of arrival typewritten or printed lists or manifests of the persons on board such vessel or aircraft. Such lists or manifests shall be prepared at such time, be in such form and shall contain such information as the Attorney General shall prescribe by regulation as being necessary for the identification of the persons transported and for the enforcement of the immigration laws. This subsection shall not require the master or commanding officer, or authorized agent, owner, or consignee of a vessel or aircraft to furnish a list or manifest relating **(1)** to an alien crewman or **(2)** to any other person arriving by air on a trip originating in foreign contiguous territory, except (with respect to such arrivals by air) as may be required by regulations issued pursuant to section 234 [8 U.S.C.A. § 1224].

(b) Departure; shipment or aircraft manifest; form and contents; exclusions

It shall be the duty of the master or commanding officer or authorized agent of every vessel or aircraft taking passengers on board at any port of the United States, who are destined to any place outside the United States, to file with the immigration officers before departure from such port a list of all such persons taken on board. Such list shall be in such form, contain such information, and be accompanied by such documents, as the Attorney General shall prescribe by regulation as necessary for the identification of the persons so transported and for the enforcement of the immigration laws. No master or commanding officer of any such vessel or aircraft shall be granted clearance papers for his vessel or aircraft until he or the authorized agent has deposited such list or lists and accompanying documents with the immigration officer at such port and made oath that they are full and complete as to the information required to be contained therein, except that in the case of vessels or aircraft which the Attorney General determines are making regular trips to ports of the United States, the Attorney General may, when expedient, arrange for the delivery of lists of outgoing persons at a later date. This subsection shall not require the master or commanding officer, or authorized agent, owner, or consignee of a vessel or aircraft to furnish a list or manifest relating **(1)** to an alien crewman or **(2)** to any other person departing by air on a trip originating in the United States who is destined to foreign contiguous territory, except (with respect to such departure by air) as may be required by regulations issued pursuant to section 234 [8 U.S.C.A. § 1224].

(c) Record of citizens and resident aliens leaving permanently for foreign countries

The Attorney General may authorize immigration officers to record the following information regarding every resident person leaving the United States by way of the Canadian or Mexican borders for permanent residence in a foreign country: Names, age, and sex; whether married or single; calling or occupation; whether able to read or write; nationality; country of birth; country of which citizen or subject; race; last permanent residence in the United States; intended future permanent residence; and time and port of last arrival in the United States; and if a United States citizen or national, the facts on which claim to that status is based.

(d) Penalties against noncomplying shipments or aircraft

If it shall appear to the satisfaction of the Attorney General that the master or commanding officer, owner, or consignee of any vessel or aircraft, or the agent of any transportation line, as the case may be, has refused or failed to deliver any list or manifest required by subsection (a) or (b), or that the list or manifest delivered is not accurate and full, such master or commanding officer, owner, or consignee, or agent, as the case may be, shall pay to the Commissioner the sum of $300 for each person concerning whom such accurate and full list or manifest is not furnished, or concerning whom the manifest or list is not prepared and sworn to as prescribed by this section or by regulations issued pursuant thereto. No vessel or aircraft shall be granted clearance pending determination of the question of the liability to the payment of such penalty, or while it remains unpaid, and no such penalty shall be remitted or refunded, except that clearance may be granted prior to the determination of such question upon the deposit with the Commissioner of a bond or undertaking approved by the Attorney General or a sum sufficient to cover such penalty.

(e) Waiver of requirements

The Attorney General is authorized to prescribe the circumstances and conditions under which the list or manifest requirements of subsections (a) and (b) may be waived.

(June 27, 1952, c. 477, Title II, ch. 4, § 231, 66 Stat. 195; Dec. 29, 1981, Pub.L. 97–116, § 18(g), 95 Stat. 1620; Nov. 29, 1990, Pub.L. 101–649, Title V, § 543(a)(1), 104 Stat. 5057; Dec. 12, 1991, Pub.L. 102–232, Title III, § 306(c)(4)(A), 105 Stat. 1752; Pub.L. 104–208, Div. C, Title III, § 308(g)(1), Sept. 30, 1996, 110 Stat. 3009–622.)

§ 232. Detention of aliens for physical and mental examination [8 U.S.C.A. § 1222]

(a) Detention of aliens

For the purpose of determining whether aliens (including alien crewmen) arriving at ports of the United States belong to any of the classes inadmissible under this Act, by reason of being afflicted with any of the diseases or mental or physical defects or disabilities set forth in section 212(a) [8 U.S.C.A. § 1182(a)], or whenever the Attorney General has received information showing that any aliens are coming from a country or have embarked at a place where any of such diseases are prevalent or epidemic, such aliens shall be detained by the Attorney General, for a sufficient time to enable the immigration officers and medical officers to subject such aliens to observation and an examination sufficient to determine whether or not they belong to the inadmissible classes.

(b) Physical and mental examination

The physical and mental examination of arriving aliens (including alien crewmen) shall be made by medical officers of the United States Public Health Service, who shall conduct all medical examinations and shall certify, for the information of the immigration officers and the immigration judges, any physical and mental defect or disease observed by such medical officers in any such alien. If medical officers of the United States Public Health Service are not available, civil surgeons of not less than four years' professional experience may be employed for such service upon such terms as may be prescribed by the Attorney General. Aliens (including alien crewmen) arriving at ports of the United States shall be examined by at least one such medical officer or civil surgeon under such administrative regulations as the Attorney General may prescribe, and under medical regulations prepared by the Secretary of Health and Human Services. Medical officers of the United States Public Health Service who have had special training in the diagnosis of insanity and mental defects shall be detailed for duty or employed at such ports of entry as the Attorney General may designate, and such medical officers shall be provided with suitable facilities for the detention and examination of all arriving aliens who it is suspected may be inadmissible under paragraph (1) of section 212(a) [8 U.S.C.A. § 1182(a)], and the services of interpreters shall be provided for such examination. Any alien certified under paragraph (1) of section 212(a) [8 U.S.C.A. § 1182(a)], may appeal to a board of medical officers of the United States Public Health Service, which shall be convened by the Secretary of Health and Human Services, and any such alien may introduce before such board one expert medical witness at his own cost and expense.

(c) Certification of certain helpless aliens

If an examining medical officer determines that an alien arriving in the United States is inadmissible, is helpless from sickness, mental or physical disability, or infancy, and is accompanied by another alien whose protection or guardianship may be required, the officer may certify such fact for purposes of applying section 212(a)(10)(B) [8 U.S.C.A. § 1182(a)(10)(B)] with respect to the other alien.

(June 27, 1952, c. 477, Title II, ch. 4, § 232, 66 Stat. 196; Oct. 18, 1986, Pub.L. 99–500, Title I, § 101(b) [Title II, § 206(a), formerly § 206], 100 Stat. 1783–56 as renumbered and amended Oct. 24, 1988, Pub.L. 100–525, § 4(b)(1), (2), (d), 102 Stat. 2615; Sept. 30, 1996, Pub.L. 104–208, Div. C, Title III, §§ 308(b)(2), (3), (c)(2)(A), (d)(3)(A), (4)(H), 371(b)(3), 110 Stat. 3009–615, 3009–616, 3009–617, 3009–618, 3009–645.)

§ 233. Entry through or from foreign territory and adjacent islands [8 U.S.C.A. § 1223]

(a) Necessity of transportation contract

The Attorney General shall have power to enter into contracts with transportation lines for the inspection and admission of aliens coming to the United States from foreign territory or from adjacent islands. No such transportation line shall be allowed to land any such alien in the United States until and unless it has entered into any such contracts which may be required by the Attorney General.

(b) Landing stations

Every transportation line engaged in carrying alien passengers for hire to the United States from foreign territory of from adjacent islands shall provide and maintain at its expense suitable landing stations, approved by the Attorney General, conveniently located at the point or points of entry. No such transportation line shall be allowed to land any alien passengers in the United States until such landing stations are provided, and unless such stations are thereafter maintained to the satisfaction of the Attorney General.

(c) Landing agreements

The Attorney General shall have power to enter into contracts including bonding agreements with transportation lines to guarantee the passage through the United States in immediate and continuous transit of aliens destined to foreign countries. Notwithstanding any other provision of this Act, such aliens may not have their classification changed under section 248 [8 U.S.C.A. § 1258].

(d) Definitions

As used in this section the terms "transportation line" and "transportation company" include, but are not limited to, the owner, charterer, consignee, or authorized agent operating any vessel or aircraft or railroad train bringing aliens to the United States, to foreign territory, or to adjacent islands.

(e) Redesignated (d)

(June 27, 1952, c. 477, Title II, ch. 4, § 233, formerly § 238, 66 Stat. 202, as amended Nov. 14, 1986, Pub.L. 99–653, § 7(b), 100 Stat. 3657; redesignated

§ 233 and amended, Sept. 30, 1996, Pub.L. 104–208, Div. C, Title III, §§ 308(b)(4), (f)(4), 362, 110 Stat. 3009–615, 3009–622, 3009–645.)

§ 234. Designation of ports of entry for aliens arriving by aircraft [8 U.S.C.A. § 1224]

The Attorney General is authorized **(1)** by regulation to designate as ports of entry for aliens arriving by aircraft any of the ports of entry for civil aircraft designated as such in accordance with law; **(2)** by regulation to provide such reasonable requirements for aircraft in civil air navigation with respect to giving notice of intention to land in advance of landing, or notice of landing, as shall be deemed necessary for purposes of administration and enforcement of this Act; and **(3)** by regulation to provide for the application to civil air navigation of the provisions of this Act where not expressly so provided in this Act to such extent and upon such conditions as he deems necessary. Any person who violates any regulation made under this section shall be subject to a civil penalty of $2,000 which may be remitted or mitigated by the Attorney General in accordance with such proceedings as the Attorney General shall by regulation prescribe. In case the violation is by the owner or person in command of the aircraft, the penalty shall be a lien upon the aircraft, and such aircraft may be libeled therefor in the appropriate United States court. The determination by the Attorney General and remission or mitigation of the civil penalty shall be final. In case the violation is by the owner or person in command of the aircraft, the penalty shall be a lien upon the aircraft and may be collected by proceedings in rem which shall conform as nearly as may be to civil suits in admiralty. The Supreme Court of the United States, and under its direction other courts of the United States, are authorized to prescribe rules regulating such proceedings against aircraft in any particular not otherwise provided by law. Any aircraft made subject to a lien by this section may be summarily seized by, and placed in the custody of such persons as the Attorney General may by regulation prescribe. The aircraft may be released from such custody upon deposit of such amount not exceeding $2000 as the Attorney General may prescribe, or of a bond in such sum and with such sureties as the Attorney General may prescribe, conditioned upon the payment of the penalty which may be finally determined by the Attorney General.

(June 27, 1952, c. 477, Title II, ch. 4, § 234, formerly § 239, 66 Stat. 203, as amended Nov. 29, 1990, Pub.L. 101–649, Title V, § 543(a)(3), 104 Stat. 5058; Dec. 12, 1991, Pub.L. 102–232, Title III, § 306(c)(2), 105 Stat. 1752; renumbered § 234, Pub.L. 104–208, Div. C, Title III, § 304(a)(1), Sept. 30, 1996, 110 Stat. 3009–587.)

§ 235. Inspection by immigration officers; expedited removal of inadmissible arriving aliens; referral for hearing [8 U.S.C.A. § 1225]

(a) Inspection

(1) Aliens treated as applicants for admission

An alien present in the United States who has not been admitted or who arrives in the United States (whether or not at a designated port of arrival and including an alien who is brought to the United States after having been interdicted in international or United States waters) shall be deemed for purposes of this Act an applicant for admission. — defined 101(a)(13)

(2) Stowaways

An arriving alien who is a stowaway is not eligible to apply for admission or to be admitted and shall be ordered removed upon inspection by an immigration officer. Upon such inspection if the alien indicates an intention to apply for asylum under section 208 [8 U.S.C.A. § 1158] or a fear of persecution, the officer shall refer the alien for an interview under subsection (b)(1)(B). A stowaway may apply for asylum only if the stowaway is found to have a credible fear of persecution under subsection (b)(1)(B). In no case may a stowaway be considered an applicant for admission or eligible for a hearing under section 240 [8 U.S.C.A. § 1229a].

(3) Inspection

All aliens (including alien crewmen) who are applicants for admission or otherwise seeking admission or readmission to or transit through the United States shall be inspected by immigration officers.

(4) Withdrawal of application for admission

An alien applying for admission may, in the discretion of the Attorney General and at any time, be permitted to withdraw the application for admission and depart immediately from the United States.

(5) Statements

An applicant for admission may be required to state under oath any information sought by an immigration officer regarding the purposes and intentions of the applicant in seeking admission to the United States, including the applicant's intended length of stay and whether the applicant intends to remain permanently or become a United States citizen, and whether the applicant is inadmissible.

(b) Inspection of applicants for admission

(1) Inspection of aliens arriving in the United States and certain other aliens who have not been admitted or paroled

(A) Screening

(i) In general

If an immigration officer determines that an alien (other than an alien described in subparagraph (F)) who is arriving in the United States or is described in clause (iii) is inadmissible under section 212(a)(6)(C) [8 U.S.C.A.

§ 1182(a)(6)(C)] or 212(a)(7) [8 U.S.C.A. § 1182(a)(7)], the officer shall order the alien removed from the United States without further hearing or review unless the alien indicates either an intention to apply for asylum under section 208 [8 U.S.C.A. § 1158] or a fear of persecution.

(ii) Claims for asylum

If an immigration officer determines that an alien (other than an alien described in subparagraph (F)) who is arriving in the United States or is described in clause (iii) is inadmissible under section 212(a)(6)(C) [8 U.S.C.A. § 1182(a)(6)(C)] or 212(a)(7) [8 U.S.C.A. § 1182(a)(7)] and the alien indicates either an intention to apply for asylum under section 208 [8 U.S.C.A. § 1158] or a fear of persecution, the officer shall refer the alien for an interview by an asylum officer under subparagraph (B).

(iii) Application to certain other aliens

(I) In general

The Attorney General may apply clauses (i) and (ii) of this subparagraph to any or all aliens described in subclause (II) as designated by the Attorney General. Such designation shall be in the sole and unreviewable discretion of the Attorney General and may be modified at any time.

(II) Aliens described

An alien described in this clause is an alien who is not described in subparagraph (F), who has not been admitted or paroled into the United States, and who has not affirmatively shown, to the satisfaction of an immigration officer, that the alien has been physically present in the United States continuously for the 2–year period immediately prior to the date of the determination of inadmissibility under this subparagraph.

(B) Asylum interviews

(i) Conduct by asylum officers

An asylum officer shall conduct interviews of aliens referred under subparagraph (A)(ii), either at a port of entry or at such other place designated by the Attorney General.

(ii) Referral of certain aliens

If the officer determines at the time of the interview that an alien has a credible fear of persecution (within the meaning of clause (v)), the alien shall be detained for further consideration of the application for asylum.

(iii) Removal without further review if no credible fear of persecution

(I) In general

Subject to subclause (III), if the officer determines that an alien does not have a credible fear of persecution, the officer shall order the alien removed from the United States without further hearing or review.

(II) Record of determination

The officer shall prepare a written record of a determination under subclause (I). Such record shall include a summary of the material facts as stated by the applicant, such additional facts (if any) relied upon by the officer, and the officer's analysis of why, in the light of such facts, the alien has not established a credible fear of persecution. A copy of the officer's interview notes shall be attached to the written summary.

(III) Review of determination

The Attorney General shall provide by regulation and upon the alien's request for prompt review by an immigration judge of a determination under subclause (I) that the alien does not have a credible fear of persecution. Such review shall include an opportunity for the alien to be heard and questioned by the immigration judge, either in person or by telephonic or video connection. Review shall be concluded as expeditiously as possible, to the maximum extent practicable within 24 hours, but in no case later than 7 days after the date of the determination under subclause (I).

(IV) Mandatory detention

Any alien subject to the procedures under this clause shall be detained pending a final determination of credible fear of persecution and, if found not to have such a fear, until removed.

(iv) Information about interviews

The Attorney General shall provide information concerning the asylum interview described in this subparagraph to aliens who may be eligible. An alien who is eligible for such interview may consult with a person or persons of the alien's choosing prior to the interview or any review thereof, according to regulations prescribed by the Attorney General. Such consultation shall be at no expense to the Government and shall not unreasonably delay the process.

(v) Credible fear of persecution defined

For purposes of this subparagraph, the term "credible fear of persecution" means that there is a significant possibility, taking into account the credibility of the statements made by the alien in support of the alien's claim and such other facts as are known to the officer, that the alien could establish eligibility for asylum under section 208 [8 U.S.C.A. § 1158].

(C) Limitation on administrative review

Except as provided in subparagraph (B)(iii)(III), a removal order entered in accordance with subparagraph (A)(i) or (B)(iii)(I) is not subject to administrative appeal, except that the Attorney General shall provide by regulation for prompt review of such an order under subparagraph (A)(i) against an alien who claims under oath, or as permitted under penalty of perjury under section 1746 of Title 28, after having been warned of the penalties for falsely making such claim under such conditions, to have been lawfully admitted for permanent residence, to have been admitted as a refugee under section 207 [8 U.S.C.A. § 1157], or to have been granted asylum under section 208 [8 U.S.C.A. § 1158].

(D) Limit on collateral attacks

In any action brought against an alien under section 275(a) [8 U.S.C.A. § 1325(a)] or section 276 [8 U.S.C.A. § 1326], the court shall not have jurisdiction to hear any claim attacking the validity of an order of removal entered under subparagraph (A)(i) or (B)(iii).

(E) Asylum officer defined

As used in this paragraph, the term "asylum officer" means an immigration officer who—

(i) has had professional training in country conditions, asylum law, and interview techniques comparable to that provided to full-time adjudicators of applications under section 208 [8 U.S.C.A. § 1158], and

(ii) is supervised by an officer who meets the condition described in clause (i) and has had substantial experience adjudicating asylum applications.

(F) Exception

Subparagraph (A) shall not apply to an alien who is a native or citizen of a country in the Western Hemisphere with whose government the United States does not have full diplomatic relations and who arrives by aircraft at a port of entry.

(2) Inspection of other aliens

(A) In general

Subject to subparagraphs (B) and (C), in the case of an alien who is an applicant for admission, if the examining immigration officer determines that an alien seeking admission is not clearly and beyond a doubt entitled to be admitted, the alien shall be detained for a proceeding under section 240 [8 U.S.C.A. § 1229a].

(B) Exception

Subparagraph (A) shall not apply to an alien—

(i) who is a crewman,

(ii) to whom paragraph (1) applies, or

(iii) who is a stowaway.

(C) Treatment of aliens arriving from contiguous territory

In the case of an alien described in subparagraph (A) who is arriving on land (whether or not at a designated port of arrival) from a foreign territory contiguous to the United States, the Attorney General may return the alien to that territory pending a proceeding under section 240 [8 U.S.C.A. § 1229a].

(3) Challenge of decision

The decision of the examining immigration officer, if favorable to the admission of any alien, shall be subject to challenge by any other immigration officer and such challenge shall operate to take the alien whose privilege to be admitted is so challenged, before an immigration judge for a proceeding under section 240 [8 U.S.C.A. § 1229a].

(c) Removal of aliens inadmissible on security and related grounds

(1) Removal without further hearing

If an immigration officer or an immigration judge suspects that an arriving alien may be inadmissible under subparagraph (A) (other than clause (ii)), (B), or (C) of section 212(a)(3) [8 U.S.C.A. § 1182(a)(3)], the officer or judge shall—

(A) order the alien removed, subject to review under paragraph (2);

(B) report the order of removal to the Attorney General; and

(C) not conduct any further inquiry or hearing until ordered by the Attorney General.

(2) Review of order

(A) The Attorney General shall review orders issued under paragraph (1).

(B) If the Attorney General—

(i) is satisfied on the basis of confidential information that the alien is inadmissible under subparagraph (A) (other than clause (ii)), (B), or (C) of section 212(a)(3) [8 U.S.C.A. § 1182(a)(3)], and

(ii) after consulting with appropriate security agencies of the United States Government, concludes that disclosure of the information would be prejudicial to the public interest, safety, or security,

the Attorney General may order the alien removed without further inquiry or hearing by an immigration judge.

(C) If the Attorney General does not order the removal of the alien under subparagraph (B), the Attorney General shall specify the further inquiry or hearing that shall be conducted in the case.

(3) Submission of statement and information

The alien or the alien's representative may submit a written statement and additional information for consideration by the Attorney General.

(d) Authority relating to inspections

(1) Authority to search conveyances

Immigration officers are authorized to board and search any vessel, aircraft, railway car, or other conveyance or vehicle in which they believe aliens are being brought into the United States.

(2) Authority to order detention and delivery of arriving aliens

Immigration officers are authorized to order an owner, agent, master, commanding officer, person in charge, purser, or consignee of a vessel or aircraft bringing an alien (except an alien crewmember) to the United States—

(A) to detain the alien on the vessel or at the airport of arrival, and

(B) to deliver the alien to an immigration officer for inspection or to a medical officer for examination.

(3) Administration of oath and consideration of evidence

The Attorney General and any immigration officer shall have power to administer oaths and to take and consider evidence of or from any person touching the privilege of any alien or person he believes or suspects to be an alien to enter, reenter, transit through, or reside in the United States or concerning any matter which is material and relevant to the enforcement of this Act and the administration of the Service.

(4) Subpoena authority

(A) The Attorney General and any immigration officer shall have power to require by subpoena the attendance and testimony of witnesses before immigration officers and the production of books, papers, and documents relating to the privilege of any person to enter, reenter, reside in, or pass through the United States or concerning any matter which is material and relevant to the enforcement of this Act and the administration of the Service, and to that end may invoke the aid of any court of the United States.

(B) Any United States district court within the jurisdiction of which investigations or inquiries are being conducted by an immigration officer may, in the event of neglect or refusal to respond to a subpoena issued under this paragraph or refusal to testify before an immigration officer, issue an order requiring such persons to appear before an immigration officer, produce books, papers, and documents if demanded, and testify, and any failure to obey such order of the court may be punished by the court as a contempt thereof.

(June 27, 1952, c. 477, Title II, ch. 4, § 235, 66 Stat. 198; Nov. 29, 1990, Pub.L. 101–649, Title VI, § 603(a)(11), 104 Stat. 5083; Apr. 24, 1996, Pub.L. 104–132, Title IV, §§ 422(a), 423(b), 110 Stat. 1270, 1272; Sept. 30, 1996, Pub.L. 104–208, Div. C, Title III, §§ 302(a), 308(d)(5), 371(b)(4), 110 Stat. 3009–579, 3009–619, 3009–645.)

§ 235A. Preinspection at foreign airports [8 U.S.C.A. § 1225a]

(a) Establishment of preinspection stations

(1) New stations

Subject to paragraph (5), not later than October 31, 1998, the Attorney General, in consultation with the Secretary of State, shall establish and maintain preinspection stations in at least 5 of the foreign airports that are among the 10 foreign airports which the Attorney General identifies as serving as last points of departure for the greatest numbers of inadmissible alien passengers who arrive from abroad by air at ports of entry within the United States. Such preinspection stations shall be in addition to any preinspection stations established prior to the date of the enactment of such Act.

(2) Report

Not later than October 31, 1998, the Attorney General shall report to the Committees on the Judiciary of the House of Representatives and of the Senate on the implementation of paragraph (1).

(3) Data collection

Not later than November 1, 1997, and each subsequent November 1, the Attorney General shall compile data identifying—

(A) the foreign airports which served as last points of departure for aliens who arrived by air at United States ports of entry without valid documentation during the preceding fiscal years;

(B) the number and nationality of such aliens arriving from each such foreign airport; and

(C) the primary routes such aliens followed from their country of origin to the United States.

(4) Additional stations

Subject to paragraph (5), not later than October 31, 2000, the Attorney General, in consultation with the Secretary of State, shall establish preinspection stations in at least 5 additional foreign airports which the Attorney General, in consultation with the Secretary of State, determines, based on the data compiled under paragraph (3) and such other information as may be available, would most effectively reduce the number of aliens who arrive from abroad by air at points of entry within the United States who are inadmissible to the United States. Such preinspection stations shall be in addition to those established prior to the date of the enactment of such Act or pursuant to paragraph (1).

(5) Conditions

Prior to the establishment of a preinspection station, the Attorney General, in consultation with the Secretary of State, shall ensure that—

(A) employees of the United States stationed at the preinspection station and their accompanying family members will receive appropriate protection;

(B) such employees and their families will not be subject to unreasonable risks to their welfare and safety; and

(C) the country in which the preinspection station is to be established maintains practices and procedures with respect to asylum seekers and refugees in accordance with the Convention Relating to the Status of Refugees (done at Geneva, July 28, 1951), or the Protocol Relating to the Status of Refugees (done at New York, January 31, 1967), or that an alien in the country otherwise has recourse to avenues of protection from return to persecution.

(b) Establishment of carrier consultant program

The Attorney General shall assign additional immigration officers to assist air carriers in the detection of fraudulent documents at foreign airports which, based on the records maintained pursuant to subsection (a)(3), served as a point of departure for a significant number of arrivals at United States ports of entry without valid documentation, but where no preinspection station exists.

(June 27, 1952, c. 477, Title II, ch. 4, § 235A, as added Sept. 30, 1996, Pub.L. 104–208, Div.C, Title I, § 123(a), 110 Stat. 3009–560.)

§ 236. Apprehension and detention of aliens [8 U.S.C.A. § 1226]

(a) Arrest, detention, and release

On a warrant issued by the Attorney General, an alien may be arrested and detained pending a decision on whether the alien is to be removed from the United States. Except as provided in subsection (c) and pending such decision, the Attorney General—

(1) may continue to detain the arrested alien; and

(2) may release the alien on—

(A) bond of at least $1,500 with security approved by, and containing conditions prescribed by, the Attorney General; or

(B) conditional parole; but

(3) may not provide the alien with work authorization (including an "employment authorized" endorsement or other appropriate work permit), unless the alien is lawfully admitted for permanent residence or otherwise would (without regard to removal proceedings) be provided such authorization.

(b) Revocation of bond or parole

The Attorney General at any time may revoke a bond or parole authorized under subsection (a), rearrest the alien under the original warrant, and detain the alien.

(c) Detention of criminal aliens

(1) Custody

The Attorney General shall take into custody any alien who—

(A) is inadmissible by reason of having committed any offense covered in section 212(a)(2) [8 U.S.C.A. § 1182(a)(2)],

(B) is deportable by reason of having committed any offense covered in section 237(a)(2)(A)(ii), (A)(iii), (B), (C), or (D) [8 U.S.C.A. § 1227(a)(2)(A)(ii), (A)(iii), (B), (C), or (D)],

(C) is deportable under section 237(a)(2)(A)(i) [8 U.S.C.A. § 1227(a)(2)(A)(i)] on the basis of an offense for which the alien has been sentence [sic] to a term of imprisonment of at least 1 year, or

(D) is inadmissible under section 212(a)(3)(B) [8 U.S.C.A. § 1182(a)(3)(B)] or deportable under section 237(a)(4)(B) [8 U.S.C.A. § 1227(a)(4)(B)],

when the alien is released, without regard to whether the alien is released on parole, supervised release, or probation, and without regard to whether the alien may be arrested or imprisoned again for the same offense.

(2) Release

The Attorney General may release an alien described in paragraph (1) only if the Attorney General decides pursuant to section 3521 of Title 18, that release of the alien from custody is necessary to provide protection to a witness, a potential witness, a person cooperating with an investigation into major criminal activity, or an immediate family member or close associate of a witness, potential witness, or person cooperating with such an investigation, and the alien satisfies the Attorney General that the alien will not pose a danger to the safety of other persons or of property and is likely to appear for any scheduled proceeding. A decision relating to such release shall take place in accordance with a procedure that considers the severity of the offense committed by the alien.

(d) Identification of criminal aliens

(1) The Attorney General shall devise and implement a system—

(A) to make available, daily (on a 24–hour basis), to Federal, State, and local authorities the investigative resources of the Service to determine whether individuals arrested by such authorities for aggravated felonies are aliens;

(B) to designate and train officers and employees of the Service to serve as a liaison to Federal, State, and local law enforcement and correctional agencies and courts with respect to the arrest, conviction, and release of any alien charged with an aggravated felony; and

(C) which uses computer resources to maintain a current record of aliens who have been convicted of an aggravated felony, and indicates those who have been removed.

(2) The record under paragraph (1)(C) shall be made available—

(A) to inspectors at ports of entry and to border patrol agents at sector headquarters for purposes of immediate identification of any alien who was previously ordered removed and is seeking to reenter the United States, and

(B) to officials of the Department of State for use in its automated visa lookout system.

(3) Upon the request of the governor or chief executive officer of any State, the Service shall provide assistance to State courts in the identification of aliens unlawfully present in the United States pending criminal prosecution.

(e) Judicial review

The Attorney General's discretionary judgment regarding the application of this section shall not be subject to review. No court may set aside any action or decision by the Attorney General under this section regarding the detention or release of any alien or the grant, revocation, or denial of bond or parole.

(June 27, 1952, c. 477, Title II, ch. 4, § 236, 66 Stat. 200; Nov. 29, 1990, Pub.L. 101–649, Title V, § 504(b), Title VI, § 603(a)(12), 104 Stat. 5050, 5083; Dec. 12, 1991, Pub.L. 102–232, Title III, § 306(a)(5), 105 Stat. 1751; Sept. 30, 1996, Pub.L. 104–208, Div. C, Title III, §§ 303(a), 371(b)(5), 110 Stat. 3009–585, 3009–645.)

§ 237. Deportable aliens [8 U.S.C.A. § 1227]

(a) Classes of deportable aliens

Any alien (including an alien crewman) in and admitted to the United States shall, upon the order of the Attorney General, be removed if the alien is within one or more of the following classes of deportable aliens:

(1) Inadmissible at time of entry or of adjustment of status or violates status

(A) Inadmissible aliens

Any alien who at the time of entry or adjustment of status was within one or more of the classes of aliens inadmissible by the law existing at such time is deportable.

(B) Present in violation of law

Any alien who is present in the United States in violation of this Act or any other law of the United States is deportable.

(C) Violated nonimmigrant status or condition of admission

(i) Nonimmigrant status violators

Any alien who was admitted as a nonimmigrant and who has failed to maintain the nonimmigrant status in which the alien was admitted or to which it was changed under section 248 [8 U.S.C.A. § 1258], or to comply with the conditions of any such status, is deportable.

(ii) Violators of conditions of admission

Any alien whom the Secretary of Health and Human Services certifies has failed to comply with terms, conditions, and controls that were imposed under section 212(g) [8 U.S.C.A. § 1182(g)] is deportable.

(D) Termination of conditional permanent residence

(i) In general

Any alien with permanent resident status on a conditional basis under section 216 [8 U.S.C.A. § 1186a] (relating to conditional permanent resident status for certain alien spouses and sons and daughters) or under section 216A [8 U.S.C.A. § 1186b] (relating to conditional permanent resident status for certain alien entrepreneurs, spouses, and children) who has had such status terminated under such respective section is deportable.

(ii) Exception

Clause (i) shall not apply in the cases described in section 216(c)(4) [8 U.S.C.A. § 1186a(c)(4)] (relating to certain hardship waivers).

(E) Smuggling

(i) In general

Any alien who (prior to the date of entry, at the time of any entry, or within 5 years of the date of any entry) knowingly has encouraged, induced, assisted, abetted, or aided any other alien to enter or to try to enter the United States in violation of law is deportable.

(ii) Special rule in the case of family reunification

Clause (i) shall not apply in the case of alien who is an eligible immigrant (as defined in section 301(b)(1) of the Immigration Act of 1990), was physically present in the United States on May 5, 1988, and is seeking admission as an immediate relative or under section 203(a)(2) [8 U.S.C.A. § 1153(a)(2)] (including under section 112 of the Immigration Act of 1990) or benefits under section 301(a) of the Immigration Act of 1990 if the alien, before May 5, 1988, has encouraged, induced, assisted, abetted, or aided only the alien's spouse, parent, son, or daughter (and no other individual) to enter the United States in violation of law.

(iii) Waiver authorized

The Attorney General may, in his discretion for humanitarian purposes, to assure family unity, or when it is otherwise in the public interest, waive application of clause (i) in the case of any alien lawfully admitted for permanent residence if the alien has encouraged, induced, assisted, abetted, or aided only an individual who at the time of the offense was the alien's spouse, parent, son, or daughter (and no other individual) to enter the United States in violation of law.

(F) Repealed. Pub.L. 104–208, Div. C, Title VI, § 671(d)(1)(C), Sept. 30, 1996, 110 Stat. 3009–723.

(G) Marriage fraud

An alien shall be considered to be deportable as having procured a visa or other documentation by fraud (within the meaning of section 212(a)(6)(C)(i) [8 U.S.C.A.

§ 1182(a)(6)(C)(i)]) and to be in the United States in violation of this Act (within the meaning of subparagraph (B)) if—

(i) the alien obtains any admission into the United States with an immigrant visa or other documentation procured on the basis of a marriage entered into less than 2 years prior to such admission of the alien and which, within 2 years subsequent to any admission of the alien in the United States, shall be judicially annulled or terminated, unless the alien establishes to the satisfaction of the Attorney General that such marriage was not contracted for the purpose of evading any provisions of the immigration laws, or

(ii) it appears to the satisfaction of the Attorney General that the alien has failed or refused to fulfill the alien's marital agreement which in the opinion of the Attorney General was made for the purpose of procuring the alien's admission as an immigrant.

(H) Waiver authorized for certain misrepresentations

The provisions of this paragraph relating to the removal of aliens within the United States on the ground that they were inadmissible at the time of admission as aliens, described in section 212(a)(6)(C)(i) [8 U.S.C.A. § 1182(a)(6)(C)(i)], whether willful or innocent, may, in the discretion of the Attorney General, be waived for any alien (other than an alien described in paragraph (4)(D)) who—

(i) is the spouse, parent, son, or daughter of a citizen of the United States or of an alien lawfully admitted to the United States for permanent residence; and

(ii) was in possession of an immigrant visa or equivalent document and was otherwise admissible to the United States at the time of such admission except for those grounds of inadmissibility specified under paragraphs (5)(A) and (7)(A) of section 212(a) [8 U.S.C.A. § 1182(a)] which were a direct result of that fraud or misrepresentation.

A waiver of removal for fraud or misrepresentation granted under this subparagraph shall also operate to waive removal based on the grounds of inadmissibility directly resulting from such fraud or misrepresentation.

(2) Criminal offenses

(A) General crimes

(i) Crimes of moral turpitude

Any alien who—

(I) is convicted of a crime involving moral turpitude committed within five years (or 10 years in the case of an alien provided lawful permanent resident status under section 245(j) [8 U.S.C.A. § 1255(j)]) after the date of admission, and

(II) is convicted of a crime for which a sentence of one year or longer may be imposed,

is deportable.

(ii) Multiple criminal convictions

Any alien who at any time after admission is convicted of two or more crimes involving moral turpitude, not arising out of a single scheme of criminal misconduct, regardless of whether confined therefor and regardless of whether the convictions were in a single trial, is deportable.

(iii) Aggravated felony

Any alien who is convicted of an aggravated felony at any time after admission is deportable.

(iv) High speed flight

Any alien who is convicted of a violation of section 758 of Title 18, (relating to high speed flight from an immigration checkpoint) is deportable.

(v) Waiver authorized

Clauses (i), (ii), (iii), and (iv) shall not apply in the case of an alien with respect to a criminal conviction if the alien subsequent to the criminal conviction has been granted a full and unconditional pardon by the President of the United States or by the Governor of any of the several States.

(B) Controlled substances

(i) Conviction

Any alien who at any time after admission has been convicted of a violation of (or a conspiracy or attempt to violate) any law or regulation of a State, the United States, or a foreign country relating to a controlled substance (as defined in section 802 of Title 21), other than a single offense involving possession for one's own use of 30 grams or less of marijuana, is deportable.

(ii) Drug abusers and addicts

Any alien who is, or at any time after admission has been, a drug abuser or addict is deportable.

(C) Certain firearm offenses

Any alien who at any time after admission is convicted under any law of purchasing, selling, offering for sale, exchanging, using, owning, possessing, or carrying, or of attempting or conspiring to purchase, sell, offer for sale, exchange, use, own, possess, or carry, any weapon, part, or accessory which is a firearm or destructive device (as defined in section 921(a) of Title 18) in violation of any law is deportable.

(D) Miscellaneous crimes

Any alien who at any time has been convicted (the judgment on such conviction becoming final) of, or has been so convicted of a conspiracy or attempt to violate—

(i) any offense under chapter 37 (relating to espionage), chapter 105 (relating to sabotage), or chapter 115 (relating to treason and sedition) of Title 18, for which a term of imprisonment of five or more years may be imposed;

(ii) any offense under section 871 or 960 of Title 18;

(iii) a violation of any provision of the Military Selective Service Act (50 U.S.C. App. 451 et seq.) or the Trading With the Enemy Act (50 U.S.C. App. 1 et seq.); or

(iv) a violation of section 215 [8 U.S.C.A. § 1185] or 278 [8 U.S.C.A. § 1328],

is deportable.

(E) Crimes of domestic violence, stalking, or violation of protection order, crimes against children and

(i) Domestic violence, stalking, and child abuse

Any alien who at any time after admission is convicted of a crime of domestic violence, a crime of stalking, or a crime of child abuse, child neglect, or child abandonment is deportable. For purposes of this clause, the term "crime of domestic violence" means any crime of violence (as defined in section 16 of Title 18) against a person committed by a current or former spouse of the person, by an individual with whom the person shares a child in common, by an individual who is cohabiting with or has cohabited with the person as a spouse, by an individual similarly situated to a spouse of the person under the domestic or family violence laws of the jurisdiction where the offense occurs, or by any other individual against a person who is protected from that individual's acts under the domestic or family violence laws of the United States or any State, Indian tribal government, or unit of local government.

(ii) Violators of protection orders

Any alien who at any time after admission is enjoined under a protection order issued by a court and whom the court determines has engaged in conduct that violates the portion of a protection order that involves protection against credible threats of violence, repeated harassment, or bodily injury to the person or persons for whom the protection order was issued is deportable. For purposes of this clause, the term "protection order" means any injunction issued for the purpose of preventing violent or threatening acts of domestic violence, including temporary or final orders issued by civil or criminal courts (other than support or child custody orders or provisions) whether obtained by filing an independent action or as a pendente lite order in another proceeding.

(3) Failure to register and falsification of documents

(A) Change of address

An alien who has failed to comply with the provisions of section 265 [8 U.S.C.A. § 1305] is deportable, unless the alien establishes to the satisfaction of the Attorney General that such failure was reasonably excusable or was not willful.

(B) Failure to register or falsification of documents

Any alien who at any time has been convicted—

(i) under section 266(c) [8 U.S.C.A. § 1306(c)] or under section 36(c) of the Alien Registration Act, 1940,

(ii) of a violation of, or an attempt or a conspiracy to violate, any provision of the Foreign Agents Registration Act of 1938 (22 U.S.C. 611 et seq.), or

(iii) of a violation of, or an attempt or a conspiracy to violate, section 1546 of Title 18 (relating to fraud and misuse of visas, permits, and other entry documents),

is deportable.

(C) Document fraud

(i) In general

An alien who is the subject of a final order for violation of section 274C [8 U.S.C.A. § 1324C] is deportable.

(ii) Waiver authorized

The Attorney General may waive clause (i) in the case of an alien lawfully admitted for permanent residence if no previous civil money penalty was imposed against the alien under section 274C [8 U.S.C.A. § 1324C] and the offense was incurred solely to assist, aid, or support the alien's spouse or child (and no other individual). No court shall have jurisdiction to review a decision of the Attorney General to grant or deny a waiver under this clause.

(D) Falsely claiming citizenship

Any alien who falsely represents, or has falsely represented, himself to be a citizen of the United States for any purpose or benefit under this Act (including section 274A [8 U.S.C.A. § 1324a]) or any Federal or State law is deportable.

(4) Security and related grounds

(A) In general

Any alien who has engaged, is engaged, or at any time after admission engages in—

(i) any activity to violate any law of the United States relating to espionage or sabotage or to violate or evade any law prohibiting the export from the United States of goods, technology, or sensitive information,

(ii) any other criminal activity which endangers public safety or national security, or

(iii) any activity a purpose of which is the opposition to, or the control or overthrow of, the Government of the United States by force, violence, or other unlawful means,

is deportable.

(B) Terrorist activities

Any alien who has engaged, is engaged, or at any time after admission engages in any terrorist activity (as defined in section 212(a)(3)(B)(iii) [8 U.S.C.A. § 1182(a)(3)(B)(iii)]) is deportable.

(C) Foreign policy

(i) In general

An alien whose presence or activities in the United States the Secretary of State has reasonable ground to believe would have potentially serious adverse foreign policy consequences for the United States is deportable.

(ii) Exceptions

The exceptions described in clauses (ii) and (iii) of section 212(a)(3)(C) [8 U.S.C.A. § 1182(a)(3)(C)] shall apply to deportability under clause (i) in the same manner as they apply to inadmissibility under section 212(a)(3)(C)(i) [8 U.S.C.A. § 1182(a)(3)(C)(i)].

(D) Assisted in Nazi persecution or engaged in genocide

Any alien described in clause (i) or (ii) of section 212(a)(3)(E) [8 U.S.C.A. § 1182(a)(3)(E)] is deportable.

(5) Public charge

Any alien who, within five years after the date of entry, has become a public charge from causes not affirmatively shown to have arisen since entry is deportable.

(6) Unlawful voters

Any alien who has voted in violation of any Federal, State, or local constitutional provision, statute, ordinance, or regulation is deportable.

(b) Deportation of certain nonimmigrants

An alien, admitted as a nonimmigrant under the provisions of either section 101(a)(15)(A)(i) [8 U.S.C.A. § 1101(a)(15)(A)(i)] or 101(a)(15)(G)(i) [8 U.S.C.A. § 1101(a)(15)(G)(i)], and who fails to maintain a status under either of those provisions, shall not be required to depart from the United States without the approval of the Secretary of State, unless such alien is subject to deportation under paragraph (4) of subsection (a).

(c) Waiver of grounds for deportation

Paragraphs (1)(A), (1)(B), (1)(C), (1)(D), and (3)(A) of subsection (a) (other than so much of paragraph (1) as relates to a ground of inadmissibility described in paragraph (2) or (3) of section 212(a) [8 U.S.C.A. § 1182(a)]) shall not apply to a special immigrant described in section 101(a)(27)(J) [8 U.S.C.A. § 1101(a)(27)(J)] based upon circumstances that existed before the date the alien was provided such special immigrant status.

(d) Repealed. Pub.L. 104–208, Div. C, Title III, § 308(d)(2)(D), Sept. 30, 1996, 110 Stat. 3009–617.

(e) Redesignated (b)

(f) and (g) Repealed. Pub.L. 101–649, § 602(b)(1), Nov. 29, 1990, 104 Stat. 5081.

(h) Redesignated (c)

(June 27, 1952, c. 477, Title II, ch. 5, § 237, formerly § 241, 66 Stat. 204; July 18, 1956, c. 629, Title III, § 301(b), (c), 70 Stat. 575; July 14, 1960, Pub.L. 86–648, § 9, 74 Stat. 505; Sept. 26, 1961, Pub.L. 87–301, § 16, 75 Stat. 655; Oct. 3, 1965, Pub.L. 89–236, § 11(e), 79 Stat. 918; Oct. 20, 1976, Pub.L. 94–571, § 7(e), 90 Stat. 2706; Oct. 30, 1978; Pub.L. 95–549, Title I, § 103, 92 Stat. 2065; Dec. 29, 1981, Pub.L. 97–116, § 8, 95 Stat. 1616; Oct. 27, 1986, Pub.L. 99–570, Title I, § 1751(b), 100 Stat. 3207–47; Nov. 6, 1986, Pub.L. 99–603, Title III, § 303(b), 100 Stat. 3431; Nov. 10, 1986, Pub.L. 99–639, § 2(b), 100 Stat. 3541; Nov. 14, 1986, Pub.L. 99–653, § 7(c), 100 Stat. 3657; Oct. 24, 1988, Pub.L. 100–525, §§ 2(n)(2), 9(m), 102 Stat. 2613, 2620; Nov. 18, 1988, Pub.L. 100–690, Title VII, §§ 7344(a), 7348(a), 102 Stat. 4471, 4473; Nov. 29, 1990, Pub.L. 101–649, Title I, § 153(b), Title V, §§ 505(a), 508(a), 544(b), Title VI, § 602(a), (b), 104 Stat. 5006, 5050, 5051, 5061, 5077, 5081; Dec. 12, 1991, Pub.L. 102–232, Title III, §§ 302(d)(3), 307(h), (k), 105 Stat. 1745, 1755, 1756; Sept. 13, 1994, Pub.L. 103–322, Title XIII, § 130003(d), 108 Stat. 2026; Oct. 25, 1994, Pub.L. 103–416, Title II, §§ 203(b), 219(g), 108 Stat. 4311, 4317; Apr. 24, 1996, Pub.L. 104–132, Title IV, §§ 414(a), 435(a), 110 Stat. 1270, 1274; renumbered § 237 and amended Sept. 30, 1996, Pub.L. 104–208, Div. C, Title I, § 108(c), Title III, §§ 301(d), 305(a)(2), 308(d)(2), (3)(A), (e)(1)(E), (2)(C), (f)(1)(L) to (N), (5), 344(b), 345(b), 347(b), 350(a), 351(b), Title VI, § 671(a)(4)(B), (d)(1)(C), 110 Stat. 3009–558,

3009–579, 3009–598, 3009–617, 3009–619 to 3009–622, 3009–637 to 3009–640, 3009–721, 3009–723.)

§ 238. Expedited removal of aliens convicted of committing aggravated felonies [8 U.S.C.A. § 1228]

(a) Removal of criminal aliens

(1) In general

The Attorney General shall provide for the availability of special removal proceedings at certain Federal, State, and local correctional facilities for aliens convicted of any criminal offense covered in section 237(a)(2)(A)(iii), (B), (C), or (D) [8 U.S.C.A. § 1227(a)(2)(A)(iii), (B), (C), or (D)], or any offense covered by section 237(a)(2)(A)(ii) [8 U.S.C.A. § 1227(a)(2)(A)(ii)] for which both predicate offenses are, without regard to the date of their commission, otherwise covered by section 237(a)(2)(A)(i) [8 U.S.C.A. § 1227(a)(2)(A)(i)]. Such proceedings shall be conducted in conformity with section 240 [8 U.S.C.A. § 1229a] (except as otherwise provided in this section), and in a manner which eliminates the need for additional detention at any processing center of the Service and in a manner which assures expeditious removal following the end of the alien's incarceration for the underlying sentence. Nothing in this section shall be construed to create any substantive or procedural right or benefit that is legally enforceable by any party against the United States or its agencies or officers or any other person.

(2) Implementation

With respect to an alien convicted of an aggravated felony who is taken into custody by the Attorney General pursuant to section 236(c) [8 U.S.C.A. § 1226(c)], the Attorney General shall, to the maximum extent practicable, detain any such felon at a facility at which other such aliens are detained. In the selection of such facility, the Attorney General shall make reasonable efforts to ensure that the alien's access to counsel and right to counsel under section 292 [8 U.S.C.A. § 1362] are not impaired.

(3) Expedited proceedings

(A) Notwithstanding any other provision of law, the Attorney General shall provide for the initiation and, to the extent possible, the completion of removal proceedings, and any administrative appeals thereof, in the case of any alien convicted of an aggravated felony before the alien's release from incarceration for the underlying aggravated felony.

(B) Nothing in this section shall be construed as requiring the Attorney General to effect the removal of any alien sentenced to actual incarceration, before release from the penitentiary or correctional institution where such alien is confined.

(4) Review

(A) The Attorney General shall review and evaluate removal proceedings conducted under this section.

(B) The Comptroller General shall monitor, review, and evaluate removal proceedings conducted under this section. Within 18 months after the effective date of this section, the Comptroller General shall submit a report to such Committees concerning the extent to which removal proceedings conducted under this section may adversely affect the ability of such aliens to contest removal effectively.

(b) Removal of aliens who are not permanent residents

(1) The Attorney General may, in the case of an alien described in paragraph (2), determine the deportability of such alien under section 237(a)(2)(A)(iii) [8 U.S.C.A. § 1227(a)(2)(A)(iii)] (relating to conviction of an aggravated felony) and issue an order of removal pursuant to the procedures set forth in this subsection or section 240 [8 U.S.C.A. § 1229a].

(2) An alien is described in this paragraph if the alien—

(A) was not lawfully admitted for permanent residence at the time at which proceedings under this section commenced; or

(B) had permanent resident status on a conditional basis (as described in section 216 [8 U.S.C.A. § 1186a]) at the time that proceedings under this section commenced.

(3) The Attorney General may not execute any order described in paragraph (1) until 14 calendar days have passed from the date that such order was issued, unless waived by the alien, in order that the alien has an opportunity to apply for judicial review under section 242 [8 U.S.C.A. § 1252].

(4) Proceedings before the Attorney General under this subsection shall be in accordance with such regulations as the Attorney General shall prescribe. The Attorney General shall provide that—

(A) the alien is given reasonable notice of the charges and of the opportunity described in subparagraph (C);

(B) the alien shall have the privilege of being represented (at no expense to the government) by such counsel, authorized to practice in such proceedings, as the alien shall choose;

(C) the alien has a reasonable opportunity to inspect the evidence and rebut the charges;

(D) a determination is made for the record that the individual upon whom the notice for the proceeding under this section is served (either in person or by mail) is, in fact, the alien named in such notice;

(E) a record is maintained for judicial review; and

(F) the final order of removal is not adjudicated by the same person who issues the charges.

(G) Redesignated (F)

(5) No alien described in this section shall be eligible for any relief from removal that the Attorney General may grant in the Attorney General's discretion.

(c) [sic] Presumption of deportability

An alien convicted of an aggravated felony shall be conclusively presumed to be deportable from the United States.

(c) [sic] Judicial removal

(1) Authority

Notwithstanding any other provision of this Act, a United States district court shall have jurisdiction to enter a judicial order of removal at the time of sentencing against an alien who is deportable, if such an order has been requested by the United States Attorney with the concurrence of the Commissioner and if the court chooses to exercise such jurisdiction.

(2) Procedure

(A) The United States Attorney shall file with the United States district court, and serve upon the defendant and the Service, prior to commencement of the trial or entry of a guilty plea a notice of intent to request judicial removal.

(B) Notwithstanding section 242B [8 U.S.C.A. § 1252b] [sic], the United States Attorney, with the concurrence of the Commissioner, shall file at least 30 days prior to the date set for sentencing a charge containing factual allegations regarding the alienage of the defendant and identifying the crime or crimes which make the defendant deportable under section 237(a)(2)(A) [8 U.S.C.A. § 1227(a)(2)(A)].

(C) If the court determines that the defendant has presented substantial evidence to establish prima facie eligibility for relief from removal under this Act, the Commissioner shall provide the court with a recommendation and report regarding the alien's eligibility for relief. The court shall either grant or deny the relief sought.

(D)(i) The alien shall have a reasonable opportunity to examine the evidence against him or her, to present evidence on his or her own behalf, and to cross-examine witnesses presented by the Government.

(ii) The court, for the purposes of determining whether to enter an order described in paragraph (1), shall only consider evidence that would be admissible in proceedings conducted pursuant to section 240 [8 U.S.C.A. § 1229a].

(iii) Nothing in this subsection shall limit the information a court of the United States may receive or consider for the purposes of imposing an appropriate sentence.

(iv) The court may order the alien removed if the Attorney General demonstrates that the alien is deportable under this Act.

(3) Notice, appeal, and execution of judicial order of removal

(A)(i) A judicial order of removal or denial of such order may be appealed by either party to the court of appeals for the circuit in which the district court is located.

(ii) Except as provided in clause (iii), such appeal shall be considered consistent with the requirements described in section 242 [8 U.S.C.A. § 1252].

(iii) Upon execution by the defendant of a valid waiver of the right to appeal the conviction on which the order of removal is based, the expiration of the period described in section 242(b)(1) [8 U.S.C.A. § 1252(b)(1)], or the final dismissal of an appeal from such conviction, the order of removal shall become final and shall be executed at the end of the prison term in accordance with the terms of the order. If the conviction is reversed on direct appeal, the order entered pursuant to this section shall be void.

(B) As soon as is practicable after entry of a judicial order of removal, the Commissioner shall provide the defendant with written notice of the order of removal, which shall designate the defendant's country of choice for removal and any alternate country pursuant to section 243(a) [8 U.S.C.A. § 1253(a)].

(4) Denial of judicial order

Denial of a request for a judicial order of removal shall not preclude the Attorney General from initiating removal proceedings pursuant to section 240 [8 U.S.C.A. § 1229a] upon the same ground of deportability or upon any other ground of deportability provided under section 237(a) [8 U.S.C.A. § 1227(a)].

(5) Stipulated judicial order of removal

The United States Attorney, with the concurrence of the Commissioner, may, pursuant to Federal Rule of Criminal Procedure 11, enter into a plea agreement which calls for the alien, who is deportable under this Act, to waive the right to notice and a hearing under this section, and stipulate to the entry of a judicial order of removal from the United States as a condition of the plea agreement or as a condition of probation or supervised release, or both. The United States district court, in both felony and misdemeanor cases, and a United States magistrate judge in misdemeanor cases, may accept such a stipulation and shall have jurisdiction to enter a judicial order of removal pursuant to the terms of such stipulation.

(d) Redesignated (c)

(June 27, 1952, c. 477, Title II, ch. 5, § 238, formerly § 242A, as added Nov. 18, 1988, Pub.L. 100–690, Title VII, § 7347(a), 102 Stat. 4471, and amended Nov. 29, 1990, Pub.L. 101–649, Title V, § 506(a), 104 Stat. 5050; Dec. 12, 1991, Pub.L. 102–232, Title III, § 309(b)(10), 105 Stat. 1759; Sept. 13, 1994, Pub.L. 103–322, Title XIII, § 130004(a), (c), 108 Stat. 2026, 2028; Oct. 25, 1994, Pub.L. 103–416, Title II, §§ 223(a), 224(a), 108 Stat. 4322; Apr. 24, 1996, Pub.L. 104–132, Title IV, §§ 440(g), 442(a), (c), 110 Stat. 1278, 1279, 1280; redesignated § 238 and amended Sept. 30, 1996, Pub.L. 104–208, Div. C, Title III, §§ 304(c)(1), 306(d), 308(b)(5), (c)(1), (4)(A), (e)(1)(F), (2)(D), (10), (g)(1), (2)(A), (C), (5)(A)(ii), (C), (D), (10)(H), 374(a), Title VI, § 671(b)(13), (c)(5), (6), 110 Stat. 3009–597, 3009–612, 3009–615, 3009–616, 3009–619, 3009–620, 3009–622, 3009–623, 3009–625, 3009–647, 3009–722, 3009–723.)

§ 239. Initiation of removal proceedings [8 U.S.C.A. § 1229]

(a) Notice to appear

(1) In general

In removal proceedings under section 240 [8 U.S.C.A. § 1229a], written notice (in this section referred to as a "notice to appear") shall be given in person to the alien (or, if personal service is not practicable, through service by mail to the alien or to the alien's counsel of record, if any) specifying the following:

(A) The nature of the proceedings against the alien.

(B) The legal authority under which the proceedings are conducted.

(C) The acts or conduct alleged to be in violation of law.

(D) The charges against the alien and the statutory provisions alleged to have been violated.

(E) The alien may be represented by counsel and the alien will be provided (i) a period of time to secure counsel under subsection (b)(1) and (ii) a current list of counsel prepared under subsection (b)(2).

(F)(i) The requirement that the alien must immediately provide (or have provided) the Attorney General with a written record of an address and telephone number (if any) at which the alien may be contacted respecting proceedings under section 240 [8 U.S.C.A. § 1229a].

(ii) The requirement that the alien must provide the Attorney General immediately with a written record of any change of the alien's address or telephone number.

(iii) The consequences under section 240(b)(5) [8 U.S.C.A. § 1229a(b)(5)] of failure to provide address and telephone information pursuant to this subparagraph.

(G)(i) The time and place at which the proceedings will be held.

(ii) The consequences under section 240(b)(5) [8 U.S.C.A. § 1229a(b)(5)] of the failure, except under exceptional circumstances, to appear at such proceedings.

(2) Notice of change in time or place of proceedings

(A) In general

In removal proceedings under section 240(b)(5) [8 U.S.C.A. § 1229a(b)(5)], in the case of any change or postponement in the time and place of such proceedings, subject to subparagraph (B) a written notice shall be given in person to the alien (or, if personal service is not practicable, through service by mail to the alien or to the alien's counsel of record, if any) specifying—

(i) the new time or place of the proceedings, and

(ii) the consequences under section 240(b)(5) [8 U.S.C.A. § 1229a(b)(5)] of failing, except under exceptional circumstances, to attend such proceedings.

(B) Exception

In the case of an alien not in detention, a written notice shall not be required under this paragraph if the alien has failed to provide the address required under paragraph (1)(F).

(3) Central address files

The Attorney General shall create a system to record and preserve on a timely basis notices of addresses and telephone numbers (and changes) provided under paragraph (1)(F).

(b) Securing of counsel

(1) In general

In order that an alien be permitted the opportunity to secure counsel before the first hearing date in proceedings under section 240 [8 U.S.C.A. § 1229a], the hearing date shall not be scheduled earlier than 10 days after the service of the notice to appear, unless the alien requests in writing an earlier hearing date.

(2) Current lists of counsel

The Attorney General shall provide for lists (updated not less often than quarterly) of persons who have indicated their availability to represent pro bono aliens in proceedings under section 240 [8 U.S.C.A. § 1229a]. Such lists shall be provided under subsection (a)(1)(E) and otherwise made generally available.

(3) Rule of construction

Nothing in this subsection may be construed to prevent the Attorney General from proceeding against an alien pursuant to section 240 [8 U.S.C.A. § 1229a] if the time period described in paragraph (1) has elapsed and the alien has failed to secure counsel.

(c) Service by mail

Service by mail under this section shall be sufficient if there is proof of attempted delivery to the last address provided by the alien in accordance with subsection (a)(1)(F).

(d) Prompt initiation of removal

(1) In the case of an alien who is convicted of an offense which makes the alien deportable, the Attorney General shall begin any removal proceeding as expeditiously as possible after the date of the conviction.

(2) Nothing in this subsection shall be construed to create any substantive or procedural right or benefit that is legally enforceable by any party against the United States or its agencies or officers or any other person.

(June 27, 1952, c. 477, Title II, § 239, as added Sept. 30, 1996, Pub.L. 104–208, Div. C, Title III, § 304(a)(3), 110 Stat. 3009–587.)

§ 240. Removal proceedings [8 U.S.C.A. § 1229a]

(a) Proceeding

(1) In general

An immigration judge shall conduct proceedings for deciding the inadmissibility or deportability of an alien.

(2) Charges

An alien placed in proceedings under this section may be charged with any applicable ground of inadmissibility under section 212(a) [8 U.S.C.A. § 1182(a)] or any applicable ground of deportability under section 237(a) [8 U.S.C.A. § 1227(a)].

(3) Exclusive procedures

Unless otherwise specified in this Act, a proceeding under this section shall be the sole and exclusive procedure for determining whether an alien may be admitted to the United States or, if the alien has been so admitted, removed from the United States. Nothing in this section shall affect proceedings conducted pursuant to section 238 [8 U.S.C.A. § 1228].

(b) Conduct of proceeding

(1) Authority of immigration judge

The immigration judge shall administer oaths, receive evidence, and interrogate, examine, and cross-examine the alien and any witnesses. The immigration judge may issue subpoenas for the attendance of witnesses and presentation of evidence. The immigration judge shall have authority (under regulations prescribed by the Attorney General) to sanction by civil money penalty any action (or inaction) in contempt of the judge's proper exercise of authority under this Act.

(2) Form of proceeding

(A) In general

The proceeding may take place—

(i) in person,

(ii) where agreed to by the parties, in the absence of the alien,

(iii) through video conference, or

(iv) subject to subparagraph (B), through telephone conference.

(B) Consent required in certain cases

An evidentiary hearing on the merits may only be conducted through a telephone conference with the consent of the alien involved after the alien has been advised of the right to proceed in person or through video conference.

(3) Presence of alien

If it is impracticable by reason of an alien's mental incompetency for the alien to be present at the proceeding, the Attorney General shall prescribe safeguards to protect the rights and privileges of the alien.

(4) Aliens [sic] rights in proceeding

In proceedings under this section, under regulations of the Attorney General—

(A) the alien shall have the privilege of being represented, at no expense to the Government, by counsel of the alien's choosing who is authorized to practice in such proceedings,

(B) the alien shall have a reasonable opportunity to examine the evidence against the alien, to present evidence on the alien's own behalf, and to cross-examine witnesses presented by the Government but these rights shall not entitle the alien to examine such national security information as the Government may proffer in opposition to the alien's admission to the United States or to an application by the alien for discretionary relief under this Act, and

(C) a complete record shall be kept of all testimony and evidence produced at the proceeding.

(5) Consequences of failure to appear

(A) In general

Any alien who, after written notice required under paragraph (1) or (2) of section 239(a) [8 U.S.C.A. § 1229(a)] has been provided to the alien or the alien's counsel of record, does not attend a proceeding under this section, shall be ordered removed in absentia if the Service establishes by clear, unequivocal, and convincing evidence that the written notice was so provided and that the alien is removable (as defined in subsection (e)(2)). The written notice by the Attorney General shall be considered sufficient for purposes of this subparagraph if provided at the most recent address provided under section 239(a)(1)(F) [8 U.S.C.A. § 1229(a)(1)(F)].

(B) No notice if failure to provide address information

No written notice shall be required under subparagraph (A) if the alien has failed to provide the address required under section 239(a)(1)(F) [8 U.S.C.A. § 1229(a)(1)(F)].

(C) Rescission of order

Such an order may be rescinded only—

(i) upon a motion to reopen filed within 180 days after the date of the order of removal if the alien demonstrates that the failure to appear was because of exceptional circumstances (as defined in subsection (e)(1)), or

(ii) upon a motion to reopen filed at any time if the alien demonstrates that the alien did not receive notice in accordance with paragraph (1) or (2) of section 239(a) [8 U.S.C.A. § 1229(a)] or the alien demonstrates that the alien was in Federal or State custody and the failure to appear was through no fault of the alien.

The filing of the motion to reopen described in clause (i) or (ii) shall stay the removal of the alien pending disposition of the motion by the immigration judge.

(D) Effect on judicial review

Any petition for review under section 242 [8 U.S.C.A. § 1252] of an order entered in absentia under this paragraph shall (except in cases described in section 242(b)(5) [8 U.S.C.A. § 1252(b)(5)]) be confined to (i) the validity of the notice provided to the alien, (ii) the reasons for the alien's not attending the proceeding, and (iii) whether or not the alien is removable.

(E) Additional application to certain aliens in contiguous territory

The preceding provisions of this paragraph shall apply to all aliens placed in proceedings under this section, including any alien who remains in a contiguous foreign territory pursuant to section 235(b)(2)(C) [8 U.S.C.A. § 1225(b)(2)(C)].

(6) Treatment of frivolous behavior

The Attorney General shall, by regulation—

(A) define in a proceeding before an immigration judge or before an appellate administrative body under this title, frivolous behavior for which attorneys may be sanctioned,

(B) specify the circumstances under which an administrative appeal of a decision or ruling will be considered frivolous and will be summarily dismissed, and

(C) impose appropriate sanctions (which may include suspension and disbarment) in the case of frivolous behavior.

Nothing in this paragraph shall be construed as limiting the authority of the Attorney General to take actions with respect to inappropriate behavior.

(7) Limitation on discretionary relief for failure to appear

Any alien against whom a final order of removal is entered in absentia under this subsection and who, at the time of the notice described in paragraph (1) or (2) of section 239(a) [8 U.S.C.A. § 1229(a)], was provided oral notice, either in the alien's native language or in another language the alien understands, of the time and place of the proceedings and of the consequences under this paragraph of failing, other than because of exceptional circumstances (as defined in subsection (e)(1)) to attend a proceeding under this section, shall not be eligible for relief under section 240A [8 U.S.C.A. § 1229b], 240B [8 U.S.C.A. § 1229c], 245 [8 U.S.C.A. § 1255], 248 [8 U.S.C.A. § 1258], or 249 [8 U.S.C.A. § 1259] for a period of 10 years after the date of the entry of the final order of removal.

(c) Decision and burden of proof

(1) Decision

(A) In general

At the conclusion of the proceeding the immigration judge shall decide whether an alien is removable from the United States. The determination of the immigration judge shall be based only on the evidence produced at the hearing.

(B) Certain medical decisions

If a medical officer or civil surgeon or board of medical officers has certified under section 232(b) [8 U.S.C.A. § 1222(b)] that an alien has a disease, illness, or addiction which would make the alien inadmissible under paragraph (1) of section 212(a) [8 U.S.C.A. § 1182(a)], the decision of the immigration judge shall be based solely upon such certification.

(2) Burden on alien

In the proceeding the alien has the burden of establishing—

(A) if the alien is an applicant for admission, that the alien is clearly and beyond doubt entitled to be admitted and is not inadmissible under section 212 [8 U.S.C.A. § 1182]; or

(B) by clear and convincing evidence, that the alien is lawfully present in the United States pursuant to a prior admission.

In meeting the burden of proof under subparagraph (B), the alien shall have access to the alien's visa or other entry document, if any, and any other records and documents, not considered by the Attorney General to be confidential, pertaining to the alien's admission or presence in the United States.

(3) Burden on service in cases of deportable aliens

(A) In general

In the proceeding the Service has the burden of establishing by clear and convincing evidence that, in the case of an alien who has been admitted to the United States, the alien is deportable. No decision on deportability shall be valid unless it is based upon reasonable, substantial, and probative evidence.

(B) Proof of convictions

In any proceeding under this Act, any of the following documents or records (or a certified copy of such an official document or record) shall constitute proof of a criminal conviction:

(i) An official record of judgment and conviction.

(ii) An official record of plea, verdict, and sentence.

(iii) A docket entry from court records that indicates the existence of the conviction.

(iv) Official minutes of a court proceeding or a transcript of a court hearing in which the court takes notice of the existence of the conviction.

(v) An abstract of a record of conviction prepared by the court in which the conviction was entered, or by a State official associated with the State's repository of criminal justice records, that indicates the charge or section of law violated, the disposition of the case, the existence and date of conviction, and the sentence.

(vi) Any document or record prepared by, or under the direction of, the court in which the conviction was entered that indicates the existence of a conviction.

(vii) Any document or record attesting to the conviction that is maintained by an official of a State or Federal penal institution, which is the basis for that institution's authority to assume custody of the individual named in the record.

(C) Electronic records

In any proceeding under this Act, any record of conviction or abstract that has been submitted by electronic means to the Service from a State or court shall be admissible as evidence to prove a criminal conviction if it is—

(i) certified by a State official associated with the State's repository of criminal justice records as an official record from its repository or by a court official from the court in which the conviction was entered as an official record from its repository, and

(ii) certified in writing by a Service official as having been received electronically from the State's record repository or the court's record repository.

A certification under clause (i) may be by means of a computer-generated signature and statement of authenticity.

(4) Notice

If the immigration judge decides that the alien is removable and orders the alien to be removed, the judge shall inform the alien of the right to appeal that decision and of the consequences for failure to depart under the order of removal, including civil and criminal penalties.

(5) Motions to reconsider

(A) In general

The alien may file one motion to reconsider a decision that the alien is removable from the United States.

(B) Deadline

The motion must be filed within 30 days of the date of entry of a final administrative order of removal.

(C) Contents

The motion shall specify the errors of law or fact in the previous order and shall be supported by pertinent authority.

(6) Motions to reopen

(A) In general

An alien may file one motion to reopen proceedings under this section.

(B) Contents

The motion to reopen shall state the new facts that will be proven at a hearing to be held if the motion is granted, and shall be supported by affidavits or other evidentiary material.

(C) Deadline

(i) In general

Except as provided in this subparagraph, the motion to reopen shall be filed within 90 days of the date of entry of a final administrative order of removal.

(ii) Asylum

There is no time limit on the filing of a motion to reopen if the basis of the motion is to apply for relief under sections 208 [8 U.S.C.A. § 1158] or 241(b)(3) [8 U.S.C.A. § 1231(b)(3)] and is based on changed country conditions arising in the country of nationality or the country to which removal has been ordered, if such evidence is material and was not available and would not have been discovered or presented at the previous proceeding.

(iii) Failure to appear

The filing of a motion to reopen an order entered pursuant to subsection (b)(5) is subject to the deadline specified in subparagraph (C) of such subsection.

(d) Stipulated removal

The Attorney General shall provide by regulation for the entry by an immigration judge of an order of removal stipulated to by the alien (or the alien's representative) and the Service. A stipulated order shall constitute a conclusive determination of the alien's removability from the United States.

(e) Definitions

In this section and section 240A [8 U.S.C.A. § 1229b]:

(1) Exceptional circumstances

The term "exceptional circumstances" refers to exceptional circumstances (such as serious illness of the alien or serious illness or death of the spouse, child, or parent of the alien, but not including less compelling circumstances) beyond the control of the alien.

(2) Removable

The term "removable" means—

(A) in the case of an alien not admitted to the United States, that the alien is inadmissible under section 212 [8 U.S.C.A. § 1182], or

(B) in the case of an alien admitted to the United States, that the alien is deportable under section 237 [8 U.S.C.A. § 1227].

(June 27, 1952, c. 477, Title II, Ch. 4, § 240 as added Sept. 30, 1996, Pub.L. 104–208, Div. C, Title III, § 304(a)(3), 110 Stat. 3009–589.)

§ 240A. Cancellation of removal; adjustment of status [8 U.S.C.A. § 1229b]

(a) Cancellation of removal for certain permanent residents

The Attorney General may cancel removal in the case of an alien who is inadmissible or deportable from the United States if the alien—

(1) has been an alien lawfully admitted for permanent residence for not less than 5 years,

(2) has resided in the United States continuously for 7 years after having been admitted in any status, and

(3) has not been convicted of any aggravated felony.

(b) Cancellation of removal and adjustment of status for certain nonpermanent residents

(1) In general

The Attorney General may cancel removal of, and adjust to the status of an alien lawfully admitted for permanent residence, an alien who is inadmissible or deportable from the United States if the alien—

(A) has been physically present in the United States for a continuous period of not less than 10 years immediately preceding the date of such application;

(B) has been a person of good moral character during such period;

(C) has not been convicted of an offense under section 212(a)(2) [8 U.S.C.A. § 1182(a)(2)], 237(a)(2) [8 U.S.C.A. § 1227(a)(2)], or 237(a)(3) [8 U.S.C.A. § 237(a)(3)]; and

(D) establishes that removal would result in exceptional and extremely unusual hardship to the alien's spouse, parent, or child, who is a citizen of the United States or an alien lawfully admitted for permanent residence.

(2) Special rule for battered spouse or child

The Attorney General may cancel removal of, and adjust to the status of an alien lawfully admitted for permanent residence, an alien who is inadmissible or deportable from the United States if the alien demonstrates that—

(A) the alien has been battered or subjected to extreme cruelty in the United States by a spouse or parent who is a United States citizen or lawful permanent resident (or is the parent of a child of a United States citizen or lawful permanent resident and the child has been battered or subjected to extreme cruelty in the United States by such citizen or permanent resident parent);

(B) the alien has been physically present in the United States for a continuous period of not less than 3 years immediately preceding the date of such application;

(C) the alien has been a person of good moral character during such period;

(D) the alien is not inadmissible under paragraph (2) or (3) of section 212(a) [8 U.S.C.A. § 1182(a)], is not deportable under paragraph (1)(G) or (2) through (4) of section 237(a) [8 U.S.C.A. § 1227(a)], and has not been convicted of an aggravated felony; and

(E) the removal would result in extreme hardship to the alien, the alien's child, or (in the case of an alien who is a child) to the alien's parent.

In acting on applications under this paragraph, the Attorney General shall consider any credible evidence relevant to the application. The determination of what evidence is credible and the weight to be given that evidence shall be within the sole discretion of the Attorney General.

(3) Recordation of date

With respect to aliens who the Attorney General adjusts to the status of an alien lawfully admitted for permanent residence under paragraph (1) or (2), the Attorney General shall record the alien's lawful admission for permanent residence as of the date of the Attorney General's cancellation of removal under paragraph (1) or (2).

(c) Aliens ineligible for relief

The provisions of subsections (a) and (b)(1) shall not apply to any of the following aliens:

(1) An alien who entered the United States as a crewman subsequent to June 30, 1964.

(2) An alien who was admitted to the United States as a nonimmigrant exchange alien as defined in section 101(a)(15)(J) [8 U.S.C.A. § 1101(a)(15)(J)], or has acquired the status of such a nonimmigrant exchange alien after admission, in order to receive graduate medical education or training, regardless of whether or not the alien is subject to or has fulfilled the two-year foreign residence requirement of section 212(c) [8 U.S.C.A. § 1182(c)].

exchange-vistor

(3) An alien who—

(A) was admitted to the United States as a nonimmigrant exchange alien as defined in section 101(a)(15)(J) [8 U.S.C.A. § 1101(a)(15)(J)] or has acquired the status of such a nonimmigrant exchange alien after admission other than to receive graduate medical education or training,

(B) is subject to the two-year foreign residence requirement of section 212(e) [8 U.S.C.A. § 1182(e)], and

(C) has not fulfilled that requirement or received a waiver thereof.

(4) An alien who is inadmissible under section 212(a)(3) [8 U.S.C.A. § 1182(a)(3)] or deportable under section 237(a)(4) [8 U.S.C.A. § 1227(a)(4)].

(5) An alien who is described in section 241(b)(3)(B)(i) [8 U.S.C.A. § 1231(b)(3)(B)(i)].

(6) An alien whose removal has previously been cancelled under this section or whose deportation was suspended under section 244(a) [8 U.S.C.A. § 1254(a)] or who has been granted relief under section 212(c) [8 U.S.C.A. § 1182(c)], as such sections were in effect before September 30, 1996.

(d) Special rules relating to continuous residence or physical presence

(1) Termination of continuous period

For purposes of this section, any period of continuous residence or continuous physical presence in the United States shall be deemed to end when the alien is served a notice to appear under section 239(a) [8 U.S.C.A. § 1229(a)] or when the alien has committed an offense referred to in section 212(a)(2) [8 U.S.C.A. § 1182(a)(2)] that renders the alien inadmissible to the United States under section 212(a)(2) [8 U.S.C.A. § 1182(a)(2)] or removable from the United States under section 237(a)(2) or (4) [8 U.S.C.A. § 1227(a)(2) or (4)], whichever is earliest.

(2) Treatment of certain breaks in presence

An alien shall be considered to have failed to maintain continuous physical presence in the United States under subsections (b)(1) and (b)(2) if the alien has departed from the United States for any period in excess of 90 days or for any periods in the aggregate exceeding 180 days.

(3) Continuity not required because of honorable service in armed forces and presence upon entry into service

The requirements of continuous residence or continuous physical presence in the United States under subsections (a) and (b) shall not apply to an alien who—

(A) has served for a minimum period of 24 months in an active-duty status in the Armed Forces of the United States and, if separated from such service, was separated under honorable conditions, and

(B) at the time of the alien's enlistment or induction was in the United States.

(e) Annual limitation

(1) Aggregate limitation

Subject to paragraphs (2) and (3), the Attorney General may not cancel the removal and adjust the status under this section, nor suspend the deportation and adjust the status under section 244(a) [8 U.S.C.A. § 1254(a)] (as in effect before the enactment of the Illegal Immigration Reform and Immigrant Responsibility Act of 1996), of a total of more than 4,000 aliens in any fiscal year. The previous sentence shall apply regardless of when an alien applied for such cancellation and adjustment, or such suspension and adjustment, and whether such an alien had previously applied for suspension of deportation under such section 244(a) [8 U.S.C.A. § 1254(a)]. The numerical limitation under this paragraph shall apply to the aggregate number of decisions in any fiscal year to cancel the removal (and adjust the status) of an alien, or suspend the deportation (and adjust the status) of an alien, under this section or such section 244(a) [8 U.S.C.A. § 1254(a)].

(2) Fiscal year 1997

For fiscal year 1997, paragraph (1) shall only apply to decisions to cancel the removal of an alien, or suspend the deportation of an alien, made after April 1, 1997. Notwithstanding any other provision of law, the Attorney General may cancel the removal or suspend the deportation, in addition to the normal allotment for fiscal year 1998, of a number of aliens equal to 4,000 less the number of such cancellations of removal and suspensions of deportation granted in fiscal year 1997 after April 1, 1997.

(3) Exception for certain aliens

Paragraph (1) shall not apply to the following:

(A) Aliens described in section 309(c)(5)(C)(i) of the Illegal Immigration Reform and Immigrant Responsibility Act of 1996 (as amended by the Nicaraguan Adjustment and Central American Relief Act).

(B) Aliens in deportation proceedings prior to April 1, 1997, who applied for suspension of deportation under section 244(a)(3) [8 U.S.C.A. § 1254(a)(3)] (as in effect before Sept. 30, 1996).

(June 27, 1952, c. 477, Title II, ch. 4, § 240A, as added Sept. 30, 1996, Pub.L. 104–208, Div. C, Title III, § 304(a)(3), 110 Stat. 3009–594; Nov. 19, 1997, Pub.L. 105–100, Title I, § 204(a) to (c), 111 Stat. 2200.)

§ 240B. Voluntary departure [8 U.S.C.A. § 1229c]

(a) Certain conditions

(1) In general

The Attorney General may permit an alien voluntarily to depart the United States at the alien's own expense under this subsection, in lieu of being subject to proceedings under section 240 [8 U.S.C.A.

§ 1229a] or prior to the completion of such proceedings, if the alien is not deportable under section 237(a)(2)(A)(iii) [8 U.S.C.A. § 1227(a)(2)(A)(iii)] or section 237(a)(4)(B) [8 U.S.C.A. § 1227(a)(4)(B)].

(2) Period

Permission to depart voluntarily under this subsection shall not be valid for a period exceeding 120 days.

(3) Bond

The Attorney General may require an alien permitted to depart voluntarily under this subsection to post a voluntary departure bond, to be surrendered upon proof that the alien has departed the United States within the time specified.

(4) Treatment of aliens arriving in the United States

In the case of an alien who is arriving in the United States and with respect to whom proceedings under section 240 [8 U.S.C.A. § 1229a] are (or would otherwise be) initiated at the time of such alien's arrival, paragraph (1) shall not apply. Nothing in this paragraph shall be construed as preventing such an alien from withdrawing the application for admission in accordance with section 235(a)(4) [8 U.S.C.A. § 1225(a)(4)].

(b) At conclusion of proceedings

(1) In general

The Attorney General may permit an alien voluntarily to depart the United States at the alien's own expense if, at the conclusion of a proceeding under section 240 [8 U.S.C.A. § 1229a], the immigration judge enters an order granting voluntary departure in lieu of removal and finds that—

(A) the alien has been physically present in the United States for a period of at least one year immediately preceding the date the notice to appear was served under section 239(a) [8 U.S.C.A. § 1229(a)];

(B) the alien is, and has been, a person of good moral character for at least 5 years immediately preceding the alien's application for voluntary departure;

(C) the alien is not deportable under section 237(a)(2)(A)(iii) [8 U.S.C.A. § 1227(a)(2)(A)(iii)] or section 237(a)(4) [8 U.S.C.A. § 1227(a)(4)]; and

(D) the alien has established by clear and convincing evidence that the alien has the means to depart the United States and intends to do so.

(2) Period

Permission to depart voluntarily under this subsection shall not be valid for a period exceeding 60 days.

(3) Bond

An alien permitted to depart voluntarily under this subsection shall be required to post a voluntary departure bond, in an amount necessary to ensure that the alien will depart, to be surrendered upon proof that the alien has departed the United States within the time specified.

(c) Aliens not eligible

The Attorney General shall not permit an alien to depart voluntarily under this section if the alien was previously permitted to so depart after having been found inadmissible under section 212(a)(6)(A) [8 U.S.C.A. § 1182(a)(6)(A)].

(d) Civil penalty for failure to depart

If an alien is permitted to depart voluntarily under this section and fails voluntarily to depart the United States within the time period specified, the alien shall be subject to a civil penalty of not less than $1,000 and not more than $5,000, and be ineligible for a period of 10 years for any further relief under this section and sections 240A [8 U.S.C.A. § 1229b], 245 [8 U.S.C.A. § 1255], 248 [8 U.S.C.A. § 1258], and 249 [8 U.S.C.A. § 1259]. The order permitting the alien to depart voluntarily shall inform the alien of the penalties under this subsection.

(e) Additional conditions

The Attorney General may by regulation limit eligibility for voluntary departure under this section for any class or classes of aliens. No court may review any regulation issued under this subsection.

(f) Judicial review

No court shall have jurisdiction over an appeal from denial of a request for an order of voluntary departure under subsection (b), nor shall any court order a stay of an alien's removal pending consideration of any claim with respect to voluntary departure.

(June 27, 1952, c. 477, Title II, ch. 4, § 240B, as added Sept. 30, 1996, Pub.L. 104–208, Div. C, Title III, § 304(a)(3), 110 Stat. 3009–596.)

§ 240C. Records of admission [8 U.S.C.A. § 1230]

(a) The Attorney General shall cause to be filed, as a record of admission of each immigrant, the immigrant visa required by section 211(e) [8 U.S.C.A. § 1201(e)] to be surrendered at the port of entry by the arriving alien to an immigration officer.

(b) The Attorney General shall cause to be filed such record of the admission into the United States of each immigrant admitted under section 211(b) [8 U.S.C.A. § 1181(b)] and of each nonimmigrant as the Attorney General deems necessary for the enforcement of the immigration laws.

(June 27, 1952, c. 477, Title II, ch. 4, § 240C, formerly § 240, 66 Stat. 204, redesignated and amended Sept. 30, 1996, Pub.L. 104–208, Div. C, Title III, §§ 304(a)(2), 308(f)(1)(K), 110 Stat. 3009–587, 3009–621.)

§ 241. Detention and removal of aliens ordered removed [8 U.S.C.A. § 1231]

(a) Detention, release, and removal of aliens ordered removed

(1) Removal period

(A) In general

Except as otherwise provided in this section, when an alien is ordered removed, the Attorney General shall remove the alien from the United States within a period of 90 days (in this section referred to as the "removal period").

(B) Beginning of period

The removal period begins on the latest of the following:

(i) The date the order of removal becomes administratively final.

(ii) If the removal order is judicially reviewed and if a court orders a stay of the removal of the alien, the date of the court's final order.

(iii) If the alien is detained or confined (except under an immigration process), the date the alien is released from detention or confinement.

(C) Suspension of period

The removal period shall be extended beyond a period of 90 days and the alien may remain in detention during such extended period if the alien fails or refuses to make timely application in good faith for travel or other documents necessary to the alien's departure or conspires or acts to prevent the alien's removal subject to an order of removal.

(2) Detention

During the removal period, the Attorney General shall detain the alien. Under no circumstance during the removal period shall the Attorney General release an alien who has been found inadmissible under section 212(a)(2) [8 U.S.C.A. § 1182(a)(2)] or 212(a)(3)(B) [8 U.S.C.A. § 1182(a)(3)(B)] or deportable under section 237(a)(2) [8 U.S.C.A. § 1227(a)(2)]or 237(a)(4)(B) [8 U.S.C.A. § 1227(a)(4)(B)].

(3) Supervision after 90–day period

If the alien does not leave or is not removed within the removal period, the alien, pending removal, shall be subject to supervision under regulations prescribed by the Attorney General. The regulations shall include provisions requiring the alien—

(A) to appear before an immigration officer periodically for identification;

(B) to submit, if necessary, to a medical and psychiatric examination at the expense of the United States Government;

(C) to give information under oath about the alien's nationality, circumstances, habits, associations, and activities, and other information the Attorney General considers appropriate; and

(D) to obey reasonable written restrictions on the alien's conduct or activities that the Attorney General prescribes for the alien.

(4) Aliens imprisoned, arrested, or on parole, supervised release, or probation

(A) In general

Except as provided in section 259(a) of Title 42 and paragraph (2), the Attorney General may not remove an alien who is sentenced to imprisonment until the alien is released from imprisonment. Parole, supervised release, probation, or possibility of arrest or further imprisonment is not a reason to defer removal.

(B) Exception for removal of nonviolent offenders prior to completion of sentence of imprisonment

The Attorney General is authorized to remove an alien in accordance with applicable procedures under this Act before the alien has completed a sentence of imprisonment—

(i) in the case of an alien in the custody of the Attorney General, if the Attorney General determines that (I) the alien is confined pursuant to a final conviction for a nonviolent offense (other than an offense related to smuggling or harboring of aliens or an offense described in section 101(a)(43)(B), (C), (E), (I), or (L) [8 U.S.C.A. § 1101(a)(43)(B), (C), (E), (I), or (L)] [sic] and (II) the removal of the alien is appropriate and in the best interest of the United States); or

(ii) in the case of an alien in the custody of a State (or a political subdivision of a State), if the chief State official exercising authority with respect to the incarceration of the alien determines that (I) the alien is confined pursuant to a final conviction for a nonviolent offense (other than an offense described in section 101(a)(43)(C) or (E) [8 U.S.C.A. § 1101(a)(43)(C) or (E)]), (II) the removal is appropriate and in the best interest of the State, and (III) submits a written request to the Attorney General that such alien be so removed.

(C) Notice

Any alien removed pursuant to this paragraph shall be notified of the penalties under the laws of the United States relating to the reentry of deported aliens, particularly the expanded penalties for aliens removed under subparagraph (B).

(D) No private right

No cause or claim may be asserted under this paragraph against any official of the United States or of any State to compel the release, removal, or consideration for release or removal of any alien.

(5) Reinstatement of removal orders against aliens illegally reentering

If the Attorney General finds that an alien has reentered the United States illegally after having been removed or having departed voluntarily, under an order of removal, the prior order of removal is reinstated from its original date and is not subject to being reopened or reviewed, the alien is not eligible and may not apply for any relief under this Act, and the alien shall be removed under the prior order at any time after the reentry.

(6) Inadmissible or criminal aliens

An alien ordered removed who is inadmissible under section 212 [8 U.S.C.A. § 1182], removable under section 237(a)(1)(C) [8 U.S.C.A. § 1227(a)(1)(C)], 237(a)(2) [8 U.S.C.A. § 1227(a)(2)], or 237(a)(4) [8 U.S.C.A. § 1227(a)(4)] or who has been determined by the Attorney General to be a risk to the community or unlikely to comply with the order of removal, may be detained beyond the removal period and, if released, shall be subject to the terms of supervision in paragraph (3).

(7) Employment authorization

No alien ordered removed shall be eligible to receive authorization to be employed in the United States unless the Attorney General makes a specific finding that—

(A) the alien cannot be removed due to the refusal of all countries designated by the alien or under this section to receive the alien, or

(B) the removal of the alien is otherwise impracticable or contrary to the public interest.

(b) Countries to which aliens may be removed

(1) Aliens arriving at the United States

Subject to paragraph (3)—

(A) In general

Except as provided by subparagraphs (B) and (C), an alien who arrives at the United States and with respect to whom proceedings under section 240 [8 U.S.C.A. § 1229a] were initiated at the time of such alien's arrival shall be removed to the country in which the alien boarded the vessel or aircraft on which the alien arrived in the United States.

(B) Travel from contiguous territory

If the alien boarded the vessel or aircraft on which the alien arrived in the United States in a foreign territory contiguous to the United States, an island adjacent to the United States, or an island adjacent to a foreign territory contiguous to the United States, and the alien is not a native, citizen, subject, or national of, or does not reside in, the territory or island, removal shall be to the country in which the alien boarded the vessel that transported the alien to the territory or island.

(C) Alternative countries

If the government of the country designated in subparagraph (A) or (B) is unwilling to accept the alien into that country's territory, removal shall be to any of the following countries, as directed by the Attorney General:

(i) The country of which the alien is a citizen, subject, or national.

(ii) The country in which the alien was born.

(iii) The country in which the alien has a residence.

(iv) A country with a government that will accept the alien into the country's territory if removal to each country described in a previous clause of this subparagraph is impracticable, inadvisable, or impossible.

(2) Other aliens

Subject to paragraph (3)—

(A) Selection of country by alien ✓

Except as otherwise provided in this paragraph—

(i) any alien not described in paragraph (1) who has been ordered removed may designate one country to which the alien wants to be removed, and

(ii) the Attorney General shall remove the alien to the country the alien so designates.

(B) Limitation on designation

An alien may designate under subparagraph (A)(i) a foreign territory contiguous to the United States, an adjacent island, or an island adjacent to a foreign territory contiguous to the United States as the place to which the alien is to be removed only if the alien is a native, citizen, subject, or national of, or has resided in, that designated territory or island.

(C) Disregarding designation

The Attorney General may disregard a designation under subparagraph (A)(i) if—

(i) the alien fails to designate a country promptly;

(ii) the government of the country does not inform the Attorney General finally, within 30 days after the date the Attorney General first inquires, whether the government will accept the alien into the country;

(iii) the government of the country is not willing to accept the alien into the country; or

(iv) the Attorney General decides that removing the alien to the country is prejudicial to the United States.

(D) Alternative country

If an alien is not removed to a country designated under subparagraph (A)(i), the Attorney General shall remove the alien to a country of which the alien is a subject, national, or citizen unless the government of the country—

(i) does not inform the Attorney General or the alien finally, within 30 days after the date the Attorney General first inquires or within another period of time the Attorney General decides is reasonable, whether the government will accept the alien into the country; or

(ii) is not willing to accept the alien into the country.

(E) Additional removal countries

If an alien is not removed to a country under the previous subparagraphs of this paragraph, the Attorney General shall remove the alien to any of the following countries:

(i) The country from which the alien was admitted to the United States.

(ii) The country in which is located the foreign port from which the alien left for the United States or for a foreign territory contiguous to the United States.

(iii) A country in which the alien resided before the alien entered the country from which the alien entered the United States.

(iv) The country in which the alien was born.

(v) The country that had sovereignty over the alien's birthplace when the alien was born.

(vi) The country in which the alien's birthplace is located when the alien is ordered removed.

(vii) If impracticable, inadvisable, or impossible to remove the alien to each country described in a previous clause of this subparagraph, another country whose government will accept the alien into that country.

(F) Removal country when United States is at war

When the United States is at war and the Attorney General decides that it is impracticable, inadvisable, inconvenient, or impossible to remove an alien under this subsection because of the war, the Attorney General may remove the alien—

(i) to the country that is host to a government in exile of the country of which the alien is a citizen or subject if the government of the host country will permit the alien's entry; or

(ii) if the recognized government of the country of which the alien is a citizen or subject is not in exile, to a country, or a political or territorial subdivision of a country, that is very near the country of which the alien is a citizen or subject, or, with the consent of the government of the country of which the alien is a citizen or subject, to another country.

(3) Restriction on removal to a country where alien's life or freedom would be threatened

(A) In general

Notwithstanding paragraphs (1) and (2), the Attorney General may not remove an alien to a country if the Attorney General decides that the alien's life or freedom would be threatened in that country because of the alien's race, religion, nationality, membership in a particular social group, or political opinion.

(B) Exception

Subparagraph (A) does not apply to an alien deportable under section 237(a)(4)(D) [8 U.S.C.A. § 1227(a)(4)(D)] or if the Attorney General decides that—

(i) the alien ordered, incited, assisted, or otherwise participated in the persecution of an individual because of the individual's race, religion, nationality, membership in a particular social group, or political opinion;

(ii) the alien, having been convicted by a final judgment of a particularly serious crime is a danger to the community of the United States;

(iii) there are serious reasons to believe that the alien committed a serious nonpolitical crime outside the United States before the alien arrived in the United States; or

(iv) there are reasonable grounds to believe that the alien is a danger to the security of the United States.

For purposes of clause (ii), an alien who has been convicted of an aggravated felony (or felonies) for which the alien has been sentenced to an aggregate term of imprisonment of at least 5 years shall be considered to have committed a particularly serious crime. The previous sentence shall not preclude the Attorney General from determining that, notwithstanding the length of sentence imposed, an alien has been convicted of a particularly serious crime. For purposes of clause (iv), an alien who is described in section 237(a)(4)(B) [8 U.S.C.A. § 1227(a)(4)(B)] shall be considered to be an alien with respect to whom there are reasonable grounds for regarding as a danger to the security of the United States.

(c) Removal of aliens arriving at port of entry

(1) Vessels and aircraft

An alien arriving at a port of entry of the United States who is ordered removed either without a hearing under section 235(b)(1) [8 U.S.C.A. § 1225(b)(1)] or 235(c) [8 U.S.C.A. § 1225(c)] or pursuant to proceedings under section 240 [8 U.S.C.A. § 1229a] initiated at the time of such alien's arrival shall be removed immediately on a vessel or aircraft owned by the owner of the vessel or aircraft on which the alien arrived in the United States, unless—

(A) it is impracticable to remove the alien on one of those vessels or aircraft within a reasonable time, or

(B) the alien is a stowaway—

(i) who has been ordered removed in accordance with section 235(a)(1) [8 U.S.C.A. § 1225(a)(1)],

(ii) who has requested asylum, and

(iii) whose application has not been adjudicated or whose asylum application has been denied but who has not exhausted all appeal rights.

(2) Stay of removal

(A) In general

The Attorney General may stay the removal of an alien under this subsection if the Attorney General decides that—

(i) immediate removal is not practicable or proper; or

(ii) the alien is needed to testify in the prosecution of a person for a violation of a law of the United States or of any State.

(B) Payment of detention costs

During the period an alien is detained because of a stay of removal under subparagraph (A)(ii), the Attorney General may pay from the appropriation "Immigration and Naturalization Service—Salaries and Expenses"—

(i) the cost of maintenance of the alien; and

(ii) a witness fee of $1 a day.

(C) Release during stay

The Attorney General may release an alien whose removal is stayed under subparagraph (A)(ii) on—

(i) the alien's filing a bond of at least $500 with security approved by the Attorney General;

(ii) condition that the alien appear when required as a witness and for removal; and

(iii) other conditions the Attorney General may prescribe.

(3) Costs of detention and maintenance pending removal

(A) In general

Except as provided in subparagraph (B) and subsection (d), an owner of a vessel or aircraft bringing an alien to the United States shall pay the costs of detaining and maintaining the alien—

(i) while the alien is detained under subsection (d)(1), and

(ii) in the case of an alien who is a stowaway, while the alien is being detained pursuant to—

(I) subsection (d)(2)(A) or (d)(2)(B)(i),

(II) subsection (d)(2)(B)(ii) or (iii) for the period of time reasonably necessary for the owner to arrange for repatriation or removal of the stowaway, including obtaining necessary travel documents, but not to extend beyond the date on which it is ascertained that such travel documents cannot be obtained from the country to which the stowaway is to be returned, or

(III) section 235(b)(1)(B)(ii), for a period not to exceed 15 days (excluding Saturdays, Sundays, and holidays) commencing on the first such day which begins on the earlier of 72 hours after the time of the initial presentation of the stowaway for inspection or at the time the stowaway is determined to have a credible fear of persecution.

(B) Nonapplication

Subparagraph (A) shall not apply if—

(i) the alien is a crewmember;

(ii) the alien has an immigrant visa;

(iii) the alien has a nonimmigrant visa or other documentation authorizing the alien to apply for temporary admission to the United States and applies for admission not later than 120 days after the date the visa or documentation was issued;

(iv) the alien has a reentry permit and applies for admission not later than 120 days after the date of the alien's last inspection and admission;

(v)(I) the alien has a nonimmigrant visa or other documentation authorizing the alien to apply for temporary admission to the United States or a reentry permit;

(II) the alien applies for admission more than 120 days after the date the visa or documentation was issued or after the date of the last inspection and admission under the reentry permit; and

(III) the owner of the vessel or aircraft satisfies the Attorney General that the existence of the condition relating to inadmissibility could not have been discovered by exercising reasonable care before the alien boarded the vessel or aircraft; or

(vi) the individual claims to be a national of the United States and has a United States passport.

(d) Requirements of persons providing transportation

(1) Removal at time of arrival

An owner, agent, master, commanding officer, person in charge, purser, or consignee of a vessel or aircraft bringing an alien (except an alien crewmember) to the United States shall—

(A) receive an alien back on the vessel or aircraft or another vessel or aircraft owned or operated by the same interests if the alien is ordered removed under this part; and

(B) take the alien to the foreign country to which the alien is ordered removed.

(2) Alien stowaways

An owner, agent, master, commanding officer, charterer, or consignee of a vessel or aircraft arriving in the United States with an alien stowaway—

(A) shall detain the alien on board the vessel or aircraft, or at such place as the Attorney General shall designate, until completion of the inspection of the alien by an immigration officer;

(B) may not permit the stowaway to land in the United States, except pursuant to regulations of the Attorney General temporarily—

(i) for medical treatment,

(ii) for detention of the stowaway by the Attorney General, or

(iii) for departure or removal of the stowaway; and

(C) if ordered by an immigration officer, shall remove the stowaway on the vessel or aircraft or on another vessel or aircraft.

The Attorney General shall grant a timely request to remove the stowaway under subparagraph (C) on a vessel or aircraft other than that on which the stowaway arrived if the requester has obtained any travel documents necessary for departure or repatriation of the stowaway and removal of the stowaway will not be unreasonably delayed.

(3) Removal upon order

An owner, agent, master, commanding officer, person in charge, purser, or consignee of a vessel, aircraft, or other transportation line shall comply with an order of the Attorney General to take on board, guard safely, and transport to the destination specified any alien ordered to be removed under this Act.

(e) Payment of expenses of removal

(1) Costs of removal at time of arrival

In the case of an alien who is a stowaway or who is ordered removed either without a hearing under section 235(a)(1) [8 U.S.C.A. § 1225(a)(1)] or 235(c) [8 U.S.C.A. § 1225(c)] or pursuant to proceedings under section 240 [8 U.S.C.A. § 1229a] initiated at the time of such alien's arrival, the owner of the vessel or aircraft (if any) on which the alien arrived in the United States shall pay the transportation cost of removing the alien. If removal is on a vessel or aircraft not owned by the owner of the vessel or aircraft on which the alien arrived in the United States, the Attorney General may—

(A) pay the cost from the appropriation "Immigration and Naturalization Service—Salaries and Expenses"; and

(B) recover the amount of the cost in a civil action from the owner, agent, or consignee of the vessel or aircraft (if any) on which the alien arrived in the United States.

(2) Costs of removal to port of removal for aliens admitted or permitted to land

In the case of an alien who has been admitted or permitted to land and is ordered removed, the cost (if any) of removal of the alien to the port of removal shall be at the expense of the appropriation for the enforcement of this Act.

(3) Costs of removal from port of removal for aliens admitted or permitted to land

(A) Through appropriation

Except as provided in subparagraph (B), in the case of an alien who has been admitted or permitted to land and is ordered removed, the cost (if any) of removal of the alien from the port of removal shall be at the expense of the appropriation for the enforcement of this Act.

(B) Through owner

(i) In general

In the case of an alien described in clause (ii), the cost of removal of the alien from the port of removal may be charged to any owner of the vessel, aircraft, or other transportation line by which the alien came to the United States.

(ii) Aliens described

An alien described in this clause is an alien who—

(I) is admitted to the United States (other than lawfully admitted for permanent residence) and is ordered removed within 5 years of the date of admission based on a ground that existed before or at the time of admission, or

(II) is an alien crewman permitted to land temporarily under section 252 [8 U.S.C.A. § 1282] and is ordered removed within 5 years of the date of landing.

(C) Costs of removal of certain aliens granted voluntary departure

In the case of an alien who has been granted voluntary departure under section 240B [8 U.S.C.A. § 1229c] and who is financially unable to depart at the alien's own expense and whose removal the Attorney General deems to be in the best interest of the United States, the expense of such removal may be paid from the appropriation for the enforcement of this Act.

(f) Aliens requiring personal care during removal

(1) In general

If the Attorney General believes that an alien being removed requires personal care because of the alien's mental or physical condition, the Attorney General may employ a suitable person for that purpose who shall accompany and care for the alien until the alien arrives at the final destination.

(2) Costs

The costs of providing the service described in paragraph (1) shall be defrayed in the same manner as the expense of removing the accompanied alien is defrayed under this section.

(g) Places of detention

(1) In general

The Attorney General shall arrange for appropriate places of detention for aliens detained pending removal or a decision on removal. When United States Government facilities are unavailable or facilities adapted or suitably located for detention are unavailable for rental, the Attorney General may expend from the appropriation "Immigration and Naturalization Service—Salaries and Expenses", without regard to section 5 of Title 41, amounts necessary to acquire land and to acquire, build, remodel, repair, and operate facilities (including living quarters for immigration officers if not otherwise available) necessary for detention.

(2) Detention facilities of the immigration and naturalization service

Prior to initiating any project for the construction of any new detention facility for the Service, the Commissioner shall consider the availability for purchase or lease of any existing prison, jail, detention center, or other comparable facility suitable for such use.

(h) Statutory construction

Nothing in this section shall be construed to create any substantive or procedural right or benefit that is legally enforceable by any party against the United States or its agencies or officers or any other person.

(i) Incarceration

(1) If the chief executive officer of a State (or, if appropriate, a political subdivision of the State) exercising authority with respect to the incarceration of an undocumented criminal alien submits a written request to the Attorney General, the Attorney General shall, as determined by the Attorney General—

(A) enter into a contractual arrangement which provides for compensation to the State or a political subdivision of the State, as may be appropriate, with respect to the incarceration of the undocumented criminal alien; or

(B) take the undocumented criminal alien into the custody of the Federal Government and incarcerate the alien.

(2) Compensation under paragraph (1)(A) shall be the average cost of incarceration of a prisoner in the relevant State as determined by the Attorney General.

(3) For purposes of this subsection, the term "undocumented criminal alien" means an alien who—

(A) has been convicted of a felony or two or more misdemeanors; and

(B)(i) entered the United States without inspection or at any time or place other than as designated by the Attorney General;

(ii) was the subject of exclusion or deportation proceedings at the time he or she was taken into custody by the State or a political subdivision of the State; or

(iii) was admitted as a nonimmigrant and at the time he or she was taken into custody by the State or a political subdivision of the State has failed to maintain the nonimmigrant status in which the alien was admitted or to which it was changed under section 248 [8 U.S.C.A. § 1258], or to comply with the conditions of any such status.

(4)(A) In carrying out paragraph (1), the Attorney General shall give priority to the Federal incarceration of undocumented criminal aliens who have committed aggravated felonies.

(B) The Attorney General shall ensure that undocumented criminal aliens incarcerated in Federal facilities pursuant to this subsection are held in facilities which provide a level of security appropriate to the crimes for which they were convicted.

(5) There are authorized to be appropriated such sums as may be necessary to carry out this subsection, of which the following amounts may be appropriated from the Violent Crime Reduction Trust Fund:

(A) $130,000,000 for fiscal year 1995;

(B) $300,000,000 for fiscal year 1996;

(C) $330,000,000 for fiscal year 1997;

(D) $350,000,000 for fiscal year 1998;

(E) $350,000,000 for fiscal year 1999; and

(F) $340,000,000 for fiscal year 2000.

(6) To the extent of available appropriations, funds otherwise made available under this section with respect to a State (or political subdivision, including a municipality) for incarceration of an undocumented criminal alien may, at the discretion of the recipient of the funds, be used for the costs of imprisonment of such alien in a State, local, or municipal prison or jail.

(June 27, 1952, c. 477, Title II, ch. 4, § 241, as added and amended Sept. 30, 1996, Pub.L. 104–208, Div. C, Title III, §§ 305(a)(3), 306(a)(1), 328(a)(1), 110 Stat. 3009–598, 3009–607, 3009–630.)

§ 242. Judicial review of orders of removal [8 U.S.C.A. § 1252]

(a) Applicable provisions

(1) General orders of removal

Judicial review of a final order of removal (other than an order of removal without a hearing pursuant to section 235(b)(1) [8 U.S.C.A. § 1225(b)(1)] is governed only by chapter 158 of Title 28, except as provided in subsection (b) and except that the court may not order the taking of additional evidence under section 2347(c) of Title 28).

(2) Matters not subject to judicial review

(A) Review relating to section 235(b)(1) [8 U.S.C.A. § 1225(b)(1)]

Notwithstanding any other provision of law, no court shall have jurisdiction to review—

(i) except as provided in subsection (e), any individual determination or to entertain any other cause or claim arising from or relating to the implementation or operation of an order of removal pursuant to section 235(b)(1) [8 U.S.C.A. § 1225(b)(1)],

(ii) except as provided in subsection (e), a decision by the Attorney General to invoke the provisions of such section,

(iii) the application of such section to individual aliens, including the determination made under section 235(b)(1)(B) [8 U.S.C.A. § 1225(b)(1)(B)], or

(iv) except as provided in subsection (e), procedures and policies adopted by the Attorney General to implement the provisions of section 235(b)(1) [8 U.S.C.A. § 1225(b)(1)].

(B) Denials of discretionary relief

Notwithstanding any other provision of law, no court shall have jurisdiction to review—

(i) any judgment regarding the granting of relief under section 212(h) [8 U.S.C.A. § 1182(h)], 212(i) [8 U.S.C.A. § 1182(i)], 240A [8 U.S.C.A. § 1229b], 240B [8 U.S.C.A. § 1229c], or 245 [8 U.S.C.A. § 1255], or

(ii) any other decision or action of the Attorney General the authority for which is specified under this title to be in the discretion of the Attorney General, other than the granting of relief under section 208(a) [8 U.S.C.A. § 1158(a)].

(C) Orders against criminal aliens

Notwithstanding any other provision of law, no court shall have jurisdiction to review any final order of removal against an alien who is removable by reason of having committed a criminal offense covered in section 212(a)(2) [8 U.S.C.A. § 1182(a)(2)] or 237(a)(2)(A)(iii), (B), (C), or (D) [8 U.S.C.A. § 1227(a)(2)(A)(iii), (B), (C), or (D)], or any offense covered by section 237(a)(2)(A)(ii) [8 U.S.C.A. § 1227(a)(2)(A)(ii)] for which both predicate offenses are, without regard to their date of commission, otherwise covered by section 237(a)(2)(A)(i) [8 U.S.C.A. § 1227(a)(2)(A)(i)].

(3) Treatment of certain decisions

No alien shall have a right to appeal from a decision of an immigration judge which is based solely on a certification described in section 240(c)(1)(B) [8 U.S.C.A. § 1229a(c)(1)(B)].

(b) Requirements for review of orders of removal

With respect to review of an order of removal under subsection (a)(1), the following requirements apply:

(1) Deadline

The petition for review must be filed not later than 30 days after the date of the final order of removal.

(2) Venue and forms

The petition for review shall be filed with the court of appeals for the judicial circuit in which the immigration judge completed the proceedings. The record and briefs do not have to be printed. The court of appeals shall review the proceeding on a typewritten record and on typewritten briefs.

(3) Service

(A) In general

The respondent is the Attorney General. The petition shall be served on the Attorney General and on the officer or employee of the Service in charge of the Service district in which the final order of removal under section 240 [8 U.S.C.A. § 1229a] was entered.

(B) Stay of order

Service of the petition on the officer or employee does not stay the removal of an alien pending the court's decision on the petition, unless the court orders otherwise.

(C) Alien's brief

The alien shall serve and file a brief in connection with a petition for judicial review not later than 40 days after the date on which the administrative record is available, and may serve and file a reply brief not later than 14 days after service of the brief of the Attorney General, and the court may not extend these deadlines except upon motion for good cause shown. If an alien fails to file a brief within the time provided in this paragraph, the court shall dismiss the appeal unless a manifest injustice would result.

(4) Scope and standard for review

Except as provided in paragraph (5)(B)—

(A) the court of appeals shall decide the petition only on the administrative record on which the order of removal is based,

(B) the administrative findings of fact are conclusive unless any reasonable adjudicator would be compelled to conclude to the contrary,

(C) a decision that an alien is not eligible for admission to the United States is conclusive unless manifestly contrary to law, and

(D) the Attorney General's discretionary judgment whether to grant relief under section 208(a) [8 U.S.C.A. § 1158(a)] shall be conclusive unless manifestly contrary to the law and an abuse of discretion.

(5) Treatment of nationality claims

(A) Court determination if no issue of fact

If the petitioner claims to be a national of the United States and the court of appeals finds from the pleadings and affidavits that no genuine issue of material fact about the petitioner's nationality is presented, the court shall decide the nationality claim.

(B) Transfer if issue of fact

If the petitioner claims to be a national of the United States and the court of appeals finds that a genuine issue of material fact about the petitioner's nationality is presented, the court shall transfer the proceeding to the district court of the United States for the judicial district in which the petitioner resides for a new hearing on the nationality claim and a decision on that claim as if an action had been brought in the district court under section 2201 of Title 28.

(C) Limitation on determination

The petitioner may have such nationality claim decided only as provided in this paragraph.

(6) Consolidation with review of motions to reopen or reconsider

When a petitioner seeks review of an order under this section, any review sought of a motion to reopen or reconsider the order shall be consolidated with the review of the order.

(7) Challenge to validity of orders in certain criminal proceedings

(A) In general

If the validity of an order of removal has not been judicially decided, a defendant in a criminal proceeding charged with violating section 243(a) [8 U.S.C.A. § 1253(a)] may challenge the validity of the order in the criminal proceeding only by filing a separate motion before trial. The district court, without a jury, shall decide the motion before trial.

(B) Claims of United States nationality

If the defendant claims in the motion to be a national of the United States and the district court finds that—

(i) no genuine issue of material fact about the defendant's nationality is presented, the court shall decide the motion only on the administrative record on which the removal order is based and the administrative findings of fact are conclusive if supported by reasonable, substantial, and probative evidence on the record considered as a whole; or

(ii) a genuine issue of material fact about the defendant's nationality is presented, the court shall hold a new hearing on the nationality claim and decide that claim as if an action had been brought under section 2201 of Title 28, United States Code.

The defendant may have such nationality claim decided only as provided in this subparagraph.

(C) Consequence of invalidation

If the district court rules that the removal order is invalid, the court shall dismiss the indictment for violation of section 243(a) [8 U.S.C.A. § 1253(a)]. The United States Government may appeal the dismissal to the court of appeals for the appropriate circuit within 30 days after the date of the dismissal.

(D) Limitation on filing petitions for review

The defendant in a criminal proceeding under section 243(a) [8 U.S.C.A. § 1253(a)] may not file a petition for review under subsection (a) during the criminal proceeding.

(8) Construction

This subsection—

(A) does not prevent the Attorney General, after a final order of removal has been issued, from detaining the alien under section 241(a) [8 U.S.C.A. § 1231(a)];

(B) does not relieve the alien from complying with section 241(a)(4) [8 U.S.C.A. § 1231(a)(4)] and section 243(g) [8 U.S.C.A. § 1253(g)]; and

(C) does not require the Attorney General to defer removal of the alien.

(9) Consolidation of questions for judicial review

Judicial review of all questions of law and fact, including interpretation and application of constitutional and statutory provisions, arising from any action taken or proceeding brought to remove an alien from the United States under this title shall be available only in judicial review of a final order under this section.

(c) Requirements for petition

A petition for review or for habeas corpus of an order of removal—

(1) shall attach a copy of such order, and

(2) shall state whether a court has upheld the validity of the order, and, if so, shall state the name of the court, the date of the court's ruling, and the kind of proceeding.

(d) Review of final orders

A court may review a final order of removal only if—

(1) the alien has exhausted all administrative remedies available to the alien as of right, and

(2) another court has not decided the validity of the order, unless the reviewing court finds that the petition presents grounds that could not have been presented in the prior judicial proceeding or that the remedy provided by the prior proceeding was inadequate or ineffective to test the validity of the order.

(e) Judicial review of orders under section 235(b)(1) [8 U.S.C.A. § 1225(b)(1)]

(1) Limitations on relief

Without regard to the nature of the action or claim and without regard to the identity of the party or parties bringing the action, no court may—

(A) enter declaratory, injunctive, or other equitable relief in any action pertaining to an order to exclude an alien in accordance with section 235(b)(1) [8 U.S.C.A. § 1225(b)(1)] except as specifically authorized in a subsequent paragraph of this subsection, or

(B) certify a class under Rule 23 of the Federal Rules of Civil Procedure in any action for which judicial review is authorized under a subsequent paragraph of this subsection.

(2) Habeas corpus proceedings

Judicial review of any determination made under section 235(b)(1) [8 U.S.C.A. § 1225(b)(1)] is available in habeas corpus proceedings, but shall be limited to determinations of—

(A) whether the petitioner is an alien,

(B) whether the petitioner was ordered removed under such section, and

(C) whether the petitioner can prove by a preponderance of the evidence that the petitioner is an alien lawfully admitted for permanent residence, has been admitted as a refugee under section 207 [8 U.S.C.A. § 1157], or has been granted asylum under section 208 [8 U.S.C.A. § 1158], such status not having been terminated, and is entitled to such further inquiry as prescribed by the Attorney General pursuant to section 235(b)(1)(C) [8 U.S.C.A. § 1225(b)(1)(C)].

(3) Challenges on validity of the system

(A) In general

Judicial review of determinations under section 235(b) [8 U.S.C.A. § 1225(b)] and its implementation is available in an action instituted in the United States District Court for the District of Columbia, but shall be limited to determinations of—

(i) whether such section, or any regulation issued to implement such section, is constitutional; or

(ii) whether such a regulation, or a written policy directive, written policy guideline, or written procedure issued by or under the authority of the Attorney General to implement such section, is not consistent with applicable provisions of this title or is otherwise in violation of law.

(B) Deadlines for bringing actions

Any action instituted under this paragraph must be filed no later than 60 days after the date the challenged section, regulation, directive, guideline, or procedure described in clause (i) or (ii) of subparagraph (A) is first implemented.

(C) Notice of appeal

A notice of appeal of an order issued by the District Court under this paragraph may be filed not later than 30 days after the date of issuance of such order.

(D) Expeditious consideration of cases

It shall be the duty of the District Court, the Court of Appeals, and the Supreme Court of the United States to advance on the docket and to expedite to the greatest possible extent the disposition of any case considered under this paragraph.

(4) Decision

In any case where the court determines that the petitioner—

(A) is an alien who was not ordered removed under section 235(b)(1) [8 U.S.C.A. § 1225(b)(1)], or

(B) has demonstrated by a preponderance of the evidence that the alien is an alien lawfully admitted for permanent residence, has been admitted as a refugee under section 207 [8 U.S.C.A. § 1157], or has been granted asylum under section 208 [8 U.S.C.A. § 1158], the court may order no remedy or relief other than to require that the petitioner be provided a hearing in accordance with section 240 [8 U.S.C.A. § 1229a]. Any alien who is provided a hearing under section 240 [8 U.S.C.A. § 1229a] pursuant to this paragraph may thereafter obtain judicial review of any resulting final order of removal pursuant to subsection (a)(1) of this section.

(5) Scope of inquiry

In determining whether an alien has been ordered removed under section 235(b)(1) [8 U.S.C.A. § 1225(b)(1)], the court's inquiry shall be limited to whether such an order in fact was issued and whether it relates to the petitioner. There shall be no review of whether the alien is actually inadmissible or entitled to any relief from removal.

(f) Limit on injunctive relief

(1) In general

Regardless of the nature of the action or claim or of the identity of the party or parties bringing the action, no court (other than the Supreme Court) shall have jurisdiction or authority to enjoin or restrain the operation of the provisions of chapter 4 of title II, as amended by the Illegal Immigration Reform and Immigrant Responsibility Act of 1996, other than with respect to the application of such provisions to an individual alien against whom proceedings under such part have been initiated.

(2) Particular cases

Notwithstanding any other provision of law, no court shall enjoin the removal of any alien pursuant to a final order under this section unless the alien shows by clear and convincing evidence that the entry or execution of such order is prohibited as a matter of law.

(g) Exclusive jurisdiction

Except as provided in this section and notwithstanding any other provision of law, no court shall have jurisdiction to hear any cause or claim by or on behalf of any alien arising from the decision or action by the Attorney General to commence proceedings, adjudicate cases, or execute removal orders against any alien under this Act.

(June 27, 1952, c. 477, Title II, ch. 5, § 242, 66 Stat. 208; Sept. 3, 1954, c. 1263, § 17, 68 Stat. 1232; Dec. 29, 1981, Pub.L. 97–116, § 18(h)(1), 95 Stat. 1620; Oct. 12, 1984, Pub.L. 98–473, Title II, § 220(b), 98 Stat. 2028; Nov. 6, 1986, Pub.L. 99–603, Title VII, § 701, 100 Stat. 3445; Oct. 24, 1988, Pub.L. 100–525, § 9(n) 102 Stat. 2620; Nov. 18, 1988, Pub.L. 100–690, Title VII, § 7343(a), 102 Stat. 4470; Nov. 29, 1990, Pub.L. 101–649, Title V, §§ 504(a), 545(e), Title VI, § 603(b)(2), 104 Stat. 5049, 5066, 5085; Dec. 12, 1991, Pub.L. 102–232, Title III, §§ 306(a)(4), (c)(7), 307(m)(2), 309(b)(9), 105 Stat. 1751, 1753, 1757, 1759; Sept. 13, 1994, Pub.L. 103–322, Title II, § 20301(a), Title XIII, § 130001(a), 108 Stat. 1823, 2023; Oct. 25, 1994, Pub.L. 103–416, Title II, §§ 219(h), 224(b), 108 Stat. 4317, 4324; Apr. 24, 1996, Pub.L. 104–132, Title IV, §§ 436(a), (b)(1), 438(a), 440(c), (h), 110 Stat. 1275, 1277, 1279; Sept. 30, 1996, Pub.L. 104–208,

Div. C, Title III, §§ 306(a), (d), 308(g)(10)(H), 371(b)(6), 110 Stat. 3009–607, 3009–612, 3009–625, 3009–645.)

§ 243. Countries to which aliens shall be deported [8 U.S.C.A. § 1253]

(a) Penalty for failure to depart

(1) In general

Any alien against whom a final order of removal is outstanding by reason of being a member of any of the classes described in section 237(a) [8 U.S.C.A. § 1227(a)], who—

(A) willfully fails or refuses to depart from the United States within a period of 90 days from the date of the final order of removal under administrative processes, or if judicial review is had, then from the date of the final order of the court,

(B) willfully fails or refuses to make timely application in good faith for travel or other documents necessary to the alien's departure,

(C) connives or conspires, or takes any other action, designed to prevent or hamper or with the purpose of preventing or hampering the alien's departure pursuant to such, or

(D) willfully fails or refuses to present himself or herself for removal at the time and place required by the Attorney General pursuant to such order,

shall be fined under Title 18, or imprisoned not more than four years (or 10 years if the alien is a member of any of the classes described in paragraph (1)(E), (2), (3), or (4) of section 237(a) [8 U.S.C.A. § 1227(a)]), or both.

(2) Exception

It is not a violation of paragraph (1) to take any proper steps for the purpose of securing cancellation of or exemption from such order of removal or for the purpose of securing the alien's release from incarceration or custody.

(3) Suspension

The court may for good cause suspend the sentence of an alien under this subsection and order the alien's release under such conditions as the court may prescribe. In determining whether good cause has been shown to justify releasing the alien, the court shall take into account such factors as—

(A) the age, health, and period of detention of the alien;

(B) the effect of the alien's release upon the national security and public peace or safety;

(C) the likelihood of the alien's resuming or following a course of conduct which made or would make the alien deportable;

(D) the character of the efforts made by such alien himself and by representatives of the country or countries to which the alien's removal is directed to expedite the alien's departure from the United States;

(E) the reason for the inability of the Government of the United States to secure passports, other travel documents, or removal facilities from the country or countries to which the alien has been ordered removed; and

(F) the eligibility of the alien for discretionary relief under the immigration laws.

(b) Willful failure to comply with terms of release under supervision

An alien who shall willfully fail to comply with regulations or requirements issued pursuant to section 241(a)(3) [8 U.S.C.A. § 1231(a)(3)] or knowingly give false information in response to an inquiry under such section shall be fined not more than $1,000 or imprisoned for not more than one year, or both.

(c) Penalties relating to vessels and aircraft

(1) Civil penalties

(A) Failure to carry out certain orders

If the Attorney General is satisfied that a person has violated subsection (d) or (e) of section 241 [8 U.S.C.A. § 1231], the person shall pay to the Commissioner the sum of $2,000 for each violation.

(B) Failure to remove alien stowaways

If the Attorney General is satisfied that a person has failed to remove an alien stowaway as required under section 241(d)(2) [8 U.S.C.A. § 1231(d)(2)], the person shall pay to the Commissioner the sum of $5,000 for each alien stowaway not removed.

(C) No compromise

The Attorney General may not compromise the amount of such penalty under this paragraph.

(2) Clearing vessels and aircraft

(A) Clearance before decision on liability

A vessel or aircraft may be granted clearance before a decision on liability is made under paragraph (1) only if a bond approved by the Attorney General or an amount sufficient to pay the civil penalty is deposited with the Commissioner.

(B) Prohibition on clearance while penalty unpaid

A vessel or aircraft may not be granted clearance if a civil penalty imposed under paragraph (1) is not paid.

(d) Discontinuing granting visas to nationals of country denying or delaying accepting alien

On being notified by the Attorney General that the government of a foreign country denies or unreasonably delays accepting an alien who is a citizen, subject, national, or resident of that country after the Attorney General asks whether the government will accept the alien under this section, the Secretary of State shall order consular officers in that foreign country to discontinue granting immigrant visas or nonimmigrant visas, or both, to citizens, subjects, nationals, and residents of that country until the Attorney General notifies the Secretary that the country has accepted the alien.

(June 27, 1952, c. 477, Title II, ch. 5, § 243, 66 Stat. 212; Oct. 3, 1965, Pub.L. 89–236, § 11(f), 79 Stat. 918; Oct. 30, 1978, Pub.L. 95–549, Title I, § 104, 92 Stat. 2066; Mar. 17, 1980, Pub.L. 96–212, Title II, § 203(e), 94 Stat. 107; Dec. 29, 1981, Pub.L. 97–116, § 18(i), 95 Stat. 1620; Nov. 29, 1990, Pub.L. 101–649, Title V, § 515(a)(2), Title VI, § 603(b)(3), 104 Stat. 5053, 5085; Apr. 24, 1996, Pub.L. 104–132, Title IV, § 413(a), (f), 110 Stat. 1269; Sept. 30, 1996, Pub.L. 104–208, Div. C, Title III, § 307(a), 110 Stat. 3009–612.)

§ 244. Temporary protected status [8 U.S.C.A. § 1254]

(a) Granting of status

(1) In general

In the case of an alien who is a national of a foreign state designated under subsection (b) (or in the case of an alien having no nationality, is a person who last habitually resided in such designated state) and who meets the requirements of subsection (c), the Attorney General, in accordance with this section—

(A) may grant the alien temporary protected status in the United States and shall not remove the alien from the United States during the period in which such status is in effect, and

(B) shall authorize the alien to engage in employment in the United States and provide the alien with an "employment authorized" endorsement or other appropriate work permit.

(2) Duration of work authorization

Work authorization provided under this section shall be effective throughout the period the alien is in temporary protected status under this section.

(3) Notice

(A) Upon the granting of temporary protected status under this section, the Attorney General shall provide the alien with information concerning such status under this section.

(B) If, at the time of initiation of a removal proceeding against an alien, the foreign state (of which the alien is a national) is designated under subsection (b), the Attorney General shall promptly notify the alien of the temporary protected status that may be available under this section.

(C) If, at the time of designation of a foreign state under subsection (b), an alien (who is a national of such state) is in a removal proceeding under this title, the Attorney General shall promptly notify the alien of the temporary protected status that may be available under this section.

(D) Notices under this paragraph shall be provided in a form and language that the alien can understand.

(4) Temporary treatment for eligible aliens

(A) In the case of an alien who can establish a prima facie case of eligibility for benefits under paragraph (1), but for the fact that the period of registration under subsection (c)(1)(A)(iv) has not begun, until the alien has had a reasonable opportunity to register during the first 30 days of such period, the Attorney General shall provide for the benefits of paragraph (1).

(B) In the case of an alien who establishes a prima facie case of eligibility for benefits under paragraph (1), until a final determination with respect to the alien's eligibility for such benefits under paragraph (1) has been made, the alien shall be provided such benefits.

(5) Clarification

Nothing in this section shall be construed as authorizing the Attorney General to deny temporary protected status to an alien based on the alien's immigration status or to require any alien, as a condition of being granted such status, either to relinquish nonimmigrant or other status the alien may have or to execute any waiver of other rights under this Act. The granting of temporary protected status under this section shall not be considered to be inconsistent with the granting of nonimmigrant status under this Act.

(b) Designations

(1) In general

The Attorney General, after consultation with appropriate agencies of the Government, may designate any foreign state (or any part of such foreign state) under this subsection only if—

(A) the Attorney General finds that there is an ongoing armed conflict within the state and, due to such conflict, requiring the return of aliens who are nationals of that state to that state (or to the part of the state) would pose a serious threat to their personal safety;

(B) the Attorney General finds that—

(i) there has been an earthquake, flood, drought, epidemic, or other environmental disaster in the state resulting in a substantial, but temporary, disruption of living conditions in the area affected,

(ii) the foreign state is unable, temporarily, to handle adequately the return to the state of aliens who are nationals of the state, and

(iii) the foreign state officially has requested designation under this subparagraph; or

(C) the Attorney General finds that there exist extraordinary and temporary conditions in the foreign state that prevent aliens who are nationals of the state from returning to the state in safety, unless the Attorney General finds that permitting the aliens to remain temporarily in the United States is contrary to the national interest of the United States.

A designation of a foreign state (or part of such foreign state) under this paragraph shall not become effective unless notice of the designation (including a statement of the findings under this paragraph and the effective date of the designation) is published in the Federal Register. In such notice, the Attorney General shall also state an estimate of the number of nationals of the foreign state designated who are (or within the effective period of the designation are likely to become) eligible for temporary protected status under this section and their immigration status in the United States.

(2) Effective period of designation for foreign states

The designation of a foreign state (or part of such foreign state) under paragraph (1) shall—

(A) take effect upon the date of publication of the designation under such paragraph, or such later date as the Attorney General may specify in the notice published under such paragraph, and

(B) shall remain in effect until the effective date of the termination of the designation under paragraph (3)(B).

For purposes of this section, the initial period of designation of a foreign state (or part thereof) under paragraph (1) is the period, specified by the Attorney General, of not less than 6 months and not more than 18 months.

(3) Periodic review, terminations, and extensions of designations

(A) Periodic review

At least 60 days before end of the initial period of designation, and any extended period of designation, of a foreign state (or part thereof) under this section the Attorney General, after consultation with appropriate agencies of the Government, shall review the conditions in the foreign state (or part of such foreign state) for which a designation is in effect under this subsection and shall determine whether the conditions for such designation under this subsection continue to be met. The Attorney General shall provide on a timely basis for the publication of notice of each such determination (including the basis for the determination, and, in the case of an affirmative determination, the period of extension of designation under subparagraph (C)) in the Federal Register.

(B) Termination of designation

If the Attorney General determines under subparagraph (A) that a foreign state (or part of such foreign state) no longer continues to meet the conditions for designation under paragraph (1), the Attorney General shall terminate the designation by publishing notice in the Federal Register of the determination under this subparagraph (including the basis for the determination). Such termination is effective in accordance with subsection (d)(3), but shall not be effective earlier than 60 days after the date the notice is published or, if later, the expiration of the most recent previous extension under subparagraph (C).

(C) Extension of designation

If the Attorney General does not determine under subparagraph (A) that a foreign state (or part of such foreign state) no longer meets the conditions for designation under paragraph (1), the period of designation of the foreign state is extended for an additional period of 6 months (or, in the discretion of the Attorney General, a period of 12 or 18 months).

(4) Information concerning protected status at time of designations

At the time of a designation of a foreign state under this subsection, the Attorney General shall make available information respecting the temporary protected status made available to aliens who are nationals of such designated foreign state.

(5) Review

(A) Designations

There is no judicial review of any determination of the Attorney General with respect to the designation, or termination or extension of a designation, of a foreign state under this subsection.

(B) Application to individuals

The Attorney General shall establish an administrative procedure for the review of the denial of benefits to aliens under this subsection. Such procedure shall not prevent an alien from asserting protection under this section in removal proceedings if the alien demonstrates that the alien is a national of a state designated under paragraph (1).

(c) Aliens eligible for temporary protected status

(1) In general

(A) Nationals of designated foreign states

Subject to paragraph (3), an alien, who is a national of a state designated under subsection (b)(1) (or in the case of an alien having no nationality, is a person who last habitually resided in such designated state) meets the requirements of this paragraph only if—

(i) the alien has been continuously physically present in the United States since the effective date of the most recent designation of that state;

(ii) the alien has continuously resided in the United States since such date as the Attorney General may designate;

(iii) the alien is admissible as an immigrant, except as otherwise provided under paragraph (2)(A), and is not ineligible for temporary protected status under paragraph (2)(B); and

(iv) to the extent and in a manner which the Attorney General establishes, the alien registers for the temporary protected status under this section during a registration period of not less than 180 days.

(B) Registration fee

The Attorney General may require payment of a reasonable fee as a condition of registering an alien under subparagraph (A)(iv) (including providing an alien with an "employment authorized" endorsement or other appropriate work permit under this section). The amount of any such fee shall not exceed $50. In the case of aliens registered pursuant to a designation under this section made after July 17, 1991, the Attorney General may impose a separate, additional fee for providing an alien with documentation of work authorization. Notwithstanding section 3302 of Title 31, all fees collected under this subparagraph shall be credited to the appropriation to be used in carrying out this section.

(2) Eligibility standards

(A) Waiver of certain grounds for inadmissibility

In the determination of an alien's admissibility for purposes of subparagraph (A)(iii) of paragraph (1)—

(i) the provisions of paragraphs (5) and (7)(A) of section 212(a) [8 U.S.C.A. § 1182(a)] shall not apply;

(ii) except as provided in clause (iii), the Attorney General may waive any other provision of section 212(a) [8 U.S.C.A. § 1182(a)] in the case of individual aliens for humanitarian purposes, to assure family unity, or when it is otherwise in the public interest; but

(iii) the Attorney General may not waive—

(I) paragraphs (2)(A) and (2)(B) (relating to criminals) of such section,

(II) paragraph (2)(C) of such section (relating to drug offenses), except for so much of such paragraph as relates to a single offense of simple possession of 30 grams or less of marijuana, or

(III) paragraphs (3)(A), (3)(B), (3)(C), and (3)(E) of such section (relating to national security and participation in the Nazi persecutions or those who have engaged in genocide).

(B) Aliens ineligible

An alien shall not be eligible for temporary protected status under this section if the Attorney General finds that—

(i) the alien has been convicted of any felony or 2 or more misdemeanors committed in the United States, or

(ii) the alien is described in section 208(b)(2)(A) [8 U.S.C.A. § 1158(b)(2)(A)].

(3) Withdrawal of temporary protected status

The Attorney General shall withdraw temporary protected status granted to an alien under this section if—

(A) the Attorney General finds that the alien was not in fact eligible for such status under this section,

(B) except as provided in paragraph (4) and permitted in subsection (f)(3), the alien has not remained continuously physically present in the United States from the date the alien first was granted temporary protected status under this section, or

(C) the alien fails, without good cause, to register with the Attorney General annually, at the end of each 12–month period after the granting of such status, in a form and manner specified by the Attorney General.

(4) Treatment of brief, casual, and innocent departures and certain other absences

(A) For purposes of paragraphs (1)(A)(i) and (3)(B), an alien shall not be considered to have failed to maintain continuous physical presence in the United States by virtue of brief, casual, and innocent absences from the United States, without regard to whether such absences were authorized by the Attorney General.

(B) For purposes of paragraph (1)(A)(ii), an alien shall not be considered to have failed to maintain continuous residence in the United States by reason of a brief, casual, and innocent absence described in subparagraph (A) or due merely to a brief temporary trip abroad required by emergency or extenuating circumstances outside the control of the alien.

(5) Construction

Nothing in this section shall be construed as authorizing an alien to apply for admission to, or to be admitted to, the Unites States in order to apply for temporary protected status under this section.

(6) Confidentiality of information

The Attorney General shall establish procedures to protect the confidentiality of information provided by aliens under this section.

(d) Documentation

(1) Initial issuance

Upon the granting of temporary protected status to an alien under this section, the Attorney General shall provide for the issuance of such temporary documentation and authorization as may be necessary to carry out the purposes of this section.

(2) Period of validity

Subject to paragraph (3), such documentation shall be valid during the initial period of designation of the foreign state (or part thereof) involved and any extension of such period. The Attorney General may stagger the periods of validity of the documentation and authorization in order to provide for an orderly renewal of such documentation and authorization and for an orderly transition (under paragraph (3)) upon the termination of a designation of a foreign state (or any part of such foreign state).

(3) Effective date of terminations

If the Attorney General terminates the designation of a foreign state (or part of such foreign state) under subsection (b)(3)(B), such termination shall only apply to documentation and authorization issued or renewed after the effective date of the publication of notice of the determination under that subsection (or, at the Attorney General's option, after such period after the effective date of the determination as the Attorney General determines to be appropriate in order to provide for an orderly transition).

(4) Detention of the alien

An alien provided temporary protected status under this section shall not be detained by the Attorney General on the basis of the alien's immigration status in the United States.

(e) Relation of period of temporary protected status to cancellation of removal

With respect to an alien granted temporary protected status under this section, the period of such status shall not be counted as a period of physical presence in the United States for purposes of section 240A(a) [8 U.S.C.A. § 1229b(a)], unless the Attorney General determines that extreme hardship exists. Such period shall not cause a break in the continuity of residence of the period before and after such period for purposes of such section.

(f) Benefits and status during period of temporary protected status

During a period in which an alien is granted temporary protected status under this section—

(1) the alien shall not be considered to be permanently residing in the United States under color of law;

(2) the alien may be deemed ineligible for public assistance by a State (as defined in section 101(a)(36) [8 U.S.C.A. § 1101(a)(36)]) or any political subdivision thereof which furnishes such assistance;

(3) the alien may travel abroad with the prior consent of the Attorney General; and

(4) for purposes of adjustment of status under section 245 [8 U.S.C.A. § 1255] and change of status under section 248 [8 U.S.C.A. § 1258], the alien shall be considered as being in, and maintaining, lawful status as a nonimmigrant.

(g) Exclusive remedy

Except as otherwise specifically provided, this section shall constitute the exclusive authority of the Attorney General under law to permit aliens who are or may become otherwise deportable or have been paroled into the United States to remain in the United States temporarily because of their particular nationality or region of foreign state of nationality.

(h) Limitation on consideration in Senate of legislation adjusting status

(1) In general

Except as provided in paragraph (2), it shall not be in order in the Senate to consider any bill, resolution, or amendment that—

(A) provides for adjustment to lawful temporary or permanent resident alien status for any alien receiving temporary protected status under this section, or

(B) has the effect of amending this subsection or limiting the application of this subsection.

(2) Supermajority required

Paragraph (1) may be waived or suspended in the Senate only by the affirmative vote of three-fifths of the Members duly chosen and sworn. An affirmative vote of three-fifths of the Members of the Senate duly chosen and sworn shall be required in the Senate to sustain an appeal of the ruling of the Chair on a point of order raised under paragraph (1).

(3) Rules

Paragraphs (1) and (2) are enacted—

(A) as an exercise of the rulemaking power of the Senate and as such they are deemed a part of the rules of the Senate, but applicable only with respect to the matters described in paragraph (1) and supersede other rules of the Senate only to the extent that such paragraphs are inconsistent therewith; and

(B) with full recognition of the constitutional right of the Senate to change such rules at any time, in the same manner as in the case of any other rule of the Senate.

(i) Annual report and review

(1) Annual report

Not later than March 1 of each year (beginning with 1992), the Attorney General, after consultation with the appropriate agencies of the Government, shall submit a report to the Committees on the Judiciary of the House of Representatives and of the Senate on the operation of this section during the previous year. Each report shall include—

(A) a listing of the foreign states or parts thereof designated under this section,

(B) the number of nationals of each such state who have been granted temporary protected status under this section and their immigration status before being granted such status, and

(C) an explanation of the reasons why foreign states or parts thereof were designated under subsection (b)(1) and, with respect to foreign states or parts thereof previously designated, why the designation was terminated or extended under subsection (b)(3).

(2) Committee report

No later than 180 days after the date of receipt of such a report, the Committee on the Judiciary of each House of Congress shall report to its respective House such oversight findings and legislation as it deems appropriate.

(June 27, 1952, c. 477, Title II, ch. 5, § 244, formerly § 244A, as added and amended Nov. 29, 1990, Pub.L. 101–649, Title III, § 302(a), Title VI, § 603(a)(24), 104 Stat. 5030, 5084; Dec. 12, 1991, Pub.L. 102–232, Title III, §§ 304(b), 307(*l*)(5), 105 Stat. 1749, 1756; Oct. 25, 1994, Pub.L. 103–416, Title II, § 219(j), (z)(2), 108 Stat. 4317, 4318; renumbered § 244 and amended Sept.

30, 1996, Pub.L. 104–208, Div. C, Title III, § 308(b)(7), (e)(1)(G), (11), (g)(7)(E)(i), (g)(8)(A)(i), 110 Stat. 3009–615, 3009–619, 3009–620, 3009–624.)

CHAPTER V—ADJUSTMENT AND CHANGE OF STATUS*

§ 245. Adjustment of status of nonimmigrant to that of person admitted for permanent residence [8 U.S.C.A. § 1255]

(a) Status as person admitted for permanent residence on application and eligibility for immigrant visa

The status of an alien who was inspected and admitted or paroled into the United States may be adjusted by the Attorney General, in his discretion and under such regulations as he may prescribe, to that of an alien lawfully admitted for permanent residence if **(1)** the alien makes an application for such adjustment, **(2)** the alien is eligible to receive an immigrant visa and is admissible to the United States for permanent residence, and **(3)** an immigrant visa is immediately available to him at the time his application is filed.

(b) Record of lawful admission for permanent residence; reduction of preference visas

Upon the approval of an application for adjustment made under subsection (a), the Attorney General shall record the alien's lawful admission for permanent residence as of the date the order of the Attorney General approving the application for the adjustment of status is made, and the Secretary of State shall reduce by one the number of the preference visas authorized to be issued under sections 202 [8 U.S.C.A. § 1152] and 203 [8 U.S.C.A. § 1153] within the class to which the alien is chargeable for the fiscal year then current.

(c) Alien crewmen, aliens continuing or accepting unauthorized employment, and aliens admitted in transit without visa

Subsection (a) shall not be applicable to **(1)** an alien crewman; **(2)** subject to subsection (k), an alien (other than an immediate relative as defined in section 201(b) [8 U.S.C.A. § 1151(b)] or a special immigrant described in section 101(a)(27)(H), (I), (J), or (K) [8 U.S.C.A. § 1101(a)(27)(H), (I), (J), or (K)] who hereafter continues in or accepts unauthorized employment prior to filing an application for adjustment of status or who is in unlawful immigration status on the date of filing the application for adjustment of status or who has failed (other than through no fault of his own or for technical reasons) to maintain continuously a lawful status since entry into the United States; or **(3)** any alien admitted in transit without visa under section 212(d)(4)(C) [8

* Pub.L. 104–208, section 308(a)(2), amended the table of contents of the Immigration and Nationality Act to show that renumbered §§ 242 to 244 are part of chapter IV, with chapter V starting with § 245. This suggests Congressional intent to move §§ 242 to 244 to chapter IV, but there is no specific directory language that actually moves these sections.

U.S.C.A. § 1182(d)(4)(C)]; **(4)** an alien (other than an immediate relative as defined in section 201(b) [8 U.S.C.A. § 1151(b)] who was admitted as a nonimmigrant visitor without a visa under section 212(*l*) [8 U.S.C.A. § 1182(*l*)] or section 217 [8 U.S.C.A. § 1187]; **(5)** an alien who was admitted as a nonimmigrant described in section 101(a)(15)(S) [8 U.S.C.A. § 1101(a)(15)(S)], [sic] **(6)** an alien who is deportable under section 237(a)(4)(B) [8 U.S.C.A. § 1227(a)(4)(B)]; **(7)** any alien who seeks adjustment of status to that of an immigrant under section 203(b) [8 U.S.C.A. § 1153(b)] and is not in a lawful nonimmigrant status; or **(8)** any alien who was employed while the alien was an unauthorized alien, as defined in section 274A(h)(3) [8 U.S.C.A. § 1324a(h)(3)], or who has otherwise violated the terms of a nonimmigrant visa.

(d) Alien admitted for permanent residence on conditional basis; fiancee or fiance of citizen

The Attorney General may not adjust, under subsection (a), the status of an alien lawfully admitted to the United States for permanent residence on a conditional basis under section 216 [8 U.S.C.A. § 1186a]. The Attorney General may not adjust, under subsection (a), the status of a nonimmigrant alien described in section 101(a)(15)(K) [8 U.S.C.A. § 1101(a)(15)(K)] (relating to an alien fiancee or fiance or the minor child of such alien) except to that of an alien lawfully admitted to the United States on a conditional basis under section 216 [8 U.S.C.A. § 1186a] as a result of the marriage of the nonimmigrant (or, in the case of a minor child, the parent) to the citizen who filed the petition to accord that alien's nonimmigrant status under section 101(a)(15)(K) [8 U.S.C.A. § 1101(a)(15)(K)].

(e) Restrictions on adjustment of status based on marriages entered while in exclusion or deportation proceedings; bona fide marriage exception

(1) Except as provided in paragraph (3), an alien who is seeking to receive an immigrant visa on the basis of a marriage which was entered into during the period described in paragraph (2) may not have the alien's status adjusted under subsection (a).

(2) The period described in this paragraph is the period during which administrative or judicial proceedings are pending regarding the alien's right to be admitted or remain in the United States.

(3) Paragraph (1) and section 204(g) [8 U.S.C.A. § 1154(g)] shall not apply with respect to a marriage if the alien establishes by clear and convincing evidence to the satisfaction of the Attorney General that the marriage was entered into in good faith and in accordance with the laws of the place where the marriage took place and the marriage was not entered into for the purpose of procuring the alien's admission as an immigrant and no fee or other consideration was given (other than a fee or other consideration to an attorney for assistance in preparation of a lawful petition) for the filing of a petition under section 204(a) [8 U.S.C.A. § 1154(a)] or

214(d) [8 U.S.C.A. § 1184(d)] with respect to the alien spouse or alien son or daughter. In accordance with regulations, there shall be only one level of administrative appellate review for each alien under the previous sentence.

(f) Limitation on adjustment of status

The Attorney General may not adjust, under subsection (a), the status of an alien lawfully admitted to the United States for permanent residence on a conditional basis under section 216A [8 U.S.C.A. § 1186b].

(g) Special immigrants

In applying this section to a special immigrant described in section 101(a)(27)(K) [8 U.S.C.A. § 1101(a)(27)(K)], such an immigrant shall be deemed, for purposes of subsection (a), to have been paroled into the United States.

(h) Application with respect to special immigrants

In applying this section to a special immigrant described in section 101(a)(27)(J) [8 U.S.C.A. § 1101(a)(27)(J)]—

(1) such an immigrant shall be deemed, for purposes of subsection (a), to have been paroled into the United States; and

(2) in determining the alien's admissibility as an immigrant—

(A) paragraphs (4), (5)(A), and (7)(A) of section 212(a) [8 U.S.C.A. § 1182(a)] shall not apply, and

(B) the Attorney General may waive other paragraphs of section 212(a) [8 U.S.C.A. § 1182(a)] (other than paragraphs (2)(A), (2)(B), (2)(C) (except for so much of such paragraph as related to a single offense of simple possession of 30 grams or less of marijuana), (3)(A), (3)(B), (3)(C), and (3)(E)) in the case of individual aliens for humanitarian purposes, family unity, or when it is otherwise in the public interest.

The relationship between an alien and the alien's natural parents or prior adoptive parents shall not be considered a factor in making a waiver under paragraph (2)(B). Nothing in this subsection or section 101(a)(27)(J) [8 U.S.C.A. § 1101(a)(27)(J)] shall be construed as authorizing an alien to apply for admission or be admitted to the United States in order to obtain special immigrant status described in such section.

(i) Adjustment of status of certain aliens physically present in United States

(1) Notwithstanding the provisions of subsections (a) and (c) of this section, an alien physically present in the United States—

(A) who—

(i) entered the United States without inspection; or

(ii) is within one of the classes enumerated in subsection (c) of this section; and

(B) who is the beneficiary (including a spouse or child of the principal alien, if eligible to receive a visa under section 203(d) [8 U.S.C.A. § 1153(d)]) of—

(i) a petition for classification under section 204 [8 U.S.C.A. § 1154] that was filed with the Attorney General on or before January 14, 1998; or

(ii) an application for a labor certification under section 212(a)(5)(A) [8 U.S.C.A. § 1182(a)(5)(A)] that was filed pursuant to the regulations of the Secretary of Labor on or before such date;

may apply to the Attorney General for the adjustment of his or her status to that of an alien lawfully admitted for permanent residence. The Attorney General may accept such application only if the alien remits with such application a sum equalling $1,000 as of the date of receipt of the application, but such sum shall not be required from a child under the age of seventeen, or an alien who is the spouse or unmarried child of an individual who obtained temporary or permanent resident status under section 210 [8 U.S.C.A. § 1160] or 245A [8 U.S.C.A. § 1255a] or section 202 of the Immigration Reform and Control Act of 1986 at any date, who—

(i) as of May 5, 1988, was the unmarried child or spouse of the individual who obtained temporary or permanent resident status under section 210 [8 U.S.C.A. § 1160] or 245A [8 U.S.C.A. § 1255a] or section 202 of the Immigration Reform and Control Act of 1986;

(ii) entered the United States before May 5, 1988, resided in the United States on May 5, 1988, and is not a lawful permanent resident; and

(iii) applied for benefits under section 301(a) of the Immigration Act of 1990. The sum specified herein shall be in addition to the fee normally required for the processing of an application under this section.

(2) Upon receipt of such an application and the sum hereby required, the Attorney General may adjust the status of the alien to that of an alien lawfully admitted for permanent residence if—

(A) the alien is eligible to receive an immigrant visa and is admissible to the United States for permanent residence; and

(B) an immigrant visa is immediately available to the alien at the time the application is filed.

(3)(A) The portion of each application fee (not to exceed $200) that the Attorney General determines is required to process an application under this section and is remitted to the Attorney General pursuant to paragraphs (1) and (2) of this subsection shall be disposed of by the Attorney General as provided in subsections (m), (n), and (*o*) of section 286 [8 U.S.C.A. § 1356].

(B) Any remaining portion of such fees remitted under such paragraphs shall be deposited by the Attorney General into the Breached Bond/Detention Fund established under section 286(r) [8 U.S.C.A. § 1356(s)].

(j) Adjustment to permanent resident status

(1) If, in the opinion of the Attorney General—

(A) a nonimmigrant admitted into the United States under section 101(a)(15)(S)(i) [8 U.S.C.A. § 1101(a)(15)(S)(i)] has supplied information described in subclause (I) of such section; and

(B) the provision of such information has substantially contributed to the success of an authorized criminal investigation or the prosecution of an individual described in subclause (III) of that section,

the Attorney General may adjust the status of the alien (and the spouse, married and unmarried sons and daughters, and parents of the alien if admitted under that section) to that of an alien lawfully admitted for permanent residence if the alien is not described in section 212(a)(3)(E) [8 U.S.C.A. § 1182(a)(3)(E)].

(2) If, in the sole discretion of the Attorney General—

(A) a nonimmigrant admitted into the United States under section 101(a)(15)(S)(ii) [8 U.S.C.A. § 1101(a)(15)(S)(ii)] has supplied information described in subclause (I) of such section, and

(B) the provision of such information has substantially contributed to—

(i) the prevention or frustration of an act of terrorism against a United States person or United States property, or

(ii) the success of an authorized criminal investigation of, or the prosecution of, an individual involved in such an act of terrorism, and

(C) the nonimmigrant has received a reward under section 2708(a) of Title 22,

the Attorney General may adjust the status of the alien (and the spouse, married and unmarried sons and daughters, and parents of the alien if admitted under such section) to that of an alien lawfully admitted for permanent residence if the alien is not described in section 212(a)(3)(E) [8 U.S.C.A. § 1182(a)(3)(E)].

(3) Upon the approval of adjustment of status under paragraph (1) or (2), the Attorney General shall record the alien's lawful admission for permanent residence as of the date of such approval and the Secretary of State shall reduce by one the number of visas authorized to be issued under sections 201(d) [8 U.S.C.A. § 1151(d)] and 203(b)(4) [8 U.S.C.A. § 1153(b)(4)] for the fiscal year then current.

(k) Inapplicability of certain provisions for certain employment-based immigrants

An alien who is eligible to receive an immigrant visa under paragraph (1), (2), or (3) of section 203(b) [8 U.S.C.A. § 1153(b)] (or, in the case of an alien who is an immigrant described in section 101(a)(27)(C) [8 U.S.C.A. § 1101(a)(27)(C)], under section 203(b)(4) [8 U.S.C.A. § 1153(b)(4)]) may adjust status pursuant to subsection (a) and notwithstanding subsection (c)(2), (c)(7), and (c)(8), if—

(1) the alien, on the date of filing an application for adjustment of status, is present in the United States pursuant to a lawful admission;

(2) the alien, subsequent to such lawful admission has not, for an aggregate period exceeding 180 days—

✓ **(A)** failed to maintain, continuously, a lawful status;

(B) engaged in unauthorized employment; or

(C) otherwise violated the terms and conditions of the alien's admission.

(June 27, 1952, c. 477, Title II, ch. 5, § 245, 66 Stat. 217; Aug. 21, 1958, Pub.L. 85–700, § 1, 72 Stat. 699; July 14, 1960, Pub.L. 86–648, § 10, 74 Stat. 505; Oct. 3, 1965, Pub.L. 89–236, § 13, 79 Stat. 918; Oct. 20, 1976, Pub.L. 94–571, § 6, 90 Stat. 2705; Dec. 29, 1981, Pub.L. 97–116, § 5(d)(2), 95 Stat. 1614; Nov. 6, 1986, Pub.L. 99–603, Title III, §§ 117, 313(c), 100 Stat. 3384, 3438; Nov. 6, 1986, Pub.L. 99–603, Title III, § 313(c), as amended Oct. 24, 1988, Pub.L. 100–525, § 2(p)(3), 102 Stat. 2613; Nov. 10, 1986, Pub.L. 99–639, §§ 2(e), 3(b), 5(a), 100 Stat. 3542, 3543; Nov. 10, 1986, Pub.L. 99–639, § 3(b), as amended Oct. 24, 1988, Pub.L. 100–525, § 7(b), 102 Stat. 2616; Oct. 24, 1988, Pub.L. 100–525, § 2(f)(1), 102 Stat. 2611; Nov. 29, 1990, Pub.L. 101–649, Title I, §§ 121(b)(4), 162(e)(3), Title VII, § 702(a), 104 Stat. 4994, 5011, 5086; Oct. 1, 1991, Pub.L. 102–110, § 2(c), 105 Stat. 556; Dec. 12, 1991, Pub.L. 102–232, Title III, §§ 302(d)(2), (e)(7), 308(a), 105 Stat. 1744, 1746, 1757; Aug. 26, 1994, Pub.L. 103–317, Title V, § 506(b), 108 Stat. 1765; Sept. 13, 1994, Pub.L. 103–322, Title XIII, § 130003(c), 108 Stat. 2025; Oct. 25, 1994, Pub.L. 103–416, Title II, § 219(k), 108 Stat. 4317; Apr. 24, 1996, Pub.L. 104–132, Title IV, § 413(d), 110 Stat. 1269; Sept. 30, 1996, Pub.L. 104–208, Div. C, Title III, §§ 308(f)(1)(O), (2)(C), (g)(10)(B), 375, 376(a), Title VI, § 671(a)(4)(A), (5), 110 Stat. 3009–621, 3009–625, 3009–648, 3009–721; Nov. 26, 1997, Pub.L. 105–119, Title I, §§ 110(3), 111(a), (c), 111 Stat. 2458.)

§ 245A. Adjustment of status of certain entrants before January 1, 1982, to that of person admitted for lawful residence [8 U.S.C.A. § 1255a]

(a) Temporary resident status

The Attorney General shall adjust the status of an alien to that of an alien lawfully admitted for temporary residence if the alien meets the following requirements:

(1) Timely application

(A) During application period

Except as provided in subparagraph (B), the alien must apply for such adjustment during the 12–month period beginning on a date (not later than 180 days after November 6, 1986) designated by the Attorney General.

(B) Application within 30 days of show-cause order

An alien who, at any time during the first 11 months of the 12–month period described in subparagraph (A) is the subject of an order to show cause issued under section 242 [8 U.S.C.A. § 1252] (as in effect before October 1, 1996), must make application under this section not later than the end of the 30–day period beginning either on the first day of such 12–month period or on the date of the issuance of such order, whichever day is later.

(C) Information included in application

Each application under this subsection shall contain such information as the Attorney General may require, including information on living relatives of the applicant with respect to whom a petition for preference or other status may be filed by the applicant at any later date under section 204(a) [8 U.S.C.A. § 1154(a)].

(2) Continuous unlawful residence since 1982

(A) In general

The alien must establish that he entered the United States before January 1, 1982, and that he has resided continuously in the United States in an unlawful status since such date and through the date the application is filed under this subsection.

(B) Nonimmigrants

In the case of an alien who entered the United States as a nonimmigrant before January 1, 1982, the alien must establish that the alien's period of authorized stay as a nonimmigrant expired before such date through the passage of time or the alien's unlawful status was known to the Government as of such date.

(C) Exchange visitors

If the alien was at any time a nonimmigrant exchange alien (as defined in section 101(a)(15)(J) [8 U.S.C.A. § 1101(a)(15)(J)]), the alien must establish that the alien was not subject to the two-year foreign residence requirement of section 212(e) [8 U.S.C.A. § 1182(e)] or has fulfilled that requirement or received a waiver thereof.

(3) Continuous physical presence since November 6, 1986

(A) In general

The alien must establish that the alien has been continuously physically present in the United States since November 6, 1986.

(B) Treatment of brief, casual, and innocent absences

An alien shall not be considered to have failed to maintain continuous physical presence in the United States for purposes of subparagraph (A) by virtue of brief, casual, and innocent absences from the United States.

(C) Admissions

Nothing in this section shall be construed as authorizing an alien to apply for admission to, or to be admitted to, the United States in order to apply for adjustment of status under this subsection.

(4) Admissible as immigrant

The alien must establish that he—

(A) is admissible to the United States as an immigrant, except as otherwise provided under subsection (d)(2),

(B) has not been convicted of any felony or of three or more misdemeanors committed in the United States,

(C) has not assisted in the persecution of any person or persons on account of race, religion, nationality, membership in a particular social group, or political opinion, and

(D) is registered or registering under the Military Selective Service Act [50 U.S.C.A.App. § 451 et seq.], if the alien is required to be so registered under that Act.

For purposes of this subsection, an alien in the status of a Cuban and Haitian entrant described in paragraph (1) or (2)(A) of section 501(e) of Public Law 96–422 [8 U.S.C.A. § 1522 note] shall be considered to have entered the United States and to be in an unlawful status in the United States.

(b) Subsequent adjustment to permanent residence and nature of temporary resident status

(1) Adjustment to permanent residence

The Attorney General shall adjust the status of any alien provided lawful temporary resident status under subsection (a) to that of an alien lawfully admitted for permanent residence if the alien meets the following requirements:

(A) Timely application after one year's residence

The alien must apply for such adjustment during the 2–year period beginning with the nineteenth month that begins after the date the alien was granted such temporary resident status.

2 YR period to apply (19 mo after temp. resd status granted)

(B) Continuous residence

(i) In general

The alien must establish that he has continuously resided in the United States since the date the alien was granted such temporary resident status.

(ii) Treatment of certain absences

An alien shall not be considered to have lost the continuous residence referred to in clause (i) by reason of an absence from the United States permitted under paragraph (3)(A).

(C) Admissible as immigrant

The alien must establish that he—

(i) is admissible to the United States as an immigrant, except as otherwise provided under subsection (d)(2), and

(ii) has not been convicted of any felony or three or more misdemeanors committed in the United States.

(D) Basic citizenship skills

(i) In general

The alien must demonstrate that he either—

(I) meets the requirements of section 312(a) [8 U.S.C.A. § 1423(a)] (relating to minimal understanding of ordinary English and a knowledge and understanding of the history and government of the United States), or

(II) is satisfactorily pursuing a course of study (recognized by the Attorney General) to achieve such an understanding of English and such a knowledge and understanding of the history and government of the United States.

(ii) Exception for elderly or developmentally disabled individuals

The Attorney General may, in his discretion, waive all or part of the requirements of clause (i) in the case of an alien who is 65 years of age or older or who is developmentally disabled.

(iii) Relation to naturalization examination

In accordance with regulations of the Attorney General, an alien who has demonstrated under clause (i)(I) that the alien meets the requirements of section 312(a) [8 U.S.C.A. § 1423(a)] may be considered to have satisfied the requirements of that section for purposes of becoming naturalized as a citizen of the United States under title III.

(2) Termination of temporary residence

The Attorney General shall provide for termination of temporary resident status granted an alien under subsection (a)—

(A) if it appears to the Attorney General that the alien was in fact not eligible for such status;

(B) if the alien commits an act that **(i)** makes the alien inadmissible to the United States as an immigrant, except as otherwise provided under subsection (d)(2), or **(ii)** is convicted of any felony or three or more misdemeanors committed in the United States; or

(C) at the end of the 43rd month beginning after the date the alien is granted such status, unless the alien has filed an application for adjustment of such status pursuant to paragraph (1) and such application has not been denied.

(3) Authorized travel and employment during temporary residence

During the period an alien is in lawful temporary resident status granted under subsection (a)—

(A) Authorization of travel abroad

The Attorney General shall, in accordance with regulations, permit the alien to return to the United States after such brief and casual trips abroad as reflect an intention on the part of the alien to adjust to lawful permanent resident status under paragraph (1) and after brief temporary trips abroad occasioned by a family obligation involving an occurrence such as the illness or death of a close relative or other family need.

(B) Authorization of employment

The Attorney General shall grant the alien authorization to engage in employment in the United States and provide to that alien an "employment authorized" endorsement or other appropriate work permit.

(c) Applications for adjustment of status

(1) To whom may be made

The Attorney General shall provide that applications for adjustment of status under subsection (a) may be filed—

(A) with the Attorney General, or

(B) with a qualified designated entity, but only if the applicant consents to the forwarding of the application to the Attorney General.

As used in this section, the term "qualified designated entity" means an organization or person designated under paragraph (2).

(2) Designation of qualified entities to receive applications

For purposes of assisting in the program of legalization provided under this section, the Attorney General—

(A) shall designate qualified voluntary organizations and other qualified State, local, and community organizations, and

(B) may designate such other persons as the Attorney General determines are qualified and have substantial experience, demonstrated competence, and traditional long-term involvement in the preparation and submittal of applications for adjustment of status under section 209 [8 U.S.C.A. § 1159] or 245 [8 U.S.C.A. § 1255], Public Law 89–732 [8 U.S.C.A. § 1255 note], or Public Law 95–145.

(3) Treatment of applications by designated entities

Each qualified designated entity must agree to forward to the Attorney General applications filed with it in accordance with paragraph (1)(B) but not to forward to the Attorney General applications filed with it unless the applicant has consented to such forwarding. No such entity may make a determination required by this section to be made by the Attorney General.

(4) Limitation on access to information

Files and records of qualified designated entities relating to an alien's seeking assistance or information with respect to filing an application under this section are confidential and the Attorney General and the Service shall not have access to such files or records relating to an alien without the consent of the alien.

(5) Confidentiality of information

(A) In general

Except as provided in this paragraph, neither the Attorney General, nor any other official or employee of the Department of Justice, or bureau or agency thereof, may—

(i) use the information furnished by the applicant pursuant to an application filed under this section for any purpose other than to make a determination on the application, for enforcement of paragraph (6), or for the preparation of reports to Congress under section 404 of the Immigration Reform and Control Act of 1986;

(ii) make any publication whereby the information furnished by any particular applicant can be identified; or

(iii) permit anyone other than the sworn officers and employees of the Department or bureau or agency or, with respect to applications filed with a designated entity, that designated entity, to examine individual applications.

(B) Required disclosures

The Attorney General shall provide the information furnished under this section, and any other information derived from such furnished information, to a duly recognized law enforcement entity in connection with a criminal investigation or prosecution, when such information is requested in writing by such entity, or to an official coroner for purposes of affirmatively identifying a deceased individual (whether or not such individual is deceased as a result of a crime).

(C) Authorized disclosures

The Attorney General may provide, in the Attorney General's discretion, for the furnishing of information furnished under this section in the same manner and circumstances as census information may be disclosed by the Secretary of Commerce under section 8 of Title 13.

(D) Construction

(i) In general

Nothing in this paragraph shall be construed to limit the use, or release, for immigration enforcement purposes or law enforcement purposes of information contained in files or records of the Service pertaining to an application filed under this section, other than information furnished by an applicant pursuant to the application, or any other information derived from the application, that is not available from any other source.

(ii) Criminal convictions

Information concerning whether the applicant has at any time been convicted of a crime may be used or released for immigration enforcement or law enforcement purposes.

(E) Crime

Whoever knowingly uses, publishes, or permits information to be examined in violation of this paragraph shall be fined not more than $10,000.

(6) Penalties for false statements in applications

Whoever files an application for adjustment of status under this section and knowingly and willfully falsifies, misrepresents, conceals, or covers up a material fact or makes any false, fictitious, or fraudulent statements or representations, or makes or uses any false writing or document knowing the same to contain any false, fictitious, or fraudulent statement or entry, shall be fined in accordance with Title 18, or imprisoned not more than five years, or both.

(7) Application fees

(A) Fee schedule

The Attorney General shall provide for a schedule of fees to be charged for the filing of applications for adjustment under subsection (a) or (b)(1). The Attorney General shall provide for an additional fee for filing an application for adjustment under subsection (b)(1) after the end of the first year of the 2-year period described in subsection (b)(1)(A).

Fee

(B) Use of fees

The Attorney General shall deposit payments received under this paragraph in a separate account and amounts in such account shall be available, without fiscal year limitation, to cover administrative and other expenses incurred in connection with the review of applications filed under this section.

(C) Immigration-related unfair employment practices

Not to exceed $3,000,000 of the unobligated balances remaining in the account established in subparagraph (B) shall be available in fiscal year 1992 and each fiscal year thereafter for grants, contracts, and cooperative agreements to community-based organizations for outreach programs, to be administered by the Office of Special Counsel for Immigration-Related Unfair Employment Practices: Provided, That such amounts shall be in addition to any funds appropriated to the Office of Special Counsel for such purposes: Provided further, That none of the funds made available by this section shall be used by the Office of Special Counsel to establish regional offices.

(d) Waiver of numerical limitations and certain grounds for exclusion

(1) Numerical limitations do not apply

The numerical limitations of sections 201 [8 U.S.C.A. § 1151] and 202 [8 U.S.C.A. § 1152] shall not apply to the adjustment of aliens to lawful permanent resident status under this section.

(2) Waiver of grounds for exclusion

In the determination of an alien's admissibility under subsections (a)(4)(A), (b)(1)(C)(i), and (b)(2)(B)—

(A) Grounds of exclusion not applicable

The provisions of paragraphs (5) and (7)(A) of section 212(a) [8 U.S.C.A. § 1182(a)] shall not apply.

(B) Waiver of other grounds

(i) In general

Except as provided in clause (ii), the Attorney General may waive any other provision of section 212(a) [8 U.S.C.A. § 1182(a)] in the case of individual aliens for humanitarian purposes, to assure family unity, or when it is otherwise in the public interest.

(ii) Grounds that may not be waived

The following provisions of section 212(a) [8 U.S.C.A. § 1182(a)] may not be waived by the Attorney General under clause (i):

(I) Paragraphs (2)(A) and (2)(B) (relating to criminals).

(II) Paragraph (2)(C) (relating to drug offenses), except for so much of such paragraph as relates to a single offense of simple possession of 30 grams or less of marihuana.

(III) Paragraph (3) (relating to security and related grounds).

(IV) Paragraph (4) (relating to aliens likely to become public charges) insofar as it relates to an application for adjustment to permanent residence.

Subclause (IV) (prohibiting the waiver of section 212(a)(4) [8 U.S.C.A. § 1182(a)(4)]) shall not apply to an alien who is or was an aged, blind, or disabled individual (as defined in section 1382c(a)(1) of Title 42).

(iii) Special rule for determination of public charge

An alien is not ineligible for adjustment of status under this section due to being inadmissible under section 212(a)(4) [8 U.S.C.A. § 1182(a)(4)] if the alien demonstrates a history of employment in the United States evidencing self-support without receipt of public cash assistance.

(C) Medical examination

The alien shall be required, at the alien's expense, to undergo such a medical examination (including a determination of immunization status) as is appropriate and conforms to generally accepted professional standards of medical practice.

(e) Temporary stay of deportation and work authorization for certain applicants

(1) Before application period

The Attorney General shall provide that in the case of an alien who is apprehended before the beginning of the application period described in subsection (a)(1)(A) and who can establish a prima facie case of eligibility to have his status adjusted under subsection (a) (but for the fact that he may not apply for such adjustment until the beginning of such period), until the alien has had the opportunity during the first 30 days of the application period to complete the filing of an application for adjustment, the alien—

(A) may not be deported, and

(B) shall be granted authorization to engage in employment in the United States and be provided an "employment authorized" endorsement or other appropriate work permit.

(2) During application period

The Attorney General shall provide that in the case of an alien who presents a prima facie application for adjustment of status under subsection (a) during the application period, and until a final determination on the application has been made in accordance with this section, the alien—

(A) may not be deported, and

(B) shall be granted authorization to engage in employment in the United States and be provided an "employment authorized" endorsement or other appropriate work permit.

(f) Administrative and judicial review

(1) Administrative and judicial review

There shall be no administrative or judicial review of a determination respecting an application for adjustment of status under this section except in accordance with this subsection.

(2) No review for late filings

No denial of adjustment of status under this section based on a late filing of an application for such adjustment may be reviewed by a court of the United States or of any State or reviewed in any administrative proceeding of the United States Government.

(3) Administrative review

(A) Single level of administrative appellate review

The Attorney General shall establish an appellate authority to provide for a single level of administrative appellate review of a determination described in paragraph (1).

(B) Standard for review

Such administrative appellate review shall be based solely upon the administrative record established at the time of the determination on the application and upon such additional or newly discovered evidence as may not have been available at the time of the determination.

(4) Judicial review

(A) Limitation to review of deportation

There shall be judicial review of such a denial only in the judicial review of an order of deportation under section 106 [8 U.S.C.A. § 1105a] (as in effect before October 1, 1996).

(B) Standard for judicial review

Such judicial review shall be based solely upon the administrative record established at the time of the review by the appellate authority and the findings of fact and determinations contained in such record shall be conclusive unless the applicant can establish abuse of discretion or that the findings are directly contrary to clear and convincing facts contained in the record considered as a whole.

(C) Jurisdiction of courts

Notwithstanding any other provision of law, no court shall have jurisdiction of any cause of action or claim by or on behalf of any person asserting an interest under this section unless such person in fact filed an application under this section within the period specified by subsection (a)(1), or attempted to file a complete application and application fee with an authorized legalization officer of the Service but had the application and fee refused by that officer.

(g) Implementation of section

(1) Regulations

The Attorney General, after consultation with the Committees on the Judiciary of the House of Representatives and of the Senate, shall prescribe—

(A) regulations establishing a definition of the term "resided continuously", as used in this section, and the evidence needed to establish that an alien has resided continuously in the United States for purposes of this section, and

(B) such other regulations as may be necessary to carry out this section.

(2) Considerations

In prescribing regulations described in paragraph (1)(A)—

(A) Periods of continuous residence

The Attorney General shall specify individual periods, and aggregate periods, of absence from the United States which will be considered to break a period of continuous residence in the United States and shall take into account absences due merely to brief and casual trips abroad.

(B) Absences caused by deportation or advanced parole

The Attorney General shall provide that—

(i) an alien shall not be considered to have resided continuously in the United States, if, during any period for which continuous residence is required, the alien was outside the United States as a result of a departure under an order of deportation, and

(ii) any period of time during which an alien is outside the United States pursuant to the advance parole procedures of the Service shall not be considered as part of the period of time during which an alien is outside the United States for purposes of this section.

(C) Waivers of certain absences

The Attorney General may provide for a waiver, in the discretion of the Attorney General, of the periods specified under subparagraph (A) in the case of an absence from the United States due merely to a brief temporary trip abroad required by emergency or extenuating circumstances outside the control of the alien.

(D) Use of certain documentation

The Attorney General shall require that—

(i) continuous residence and physical presence in the United States must be established through documents, together with independent corroboration of the information contained in such documents, and

(ii) the documents provided under clause (i) be employment-related if employment-related documents with respect to the alien are available to the applicant.

(3) Interim final regulations

Regulations prescribed under this section may be prescribed to take effect on an interim final basis if the Attorney General determines that this is necessary in order to implement this section in a timely manner.

(h) Temporary disqualification of newly legalized aliens from receiving certain public welfare assistance

(1) In general

During the five-year period beginning on the date an alien was granted lawful temporary resident status under subsection (a), and notwithstanding any other provision of law—

(A) except as provided in paragraphs (2) and (3), the alien is not eligible for—

(i) any program of financial assistance furnished under Federal law (whether through grant, loan, guarantee, or otherwise) on the basis of financial need, as such programs are identified by the Attorney General in consultation with other appropriate heads of the various departments and agencies of Government (but in any event including the program of aid to families with dependent children under part A of title IV of the Social Security Act [42 U.S.C.A. § 601 et seq.]),

(ii) medical assistance under a State plan approved under title XIX of the Social Security Act [42 U.S.C.A. § 1396 et seq.], and

(iii) assistance under the Food Stamp Act of 1977 [7 U.S.C.A. § 2011 et seq.]; and

(B) a State or political subdivision therein may, to the extent consistent with subparagraph (A) and paragraphs (2) and (3), provide that the alien is not eligible for the programs of financial assistance or for medical assistance described in subparagraph (A)(ii) furnished under the law of that State or political subdivision.

Unless otherwise specifically provided by this section or other law, an alien in temporary lawful residence status granted under subsection (a) shall not be considered (for purposes of any law of a State or political subdivision providing for a program of financial assistance) to be permanently residing in the United States under color of law.

(2) Exceptions

Paragraph (1) shall not apply—

(A) to a Cuban and Haitian entrant (as defined in paragraph (1) or (2)(A) of section 501(e) of Public Law 96–422 [8 U.S.C.A. § 1522 note], as in effect on April 1, 1983), or

(B) in the case of assistance (other than aid to families with dependent children) which is furnished to an alien who is an aged, blind, or disabled individual (as defined in section 1614(a)(1) of the Social Security Act [42 U.S.C.A. § 1382c(a)(1)]).

(3) Restricted medicaid benefits

(A) Clarification of entitlement

Subject to the restrictions under subparagraph (B), for the purpose of providing aliens with eligibility to receive medical assistance—

(i) paragraph (1) shall not apply,

(ii) aliens who would be eligible for medical assistance but for the provisions of paragraph (1) shall be deemed, for purposes of title XIX of the Social Security Act [42 U.S.C.A. § 1396 et seq.], to be so eligible, and

(iii) aliens lawfully admitted for temporary residence under this section, such status not having changed, shall be considered to be permanently residing in the United States under color of law.

(B) Restriction of benefits

(i) Limitation to emergency services and services for pregnant women

Notwithstanding any provision of title XIX of the Social Security Act (including subparagraphs (B) and (C) of section 1902(a)(10) of such Act [42 U.S.C.A. § 1396a(a)(10)]) aliens who, but for subparagraph (A), would be ineligible for medical assistance under paragraph (1), are only eligible for such assistance with respect to—

(I) emergency services (as defined for purposes of section 1916(a)(2)(D) of the Social Security Act [42 U.S.C.A. § 1396o(a)(2)(D)]), and

(II) services described in section 1916(a)(2)(B) of such Act [42 U.S.C.A. § 1396o(a)(2)(B)] (relating to service for pregnant women).

(ii) No restriction for exempt aliens and children

The restrictions of clause (i) shall not apply to aliens who are described in paragraph (2) or who are under 18 years of age.

(C) Definition of medical assistance

In this paragraph, the term "medical assistance" refers to medical assistance under a State plan approved under title XIX of the Social Security Act.

(4) Treatment of certain programs

Assistance furnished under any of the following provisions of law shall not be construed to be financial assistance described in paragraph (1)(A)(i):

(A) The Richard B. Russell National School Lunch Act [42 U.S.C.A. § 1751 et seq.].

(B) The Child Nutrition Act of 1966 [42 U.S.C.A. § 1771 et seq.].

(C) Carl D. Perkins Vocational and Technical Education Act of 1998 [20 U.S.C.A. § 2301 et seq.].

(D) Title I of the Elementary and Secondary Education Act of 1965 [20U.S.C.A. § 6301 et seq.].

(E) The Headstart–Follow Through Act.

(F) The Job Training Partnership Act or title I of the Workforce Investment Act of 1998 [29 U.S.C.A. § 2801 et seq.].

(G) Title IV of the Higher Education Act of 1965 [20 U.S.C.A. § 1070 et seq.].

(H) The Public Health Service Act [42 U.S.C.A. § 1201 et seq.].

(I) Titles V, XVI, and XX, and parts B, D, and E of title IV, of the Social Security Act [42 U.S.C.A. §§ 701 et seq., 1381 et seq., 1391 et seq., 620 et seq., 651 et seq., and 670 et seq., respectively] (and titles I, X, XIV, and XVI of such Act [42

U.S.C.A. §§ 301 et seq., 1201 et seq., 1351 et seq., and 1381 et seq., respectively] as in effect without regard to the amendment made by section 301 of the Social Security Amendments of 1972).

(5) Adjustment not affecting Fascell–Stone benefits

For the purpose of section 501 of the Refugee Education Assistance Act of 1980 (Public Law 96–122) [sic] [8 U.S.C.A. § 1522 note]; assistance shall be continued under such section with respect to an alien without regard to the alien's adjustment of status under this section.

(i) Dissemination of information on legalization program

Beginning not later than the date designated by the Attorney General under subsection (a)(1)(A), the Attorney General, in cooperation with qualified designated entities, shall broadly disseminate information respecting the benefits which aliens may receive under this section and the requirements to obtain such benefits.

(June 27, 1952, c. 477, Title II, ch. 5, § 245A, as added Nov. 6, 1986, Pub.L. 99–603, Title II, § 201(a), 100 Stat. 3394, and amended Oct. 24, 1988, Pub.L. 100–525, § 2(h)(1), 102 Stat. 2611; Nov. 5, 1990, Pub.L. 101–649, Title VI, § 603(a)(13), Title VII, § 703, 104 Stat. 5083, 5086; Oct. 28, 1991, Pub.L. 102–140, Title I, 105 Stat. 785; Dec. 12, 1991, Pub.L. 102–232, Title III, § 307(*l*)(6), 105 Stat. 1756; Oct. 20, 1994, Pub.L. 103–382, Title III, § 394(g), 108 Stat. 4028; Oct. 25, 1994, Pub.L. 103–416, Title I, § 108(b), Title II, § 219(*l*)(1), 108 Stat. 4310, 4317; Apr. 24, 1996, Pub.L. 104–132, Title IV, § 431(a), 110 Stat. 1273; Aug. 22, 1996, Pub.L. 104–193, Title I, § 110(s)(2), 110 Stat. 2175; Sept. 30, 1996, Pub.L. 104–208, Div. C, Title III, §§ 308(g)(2)(B), (5)(A)(iii), 377(a), 384(d)(1), Title VI, § 623(a), 110 Stat. 3009–622, 3009–623, 3009–649, 3009–653, 3009–696; Oct. 21, 1998, 112 Stat. 2681–419, 2681–430; Oct. 31, 1998, Pub.L. 105–332, § 3(a), 112 Stat. 3125, Pub.L. 105–277, Div. A, § 101(f) [Title VIII, § 405(d)(4)]; Oct. 22, 1999, Pub.L. 106–78, Title VII, § 752(b)(5), 113 Stat. 1169.)

§ 246. Rescission of adjustment of status; effect upon naturalized citizen [8 U.S.C.A. § 1256]

(a) If, at any time within five years after the status of a person has been otherwise adjusted under the provisions of section 245 [8 U.S.C.A. § 1255] or 249 [8 U.S.C.A. § 1259] or any other provision of law to that of an alien lawfully admitted for permanent residence, it shall appear to the satisfaction of the Attorney General that the person was not in fact eligible for such adjustment of status, the Attorney General shall rescind the action taken granting an adjustment of status to such person and cancelling removal in the case of such person if that occurred and the person shall thereupon be subject to all provisions of this Act to the same extent as if the adjustment of status had not been made. Nothing in this subsection shall require the Attorney General to rescind the alien's status prior to commencement of procedures to remove the alien under section 240 [8 U.S.C.A. § 1229a], and an order of removal issued by an immigration judge shall be sufficient to rescind the alien's status.

(b) Any person who has become a naturalized citizen of the United States upon the basis of a record of a lawful admission for permanent residence, created as a result of an adjustment of status for which such person was not in fact eligible, and which is subsequently rescinded under subsection (a) of this section, shall be subject to the provisions of section 340 of this Act [8 U.S.C.A. § 1451] as a person whose naturalization was procured by concealment of a material fact or by willful misrepresentation.

(June 27, 1952, c. 477, Title II, ch. 5, § 246, 66 Stat. 217; Oct. 25, 1994, Pub.L. 103–416, Title II, § 219(m), 108 Stat. 4317; Sept. 30, 1996, Pub.L. 104–208, Div. C, Title III, §§ 308(e)(1)(H), 378(a), 110 Stat. 3009–619, 3009–649.)

§ 247. Adjustment of status of certain resident aliens to nonimmigrant status; exceptions [8 U.S.C.A. § 1257]

(a) The status of an alien lawfully admitted for permanent residence shall be adjusted by the Attorney General, under such regulations as he may prescribe, to that of a nonimmigrant under paragraph (15)(A), (E), or (G) of section 101(a) [8 U.S.C.A. § 1101(a)], if such alien had at the time of admission or subsequently acquires an occupational status which would, if he were seeking admission to the United States, entitle him to a nonimmigrant status under such paragraphs. As of the date of the Attorney General's order making such adjustment of status, the Attorney General shall cancel the record of the alien's admission for permanent residence, and the immigrant status of such alien shall thereby be terminated.

(b) The adjustment of status required by subsection (a) shall not be applicable in the case of any alien who requests that he be permitted to retain his status as an immigrant and who, in such form as the Attorney General may require, executes and files with the Attorney General a written waiver of all rights, privileges, exemptions, and immunities under any law or any executive order which would otherwise accrue to him because of the acquisition of an occupational status entitling him to a nonimmigrant status under paragraph (15)(A), (E), or (G) of section 101(a) [8 U.S.C.A. § 1101(a)].

(June 27, 1952, c. 477, Title II, ch. 5, § 247, 66 Stat. 218; Sept. 30, 1996, Pub.L. 104–208, Div. C, Title III, § 308(f)(1)(P), 110 Stat. 3009–621.)

§ 248. Change of nonimmigrant classification [8 U.S.C.A. § 1258]

The Attorney General may, under such conditions as he may prescribe, authorize a change from any nonimmigrant classification to any other nonimmigrant classification in the case of any alien lawfully admitted to the United States as a nonimmigrant who is continuing to maintain that status and who is not inadmissible under section 212(a)(9)(B)(i) [8 U.S.C.A. § 1182(a)(9)(B)(i)] (or whose inadmissibility under such section is waived under section 212(a)(9)(B)(v)) [8 U.S.C.A. § 1182(a)(9)(B)(v)], except in the case of—

(1) an alien classified as a nonimmigrant under subparagraph (C), (D), (K), or (S) of section 101(a)(15) [8 U.S.C.A. § 1101(a)(15)],

(2) an alien classified as a nonimmigrant under subparagraph (J) of section 101(a)(15) [8 U.S.C.A. § 1101(a)(15)] who came to the United States or acquired such classification in order to receive graduate medical education or training,

(3) an alien (other than an alien described in paragraph (2)) classified as a nonimmigrant under subparagraph (J) of section 101(a)(15) [8 U.S.C.A. § 1101(a)(15)] who is subject to the two-year foreign residence requirement of section 212(e) [8 U.S.C.A. § 1182(e)] and has not received a waiver thereof, unless such alien applies to have the alien's classification changed from classification under subparagraph (J) of section 101(a)(15) [8 U.S.C.A. § 1101(a)(15)] to a classification under subparagraph (A) or (G) of such section and

(4) an alien admitted as a nonimmigrant visitor without a visa under section 212(*l*) [8 U.S.C.A. § 1182(*l*)] or section 217 [8 U.S.C.A. § 1187].

(June 27, 1952, c. 477, Title II, ch. 5, § 248, 66 Stat. 218; Sept. 21, 1961, Pub.L. 87–256, § 109(d), 75 Stat. 535; Dec. 29, 1981, Pub.L. 97–116, § 10, 95 Stat. 1617; Nov. 6, 1986, Pub.L. 99–603, Title III, § 313(d), 100 Stat. 3439; Sept. 13, 1994, Pub.L. 103–322, Title XIII, § 130003(b)(3), 108 Stat. 2025; Sept. 30, 1996, Pub.L. 104–208, Div. C, Title III, § 301(b)(2), Title VI, § 671(a)(2), 110 Stat. 3009–578, 3009–721.)

§ 249. Record of admission for permanent residence in the case of certain aliens who entered the United States prior to January 1, 1972 [8 U.S.C.A. § 1259]

A record of lawful admission for permanent residence may, in the discretion of the Attorney General and under such regulations as he may prescribe, be made in the case of any alien, as of the date of the approval of his application or, if entry occurred prior to July 1, 1924, as of the date of such entry, if no such record is otherwise available and such alien shall satisfy the Attorney General that he is not inadmissible under section 212(a)(3)(E) [8 U.S.C.A. § 1182(a)(3)(E)] or under section 212(a) [8 U.S.C.A. § 1182(a)] insofar as it relates to criminals, procurers and other immoral persons, subversives, violators of the narcotic laws or smugglers of aliens, and he establishes that he—

(a) entered the United States prior to January 1, 1972;

(b) has had his residence in the United States continuously since such entry;

(c) is a person of good moral character; and

(d) is not ineligible to citizenship and is not deportable under section 237(a)(4)(B) [8 U.S.C.A. § 1227(a)(4)(B)].

(June 27, 1952, c. 477, Title II, ch. 5, § 249, 66 Stat. 219; Aug. 8, 1958, Pub.L. 85–616, 72 Stat. 546; Oct. 3, 1965, Pub.L. 89–236, § 19, 79 Stat. 920; Nov. 6, 1986, Pub.L. 99–603, Title II, § 203(a), 100 Stat. 3405; Oct. 24, 1988, Pub.L. 100–525, § 2(j), 102 Stat. 2612; Nov. 29, 1990, Pub.L. 101–649, Title VI, § 603(a)(14), 104 Stat. 5083; Apr. 24, 1996, Pub.L. 104–132, Title IV, § 413(e), 110 Stat. 1269; Sept. 30, 1996, Pub.L. 104–208, Div. C, Title III, § 308(g)(10)(C), 110 Stat. 3009–625.)

§ 250. Removal of aliens falling into distress [8 U.S.C.A. § 1260]

The Attorney General may remove from the United States any alien who falls into distress or who needs public aid from causes arising subsequent to his entry, and is desirous of being so removed, to the native country of such alien, or to the country from which he came, or to the country of which he is a citizen or subject, or to any other country to which he wishes to go and which will receive him, at the expense of the appropriation for the enforcement of this Act. Any alien so removed shall be ineligible to apply for or receive a visa or other documentation for readmission, or to apply for admission to the United States except with the prior approval of the Attorney General.

(June 27, 1952, c. 477, Title II, ch. 5, § 250, 66 Stat. 219.)

Chapter VI—Special Provisions Relating to Alien Crewmen

§ 251. Alien crewmen [8 U.S.C.A. § 1281]

(a) Arrival; submission of list; exceptions

Upon arrival of any vessel or aircraft in the United States from any place outside the United States it shall be the duty of the owner, agent, consignee, master, or commanding officer thereof to deliver to an immigration officer at the port of arrival **(1)** a complete, true, and correct list containing the names of all aliens employed on such vessel or aircraft, the positions they respectively hold in the crew of the vessel or aircraft, when and where they were respectively shipped or engaged, and those to be paid off or discharged in the port of arrival; or **(2)** in the discretion of the Attorney General, such a list containing so much of such information, or such additional or supplemental information, as the Attorney General shall by regulations prescribe. In the case of a vessel engaged solely in traffic on the Great Lakes, Saint Lawrence River, and connecting waterways, such lists shall be furnished at such times as the Attorney General may require.

(b) Reports of illegal landings

It shall be the duty of any owner, agent, consignee, master, or commanding officer of any vessel or aircraft to report to an immigration officer, in writing, as soon as discovered, all cases in which any alien crewman has illegally landed in the United States from the vessel or aircraft, together with a description of such alien and any information likely to lead to his apprehension.

(c) Departure; submission of list; exceptions

Before the departure of any vessel or aircraft from any port in the United States, it shall be the duty of the owner, agent, consignee, master, or commanding officer thereof, to deliver to an immigration officer at that port **(1)** a list containing the names of all alien employees who were not employed thereon at the time of the arrival at that port but who will leave such port thereon at the time of the departure of such vessel or aircraft and the names of those, if any, who have been paid off or discharged, and of those, if any, who have deserted or landed at that port, or **(2)** in the discretion of the Attorney General, such a list containing so much of such information, or such additional or supplemental information, as the Attorney General shall by regulations prescribe. In the case of a vessel engaged solely in traffic on the Great Lakes, Saint Lawrence River, and connecting waterways, such lists shall be furnished at such times as the Attorney General may require.

(d) Violations

In case any owner, agent, consignee, master, or commanding officer shall fail to deliver complete, true, and correct lists or reports of aliens, or to report cases of desertion or landing, as required by subsections (a), (b), and (c), such owner, agent, consignee, master, or commanding officer, shall, if required by the Attorney General, pay to the Commissioner the sum of $200 for each alien concerning whom such lists are not delivered or such reports are not made as required in the preceding subsections. In the case that any owner, agent, consignee, master, or commanding officer of a vessel shall secure services of an alien crewman described in section 101(a)(15)(D)(i) [8 U.S.C.A. § 1101(a)(15)(D)(i)] to perform longshore work not included in the normal operation and service on board the vessel under section 258 [8 U.S.C.A. § 1288], the owner, agent, consignee, master, or commanding officer shall pay to the Commissioner the sum of $5,000, and such fine shall be a lien against the vessel. No such vessel or aircraft shall be granted clearance from any port at which it arrives pending the determination of the question of the liability to the payment of such fine, and if such fine is imposed, while it remains unpaid. No such fine shall be remitted or refunded. Clearance may be granted prior to the determination of such question upon deposit of a bond or a sum sufficient to cover such fine.

(e) Regulations

The Attorney General is authorized to prescribe by regulations the circumstances under which a vessel or aircraft shall be deemed to be arriving in, or departing from the United States or any port thereof within the meaning of any provision of this chapter.

(June 27, 1952, c. 477, Title II, ch. 6, § 251, 66 Stat. 219; Nov. 29, 1990, Pub.L. 101–649, Title II, § 203(b), 104 Stat. 5018; Dec. 12, 1991, Pub.L. 102–232, Title III, § 303(a)(3), 105 Stat. 1746.)

§ 252. Conditional permits to land temporarily [8 U.S.C.A. § 1282]

(a) Period of time

No alien crewman shall be permitted to land temporarily in the United States except as provided in this section and sections 212(d)(3), (5) [8 U.S.C.A. § 1182(d)(3), (5)] and 253 [8 U.S.C.A. § 1283]. If an immigration officer finds upon examination that an alien crewman is a nonimmigrant under paragraph (15)(D) of section 101(a) [8 U.S.C.A. § 1101(a)] and is otherwise admissible and has agreed to accept such permit, he may, in his discretion, grant the crewman a conditional permit to land temporarily pursuant to regulations prescribed by the Attorney General, subject to revocation in subsequent proceedings as provided in subsection (b), and for a period of time, in any event, not to exceed—

(1) the period of time (not exceeding twenty-nine days) during which the vessel or aircraft on which he arrived remains in port, if the immigration officer is satisfied that the crewman intends to depart on the vessel or aircraft on which he arrived; or

(2) twenty-nine days, if the immigration officer is satisfied that the crewman intends to depart, within the period for which he is permitted to land, on a vessel or aircraft other than the one on which he arrived.

(b) Revocation; expenses of detention

Pursuant to regulations prescribed by the Attorney General, any immigration officer may, in his discretion, if he determines that an alien is not a bona fide crewman, or does not intend to depart on the vessel or aircraft which brought him, revoke the conditional permit to land which was granted such crewman under the provisions of subsection (a)(1), take such crewman into custody, and require the master or commanding officer of the vessel or aircraft on which the crewman arrived to receive and detain him on board such vessel or aircraft, if practicable, and such crewman shall be removed from the United States at the expense of the transportation line which brought him to the United States. Until such alien is so removed, any expenses of his detention shall be borne by such transportation company. Nothing in this section shall be construed to require the procedure prescribed in section 240 [8 U.S.C.A. § 1229a] to cases falling within the provisions of this subsection.

(c) Penalties

Any alien crewman who willfully remains in the United States in excess of the number of days allowed in any conditional permit issued under subsection (a) shall be fined under Title 18 or imprisoned not more than 6 months, or both.

(June 27, 1952, c. 477, Title II, ch. 6, § 252, 66 Stat. 220; Nov. 29, 1990, Pub.L. 101–649, Title V, § 543(b)(1), 104 Stat. 5059; Dec. 12, 1991, Pub.L. 102–232, Title III, § 306(c)(3), 105 Stat. 1752; Sept. 30, 1996, Pub.L. 104–208, Div. C, Title III, § 308(e)(2)(E), (g)(5)(A)(i), 110 Stat. 3009–620, 3009–623.)

§ 253. Hospital treatment of alien crewmen afflicted with certain diseases [8 U.S.C.A. § 1283]

An alien crewman, including an alien crewman ineligible for a conditional permit to land under section 252(a) [8 U.S.C.A. § 1282(a)], who is found on arrival in a port of the United States to be afflicted with any of the disabilities or diseases mentioned in section 255 [8 U.S.C.A. § 1285], shall be placed in a hospital designated by the immigration officer in charge at the port of arrival and treated, all expenses connected therewith, including burial in the event of death, to be borne by the owner, agent, consignee, commanding officer, or master of the vessel or aircraft, and not to be deducted from the crewman's wages. No such vessel or aircraft shall be granted clearance until such expenses are paid, or their payment appropriately guaranteed, and the collector of customs is so notified by the immigration officer in charge. An alien crewman suspected of being afflicted with any such disability or disease may be removed from the vessel or aircraft on which he arrived to an immigration station, or other appropriate place, for such observation as will enable the examining surgeons to determine definitely whether or not he is so afflicted, all expenses connected therewith to be borne in the manner hereinbefore prescribed. In cases in which it appears to the satisfaction of the immigration officer in charge that it will not be possible within a reasonable time to effect a cure, the return of the alien crewman shall be enforced on, or at the expense of, the transportation line on which he came, upon such conditions as the Attorney General shall prescribe, to insure that the alien shall be properly cared for and protected, and that the spread of contagion shall be guarded against.

(June 27, 1952, c. 477, Title II, ch. 6, § 253, 66 Stat. 221.)

§ 254. Control of alien crewmen [8 U.S.C.A. § 1284]

(a) Penalties for failure

The owner, agent, consignee, charterer, master, or commanding officer of any vessel or aircraft arriving in the United States from any place outside thereof who fails **(1)** to detain on board the vessel, or in the case of an aircraft to detain at a place specified by an immigration officer at the expense of the airline, any alien crewman employed thereon until an immigration officer has completely inspected such alien crewman, including a physical examination by the medical examiner, or **(2)** to detain any alien crewman on board the vessel, or in the case of an aircraft at a place specified by an immigration officer at the expense of the airline, after such inspection unless a conditional permit to land temporarily has been granted such alien crewman under section 252 [8 U.S.C.A. § 1282] or unless an alien crewman has been permitted to land temporarily under section 212(d)(5) [8 U.S.C.A. § 1182(d)(5)] or 253 [8 U.S.C.A. § 1283] for medical or hospital treatment, or **(3)** to remove such alien crewman if required to do so by an immigration officer, whether such removal requirement is imposed before or after the crewman is permitted to land temporarily under section 212(d)(5) [8 U.S.C.A. § 1182(d)(5)], 252 [8 U.S.C.A. § 1282], or 253 [8 U.S.C.A. § 1283], shall pay to the Commissioner the sum of $3,000 for each alien crewman in respect to whom any such failure occurs. No such vessel or aircraft shall be granted clearance pending the determination of the liability to the payment of such fine, or while the fine remains unpaid, except that clearance may be granted prior to the determination of such question upon the deposit of a sum sufficient to cover such fine, or of a bond with sufficient surety to secure the payment thereof approved by the Commissioner. The Attorney General may, upon application in writing therefor, mitigate such penalty to not less than $500 for each alien crewman in respect of whom such failure occurs, upon such terms as he shall think proper.

(b) Prima facie evidence against transportation line

Except as may be otherwise prescribed by regulations issued by the Attorney General, proof that an alien crewman did not appear upon the outgoing manifest of the vessel or aircraft on which he arrived in the United States from any place outside thereof, or that he was reported by the master or commanding officer of such vessel or aircraft as a deserter, shall be prima facie evidence of a failure to detain or remove such alien crewman.

(c) Removal on other than arriving vessel or aircraft; expenses

If the Attorney General finds that removal of an alien crewman under this section on the vessel or aircraft on which he arrived is impracticable or impossible, or would cause undue hardship to such alien crewman, he may cause the alien crewman to be removed from the port of arrival or any other port on another vessel or aircraft of the same transportation line, unless the Attorney General finds this to be impracticable. All expenses incurred in connection with such removal, including expenses incurred in transferring an alien crewman from one place in the United States to another under such conditions and safeguards as the Attorney General shall impose, shall be paid by the owner or owners of the vessel or aircraft on which the alien arrived in the United States. The vessel or aircraft on which the alien arrived shall not be granted clearance until such expenses have been paid or their payment guaranteed to the satisfaction of the Attorney General. An alien crewman who is transferred within the United States in accordance with this subsection shall not be regarded as having been landed in the United States.

(June 27, 1952, c. 477, Title II, ch. 6, § 254, 66 Stat. 221; Nov. 29, 1990, Pub.L. 101–649, Title V, § 543(a)(4), 104 Stat. 5058; Dec. 12, 1991, Pub.L. 102–232, Title III, § 306(c)(4)(C), 105 Stat. 1752; Sept. 30, 1996, Pub.L. 104–208, Div. C, Title III, § 308(e)(1)(I), (2)(F), (12), 110 Stat. 3009–619, 3009–620.)

§ 255. Employment on passenger vessels of aliens afflicted with certain disabilities [8 U.S.C.A. § 1285]

It shall be unlawful for any vessel or aircraft carrying passengers between a port of the United States and a port outside thereof to have employed on board upon arrival in the United States any alien afflicted with feeble-mindedness, insanity, epilepsy, tuberculosis in any form, leprosy, or any dangerous contagious disease. If it appears to the satisfaction of the Attorney General, from an examination made by a medical officer of the United States Public Health Service, and is so certified by such officer, that any such alien was so afflicted at the time he was shipped or engaged and taken on board such vessel or aircraft and that the existence of such affliction might have been detected by means of a competent medical examination at such time, the owner, commanding officer, agent, consignee, or master thereof shall pay for each alien so afflicted to the Commissioner the sum of $1,000. No vessel or aircraft shall be granted clearance pending the determination of the question of the liability to the payment of such sums, or while such sums remain unpaid, except that clearance may be granted prior to the determination of such question upon the deposit of an amount sufficient to cover such sums or of a bond approved by the Commissioner with sufficient surety to secure the payment thereof. Any such fine may, in the discretion of the Attorney General, be mitigated or remitted.

(June 27, 1952, c. 477, Title II, ch. 6, § 255, 66 Stat. 222; Nov. 29, 1990, Pub.L. 101–649, Title V, § 543(a)(5), 104 Stat. 5058.)

§ 256. Discharge of alien crewmen; penalties [8 U.S.C.A. § 1286]

It shall be unlawful for any person, including the owner, agent, consignee, charterer, master, or commanding officer of any vessel or aircraft, to pay off or discharge any alien crewman, except an alien lawfully admitted for permanent residence, employed on board a vessel or aircraft arriving in the United States without first having obtained the consent of the Attorney General. If it shall appear to the satisfaction of the Attorney General that any alien crewman has been paid off or discharged in the United States in violation of the provisions of this section, such owner, agent, consignee, charterer, master, commanding officer, or other person, shall pay to the Commissioner the sum of $3,000 for each such violation. No vessel or aircraft shall be granted clearance pending the determination of the question of the liability to the payment of such sums, or while such sums remain unpaid, except that clearance may be granted prior to the determination of such question upon the deposit of an amount sufficient to cover such sums, or of a bond approved by the Commissioner with sufficient surety to secure the payment thereof. Such fine may, in the discretion of the Attorney General, be mitigated to not less than $1,500 for each violation, upon such terms as he shall think proper.

(June 27, 1952, c. 477, Title II, ch. 6, § 256, 66 Stat. 223; Nov. 29, 1990, Pub.L. 101–649, Title V, § 543(a)(6), 104 Stat. 5058.)

§ 257. Alien crewmen brought into the United States with intent to evade immigration laws; penalties [8 U.S.C.A. § 1287]

Any person, including the owner, agent, consignee, master, or commanding officer of any vessel or aircraft arriving in the United States from any place outside thereof, who shall knowingly sign on the vessel's articles, or bring to the United States as one of the crew of such vessel or aircraft, any alien, with intent to permit or assist such alien to enter or land in the United States in violation of law, or who shall falsely and knowingly represent to a consular officer at the time of application for visa, or to the immigration officer at the port of arrival in the United States, that such alien is a bona fide member of the crew employed in any capacity regularly required for normal operation and services aboard such vessel or aircraft, shall be liable to a penalty not exceeding $10,000 for each such violation, for which sum such vessel or aircraft shall be liable and may be seized and proceeded against by way of libel in any district court of the United States having jurisdiction of the offense.

(June 27, 1952, c. 477, Title II, ch. 6, § 257, 66 Stat. 223; Nov. 29, 1990, Pub.L. 101–649, Title V, § 543(a)(7), 104 Stat. 5058.)

§ 258. Limitations on performance of longshore work by alien crewmen [8 U.S.C.A. § 1288]

(a) In general

For purposes of section 101(a)(15)(D)(i) [8 U.S.C.A. § 1101(a)(15)(D)(i)], the term "normal operation and service on board a vessel" does not include any activity that is longshore work (as defined in subsection (b)), except as provided under subsection (c), (d), or (e).

(b) Longshore work defined

(1) In general

In this section, except as provided in paragraph (2), the term "longshore work" means any activity relating to the loading or unloading of cargo, the operation of cargo-related equipment (whether or not integral to the vessel), and the handling of mooring lines on the dock when the vessel is made fast or let go, in the United States or the coastal waters thereof.

(2) Exception for safety and environmental protection

The term "longshore work" does not include the loading or unloading of any cargo for which the Secretary of Transportation has, under the authority contained in chapter 37 of Title 46 (relating to Carriage of Liquid Bulk Dangerous Cargoes), section 311 of the Federal Water Pollution Control Act (33 U.S.C. 1321), section 4106 of the Oil Pollution Act of 1990, or section 5103(b), 5104, 5106, 5107, or 5110 of Title 49 prescribed regulations which govern—

(A) the handling or stowage of such cargo,

(B) the manning of vessels and the duties, qualifications, and training of the officers and crew of vessels carrying such cargo, and

(C) the reduction or elimination of discharge during ballasting, tank cleaning, handling of such cargo.

(3) Construction

Nothing in this section shall be construed as broadening, limiting, or otherwise modifying the meaning or scope of longshore work for purposes of any other law, collective bargaining agreement, or international agreement.

(c) Prevailing practice exception

(1) Subsection (a) shall not apply to a particular activity of longshore work in and about a local port if—

(A) (i) there is in effect in the local port one or more collective bargaining agreements each covering at least 30 percent of the number of individuals employed in performing longshore work and **(ii)** each such agreement (covering such percentage of longshore workers) permits the activity to be performed by alien crewmen under the terms of such agreement; or

(B) there is no collective bargaining agreement in effect in the local port covering at least 30 percent of the number of individuals employed in performing longshore work, and an employer of alien crewmen (or the employer's designated agent or representative) has filed with the Secretary of Labor at least 14 days before the date of performance of the activity (or later, if necessary due to an unanticipated emergency, but not later than the date of performance of the activity) an attestation setting forth facts and evidence to show that—

(i) the performance of the activity by alien crewmen is permitted under the prevailing practice of the particular port as of the date of filing of the attestation and that the use of alien crewmen for such activity—

(I) is not during a strike or lockout in the course of a labor dispute, and

(II) is not intended or designed to influence an election of a bargaining representative for workers in the local port; and

(ii) notice of the attestation has been provided by the owner, agent, consignee, master, or commanding officer to the bargaining representative of longshore workers in the local port, or, where there is no such bargaining representative, notice of the attestation has been provided to longshore workers employed at the local port.

In applying subparagraph (B) in the case of a particular activity of longshore work consisting of the use of an automated self-unloading conveyor belt or vacuum-actuated system on a vessel, the attestation shall be required to be filed only if the Secretary of Labor finds, based on a preponderance of the evidence which may be submitted by any interested party, that the performance of such particular activity is not described in clause (i) of such subparagraph.

(2) Subject to paragraph (4), an attestation under paragraph (1) shall—

(A) expire at the end of the 1–year period beginning on the date of its filing with the Secretary of Labor, and

(B) apply to aliens arriving in the United States during such 1–year period if the owner, agent, consignee, master, or commanding officer states in each list under section 251 [8 U.S.C.A. § 1281] that it continues to comply with the conditions in the attestation.

(3) An owner, agent, consignee, master, or commanding officer may meet the requirements under this subsection with respect to more than one alien crewman in a single list.

(4)(A) The Secretary of Labor shall compile and make available for public examination in a timely manner in Washington, D.C., a list identifying owners, agents, consignees, masters, or commanding officers which have filed lists for nonimmigrants described in section 101(a)(15)(D)(i) [8 U.S.C.A. § 1101(a)(15)(D)(i)] with respect to whom an attestation under paragraph (1) or subsection (d)(1) is made and, for each such entity, a copy of the entity's attestation under paragraph (1) or subsection (d)(1) (and accompanying documentation) and each such list filed by the entity.

(B)(i) The Secretary of Labor shall establish a process for the receipt, investigation, and disposition of complaints respecting an entity's failure to meet conditions attested to, an entity's misrepresentation of a material fact in an attestation, or, in the case described in the last sentence of paragraph (1), whether the performance of the particular activity is or is not described in paragraph (1)(B)(i).

(ii) Complaints may be filed by any aggrieved person or organization (including bargaining representatives, associations deemed appropriate by the Secretary, and other aggrieved parties as determined under regulations of the Secretary).

(iii) The Secretary shall promptly conduct an investigation under this subparagraph if there is reasonable cause to believe that an entity fails to meet conditions attested to, an entity has misrepresented a material fact in the attestation, or, in the case described in the last sentence of paragraph (1), the performance of the particular activity is not described in paragraph (1)(B)(i).

(C)(i) If the Secretary determines that reasonable cause exists to conduct an investigation with respect to an attestation, a complaining party may request that the activities attested to by the employer cease during the hearing process described in subparagraph (D). If such a request is made, the attesting employer shall be issued notice of such request and shall respond within 14 days to the notice. If the Secretary makes an initial determination that the complaining party's position is supported by a preponderance of the evidence submitted, the Secretary shall require immediately that the employer cease and desist from such activities until completion of the process described in subparagraph (D).

(ii) If the Secretary determines that reasonable cause exists to conduct an investigation with respect to a matter under the last sentence of paragraph (1), a complaining party may request that the activities of the employer cease during the hearing process described in subparagraph (D) unless the employer files with the Secretary of Labor an attestation under paragraph (1). If such a request is made, the employer shall be issued notice of such request and shall respond within 14 days to the notice. If the Secretary makes an initial determination that the complaining party's position is supported by a preponderance of the evidence submitted, the Secretary shall require immediately that the employer cease and desist from such activities until completion of the process described in subparagraph (D) unless the employer files with the Secretary of Labor an attestation under paragraph (1).

(D) Under the process established under subparagraph (B), the Secretary shall provide, within 180 days after the date a complaint is filed (or later for good cause shown), for a determination as to whether or not a basis exists to make a finding described in subparagraph (E). The Secretary shall provide notice of such determination to the interested parties and an opportunity for a hearing on the complaint within 60 days of the date of the determination.

(E)(i) If the Secretary of Labor finds, after notice and opportunity for a hearing, that an entity has failed to meet a condition attested to or has made a misrepresentation of material fact in the attestation, the Secretary shall notify the Attorney General of such finding and may, in addition, impose such other administrative remedies (including civil monetary penalties in an amount not to exceed $5,000 for each alien crewman performing unauthorized longshore work) as the Secretary determines to be appropriate. Upon receipt of such notice, the Attorney General shall not permit the vessels owned or chartered by such entity to enter any port of the United States during a period of up to 1 year.

(ii) If the Secretary of Labor finds, after notice and opportunity for a hearing, that, in the case described in the last sentence of paragraph (1), the performance of the particular activity is not described in subparagraph (B)(i), the Secretary shall notify the Attorney General of such finding and, thereafter, the attestation described in paragraph (1) shall be required of the employer for the performance of the particular activity.

(F) A finding by the Secretary of Labor under this paragraph that the performance of an activity by alien crewmen is not permitted under the prevailing practice of a local port shall preclude for one year the filing of a subsequent attestation concerning such activity in the port under paragraph (1).

(5) Except as provided in paragraph (5) of subsection (d), this subsection shall not apply to longshore work performed in the State of Alaska.

(d) State of Alaska exception

(1) Subsection (a) shall not apply to a particular activity of longshore work at a particular location in the State of Alaska if an employer of alien crewmen has filed an attestation with the Secretary of Labor at least 30 days before the date of the first performance of the activity (or anytime up to 24 hours before the first performance of the activity, upon a showing that the employer could not have reasonably anticipated the need to file an attestation for that location at that time) setting forth facts and evidence to show that—

(A) the employer will make a bona fide request for United States longshore workers who are qualified and available in sufficient numbers to perform the activity at the particular time and location from the parties to whom notice has been provided under clauses (ii) and (iii) of subparagraph (D), except that—

(i) wherever two or more contract stevedoring companies have signed a joint collective bargaining agreement with a single labor organization described in subparagraph (D)(i), the employer may request longshore workers from only one of such contract stevedoring companies, and

(ii) a request for longshore workers to an operator of a private dock may be made only for longshore work to be performed at that dock and only if the operator meets the requirements of section 932 of Title 33;

(B) the employer will employ all those United States longshore workers made available in response to the request made pursuant to subparagraph (A) who are qualified and available in sufficient numbers and who are needed to perform the longshore activity at the particular time and location;

(C) the use of alien crewmembers for such activity is not intended or designed to influence an election of a bargaining representative for workers in the State of Alaska; and

(D) notice of the attestation has been provided by the employer to—

(i) labor organizations which have been recognized as exclusive bargaining representatives of United States longshore workers within the meaning of the National Labor Relations Act [29 U.S.C.A. § 151 et seq.] and which make available or intend to make available workers to the particular location where the longshore work is to be performed,

(ii) contract stevedoring companies which employ or intend to employ United States longshore workers at that location, and

(iii) operators of private docks at which the employer will use longshore workers.

(2)(A) An employer filing an attestation under paragraph (1) who seeks to use alien crewmen to perform longshore work shall be responsible while the attestation is valid to make bona fide requests for United States longshore workers under paragraph (1)(A) and to employ United States longshore workers, as provided in paragraph (1)(B), before using alien crewmen to perform the activity or activities specified in the attestation, except that an employer shall not be required to request longshore workers from a party if that party has notified the employer in writing that it does not intend to make available United States longshore workers to the location at which the longshore work is to be performed.

(B) If a party that has provided such notice subsequently notifies the employer in writing that it is prepared to make available United States longshore workers who are qualified and available in sufficient numbers to perform the longshore activity to the location at which the longshore work is to be performed, then the employer's obligations to that party under subparagraphs (A) and (B) of paragraph (1) shall begin 60 days following the issuance of such notice.

(3)(A) In no case shall an employer filing an attestation be required—

(i) to hire less than a full work unit of United States longshore workers needed to perform the longshore activity;

(ii) to provide overnight accommodations for the longshore workers while employed; or

(iii) to provide transportation to the place of work, except where—

(I) surface transportation is available;

(II) such transportation may be safely accomplished;

(III) travel time to the vessel does not exceed one-half hour each way; and

(IV) travel distance to the vessel from the point of embarkation does not exceed 5 miles.

(B) In the cases of Wide Bay, Alaska, and Klawock/Craig, Alaska, the travel times and travel distances specified in subclauses (III) and (IV) of subparagraph (A)(iii) shall be extended to 45 minutes and 7.5 miles, respectively, unless the party responding to the request for longshore workers agrees to the lesser time and distance limitations specified in those subclauses.

(4) Subject to subparagraphs (A) through (D) of subsection (c)(4), attestations filed under paragraph (1) of this subsection shall—

(A) expire at the end of the 1–year period beginning on the date the employer anticipates the longshore work to begin, as specified in the attestation filed with the Secretary of Labor, and

(B) apply to aliens arriving in the United States during such 1–year period if the owner, agent, consignee, master, or commanding officer states in each list under section 251 [8 U.S.C.A. § 1281] that it continues to comply with the conditions in the attestation.

(5)(A) Except as otherwise provided by subparagraph (B), subsection (c)(3) and subparagraphs (A) through (E) of subsection (c)(4) shall apply to attestations filed under this subsection.

(B) The use of alien crewmen to perform longshore work in Alaska consisting of the use of an automated self-unloading conveyor belt or vacuum-actuated system on a vessel shall be governed by the provisions of subsection (c).

(6) For purposes of this subsection—

(A) the term "contract stevedoring companies" means those stevedoring companies licensed to do business in the State of Alaska that meet the requirements of section 932 of Title 33;

(B) the term "employer" includes any agent or representative designated by the employer; and

(C) the terms "qualified" and "available in sufficient numbers" shall be defined by reference to industry standards in the State of Alaska, including safety considerations.

(e) Reciprocity exception

(1) In general

Subject to the determination of the Secretary of State pursuant to paragraph (2), the Attorney General shall permit an alien crewman to perform an activity constituting longshore work if—

(A) the vessel is registered in a country that by law, regulation, or in practice does not prohibit such activity by crewmembers aboard United States vessels; and

(B) nationals of a country (or countries) which by law, regulation, or in practice does not prohibit such activity by crewmembers aboard United States vessels hold a majority of the ownership interest in the vessel.

(2) Establishment of list

The Secretary of State shall, in accordance with section 553 of Title 5, compile and annually maintain a list, of longshore work by particular activity, or countries where performance of such a particular activity by crewmembers aboard United States vessels is prohibited by law, regulation, or in practice in the country. By not later than 90 days after November 29, 1990, the Secretary shall publish a notice of proposed rulemaking to establish such list. The Secretary shall first establish such list by not later than 180 days after November 29, 1990.

(3) In practice defined

For purposes of this subsection, the term "in practice" refers to an activity normally performed in such country during the one-year period preceding the arrival of such vessel into the United States or coastal waters thereof.

(June 27, 1952, c. 477, Title II, ch. 6, § 258, as added Nov. 29, 1990, Pub.L. 101–649, Title II, § 203(a)(1), 104 Stat. 5015, and amended Dec. 12, 1991, Pub.L. 102–232, Title III, § 303(a)(4), 105 Stat. 1747; Dec. 17, 1993, Pub.L. 103–198, § 8(a), (b), 107 Stat. 2313, 2315; Dec. 20, 1993, Pub.L. 103–206, Title III, § 323(a), (b), 107 Stat. 2428, 2430; Oct. 25, 1994, Pub.L. 103–416, Title II, § 219(f), (gg), 108 Stat. 4317, 4319; Sept. 30, 1996, Pub.L. 104–208, Div. C, Title VI, § 671(e)(4)(B), 110 Stat. 3009–723.)

Chapter VII—Registration of Aliens

§ 261. Alien seeking entry; contents [8 U.S.C.A. § 1301]

No visa shall be issued to any alien seeking to enter the United States until such alien has been registered in accordance with section 221(b) [8 U.S.C.A. § 1201(b)].

(June 27, 1952, c. 477, Title II, ch. 7, § 261, 66 Stat. 223; Pub.L. 99–653, § 8, Nov. 14, 1986, 100 Stat. 3657, as amended Pub.L. 100–525, § 8(g), Oct. 24, 1988, 102 Stat. 2617.)

§ 262. Registration of aliens [8 U.S.C.A. § 1302]

(a) It shall be the duty of every alien now or hereafter in the United States, who **(1)** is fourteen years of age or older, **(2)** has not been registered and fingerprinted under section 221(b) [8 U.S.C.A. § 1201(b)] or section 30 or 31 of the Alien Registration Act, 1940, and **(3)** remains in the United States for thirty days or longer, to apply for registration and to be fingerprinted before the expiration of such thirty days.

(b) It shall be the duty of every parent or legal guardian of any alien now or hereafter in the United States, who **(1)** is less than fourteen years of age, **(2)** has not been registered under section 221(b) [8 U.S.C.A. § 1201(b)] or section 30 or 31 of the Alien Registration Act, 1940, and **(3)** remains in the United States for thirty days or longer, to apply for the registration of such alien before the expiration of such thirty days. Whenever any alien attains his fourteenth birthday in the United States he shall, within thirty days thereafter, apply in person for registration and to be fingerprinted.

(c) The Attorney General may, in his discretion and on the basis of reciprocity pursuant to such regulations as he may prescribe, waive the requirement of fingerprinting specified in subsections (a) and (b) in the case of any nonimmigrant.

(June 27, 1952, c. 477, Title II, ch. 7, § 262, 66 Stat. 224; Nov. 14, 1986, Pub.L. 99–653, § 9, 100 Stat. 3657; Oct. 24, 1988, Pub.L. 100–525, § 8(h), 102 Stat. 2617; Oct. 25, 1994, Pub.L. 103–416, Title II, § 219(n), 108 Stat. 4317.)

§ 263. Registration of special groups [8 U.S.C.A. § 1303]

(a) Notwithstanding the provisions of sections 261 [8 U.S.C.A. § 1301] and 262 [8 U.S.C.A. § 1302], the Attorney General is authorized to prescribe special regulations and forms for the registration and fingerprinting of **(1)** alien crewmen, **(2)** holders of border-crossing identification cards, **(3)** aliens confined in institutions within the United States, **(4)** aliens under order of removal, **(5)** aliens who are or have been on criminal probation or criminal parole within the United States, and **(6)** aliens of any other class not lawfully admitted to the United States for permanent residence.

(b) The provisions of section 262 [8 U.S.C.A. § 1302] and of this section shall not be applicable to any alien who is in the United States as a nonimmigrant under section 101(a)(15)(A) or (a)(15)(G) [8 U.S.C.A. § 1101(a)(15)(A) or (a)(15)(G)] until the alien ceases to be entitled to such a nonimmigrant status.

(June 27, 1952, c. 477, Title II, ch. 7, § 263, 66 Stat. 224; Sept. 30, 1996, Pub.L. 104–208, Div. C, Title III, §§ 308(e)(1)(J), 323, 110 Stat. 3009–619, 3009–629.)

§ 264. Forms for registration and fingerprinting [8 U.S.C.A. § 1304]

(a) Preparation; contents

The Attorney General and the Secretary of State jointly are authorized and directed to prepare forms for the registration of aliens under section 261 [8 U.S.C.A. § 1301], and the Attorney General is authorized and directed to prepare forms for the registration and fingerprinting of aliens under section 262 [8 U.S.C.A. § 1302]. Such forms shall contain inquiries with respect to **(1)** the date and place of entry of the alien into the United States; **(2)** activities in which he has been and intends to be engaged; **(3)** the length of time he expects to remain in the United States; **(4)** the police and criminal record, if any, of such alien; and **(5)** such additional matters as may be prescribed.

(b) Confidential nature

All registration and fingerprint records made under the provisions of this title shall be confidential, and shall be made available only **(1)** pursuant to section 287(f)(2) [8 U.S.C.A. § 1357(f)(2)], and **(2)** to such persons or agencies as may be designated by the Attorney General.

(c) Information under oath

Every person required to apply for the registration of himself or another under this title shall submit under oath the information required for such registration. Any person authorized under regulations issued by the Attorney General to register aliens under this title shall be authorized to administer oaths for such purpose.

(d) Certificate of alien registration or alien receipt card

Every alien in the United States who has been registered and fingerprinted under the provisions of the Alien Registration Act, 1940, or under the provisions of this Act shall be issued a certificate of alien registration or an alien registration receipt card in such form and manner and at such time as shall be prescribed under regulations issued by the Attorney General.

(e) Personal possession of registration or receipt card; penalties

Every alien, eighteen years of age and over, shall at all times carry with him and have in his personal possession any certificate of alien registration or alien registration receipt card issued to him pursuant to subsection (d). Any alien who fails to comply with the provisions of this subsection shall be guilty of a misdemeanor and shall upon conviction for each offense be fined not to exceed $100 or be imprisoned not more than thirty days, or both.

(f) Social security account number

Notwithstanding any other provision of law, the Attorney General is authorized to require any alien to provide the alien's social security account number for purposes of inclusion in any record of the alien maintained by the Attorney General or the Service.

(June 27, 1952, c. 477, Title II, ch. 7, § 264, 66 Stat. 224; Nov. 14, 1986, Pub.L. 99–653, § 10, 100 Stat. 3657; Oct. 24, 1988, Pub.L. 100–525, § 8(i), 102

Stat. 2617; Nov. 29, 1990, Pub.L. 101–649, Title V, § 503(b)(2), 104 Stat. 5049; Sept. 30, 1996, Pub.L. 104–208, Div. C, Title IV, § 415, 110 Stat. 3009–669.)

§ 265. Notices of change of address [8 U.S.C.A. § 1305]

(a) Notification of change

Each alien required to be registered under this title who is within the United States shall notify the Attorney General in writing of each change of address and new address within ten days from the date of such change and furnish with such notice such additional information as the Attorney General may require by regulation.

(b) Current address of natives of any one or more foreign states

The Attorney General may in his discretion, upon ten days notice, require the natives of any one or more foreign states, or any class or group thereof, who are within the United States and who are required to be registered under this title, to notify the Attorney General of their current addresses and furnish such additional information as the Attorney General may require.

(c) Notice to parent or legal guardian

In the case of an alien for whom a parent or legal guardian is required to apply for registration, the notice required by this section shall be given to such parent or legal guardian.

(June 27, 1952, c. 477, Title II, c. 7, § 265, 66 Stat. 225; Pub.L. 97–116, § 11, Dec. 29, 1981, 95 Stat. 1617; Pub.L. 100–525, § 9(*o*), Oct. 24, 1988, 102 Stat. 2620.)

§ 266. Penalties [8 U.S.C.A. § 1306]

(a) Willful failure to register

Any alien required to apply for registration and to be fingerprinted in the United States who willfully fails or refuses to make such application or to be fingerprinted, and any parent or legal guardian required to apply for the registration of any alien who willfully fails or refuses to file application for the registration of such alien shall be guilty of a misdemeanor and shall, upon conviction thereof, be fined not to exceed $1,000 or be imprisoned not more than six months, or both.

(b) Failure to notify change of address

Any alien or any parent or legal guardian in the United States of any alien who fails to give written notice to the Attorney General, as required by section 265 [8 U.S.C.A. § 1305], shall be guilty of a misdemeanor and shall, upon conviction thereof, be fined not to exceed $200 or be imprisoned not more than thirty days, or both. Irrespective of whether an alien is convicted and punished as herein provided, any alien who fails to give written notice to the Attorney General, as required by section 265 [8 U.S.C.A. § 1305], shall be taken into custody and removed in the manner provided by chapter 4 of the title, unless such alien establishes to the satisfaction of the Attorney General that such failure was reasonably excusable or was not willful.

(c) Fraudulent statements

Any alien or any parent or legal guardian of any alien, who files an application for registration containing statements known by him to be false, or who procures or attempts to procure registration of himself or another person through fraud, shall be guilty of a misdemeanor and shall, upon conviction thereof, be fined not to exceed $1,000, or be imprisoned not more than six months, or both; and any alien so convicted shall, upon the warrant of the Attorney General, be taken into custody and be removed in the manner provided in part IV of this title.

(d) Counterfeiting

Any person who with unlawful intent photographs, prints, or in any other manner makes, or executes, any engraving, photograph, print, or impression in the likeness of any certificate of alien registration or an alien registration receipt card or any colorable imitation thereof, except when and as authorized under such rules and regulations as may be prescribed by the Attorney General, shall upon conviction be fined not to exceed $5,000 or be imprisoned not more than five years, or both.

(June 27, 1952, c. 477, Title II, ch. 7, § 266, 66 Stat. 225; Sept. 30, 1996, Pub.L. 104–208, Div. C, Title III, § 308(e)(2)(G), (g)(9)(A), 110 Stat. 3009–620, 3009–624.)

Chapter VIII—General Penalty Provisions

§ 271. Prevention of unauthorized landing of aliens [8 U.S.C.A. § 1321]

(a) Failure to report; penalties

It shall be the duty of every person, including the owners, masters, officers, and agents of vessels, aircraft, transportation lines, or international bridges or toll roads, other than transportation lines which may enter into a contract as provided in section 233 [8 U.S.C.A. § 1223], bringing an alien to, or providing a means for an alien to come to, the United States (including an alien crewman whose case is not covered by section 254(a) [8 U.S.C.A. § 1284(a)]) to prevent the landing of such alien in the United States at a port of entry other than as designated by the Attorney General or at any time or place other than as designated by the immigration officers. Any such person, owner, master, officer, or agent who fails to comply with the foregoing requirements shall be liable to a penalty to be imposed by the Attorney General of $3,000 for each such violation, which may, in the discretion of the Attorney General, be remitted or mitigated by him in accordance with such proceedings as he shall by regulation prescribe. Such penalty shall be a lien upon the vessel or aircraft whose owner, master, officer, or agent violates the provisions of this section, and such vessel or aircraft may be libeled therefor in the appropriate United States court.

(b) Prima facie evidence

Proof that the alien failed to present himself at the time and place designated by the immigration officers shall be prima facie evidence that such alien has landed in the United States at a time or place other than as designated by the immigration officers.

(c) Liability of owners and operators of international bridges and toll roads

(1) Any owner or operator of a railroad line, international bridge, or toll road who establishes to the satisfaction of the Attorney General that the person has acted diligently and reasonably to fulfill the duty imposed by subsection (a) shall not be liable for the penalty described in such subsection, notwithstanding the failure of the person to prevent the unauthorized landing of any alien.

(2)(A) At the request of any person described in paragraph (1), the Attorney General shall inspect any facility established, or any method utilized, at a point of entry into the United States by such person for the purpose of complying with subsection (a). The Attorney General shall approve any such facility or method (for such period of time as the Attorney General may prescribe) which the Attorney General determines is satisfactory for such purpose.

(B) Proof that any person described in paragraph (1) has diligently maintained any facility, or utilized any method, which has been approved by the Attorney General under subparagraph (A) (within the period for which the approval is effective) shall be prima facie evidence that such person acted diligently and reasonably to fulfill the duty imposed by subsection (a) (within the meaning of paragraph (1) of this subsection).

(June 27, 1952, c. 477, Title II, ch. 8, § 271, 66 Stat. 226; Nov. 6, 1986, Pub.L. 99–603, Title I, § 114, 100 Stat. 3383; Nov. 29, 1990, Pub.L. 101–649, Title V, § 543(a)(8), 104 Stat. 5058; Sept. 30, 1996, Pub.L. 104–208, Div. C, Title III, § 308(g)(1), 110 Stat. 3009–622.)

§ 272. Bringing in aliens subject to denial of admission on a health-related ground; persons liable; clearance papers; exceptions; "person" defined [8 U.S.C.A. § 1322]

(a) Any person who shall bring to the United States an alien (other than an alien crewman) who is inadmissible under section 212(a)(1) [8 U.S.C.A. § 1182(a)(1)] shall pay to the Commissioner for each and every alien so afflicted the sum of $3,000 unless (1) the alien was in possession of a valid, unexpired immigrant visa, or **(2)** the alien was allowed to land in the United States, or **(3)** the alien was in possession of a valid unexpired non-immigrant visa or other document authorizing such alien to apply for temporary admission to the United States or an unexpired reentry permit issued to him, and **(A)** such application was made within one hundred and twenty days of the date of issuance of the visa or other document, or in the case of an alien in possession of a reentry permit, within one hundred and twenty days of the date on which the alien was last examined and admitted by the Service, or **(B)** in the event the application was made later than one hundred and twenty days of the date of issuance of the visa or other document or such examination and admission, if such person establishes to the satisfaction of the Attorney General that the existence of the condition causing inadmissibility could not have been detected by the exercise of due diligence prior to the alien's embarkation.

(b) No vessel or aircraft shall be granted clearance papers pending determination of the question of liability to the payment of any fine under this section, or while the fines remain unpaid, nor shall such fines be remitted or refunded; but clearance may be granted prior to the determination of such question upon the deposit of a sum sufficient to cover such fines or of a bond with sufficient surety to secure the payment thereof, approved by the Commissioner.

(c) Nothing contained in this section shall be construed to subject transportation companies to a fine for bringing to ports of entry in the United States aliens who are entitled by law to exemption from the provisions of section 212(a) [8 U.S.C.A. § 1182(a)].

(d) As used in this section, the term "person" means the owner, master, agent, commanding officer, charterer, or consignee of any vessel or aircraft.

(June 27, 1952, c. 477, Title II, ch. 8, § 272, 66 Stat. 226; Oct. 3, 1965, Pub.L. 89–236, § 18, 79 Stat. 920; Nov. 29, 1990, Pub.L. 101–649, Title V, § 543(a)(9), Title VI, § 603(a)(15), 104 Stat. 5058, 5084; Dec. 12, 1991, Pub.L. 102–232, Title III, § 307(*l*)(7), 105 Stat. 1757; Oct. 25, 1994, Pub.L. 103–416, Title II, § 219(*o*), 108 Stat. 4317; Sept. 30, 1996, Pub.L. 104–208, Div. C, Title III, § 308(d)(3)(A), (4)(I)(i), 110 Stat. 3009–617, 3009–618.)

§ 273. Unlawful bringing of aliens into United States [8 U.S.C.A. § 1323]

(a) Persons liable

(1) It shall be unlawful for any person, including any transportation company, or the owner, master, commanding officer, agent, charterer, or consignee of any vessel or aircraft, to bring to the United States from any place outside thereof (other than from foreign contiguous territory) any alien who does not have a valid passport and an unexpired visa, if a visa was required under this Act or regulations issued thereunder.

(2) It is unlawful for an owner, agent, master, commanding officer, person in charge, purser, or consignee of a vessel or aircraft who is bringing an alien (except an alien crewmember) to the United

States to take any consideration to be kept or returned contingent on whether an alien is admitted to, or ordered removed from, the United States.

(b) Evidence

If it appears to the satisfaction of the Attorney General that any alien has been so brought, such person, or transportation company, or the master, commanding officer, agent, owner, charterer, or consignee of any such vessel or aircraft, shall pay to the Commissioner a fine of $3,000 for each alien so brought and, except in the case of any such alien who is admitted, or permitted to land temporarily, in addition, an amount equal to that paid by such alien for his transportation from the initial point of departure, indicated in his ticket, to the port of the arrival, such latter fine to be delivered by the Commissioner to the alien on whose account the assessment is made. No vessel or aircraft shall be granted clearance pending the determination of the liability to the payment of such fine or while such fine remains unpaid, except that clearance may be granted prior to the determination of such question upon the deposit of an amount sufficient to cover such fine, or of a bond with sufficient surety to secure the payment thereof approved by the Commissioner.

(c) Remission or refund

Except as provided in subsection (e), such fine shall not be remitted or refunded, unless it appears to the satisfaction of the Attorney General that such person, and the owner, master, commanding officer, agent, charterer, and consignee of the vessel or aircraft, prior to the departure of the vessel or aircraft from the last port outside the United States, did not know, and could not have ascertained by the exercise of reasonable diligence, that the individual transported was an alien and that a valid passport or visa was required.

(d) Repealed. Pub.L. 104–208, Div. C, Title III, § 308(e)(13), Sept. 30, 1996, 110 Stat. 3009–620.

(e) Reduction, refund, or waiver

A fine under this section may be reduced, refunded, or waived under such regulations as the Attorney General shall prescribe in cases in which—

(1) the carrier demonstrates that it had screened all passengers on the vessel or aircraft in accordance with procedures prescribed by the Attorney General, or

(2) circumstances exist that the Attorney General determines would justify such reduction, refund, or waiver.

(June 27, 1952, c. 477, Title II, ch. 8, § 273, 66 Stat. 227; Nov. 29, 1990, Pub.L. 101–649, Title II, § 201(b), Title V, § 543(a)(10), 104 Stat. 5014, 5058; Dec. 12, 1991, Pub.L. 102–232, Title III, § 306(c)(4)(D), 105 Stat. 1752; Oct. 25, 1994, Pub.L. 103–416, Title II, §§ 209(a), 216, 219(p), 108 Stat. 4312, 4315, 4317; Sept. 30, 1996, Pub.L. 104–208, Div. C, Title III, §§ 308(c)(3), (e)(13), 371(b)(8), Title VI, § 671(b)(6), (7), 110 Stat. 3009–616, 3009–620, 3009–645, 3009–722.)

§ 274. Bringing in and harboring certain aliens [8 U.S.C.A. § 1324]

(a) Criminal penalties

(1)(A) Any person who—

(i) knowing that a person is an alien, brings to or attempts to bring to the United States in any manner whatsoever such person at a place other than a designated port of entry or place other than as designated by the Commissioner, regardless of whether such alien has received prior official authorization to come to, enter, or reside in the United States and regardless of any future official action which may be taken with respect to such alien;

(ii) knowing or in reckless disregard of the fact that an alien has come to, entered, or remains in the United States in violation of law, transports, or moves or attempts to transport or move such alien within the United States by means of transportation or otherwise, in furtherance of such violation of law;

(iii) knowing or in reckless disregard of the fact that an alien has come to, entered, or remains in the United States in violation of law, conceals, harbors, or shields from detection, or attempts to conceal, harbor, or shield from detection, such alien in any place, including any building or any means of transportation;

(iv) encourages or induces an alien to come to, enter, or reside in the United States, knowing or in reckless disregard of the fact that such coming to, entry, or residence is or will be in violation of law; or

(v)(I) engages in any conspiracy to commit any of the preceding acts, or

(II) aids or abets the commission of any of the preceding acts,

shall be punished as provided in subparagraph (B).

(B) A person who violates subparagraph (A) shall, for each alien in respect to whom such a violation occurs—

(i) in the case of a violation of subparagraph (A)(i) or (v)(I) or in the case of a violation of subparagraph (A)(ii), (iii), or (iv) in which the offense was done for the purpose of commercial advantage or private financial gain, be fined under Title 18, imprisoned not more than 10 years, or both;

(ii) in the case of a violation of subparagraph (A) (ii), (iii), (iv), or (v)(II), be fined under Title 18, imprisoned not more than 5 years, or both;

(iii) in the case of a violation of subparagraph (A) (i), (ii), (iii), (iv), or (v) during and in relation to which the person causes serious bodily injury (as defined in section 1365 of Title 18) to, or places in jeopardy the life of, any person, be fined under Title 18, imprisoned not more than 20 years, or both; and

(iv) in the case of a violation of subparagraph (A) (i), (ii), (iii), (iv), or (v) resulting in the death of any person, be punished by death or imprisoned for any term of years or for life, fined under Title 18, or both.

(2) Any person who, knowing or in reckless disregard of the fact that an alien has not received prior official authorization to come to, enter, or reside in the United States, brings to or attempts to bring to the United States in any manner whatsoever, such alien, regardless of any official action which may later be taken with respect to such alien shall, for each alien in respect to whom a violation of this paragraph occurs—

(A) be fined in accordance with Title 18, or imprisoned not more than one year, or both; or

(B) in the case of—

(i) an offense committed with the intent or with reason to believe that the alien unlawfully brought into the United States will commit an offense against the United States or any State punishable by imprisonment for more than 1 year,

(ii) an offense done for the purpose of commercial advantage or private financial gain, or

(iii) an offense in which the alien is not upon arrival immediately brought and presented to an appropriate immigration officer at a designated port of entry,

be fined under Title 18, and shall be imprisoned, in the case of a first or second violation of subparagraph (B)(iii), not more than 10 years, in the case of a first or second violation of subparagraph (B)(i) or (B)(ii), not less than 3 nor more than 10 years, and for any other violation, not less than 5 nor more than 15 years.

(3)(A) Any person who, during any 12–month period, knowingly hires for employment at least 10 individuals with actual knowledge that the individuals are aliens described in subparagraph (B) shall be fined under Title 18, or imprisoned for not more than 5 years, or both.

(B) An alien described in this subparagraph is an alien who—

(i) is an unauthorized alien (as defined in section 274A(h)(3) [8 U.S.C.A. § 1324a(h)(3)]), and

(ii) has been brought into the United States in violation of this subsection.

(b) Seizure and forfeiture

(1) Any conveyance, including any vessel, vehicle, or aircraft, that has been or is being used in the commission of a violation of subsection (a), the gross proceeds of such violation, and any property traceable to such conveyance or proceeds, shall be seized and subject to forfeiture.

(2) Seizures and forfeitures under this subsection shall be governed by the provisions of chapter 46 of title 18, United States Code, relating to civil forfeitures, including section 981(d) of such title, except that such duties as are imposed upon the Secretary of the Treasury under the customs laws described in that section shall be performed by such officers, agents, and other persons as may be designated for that purpose by the Attorney General.

(3) In determining whether a violation of subsection (a) has occurred, any of the following shall be prima facie evidence that an alien involved in the alleged violation had not received prior official authorization to come to, enter, or reside in the United States or that such alien had come to, entered, or remained in the United States in violation of law:

(A) Records of any judicial or administrative proceeding in which that alien's status was an issue and in which it was determined that the alien had not received prior official authorization to come to, enter, or reside in the United States or that such alien had come to, entered, or remained in the United States in violation of law.

(B) Official records of the Service or of the Department of State showing that the alien had not received prior official authorization to come to, enter, or reside in the United States or that such alien had come to, entered, or remained in the United States in violation of law.

(C) Testimony, by an immigration officer having personal knowledge of the facts concerning that alien's status, that the alien had not received prior official authorization to come to, enter, or reside in the United States or that such alien had come to, entered, or remained in the United States in violation of law.

(c) Authority to arrest

No officer or person shall have authority to make any arrest for a violation of any provision of this section except officers and employees of the Service designated by the Attorney General, either individually or as a member of a class, and all other officers whose duty it is to enforce criminal laws.

(d) Admissibility of videotaped witness testimony

Notwithstanding any provision of the Federal Rules of Evidence, the videotaped (or otherwise audiovisually preserved) deposition of a witness to a violation of subsection (a) who has been deported or otherwise expelled from the United States, or is otherwise unable to testify, may be admitted into evidence in an action brought for that violation if the witness was available for cross examination and the deposition otherwise complies with the Federal Rules of Evidence.

(June 27, 1952, c. 477, Title II, ch. 8, § 274, 66 Stat. 228; Nov. 2, 1978, Pub.L. 95–582, § 2, 92 Stat. 2479; Dec. 29, 1981, Pub.L. 97–116, § 12, 95 Stat. 1617; Nov. 6, 1986, Pub.L. 99–603, § 112, 100 Stat. 3381; Oct. 24, 1988, Pub.L. 100–525, § 2(d), 102 Stat. 2610; Sept. 13, 1994, Pub.L. 103–322, Title VI, § 60024, 108 Stat. 1981; Sept. 30, 1996, Pub.L. 104–208, Div. C, Title II, §§ 203(a) to (d), 219, Title VI, § 671(a)(1), 110 Stat. 3009–565, 3009–566, 3009–574, 3009–721; April 25, 2000, Pub.L. 106–185, § 18, 114 Stat. 222.)

§ 274A. Unlawful employment of aliens [8 U.S.C.A. § 1324a]

(a) Making employment of unauthorized aliens unlawful

(1) In general

It is unlawful for a person or other entity—

(A) to hire, or to recruit or refer for a fee, for employment in the United States an alien knowing the alien is an unauthorized alien (as defined in subsection (h)(3)) with respect to such employment, or

(B) **(i)** to hire for employment in the United States an individual without complying with the requirements of subsection (b) or **(ii)** if the person or entity is an agricultural association, agricultural employer, or farm labor contractor (as defined in section 1802 of Title 29) to hire, or to recruit or refer for a fee, for employment in the United States an individual without complying with the requirements of subsection (b).

(2) Continuing employment

It is unlawful for a person or other entity, after hiring an alien for employment in accordance with paragraph (1), to continue to employ the alien in the United States knowing the alien is (or has become) an unauthorized alien with respect to such employment.

(3) Defense

A person or entity that establishes that it has complied in good faith with the requirements of subsection (b) with respect to the hiring, recruiting, or referral for employment of an alien in the United States has established an affirmative defense that the person or entity has not violated paragraph (1)(A) with respect to such hiring, recruiting, or referral.

(4) Use of labor through contract

For purposes of this section, a person or other entity who uses a contract, subcontract, or exchange, entered into, renegotiated, or extended after the date of the enactment of this section, to obtain the labor of an alien in the United States knowing that the alien is an unauthorized alien (as defined in subsection (h)(3)) with respect to performing such labor, shall be considered to have hired the alien for employment in the United States in violation of paragraph (1)(A).

(5) Use of State employment agency documentation

For purposes of paragraphs (1)(B) and (3), a person or entity shall be deemed to have complied with the requirements of subsection (b) with respect to the hiring of an individual who was referred for such employment by a State employment agency (as defined by the Attorney General), if the person or entity has and retains (for the period and in the manner described in subsection (b)(3)) appropriate documentation of such referral by that agency, which documentation certifies that the agency has complied with the procedures specified in subsection (b) with respect to the individual's referral.

(6) Treatment of documentation for certain employees

(A) In general

For purposes of this section, if—

(i) an individual is a member of a collective-bargaining unit and is employed, under a collective bargaining agreement entered into between one or more employee organizations and an association of two or more employers, by an employer that is a member of such association, and

(ii) within the period specified in subparagraph (B), another employer that is a member of the association (or an agent of such association on behalf of the employer) has complied with the requirements of subsection (b) with respect to the employment of the individual,

the subsequent employer shall be deemed to have complied with the requirements of subsection (b) with respect to the hiring of the employee and shall not be liable for civil penalties described in subsection (e)(5).

(B) Period

The period described in this subparagraph is 3 years, or, if less, the period of time that the individual is authorized to be employed in the United States.

(C) Liability

(i) In general

If any employer that is a member of an association hires for employment in the United States an individual and relies upon the provisions of subparagraph (A) to comply with the requirements of subsection (b) and the individual is an alien not authorized to work in the United States, then for the purposes of paragraph (1)(A), subject to clause (ii), the employer shall be presumed to have known at the time of hiring or afterward that the individual was an alien not authorized to work in the United States.

(ii) Rebuttal of presumption

The presumption established by clause (i) may be rebutted by the employer only through the presentation of clear and convincing evidence that the employer did not know (and could not reasonably have known) that the individual at the time of hiring or afterward was an alien not authorized to work in the United States.

(iii) Exception

Clause (i) shall not apply in any prosecution under subsection (f)(1).

(7) Application to Federal Government

For purposes of this section, the term "entity" includes an entity in any branch of the Federal Government.

(b) Employment verification system

The requirements referred to in paragraphs (1)(B) and (3) of subsection (a) are, in the case of a person or other entity hiring, recruiting, or referring an individual for employment in the United States, the requirements specified in the following three paragraphs:

(1) Attestation after examination of documentation

(A) In general

The person or entity must attest, under penalty of perjury and on a form designated or established by the Attorney General by regulation, that it has verified that the individual is not an unauthorized alien by examining—

(i) a document described in subparagraph (B), or

(ii) a document described in subparagraph (C) and a document described in subparagraph (D).

A person or entity has complied with the requirement of this paragraph with respect to examination of a document if the document reasonably appears on its face to be genuine. If an individual provides a document or combination of documents that reasonably appears on its face to be genuine and that is sufficient to meet the requirements of the first sentence of this paragraph, nothing in this paragraph shall be construed as requiring the person or entity to solicit the production of any other document or as requiring the individual to produce such another document.

(B) Documents establishing both employment authorization and identity

A document described in this subparagraph is an individual's—

(i) United States passport;

(ii) resident alien card, alien registration card, or other document designated by the Attorney General, if the document—

(I) contains a photograph of the individual and such other personal identifying information relating to the individual as the Attorney General finds, by regulation, sufficient for purposes of this subsection,

(II) is evidence of authorization of employment in the United States, and

(III) contains security features to make it resistant to tampering, counterfeiting, and fraudulent use.

(iii), (iv) Repealed. Pub.L. 104–208, Div. C, Title IV, § 412(a)(1)(A), Sept. 30, 1996, 110 Stat. 3009–666.

(v) Redesignated (ii)

(C) Documents evidencing employment authorization

A document described in this subparagraph is an individual's—

(i) social security account number card (other than such a card which specifies on the face that the issuance of the card does not authorize employment in the United States); or

(ii) other documentation evidencing authorization of employment in the United States which the Attorney General finds, by regulation, to be acceptable for purposes of this section.

(iii) Redesignated (ii)

(D) Documents establishing identity of individual

A document described in this subparagraph is an individual's—

(i) driver's license or similar document issued for the purpose of identification by a State, if it contains a photograph of the individual or such other personal identifying information relating to the individual as the Attorney General finds, by regulation, sufficient for purposes of this section; or

(ii) in the case of individuals under 16 years of age or in a State which does not provide for issuance of an identification document (other than a driver's license) referred to in clause (i), documentation of personal identity of such other type as the Attorney General finds, by regulation, provides a reliable means of identification.

(E) Authority to prohibit use of certain documents

If the Attorney General finds, by regulation, that any document described in subparagraph (B), (C), or (D) as establishing employment authorization or identity does not reliably establish such authorization or identity or is being used fraudulently to an unacceptable degree, the Attorney General may prohibit or place conditions on its use for purposes of this subsection.

(2) Individual attestation of employment authorization

The individual must attest, under penalty of perjury on the form designated or established for purposes of paragraph (1), that the individual is a citizen or national of the United States, an alien lawfully admitted for permanent residence, or an alien who is authorized under this Act or by the Attorney General to be hired, recruited, or referred for such employment.

(3) Retention of verification form

After completion of such form in accordance with paragraphs (1) and (2), the person or entity must retain the form and make it available for inspection by officers of the Service, the Special Counsel for Immigration–Related Unfair Employment Practices, or the Department of Labor during a period beginning on the date of the hiring, recruiting, or referral of the individual and ending—

(A) in the case of the recruiting or referral for a fee (without hiring) of an individual, three years after the date of the recruiting or referral, and

(B) in the case of the hiring of an individual—

(i) three years after the date of such hiring, or

(ii) one year after the date the individual's employment is terminated,

whichever is later.

(4) Copying of documentation permitted

Notwithstanding any other provision of law, the person or entity may copy a document presented by an individual pursuant to this subsection and may retain the copy, but only (except as otherwise permitted under law) for the purpose of complying with the requirements of this subsection.

(5) Limitation on use of attestation form

A form designated or established by the Attorney General under this subsection and any information contained in or appended to such form, may not be used for purposes other than for enforcement of this Act and sections 1001, 1028, 1546, and 1621 of Title 18.

(6) Good faith compliance

(A) In general

Except as provided in subparagraphs (B) and (C), a person or entity is considered to have complied with a requirement of this subsection notwithstanding a technical or procedural failure to meet such requirement if there was a good faith attempt to comply with the requirement.

(B) Exception if failure to correct after notice

Subparagraph (A) shall not apply if—

(i) the Service (or another enforcement agency) has explained to the person or entity the basis for the failure,

(ii) the person or entity has been provided a period of not less than 10 business days (beginning after the date of the explanation) within which to correct the failure, and

(iii) the person or entity has not corrected the failure voluntarily within such period.

(C) Exception for pattern or practice violators

Subparagraph (A) shall not apply to a person or entity that has or is engaging in a pattern or practice of violations of subsection (a)(1)(A) or (a)(2).

(c) No authorization of national identification cards

Nothing in this section shall be construed to authorize, directly or indirectly, the issuance or use of national identification cards or the establishment of a national identification card.

(d) Evaluation and changes in employment verification system

(1) Presidential monitoring and improvements in system

(A) Monitoring

The President shall provide for the monitoring and evaluation of the degree to which the employment verification system established under subsection (b) provides a secure system to determine employment eligibility in the United States and shall examine the suitability of existing Federal and State identification systems for use for this purpose.

(B) Improvements to establish secure system

To the extent that the system established under subsection (b) is found not to be a secure system to determine employment eligibility in the United States, the President shall, subject to paragraph (3) and taking into account the results of any demonstration projects conducted under paragraph (4), implement such changes in (including additions to) the requirements of subsection (b) as may be necessary to establish a secure system to determine employment eligibility in the United States. Such changes in the system may be implemented only if the changes conform to the requirements of paragraph (2).

(2) Restrictions on changes in system

Any change the President proposes to implement under paragraph (1) in the verification system must be designed in a manner so the verification system, as so changed, meets the following requirements:

(A) Reliable determination of identity

The system must be capable of reliably determining whether—

(i) a person with the identity claimed by an employee or prospective employee is eligible to work, and

(ii) the employee or prospective employee is claiming the identity of another individual.

(B) Using of counterfeit-resistant documents

If the system requires that a document be presented to or examined by an employer, the document must be in a form which is resistant to counterfeiting and tampering.

(C) Limited use of system

Any personal information utilized by the system may not be made available to Government agencies, employers, and other persons except to the extent necessary to verify that an individual is not an unauthorized alien.

(D) Privacy of information

The system must protect the privacy and security of personal information and identifiers utilized in the system.

(E) Limited denial of verification

A verification that an employee or prospective employee is eligible to be employed in the United States may not be withheld or revoked under the system for any reason other than that the employee or prospective employee is an unauthorized alien.

(F) Limited use for law enforcement purposes

The system may not be used for law enforcement purposes, other than for enforcement of this Act or sections 1001, 1028, 1546, and 1621 of Title 18.

(G) Restriction on use of new documents

If the system requires individuals to present a new card or other document (designed specifically for use for this purpose) at the time of hiring, recruitment, or referral, then such document may not be required to be presented for any purpose other than under this Act (or enforcement of sections 1001, 1028, 1546, and 1621 of Title 18) nor to be carried on one's person.

(3) Notice to Congress before implementing changes

(A) In general

The President may not implement any change under paragraph (1) unless at least—

(i) 60 days,

(ii) one year, in the case of a major change described in subparagraph (D)(iii), or

(iii) two years, in the case of a major change described in clause (i) or (ii) of subparagraph (D),

before the date of implementation of the change, the President has prepared and transmitted to the Committee on the Judiciary of the House of Representatives and to the Committee on the Judiciary of the Senate a written report setting forth the proposed change. If the President proposes to make any change regarding social security account number cards, the President shall transmit to the Committee on Ways and Means of the House of Representatives and to the Committee on Finance of the Senate a written report setting forth the proposed change. The President promptly shall cause to have printed in the Federal Register the substance of any major change (described in subparagraph (D)) proposed and reported to Congress.

(B) Contents of report

In any report under subparagraph (A) the President shall include recommendations for the establishment of civil and criminal sanctions for unauthorized use or disclosure of the information or identifiers contained in such system.

(C) Congressional review of major changes

(i) Hearings and review

The Committees on the Judiciary of the House of Representatives and of the Senate shall cause to have printed in the Congressional Record the substance of any major change described in subparagraph (D), shall hold hearings respecting the feasibility and desirability of implementing such a change, and, within the two year period before implementation, shall report to their respective Houses findings on whether or not such a change should be implemented.

(ii) Congressional action

No major change may be implemented unless the Congress specifically provides, in an appropriations or other Act, for funds for implementation of the change.

(D) Major changes defined

As used in this paragraph, the term "major change" means a change which would—

(i) require an individual to present a new card or other document (designed specifically for use for this purpose) at the time of hiring, recruitment, or referral,

(ii) provide for a telephone verification system under which an employer, recruiter, or referrer must transmit to a Federal official information concerning the immigration status of prospective employees and the official transmits to the person, and the person must record, a verification code, or

(iii) require any change in any card used for accounting purposes under the Social Security Act [42 U.S.C.A. § 301 et seq.]; including any change requiring that the only social security account number cards which may be presented in order to comply with subsection (b)(1)(C)(i) are such cards as are in a counterfeit-resistant form consistent with the second sentence of section 205(c)(2)(D) of the Social Security Act [42 U.S.C.A. § 405(c)(2)(D)].

(E) General revenue funding of social security card changes

Any costs incurred in developing and implementing any change described in subparagraph (D)(iii) for purposes of this subsection shall not be paid for out of any trust fund established under the Social Security Act.

(4) Demonstration projects

(A) Authority

The President may undertake demonstration projects (consistent with paragraph (2)) of different changes in the requirements of subsection (b). No such project may extend over a period of longer than five years.

(B) Reports on projects

The President shall report to the Congress on the results of demonstration projects conducted under this paragraph.

(e) Compliance

(1) Complaints and investigations

The Attorney General shall establish procedures—

(A) for individuals and entities to file written, signed complaints respecting potential violations of subsection (a) or (g)(1),

(B) for the investigation of those complaints which, on their face, have a substantial probability of validity,

(C) for the investigation of such other violations of subsection (a) or (g)(1) as the Attorney General determines to be appropriate, and

(D) for the designation in the Service of a unit which has, as its primary duty, the prosecution of cases of violations of subsection (a) or (g)(1) under this subsection.

(2) Authority in investigations

In conducting investigations and hearings under this subsection—

(A) immigration officers and administrative law judges shall have reasonable access to examine evidence of any person or entity being investigated,

(B) administrative law judges may, if necessary, compel by subpoena the attendance of witnesses and the production of evidence at any designated place or hearing, and

(C) immigration officers designated by the Commissioner may compel by subpoena the attendance of witnesses and the production of evidence at any designated place prior to the filing of a complaint in a case under paragraph (2).

In case of contumacy or refusal to obey a subpoena lawfully issued under this paragraph and upon application of the Attorney General, an appropriate district court of the United States may issue an order requiring compliance with such subpoena and any failure to obey such order may be punished by such court as a contempt thereof.

(3) Hearing

(A) In general

Before imposing an order described in paragraph (4), (5), or (6) against a person or entity under this subsection for a violation of subsection (a) or (g)(1), the Attorney General shall provide the person or entity with notice and, upon request made within a reasonable time (of not less than 30 days, as established by the Attorney General) of the date of the notice, a hearing respecting the violation.

(B) Conduct of hearing

Any hearing so requested shall be conducted before an administrative law judge. The hearing shall be conducted in accordance with the requirements of section 554 of Title 5. The hearing shall be held at the nearest practicable place to the place where the person or entity resides or of the place where the alleged violation occurred. If no hearing is so requested, the Attorney General's imposition of the order shall constitute a final and unappealable order.

(C) Issuance of orders

If the administrative law judge determines, upon the preponderance of the evidence received, that a person or entity named in the complaint has violated subsection (a) or (g)(1), the administrative law judge shall state his findings of fact and issue and cause to be served on such person or entity an order described in paragraph (4), (5), or (6).

(4) Cease and desist order with civil money penalty for hiring, recruiting, and referral violations

With respect to a violation of subsection (a)(1)(A) or (a)(2), the order under this subsection—

(A) shall require the person or entity to cease and desist from such violations and to pay a civil penalty in an amount of—

(i) not less than $250 and not more than $2,000 for each unauthorized alien with respect to whom a violation of either such subsection occurred.

(ii) not less than $2,000 and not more than $5,000 for each such alien in the case of a person or entity previously subject to one order under this paragraph, or

(iii) not less than $3,000 and not more than $10,000 for each such alien in the case of a person or entity previously subject to more than one order under this paragraph; and

(B) may require the person or entity—

(i) to comply with the requirements of subsection (b) (or subsection (d) if applicable) with respect to individuals hired (or recruited or referred for employment for a fee) during a period of up to three years, and

(ii) to take such other remedial action as is appropriate.

In applying this subsection in the case of a person or entity composed of distinct, physically separate subdivisions each of which provides separately for the hiring, recruiting, or referring for employment, without reference to the practices of, and not under the control of or common control with, another subdivision, each such subdivision shall be considered a separate person or entity.

(5) Order for civil money penalty for paperwork violations

With respect to a violation of subsection (a)(1)(B), the order under this subsection shall require the person or entity to pay a civil penalty in an amount of not less than $100 and not more than $1,000 for each individual with respect to whom such violation occurred. In determining the amount of the penalty, due consideration shall be given to the size of the business of the employer being charged, the good faith of the employer, the seriousness of the violation, whether or not the individual was an unauthorized alien, and the history of previous violations.

(6) Order for prohibited indemnity bonds

With respect to a violation of subsection (g)(1), the order under this subsection may provide for the remedy described in subsection (g)(2).

(7) Administrative appellate review

The decision and order of an administrative law judge shall become the final agency decision and order of the Attorney General unless either **(A)** within 30 days, an official delegated by regulation to exercise review authority over the decision and order modifies or vacates the decision and order, or **(B)** within 30 days of the date of such a modification or vacation (or within 60 days of the date of decision and order of an administrative law judge if not so modified or vacated) the decision and order is referred to the Attorney General pursuant to regulations, in which case the decision and order of the Attorney General shall become the final agency decision and order under this subsection. The Attorney General may not delegate the Attorney General's authority under this paragraph to any entity which has review authority over immigration-related matters.

(8) Judicial review

A person or entity adversely affected by a final order respecting an assessment may, within 45 days after the date the final order is issued, file a petition in the Court of Appeals for the appropriate circuit for review of the order.

(9) Enforcement of orders

If a person or entity fails to comply with a final order issued under this subsection against the person or entity, the Attorney General shall file a suit to seek compliance with the order in any appropriate district court of the United States. In any such suit, the validity and appropriateness of the final order shall not be subject to review.

(f) Criminal penalties and injunctions for pattern or practice violations

(1) Criminal penalty

Any person or entity which engages in a pattern or practice of violations of subsection (a)(1)(A) or (a)(2) shall be fined not more than $3,000 for each unauthorized alien with respect to whom such a violation occurs, imprisoned for not more than six months for the entire pattern or practice, or both, notwithstanding the provisions of any other Federal law relating to fine levels.

(2) Enjoining of pattern or practice violations

Whenever the Attorney General has reasonable cause to believe that a person or entity is engaged in a pattern or practice of employment, recruitment, or referral in violation of paragraph (1)(A) or (2) of subsection (a), the Attorney General may bring a civil action in the appropriate district court of the United States requesting such relief, including a permanent or temporary injunction, restraining order, or other order against the person or entity, as the Attorney General deems necessary.

(g) Prohibition of indemnity bonds

(1) Prohibition

It is unlawful for a person or other entity, in the hiring, recruiting, or referring for employment of any individual, to require the individual to post a bond or security, to pay or agree to pay an amount, or otherwise to provide a financial guarantee or indemnity, against any potential liability arising under this section relating to such hiring, recruiting, or referring of the individual.

(2) Civil penalty

Any person or entity which is determined, after notice and opportunity for an administrative hearing under subsection (e), to have violated paragraph (1) shall be subject to a civil penalty of $1,000 for each violation and to an administrative order requiring the return of any amounts received in violation of such paragraph to the employee or, if the employee cannot be located, to the general fund of the Treasury.

(h) Miscellaneous provisions

(1) Documentation

In providing documentation or endorsement of authorization of aliens (other than aliens lawfully admitted for permanent residence) authorized to be employed in the United States, the Attorney General shall provide that any limitations with respect to the period or type of employment or employer shall be conspicuously stated on the documentation or endorsement.

(2) Preemption

The provisions of this section preempt any State or local law imposing civil or criminal sanctions (other than through licensing and similar laws) upon those who employ, or recruit or refer for a fee for employment, unauthorized aliens.

(3) Definition of unauthorized alien

As used in this section, the term "unauthorized alien" means, with respect to the employment of an alien at a particular time, that the alien is not at that time either (A) an alien lawfully admitted for permanent residence, or (B) authorized to be so employed by this Act or by the Attorney General.

(i) to (n) Repealed. Pub.L. 104–208, Div. C, Title IV, § 412(c), Sept. 30, 1996, 110 Stat. 3009–668.

(June 27, 1952, c. 477, Title II, ch. 8, § 274A, as added Nov. 6, 1986, Pub.L. 99–603, Title I, § 101(a)(1), 100 Stat. 3360, and amended Oct. 24, 1988, Pub.L. 100–525, § 2(a)(1), 102 Stat. 2609; Nov. 29, 1990, Pub.L. 101–649, Title V, §§ 521(a), 538(a), 104 Stat. 5053, 5056; Dec. 12, 1991, Pub.L. 102–232, Title III, §§ 306(b)(2), 309(b)(11), 105 Stat. 1752, 1759; Oct. 25, 1994, Pub.L. 103–416, Title II, §§ 213, 219(z)(4), 108 Stat. 4314, 4318; Sept. 30, 1996, Pub.L. 104–208, Div. C, Title III, § 379(a), Title IV, §§ 411(a), 412(a) to (d), 416, 110 Stat. 3009–649, 3009–666 to 3009–669.)

§ 274B. Unfair immigration-related employment practices [8 U.S.C.A. § 1324b]

(a) Prohibition of discrimination based on national origin or citizenship status

(1) General rule

It is an unfair immigration-related employment practice for a person or other entity to discriminate against any individual (other than an unauthorized alien, as defined in section 274A(h)(3) [8 U.S.C.A. § 1324a(h)(3)]) with respect to the hiring, or recruitment or referral for a fee, of the individual for employment or the discharging of the individual from employment—

(A) because of such individual's national origin, or

(B) in the case of a protected individual (as defined in paragraph (3)), because of such individual's citizenship status.

(2) Exceptions

Paragraph (1) shall not apply to—

(A) a person or other entity that employs three or fewer employees,

(B) a person's or entity's discrimination because of an individual's national origin if the discrimination with respect to that person or entity and that individual is covered under section 2000e–2 of Title 42, or

(C) discrimination because of citizenship status which is otherwise required in order to comply with law, regulation, or executive order, or required by Federal, State, or local government contract, or which the Attorney General determines to be essential for an employer to do business with an agency or department of the Federal, State, or local government.

(3) Definition of protected individual

As used in paragraph (1), the term "protected individual" means an individual who—

(A) is a citizen or national of the United States, or

(B) is an alien who is lawfully admitted for permanent residence, is granted the status of an alien lawfully admitted for temporary residence under section 210(a) [8 U.S.C.A. § 1160(a)] or 245A(a)(1) [8 U.S.C.A. § 1255a(a)(1)], is admitted as a refugee under section 207 [8 U.S.C.A. § 1157], or is granted asylum under section 208 [8 U.S.C.A. § 1158]; but does not include **(i)** an alien who fails to apply for naturalization within six months of the date the alien first becomes eligible (by virtue of period of lawful permanent residence) to apply for naturalization or, if later, within six months after November 6, 1986 and **(ii)** an alien who has applied on a timely basis, but has not been naturalized as a citizen within 2 years after the date of the application, unless the alien can establish that the alien is actively pursuing naturalization, except that time consumed in the Service's processing the application shall not be counted toward the 2-year period.

(4) Additional exception providing right to prefer equally qualified citizens

Notwithstanding any other provision of this section, it is not an unfair immigration-related employment practice for a person or other entity to prefer to hire, recruit, or refer an individual who is a citizen or national of the United States over another individual who is an alien if the two individuals are equally qualified.

(5) Prohibition of intimidation or retaliation

It is also an unfair immigration-related employment practice for a person or other entity to intimidate, threaten, coerce, or retaliate against any individual for the purpose of interfering with any right or privilege secured under this section or because the individual intends to file or has filed a charge or a complaint, testified, assisted, or participated in any manner in an investigation, proceeding, or hearing under this section. An individual so intimidated, threatened, coerced, or retaliated against shall be considered, for purposes of subsections (d) and (g), to have been discriminated against.

(6) Treatment of certain documentary practices as employment practices

A person's or other entity's request, for purposes of satisfying the requirements of section 274A(b) [8 U.S.C.A. § 1324a(b)], for more or different documents than are required under such section or refusing to honor documents tendered that on their face reasonably appear to be genuine shall be treated as an unfair immigration-related employment practice if made for the purpose or with the intent of discriminating against an individual in violation of paragraph (1).

(b) Charges of violations

(1) In general

Except as provided in paragraph (2), any person alleging that the person is adversely affected directly by an unfair immigration-related employment practice (or a person on that person's behalf) or an officer of the Service alleging that an unfair immigration-related employment practice has occurred or is occurring may file a charge respecting such practice or violation with the Special Counsel (appointed under subsection (c)). Charges shall be in writing under oath or affirmation and shall contain such information as the Attorney General requires. The Special Counsel by certified mail shall serve a notice of the charge (including the date, place, and circumstances of the alleged unfair immigration-related employment practice) on the person or entity involved within 10 days.

(2) No overlap with EEOC complaints

No charge may be filed respecting an unfair immigration-related employment practice described in subsection (a)(1)(A) if a charge with respect to that practice based on the same set of facts has been filed with the Equal Employment Opportunity Commission under title VII of the Civil Rights Act of 1964 [42 U.S.C.A. § 2000e et seq.], unless the charge is dismissed as being outside the scope of such title. No charge respecting an employment practice may be filed with the Equal Employment Opportunity Commission under such title if a charge with respect to such practice based on the same set of facts has been filed under this subsection, unless the charge is dismissed under this section as being outside the scope of this section.

(c) Special Counsel

(1) Appointment

The President shall appoint, by and with the advice and consent of the Senate, a Special Counsel for Immigration–Related Unfair Employment Practices (hereinafter in this section referred to as the "Special Counsel") within the Department of Justice to serve for a term of four years. In the case of a vacancy in the office of the Special Counsel the President may designate the officer or employee who shall act as Special Counsel during such vacancy.

(2) Duties

The Special Counsel shall be responsible for investigation of charges and issuance of complaints under this section and in respect of the prosecution of all such complaints before administrative law judges and the exercise of certain functions under subsection (j)(1).

(3) Compensation

The Special Counsel is entitled to receive compensation at a rate not to exceed the rate now or hereafter provided for grade GS–17 of the General Schedule, under section 5332 of Title 5.

(4) Regional offices

The Special Counsel, in accordance with regulations of the Attorney General, shall establish such regional offices as may be necessary to carry out his duties.

(d) Investigation of charges

(1) By Special Counsel

The Special Counsel shall investigate each charge received and, within 120 days of the date of the receipt of the charge, determine whether or not there is reasonable cause to believe that the charge is true and whether nor not to bring a complaint with respect to the charge before an administrative law judge. The Special Counsel may, on his own initiative, conduct investigations respecting unfair immigration-related employment practices and, based on such an investigation and subject to paragraph (3), file a complaint before such a judge.

(2) Private actions

If the Special Counsel, after receiving such a charge respecting an unfair immigration-related employment practice which alleges knowing and intentional discriminatory activity or a pattern or practice of discriminatory activity, has not filed a complaint before an administrative law judge with respect to such charge within such 120–day period, the Special Counsel shall notify the person making the charge of the determination not to file such a complaint during such period and the person making the charge may (subject to paragraph (3)) file a complaint directly before such a judge within 90 days after the date of receipt of the notice. The Special Counsel's failure to file such a complaint within such 120–day period shall not affect the right of the Special Counsel to investigate the charge or to bring a complaint before an administrative law judge during such 90–day period.

(3) Time limitations on complaints

No complaint may be filed respecting any unfair immigration-related employment practice occurring more than 180 days prior to the date of the filing of the charge with the Special Counsel. This subparagraph shall not prevent the subsequent amending of a charge or complaint under subsection (e)(1).

(e) Hearings

(1) Notice

Whenever a complaint is made that a person or entity has engaged in or is engaging in any such unfair immigration-related employment practice, an administrative law judge shall have power to issue and cause to be served upon such person or entity a copy of the complaint and a notice of hearing before the judge at a place therein fixed, not less than five days after the serving of the complaint. Any such complaint may be amended by the judge conducting the hearing, upon the motion of the party filing the complaint, in the judge's discretion at any time prior to the issuance of an order based thereon. The person or entity so complained of shall have the right to file an answer to the original or amended complaint and to appear in person or otherwise and give testimony at the place and time fixed in the complaint.

(2) Judges hearing cases

Hearings on complaints under this subsection shall be considered before administrative law judges who are specially designated by the Attorney General as having special training respecting employment discrimination and, to the extent practicable, before such judges who only consider cases under this section.

(3) Complainant as party

Any person filing a charge with the Special Counsel respecting an unfair immigration-related employment practice shall be considered a party to any complaint before an administrative law judge respecting such practice and any subsequent appeal respecting that complaint. In the discretion of the judge conducting the hearing, any other person may be allowed to intervene in the proceeding and to present testimony.

(f) Testimony and authority of hearing officers

(1) Testimony

The testimony taken by the administrative law judge shall be reduced to writing. Thereafter, the judge, in his discretion, upon notice may provide for the taking of further testimony or hear argument.

(2) Authority of administrative law judges

In conducting investigations and hearings under this subsection and in accordance with regulations of the Attorney General, the Special Counsel and administrative law judges shall have reasonable access to examine evidence of any person or entity being investigated. The administrative law judges by subpoena may compel the attendance of witnesses and the production of evidence at any designated place or hearing. In case of contumacy or refusal to obey a subpoena lawfully issued under this paragraph and upon application of the administrative law judge, an appropriate district court of the United States may issue an order requiring compliance with such subpoena and any failure to obey such order may be punished by such court as a contempt thereof.

(g) Determinations

(1) Order

The administrative law judge shall issue and cause to be served on the parties to the proceeding an order, which shall be final unless appealed as provided under subsection (i).

(2) Orders finding violations

(A) In general

If, upon the preponderance of the evidence, an administrative law judge determines that any person or entity named in the complaint has engaged in or is engaging in any such unfair immigration-related employment practice, then the judge shall state his findings of fact and shall issue and cause to be served on such person or entity an order which requires such person or entity to cease and desist from such unfair immigration-related employment practice.

(B) Contents of order

Such an order also may require the person or entity—

(i) to comply with the requirements of section 274A(b) [8 U.S.C.A. § 1324a(b)] with respect to individuals hired (or recruited or referred for employment for a fee) during a period of up to three years;

(ii) to retain for the period referred to in clause (i) and only for purposes consistent with section 274A(b)(5) [8 U.S.C.A. § 1324a(b)(5)], the name and address of each individual who applies, in person or in writing, for hiring for an existing position, or for recruiting or referring for a fee, for employment in the United States;

(iii) to hire individuals directly and adversely affected, with or without back pay;

(iv)(I) except as provided in subclauses (III) through (IV), to pay a civil penalty of not less than $250 and not more than $2,000 for each individual discriminated against,

(II) except as provided in subclauses (III) and (IV), in the case of a person or entity previously subject to a single order under this paragraph, to pay a civil penalty of not less than $2,000 and not more than $5,000 for each individual discriminated against,

(III) except as provided in subclause (IV), in the case of a person or entity previously subject to more than one order under this paragraph, to pay a civil penalty of not less than $3,000 and not more than $10,000 for each individual discriminated against, and

(IV) in the case of an unfair immigration-related employment practice described in subsection (a)(6) of this section, to pay a civil penalty of not less than $100 and not more than $1,000 for each individual discriminated against;

(v) to post notices to employees about their rights under this section and employers' obligations under section 274A [8 U.S.C.A. § 1324a];

(vi) to educate all personnel involved in hiring and complying with this section or section 274A [8 U.S.C.A. § 1324a] about the requirements of this section or such section;

(vii) to remove (in an appropriate case) a false performance review or false warning from an employee's personnel file; and

(viii) to lift (in an appropriate case) any restrictions on an employee's assignments, work shifts, or movements.

(C) Limitation on back pay remedy

In providing a remedy under subparagraph (B)(iii), back pay liability shall not accrue from a date more than two years prior to the date of the filing of a charge with the Special Counsel. Interim earnings or amounts earnable with reasonable diligence by the individual or individuals discriminated against shall operate to reduce the back pay otherwise allowable under such subparagraph. No order shall require the hiring of an individual as an employee or the payment to an individual of any back pay, if the individual was refused employment for any reason other than discrimination on account of national origin or citizenship status.

(D) Treatment of distinct entities

In applying this subsection in the case of a person or entity composed of distinct, physically separate subdivisions each of which provides separately for the hiring, recruiting, or referring for employment, without reference to the practices of, and not under the control of or common control with, another subdivision, each such subdivision shall be considered a separate person or entity.

(3) Orders not finding violations

If upon the preponderance of the evidence an administrative law judge determines that the person or entity named in the complaint has not engaged and is not engaging in any such unfair immigration-related employment practice, then the judge shall state his findings of fact and shall issue an order dismissing the complaint.

(h) Awarding of attorney's fees

In any complaint respecting an unfair immigration-related employment practice, an administrative law judge, in the judge's discretion, may allow a prevailing party, other than the United States, a reasonable attorney's fee, if the losing party's argument is without reasonable foundation in law and fact.

(i) Review of final orders

(1) In general

Not later than 60 days after the entry of such final order, any person aggrieved by such final order may seek a review of such order in the United States court of appeals for the circuit in which the violation is alleged to have occurred or in which the employer resides or transacts business.

(2) Further review

Upon the filing of the record with the court, the jurisdiction of the court shall be exclusive and its judgment shall be final, except that the same shall be subject to review by the Supreme Court of the United States upon writ of certiorari or certification as provided in section 1254 of Title 28.

(j) Court enforcement of administrative orders

(1) In general

If an order of the agency is not appealed under subsection (i)(1), the Special Counsel (or, if the Special Counsel fails to act, the person filing the charge) may petition the United States district court for the district in which a violation of the order is alleged to have occurred, or in which the respondent resides or transacts business, for the enforcement of the order of the administrative law judge, by filing in such court a written petition praying that such order be enforced.

(2) Court enforcement order

Upon the filing of such petition, the court shall have jurisdiction to make and enter a decree enforcing the order of the administrative law judge. In such a proceeding, the order of the administrative law judge shall not be subject to review.

(3) Enforcement decree in original review

If, upon appeal of an order under subsection (i)(1), the United States court of appeals does not reverse such order, such court shall have the jurisdiction to make and enter a decree enforcing the order of the administrative law judge.

(4) Awarding of attorney's fees

In any judicial proceeding under subsection (i) or this subsection, the court, in its discretion, may allow a prevailing party, other than the United States, a reasonable attorney's fee as part of costs but only if the losing party's argument is without reasonable foundation in law and fact.

(k) Termination dates

(1) This section shall not apply to discrimination in hiring, recruiting, referring, or discharging of individuals occurring after the date of any termination of the provisions of section 274A [8 U.S.C.A. § 1324a], under subsection (*l*) of that section.

(2) The provisions of this section shall terminate 30 calendar days after receipt of the last report required to be transmitted under section 274A(i) [8 U.S.C.A. § 1324a(i)] if—

(A) the Comptroller General determines, and so reports in such report that—

(i) no significant discrimination has resulted, against citizens or nationals of the United States or against any eligible workers seeking employment, from the implementation of section 274A [8 U.S.C.A. § 1324a], or

(ii) such section has created an unreasonable burden on employers hiring such workers; and

(B) there has been enacted, within such period of 30 calendar days, a joint resolution stating in substance that the Congress approves the findings of the Comptroller General contained in such report.

The provisions of subsections (m) and (n) of section 274A [8 U.S.C.A. § 1324a] shall apply to any joint resolution under subparagraph (B) in the same manner as they apply to a joint resolution under subsection (*l*) of such section.

(*l*) Dissemination of information concerning anti-discrimination provisions

(1) Not later than 3 months after November 29, 1990, the Special Counsel, in cooperation with the chairman of the Equal Employment Opportunity Commission, the Secretary of Labor, and the Administrator of the Small Business Administration, shall conduct a campaign to disseminate information respecting the rights and remedies prescribed under this section and under title VII of the Civil Rights Act of 1964 [42 U.S.C.A. § 2000e et seq.] in connection with unfair immigration-related employment practices. Such campaign shall be aimed at increasing the knowledge of employers, employees, and the general public concerning employer and employee rights, responsibilities, and remedies under this section and such title.

(2) In order to carry out the campaign under this subsection, the Special Counsel—

(A) may, to the extent deemed appropriate and subject to the availability of appropriations, contract with public and private organizations for outreach activities under the campaign, and

(B) shall consult with the Secretary of Labor, the chairman of the Equal Employment Opportunity Commission, and the heads of such other agencies as may be appropriate.

(3) There are authorized to be appropriated to carry out this subsection $10,000,000 for each fiscal year (beginning with fiscal year 1991).

(June 27, 1952, c. 477, Title II, ch. 8, § 274B, as added Nov. 6, 1986, Pub.L. 99–603, Title I, 102(a), 100 Stat. 3374, and amended Oct. 24, 1988, Pub.L. 100–525, § 2(b), 102 Stat. 2610; Nov. 29, 1990, Pub.L. 101–649, Title V, §§ 531, 532(a), 533(a), 534(a), 535(a), 536(a), 537(a), 539(a), 104 Stat. 5054, 5055, 5056; Dec. 12, 1991, Pub.L. 102–232, Title III, § 306(b)(1),(3),(c)(1), 105 Stat. 1752; Oct. 25, 1994, Pub.L. 103–416, Title II, § 219(q), 108 Stat. 4317; Sept. 30, 1996, Pub.L. 104–208, Div. C, Title IV, § 421(a), Title VI, § 671(d)(1)(B), 110 Stat. 3009–670, 3009–723.)

§ 274C. Penalties for document fraud [8 U.S.C.A. § 1324c]

(a) Activities prohibited

It is unlawful for any person or entity knowingly—

(1) to forge, counterfeit, alter, or falsely make any document for the purpose of satisfying a requirement of this Act or to obtain a benefit under this Act,

(2) to use, attempt to use, possess, obtain, accept, or receive or to provide any forged, counterfeit, altered, or falsely made document in order to satisfy any requirement of this Act or to obtain a benefit under this Act,

(3) to use or attempt to use or to provide or attempt to provide any document lawfully issued to or with respect to a person other than the possessor (including a deceased individual) for the purpose of satisfying a requirement of this Act or obtaining a benefit under this Act,

(4) to accept or receive or to provide any document lawfully issued to or with respect to a person other than the possessor (including a deceased individual) for the purpose of complying with section 274A(b) [8 U.S.C.A. § 1324a(b)] or obtaining a benefit under this Act, or

(5) to prepare, file, or assist another in preparing or filing, any application for benefits under this Act, or any document required under this Act, or any document submitted in connection with such application or document, with knowledge or in reckless disregard of the fact that such application or document was falsely made or, in whole or in part, does not relate to the person on whose behalf it was or is being submitted, or

(6) (A) to present before boarding a common carrier for the purpose of coming to the United States a document which relates to the alien's eligibility to enter the United States, and (B) to fail to present such document to an immigration officer upon arrival at a United States port of entry.

(b) Exception

This section does not prohibit any lawfully authorized investigative, protective, or intelligence activity of a law enforcement agency of the

United States, a State, or a subdivision of a State, or of an intelligence agency of the United States, or any activity authorized under chapter 224 of Title 18.

(c) Construction

Nothing in this section shall be construed to diminish or qualify any of the penalties available for activities prohibited by this section but proscribed as well in Title 18.

(d) Enforcement

(1) Authority in investigations

In conducting investigations and hearings under this subsection—

(A) immigration officers and administrative law judges shall have reasonable access to examine evidence of any person or entity being investigated,

(B) administrative law judges, may, if necessary, compel by subpoena the attendance of witnesses and the production of evidence at any designated place or hearing, and

(C) immigration officers designated by the Commissioner may compel by subpoena the attendance of witnesses and the production of evidence at any designated place prior to the filing of a complaint in a case under paragraph (2).

In case of contumacy or refusal to obey a subpoena lawfully issued under this paragraph and upon application of the Attorney General, an appropriate district court of the United States may issue an order requiring compliance with such subpoena and any failure to obey such order may be punished by such court as a contempt thereof.

(2) Hearing

(A) In general

Before imposing an order described in paragraph (3) against a person or entity under this subsection for a violation of subsection (a), the Attorney General shall provide the person or entity with notice and, upon request made within a reasonable time (of not less than 30 days, as established by the Attorney General) of the date of the notice, a hearing respecting the violation.

(B) Conduct of hearing

Any hearing so requested shall be conducted before an administrative law judge. The hearing shall be conducted in accordance with the requirements of section 554 of Title 5. The hearing shall be held at the nearest practicable place to the place where the person or entity resides or of the place where the alleged violation occurred. If no hearing is so requested, the Attorney General's imposition of the order shall constitute a final and unappealable order.

(C) Issuance of orders

If the administrative law judge determines, upon the preponderance of the evidence received, that a person or entity has violated subsection (a), the administrative law judge shall state his findings of fact and issue and cause to be served on such person or entity an order described in paragraph (3).

(3) Cease and desist order with civil money penalty

With respect to a violation of subsection (a), the order under this subsection shall require the person or entity to cease and desist from such violations and to pay a civil penalty in an amount of—

(A) not less than $250 and not more than $2,000 for each document that is the subject of a violation under subsection (a), or

(B) in the case of a person or entity previously subject to an order under this paragraph, not less than $2,000 and not more than $5,000 for each document that is the subject of a violation under subsection (a).

In applying this subsection in the case of a person or entity composed of distinct, physically separate subdivisions each of which provides separately for the hiring, recruiting, or referring for employment, without reference to the practices of, and not under the control of or common control with, another subdivision, each such subdivision shall be considered a separate person or entity.

(4) Administrative appellate review

The decision and order of an administrative law judge shall become the final agency decision and order of the Attorney General unless either **(A)** within 30 days, an official delegated by regulation to exercise review authority over the decision and order modifies or vacates the decision and order, or **(B)** within 30 days of the date of such a modification or vacation (or within 60 days of the date of decision and order of an administrative law judge if not so modified or vacated) the decision and order is referred to the Attorney General pursuant to regulations, in which case the decision and order of the Attorney General shall become the final agency decision and order under this subsection.

(5) Judicial review

A person or entity adversely affected by a final order under this section may, within 45 days after the date the final order is issued, file a petition in the Court of Appeals for the appropriate circuit for review of the order.

(6) Enforcement of orders

If a person or entity fails to comply with a final order issued under this section against the person or entity, the Attorney General shall file a suit to seek compliance with the order in any appropriate district court of the United States. In any such suit, the validity and appropriateness of the final order shall not be subject to review.

(7) Waiver by Attorney General

The Attorney General may waive the penalties imposed by this section with respect to an alien who knowingly violates subsection (a)(6) if the alien is granted asylum under section 208 [8 U.S.C.A. § 1158] or withholding of removal under section 241(b)(3) [8 U.S.C.A. § 1231(b)(3)].

(e) Criminal penalties for failure to disclose role as document preparer

(1) Whoever, in any matter within the jurisdiction of the Service, knowingly and willfully fails to disclose, conceals, or covers up the fact that they have, on behalf of any person and for a fee or other remuneration, prepared or assisted in preparing an application which was falsely made (as defined in subsection (f)) for immigration benefits, shall be fined in accordance with Title 18, imprisoned for not more than 5 years, or both, and prohibited from preparing or assisting in preparing, whether or not for a fee or other remuneration, any other such application.

(2) Whoever, having been convicted of a violation of paragraph (1), knowingly and willfully prepares or assists in preparing an application for immigration benefits pursuant to this Act, or the regulations promulgated thereunder, whether or not for a fee or other remuneration and regardless of whether in any matter within the jurisdiction of the Service, shall be fined in accordance with Title 18, imprisoned for not more than 15 years, or both, and prohibited from preparing or assisting in preparing any other such application.

(f) Falsely make

For purposes of this section, the term "falsely make" means to prepare or provide an application or document, with knowledge or in reckless disregard of the fact that the application or document contains a false, fictitious, or fraudulent statement or material representation, or has no basis in law or fact, or otherwise fails to state a fact which is material to the purpose for which it was submitted.

(June 27, 1952, c. 477, Title II, ch. 8, § 274C, as added Nov. 29, 1990, Pub.L. 101–649, Title V, § 544(a), 104 Stat. 5059, and amended Dec. 12, 1991, Pub.L. 102–232, Title III, § 306(c)(5)(A), 105 Stat. 1752; Oct. 25, 1994, Pub.L. 103–416, Title II, § 219(r), 108 Stat. 4317; Sept. 30, 1996, Pub.L. 104–208, Div. C, Title II, §§ 212(a) to (d), 213, 220, Title III, §§ 308(g)(10)(D), 379(a), 110 Stat. 3009–570, 3009–571, 3009–575, 3009–625, 3009–649.)

§ 274D. Civil penalties for failure to depart [8 U.S.C.A. § 1324d]

(a) In general

Any alien subject to a final order of removal who—

(1) willfully fails or refuses to—

(A) depart from the United States pursuant to the order,

(B) make timely application in good faith for travel or other documents necessary for departure, or

(C) present for removal at the time and place required by the Attorney General; or

(2) conspires to or takes any action designed to prevent or hamper the alien's departure pursuant to the order,

shall pay a civil penalty of not more than $500 to the Commissioner for each day the alien is in violation of this section.

(b) Construction

Nothing in this section shall be construed to diminish or qualify any penalties to which an alien may be subject for activities proscribed by section 243(a) [8 U.S.C.A. § 1253(a)] or any other section of this Act.

(June 27, 1952, c. 477, Title II, ch. 8, § 274D, as added Sept. 30, 1996, Pub.L. 104–208, Div. C, Title III, § 380(a), 110 Stat. 3009–650.)

§ 275. Improper entry by alien [8 U.S.C.A. § 1325]

(a) Improper time or place; avoidance of examination or inspection; misrepresentation and concealment of facts

Any alien who **(1)** enters or attempts to enter the United States at any time or place other than as designated by immigration officers, or **(2)** eludes examination or inspection by immigration officers, or **(3)** attempts to enter or obtains entry to the United States by a willfully false or misleading representation or the willful concealment of a material fact, shall, for the first commission of any such offense, be fined under Title 18 or imprisoned not more than 6 months, or both, and, for a subsequent commission of any such offense, be fined under Title 18, or imprisoned not more than 2 years, or both.

(b) Civil penalty for illegal entry

Any alien who is apprehended while entering (or attempting to enter) the United States at a time or place other than as designated by immigration officers shall be subject to a civil penalty of—

(1) at least $50 and not more than $250 for each such entry (or attempted entry); or

(2) twice the amount specified in paragraph (1) in the case of an alien who has been previously subject to a civil penalty under this subsection.

Civil penalties under this subsection are in addition to, and not in lieu of, any criminal or other civil penalties that may be imposed.

(c) Marriage fraud

Any individual who knowingly enters into a marriage for the purpose of evading any provision of the immigration laws shall be imprisoned for not more than 5 years, or fined not more than $250,000, or both.

(d) Immigration-related entrepreneurship fraud

Any individual who knowingly establishes a commercial enterprise for the purpose of evading any provision of the immigration laws shall be imprisoned for not more than 5 years, fined in accordance with Title 18, or both.

(June 27, 1952, c. 477, Title II, ch. 8, § 275, 66 Stat. 229; Nov. 10, 1986, Pub.L. 99–639, § 2(d), 100 Stat. 3542; Nov. 29, 1990, Pub.L. 101–649, Title I, § 121(b)(3), Title V, § 543(b)(2), 104 Stat. 4994, 5059; Dec. 12, 1991, Pub.L. 102–232, Title III, § 306(c)(3), 105 Stat. 1752; Sept. 30, 1996, Pub.L. 104–208, Div C, Title I, § 105(a), 110 Stat. 3009–556.)

§ 276. Reentry of deported alien; criminal penalties for reentry of certain deported aliens [8 U.S.C.A. § 1326]

(a) Subject to subsection (b), any alien who—

(1) has been denied admission, excluded, deported, or removed or has departed the United States while an order of exclusion, deportation, or removal is outstanding, and thereafter.

(2) enters, attempts to enter, or is at any time found in, the United States, unless **(A)** prior to his reembarkation at a place outside the United States or his application for admission from foreign contiguous territory, the Attorney General has expressly consented to such alien's reapplying for admission; or **(B)** with respect to an alien previously denied admission and removed, unless such alien shall establish that he was not required to obtain such advance consent under this or any prior Act,

shall be fined under Title 18, or imprisoned not more than 2 years, or both.

(b) Notwithstanding subsection (a), in the case of any alien described in such subsection—

(1) whose removal was subsequent to a conviction for commission of three or more misdemeanors involving drugs, crimes against the person, or both, or a felony (other than an aggravated felony), such alien shall be fined under Title 18, imprisoned not more than 10 years, or both;

(2) whose removal was subsequent to a conviction for commission of an aggravated felony, such alien shall be fined under such Title, imprisoned not more than 20 years, or both;

(3) who has been excluded from the United States pursuant to section 235(c) [8 U.S.C.A. § 1225(c)] because the alien was excludable under section 212(a)(3)(B) [8 U.S.C.A. § 1182(a)(3)(B)] or who has been removed from the United States pursuant to the provisions of title V, and who thereafter, without the permission of the Attorney General, enters the United States, or attempts to do so, shall be fined under Title 18, and imprisoned for a period of 10 years, which sentence shall not run concurrently with any other sentence; or

(4) who was removed from the United States pursuant to section 241(a)(4)(B) [8 U.S.C.A. § 1231(a)(4)(B)] who thereafter, without the permission of the Attorney General, enters, attempts to enter, or is at any time found in, the United States (unless the Attorney General has expressly consented to such alien's reentry) shall be fined under Title 18, imprisoned for not more than 10 years, or both.

For the purposes of this subsection, the term "removal" includes any agreement in which an alien stipulates to removal during (or not during) a criminal trial under either Federal or State law.

(c) Any alien deported pursuant to section 242(h)(2) [8 U.S.C.A. § 1252(h)(2)] who enters, attempts to enter, or is at any time found in, the United States (unless the Attorney General has expressly consented to such alien's reentry) shall be incarcerated for the remainder of the sentence of imprisonment which was pending at the time of deportation without any reduction for parole or supervised release. Such alien shall be subject to such other penalties relating to the reentry of deported aliens as may be available under this section or any other provision of law.

(d) In a criminal proceeding under this section, an alien may not challenge the validity of the deportation order described in subsection (a)(1) or subsection (b) unless the alien demonstrates that—

(1) the alien exhausted any administrative remedies that may have been available to seek relief against the order;

(2) the deportation proceedings at which the order was issued improperly deprived the alien of the opportunity for judicial review; and

(3) the entry of the order was fundamentally unfair.

(June 27, 1952, c. 477, Title II, ch. 8, § 276, 66 Stat. 229; Nov. 18, 1988, Pub.L. 100–690, Title VII, § 7345(a), 102 Stat. 4471; Nov. 29, 1990, Pub.L. 101–649, Title V, § 543(b)(3), 104 Stat. 5059; Sept. 13, 1994, Pub.L. 103–322, Title XIII, § 130001(b), 108 Stat. 2023; Apr. 24, 1996, Pub.L. 104–132, Title IV, §§ 401(c), 438(b), 441(a), 110 Stat. 1267, 1276, 1279; Sept. 30, 1996, Pub.L. 104–208, Div. C, Title III, §§ 305(b), 308(d)(4)(J), (e)(1)(K), (14)(A), 324(a), (b), 110 Stat. 3009–606, 3009–618, 3009–619, 3009–620, 3009–629.)

§ 277. Aiding or assisting certain aliens to enter [8 U.S.C.A. § 1327]

Any person who knowingly aids or assists any alien inadmissible under section 212(a)(2) [8 U.S.C.A. § 1182(a)(2)] (insofar as an alien inadmissible under such section has been convicted of an aggravated felony) or 212(a)(3) [8 U.S.C.A. § 1182(a)(3)] (other than subparagraph (E) thereof) to enter the United States, or who connives or conspires with any person or persons to allow, procure, or permit any such alien to enter the United States, shall be fined under Title 18, or imprisoned not more than 10 years, or both.

(June 27, 1952, c. 477, Title II, ch. 8, § 277, 66 Stat. 229; Nov. 18, 1988, Pub.L. 100–690, Title VII, § 7346(a), (c)(1), 102 Stat. 4471; Nov. 29, 1990, Pub.L. 101–649, Title V, § 543(b)(4), Title VI, § 603(a)(16), 104 Stat. 5059, 5084; Sept. 30, 1996, Pub.L. 104–208, Div. C, Title III, § 308(d)(3)(A), 110 Stat. 3009–617.)

§ 278. Importation of alien for immoral purpose [8 U.S.C.A. § 1328]

The importation into the United States of any alien for the purpose of prostitution, or for any other immoral purpose, is forbidden. Whoever shall, directly or indirectly, import, or attempt to import into the United States any alien for the purpose of prostitution or for any other immoral purpose, or shall hold or attempt to hold any alien for any such purpose in pursuance of such illegal importation, or shall keep, maintain, control, support, employ, or harbor in any house or other place, for the purpose of prostitution or for any other immoral purpose, any alien, in pursuance of such illegal importation, shall be fined under Title 18, or imprisoned not more than 10 years, or both. The trial and punishment of offenses under this section may be in any district to or into which such alien is brought in pursuance of importation by the person or persons accused, or in any district in which a violation of any of the provisions of this section occurs. In all prosecutions under this section, the testimony of a husband or wife shall be admissible and competent evidence against each other.

(June 27, 1952, c. 477, Title II, ch. 8, § 278, 66 Stat. 230; Nov. 29, 1990, Pub.L. 101–649, Title V, § 543(b)(5), 104 Stat. 5059.)

§ 279. Jurisdiction of district courts [8 U.S.C.A. § 1329]

The district courts of the United States shall have jurisdiction of all causes, civil and criminal, brought by the United States that arise under the provisions of this title. It shall be the duty of the United States attorney of the proper district to prosecute every such suit when brought by the United States. Notwithstanding any other law, such prosecutions or suits may be instituted at any place in the United States at which the violation may occur or at which the person charged with a violation under section 275 [8 U.S.C.A. § 1325] or 276 [8 U.S.C.A. § 1326] may be apprehended. No suit or proceeding for a violation of any of the provisions of this title shall be settled, compromised, or discontinued without the consent of the court in which it is pending and any such settlement, compromise, or discontinuance shall be entered of record with the reasons therefor. Nothing in this section shall be construed as providing jurisdiction for suits against the United States or its agencies or officers.

(June 27, 1952, c. 477, Title II, ch. 8, § 279, 66 Stat. 230; Sept. 30, 1996, Pub.L. 104–208, Div. C, Title III, § 381(a), 110 Stat. 3009–650.)

§ 280. Collection of penalties and expenses [8 U.S.C.A. § 1330]

(a) Notwithstanding any other provisions of this title, the withholding or denial of clearance of or a lien upon any vessel or aircraft provided for in section 231 [8 U.S.C.A. § 1221], 234 [8 U.S.C.A. § 1224], 243(c)(2) [8 U.S.C.A. § 1253(c)(2)], 251 [8 U.S.C.A. § 1281], 253 [8 U.S.C.A. § 1283], 254 [8 U.S.C.A. § 1284], 255 [8 U.S.C.A. § 1285], 256 [8 U.S.C.A. § 1286], 271 [8 U.S.C.A. § 1321], 272 [8 U.S.C.A. § 1322], or 273 [8 U.S.C.A. § 1323] shall not be regarded as the sole and exclusive means or remedy for the enforcement of payments of any fine, penalty or expenses imposed or incurred under such sections, but, in the discretion of the Attorney General, the amount thereof may be recovered by civil suit, in the name of the United States, from any person made liable under any of such sections.

(b)(1) There is established in the general fund of the Treasury a separate account which shall be known as the "Immigration Enforcement Account". Notwithstanding any other section of this title, there shall be deposited as offsetting receipts into the Immigration Enforcement Account amounts described in paragraph (2) to remain available until expended.

(2) The amounts described in this paragraph are the following:

(A) The increase in penalties collected resulting from the amendments made by sections 203(b) and 543(a) of the Immigration Act of 1990.

(B) Civil penalties collected under sections 240B(d) [8 U.S.C.A. § 1229c(d)], 274C [8 U.S.C.A. § 1324c], 274D [8 U.S.C.A. § 1324d], and 275(b) [8 U.S.C.A. § 1325(b)].

(3)(A) The Secretary of the Treasury shall refund out of the Immigration Enforcement Account to any appropriation the amount paid out of such appropriation for expenses incurred by the Attorney General for activities that enhance enforcement of provisions of this title. Such activities include—

(i) the identification, investigation, apprehension, detention, and removal of criminal aliens;

(ii) the maintenance and updating of a system to identify and track criminal aliens, deportable aliens, inadmissible aliens, and aliens illegally entering the United States; and

(iii) for the repair, maintenance, or construction on the United States border, in areas experiencing high levels of apprehensions of illegal aliens, of structures to deter illegal entry into the United States.

(B) The amounts which are required to be refunded under subparagraph (A) shall be refunded at least quarterly on the basis of estimates made by the Attorney General of the expenses referred to in subparagraph (A). Proper adjustments shall be made in the amounts subsequently refunded under subparagraph (A) to the extent prior estimates were in excess of, or less than, the amount required to be refunded under subparagraph (A).

(C) The amounts required to be refunded from the Immigration Enforcement Account for fiscal year 1996 and thereafter shall be refunded in accordance with estimates made in the budget request of the Attorney General for those fiscal years. Any proposed changes in the amounts designated in such budget requests shall only be made after notification to the Committees on Appropriations of the House of Representatives and the Senate in accordance with section 605 of Public Law 104–134.

(D) The Attorney General shall prepare and submit annually to the Congress statements of financial condition of the Immigration Enforcement Account, including beginning account balance, revenues, withdrawals, and ending account balance and projection for the ensuing fiscal year.

(June 27, 1952, c. 477, Title II, ch. 8, § 280, 66 Stat. 230; Nov. 29, 1990, Pub.L. 101–649, Title V, § 542(a), 104 Stat. 5057; Oct. 25, 1994, Pub.L. 103–416, Title II, § 219(s), 108 Stat. 4317; Sept. 30, 1996, Pub.L. 104–208, Div. C, Title III, §§ 308(g)(4)(C), 382(a), 110 Stat. 3009–623, 3009–651.)

Chapter IX. Miscellaneous

§ 281. Nonimmigrant visa fees [8 U.S.C.A. § 1351]

The fees for the furnishing and verification of applications for visas by nonimmigrants of each foreign country and for the issuance of visas to nonimmigrants of each foreign country shall be prescribed by the Secretary of State, if practicable, in amounts corresponding to the total of all visa, entry, residence, or other similar fees, taxes, or charges assessed or levied against nationals of the United States by the foreign countries of which such nonimmigrants are nationals or stateless residents: *Provided,* That nonimmigrant visas issued to aliens coming to the United States in transit to and from the headquarters district of the United Nations in accordance with the provisions of the Headquarters Agreement shall be gratis. Subject to such criteria as the Secretary of State may prescribe, including the duration of stay of the alien and the financial burden upon the charitable organization, the Secretary of State shall waive or reduce the fee for application and issuance of a nonimmigrant visa for any alien coming to the United States primarily for, or in activities related to, a charitable purpose involving health or nursing care, the provision of food or housing, job training, or any other similar direct service or assistance to poor or otherwise needy individuals in the United States.

(June 27, 1952, c. 477, Title II, ch. 9, § 281, 66 Stat. 230; Oct. 3, 1965, Pub. L. 89–236, § 14, 79 Stat. 919; Oct. 21, 1968, Pub. L. 90–609, § 1, 82 Stat. 1199; Oct. 6, 1997, Pub.L. 105–54, § 2(a), 111 Stat. 1175.)

§ 282. Printing of reentry permits and blank forms of manifest and crew lists; sale to public [8 U.S.C.A. § 1352]

(a) Reentry permits issued under section 223 [8 U.S.C.A. § 1203] shall be printed on distinctive safety paper and shall be prepared and issued under regulations prescribed by the Attorney General.

(b) The Public Printer is authorized to print for sale to the public by the Superintendent of Documents, upon prepayment, copies of blank forms of manifests and crew lists and such other forms as may be prescribed and authorized by the Attorney General to be sold pursuant to the provisions of this title.

(June 27, 1952, c. 477, Title II, ch. 9, § 282, 66 Stat. 231.)

§ 283. Travel expenses and expense of transporting remains of officers and employees dying outside of United States [8 U.S.C.A. § 1353]

When officers, inspectors, or other employees of the Service are ordered to perform duties in a foreign country, or are transferred from one station to another, in the United States or in a foreign country, or while performing duties in any foreign country become eligible for voluntary retirement and return to the United States, they shall be allowed their traveling expenses in accordance with such regulations as the Attorney General may deem advisable, and they may also be allowed, within the discretion and under written orders of the Attorney General, the expenses incurred for the transfer of their wives and dependent children, their household effects and other personal property, including the expenses for packing, crating, freight, unpacking, temporary storage, and drayage thereof in accordance with subchapter II of chapter 57 of Title 5. The expense of transporting the remains of such officers, inspectors, or other employees who die while in, or in transit to, a foreign country in the discharge of their official duties, to their former homes in this country for interment, and the ordinary and necessary expenses of such interment and of preparation for shipment, are authorized to be paid on the written order of the Attorney General.

(June 27, 1952, c. 477, Title II, ch. 9, § 283, 66 Stat. 231; Pub.L. 100–525, § 9(p), Oct. 24, 1988, 102 Stat. 2621.)

§ 284. Applicability to members of the armed forces [8 U.S.C.A. § 1354]

Nothing contained in this title shall be construed so as to limit, restrict, deny, or affect the coming into or departure from the United States of an alien member of the Armed Forces of the United States who is in the uniform of, or who bears documents identifying him as a member of, such Armed Forces, and who is coming to or departing from the United States under official orders or permit of such Armed Forces: *Provided,* That nothing contained in this section shall be construed to give to or confer upon any such alien any other privileges, rights, benefits, exemptions, or immunities under this Act, which are not otherwise specifically granted by this Act.

(June 27, 1952, c. 477, Title II, ch. 9, § 284, 66 Stat. 232.)

§ 285. Disposal of privileges at immigrant stations; rentals; retail sale; disposition of receipts [8 U.S.C.A. § 1355]

(a) Subject to such conditions and limitations as the Attorney General shall prescribe, all exclusive privileges of exchanging money, transporting passengers or baggage, keeping eating houses, or other like privileges in connection with any United States immigrant station, shall be disposed of to the lowest responsible and capable bidder (other than an alien) in accordance with the provisions of section 5 of Title 41 and for the use of Government property in connection with the exercise of such exclusive privileges a reasonable rental may be charged. The feeding of aliens, or the furnishing of any other necessary service in connection with any United States immigrant station, may be performed by the Service without regard to the foregoing provisions of this subsection if the Attorney General shall find that it would be advantageous to the Government in terms of economy and efficiency. No intoxicating liquors shall be sold at any immigrant station.

(b) Such articles determined by the Attorney General to be necessary to the health and welfare of aliens detained at any immigrant station, when not otherwise readily procurable by such aliens, may be sold at reasonable prices to such aliens through Government canteens operated by the Service, under such conditions and limitations as the Attorney General shall prescribe.

(c) All rentals or other receipts accruing from the disposal of privileges, and all moneys arising from the sale of articles through Service-operated canteens, authorized by this section, shall be covered into the Treasury to the credit of the appropriation for the enforcement of this title.

(June 27, 1952, c. 477, Title II, ch. 9, § 285, 66 Stat. 232.)

§ 286. Disposition of monies collected under the provisions of this title [8 U.S.C.A. § 1356]

(a) Detention, transportation, hospitalization, and all other expenses of detained aliens; expenses of landing stations

All moneys paid into the Treasury to reimburse the Service for detention, transportation, hospitalization, and all other expenses of detained aliens paid from the appropriation for the enforcement of this Act, and all moneys paid into the Treasury to reimburse the Service for expenses of landing stations referred to in section 233(b) [8 U.S.C.A. § 1223(b)] paid by the Service from the appropriation for the enforcement of this Act, shall be credited to the appropriation for the enforcement of this Act for the fiscal year in which the expenses were incurred.

(b) Purchase of evidence

Moneys expended from appropriations for the Service for the purchase of evidence and subsequently recovered shall be reimbursed to the current appropriation for the Service.

(c) Fees and administrative fines and penalties; exception

Except as otherwise provided in subsection (a) and subsection (b), or in any other provision of this title, all moneys received in payment of fees and administrative fines and penalties under this title shall be covered into the Treasury as miscellaneous receipts: Provided, however, That all fees received from applicants residing in the Virgin Islands of the United States, and in Guam, required to be paid under section 281 [8 U.S.C.A. § 1351], shall be paid over to the Treasury of the Virgin Islands and to the Treasury of Guam, respectively.

(d) Schedule of fees

In addition to any other fee authorized by law, the Attorney General shall charge and collect $6 per individual for the immigration inspection of each passenger arriving at a port of entry in the United States, or for the preinspection of a passenger in a place outside of the United States prior to such arrival, aboard a commercial aircraft or commercial vessel.

(e) Limitations on fees

(1) No fee shall be charged under subsection (d) for immigration inspection or preinspection provided in connection with the arrival of any passenger, other than aircraft passengers, whose journey originated in the following:

(A) Canada,

(B) Mexico,

(C) a State, territory or possession of the United States, or

(D) any adjacent island (within the meaning of section 101(b)(5) [8 U.S.C.A. § 1101(b)(5)]).

(2) No fee may be charged under subsection (d) with respect to the arrival of any passenger—

(A) who is in transit to a destination outside the United States, and

(B) for whom immigration inspection services are not provided.

(f) Collection

(1) Each person that issues a document or ticket to an individual for transportation by a commercial vessel or commercial aircraft into the United States shall—

(A) collect from that individual the fee charged under subsection (d) at the time the document or ticket is issued; and

(B) identify on that document or ticket the fee charged under subsection (d) as a Federal inspection fee.

(2) If—

(A) a document or ticket for transportation of a passenger into the United States is issued in a foreign country; and

(B) the fee charged under subsection (d) is not collected at the time such document or ticket is issued;

the person providing transportation to such passenger shall collect such fee at the time such passenger departs from the United States and shall provide such passenger a receipt for the payment of such fee.

(3) The person who collects fees under paragraph (1) or (2) shall remit those fees to the Attorney General at any time before the date that is thirty-one days after the close of the calendar quarter in which the fees are collected, except the fourth quarter payment for fees collected from airline passengers shall be made on the date that is ten days before the end of the fiscal year, and the first quarter payment shall include any collections made in the preceding quarter that were not remitted with the previous payment. Regulations issued by the Attorney General under this subsection with respect to the collection of the fees charged under subsection (d) and the remittance of such fees to the Treasury of the United States shall be consistent with the regulations issued by the Secretary of the Treasury for the collection and remittance of the taxes imposed by subchapter C of chapter 33 of Title 26, but only to the extent the regulations issued with respect to such taxes do not conflict with the provisions of this section.

(g) Provision of immigration inspection and preinspection services

Notwithstanding the Act of March 2, 1931, 46 Stat. 1467 [8 U.S.C.A. § 1353b] or any other provision of law, the immigration services required to be provided to passengers upon arrival in the United States on scheduled airline flights shall be adequately provided, within forty-five minutes of their presentation for inspection, when needed and at no cost (other than the fees imposed under subsection (d)) to airlines and airline passengers at:

(1) immigration serviced airports, and

(2) places located outside of the United States at which an immigration officer is stationed for the purpose of providing such immigration services.

(h) Disposition of receipts

(1)(A) There is established in the general fund of the Treasury a separate account which shall be known as the "Immigration User Fee Account". Notwithstanding any other section of this title, there shall be deposited as offsetting receipts into the Immigration User Fee Account all fees collected under subsection (d) of this section, to remain available until expended. At the end of each 2–year period, beginning with the creation of this account, the Attorney General, following a public rulemaking with opportunity for notice and comment, shall submit a report to the Congress concerning the status of the account, including any balances therein, and recommend any adjustment in the prescribed fee that may be required to ensure that the receipts collected from the fee charged for the succeeding two years equal, as closely as possible, the cost of providing these services.

(B) Notwithstanding any other provisions of law, all civil fines or penalties collected pursuant to sections 243(c) [8 U.S.C.A. § 1253(c)], 271 [8 U.S.C.A. § 1321], and 273 [8 U.S.C.A. § 1323] and all liquidated damages and expenses collected pursuant to this Act shall be deposited in the Immigration User Fee Account.

(2)(A) The Secretary of the Treasury shall refund out of the Immigration User Fee Account to any appropriation the amount paid out of such appropriation for expenses incurred by the Attorney General in providing immigration inspection and preinspection services for commercial aircraft or vessels and in—

(i) providing overtime immigration inspection services for commercial aircraft or vessels;

(ii) administration of debt recovery, including the establishment and operation of a national collections office;

(iii) expansion, operation and maintenance of information systems for nonimmigrant control and debt collection;

(iv) detection of fraudulent documents used by passengers traveling to the United States, including training of, and technical assistance to, commercial airline personnel regarding such detection;

(v) providing detention and removal services for inadmissible aliens arriving on commercial aircraft and vessels and for any alien who is inadmissible under section 212(a) [8 U.S.C.A. § 1182(a)] who has attempted illegal entry into the United States through avoidance of immigration inspection at air or sea ports-of-entry; and

(vi) providing removal and asylum proceedings at air or sea ports-of-entry for inadmissible aliens arriving on commercial aircraft and vessels including immigration removal proceedings resulting from presentation of fraudulent documents and failure to present documentation and for any alien who is inadmissible under section 212(a) [8 U.S.C.A. § 1182(a)] who has attempted illegal entry into the United States through avoidance of immigration inspection at air or sea ports-of-entry.

(B) The amounts which are required to be refunded under subparagraph (A) shall be refunded at least quarterly on the basis of estimates made by the Attorney General of the expenses referred to in subparagraph (A). Proper adjustments shall be made in the amounts subsequently refunded under subparagraph (A) to the extent prior estimates were in excess of, or less than, the amount required to be refunded under subparagraph (A).

The Attorney General shall provide for expenditures for training and assistance described in clause (iv) in an amount, for any fiscal year, not less than 5 percent of the total of the expenses incurred that are described in the previous sentence.

(i) Reimbursement

Notwithstanding any other provision of law, the Attorney General is authorized to receive reimbursement from the owner, operator, or agent of a private or commercial aircraft or vessel, or from any airport or seaport authority for expenses incurred by the Attorney General in providing immigration inspection services which are rendered at the request of such person or authority (including the salary and expenses of individuals employed by the Attorney General to provide such immigration inspection services). The Attorney General's authority to receive such reimbursement shall terminate immediately upon the provision for such services by appropriation.

(j) Regulations

The Attorney General may prescribe such rules and regulations as may be necessary to carry out the provisions of this section.

(k) Advisory committee

In accordance with the provisions of the Federal Advisory Committee Act [5 U.S.C.A.App. § 1 et seq.], the Attorney General shall establish an advisory committee, whose membership shall consist of representatives from the airline and other transportation industries who may be subject to any fee or charge authorized by law or proposed by the Immigration and Naturalization Service for the purpose of covering expenses incurred by the Immigration and Naturalization Service. The advisory committee shall meet on a periodic basis and shall advise the Attorney General on issues related to the performance of the inspectional services of the Immigration and Naturalization Service. This advice shall include, but not be limited to, such issues as the time periods during which such services should be performed, the proper number and deployment of inspection officers, the level of fees, and the appropriateness of any proposed fee. The Attorney General shall give substantial consideration to the views of the advisory committee in the exercise of his duties.

(*l*) Report to Congress

In addition to the reporting requirements established pursuant to subsection (h), the Attorney General shall prepare and submit annually to the Congress, not later than March 31st of each year, a statement of the financial condition of the "Immigration User Fee Account" including beginning account balance, revenues, withdrawals and their purpose, ending balance, projections for the ensuing fiscal year and a full and complete workload analysis showing on a port by port basis the current and projected need for inspectors. The statement shall indicate the success rate of the Immigration and Naturalization Service in meeting the forty-five minute inspection standard and shall provide detailed statistics regarding the number of passengers inspected within the standard, progress that is being made to expand the utilization of United States citizen by-pass, the number of passengers for whom the standard is not met and the length of their delay, locational breakdown of these statistics and the steps being taken to correct any nonconformity.

(m) Immigration Examinations Fee Account

Notwithstanding any other provisions of law, all adjudication fees as are designated by the Attorney General in regulations shall be deposited as offsetting receipts into a separate account entitled "Immigration Examinations Fee Account" in the Treasury of the United States, whether collected directly by the Attorney General or through clerks of courts: Provided, however, That all fees received by the Attorney General from applicants residing in the Virgin Islands of the United States, and in Guam, under this subsection shall be paid over to the treasury of the Virgin Islands and to the treasury of Guam: Provided further, That fees for providing adjudication and naturalization services may be set at a level that will ensure recovery of the full costs of providing all such services, including the costs of similar services provided without charge to asylum applicants or other immigrants. Such fees may also be set at a level that will recover any additional costs associated with the administration of the fees collected.

(n) Reimbursement of administrative expenses; transfer of deposits to General Fund of United States Treasury

All deposits into the "Immigration Examinations Fee Account" shall remain available until expended to the Attorney General to reimburse any appropriation the amount paid out of such appropriation for expenses in providing immigration adjudication and naturalization services and the collection, safeguarding and accounting for fees deposited in and funds reimbursed from the "Immigration Examinations Fee Account". [sic]

(*o*) Annual financial reports to Congress

The Attorney General shall prepare and submit annually to Congress statements of financial condition of the "Immigration Examinations Fee Account", including beginning account balance, revenues, withdrawals, and ending account balance and projections for the ensuing fiscal year.

(p) Additional effective dates

The provisions set forth in subsections (m), (n), and (*o*) apply to adjudication and naturalization services performed and to related fees collected on or after October 1, 1988.

(q) Land Border Inspection Fee Account

(1)(A)(i) Notwithstanding any other provision of law, the Attorney General is authorized to establish, by regulation, not more than 6 projects under which a fee may be charged and collected for inspection services provided at one or more land border points of entry. Such projects may include the establishment of commuter lanes to be made available to qualified United States citizens and aliens, as determined by the Attorney General.

(ii) This subparagraph shall take effect, with respect to any project described in clause (1) [sic] that was not authorized to be commenced before September 30, 1996, 30 days after submission of a written plan by the Attorney General detailing the proposed implementation of such project.

(iii) The Attorney General shall prepare and submit on a quarterly basis a status report on each land border inspection project implemented under this subparagraph.

(iv) Redesignated (iii).

(B) The Attorney General, in consultation with the Secretary of the Treasury, may conduct pilot projects to demonstrate the use of designated ports of entry after working hours through the use of card reading machines or other appropriate technology.

(2) All of the fees collected under this subsection shall be deposited as offsetting receipts in a separate account within the general fund of the Treasury of the United States, to remain available until expended. Such account shall be known as the Land Border Inspection Fee Account.

(3)(A) The Secretary of the Treasury shall refund, at least on a quarterly basis amounts to any appropriations for expenses incurred in providing inspection services at land border points of entry. Such expenses shall include—

(i) the providing of overtime inspection services;

(ii) the expansion, operation and maintenance of information systems for nonimmigrant control;

(iii) the hire of additional permanent and temporary inspectors;

(iv) the minor construction costs associated with the addition of new traffic lanes (with the concurrence of the General Services Administration);

(v) the detection of fraudulent documents used by passengers travelling to the United States;

(vi) providing for the administration of said account.

(B) The amounts required to be refunded from the Land Border Inspection Fee Account for fiscal years 1992 and thereafter shall be refunded in accordance with estimates made in the budget request of the Attorney General for those fiscal years: Provided, That any proposed changes in the amounts designated in said budget requests shall only be made after notification to the Committees on Appropriations of the House of Representatives and the Senate in accordance with section 606 of Public Law 101–162.

(4) The Attorney General will prepare and submit annually to the Congress statements of financial condition of the Land Border Immigration Fee Account, including beginning account balance, revenues, withdrawals, and ending account balance and projection for the ensuing fiscal year.

(5) Repealed. Pub.L. 104–208, Div. C, Title I, § 122(a)(2), Sept. 30, 1996, 110 Stat. 3009–560.

(r) Breached Bond/Detention Fund

(1) Notwithstanding any other provision of law, there is established in the general fund of the Treasury a separate account which shall be known as the Breached Bond/Detention Fund (in this subsection referred to as the "Fund").

(2) There shall be deposited as offsetting receipts into the Fund all breached cash and surety bonds, in excess of $8,000,000, posted under this Act, which are recovered by the Department of Justice, and amount [sic] described in section 245(i)(3)(B) [8 U.S.C.A. § 1255(i)(3)(B)].

(3) Such amounts as are deposited into the Fund shall remain available until expended and shall be refunded out of the Fund by the Secretary of the Treasury, at least on a quarterly basis, to the Attorney General for the following purposes—

(i) for expenses incurred in the collection of breached bonds, and

(ii) for expenses associated with the detention of illegal aliens.

(4) The amounts required to be refunded from the Fund for fiscal year 1998 and thereafter shall be refunded in accordance with estimates made in the budget request of the President for those fiscal years. Any proposed changes in the amounts designated in such budget requests shall only be made after Congressional reprogramming notification in accordance with the reprogramming guidelines for the applicable fiscal year.

(5) The Attorney General shall prepare and submit annually to the Congress, statements of financial condition of the Fund, including the beginning balance, receipts, refunds to appropriations, transfers to the general fund, and the ending balance.

(6) For fiscal year 1993 only, the Attorney General may transfer up to $1,000,000 from the Immigration User Fee Account to the Fund for initial expenses necessary to enhance collection efforts: Provided, That any such transfers shall be refunded from the Fund back to the Immigration User Fee Account by December 31, 1993.

(s) H–1B nonimmigrant petitioner account

(1) In general

There is established in the general fund of the Treasury a separate account, which shall be known as the "H–1B Nonimmigrant Petitioner Account". Notwithstanding any other section of this title, there shall be deposited as offsetting receipts into the account all fees collected under section 214(c)(9) [8 U.S.C.A. § 1184(c)(9)].

(2) Use of fees for job training

56.3 percent of amounts deposited into the H–1B Nonimmigrant Petitioner Account shall remain available to the Secretary of Labor until expended for demonstration programs and projects described in section 414(c) of the American Competitiveness and Workforce Improvement Act of 1998.

(3) Use of fees for low-income scholarship program

28.2 percent of the amounts deposited into the H–1B Nonimmigrant Petitioner Account shall remain available to the Director of the National Science Foundation until expended for scholarships described in section 414(d) of the American Competitiveness and Workforce Improvement Act of 1998 for low-income students enrolled in a program of study leading to a degree in mathematics, engineering, or computer science.

(4) Additional uses

(A) Grants for mathematics, engineering, or science enrichment courses

4 percent of the amounts deposited into the H–1B Nonimmigrant Petitioner Account shall remain available to the Director of the National Science Foundation until expended to make merit-reviewed grants, under section 3(a)(1) of the National Science Foundation Act of 1950 (42 U.S.C. 1862(a)(1)), for programs that provide opportunities for enrollment in year-round academic enrichment courses in mathematics, engineering, or science.

(B) Systemic reform activities

4 percent of the amounts deposited into the H–1B Nonimmigrant Petitioner Account shall remain available to the Director of the National Science Foundation until expended to carry out systemic reform activities administered by the Nation-

al Science Foundation under section 3(a)(1) of the National Science Foundation Act of 1950 (42 U.S.C. 1862(a)(1)).

(5) Use of fees for duties relating to petitions

1.5 percent of the amounts deposited into the H–1B Nonimmigrant Petitioner Account shall remain available to the Attorney General until expended to carry out duties under paragraphs (1) and (9) of section 214(c) [8 U.S.C.A. § 1184(c)] related to petitions made for nonimmigrants described in section 101(a)(15)(H)(i)(b) [8 U.S.C.A. § 1101(a)(15)(H)(i)(b)], to decrease the processing time for such petitions, and to carry out duties under section 416 of the American Competitiveness and Workforce Improvement Act of 1998. Such amounts shall be available in addition to any other fees authorized to be collected by the Attorney General with respect to such petitions.

(6) Use of fees for application processing and enforcement

For fiscal year 1999, 6 percent of the amounts deposited into the H–1B Nonimmigrant Petitioner Account shall remain available to the Secretary of Labor until expended for decreasing the processing time for applications under section 212(n)(1) [8 U.S.C.A. § 1182(n)(1)] and for carrying out section 212(n)(2) [8 U.S.C.A. § 1182(n)(2)]. Beginning with fiscal year 2000, 3 percent of the amounts deposited into the H–1B Nonimmigrant Petitioner Account shall remain available to the Secretary of Labor until expended for decreasing the processing time for applications under section 212(n)(1) [8 U.S.C.A. § 1182(n)(1)], and 3 percent of such amounts shall remain available to such Secretary until expended for carrying out section 212(n)(2) [8 U.S.C.A. § 1182(n)(2)]. Notwithstanding the preceding sentence, both of the amounts made available for any fiscal year (beginning with fiscal year 2000) pursuant to the preceding sentence shall be available to such Secretary, and shall remain available until expended, only for decreasing the processing time for applications under section 212(n)(1) [8 U.S.C.A. § 1182(n)(1)] until the Secretary submits to the Congress a report containing a certification that, during the most recently concluded calendar year, the Secretary substantially complied with the requirement in section 212(n)(1) [8 U.S.C.A. § 1182(n)(1)] relating to the provision of the certification described in section 101(a)(15)(H)(i)(b) [8 U.S.C.A. § 1101(a)(15)(H)(i)(b)] within a 7–day period.

(June 27, 1952, c. 477, Title II, ch. 9, § 286, 66 Stat. 232; Dec. 29, 1981, Pub.L. 97–116, § 13, 95 Stat. 1618; Oct. 18, 1986, Pub.L. 99–500, Title I, § 101(b) [Title II, § 205(a), formerly § 205], 100 Stat. 1783–39, 1783–53, as amended Oct. 24, 1988, Pub.L. 100–525, § 4(a)(2)(A), 102 Stat. 2615; Nov. 14, 1986, Pub.L. 99–653, § 7(d)(1), as added Oct. 24, 1988, Pub.L. 100–525, § 8(f), 102 Stat. 2617; July 11, 1987, Pub.L. 100–71, Title I, § 1, 101 Stat. 394; Oct. 1, 1988, Pub.L. 100–459, § 209(a), 102 Stat. 2203, as amended Dec. 12, 1991, Pub.L. 102–232, Title III, § 309(a)(1)(A)(i)(I), 105 Stat. 1757; Oct. 24, 1988,

Pub.L. 100–525, § 4(a)(1), 102 Stat. 2614; Nov. 21, 1989, Pub. L. 101–162, Title II, 103 Stat. 1000, as amended Dec. 12, 1991, Pub.L. 102–232, Title III, § 309(a)(1)(B), 105 Stat. 1758; Nov. 5, 1990, Pub.L. 101–515, Title II, § 210(a), (d), 104 Stat. 2120, 2121; Dec. 12, 1991, Pub.L. 102–232, Title III, § 309(a)(1)(A)(i), (B), (2), (b)(12), 105 Stat. 1758, 1759; Oct. 6, 1992, Pub.L. 102–395, Title I, § 112, 106 Stat. 1843; Oct. 27, 1993, Pub.L. 103–121, Title I, 107 Stat. 1161; Oct. 25, 1994, Pub.L. 103–416, Title II, § 219(t), 108 Stat. 4317; Sept. 30, 1996, Pub.L. 104–208, Div. C, Title I, §§ 122(a), 124(a)(1), Title III, §§ 308(d)(3)(A), (4)(K), (e)(1)(L), (g)(1), 376(b), 382(b), Title VI, § 671(b)(11), (e)(5), (6), 110 Stat. 3009–560, 3009–562, 3009–617 to 3009–619, 3009–622, 3009–648, 3009–651, 3009–722, 3009–723; Nov. 26, 1997, Pub.L. 105–119, Title I, § 110(1), (2), 111 Stat. 2457; Oct. 21, 1998, Pub.L. 105–277, Div. A, § 101(b) [Title I, § 114], Div. C, Title IV, § 414(b), 112 Stat. 2681–68, 2681–652; Nov. 29, 1999, Pub.L. 106–113, Div. B, § 1000(a)(1) [H.R. 3421, Title I, § 118], 113 Stat. 1535, 1537.)

§ 287. Powers of immigration officers and employees [8 U.S.C.A. § 1357]

(a) Powers without warrant

Any officer or employee of the Service authorized under regulations prescribed by the Attorney General shall have power without warrant—

(1) to interrogate any alien or person believed to be an alien as to his right to be or to remain in the United States;

(2) to arrest any alien who in his presence or view is entering or attempting to enter the United States in violation of any law or regulation made in pursuance of law regulating the admission, exclusion, expulsion, or removal of aliens, or to arrest any alien in the United States, if he has reason to believe that the alien so arrested is in the United States in violation of any such law or regulation and is likely to escape before a warrant can be obtained for his arrest, but the alien arrested shall be taken without unnecessary delay for examination before an officer of the Service having authority to examine aliens as to their right to enter or remain in the United States;

(3) within a reasonable distance from any external boundary of the United States, to board and search for aliens any vessel within the territorial waters of the United States and any railway car, aircraft, conveyance, or vehicle, and within a distance of twenty-five miles from any such external boundary to have access to private lands, but not dwellings, for the purpose of patrolling the border to prevent the illegal entry of aliens into the United States;

(4) to make arrests for felonies which have been committed and which are cognizable under any law of the United States regulating the admission, exclusion, expulsion, or removal of aliens, if he has reason to believe that the person so arrested is guilty of such felony and if there is likelihood of the person escaping before a warrant can be obtained for his arrest, but the person arrested shall be taken without unnecessary delay before the nearest available officer empowered to commit persons charged with offenses against the laws of the United States; and

(5) to make arrests—

(A) for any offense against the United States, if the offense is committed in the officer's or employee's presence, or

(B) for any felony cognizable under the laws of the United States, if the officer or employee has reasonable grounds to believe that the person to be arrested has committed or is committing such a felony,

if the officer or employee is performing duties relating to the enforcement of the immigration laws at the time of the arrest and if there is a likelihood of the person escaping before a warrant can be obtained for his arrest.

Under regulations prescribed by the Attorney General, an officer or employee of the Service may carry a firearm and may execute and serve any order, warrant, subpoena, summons, or other process issued under the authority of the United States. The authority to make arrests under paragraph (5)(B) shall only be effective on and after the date on which the Attorney General publishes final regulations which **(i)** prescribe the categories of officers and employees of the Service who may use force (including deadly force) and the circumstances under which such force may be used, **(ii)** establish standards with respect to enforcement activities of the Service, **(iii)** require that any officer or employee of the Service is not authorized to make arrests under paragraph (5)(B) unless the officer or employee has received certification as having completed a training program which covers such arrests and standards described in clause (ii), and **(iv)** establish an expedited, internal review process for violations of such standards, which process is consistent with standard agency procedure regarding confidentiality of matters related to internal investigations.

(b) Administration of oath; taking of evidence

Any officer or employee of the Service designated by the Attorney General, whether individually or as one of a class, shall have power and authority to administer oaths and to take and consider evidence concerning the privilege of any person to enter, reenter, pass through, or reside in the United States, or concerning any matter which is material or relevant to the enforcement of this Act and the administration of the Service; and any person to whom such oath has been administered (or who has executed an unsworn declaration, certificate, verification, or statement under penalty of perjury as permitted under section 1746 of Title 28), under the provisions of this Act, who shall knowingly or willfully give false evidence or swear (or subscribe under penalty of perjury as permitted under section 1746 of Title 28) to any false statement concerning any matter referred to in this subsection shall be guilty of perjury and shall be punished as provided by section 1621 of Title 18.

(c) Search without warrant

Any officer or employee of the Service authorized and designated under regulations prescribed by the Attorney General, whether individually or as one of a class, shall have power to conduct a search, without warrant, of the person, and of the personal effects in the possession of any person seeking admission to the United States, concerning whom such officer or employee may have reasonable cause to suspect that grounds exist for denial of admission to the United States under this Act which would be disclosed by such search.

(d) Detainer of aliens for violation of controlled substances laws

In the case of an alien who is arrested by a Federal, State, or local law enforcement official for a violation of any law relating to controlled substances, if the official (or another official)—

(1) has reason to believe that the alien may not have been lawfully admitted to the United States or otherwise is not lawfully present in the United States,

(2) expeditiously informs an appropriate officer or employee of the Service authorized and designated by the Attorney General of the arrest and of facts concerning the status of the alien, and

(3) requests the Service to determine promptly whether or not to issue a detainer to detain the alien,

the officer or employee of the Service shall promptly determine whether or not to issue such a detainer. If such a detainer is issued and the alien is not otherwise detained by Federal, State, or local officials, the Attorney General shall effectively and expeditiously take custody of the alien.

(e) Restriction on warrantless entry in case of outdoor agricultural operations

Notwithstanding any other provision of this section other than paragraph (3) of subsection (a) an officer or employee of the Service may not enter without the consent of the owner (or agent thereof) or a properly executed warrant onto the premises of a farm or other outdoor agricultural operation for the purpose of interrogating a person believed to be an alien as to the person's right to be or to remain in the United States.

(f) Fingerprinting and photographing of certain aliens

(1) Under regulations of the Attorney General, the Commissioner shall provide for the fingerprinting and photographing of each alien 14 years of age or older against whom a proceeding is commenced under section 240 [8 U.S.C.A. § 1229a].

(2) Such fingerprints and photographs shall be made available to Federal, State, and local law enforcement agencies, upon request.

(g) Acceptance of State services to carry out immigration enforcement

(1) Notwithstanding section 1342 of Title 31, the Attorney General may enter into a written agreement with a State, or any political subdivision of a State, pursuant to which an officer or employee of the State or subdivision, who is determined by the Attorney General to be qualified to perform a function of an immigration officer in relation to the investigation, apprehension, or detention of aliens in the United States (including the transportation of such aliens across State lines to detention centers), may carry out such function at the expense of the State or political subdivision and to the extent consistent with State and local law.

(2) An agreement under this subsection shall require that an officer or employee of a State or political subdivision of a State performing a function under the agreement shall have knowledge of, and adhere to, Federal law relating to the function, and shall contain a written certification that the officers or employees performing the function under the agreement have received adequate training regarding the enforcement of relevant Federal immigration laws.

(3) In performing a function under this subsection, an officer or employee of a State or political subdivision of a State shall be subject to the direction and supervision of the Attorney General.

(4) In performing a function under this subsection, an officer or employee of a State or political subdivision of a State may use Federal property or facilities, as provided in a written agreement between the Attorney General and the State or subdivision.

(5) With respect to each officer or employee of a State or political subdivision who is authorized to perform a function under this subsection, the specific powers and duties that may be, or are required to be, exercised or performed by the individual, the duration of the authority of the individual, and the position of the agency of the Attorney General who is required to supervise and direct the individual, shall be set forth in a written agreement between the Attorney General and the State or political subdivision.

(6) The Attorney General may not accept a service under this subsection if the service will be used to displace any Federal employee.

(7) Except as provided in paragraph (8), an officer or employee of a State or political subdivision of a State performing functions under this subsection shall not be treated as a Federal employee for any purpose other than for purposes of chapter 81 of Title 5 (relating to compensation for injury) and sections 2671 through 2680 of Title 28 (relating to tort claims).

(8) An officer or employee of a State or political subdivision of a State acting under color of authority under this subsection, or any agreement entered into under this subsection, shall be considered to be acting under color of Federal authority for purposes of determining the liability, and immunity from suit, of the officer or employee in a civil action brought under Federal or State law.

(9) Nothing in this subsection shall be construed to require any State or political subdivision of a State to enter into an agreement with the Attorney General under this subsection.

(10) Nothing in this subsection shall be construed to require an agreement under this subsection in order for any officer or employee of a State or political subdivision of a State—

(A) to communicate with the Attorney General regarding the immigration status of any individual, including reporting knowledge that a particular alien is not lawfully present in the United States; or

(B) otherwise to cooperate with the Attorney General in the identification, apprehension, detention, or removal of aliens not lawfully present in the United States.

(June 27, 1952, c. 477, Title II, ch. 9, § 287, 66 Stat. 233; Oct. 18, 1976, Pub.L. 94–550, § 7, 90 Stat. 2535; Oct. 27, 1986, Pub.L. 99–570, Title I, § 1751(d), 100 Stat. 3207–47; Nov. 6, 1986, Pub.L. 99–603, Title I, § 116, 100 Stat. 3384; Oct. 24, 1988, Pub.L. 100–525, §§ 2(e), 5, 102 Stat. 2610, 2615; Nov. 29, 1990, Pub.L. 101–649, Title V, § 503(a), (b)(1), 104 Stat. 5048; Dec. 12, 1991, Pub.L. 102–232, Title III, § 306(a)(3), 105 Stat. 1751; Sept. 30, 1996, Pub.L. 104–208, Div. C, Title I, § 133, Title III, § 308(d)(4)(L), (e)(1)(M), (g)(5)(A)(i), 110 Stat. 3009–563, 3009–618, 3009–619, 3009–623.)

§ 288. Local jurisdiction over immigrant stations [8 U.S.C.A. § 1358]

The officers in charge of the various immigrant stations shall admit therein the proper State and local officers charged with the enforcement of the laws of the State or Territory of the United States in which any such immigrant station is located in order that such State and local officers may preserve the peace and make arrests for crimes under the laws of the States and Territories. For the purpose of this section the jurisdiction of such State and local officers and of the State and local courts shall extend over such immigrant stations.

(June 27, 1952, c. 477, Title II, ch. 9, § 288, 66 Stat. 234.)

§ 289. Application to American Indians born in Canada [8 U.S.C.A. § 1359]

Nothing in this title shall be construed to affect the right of American Indians born in Canada to pass the borders of the United States, but such right shall extend only to persons who possess at least 50 per centum of blood of the American Indian race.

(June 27, 1952, c. 477, Title II, ch. 9, § 289, 66 Stat. 234.)

§ 290. Establishment of central file; information from other departments and agencies [8 U.S.C.A. § 1360]

(a) There shall be established in the office of the Commissioner, for the use of security and enforcement agencies of the Government of the United States, a central index, which shall contain the names of all aliens heretofore admitted or denied admission to the United States, insofar as such information is available from the existing records of the Service, and the names of all aliens hereafter admitted or denied admission to the United States, the names of their sponsors of record, if any, and such other relevant information as the Attorney General shall require as an aid to the proper enforcement of this Act.

(b) Any information in any records kept by any department or agency of the Government as to the identity and location of aliens in the United States shall be made available to the Service upon request made by the Attorney General to the head of any such department or agency.

(c)(1) Not later than 3 months after the end of each fiscal year (beginning with fiscal year 1996), the Commissioner of Social Security shall report to the Committees on the Judiciary of the House of Representatives and the Senate on the aggregate quantity of social security account numbers issued to aliens not authorized to be employed, with respect to which, in such fiscal year, earnings were reported to the Social Security Administration.

(2) If earnings are reported on or after January 1, 1997, to the Social Security Administration on a social security account number issued to an alien not authorized to work in the United States, the Commissioner of Social Security shall provide the Attorney General with information regarding the name and address of the alien, the name and address of the person reporting the earnings, and the amount of the earnings. The information shall be provided in an electronic form agreed upon by the Commissioner and the Attorney General.

(d) A written certification signed by the Attorney General or by any officer of the Service designated by the Attorney General to make such certification, that after diligent search no record or entry of a specified nature is found to exist in the records of the Service, shall be admissible as evidence in any proceeding as evidence that the records of the Service contain no such record or entry, and shall have the same effect as the testimony of a witness given in open court.

(June 27, 1952, c. 477, Title II, ch. 9, § 290, 66 Stat. 234; 1953 Reorg. Plan No. 1, §§ 5, 8, eff. Apr. 11, 1953, 18 F.R. 2053, 67 Stat. 631; Oct. 24, 1988, Pub.L. 100–525, § 9(q), 102 Stat. 2621; Sept. 30, 1996, Pub.L. 104–208, Div. C, Title III, § 308(d)(4)(M), Title IV, § 414(a), 110 Stat. 3009–618, 3009–669.)

§ 291. Burden of proof upon alien [8 U.S.C.A. § 1361]

Whenever any person makes application for a visa or any other document required for entry, or makes application for admission, or otherwise attempts to enter the United States, the burden of proof shall be upon such person to establish that he is eligible to receive such visa or such document, or is not inadmissible under any provision of this Act, and, if an alien, that he is entitled to the nonimmigrant, immigrant, special immigrant, immediate relative, or refugee status claimed, as the case may be. If such person fails to establish to the satisfaction of the consular officer that he is eligible to receive a visa or other document required for entry, no visa or other document required for entry shall be issued to such person, nor shall such person be admitted to the United States unless he establishes to the satisfaction of the Attorney General that he is not inadmissible under any provision of this Act. In any removal proceeding under chapter 4 against any person, the burden of proof shall be upon such person to show the time, place, and manner of his entry into the United States, but in presenting such proof he shall be entitled to the production of his visa or other entry document, if any, and of any other documents and records, not considered by the Attorney General to be confidential, pertaining to such entry in the custody of the Service. If such burden of proof is not sustained, such person shall be presumed to be in the United States in violation of law.

(June 27, 1952, c. 477, Title II, ch. 9, § 291, 66 Stat. 234; Dec. 29, 1981, Pub.L. 97–116, § 18(k)(1), 95 Stat. 1620; Sept. 30, 1996, Pub.L. 104–208, Div. C, Title III, § 308(d)(4)(N), (e)(1)(N), (g)(9)(A), 110 Stat. 3009–618, 3009–619, 3009–624.)

§ 292. Right to counsel [8 U.S.C.A. § 1362]

In any removal proceedings before an immigration judge and in any appeal proceedings before the Attorney General from any such removal proceedings, the person concerned shall have the privilege of being represented (at no expense to the Government) by such counsel, authorized to practice in such proceedings, as he shall choose.

(June 27, 1952, c. 477, Title II, ch. 9, § 292, 66 Stat. 235; Sept. 30, 1996, Pub.L. 104–208, Div. C, Title III, §§ 308(d)(4)(O), 371(b)(9), 110 Stat. 3009–619, 3009–645.)

§ 293. Deposit of and interest on cash received to secure immigration bonds [8 U.S.C.A. § 1363]

(a) Cash received by the Attorney General as security on an immigration bond shall be deposited in the Treasury of the United States in trust for the obligor on the bond, and shall bear interest payable at a rate determined by the Secretary of the Treasury, except that in no case shall the interest rate exceed 3 per centum per annum. Such interest shall accrue from date of deposit occurring after April 27, 1966, to and including date of withdrawal or date of breach of the immigration bond, whichever occurs first: *Provided,* That cash received by the Attorney General as security on an immigration bond, and deposited by him in the postal savings system prior to discontinuance of the system, shall accrue interest as provided in this section from the date such cash ceased to accrue interest under the system. Appropriations to the Treasury Department for interest on uninvested funds shall be available for payment of said interest.

(b) The interest accruing on cash received by the Attorney General as security on an immigration bond shall be subject to the same disposition as prescribed for the principal cash, except that interest accruing to the date of breach of the immigration bond shall be paid to the obligor on the bond.

(June 27, 1952, c. 477, Title II, ch. 9, § 293; as added Pub.L. 91–313, § 2, July 10, 1970, 84 Stat. 413.)

§ 294. Undercover investigation authority [8 U.S.C.A. § 1363a]

(a) In general

With respect to any undercover investigative operation of the Service which is necessary for the detection and prosecution of crimes against the United States—

(1) sums appropriated for the Service may be used for leasing space within the United States and the territories and possessions of the United States without regard to the following provisions of law:

(A) section 3679(a) of the Revised Statutes (31 U.S.C. 1341),

(B) section 3732(a) of the Revised Statutes (41 U.S.C. 11(a)),

(C) section 305 of the Act of June 30, 1949 (63 Stat. 396; 41 U.S.C. 255),

(D) the third undesignated paragraph under the heading "Miscellaneous" of the Act of March 3, 1877 (19 Stat. 370; 40 U.S.C. 34),

(E) section 3648 of the Revised Statutes (31 U.S.C. 3324),

(F) section 3741 of the Revised Statutes (41 U.S.C. 22), and

(G) subsections (a) and (c) of section 304 of the Federal Property and Administrative Services Act of 1949 (63 Stat. 395; 41 U.S.C. 254(a) and (c));

(2) sums appropriated for the Service may be used to establish or to acquire proprietary corporations or business entities as part of an undercover operation, and to operate such corporations or business entities on a commercial basis, without regard to the provisions of section 304 of the Government Corporation Control Act (31 U.S.C. 9102);

(3) sums appropriated for the Service, and the proceeds from the undercover operation, may be deposited in banks or other financial institutions without regard to the provisions of section 648

of Title 18, and of section 3639 of the Revised Statutes (31 U.S.C. 3302); and

(4) the proceeds from the undercover operation may be used to offset necessary and reasonable expenses incurred in such operation without regard to the provisions of section 3617 of the Revised Statutes (31 U.S.C. 3302).

The authority set forth in this subsection may be exercised only upon written certification of the Commissioner, in consultation with the Deputy Attorney General, that any action authorized by paragraph (1), (2), (3), or (4) is necessary for the conduct of the undercover operation.

(b) Disposition of proceeds no longer required

As soon as practicable after the proceeds from an undercover investigative operation, carried out under paragraphs (3) and (4) of subsection (a), are no longer necessary for the conduct of the operation, the proceeds or the balance of the proceeds remaining at the time shall be deposited into the Treasury of the United States as miscellaneous receipts.

(c) Disposition of certain corporations and business entities

If a corporation or business entity established or acquired as part of an undercover operation under paragraph (2) of subsection (a) with a net value of over $50,000 is to be liquidated, sold, or otherwise disposed of, the Service, as much in advance as the Commissioner or Commissioner's designee determines practicable, shall report the circumstances to the Attorney General, the Director of the Office of Management and Budget, and the Comptroller General. The proceeds of the liquidation, sale, or other disposition, after obligations are met, shall be deposited in the Treasury of the United States as miscellaneous receipts.

(d) Financial audits

The Service shall conduct detailed financial audits of closed undercover operations on a quarterly basis and shall report the results of the audits in writing to the Deputy Attorney General.

(June 27, 1952, c. 477, Title II, ch. 9, § 294, as added Sept. 30, 1996, Pub.L. 104–208, Div. C, Title II, § 205(a), 110 Stat. 3009–567.)

TITLE III

NATIONALITY AND NATURALIZATION

CHAPTER I—NATIONALITY AT BIRTH AND COLLECTIVE NATURALIZATION

§ 301. Nationals and citizens of United States at birth [8 U.S.C.A. § 1401]

The following shall be nationals and citizens of the United States at birth:

(a) a person born in the United States, and subject to the jurisdiction thereof;

(b) a person born in the United States to a member of an Indian, Eskimo, Aleutian, or other aboriginal tribe: Provided, That the granting of citizenship under this subsection shall not in any manner impair or otherwise affect the right of such person to tribal or other property;

(c) a person born outside of the United States and its outlying possessions of parents both of whom are citizens of the United States and one of whom has had a residence in the United States or one of its outlying possessions, prior to the birth of such person;

(d) a person born outside of the United States and its outlying possessions of parents one of whom is a citizen of the United States who has been physically present in the United States or one of its outlying possessions for a continuous period of one year prior to the birth of such person, and the other of whom is a national, but not a citizen of the United States;

(e) a person born in an outlying possession of the United States of parents one of whom is a citizen of the United States who has been physically present in the United States or one of its outlying possessions for a continuous period of one year at any time prior to the birth of such person;

(f) a person of unknown parentage found in the United States while under the age of five years, until shown, prior to his attaining the age of twenty-one years, not to have been born in the United States;

(g) a person born outside the geographical limits of the United States and its outlying possessions of parents one of whom is an alien, and the other a citizen of the United States who, prior to the birth of such person, was physically present in the United States or its outlying possessions for a period or periods totaling not less than five years, at least two of which were after attaining the age of fourteen years: Provided, That any periods of honorable service in the Armed Forces of the United States, or periods of employment with the United States Government or with an international organization as that term is defined in section 288 of Title 22 by such citizen parent, or any periods during which such citizen parent is physically present abroad as the dependent unmarried son or daughter and a member of the household of a person **(A)** honorably serving with the Armed Forces of the United States, or **(B)** employed by the United States Government or an international organization as defined in section 288 of Title 22, may be included in order to satisfy the physical-presence requirement of this paragraph. This proviso shall be applicable to persons born on or after December 24, 1952, to the same extent as if it had become effective in its present form on that date; and

(h) a person born before noon (Eastern Standard Time) May 24, 1934, outside the limits and jurisdiction of the United States of an alien father and a mother who is a citizen of the United States who, prior to the birth of such person, had resided in the United States.

(June 27, 1952, c. 477, Title III, ch. 1, § 301, 66 Stat. 235; Nov. 6, 1966, Pub.L. 89–770, 80 Stat. 1322; Oct. 27, 1972, Pub.L. 92–584, §§ 1, 3, 86 Stat. 1289; Oct. 10, 1978, Pub.L. 95–432, §§ 1, 3, 92 Stat. 1046; Nov. 14, 1986, Pub.L. 99–653, § 12, 100 Stat. 3657; Oct. 25, 1994, Pub.L. 103–416, Title I, § 101(a), 108 Stat. 4306.)

§ 302. Persons born in Puerto Rico on or after April 11, 1899 [8 U.S.C.A. § 1402]

All persons born in Puerto Rico on or after April 11, 1899, and prior to January 13, 1941, subject to the jurisdiction of the United States, residing on January 13, 1941, in Puerto Rico or other territory over which the United States exercises rights of sovereignty and not citizens of the United States under any other Act, are declared to be citizens of the United States as of January 13, 1941. All persons born in Puerto Rico on or after January 13, 1941, and subject to the jurisdiction of the United States, are citizens of the United States at birth.

(June 27, 1952, c. 477, Title III, ch. 1, § 302, 66 Stat. 236.)

§ 303. Persons born in the Canal Zone or Republic of Panama on or after February 26, 1904 [8 U.S.C.A. § 1403]

(a) Any person born in the Canal Zone on or after February 26, 1904, and whether before or after the effective date of this Act, whose father or mother or both at the time of the birth of such person was or is a citizen of the United States, is declared to be a citizen of the United States.

(b) Any person born in the Republic of Panama on or after February 26, 1904, and whether before or after the effective date of this Act, whose father or mother or both at the time of the birth of such person was or is a citizen of the United States employed by the Government of the United States or by the Panama Railroad Company, or its successor in title, is declared to be a citizen of the United States.

(June 27, 1952, c. 477, Title III, ch. 1, § 303, 66 Stat. 236.)

§ 304. Persons born in Alaska on or after March 30, 1867 [8 U.S.C.A. § 1404]

A person born in Alaska on or after March 30, 1867, except a noncitizen Indian, is a citizen of the United States at birth. A noncitizen Indian born in Alaska on or after March 30, 1867, and prior to June 2, 1924, is declared to be a citizen of the United States as of June 2, 1924. An Indian born in Alaska on or after June 2, 1924, is a citizen of the United States at birth.

(June 27, 1952, c. 477, Title III, ch. 1, § 304, 66 Stat. 237.)

§ 305. Persons born in Hawaii [8 U.S.C.A. § 1405]

A person born in Hawaii on or after August 12, 1898, and before April 30, 1900, is declared to be a citizen of the United States as of April 30, 1900. A person born in Hawaii on or after April 30, 1900, is a citizen of the United States at birth. A person who was a citizen of the Republic of Hawaii on August 12, 1898, is declared to be a citizen of the United States as of April 30, 1900.

(June 27, 1952, c. 477, Title III, ch. 1, § 305, 66 Stat. 237.)

§ 306. Persons living in and born in the Virgin Islands [8 U.S.C.A. § 1406]

(a) The following persons and their children born subsequent to January 17, 1917, and prior to February 25,1927, are declared to be citizens of the United States as of February 25, 1927:

(1) All former Danish citizens who, on January 17, 1917, resided in the Virgin Islands of the United States, and were residing in those islands or in the United States or Puerto Rico on February 25, 1927, and who did not make the declaration required to preserve their Danish citizenship by article 6 of the treaty entered into on August 4, 1916, between the United States and Denmark, or who, having made such a declaration have heretofore renounced or may hereafter renounce it by a declaration before a court of record;

(2) All natives of the Virgin Islands of the United States who, on January 17, 1917, resided in those islands, and were residing in those islands or in the United States or Puerto Rico on February 25, 1927, and who were not on February 25, 1927, citizens or subjects of any foreign country;

(3) All natives of the Virgin Islands of the United States who, on January 17, 1917, resided in the United States, and were residing in those islands on February 25, 1927, and who were not on February 25, 1927, citizens or subjects of any foreign country; and

(4) All natives of the Virgin Islands of the United States who, on June 28, 1932, were residing in continental United States, the Virgin Islands of the United States, Puerto Rico, the Canal Zone, or any other insular possession or territory of the United States, and who, on June 28, 1932, were not citizens or subjects of any foreign country, regardless of their place of residence on January 17, 1917.

(b) All persons born in the Virgin Islands of the United States on or after January 17, 1917, and prior to February 25, 1927, and subject to the jurisdiction of the United States are declared to be citizens of the United States as of February 25, 1927; and all persons born in those islands on or after February 25, 1927, and subject to the jurisdiction of the United States, are declared to be citizens of the United States at birth.

(June 27, 1952, c. 477, Title III, ch. 1, § 306, 66 Stat. 237.)

§ 307. Persons living in and born in Guam [8 U.S.C.A. § 1407]

(a) The following persons, and their children born after April 11, 1899, are declared to be citizens of the United States as of August 1, 1950, if they were residing on August 1, 1950, on the island of Guam or other territory over which the United States exercises rights of sovereignty:

(1) All inhabitants of the island of Guam on April 11, 1899, including those temporarily absent from the island on that date, who were Spanish subjects, who after that date continued to reside in Guam or other territory over which the United States exercises sovereignty, and who have taken no affirmative steps to preserve or acquire foreign nationality; and

(2) All persons born in the island of Guam who resided in Guam on April 11, 1899, including those temporarily absent from the island on that date, who after that date continued to reside in Guam or other territory over which the United States exercises sovereignty, and who have taken no affirmative steps to preserve or acquire foreign nationality.

(b) All persons born in the island of Guam on or after April 11, 1899 (whether before or after August 1, 1950) subject to the jurisdiction of the United States, are declared to be citizens of the United States: *Provided,* That in the case of any person born before August 1, 1950, he has taken no affirmative steps to preserve or acquire foreign nationality.

(c) Any person hereinbefore described who is a citizen or national of a country other than the United States and desires to retain his present political status shall have made, prior to August 1, 1952, a declaration under oath of such desire, said declaration to be in form and executed in the manner prescribed by regulations. From and after the making of such a declaration any such person shall be held not to be a national of the United States by virtue of this Act.

(June 27, 1952, c. 477, Title III, ch. 1, § 307, 66 Stat. 237.)

§ 308. Nationals but not citizens of the United States at birth [8 U.S.C.A. § 1408]

Unless otherwise provided in section 301 [8 U.S.C.A. § 1401], the following shall be nationals, but not citizens, of the United States at birth:

(1) A person born in an outlying possession of the United States on or after the date of formal acquisition of such possession;

(2) A person born outside the United States and its outlying possessions of parents both of whom are nationals, but not citizens, of the United States, and have had a residence in the United States, or one of its outlying possessions prior to the birth of such person;

(3) A person of unknown parentage found in an outlying possession of the United States while under the age of five years, until shown, prior to his attaining the age of twenty-one years, not to have been born in such outlying possession; and

(4) A person born outside the United States and its outlying possessions of parents one of whom is an alien, and the other a national, but not a citizen, of the United States who, prior to the birth of such person, was physically present in the United States or its outlying possessions for a period or periods totaling not less than seven years in any continuous period of ten years—

(A) during which the national parent was not outside the United States or its outlying possessions for a continuous period of more than one year, and

(B) at least five years of which were after attaining the age of fourteen years.

The proviso of section 301(g) [8 U.S.C.A. § 1401(g)] shall apply to the national parent under this paragraph in the same manner as it applies to the citizen parent under that section.

(June 27, 1952, c. 477, Title III, ch. 1, § 308, 66 Stat. 238; Pub. L. 99–396, § 15(a), Aug. 27, 1986, 100 Stat. 842, as amended Pub.L. 100–525, § 3(2), Oct. 24, 1988, 102 Stat. 2614.)

§ 309. Children born out of wedlock [8 U.S.C.A. § 1409]

(a) The provisions of paragraphs (c), (d), (e), and (g) of section 301 [8 U.S.C.A. § 1401(c), (d), (e), and (g)], and of paragraph (2) of section 308 [8 U.S.C.A. § 1408], shall apply as of the date of birth to a person born out of wedlock if—

(1) a blood relationship between the person and the father is established by clear and convincing evidence,

(2) the father had the nationality of the United States at the time of the person's birth,

(3) the father (unless deceased) has agreed in writing to provide financial support for the person until the person reaches the age of 18 years, and

(4) while the person is under the age of 18 years—

(A) the person is legitimated under the law of the person's residence or domicile,

(B) the father acknowledges paternity of the person in writing under oath, or

(C) the paternity of the person is established by adjudication of a competent court.

(b) Except as otherwise provided in section 405 of this Act, the provisions of section 301(g) [8 U.S.C.A. § 1401(g)] shall apply to a child born out of wedlock on or after January 13, 1941, and before December 24, 1952, as of the date of birth, if the paternity of such child is established at any time and while such child is under the age of twenty-one years by legitimation.

(c) Notwithstanding the provision of subsection (a) of this section, a person born after December 23, 1952, outside the United States and out of wedlock shall be held to have acquired at birth the nationality status of his mother, if the mother had the nationality of the United States at the time of such person's birth, and if the mother had previously been physically present in the United States or one of its outlying possessions for a continuous period of one year.

(June 27, 1952, c. 477, Title III, ch. 1, § 309, 66 Stat. 238; Pub. L. 97–116, § 18(*l*), Dec. 29, 1981, 95 Stat. 1620; Pub.L. 99–653, § 13, Nov. 14, 1986, 100 Stat. 3657, as amended Pub.L. 100–525, § 8(k), Oct. 24, 1988, 102 Stat. 2617; Pub.L. 100–525, § 9(r), Oct. 24, 1988, 102 Stat. 2621.)

CHAPTER II—NATIONALITY THROUGH NATURALIZATION

§ 310. Naturalization authority [8 U.S.C.A. § 1421]

(a) Authority in Attorney General

The sole authority to naturalize persons as citizens of the United States is conferred upon the Attorney General.

(b) Court authority to administer oaths

(1) Jurisdiction

Subject to section 337(c) [8 U.S.C.A. § 1448(c)]—

(A) General jurisdiction

Except as provided in subparagraph (B), each applicant for naturalization may choose to have the oath of allegiance under section 337(a) [8 U.S.C.A. § 1448(a)] administered by the Attorney General or by an eligible court described in paragraph (5). Each such eligible court shall have authority to administer such oath of allegiance to persons residing within the jurisdiction of the court.

(B) Exclusive authority

An eligible court described in paragraph (5) that wishes to have exclusive authority to administer the oath of allegiance under section 337(a) [8 U.S.C.A. § 1448(a)] to persons residing within the jurisdiction of the court during the period described in paragraph (3)(A)(i) shall notify the Attorney General of such wish and, subject to this subsection, shall have such exclusive authority with respect to such persons during such period.

(2) Information

(A) General information

In the case of a court exercising authority under paragraph (1), in accordance with procedures established by the Attorney General—

(i) the applicant for naturalization shall notify the Attorney General of the intent to be naturalized before the court, and

(ii) the Attorney General—

(I) shall forward to the court (not later than 10 days after the date of approval of an application for naturalization in the case of a court which has provided notice under paragraph (1)(B)) such information as may be necessary to administer the oath of allegiance under section 337(a) [8 U.S.C.A. § 1448(a)] , and

(II) shall promptly forward to the court a certificate of naturalization (prepared by the Attorney General).

(B) Assignment of individuals in the case of exclusive authority

If an eligible court has provided notice under paragraph (1)(B), the Attorney General shall inform each person (residing within the jurisdiction of the court), at the time of the approval of the person's application for naturalization, of—

(i) the court's exclusive authority to administer the oath of allegiance under section 337(a) [8 U.S.C.A. § 1448(a)] to such a person during the period specified in paragraph (3)(A)(i), and

(ii) the date or dates (if any) under paragraph (3)(B) on which the court has scheduled oath administration ceremonics.

If more than one eligible court in an area has provided notice under paragraph (1)(B), the Attorney General shall permit the person, at the time of the approval, to choose the court to which the information will be forwarded for administration of the oath of allegiance under this section.

(3) Scope of exclusive authority

(A) Limited period and advance notice required

The exclusive authority of a court to administer the oath of allegiance under paragraph (1)(B) shall apply with respect to a person—

(i) only during the 45–day period beginning on the date on which the Attorney General certifies to the court that an applicant is eligible for naturalization, and

(ii) only if the court has notified the Attorney General, prior to the date of certification of eligibility, of the day or days (during such 45–day period) on which the court has scheduled oath administration ceremonies.

(B) Authority of attorney general

Subject to subparagraph (C), the Attorney General shall not administer the oath of allegiance to a person under subsection (a) during the period in which exclusive authority to administer the oath of allegiance may be exercised by an eligible court under this subsection with respect to that person.

(C) Waiver of exclusive authority

Notwithstanding the previous provisions of this paragraph, a court may waive exclusive authority to administer the oath of allegiance under section 337(a) [8 U.S.C.A. § 1448(a)] to a person under this subsection if the Attorney General has not provided the court with the certification described in subparagraph (A)(i) within a reasonable time before the date scheduled by the court for oath administration ceremonies. Upon notification of a court's waiver of jurisdiction, the Attorney General shall promptly notify the applicant.

(4) Issuance of certificates

The Attorney General shall provide for the issuance of certificates of naturalization at the time of administration of the oath of allegiance.

(5) Eligible courts

For purposes of this section, the term "eligible court" means—

(A) a district court of the United States in any State, or

(B) any court of record in any State having a seal, a clerk, and jurisdiction in actions in law or equity, or law and equity, in which the amount in controversy is unlimited.

(c) Judicial review

A person whose application for naturalization under this title is denied, after a hearing before an immigration officer under section 336(a) [8 U.S.C.A. § 1447(a)], may seek review of such denial before the United States district court for the district in which such person resides in accordance with chapter 7 of Title 5. Such review shall be de novo, and the court shall make its own findings of fact and conclusions of law and shall, at the request of the petitioner, conduct a hearing de novo on the application.

(d) Sole procedure

A person may only be naturalized as a citizen of the United States in the manner and under the conditions prescribed in this title and not otherwise.

(June 27, 1952, c. 477, Title III, ch. 2, § 310, 66 Stat. 239; July 7, 1958, Pub.L. 85–508, § 25, 72 Stat. 351; Mar. 18, 1959, Pub.L. 86–3, § 20(c), 73 Stat. 13; Sept. 26, 1961, Pub.L. 87–301, § 17, 75 Stat. 656; Oct. 24, 1988, Pub.L. 100–525, § 9(s), 102 Stat. 2621; Nov. 29, 1990, Pub.L. 101–649, Title IV, § 401(a), 104 Stat. 5038; Dec. 12, 1991, Pub.L. 102–232, Title I, § 102(a), Title III, § 305(a), 105 Stat. 1734, 1749; Oct. 25, 1994, Pub.L. 103–416, Title II, § 219(u), 108 Stat. 4318.)

§ 311. Eligibility for naturalization [8 U.S.C.A. § 1422]

The right of a person to become a naturalized citizen of the United States shall not be denied or abridged because of race or sex or because such person is married.

(June 27, 1952, c. 477, Title III, ch. 2, § 311, 66 Stat. 239; Pub.L. 100–525, § 9(t), Oct. 24, 1988, 102 Stat. 2621.)

§ 312. Requirements as to understanding the English language, history, principles and form of government of the United States [8 U.S.C.A. § 1423]

(a) No person except as otherwise provided in this title shall hereafter be naturalized as a citizen of the United States upon his own application who cannot demonstrate—

(1) an understanding of the English language, including an ability to read, write, and speak words in ordinary usage in the English language: Provided, That the requirements of this paragraph relating to ability to read and write shall be met if the applicant can read or write simple words and phrases to the end that a reasonable test of his literacy shall be made and that no extraordinary or unreasonable condition shall be imposed upon the applicant; and

(2) a knowledge and understanding of the fundamentals of the history, and of the principles and form of government, of the United States.

(b)(1) The requirements of subsection (a) shall not apply to any person who is unable because of physical or developmental disability or mental impairment to comply therewith.

(2) The requirement of subsection (a)(1) shall not apply to any person who, on the date of the filing of the person's application for naturalization as provided in section 334 [8 U.S.C.A. § 1445], either—

(A) is over fifty years of age and has been living in the United States for periods totaling at least twenty years subsequent to a lawful admission for permanent residence, or

(B) is over fifty-five years of age and has been living in the United States for periods totaling at least fifteen years subsequent to a lawful admission for permanent residence.

(3) The Attorney General, pursuant to regulations, shall provide for special consideration, as determined by the Attorney General, concerning the requirement of subsection (a)(2) with respect to any person who, on the date of the filing of the person's application for naturalization as provided in section 334 [8 U.S.C.A. § 1445], is over sixty-five years of age and has been living in the United States for periods totaling at least twenty years subsequent to a lawful admission for permanent residence.

(June 27, 1952, c. 477, Title III, ch. 2, § 312, 66 Stat. 239; Nov. 2, 1978, Pub.L. 95–579, § 3, 92 Stat. 2474; Nov. 29, 1990, Pub.L. 101–649, Title IV, § 403, 104 Stat. 5039; Dec. 12, 1991, Pub.L. 102–232, Title III, § 305(m)(2), 105 Stat. 1750; Oct. 25, 1994, Pub.L. 103–416, Title I, § 108(a), 108 Stat. 4309.)

§ 313. Prohibition upon the naturalization of persons opposed to government or law, or who favor totalitarian forms of government [8 U.S.C.A. § 1424]

(a) Notwithstanding the provisions of section 405(b) of this Act [8 U.S.C.A. § 1101 note], no person shall hereafter be naturalized as a citizen of the United States—

(1) who advocates or teaches, or who is a member of or affiliated with any organization that advocates or teaches, opposition to all organized government; or

(2) who is a member of or affiliated with **(A)** the Communist Party of the United States; **(B)** any other totalitarian party of the United States; **(C)** the Communist Political Association; **(D)** the Communist or other totalitarian party of any State of the United States, of any foreign state, or of any political or geographical subdivision of any foreign state; **(E)** any section, subsidiary, branch, affiliate, or subdivision of any such association or party; or **(F)** the direct predecessors or successors of any such association or party, regardless of what name such group or organization may have used, may now bear, or may hereafter adopt, unless such alien establishes that he did not have knowledge or reason to believe at the time he became a member of or affiliated with such an organization (and did not thereafter and prior to the date upon which such organization was so registered or so required to be registered have such knowledge or reason to believe) that such organization was a Communist-front organization; or

(3) who, although not within any of the other provisions of this section, advocates the economic, international, and governmental doctrines of world communism or the establishment in the United States of a totalitarian dictatorship, or who is a member of or affiliated with any organization that advocates the economic, international, and governmental doctrines of world communism or the establishment in the United States of a totalitarian dictatorship, either through its own utterances or through any written or printed publications issued or published by or with the permission or consent of or under authority of such organization or paid for by the funds of such organization; or

(4) who advocates or teaches or who is a member of or affiliated with any organization that advocates or teaches **(A)** the overthrow by force or violence or other unconstitutional means of the Government of the United States or of all forms of law; or **(B)** the duty, necessity, or propriety of the unlawful assaulting or killing of any officer or officers (either of specific individuals or of officers generally) of the Government of the United States or of any other organized government because of his or their official character; or **(C)** the unlawful damage, injury, or destruction of property; or **(D)** sabotage; or

(5) who writes or publishes or causes to be written or published, or who knowingly circulates, distributes, prints, or displays, or knowingly causes to be circulated, distributed, printed, published, or displayed, or who knowingly has in his possession for the purpose of circulation, publication, distribution, or display, any written or printed matter, advocating or teaching opposition to all organized government, or advocating **(A)** the overthrow by force, violence, or other unconstitutional means of the Government of the United States or of all forms of law; or **(B)** the duty, necessity, or propriety of the unlawful assaulting or killing of any officer or officers (either of specific individuals or of officers generally) of the Government of the United States or of any other organized government, because of his or their official character; or **(C)** the unlawful damage, injury, or destruction of property; or **(D)** sabotage; or **(E)** the economic, international, and governmental doctrines of world communism or the establishment in the United States of a totalitarian dictatorship; or

(6) who is a member of or affiliated with any organization that writes, circulates, distributes, prints, publishes, or displays, or causes to be written, circulated, distributed, printed, published, or displayed, or that has in its possession for the purpose of circulation, distribution, publication, issue, or display, any written or printed matter of the character described in subparagraph (5) of this subsection.

(b) The provisions of this section or of any other section of this title shall not be construed as declaring that any of the organizations referred to in this section or in any other section of this title do not advocate the overthrow of the Government of the United States by force, violence, or other unconstitutional means.

(c) The provisions of this section shall be applicable to any applicant for naturalization who at any time within a period of ten years immediately preceding the filing of the application for naturalization or after such filing and before taking the final oath of citizenship is, or has been found to be within any of the classes enumerated within this section, notwithstanding that at the time the application is filed he may not be included within such classes.

(d) Any person who is within any of the classes described in subsection (a) solely because of past membership in, or past affiliation with, a party or organization may be naturalized without regard to the provisions of subsection (c) if such person establishes that such membership or affiliation is or was involuntary, or occurred and terminated prior to the attainment by such alien of the age of sixteen years, or that such membership or affiliation is or was by operation of law, or was for purposes of obtaining employment, food rations, or other essentials of living and where necessary for such purposes.

(e) A person may be naturalized under this title without regard to the prohibitions in subsections (a)(2) and (c) of this section if the person—

(1) is otherwise eligible for naturalization;

(2) is within the class described in subsection (a)(2) solely because of past membership in, or past affiliation with, a party or organization described in that subsection;

(3) does not fall within any other of the classes described in that subsection; and

(4) is determined by the Director of Central Intelligence, in consultation with the Secretary of Defense, and with the concurrence of the Attorney General, to have made a contribution to the national security or to the national intelligence mission of the United States.

(June 27, 1952, c. 477, Title III, ch. 2, § 313, 66 Stat. 240; Oct. 24, 1988, Pub.L. 100–525, § 9(u), 102 Stat. 2621; Nov. 29, 1990, Pub.L. 101–649, Title IV, § 407(c), 104 Stat. 5041; Dec. 12, 1991, Pub.L. 102–232, Title III, § 309(b)(13),

105 Stat. 1759; Oct. 25, 1994, Pub.L. 103–416, Title II, § 219(v), 108 Stat. 4318; Dec. 3, 1999, Pub.L. 106–120, Title III, § 306, 113 Stat. 1612.)

§ 314. Ineligibility to naturalization of deserters from the armed forces [8 U.S.C.A. § 1425]

A person who, at any time during which the United States has been or shall be at war, deserted or shall desert the military, air, or naval forces of the United States, or who, having been duly enrolled, departed, or shall depart from the jurisdiction of the district in which enrolled, or who, whether or not having been duly enrolled, went or shall go beyond the limits of the United States, with intent to avoid any draft into the military, air, or naval service, lawfully ordered, shall, upon conviction thereof by a court martial or a court of competent jurisdiction, be permanently ineligible to become a citizen of the United States; and such deserters and evaders shall be forever incapable of holding any office of trust or of profit under the United States, or of exercising any rights of citizens thereof.

(June 27, 1952, c. 477, Title III, ch. 2, § 314, 66 Stat. 241.)

§ 315. Citizenship denied alien relieved of service in armed forces because of alienage [8 U.S.C.A. § 1426]

(a) Permanent ineligibility

Notwithstanding the provisions of section 405(b) of this Act but subject to subsection (c), any alien who applies or has applied for exemption or discharge from training or service in the Armed Forces or in the National Security Training Corps of the United States on the ground that he is an alien, and is or was relieved or discharged from such training or service on such ground, shall be permanently ineligible to become a citizen of the United States.

(b) Conclusiveness of records

The records of the Selective Service System or of the Department of Defense shall be conclusive as to whether an alien was relieved or discharged from such liability for training or service because he was an alien.

(c) Service in armed forces of a foreign country

An alien shall not be ineligible for citizenship under this section or otherwise because of an exemption from training or service in the Armed Forces of the United States pursuant to the exercise of rights under a treaty, if before the time of the exercise of such rights the alien served in the Armed Forces of a foreign country of which the alien was a national.

(June 27, 1952, c. 477, Title III, ch. 2, § 315, 66 Stat. 242; Pub.L. 100–525, § 9(v), Oct. 24, 1988, 102 Stat. 2621; Pub.L. 101–649, Title IV, § 404, Nov. 29, 1990, 104 Stat. 5039.)

§ 316. Requirements of naturalization [8 U.S.C.A. § 1427]

(a) Residence

No person, except as otherwise provided in this title, shall be naturalized unless such applicant, **(1)** immediately preceding the date of filing his application for naturalization has resided continuously, after being lawfully admitted for permanent residence, within the United States for at least five years and during the five years immediately preceding the date of filing his application has been physically present therein for periods totaling at least half of that time, and who has resided within the State or within the district of the Service in the United States in which the applicant filed the application for at least three months, **(2)** has resided continuously within the United States from the date of the application up to the time of admission to citizenship, and **(3)** during all the period referred to in this subsection has been and still is a person of good moral character, attached to the principles of the Constitution of the United States, and well disposed to the good order and happiness of the United States.

(b) Absences

Absence from the United States of more than six months but less than one year during the period for which continuous residence is required for admission to citizenship, immediately preceding the date of filing the application for naturalization, or during the period between the date of filing the application and the date of any hearing under section 336(a) [8 U.S.C.A. § 1447(a)], shall break the continuity of such residence, unless the applicant shall establish to the satisfaction of the Attorney General that he did not in fact abandon his residence in the United States during such period.

Absence from the United States for a continuous period of one year or more during the period for which continuous residence is required for admission to citizenship (whether preceding or subsequent to the filing of the application for naturalization) shall break the continuity of such residence, except that in the case of a person who has been physically present and residing in the United States, after being lawfully admitted for permanent residence, for an uninterrupted period of at least one year, and who thereafter is employed by or under contract with the Government of the United States or an American institution of research recognized as such by the Attorney General, or is employed by an American firm or corporation engaged in whole or in part in the development of foreign trade and commerce of the United States, or a subsidiary thereof more than 50 per centum of whose stock is owned by an American firm or corporation, or is employed by a public international organization of which the United States is a member by treaty or statute and by which the alien was not employed until after being lawfully admitted for permanent residence, no period of absence from the United States shall break the continuity of residence if—

(1) prior to the beginning of such period of employment (whether such period begins before or after his departure from the United States), but prior to the expiration of one year of continuous absence from the United States, the person has established to the satisfaction of the Attorney General that his absence from the United States for such period is to be on behalf of such Government, or for the purpose of carrying on scientific research on behalf of such institution, or to be engaged in the development of such foreign trade and commerce or whose residence abroad is necessary to the protection of the property rights in such countries in such firm or corporation, or to be employed by a public international organization of which the United States is a member by treaty or statute and by which the alien was not employed until after being lawfully admitted for permanent residence; and

(2) such person proves to the satisfaction of the Attorney General that his absence from the United States for such period has been for such purpose.

The spouse and dependent unmarried sons and daughters who are members of the household of a person who qualifies for the benefits of this subsection shall also be entitled to such benefits during the period for which they were residing abroad as dependent members of the household of the person.

(c) Physical presence

The granting of the benefits of subsection (b) of this section shall not relieve the applicant from the requirement of physical presence within the United States for the period specified in subsection (a) of this section, except in the case of those persons who are employed by, or under contract with, the Government of the United States. In the case of a person employed by or under contract with Central Intelligence Agency, the requirement in subsection (b) of an uninterrupted period of at least one year of physical presence in the United States may be complied with by such person at any time prior to filing an application for naturalization.

(d) Moral character

No finding by the Attorney General that the applicant is not deportable shall be accepted as conclusive evidence of good moral character.

(e) Determination

In determining whether the applicant has sustained the burden of establishing good moral character and the other qualifications for citizenship specified in subsection (a) of this section, the Attorney General shall not be limited to the applicant's conduct during the five years preceding the filing of the application, but may take into consideration as a basis for such determination the applicant's conduct and acts at any time prior to that period.

(f) Persons making extraordinary contributions to national security

(1) Whenever the Director of Central Intelligence, the Attorney General and the Commissioner of Immigration determine that an applicant otherwise eligible for naturalization has made an extraordinary contribution to the national security of the United States or to the conduct of United States intelligence activities, the applicant may be naturalized without regard to the residence and physical presence requirements of this section, or to the prohibitions of section 313 [8 U.S.C.A. § 1424], and no residence within a particular State or district of the Service in the United States shall be required: Provided, That the applicant has continuously resided in the United States for at least one year prior to naturalization: Provided, further, That the provisions of this subsection shall not apply to any alien described in clauses (i) through (iv) of section 208(b)(2)(A) [8 U.S.C.A. § 1158(b)(2)(A)].

(2) An applicant for naturalization under this subsection may be administered the oath of allegiance under section 337(a) [8 U.S.C.A. § 1448(a)] by any district court of the United States, without regard to the residence of the applicant. Proceedings under this subsection shall be conducted in a manner consistent with the protection of intelligence sources, methods and activities.

(3) The number of aliens naturalized pursuant to this subsection in any fiscal year shall not exceed five. The Director of Central Intelligence shall inform the Select Committee on Intelligence and the Committee on the Judiciary of the Senate and the Permanent Select Committee on Intelligence and the Committee on the Judiciary of the House of Representatives within a reasonable time prior to the filing of each application under the provisions of this subsection.

(June 27, 1952, c. 477, Title III, ch. 2, § 316, 66 Stat. 242; Dec. 29, 1981, Pub.L. 97–116, § 14, 95 Stat. 1619; Dec. 4, 1985, Pub.L. 99–169, Title VI, § 601, 99 Stat. 1007; Nov. 29, 1990, Pub.L. 101–649, Title IV, §§ 402, 407(c)(2), (d)(1), (e)(1), 104 Stat. 5038, 5041, 5046; Sept. 30, 1996, Pub.L. 104–208, Div. C, Title III, § 308(g)(7)(F), 110 Stat. 3009–624.)

§ 317. Temporary absence of persons performing religious duties [8 U.S.C.A. § 1428]

Any person who is authorized to perform the ministerial or priestly functions of a religious denomination having a bona fide organization within the United States, or any person who is engaged solely by a religious denomination or by an interdenominational mission organization having a bona fide organization within the United States as a missionary, brother, nun, or sister, who **(1)** has been lawfully admitted to the United States for permanent residence, **(2)** has at any time thereafter and before filing an application for naturalization been physically present and residing within the United States for an uninterrupted period of at least one year, and **(3)** has heretofore been or may hereafter be absent temporarily from the United States in connection with or for the purpose of performing the ministerial or priestly functions of such religious denomination, or serving as a missionary, brother, nun, or sister, shall be considered as being physically present and residing in the United States for the purpose of naturalization within the meaning of section 316(a) [8 U.S.C.A. § 1427(a)], notwithstanding any such absence from the United States, if he shall in all other respects comply with the requirements of the naturalization law. Such person shall prove to the satisfaction of the Attorney General that his absence from the United States has been solely for the purpose of performing the ministerial or priestly functions of such religious denomination, or of serving as a missionary, brother, nun, or sister.

(June 27, 1952, c. 477, Title III, ch. 2, § 317, 66 Stat. 243; Nov. 29, 1990, Pub.L. 101–649, Title IV, § 407(c), (d)(2), 104 Stat. 5041.)

§ 318. Prerequisite to naturalization; burden of proof [8 U.S.C.A. § 1429]

Except as otherwise provided in this title, no person shall be naturalized unless he has been lawfully admitted to the United States for permanent residence in accordance with all applicable provisions of this Act. The burden of proof shall be upon such person to show that he entered the United States lawfully, and the time, place, and manner of such entry into the United States, but in presenting such proof he shall be entitled to the production of his immigrant visa, if any, or of other entry document, if any, and of any other documents and records, not considered by the Attorney General to be confidential, pertaining to such entry, in the custody of the Service. Notwithstanding the provisions of section 405(b) of this Act, and except as provided in sections 328 [8 U.S.C.A. § 1439] and 329 [8 U.S.C.A. § 1440] no person shall be naturalized against whom there is outstanding a final finding of deportability pursuant to a warrant of arrest issued under the provisions of this or any other Act; and no application for naturalization shall be considered by the Attorney General if there is pending against the applicant a removal proceeding pursuant to a warrant of arrest issued under the provisions of this or any other Act: Provided, That the findings of the Attorney General in terminating removal proceedings or in canceling the removal of an alien pursuant to the provisions of this Act, shall not be deemed binding in any way upon the Attorney General with respect to the question of whether such person has established his eligibility for naturalization as required by this title.

(June 27, 1952, c. 477, Title III, ch. 2, § 318, 66 Stat. 244; Oct. 24, 1968, Pub.L. 90–633, § 4, 82 Stat. 1344; Nov. 29, 1990, Pub.L. 101–649, Title IV, § 407(c)(4), (d)(3), 104 Stat. 5041; Sept. 30, 1996, Pub.L. 104–208, Div. C, Title III, § 308(e)(1)(O), (15), 110 Stat. 3009–620, 3009–621.)

§ 319. Married persons and employees of certain nonprofit organizations [8 U.S.C.A. § 1430]

(a) Any person whose spouse is a citizen of the United States may be naturalized upon compliance with all the requirements of this title except the provisions of paragraph (1) of section 316(a) [8 U.S.C.A. § 1427(a)(1)] if such person immediately preceding the date of filing his application for naturalization has resided continuously, after being lawfully admitted for permanent residence, within the United States for at least three years, and during the three years immediately preceding the date of filing his application has been living in marital union with the citizen spouse, who has been a United States citizen during all of such period, and has been physically present in the United States for periods totaling at least half of that time and has resided within the State or the district of the Service in the United States in which the applicant filed his application for at least three months.

(b) Any person, **(1)** whose spouse is **(A)** a citizen of the United States, **(B)** in the employment of the Government of the United States, or of an American institution of research recognized as such by the Attorney General, or of an American firm or corporation engaged in whole or in part in the development of foreign trade and commerce of the United States, or a subsidiary thereof, or of a public international organization in which the United States participates by treaty or statute, or is authorized to perform the ministerial or priestly functions of a religious denomination having a bona fide organization within the United States, or is engaged solely as a missionary by a religious denomination or by an interdenominational mission organization having a bona fide organization within the United States, and **(C)** regularly stationed abroad in such employment, and **(2)** who is in the United States at the time of naturalization, and **(3)** who declares before the Attorney General in good faith an intention to take up residence within the United States immediately upon the termination of such employment abroad of the citizen spouse, may be naturalized upon compliance with all the requirements of the naturalization laws, except that no prior residence or specified period of physical presence within the United States or within a State or a district of the Service in the United States or proof thereof shall be required.

(c) Any person who **(1)** is employed by a bona fide United States incorporated nonprofit organization which is principally engaged in conducting abroad through communications media the dissemination of information which significantly promotes United States interests abroad and which is recognized as such by the Attorney General, and **(2)** has been so employed continuously for a period of not less than five years after a lawful admission for permanent residence, and **(3)** who files his application for naturalization while so employed or within six months following the termination thereof, and **(4)** who is in the United States at the time of naturalization, and **(5)** who declares before the Attorney General in good faith an intention to take up residence within the United States immediately upon termination of such employment, may be naturalized upon compliance with all the requirements of this title except that no prior residence or specified period of physical presence within the United States or any State or district of the Service in the United States, or proof thereof, shall be required.

(d) Any person who is the surviving spouse of a United States citizen, whose citizen spouse dies during a period of honorable service in an active duty status in the Armed Forces of the United States and who was living in marital union with the citizen spouse at the time of his death, may be naturalized upon compliance with all the requirements of this title except that no prior residence or specified physical presence within the United States, or within a State or a district of the Service in the United States shall be required.

(June 27, 1952, c. 477, Title III, ch. 2, § 319, 66 Stat. 244; Pub. L. 85–697, § 2, Aug. 20, 1958, 72 Stat. 687; Pub. L. 90–215, § 1(a), Dec. 18, 1967, 81 Stat. 661; Pub. L. 90–369, June 29, 1968, 82 Stat. 279; Pub.L. 101–649, Title IV, § 407(b)(1), (c), (d)(4), 104 Stat. 5040, 5041.)

§ 320. Children born outside United States of one alien and one citizen parent; conditions for automatic citizenship [8 U.S.C.A. § 1431]

(a) A child born outside of the United States, one of whose parents at the time of the child's birth was an alien and the other of whose parents then was and never thereafter ceased to be a citizen of the United States, shall, if such alien parent is naturalized, become a citizen of the United States, when—

(1) such naturalization takes place while such child is under the age of eighteen years; and

(2) such child is residing in the United States pursuant to a lawful admission for permanent residence at the time of naturalization or thereafter and begins to reside permanently in the United States while under the age of eighteen years.

(b) Subsection (a) of this section shall apply to an adopted child only if the child is residing in the United States at the time of naturalization of such adoptive parent, in the custody of his adoptive parents, pursuant to a lawful admission for permanent residence.

(June 27, 1952, c. 477, Title III, ch. 2, § 320, 66 Stat. 245; Pub. L. 95–417, § 4, Oct. 5, 1978, 92 Stat. 917; Pub. L. 97–116, § 18(m), Dec. 29, 1981, 95 Stat. 1620; Pub.L. 99–653, § 14, Nov. 14, 1986, 100 Stat. 3658; Pub.L. 100–525, §§ 8(*l*), 9(w), Oct. 24, 1988, 102 Stat. 2618, 2621.)

§ 321. Children born outside of United States of alien parents; conditions for automatic citizenship [8 U.S.C.A. § 1432]

(a) A child born outside of the United States of alien parents, or of an alien parent and a citizen parent who has subsequently lost citizenship of the United States, becomes a citizen of the United States upon fulfillment of the following conditions:

(1) The naturalization of both parents; or

(2) The naturalization of the surviving parent if one of the parents is deceased; or

(3) The naturalization of the parent having legal custody of the child when there has been a legal separation of the parents or the naturalization of the mother if the child was born out of wedlock and the paternity of the child has not been established by legitimation; and if

(4) Such naturalization takes place while such child is under the age of eighteen years; and

(5) Such child is residing in the United States pursuant to a lawful admission for permanent residence at the time of the naturalization of the parent last naturalized under clause (1) of this subsection, or the parent naturalized under clause (2) or (3) of this subsection, or thereafter begins to reside permanently in the United States while under the age of eighteen years.

(b) Subsection (a) of this section shall apply to an adopted child only if the child is residing in the United States at the time of naturalization of such adoptive parent or parents, in the custody of his adoptive parent or parents, pursuant to a lawful admission for permanent residence.

(June 27, 1952, c. 477, Title III, ch. 2, § 321, 66 Stat. 245; Pub. L. 95–417, § 5, Oct. 5, 1978, 92 Stat. 918; Pub. L. 97–116, § 18(m), Dec. 29, 1981, 95 Stat. 1620; Pub.L. 99–653, § 15, Nov. 14, 1986, 100 Stat. 3658; Pub.L. 100–525, § 8(*l*), Oct. 24, 1988, 102 Stat. 2618.)

§ 322. Child born outside United States; application for certificate of citizenship requirements [8 U.S.C.A. § 1433]

(a) Naturalization on application of citizen parents; requirements

A parent who is a citizen of the United States may apply to the Attorney General for a certificate of citizenship on behalf of a child born outside the United States. The Attorney General shall issue such a certificate of citizenship upon proof to the satisfaction of the Attorney General that the following conditions have been fulfilled:

(1) At least one parent is a citizen of the United States, whether by birth or naturalization.

(2) The child is physically present in the United States pursuant to a lawful admission.

(3) The child is under the age of 18 years and in the legal custody of the citizen parent.

(4) If the citizen parent is an adoptive parent of the child, the child was adopted by the citizen parent before the child reached the age of 16 years (except to the extent that the child is described in clause (ii) of subparagraph (E) or (F) of section 101(b)(1) [8 U.S.C.A.

§ 1101(b)(1)]) and the child meets the requirements for being a child under either of such subparagraphs.

(5) If the citizen parent has not been physically present in the United States or its outlying possessions for a period or periods totaling not less than five years, at least two of which were after attaining the age of fourteen years—

(A) the child is residing permanently in the United States with the citizen parent, pursuant to a lawful admission for permanent residence, or

(B) a citizen parent of the citizen parent has been physically present in the United States or its outlying possessions for a period or periods totaling not less than five years, at least two of which were after attaining the age of fourteen years.

(b) Attainment of citizenship status; receipt of certificate

Upon approval of the application (which may be filed abroad) and, except as provided in the last sentence of section 337(a) [8 U.S.C.A. § 1448(a)] , upon taking and subscribing before an officer of the Service within the United States to the oath of allegiance required by this Act of an applicant for naturalization, the child shall become a citizen of the United States and shall be furnished by the Attorney General with a certificate of citizenship.

(c) Adopted children

Subsection (a) of this section shall apply to the adopted child of a United States citizen adoptive parent if the conditions specified in such subsection have been fulfilled.

(June 27, 1952, c. 477, Title III, ch. 2, § 322, 66 Stat. 246; Oct. 5, 1978, Pub.L. 95–417, § 6, 92 Stat. 918; Dec. 29, 1981, Pub.L. 97–116, § 18(m), (n), 95 Stat. 1620, 1621; Nov. 14, 1986, Pub.L. 99–653, § 16, 100 Stat. 3658; Oct. 24, 1988, Pub.L. 100–525, § 8(*l*), 102 Stat. 2618; Nov. 29, 1990, Pub.L. 101–649, Title IV, § 407(b)(2), (c)(6), (d)(5), 104 Stat. 5040–5042; Dec. 12, 1991, Pub.L. 102–232, Title III, § 305(m)(3), 105 Stat. 1750; Oct. 25, 1994, Pub.L. 103–416, Title I, § 102(a), 108 Stat. 4306; Dec. 7, 1999, Pub.L. 106–139, § 1(b)(2), 113 Stat. 1697.)

§ 323. Repealed. Pub. L. 95–417, § 7, Oct. 5, 1978, 92 Stat. 918 [8 U.S.C.A. § 1434]

§ 324. Former citizens regaining citizenship [8 U.S.C.A. § 1435]

(a) Requirements

Any person formerly a citizen of the United States who **(1)** prior to September 22, 1922, lost United States citizenship by marriage to an alien, or by the loss of United States citizenship of such person's spouse, or **(2)** on or after September 22, 1922, lost United States citizenship by marriage to an alien ineligible to citizenship, may if no other nationality was acquired by an affirmative act of such person other than by marriage be naturalized upon compliance with all requirements of this title, except—

(1) no period of residence or specified period of physical presence within the United States or within the State or district of the Service in the United States where the application is filed shall be required; and

(2) the application need not set forth that it is the intention of the applicant to reside permanently within the United States.

Such person, or any person who was naturalized in accordance with the provisions of section 317(a) of the Nationality Act of 1940, shall have, from and after her naturalization, the status of a native-born or naturalized citizen of the United States, whichever status existed in the case of such person prior to the loss of citizenship: Provided, That nothing contained herein or in any other provision of law shall be construed as conferring United States citizenship retroactively upon such person, or upon any person who was naturalized in accordance with the provisions of section 317(a) of the Nationality Act of 1940, during any period in which such person was not a citizen.

(b) Additional requirements

No person who is otherwise eligible for naturalization in accordance with the provisions of subsection (a) of this section shall be naturalized unless such person shall establish to the satisfaction of the Attorney General that she has been a person of good moral character, attached to the principles of the Constitution of the United States, and well disposed to the good order and happiness of the United States for a period of not less than five years immediately preceding the date of filing an application for naturalization and up to the time of admission to citizenship, and, unless she has resided continuously in the United States since the date of her marriage, has been lawfully admitted for permanent residence prior to filing her application for naturalization.

(c) Oath of allegiance

(1) A woman who was a citizen of the United States at birth and **(A)** who has or is believed to have lost her United States citizenship solely by reason of her marriage prior to September 22, 1922, to an alien, or by her marriage on or after such date to an alien ineligible to citizenship, **(B)** whose marriage to such alien shall have terminated subsequent to January 12, 1941, and **(C)** who has not acquired by an affirmative act other than by marriage any other nationality, shall, from and after taking the oath of allegiance required by section 337 [8 U.S.C.A. § 1448], be a citizen of the United States and have the status of a citizen of the United States by birth, without filing an application for naturalization, and notwithstanding any of the other provisions of this title except the provisions of section 313 [8 U.S.C.A. § 1424]: Provided, That nothing contained herein or in any other provision of law shall be construed as conferring United States citizenship retroactively upon such person, or upon any person who was naturalized in accordance with the provisions of section 317(b) of the Nationality Act of 1940, during any period in which such person was not a citizen.

(2) Such oath of allegiance may be taken abroad before a diplomatic or consular officer of the United States, or in the United States before the Attorney General or the judge or clerk of a court described in section 310(b) [8 U.S.C.A. § 1421(b)] .

(3) Such oath of allegiance shall be entered in the records of the appropriate embassy, legation, consulate, court, or the Attorney General, and, upon demand, a certified copy of the proceedings, including a copy of the oath administered, under the seal of the embassy, legation, consulate, court, or the Attorney General, shall be delivered to such woman at a cost not exceeding $5, which certified copy shall be evidence of the facts stated therein before any court of record or judicial tribunal and in any department or agency of the Government of the United States.

(d) Persons losing citizenship for failure to meet physical presence retention requirement

(1) A person who was a citizen of the United States at birth and lost such citizenship for failure to meet the physical presence retention requirements under section 301(b) [8 U.S.C.A. § 1401(b)] (as in effect before October 10, 1978), shall, from and after taking the oath of allegiance required by section 337 [8 U.S.C.A. § 1448] be a citizen of the United States and have the status of a citizen of the United States by birth, without filing an application for naturalization, and notwithstanding any of the other provisions of this title except the provisions of section 313 [8 U.S.C.A. § 1424]. Nothing in this subsection or any other provision of law shall be construed as conferring United States citizenship retroactively upon such person during any period in which such person was not a citizen.

(2) The provisions of paragraphs (2) and (3) of subsection (c) shall apply to a person regaining citizenship under paragraph (1) in the same manner as they apply under subsection (c)(1).

(June 27, 1952, c. 477, Title III, ch. 2, § 324, 66 Stat. 246; Oct. 24, 1988, Pub.L. 100–525, § 9(x), 102 Stat. 2621; Nov. 29, 1990, Pub.L. 101–649, Title IV, § 407(b)(3), (c)(7), (d)(6), 104 Stat. 5040–5042; Oct. 25, 1994, Pub.L. 103–416, Title I, § 103(a), 108 Stat. 4307.)

§ 325. Nationals but not citizens; residence within outlying possessions [8 U.S.C.A. § 1436]

A person not a citizen who owes permanent allegiance to the United States, and who is otherwise qualified, may, if he becomes a resident of any State, be naturalized upon compliance with the applicable requirements of this title, except that in applications for naturalization filed under the provisions of this section residence and physical presence within the United States within the meaning of this title shall include residence and physical presence within any of the outlying possessions of the United States.

(June 27, 1952, c. 477, Title III, ch. 2, § 325, 66 Stat. 248; Nov. 29, 1990, Pub.L. 101–649, Title IV, § 407(c)(8), 104 Stat. 5041.)

§ 326. Resident Philippine citizens excepted from certain requirements [8 U.S.C.A. § 1437]

Any person who **(1)** was a citizen of the Commonwealth of the Philippines on July 2, 1946, **(2)** entered the United States prior to May 1, 1934, and **(3)** has, since such entry, resided continuously in the United States shall be regarded as having been lawfully admitted to the United States for permanent residence for the purpose of applying for naturalization under this title.

(June 27, 1952, c. 477, Title III, ch. 2, § 326, 66 Stat. 248; Nov. 29, 1990, Pub.L. 101–649, Title IV, § 407(c)(9), 104 Stat. 5041.)

§ 327. Former citizens losing citizenship by entering armed forces of foreign countries during World War II [8 U.S.C.A. § 1438]

(a) Requirements; oath; certified copies of oath

Any person who, **(1)** during World War II and while a citizen of the United States, served in the military, air, or naval forces of any country at war with a country with which the United States was at war after December 7, 1941, and before September 2, 1945, and **(2)** has lost United States citizenship by reason of entering or serving in such forces, or taking an oath or obligation for the purpose of entering such forces, may, upon compliance with all the provisions of title III of this Act, except section 316(a) [8 U.S.C.A. § 1427(a)], and except as otherwise provided in subsection (b), be naturalized by taking before the Attorney General or before a court described in section 310(b) [8 U.S.C.A. § 1421(b)] the oath required by section 337 [8 U.S.C.A. § 1448]. Certified copies of such oath shall be sent by such court to the Department of State and to the Department of Justice and by the Attorney General to the Secretary of State.

(b) Exceptions

No person shall be naturalized under subsection (a) of this section unless he—

(1) is, and has been for a period of at least five years immediately preceding taking the oath required in subsection (a), a person of good moral character, attached to the principles of the Constitution of the United States and well disposed to the good order and happiness of the United States; and

(2) has been lawfully admitted to the United States for permanent residence and intends to reside permanently in the United States.

(c) Status

Any person naturalized in accordance with the provisions of this section, or any person who was naturalized in accordance with the provisions of section 323 of the Nationality Act of 1940, shall have, from and after such naturalization, the status of a native-born, or naturalized, citizen of the United States, whichever status existed in the case of such person prior to the loss of citizenship: *Provided,* That nothing contained herein, or in any other provision of law, shall be construed as conferring United States citizenship retroactively upon any such person during any period in which such person was not a citizen.

(d) Span of World War II

For the purposes of this section, World War II shall be deemed to have begun on September 1, 1939, and to have terminated on September 2, 1945.

(e) Inapplicability to certain persons

This section shall not apply to any person who during World War II served in the armed forces of a country while such country was at war with the United States.

(June 27, 1952, c. 477, Title III, ch. 2, § 327, 66 Stat. 248; Nov. 29, 1990, Pub.L. 101–649, Title IV, § 407(d)(7), 104 Stat. 5042.)

§ 328. Naturalization through service in the armed forces [8 U.S.C.A. § 1439]

(a) Requirements

A person who has served honorably at any time in the armed forces of the United States for a period or periods aggregating three years, and, who, if separated from such service, was never separated except under honorable conditions, may be naturalized without having resided, continuously immediately preceding the date of filing such person's application, in the United States for at least five years, and in the State or district of the Service in the United States in which the application for naturalization is filed for at least three months, and without having been physically present in the United States for any specified period, if such application is filed while the applicant is still in the service or within six months after the termination of such service.

(b) Exceptions

A person filing an application under subsection (a) of this section shall comply in all other respects with the requirements of this subchapter, except that—

(1) no residence within a State or district of the Service in the United States shall be required;

(2) notwithstanding section 318 [8 U.S.C.A. § 1429] insofar as it relates to deportability, such applicant may be naturalized immediately if the applicant be then actually in the Armed Forces of the

United States, and if prior to the filing of the application, the applicant shall have appeared before and been examined by a representative of the Service;

(3) the applicant shall furnish to the Attorney General, prior to any hearing upon his application, a certified statement from the proper executive department for each period of his service upon which he relies for the benefits of this section, clearly showing that such service was honorable and that no discharges from service, including periods of service not relied upon by him for the benefits of this section, were other than honorable. The certificate or certificates herein provided for shall be conclusive evidence of such service and discharge.

(c) Periods when not in service

In the case such applicant's service was not continuous, the applicant's residence in the United States and State or district of the Service in the United States, good moral character, attachment to the principles of the Constitution of the United States, and favorable disposition toward the good order and happiness of the United States, during any period within five years immediately preceding the date of filing such application between the periods of applicant's service in the Armed Forces, shall be alleged in the application filed under the provisions of subsection (a) of this section, and proved at any hearing thereon. Such allegation and proof shall also be made as to any period between the termination of applicant's service and the filing of the application for naturalization.

(d) Residence requirements

The applicant shall comply with the requirements of section 316(a) [8 U.S.C.A. § 1427(a)], if the termination of such service has been more than six months preceding the date of filing the application for naturalization, except that such service within five years immediately preceding the date of filing such application shall be considered as residence and physical presence within the United States.

(e) Moral character

Any such period or periods of service under honorable conditions, and good moral character, attachment to the principles of the Constitution of the United States, and favorable disposition toward the good order and happiness of the United States, during such service, shall be proved by duly authenticated copies of the records of the executive departments having custody of the records of such service, and such authenticated copies of records shall be accepted in lieu of compliance with the provisions of section 316(a) [8 U.S.C.A. § 1427(a)].

(June 27, 1952, c. 477, Title III, ch. 2, § 328, 66 Stat. 249; Oct. 24, 1968, Pub.L. 90–633, § 5, 82 Stat. 1344; Dec. 29, 1981, Pub.L. 97–116, § 15(e), 95 Stat. 1619; Nov. 29, 1990, Pub.L. 101–649, Title IV, § 407(b)(4), (c)(10), (d)(8), 104 Stat. 5040 to 5042; Nov. 29, 1990, Pub.L. 101–649, Title IV, § 407(d)(8); Dec. 12, 1991, Pub.L. 102–232, Title III, § 305(c), 105 Stat. 1750.)

§ 329. Naturalization through active-duty service in the armed forces during World War I, World War II, Korean hostilities, Vietnam hostilities, or other periods of military hostilities [8 U.S.C.A. § 1440]

(a) Requirements

Any person who, while an alien or a noncitizen national of the United States, has served honorably in an active-duty status in the military, air, or naval forces of the United States during either World War I or during a period beginning September 1, 1939, and ending December 31, 1946, or during a period beginning June 25, 1950, and ending July 1, 1955, or during a period beginning February 28, 1961, and ending on a date designated by the President by Executive order as of the date of termination of the Vietnam hostilities, or thereafter during any other period which the President by Executive order shall designate as a period in which Armed Forces of the United States are or were engaged in military operations involving armed conflict with a hostile foreign force, and who, if separated from such service, was separated under honorable conditions, may be naturalized as provided in this section if **(1)** at the time of enlistment, reenlistment, extension of enlistment, or induction such person shall have been in the United States, the Canal Zone, American Samoa, or Swains Island, or on board a public vessel owned or operated by the United States for noncommercial service, whether or not he has been lawfully admitted to the United States for permanent residence, or **(2)** at any time subsequent to enlistment or induction such person shall have been lawfully admitted to the United States for permanent residence. The executive department under which such person served shall determine whether persons have served honorably in an active-duty status, and whether separation from such service was under honorable conditions: Provided, however, That no person who is or has been separated from such service on account of alienage, or who was a conscientious objector who performed no military, air, or naval duty whatever or refused to wear the uniform, shall be regarded as having served honorably or having been separated under honorable conditions for the purposes of this section. No period of service in the Armed Forces shall be made the basis of an application for naturalization under this section if the applicant has previously been naturalized on the basis of the same period of service.

(b) Exceptions

A person filing an application under subsection (a) of this section shall comply in all other respects with the requirements of this title, except that—

(1) he may be naturalized regardless of age, and notwithstanding the provisions of section 318 [8 U.S.C.A. § 1429] as they relate to deportability and the provisions of section 331 [8 U.S.C.A. § 1442];

(2) no period of residence or specified period of physical presence within the United States or any State or district of the Service in the United States shall be required; and

(3) service in the military, air, or naval forces of the United States shall be proved by a duly authenticated certification from the executive department under which the applicant served or is serving, which shall state whether the applicant served honorably in an active-duty status during either World War I or during a period beginning September 1, 1939, and ending December 31, 1946, or during a period beginning June 25, 1950, and ending July 1, 1955, or during a period beginning February 28, 1961, and ending on a date designated by the President by Executive order as the date of termination of the Vietnam hostilities, or thereafter during any other period which the President by Executive order shall designate as a period in which Armed Forces of the United States are or were engaged in military operations involving armed conflict with a hostile foreign force, and was separated from such service under honorable conditions.

(4) Redesignated (3).

(5) Repealed.

(c) Revocation

Citizenship granted pursuant to this section may be revoked in accordance with section 340 [8 U.S.C.A. § 1451] if at any time subsequent to naturalization the person is separated from the military, air, or naval forces under other than honorable conditions, and such ground for revocation shall be in addition to any other provided by law. The fact that the naturalized person was separated from the service under other than honorable conditions shall be proved by a duly authenticated certification from the executive department under which the person was serving at the time of separation.

(d) Repealed.

(June 27, 1952, c. 477, Title III, ch. 2, § 329, 66 Stat. 250; Pub. L. 87–301, § 8, Sept. 26, 1961, 75 Stat. 654; Pub. L. 90–633, §§ 1, 2, 6, Oct. 24, 1968, 82 Stat. 1343, 1344; Pub. L. 97–116, § 15(a), Dec. 29, 1981, 95 Stat. 1619; Pub.L. 100–525, § 9(y), Oct. 24, 1988, 102 Stat. 2621; Pub.L. 101–649, Title IV, § 407(b)(5), (c)(11), Nov. 29, 1990, 104 Stat. 5040, 5041; Dec. 12, 1991, Pub.L. 102–232, Title III, § 305(b), 105 Stat. 1749; Nov. 18, 1997, Pub.L. 105–85, Div. A, Title X, § 1080(a), 111 Stat. 1916.)

§ 329A. Posthumous citizenship through death while on active-duty service in the armed forces during World War I, World War II, the Korean hostilities, the Vietnam hostilities, or in other periods of military hostilities [8 U.S.C.A. § 1440–1]

(a) Permitting granting of posthumous citizenship. Notwithstanding any other provision of this title, the Attorney General shall provide, in accordance with this section, for the granting of posthumous citizenship at the time of death to a person described in subsection (b) if the Attorney General approves an application for that posthumous citizenship under subsection (c).

(b) Noncitizens eligible for posthumous citizenship. A person referred to in subsection (a) is a person who, while an alien or a noncitizen national of the United States—

(1) served honorably in an active-duty status in the military, air, or naval forces of the United States during any period described in the first sentence of section 329(a) [8 U.S.C.A. § 1440(a)],

(2) died as a result of injury or disease incurred in or aggravated by that service, and

(3) satisfied the requirements of clause (1) or (2) of the first sentence of section 329(a) [8 U.S.C.A. § 1440(a)(1) or (2)] .

The executive department under which the person so served shall determine whether the person satisfied the requirements of paragraphs (1) and (2).

(c) Requests for posthumous citizenship. A request for the granting of posthumous citizenship to a person described in subsection (b) may be filed on behalf of the person only by the next-of-kin (as defined by the Attorney General) or another representative (as defined by the Attorney General). The Attorney General shall approve such a request respecting a person if—

(1) the request is filed not later than 2 years after—

(A) March 6, 1990, or

(B) the date of the person's death, whichever date is later;

(2) the request is accompanied by a duly authenticated certificate from the executive department under which the person served which states that the person satisfied the requirements of paragraphs (1) and (2) of subsection (b); and

(3) the Attorney General finds that the person satisfied the requirement of subsection (b)(3).

(d) Documentation of posthumous citizenship. If the Attorney General approves such a request to grant a person posthumous citizenship, the Attorney General shall send to the individual who filed the request a suitable document which states that the United States considers the person to have been a citizen of the United States at the time of the person's death.

(e) No benefits to survivors. Nothing in this section or section 319(d) [8 U.S.C.A. § 1430(d)] shall be construed as providing for any benefits under this Act for any spouse, son, daughter, or other relative of a person granted posthumous citizenship under this section.

(June 27, 1952, c. 477, Title III, ch. 2, § 329A, as added Mar. 6, 1990, Pub.L. 101–249, § 2(a), 104 Stat. 94.)

§ 330. Constructive residence through service on certain United States vessels [8 U.S.C.A. § 1441]

Any periods of time during all of which a person who was previously lawfully admitted for permanent residence has served honorably or with good conduct, in any capacity other than as a member of the Armed Forces of the United States, **(A)** on board a vessel operated by the United States, or an agency thereof, the full legal and equitable title to which is in the United States; or **(B)** on board a vessel whose home port is in the United States, and **(i)** which is registered under the laws of the United States, or **(ii)** the full legal and equitable title to which is in a citizen of the United States, or a corporation organized under the laws of any of the several States of the United States, shall be deemed residence and physical presence within the United States within the meaning of section 316(a) [8 U.S.C.A. § 1427(a)], if such service occurred within five years immediately preceding the date such person shall file an application for naturalization. Service on vessels described in clause (A) of this section shall be proved by duly authenticated copies of the records of the executive departments or agency having custody of the records of such service. Service on vessels described in clause (B) of this section may be proved by certificates from the masters of such vessels.

(June 27, 1952, c. 477, Title III, ch. 2, § 330, 66 Stat. 251; Pub.L. 100–525, § 9(z), Oct. 24, 1988, 102 Stat. 2621; Pub.L. 101–649, Title IV, § 407(c)(12), Nov. 29, 1990, 104 Stat. 5041; Pub.L. 102–232, Title III, § 305(m)(5), Dec. 12, 1991, 105 Stat. 1750.)

§ 331. Alien enemies [8 U.S.C.A. § 1442]

(a) Naturalization under specified conditions

An alien who is a native, citizen, subject, or denizen of any country, state, or sovereignty with which the United States is at war may, after his loyalty has been fully established upon investigation by the Attorney General, be naturalized as a citizen of the United States if such alien's application for naturalization shall be pending at the beginning of the state of war and the applicant is otherwise entitled to admission to citizenship.

(b) Procedure

An alien embraced within this section shall not have his application for naturalization considered or heard except after 90 days' notice to the Attorney General to be considered at the examination or hearing, and the Attorney General's objection to such consideration shall cause the application to be continued from time to time for so long as the Attorney General may require.

(c) Exceptions from classification

The Attorney General may, in his discretion, upon investigation fully establishing the loyalty of any alien enemy who did not have an application for naturalization pending at the beginning of the state of war, except such alien enemy from the classification of alien enemy for the purposes of this title, and thereupon such alien shall have the privilege of filing an application for naturalization.

(d) Effect of cessation of hostilities

An alien who is a native, citizen, subject, or denizen of any country, state, or sovereignty with which the United States is at war shall cease to be an alien enemy within the meaning of this section upon the determination by proclamation of the President, or by concurrent resolution of the Congress, that hostilities between the United States and such country, state, or sovereignty have ended.

(e) Apprehension and removal

Nothing contained herein shall be taken or construed to interfere with or prevent the apprehension and removal, consistent with law, of any alien enemy at any time prior to the actual naturalization of such alien.

(June 27, 1952, c. 477, Title III, ch. 2, § 331, 66 Stat. 252; Nov. 29, 1990, Pub.L. 101–649, Title IV, § 407(c)(13), (d)(9), (e)(2), 104 Stat. 5041, 5042, 5046.)

§ 332. Administration [8 U.S.C.A. § 1443]

(a) Rules and regulations governing examination of petitioners

The Attorney General shall make such rules and regulations as may be necessary to carry into effect the provisions of this part and is authorized to prescribe the scope and nature of the examination of applicants for naturalization as to their admissibility to citizenship. Such examination shall be limited to inquiry concerning the applicant's residence, physical presence in the United States, good moral character, understanding of and attachment to the fundamental principles of the Constitution of the United States, ability to read, write, and speak English, and other qualifications to become a naturalized citizen as required by law, and shall be uniform throughout the United States.

(b) Instruction in citizenship

The Attorney General is authorized to promote instruction and training in citizenship responsibilities of applicants for naturalization including the sending of names of candidates for naturalization to the public schools, preparing and distributing citizenship textbooks to such candidates as are receiving instruction in preparation for citizenship within or under the supervision of the public schools, preparing and distributing monthly an immigration and naturalization bulletin and securing the aid of and cooperating with official State and national organizations, including those concerned with vocational education.

(c) Prescription of forms

The Attorney General shall prescribe and furnish such forms as may be required to give effect to the provisions of this part, and only such forms as may be so provided shall be legal. All certificates of naturalization and of citizenship shall be printed on safety paper and shall be consecutively numbered in separate series.

(d) Administration of oaths and depositions

Employees of the Service may be designated by the Attorney General to administer oaths and to take depositions without charge in matters relating to the administration of the naturalization and citizenship laws. In cases where there is a likelihood of unusual delay or of hardship, the Attorney General may, in his discretion, authorize such depositions to be taken before a postmaster without charge, or before a notary public or other person authorized to administer oaths for general purposes.

(e) Issuance of certificate of naturalization or citizenship

A certificate of naturalization or of citizenship issued by the Attorney General under the authority of this title shall have the same effect in all courts, tribunals, and public offices of the United States, at home and abroad, of the District of Columbia, and of each State, Territory, and outlying possession of the United States, as a certificate of naturalization or of citizenship issued by a court having naturalization jurisdiction.

(f) Copies of records

Certifications and certified copies of all papers, documents, certificates, and records required or authorized to be issued, used, filed, recorded, or kept under any and all provisions of this Act shall be admitted in evidence equally with the originals in any and all cases and proceedings under this Act and in all cases and proceedings in which the originals thereof might be admissible as evidence.

(g) Furnished quarters for photographic studios

The officers in charge of property owned or leased by the Government are authorized, upon the recommendation of the Attorney General, to provide quarters, without payment of rent, in any building occupied by the Service, for a photographic studio, operated by welfare organizations without profit and solely for the benefit of persons seeking to comply with requirements under the immigration and nationality laws. Such studio shall be under the supervision of the Attorney General.

(h) Public education regarding naturalization benefits

In order to promote the opportunities and responsibilities of United States citizenship, the Attorney General shall broadly distribute information concerning the benefits which persons may receive under this title and the requirements to obtain such benefits. In carrying out this subsection, the Attorney General shall seek the assistance of appropriate community groups, private voluntary agencies, and other relevant organizations. There are authorized to be appropriated (for each fiscal year beginning with fiscal year 1991) such sums as may be necessary to carry out this subsection.

(June 27, 1952, c. 477, Title III, ch. 2, § 332, 66 Stat. 252; Nov. 29, 1990, Pub.L. 101–649, Title IV, §§ 406, 407(d)(10), 104 Stat. 5040, 5042; Dec. 12, 1991, Pub.L. 102–232, Title III, § 305(m)(6), 105 Stat. 1750.)

§ 333. Photographs; number [8 U.S.C.A. § 1444]

(a) Three identical photographs of the applicant shall be signed by and furnished by each applicant for naturalization or citizenship. One of such photographs shall be affixed by the Attorney General to the original certificate of naturalization issued to the naturalized citizen and one to the duplicate certificate of naturalization required to be forwarded to the Service.

(b) Three identical photographs of the applicant shall be furnished by each applicant for—

(1) a record of lawful admission for permanent residence to be made under section 249 [8 U.S.C.A. § 1259];

(2) a certificate of derivative citizenship;

(3) a certificate of naturalization or of citizenship;

(4) a special certificate of naturalization;

(5) a certificate of naturalization or of citizenship, in lieu of one lost, mutilated, or destroyed;

(6) a new certificate of citizenship in the new name of any naturalized citizen who, subsequent to naturalization, has had his name changed by order of a court of competent jurisdiction or by marriage; and

(7) a declaration of intention.

One such photograph shall be affixed to each such certificate issued by the Attorney General and one shall be affixed to the copy of such certificate retained by the Service.

(June 27, 1952, c. 477, Title III, ch. 2, § 333, 66 Stat. 253; Nov. 29, 1990, Pub.L. 101–649, Title IV, § 407(c)(14), (d)(11), 104 Stat. 5041, 5042; Oct. 25, 1994, Pub.L. 103–416, Title II, § 219(w), 108 Stat. 4318.)

§ 334. Application for naturalization; declaration of intention [8 U.S.C.A. § 1445]

(a) Evidence and form

An applicant for naturalization shall make and file with the Attorney General a sworn application in writing, signed by the applicant in the applicant's own handwriting if physically able to write, which application shall be on a form prescribed by the Attorney General and shall include averments of all facts which in the opinion of the Attorney General may be material to the applicant's naturalization, and required to be proved under this title. In the case of an applicant subject to a requirement of continuous residence under section 316(a) or 319(a) [8 U.S.C.A. §§ 1427(a) or 1430(a)], the application for naturalization may be filed up to 3 months before the date the applicant would first otherwise meet such continuous residence requirement.

(b) Who may file

No person shall file a valid application for naturalization unless he shall have attained the age of eighteen years. An application for naturalization by an alien shall contain an averment of lawful admission for permanent residence.

(c) Hearings

Hearings under section 336(a) [8 U.S.C.A. § 1447(a)] on applications for naturalization shall be held at regular intervals specified by the Attorney General.

(d) Filing of application

Except as provided in subsection (e), an application for naturalization shall be filed in the office of the Attorney General.

(e) Substitute filing place and administering oath other than before Attorney General

A person may file an application for naturalization other than in the office of the Attorney General, and an oath of allegiance administered other than in a public ceremony before the Attorney General or a court, if the Attorney General determines that the person has an illness or other disability which—

(1) is of a permanent nature and is sufficiently serious to prevent the person's personal appearance, or

(2) is of a nature which so incapacitates the person as to prevent him from personally appearing.

(f) Declaration of intention

An alien over 18 years of age who is residing in the United States pursuant to a lawful admission for permanent residence may file with the Attorney General a declaration of intention to become a citizen of the United States. Such a declaration shall be filed in duplicate and in a form prescribed by the Attorney General and shall be accompanied by an application prescribed and approved by the Attorney General. Nothing in this subsection shall be construed as requiring any such alien to make and file a declaration of intention as a condition precedent to filing an application for naturalization nor shall any such declaration of intention be regarded as conferring or having conferred upon any such alien United States citizenship or nationality or the right to United States citizenship or nationality, nor shall such declaration be regarded as evidence of such alien's lawful admission for permanent residence in any proceeding, action, or matter arising under this or any other Act.

(June 27, 1952, c. 477, Title III, ch. 2, § 334, 66 Stat. 254; Pub. L. 97–116, § 15(b), Dec. 29, 1981, 95 Stat. 1619; Pub.L. 101–649, Title IV, §§ 401(b), 407(c)(15), (d)(12), Nov. 29, 1990, 104 Stat. 5038, 5041, 5042; Pub.L. 102–232, Title III, § 305(d), (e), (m)(7), Dec. 12, 1991, 105 Stat. 1750.)

§ 335. Investigation of applicants; examination of applications [8 U.S.C.A. § 1446]

(a) Waiver

Before a person may be naturalized, an employee of the Service, or of the United States designated by the Attorney General, shall conduct a personal investigation of the person applying for naturalization in the vicinity or vicinities in which such person has maintained his actual place of abode and in the vicinity or vicinities in which such person has been employed or has engaged in business or work for at least five years immediately preceding the filing of his application for naturalization. The Attorney General may, in his discretion, waive a personal investigation in an individual case or in such cases or classes of cases as may be designated by him.

(b) Conduct of examinations; authority of designees; record

The Attorney General shall designate employees of the Service to conduct examinations upon petitions for naturalization. For such purposes any such employee so designated is authorized to take testimony concerning any matter touching or in any way affecting the admissibility of any applicant for naturalization, to administer oaths, including the oath of the applicant for naturalization, and to require by subpena the attendance and testimony of witnesses, including applicant, before such employee so designated and the production of relevant books, papers, and documents, and to that end may invoke the aid of any district court of the United States; and any such court may, in the event of neglect or refusal to respond to a subpena issued by any such employee so designated or refusal to testify before such employee so designated issue an order requiring such person to appear before such employee so designated, produce relevant books, papers, and documents if demanded, and testify; and any failure to obey such order of the court may be punished by the court as a contempt thereof. The record of the examination authorized by this subsection shall be admissible as evidence in any hearing conducted by an immigration officer under section 336(a) [8 U.S.C.A. § 1447(a)]. Any such employee shall, at the examination, inform the petitioner of the remedies available to the petitioner under section 336 [8 U.S.C.A. § 1447].

(c) Transmittal of record of examination

The record of the examination upon any application for naturalization may, in the discretion of the Attorney General be transmitted to the Attorney General and the determination with respect thereto of the employee designated to conduct such examination shall when made also be transmitted to the Attorney General.

(d) Determination to grant or deny application

The employee designated to conduct any such examination shall make a determination as to whether the application should be granted or denied, with reasons therefor.

(e) Withdrawal of application

After an application for naturalization has been filed with the Attorney General, the applicant shall not be permitted to withdraw his application, except with the consent of the Attorney General. In cases where the Attorney General does not consent to the withdrawal of the application, the application shall be determined on its merits and a final order determination made accordingly. In cases where the applicant fails to prosecute his application, the application shall be decided on the merits unless the Attorney General dismisses it for lack of prosecution.

(f) Transfer of application

An applicant for naturalization who moves from the district of the Service in the United States in which the application is pending may, at any time thereafter, request the Service to transfer the application to any district of the Service in the United States which may act on the application. The transfer shall not be made without the consent of the Attorney General. In the case of such a transfer, the proceedings on the application shall continue as though the application had originally been filed in the district of the Service to which the application is transferred.

(g), (h) Repealed. Pub. L. 97–116, § 15(c)(2), Dec. 29, 1981, 95 Stat. 1619.

(i) Redesignated (f)

(June 27, 1952, c. 477, Title III, ch. 2, § 335, 66 Stat. 255; Pub. L. 97–116, § 15(c), Dec. 29, 1981, 95 Stat. 1619; Pub.L. 100–525, § 9(aa), (bb), Oct. 24, 1988, 102 Stat. 2621; Pub.L. 101–649, Title IV, §§ 401(c), 407(c)(16), (d)(13), Nov. 29, 1990, 104 Stat. 5038, 5041, 5043; Dec. 12, 1991, Pub.L. 102–232, Title III, § 305(f), 105 Stat. 1750.)

§ 336. Hearings on denials of applications for naturalization [8 U.S.C.A. § 1447]

(a) Request for hearing before immigration officer

If, after an examination under section 335 [8 U.S.C.A. § 1446], an application for naturalization is denied, the applicant may request a hearing before an immigration officer.

(b) Request for hearing before district court

If there is a failure to make a determination under section 335 [8 U.S.C.A. § 1446] before the end of the 120–day period after the date on which the examination is conducted under such section, the applicant may apply to the United States district court for the district in which the applicant resides for a hearing on the matter. Such court has jurisdiction over the matter and may either determine the matter or remand the matter, with appropriate instructions, to the Service to determine the matter.

(c) Appearance of Attorney General

The Attorney General shall have the right to appear before any immigration officer in any naturalization proceedings for the purpose of cross-examining the applicant and the witnesses produced in support of the application concerning any matter touching or in any way affecting the applicant's right to admission to citizenship, and shall have the right to call witnesses, including the applicant, produce evidence, and be heard in opposition to, or in favor of, the granting of any application in naturalization proceedings.

(d) Subpena of witness

The immigration officer shall, if the applicant requests it at the time of filing the request for the hearing, issue a subpena for the witnesses named by such applicant to appear upon the day set for the hearing, but in case such witnesses cannot be produced upon the hearing other witnesses may be summoned upon notice to the Attorney General, in such manner and at such time as the Attorney General may by regulation prescribe. Such subpenas may be enforced in the same manner as subpenas under section 335(b) [8 U.S.C.A. § 1446(b)] may be enforced.

(e) Change of name of applicant

It shall be lawful at the time and as a part of the administration by a court of the oath of allegiance under section 337(a) [8 U.S.C.A. § 1448(a)] for the court, in its discretion, upon the bona fide prayer of the applicant included in an appropriate petition to the court, to make a decree changing the name of said person, and the certificate of naturalization shall be issued in accordance therewith.

(f) Redesignated (e)

(June 27, 1952, c. 477, Title III, ch. 2, § 336, 66 Stat. 257; Pub. L. 91–136, Dec. 5, 1969, 83 Stat. 283; Pub. L. 97–116, § 15(d), Dec. 29, 1981, 95 Stat. 1619; Pub.L. 100–525, § 9(cc), Oct. 24, 1988, 102 Stat. 2621; Pub.L. 101–649, Title IV, § 407(c)(17), (d)(14), Nov. 29, 1990, 104 Stat. 5041, 5044; Dec. 12, 1991, Pub.L. 102–232, Title III, § 305(g), (h), 105 Stat. 1750.)

§ 337. Oath of renunciation and allegiance [8 U.S.C.A. § 1448]

(a) Public ceremony

A person who has applied for naturalization shall, in order to be and before being admitted to citizenship, take in a public ceremony before the Attorney General or a court with jurisdiction under section 310(b) [8 U.S.C.A. § 1421(b)] an oath **(1)** to support the Constitution of the United States; **(2)** to renounce and abjure absolutely and entirely all allegiance and fidelity to any foreign prince, potentate, state, or sovereignty of whom or which the applicant was before a subject or citizen; **(3)** to support and defend the Constitution and the laws of the United States against all enemies, foreign and domestic; **(4)** to bear true faith and allegiance to the same; and **(5)(A)** to bear arms on behalf of the United States when required by the law, or **(B)** to perform noncombatant service in the Armed Forces of the United States when required by the law, or **(C)** to perform work of national importance under civilian direction when required by the law. Any such person shall be required to take an oath containing the substance of clauses (1) to (5) of the preceding sentence, except that a person who shows by clear and convincing evidence to the satisfaction of the Attorney General that he is opposed to the bearing of arms in the Armed Forces of the United States by reason of religious training and belief shall be required to take an oath containing the substance of clauses (1) to (4) and clauses (5)(B) and (5)(C) of this subsection, and a person who shows by clear and convincing evidence to the satisfaction of the Attorney General that he is opposed to any type of service in the Armed Forces of the United States by reason of religious training and belief shall be required to take an oath containing the substance of said clauses (1) to (4) and clause (5)(C). The term "religious training and belief" as used in this section shall mean an individual's belief in a relation to a Supreme Being involving duties superior to those arising from any human relation, but does not include essentially political, sociological, or philosophical views or a merely personal moral code. In the case of the naturalization of a child under the provisions of section 322 [8 U.S.C.A. § 1433] the Attorney General may waive the taking of the oath if in the opinion of the Attorney General the child is unable to understand its meaning.

(b) Hereditary titles or orders of nobility

In case the person applying for naturalization has borne any hereditary title, or has been of any of the orders of nobility in any foreign state, the applicant shall in addition to complying with the requirements of subsection (a) of this section, make under oath in the same public ceremony in which the oath of allegiance is administered, an express renunciation of such title or order of nobility, and such renunciation shall be recorded as a part of such proceedings.

(c) Expedited administration of oath

Notwithstanding section 310(b) [8 U.S.C.A. § 1421(b)] , an individual may be granted an expedited judicial oath administration ceremony or administrative naturalization by the Attorney General upon demonstrating sufficient cause. In determining whether to grant an expedited judicial oath administration ceremony, a court shall consider special circumstances (such as serious illness of the applicant or a member of the applicant's immediate family, permanent disability sufficiently incapacitating as to prevent the applicant's personal appearance at the scheduled ceremony, developmental disability or advanced age, or exigent circumstances relating to travel or employment). If an expedited judicial oath administration ceremony is impracticable, the court shall refer such individual to the Attorney General who may provide for immediate administrative naturalization.

(d) Rules and regulations

The Attorney General shall prescribe rules and procedures to ensure that the ceremonies conducted by the Attorney General for the administration of oaths of allegiance under this section are public, conducted frequently and at regular intervals, and are in keeping with the dignity of the occasion.

(June 27, 1952, c. 477, Title III, ch. 2, § 337, 66 Stat. 258; Pub. L. 97–116, § 18(*o*), Dec. 29, 1981, 95 Stat. 1621; Pub.L. 101–649, Title IV, § 407(c)(18), (d)(15), Nov. 29, 1990, 104 Stat. 5041, 5044; Pub.L. 102–232, Title I, § 102(b)(2), Title III, § 305(i), Dec. 12, 1991, 105 Stat. 1736, 1750.)

§ 338. Certificate of naturalization; contents [8 U.S.C.A. § 1449]

A person admitted to citizenship in conformity with the provisions of this title shall be entitled upon such admission to receive from the Attorney General a certificate of naturalization, which shall contain substantially the following information: Number of application for naturalization; number of certificate of naturalization; date of naturalization; name, signature, place of residence, autographed photograph, and personal description of the naturalized person, including age, sex, marital status, and country of former nationality; location of the district office of the Service in which the application was filed and the title, authority, and location of the official or court administering the oath of allegiance; statement that the Attorney General having found that the applicant had complied in all respects with all of the applicable provisions of the naturalization laws of the United States, and was entitled to be admitted a citizen of the United States of America, thereupon ordered that the applicant be admitted as a citizen of the United States of America; attestation of an immigration officer; and the seal of the Department of Justice.

(June 27, 1952, c. 447, Title III, ch. 2, § 338, 66 Stat. 259; Nov. 29, 1990, Pub.L. 101–649, Title IV, § 407(c)(19), (d)(16), 104 Stat. 5041, 5045; Dec. 12, 1991, Pub.L. 102–232, Title III, § 305(j), 105 Stat. 1750; Oct. 25, 1994, Pub.L. 103–416, Title I, § 104(a), Title II, § 219(z)(3), 108 Stat. 4308, 4318.)

§ 339. Functions and duties of clerks and records of declarations of intention and applications for naturalization [8 U.S.C.A. § 1450]

(a) The clerk of each court that administers oaths of allegiance under section 337 [8 U.S.C.A. § 1448] shall—

(1) deliver to each person administered the oath of allegiance by the court pursuant to section 337(a) [8 U.S.C.A. § 1448(a)] the certificate of naturalization prepared by the Attorney General pursuant to section 310(b)(2)(A)(ii) [8 U.S.C.A. § 1421(b)(2)(A)(ii)] ,

(2) forward to the Attorney General a list of applicants actually taking the oath as each scheduled ceremony and information concerning each person to whom such an oath is administered by the court, within 30 days after the close of the month in which the oath was administered,

(3) forward to the Attorney General certified copies of such other proceedings and orders instituted in or issued out of the court affecting or relating to the naturalization of persons as may be required from time to time by the Attorney General, and

(4) be responsible for all blank certificates of naturalization received by them from time to time from the Attorney General and shall account to the Attorney General for them whenever required to do so.

No certificate of naturalization received by any clerk of court which may be defaced or injured in such manner as to prevent its use as herein provided shall in any case be destroyed, but such certificates shall be returned to the Attorney General.

(b) Each district office of the Service in the United States shall maintain, in chronological order, indexed, and consecutively numbered, as part of its permanent records, all declarations of intention and applications for naturalization filed with the office.

(June 27, 1952, c. 477, Title III, ch. 2, § 339, 66 Stat. 259; Nov. 29, 1990, Pub.L. 101–649, Title IV, § 407(d)(17), 104 Stat. 5045; Dec. 12, 1991, Pub.L. 102–232, Title I, § 102(b)(1), 105 Stat. 1735.)

§ 340. Revocation of naturalization [8 U.S.C.A. § 1451]

(a) Concealment of material evidence; refusal to testify

It shall be the duty of the United States attorneys for the respective districts, upon affidavit showing good cause therefor, to institute proceedings in any district court of the United States in the judicial district in which the naturalized citizen may reside at the time of bringing suit, for the purpose of revoking and setting aside the order admitting such person to citizenship and canceling the certificate of naturalization on the ground that such order and certificate of naturalization were illegally procured or were procured by concealment of a material fact or by willful misrepresentation, and such revocation and setting aside of the order admitting such person to citizenship and such canceling of certificate of naturalization shall be effective as of the original date of the order and certificate, respectively: Provided, That refusal on the part of a naturalized citizen within a period of ten years following his naturalization to testify as a witness in any proceeding before a congressional committee concerning his subversive activities, in a case where such person has been convicted of contempt for such refusal, shall be held to constitute a ground for revocation of such person's naturalization under this subsection as having been procured by concealment of a material fact or by willful misrepresentation. If the naturalized citizen does not reside in any judicial district in the United States at the time of bringing such suit, the proceedings may be instituted in the United States District Court for the District of Columbia or in the United States district court in the judicial district in which such person last had his residence.

(b) Notice to party

The party to whom was granted the naturalization alleged to have been illegally procured or procured by concealment of a material fact or by willful misrepresentation shall, in any such proceedings under subsection (a) of this section, have sixty days' personal notice, unless waived by such party, in which to make answers to the petition of the United States; and if such naturalized person be absent from the United States or from the judicial district in which such person last had his residence, such notice shall be given either by personal service upon him or by publication in the manner provided for the service of summons by publication or upon absentees by the laws of the State or the place where such suit is brought.

(c) Membership in certain organizations; prima facie evidence

If a person who shall have been naturalized after December 24, 1952 shall within five years next following such naturalization become a member of or affiliated with any organization, membership in or affiliation with which at the time of naturalization would have precluded such person from naturalization under the provisions of section 313 [8 U.S.C.A. § 1424], it shall be considered prima facie evidence that such person was not attached to the principles of the Constitution of the United States and was not well disposed to the good order and happiness of the United States at the time of naturalization, and, in the absence of countervailing evidence, it shall be sufficient in the proper proceeding to authorize the revocation and setting aside of the order admitting such person to citizenship and the cancellation of the certificate of naturalization as having been obtained by concealment of a material fact or by willful misrepresentation, and such revocation and setting aside of the order admitting such person to citizenship and such canceling of certificate of naturalization shall be effective as of the original date of the order and certificate, respectively.

(d) Applicability to citizenship through naturalization of parent or spouse

Any person who claims United States citizenship through the naturalization of a parent or spouse in whose case there is a revocation and setting aside of the order admitting such parent or spouse to citizenship under the provisions of subsection (a) of this section on the ground that the order and certificate of naturalization were procured by concealment of a material fact or by willful misrepresentation shall be deemed to have lost and to lose his citizenship and any right or privilege of citizenship which he may have, now has, or may hereafter acquire under and by virtue of such naturalization of such parent or spouse, regardless of whether such person is residing within or without the United States at the time of the revocation and setting aside of the order admitting such parent or spouse to citizenship. Any person who claims United States citizenship through the naturalization of a parent or spouse in whose case there is a revocation and setting aside of the order admitting such parent or spouse to citizenship and the cancellation of the certificate of naturalization under the provisions of subsection (c) of this section, or under the provisions of section 329(c) [8 U.S.C.A. § 1440 (c)] on any ground other than that the order and certificate of naturalization were procured by concealment of a material fact or by willful misrepresentation, shall be deemed to have lost and to lose his citizenship and any right or privilege of citizenship which would have been enjoyed by such person had there not been a revocation and setting aside of the order admitting such parent or spouse to citizenship and the cancellation of the certificate of naturalization, unless such person is residing in the United States at the time of the revocation and setting aside of the order admitting such parent or spouse to citizenship and the cancellation of the certificate of naturalization.

(e) Citizenship unlawfully procured

When a person shall be convicted under section 1425 of Title 18 of knowingly procuring naturalization in violation of law, the court in which such conviction is had shall thereupon revoke, set aside, and declare void the final order admitting such person to citizenship, and shall declare the certificate of naturalization of such person to be canceled. Jurisdiction is conferred on the courts having jurisdiction of the trial of such offense to make such adjudication.

(f) Cancellation of certificate of naturalization

Whenever an order admitting an alien to citizenship shall be revoked and set aside or a certificate of naturalization shall be canceled, or both, as provided in this section, the court in which such judgment or decree is rendered shall make an order canceling such certificate and shall send a certified copy of such order to the Attorney General. The clerk of court shall transmit a copy of such order and judgment to the Attorney General. A person holding a certificate of naturalization or citizenship which has been canceled as provided by this section shall upon notice by the court by which the decree of cancellation was made, or by the Attorney General, surrender the same to the Attorney General.

(g) Applicability of certificates of naturalization and citizenship

The provisions of this section shall apply not only to any naturalization granted and to certificates of naturalization and citizenship issued under the provisions of this title, but to any naturalization heretofore granted by any court, and to all certificates of naturalization and citizenship which may have been issued heretofore by any court or by the Commissioner based upon naturalization granted by any court, or by a designated representative of the Commissioner under the provisions of section 702 of the Nationality Act of 1940, as amended, or by such designated representative under any other act.

(h) Power to correct, reopen, alter, modify, or vacate order

Nothing contained in this section shall be regarded as limiting, denying, or restricting the power of the Attorney General to correct, reopen, alter, modify, or vacate an order naturalizing the person.

(June 27, 1952, c. 477, Title III, ch. 2, § 340, 66 Stat. 260; Sept. 3, 1954, c. 1263, § 18, 68 Stat. 1232; Sept. 26, 1961, Pub.L. 87–301, § 18, 75 Stat. 656; Nov. 14, 1986, Pub.L. 99–653, § 17, 100 Stat. 3658; Oct. 24, 1988, Pub.L. 100–525, § 9(dd), 102 Stat. 2621; Nov. 29, 1990, Pub.L. 101–649, Title IV, § 407(d)(18), 104 Stat. 5046; Dec. 12, 1991, Pub.L. 102–232, Title III, § 305(k), 105 Stat. 1750; Oct. 25, 1994, Pub.L. 103–416, Title I, § 104(b), (c), 108 Stat. 4308.)

§ 341. Certificates of citizenship or U.S. non-citizen national status; procedure [8 U.S.C.A. § 1452]

(a) A person who claims to have derived United States citizenship through the naturalization of a parent or through the naturalization or citizenship of a husband, or who is a citizen of the United States by virtue of the provisions of section 1993 of the United States Revised Statutes, or of section 1993 of the United States Revised Statutes, as amended by section 1 of the Act of May 24, 1934 (48 Stat. 797), or who is a citizen of the United States by virtue of the provisions of subsection (c), (d), (e), (g), or (i) of section 201 of the Nationality Act of 1940, as amended (54 Stat. 1138), or of the Act of May 7, 1934 (48 Stat. 667), or of paragraph (c), (d), (e), or (g) of section 301 [8 U.S.C.A. § 1401], or under the provisions of the Act of August 4, 1937 (50 Stat. 558), or under the provisions of section 203 or 205 of the Nationality Act of 1940 (54 Stat. 1139), or under the provisions of section 303 [8 U.S.C.A. § 1403], may apply to the Attorney General for a certificate of citizenship. Upon proof to the satisfaction of the Attorney General that the applicant is a citizen, and that the applicant's alleged citizenship was derived as claimed, or acquired, as the case may be, and upon taking and subscribing before a member of the Service within the United States to the oath of allegiance required by this Act of an applicant for naturalization, such individual shall be furnished by the Attorney General with a certificate of citizenship, but only if such individual is at the time within the United States.

(b) A person who claims to be a national, but not a citizen, of the United States may apply to the Secretary of State for a certificate of non-citizen national status. Upon—

(1) proof to the satisfaction of the Secretary of State that the applicant is a national, but not a citizen, of the United States, and

(2) in the case of such a person born outside of the United States or its outlying possessions, taking and subscribing, before an immigration officer within the United States or its outlying possessions, to the oath of allegiance required by this Act of a petitioner for naturalization, the individual shall be furnished by the Secretary of State with a certificate of non-citizen national status, but only if the individual is at the time within the United States or its outlying possessions.

(June 27, 1952, c. 477, Title III, ch. 2, § 341, 66 Stat. 263; Dec. 29, 1981, Pub.L. 97–116, § 18(p), 95 Stat. 1621; Aug. 27, 1986, Pub.L. 99–396, § 16(a), 100 Stat. 843; Nov. 14, 1986, Pub.L. 99–653, § 22, 100 Stat. 3658; Oct. 24, 1988, Pub.L. 100–525, § 8(q), 102 Stat. 2618; Dec. 12, 1991, Pub.L. 102–232, Title III, § 305(m)(8), 105 Stat. 1750; Oct. 25, 1994, Pub.L. 103–416, Title I, § 102(b), 108 Stat. 4307.)

§ 342. Cancellation of certificates issued by Attorney General, the Commissioner or a Deputy Commissioner; action not to affect citizenship status [8 U.S.C.A. § 1453]

The Attorney General is authorized to cancel any certificate of citizenship, certificate of naturalization, copy of a declaration of intention, or other certificate, document or record heretofore issued or made by the Commissioner or a Deputy Commissioner or hereafter made by the Attorney General if it shall appear to the Attorney General's satisfaction that such document or record was illegally or fraudulently obtained from, or was created through illegality or by fraud practiced upon, him or the Commissioner or a Deputy Commissioner; but the person for or to whom such document or record has been issued or made shall be given at such person's last-known place of address written notice of the intention to cancel such document or record with the reasons therefor and shall be given at least sixty days in which to show cause why such document or record should not be canceled. The cancellation under this section of any document purporting to show the citizenship status of the person to whom it was issued shall affect only the document and not the citizenship status of the person in whose name the document was issued.

(June 27, 1952, c. 477, Title III, ch. 2, § 342, 66 Stat. 263.)

§ 343. Documents and copies issued by Attorney General [8 U.S.C.A. § 1454]

(a) If any certificate of naturalization or citizenship issued to any citizen or any declaration of intention furnished to any declarant is lost, mutilated, or destroyed, the citizen or declarant may make application to the Attorney General for a new certificate or declaration. If the Attorney General finds that the certificate or declaration is lost, mutilated, or destroyed, he shall issue to the applicant a new certificate or declaration. If the certificate or declaration has been mutilated, it shall be surrendered to the Attorney General before the applicant may receive such new certificate or declaration. If the certificate or declaration has been lost, the applicant or any other person who shall have, or may come into possession of it is required to surrender it to the Attorney General.

(b) The Attorney General shall issue for any naturalized citizen, on such citizen's application therefor, a special certificate of naturalization for use by such citizen only for the purpose of obtaining recognition as a citizen of the United States by a foreign state. Such certificate when issued shall be furnished to the Secretary of State for transmission to the proper authority in such foreign state.

(c) If the name of any naturalized citizen has, subsequent to naturalization, been changed by order of any court of competent jurisdiction, or by marriage, the citizen may make application for a new certificate of naturalization in the new name of such citizen. If the Attorney General finds the name of the applicant to have been changed as claimed, the Attorney General shall issue to the applicant a new certificate and shall notify the naturalization court of such action.

(d) The Attorney General is authorized to make and issue certifications of any part of the naturalization records of any court, or of any certificate of naturalization or citizenship, for use in complying with any statute, State or Federal, or in any judicial proceeding. No such certification shall be made by any clerk of court except upon order of the court.

(June 27, 1952, c. 477, Title III, ch. 2, § 343, 66 Stat. 263; Pub.L. 100–525, § 9(ee), Oct. 24, 1988, 102 Stat. 2621.)

§ 344. Fiscal provisions [8 U.S.C.A. § 1455]

(a) The Attorney General shall charge, collect, and account for fees prescribed by the Attorney General pursuant to section 9701 of Title 31 for the following:

(1) Making, filing, and docketing an application for naturalization, including the hearing on such application, if such hearing be held, and a certificate of naturalization, if the issuance of such certificate is authorized by the Attorney General.

(2) Receiving and filing a declaration of intention, and issuing a duplicate thereof.

(b) Notwithstanding the provisions of this Act or any other law, no fee shall be charged or collected for an application for declaration of intention or a certificate of naturalization in lieu of a declaration or a certificate alleged to have been lost, mutilated, or destroyed, submitted by a person who was a member of the military or naval forces of the United States at any time after April 20, 1898, and before July 5, 1902; or at any time after April 5, 1917, and before November 12, 1918; or who served on the Mexican border as a member of the Regular Army or National Guard between June 1916 and April 1917; or who has served or hereafter serves in the military, air, or naval forces of the United States after September 16, 1940, and who was not at any time during such period or thereafter separated from such forces under other than honorable conditions, who was not a conscientious objector who performed no military duty whatever or refused to wear the uniform, or who was not at any time during such period or thereafter discharged from such military, air, or naval forces on account of alienage.

(c) All fees collected by the Attorney General shall be deposited by the Attorney General in the Treasury of the United States except that all fees collected or paid over on or after October 1, 1988, shall be deposited in the Immigration Examinations Fee Account established under section 286(m) [8 U.S.C.A. 1356(m)]: *Provided, however,* That all fees received by the Attorney General from applicants residing in the Virgin Islands of the United States, and in Guam, under this title, shall be paid over to the treasury of the Virgin Islands and to the treasury of Guam, respectively.

(d) During the time when the United States is at war the Attorney General may not charge or collect a naturalization fee from an alien in the military, air, or naval service of the United States for filing an application for naturalization or issuing a certificate of naturalization upon admission to citizenship.

(e) In addition to the other fees required by this title, the applicant for naturalization shall, upon the filing of an application for naturalization, deposit with and pay to the Attorney General a sum of money sufficient to cover the expenses of subpenaing and paying the legal fees of any witnesses for whom such applicant may request a subpena, and upon the final discharge of such witnesses, they shall receive, if they demand the same from the Attorney General, the customary and usual witness fees from the moneys which the applicant shall have paid to the Attorney General for such purpose, and the residue, if any, shall be returned by the Attorney General to the applicant.

(f)(1) The Attorney General shall pay over to courts administering oaths of allegiance to persons under this title a specified percentage of all fees described in subsection (a)(1) collected by the Attorney General with respect to persons administered the oath of allegiance by the respective courts. The Attorney General, annually and in consultation with the courts, shall determine the specified percentage based on the proportion, of the total costs incurred by the Service and courts for essential services directly related to the naturalization process, which are incurred by courts.

(2) The Attorney General shall provide on an annual basis to the Committees on the Judiciary of the House of Representatives and of the Senate a detailed report on the use of the fees described in paragraph (1) and shall consult with such Committees before increasing such fees.

(g) to (i) Redesignated (c) to (e)

(June 27, 1952, c. 477, Title III, ch. 2, § 344, 66 Stat. 264; Pub. L. 85–508, § 26, July 7, 1958, 72 Stat. 351; Pub. L. 90–609, § 3, Oct. 21, 1968, 82 Stat. 1200; Pub. L. 97–116, § 16, Dec. 29, 1981, 95 Stat. 1619; Pub.L. 100–459, Title II, § 209(b), Oct. 1, 1988, 102 Stat. 2203; Pub.L. 100–525, § 9(ff), Oct. 24, 1988, 102 Stat. 2621; Pub.L. 101–649, Title IV, § 407(c)(20), (d)(19), Nov. 29, 1990, 104 Stat. 5041, 5046; Pub.L. 100–459, Title II, § 209(b), amended Pub.L. 102–232, Title I, § 102(b)(3), Title III, §§ 305(*l*),309(a)(1)(A)(ii), Dec. 12, 1991, 105 Stat.

1758; Pub.L. 102–232 309(b)(14), Dec. 12, 1991, 105 Stat. 1736, 1750, 1758, 1759.)

§ 345. Repealed. Pub. L. 86–682, § 12(c), Sept. 2, 1960, 74 Stat. 708, eff. Sept. 1, 1960 [8 U.S.C.A. § 1456]

§ 346. Publication and distribution of citizenship textbooks; use of naturalization fees [8 U.S.C.A. § 1457]

Authorization is granted for the publication and distribution of the citizenship textbook described in subsection (b) of section 332 [8 U.S.C.A. § 1443(b)] and for the reimbursement of the appropriation of the Department of Justice upon the records of the Treasury Department from the naturalization fees deposited in the Treasury through the Service for the cost of such publication and distribution, such reimbursement to be made upon statements by the Attorney General of books so published and distributed.

(June 27, 1952, c. 477, Title III, ch. 2, § 346, 66 Stat. 266.)

§ 347. Compilation of naturalization statistics and payment for equipment [8 U.S.C.A. § 1458]

The Attorney General is authorized and directed to prepare from the records in the custody of the Service a report upon those heretofore seeking citizenship to show by nationalities their relation to the numbers of aliens annually arriving and to the prevailing census populations of the foreign-born, their economic, vocational, and other classification, in statistical form, with analytical comment thereon, and to prepare such report annually hereafter. Payment for the equipment used in preparing such compilation shall be made from the appropriation for the enforcement of this Act by the Service.

(June 27, 1952, c. 477, Title III, ch. 2, § 347, 66 Stat. 266.)

§ 348. [8 U.S.C.A. § 1459] Repealed.

Chapter III—Loss of Nationality

§ 349. Loss of nationality by native-born or naturalized citizen; voluntary action; burden of proof; presumptions [8 U.S.C.A. § 1481]

(a) A person who is a national of the United States whether by birth or naturalization, shall lose his nationality by voluntarily performing any of the following acts with the intention of relinquishing United States nationality—

(1) obtaining naturalization in a foreign state upon his own application, or upon an application filed by a duly authorized agent, after having attained the age of eighteen years; or

(2) taking an oath or making an affirmation or other formal declaration of allegiance to a foreign state or a political subdivision thereof, after having attained the age of eighteen years; or

(3) entering, or serving in, the armed forces of a foreign state if **(A)** such armed forces are engaged in hostilities against the United States, or **(B)** such persons serve as a commissioned or noncommissioned officer; or

(4)(A) accepting, serving in, or performing the duties of any office, post, or employment under the government of a foreign state or a political subdivision thereof, after attaining the age of eighteen years, if he has or acquires the nationality of such foreign state; or

(B) accepting, serving in, or performing the duties of any office, post, or employment under the government of a foreign state or a political subdivision thereof, after attaining the age of eighteen years for which office, post, or employment an oath, affirmation, or declaration of allegiance is required; or

(5) making a formal renunciation of nationality before a diplomatic or consular officer of the United States in a foreign state, in such form as may be prescribed by the Secretary of State; or

(6) making in the United States a formal written renunciation of nationality in such form as may be prescribed by, and before such officer as may be designated by, the Attorney General, whenever the United States shall be in a state of war and the Attorney General shall approve such renunciation as not contrary to the interests of national defense; or

(7) committing any act of treason against, or attempting by force to overthrow, or bearing arms against, the United States, violating or conspiring to violate any of the provisions of section 2383 of Title 18, or willfully performing any act in violation of section 2385 of Title 18, or violating section 2384 of Title 18 by engaging in a conspiracy to overthrow, put down, or to destroy by force the Government of the United States, or to levy war against them, if and when he is convicted thereof by a court martial or by a court of competent jurisdiction.

(b) Whenever the loss of United States nationality is put in issue in any action or proceeding commenced on or after September 26, 1961 under, or by virtue of, the provisions of this Act or any other Act, the burden shall be upon the person or party claiming that such loss occurred, to establish such claim by a preponderance of the evidence. Any person who commits or performs, or who has committed or performed, any act of expatriation under the provisions of this or any other Act shall be presumed to have done so voluntarily, but such presumption may be rebutted upon a showing, by a preponderance of the evidence, that the act or acts committed or performed were not done voluntarily.

(June 27, 1952, c. 477, Title III, ch. 3, § 349, 66 Stat. 267; Sept. 3, 1954, c. 1256, § 2, 68 Stat. 1146; Pub.L. 87–301, § 19, Sept. 26, 1961, 75 Stat. 656; Pub.L. 94–412, Title V, § 501(a), Sept. 14, 1976, 90 Stat. 1258; Pub.L. 95–432, §§ 2, 4, Oct. 10, 1978, 92 Stat. 1046; Pub.L. 97–116, § 18(k)(2), (q), Dec. 29, 1981, 95 Stat. 1620, 1621; Pub.L. 99–653, §§ 18, 19, Nov. 14, 1986, 100 Stat. 3658, as amended Pub.L. 100–525, §§ 8(m), (n), 9(hh), Oct. 24, 1988, 102 Stat. 2618, 2622.)

§ 350. Repealed. Pub. L. 95–432, § 1, Oct. 10, 1978, 92 Stat. 1046 [8 U.S.C.A. § 1482]

§ 351. Restrictions on loss of nationality [8 U.S.C.A. § 1483]

(a) Except as provided in paragraphs (6) and (7) of section 349(a) of this title [8 U.S.C.A. § 1481(a)], no national of the United States can lose United States nationality under this Act while within the United States or any of its outlying possessions, but loss of nationality shall result from the performance within the United States or any of its outlying possessions of any of the acts or the fulfillment of any of the conditions specified in this part if and when the national thereafter takes up a residence outside the United States and its outlying possessions.

(b) A national who within six months after attaining the age of eighteen years asserts his claim to United States nationality, in such manner as the Secretary of State shall by regulation prescribe, shall not be deemed to have lost United States nationality by the commission, prior to his eighteenth birthday, of any of the acts specified in paragraphs (3) and (5) of section 349(a) [8 U.S.C.A. § 1481(a)].

(June 27, 1952, c. 477, Title III, ch. 3, § 351, 66 Stat. 269; Dec. 29, 1981, Pub.L. 97–116, § 18(r), 95 Stat. 1621; Nov. 14, 1986, Pub.L. 99–653, § 20, 100 Stat. 3658; Oct. 24, 1988, Pub.L. 100–525, § 8(*o*), 102 Stat. 2618; Oct. 25, 1994, Pub.L. 103–416, Title I, § 105(a), 108 Stat. 4308; Sept. 30, 1996, Pub.L. 104–208, Div. C, Title VI, § 671(b)(3), 110 Stat. 3009–721.)

§§ 352 to 355. Repealed. Pub. L. 95–432, § 2, Oct. 10, 1978, 92 Stat. 1046 [8 U.S.C.A. §§ 1484 to 1487]

§ 356. Nationality lost solely from performance of acts or fulfillment of conditions [8 U.S.C.A. § 1488]

The loss of nationality under this part shall result solely from the performance by a national of the acts or fulfillment of the conditions specified in this Part.

(June 27, 1952, c. 477, Title III, ch. 3, § 356, 66 Stat. 272.)

§ 357. Application of treaties; exceptions [8 U.S.C.A. § 1489]

Nothing in this title shall be applied in contravention of the provisions of any treaty or convention to which the United States is a party and which has been ratified by the Senate before December 25, 1952: *Provided, however,* That no woman who was a national of the United States shall be deemed to have lost her nationality solely by reason of her marriage to an alien on or after September 22, 1922, or to an alien racially ineligible to citizenship on or after March 3, 1931, or, in the case of a woman who was a United States citizen at birth, through residence abroad following such marriage, notwithstanding the provisions of any existing treaty or convention.

(June 27, 1952, c. 477, Title III, ch. 3, § 357, 66 Stat. 272; Pub.L. 100–525, § 9(ii), Oct. 24, 1988, 102 Stat. 2622.)

CHAPTER IV—MISCELLANEOUS

§ 358. Certificate of diplomatic or consular officer of United States as to loss of American nationality [8 U.S.C.A. § 1501]

Whenever a diplomatic or consular officer of the United States has reason to believe that a person while in a foreign state has lost his United States nationality under any provision of chapter 3 of this title, or under any provision of chapter IV of the Nationality Act of 1940, as amended, he shall certify the facts upon which such belief is based to the Department of State, in writing, under regulations prescribed by the Secretary of State. If the report of the diplomatic or consular officer is approved by the Secretary of State, a copy of the certificate shall be forwarded to the Attorney General, for his information, and the diplomatic or consular office in which the report was made shall be directed to forward a copy of the certificate to the person to whom it relates. Approval by the Secretary of State of a certificate under this section shall constitute a final administrative determination of loss of United States nationality under this Act, subject to such procedures for administrative appeal as the Secretary may prescribe by regulation, and also shall constitute a denial of a right or privilege of United States nationality for purposes of section 360 [8 U.S.C.A. § 1503].

(June 27, 1952, c. 477, Title III, ch. 3, § 358, 66 Stat. 272; Oct. 25, 1994, Pub.L. 103–416, Title I, § 106, 108 Stat. 4309.)

§ 359. Certificate of nationality issued by Secretary of State for person not a naturalized citizen of United States for use in proceedings of a foreign state [8 U.S.C.A. § 1502]

The Secretary of State is authorized to issue, in his discretion and in accordance with rules and regulations prescribed by him, a certificate of nationality for any person not a naturalized citizen of the United States who presents satisfactory evidence that he is an American national and that such certificate is needed for use in judicial or administrative proceedings in a foreign state. Such certificate shall be solely for use in the case for which it was issued and shall be transmitted by the Secretary of State through appropriate official channels to the judicial or administrative officers of the foreign state in which it is to be used.

(June 27, 1952, c. 477, Title III, ch. 4, § 359, 66 Stat. 273.)

§ 360. Denial of rights and privileges as national [8 U.S.C.A. § 1503]

(a) Proceedings for declaration of United States nationality

If any person who is within the United States claims a right or privilege as a national of the United States and is denied such right or privilege by any department or independent agency, or official thereof, upon the ground that he is not a national of the United States, such person may institute an action under the provisions of section 2201 of Title 28 against the head of such department or independent agency for a judgment declaring him to be a national of the United States, except that no such action may be instituted in any case if the issue of such person's status as a national of the United States **(1)** arose by reason of, or in connection with any removal proceeding under the provisions of this or any other act, or **(2)** is in issue in any such removal proceeding. An action under this subsection may be instituted only within five years after the final administrative denial of such right or privilege and shall be filed in the district court of the United States for the district in which such person resides or claims a residence, and jurisdiction over such officials in such cases is conferred upon those courts.

(b) Application for certificate of identity; appeal

If any person who is not within the United States claims a right or privilege as a national of the United States and is denied such right or privilege by any department or independent agency, or official thereof, upon the ground that he is not a national of the United States, such person may make application to a diplomatic or consular officer of the United States in the foreign country in which he is residing for a certificate of identity for the purpose of traveling to a port of entry in the United States and applying for admission. Upon proof to the satisfaction of such diplomatic or consular officer that such application is made in good faith and has a substantial basis, he shall issue to such person a certificate of identity. From any denial of an application for such certificate the applicant shall be entitled to an appeal to the Secretary of State, who, if he approves the denial, shall state in writing his reasons for his decision. The Secretary of State shall prescribe rules and regulations for the issuance of certificates of identity as above provided. The provisions of this subsection shall be applicable only to a person who at some time prior to his application for the certificate of identity has been physically present in the United States, or to a person under sixteen years of age who was born abroad of a United States citizen parent.

(c) Application for admission to United States under certificate of identity; revision of determination

A person who has been issued a certificate of identity under the provisions of subsection (b), and while in possession thereof, may apply for admission to the United States at any port of entry, and shall be subject to all the provisions of this Act relating to the conduct of proceedings involving aliens seeking admission to the United States. A final determination by the Attorney General that any such person is not entitled to admission to the United States shall be subject to review by any court of competent jurisdiction in habeas corpus proceedings and not otherwise. Any person described in this section who is finally denied admission to the United States shall be subject to all the provisions of this Act relating to aliens seeking admission to the United States.

(June 27, 1952, c. 477, Title III, ch. 3, § 360, 66 Stat. 273; Sept. 30, 1996, Pub.L. 104–208, Div. C, Title III, § 308(d)(4)(P), 110 Stat. 3009–619.)

§ 361. Cancellation of United States passports and Consular Reports of Birth [8 U.S.C.A. § 1504]

(a) The Secretary of State is authorized to cancel any United States passport or Consular Report of Birth, or certified copy thereof, if it appears that such document was illegally, fraudulently, or erroneously obtained from, or was created through illegality or fraud practiced upon, the Secretary. The person for or to whom such document has been issued or made shall be given, at such person's last known address, written notice of the cancellation of such document, together with the procedures for seeking a prompt post-cancellation hearing. The cancellation under this section of any document purporting to show the citizenship status of the person to whom it was issued shall affect only the document and not the citizenship status of the person in whose name the document was issued.

(b) For purposes of this section, the term "Consular Report of Birth" refers to the report, designated as a "Report of Birth Abroad of a Citizen of the United States", issued by a consular officer to document a citizen born abroad.

(June 27, 1952, c. 477, Title III, ch. 3, § 361, as added Oct. 25, 1994, Pub.L. 103–416, Title I, § 107(a), 108 Stat. 4309.)

TITLE IV

MISCELLANEOUS AND REFUGEE ASSISTANCE

§ 404. Authorization of appropriations [8 U.S.C.A. § 1101, note]

(a) There are authorized to be appropriated such sums as may be necessary to carry out the provisions of this Act (other than chapter 2 of title IV).

(b)(1) There are authorized to be appropriated (for fiscal year 1991 and any subsequent fiscal year) to an immigration emergency fund, to be established in the Treasury, an amount sufficient to provide for a balance of $35,000,000 in such fund, to be used to carry out paragraph (2) and to provide for an increase in border patrol or other enforcement activities of the Service and for reimbursement of State and localities in providing assistance as requested by the Attorney General in meeting an immigration emergency, except that no amounts may be withdrawn from such fund with respect to an emergency unless the President has determined that the immigration emergency exists and has certified such fact to the Judiciary Committees of the House of Representatives and of the Senate.

(2)(A) Funds which are authorized to be appropriated by paragraph (1), subject to the dollar limitation contained in subparagraph (B), shall be available, by application for the reimbursement of States and localities providing assistance as required by the Attorney General, to States and localities whenever—

> **(i)** a district director of the Service certifies to the Commissioner that the number of asylum applications filed in the respective district during a calendar quarter exceeds by at least 1,000 the number of such applications filed in that district during the preceding calendar quarter,
>
> **(ii)** the lives, property, safety, or welfare of the residents of a State or locality are endangered, or
>
> **(iii)** in any other circumstances as determined by the Attorney General.

In applying clause (i), the providing of parole at a point of entry in a district shall be deemed to constitute an application for asylum in the district.

(B) Not more than $20,000,000 shall be made available for all localities under this paragraph.

(C) For purposes of subparagraph (A), the requirement of paragraph (1) that an immigration emergency be determined shall not apply.

(D) A decision with respect to an application for reimbursement under subparagraph (A) shall be made by the Attorney General within 15 days after the date of receipt of the application.

(June 27, 1952, c. 477, Title IV, ch. 2, § 404, as amended Pub.L. 97–116, § 18(s), Dec. 29, 1981, 95 Stat. 1621; Pub.L. 99–603, Title I, § 113, Nov. 6, 1986, 100 Stat. 3383; Pub.L. 101–649, Title VII, § 705(a), Nov. 29, 1990, 104 Stat. 5087; Pub.L. 102–232, Title III, § 308(d), Dec. 12, 1991, 105 Stat. 1757.)

§ 405. Savings clause [8 U.S.C.A. § 1101, note]

(a) Nothing contained in this Act, unless otherwise specifically provided therein, shall be construed to affect the validity of any declaration of intention, petition for naturalization, certificate of naturalization, certificate of citizenship, warrant of arrest, order or warrant of deportation, order of exclusion, or other document or proceeding which shall be valid at the time this Act shall take effect; or to affect any prosecution, suit, action, or proceedings, civil or criminal, brought, or any status, condition, right in process of acquisition, act, thing, liability, obligation, or matter, civil or criminal, done or existing, at the time this Act shall take effect; but as to all such prosecutions, suits, actions, proceedings, statutes [sic] conditions, rights, acts, things, liabilities, obligations, or matters the statutes or parts of statutes repealed by this Act are, unless otherwise specifically provided therein, hereby continued in force and effect. When an immigrant, in possession of an unexpired immigrant visa issued prior to the effective date of this Act, makes application for admission, his admissibility shall be determined under the provisions of law in effect on the date of the issuance of such visa. An application for suspension of deportation under § 19 of the Immigration Act of 1917, as amended, or for adjustment of status under § 4 of the Displaced Persons Act of 1948, as amended, which is pending on the date of enactment of this Act [June 27, 1952], shall be regarded as a proceeding within the meaning of this subsection.

(b) Except as otherwise specifically provided in title III, any petition for naturalization heretofore filed which may be pending at the time this Act shall take effect shall be heard and determined in accordance with the requirements of law in effect when such petition was filed.

(c) Except as otherwise specifically provided in this Act, the repeal of any statute by this Act shall not terminate nationality heretofore lawfully acquired nor restore nationality heretofore lost under any law of the United States or any treaty to which the United States may have been a party.

(d) Except as otherwise specifically provided in this Act, or any amendment thereto, fees, charges and prices for purposes specified in title V of the Independent Offices Appropriation Act, 1952 (Public Law 137, Eighty-second Congress, approved August 31, 1951), may be fixed and established in the manner and by the head of any Federal Agency as specified in that Act.

(e) This Act shall not be construed to repeal, alter, or amend section 231(a) of the Act of April 30, 1946 (60 Stat. 148; 22 U.S.C. 1281(a)), the Act of June 20, 1949 (Public Law 110, section 8, Eighty-first Congress, first session; 63 Stat. 208 [section 403h of Title 50]), the Act of June 5, 1950 (Public Law 535, Eighty-first Congress, second session [former section 1501 et seq. of Title 22]), nor Title V of the Agricultural Act of 1949, as amended (Public Law 78, Eighty-second Congress, first session [sections 1461 to 1468 of Title 7]).

(June 27, 1952, c. 477, Title IV, ch. 2, § 405, 66 Stat. 274.)

§ 406. Separability clause [8 U.S.C.A. § 1101, note]

If any particular provision of this Act, or the application thereof to any person or circumstance, is held invalid, the remainder of the Act and the application of such provision to other persons or circumstances shall not be affected thereby.

(June 27, 1952, c. 477, Title IV, ch. 2, § 406, 66 Stat. 275.)

§ 411. Office of Refugee Resettlement; establishment; appointment of Director; functions [8 U.S.C.A. § 1521]

(a) There is established, within the Department of Health and Human Services, an office to be known as the Office of Refugee Resettlement (hereinafter in this chapter referred to as the "Office"). The head of the Office shall be a Director (hereinafter in this chapter referred to as the "Director"), to be appointed by the Secretary of Health and Human Services (hereinafter in this chapter referred to as the "Secretary").

(b) The function of the Office and its Director is to fund and administer (directly or through arrangements with other Federal agencies), in consultation with the Secretary of State, programs of the Federal Government under this chapter.

(June 27, 1952, c. 477, Title IV, ch. 2, § 411, as added Mar. 17, 1980, Pub.L. 96–212, Title III, § 311(a) (2), 94 Stat. 110, and amended Apr. 30, 1994, Pub.L. 103–236, Title I, § 162(n)(1), 108 Stat. 409.)

§ 412. Authorization for programs for domestic resettlement of and assistance to refugees [8 U.S.C.A. § 1522]

(a) Conditions and considerations

(1)(A) In providing assistance under this section, the Director shall, to the extent of available appropriations, **(i)** make available sufficient resources for employment training and placement in order to achieve economic self-sufficiency among refugees as quickly as possible, **(ii)** provide refugees with the opportunity to acquire sufficient English language training to enable them to become effectively resettled as quickly as possible, **(iii)** insure that cash assistance is made available to refugees in such a manner as not to discourage their economic self-sufficiency, in accordance with subsection (e)(2), and **(iv)** insure that women have the same opportunities as men to participate in training and instruction.

(B) it is the intent of Congress that in providing refugee assistance under this section—

(i) employable refugees should be placed on jobs as soon as possible after their arrival in the United States;

(ii) social service funds should be focused on employment-related services, English-as-a-second-language training (in non-work hours where possible), and case-management services; and

(iii) local voluntary agency activities should be conducted in close cooperation and advance consultation with State and local governments.

(2)(A) The Director and the Federal agency administering subsection (b)(1) shall consult regularly (not less often than quarterly) with State and local governments and private nonprofit voluntary agencies concerning the sponsorship process and the intended distribution of refugees among the States and localities before their placement in those States and localities.

(B) The Director shall develop and implement, in consultation with representatives of voluntary agencies and State and local governments, policies and strategies for the placement and resettlement of refugees within the United States.

(C) Such policies and strategies, to the extent practicable and except under such unusual circumstances as the Director may recognize, shall—

(i) insure that a refugee is not initially placed or resettled in an area highly impacted (as determined under regulations prescribed by the Director after consultation with such agencies and governments) by the presence of refugees or comparable populations unless the refugee has a spouse, parent, sibling, son, or daughter residing in that area,

(ii) provide for a mechanism whereby representatives of local affiliates of voluntary agencies regularly (not less often than quarterly) meet with representatives of State and local governments to plan and coordinate in advance of their arrival the appropriate placement of refugees among the various States and localities, and

(iii) take into account—

(I) the proportion of refugees and comparable entrants in the population in the area,

(II) the availability of employment opportunities, affordable housing, and public and private resources (including educational, health care, and mental health services) for refugees in the area,

(III) the likelihood of refugees placed in the area becoming self-sufficient and free from long-term dependence on public assistance, and

(IV) the secondary migration of refugees to and from the area that is likely to occur.

(D) With respect to the location of placement of refugees within a State, the Federal agency administering subsection (b)(1) shall, consistent with such policies and strategies and to the maximum extent possible, take into account recommendations of the State.

(3) In the provision of domestic assistance under this section, the Director shall make a periodic assessment, based on refugee population and other relevant factors, of the relative needs of refugees for assistance and services under this chapter and the resources available to meet such needs. The Director shall compile and maintain data on secondary migration of refugees within the United States and, by State of residence and nationality, on the proportion of refugees receiving cash or medical assistance described in subsection (e). In allocating resources, the Director shall avoid duplication of services and provide for maximum coordination between agencies providing related services.

(4)(A) No grant or contract may be awarded under this section unless an appropriate proposal and application (including a description of the agency's ability to perform the services specified in the proposal) are submitted to, and approved by, the appropriate administering official. Grants and contracts under this section shall be made to those agencies which the appropriate administering official determines can best perform the services. Payments may be made for activities authorized under this chapter in advance or by way of reimbursement. In carrying out this section, the Director, the Secretary of State, and any such other appropriate administering official are authorized—

(i) to make loans, and

(ii) to accept and use money, funds, property, and services of any kind made available by gift, devise, bequest, grant, or otherwise for the purpose of carrying out this section.

(B) No funds may be made available under this chapter (other than under subsection (b)(1)) to States or political subdivisions in the form of block grants, per capita grants, or similar consolidated grants or contracts. Such funds shall be made available under separate grants or contracts—

(i) for medical screening and initial medical treatment under subsection (b)(5),

(ii) for services for refugees under subsection (c)(1),

(iii) for targeted assistance project grants under subsection (c)(2), and

(iv) for assistance for refugee children under subsection (d)(2).

(C) The Director may not delegate to a State or political subdivision his authority to review or approve grants or contracts under this chapter or the terms under which such grants or contracts are made.

(5) Assistance and services funded under this section shall be provided to refugees without regard to race, religion, nationality, sex, or political opinion.

(6) As a condition for receiving assistance under this section, a State must—

(A) submit to the Director a plan which provides—

(i) a description of how the State intends to encourage effective refugee resettlement and to promote economic self-sufficiency as quickly as possible,

(ii) a description of how the State will insure that language training and employment services are made available to refugees receiving cash assistance,

(iii) for the designation of an individual, employed by the State, who will be responsible for insuring coordination of public and private resources in refugee resettlement,

(iv) for the care and supervision of and legal responsibility for unaccompanied refugee children in the State, and

(v) for the identification of refugees who at the time of resettlement in the State are determined to have medical conditions requiring, or medical histories indicating a need for, treatment or observation and such monitoring of such treatment or observation as may be necessary;

(B) meet standards, goals, and priorities, developed by the Director, which assure the effective resettlement of refugees and which promote their economic self-sufficiency as quickly as possible and the efficient provision of services; and

(C) submit to the Director, within a reasonable period of time after the end of each fiscal year, a report on the uses of funds provided under this chapter which the State is responsible for administering.

(7) The Secretary, together with the Secretary of State with respect to assistance provided by the Secretary of State under subsection (b), shall develop a system of monitoring the assistance provided under this section. This system shall include—

(A) evaluations of the effectiveness of the programs funded under this section and the performance of States, grantees, and contractors;

(B) financial auditing and other appropriate monitoring to detect any fraud, abuse, or mismanagement in the operation of such programs; and

(C) data collection on the services provided and the results achieved.

(8) The Attorney General shall provide the Director with information supplied by refugees in conjunction with their applications to the Attorney General for adjustment of status, and the Director shall compile, summarize, and evaluate such information.

(9) The Secretary, the Secretary of Education, the Attorney General, and the Secretary of State may issue such regulations as each deems appropriate to carry out this chapter.

(10) For purposes of this chapter, the term "refugee" includes any alien described in section 207(c)(2) [8 U.S.C.A. § 1157(c)(2)].

(b) Program of initial resettlement

(1)(A) For—

(i) fiscal years 1980 and 1981, the Secretary of State is authorized, and

(ii) fiscal year 1982 and succeeding fiscal years, the Director (except as provided in subparagraph (B)) is authorized,

to make grants to, and contracts with, public or private nonprofit agencies for initial resettlement (including initial reception and placement with sponsors) of refugees in the United States. Grants to, or contracts with, private nonprofit voluntary agencies under this paragraph shall be made consistent with the objectives of this chapter, taking into account the different resettlement approaches and practices of such agencies. Resettlement assistance under this paragraph shall be provided in coordination with the Director's provision of other assistance under this chapter. Funds provided to agencies under such grants and contracts may only be obligated or expended during the fiscal year in which they are provided (or the subsequent fiscal year or such subsequent fiscal period as the Federal contracting agency may approve) to carry out the purposes of this subsection.

(B) If the President determines that the Director should not administer the program under this paragraph, the authority of the Director under the first sentence of subparagraph (A) shall be exercised by such officer as the President shall from time to time specify.

(2) The Director is authorized to develop programs for such orientation, instruction in English, and job training for refugees, and such other education and training of refugees, as facilitates their resettlement in the United States. The Director is authorized to implement such programs, in accordance with the provisions of this section, with respect to refugees in the United States. The Secretary of State is authorized to implement such programs with respect to refugees awaiting entry into the United States.

(3) The Secretary is authorized to make arrangements (including cooperative arrangements with other Federal agencies) for the temporary care of refugees in the United States in emergency circumstances, including the establishment of processing centers, if necessary, without regard to such provisions of law (other than the Renegotiation Act of 1951 [50 App. U.S.C.A. § 1211 et seq.] and section 414(b) [8 U.S.C.A. § 1524(b)]) regulating the making, performance amendment, or modification of contracts and the expenditure of funds of the United States Government as the Secretary may specify.

(4) The Secretary shall—

(A) assure that an adequate number of trained staff are available at the location at which the refugees enter the United States to assure that all necessary medical records are available and in proper order;

(B) provide for the identification of refugees who have been determined to have medical conditions affecting the public health and requiring treatment;

(C) assure that State or local health officials at the resettlement destination within the United States of each refugee are promptly notified of the refugee's arrival and provided with all applicable medical records; and

(D) provide for such monitoring of refugees identified under subparagraph (B) as will insure that they receive appropriate and timely treatment.

The Secretary shall develop and implement methods for monitoring and assessing the quality of medical screening and related health services provided to refugees awaiting resettlement in the United States.

(5) The Director is authorized to make grants to, and enter into contracts with, State and local health agencies for payments to meet their costs of providing medical screening and initial medical treatment to refugees.

(6) The Comptroller General shall directly conduct an annual financial audit of funds expended under each grant or contract made under paragraph (1) for fiscal year 1986 and for fiscal year 1987.

(7) Each grant or contract with an agency under paragraph (1) shall require the agency to do the following:

(A) To provide quarterly performance and financial status reports to the Federal agency administering paragraph (1).

(B)(i) To provide, directly or through its local affiliate, notice to the appropriate county or other local welfare office at the time that the agency becomes aware that a refugee is offered employment and to provide notice to the refugee that such notice has been provided, and

(ii) upon request of such a welfare office to which a refugee has applied for cash assistance, to furnish that office with documentation respecting any cash or other resources provided directly by the agency to the refugee under this subsection.

(C) To assure that refugees, known to the agency as having been identified pursuant to paragraph (4)(B) as having medical conditions affecting the public health and requiring treatment, report to the appropriate county or other health agency upon their resettlement in an area.

(D) To fulfill its responsibility to provide for the basic needs (including food, clothing, shelter, and transportation for job interviews and training) of each refugee resettled and to develop and implement a resettlement plan including the early employment of each refugee resettled and to monitor the implementation of such plan.

(E) To transmit to the Federal agency administering paragraph (1) an annual report describing the following:

(i) The number of refugees placed (by county of placement) and the expenditures made in the year under the grant or contract, including the proportion of such expenditures used for administrative purposes and for provision of services.

(ii) The proportion of refugees placed by the agency in the previous year who are receiving cash or medical assistance described in subsection (e).

(iii) The efforts made by the agency to monitor placement of the refugees and the activities of local affiliates of the agency.

(iv) The extent to which the agency has coordinated its activities with local social service providers in a manner which avoids duplication of activities and has provided notices to local welfare offices and the reporting of medical conditions of certain aliens to local health departments in accordance with subparagraphs (B)(i) and (C).

(v) Such other information as the agency administering paragraph (1) deems to be appropriate in monitoring the effectiveness of agencies in carrying out their functions under such grants and contracts.

The agency administering paragraph (1) shall promptly forward a copy of each annual report transmitted under subparagraph (E) to the Committees on the Judiciary of the House of Representatives and of the Senate.

(8) The Federal agency administering paragraph (1) shall establish criteria for the performance of agencies under grants and contracts under that paragraph, and shall include criteria relating to an agency's—

(A) efforts to reduce welfare dependency among refugees resettled by that agency,

(B) collection of travel loans made to refugees resettled by that agency for travel to the United States,

(C) arranging for effective local sponsorship and other non-public assistance for refugees resettled by that agency,

(D) cooperation with refugee mutual assistance associations, local social service providers, health agencies, and welfare offices,

(E) compliance with the guidelines established by the Director for the placement and resettlement of refugees within the United States, and

(F) compliance with other requirements contained in the grant or contract, including the reporting and other requirements under subsection (b)(7).

The Federal administering agency shall use the criteria in the process of awarding or renewing grants and contracts under paragraph (1).

(c) Project grants and contracts for services for refugees

(1)(A) The Director is authorized to make grants to, and enter into contracts with, public or private nonprofit agencies for projects specifically designed—

(i) to assist refugees in obtaining the skills which are necessary for economic self-sufficiency, including projects for job training, employment services, day care, professional refresher training, and other recertification services;

(ii) to provide training in English where necessary (regardless of whether the refugees are employed or receiving cash or other assistance); and

(iii) to provide where specific needs have been shown and recognized by the Director, health (including mental health) services, social services, educational and other services.

(B) The funds available for a fiscal year for grants and contracts under subparagraph (A) shall be allocated among the States based on the total number or refugees (including children and adults) who arrived in the United States not more than 36 months before the beginning of such fiscal year and who are actually residing in each State (taking into account secondary migration) as of the beginning of the fiscal year.

(C) Any limitation which the Director establishes on the proportion of funds allocated to a State under this paragraph that the State may use for services other than those described in subsection (a)(1)(B)(ii) shall not apply if the Director receives a plan (established by or in consultation with local governments) and determines that the plan provides for the maximum appropriate provision of employment-related services for, and the maximum placement of, employable refugees consistent with performance standards established under section 1516 of Title 29.

(2)(A) The Director is authorized to make grants to States for assistance to counties and similar areas in the States where, because of factors such as unusually large refugee populations (including secondary migration), high refugee concentrations, and high use of public assistance by refugees, there exists and can be demonstrated a specific need for supplementation of available resources for services to refugees.

(B) Grants shall be made available under this paragraph—

(i) primarily for the purpose of facilitating refugee employment and achievement of self-sufficiency,

(ii) in a manner that does not supplant other refugee program funds and that assures that not less than 95 percent of the amount of the grant award is made available to the county or other local entity.

(d) Assistance for refugee children

(1) The Secretary of Education is authorized to make grants, and enter into contracts, for payments for projects to provide special educational services (including English language training) to refugee children in elementary and secondary schools where a demonstrated need has been shown.

(2)(A) The Director is authorized to provide assistance, reimbursement to States, and grants to and contracts with public and private nonprofit agencies, for the provision of child welfare services, including foster care maintenance payments and services and health care, furnished to any refugee child (except as provided in subparagraph (B)) during the thirty-six month period beginning with the first month in which such refugee child is in the United States.

(B)(i) In the case of a refugee child who is unaccompanied by a parent or other close adult relative (as defined by the Director), the services described in subparagraph (A) may be furnished until the month after the child attains eighteen years of age (or such higher age as the State's child welfare services plan under part B of title IV of the Social Security Act [42 U.S.C.A. § 620 et seq.] prescribes for the availability of such services to any other child in that State).

(ii) The Director shall attempt to arrange for the placement under the laws of the States of such unaccompanied refugee children, who have been accepted for admission to the United States, before (or as soon as possible after) their arrival in the United States. During any interim period while such a child is in the United States or in transit to the United States but before the child is so placed, the Director shall assume legal responsibility (including financial responsibility) for the child, if necessary, and is authorized to make necessary decisions to provide for the child's immediate care.

(iii) In carrying out the Director's responsibilities under clause (ii), the Director is authorized to enter into contracts with appropriate public or private nonprofit agencies under such conditions as the Director determines to be appropriate.

(iv) The Director shall prepare and maintain a list of (I) all such unaccompanied children who have entered the United States after April 1, 1975, (II) the names and last known residences of their parents (if living) at the time of arrival, and (III) the children's location, status, and progress.

(e) Cash assistance and medical assistance to refugees

(1) The Director is authorized to provide assistance, reimbursement to States, and grants to, and contracts with, public or private nonprofit agencies for 100 per centum of the cash assistance and medical assistance provided to any refugee during the thirty-six month period beginning with the first month in which such refugee has entered the United States and for the identifiable and reasonable administrative costs of providing this assistance.

(2)(A) Cash assistance provided under this subsection to an employable refugee is conditioned, except for good cause shown—

(i) on the refugee's registration with an appropriate agency providing employment services described in subsection (c)(1)(A)(i), or, if there is no such agency available, with an appropriate State or local employment service;

(ii) on the refugee's participation in any available and appropriate social service or targeted assistance program (funded under subsection (c)) providing job or language training in the area in which the refugee resides; and

(iii) on the refugee's acceptance of appropriate offers of employment.

(B) Cash assistance shall not be made available to refugees who are full-time students in institutions of higher education (as defined by the Director after consultation with the Secretary of Education).

(C) In the case of a refugee who—

(i) refuses an offer of employment which has been determined to be appropriate either by the agency responsible for the initial resettlement of the refugee under subsection (b) or by the appropriate State or local employment service,

(ii) refuses to go to a job interview which has been arranged through such agency or service, or

(iii) refuses to participate in a social service or targeted assistance program referred to in subparagraph (A)(ii) which such agency or service determines to be available and appropriate,

cash assistance to the refugee shall be terminated (after opportunity for an administrative hearing) for a period of three months (for the first such refusal) or for a period of six months for any subsequent refusal.

(3) The Director shall develop plans to provide English training and other appropriate services and training to refugees receiving cash assistance.

(4) If a refugee is eligible for aid or assistance under a State plan approved under part A of title IV or under title XIX of the Social Security Act [42 U.S.C.A §§ 601 et seq., 1396 et seq.], or for supplemental security income benefits (including State supplementary payments) under the program established under title XVI of that Act [42 U.S.C.A. § 1381 et seq.], funds authorized under this subsection shall only be used for the non-Federal share of such aid or assistance, or for such supplementary payments, with respect to cash and medical assistance provided with respect to such refugee under this paragraph.

(5) The Director is authorized to allow for the provision of medical assistance under paragraph (1) to any refugee, during the one-year period after entry, who does not qualify for assistance under a State plan approved under title XIX of the Social Security Act [42 U.S.C.A. § 1396 et seq.] on account of any resources or income requirement of such plan, but only if the Director determines that—

(A) this will (i) encourage economic self-sufficiency, or (ii) avoid a significant burden on State and local governments; and

(B) the refugee meets such alternative financial resources and income requirements as the Director shall establish.

(6) As a condition for receiving assistance, reimbursement, or a contract under this subsection and notwithstanding any other provision of law, a State or agency must provide assurances that whenever a refugee applies for cash or medical assistance for which assistance or reimbursement is provided under this subsection, the State or agency must notify promptly the agency (or local affiliate) which provided for the initial resettlement of the refugee under subsection (b) of the fact that the refugee has so applied.

(7)(A) The Secretary shall develop and implement alternative projects for refugees who have been in the United States less than thirty-six months, under which refugees are provided interim support, medical services, support services, and case management, as needed, in a manner that encourages self-sufficiency, reduces welfare dependency, and fosters greater coordination among the resettlement agencies and service providers. The Secretary may permit alternative projects to cover specific groups of refugees who have been in the United States 36 months or longer if the Secretary determines that refugees in the group have been significantly and disproportionately dependent on welfare and need the services provided under the project in order to become self-sufficient and that their coverage under the projects would be cost-effective.

(B) Refugees covered under such alternative projects shall be precluded from receiving cash or medical assistance under any other paragraph of this subsection or under title XIX or part A of title IV of the Social Security Act [42 U.S.C.A. §§ 601 et seq., 1396 et seq.].

(C) The Secretary shall report to Congress not later than October 31, 1985, on the results of these projects and on any recommendations respecting changes in the refugee assistance program under this section to take into account such results.

(D) To the extent that the use of such funds is consistent with the purposes of such provisions, funds appropriated under section 414(a) [8 U.S.C.A. § 1524(a)], part A of title IV of the Social Security Act [42 U.S.C.A. § 601 et seq.], or title XIX of such Act [42 U.S.C.A. § 1396 et seq.], may be used for the purpose of implementing and evaluating alternative projects under this paragraph.

(8) In its provision of assistance to refugees, a State or political subdivision shall consider the recommendations of, and assistance provided by, agencies with grants or contracts under subsection (b)(1).

(f) Assistance to States and counties for incarceration of certain Cuban nationals; priority for removal and return to Cuba

(1) The Attorney General shall pay compensation to States and to counties for costs incurred by the States and counties to confine in prisons, during the fiscal year for which such payment is made, nationals of Cuba who—

(A) were paroled into the United States in 1980 by the Attorney General,

(B) after such parole committed any violation of State or county law for which a term of imprisonment was imposed, and

(C) at the time of such parole and such violation were not aliens lawfully admitted to the United States—

(i) for permanent residence, or

(ii) under the terms of an immigrant or a nonimmigrant visa issued,

under this Act.

(2) For a State or county to be eligible to receive compensation under this subsection, the chief executive officer of the State or county shall submit to the Attorney General, in accordance with rules to be issued by the Attorney General, an application containing—

(A) the number and names of the Cuban nationals with respect to whom the State or county is entitled to such compensation, and

(B) such other information as the Attorney General may require.

(3) For a fiscal year the Attorney General shall pay the costs described in paragraph (1) to each State and county determined by the Attorney General to be eligible under paragraph (2); except that if the amounts appropriated for the fiscal year to carry out this subsection are insufficient to cover all such payments, each of such payments shall be ratably reduced so that the total of such payments equals the amount so appropriated.

(4) The authority of the Attorney General to pay compensation under this subsection shall be effective for any fiscal year only to the extent and in such amounts as may be provided in advance in appropriation Acts.

(5) Priority for removal and return to Cuba of certain Cuban nationals.

It shall be the policy of the United States Government that the President, in consultation with the Attorney General and all other appropriate Federal officials and all appropriate State and county officials referred to in paragraph (2), shall place top priority on seeking the expeditious removal from this country and the return to Cuba of Cuban nationals described in paragraph (1) by any reasonable and responsible means, and to this end the Attorney General may use the funds authorized to carry out this subsection to conduct such policy.

(June 27, 1952, c. 477, Title IV, ch. 2, § 412, as added Mar. 17, 1980, Pub.L. 96–212, Title III, § 311(a)(2), 94 Stat. 111, and amended Oct. 25, 1982, Pub.L. 97–363, §§ 3(a), 4 to 6, 96 Stat. 1734 to 1736; Nov. 22, 1983, Pub.L. 98–164, Title X, § 1011 (b), 97 Stat. 1061; Oct. 12, 1984, Pub.L. 98–473 Title I, § 101(d), 98 Stat. 1877; Pub.L. 99–605, §§ 3, 4, 5(a), (b), (c), 6(a), (b), (d), 8, 9(a), (b), 10, 12,

13, Nov. 6, 1986, 100 Stat. 3449 to 3451, 3453 to 3455; Oct. 24, 1988, Pub.L. 100–525, § 6(b), 102 Stat. 2616; Apr. 30, 1994, Pub.L. 103–236, Title I, § 162(n)(2), 108 Stat. 409; Oct. 25, 1994, Pub.L. 103–416, Title II, § 219(x), 108 Stat. 4318; Aug. 22, 1996, Pub.L. 104–193, Title I, § 110(s)(3), 110 Stat. 2175; Sept. 30, 1996, Pub.L. 104–208, Div. C, Title VI, § 671(e)(7), 110 Stat. 3009–723.)

§ 413. Congressional reports [8 U.S.C.A. § 1523]

(a) The Secretary shall submit a report on activities under this chapter to the Committees on the Judiciary of the House of Representatives and of the Senate not later than the January 31 following the end of each fiscal year, beginning with fiscal year 1980.

(b) Each such report shall contain—

(1) an updated profile of the employment and labor force statistics for refugees who have entered the United States within the five-fiscal-year period immediately preceding the fiscal year within which the report is to be made and for refugees who entered earlier and who have shown themselves to be significantly and disproportionately dependent on welfare, as well as a description of the extent to which refugees received the forms of assistance or services under this chapter during that period;

(2) a description of the geographic location of refugees;

(3) a summary of the results of the monitoring and evaluation conducted under section 412(a)(7) [8 U.S.C.A. § 1522(a)(7)] during the period for which the report is submitted;

(4) a description of **(A)** the activities, expenditures, and policies of the Office under this chapter and of the activities of States, voluntary agencies, and sponsors, and **(B)** the Director's plans for improvement of refugee resettlement;

(5) evaluations of the extent to which **(A)** the services provided under this chapter are assisting refugees in achieving economic self-sufficiency, achieving ability in English, and achieving employment commensurate with their skills and abilities, and **(B)** any fraud, abuse, or mismanagement has been reported in the provisions of services or assistance;

(6) a description of any assistance provided by the Director pursuant to section 412(e)(5) [8 U.S.C.A. § 1522(e)(5)] ;

(7) a summary of the location and status of unaccompanied refugee children admitted to the United States; and

(8) a summary of the information compiled and evaluation made under section 412(a)(8) [8 U.S.C.A. § 1522(a)(8)] .

(June 27, 1952, c. 477, Title IV, ch. 2, § 413, as added Mar. 17, 1980, Pub.L. 96–212, Title III, § 311(a) (2), 94 Stat. 115, and amended Oct. 25, 1982, Pub.L. 97–363, §§ 3(b), 7, 96 Stat. 1734, 1737; Pub.L. 99–605, § 11, Nov. 6, 1986, 100 Stat. 3455; Oct. 24, 1988, Pub.L. 100–525, § 9(jj), 102 Stat. 2622; Apr. 30, 1994, Pub.L. 103–236, Title I, § 162(n)(3), 108 Stat. 409.)

§ 414. Authorization of appropriations [8 U.S.C.A. § 1524]

(a) There are authorized to be appropriated for each of fiscal years 2000 through 2002 such sums as may be necessary to carry out this chapter.

(b) The authority to enter into contracts under this chapter shall be effective for any fiscal year only to such extent or in such amounts as are provided in advance in appropriation Acts.

(June 27, 1952, c. 477, Title IV, ch. 2, § 414, as added Mar. 17, 1980, Pub.L. 96–212, Title III, § 311(a)(2), 94 Stat. 116, and amended Oct. 25, 1982, Pub.L. 97–363, § 2, 96 Stat. 1734; Nov. 6, 1986, Pub.L. 99–605, § 2, 100 Stat. 3449; Oct. 24, 1988, Pub.L. 100–525, § 6(a), 102 Stat. 2616; Oct. 1, 1991, Pub.L. 102–110, § 5, 105 Stat. 558; June 8, 1993, Pub.L. 103–37, § 1, 107 Stat. 107; Oct. 25, 1994, Pub.L. 103–416, Title II, § 208, 108 Stat. 4312; Nov. 13, 1997, Pub.L. 105–78, Title VI, § 604(a), 111 Stat. 1521; Dec. 2, 1997, Pub.L. 105–136, § 1(a), 111 Stat. 2639; Nov. 13, 1999, Pub.L. 106–104, § 3, 113 Stat. 1483.)

TITLE V

ALIEN TERRORIST REMOVAL PROCEDURES

§ 501. Definitions [8 U.S.C.A. § 1531]

As used in this title—

(1) the term "alien terrorist" means any alien described in section 237(a)(4)(B) [8 U.S.C.A. § 1227(a)(4)(B)];

(2) the term "classified information" has the same meaning as in section 1(a) of the Classified Information Procedures Act (18 U.S.C. App.);

(3) the term "national security" has the same meaning as in section 1(b) of the Classified Information Procedures Act (18 U.S.C. App.);

(4) the term "removal court" means the court described in section 502 [8 U.S.C.A. § 1532];

(5) the term "removal hearing" means the hearing described in section 504 [8 U.S.C.A. § 1534];

(6) the term "removal proceeding" means a proceeding under this title; and

(7) the term "special attorney" means an attorney who is on the panel established under section 502(e) [8 U.S.C.A. § 1532(e)].

(June 27, 1952, c. 477, Title V, § 501, as added Apr. 24, 1996, Pub.L. 104–132, Title IV, § 401(a), 110 Stat. 1259, and amended Sept. 30, 1996, Pub.L. 104–208, Title III, §§ 308(g)(1), 354(a)(5), 110 Stat. 3009–622, 3009–643.)

§ 502. Establishment of removal court [8 U.S.C.A. § 1532]

(a) Designation of judges

The Chief Justice of the United States shall publicly designate 5 district court judges from 5 of the United States judicial circuits who shall constitute a court that shall have jurisdiction to conduct all removal proceedings. The Chief Justice may, in the Chief Justice's discretion, designate the same judges under this section as are designated pursuant to section 103(a) of the Foreign Intelligence Surveillance Act of 1978 (50 U.S.C. 1803(a)).

(b) Terms

Each judge designated under subsection (a) shall serve for a term of 5 years and shall be eligible for redesignation, except that of the members first designated—

(1) 1 member shall serve for a term of 1 year;

(2) 1 member shall serve for a term of 2 years;

(3) 1 member shall serve for a term of 3 years; and

(4) 1 member shall serve for a term of 4 years.

(c) Chief judge

(1) Designation

The Chief Justice shall publicly designate one of the judges of the removal court to be the chief judge of the removal court.

(2) Responsibilities

The chief judge shall—

(A) promulgate rules to facilitate the functioning of the removal court; and

(B) assign the consideration of cases to the various judges on the removal court.

(d) Expeditious and confidential nature of proceedings

The provisions of section 103(c) of the Foreign Intelligence Surveillance Act of 1978 (50 U.S.C. 1803(c)) shall apply to removal proceedings in the same manner as they apply to proceedings under that Act.

(e) Establishment of panel of special attorneys

The removal court shall provide for the designation of a panel of attorneys each of whom—

(1) has a security clearance which affords the attorney access to classified information, and

(2) has agreed to represent permanent resident aliens with respect to classified information under section 504(e)(3) [8 U.S.C.A. § 1534(e)(3)] in accordance with (and subject to the penalties under) this title.

(June 27, 1952, c. 477, Title V, § 502, as added Apr. 24, 1996, Pub.L. 104–132, Title IV, § 401(a), 110 Stat. 1259, and amended Sept. 30, 1996, Pub.L. 104–208, Div. C, Title III, § 354(a)(4), 110 Stat. 3009–643.)

§ 503. Removal court procedure [8 U.S.C.A. § 1533]

(a) Application

(1) In general

In any case in which the Attorney General has classified information that an alien is an alien terrorist, the Attorney General may seek removal of the alien under this title by filing an application with the removal court that contains—

(A) the identity of the attorney in the Department of Justice making the application;

(B) a certification by the Attorney General or the Deputy Attorney General that the application satisfies the criteria and requirements of this section;

(C) the identity of the alien for whom authorization for the removal proceeding is sought; and

(D) a statement of the facts and circumstances relied on by the Department of Justice to establish probable cause that—

(i) the alien is an alien terrorist;

(ii) the alien is physically present in the United States; and

(iii) with respect to such alien, removal under title II would pose a risk to the national security of the United States.

(2) Filing

An application under this section shall be submitted ex parte and in camera, and shall be filed under seal with the removal court.

(b) Right to dismiss

The Attorney General may dismiss a removal action under this title at any stage of the proceeding.

(c) Consideration of application

(1) Basis for decision

In determining whether to grant an application under this section, a single judge of the removal court may consider, ex parte and in camera, in addition to the information contained in the application—

(A) other information, including classified information, presented under oath or affirmation; and

(B) testimony received in any hearing on the application, of which a verbatim record shall be kept.

(2) Approval of order

The judge shall issue an order granting the application, if the judge finds that there is probable cause to believe that—

(A) the alien who is the subject of the application has been correctly identified and is an alien terrorist present in the United States; and

(B) removal under title II would pose a risk to the national security of the United States.

(3) Denial of order

If the judge denies the order requested in the application, the judge shall prepare a written statement of the reasons for the denial, taking all necessary precautions not to disclose any classified information contained in the Government's application.

(d) Exclusive provisions

If an order is issued under this section granting an application, the rights of the alien regarding removal and expulsion shall be governed solely by this title, and except as they are specifically referenced in this title, no other provisions of this Act shall be applicable.

(June 27, 1952, c. 477, Title V, § 503, as added Apr. 24, 1996, Pub.L. 104–132, Title IV, § 401(a), 110 Stat. 1259.)

§ 504. Removal hearing [8 U.S.C.A. § 1534]

(a) In general

(1) Expeditious hearing

In any case in which an application for an order is approved under section 503(c)(2) [8 U.S.C.A. § 1533(c)(2)], a removal hearing shall be conducted under this section as expeditiously as practicable for the purpose of determining whether the alien to whom the order pertains should be removed from the United States on the grounds that the alien is an alien terrorist.

(2) Public hearing

The removal hearing shall be open to the public.

(b) Notice

An alien who is the subject of a removal hearing under this title shall be given reasonable notice of—

(1) the nature of the charges against the alien, including a general account of the basis for the charges; and

(2) the time and place at which the hearing will be held.

(c) Rights in hearing

(1) Right of counsel

The alien shall have a right to be present at such hearing and to be represented by counsel. Any alien financially unable to obtain counsel shall be entitled to have counsel assigned to represent the alien. Such counsel shall be appointed by the judge pursuant to the plan for furnishing representation for any person financially unable to obtain adequate representation for the district in which the hearing is conducted, as provided for in section 3006A of Title 18. All provisions of that section shall apply and, for purposes of determining the maximum amount of compensation, the matter shall be treated as if a felony was charged.

(2) Introduction of evidence

Subject to the limitations in subsection (e), the alien shall have a reasonable opportunity to introduce evidence on the alien's own behalf.

(3) Examination of witnesses

Subject to the limitations in subsection (e), the alien shall have a reasonable opportunity to examine the evidence against the alien and to cross-examine any witness.

(4) Record

A verbatim record of the proceedings and of all testimony and evidence offered or produced at such a hearing shall be kept.

(5) Removal decision based on evidence at hearing

The decision of the judge regarding removal shall be based only on that evidence introduced at the removal hearing.

(d) Subpoenas

(1) Request

At any time prior to the conclusion of the removal hearing, either the alien or the Department of Justice may request the judge to issue a subpoena for the presence of a named witness (which subpoena may also command the person to whom it is directed to produce books, papers, documents, or other objects designated therein) upon a satisfactory showing that the presence of the witness is necessary for the determination of any material matter. Such a request may be made ex parte except that the judge shall inform the Department of Justice of any request for a subpoena by the alien for a witness or material if compliance with such a subpoena would reveal classified evidence or the source of that evidence. The Department of Justice shall be given a reasonable opportunity to oppose the issuance of such a subpoena.

(2) Payment for attendance

If an application for a subpoena by the alien also makes a showing that the alien is financially unable to pay for the attendance of a witness so requested, the court may order the costs incurred by the process and the fees of the witness so subpoenaed to be paid from funds appropriated for the enforcement of title II.

(3) Nationwide service

A subpoena under this subsection may be served anywhere in the United States.

(4) Witness fees

A witness subpoenaed under this subsection shall receive the same fees and expenses as a witness subpoenaed in connection with a civil proceeding in a court of the United States.

(5) No access to classified information

Nothing in this subsection is intended to allow an alien to have access to classified information.

(e) Discovery

(1) In general

For purposes of this title—

(A) the Government is authorized to use in a removal proceedings [sic] the fruits of electronic surveillance and unconsented physical searches authorized under the Foreign Intelligence Surveillance Act of 1978 (50 U.S.C. 1801 et seq.) without regard to subsections (c), (e), (f), (g), and (h) of section 106 of that Act [50 U.S.C.A. § 1806(c), (e), (f), (g), (h)] and discovery of information derived pursuant to such Act, or otherwise collected for national security purposes, shall not be authorized if disclosure would present a risk to the national security of the United States;

(B) an alien subject to removal under this title shall not be entitled to suppress evidence that the alien alleges was unlawfully obtained; and

(C) section 3504 of Title 18, and section 1806(c) of Title 50, shall not apply if the Attorney General determines that public disclosure would pose a risk to the national security of the United States because it would disclose classified information or otherwise threaten the integrity of a pending investigation.

(2) Protective orders

Nothing in this title shall prevent the United States from seeking protective orders and from asserting privileges ordinarily available to the United States to protect against the disclosure of classified information, including the invocation of the military and State secrets privileges.

(3) Treatment of classified information

(A) Use

The judge shall examine, ex parte and in camera, any evidence for which the Attorney General determines that public disclosure would pose a risk to the national security of the United States or to the security of any individual because it would disclose classified information and neither the alien nor the public shall be informed of such evidence or its sources other than through reference to the summary provided pursuant to this paragraph. Notwithstanding the previous sentence, the Department of Justice may, in its discretion and, in the case of classified information, after coordination with the originating agency, elect to introduce such evidence in open session.

(B) Submission

With respect to such information, the Government shall submit to the removal court an unclassified summary of the specific evidence that does not pose that risk.

(C) Approval

Not later than 15 days after submission, the judge shall approve the summary if the judge finds that it is sufficient to enable the alien to prepare a defense. The Government shall deliver to the alien a copy of the unclassified summary approved under this subparagraph.

(D) Disapproval

(i) In general

If an unclassified summary is not approved by the removal court under subparagraph (C), the Government shall be afforded 15 days to correct the deficiencies identified by the court and submit a revised unclassified summary.

(ii) Revised summary

If the revised unclassified summary is not approved by the court within 15 days of its submission pursuant to subparagraph (C), the removal hearing shall be terminated unless the judge makes the findings under clause (iii).

(iii) Findings

The findings described in this clause are, with respect to an alien, that—

(I) the continued presence of the alien in the United States would likely cause serious and irreparable harm to the national security or death or serious bodily injury to any person, and

(II) the provision of the summary would likely cause serious and irreparable harm to the national security or death or serious bodily injury to any person.

(E) Continuation of hearing without summary

If a judge makes the findings described in subparagraph (D)(iii)—

(i) if the alien involved is an alien lawfully admitted for permanent residence, the procedures described in subparagraph (F) shall apply; and

(ii) in all cases the special removal hearing shall continue, the Department of Justice shall cause to be delivered to the alien a statement that no summary is possible, and the classified information submitted in camera and ex parte may be used pursuant to this paragraph.

(F) Special procedures for access and challenges to classified information by special attorneys in case of lawful permanent aliens

(i) In general

The procedures described in this subparagraph are that the judge (under rules of the removal court) shall designate a special attorney to assist the alien—

(I) by reviewing in camera the classified information on behalf of the alien, and

(II) by challenging through an in camera proceeding the veracity of the evidence contained in the classified information.

(ii) Restrictions on disclosure

A special attorney receiving classified information under clause (i)—

(I) shall not disclose the information to the alien or to any other attorney representing the alien, and

(II) who discloses such information in violation of subclause (I) shall be subject to a fine under Title 18, imprisoned for not less than 10 years nor more than 25 years, or both.

(f) Arguments

Following the receipt of evidence, the Government and the alien shall be given fair opportunity to present argument as to whether the evidence is sufficient to justify the removal of the alien. The Government shall open the argument. The alien shall be permitted to reply. The Government shall then be permitted to reply in rebuttal. The judge may allow any part of the argument that refers to evidence received in camera and ex parte to be heard in camera and ex parte.

(g) Burden of proof

In the hearing, it is the Government's burden to prove, by the preponderance of the evidence, that the alien is subject to removal because the alien is an alien terrorist.

(h) Rules of evidence

The Federal Rules of Evidence shall not apply in a removal hearing.

(i) Determination of deportation

If the judge, after considering the evidence on the record as a whole, finds that the Government has met its burden, the judge shall order the alien removed and detained pending removal from the United States. If the alien was released pending the removal hearing, the judge shall order the Attorney General to take the alien into custody.

(j) Written order

At the time of issuing a decision as to whether the alien shall be removed, the judge shall prepare a written order containing a statement of facts found and conclusions of law. Any portion of the order that would reveal the substance or source of information received in camera and ex parte pursuant to subsection (e) shall not be made available to the alien or the public.

(k) No right to ancillary relief

At no time shall the judge consider or provide for relief from removal based on—

(1) asylum under section 208 [8 U.S.C.A. § 1158];

(2) by [sic] withholding of removal under section 237(b)(3) [8 U.S.C.A. § 1227(b)(3)];

(3) cancellation of removal under section 240A [8 U.S.C.A. § 1229b];

(4) voluntary departure under section 244(e) [8 U.S.C.A. § 1254(e)];

(5) adjustment of status under section 245 [8 U.S.C.A. § 1255]; or

(6) registry under section 249 [8 U.S.C.A. § 1259].

(June 27, 1952, c. 477, Title V, § 504, as added Apr. 24, 1996, Pub.L. 104–132, Title IV, § 401(a), 110 Stat. 1260, and amended Sept. 30, 1996, Pub.L. 104–208, Div. C, Title III, §§ 308(g)(7)(B), (8)(B), 354(a)(1), (2), (b), 357, 110 Stat. 3009–623, 3009–624, 3009–641 to 3009–644.)

§ 505. Appeals [8 U.S.C.A. § 1535]

(a) Appeal of denial of application for removal proceedings

(1) In general

The Attorney General may seek a review of the denial of an order sought in an application filed pursuant to section 503 [8 U.S.C.A. § 1533]. The appeal shall be filed in the United States Court of Appeals for the District of Columbia Circuit by notice of appeal filed not later than 20 days after the date of such denial.

(2) Record on appeal

The entire record of the proceeding shall be transmitted to the Court of Appeals under seal, and the Court of Appeals shall hear the matter ex parte.

(3) Standard of review

The Court of Appeals shall—

(A) review questions of law de novo; and

(B) set aside a finding of fact only if such finding was clearly erroneous.

(b) Appeal of determination regarding summary of classified information

(1) In general

The United States may take an interlocutory appeal to the United States Court of Appeals for the District of Columbia Circuit of—

(A) any determination by the judge pursuant to section 504(e)(3) [8 U.S.C.A. § 1534(e)(3)]; or

(B) the refusal of the court to make the findings permitted by section 504(e)(3) [8 U.S.C.A. § 1534(e)(3)].

(2) Record

In any interlocutory appeal taken pursuant to this subsection, the entire record, including any proposed order of the judge, any classified information and the summary of evidence, shall be transmitted to the Court of Appeals. The classified information shall be transmitted under seal. A verbatim record of such appeal shall be kept under seal in the event of any other judicial review.

(c) Appeal of decision in hearing

(1) In general

Subject to paragraph (2), the decision of the judge after a removal hearing may be appealed by either the alien or the Attorney General to the United States Court of Appeals for the District of Columbia Circuit by notice of appeal filed not later than 20 days after the date on which the order is issued. The order shall not be enforced during the pendency of an appeal under this subsection.

(2) Automatic appeals in cases of permanent resident aliens in which no summary provided

(A) In general

Unless the alien waives the right to a review under this paragraph, in any case involving an alien lawfully admitted for permanent residence who is denied a written summary of classified information under section 504(e)(3) [8 U.S.C.A. § 1534(e)(3)] and with respect to which the procedures described in section 504(e)(3)(F) [8 U.S.C.A. § 1534(e)(3)(F)] apply, any order issued by the judge shall be reviewed by the Court of Appeals for the District of Columbia Circuit.

(B) Use of special attorney

With respect to any issue relating to classified information that arises in such review, the alien shall be represented only by the special attorney designated under section 504(e)(3)(F)(i) [8 U.S.C.A. § 1534(e)(3)(F)(i)] on behalf of the alien.

(3) Transmittal of record

In an appeal or review to the Court of Appeals pursuant to this subsection—

(A) the entire record shall be transmitted to the Court of Appeals; and

(B) information received in camera and ex parte, and any portion of the order that would reveal the substance or source of such information, shall be transmitted under seal.

(4) Expedited appellate proceeding

In an appeal or review to the Court of Appeals under this subsection—

(A) the appeal or review shall be heard as expeditiously as practicable and the court may dispense with full briefing and hear the matter solely on the record of the judge of the removal court and on such briefs or motions as the court may require to be filed by the parties;

(B) the Court of Appeals shall issue an opinion not later than 60 days after the date of the issuance of the final order of the district court;

(C) the court shall review all questions of law de novo; and

(D) a finding of fact shall be accorded deference by the reviewing court and shall not be set aside unless such finding was clearly erroneous, except that in the case of a review under paragraph (2) in which an alien lawfully admitted for permanent residence was denied a written summary of classified information under section 504(c)(3) [8 U.S.C.A. § 1534(c)(3)], the Court of Appeals shall review questions of fact de novo.

(d) Certiorari

Following a decision by the Court of Appeals pursuant to subsection (c), the alien or the Attorney General may petition the Supreme Court for a writ of certiorari. In any such case, any information transmitted to the Court of Appeals under seal shall, if such information is also submitted to the Supreme Court, be transmitted under seal. Any order of removal shall not be stayed pending disposition of a writ of certiorari, except as provided by the Court of Appeals or a Justice of the Supreme Court.

(e) Appeal of detention order

(1) In general

Sections 3145 through 3148 of Title 18, pertaining to review and appeal of a release or detention order, penalties for failure to appear, penalties for an offense committed while on release, and sanctions for violation of a release condition shall apply to an alien to whom section 507(b)(1) [8 U.S.C.A. § 1537(b)(1)] applies. In applying the previous sentence—

(A) for purposes of section 3145 of Title 18 an appeal shall be taken to the United States Court of Appeals for the District of Columbia Circuit; and

(B) for purposes of section 3146 of Title 18 the alien shall be considered released in connection with a charge of an offense punishable by life imprisonment.

(2) No review of continued detention

The determinations and actions of the Attorney General pursuant to section 507(b)(2)(C) [8 U.S.C.A. § 1537(b)(2)(C)] shall not be subject to judicial review, including application for a writ of habeas corpus, except for a claim by the alien that continued detention violates the alien's rights under the Constitution. Jurisdiction over any such challenge shall lie exclusively in the United States Court of Appeals for the District of Columbia Circuit.

(June 27, 1952, c. 477, Title V, § 505, as added Apr. 24, 1996, Pub.L. 104–132, Title IV, § 401(a), 110 Stat. 1263, and amended Sept. 30, 1996, Pub.L. 104–208, Div. C, Title III, § 354(a)(3), 110 Stat. 3009–642.)

§ 506. Custody and release pending removal hearing [8 U.S.C.A. § 1536]

(a) Upon filing application

(1) In general

Subject to paragraphs (2) and (3), the Attorney General may—

(A) take into custody any alien with respect to whom an application under section 503 [8 U.S.C.A. § 1533] has been filed; and

(B) retain such an alien in custody in accordance with the procedures authorized by this title.

(2) Special rules for permanent resident aliens

(A) Release hearing

An alien lawfully admitted for permanent residence shall be entitled to a release hearing before the judge assigned to hear the removal hearing. Such an alien shall be detained pending the removal hearing, unless the alien demonstrates to the court that the alien—

(i) is a person lawfully admitted for permanent residence in the United States;

(ii) if released upon such terms and conditions as the court may prescribe (including the posting of any monetary amount), is not likely to flee; and

(iii) will not endanger national security, or the safety of any person or the community, if released.

(B) Information considered

The judge may consider classified information submitted in camera and ex parte in making a determination whether to release an alien pending the removal hearing.

(3) Release if order denied and no review sought

(A) In general

Subject to subparagraph (B), if a judge of the removal court denies the order sought in an application filed pursuant to section 503 [8 U.S.C.A. § 1533], and the Attorney General does not seek review of such denial, the alien shall be released from custody.

(B) Application of regular procedures

Subparagraph (A) shall not prevent the arrest and detention of the alien pursuant to title II.

(b) Conditional release if order denied and review sought

(1) In general

If a judge of the removal court denies the order sought in an application filed pursuant to section 503 [8 U.S.C.A. § 1533] and the Attorney General seeks review of such denial, the judge shall release the alien from custody subject to the least restrictive condition, or combination of conditions, of release described in section 3142(b) and clauses (i) through (xiv) of section 3142(c)(1)(B) of Title 18, that—

(A) will reasonably assure the appearance of the alien at any future proceeding pursuant to this title; and

(B) will not endanger the safety of any other person or the community.

(2) No release for certain aliens

If the judge finds no such condition or combination of conditions, as described in paragraph (1), the alien shall remain in custody until the completion of any appeal authorized by this title.

(June 27, 1952, c. 477, Title V, § 506, as added Apr. 24, 1996, Pub.L. 104–132, Title IV, § 401(a), 110 Stat. 1265.)

§ 507. Custody and release after removal hearing [8 U.S.C.A. § 1537]

(a) Release

(1) In general

Subject to paragraph (2), if the judge decides that an alien should not be removed, the alien shall be released from custody.

(2) Custody pending appeal

If the Attorney General takes an appeal from such decision, the alien shall remain in custody, subject to the provisions of section 3142 of Title 18.

(b) Custody and removal

(1) Custody

If the judge decides that an alien shall be removed, the alien shall be detained pending the outcome of any appeal. After the conclusion of any judicial review thereof which affirms the removal order, the Attorney General shall retain the alien in custody and remove the alien to a country specified under paragraph (2).

(2) Removal

(A) In general

The removal of an alien shall be to any country which the alien shall designate if such designation does not, in the judgment of the Attorney General, in consultation with the Secretary of State, impair the obligation of the United States under any treaty (including a treaty pertaining to extradition) or otherwise adversely affect the foreign policy of the United States.

(B) Alternate countries

If the alien refuses to designate a country to which the alien wishes to be removed or if the Attorney General, in consultation with the Secretary of State, determines that removal of the alien to the country so designated would impair a treaty obligation or adversely affect United States foreign policy, the Attorney General shall cause the alien to be removed to any country willing to receive such alien.

(C) Continued detention

If no country is willing to receive such an alien, the Attorney General may, notwithstanding any other provision of law, retain the alien in custody. The Attorney General, in coordination with the Secretary of State, shall make periodic efforts to reach agreement with other countries to accept such an alien and at least every 6 months shall provide to the attorney representing the alien at the removal hearing a written report on the Attorney General's efforts. Any alien in custody pursuant to this subparagraph shall be released from custody solely at the discretion of the Attorney General and subject to such conditions as the Attorney General shall deem appropriate.

(D) Fingerprinting

Before an alien is removed from the United States pursuant to this subsection, or pursuant to an order of removal because such alien is inadmissible under section 212(a)(3)(B) [8 U.S.C.A. § 1182(a)(3)(B)], the alien shall be photographed and fingerprinted, and shall be advised of the provisions of section 276(b) [8 U.S.C.A. § 1326(b)].

(c) Continued detention pending trial

(1) Delay in removal

The Attorney General may hold in abeyance the removal of an alien who has been ordered removed, pursuant to this title, to allow the trial of such alien on any Federal or State criminal charge and the service of any sentence of confinement resulting from such a trial.

(2) Maintenance of custody

Pending the commencement of any service of a sentence of confinement by an alien described in paragraph (1), such an alien shall remain in the custody of the Attorney General, unless the Attorney General determines that temporary release of the alien to the custody of State authorities for confinement in a State facility is appropriate and would not endanger national security or public safety.

(3) Subsequent removal

Following the completion of a sentence of confinement by an alien described in paragraph (1), or following the completion of State criminal proceedings which do not result in a sentence of confinement of an alien released to the custody of State authorities pursuant to paragraph (2), such an alien shall be returned to the custody of the Attorney General who shall proceed to the removal of the alien under this title.

(d) Application of certain provisions relating to escape of prisoners

For purposes of sections 751 and 752 of Title 18, an alien in the custody of the Attorney General pursuant to this title shall be subject to the penalties provided by those sections in relation to a person committed to the custody of the Attorney General by virtue of an arrest on a charge of a felony.

(e) Rights of aliens in custody

(1) Family and attorney visits

An alien in the custody of the Attorney General pursuant to this title shall be given reasonable opportunity, as determined by the Attorney General, to communicate with and receive visits from members of the alien's family, and to contact, retain, and communicate with an attorney.

(2) Diplomatic contact

An alien in the custody of the Attorney General pursuant to this title shall have the right to contact an appropriate diplomatic or consular official of the alien's country of citizenship or nationality or of any country providing representation services therefore. The Attorney General shall notify the appropriate embassy, mission, or consular office of the alien's detention.

(June 27, 1952, c. 477, Title V, § 507, as added Apr. 24, 1996, Pub.L. 104–132, Title IV, § 401(a), 110 Stat. 1266, and amended Pub.L. 104–208, Div. C, Title III, § 308(d)(4)(Q), Sept. 30, 1996, 110 Stat. 3009–619.)

II. ADDITIONAL STATUTES

TITLE 5. GOVERNMENT ORGANIZATION AND EMPLOYEES

The Administrative Procedure Act

Sec.

551. Definitions.
553. Rule making.
701. Application; definitions.
702. Right of review.
703. Form and venue of proceeding.
704. Actions reviewable.
705. Relief pending review.
706. Scope of review.

ADDITIONAL IMMIGRATION STATUTORY PROVISIONS

Designation and Adjustment of Soviet and Indochinese Refugees

599D. Establishing Categories of Aliens for Purposes of Refugee Determinations

599E. Adjustment of Status for Certain Soviet and Indochinese Parolees

Personal Responsibility and Work Opportunity Reconciliation Act of 1996

400. Statements of national policy concerning welfare and immigration
401. Aliens who are not qualified aliens ineligible for Federal public benefits
402. Limited eligibility of qualified aliens for certain Federal programs
403. Five-year limited eligibility of qualified aliens for Federal means-tested public benefit

404(a). Notification and information reporting

411. Aliens who are not qualified aliens or nonimmigrants ineligible for State and local public benefits
412. State authority to limit eligibility of qualified aliens for State public benefits
421. Federal attribution of sponsor's income and resources to alien
431. Definitions
432. Verification of eligibility for Federal public benefits
433. Statutory construction
434. Communication between State and local government agencies and the Immigration and Naturalization Service
435. Qualifying quarters
742. Requirements relating to provision of benefits based on citizenship, alienage, or immigration status under the National School Lunch Act, the Child Nutrition Act of 1966, and certain other Acts

Illegal Immigration Reform and Immigrant Responsibility Act of 1996

303. Apprehension and Detention of Aliens

306(c). Effective date (judicial review)

309. Effective dates, transition

Sec.
553. Authority of States and political subdivisions of States to limit assistance to aliens and to distinguish among classes of aliens in providing general cash public assistance
642. Communication between Government agencies and the Immigration and Naturalization Service
644. Information regarding female genital mutilation

Nicaraguan Adjustment and Central American Relief Act

201. Short title
202. Adjustment of status of certain Nicaraguans and Cubans
203. Modification of certain transitional rules
204. Limitation on cancellation of removal and suspensions of deportation

Haitian Refugee Immigration Fairness Act of 1998

902. Adjustment of Status for Certain Haitian Nationals

Admiral James W. Nance and Meg Donovan Foreign Relations Authorization Act

251. United States Policy Regarding Involuntary Return of Refugees

Foreign Affairs Reform and Restructuring Act

2242. United States Policy with Respect to the Involuntary Return of Persons in Danger of Subjection to Torture

---

TITLE 5

GOVERNMENT ORGANIZATION AND EMPLOYEES

[Excerpts From the Administrative Procedure Act]

§ 551. Definitions

For the purpose of this subchapter—

(1) "agency" means each authority of the Government of the United States, whether or not it is within or subject to review by another agency, but does not include—

(A) the Congress;

(B) the courts of the United States;

(C) the governments of the territories or possessions of the United States;

(D) the government of the District of Columbia;

or except as to the requirements of section 552 of this title—

(E) agencies composed of representatives of the parties or of representatives of organizations of the parties to the disputes determined by them;

(F) courts martial and military commissions;

(G) military authority exercised in the field in time of war or in occupied territory; or

(H) functions conferred by sections 1738, 1739, 1743, and 1744 of title 12; chapter 2 of title 41; subchapter II of chapter 471 of title 49; or sections 1884, 1891–1902, and former section 1641(b)(2), of title 50, appendix;

(2) "person" includes an individual, partnership, corporation, association, or public or private organization other than an agency;

(3) "party" includes a person or agency named or admitted as a party, or properly seeking and entitled as of right to be admitted as a party, in an agency proceeding, and a person or agency admitted by an agency as a party for limited purposes;

(4) "rule" means the whole or a part of an agency statement of general or particular applicability and future effect designed to implement, interpret, or prescribe law or policy or describing the organization, procedure, or practice requirements of an agency and includes the approval or prescription for the future of rates, wages, corporate or financial structures or reorganizations thereof, prices, facilities, appliances, services or allowances therefor or of valuations, costs, or accounting, or practices bearing on any of the foregoing;

(5) "rule making" means agency process for formulating, amending, or repealing a rule;

(6) "order" means the whole or a part of a final disposition, whether affirmative, negative, injunctive, or declaratory in form, of an agency in a matter other than rule making but including licensing;

(7) "adjudication" means agency process for the formulation of an order;

(8) "license" includes the whole or a part of an agency permit, certificate, approval, registration, charter, membership, statutory exemption or other form of permission;

(9) "licensing" includes agency process respecting the grant, renewal, denial, revocation, suspension, annulment, withdrawal, limitation, amendment, modification, or conditioning of a license;

(10) "sanction" includes the whole or a part of an agency—

(A) prohibition, requirement, limitation, or other condition affecting the freedom of a person;

(B) withholding of relief;

(C) imposition of penalty or fine;

(D) destruction, taking, seizure, or withholding of property;

(E) assessment of damages, reimbursement, restitution, compensation, costs, charges, or fees;

(F) requirement, revocation, or suspension of a license; or

(G) taking other compulsory or restrictive action;

(11) "relief" includes the whole or a part of an agency—

(A) grant of money, assistance, license, authority, exemption, exception, privilege, or remedy;

(B) recognition of a claim, right, immunity, privilege, exemption, or exception; or

(C) taking of other action on the application or petition of, and beneficial to, a person;

(12) "agency proceeding" means an agency process as defined by paragraphs (5), (7), and (9) of this section;

(13) "agency action" includes the whole or a part of an agency rule, order, license, sanction, relief, or the equivalent or denial thereof, or failure to act; and

(14) "ex parte communication" means an oral or written communication not on the public record with respect to which reasonable prior notice to all parties is not given, but it shall not include requests for status reports on any matter or proceeding covered by this subchapter.

(Pub.L. 89–554, Sept. 6, 1966, 80 Stat. 381; Pub.L. 94–409, § 4(b), Sept. 13, 1976, 90 Stat. 1247; Pub.L. 103–272, § 5(a), July 5, 1994, 108 Stat. 1373.)

§ 553. Rule making

(a) This section applies, according to the provisions thereof, except to the extent that there is involved—

(1) a military or foreign affairs function of the United States; or

(2) a matter relating to agency management or personnel or to public property, loans, grants, benefits, or contracts.

(b) General notice of proposed rule making shall be published in the Federal Register, unless persons subject thereto are named and either personally served or otherwise have actual notice thereof in accordance with law. The notice shall include—

(1) a statement of the time, place, and nature of public rule making proceedings;

(2) reference to the legal authority under which the rule is proposed; and

(3) either the terms or substance of the proposed rule or a description of the subjects and issues involved.

Except when notice or hearing is required by statute, this subsection does not apply—

(A) to interpretative rules, general statements of policy, or rules of agency organization, procedure, or practice; or

(B) when the agency for good cause finds (and incorporates the finding and a brief statement of reasons therefor in the rules issued)

that notice and public procedure thereon are impracticable, unnecessary, or contrary to the public interest.

(c) After notice required by this section, the agency shall give interested persons an opportunity to participate in the rule making through submission of written data, views, or arguments with or without opportunity for oral presentation. After consideration of the relevant matter presented, the agency shall incorporate in the rules adopted a concise general statement of their basis and purpose. When rules are required by statute to be made on the record after opportunity for an agency hearing, sections 556 and 557 of this title apply instead of this subsection.

(d) The required publication or service of a substantive rule shall be made not less than 30 days before its effective date, except—

(1) a substantive rule which grants or recognizes an exemption or relieves a restriction;

(2) interpretative rules and statements of policy; or

(3) as otherwise provided by the agency for good cause found and published with the rule.

(e) Each agency shall give an interested person the right to petition for the issuance, amendment, or repeal of a rule.

(Pub.L. 89–554, Sept. 6, 1966, 80 Stat. 383.)

§ 701. Application; definitions

(a) This chapter applies, according to the provisions thereof, except to the extent that—

(1) statutes preclude judicial review; or

(2) agency action is committed to agency discretion by law.

(b) For the purpose of this chapter—

(1) "agency" means each authority of the Government of the United States, whether or not it is within or subject to review by another agency, but does not include—

(A) the Congress;

(B) the courts of the United States;

(C) the governments of the territories or possessions of the United States;

(D) the government of the District of Columbia;

(E) agencies composed of representatives of the parties or of representatives of organizations of the parties to the disputes determined by them;

(F) courts martial and military commissions;

(G) military authority exercised in the field in time of war or in occupied territory; or

(H) functions conferred by sections 1738, 1739, 1743, and 1744 of title 12; chapter 2 of title 41; subchapter II of chapter 471 of title 49; or sections 1884, 1891–1902, and former section 1641(b)(2), of title 50, appendix; and

(2) "person", "rule", "order", "license", "sanction", "relief", and "agency action" have the meanings given them by section 551 of this title.

(Pub.L. 89–554, Sept. 6, 1966, 80 Stat. 392; Pub.L. 103–272, § 5(a), July 5, 1994, 108 Stat. 1373.)

§ 702. Right of review

A person suffering legal wrong because of agency action, or adversely affected or aggrieved by agency action within the meaning of a relevant statute, is entitled to judicial review thereof. An action in a court of the United States seeking relief other than money damages and stating a claim that an agency or an officer or employee thereof acted or failed to act in an official capacity or under color of legal authority shall not be dismissed nor relief therein be denied on the ground that it is against the United States or that the United States is an indispensable party. The United States may be named as a defendant in any such action, and a judgment or decree may be entered against the United States: *Provided,* That any mandatory or injunctive decree shall specify the Federal officer or officers (by name or by title), and their successors in office, personally responsible for compliance. Nothing herein **(1)** affects other limitations on judicial review or the power or duty of the court to dismiss any action or deny relief on any other appropriate legal or equitable ground; or **(2)** confers authority to grant relief if any other statute that grants consent to suit expressly or impliedly forbids the relief which is sought.

(Pub.L. 89–554, Sept. 6, 1966, 80 Stat. 392; Pub.L. 94–574, § 1, Oct. 21, 1976, 90 Stat. 2721.)

§ 703. Form and venue of proceeding

The form of proceeding for judicial review is the special statutory review proceeding relevant to the subject matter in a court specified by statute or, in the absence or inadequacy thereof, any applicable form of legal action, including actions for declaratory judgments or writs of prohibitory or mandatory injunction or habeas corpus, in a court of competent jurisdiction. If no special statutory review proceeding is applicable, the action for judicial review may be brought against the United States, the agency by its official title, or the appropriate officer. Except to the extent that prior, adequate, and exclusive opportunity for judicial review is provided by law, agency action is subject to judicial review in civil or criminal proceedings for judicial enforcement.

(Pub.L. 89–554, Sept. 6, 1966, 80 Stat. 392; Pub.L. 94–574, § 1, Oct. 21, 1976, 90 Stat. 2721.)

§ 704. Actions reviewable

Agency action made reviewable by statute and final agency action for which there is no other adequate remedy in a court are subject to judicial review. A preliminary, procedural, or intermediate agency action or ruling not directly reviewable is subject to review on the review of the final agency action. Except as otherwise expressly required by statute, agency action otherwise final is final for the purposes of this section whether or not there has been presented or determined an application for a declaratory order, for any form of reconsiderations, or, unless the agency otherwise requires by rule and provides that the action meanwhile is inoperative, for an appeal to superior agency authority.

(Pub.L. 89–554, Sept. 6, 1966, 80 Stat. 392.)

§ 705. Relief pending review

When an agency finds that justice so requires, it may postpone the effective date of action taken by it, pending judicial review. On such conditions as may be required and to the extent necessary to prevent irreparable injury, the reviewing court, including the court to which a case may be taken on appeal from or on application for certiorari or other writ to a reviewing court, may issue all necessary and appropriate process to postpone the effective date of an agency action or to preserve status or rights pending conclusion of the review proceedings.

(Pub.L. 89–554, Sept. 6, 1966, 80 Stat. 393.)

§ 706. Scope of review

To the extent necessary to decision and when presented, the reviewing court shall decide all relevant questions of law, interpret constitutional and statutory provisions, and determine the meaning or applicability of the terms of an agency action. The reviewing court shall—

(1) compel agency action unlawfully withheld or unreasonably delayed; and

(2) hold unlawful and set aside agency action, findings, and conclusions found to be—

(A) arbitrary, capricious, an abuse of discretion, or otherwise not in accordance with law;

(B) contrary to constitutional right, power, privilege, or immunity;

(C) in excess of statutory jurisdiction, authority, or limitations, or short of statutory right;

(D) without observance of procedure required by law;

(E) unsupported by substantial evidence in a case subject to sections 556 and 557 of this title or otherwise reviewed on the record of an agency hearing provided by statute; or

(F) unwarranted by the facts to the extent that the facts are subject to trial de novo by the reviewing court.

In making the foregoing determinations, the court shall review the whole record or those parts of it cited by a party, and due account shall be taken of the rule of prejudicial error.

(Pub.L. 89–554, Sept. 6, 1966, 80 Stat. 393.)

ADDITIONAL IMMIGRATION STATUTORY PROVISIONS

DESIGNATION AND ADJUSTMENT OF SOVIET AND INDOCHINESE REFUGEES

§ 599D. Establishing Categories of Aliens for Purposes of Refugee Determinations [8 U.S.C.A. § 1157, Note]

(a) In General.—In the case of an alien who is within a category of aliens established under subsection (b), the alien may establish, for purposes of admission as a refugee under section 207 of the Immigration and Nationality Act, that the alien has a well-founded fear of persecution on account of race, religion, nationality, membership in a particular social group, or political opinion by asserting such a fear and asserting a credible basis for concern about the possibility of such persecution.

(b) Establishment of Categories.—

(1) For purposes of subsection (a), the Attorney General, in consultation with the Secretary of State and the Coordinator for Refugee Affairs, shall establish—

(A) one or more categories of aliens who are or were nationals and residents of an independent state of the former Soviet Union or of Estonia, Latvia, or Lithuania and who share common characteristics that identify them as targets of persecution in that state on account of race, religion, nationality, membership in a particular social group, or political opinion, and

(B) one or more categories of aliens who are or were nationals and residents of Vietnam, Laos, or Cambodia and who share common characteristics that identify them as targets of persecution in such respective foreign state on such an account.

(2)(A) Aliens who are (or were) nationals and residents of an independent state of the former Soviet Union or of Estonia, Latvia, or Lithuania and who are Jews or Evangelical Christians shall be deemed a category of alien established under paragraph (1)(A).

(B) Aliens who are (or were) nationals of an independent state of the former Soviet Union or of Estonia, Latvia, or Lithuania and who are current members of, and demonstrate public, active, and continuous participation (or attempted participation) in the religious activities of, the Ukrainian Catholic Church or the Ukrainian Orthodox Church, shall be deemed a category of alien established under paragraph (1)(A).

(C) Aliens who are (or were) nationals and residents of Vietnam, Laos, or Cambodia and who are members of categories of individuals determined, by the Attorney General in accordance with 'Immigration and Naturalization Service Worldwide Guidelines for Overseas Refugee Processing' (issued by the Immigration and Naturalization Service in August 1983) shall be deemed a category of alien established under paragraph (1)(B).

(3) Within the number of admissions of refugees allocated for each of fiscal years 1990, 1991, and 1992 for refugees who are nationals of the Soviet Union under section 207(a)(3) of the Immigration and Nationality Act and within the number of such admissions allocated for each of fiscal years 1993, 1994, 1995, 1996, 1997, 1998, 1999, and 2000 for refugees who are nationals of the independent states of the former Soviet Union, Estonia, Latvia, and Lithuania under such section, notwithstanding any other provision of law, the President shall allocate one thousand of such admissions for such fiscal year to refugees who are within the category of aliens described in paragraph (2)(B).

(c) Written Reasons for Denials of Refugee Status.—Each decision to deny an application for refugee status of an alien who is within a category established under this section shall be in writing and shall state, to the maximum extent feasible, the reason for the denial.

(d) Permitting Certain Aliens Within Categories to Reapply for Refugee Status.—Each alien who is within a category established under this section and who (after August 14, 1988, and before the date of the enactment of this Act [Nov. 21, 1989]) was denied refugee status shall be permitted to reapply for such status. Such an application shall be determined taking into account the application of this section.

(e) Period of Application.—

(1) Subsections (a) and (b) shall take effect on the date of the enactment of this Act [Nov. 21, 1989] and shall only apply to applications for refugee status submitted before October 1, 2000.

(2) Subsection (c) shall apply to decisions made after the date of the enactment of this Act [Nov. 21, 1989] and before October 1, 2000.

(3) Subsection (d) shall take effect on the date of the enactment of this Act [Nov. 21, 1989] and shall only apply to reapplications for refugee status submitted before October 1, 1992.

(f) Repealed. Pub.L. 102–391, Title V, § 582(c), Oct. 6, 1992, 106 Stat. 1686; Pub.L. 102–511, Title IX, § 905(c), Oct. 24, 1992, 106 Stat. 3356.

(Pub.L. 101–167, Title V, § 599D, Nov. 21, 1989, 103 Stat. 1261, as amended Pub.L. 101–513, Title V, § 598(a), Nov. 5, 1990, 104 Stat. 2063; Pub.L. 102–391,

Title V, § 582(a)(1), (b)(1), and (c), Oct. 6, 1992, 106 Stat. 1686; Pub.L. 102–511, Title IX, § 905(a), (b)(1), and (c), Oct. 24, 1992, 106 Stat. 3356; Pub.L. 103–236, Title V, § 512(1), Apr. 30, 1994, 108 Stat. 466; Pub.L. 104–208, Div. A, Title I, § 101(c) [Title V, § 575(1)], Sept. 30, 1996, 110 Stat. 3009–168; Pub.L. 104–319, Title I, § 101(1), Oct. 19, 1996, 110 Stat. 3865; Pub.L. 105–118, Title V, § 574(1), Nov. 26, 1997, 111 Stat. 2432; Pub.L. 105–277, Div. A, § 101(f) [Title VII, § 705(1)], Oct. 21, 1998, 112 Stat. 2681–389; Nov. 29, 1999, Pub.L. 106–113, Div. B, § 1000(a)(4) [H.R. 3424, Title II, § 214(1)], 113 Stat. 1535, 1537.)

§ 599E. Adjustment of Status for Certain Soviet and Indochinese Parolees [8 U.S.C.A. § 1255, Note]

(a) In general.—The Attorney General shall adjust the status of an alien described in subsection (b) to that of an alien lawfully admitted for permanent residence if the alien—

(1) applies for such adjustment,

(2) has been physically present in the United States for at least 1 year and is physically present in the United States on the date the application for such adjustment is filed,

(3) is admissible to the United States as an immigrant, except as provided in subsection (c), and

(4) pays a fee (determined by the Attorney General) for the processing of such application.

(b) Aliens eligible for adjustment of status.—The benefits provided in subsection (a) shall only apply to an alien who—

(1) was a national of an independent state of the former Soviet Union, Estonia, Latvia, Lithuania, Vietnam, Laos, or Cambodia, and

(2) was inspected and granted parole into the United States during the period beginning on August 15, 1988, and ending on September 30, 2000, after being denied refugee status.

(c) Waiver of certain grounds for inadmissibility.—The provisions of paragraphs (4), (5), and (7)(A) of section 212(a) of the Immigration and Nationality Act [8 U.S.C.A. § 1182(a)] shall not apply to adjustment of status under this section and the Attorney General may waive any other provision of such section (other than paragraph (2)(C) or subparagraph (A), (B), (C), or (E) of paragraph (3)) with respect to such an adjustment for humanitarian purposes, to assure family unity, or when it is otherwise in the public interest.

(d) Date of approval.—Upon the approval of such an application for adjustment of status, the Attorney General shall create a record of the alien's admission as a lawful permanent resident as of the date of the alien's inspection and parole described in subsection (b)(2).

(e) No offset in number of visas available.—When an alien is granted the status of having been lawfully admitted for permanent residence under this section, the Secretary of State shall not be required to reduce the number of immigrant visas authorized to be issued under the Immigration and Nationality Act.

(Pub.L. 101–167, Title V, § 599E, Nov. 21, 1989, 103 Stat. 1263, as amended Pub.L. 101–513, Title V, § 598(b), Nov. 5, 1990, 104 Stat. 2063, Pub.L. 101–649, Title VI, § 603(a)(22), Nov. 29, 1990, 104 Stat. 5084; Pub.L. 102–232, Title III, 307(*l*)(9), Dec. 12, 1991, 105 Stat. 1757; Pub.L. 102–391, Title V, § 582(a)(2), (b)(2), Oct. 6, 1992, 106 Stat. 1686; Pub.L. 102–511, Title IX, § 905(b)(2), Oct. 24, 1992, 106 Stat. 3356; Pub.L. 103–236, Title V, § 512(2), Apr. 30, 1994, 108 Stat. 466; Pub.L. 103–416, Title II, § 219(bb), Oct. 25, 1994, 108 Stat. 4319; Pub.L. 104–208, Div. A, Title I, § 101(c) [Title V, § 575(2)], Sept. 30, 1996, 110 Stat. 3009–168; Pub.L. 104–319, Title I, § 101(2), Oct. 19, 1996, 110 Stat. 3865; Pub.L. 105–118, Title V, § 574(2), Nov. 26, 1997, 111 Stat. 2432; Pub.L. 105–277, Div. A, § 101(f) [Title VII, § 705(2)], Oct. 21, 1998, 112 Stat. 2681; Nov. 29, 1999, Pub.L. 106–113, Div. B, § 1000(a)(4) [H.R. 3424, Title I, § 214(2)], 113 Stat. 1535, 1537.)

PERSONAL RESPONSIBILITY AND WORK OPPORTUNITY RECONCILIATION ACT OF 1996

§ 400. Statements of national policy concerning welfare and immigration [8 U.S.C.A. § 1601]

The Congress makes the following statements concerning national policy with respect to welfare and immigration:

(1) Self-sufficiency has been a basic principle of United States immigration law since this country's earliest immigration statutes.

(2) It continues to be the immigration policy of the United States that—

(A) aliens within the Nation's borders not depend on public resources to meet their needs, but rather rely on their own capabilities and the resources of their families, their sponsors, and private organizations, and

(B) the availability of public benefits not constitute an incentive for immigration to the United States.

(3) Despite the principle of self-sufficiency, aliens have been applying for and receiving public benefits from Federal, State, and local governments at increasing rates.

(4) Current eligibility rules for public assistance and unenforceable financial support agreements have proved wholly incapable of assuring that individual aliens not burden the public benefits system.

(5) It is a compelling government interest to enact new rules for eligibility and sponsorship agreements in order to assure that aliens be self-reliant in accordance with national immigration policy.

(6) It is a compelling government interest to remove the incentive for illegal immigration provided by the availability of public benefits.

(7) With respect to the State authority to make determinations concerning the eligibility of qualified aliens for public benefits in this chapter, a State that chooses to follow the Federal classification in determining the eligibility of such aliens for public assistance shall be considered to have chosen the least restrictive means available for achieving the compelling governmental interest of assuring that aliens be self-reliant in accordance with national immigration policy.

(Pub.L. 104–193, Title IV, § 400, Aug. 22, 1996, 110 Stat. 2260.)

§ 401. Aliens who are not qualified aliens ineligible for Federal public benefits [8 U.S.C.A. § 1611]

(a) In general

Notwithstanding any other provision of law and except as provided in subsection (b) of this section, an alien who is not a qualified alien (as defined in section 1641 of this title [8 U.S.C.A. § 1641]) is not eligible for any Federal public benefit (as defined in subsection (c) of this section).

(b) Exceptions

(1) Subsection (a) of this section shall not apply with respect to the following Federal public benefits:

(A) Medical assistance under title XIX of the Social Security Act [42 U.S.C.A § 1396 et seq.] (or any successor program to such title) for care and services that are necessary for the treatment of an emergency medical condition (as defined in section 1903(v)(3) of such Act [42 U.S.C.A. § 1396b(v)(3)]) of the alien involved and are not related to an organ transplant procedure, if the alien involved otherwise meets the eligibility requirements for medical assistance under the State plan approved under such title (other than the requirement of the receipt of aid or assistance under title IV of such Act [42 U.S.C.A § 601 et seq.], supplemental security income benefits under title XVI of such Act [42 U.S.C.A. § 1381 et seq.], or a State supplementary payment).

(B) Short-term, non-cash, in-kind emergency disaster relief.

(C) Public health assistance (not including any assistance under title XIX of the Social Security Act [42 U.S.C.A. § 1396 et seq.]) for immunizations with respect to immunizable diseases and for testing and treatment of symptoms of communicable diseases whether or not such symptoms are caused by a communicable disease.

(D) Programs, services, or assistance (such as soup kitchens, crisis counseling and intervention, and short-term shelter) specified by the Attorney General, in the Attorney General's sole and unreviewable discretion after consultation with appropriate Federal agencies and departments, which (i) deliver in-kind services at the community level, including through public or private nonprofit agencies; (ii) do not condition the provision of assistance, the amount of assistance provided, or the cost of assistance provided on the individual recipient's income or resources; and (iii) are necessary for the protection of life or safety.

(E) Programs for housing or community development assistance or financial assistance administered by the Secretary of

Housing and Urban Development, any program under title V of the Housing Act of 1949 [42 U.S.C.A. § 1471 et seq.], or any assistance under section 1926C of Title 7, to the extent that the alien is receiving such a benefit on August 22, 1996.

(2) Subsection (a) of this section shall not apply to any benefit payable under title II of the Social Security Act [42 U.S.C.A. § 401 et seq.] to an alien who is lawfully present in the United States as determined by the Attorney General, to any benefit if nonpayment of such benefit would contravene an international agreement described in section 233 of the Social Security Act [42 U.S.C.A. § 433], to any benefit if nonpayment would be contrary to section 202(t) of the Social Security Act [42 U.S.C.A. § 402(t)], or to any benefit payable under title II of the Social Security Act [42 U.S.C.A. § 401 et seq.] to which entitlement is based on an application filed in or before the month in which this Act becomes law.

(3) Subsection (a) of this section shall not apply to any benefit payable under title XVIII of the Social Security Act (relating to the medicare program) [42 U.S.C.A. § 1395 et seq.] to an alien who is lawfully present in the United States as determined by the Attorney General and, with respect to benefits payable under part A of such title, who was authorized to be employed with respect to any wages attributable to employment which are counted for purposes of eligibility for such benefits.

(4) Subsection (a) of this section shall not apply to any benefit payable under the Railroad Retirement Act of 1974 [45 U.S.C.A. § 231 et seq.] or the Railroad Unemployment Insurance Act [45 U.S.C.A. § 351 et seq.] to an alien who is lawfully present in the United States as determined by the Attorney General or to an alien residing outside the United States.

(5) Subsection (a) shall not apply to eligibility for benefits for the program defined in section 1612(a)(3)(A) of this title [8 U.S.C.A. § 1612(a)(3)(A)] (relating to the supplemental security income program), or to eligibility for benefits under any other program that is based on eligibility for benefits under the program so defined, for an alien who was receiving such benefits on August 22, 1996.

(c) "Federal public benefit" defined

(1) Except as provided in paragraph (2), for purposes of this chapter the term "Federal public benefit" means—

(A) any grant, contract, loan, professional license, or commercial license provided by an agency of the United States or by appropriated funds of the United States; and

(B) any retirement, welfare, health, disability, public or assisted housing, postsecondary education, food assistance, unemployment benefit, or any other similar benefit for which payments or assistance are provided to an individual, household, or family eligibility unit by an agency of the United States or by appropriated funds of the United States.

(2) Such term shall not apply—

(A) to any contract, professional license, or commercial license for a nonimmigrant whose visa for entry is related to such employment in the United States, or to a citizen of a freely associated state, if section 141 of the applicable compact of free association approved in Public Law 99–239 [48 U.S.C.A. § 1901 note] or 99–658 [48 U.S.C.A. § 1931 note] (or a successor provision) is in effect;

(B) with respect to benefits for an alien who as a work authorized nonimmigrant or as an alien lawfully admitted for permanent residence under the Immigration and Nationality Act [8 U.S.C.A. § 1101 et seq.] qualified for such benefits and for whom the United States under reciprocal treaty agreements is required to pay benefits, as determined by the Attorney General, after consultation with the Secretary of State; or

(C) to the issuance of a professional license to, or the renewal of a professional license by, a foreign national not physically present in the United States.

(Pub.L. 104–193, Title IV, § 401, Aug. 22, 1996, 110 Stat. 2261; Pub.L. 105–33, Title V, §§ 5561, 5565, Aug. 5, 1997, 111 Stat. 638, 639; Pub.L. 105–306, §§ 2, 5(a), Oct. 28, 1998, 112 Stat. 2926, 2927.)

§ 402. Limited eligibility of qualified aliens for certain Federal programs [8 U.S.C.A. § 1612]

(a) Limited eligibility for specified Federal programs

(1) In general

Notwithstanding any other provision of law and except as provided in paragraph (2), an alien who is a qualified alien (as defined in section 1641 of this title [8 U.S.C.A. § 1641]) is not eligible for any specified Federal program (as defined in paragraph (3)).

(2) Exceptions

(A) Time-limited exception for refugees and asylees

With respect to the specified Federal programs described in paragraph (3), paragraph (1) shall not apply to an alien until 7 years after the date—

(i) an alien is admitted to the United States as a refugee under section 207 of the Immigration and Nationality Act [8 U.S.C.A. § 1157];

(ii) an alien is granted asylum under section 208 of such Act [8 U.S.C.A. § 1158];

(iii) an alien's deportation is withheld under section 243(h) of such Act [8 U.S.C.A. § 1253(h)] (as in effect immediately before the effective date [April 1, 1997] of section 307 of division C of Public Law 104–208) or section 241(b)(3) [8 U.S.C.A. § 1251(b)(3)] of such Act (as amended by section 305(a) of division C of Public Law 104–208);

(iv) an alien is granted status as a Cuban and Haitian entrant (as defined in section 501(e) of the Refugee Education Assistance Act of 1980); or

(v) an alien is admitted to the United States as an Amerasian immigrant pursuant to section 584 of the Foreign Operations, Export Financing, and Related Programs Appropriations Act, 1988 (as contained in section 101(e) of Public Law 100–202 and amended by the 9th proviso under MIGRATION AND REFUGEE ASSISTANCE in title II of the Foreign Operations, Export Financing, and Related Programs Appropriations Act, 1989, Public Law 100–461, as amended).

(B) Certain permanent resident aliens

Paragraph (1) shall not apply to an alien who—

(i) is lawfully admitted to the United States for permanent residence under the Immigration and Nationality Act [8 U.S.C.A. § 1101 et seq.]; and

(ii) (I) has worked 40 qualifying quarters of coverage as defined under title II of the Social Security Act [42 U.S.C.A. § 401 et seq.] or can be credited with such qualifying quarters as provided under section 1645 of this title, and **(II)** in the case of any such qualifying quarter creditable for any period beginning after December 31, 1996, did not receive any Federal means-tested public benefit (as provided under section 1613 of this title) during any such period.

(C) Veteran and active duty exception

Paragraph (1) shall not apply to an alien who is lawfully residing in any State and is—

(i) a veteran (as defined in section 101, 1101, or 1301, or as described in section 107 of Title 38) with a discharge characterized as an honorable discharge and not on account of alienage and who fulfills the minimum active-duty service requirements of section 5303A(d) of title 38, United States Code,

(ii) on active duty (other than active duty for training) in the Armed Forces of the United States, or

(iii) the spouse or unmarried dependent child of an individual described in clause (i) or (ii) or the unremarried surviving spouse of an individual described in clause (i) or (ii) who is deceased if the marriage fulfills the requirements of section 1304 of title 38, United States Code.

(D) Transition for aliens currently receiving benefits

(i) SSI

(I) In general

With respect to the specified Federal program described in paragraph (3)(A), during the period beginning on August 22, 1996 and ending on September 30, 1998, the Commissioner of Social Security shall redetermine the eligibility of any individual who is receiving benefits under such program as of August 22, 1996 and whose eligibility for such benefits may terminate by reason of the provisions of this subsection.

(II) Redetermination criteria

With respect to any redetermination under subclause (I), the Commissioner of Social Security shall apply the eligibility criteria for new applicants for benefits under such program.

(III) Grandfather provision

The provisions of this subsection and the redetermination under subclause (I), shall only apply with respect to the benefits of an individual described in subclause (I) for months beginning on or after September 30, 1998.

(IV) Notice

Not later than March 31, 1997, the Commissioner of Social Security shall notify an individual described in subclause (I) of the provisions of this clause.

(ii) Food stamps

(I) In general

With respect to the specified Federal program described in paragraph (3)(B), ineligibility under paragraph (1) shall not apply until April 1, 1997, to an alien who received benefits under such program on August 22, 1996, unless such alien is determined to be ineligible to receive such benefits under the Food Stamp Act of 1977 [7 U.S.C.A. § 2011 et seq.]. The State agency shall recertify the eligibility of all such aliens during the period beginning April 1, 1997, and ending August 22, 1997.

(II) recertification criteria

With respect to any recertification under subclause (I), the State agency shall apply the eligibility criteria for applicants for benefits under such program.

(III) Grandfather provision

The provisions of this subsection and the recertification under subclause (I) shall only apply with respect to the eligibility of an alien for a program for months beginning on or after the date of recertification, if on August 22, 1996 the alien is lawfully residing in any State and is receiving benefits under such program on August 22, 1996.

(E) Aliens receiving SSI on August 22, 1996

With respect to eligibility for benefits for the program defined in paragraph (3)(A) (relating to the supplemental security income program), paragraph (1) shall not apply to an alien who is lawfully residing in the United States and who was receiving such benefits on August 22, 1996.

(F) Disabled aliens lawfully residing in the United States on August 22, 1996

With respect to eligibility for benefits for the specified Federal programs described in paragraph (3), paragraph (1) shall not apply to an alien who—

(i) was lawfully residing in the United States on August 22, 1996; and

(ii)(I) in the case of the specified Federal program described in paragraph (3)(A), is blind or disabled, as defined in section 1382(a)(2) or 1382(a)(3) of Title 42; and

(II) in the case of the specified Federal programs described in paragraph (3)(B), is receiving benefits or assistance for blindness or disability (within the meaning of section 3(r) of the Food Stamp Act of 1977 (7 U.S.C. 2012(r))).

(G) Exception for certain Indians

With respect to eligibility for benefits for the specified Federal programs defined in paragraph (3), section 1611(a) of this title [8 U.S.C.A. § 1611(a)] and paragraph (1) shall not apply to any individual—

(i) who is an American Indian born in Canada to whom the provisions of section 1359 of this title [INA § 289] apply; or

(ii) who is a member of an Indian tribe (as defined in section 450b(e) of Title 25).

(H) SSI exception for certain recipients on the basis of very old applications

With respect to eligibility for benefits for the program defined in paragraph (3)(A) (relating to the supplemental security income program), paragraph (1) shall not apply to any individual—

(i) who is receiving benefits under such program for months after July 1996 on the basis of an application filed before January 1, 1979; and

(ii) with respect to whom the Commissioner of Social Security lacks clear and convincing evidence that such individual is an alien ineligible for such benefits as a result of the application of this section.

(I) Food stamp exception for certain elderly individuals

With respect to eligibility for benefits for the specified Federal program described in paragraph (3)(B), paragraph (1) shall not apply to any individual who on August 22, 1996—

(i) was lawfully residing in the United States; and

(ii) was 65 years of age or older.

(J) Food stamp exception for certain children

With respect to eligibility for benefits for the specified Federal program described in paragraph (3)(B), paragraph (1) shall not apply to any individual who—

(i) was lawfully residing in the United States on August 22, 1996; and

(ii) is under 18 years of age.

(K) Food stamp exception for certain Hmong and Highland Laotians

With respect to eligibility for benefits for the specified Federal program described in paragraph (3)(B), paragraph (1) shall not apply to—

(i) any individual who—

(I) is lawfully residing in the United States; and

(II) was a member of a Hmong or Highland Laotian tribe at the time that the tribe rendered assistance to United States personnel by taking part in a military or rescue operation during the Vietnam era (as defined in section 101 of Title 38);

(ii) the spouse, or an unmarried dependent child, of such an individual; or

(iii) the unremarried surviving spouse of such an individual who is deceased.

(3) Specified Federal program defined

For purposes of this chapter, the term "specified Federal program" means any of the following:

(A) SSI

The supplemental security income program under title XVI of the Social Security Act [42 U.S.C.A. § 1381 et seq.], including supplementary payments pursuant to an agreement for Federal administration under section 1616(a) of the Social Security Act [42 U.S.C.A. § 1382e(a)] and payments pursuant to an agreement entered into under section 212(b) of Public Law 93–66.

(B) Food stamps

The food stamp program as defined in section 2012(h) of Title 7.

(b) Limited eligibility for designated Federal programs

(1) In general

Notwithstanding any other provision of law and except as provided in section 1613 of this title and paragraph (2), a State is authorized to determine the eligibility of an alien who is a qualified alien (as defined in section 1641 of this title) for any designated Federal program (as defined in paragraph (3)).

(2) Exceptions

Qualified aliens under this paragraph shall be eligible for any designated Federal program.

(A) Time-limited exception for refugees and asylees

(i) Medicaid

With respect to the designated Federal program described in paragraph (3)(C), paragraph (1) shall not apply to an alien until 7 years after the date—

(I) an alien is admitted to the United States as a refugee under section 207 of the Immigration and Nationality Act [8 U.S.C.A. § 1157];

(II) an alien is granted asylum under section 208 of such Act [8 U.S.C.A. § 1158];

(III) an alien's deportation is withheld under section 243 of such Act [8 U.S.C.A. § 1253(h)] (as in effect immediately before the effective date [April 1, 1997] of section 307 of division C of Public Law 104–208) or section 241(b)(3) of such Act [8 U.S.C.A. § 1251(b)(3)](as amended by section 305(a) of division C of Public Law 104–208);

(IV) an alien is granted status as a Cuban and Haitian entrant (as defined in section 501(e) of the Refugee Education Assistance Act of 1980); or

(V) an alien admitted to the United States as an Amerasian immigrant as described in subsection (a)(2)(A)(i)(V) until 5 years after the date of such alien's entry into the United States.

(ii) Other designated Federal programs

With respect to the designated Federal programs under paragraph (3) (other than subparagraph (C)), paragraph (1) shall not apply to an alien until 5 years after the date—

(I) an alien is admitted to the United States as a refugee under section 207 of the Immigration and Nationality Act [8 U.S.C.A. § 1157];

(II) an alien is granted asylum under section 208 of such Act [8 U.S.C.A. § 1158];

(III) an alien's deportation is withheld under section 243(h) of such Act [8 U.S.C.A. § 1253(h)] (as in effect immediately before the effective date [April 1, 1997] of section 307 of division C of Public Law 104–208) or section 241(b)(3) of such Act [8 U.S.C.A. § 1251(b)(3)] (as amended by section 305(a) of division C of Public Law 104–208);

(IV) an alien is granted status as a Cuban and Haitian entrant (as defined in section 501(e) of the Refugee Education Assistance Act of 1980); or

(V) an alien admitted to the United States as an Amerasian immigrant as described in subsection (a)(2)(A)(i)(V) until 5 years after the date of such alien's entry into the United States.

(B) Certain permanent resident aliens

An alien who—

(i) is lawfully admitted to the United States for permanent residence under the Immigration and Nationality Act [8 U.S.C.A. § 1101 et seq.]; and

(ii)(I) has worked 40 qualifying quarters of coverage as defined under title II of the Social Security Act [42 U.S.C.A. § 401 et seq.] or can be credited with such qualifying quarters as provided under section 1645 of this title, and **(II)** in the case of any such qualifying quarter creditable for any period beginning after December 31, 1996, did not receive any Federal means-tested public benefit (as provided under section 1613 of this title) during any such period.

(C) Veteran and active duty exception

An alien who is lawfully residing in any State and is—

(i) a veteran (as defined in section 101, 1101, or 1301, or as described in section 107 of Title 38) with a discharge characterized as an honorable discharge and not on account of alienage, and who fulfills the minimum active-duty service requirements of section 5303A(d) of title 38, United States Code

(ii) on active duty (other than active duty for training) in the Armed Forces of the United States, or

(iii) the spouse or unmarried dependent child of an individual described in clause (i) or (ii) or the unremarried surviving spouse of an individual described in clause (i) or (ii) who is deceased if the marriage fulfills the requirements of section 1304 of title 38, United States Code.

(D) Transition for those currently receiving benefits

An alien who on August 22, 1996 is lawfully residing in any State and is receiving benefits under such program on August 22, 1996 shall continue to be eligible to receive such benefits until January 1, 1997.

(E) Medicaid exception for certain Indians

With respect to eligibility for benefits for the program defined in paragraph (3)(C) (relating to the medicaid program), section 1611(a) of this title [8 U.S.C.A. § 1611(a)] and paragraph (1) shall not apply to any individual described in subsection (a)(2)(G) of this section.

(F) Medicaid exception for aliens receiving SSI

An alien who is receiving benefits under the program defined in subsection (a)(3)(A) of this section (relating to the supplemental security income program) shall be eligible for medical assistance under a State plan under title XIX of the Social Security Act (42 U.S.C. § 1396 et seq.) under the same terms and conditions that apply to other recipients of benefits under the program defined in such subsection.

(3) "Designated Federal program" defined

For purposes of this title, the term "designated Federal program" means any of the following:

(A) Temporary assistance for needy families

The program of block grants to States for temporary assistance for needy families under part A of title IV of the Social Security Act [42 U.S.C.A. § 601 et seq.].

(B) Social services block grant

The program of block grants to States for social services under title XX of the Social Security Act [42 U.S.C.A. § 1397 et seq.].

(C) Medicaid

A State plan approved under title XIX of the Social Security Act [42 U.S.C.A. § 1396 et seq.], other than medical assistance described in section 1611(b)(1)(A) of this title.

(Pub.L. 104–193, Title IV, § 402, Aug. 22, 1996, 110 Stat. 2262; Pub.L. 104–208, Div. C, Title V, § 510, Sept. 30, 1996, 110 Stat. 3009–673; Pub.L. 105–18, Title II, § 6005, June 12, 1997, 111 Stat. 191; Pub.L. 105–33, Title V, §§ 5301, 5302(a), (b), 5303(a), (b), 5304, 5305(b), 5306(a), (b), 5562, 5563, Aug. 5, 1997, 111 Stat. 597, 598, 600, 601, 602, 638, 639; Pub.L. 105–185, Title V, §§ 503–508, June 23, 1998, 112 Stat. 578, 579.)

§ 403. Five-year limited eligibility of qualified aliens for Federal means-tested public benefit [8 U.S.C.A. § 1613]

(a) In general

Notwithstanding any other provision of law and except as provided in subsections (b), (c), and (d) of this section, an alien who is a qualified alien (as defined in section 1641 of this title) and who enters the United States on or after August 22, 1996 is not eligible for any Federal means-tested public benefit for a period of 5 years beginning on the date of the alien's entry into the United States with a status within the meaning of the term "qualified alien".

(b) Exceptions

The limitation under subsection (a) of this section shall not apply to the following aliens:

(1) Exception for refugees and asylees

(A) An alien who is admitted to the United States as a refugee under section 207 of the Immigration and Nationality Act [8 U.S.C.A. § 1157].

(B) An alien who is granted asylum under section 208 of such Act [8 U.S.C.A. § 1158].

(C) An alien whose deportation is being withheld under section 243(h) of such Act [8 U.S.C.A. § 1253(h)] (as in effect immediately before the effective date [April 1, 1997] of section 307 of division C of Public Law 104–208) or section 241(b)(3) of such Act [8 U.S.C.A. § 1251(b)(3)] (as amended by section 305(a) of division C of Public Law 104–208).

(D) An alien who is a Cuban and Haitian entrant as defined in section 501(e) of the Refugee Education Assistance Act of 1980.

(E) An alien admitted to the United States as an Amerasian immigrant as described in section 1612(a)(2)(A)(i)(V) of this title [8 U.S.C.A. § 1612(a)(2)(A)(i)(V)].

(2) Veteran and active duty exception

An alien who is lawfully residing in any State and is—

(A) a veteran (as defined in section 101, 1101, or 1301, or as described in section 107 of Title 38) with a discharge characterized as an honorable discharge and not on account of alienage and who fulfills the minimum active-duty service requirements of section 5303A(d) of title 38, United States Code.

(B) on active duty (other than active duty for training) in the Armed Forces of the United States, or

(C) the spouse or unmarried dependent child of an individual described in subparagraph (A) or (B) or the unremarried surviving spouse of an individual described in clause (i) or (ii) who is deceased if the marriage fulfills the requirements of section 1304 of title 38, United States Code.

(c) Application of term Federal means-tested public benefit

(1) The limitation under subsection (a) of this section shall not apply to assistance or benefits under paragraph (2).

(2) Assistance and benefits under this paragraph are as follows:

(A) Medical assistance described in section 1611(b)(1)(A) of this title.

(B) Short-term, non-cash, in-kind emergency disaster relief.

(C) Assistance or benefits under the Richard B. Russell National School Lunch Act [42 U.S.C.A. § 1751 et seq.].

(D) Assistance or benefits under the Child Nutrition Act of 1966 [42 U.S.C.A. § 1771 et seq.].

(E) Public health assistance (not including any assistance under title XIX of the Social Security Act [42 U.S.C.A. § 1396 et seq.]) for immunizations with respect to immunizable diseases and for testing and treatment of symptoms of communicable diseases whether or not such symptoms are caused by a communicable disease.

(F) Payments for foster care and adoption assistance under parts B and E of title IV of the Social Security Act [42 U.S.C.A. § 620 et seq. and § 670 et seq.] for a parent or a child who would, in the absence of subsection (a) of this section, be eligible to have such payments made on the child's behalf under such part, but only if the foster or adoptive parent (or parents) of such child is a qualified alien (as defined in section 1641 of this title [8 U.S.C.A. § 1641]).

(G) Programs, services, or assistance (such as soup kitchens, crisis counseling and intervention, and short-term shelter) specified by the Attorney General, in the Attorney General's sole and unreviewable discretion after consultation with appropriate Federal agencies and departments, which (i) deliver in-kind services at the community level, including through public or private nonprofit agencies; (ii) do not condition the provision of assistance, the amount of assistance provided, or the cost of assistance provided on the individual recipient's income or resources; and (iii) are necessary for the protection of life or safety.

(H) Programs of student assistance under titles IV, V, IX, and X of the Higher Education Act of 1965 [20 U.S.C.A. § 1070 et seq., § 1101 et seq., § 1134 et seq., and § 1135 et seq.], and titles III, VII, and VIII of the Public Health Service Act [42 U.S.C.A. § 241 et seq., § 292 et seq., and § 296 et seq.].

(I) Means-tested programs under the Elementary and Secondary Education Act of 1965 [20 U.S.C.A. § 6301 et seq.].

(J) Benefits under the Head Start Act [42 U.S.C.A. § 9831 et seq.].

(K) Benefits under the Job Training Partnership Act or title I of the Workforce Investment Act of 1998 [29 U.S.C.A. § 2801 et seq.].

(d) Benefits for certain groups

Notwithstanding any other provision of law, the limitations under section 1611(a) of this title and subsection (a) of this section shall not apply to—

(1) an individual described in section 1612(a)(2)(G) of this title [8 U.S.C.A. § 1612(a)(2)(G)], but only with respect to the programs specified in subsections (a)(3) and (b)(3)(C) of section 1612 of this title [8 U.S.C.A. § 1612]; or

(2) an individual, spouse, or dependent described in section 1612(a)(2)(K) of this title [8 U.S.C.A. § 1612(a)(2)(K)], but only with respect to the specified Federal program described in section 1612(a)(3)(B) of this title [8 U.S.C.A. § 1612(a)(3)(B)].

(Pub.L. 104–193, Title IV, § 403, Aug. 22, 1996, 110 Stat. 2265; Pub.L. 105–33, Title V, §§ 5302(c)(1), 5303(c), 5306(c), 5562, 5563(a), (b), Aug. 5, 1997, 111 Stat. 638, 639, 599, 600, 602; Pub.L. 105–185, Title V, § 509, June 23, 1998, 112 Stat. 580; Pub.L. 105–277, Div. A, § 101(f) [Title VIII, § 405(d)(3)(A)], Oct. 21, 1998, 112 Stat. 2681–419; Oct. 22, 1999, Pub.L. 106–78, Title VII, § 752(b)(6), 113 Stat. 1169.)

§ 404(a). Notification and information reporting [8 U.S.C.A. § 1614]

Each Federal agency that administers a program to which section 1611, 1612 or 1613 of this title [8 U.S.C.A. § 1611, 1612 or 1613] applies shall, directly or through the States, post information and provide general notification to the public and to program recipients of the changes regarding eligibility for any such program pursuant to this subchapter.

(Pub.L. 104–193, Title IV, § 404(a), Aug. 22, 1996, 110 Stat. 2267.)

§ 411. Aliens who are not qualified aliens or nonimmigrants ineligible for State and local public benefits [8 U.S.C.A. § 1621]

(a) In general

Notwithstanding any other provision of law and except as provided in subsections (b) and (d) of this section, an alien who is not—

(1) a qualified alien (as defined in section 1641 of this title [8 U.S.C.A. § 1641]),

(2) a nonimmigrant under the Immigration and Nationality Act [8 U.S.C.A. § 1101 et seq.], or

(3) an alien who is paroled into the United States under section 212(d)(5) of such Act [8 U.S.C.A. § 1182(d)(5)] for less than one year,

is not eligible for any State or local public benefit (as defined in subsection (c) of this section).

(b) Exceptions

Subsection (a) of this section shall not apply with respect to the following State or local public benefits:

(1) Assistance for health care items and services that are necessary for the treatment of an emergency medical condition (as defined in section 1396b(v)(3) of Title 42) of the alien involved and are not related to an organ transplant procedure.

(2) Short-term, non-cash, in-kind emergency disaster relief.

(3) Public health assistance for immunizations with respect to immunizable diseases and for testing and treatment of symptoms of communicable diseases whether or not such symptoms are caused by a communicable disease.

(4) Programs, services, or assistance (such as soup kitchens, crisis counseling and intervention, and short-term shelter) specified by the Attorney General, in the Attorney General's sole and unreviewable discretion after consultation with appropriate Federal agencies and departments, which **(A)** deliver in-kind services at the community level, including through public or private nonprofit agencies; **(B)** do not condition the provision of assistance, the amount of assistance provided, or the cost of assistance provided on the individual recipient's income or resources; and **(C)** are necessary for the protection of life or safety.

(c) "State or local public benefit" defined

(1) Except as provided in paragraphs (2) and (3), for purposes of this subchapter the term "State or local public benefit" means—

(A) any grant, contract, loan, professional license, or commercial license provided by an agency of a State or local government or by appropriated funds of a State or local government; and

(B) any retirement, welfare, health, disability, public or assisted housing, postsecondary education, food assistance, unemployment benefit, or any other similar benefit for which payments or assistance are provided to an individual, household, or family eligibility unit by an agency of a State or local government or by appropriated funds of a State or local government.

(2) Such term shall not apply—

(A) to any contract, professional license, or commercial license for a nonimmigrant whose visa for entry is related to such employment in the United States, or to a citizen of a freely associated state, if section 141 of the applicable compact of free association approved in Public Law 99–239 [48 U.S.C.A. § 1901 note] or 99–658 [48 U.S.C.A. § 1931 note] (or a successor provision) is in effect;

(B) with respect to benefits for an alien who as a work authorized nonimmigrant or as an alien lawfully admitted for permanent residence under the Immigration and Nationality Act qualified for such benefits and for whom the United States under reciprocal treaty agreements is required to pay benefits, as determined by the Secretary of State, after consultation with the Attorney General; or

(C) to the issuance of a professional license to, or the renewal of a professional license by, a foreign national not physically present in the United States.

(3) Such term does not include any Federal public benefit under section 1611(c) of this title [8 U.S.C.A. § 1611(c)].

(d) State authority to provide for eligibility of illegal aliens for State and local public benefits

A State may provide that an alien who is not lawfully present in the United States is eligible for any State or local public benefit for which such alien would otherwise be ineligible under subsection (a) of this section only through the enactment of a State law after August 22, 1996 which affirmatively provides for such eligibility.

(Pub.L. 104–193, Title IV, § 411, Aug. 22, 1996, 110 Stat. 2268; Pub.L. 105–33, Title V, §§ 5565, 5581(b)(1), Aug. 5, 1997, 111 Stat. 639, 642; Pub.L. 105–306, § 5(b), Oct. 28, 1998, 112 Stat. 2927.)

§ 412. State authority to limit eligibility of qualified aliens for State public benefits [8 U.S.C.A. § 1622]

(a) In general

Notwithstanding any other provision of law and except as provided in subsection (b) of this section, a State is authorized to determine the lic eligibility for any State public benefits of an alien who is a qualified alien (as defined in section 1641 of this title [8 U.S.C.A. § 1641]), a non-immigrant under the Immigration and Nationality Act [8 U.S.C.A. § 1101 et seq.] or an alien who is paroled into the United States under section 212(d)(5) of such Act [8 U.S.C.A. § 1182(d)(5)] for less than one year.

(b) Exceptions

Qualified aliens under this subsection shall be eligible for any State public benefits.

(1) Time-limited exception for refugees and asylees

(A) An alien who is admitted to the United States as a refugee under section 207 of the Immigration and Nationality Act [8 U.S.C.A. § 1157] until 5 years after the date of an alien's entry into the United States.

(B) An alien who is granted asylum under section 208 of such Act [8 U.S.C.A. § 1158] until 5 years after the date of such grant of asylum.

(C) An alien whose deportation is being withheld under section 243(h) of such Act [8 U.S.C.A. § 1253(h)] (as in effect immediately before the effective date [April 1, 1997] of section 307 of division C of Public Law 104–208) or section 241(b)(3) of such Act [8 U.S.C.A. § 1251(b)(3)] (as amended by section 305(a) of division C of Public Law 104–208) until 5 years after such withholding.

(D) An alien who is a Cuban and Haitian entrant as defined in section 501(e) of the Refugee Education Assistance Act of 1980 until 5 years after the alien is granted such status.

(E) An alien admitted to the United States as an Amerasian immigrant as described in section 1612(a)(2)(A)(i)(V) of this title [8 U.S.C.A. § 1612(a)(2)(A)(i)(V)].

(2) Certain permanent resident aliens

An alien who—

(A) is lawfully admitted to the United States for permanent residence under the Immigration and Nationality Act [8 U.S.C.A. § 1101 et seq.]; and

(B)(i) has worked 40 qualifying quarters of coverage as defined under title II of the Social Security Act [42 U.S.C.A. § 401 et seq.] or can be credited with such qualifying quarters as provided under section 1645 of this title [8 U.S.C.A. § 1645], and (ii) in the case of any such qualifying quarter creditable for any period beginning after December 31, 1996, did not receive any Federal means-tested public benefit (as provided under section 1613 of this title [8 U.S.C.A. § 1613]) during any such period.

(3) Veteran and active duty exception

An alien who is lawfully residing in any State and is—

(A) a veteran (as defined in section 101, 1101, or 1301, or as described in section 107 of Title 38) with a discharge characterized as an honorable discharge and not on account of alienage and who fulfills the minimum active-duty service requirements of section 5303A(d) of title 38, United States Code,

(B) on active duty (other than active duty for training) in the Armed Forces of the United States, or

(C) the spouse or unmarried dependent child of an individual described in subparagraph (A) or (B) or the unremarried surviving spouse of an individual described in clause (i) or (ii) who is deceased if the marriage fulfills the requirements of section 1304 of title 38, United States Code.

(4) Transition for those currently receiving benefits

An alien who on August 22, 1996 is lawfully residing in any State and is receiving benefits on August 22, 1996 shall continue to be eligible to receive such benefits until January 1, 1997.

(Pub.L. 104–193, Title IV, § 412, Aug. 22, 1996, 110 Stat. 2269; Pub.L. 105–33, Title V, §§ 5302(c)(2), 5306(d), 5562, 5563, 5581(b)(3), Aug. 5, 1997, 111 Stat. 599, 602, 638, 639, 643.)

§ 421. Federal attribution of sponsor's income and resources to alien [8 U.S.C.A. § 1631]

(a) In general

Notwithstanding any other provision of law, in determining the eligibility and the amount of benefits of an alien for any Federal means-tested public benefits program (as provided under section 1613 of this title [8 U.S.C.A. § 1613]), the income and resources of the alien shall be deemed to include the following:

(1) The income and resources of any person who executed an affidavit of support pursuant to section 213A of the Immigration and Nationality Act [8 U.S.C.A. § 1183a] (as added by section 423) and as amended by section 551(a) of the Illegal Immigration Reform and Immigrant Responsibility Act of 1996 on behalf of such alien.

(2) The income and resources of the spouse (if any) of the person.

(b) Duration of attribution period

Subsection (a) of this section shall apply with respect to an alien until such time as the alien—

(1) achieves United States citizenship through naturalization pursuant to chapter 2 of title III of the Immigration and Nationality Act [8 U.S.C.A. § 1421 et seq.]; or

(2)(A) has worked 40 qualifying quarters of coverage as defined under title II of the Social Security Act [42 U.S.C.A. § 401 et seq.] or can be credited with such qualifying quarters as provided under section 1645 of this title [8 U.S.C.A. § 1645], and (B) in the case of any such qualifying quarter creditable for any period beginning after December 31, 1996, did not receive any Federal means-tested public benefit (as provided under section 1613 of this title [8 U.S.C.A. § 1613]) during any such period.

(c) Review of income and resources of alien upon reapplication

Whenever an alien is required to reapply for benefits under any Federal means-tested public benefits program, the applicable agency shall review the income and resources attributed to the alien under subsection (a) of this section.

(d) Application

(1) If on August 22, 1996, a Federal means-tested public benefits program attributes a sponsor's income and resources to an alien in determining the alien's eligibility and the amount of benefits for an alien, this section shall apply to any such determination beginning on the day after August 22, 1996.

(2) If on August 22, 1996, a Federal means-tested public benefits program does not attribute a sponsor's income and resources to an alien in determining the alien's eligibility and the amount of benefits for an alien, this section shall apply to any such determination beginning 180 days after August 22, 1996.

(e) Indigence exception

(1) In general

For an alien for whom an affidavit of support under section 213A of the Immigration and Nationality Act [8 U.S.C.A. § 1183a] has been executed, if a determination described in paragraph (2) is made, the amount of income and resources of the sponsor or the sponsor's spouse which shall be attributed to the sponsored alien shall not exceed the amount actually provided for a period beginning on the date of such determination and ending 12 months after such date.

(2) Determination described

A determination described in this paragraph is a determination by an agency that a sponsored alien would, in the absence of the assistance provided by the agency, be unable to obtain food and shelter, taking into account the alien's own income, plus any cash, food, housing, or other assistance provided by other individuals, including the sponsor. The agency shall notify the Attorney General of each such determination, including the names of the sponsor and the sponsored alien involved.

(f) Special rule for battered spouse and child

(1) In general

Subject to paragraph (2) and notwithstanding any other provision of this section, subsection (a) of this section shall not apply to benefits—

(A) during a 12 month period if the alien demonstrates that (i) the alien has been battered or subjected to extreme cruelty in the United States by a spouse or a parent, or by a member of the spouse or parent's family residing in the same household as the alien and the spouse or parent consented to or acquiesced to such battery or cruelty, (ii) the alien's child has been battered or subjected to extreme cruelty in the United States by the spouse or parent of the alien (without the active participation of the alien in the battery or cruelty), or by a member of the spouse's or parent's family residing in the same household as the alien when the spouse or parent consented or acquiesced to and the alien did not actively participate in such battery or cruelty, or (iii) the alien is a child whose parent (who resides in the same household as the alien child) has been battered or subjected to extreme cruelty in the United States by that parent's spouse, or by a member of the spouse's family residing in the same household as the parent and the spouse consented to, or acquiesced in, such battery or cruelty, and the battery or cruelty described in clause (i), (ii), or (iii) (in the opinion of the agency providing such public benefits, which opinion is not subject to review by any court) has a substantial connection to the need for the public benefits applied for; and

(B) after a 12 month period (regarding the batterer's income and resources only) if the alien demonstrates that such battery or cruelty under subparagraph (A) has been recognized in an order of a judge or administrative law judge or a prior determination of the Immigration and Naturalization Service, and that such battery or cruelty (in the opinion of the agency providing such public benefits, which opinion is not subject to review by any court) has a substantial connection to the need for the benefits.

(2) Limitation

The exception under paragraph (1) shall not apply to benefits for an alien during any period in which the individual responsible for such battery or cruelty resides in the same household or family eligibility unit as the individual who was subjected to such battery or cruelty.

(Pub.L. 104–193, Title IV, § 421, Aug. 22, 1996, 110 Stat. 2270; Pub.L. 104–208, Div. C, Title V, §§ 551(b)(1), 552, Sept. 30, 1996, 110 Stat. 3009–679, 3009–680; Pub.L. 105–33, Title V, § 5571(d), Aug. 5, 1997, 111 Stat. 641.)

§ 422. Authority for States to provide for attribution of sponsors income and resources to the alien with respect to State programs [8 U.S.C.A. § 1632]

(a) Optional application to State programs

Except as provided in subsection (b) of this section, in determining the eligibility and the amount of benefits of an alien for any State public benefits, the State or political subdivision that offers the benefits is authorized to provide that the income and resources of the alien shall be deemed to include—

(1) the income and resources of any individual who executed an affidavit of support pursuant to section 1183a of this title [INA § 213A, 8 U.S.C.A. § 1183a] and as amended by section 551(a) of the Illegal Immigration Reform and Immigrant Responsibility Act of 1996 on behalf of such alien, and

(2) the income and resources of the spouse (if any) of the individual.

(b) Exceptions

Subsection (a) of this section shall not apply with respect to the following State public benefits:

(1) Assistance described in section 1621(b)(1) of this title [8 U.S.C.A. § 1621(b)(1)].

(2) Short-term, non-cash, in-kind emergency disaster relief.

(3) Programs comparable to assistance or benefits under the Richard B. Russell National School Lunch Act [42 U.S.C.A. § 1751 et seq.].

(4) Programs comparable to assistance or benefits under the Child Nutrition Act of 1966 [42 U.S.C.A. § 1771 et seq.].

(5) Public health assistance for immunizations with respect to immunizable diseases and for testing and treatment of symptoms of communicable diseases whether or not such symptoms are caused by a communicable disease.

(6) Payments for foster care and adoption assistance.

(7) Programs, services, or assistance (such as soup kitchens, crisis counseling and intervention, and short-term shelter) specified by the Attorney General of a State, after consultation with appropriate agencies and departments, which **(A)** deliver in-kind services at the community level, including through public or private nonprofit agencies; **(B)** do not condition the provision of assistance, the amount of assistance provided, or the cost of assistance provided on the individual recipient's income or resources; and **(C)** are necessary for the protection of life or safety.

(Pub.L. 104–193, Title IV, § 422, Aug. 22, 1996, 110 Stat. 2271; Pub.L. 104–208, Div. C, Title V, § 551(b)(1), Sept. 30, 1996, 110 Stat. 3009–679; Pub.L. 105–33, Title V, § 5581(b)(2), Aug. 5, 1997, 111 Stat. 643; Oct. 22, 1999, Pub.L. 106–78, Title VII, § 752(b)(6), 113 Stat. 1169.)

§ 431. Definitions [8 U.S.C.A. § 1641]

(a) In general

Except as otherwise provided in this chapter, the terms used in this chapter have the same meaning given such terms in section 101(a) of the Immigration and Nationality Act [8 U.S.C.A. § 1101(a)].

(b) Qualified alien

For purposes of this chapter, the term "qualified alien" means an alien who, at the time the alien applies for, receives, or attempts to receive a Federal public benefit, is—

(1) an alien who is lawfully admitted for permanent residence under the Immigration and Nationality Act [8 U.S.C.A. § 1101 et seq.],

(2) an alien who is granted asylum under section 208 of such Act [8 U.S.C.A. § 1158],

(3) a refugee who is admitted to the United States under section 207 of such Act [8 U.S.C.A. § 1157],

(4) an alien who is paroled into the United States under section 212(d)(5) of such Act [8 U.S.C.A. § 1182(d)(5)] for a period of at least 1 year,

(5) an alien whose deportation is being withheld under section 243(h) of such Act [8 U.S.C.A. § 1253(h)] (as in effect immediately before the effective date [April 1, 1997] of section 307 of division C of Public Law 104–208) or section 241(b)(3) of such Act [8 U.S.C.A. § 1251(b)(3)] (as amended by section 305(a) of division C of Public Law 104–208).

(6) an alien who is granted conditional entry pursuant to section 203(a)(7) of such Act as in effect prior to April 1, 1980 [8 U.S.C.A. § 1153(a)(7)]; or

(7) an alien who is a Cuban and Haitian entrant (as defined in section 501(e) of the Refugee Education Assistance Act of 1980).

(c) Treatment of certain battered aliens as qualified aliens

For purposes of this chapter, the term "qualified alien" includes—

(1) an alien who—

(A) has been battered or subjected to extreme cruelty in the United States by a spouse or a parent, or by a member of the spouse or parent's family residing in the same household as the alien and the spouse or parent consented to, or acquiesced in, such battery or cruelty, but only if (in the opinion of the agency providing such benefits) there is a substantial connection between such battery or cruelty and the need for the benefits to be provided; and

(B) has been approved or has a petition pending which sets forth a prima facie case for—

(i) status as a spouse or a child of a United States citizen pursuant to clause (ii), (iii), or (iv) of section 204(a)(1)(A) of the Immigration and Nationality Act [8 U.S.C.A. § 1154(a)(1)(A)(ii), (iii) or (iv)],

(ii) classification pursuant to clause (ii) or (iii) of section 204(a)(1)(B) of the Act [8 U.S.C.A. § 1154(a)(1)(B)(ii) or (iii)],

(iii) cancellation of removal under section 1229b of this title [INA § 240A, 8 U.S.C.A. § 1229b] (as in effect prior to April 1, 1997),

(iv) status as a spouse or child of a United States citizen pursuant to clause (i) of section 204(a)(1)(A) of such Act [8 U.S.C.A. § 1154(a)(1)(A)(i)], or classification pursuant to clause (i) of section 204(a)(1)(B) of such Act [8 U.S.C.A. § 1154(a)(1)(B)(i)];

(v) cancellation of removal pursuant to section 1229b(b)(2) of this title [INA § 240A(b)(2), 8 U.S.C.A. § 1229b(b)(2)];

(2) an alien—

(A) whose child has been battered or subjected to extreme cruelty in the United States by a spouse or a parent of the alien (without the active participation of the alien in the battery or cruelty), or by a member of the spouse or parent's family residing in the same household as the alien and the spouse or parent consented or acquiesced to such battery or cruelty, and the alien did not actively participate in such battery or cruelty, but only if (in the opinion of the agency providing such benefits) there is a substantial connection between such battery or cruelty and the need for the benefits to be provided; and

(B) who meets the requirement of subparagraph (B) of paragraph (1); or

(3) an alien child who—

(A) resides in the same household as a parent who has been battered or subjected to extreme cruelty in the United States by that parent's spouse or by a member of the spouse's family residing in the same household as the parent and the spouse consented or acquiesced to such battery or cruelty, but only if (in the opinion of the agency providing such benefits) there is a substantial connection between such battery or cruelty and the need for the benefits to be provided; and

(B) who meets the requirement of subparagraph (B) of paragraph (1).

This subsection shall not apply to an alien during any period in which the individual responsible for such battery or cruelty resides in the same household or family eligibility unit as the individual subjected to such battery or cruelty.

After consultation with the Secretaries of Health and Human Services, Agriculture, and Housing and Urban Development, the Commissioner of Social Security, and with the heads of such Federal agencies administering benefits as the Attorney General considers appropriate, the Attorney General shall issue guidance (in the Attorney General's sole and unreviewable discretion) for purposes of this subsection and section 1631(f) of this title [8 U.S.C.A. § 1631(f)], concerning the meaning of the terms "battery" and "extreme cruelty", and the standards and methods to be used for determining whether a substantial connection exists between battery or cruelty suffered and an individual's need for benefits under a specific Federal, State, or local program.

(Pub.L. 104–193, Title IV, § 431, Aug. 22, 1996, 110 Stat. 2274; Pub.L. 104–208, Div. C, Title III, § 308(g)(8)(E), Title V, § 501, Sept. 30, 1996, 110 Stat. 3009–624, 3009–670; Pub.L. 105–33, Title V, §§ 5302(c)(3), 5562, 5571(a) to (c), 5581(b)(6), (7), Aug. 5, 1997, 111 Stat. 599, 638, 640, 643.)

§ 432. Verification of eligibility for Federal public benefits [8 U.S.C.A. § 1642]

(a) In general

(1) Not later than 18 months after August 22, 1996, the Attorney General of the United States, after consultation with the Secretary of Health and Human Services, shall promulgate regulations requiring verification that a person applying for a Federal public benefit (as defined in section 1611(c) of this title), to which the limitation under section 1611 of this title [8 U.S.C.A. § 1611] applies, is a qualified alien and is eligible to receive such benefit. Such regulations shall, to the extent feasible, require that information requested and exchanged be similar in form and manner to information requested and exchanged under section 1320b–7 of Title 42. Not later than 90 days after the date of the enactment of the Balanced Budget Act of 1997 [Aug. 5, 1997], the Attorney General of the United States, after consultation with the Secretary of Health and Human Services, shall issue interim verification guidance.

(2) Not later than 18 months after August 22, 1996, the Attorney General, in consultation with the Secretary of Health and Human Services, shall also establish procedures for a person applying for a Federal public benefit (as defined in section 1611(c) of this title [8 U.S.C.A. § 1611(c)]) to provide proof of citizenship in a fair and nondiscriminatory manner.

(3) Not later than 90 days after the date of the enactment of the Balanced Budget Act of 1997 [Aug. 5, 1997], the Attorney General shall promulgate regulations which set forth the procedures by which a State or local government can verify whether an alien applying for a State or local public benefit is a qualified alien, a nonimmigrant under the Immigration and Nationality Act, or an alien paroled into the United States under section 1182(d)(5) of this title [INA § 212(d)(5), 8 U.S.C.A. § 1182(d)(5)] for less than 1 year, for purposes of determining whether the alien is ineligible for benefits under section 1621 of this title [8 U.S.C.A. § 1621].

(b) State compliance

Not later than 24 months after the date the regulations described in subsection (a) of this section are adopted, a State that administers a program that provides a Federal public benefit shall have in effect a verification system that complies with the regulations.

(c) Authorization of appropriations

There are authorized to be appropriated such sums as may be necessary to carry out the purpose of this section.

(d) No verification requirement for nonprofit charitable organizations

Subject to subsection (a) of this section, a nonprofit charitable organization, in providing any Federal public benefit (as defined in section 1611(c) of this title [8 U.S.C.A. § 1611(c)]) or any State or local public benefit (as defined in section 1621(c) of this title [8 U.S.C.A. § 1621(c)]), is not required under this chapter to determine, verify, or otherwise require proof of eligibility of any applicant for such benefits.

(Pub.L. 104–193, Title IV, § 432, Aug. 22, 1996, 110 Stat. 2274; Pub.L. 104–208, Div. C, Title V, §§ 504, 508, Sept. 30, 1996, 110 Stat. 3009–672, 3009–673; Pub.L. 105–33, Title V, § 5572(a), Aug. 5, 1997, 111 Stat. 641.)

§ 433. Statutory construction [8 U.S.C.A. § 1643]

(a) Limitation

(1) Nothing in this chapter may be construed as an entitlement or a determination of an individual's eligibility or fulfillment of the requisite requirements for any Federal, State, or local governmental program, assistance, or benefits. For purposes of this chapter, eligibility relates only to the general issue of eligibility or ineligibility on the basis of alienage.

(2) Nothing in this chapter may be construed as addressing alien eligibility for a basic public education as determined by the Supreme Court of the United States under Plyler v. Doe (457 U.S. 202) (1982).

(b) Benefit eligibility limitations applicable only with respect to aliens present in the United States

Notwithstanding any other provision of this title, the limitations on eligibility for benefits under this title shall not apply to eligibility for benefits of aliens who are not residing, or present, in the United States with respect to—

(1) wages, pensions, annuities, and other earned payments to which an alien is entitled resulting from employment by, or on behalf of, a Federal, State, or local government agency which was not prohibited during the period of such employment or service under section 1324a of this title [INA § 274A, 8 U.S.C.A. § 1324a] or other applicable provision of the Immigration and Nationality Act; or

(2) benefits under laws administered by the Secretary of Veterans Affairs.

(c) Not applicable to foreign assistance

This chapter does not apply to any Federal, State, or local governmental program, assistance, or benefits provided to an alien under any program of foreign assistance as determined by the Secretary of State in consultation with the Attorney General.

(d) Severability

If any provision of this chapter or the application of such provision to any person or circumstance is held to be unconstitutional, the remainder of this chapter and the application of the provisions of such to any person or circumstance shall not be affected thereby.

(Pub.L. 104–193, Title IV, § 433, Aug. 22, 1996, 110 Stat. 2275; Pub.L. 105–33, Title V, § 5574, Aug. 5, 1997, 111 Stat. 642.)

§ 434. Communication between State and local government agencies and the Immigration and Naturalization Service [8 U.S.C.A. § 1644]

Notwithstanding any other provision of Federal, State, or local law, no State or local government entity may be prohibited, or in any way restricted, from sending to or receiving from the Immigration and Naturalization Service information regarding the immigration status, lawful or unlawful, of an alien in the United States.

(Pub.L. 104–193, Title IV, § 434, Aug. 22, 1996, 110 Stat. 2275.)

§ 435. Qualifying quarters [8 U.S.C.A. § 1645]

For purposes of this chapter, in determining the number of qualifying quarters of coverage under Title II of the Social Security Act [42 U.S.C.A. § 401 et seq.] an alien shall be credited with—

(1) all of the qualifying quarters of coverage as defined under Title II of the Social Security Act [42 U.S.C.A. § 401 et seq.] worked by a parent of such alien before the date on which the alien attains age 18, and

(2) all of the qualifying quarters worked by a spouse of such alien during their marriage and the alien remains married to such spouse or such spouse is deceased.

No such qualifying quarter of coverage that is creditable under Title II of the Social Security Act [42 U.S.C.A. § 401 et seq.] for any period beginning after December 31, 1996, may be credited to an alien under paragraph (1) or (2) if the parent or spouse (as the case may be) of such alien received any Federal means-tested public benefit (as provided under section 1613 of this title [8 U.S.C.A. § 1613]) during the period for which such qualifying quarter of coverage is so credited. Notwithstanding section 6103 of the Internal Revenue Code of 1986, the Commissioner of Social Security is authorized to disclose quarters of coverage information concerning an alien and an alien's spouse or parents to a government agency for the purposes of this title.

(Pub.L. 104–193, Title IV, § 435, Aug. 22, 1996, 110 Stat. 2275; Pub.L. 105–33, Title V, § 5573, Aug. 5, 1997, 111 Stat. 641.)

§ 742. Requirements relating to provision of benefits based on citizenship, alienage, or immigration status under the Richard B. Russell National School Lunch Act, the Child Nutrition Act of 1966, and certain other Acts [8 U.S.C.A. § 1615]

(a) School lunch and breakfast programs

Notwithstanding any other provision of this Act, an individual who is eligible to receive free public education benefits under State or local law shall not be ineligible to receive benefits provided under the school lunch program under the Richard B. Russell National School Lunch Act (42 U.S.C. 1751 et seq.) or the school breakfast program under section 4 of the Child Nutrition Act of 1966 (42 U.S.C. 1773) on the basis of citizenship, alienage, or immigration status.

(b) Other programs

(1) In general

Nothing in this Act shall prohibit or require a State to provide to an individual who is not a citizen or a qualified alien, as defined in section 1614(b) of this title [8 U.S.C.A. § 1614(b)], benefits under programs established under the provisions of law described in paragraph (2).

(2) Provisions of law described

The provisions of law described in this paragraph are the following:

(A) Programs (other than the school lunch program and the school breakfast program) under the Richard B. Russell National School Lunch Act (42 U.S.C. 1751 et seq.) and the Child Nutrition Act of 1966 (42 U.S.C. 1771 et seq.).

(B) Section 4 of the Agriculture and Consumer Protection Act of 1973 (7 U.S.C. 612c note).

(C) The Emergency Food Assistance Act of 1983 (7 U.S.C. 612c note).

(D) The food distribution program on Indian reservations established under section 2013(b) of Title 7.

(Pub.L. 104–193, Title VII, § 742, Aug. 22, 1996, 110 Stat. 2307; Oct. 22, 1999, Pub.L. 106–78, Title VII, § 752(b)(6), 113 Stat. 1169.)

ILLEGAL IMMIGRATION REFORM AND IMMIGRANT RESPONSIBILITY ACT OF 1996

§ 303. Apprehension and Detention of Aliens [8 U.S.C.A. § 1226, Note]

* * *

(b) Effective date

(1) In general.—The amendment made by subsection (a) shall become effective on the title III–A effective date [April 1, 1997].

(2) Notification regarding custody.—If the Attorney General, not later than 10 days after the date of the enactment of this Act, notifies in writing the Committees on the Judiciary of the House of Representatives and the Senate that there is insufficient detention space and Immigration and Naturalization Service personnel available to carry out section 236(c) of the Immigration and Nationality Act, as amended by subsection (a), or the amendments made by section 440(c) of Public Law 104–132, the provisions in paragraph (3) shall be in effect for a 1–year period beginning on the date of such notification, instead of such section or such amendments. The Attorney General may extend such 1–year period for an additional year if the Attorney General provides the same notice not later than 10 days before the end of the first 1–year period. After the end of such 1–year or 2–year periods, the provisions of such section 236(c) shall apply to individuals released after such periods.

(3) Transition period custody rules.—

(A) In general.—During the period in which this paragraph is in effect pursuant to paragraph (2), the Attorney General shall take into custody any alien who—

(i) has been convicted of an aggravated felony (as defined under section 101(a)(43) of the Immigration and Nationality Act, as amended by section 321 of this division),

(ii) is inadmissible by reason of having committed any offense covered in section 212(a)(2) of such Act,

(iii) is deportable by reason of having committed any offense covered in section 241(a)(2)(A)(ii), (A)(iii), (B), (C), or (D) of such Act (before redesignation under this subtitle), or

(iv) is inadmissible under section 212(a)(3)(B) of such Act or deportable under section 241(a)(4)(B) of such Act (before redesignation under this subtitle),

when the alien is released, without regard to whether the alien is released on parole, supervised release, or probation, and without regard to whether the alien may be arrested or imprisoned again for the same offense.

(B) Release.—The Attorney General may release the alien only if the alien is an alien described in subparagraph (A)(ii) or (A)(iii) and—

(i) the alien was lawfully admitted to the United States and satisfies the Attorney General that the alien will not pose a danger to the safety of other persons or of property and is likely to appear for any scheduled proceeding, or

(ii) the alien was not lawfully admitted to the United States, cannot be removed because the designated country of removal will not accept the alien, and satisfies the Attorney General that the alien will not pose a danger to the safety of other persons or of property and is likely to appear for any scheduled proceeding.

(Pub.L. 104–208, Div. C, Title III, § 303(b), Sept. 30, 1996, 110 Stat. 3009–586.)

§ 306(c). Effective date (judicial review) [8 U.S.C.A. § 1252, Note]

(1) In general.—Subject to paragraph (2), the amendments made by subsections (a) and (b) shall apply as provided under section 309, except that subsection (g) of section 242 of the Immigration and Nationality Act (as added by subsection (a)), shall apply without limitation to claims arising from all past, pending, or future exclusion, deportation, or removal proceedings under such Act.

(2) Limitation.—Paragraph (1) shall not be considered to invalidate or to require the reconsideration of any judgment or order entered under section 106 of the Immigration and Nationality Act, as amended by section 440 of Public Law 104–132 [former 8 U.S.C.A. § 1105a].

(Pub.L. 104–208, Div. C, Title III, § 306(c), as amended Pub.L. 104–302, § 2(1), Oct. 11, 1996, 110 Stat. 3657.)

§ 309. Effective dates, transition [8 U.S.C.A. § 1101, Note]

(a) In general.—Except as provided in this section and sections 303(b)(2), 306(c), 308(d)(2)(D), or 308(d)(5) of this division, this subtitle and the amendments made by this subtitle [subtitle A of Title III [sections 301 to 309] of Div. C of Pub.L. 104–208] shall take effect on the first day of the first month beginning more than 180 days after the date of the enactment of this Act [Sept. 30, 1996] (in this title referred to as the 'title III–A effective date').

(b) Promulgation of regulations.—The Attorney General shall first promulgate regulations to carry out this subtitle by not later than 30 days before the title III–A effective date.

(c) Transition for certain aliens.—

(1) General rule that new rules do not apply.—Subject to the succeeding provisions of this subsection, in the case of an alien who is in exclusion or deportation proceedings before the title III–A effective date—

(A) the amendments made by this subtitle shall not apply, and

(B) the proceedings (including judicial review thereof) shall continue to be conducted without regard to such amendments.

(2) Attorney General option to elect to apply new procedures.—In a case described in paragraph (1) in which an evidentiary hearing under section 236 or 242 and 242B of the Immigration and Nationality Act [8 U.S.C.A. § 1226 or 1252 and 1252b] has not commenced as of the title III–A effective date, the Attorney General may elect to proceed under chapter 4 of title II of such Act (as amended by this subtitle). The Attorney General shall provide notice of such election to the alien involved not later than 30 days before the date any evidentiary hearing is commenced. If the Attorney General makes such election, the notice of hearing provided to the alien under section 235 or 242(a) of such Act [8 U.S.C.A. § 1225 or 1252(a)] shall be valid as if provided under section 239 of such Act (as amended by this subtitle) [8 U.S.C.A. § 1229] to confer jurisdiction on the immigration judge.

(3) Attorney General option to terminate and reinitiate proceedings.—In the case described in paragraph (1), the Attorney General may elect to terminate proceedings in which there has not been a final administrative decision and to reinitiate proceedings under chapter 4 of title II the Immigration and Nationality Act (as amended by this subtitle). Any determination in the terminated proceeding shall not be binding in the reinitiated proceeding.

(4) Transitional changes in judicial review.—In the case in which a final order of exclusion or deportation is entered more than 30 days after the date of the enactment of this Act [Sept. 30, 1996], notwithstanding any provision of section 106 of the Immigration and Nationality Act [8 U.S.C.A. § 1105a] (as in effect as of the date of the enactment of this Act [Sept. 30, 1996]) to the contrary—

(A) in the case of judicial review of a final order of exclusion, subsection (b) of such section shall not apply and the action for judicial review shall be governed by the provisions of subsections (a) and (c) of such in the same manner as they apply to judicial review of orders of deportation;

(B) a court may not order the taking of additional evidence under section 2347(c) of title 28, United States Code;

(C) the petition for judicial review must be filed not later than 30 days after the date of the final order of exclusion or deportation;

(D) the petition for review shall be filed with the court of appeals for the judicial circuit in which the administrative proceedings before the special inquiry officer or immigration judge were completed;

(E) there shall be no appeal of any discretionary decision under section 212(c), 212(h), 212(i), 244, or 245 of the Immigration and Nationality Act [8 U.S.C.A. § 1182(c), 1182(h), 1182(i), 1254, or 1255] (as in effect as of the date of the enactment of this Act [Sept. 30, 1996]);

(F) service of the petition for review shall not stay the deportation of an alien pending the court's decision on the petition, unless the court orders otherwise; and

(G) there shall be no appeal permitted in the case of an alien who is inadmissible or deportable by reason of having committed a criminal offense covered in section 212(a)(2) or section 241(a)(2)(A)(iii), (B), (C), or (D) of the Immigration and Nationality Act [8 U.S.C.A. § 1182(a)(2) or 1251(a)(2)(A)(iii), (B), (C), or (D)] (as in effect as of the date of the enactment of this Act) [Sept. 30, 1996], or any offense covered by section 241(a)(2)(A)(ii) of such Act [8 U.S.C.A. § 1251(a)(2)(A)(ii)] (as in effect on such date) for which both predicate offenses are, without regard to their date of commission, otherwise covered by section 241(a)(2)(A)(i) of such Act [8 U.S.C.A. § 1251(a)(2)(A)(i)] (as so in effect).

(5) Transitional rules with regard to suspension of deportation.—

(A) In general.—Subject to subparagraphs (B) and (C), paragraphs (1) and (2) of section 240A(d) of the Immigration and Nationality Act [8 U.S.C.A. § 1229b(d)] (relating to continuous residence or physical presence) shall apply to orders to show cause (including those referred to in section 242B(a)(1) of the Immigration and Nationality Act [8 U.S.C.A. § 1252b(a)(1)], as in effect before the title III–A effective date), issued before, on, or after the date of the enactment of this Act [Nov. 19, 1997].

(B) Exception for certain orders.—In any case in which the Attorney General elects to terminate and reinitiate proceedings in accordance with paragraph (3) of this subsection, paragraphs (1) and (2) of section 240A(d) of the Immigration and Nationality Act [8 U.S.C.A. § 1229b(d)] shall not apply to an order to show cause issued before April 1, 1997.

(C) Special rule for certain aliens granted temporary protection from deportation.—

(i) In general.—For purposes of calculating the period of continuous physical presence under section 244(a) of the Immigration and Nationality Act [8 U.S.C.A. § 1254(a)] (as in effect before the title III–A effective date) or section 240A of such Act [8 U.S.C.A. § 1229b] (as in effect after the title III–A effective date), subparagraph (A) of this paragraph and paragraphs (1) and (2) of section 240A(d) of the Immigration and Nationality Act [8 U.S.C.A. § 1229b(d)] shall not apply in the case of an alien, regardless of whether the alien is in exclusion or deportation proceedings before the title III–A effective date, who has not been convicted at any time of an aggravated felony (as defined in section 101(a) of the Immigration and Nationality Act [8 U.S.C.A. § 1101(a)]) and—

(I) was not apprehended after December 19, 1990, at the time of entry, and is—

(aa) a Salvadoran national who first entered the United States on or before September 19, 1990, and who registered for benefits pursuant to the settlement agreement in American Baptist Churches, et al. v. Thornburgh (ABC), 760 F.Supp. 796 (N.D.Cal.1991) on or before October 31, 1991, or applied for temporary protected status on or before October 31, 1991; or

(bb) a Guatemalan national who first entered the United States on or before October 1, 1990, and who registered for benefits pursuant to such settlement agreement on or before December 31, 1991;

(II) is a Guatemalan or Salvadoran national who filed an application for asylum with the Immigration and Naturalization Service on or before April 1, 1990;

(III) is the spouse or child (as defined in section 101(b)(1) of the Immigration and Nationality Act [8 U.S.C.A. § 1101(b)(1)]) of an individual, at the time a decision is rendered to suspend the deportation, or cancel the removal, of such individual, if the individual has been determined to be described in this clause (excluding this subclause and subclause (IV));

(IV) is the unmarried son or daughter of an alien parent, at the time a decision is rendered to suspend the deportation, or cancel the removal, of such alien parent, if—

(aa) the alien parent has been determined to be described in this clause (excluding this subclause and subclause (III)); and

(bb) in the case of a son or daughter who is 21 years of age or older at the time such decision is rendered, the son or daughter entered the United States on or before October 1, 1990; or

(V) is an alien who entered the United States on or before December 31, 1990, who filed an application for asylum on or before December 31, 1991, and who, at the time of filing such application, was a national of the Soviet Union, Russia, any republic of the former Soviet Union, Latvia, Estonia, Lithuania, Poland, Czechoslovakia, Romania, Hungary, Bulgaria, Albania, East Germany, Yugoslavia, or any state of the former Yugoslavia.

(ii) Limitation on judicial review.—A determination by the Attorney General as to whether an alien satisfies the requirements of clause (i) is final and shall not be subject to review by any court. Nothing in the preceding sentence shall be construed as limiting the application of section 242(a)(2)(B) of the Immigration and Nationality Act [8 U.S.C.A. § 1252(a)(2)(B)] (as in effect after the title III–A effective date) to other eligibility determinations pertaining to discretionary relief under this Act.

(6) Transition for certain family unity aliens.—The Attorney General may waive the application of section 212(a)(9) of the Immigration and Nationality Act [8 U.S.C.A. § 1182(a)(9)], as inserted by section 301(b)(1) of this division [8 U.S.C.A. § 1182(a)(9)], in the case of an alien who is provided benefits under the provisions of section 301 of the Immigration Act of 1990 (relating to family unity) [Pub.L. 101–649].

(7) Limitation on suspension of deportation.—After April 1, 1997, the Attorney General may not suspend the deportation and adjust the status under section 244 of the Immigration and Nationality Act [8 U.S.C.A. § 1254] (as in effect before the title III–A effective date) of any alien in any fiscal year, except in accordance with section 240A(e) of such Act [8 U.S.C.A. § 1229b(e)]. The previous sentence shall apply regardless of when an alien applied for such suspension and adjustment.

(d) Transitional references.—For purposes of carrying out the Immigration and Nationality Act, as amended by this subtitle—

(1) any reference in section 212(a)(1)(A) of such Act [8 U.S.C.A. § 1182(a)(1)(A)] to the term 'inadmissible' is deemed to include a reference to the term 'excludable', and

(2) any reference in law to an order of removal shall be deemed to include a reference to an order of exclusion and deportation or an order of deportation.

(e) Transition.—No period of time before the date of the enactment of this Act [Sept. 30, 1996] shall be included in the period of 1 year described in section 212(a)(6)(B)(i) of the Immigration and Nationality Act [8 U.S.C.A. § 1182(a)(6)(B)(i)] (as amended by section 301(c) of this division).

(f) Special rule for cancellation of removal.—

(1) In general.—Subject to the provisions of the Immigration and Nationality Act (as in effect after the title III–A effective date), other than subsections (b)(1), (d)(1), and (e) of section 240A of such Act [8 U.S.C.A. § 1229b] (but including section 242(a)(2)(B) of such Act [8 U.S.C.A. § 1252(a)(2)(B)]), the Attorney General may, under section 240A of such Act [8 U.S.C.A. § 1229b], cancel removal of, and adjust to the status of an alien lawfully admitted for permanent residence, an alien who is inadmissible or deportable from the United States, if the alien applies for such relief, the alien is described in subsection (c)(5)(C)(i) of this section, and—

(A) the alien—

(i) is not inadmissible or deportable under paragraph (2) or (3) of section 212(a) [8 U.S.C.A. § 1182(a)] or paragraph (2), (3), or (4) of section 237(a) of the Immigration and Nationality Act [8 U.S.C.A. § 1227(a)] and is not an alien described in section 241(b)(3)(B)(i) of such Act [8 U.S.C.A. § 1231(b)(3)(B)(i)];

(ii) has been physically present in the United States for a continuous period of not less than 7 years immediately preceding the date of such application;

(iii) has been a person of good moral character during such period; and

(iv) establishes that removal would result in extreme hardship to the alien or to the alien's spouse, parent, or child, who is a citizen of the United States or an alien lawfully admitted for permanent residence; or

(B) the alien—

(i) is inadmissible or deportable under section 212(a)(2), 237(a)(2) (other than 237(a)(2)(A)(iii)), or 237(a)(3) of the Immigration and Nationality Act [8 U.S.C.A. § 1182(a)(2), 1227(a)(2) (other than 1227(a)(2)(A)(iii)), or 1227(a)(3)];

(ii) is not an alien described in section 241(b)(3)(B)(i) or 101(a)(43) of such Act [8 U.S.C.A. § 1231(b)(3)(B)(i) or section 1101(a)(43)];

(iii) has been physically present in the United States for a continuous period of not less than 10 years immediately following the commission of an act, or the assumption of a status, constituting a ground for removal;

(iv) has been a person of good moral character during such period; and

(v) establishes that removal would result in exceptional and extremely unusual hardship to the alien or to the alien's spouse, parent, or child, who is a citizen of the United States or an alien lawfully admitted for permanent residence.

(2) Treatment of certain breaks in presence.—Section 240A(d)(2) [8 U.S.C.A. § 1229b(d)(2)] shall apply for purposes of calculating any period of continuous physical presence under this subsection, except that the reference to subsection (b)(1) in such section shall be considered to be a reference to paragraph (1) of this section.

(g) Motions to reopen deportation or removal proceedings.— Notwithstanding any limitation imposed by law on motions to reopen removal or deportation proceedings (except limitations premised on an alien's conviction of an aggravated felony (as defined in section 101(a) of the Immigration and Nationality Act [8 U.S.C.A. § 1101(a)])), any alien who has become eligible for cancellation of removal or suspension of deportation as a result of the amendments made by section 203 of the Nicaraguan Adjustment and Central American Relief Act [Pub.L. 105–100, Title II, Nov. 19, 1997, 111 Stat. 2196] may file one motion to reopen removal or deportation proceedings to apply for cancellation of removal or suspension of deportation. The Attorney General shall designate a specific time period in which all such motions to reopen are required to be filed. The period shall begin not later than 60 days after the date of the enactment of the Nicaraguan Adjustment and Central American Relief Act [Pub.L. 105–100, Title II, Nov. 19, 1997, 111 Stat. 2193] and shall extend for a period not to exceed 240 days.

(Section 309 of Div. C of Pub.L. 104–208, as amended Pub.L. 104–302, § 2(2), (3), Oct. 11, 1996, 110 Stat. 3657; Pub. L. 105–100, Title II, §§ 203(a) to (c), 204(d), Nov. 19, 1997, 111 Stat. 2196, 2201; Pub.L. 105–139, § 1(c), Dec. 2, 1997, 111 Stat. 2644.)

§ 553. Authority of States and political subdivisions of States to limit assistance to aliens and to distinguish among classes of aliens in providing general cash public assistance [8 U.S.C.A. § 1624]

(a) In general

Subject to subsection (b) of this section and notwithstanding any other provision of law, a State or political subdivision of a State is authorized to prohibit or otherwise limit or restrict the eligibility of aliens or classes of aliens for programs of general cash public assistance furnished under the law of the State or a political subdivision of a State.

(b) Limitation

The authority provided for under subsection (a) of this section may be exercised only to the extent that any prohibitions, limitations, or restrictions imposed by a State or political subdivision of a State are not more restrictive than the prohibitions, limitations, or restrictions imposed under comparable Federal programs. For purposes of this section, attribution to an alien of a sponsor's income and resources (as described in section 1631 of this title) for purposes of determining eligibility for, and the amount of, benefits shall be considered less restrictive than a prohibition of eligibility for such benefits.

(Pub.L. 104–208, Div. C, Title V, § 553, Sept. 30, 1996, 110 Stat. 3009–681.)

§ 642. Communication between Government agencies and the Immigration and Naturalization Service [Title 8, U.S.C.A. § 1373]

(a) In general

Notwithstanding any other provision of Federal, State, or local law, a Federal, State, or local government entity or official may not prohibit, or in any way restrict, any government entity or official from sending to, or receiving from, the Immigration and Naturalization Service information regarding the citizenship or immigration status, lawful or unlawful, of any individual.

(b) Additional authority of Government entities

Notwithstanding any other provision of Federal, State, or local law, no person or agency may prohibit, or in any way restrict, a Federal, State, or local government entity from doing any of the following with respect to information regarding the immigration status, lawful or unlawful, of any individual:

(1) Sending such information to, or requesting or receiving such information from, the Immigration and Naturalization Service.

(2) Maintaining such information.

(3) Exchanging such information with any other Federal, State, or local government entity.

(c) Obligation to respond to inquiries

The Immigration and Naturalization Service shall respond to an inquiry by a Federal, State, or local government agency, seeking to verify or ascertain the citizenship or immigration status of any individual within the jurisdiction of the agency for any purpose authorized by law, by providing the requested verification or status information.

(Pub.L. 104–208, Div. C, Title VI, § 642, Sept. 30, 1996, 110 Stat. 3009–707.)

§ 644. Information regarding female genital mutilation [Title 8, U.S.C.A. § 1374]

(a) Provision of information regarding female genital mutilation

The Immigration and Naturalization Service (in cooperation with the Department of State) shall make available for all aliens who are issued immigrant or nonimmigrant visas, prior to or at the time of entry into the United States, the following information:

(1) Information on the severe harm to physical and psychological health caused by female genital mutilation which is compiled and presented in a manner which is limited to the practice itself and respectful to the cultural values of the societies in which such practice takes place.

(2) Information concerning potential legal consequences in the United States for **(A)** performing female genital mutilation, or **(B)** allowing a child under his or her care to be subjected to female genital mutilation, under criminal or child protection statutes or as a form of child abuse.

(b) Limitation

In consultation with the Secretary of State, the Commissioner of Immigration and Naturalization shall identify those countries in which female genital mutilation is commonly practiced and, to the extent practicable, limit the provision of information under subsection (a) of this section to aliens from such countries.

(c) Definition

For purposes of this section, the term "female genital mutilation" means the removal or infibulation (or both) of the whole or part of the clitoris, the labia minora, or labia majora.

(Pub.L. 104–208, Div. C, Title VI, § 644, Sept. 30, 1996, 110 Stat. 3009–708.)

NICARAGUAN ADJUSTMENT AND CENTRAL AMERICAN RELIEF ACT

§ 201. Short title [8 U.S.C.A. § 1101, Note]

This title may be cited as the "Nicaraguan Adjustment and Central American Relief Act.".

(Nov. 19, 1997, Pub. L. 105–100, Title II, § 201–204, 111 Stat. 2130).

§ 202. Adjustment of status of certain Nicaraguans and Cubans [8 U.S.C.A. § 1255, Note]

(a) Adjustment of status—

(1) In general—The status of any alien described in subsection (b) shall be adjusted by the Attorney General to that of an alien lawfully admitted for permanent residence, if the alien—

(A) applies for such adjustment before April 1, 2000; and

(B) is otherwise admissible to the United States for permanent residence, except in determining such admissibility the grounds for inadmissibility specified in paragraphs (4), (5), (6)(A), (7)(A), and (9)(B) of section 212(a) of the Immigration and Nationality Act [8 U.S.C.A. § 1182] shall not apply.

(2) Relationship of application to certain orders—An alien present in the United States who has been ordered excluded, deported, removed, or ordered to depart voluntarily from the United States under any provision of the Immigration and Nationality Act may, notwithstanding such order, apply for adjustment of status under paragraph (1). Such an alien may not be required, as a condition of submitting or granting such application, to file a separate motion to reopen, reconsider, or vacate such order. If the Attorney General grants the application, the Attorney General shall cancel the order. If the Attorney General renders a final administrative decision to deny the application, the order shall be effective and enforceable to the same extent as if the application had not been made.

(b) Aliens eligible for adjustment of status—

(1) In general—The benefits provided by subsection (a) shall apply to any alien who is a national of Nicaragua or Cuba and who has been physically present in the United States for a continuous period, beginning not later than December 1, 1995, and ending not earlier than the date the application for adjustment under such subsection is filed, except an alien shall not be considered to have failed to maintain continuous physical presence by reason of an absence, or absences, from the United States for any periods in the aggregate not exceeding 180 days.

(2) Proof of commencement of continuous presence—For purposes of establishing that the period of continuous physical presence referred to in paragraph (1) commenced not later than December 1, 1995, an alien—

(A) shall demonstrate that the alien, prior to December 1, 1995

(i) applied to the Attorney General for asylum;

(ii) was issued an order to show cause under section 242 or 242B of the Immigration and Nationality Act [8 U.S.C.A. § 1252 or 1252b] (as in effect prior to April 1, 1997);

(iii) was placed in exclusion proceedings under section 236 of such Act [8 U.S.C.A. § 1226] (as so in effect);

(iv) applied for adjustment of status under section 245 of such Act [8 U.S.C.A. § 1255];

(v) applied to the Attorney General for employment authorization;

(vi) performed service, or engaged in a trade or business, within the United States which is evidenced by records maintained by the Commissioner of Social Security; or

(vii) applied for any other benefit under the Immigration and Nationality Act by means of an application establishing the alien's presence in the United States prior to December 1, 1995; or

(B) shall make such other demonstration of physical presence as the Attorney General may provide for by regulation.

(c) Stay of removal; work authorization—

(1) In general—The Attorney General shall provide by regulation for an alien subject to a final order of deportation or removal to seek a stay of such order based on the filing of an application under subsection (a).

(2) During certain proceedings—Notwithstanding any provision of the Immigration and Nationality Act, the Attorney General shall not order any alien to be removed from the United States, if the alien is in exclusion, deportation, or removal proceedings under any provision of such Act and has applied for adjustment of status under subsection (a), except where the Attorney General has rendered a final administrative determination to deny the application.

(3) Work authorization—The Attorney General may authorize an alien who has applied for adjustment of status under subsection (a) to engage in employment in the United States during the pendency of such application and may provide the alien with an "employment authorized" endorsement or other appropriate document signifying authorization of employment, except that if such application is pending for a period exceeding 180 days, and has not been denied, the Attorney General shall authorize such employment.

(d) Adjustment of status for spouses and children—

(1) In general—The status of an alien shall be adjusted by the Attorney General to that of an alien lawfully admitted for permanent residence, if—

(A) the alien is a national of Nicaragua or Cuba;

(B) the alien is the spouse, child, or unmarried son or daughter, of an alien whose status is adjusted to that of an alien lawfully admitted for permanent residence under subsection (a), except that in the case of such an unmarried son or daughter, the son or daughter shall be required to establish that they have been physically present in the United States for a continuous period, beginning not later than December 1, 1995, and ending not earlier than the date the application for adjustment under this subsection is filed;

(C) the alien applies for such adjustment and is physically present in the United States on the date the application is filed;

(D) the alien is otherwise admissible to the United States for permanent residence, except in determining such admissibility the grounds for inadmissibility specified in paragraphs (4), (5), (6)(A), (7)(A), and (9)(B) of section 212(a) of the Immigration and Nationality Act [8 U.S.C.A. § 1182] shall not apply; and

(E) applies for such adjustment before April 1, 2000.

(2) Proof of continuous presence—For purposes of establishing the period of continuous physical presence referred to in paragraph (1)(B), an alien—

(A) shall demonstrate that such period commenced not later than December 1, 1995, in a manner consistent with subsection (b)(2); and

(B) shall not be considered to have failed to maintain continuous physical presence by reason of an absence, or absences, from the United States for any period in the aggregate not exceeding 180 days.

(e) Availability of administrative review—The Attorney General shall provide to applicants for adjustment of status under subsection (a) the same right to, and procedures for, administrative review as are provided to—

(1) applicants for adjustment of status under section 245 of the Immigration and Nationality Act [8 U.S.C.A. § 1255]; or

(2) aliens subject to removal proceedings under section 240 of such Act [8 U.S.C.A. § 1229a].

(f) Limitation on judicial review—A determination by the Attorney General as to whether the status of any alien should be adjusted under this section is final and shall not be subject to review by any court.

(g) No offset in number of visas available—When an alien is granted the status of having been lawfully admitted for permanent residence pursuant to this section, the Secretary of State shall not be required to reduce the number of immigrant visas authorized to be issued under any provision of the Immigration and Nationality Act.

(h) Application of Immigration and Nationality Act provisions—Except as otherwise specifically provided in this section, the definitions contained in the Immigration and Nationality Act shall apply in the administration of this section. Nothing contained in this section shall be held to repeal, amend, alter, modify, affect, or restrict the powers, duties, functions, or authority of the Attorney General in the administration and enforcement of such Act or any other law relating to immigration, nationality, or naturalization. The fact that an alien may be eligible to be granted the status of having been lawfully admitted for permanent residence under this section shall not preclude the alien from seeking such status under any other provision of law for which the alien may be eligible.

(Nov. 19, 1997, Pub. L. 105–100, Title II, § 201–204, 111 Stat. 2130; Dec. 2, 1997, Pub. L. 105–139, 111 Stat. 2644).

§ 203. Modification of certain transitional rules

(a) Transitional rules with regard to suspension of deportation [8 U.S.C.A. § 1101, Note]—

(1) In general—Section 309(c)(5) of the Illegal Immigration Reform and Immigration Responsibility Act of 1996 (Public Law 104–208; division C; 110 Stat. 3009–627) is amended to read as follows:

"(5) Transitional rules with regard to suspension of deportation—

"(A) In general—Subject to subparagraphs (B) and (C), paragraphs (1) and (2) of section 240A(d) of the Immigration and Nationality Act [8 U.S.C.A. § 1229b(d)] (relating to continuous residence or physical presence) shall apply to orders to show cause (including those referred to in section 242B(a)(1) of the Immigration and Nationality Act [8 U.S.C.A. § 1252b(a)(1)], as in effect before the title III–A effective date), issued before, on, or after the date of the enactment of this Act [Nov. 19, 1997].

"(B) Exception for certain orders—In any case in which the Attorney General elects to terminate and reinitiate proceedings in accordance with paragraph (3) of this subsection, paragraphs (1) and (2) of section 240A(d) of the Immigration and Nationality Act [8 U.S.C.A. § 1229b(d)] shall not apply to an order to show cause issued before April 1, 1997.

"(C) Special rule for certain aliens granted temporary protection from deportation—

"(i) In general—For purposes of calculating the period of continuous physical presence under section 244(a) of the Immigration and Nationality Act [8 U.S.C.A. § 1254(a)] (as in effect before the title III–A effective date) or section 240A of such Act [8 U.S.C.A. § 1229b] (as in effect after the title III–A effective date), subparagraph (A) of this paragraph and paragraphs (1) and (2) of section 240A(d) of the Immigration and Nationality Act [8 U.S.C.A. § 1229b(d)] shall not apply in the case of an alien, regardless of whether the alien is in exclusion or deportation proceedings before the title III–A effective date, who has not been convicted at any time of an aggravated felony (as defined in section 101(a) of the Immigration and Nationality Act [8 U.S.C.A. § 1101(a)]) and—

"**(I)** was not apprehended after December 19, 1990, at the time of entry, and is—

"**(aa)** a Salvadoran national who first entered the United States on or before September 19, 1990, and who registered for benefits pursuant to the settlement agreement in American Baptist Churches, et al. v. Thornburgh (ABC), 760 F.Supp. 796 (N.D.Cal.1991) on or before October 31, 1991, or applied for temporary protected status on or before October 31, 1991; or

"**(bb)** a Guatemalan national who first entered the United States on or before October 1, 1990, and who registered for benefits pursuant to such settlement agreement on or before December 31, 1991;

"**(II)** is a Guatemalan or Salvadoran national who filed an application for asylum with the Immigration and Naturalization Service on or before April 1, 1990;

"**(III)** is the spouse or child (as defined in section 101(b)(1) of the Immigration and Nationality Act [8 U.S.C.A. § 1101(b)(1)]) of an individual, at the time a decision is rendered to suspend the deportation, or cancel the removal, of such individual, if the individual has been determined to be described in this clause (excluding this subclause and subclause (IV));

"**(IV)** is the unmarried son or daughter of an alien parent, at the time a decision is rendered to suspend the deportation, or cancel the removal, of such alien parent, if—

"**(aa)** the alien parent has been determined to be described in this clause (excluding this subclause and subclause (III)); and

"**(bb)** in the case of a son or daughter who is 21 years of age or older at the time such decision is rendered, the son or daughter entered the United States on or before October 1, 1990; or

"**(V)** is an alien who entered the United States on or before December 31, 1990, who filed an application for asylum on or before December 31, 1991, and who, at the time of filing such application, was a national of the Soviet Union, Russia, any republic of the former Soviet Union, Latvia, Estonia, Lithuania, Poland, Czechoslovakia, Romania, Hungary, Bulgaria, Albania, East Germany, Yugoslavia, or any state of the former Yugoslavia.

"(ii) Limitation on judicial review—A determination by the Attorney General as to whether an alien satisfies the requirements of clause (i) is final and shall not be subject to review by any court. Nothing in the preceding sentence shall be construed as limiting the application of section 242(a)(2)(B) of the Immigration and Nationality Act [8 U.S.C.A. § 1252(a)(2)(B)] (as in effect after the title III–A effective date) to other eligibility determinations pertaining to discretionary relief under this Act.".

(2) Conforming amendment—Subsection (c) of section 309 of the Illegal Immigration Reform and Immigrant Responsibility Act of 1996 (Public Law 104–208; division C; 110 Stat. 3009–625) is amended by striking the subsection designation and the subsection heading and inserting the following:

"(c) Transition for certain aliens.—".

(b) Special rule for cancellation of removal [8 U.S.C.A. § 1101, Note]—Section 309 of the Illegal Immigration Reform and Immigrant Responsibility Act of 1996 (Public Law 104–208; 110 Stat. 3009–625) is amended by adding at the end the following:

"(f) Special rule for cancellation of removal—

"(1) In general—Subject to the provisions of the Immigration and Nationality Act (as in effect after the title III–A effective date), other than subsections (b)(1), (d)(1), and (e) of section 240A of such Act [8 U.S.C.A. § 1229b] (but including section 242(a)(2)(B) of such Act [8 U.S.C.A. § 1252(a)(2)(B)]), the Attorney General may, under section 240A of such Act [8 U.S.C.A. § 1229b], cancel removal of, and adjust to the status of an alien lawfully admitted for permanent residence, an alien who is inadmissible or deportable from the United States, if the alien applies for such relief, the alien is described in subsection (c)(5)(C)(i) of this section, and—

"**(A)** the alien—

"**(i)** is not inadmissible or deportable under paragraph (2) or (3) of section 212(a) [8 U.S.C.A. § 1182(a)] or paragraph (2), (3), or (4) of section 237(a) of the Immigration and Nationality Act [8 U.S.C.A. § 1227(a)] and is not an alien described in section 241(b)(3)(B)(i) of such Act;

"**(ii)** has been physically present in the United States for a continuous period of not less than 7 years immediately preceding the date of such application;

"**(iii)** has been a person of good moral character during such period; and

"**(iv)** establishes that removal would result in extreme hardship to the alien or to the alien's spouse, parent, or child, who is a citizen of the United States or an alien lawfully admitted for permanent residence; or

"**(B)** the alien—

"**(i)** is inadmissible or deportable under section 212(a)(2), 237(a)(2) (other than 237(a)(2)(A)(iii)), or 237(a)(3) of the Immigration and Nationality Act [8 U.S.C.A. § 1182(a)(2), 1227(a)(2) (other than 1227(a)(2)(A)(iii)), or 1227(a)(3)];

"**(ii)** is not an alien described in section 241(b)(3)(B)(i) or 101(a)(43) of such Act [8 U.S.C.A. § 1231(b)(3)(B)(i) or section 1101(a)(43)];

"**(iii)** has been physically present in the United States for a continuous period of not less than 10 years immediately following the commission of an act, or the assumption of a status, constituting a ground for removal;

"**(iv)** has been a person of good moral character during such period; and

"**(v)** establishes that removal would result in exceptional and extremely unusual hardship to the alien or to the alien's spouse, parent, or child, who is a citizen of the United States or an alien lawfully admitted for permanent residence.

"**(2) Treatment of certain breaks in presence**— Section 240A(d)(2) [8 U.S.C.A. § 1229b(d)(2)] shall apply for purposes of calculating any period of continuous physical presence under this subsection, except that the reference to subsection (b)(1) in such section shall be considered to be a reference to paragraph (1) of this section.".

(c) Motions to reopen deportation or removal proceedings [8 U.S.C.A. § 1101, Note]—Section 309 of the Illegal Immigration Reform and Immigrant Responsibility Act of 1996 (Public Law 104–208; 110 Stat. 3009–625), as amended by subsection (b), is further amended by adding at the end the following:

"**(g) Motions to reopen deportation or removal proceedings**—"Notwithstanding any limitation imposed by law on motions to reopen removal or deportation proceedings (except limitations premised on an alien's conviction of an aggravated felony (as defined in section 101(a) of the Immigration and Nationality Act [8 U.S.C.A. § 1101(a)])), any alien who has become eligible for cancellation of removal or suspension of deportation as a result of the amendments made by section 203 of the Nicaraguan Adjustment and Central American Relief Act may file one motion to reopen removal or deportation proceedings to apply for cancellation of removal or suspension of deportation. The Attorney General shall designate a specific time period in which all such motions to reopen are required to be filed. The period shall begin not later than 60 days after the date of the enactment of the Nicaraguan Adjustment and Central American Relief Act and shall extend for a period not to exceed 240 days.".

(d) Temporary reduction in diversity visas—[8 U.S.C.A. § 1151, Note]

(1) Beginning in fiscal year 1999, subject to paragraph (2), the number of visas available for a fiscal year under section 201(e) of the Immigration and Nationality Act [8 U.S.C.A. § 1151(e)] shall be reduced by 5,000 from the number of visas otherwise available under that section for such fiscal year.

(2) In no case shall the reduction under paragraph (1) for a fiscal year exceed the amount by which—

(A) one-half of the total number of individuals described in subclauses (I), (II), (III), and (IV) of section 309(c)(5)(C)(i) of the Illegal Immigration Reform and Immigrant Responsibility Act of 1996 who have adjusted their status to that of aliens lawfully admitted for permanent residence under the Nicaraguan Adjustment and Central American Relief Act as of the end of the previous fiscal year; exceeds

(B) the total of the reductions in available visas under this subsection for all previous fiscal years.

(e) Temporary reduction in other workers' visas—[8 U.S.C.A. § 1153, Note]

(1) Beginning in the fiscal year following the fiscal year in which a visa has been made available under section 203(b)(3)(A)(iii) of the Immigration and Nationality Act [8 U.S.C.A. § 1153(b)(3)(A)(iii)] for all aliens who are the beneficiary of a petition approved under section 204 of such Act [8 U.S.C.A. § 1154] as of the date of the enactment of this Act for classification under section 203(b)(3)(A)(iii) of such Act [8 U.S.C.A. § 1153(b)(3)(A)(iii)], subject to paragraph (2), visas available under section 203(b)(3)(A)(iii) of that Act [8 U.S.C.A. § 1153(b)(3)(A)(iii)] shall be reduced by 5,000 from the number of visas otherwise available under that section for such fiscal year.

(2) In no case shall the reduction under paragraph (1) for a fiscal year exceed the amount by which—

(A) the number computed under subsection (d)(2)(A); exceeds—

(B) the total of the reductions in available visas under this subsection for all previous fiscal years.

(f) Effective date [Title 8, U.S.C.A. § 1101, Note]—The amendments made by this section to the Illegal Immigration Reform and Immigrant Responsibility Act of 1996 shall take effect as if included in the enactment of such Act.

(Nov. 19, 1997, Pub. L. 105–100, Title II, § 201–204, 111 Stat. 2130; Dec. 2, 1997, Pub. L. 105–139, 111 Stat. 2644).

§ 204. Limitation on cancellation of removal and suspensions of deportation

(a) Annual limitation [8 U.S.C.A. § 1229b, Note]—Section 240A(e) of the Immigration and Nationality Act [8 U.S.C.A § 1229b(e)] is amended to read as follows:

"(e) Annual limitation—

"**(1) Aggregate limitation**—Subject to paragraphs (2) and (3), the Attorney General may not cancel the removal and adjust the status under this section, nor suspend the deportation and adjust the status under section 244(a) [8 U.S.C.A. § 1254(a)] (as in effect before the enactment of the Illegal Immigration Reform and Immigrant Responsibility Act of 1996), of a total of more than 4,000 aliens in any fiscal year. The previous sentence shall apply regardless of when an alien applied for such cancellation and adjustment, or such suspension and adjustment, and whether such an alien had previously applied for suspension of deportation under such section 244(a) [8 U.S.C.A. § 1254(a)]. The numerical limitation under this paragraph shall apply to the aggregate number of decisions in any fiscal year to cancel the removal (and adjust the status) of an alien, or suspend the deportation (and adjust the status) of an alien, under this section or such section 244(a) [8 U.S.C.A. § 1254(a)].

"**(2) Fiscal year 1997**—For fiscal year 1997, paragraph (1) shall only apply to decisions to cancel the removal of an alien, or suspend the deportation of an alien, made after April 1, 1997. Notwithstanding any other provision of law, the Attorney General may cancel the removal or suspend the deportation, in addition to the normal allotment for fiscal year 1998, of a number of aliens equal to 4,000 less the number of such cancellations of removal and suspensions of deportation granted in fiscal year 1997 after April 1, 1997.

"**(3) Exception for certain aliens**—Paragraph (1) shall not apply to the following:

"**(A)** Aliens described in section 309(c)(5)(C)(i) of the Illegal Immigration Reform and Immigrant Responsibility Act of 1996 (as amended by the Nicaraguan Adjustment and Central American Relief Act).

"**(B)** Aliens in deportation proceedings prior to April 1, 1997, who applied for suspension of deportation under section 244(a)(3) [8 U.S.C.A. § 1254(a)(3)] (as in effect before the date of the enactment of the Illegal Immigration Reform and Immigrant Responsibility Act of 1996).".

(b) Cancellation of removal and adjustment of status for certain nonpermanent residents [8 U.S.C.A. § 1229b, Note]—Section 240A(b) of the Immigration and Nationality Act (8 U.S.C. 1229b(b)) is amended in each of paragraphs (1) and (2) by striking "may cancel removal in the case of an alien" and inserting "may cancel removal of, and adjust to the status of an alien lawfully admitted for permanent residence, an alien".

(c) Recordation of date [8 U.S.C.A. § 1229b, Note]—Section 240A(b)(3) of the Immigration and Nationality Act (8 U.S.C. 1229b(b)(3)) is amended to read as follows:

"**(3) Recordation of date**—With respect to aliens who the Attorney General adjusts to the status of an alien lawfully admitted for permanent residence under paragraph (1) or (2), the Attorney General shall record the alien's lawful admission for permanent residence as of the date of the Attorney General's cancellation of removal under paragraph (1) or (2).".

(d) April 1 effective date for aggregate limitation [Title 8, U.S.C.A. § 1101, Note]—Section 309(c)(7) of the Illegal Immigration Reform and Immigrant Responsibility Act of 1996 (Public Law 104–208; division C; 110 Stat. 3009–627) is amended to read as follows:

"**(7) Limitation on suspension of deportation**—After April 1, 1997, the Attorney General may not suspend the deportation and adjust the status under section 244 of the Immigration and Nationality Act (as in effect before the title III–A effective date) of any alien in any fiscal year, except in accordance with section 240A(e) of such Act [8 U.S.C.A. § 1229b(e)]. The previous sentence shall apply regardless of when an alien applied for such suspension and adjustment.".

(e) Effective date [8 U.S.C.A. § 1229b, Note]

The amendments made by this section shall take effect as if included in the enactment of the Illegal Immigration Reform and Immigrant Responsibility Act of 1996 (Public Law 104–208; 110 Stat. 3009–546).

(Nov. 19, 1997, Pub. L. 105–100, Title II, § 201–204, 111 Stat. 2130).

HAITIAN REFUGEE IMMIGRATION FAIRNESS ACT OF 1998

§ 902. Adjustment of Status for Certain Haitian Nationals [8 U.S.C.A § 1255, Note]

(a) Adjustment of status.—

(1) In general.—The status of any alien described in subsection (b) shall be adjusted by the Attorney General to that of an alien lawfully admitted for permanent residence, if the alien—

(A) applies for such adjustment before April 1, 2000; and

(B) is otherwise admissible to the United States for permanent residence, except that, in determining such admissibility, the grounds for inadmissibility specified in paragraphs (4), (5), (6)(A), (7)(A), and (9)(B) of section 212(a) [8 U.S.C.A. § 1182(a)] of the Immigration and Nationality Act shall not apply.

(2) Relationship of application to certain orders.—An alien present in the United States who has been ordered excluded, deported, removed, or ordered to depart voluntarily from the United States under any provision of the Immigration and Nationality Act may, notwithstanding such order, apply for adjustment of status under paragraph (1). Such an alien may not be required, as a condition on submitting or granting such application, to file a separate motion to reopen, reconsider, or vacate such order. If the Attorney General grants the application, the Attorney General shall cancel the order. If the Attorney General makes a final decision to deny the application, the order shall be effective and enforceable to the same extent as if the application had not been made.

(b) Aliens eligible for adjustment of status.—The benefits provided by subsection (a) shall apply to any alien who is a national of Haiti who—

(1) was present in the United States on December 31, 1995, who—

(A) filed for asylum before December 31, 1995,

(B) was paroled into the United States prior to December 31, 1995, after having been identified as having a credible fear of persecution, or paroled for emergent reasons or reasons deemed strictly in the public interest, or

(C) was a child (as defined in the text above subparagraph (A) of section 101(b)(1) of the Immigration and Nationality Act (8 U.S.C. 1101(b)(1)) at the time of arrival in the United States and on December 31, 1995, and who)—

(i) arrived in the United States without parents in the United States and has remained without parents in the United States since such arrival,

(ii) became orphaned subsequent to arrival in the United States, or

(iii) was abandoned by parents or guardians prior to April 1, 1998 and has remained abandoned since such abandonment; and

(2) has been physically present in the United States for a continuous period beginning not later than December 31, 1995, and ending not earlier than the date the application for such adjustment is filed, except that an alien shall not be considered to have failed to maintain continuous physical presence by reason of an absence, or absences, from the United States for any period or periods amounting in the aggregate to not more than 180 days.

(c) Stay of removal.—

(1) In general.—The Attorney General shall provide by regulation for an alien who is subject to a final order of deportation or removal or exclusion to seek a stay of such order based on the filing of an application under subsection (a).

(2) During certain proceedings.—Notwithstanding any provision of the Immigration and Nationality Act, the Attorney General shall not order any alien to be removed from the United States, if the alien is in exclusion, deportation, or removal proceedings under any provision of such Act applied for adjustment of status under subsection (a), except where the Attorney General has made a final determination to deny the application.

(3) Work authorization.—The Attorney General may authorize an alien who has applied for adjustment of status under subsection (a) to engage in employment in the United States during the pendency of such application and may provide the alien with an 'employment authorized' endorsement or other appropriate document signifying authorization of employment, except that if such application is pending for a period exceeding 180 days, and has not been denied, the Attorney General shall authorize such employment.

(d) Adjustment of status for spouses and children.—

(1) In general.—The status of an alien shall be adjusted by the Attorney General to that of an alien lawfully admitted for permanent residence, if—

(A) the alien is a national of Haiti;

(B) the alien is the spouse, child, or unmarried son or daughter, of an alien whose status is adjusted to that of an alien lawfully admitted for permanent residence under subsection (a), except that, in the case of such an unmarried son or daughter, the son or daughter shall be required to establish that he or she has been physically present in the United States for a continuous period beginning not later than December 31, 1995, and ending not earlier than the date the application for such adjustment is filed;

(C) the alien applies for such adjustment and is physically present in the United States on the date the application is filed; and

(D) the alien is otherwise admissible to the United States for permanent residence, except that, in determining such admissibility, the grounds for inadmissibility specified in paragraphs (4), (5), (6)(A), (7)(A), and (9)(B) of section 212(a) of the Immigration and Nationality Act [8 U.S.C.A. § 1182(a)] shall not apply.

(2) Proof of continuous presence.—For purposes of establishing the period of continuous physical presence referred to in paragraph (1)(B), an alien shall not be considered to have failed to maintain continuous physical presence by reason of an absence, or absences, from the United States for any period or periods amounting in the aggregate to not more than 180 days.

(e) Availability of administrative review.—The Attorney General shall provide to applicants for adjustment of status under subsection (a) the same right to, and procedures for, administrative review as are provided to—

(1) applicants for adjustment of status under section 245 of the Immigration and Nationality Act [8 U.S.C.A. § 1255]; or

(2) aliens subject to removal proceedings under section 240 of such Act [8 U.S.C.A. § 1229b].

(f) Limitation on judicial review.—A determination by the Attorney General as to whether the status of any alien should be adjusted under this section is final and shall not be subject to review by any court.

(g) No offset in number of visas available.—When an alien is granted the status of having been lawfully admitted for permanent resident pursuant to this section, the Secretary of State shall not be required to reduce the number of immigrant visas authorized to be issued under any provision of the Immigration and Nationality Act.

(h) Application of Immigration and Nationality Act provisions.—Except as otherwise specifically provided in this title [Haitian Refugee Immigration Fairness Act of 1998], the definitions contained in the Immigration and Nationality Act shall apply in the administration of this section. Nothing contained in this title shall be held to repeal, amend, alter, modify, effect, or restrict the powers, duties, functions, or authority of the Attorney General in the administration and enforcement of such Act or any other law relating to immigration, nationality, or naturalization. The fact that an alien may be eligible to be granted the status of having been lawfully admitted for permanent residence under this section shall not preclude the alien from seeking such status under any other provision of law for which the alien may be eligible.

(i) Adjustment of status has no effect on eligibility for welfare and public benefits.—No alien whose status has been adjusted in accordance with this section and who was not a qualified alien on the date of enactment of this Act [Oct. 21, 1998] may, solely on the basis of such adjusted status, be considered to be a qualified alien under section 431(b) of the Personal Responsibility and Work Opportunity Reconciliation Act of 1996 (8 U.S.C. 1641(b)), as amended by section 5302 of the Balanced Budget Act of 1997 (Public Law 105–33; 111 Stat. 598), for purposes of determining the alien's eligibility for supplemental security income benefits under title XVI of the Social Security Act (42 U.S.C. 1381 et seq.) or medical assistance under title XIX of such Act (42 U.S.C. 1396 et seq.).

(j) Period of applicability.—Subsection (i) shall not apply after October 1, 2003.

(k) Not later than 6 Months after the date of the enactment of this Act [Oct. 21, 1998], and every 6 months thereafter (until all applications for adjustment of status under this section have been finally adjudicated), the Comptroller General of the United States shall submit to the Committees on the Judiciary and the Committees on Appropriations of the United States House of Representatives and the United States Senate a report containing the following:

(1)(A) The number of aliens who applied for adjustment of status under subsection (a), including a breakdown specifying the number of such applicants who are described in subparagraph (A), (B), or (C) of subsection (b)(1), respectively.

(B) the number of aliens described in subparagraph (A) whose status was adjusted under this section, including a breakdown described in the subparagraph.

(2)(A) The number of aliens who applied for adjustment of status under subsection (d), including a breakdown specifying the number of such applicants who are sponsors, children, or unmarried sons or daughters described in such subsection, respectively.

(B) The number of aliens described in subparagraph (A) whose status was adjusted under this section, including a breakdown described in the subparagraph.

(Pub.L. 105–277, Div. A, § 101(h) [Title IX, § 902], Oct. 21, 1998, 112 Stat. 2681–538.)

ADMIRAL JAMES W. NANCE AND MEG DONOVAN FOREIGN RELATIONS AUTHORIZATION ACT

§ 251. United States Policy Regarding the Involuntary Return of Refugees [22 U.S.C.A. § 2601, Note]

(a) In general.—None of the funds made available by this Act or by section 2(c) of the Migration and Refugee Assistance Act of 1962 (22 U.S.C. 2601(c)) shall be available to effect the involuntary return by the United States of any person to a country in which the person has a well-founded fear of persecution on account of race, religion, nationality, membership in a particular social group, or political opinion, except on grounds recognized as precluding protection as a refugee under the United Nations Convention Relating to the Status of Refugees of July 28, 1951, and the Protocol Relating to the Status of Refugees of January 31, 1967, subject to the reservations contained in the United States Senate Resolution of Ratification.

(b) Migration and Refugee Assistance.—None of the funds made available by this Act or by section 2(c) of the Migration and Refugee Assistance Act of 1962 (22 U.S.C. 2601(c)) shall be available to effect the involuntary return of any person to any country unless the Secretary of State first notifies the appropriate congressional committees, except that in the case of an emergency involving a threat to human life the Secretary of State shall notify the appropriate congressional committees as soon as practicable.

(c) Involuntary return defined.—As used in this section, the term "to effect the involuntary return" means to require, by means of physical force or circumstances amounting to a threat thereof, a person to return to a country against the person's will, regardless of whether the person is physically present in the United States and regardless of whether the United States acts directly or through an agent.

(Pub.L. 106–113, Div. B, § 1000(a)(7) [H.R. 3427, Div. A, Title II, § 251], Nov. 29, 1999, 113 Stat. 1536, 1537.)

FOREIGN AFFAIRS REFORM AND RESTRUCTURING ACT

§ 2242. United States Policy with Respect to the Involuntary Return of Persons in Danger of Subjection to Torture [8 U.S.C.A § 1231, Note]

(a) Policy.—It shall be the policy of the United States not to expel, extradite, or otherwise effect the involuntary return of any person to a country in which there are substantial grounds for believing the person would be in danger of being subjected to torture, regardless of whether the person is physically present in the United States.

(b) Regulations.—Not later than 120 days after the date of enactment of this Act [Oct. 21, 1998], the heads of the appropriate agencies shall prescribe regulations to implement the obligations of the United States under Article 3 of the United Nations Convention Against Torture and Other Forms of Cruel, Inhuman or Degrading Treatment or Punishment, subject to any reservations, understandings, declarations, and provisos contained in the United States Senate resolution of ratification of the Convention.

(c) Exclusion of certain aliens.—To the maximum extent consistent with the obligations of the United States under the Convention, subject to any reservations, understandings, declarations, and provisos contained in the United States Senate resolution of ratification of the Convention, the regulations described in subsection (b) shall exclude from the protection of such regulations aliens described in section 241(b)(3)(B) of the Immigration and Nationality Act (8 U.S.C. 1231(b)(3)(B)).

(d) Review and construction.—Notwithstanding any other provision of law, and except as provided in the regulations described in subsection (b), no court shall have jurisdiction to review the regulations adopted to implement this section, and nothing in this section shall be construed as providing any court jurisdiction to consider or review claims raised under the Convention or this section, or any other determination made with respect to the application of the policy set forth in subsection (a), except as part of the review of a final order of removal pursuant to section 242 of the Immigration and Nationality Act (8 U.S.C. 1252).

(e) Authority to detain.—Nothing in this section shall be construed as limiting the authority of the Attorney General to detain any person under any provision of law, including, but not limited to, any provision of the Immigration and Nationality Act.

(f) Definitions.—

(1) Convention defined.—In this section, the term "Convention" means the United Nations Convention Against Torture and Other Forms of Cruel, Inhuman or Degrading Treatment or Punishment, done at New York on December 10, 1984.

(2) Same terms as in the Convention.—Except as otherwise provided, the terms used in this section have the meanings given those terms in the Convention, subject to any reservations, understandings, declarations, and provisos contained in the United States Senate resolution of ratification of the Convention.

(Pub.L. 105–277, Div. G, Title XXII, § 2242, Oct. 21, 1998, 112 Stat. 2681–822.)

III. EXCERPTS FROM CODE OF FEDERAL REGULATIONS

TITLE 8

ALIENS AND NATIONALITY

Part 204—Immigrant Petitions

Sec.

204.5 Petitions for employment-based immigrants.

Part 208—Procedures for Asylum and Withholding of Removal

Subpart A—Asylum and Withholding of Removal

208.1 General.
208.2 Jurisdiction.
208.3 Form of application.
208.4 Filing the application.
208.5 Special duties toward aliens in custody of the Service.
208.6 Disclosure to third parties.
208.7 Employment authorization.
208.8 Limitations on travel outside the United States.
208.9 Procedure for interview before an asylum officer.
208.10 Failure to appear at an interview before an asylum officer.
208.11 Comments from the Department of State.
208.12 Reliance on information compiled by other sources.
208.13 Establishing asylum eligibility.
208.14 Approval, denial, referral, or dismissal of application.
208.15 Definition of "firm resettlement."
208.16 Withholding of removal under section 241(b)(3)(B) of the Act and withholding of removal under the Convention Against Torture.
208.17 Deferral of removal under the Convention Against Torture.
208.18 Implementation of the Convention Against Torture.
208.19 Determining if an asylum application is frivolous.
208.20 Admission of the asylee's spouse and children.
208.21 Effect on exclusion, deportation, and removal proceedings.
208.22 Restoration of status.
208.23 Termination of asylum or withholding of removal or deportation.
208.24–29 [Reserved.]

Subpart B—Credible Fear of Persecution

208.30 Credible fear determinations involving stowaways and applicants for admission found inadmissible pursuant to section 212(a)(6)(C) or 212(a)(7) of the Act.
208.31 Reasonable fear of persecution or torture determinations involving aliens ordered removed under section 238(b) of the Act and aliens whose removal is reinstated under section 241(a)(5) of the Act.

Part 216—Conditional Basis of Lawful Permanent Residence Status

216.1 Definition of conditional permanent resident.

Sec.
216.2 Notification requirements.
216.3 Termination of conditional resident status.
216.4 Joint petition to remove conditional basis of lawful permanent resident status for alien spouse.
216.5 Waiver of requirement to file joint petition to remove conditions by alien spouse.

Part 235—Inspection of Persons Applying for Admission

235.1 Scope of examination.
235.2 Parole for deferred inspection.
235.3 Inadmissible aliens and expedited removal.
235.4 Withdrawal of application for admission.
235.5 Preinspection.
235.6 Referral to immigration judge.

Part 274a—Control of Employment of Aliens

Subpart A—Employer Requirements

274a.1 Definitions.
274a.2 Verification of employment eligibility.
274a.3 Continuing employment of authorized aliens.
274a.4 Good faith defense.
274a.5 Use of labor through contract.
274a.6 State employment agencies.
274a.7 Pre-enactment provisions for employees hired prior to November 7, 1986.
274a.8 Prohibition of indemnity bonds.
274a.9 Enforcement procedures.
274a.10 Penalties.
274a.11 [Reserved.]

Subpart B—Employment authorization

274a.12 Classes of aliens authorized to accept employment.
274a.13 Application for employment authorization.
274a.14 Termination of employment authorization.

Part 292—Representation and Appearances

292.1 Representation of others.
292.2 Organizations qualified for recognition; requests for recognition; withdrawal of recognition; accreditation of representatives; roster.

PART 204—IMMIGRANT PETITIONS

§ 204.5 Petitions for employment-based immigrants.

(a) General. A petition to classify an alien under section 203(b)(1), 203(b)(2), or 203(b)(3) of the Act must be filed on Form I–140, Petition for Immigrant Worker. A petition to classify an alien under section 203(b)(4) (as it relates to special immigrants under section 101(a)(27)(C)) must be filed on Form I–360, Petition for Amerasian, Widow, or Special Immigrant. A separate Form I–140 or I–360 must be filed for each beneficiary, accompanied by the applicable fee. A petition is considered properly filed if it is:

(1) Accepted for processing under the provisions of part 103;

(2) Accompanied by any required individual labor certification, application for Schedule A designation, or evidence that the alien's occupation qualifies as a shortage occupation within the Department of Labor's Labor Market Information Pilot Program; and

(3) Accompanied by any other required supporting documentation.

(b) Jurisdiction. Form I–140 or I–360 must be filed with the Service Center having jurisdiction over the intended place of employment, unless specifically designated for local filing by the Associate Commissioner for Examinations.

(c) Filing petition. Any United States employer desiring and intending to employ an alien may file a petition for classification of the alien under section 203(b)(1)(B), 203(b)(1)(C), 203(b)(2), or 203(b)(3) of the Act. An alien, or any person in the alien's behalf, may file a petition for classification under section 203(b)(1)(A) or 203(b)(4) of the Act (as it relates to special immigrants under section 101(a)(27)(C) of the Act).

(d) Priority date. The priority date of any petition filed for classification under section 203(b) of the Act which is accompanied by an individual labor certification from the Department of Labor shall be the date the request for certification was accepted for processing by any office within the employment service system of the Department of Labor. The priority date of any petition filed for classification under section 203(b) of the Act which is accompanied by an application for Schedule A designation or with evidence that the alien's occupation is a shortage occupation within the Department of Labor's Labor Market Information Pilot Program shall be the date the completed, signed petition (including all initial evidence and the correct fee) is properly filed with the Service. The priority date of a petition filed for classification as a special immigrant under section 203(b)(4) of the Act shall be the date the completed, signed petition (including all initial evidence and the correct fee) is properly filed with the Service. The priority date of an alien who filed for classification as a special immigrant prior to October 1, 1991, and who is the beneficiary of an approved I–360 petition after October 1, 1991, shall be the date the alien applied for an immigrant visa or adjustment of status. In the case of a special immigrant alien who applied for adjustment before October 1, 1991, Form I–360 may be accepted and adjudicated at a Service District Office or sub-office.

(e) Retention of section 203(b) (1), (2), or (3) priority date.— A petition approved on behalf of an alien under sections 203(b) (1), (2), or (3) of the Act accords the alien the priority date of the approved petition for any subsequently filed petition for any classification under sections 203(b) (1), (2), or (3) of the Act for which the alien may qualify. In the event that the alien is the beneficiary of multiple petitions under sections 203(b) (1), (2), or (3) of the Act, the alien shall be entitled to the earliest priority date. A petition revoked under sections 204(e) or 205 of the Act will not confer a priority date, nor will any priority date be established as a result of a denied petition. A priority date is not transferable to another alien.

(f) Maintaining the priority date of a third or sixth preference petition filed prior to October 1, 1991—Any petition filed before October 1, 1991, and approved on any date, to accord status under section 203(a)(3) or 203(a)(6) of the Act, as in effect before October 1, 1991, shall be deemed a petition approved to accord status under section 203(b)(2) or within the appropriate classification under section 203(b)(3), respectively, of the Act as in effect on or after October 1, 1991, provided that the alien applies for an immigrant visa or adjustment of status within the two years following notification that an immigrant visa is immediately available for his or her use.

(g) Initial evidence—

(1) General. Specific requirements for initial supporting documents for the various employment-based immigrant classifications are set forth in this section. In general, ordinary legible photocopies of such documents (except for labor certifications from the Department of Labor) will be acceptable for initial filing and approval. However, at the discretion of the director, original documents may be required in individual cases. Evidence relating to qualifying experience or training shall be in the form of letter(s) from current or former employer(s) or trainer(s) and shall include the name, address, and title of the writer, and a specific description of the duties performed by the alien or of the training received. If such evidence is unavailable, other documentation relating to the alien's experience or training will be considered.

(2) Ability of prospective employer to pay wage. Any petition filed by or for an employment-based immigrant which requires an offer of employment must be accompanied by evidence that the prospective United States employer has the ability to pay the proffered wage. The petitioner must demonstrate this ability at the time the priority date is established and continuing until the beneficiary obtains lawful permanent residence. Evidence of this ability shall be either in the form of copies of annual reports, federal tax returns, or audited financial statements. In a case where the prospective United States employer employs 100 or more workers, the director may accept a statement from a financial officer of the organization which establishes the prospective employer's ability to pay the proffered wage. In appropriate cases, additional evidence, such as profit/loss statements, bank account records, or personnel records, may be submitted by the petitioner or requested by the Service.

(h) Aliens with extraordinary ability—

(1) An alien, or any person on behalf of the alien, may file an I-140 visa petition for classification under section 203(b)(1)(A) of the Act as an alien of extraordinary ability in the sciences, arts, education, business, or athletics.

(2) Definition. As used in this section:

Extraordinary ability means a level of expertise indicating that the individual is one of that small percentage who have risen to the very top of the field of endeavor.

(3) Initial evidence. A petition for an alien of extraordinary ability must be accompanied by evidence that the alien has sustained national or international acclaim and that his or her achievements have been recognized in the field of expertise. Such evidence shall include evidence of a one-time achievement (that is, a major, international recognized award), or at least three of the following:

(i) Documentation of the alien's receipt of lesser nationally or internationally recognized prizes or awards for excellence in the field of endeavor;

(ii) Documentation of the alien's membership in associations in the field for which classification is sought, which require outstanding achievements of their members, as judged by recognized national or international experts in their disciplines or fields;

(iii) Published material about the alien in professional or major trade publications or other major media, relating to the alien's work in the field for which classification is sought. Such evidence shall include the title, date, and author of the material, and any necessary translation;

(iv) Evidence of the alien's participation, either individually or on a panel, as a judge of the work of others in the same or an allied field of specification for which classification is sought;

(v) Evidence of the alien's original scientific, scholarly, artistic, athletic, or business-related contributions of major significance in the field;

(vi) Evidence of the alien's authorship of scholarly articles in the field, in professional or major trade publications or other major media;

(vii) Evidence of the display of the alien's work in the field at artistic exhibitions or showcases;

(viii) Evidence that the alien has performed in a leading or critical role for organizations or establishments that have a distinguished reputation;

(ix) Evidence that the alien has commanded a high salary or other significantly high remuneration for services, in relation to others in the field; or

(x) Evidence of commercial successes in the performing arts, as shown by box office receipts or record, cassette, compact disk, or video sales.

(4) If the above standards do not readily apply to the beneficiary's occupation, the petitioner may submit comparable evidence to establish the beneficiary's eligibility.

(5) No offer of employment required. Neither an offer for employment in the United States nor a labor certification is required for this classification; however, the petition must be accompanied by clear evidence that the alien is coming to the United States to continue work in the area of expertise. Such evidence may include letter(s) from prospective employer(s), evidence of prearranged commitments such as contracts, or a statement from the beneficiary detailing plans on how he or she intends to continue his or her work in the United States.

(i) Outstanding professors and researchers.

(1) Any United States employer desiring and intending to employ a professor or researcher who is outstanding in an academic field under section 203(b)(1)(B) of the Act may file an I–140 visa petition for such classification.

(2) Definitions. As used in this section:

Academic field means a body of specialized knowledge offered for study at an accredited United States university or institution of higher education.

Permanent, in reference to a research position, means either tenured, tenure-track, or for a term of indefinite or unlimited duration, and in which the employee will ordinarily have an expectation of continued employment unless there is good cause for termination.

(3) Initial evidence. A petition for an outstanding professor or researcher must be accompanied by:

(i) Evidence that the professor or researcher is recognized internationally as outstanding in the academic field specified in the petition. Such evidence shall consist of at least two of the following:

(A) Documentation of the alien's receipt of major prizes or awards for outstanding achievement in the academic field;

(B) Documentation of the alien's membership in associations in the academic field which require outstanding achievements of their members;

(C) Published material in professional publications written by others about the alien's work in the academic field. Such material shall include the title, date, and author of the material, and any necessary translation;

(D) Evidence of the alien's participation, either individually or on a panel, as the judge of the work of others in the same or an allied academic field;

(E) Evidence of the alien's original scientific or scholarly research contributions to the academic field; or

(F) Evidence of the alien's authorship of scholarly books or articles (in scholarly journals with international circulation) in the academic field;

(ii) Evidence that the alien has at least three years of experience in teaching and/or research in the academic field. Experience in teaching or research while working on an advanced degree will only be acceptable if the alien has acquired the degree, and if the teaching duties were such that he or she had full responsibility for the class taught or if the research conducted toward the degree has been recognized within the academic field as outstanding. Evidence of teaching and/or research experience shall be in the form of letter(s) from current or former employer(s) and shall include the name, address, and title of the writer, and a specific description of the duties performed by the alien; and

(iii) An offer of employment from a prospective United States employer. A labor certification is not required for this classification. The offer of employment shall be in the form of a letter from:

(A) A United States university or institution of higher learning offering the alien a tenured or tenure-track teaching position in the alien's academic field;

(B) A United States university or institution of higher learning offering the alien a permanent research position in the alien's academic field; or

(C) A department, division, or institute of a private employer offering the alien a permanent research position in the alien's academic field. The department, division, or institute must demonstrate that it employs at least three persons full-time in research positions, and that it has achieved documented accomplishments in an academic field.

(j) Certain multinational executives and managers.

(1) A United States employer may file a petition on Form I–140 for classification of an alien under section 203(b)(1)(C) of the Act as a multinational executive or manager.

(2) Definitions. As used in this section:

Affiliate means:

(A) One of two subsidiaries both of which are owned and controlled by the same parent or individual;

(B) One of two legal entities owned and controlled by the same group of individuals, each individual owning and controlling approximately the same share or proportion of each entity; or

(C) In the case of a partnership that is organized in the United States to provide accounting services, along with managerial and/or consulting services, and markets its accounting services under an internationally recognized name under an agreement with a worldwide coordinating organization that is owned and controlled by the member accounting firms, a partnership (or similar organization) that is organized outside the United States to provide accounting' services shall be considered to be an affiliate of the United States partnership if it markets its accounting services under the same internationally recognized name under the agreement with the worldwide coordinating organization of which the United States partnership is also a member.

Doing business means the regular, systematic, and continuous provision of goods and/or services by a firm, corporation, or other entity and does not include the mere presence of an agent or office.

Executive capacity means an assignment within an organization in which the employee primarily:

(A) Directs the management of the organization or a major component or function of the organization;

(B) Establishes the goals and policies of the organization, component, or function;

(C) Exercises wide latitude in discretionary decisionmaking; and

(D) Receives only general supervision or direction from higher level executives, the board of directors, or stockholders of the organization.

Managerial capacity means an assignment within an organization in which the employee primarily:

(A) Manages the organization, or a department, subdivision, function, or component of the organization;

(B) Supervises and controls the work of other supervisory, professional, or managerial employees, or manages an essential function within the organization, or a department or subdivision of the organization;

(C) If another employee or other employees are directly supervised, has the authority to hire and fire or recommend those as well as other personnel actions (such as promotion and leave authorization), or, if no other employee is directly supervised, functions at a senior level within the organizational hierarchy or with respect to the function managed; and

(D) Exercises direction over the day-to-day operations of the activity or function for which the employee has authority.

Multinational means that the qualifying entity, or its affiliate, or subsidiary, conducts business in two or more countries, one of which is the United States.

Subsidiary means a firm, corporation, or other legal entity of which a parent owns, directly or indirectly, more than half of the entity and controls the entity; or owns, directly or indirectly, half of the entity and controls the entity; or owns, directly or indirectly, 50 percent of a 50–50 joint venture and has equal control and veto power over the entity; or owns, directly or indirectly, less than half of the entity, but in fact controls the entity.

(3) Initial evidence—

(i) Required evidence. A petition for a multinational executive or manager must be accompanied by a statement from an authorized official of the petitioning United States employer which demonstrates that:

(A) If the alien is outside the United States, in the three years immediately preceding the filing of the petition the alien has been employed outside the United States for at least one year in a managerial or executive capacity by a firm or corporation, or other legal entity, or by an affiliate or subsidiary of such a firm or corporation or other legal entity; or

(B) If the alien is already in the United States working for the same employer or a subsidiary or affiliate of the firm or corporation, or other legal entity by which the alien was employed overseas, in the three years preceding entry as a nonimmigrant, the alien was employed by the entity abroad for at least one year in a managerial or executive capacity;

(C) The prospective employer in the United States is the same employer or a subsidiary or affiliate of the firm or corporation or other legal entity by which the alien was employed overseas; and

(D) The prospective United States employer has been doing business for at least one year.

(ii) Appropriate additional evidence. In appropriate cases, the director may request additional evidence.

(4) Determining managerial or executive capacities.—

(i) Supervisors as managers. A first-line supervisor is not considered to be acting in a managerial capacity merely by virtue of his or her supervisory duties unless the employees supervised are professional.

(ii) Staffing levels. If staffing levels are used as a factor in determining whether an individual is acting in a managerial or executive capacity, the reasonable needs of the organization, component, or function, in light of the overall purpose and stage of development of the organization, component, or function, shall be taken into account. An individual shall not be considered to be acting in a managerial or executive capacity merely on the basis of the number of employees that the individual supervises or has supervised or directs or has directed.

(5) Offer of employment. No labor certification is required for this classification; however, the prospective employer in the United States must furnish a job offer in the form of a statement which indicates that the alien is to be employed in the United States in a managerial or executive capacity. Such letter must clearly describe the duties to be performed by the alien.

(k) Aliens who are members of the professions holding advanced degrees or aliens of exceptional ability.

(1) Any United States employer may file a petition on Form I–140 for classification of an alien under section 203(b)(2) of the Act as an alien who is a member of the professions holding an advanced degree or an alien of exceptional ability in the sciences, arts, or business. If an alien is claiming exceptional ability in the sciences, arts, or business and is seeking an exemption from the requirement of a job offer in the United States pursuant to section 203(b)(2)(B) of the Act, then the alien, or anyone in the alien's behalf, may be the petitioner.

(2) Definitions. As used in this section: Advanced degree means any United States academic or professional degree or a foreign equivalent degree above that of baccalaureate. A United States baccalaureate degree or a foreign equivalent degree followed by at least five years of progressive experience in the specialty shall be considered the equivalent of a master's degree. If a doctoral degree is customarily required by the specialty, the alien must have a United States doctorate or a foreign equivalent degree.

Exceptional ability in the sciences, arts, or business means a degree of expertise significantly above that ordinarily encountered in the sciences, arts, or business.

Profession means one of the occupations listed in section 101(a)(32) of the Act, as well as any occupation for which a United States baccalaureate degree or its foreign equivalent is the minimum requirement for entry into the occupation.

(3) Initial evidence. The petition must be accompanied by documentation showing that the alien is a professional holding an advanced degree or an alien of exceptional ability in the sciences, the arts, or business.

(i) To show that the alien is a professional holding an advanced degree, the petition must be accompanied by:

(A) An official academic record showing that the alien has a United States advanced degree or a foreign equivalent degree; or

(B) An official academic record showing that the alien has a United States baccalaureate degree or a foreign equivalent degree, and evidence in the form of letters from current or former employer(s) showing that the alien has at least five years of progressive post-baccalaureate experience in the specialty.

(ii) To show that the alien is an alien of exceptional ability in the sciences, arts, or business, the petition must be accompanied by at least three of the following:

(A) An official academic record showing that the alien has a degree, diploma, certificate, or similar award from a college, university, school, or other institution of learning relating to the area of exceptional ability;

(B) Evidence in the form of letter(s) from current or former employer(s) showing that the alien has at least ten years of full-time experience in the occupation for which he or she is being sought;

(C) A license to practice the profession or certification for a particular profession or occupation;

(D) Evidence that the alien has commanded a salary, or other remuneration for services, which demonstrates exceptional ability;

(E) Evidence of membership in professional associations; or

(F) Evidence of recognition for achievements and significant contributions to the industry or field by peers, governmental entities, or professional or business organizations.

(iii) If the above standards do not readily apply to the beneficiary's occupation, the petitioner may submit comparable evidence to establish the beneficiary's eligibility.

(4) Labor certification or evidence that alien qualifies for Labor Market Information Pilot Program—

(i) General. Every petition under this classification must be accompanied by an individual labor certification from the Department of Labor, by an application for Schedule A designation (if applicable), or by documentation to establish that the alien qualifies for one of the shortage occupations in the Department of Labor's Labor Market Information Pilot Program. To apply for Schedule A designation or to establish that the alien's occupation is within the Labor Market Information Program, a fully executed uncertified Form ETA–750 in duplicate must accompany the petition. The job offer portion of the individual labor certification, Schedule A application, or Pilot Program application must demonstrate that the job requires a professional holding an advanced degree or the equivalent or an alien of exceptional ability.

(ii) Exemption from job offer. The director may exempt the requirement of a job offer, and thus of a labor certification, for aliens of exceptional ability in the sciences, arts, or business if exemption would be in the national interest. To apply for the exemption, the petitioner must submit Form ETA–750B, Statement of Qualifications of Alien, in duplicate, as well as evidence to support the claim that such exemption would be in the national interest.

(*l*) Skilled workers, professionals, and other workers.

(1) Any United States employer may file a petition on Form I–140 for classification of an alien under section 203(b)(3) as a skilled worker, professional, or other (unskilled) worker.

(2) Definitions. As used in this part:

Other worker means a qualified alien who is capable, at the time of petitioning for this classification, of performing unskilled labor (requiring less than two years training or experience), not of a temporary or seasonal nature, for which qualified workers are not available in the United States.

Professional means a qualified alien who holds at least a United States baccalaureate degree or a foreign equivalent degree and who is a member of the professions.

Skilled worker means an alien who is capable, at the time of petitioning for this classification, of performing skilled labor (requiring at least two years training or experience), not of a temporary or seasonal nature, for which qualified workers are not available in the United States. Relevant post-secondary education may be considered as training for the purposes of this provision.

(3) Initial evidence—

(i) Labor certification or evidence that alien qualifies for Labor Market Information Pilot Program. Every petition under this classification must be accompanied by an individual labor certification from the Department of Labor, by an application for Schedule A designation, or by documentation to establish that the alien qualifies for one of the shortage occupations in the Department of Labor's Labor Market Information Pilot Program. To apply for Schedule A designation or to establish that the alien's occupation is a shortage occupation with the Labor Market Pilot Program, a fully executed uncertified Form ETA–750 in duplicate must accompany the petition. The job offer portion of an individual labor certification, Schedule A application, or Pilot Program application for a professional must demonstrate that the job requires the minimum of a baccalaureate degree.

(ii) Other documentation—

(A) General. Any requirements of training or experience for skilled workers, professionals, or other workers must be supported by letters from trainers or employers giving the name, address, and title of the trainer or employer, and a description of the training received or the experience of the alien.

(B) Skilled workers. If the petition is for a skilled worker, the petition must be accompanied by evidence that the alien meets the educational, training or experience, and any other requirements of the individual labor certification, meets the requirements for Schedule A designation, or meets the requirements for the Labor Market Information Pilot Program occupation designation. The minimum requirements for this classification are at least two years of training or experience.

(C) Professionals. If the petition is for a professional, the petition must be accompanied by evidence that the alien holds a United States baccalaureate degree or a foreign equivalent degree and by evidence that the alien is a member of the professions. Evidence of a baccalaureate degree shall be in the form of an official college or university record showing the date the baccalaureate degree was awarded and the area of concentration of study. To show that the alien is a member of the professions, the petitioner must submit evidence showing that the minimum of a baccalaureate degree is required for entry into the occupation.

(D) Other workers. If the petition is for an unskilled (other) worker, it must be accompanied by evidence that the alien meets any educational, training and experience, and other requirements of the labor certification.

(4) Differentiating between skilled and other workers. The determination of whether a worker is a skilled or other worker will be based on the requirements of training and/or experience placed on the job by the prospective employer, as certified by the Department of Labor. In the case of a Schedule A occupation or a shortage occupation within the Labor Market Pilot Program, the petitioner will be required to establish to the director that the job is a skilled job, i.e., one which requires at least two years of training and/or experience.

(m) Religious workers—

(1) An alien, or any person in behalf of the alien, may file an I–360 visa petition for classification under section 203(b)(4) of the Act as a section 101(a)(27)(C) special immigrant religious worker. Such a petition may be filed by or for an alien, who (either abroad or in the United States) for at least the two years immediately preceding the filing of the petition has been a member of a religious denomination which has a bona fide nonprofit religious organization in the United States. The alien must be coming to the United States solely for the purpose of carrying on the vocation of a minister of that religious denomination, working for the organization at the organization's request in a professional capacity in a religious vocation or occupation for the organization or a bona fide organization which is affiliated with the religious denomination and is exempt from taxation as an organization described in section 501(c)(3) of the Internal Revenue Code of 1986 at the request of the organization. All three types of religious workers must have been performing the vocation, professional work, or other work continuously (either abroad or in the United States) for at least the two-year period immediately preceding the filing of the petition. Professional workers and other workers must obtain permanent resident status through immigration or adjustment of status on or before September 30, 1997, in order to immigrate under section 203(b)(4) of the Act as section 101(a)(27)(C) special immigrant religious workers.

(2) Definitions. As used in this section:

Bona fide nonprofit religious organization in the United States means an organization exempt from taxation as described in section 501(c)(3) of the Internal Revenue Code of 1986 as it relates to religious organizations, or one that has never sought such exemption but establishes to the satisfaction of the Service that it would be eligible therefor if it had applied for tax exempt status.

Bona fide organization which is affiliated with the religious denomination means an organization which is closely associated with the religious denomination and which is exempt from taxation as described in section 501(c)(3) of the Internal Revenue Code of 1986 as it relates to religious organizations.

Minister means an individual duly authorized by a recognized religious denomination to conduct religious worship and to perform other duties usually performed by authorized members of the clergy of that religion. In all cases, there must be a reasonable connection between the activities performed and the religious calling of the minister. The term does not include a lay preacher not authorized to perform such duties.

Professional capacity means an activity in a religious vocation or occupation for which the minimum of a United States baccalaureate degree or a foreign equivalent degree is required.

Religious denomination means a religious group or community of believers having some form of ecclesiastical government, a creed or statement of faith, some form of worship, a formal or informal code of doctrine and discipline, religious services and ceremonies, established places of religious worship, religious congregations, or comparable indicia of a bona fide religious denomination. For the purposes of this definition, an inter-denominational religious organization which is exempt from taxation pursuant to section 501(c)(3) of the Internal Revenue Code of 1986 will be treated as a religious denomination.

Religious occupation means an activity which relates to a traditional religious function. Examples of individuals in religious occupations include, but are not limited to, liturgical workers, religious instructors, religious counselors, cantors, catechists, workers in religious hospitals or religious health care facilities, missionaries, religious translators, or religious broadcasters. This group does not include janitors, maintenance workers, clerks, fund raisers, or persons solely involved in the solicitation of donations.

Religious vocation means a calling to religious life evidenced by the demonstration of commitment practiced in the religious denomination, such as the taking of vows. Examples of individuals with a religious vocation include, but are not limited to, nuns, monks, and religious brothers and sisters.

(3) Initial evidence. Unless otherwise specified, each petition for a religious worker must be accompanied by:

(i) Evidence that the organization qualifies as a nonprofit organization in the form of either:

(A) Documentation showing that it is exempt from taxation in accordance with section 501(c)(3) of the Internal Revenue Code of 1986 as it relates to religious organizations (in appropriate cases, evidence of the organization's assets and methods of operation and the organization's papers of incorporation under applicable state law may be requested); or

(B) Such documentation as is required by the Internal Revenue Service to establish eligibility for exemption under section 501(c)(3) of the Internal Revenue Code of 1986 as it relates to religious organizations; and

(ii) A letter from an authorized official of the religious organization in the United States which (as applicable to the particular alien) establishes:

(A) That, immediately prior to the filing of the petition, the alien has the required two years of membership in the denomination and the required two years of experience in the religious vocation, professional religious work, or other religious work; and

(B) That, if the alien is a minister, he or she has authorization to conduct religious worship and to perform other duties usually performed by authorized members of the clergy, including a detailed description of such authorized duties. In appropriate cases, the certificate of ordination or authorization may be requested; or

(C) That, if the alien is a religious professional, he or she has at least a United States baccalaureate or its foreign equivalent required for entry into the religious profession. In all professional cases, an official academic record showing that the alien has the required degree must be submitted; or

(D) That, if the alien is to work in another religious vocation or occupation, he or she is qualified in the religious vocation or occupation. Evidence of such qualifications may include, but need not be limited to, evidence establishing that the alien is a nun, monk, or religious brother, or that the type of work to be done relates to a traditional religious function.

(iii) If the alien is to work in a non-ministerial and nonprofessional capacity for a bona fide religious organization which is affiliated with the religious denomination, the letter from the authorized official must explain how the affiliation exists. A tax-exempt certificate indicating that the affiliated organization is exempt from taxation in accordance with section 501(c)(3) of the Internal Revenue Code of 1986 as it relates to religious organizations is required in this instance.

(iv) In appropriate cases, the director may request appropriate additional evidence relating to the eligibility under section 203(b)(4) of the Act of the religious organization, the alien, or the affiliated organization.

(4) Job offer. The letter from the authorized official of the religious organization in the United States must also state how the alien will be solely carrying on the vocation of a minister (including any terms of payment for services or other remuneration), or how the alien will be paid or remunerated if the alien will work in a professional religious capacity or in other religious work. The documentation should clearly indicate that the alien will not be solely dependent on supplemental employment or solicitation of funds for support. In doubtful cases, additional evidence such as bank letters, recent audits, church membership figures, and/or the number of individuals currently receiving compensation may be requested.

(n) Closing action—

(1) Approval. An approved employment-based petition will be forwarded to the United States Consulate selected by the petitioner and indicated on the petition. If a United States Consulate is not designated, the petition will be forwarded to the consulate having jurisdiction over the place of the alien's last residence abroad. If the petition indicates that the alien will apply for adjustment to permanent residence in the United States, the approved petition will be retained by the Service for consideration with the application for permanent resident (Form I–485).

(2) Denial. The denial of a petition for classification under section 203(b)(1), 203(b)(2), 203(b)(3), or 203(b)(4) of the Act (as it relates to special immigrants under section 101(a)(27)(C) of the Act) shall be appealable to the Associate Commissioner for Examinations. The petitioner shall be informed in plain language of the reasons for denial and of his or her right to appeal.

(3) Validity of approved petitions. Unless revoked under section 203(e) or 205 of the Act, an employment-based petition is valid indefinitely.

[30 FR 14775, Nov. 30, 1965, as amended at 41 FR 55849, Dec. 23, 1976; 52 FR 33797, Sept. 8, 1987; 53 FR 2824, Feb. 2, 1988; 56 FR 60905, Nov. 29, 1991; 59 FR 502, Jan. 5, 1994; 59 FR 27229, May 26, 1994; 59 FR 51360, Oct. 11, 1994; 60 FR 29753, June 6, 1995; 61 FR 33305, June 27, 1996; 62 FR 4631, Jan. 31, 1997]

PART 208—PROCEDURES FOR ASYLUM AND WITHHOLDING OF REMOVAL

SUBPART A—ASYLUM AND WITHHOLDING OF REMOVAL

§ 208.1 General.

(a) Applicability. Unless otherwise provided in this chapter, this subpart shall apply to all applications for asylum under section 208 of the Act or for withholding of deportation or withholding of removal under section 241(b)(3) of the Act, or under the Convention Against Torture, whether before an asylum officer or an immigration judge, regardless of the date of filing. For purposes of this chapter, withholding of removal shall also mean withholding of deportation under section 243(h) of the Act, as it appeared prior to April 1, 1997, except as provided in § 208.16(d). Such applications are hereinafter referred to as "asylum applications." The provisions of this part shall not affect the finality or validity of any decision made by a district director, an immigration judge, or the Board of Immigration Appeals in any such case prior to April 1, 1997. No asylum application that was filed with a district director, asylum officer, or immigration judge prior to April 1, 1997, may be reopened or otherwise reconsidered under the provisions of this part except by motion granted in the exercise of discretion by the Board of Immigration Appeals, an immigration judge, or an asylum officer for proper cause shown. Motions to reopen or reconsider must meet the requirements of sections 240(c)(5) and (c)(6) of the Act, and 8 CFR parts 3 and 103, where applicable.

(b) Training of asylum officers. The Director of International Affairs shall ensure that asylum officers receive special training in international human rights law, nonadversarial interview techniques, and other relevant national and international refugee laws and principles. The Director of International Affairs shall also, in cooperation with the Department of State and other appropriate sources, compile and disseminate to asylum officers information concerning the persecution of persons in other countries on account of race, religion, nationality, membership in a particular social group, or political opinion, torture of persons in other countries, and other information relevant to asylum determinations, and shall maintain a documentation center with information on human rights conditions.

[64 FR 8487, Feb. 19, 1999]

§ 208.2 Jurisdiction.

(a) Office of International Affairs. Except as provided in paragraph (b) of this section, the Office of International Affairs shall have initial jurisdiction over an asylum application filed by, or a credible fear determination pertaining to, an alien physically present in the United States or seeking admission at a port-of-entry. The Office of International Affairs shall also have initial jurisdiction to consider applications for withholding of removal under § 208.31. An application that is complete within the meaning of § 208.3(c)(3) shall either be adjudicated or referred by asylum officers under this part in accordance with § 208.14. An application that is incomplete within the meaning of § 208.3(c)(3) shall be returned to the applicant.

(b) Immigration Court—

(1) Certain aliens not entitled to proceedings under section 240 of the Act. After Form I–863, Notice of Referral to Immigration Judge, has been filed with the Immigration Court, an immigration judge shall have exclusive jurisdiction over any asylum application filed on or after April 1, 1997, by:

(i) An alien crewmember who:

(A) Is an applicant for a landing permit;

(B) Has been refused permission to land under section 252 of the Act; or

(C) On or after April 1, 1997, was granted permission to land under section 252 of the Act, regardless of whether the alien has remained in the United States longer than authorized;

(ii) An alien stowaway who has been found to have a credible fear of persecution or torture pursuant to the procedures set forth in subpart B of this part;

(iii) An alien who is an applicant for admission pursuant to the Visa Waiver Pilot Program under section 217 of the Act;

(iv) An alien who was admitted to the United States pursuant to the Visa Waiver Pilot Program under section 217 of the Act and has remained longer than authorized or has otherwise violated his or her immigration status;

(v) An alien who has been ordered removed under section 235(c) of the Act; or

(vi) An alien who is an applicant for admission, or has been admitted, as an alien classified under section 101(a)(15)(S) of the Act.

(2) Rules of procedure.

(i) General. Except as provided in this section proceedings falling under the jurisdiction of the immigration judge pursuant to paragraph (b)(1) of this section shall be conducted in accordance with the same rules of procedure as proceedings conducted under 8 CFR part 240, except the scope of review shall be limited to a determination of whether the alien is eligible for asylum or withholding of removal and whether asylum shall be granted in the exercise of discretion. During such proceedings all parties are prohibited from raising or considering any other issues, including but not limited to issues of admissibility, removability, eligibility for waivers, and eligibility for any form of relief other than asylum or withholding of removal.

(ii) Notice of hearing procedures and in-absentia decisions. The alien will be provided with notice of the time and place of the proceeding. The request for asylum and withholding of removal submitted by an alien who fails to appear for the hearing shall be denied. The denial of asylum and withholding of removal for failure to appear may be reopened only upon a motion filed with the immigration judge with jurisdiction over the case. Only one motion to reopen may be filed, and it must be filed within 90 days, unless the alien establishes that he or she did not receive notice of the hearing date or was in Federal or State custody on the date directed to appear. The motion must include documentary evidence which demonstrates that:

(A) The alien did not receive the notice;

(B) The alien was in Federal or State custody and the failure to appear was through no fault of the alien; or

(C) "Exceptional circumstances," as defined in section 240(e)(1) of the Act, caused the failure to appear.

(iii) Relief. The filing of a motion to reopen shall not stay removal of the alien unless the immigration judge grants a written request for a stay pending disposition of the motion. An alien who fails to appear for a proceeding under this section shall not be eligible for relief under section 208, 212(h), 212(i), 240A, 240B, 245, 248, or 249 for a period of 10 years after the date of the denial.

(3) Other aliens. Immigration judges shall have exclusive jurisdiction over asylum applications filed by an alien who has been served Form I–221, Order to Show Cause; Form I–122, Notice to Applicant for Admission Detained for a Hearing before an Immigration Judge; or Form I–862, Notice to Appear, after a copy of the charging document has been filed with the Immigration Court. Immigration judges shall also have jurisdiction over any asylum applications filed prior to April 1, 1997, by alien crewmembers who have remained in the United States longer than authorized, by applicants for admission under the Visa Waiver Pilot Program, and by aliens who have been admitted to the United States under the Visa Waiver Pilot Program. Immigration judges shall also have the authority to review reasonable fear determinations referred to the Executive Office for Immigration Review under § 208.31.

[62 FR 15362, April 1, 1997; 64 FR 8487, Feb. 19, 1999]

§ 208.3 Form of application.

(a) An asylum applicant must file Form I–589, Application for Asylum or Withholding of Removal, together with any additional supporting evidence in accordance with the instructions on the form. The applicant's spouse and children shall be listed on the application and may be included in the request for asylum if they are in the United States. One additional copy of the principal applicant's Form I–589 must be submitted for each dependent included in the principal's application.

(b) An asylum application shall be deemed to constitute at the same time an application for withholding of removal, unless adjudicated in deportation or exclusion proceedings commenced prior to April 1, 1997. In such instances, the asylum application shall be deemed to constitute an application for withholding of deportation under section 243(h) of the Act, as that section existed prior to April 1, 1997. Where a determination is made that an applicant is ineligible to apply for asylum under section 208(a)(2) of the Act, an asylum application shall be construed as an application for withholding of removal.

(c) Form I–589 shall be filed under the following conditions and shall have the following consequences:

(1) If the application was filed on or after January 4, 1995, information provided in the application may be used as a basis for the initiation of removal proceedings, or to satisfy any burden of proof in exclusion, deportation, or removal proceedings;

(2) The applicant and anyone other than a spouse, parent, son, or daughter of the applicant who assists the applicant in preparing the application must sign the application under penalty of perjury. The applicant's signature establishes a presumption that the applicant is aware of the contents of the application. A person other than a relative specified in this paragraph who assists the applicant in preparing the application also must provide his or her full mailing address;

(3) An asylum application that does not include a response to each of the questions contained in the Form I–589, is unsigned, or is unaccompanied by the required materials specified in paragraph (a) of this section is incomplete. The filing of an incomplete application shall not commence the 150–day period after which the applicant may file an application for employment authorization in accordance with § 208.7. An application that is incomplete shall be returned by mail to the applicant within 30 days of the receipt of the application by the Service. If the Service has not mailed the incomplete application back to the applicant within 30 days, it shall be deemed complete. An application returned to the applicant as incomplete shall be resubmitted by the applicant with the additional information if he or she wishes to have the application considered;

(4) Knowing placement of false information on the application may subject the person placing that information on the application to criminal penalties under title 18 of the United States Code and to civil penalties under section 274C of the Act; and

(5) Knowingly filing a frivolous application on or after April 1, 1997, so long as the applicant has received the notice required by section 208(d)(4) of the Act, shall render the applicant permanently ineligible for any benefits under the Act pursuant to § 208.18.

[62 FR 10338, March 6, 1997]

§ 208.4 Filing the application.

Except as prohibited in paragraph (a) of this section, asylum applications shall be filed in accordance with paragraph (b) of this section.

(a) Prohibitions on filing. Section 208(a)(2) of the Act prohibits certain aliens from filing for asylum on or after April 1, 1997, unless the alien can demonstrate to the satisfaction of the Attorney General that one of the exceptions in section 208(a)(2)(D) of the Act applies. Such prohibition applies only to asylum applications under section 208 of the Act and not to applications for withholding of removal under § 208.16 of this part. If an applicant submits an asylum application and it appears that one or more of the prohibitions contained in section 208(a)(2) of the Act apply, an asylum officer or an immigration judge shall review the application to determine if the application should be rejected or denied.

For the purpose of making determinations under section 208(a)(2) of the Act, the following rules shall apply:

(1) Authority. Only an asylum officer, an immigration judge, or the Board of Immigration Appeals is authorized to make determinations regarding the prohibitions contained in section 208(a)(2)(B) or (C) of the Act;

(2) One-year filing deadline.

(i) For purposes of section 208(a)(2)(B) of the Act, an applicant has the burden of proving

(A) By clear and convincing evidence that he or she applied within one year of the alien's arrival in the United States or

(B) To the satisfaction of the asylum officer, immigration judge, or Board of Immigration Appeals that he or she qualifies for an exception to the one-year deadline.

(ii) The one-year period shall be calculated from the date of the alien's last arrival in the United States or April 1, 1997, whichever is later. In the case of an application that appears to have been filed more than a year after the applicant arrived in the United States, an asylum officer or immigration judge will determine whether the applicant qualifies under one of the exceptions to the deadline;

(3) Prior denial of application. For purposes of section 208(a)(2)(C) of the Act, an asylum application has not been denied unless denied by an immigration judge or the Board of Immigration Appeals;

(4) Changed circumstances.

(i) The term "changed circumstances" in section 208(a)(2)(D) of the Act shall refer to circumstances materially affecting the applicant's eligibility for asylum. They may include:

(A) Changes in conditions in the applicant's country of nationality or, if the person is stateless, country of last habitual residence or

(B) Changes in objective circumstances relating to the applicant in the United States, including changes in applicable U.S. law, that create a reasonable possibility that applicant may qualify for asylum.

(ii) The applicant shall apply for asylum within a reasonable period given those "changed circumstances."

(5) The term extraordinary circumstances in section 208(a)(2)(D) of the Act shall refer to events or factors beyond the alien's control that caused the failure to meet the 1–year deadline. Such circumstances shall excuse the failure to file within the 1–year period so long as the alien filed the application within a reasonable period given those circumstances. The burden of proof is on the applicant to establish to the satisfaction of the asylum officer or immigration judge that the circumstances were both beyond his or her control and that, but for those circumstances, he or she would have filed within the 1–year period. These circumstances may include:

(i) Serious illness or mental or physical disability of significant duration, including any effects of persecution or violent harm suffered in the past, during the 1–year period after arrival;

(ii) Legal disability (e.g., the applicant was an unaccompanied minor or suffered from a mental impairment) during the first year after arrival;

(iii) Ineffective assistance of counsel, provided that:

(A) The alien files an affidavit setting forth in detail the agreement that was entered into with counsel with respect to the actions to be taken and what representations counsel did or did not make to the respondent in this regard;

(B) The counsel whose integrity or competence is being impugned has been informed of the allegations leveled against him or her and given an opportunity to respond; and

(C) The alien indicates whether a complaint has been filed with appropriate disciplinary authorities with respect to any violation of counsel's ethical or legal responsibilities, and if not, why not;

(iv) The applicant maintained Temporary Protected Status until a reasonable period before the filing of the asylum application; and

(v) The applicant submitted an asylum application prior to the expiration of the 1–year deadline, but that application was rejected by the Service as not properly filed, was returned to the applicant for corrections, and was refiled within a reasonable period thereafter.

(b) Filing location—

(1) With the service center by mail. Except as provided in paragraphs (b)(2), (b)(3), (b)(4) and (b)(5) of this section, asylum applications shall be filed directly by mail with the service center servicing the asylum office with jurisdiction over the place of the applicant's residence or, in the case of an alien without a United States residence, the applicant's current lodging or the land border port-of-entry through which the alien seeks admission to the United States.

(2) With the asylum office. Asylum applications shall be filed directly with the asylum office having jurisdiction over the matter in the case of an alien who has received the express consent of the Director of Asylum to do so.

(3) With the immigration judge. Asylum applications shall be filed directly with the Immigration Court having jurisdiction over the case in the following circumstances:

(i) During exclusion, deportation, or removal proceedings, with the Immigration Court having jurisdiction over the port, district office, or sector after service and filing of the appropriate charging document.

(ii) After completion of exclusion, deportation, or removal proceedings, and in conjunction with a motion to reopen pursuant to 8 CFR part 3 where applicable, with the Immigration Court having jurisdiction over the prior proceeding. Any such motion must reasonably explain the failure to request asylum prior to the completion of the proceedings.

(iii) In asylum proceedings pursuant to § 208.2(b)(1) and after the Notice of Referral to Immigration Judge has been served on the alien and filed with the Immigration Court having jurisdiction over the case.

(4) With the Board of Immigration Appeals. In conjunction with a motion to remand or reopen pursuant to §§ 3.2 and 3.8 of this chapter where applicable, an initial asylum application shall be filed with the Board of Immigration Appeals if jurisdiction over the proceedings is vested in the Board of Immigration Appeals under 8 CFR part 3. Any such motion must reasonably explain the failure to request asylum prior to the completion of the proceedings.

(5) With the district director. In the case of any alien described in § 208.2(b)(1) and prior to the service on the alien of Form I–863, any asylum application shall be submitted to the district director having jurisdiction pursuant to 8 CFR part 103. The district director shall forward such asylum application to the appropriate Immigration Court with the Form I–863 being filed with that Immigration Court.

(c) Amending an application after filing. Upon request of the alien and as a matter of discretion, the asylum officer or immigration judge having jurisdiction may permit an asylum applicant to amend or supplement the application, but any delay caused by such request shall extend the period within which the applicant may not apply for employment authorization in accordance with § 208.7(a).

[64 FR 8488, Feb. 19, 1999; 64 FR 13881, March 23, 1999]

§ 208.5 Special duties toward aliens in custody of the Service.

(a) General. When an alien in the custody of the Service requests asylum or withholding of removal or expresses a fear of persecution or harm upon return to his or her country of origin or to agents thereof, the Service shall make available the appropriate application forms and shall provide the applicant with the information required by section 208(d)(4) of the Act, except in the case of an alien who is in custody pending a credible fear of persecution determination under section 235(b)(1)(B) of the Act. Where possible, expedited consideration shall be given to applications of detained aliens. Except as provided in paragraph (c) of this section, such alien shall not be excluded, deported, or removed before a decision is rendered on his or her asylum application.

(b) Certain aliens aboard vessels.

(1) If an alien crewmember or alien stowaway on board a vessel or other conveyance alleges, claims, or otherwise makes known to an immigration inspector or other official making an examination on the conveyance that he or she is unable or unwilling to return to his or her country of nationality or last habitual residence (if not a national of any country) because of persecution or a fear of persecution in that country on account of race, religion, nationality, membership in a particular social group, or political opinion, or if the alien expresses a fear of torture upon return to that country, the alien shall be promptly removed from the conveyance. If the alien makes such fear known to an official while off such conveyance, the alien shall not be returned to the conveyance but shall be retained in or transferred to the custody of the Service.

(i) An alien stowaway will be referred to an asylum officer for a credible fear determination under § 208.30.

(ii) An alien crewmember shall be provided the appropriate application forms and information required by section 208(d)(4) of the Act and may then have 10 days within which to submit an asylum application to the district director having jurisdiction over the port of entry. The district director, pursuant to § 208.4(b), shall serve Form I–863 on the alien and immediately forward any such application to the appropriate Immigration Court with a copy of the Form I–863 being filed with that court.

(2) Pending adjudication of the application, and, in the case of a stowaway the credible fear determination and any review thereof, the alien may be detained by the Service or otherwise paroled in accordance with § 212.5 of this chapter. However, pending the credible fear determination, parole of an alien stowaway may be permitted only when the Attorney General determines, in the exercise of discretion, that parole is required to meet a medical emergency or is necessary for a legitimate law enforcement objective.

(c) Exception to prohibition on removal. A motion to reopen or an order to remand accompanied by an asylum application pursuant to § 208.4(b)(3)(iii) shall not stay execution of a final exclusion, deportation, or removal order unless such stay is specifically granted by the

Board of Immigration Appeals or the immigration judge having jurisdiction over the motion.

[64 FR 8488, Feb. 19, 1999]

§ 208.6 Disclosure to third parties.

(a) Information contained in or pertaining to any asylum application shall not be disclosed without the written consent of the applicant, except as permitted by this section or at the discretion of the Attorney General.

(b) The confidentiality of other records kept by the Service that indicate that a specific alien has applied for asylum shall also be protected from disclosure. The Service will coordinate with the Department of State to ensure that the confidentiality of these records is maintained if they are transmitted to Department of State offices in other countries.

(c) This section shall not apply to any disclosure to:

(1) Any United States Government official or contractor having a need to examine information in connection with:

(i) The adjudication of asylum applications;

(ii) The defense of any legal action arising from the adjudication of or failure to adjudicate the asylum application;

(iii) The defense of any legal action of which the asylum application is a part; or

(iv) Any United States Government investigation concerning any criminal or civil matter; or

(2) Any Federal, state, or local court in the United States considering any legal action:

(i) Arising from the adjudication of or failure to adjudicate the asylum application; or

(ii) Arising from the proceedings of which the asylum application is a part.

[62 FR 10340, March 6, 1997]

§ 208.7 Employment authorization.

(a) Application and approval.

(1) Subject to the restrictions contained in sections 208(d) and 236(a) of the Act, an applicant for asylum who is not an aggravated felon shall be eligible pursuant to §§ 274a.12(c)(8) and 274a.13(a) of this chapter to submit a Form I–765, Application for Employment Authorization. Except in the case of an alien whose asylum application has been recommended for approval, or in the case of an alien who filed an asylum application prior to January 4, 1995, the application shall be submitted no earlier than 150 days after the date on which a complete asylum application submitted in accordance with §§ 208.3 and 208.4 has been received. In the case of an applicant whose asylum application has been recommended for approval, the applicant may apply for employment authorization when he or she receives notice of the recommended approval. If an asylum application has been returned as incomplete in accordance with § 208.3(c)(3), the 150–day period will commence upon receipt by the Service of a complete asylum application. An applicant whose asylum application has been denied by an asylum officer or by an immigration judge within the 150–day period shall not be eligible to apply for employment authorization. If an asylum application is denied prior to a decision on the application for employment authorization, the application for employment authorization shall be denied. If the asylum application is not so denied, the Service shall have 30 days from the date of filing of the Form I–765 to grant or deny that application, except that no employment authorization shall be issued to an asylum applicant prior to the expiration of the 180–day period following the filing of the asylum application filed on or after April 1, 1997.

(2) The time periods within which the alien may not apply for employment authorization and within which the Service must respond to any such application and within which the asylum application must be adjudicated pursuant to section 208(d)(5)(A)(iii) of the Act shall begin when the alien has filed a complete asylum application in accordance with SS208.3 and 208.4. Any delay requested or caused by the applicant shall not be counted as part of these time periods, including delays caused by failure without good cause to follow the requirements for fingerprint processing. Such time periods shall also be extended by the equivalent of the time between issuance of a request for evidence pursuant to § 103.2(b)(8) of this chapter and the receipt of the applicant's response to such request.

(3) The provisions of paragraphs (a)(1) and (a)(2) of this section apply to applications for asylum filed on or after January 4, 1995.

(4) Employment authorization pursuant to § 274a.12(c)(8) of this chapter may not be granted to an alien who fails to appear for a scheduled interview before an asylum officer or a hearing before an immigration judge, unless the applicant demonstrates that the failure to appear was the result of exceptional circumstances.

(b) Renewal and termination. Employment authorization shall be renewable, in increments to be determined by the Commissioner, for the continuous period of time necessary for the asylum officer or immigration judge to decide the asylum application and, if necessary, for completion of any administrative or judicial review.

(1) If the asylum application is denied by the asylum officer, the employment authorization shall terminate at the expiration of the employment authorization document or 60 days after the denial of asylum, whichever is longer.

(2) If the application is denied by the immigration judge, the Board of Immigration Appeals, or a Federal court, the employment authorization terminates upon the expiration of the employment authorization document, unless the applicant has filed an appropriate request for administrative or judicial review.

(c) Supporting evidence for renewal of employment authorization. In order for employment authorization to be renewed under this section, the alien must provide the Service (in accordance with the instructions on or attached to the employment authorization application) with a Form I–765, the required fee (unless waived in accordance with § 103.7(c) of this chapter), and (if applicable) proof that he or she has continued to pursue his or her asylum application before an immigration judge or sought administrative or judicial review. For purposes of employment authorization, pursuit of an asylum application is established by presenting to the Service one of the following, depending on the stage of the alien's immigration proceedings:

(1) If the alien's case is pending in proceedings before the immigration judge, and the alien wishes to continue to pursue his or her asylum application, a copy of any asylum denial, referral notice, or charging document placing the alien in such proceedings;

(2) If the immigration judge has denied asylum, a copy of the document issued by the Board of Immigration Appeals to show that a timely appeal has been filed from a denial of the asylum application by the immigration judge; or

(3) If the Board of Immigration Appeals has dismissed the alien's appeal of a denial of asylum, or sustained an appeal by the Service of a grant of asylum, a copy of the petition for judicial review or for habeas corpus pursuant to section 242 of the Act, date stamped by the appropriate court.

(d) In order for employment authorization to be renewed before its expiration, the application for renewal must be received by the Service 90 days prior to expiration of the employment authorization.

[62 FR 10340, March 6, 1997; as amended at 63 FR 12986, March 17, 1998]

§ 208.8 Limitations on travel outside the United States.

(a) An applicant who leaves the United States without first obtaining advance parole under § 212.5(e) of this chapter shall be presumed to have abandoned his or her application under this section.

(b) An applicant who leaves the United States pursuant to advance parole under § 212.5(e) of this chapter and returns to the country of claimed persecution shall be presumed to have abandoned his or her application, unless the applicant is able to establish compelling reasons for such return.

[62 FR 10341, March 6, 1997]

§ 208.9 Procedure for interview before an asylum officer.

(a) The Service shall adjudicate the claim of each asylum applicant whose application is complete within the meaning of § 208.3(c)(3) and is within the jurisdiction of the Service.

(b) The asylum officer shall conduct the interview in a nonadversarial manner and, except at the request of the applicant, separate and apart from the general public. The purpose of the interview shall be to elicit all relevant and useful information bearing on the applicant's eligibility for asylum. At the time of the interview, the applicant must provide complete information regarding his or her identity, including name, date and place of birth, and nationality, and may be required to register this identity electronically or through any other means designated by the Attorney General. The applicant may have counsel or a representative present, may present witnesses, and may submit affidavits of witnesses and other evidence.

(c) The asylum officer shall have authority to administer oaths, verify the identity of the applicant (including through the use of electronic means), verify the identity of any interpreter, present and receive evidence, and question the applicant and any witnesses.

(d) Upon completion of the interview, the applicant or the applicant's representative shall have an opportunity to make a statement or comment on the evidence presented. The asylum officer may, in his or her discretion, limit the length of such statement or comment and may require its submission in writing. Upon completion of the interview, the applicant shall be informed that he or she must appear in person to receive and to acknowledge receipt of the decision of the asylum officer and any other accompanying material at a time and place designated by the asylum officer, except as otherwise provided by the asylum officer. An applicant's failure to appear to receive and acknowledge receipt of the decision shall be treated as delay caused by the applicant for purposes of § 208.7(a)(3) and shall extend the period within which the applicant may not apply for employment authorization by the number of days until the applicant does appear to receive and acknowledge receipt of the decision or until the applicant appears before an immigration judge in response to the issuance of a charging document under § 208.14(b).

(e) The asylum officer shall consider evidence submitted by the applicant together with his or her asylum application, as well as any evidence submitted by the applicant before or at the interview. As a matter of discretion, the asylum officer may grant the applicant a brief extension of time following an interview during which the applicant may submit additional evidence. Any such extension shall extend by an equivalent time the periods specified by § 208.7 for the filing and adjudication of any employment authorization application.

(f) The asylum application, all supporting information provided by the applicant, any comments submitted by the Department of State or by the Service, and any other information specific to the applicant's case and considered by the asylum officer shall comprise the record.

(g) An applicant unable to proceed with the interview in English must provide, at no expense to the Service, a competent interpreter fluent in both English and the applicant's native language or any other language in which the applicant is fluent. The interpreter must be at least 18 years of age. Neither the applicant's attorney or representative of record, a witness testifying on the applicant's behalf, nor a representative or employee of the applicant's country of nationality, or if stateless, country of last habitual residence, may serve as the applicant's interpreter. Failure without good cause to comply with this paragraph may be considered a failure to appear for the interview for purposes of § 208.10.

[62 FR 10341, March 6, 1997]

§ 208.10 Failure to appear at an interview before an asylum officer or failure to follow requirements for fingerprint processing.

Failure to appear for a scheduled interview without prior authorization may result in dismissal of the application or waiver of the right to an interview. Failure to comply with fingerprint processing requirements without good cause may result in dismissal of the application or waiver of the right to an adjudication by an asylum officer. Failure to appear shall be excused if the notice of the interview or fingerprint appointment was not mailed to the applicant's current address and such address had been provided to the Office of International Affairs by the applicant prior to the date of mailing in accordance with section 265 of the Act and regulations promulgated thereunder, unless the asylum officer determines that the applicant received reasonable notice of the interview or fingerprinting appointment. Failure to appear at the interview or fingerprint appointment will be excused if the applicant demonstrates that such failure was the result of exceptional circumstances.

[62 FR 10341, March 6, 1997; as amended at 63 FR 12986, March 17, 1998]

§ 208.11 Comments from the Department of State.

(a) The Service shall forward to the Department of State a copy of each completed application it receives. At its option, the Department of State may provide detailed country conditions information relevant to eligibility for asylum or withholding of removal.

(b) At its option, the Department of State may also provide:

(1) An assessment of the accuracy of the applicant's assertions about conditions in his or her country of nationality or habitual residence and his or her particular situation;

(2) Information about whether persons who are similarly situated to the applicant are persecuted or tortured in his or her country of nationality or habitual residence and the frequency of such persecution or torture; or

(3) Such other information as it deems relevant.

(c) Asylum officers and immigration judges may request specific comments from the Department of State regarding individual cases or types of claims under consideration, or such other information as they deem appropriate.

(d) Any such comments received pursuant to paragraphs (b) and (c) of this section shall be made part of the record. Unless the comments are classified under the applicable Executive Order, the applicant shall be provided an opportunity to review and respond to such comments prior to the issuance of any decision to deny the application.

[64 FR 8488, Feb. 19, 1999]

§ 208.12 Reliance on information compiled by other sources.

(a) In deciding an asylum application, or in deciding whether the alien has a credible fear of persecution or torture pursuant to § 208.30 of this part, or a reasonable fear of persecution or torture pursuant to § 208.31, the asylum officer may rely on material provided by the Department of State, the Office of International Affairs, other Service offices, or other credible sources, such as international organizations, private voluntary agencies, news organizations, or academic institutions.

(b) Nothing in this part shall be construed to entitle the applicant to conduct discovery directed toward the records, officers, agents, or employees of the Service, the Department of Justice, or the Department of State.

[64 FR 8488, Feb. 19, 1999]

§ 208.13 Establishing asylum eligibility.

(a) Burden of proof. The burden of proof is on the applicant for asylum to establish that he or she is a refugee as defined in section 101(a)(42) of the Act. The testimony of the applicant, if credible, may be sufficient to sustain the burden of proof without corroboration. The fact that the applicant previously established a credible fear of persecution for purposes of section 235(b)(1)(B) of the Act does not relieve the alien of the additional burden of establishing eligibility for asylum.

(b) Persecution. The applicant may qualify as a refugee either because he or she has suffered past persecution or because he or she has a well-founded fear of future persecution.

(1) Past persecution. An applicant shall be found to be a refugee on the basis of past persecution if he or she can establish that he or she has suffered persecution in the past in his or her country of nationality or last habitual residence on account of race, religion, nationality, membership in a particular social group, or political opinion, and that he or she is unable or unwilling to return to or avail himself or herself of the protection of that country owing to such persecution.

(i) If it is determined that the applicant has established past persecution, he or she shall be presumed also to have a well-founded fear of persecution unless a preponderance of the evidence establishes that since the time the persecution occurred conditions in the applicant's country of nationality or last habitual residence have changed to such an extent that the applicant no longer has a well-founded fear of being persecuted if he or she were to return.

(ii) An application for asylum shall be denied if the applicant establishes past persecution under this paragraph but it is also determined that he or she does not have a well-founded fear of future persecution under paragraph (b)(2) of this section, unless it is determined that the applicant has demonstrated compelling reasons for being unwilling to return to his or her country of nationality or last habitual residence arising out of the severity of the past persecution. If the applicant demonstrates such compelling reasons, he or she may be granted asylum unless such a grant is barred by paragraph (c) of this section .

(2) Well-founded fear of persecution. An applicant shall be found to have a well-founded fear of persecution if he or she can establish first, that he or she has a fear of persecution in his or her country of nationality or last habitual residence on account of race, religion, nationality, membership in a particular social group, or political opinion; second, that there is a reasonable possibility of suffering such persecution if he or she were to return to that country; and third, that he or she is unable or unwilling to return to or avail himself or herself of the protection of that country because of such fear. In evaluating whether the applicant has sustained his or her burden of proving that he or she has a well-founded fear of persecution, the asylum officer or immigration judge shall not require the applicant to provide evidence that he or she would be singled out individually for persecution if:

(i) The applicant establishes that there is a pattern or practice in his or her country of nationality or last habitual residence of persecution of a group of persons similarly situated to the applicant on account of race, religion, nationality, membership in a particular social group, or political opinion; and

(ii) The applicant establishes his or her own inclusion in and identification with such group of persons such that his or her fear of persecution upon return is reasonable.

(c) Mandatory denials.

(1) Applications filed on or after April 1, 1997. For applications filed on or after April 1, 1997, an applicant shall not qualify for asylum if section 208(a)(2) or 208(b)(2) of the Act applies to the applicant. If the applicant is found to be ineligible for asylum under either section 208(a)(2) or 208(b)(2) of the Act, the applicant shall be considered for eligibility for withholding of removal under section 241(b)(3) of the Act. The applicant shall also be considered for eligibility for withholding of removal under the Convention Against Torture if the applicant requests such consideration or if the evidence presented by the alien indicates that the alien may be tortured in the country of removal.

(2) Applications filed before April 1, 1997.

(i) An immigration judge or asylum officer shall not grant asylum to any applicant who filed his or her application before April 1, 1997, if the alien:

(A) Having been convicted by a final judgment of a particularly serious crime in the United States, constitutes a danger to the community;

(B) Has been firmly resettled within the meaning of § 208.15;

(C) Can reasonably be regarded as a danger to the security of the United States;

(D) Has been convicted of an aggravated felony, as defined in section 101(a)(43) of the Act; or

(E) Ordered, incited, assisted, or otherwise participated in the persecution of any person on account of race, religion, nationality, membership in a particular social group, or political opinion.

(ii) If the evidence indicates that one of the above grounds apply to the applicant, he or she shall have the burden of proving by a preponderance of the evidence that he or she did not so act.

(d) Discretionary denial. An asylum application may be denied in the discretion of the Attorney General if the alien can be removed to a third country which has offered resettlement and in which the alien would not face harm or persecution.

[64 FR 8488, Feb. 19, 1999]

§ 208.14 Approval, denial, referral, or dismissal of application.

(a) By an immigration judge. Unless otherwise prohibited in § 208.13(c), an immigration judge may grant or deny asylum in the exercise of discretion to an applicant who qualifies as a refugee under section 101(a)(42) of the Act.

(b) By an asylum officer. Unless otherwise prohibited in § 208.13(c):

(1) An asylum officer may grant asylum in the exercise of discretion to an applicant who qualifies as a refugee under section 101(a)(42) of the Act.

(2) If the alien appears to be deportable, excludable or removable under section 240 of the Act, the asylum officer shall either grant asylum or refer the application to an immigration judge for adjudication in deportation, exclusion, or removal proceedings. An asylum officer may refer such an application after an interview conducted in accordance with § 208.9, or if, in accordance with § 208.10, the applicant is deemed to have waived his or her right to an interview or an adjudication by an asylum officer.

(3) If the applicant is maintaining valid nonimmigrant status at the time the application is decided, the asylum officer may grant or deny asylum, except in the case of an applicant described in § 208.2(b)(1).

(c) Applicability of § 103.2(b) of this chapter. No application for asylum or withholding of deportation shall be subject to denial pursuant to § 103.2(b) of this chapter.

(d) Duration. If the alien's asylum application is granted, the grant will be effective for an indefinite period, subject to termination as provided in § 208.22.

(e) Effect of denial of principal's application on separate applications by dependents. The denial of an asylum application filed by a principal applicant for asylum shall also result in the denial of asylum status to any dependents of that principal applicant who are included in that same application. Such denial shall not preclude a grant of asylum for an otherwise eligible dependent who has filed a separate asylum application, nor shall such denial result in an otherwise eligible dependent becoming ineligible to apply for asylum due to the provisions of section 208(a)(2)(C) of the Act.

(f) If an asylum applicant is granted adjustment of status to lawful permanent resident, the Service may provide written notice to the applicant that his or her asylum application will be presumed abandoned and dismissed without prejudice, unless the applicant submits a written request within 30 days of the notice, that the asylum application be adjudicated. If an applicant does not respond within 30 days of the date the written notice was sent or served, the Service may presume the asylum application abandoned and dismiss it without prejudice.

[62 FR 10342, March 6, 1997; as amended at 63 FR 12986, March 17, 1998; 64 FR 27875, May 21, 1999.]

§ 208.15 Definition of "firm resettlement."

An alien is considered to be firmly resettled if, prior to arrival in the United States, he or she entered into another nation with, or while in that nation received, an offer of permanent resident status, citizenship, or some other type of permanent resettlement unless he or she establishes:

(a) That his or her entry into that nation was a necessary consequence of his or her flight from persecution, that he or she remained in that nation only as long as was necessary to arrange onward travel, and that he or she did not establish significant ties in that nation; or

(b) That the conditions of his or her residence in that nation were so substantially and consciously restricted by the authority of the country of refuge that he or she was not in fact resettled. In making his or her determination, the Asylum Officer or Immigration Judge shall consider the conditions under which other residents of the country live, the type of housing made available to the refugee, whether permanent or temporary, the types and extent of employment available to the refugee, and the extent to which the refugee received permission to hold property and to enjoy other rights and privileges, such as travel documentation including a right of entry or reentry, education, public relief, or naturalization, ordinarily available to others resident in the country.

[62 FR 10343, March 6, 1997]

§ 208.16 Withholding of removal under section 241(b)(3)(B) of the Act and withholding of removal under the Convention Against Torture.

(a) Consideration of application for withholding of removal. An asylum officer shall not decide whether the exclusion, deportation, or removal of an alien to a country where the alien's life or freedom would be threatened must be withheld, except in the case of an alien who is otherwise eligible for asylum but is precluded from being granted such status due solely to section 207(a)(5) of the Act. In exclusion, deportation, or removal proceedings, an immigration judge may adjudicate both an asylum claim and a request for withholding of removal whether or not asylum is granted.

(b) Eligibility for withholding of removal under section 241(b)(3) of the Act; burden of proof. The burden of proof is on the applicant for withholding of removal under section 241(b)(3) of the Act to establish that his or her life or freedom would be threatened in the proposed country of removal on account of race, religion, nationality, membership in a particular social group, or political opinion. The testimony of the applicant, if credible, may be sufficient to sustain the burden of proof without corroboration. The evidence shall be evaluated as follows:

(1) The applicant's life or freedom shall be found to be threatened if it is more likely than not that he or she would be persecuted on account of race, religion, nationality, membership in a particular social group, or political opinion.

(2) If the applicant is determined to have suffered persecution in the past such that his or her life or freedom was threatened in the proposed country of removal on account of race, religion, nationality, membership in a particular social group, or political opinion, it shall be presumed that his or her life or freedom would be threatened on return to that country unless a preponderance of the evidence establishes that conditions in the country have changed to such an extent that it is no longer more likely than not that the applicant would be so persecuted there.

(3) In evaluating whether the applicant has sustained the burden of proving that his or her life or freedom would be threatened in a particular country on account of race, religion, nationality, membership in a particular social group, or political opinion, the asylum officer or immigration judge shall not require the applicant to provide evidence that he or she would be singled out individually for such persecution if:

(i) The applicant establishes that there is a pattern or practice in the country of proposed removal of persecution of a group of persons similarly situated to the applicant on account of race, religion, nationality, membership in a particular social group, or political opinion; and

(ii) The applicant establishes his or her own inclusion in and identification with such group of persons such that it is more likely than not that his or her life or freedom would be threatened upon return.

(c) Eligibility for withholding of removal under the Convention Against Torture.

(1) For purposes of regulations under Title II of the Act, "Convention Against Torture" shall refer to the United Nations Convention Against Torture and Other Cruel, Inhuman or Degrading Treatment or Punishment, subject to any reservations, understandings, declarations, and provisos contained in the United States Senate resolution of ratification of the Convention, as implemented by section 2242 of the Foreign Affairs Reform and Restructuring Act of 1998 (Pub.L. 105–277, 112 Stat. 2681, 2681–821). The definition of torture contained in § 208.18(a) of this part shall govern all decisions made under regulations under Title II of the Act about the applicability of Article 3 of the Convention Against Torture.

(2) The burden of proof is on the applicant for withholding of removal under this paragraph to establish that it is more likely than not that he or she would be tortured if removed to the proposed country of removal. The testimony of the applicant, if credible, may be sufficient to sustain the burden of proof without corroboration.

(3) In assessing whether it is more likely than not that an applicant would be tortured in the proposed country of removal, all evidence relevant to the possibility of future torture shall be considered, including, but not limited to:

(i) Evidence of past torture inflicted upon the applicant;

(ii) Evidence that the applicant could relocate to a part of the country of removal where he or she is not likely to be tortured;

(iii) Evidence of gross, flagrant or mass violations of human rights within the country of removal, where applicable; and

(iv) Other relevant information regarding conditions in the country of removal.

(4) In considering an application for withholding of removal under the Convention Against Torture, the immigration judge shall first determine whether the alien is more likely than not to be tortured in the country of removal. If the immigration judge determines that the alien is more likely than not to be tortured in the country of removal, the alien is entitled to protection under the Convention Against Torture. Protection under the Convention Against Torture will be granted either in the form of withholding of removal or in the form of deferral of removal. An alien entitled to such protection shall be granted withholding of removal unless the alien is subject to mandatory denial of withholding of removal under paragraphs (d)(2) or (d)(3) of this section. If an alien entitled to such protection is subject to mandatory denial of withholding of removal under paragraphs (d)(2) or (d)(3) of this section, the alien's removal shall be deferred under § 208.17(a).

(d) Approval or denial of application.

(1) General. Subject to paragraphs (d)(2) and (d)(3) of this section, an application for withholding of deportation or removal to a country of proposed removal shall be granted if the applicant's eligibility for withholding is established pursuant to paragraphs (b) or (c) of this section.

(2) Mandatory denials. Except as provided in paragraph (d)(3) of this section, an application for withholding of removal under section 241(b)(3) of the Act or under the Convention Against Torture shall be denied if the applicant falls within section 241(b)(3)(B) of the Act or, for applications for withholding of deportation adjudicated in proceedings commenced prior to April 1, 1997, within section 243(h)(2) of the Act as it appeared prior to that date. For purposes of section 241(b)(3)(B)(ii) of the Act, or section 243(h)(2)(B) of the Act as it appeared prior to April 1, 1997, an alien who has been convicted of a particularly serious crime shall be considered to constitute a danger to the community. If the evidence indicates the applicability of one or more of the grounds for denial of withholding enumerated in the Act, the applicant shall have the burden of proving by a preponderance of the evidence that such grounds do not apply.

(3) Exception to the prohibition on withholding of deportation in certain cases. Section 243(h)(3) of the Act, as added by section 413 of Pub.L. 104–132 (110 Stat. 1214), shall apply only to applications adjudicated in proceedings commenced before April 1, 1997, and in which final action had not been taken before April 24, 1996. The discretion permitted by that section to override section 243(h)(2) of the Act shall be exercised only in the case of an applicant convicted of an aggravated felony (or felonies) where he or she was sentenced to an aggregate term of imprisonment of less than 5 years and the immigration judge determines on an individual basis that the crime (or crimes) of which the applicant was convicted does not constitute a particularly serious crime. Nevertheless, it shall be presumed that an alien convicted of an aggravated felony has been convicted of a particularly serious crime. Except in the cases specified in this paragraph, the grounds for denial of withholding of deportation in section 243(h)(2) of the Act as it appeared prior to April 1, 1997, shall be deemed to comply with the Protocol Relating to the Status of Refugees, Jan. 31, 1967, T.I.A.S. No. 6577.

(e) Reconsideration of discretionary denial of asylum. In the event that an applicant is denied asylum solely in the exercise of discretion, and the applicant is subsequently granted withholding of deportation or removal under this section, thereby effectively precluding admission of the applicant's spouse or minor children following to join him or her, the denial of asylum shall be reconsidered. Factors to be considered will include the reasons for the denial and reasonable alternatives available to the applicant such as reunification with his or her spouse or minor children in a third country.

(f) Removal to third country. Nothing in this section or § 208.17 shall prevent the Service from removing an alien to a third country other than the country to which removal has been withheld or deferred.

[64 FR 8488, Feb. 19, 1999]

§ 208.17 Deferral of removal under the Convention Against Torture.

(a) Grant of deferral of removal. An alien who: has been ordered removed; has been found under § 208.16(c)(3) to be entitled to protection under the Convention Against Torture; and is subject to the provisions for mandatory denial of withholding of removal under § 208.16(d)(2) or (d)(3), shall be granted deferral of removal to the country where he or she is more likely than not to be tortured.

(b) Notice to Alien.

(1) After an immigration judge orders an alien described in paragraph (a) of this section removed, the immigration judge shall inform the alien that his or her removal to the country where he or she is more likely than not to be tortured shall be deferred until such time as the deferral is terminated under this section. The immigration judge shall inform the alien that deferral of removal:

(i) Does not confer upon the alien any lawful or permanent immigration status in the United States;

(ii) Will not necessarily result in the alien being released from the custody of the Service if the alien is subject to such custody;

(iii) Is effective only until terminated; and

(iv) Is subject to review and termination if the immigration judge determines that it is not likely that the alien would be tortured in the country to which removal has been deferred, or if the alien requests that deferral be terminated.

(2) The immigration judge shall also inform the alien that removal has been deferred only to the country in which it has been determined that the alien is likely to be tortured, and that the alien may be removed at any time to another country where he or she is not likely to be tortured.

(c) Detention of an alien granted deferral of removal under this section. Nothing in this section shall alter the authority of the Service to detain an alien whose removal has been deferred under this section and who is otherwise subject to detention. In the case of such an alien, decisions about the alien's release shall be made according to part 241 of this chapter.

(d) Termination of deferral of removal.

(1) At any time while deferral of removal is in effect, the INS District Counsel for the District with jurisdiction over an alien whose removal has been deferred under paragraph (a) of this section may file a motion with the Immigration Court having administrative control pursuant to § 3.11 of this chapter to schedule a hearing to consider whether deferral of removal should be terminated. The Service motion shall be granted if it is accompanied by evidence that is relevant to the possibility that the alien would be tortured in the country to which removal has been deferred and that was not presented at the previous hearing. The Service motion shall not be subject to the requirements for reopening in §§ 3.2 and 3.23 of this chapter.

(2) The Immigration Court shall provide notice to the alien and the Service of the time, place, and date of the termination hearing. Such notice shall inform the alien that the alien may supplement the information in his or her initial application for withholding of removal under the Convention Against Torture and shall provide that the alien must submit any such supplemental information within 10 calendar days of service of such notice (or 13 calendar days if service of such notice was by mail). At the expiration of this 10 or 13 day period, the Immigration Court shall forward a copy of the original application, and any supplemental information the alien or the Service has submitted, to the Department of State, together with notice to the Department of State of the time, place and date of the termination hearing. At its option, the Department of State may provide comments on the case, according to the provisions of § 208.11 of this part.

(3) The immigration judge shall conduct a hearing and make a de novo determination, based on the record of proceeding and initial application in addition to any new evidence submitted by the Service or the alien, as to whether the alien is more likely than not to be tortured in the country to which removal has been deferred. This determination shall be made under the standards for eligibility set out in § 208.16(c). The burden is on the alien to establish that it is more likely than not that he or she would be tortured in the country to which removal has been deferred.

(4) If the immigration judge determines that the alien is more likely than not to be tortured in the country to which removal has been deferred, the order of deferral shall remain in place. If the immigration judge determines that the alien has not established that he or she is more likely than not to be tortured in the country to which removal has been deferred, the deferral of removal shall be terminated and the alien may be removed to that country. Appeal of the immigration judge's decision shall lie to the Board.

(e) Termination at the request of the alien.

(1) At any time while deferral of removal is in effect, the alien may make a written request to the Immigration Court having administrative control pursuant to § 3.11 of this chapter to terminate the deferral order. If satisfied on the basis of the written submission that the alien's request is knowing and voluntary, the immigration judge shall terminate the order of deferral and the alien may be removed.

(2) If necessary the immigration judge may calendar a hearing for the sole purpose of determining whether the alien's request is knowing and voluntary. If the immigration judge determines that the alien's request is knowing and voluntary, the order of deferral shall be terminated. If the immigration judge determines that the alien's request is not knowing and voluntary, the alien's request shall not serve as the basis for terminating the order of deferral.

(f) Termination pursuant to § 208.18(c). At any time while deferral of removal is in effect, the Attorney General may determine whether deferral should be terminated based on diplomatic assurances forwarded by the Secretary of State pursuant to the procedures in § 208.18(c).

[64 FR 8489, Feb. 19, 1999]

§ 208.18 Implementation of the Convention Against Torture.

(a) Definitions. The definitions in this subsection incorporate the definition of torture contained in Article 1 of the Convention Against Torture, subject to the reservations, understandings, declarations, and provisos contained in the United States Senate resolution of ratification of the Convention.

(1) Torture is defined as any act by which severe pain or suffering, whether physical or mental, is intentionally inflicted on a person for such purposes as obtaining from him or her or a third person information or a confession, punishing him or her for an act he or she or a third person has committed or is suspected of having committed, or intimidating or coercing him or her or a third person, or for any reason based on discrimination of any kind, when such pain or suffering is inflicted by or at the instigation of or with the consent or acquiescence of a public official or other person acting in an official capacity.

(2) Torture is an extreme form of cruel and inhuman treatment and does not include lesser forms of cruel, inhuman or degrading treatment or punishment that do not amount to torture.

(3) Torture does not include pain or suffering arising only from, inherent in or incidental to lawful sanctions. Lawful sanctions include judicially imposed sanctions and other enforcement actions authorized by law, including the death penalty, but do not include sanctions that defeat the object and purpose of the Convention Against Torture to prohibit torture.

(4) In order to constitute torture, mental pain or suffering must be prolonged mental harm caused by or resulting from:

(i) The intentional infliction or threatened infliction of severe physical pain or suffering;

(ii) The administration or application, or threatened administration or application, of mind altering substances or other procedures calculated to disrupt profoundly the senses or the personality;

(iii) The threat of imminent death; or

(iv) The threat that another person will imminently be subjected to death, severe physical pain or suffering, or the administration or application of mind altering substances or other procedures calculated to disrupt profoundly the sense or personality.

(5) In order to constitute torture, an act must be specifically intended to inflict severe physical or mental pain or suffering. An act that results in unanticipated or unintended severity of pain and suffering is not torture.

(6) In order to constitute torture an act must be directed against a person in the offender's custody or physical control.

(7) Acquiescence of a public official requires that the public official, prior to the activity constituting torture, have awareness of such activity and thereafter breach his or her legal responsibility to intervene to prevent such activity.

(8) Noncompliance with applicable legal procedural standards does not per se constitute torture.

(b) Applicability of §§ 208.16(c) and 208.17(a).

(1) Aliens in proceedings on or after March 22, 1999. An alien who is in exclusion, deportation, or removal proceedings on or after March 22, 1999 may apply for withholding of removal under § 208.16(c), and, if applicable, may be considered for deferral of removal under § 208.17(a).

(2) Aliens who were ordered removed, or whose removal orders became final, before March 22, 1999. An alien under a final order of deportation, exclusion, or removal that became final prior to March 22, 1999 may move to reopen proceedings for the sole purpose of seeking protection under § 208.16(c). Such motions shall be governed by §§ 3.23 and 3.2 of this chapter, except that the time and numerical limitations on motions to reopen shall not apply and the alien shall not be required to demonstrate that the evidence sought to be offered was unavailable and could not have been discovered or presented at the former hearing. The motion to reopen shall not be granted unless:

(i) The motion is filed within June 21, 1999; and

(ii) The evidence sought to be offered establishes a prima facie case that the applicant's removal must be withheld or deferred under §§ 208.16(c) or 208.17(a).

(3) Aliens who, on March 22, 1999, have requests pending with the Service for protection under Article 3 of the Convention Against Torture.

(i) Except as otherwise provided, after March 22, 1999, the Service will not:

(A) Consider, under its pre-regulatory administrative policy to ensure compliance with the Convention Against Torture, whether Article 3 of that Convention prohibits the removal of an alien to a particular country, or

(B) Stay the removal of an alien based on a request filed with the Service for protection under Article 3 of that Convention.

(ii) For each alien who, on or before March 22, 1999, filed a request with the Service for protection under Article 3 of the Convention Against Torture, and whose request has not been finally decided by the Service, the Service shall provide written notice that, after March 22, 1999, consideration for protection under Article 3 can be obtained only through the provisions of this rule.

(A) The notice shall inform an alien who is under an order of removal issued by EOIR that, in order to seek consideration of a claim under §§ 208.16(c) or 208.17(a), such an alien must file a motion to reopen with the immigration court or the Board of Immigration Appeals. This notice shall be accompanied by a stay of removal, effective until 30 days after service of the notice on the alien. A motion to reopen filed under this paragraph for the limited purpose of asserting a claim under §§ 208.16(c) or 208.17(a) shall not be subject to the requirements for reopening in §§ 3.2 and 3.23 of this chapter. Such a motion shall be granted if it is accompanied by a copy of the notice described in paragraph (b)(3)(ii) or by other convincing evidence that the alien had a request pending with the Service for protection under Article 3 of the Convention Against Torture on March 22, 1999. The filing of such a motion shall extend the stay of removal during the pendency of the adjudication of this motion.

(B) The notice shall inform an alien who is under an administrative order of removal issued by the Service under section 238(b) of the Act or an exclusion, deportation, or removal order reinstated by the Service under section 241(a)(5) of the Act that the alien's claim to withholding of removal under § 208.16(c) or deferral of removal under § 208.17(a) will be considered under § 208.31.

(C) The notice shall inform an alien who is under an administrative order of removal issued by the Service under section 235(c) of the Act that the alien's claim to protection under the Convention Against Torture will be decided by the Service as provided in § 208.18(d) and 235.8(b)(4) and will not be considered under the provisions of this part relating to consideration or review by an immigration judge, the Board of Immigration Appeals, or an asylum officer.

(4) Aliens whose claims to protection under the Convention Against Torture were finally decided by the Service prior to March 22, 1999. Sections 208.16(c) and 208.17 (a) and paragraphs (b)(1) through (b)(3) of this section do not apply to cases in which, prior to March 22, 1999, the Service has made a final administrative determination about the applicability of Article 3 of the Convention Against Torture to the case of an alien who filed a request with the Service for protection under Article 3. If, prior to March 22, 1999, the Service determined that an applicant cannot be removed consistent with the Convention Against Torture, the alien shall be considered to have been granted withholding of removal under § 208.16(c), unless the alien is subject to mandatory denial of withholding of removal under § 208.16(d)(2) or (d)(3), in which case the alien will be considered to have been granted deferral of removal under 208.17(a). If, prior to March 22, 1999, the Service determined that an alien can be removed consistent with the Convention Against Torture, the alien will be considered to have been finally denied withholding of removal under § 208.16(c) and deferral of removal under § 208.17(a).

(c) Diplomatic assurances against torture obtained by the Secretary of State.

(1) The Secretary of State may forward to the Attorney General assurances that the Secretary has obtained from the government of a specific country that an alien would not be tortured there if the alien were removed to that country.

(2) If the Secretary of State forwards assurances described in paragraph (c)(1) of this section to the Attorney General for consideration by the Attorney General or her delegates under this paragraph, the Attorney General shall determine, in consultation with the Secretary of State, whether the assurances are sufficiently reliable to allow the alien's removal to that country consistent with Article 3 of the Convention Against Torture. The Attorney General's authority under this paragraph may be exercised by the Deputy Attorney General or by the Commissioner, Immigration and Naturalization Service, but may not be further delegated.

(3) Once assurances are provided under paragraph (c)(2) of this section, the alien's claim for protection under the Convention Against Torture shall not be considered further by an immigration judge, the Board of Immigration Appeals, or an asylum officer.

(d) Cases involving aliens ordered removed under section 235(c) of the Act. With respect to an alien terrorist or other alien subject to administrative removal under section 235(c) of the Act who requests protection under Article 3 of the Convention Against Torture, the Service will assess the applicability of Article 3 through the removal process to ensure that a removal order will not be executed under circumstances that would violate the obligations of the United States under Article 3. In such cases, the provisions of Part 208 relating to consideration or review by an immigration judge, the Board of Immigration Appeals, or an asylum officer shall not apply.

(e) Judicial review of claims for protection from removal under Article 3 of the Convention Against Torture.

(1) Pursuant to the provisions of section 2242(d) of the Foreign Affairs Reform and Restructuring Act of 1998, there shall be no judicial appeal or review of any action, decision, or claim raised under the Convention or that section, except as part of the review of a final order of removal pursuant to section 242 of the Act; provided however, that any appeal or petition regarding an action, decision, or claim under the Convention or under section 2242 of the Foreign Affairs Reform and Restructuring Act of 1998 shall not be deemed to include or authorize the consideration of any administrative order or decision, or portion thereof, the appeal or review of which is restricted or prohibited by the Act.

(2) Except as otherwise expressly provided, nothing in this paragraph shall be construed to create a private right of action or to authorize the consideration or issuance of administrative or judicial relief.

[64 FR 8490, Feb. 19, 1999; 64 FR 13881, March 23, 1999]

§ 208.19 Determining if an asylum application is frivolous.

For applications filed on or after April 1, 1997, an applicant is subject to the provisions of section 208(d)(6) of the Act only if a final order by an immigration judge or the Board of Immigration Appeals specifically finds that the alien knowingly filed a frivolous asylum application. For purposes of this section, an asylum application is frivolous if any of its material elements is deliberately fabricated. Such finding shall only be made if the immigration judge or the Board is satisfied that the applicant, during the course of the proceedings, has had sufficient opportunity to account for any discrepancies or implausible aspects of the claim. For purposes of this section, a finding that an alien filed a frivolous asylum application shall not preclude the alien from seeking withholding of removal.

[64 FR 8490, 8492, Feb. 19, 1999]

§ 208.20 Admission of the asylee's spouse and children.

(a) Eligibility. A spouse, as defined in section 101(a)(35) of the Act, 8 U.S.C. 1101(a)(35), or child, as defined in section 101(b)(1)(A), (B), (C), (D), (E), or (F) of the Act, also may be granted asylum if accompanying or following to join the principal alien who was granted asylum, unless it is determined that:

(1) The spouse or child ordered, incited, assisted, or otherwise participated in the persecution of any persons on account of race, religion, nationality, membership in a particular social group, or political opinion;

(2) The spouse or child, having been convicted by a final judgment of a particularly serious crime in the United States, constitutes a danger to the community of the United States;

(3) The spouse or child has been convicted of an aggravated felony, as defined in section 101(a)(43) of the Act; or

(4) There are reasonable grounds for regarding the spouse or child a danger to the security of the United States.

(b) Relationship. The relationship of spouse and child as defined in sections 101(a)(35) and 101(b)(1) of the Act must have existed at the time the principal alien's asylum application was approved and must continue to exist at the time of filing for accompanying or following-to-join benefits and at the time of the spouse or child's subsequent admission to the United States. If the asylee proves that the asylee is the parent of a child who was born after asylum was granted, but who was in utero on the date of the asylum grant, the child shall be eligible to accompany or follow-to-join the asylee. The child's mother, if not the principal asylee, shall not be eligible to accompany or follow-to-join the principal asylee unless the child's mother was the principal asylee's spouse on the date the principal asylee was granted asylum.

(c) Spouse or child in the United States. When a spouse or child of an alien granted asylum is in the United States, but was not included in the asylee's application, the asylee may request accompanying or following-to-join benefits for his/her spouse or child by filing for each qualifying family member a separate Form I–730, Refugee/Asylee Relative Petition, and supporting evidence, with the designated Service office, regardless of the status of that spouse or child in the United States. A recent photograph of each derivative must accompany the Form I–730. The photograph must clearly identify the derivative, and will be made part of the derivative's immigration record for identification purposes. Additionally, a separate Form I–730 must be filed by the asylee for each qualifying family member before February 28, 2000, or within 2 years of the date in which he/she was granted asylum status, whichever is later, unless it is determined by the Service that this period should be extended for humanitarian reasons. Upon approval of the Form I–730, the Service will notify the asylee of such approval on Form I–797, Notice of Action. Employment will be authorized incident to status. To demonstrate employment authorization, the Service will issue a Form I–94, Arrival–Departure Record, which also reflects the derivative's current status as an asylee, or the derivative may apply under § 274a.12(a) of this chapter, using Form I–765, Application for Employment Authorization, and a copy of the Form I–797. The approval of the Form I–730 shall remain valid for the duration of the relationship to the asylee and, in the case of a child, while the child is under 21 years of age and unmarried, provided also that the principal's status has not been revoked. However, the approved Form I–730 will cease to confer immigration benefits after it has been used by the beneficiary for admission to the United States as a derivative of an asylee.

(d) Spouse or child outside the United States. When a spouse or child of an alien granted asylum is outside the United States, the asylee may request accompanying or following-to-join benefits for his/her spouse or child(ren) by filing a separate Form I–730 for each qualifying family member with the designated Service office, setting forth the full name, relationship, date and place of birth, and current location of each such person. A recent photograph of each derivative must accompany the Form I–730. The photograph must clearly identify the derivative, and will be made part of the derivative's immigration record for identification purposes. A separate Form I–730 for each qualifying family member must be filed before February 28, 2000, or within 2 years of the date in which the asylee was granted asylum status, whichever is later, unless the Service determines that the filing period should be extended for humanitarian reasons. When the Form I–730 is approved, the Service will notify the asylee of such approval on Form I–797. The approved Form I–730 shall be forwarded by the Service to the Department of State for delivery to the American Embassy or Consulate having jurisdiction over the area in which the asylee's spouse or child is located. The approval of the Form I–730 shall remain valid for the duration of the relationship to the asylee and, in the case of a child, while the child is under 21 years of age and unmarried, provided also that the principal's status has not been revoked. However, the approved Form I–730 will cease to confer immigration benefits after it has been used by the beneficiary for admission to the United States as a derivative of an asylee.

(e) Denial. If the spouse or child is found to be ineligible for the status accorded under section 208(c) of the Act, a written notice stating the basis for denial shall be forwarded to the principal alien. No appeal shall lie from this decision.

(f) Burden of proof. To establish the claimed relationship of spouse or child as defined in sections 101(a)(35) and 101(b)(1) of the Act, evidence must be submitted with the request as set forth in part 204 of this chapter. Where possible this will consist of the documents specified in § 204.2 (a)(1)(i)(B), (a)(1)(iii)(B), (a)(2), (d)(2), and (d)(5) of this chapter. The burden of proof is on the principal alien to establish by a preponderance of the evidence that any person on whose behalf he or she is making a request under this section is an eligible spouse or child.

(g) Duration. The spouse or child qualifying under section 208(c) of the Act shall be granted asylum for an indefinite period unless the principal's status is revoked.

[63 FR 3796, Jan. 27, 1998; 64 FR 8490, Feb. 19, 1999]

§ 208.21 Effect on exclusion, deportation, and removal proceedings.

(a) An alien who has been granted asylum may not be deported or removed unless his or her asylum status is terminated pursuant to § 208.23 of this part. An alien in exclusion, deportation, or removal proceedings who is granted withholding of removal or deportation or deferral of removal may not be deported or removed to the country to which his or her deportation or removal is ordered withheld or deferred unless the withholding order is terminated pursuant to § 208.23 or deferral is terminated pursuant to § 208.17(d) or (e).

(b) When an alien's asylum status or withholding of removal or deportation is terminated under this part, the Service shall initiate removal proceedings under section 235 or 240 of the Act, as appropriate, if the alien is not already in exclusion, deportation, or removal proceedings or subject to a final order of removal. Removal proceedings may also be in conjunction with a termination hearing scheduled under § 208.23(e).

[64 FR 8490, 8492, Feb. 19, 1999]

§ 208.22 Restoration of status.

An alien who was maintaining his or her nonimmigrant status at the time of filing an asylum application and has such application denied may continue in or be restored to that status, if it has not expired.

[64 FR 8490, Feb. 19, 1999]

§ 208.23 Termination of asylum or withholding of removal or deportation.

(a) Termination of asylum by the Service. Except as provided in paragraph (e) of this section, an asylum officer may terminate a grant of asylum made under the jurisdiction of an asylum officer or a district director if following an interview, the asylum officer determines that:

(1) There is a showing of fraud in the alien's application such that he or she was not eligible for asylum at the time it was granted;

(2) As to applications filed on or after April 1, 1997, one or more of the conditions described in section 208(c)(2) of the Act exist; or

(3) As to applications filed before April 1, 1997, the alien no longer has a well-founded fear of persecution upon return due to a change of country conditions in the alien's country of nationality or habitual residence or the alien has committed any act that would have been grounds for denial of asylum under § 208.13(c)(2).

(b) Termination of withholding of deportation or removal by the Service. Except as provided in paragraph (e) of this section, an asylum officer may terminate a grant of withholding of deportation or removal made under the jurisdiction of an asylum officer or a district director if the asylum officer determines, following an interview, that:

(1) The alien is no longer entitled to withholding of deportation or removal due to a change of conditions in the country to which removal was withheld;

(2) There is a showing of fraud in the alien's application such that the alien was not eligible for withholding of removal at the time it was granted;

(3) The alien has committed any other act that would have been grounds for denial of withholding of removal under section 241(b)(3)(B) of the Act had it occurred prior to the grant of withholding of removal; or

(4) For applications filed in proceedings commenced before April 1, 1997, the alien has committed any act that would have been grounds for denial of withholding of deportation under section 243(h)(2) of the Act.

(c) Procedure. Prior to the termination of a grant of asylum or withholding of deportation or removal, the alien shall be given notice of intent to terminate, with the reasons therefor, at least 30 days prior to the interview specified in paragraph (a) of this section before an asylum officer. The alien shall be provided the opportunity to present evidence showing that he or she is still eligible for asylum or withholding of deportation or removal. If the asylum officer determines that the alien is no longer eligible for asylum or withholding of deportation or removal, the alien shall be given written notice that asylum status or withholding of deportation or removal and any employment authorization issued pursuant thereto, are terminated.

(d) Termination of derivative status. The termination of asylum status for a person who was the principal applicant shall result in termination of the asylum status of a spouse or child whose status was based on the asylum application of the principal. Such termination shall not preclude the spouse or child of such alien from separately asserting an asylum or withholding of deportation or removal claim.

(e) Termination of asylum or withholding of deportation or removal by the Executive Office for Immigration Review. An immigration judge or the Board of Immigration Appeals may reopen a case pursuant to § 3.2 or § 3.23 of this chapter for the purpose of terminating a grant of asylum or withholding of deportation or removal made under the jurisdiction of an immigration judge. In such a reopened proceeding, the Service must establish, by a preponderance of evidence, one or more of the grounds set forth in paragraphs (a) or (b) of this section. In addition, an immigration judge may terminate a grant of asylum or withholding of deportation or removal made under the jurisdiction of the Service at any time after the alien has been provided a notice of intent to terminate by the Service. Any termination under this paragraph may occur in conjunction with an exclusion, deportation or removal proceeding.

(f) Termination of asylum for arriving aliens. If the Service determines that an applicant for admission who had previously been granted asylum in the United States falls within conditions set forth in section 208(c)(2) of the Act and is inadmissible, the Service shall issue a notice of intent to terminate asylum and initiate removal proceedings under section 240 of the Act. The alien shall present his or her response to the intent to terminate during proceedings before the immigration judge.

[64 FR 8490, Feb. 19, 1999]

§ 208.24 to 208.29 [Reserved]

Subpart B—Credible Fear of Persecution

§ 208.30 Credible fear determinations involving stowaways and applicants for admission found inadmissible pursuant to section 212(a)(6)(C) or 212(a)(7) of the Act.

(a) Jurisdiction. The provisions of this subpart apply to aliens subject to sections 235(a)(2) and 235(b)(1) of the Act. Pursuant to section 235(b)(1)(B) of the Act, the Service has exclusive jurisdiction to make credible fear determinations, and the Executive Office for Immigration Review has exclusive jurisdiction to review such determinations. Except as otherwise provided in this subpart, paragraphs (b) through (e) of this section are the exclusive procedures applicable to credible fear interviews, determinations, and review under section 235(b)(1)(B) of the Act.

(b) Interview and procedure. The asylum officer, as defined in section 235(b)(1)(E) of the Act, will conduct the interview in a nonadversarial manner, separate and apart from the general public. At the time of the interview, the asylum officer shall verify that the alien has received Form M–444, Information about Credible Fear Interview in Expedited Removal Cases. The officer shall also determine that the alien has an understanding of the credible fear determination process. The alien may be required to register his or her identity electronically or through any other means designated by the Attorney General. The alien may consult with a person or persons of the alien's choosing prior to the interview or any review thereof, and may present other evidence, if available. Such consultation shall be at no expense to the Government and shall not unreasonably delay the process. Any person or persons with whom the alien chooses to consult may be present at the interview and may be permitted, in the discretion of the asylum officer, to present a statement at the end of the interview. The asylum officer, in his or her discretion, may place reasonable limits on the number of such persons who may be present at the interview and on the length of statement or statements made. If the alien is unable to proceed effectively in English, and if the asylum officer is unable to proceed competently in a language chosen by the alien, the asylum officer shall arrange for the assistance of an interpreter in conducting the interview. The interpreter may not be a representative or employee of the applicant's country of nationality or, if the applicant is stateless, the applicant's country of last habitual residence. The asylum officer shall create a summary of the material facts as stated by the applicant. At the conclusion of the interview, the officer shall review the summary with the alien and provide the alien with an opportunity to correct errors therein. The asylum officer shall create a written record of his or her determination, including a summary of the material facts as stated by the applicant, any additional facts relied on by the officer, and the officer's determination of whether, in light of such facts, the alien has established a credible fear of persecution or torture. The decision shall not become final until reviewed by a supervisory asylum officer.

(c) Authority. Asylum officers conducting credible fear interviews shall have the authorities described in § 208.9(c).

(d) Referral for an asylum hearing. If an alien, other than an alien stowaway, is found to have a credible fear of persecution or torture, the asylum officer will so inform the alien and issue a Form I–862, Notice to Appear, for full consideration of the asylum and withholding of removal claim in proceedings under section 240 of the Act. Parole of the alien may only be considered in accordance with section 212(d)(5) of the Act and § 212.5 of this chapter. If an alien stowaway is found to have a credible fear of persecution or torture, the asylum officer will so inform the alien and issue a Form I–863, Notice to Referral to Immigration Judge, for full consideration of the asylum and withholding of removal claim in proceedings under § 208.2(b)(1).

(e) Removal of aliens with no credible fear of persecution or torture. If an alien is found not to have a credible fear of persecution or torture, the asylum officer shall provide the alien with a written notice of decision and inquire whether the alien wishes to have an immigration judge review the negative decision, using Form I–869, Record of Negative Credible Fear Finding and Request for Review by Immigration Judge, on which the alien shall indicate whether he or she desires such review. If the alien is not a stowaway, the officer shall also order the alien removed and issue a Form I–860, Notice and Order of Expedited Removal. If the alien is a stowaway and the alien does not request a review by an immigration judge, the asylum officer shall also refer the alien to the district director for completion of removal proceedings in accordance with section 235(a)(2) of the Act.

(f) Review by immigration judge. The asylum officer's negative decision regarding credible fear shall be subject to review by an immigration judge upon the applicant's request, in accordance with section 235(b)(1)(B)(iii)(III) of the Act. If the alien requests such review, the asylum officer shall arrange for the detention of the alien and serve him or her with a Form I–863, Notice of Referral to Immigration Judge. The record of determination, including copies of the Form I–863, the asylum officer's notes, the summary of the material facts, and other materials upon which the determination was based shall be provided to the immigration judge with the negative determination. Upon review of the asylum officer's negative credible fear determination:

(1) If the immigration judge concurs with the determination of the asylum officer that the alien does not have a credible fear of persecution or torture, the case shall be returned to the Service for removal of the alien. The immigration judge's decision is final and may not be appealed.

(2) If the immigration judge finds that the alien, other than an alien stowaway, possesses a credible fear of persecution or torture, the immigration judge shall vacate the order of the asylum officer issued on Form I–860 and the Service may commence removal proceedings under section 240 of the Act, during which time the alien may file an application for asylum and withholding of removal in accordance with § 208.4(b)(3)(i).

(3) If the immigration judge finds that an alien stowaway possesses a credible fear of persecution or torture, the alien shall be allowed to file an application for asylum and withholding of removal before the immigration judge in accordance with § 208.4(b)(3)(iii). The immigration judge shall decide the application as provided in that section. Such decision may be appealed by either the stowaway or the Service to the Board of Immigration Appeals. If and when a denial of the application for asylum or withholding of removal becomes final, the alien shall be removed from the United States in accordance with section 235(a)(2) of the Act. If and when an approval of the application for asylum or withholding of removal becomes final, the Service shall terminate removal proceedings under section 235(a)(2) of the Act.

[64 FR 8492, Feb. 19, 1999]

§ 208.31 Reasonable fear of persecution or torture determinations involving aliens ordered removed under section 238(b) of the Act and aliens whose removal is reinstated under section 241(a)(5) of the Act.

(a) Jurisdiction. This section shall apply to any alien ordered removed under section 238(b) of the Act or whose deportation, exclusion, or removal order is reinstated under section 241(a)(5) of the Act who, in the course of the administrative removal or reinstatement process, expresses a fear of returning to the country of removal. The Service has exclusive jurisdiction to make reasonable fear determinations, and EOIR has exclusive jurisdiction to review such determinations.

(b) Initiation of reasonable fear determination process. Upon issuance of a Final Administrative Removal Order under § 238.1 of this chapter, or notice under § 241.8(b) of this chapter that an alien is subject to removal, an alien described in paragraph (a) of this section shall be referred to an asylum officer for a reasonable fear determination. In the absence of exceptional circumstances, this determination will be conducted within 10 days of the referral.

(c) Interview and Procedure. The asylum officer shall conduct the interview in a non-adversarial manner, separate and apart from the general public. At the time of the interview, the asylum officer shall determine that the alien has an understanding of the reasonable fear determination process. The alien may be represented by counsel or an accredited representative at the interview, at no expense to the Government, and may present evidence, if available, relevant to the possibility of persecution or torture. The alien's representative may present a statement at the end of the interview. The asylum officer, in his or her discretion, may place reasonable limits on the number of persons who may be present at the interview and the length of the statement. If the alien is unable to proceed effectively in English, and if the asylum officer is unable to proceed competently in a language chosen by the alien, the asylum officer shall arrange for the assistance of an interpreter in conducting the interview. The interpreter may not be a representative or employee of the applicant's country or nationality, or if the applicant is stateless, the applicant's country of last habitual residence. The asylum officer shall create a summary of the material facts as stated by the applicant. At the conclusion of the interview, the officer shall review the summary with the alien and provide the alien with an opportunity to correct errors therein. The asylum officer shall create a written record of his or her determination, including a summary of the material facts as stated by the applicant, any additional facts relied on by the officers, and the officer's determination of whether, in light of such facts, the alien has established a reasonable fear of persecution or torture. The alien shall be determined to have a reasonable fear of persecution or torture if the alien establishes a reasonable possibility that he or she would be persecuted on account of his or her race, religion, nationality, membership in a particular social group or political opinion, or a reasonable possibility that he or she would be tortured in the country of removal. For purposes of the screening determination, the bars to eligibility for withholding of removal under section 241(b)(3)(B) of the Act shall not be considered.

(d) Authority. Asylum officers conducting screening determinations under this section shall have the authority described in § 208.9(c).

(e) Referral to Immigration Judge. If an asylum officer determines that an alien described in this section has a reasonable fear of persecution or torture, the officer shall so inform the alien and issue a Form I–863, Notice of Referral to the Immigration Judge, for full consideration of the request for withholding of removal only. Such cases shall be adjudicated by the immigration judge in accordance with the provisions of § 208.16. Appeal of the immigration judge's decision shall lie to the Board of Immigration Appeals.

(f) Removal of aliens with no reasonable fear of persecution or torture. If the asylum officer determines that the alien has not established a reasonable fear of persecution or torture, the asylum officer shall inform the alien in writing of the decision and shall inquire whether the alien wishes to have an immigration judge review the negative decision, using Form I–898, Record of Negative Reasonable Fear Finding and Request for Review by Immigration Judge, on which the alien shall indicate whether he or she desires such review.

(g) Review by immigration judge. The asylum officer's negative decision regarding reasonable fear shall be subject to review by an immigration judge upon the alien's request. If the alien requests such review, the asylum officer shall serve him or her with a Form I–863. The record of determination, including copies of the Form I–863, the asylum officer's notes, the summary of the material facts, and other materials upon which the determination was based shall be provided to the immigration judge with the negative determination. In the absence of exceptional circumstances, such review shall be conducted by the immigration judge within 10 days of the filing of the Form I–863 with the immigration court. Upon review of the asylum officer's negative reasonable fear determination:

(1) If the immigration judge concurs with the asylum officer's determination that the alien does not have a reasonable fear of persecution or torture, the case shall be returned to the Service for removal of the alien. No appeal shall lie from the immigration judge's decision.

(2) If the immigration judge finds that the alien has a reasonable fear of persecution or torture, the alien may submit Form I–589, Application for Asylum and Withholding of Removal.

(i) The immigration judge shall consider only the alien's application for withholding of removal under § 208.16 and shall determine whether the alien's removal to the country of removal must be withheld or deferred.

(ii) Appeal of the immigration judge's decision whether removal must be withheld or deferred lies to the Board of Immigration Appeals. If the alien or the Service appeals the immigration judge's decision, the Board shall review only the immigration judge's decision regarding the alien's eligibility for withholding or deferral of removal under § 208.16.

[64 FR 8493, Feb. 19, 1999; 64 FR 13881, March 23, 1999]

PART 216—CONDITIONAL BASIS OF LAWFUL PERMANENT RESIDENCE STATUS

§ 216.1 Definition of conditional permanent resident.

A conditional permanent resident is an alien who has been lawfully admitted for permanent residence within the meaning of section

101(a)(20) of the Act, except that a conditional permanent resident is also subject to the conditions and responsibilities set forth in section 216 or 216A of the Act, whichever is applicable, and Part 216 of this chapter. Unless otherwise specified, the rights, privileges, responsibilities and duties which apply to all other lawful permanent residents apply equally to conditional permanent residents, including but not limited to the right to apply for naturalization (if otherwise eligible), the right to file petitions on behalf of qualifying relatives, the privilege of residing permanently in the United States as an immigrant in accordance with the immigration laws, such status not having changed; the duty to register with the Selective Service System, when required; and the responsibility for complying with all laws and regulations of the United States. All references within this chapter to lawful permanent residents apply equally to conditional permanent residents, unless otherwise specified. The conditions of section 216 of the Act shall not apply to lawful permanent resident status based on a self-petitioning relationship under section 204(a)(1)(A)(iii), 204(a)(1)(A)(iv), 204(a)(1)(b)(ii), or 204(a)(1)(B)(iii) of the Act or based on eligibility as the derivative child of a self-petitioning spouse under section 204(a)(1)(A)(iii) or 204(a)(1)(B)(ii) of the Act, regardless of the date on which the marriage to the abusive citizen or lawful permanent resident occurred.

[59 FR 26590, May 23, 1994; 61 FR 13079, March 26, 1996]

§ 216.2 Notification requirements.

(a) When alien acquires status of conditional permanent resident. At the time an alien acquires conditional permanent residence through admission to the United States with an immigrant visa or adjustment of status under section 245 of the Act, the Service shall notify the alien of the conditional basis of the alien's status, of the requirement that the alien apply for removal of the conditions within the ninety days immediately preceding the second anniversary of the alien's having been granted such status, and that failure to apply for removal of the conditions will result in automatic termination of the alien's lawful status in the United States.

(b) When alien is required to apply for removal of the conditional basis of lawful permanent resident status. Approximately 90 days before the second anniversary of the date on which the alien obtained conditional permanent residence, the Service should notify the alien a second time of the requirement that the alien and the petitioning spouse or the alien entrepreneur must file a petition to remove the conditional basis of the alien's lawful permanent residence. Such notification shall be mailed to the alien's last known address.

(c) Effect of failure to provide notification. Failure of the Service to provide notification as required by either paragraph (a) or (b) of this section does not relieve the alien and the petitioning spouse, or the alien entrepreneur of the requirement to file a petition to remove conditions within the 90 days immediately preceding the second anniversary of the date on which the alien obtained permanent residence.

[53 FR 30018, Aug. 10, 1988, as amended at 59 FR 26590, May 23, 1994]

§ 216.3 Termination of conditional resident status.

(a) During the two-year conditional period. The director shall send a formal written notice to the conditional permanent resident of the termination of the alien's conditional permanent resident status if the director determines that any of the conditions set forth in section 216(b)(1) or 216A(b)(1) of the Act, whichever is applicable, are true, or it becomes known to the government that an alien entrepreneur who was admitted pursuant to section 203(b)(5) of the Act obtained his or her investment capital through other than legal means (such as through the sale of illegal drugs). If the Service issues a notice of intent to terminate an alien's conditional resident status, the director shall not adjudicate Form I–751 or Form I–829 until it has been determined that the alien's status will not be terminated. During this time, the alien shall continue to be a lawful conditional permanent resident with all the rights, privileges, and responsibilities provided to persons possessing such status. Prior to issuing the notice of termination, the director shall provide the alien with an opportunity to review and rebut the evidence upon which the decision is to be based, in accordance with § 103.2(b)(2) of this chapter. The termination of status, and all of the rights and privileges concomitant thereto (including authorization to accept or continue in employment in this country), shall take effect as of the date of such determination by the director, although the alien may request a review of such determination in removal proceedings. In addition to the notice of termination, the director shall issue a notice to appear in accordance with 8 CFR part 239. During the ensuing removal proceedings, the alien may submit evidence to rebut the determination of the director. The burden of proof shall be on the Service to establish, by a preponderance of the evidence, that one or more of the conditions in section 216(b)(1) or 216A(b)(1) of the Act, whichever is applicable, are true, or that an alien entrepreneur who was admitted pursuant to section 203(b)(5) of the Act obtained his or her investment capital through other than legal means (such as through the sale of illegal drugs).

(b) Determination of fraud after two years. If, subsequent to the removal of the conditional basis of an alien's permanent resident status, the director determines that an alien spouse obtained permanent resident status through a marriage which was entered into for the purpose of evading the immigration laws or an alien entrepreneur obtained permanent resident status through a commercial enterprise which was improper under section 216A(b)(1) of the Act, the director may institute rescission proceedings pursuant to section 246 of the Act (if otherwise appropriate) or removal proceedings under section 240 of the Act.

[53 FR 30019, Aug. 10, 1988; as amended at 59 FR 26590, May 23, 1994; 62 FR 10349, March 6, 1997]

§ 216.4 Joint petition to remove conditional basis of lawful permanent resident status for alien spouse.

(a) Filing the petition—

(1) General procedures. Within the 90–day period immediately preceding the second anniversary of the date on which the alien obtained permanent residence, the alien and the alien's spouse who filed the original immigrant visa petition or fiance/fiancee petition through which the alien obtained permanent residence must file a Petition to Remove the Conditions on Residence (Form I–751) with the Service. The petition shall be filed within this time period regardless of the amount of physical presence which the alien has accumulated in the United States. Before Form I–751 may be considered as properly filed, it must be accompanied by the fee required under § 103.7(b) of this chapter and by documentation as described in paragraph (a)(5) of this section, and it must be properly signed by the alien and the alien's spouse. If the joint petition cannot be filed due to the termination of the marriage through annulment, divorce, or the death of the petitioning spouse, or if the petitioning spouse refuses to join in the filing of the petition, the conditional permanent resident may apply for a waiver of the requirement to file the joint petition in accordance with the provisions of § 216.5 of this part. Upon receipt of a properly filed Form I–751, the alien's conditional permanent resident status shall be extended automatically, if necessary, until such time as the director has adjudicated the petition.

(2) Dependent children. Dependent children of a conditional permanent resident who acquired conditional permanent resident status concurrently with the parent may be included in the joint petition filed by the parent and the parent's petitioning spouse. A child shall be deemed to have acquired conditional residence status concurrently with the parent if the child's residence was acquired on the same date or within 90 days thereafter. Children who cannot be included in a joint petition filed by the parent and parent's petitioning spouse due to the child's not having acquired conditional resident status concurrently with the parent, the death of the parent, or other reasons may file a separate Petition to Remove the Conditions on Residence (Form I–751).

(3) Jurisdiction. Form I–751 shall be filed with the director of the regional service center having jurisdiction over the alien's place of residence.

(4) Physical presence at time of filing. A petition may be filed regardless of whether the alien is physically present in the

United States. However, if the alien is outside the United States at the time of filing, he or she must return to the United States, with his or her spouse and dependent children, to comply with the interview requirements contained in the Act. Furthermore, if the documentation submitted in support of the petition includes affidavits of third parties having knowledge of the bona fides of the marital relationship, the petitioner must arrange for the affiants to be present at the interview, at no expense to the government. Once the petition has been properly filed, the alien may travel outside the United States and return if in possession of documentation as set forth in § 211.1(b)(1) of this chapter, provided the alien and the petitioning spouse comply with the interview requirements described in § 216.4(b). An alien who is not physically present in the United States during the filing period but subsequently applies for admission to the United States shall be processed in accordance with § 235.11 of this chapter.

(5) Documentation. Form I–751 shall be accompanied by evidence that the marriage was not entered into for the purpose of evading the immigration laws of the United States. Such evidence may include:

(i) Documentation showing joint ownership of property;

(ii) Lease showing joint tenancy of a common residence;

(iii) Documentation showing commingling of financial resources;

(iv) Birth certificates of children born to the marriage;

(v) Affidavits of third parties having knowledge of the bona fides of the marital relationship, or

(vi) Other documentation establishing that the marriage was not entered into in order to evade the immigration laws of the United States.

(6) Termination of status for failure to file petition. Failure to properly file Form I–751 within the 90–day period immediately preceding the second anniversary of the date on which the alien obtained lawful permanent residence on a conditional basis shall result in the automatic termination of the alien's permanent residence status and the initiation of proceedings to remove the alien from the United States. In such proceedings the burden shall be on the alien to establish that he or she complied with the requirement to file the joint petition within the designated period. Form I–751 may be filed after the expiration of the 90–day period only if the alien establishes to the satisfaction of the director, in writing, that there was good cause for the failure to file Form I–751 within the required time period. If the joint petition is filed prior to the jurisdiction vesting with the immigration judge in removal proceedings and the director excuses the late filing and approves the petition, he or she shall restore the alien's permanent residence status, remove the conditional basis of such status and cancel any outstanding notice to appear in accordance with § 239.2 of this chapter. If the joint petition is not filed until after jurisdiction vests with the immigration judge, the immigration judge may terminate the matter upon joint motion by the alien and the Service.

(b) Interview—

(1) Authority to waive interview. The director of the regional service center shall review the Form I–751 filed by the alien and the alien's spouse to determine whether to waive the interview required by the Act. If satisfied that the marriage was not for the purpose of evading the immigration laws, the regional service center director may waive the interview and approve the petition. If not so satisfied, then the regional service center director shall forward the petition to the district director having jurisdiction over the place of the alien's residence so that an interview of both the alien and the alien's spouse may be conducted. The director must either waive the requirement for an interview and adjudicate the petition or arrange for an interview within 90 days of the date on which the petition was properly filed.

(2) Location of interview. Unless waived, an interview on the Form I–751 shall be conducted by an immigration examiner or other officer so designated by the district director at the district office, files control office or suboffice having jurisdiction over the residence of the joint petitioners.

(3) Termination of status for failure to appear for interview. If the conditional resident alien and/or the petitioning spouse fail to appear for an interview in connection with the joint petition required by section 216(c) of the Act, the alien's permanent residence status will be automatically terminated as of the second anniversary of the date on which the alien obtained permanent residence. The alien shall be provided with written notification of the termination and the reasons therefor, and a notice to appear shall be issued placing the alien under removal proceedings. The alien may seek review of the decision to terminate his or her status in such proceedings, but the burden shall be on the alien to establish compliance with the interview requirements. If the alien submits a written request that the interview be rescheduled or that the interview be waived, and the director determines that there is good cause for granting the request, the interview may be rescheduled or waived, as appropriate. If the interview is rescheduled at the request of the petitioners, the Service shall not be required to conduct the interview within the 90–day period following the filing of the petition.

(c) Adjudication of petition. The director shall adjudicate the petition within 90 days of the date of the interview, unless the interview is waived in accordance with paragraph (b)(1) of this section. In adjudicating the petition the director shall determine whether—

(1) The qualifying marriage was entered into in accordance with the laws of the place where the marriage took place;

(2) The qualifying marriage has been judicially annulled or terminated, other than through the death of a spouse;

(3) The qualifying marriage was entered into for the purpose of procuring permanent residence status for the alien; or

(4) A fee or other consideration was given (other than a fee or other consideration to an attorney for assistance in preparation of a lawful petition) in connection with the filing of the petition through which the alien obtained conditional permanent residence. If derogatory information is determined regarding any of these issues, the director shall offer the petitioners the opportunity to rebut such information. If the petitioners fail to overcome such derogatory information the director may deny the joint petition, terminate the alien's permanent residence, and issue a notice to appear to initiate removal proceedings. If derogatory information not relating to any of these issues is determined during the course of the interview, such information shall be forwarded to the investigations unit for appropriate action. If no unresolved derogatory information is determined relating to these issues, the petition shall be approved and the conditional basis of the alien's permanent residence status removed, regardless of any action taken or contemplated regarding other possible grounds for removal.

(d) Decision—

(1) Approval. If the director approves the joint petition he or she shall provide written notice of the decision to the alien and shall require the alien to report to the appropriate office of the Service for processing for a new Permanent Resident Card (if necessary), at which time the alien shall surrender any Permanent Resident Card previously issued.

(2) Denial. If the director denies the joint petition, he or she shall provide written notice to the alien of the decision and the reason(s) therefor and shall issue a notice to appear under section 239 of the Act and 8 CFR part 239. The alien's lawful permanent resident status shall be terminated as of the date of the director's written decision. The alien shall also be instructed to surrender any Permanent Resident Card previously issued by the Service. No appeal shall lie from the decision of the director; however, the alien may seek review of the decision in removal proceedings. In such proceedings the burden of proof shall be on the Service to establish, by a preponderance of the evidence, that the facts and information set forth by the petitioners are not true or that the petition was properly denied.

[54 FR 30369, July 20, 1989; 59 FR 26590, 26591, May 23, 1994; 62 FR 10349, March 6, 1997; 63 FR 70315, Dec. 21, 1998]

§ 216.5 Waiver of requirement to file joint petition to remove conditions by alien spouse.

(a) General.

(1) A conditional resident alien who is unable to meet the requirements under section 216 of the Act for a joint petition for removal of the conditional basis of his or her permanent resident status may file Form I–751, Petition to Remove the Conditions on Residence, if the alien requests a waiver, was not at fault in failing to meet the filing requirement, and the conditional resident alien is able to establish that:

(i) Deportation or removal from the United States would result in extreme hardship;

(ii) The marriage upon which his or her status was based was entered into in good faith by the conditional resident alien, but the marriage was terminated other than by death, and the conditional resident was not at fault in failing to file a timely petition; or

(iii) The qualifying marriage was entered into in good faith by the conditional resident but during the marriage the alien spouse or child was battered by or subjected to extreme cruelty committed by the citizen or permanent resident spouse or parent.

(2) A conditional resident who is in exclusion, deportation, or removal proceedings may apply for the waiver only until such time as there is a final order of exclusion, deportation or removal.

(b) Fee. Form I–751 shall be accompanied by the appropriate fee required under § 103.7(b) of this Chapter.

(c) Jurisdiction. Form I–751 shall be filed with the regional service center director having jurisdiction over the alien's place of residence.

(d) Interview. The service center director may refer the application to the appropriate local office and require that the alien appear for an interview in connection with the application for a waiver. The director shall deny the application and initiate removal proceedings if the alien fails to appear for the interview as required, unless the alien establishes good cause for such failure and the interview is rescheduled.

(e) Adjudication of waiver application.

(1) Application based on claim of hardship. In considering an application for a waiver based upon an alien's claim that extreme hardship would result from the alien's removal from the United States, the director shall take into account only those factors that arose subsequent to the alien's entry as a conditional permanent resident. The director shall bear in mind that any removal from the United States is likely to result in a certain degree of hardship, and that only in those cases where the hardship is extreme should the application for a waiver be granted. The burden of establishing that extreme hardship exists rests solely with the applicant.

(2) Application for waiver based upon the alien's claim that the marriage was entered into in good faith. In considering whether an alien entered into a qualifying marriage in good faith, the director shall consider evidence relating to the amount of commitment by both parties to the marital relationship. Such evidence may include—

(i) Documentation relating to the degree to which the financial assets and liabilities of the parties were combined;

(ii) Documentation concerning the length of time during which the parties cohabited after the marriage and after the alien obtained permanent residence;

(iii) Birth certificates of children born to the marriage; and

(iv) Other evidence deemed pertinent by the director.

(3) Application for waiver based on alien's claim of having been battered or subjected to extreme mental cruelty. A conditional resident who entered into the qualifying marriage in good faith, and who was battered or was the subject of extreme cruelty or whose child was battered by or was the subject of extreme cruelty perpetrated by the United States citizen or permanent resident spouse during the marriage, may request a waiver of the joint filing requirement. The conditional resident parent of a battered or abused child may apply for the waiver regardless of the child's citizenship or immigration status.

(i) For the purpose of this chapter the phrase "was battered by or was the subject of extreme cruelty" includes, but is not limited to, being the victim of any act or threatened act of violence, including any forceful detention, which results or threatens to result in physical or mental injury. Psychological or sexual abuse or exploitation, including rape, molestation, incest (if the victim is a minor) or forced prostitution shall be considered acts of violence.

(ii) A conditional resident or former conditional resident who has not departed the United States after termination of resident status may apply for the waiver. The conditional resident may apply for the waiver regardless of his or her present marital status. The conditional resident may still be residing with the citizen or permanent resident spouse, or may be divorced or separated.

(iii) Evidence of physical abuse may include, but is not limited to, expert testimony in the form of reports and affidavits from police, judges, medical personnel, school officials and social service agency personnel. The Service must be satisfied with the credibility of the sources of documentation submitted in support of the application.

(iv) The Service is not in a position to evaluate testimony regarding a claim of extreme mental cruelty provided by unlicensed or untrained individuals. Therefore, all waiver applications based upon claims of extreme mental cruelty must be supported by the evaluation of a professional recognized by the Service as an expert in the field. An evaluation which was obtained in the course of the divorce proceedings may be submitted if it was provided by a professional recognized by the Service as an expert in the field.

(v) The evaluation must contain the professional's full name, professional address and license number. It must also identify the licensing, certifying, or registering authority. The Service retains the right to verify the professional's license.

(vi) The Service's decision on extreme mental cruelty waivers will be based upon the evaluation of the recognized professional. The Service reserves the right to request additional evaluations from expert witnesses chosen by the Service. Requests for additional evaluations must be authorized by the Assistant Regional Commissioner for Adjudications.

(vii) Licensed clinical social workers, psychologists, and psychiatrists are professionals recognized by the Service for the purpose of this section. A clinical social worker who is not licensed only because the state in which he or she practices does not provide for licensing will be considered a licensed professional recognized by the Service if he or she is included in the Register of Clinical Social Workers published by the National Association of Social Workers or is certified by the American Board of Examiners in Clinical Social Work.

(viii) As directed by the statute, the information contained in the application and supporting documents shall not be released without a court order or the written consent of the applicant; or, in the case of a child, the written consent of the parent or legal guardian who filed the waiver application on the child's behalf. Information may be released only to the applicant, his or her authorized representative, an officer of the Department of Justice, or any federal or State law enforcement agency. Any information provided under this part may be used for the purposes of enforcement of the Act or in any criminal proceeding.

(f) Decision. The director shall provide the alien with written notice of the decision on the application for waiver. If the decision is adverse, the director shall advise the alien of the reasons therefor, notify the alien of the termination of his or her permanent residence status, instruct the alien to surrender any Permanent Resident Card issued by the Service and issue a notice to appear placing the alien in removal proceedings. No appeal shall lie from the decision of the director; however, the alien may seek review of such decision in removal proceedings.

[56 FR 22637, May 16, 1991; 59 FR 26591, May 23, 1994; 62 FR 10350, March 6, 1997; 63 FR 70315, Dec. 21, 1998]

PART 235—INSPECTION OF PERSONS APPLYING FOR ADMISSION

§ 235.1 Scope of examination.

(a) General. Application to lawfully enter the United States shall be made in person to an immigration officer at a U.S. port-of-entry when the port is open for inspection, or as otherwise designated in this section.

(b) U.S. citizens. A person claiming U.S. citizenship must establish that fact to the examining officer's satisfaction and must present a U.S. passport if such passport is required under the provisions of 22 CFR part 53. If such applicant for admission fails to satisfy the examining immigration officer that he or she is a U.S. citizen, he or she shall thereafter be inspected as an alien.

(c) Alien members of United States Armed Forces and members of a force of a NATO country. Any alien member of the United States Armed Forces who is in the uniform of, or bears documents identifying him or her as a member of, such Armed Forces, and who is coming to or departing from the United States under official orders or permit of such Armed Forces is not subject to the removal provisions of the Act. A member of the force of a NATO country signatory to Article III of the Status of Forces Agreement seeking to enter the United States under official orders is exempt from the control provision of the Act. Any alien who is a member of either of the foregoing classes may, upon request, be inspected and his or her entry as an alien may be recorded. If the alien does not appear to the examining immigration officer to be clearly and beyond a doubt entitled to enter the United States under the provisions of the Act, the alien shall be so informed and his or her entry shall not be recorded.

(d) Alien applicants for admission.

(1) Each alien seeking admission at a United States port-of-entry shall present whatever documents are required and shall establish to the satisfaction of the immigration officer that he or she is not subject to removal under the immigration laws, Executive Orders, or Presidential Proclamations and is entitled under all of the applicable provisions of the immigration laws and this chapter to enter the United States. A person claiming to have been lawfully admitted for permanent residence must establish that fact to the satisfaction of the inspecting immigration officer and must present proper documents in accordance with § 211.1 of this chapter.

(2) An alien present in the United States who has not been admitted or paroled or an alien who seeks entry at other than an open, designated port-of-entry, except as otherwise permitted in this section, is subject to the provisions of section 212(a) of the Act and to removal under section 235(b) or 240 of the Act.

(3) An alien who is brought to the United States, whether or not to a designated port-of-entry and regardless of the means of transportation, after having been interdicted in international or United States waters, is considered an applicant for admission and shall be examined under section 235(b) of the Act.

(4) An alien stowaway is not an applicant for admission and may not be admitted to the United States. A stowaway shall be removed from the United States under section 235(a)(2) of the Act. The provisions of section 240 of the Act are not applicable to stowaways, nor is the stowaway entitled to further hearing or review of the removal, except that an alien stowaway who indicates an intention to apply for asylum, or expresses a fear of persecution, a fear of torture, or a fear of return to the country of proposed removal shall be referred to an asylum officer for a determination of credible fear of persecution or torture in accordance with section 235(b)(1)(B) of the Act and § 208.30 of this chapter. An alien stowaway who is determined to have a credible fear of persecution or torture shall have his or her asylum application adjudicated in accordance with § 208.2(b)(2) of this chapter.

(e) U.S. citizens, lawful permanent residents of the United States, and other aliens, entering the United States along the northern border, other than at a Port-of-Entry. A citizen or lawful permanent resident of the United States, a Canadian national or landed immigrant of Canada having a common nationality with nationals of Canada, or a landed immigrant of Canada who is a national of a country listed in § 217.2(a), may, if in possession of a valid, unexpired, Canadian Border Boat Landing Permit (Form I–68) or evidence of enrollment in any other Service Alternative Inspections program (e.g., the Immigration and Naturalization Service Passenger Accelerated Service System (INSPASS) or the Port Passenger Accelerated Service System (PORTPASS)), enter the United States by means of a pleasure craft along the northern border of the United States from time-to-time without further inspection. No persons other than those described in this paragraph may participate in this program. Landed immigrants of Canada who do not share a common nationality with nationals of Canada, but who are nationals of a designated country listed in § 217.2(a) of this chapter (Visa Waiver Pilot Program) must be in possession of a valid, unexpired passport issued by his or her country of nationality, and an unexpired multiple entry Form I–94 or I–94W, Nonimmigrant Visa Waiver Arrival/Departure Form, and a valid unexpired United States visa (if the alien is not in possession of a valid unexpired Form I–94W). When an entry to the United States is made by a person who is a Canadian citizen or a landed immigrant of Canada, entry may be made under this program only for a purpose as described in section 101(a)(15)(B)(ii) of the Act. Persons seeking to enter the United States for any other purpose must do so at a staffed Port-of-Entry. Persons aboard a vessel which has crossed the international boundary between the United States and Canada and who do not intend to land in the United States, other than at a staffed Port-of-Entry, are not required to be in possession of Form I–68 or evidence of enrollment in an Alternative Inspections program merely because they have crossed the international boundary. However, the Service retains the right to conduct inspections or examinations of all persons applying for admission or readmission to or seeking transit through the United States in accordance with the Act.

(1) Application. An eligible applicant may apply for a Canadian Border Boat Landing Permit by completing the Form I–68 in triplicate. Application forms will be made readily available through the Internet, from a Service office, or by mail. A family may apply on a single application. For the purposes of this paragraph, a family is defined as a husband, wife, unmarried children under the age of 21, and the parents of either husband or wife, who reside at the same address. In order for the I–68 application to be considered complete, it must be accompanied by the following:

(i) For each person included on the application, evidence of citizenship, and, if not a citizen of the United States or Canada, evidence of legal permanent resident status in either the United States or Canada. Evidence of residency must be submitted by all applicants. It is not required that all persons on the application be of the same nationality; however, they must all be individually eligible to participate in this program.

(ii) If multiple members of a family, as defined in paragraph (e)(1) of this section, are included on a single application, evidence of the familial relationship.

(iii) A fee as prescribed in § 103.7(b)(1) of this chapter.

(iv) A copy of any previously approved Form I–68.

(v) A landed immigrant of Canada who does not have a common nationality with nationals of Canada, but who is a national of a designated country listed in § 217.2(a) of this chapter (Visa Waiver Pilot Program) must also present his or her passport, a valid unexpired multiple entry Form I–94 or I–94W and valid, unexpired nonimmigrant visa if he or she is not in possession of a valid, unexpired multiple entry Form I–94W. Such a landed immigrant of Canada may apply for admission simultaneously with the I–68 application and thereby obtain a Form I–94 or I–94W.

(2) Submission of Form I–68. Except as indicated in this paragraph, Form I–68 shall be properly completed and submitted in person, along with the documentary evidence and the required fee as specified in § 103.7(b)(1) of this chapter, to a United States immigration officer at a Canadian border Port-of-Entry located within the district having jurisdiction over the applicant's residence or intended place of landing. Persons previously granted Form I–68 approval may apply by mail to the issuing Service office for renewal if a copy of the previous Form I–68 is included in the application. At the discretion of the district director concerned, any applicant for renewal of Form I–68 may be required to appear for an interview in person if the applicant does not appear to be clearly eligible for renewal.

(3) Denial of Form I–68. If the applicant has committed a violation of any immigration or customs regulation or, in the case of an alien, is inadmissible to the United States, approval of the Form I–68 shall be denied. However, if, in the exercise of discretion, the district director waives under section 212(d)(3) of the Act all applicable grounds of inadmissibility, the I–68 application may be approved for such non-citizens. If the Form I–68 application is denied, the applicant shall be given written notice of and the reasons for the denial by letter from the district director. There is no appeal from the denial of the Form I–68 application, but the denial is without prejudice to a subsequent application for this program or any other Service benefit, except that the applicant may not submit a subsequent Form I–68 application for 90 days after the date of the last denial.

(4) Validity. Form I–68 shall be valid for 1 year from the date of issuance, or until revoked or violated [sic] by the Service.

(5) Conditions for participation in the I–68 program.Upon being inspected and positively identified by an immigration officer and found admissible and eligible for participation in the I–68 program, a participant must agree to abide by the following conditions:

> **(i)** Form I–68 may be used only when entering the United States by means of a vessel exclusively used for pleasure, including chartered vessels when such vessel has been chartered by an approved Form I–68 holder. When used by a person who is a not a citizen or a lawful permanent resident of the United States, admission shall be for a period not to exceed 72 hours to visit within 25 miles of the shore line along the northern border of the United States, including the shore line of Lake Michigan and Puget Sound.
>
> **(ii)** Participants must be in possession of any authorization documents issued for participation in this program or another Service Alternative Inspections program (INSPASS or PORTPASS). Participants over the age of 15 years and who are not in possession of an INSPASS or PORTPASS enrollment card must also be in possession of a photographic identification document

issued by a governmental agency. Participants who are landed immigrants of Canada and do not have a common nationality with nationals of Canada, but who are nationals of a designated country listed in § 217.2(a) of this chapter must also be in possession of proper documentation as described in paragraph (e) of this section.

(iii) Participants may not import merchandise or transport controlled or restricted items while entering the United States under this program. The entry of any merchandise or goods must be in accordance with the laws and regulations of all Federal Inspection Services.

(iv) Participants must agree to random checks or inspections that may be conducted by the Service, at any time and at any location, to ensure compliance.

(v) Participants must abide by all Federal, state, and local laws regarding the importation of alcohol or agricultural products or the importation or possession of controlled substances as defined in section 101 of the Controlled Substance Act (21 U.S.C. 802).

(vi) Participants acknowledge that all devices, decals, cards, or other Federal Government supplied identification or technology used to identify or inspect persons or vessels seeking entry via this program remain the property of the United States Government at all times, and must be surrendered upon request by a Border Patrol Agent or any other officer of a Federal Inspection Service.

(vii) The captain, charterer, master, or owner (if aboard) of each vessel bringing persons into the United States is responsible for determining that all persons aboard the vessel are in possession of a valid, unexpired Form I–68 or other evidence of participation in a Service Alternative Inspections program (INSPASS or PORTPASS) prior to entry into the territorial waters of the United States. If any person on board is not in possession of such evidence, the captain, charterer, master, or owner must transport such person to a staffed United States Port-of-Entry for an in-person immigration inspection.

(6) Revocation. The district director, the chief patrol agent, or their designated representatives may revoke the designation of any participant who violates any condition of this program, as contained in paragraph (e)(5) of this section, or who has violated any immigration law or regulation, or a law or regulation of the United States Customs Service or other Federal Inspection Service, has abandoned his or her residence in the United States or Canada, is inadmissible to the United States, or who is otherwise determined by an immigration officer to be ineligible for continued participation in this program. Such persons may be subject to other applicable sanctions, such as criminal and/or administrative prosecution or deportation, as well as possible seizure of goods and/or vessels. If permission to participate is revoked, a written request to the district director for restoration of permission to participate may be made. The district director will notify the person of his or her decision and the reasons therefore in writing.

(7) Compliance checking. Participation in this program does not relieve the holder from responsibility to comply with all other aspects of United States Immigration, Customs, or other Federal inspection service laws or regulations. To prevent abuse, the United States Immigration and Naturalization Service retains the right to conduct inspections or examinations of all persons applying for admission or readmission to or seeking transit through the United States in accordance with the Immigration and Nationality Act.

(f) Form I–94, Arrival Departure Record.

(1) Unless otherwise exempted, each arriving nonimmigrant who is admitted to the United States shall be issued, upon payment of a fee prescribed in § 103.7(b)(1) of this chapter for land border admissions, a Form I–94 as evidence of the terms of admission. A Form I–94 issued at a land border port-of-entry shall be considered issued for multiple entries unless specifically annotated for a limited number of entries. A Form I–94 issued at other than a land border port-of-entry, unless issued for multiple entries, must be surrendered upon departure from the United States in accordance with the instructions on the form. Form I–94 is not required by:

(i) Any nonimmigrant alien described in § 212.1(a) of this chapter and 22 CFR 41.33 who is admitted as a visitor for business or pleasure or admitted to proceed in direct transit through the United States;

(ii) Any nonimmigrant alien residing in the British Virgin Islands who was admitted only to the U.S. Virgin Islands as a visitor for business or pleasure under § 212.1(b) of this chapter;

(iii) Except as provided in paragraph (f)(1)(v) of this section, any Mexican national who is exempt from a visa and passport pursuant to § 212.1(c)(1) of this chapter, or who is in possession of a passport and valid visa who is admitted as a nonimmigrant visitor for a period not to exceed 72 hours to visit within 25 miles of the border;

(iv) Bearers of Mexican diplomatic or official passports described in § 212.1(c–1) of this chapter; or

(v) Any Mexican national who is exempt from a visa and passport pursuant to § 212.1(c)(1) of this chapter, or is in possession of a passport and valid visa who is admitted as a nonimmigrant visitor at the Mexican border POEs in the State of Arizona at Sasabe, Nogales, Mariposa, Naco, or Douglas for a period not to exceed 72 hours to visit within the State of Arizona and within 75 miles of the border.

(2) Paroled aliens. Any alien paroled into the United States under section 212(d)(5) of the Act, including any alien crewmember, shall be issued a completely executed Form I–94, endorsed with the parole stamp.

[32 FR 9627, July 4, 1967; 32 FR 11628, Aug. 11, 1967; 42 FR 41848, Aug. 19, 1977; 45 FR 19545, March 26, 1980; 45 FR 63483, Sept. 25, 1980; 45 FR 70428, Oct. 24, 1980; 46 FR 43826, Sept. 1, 1981; 47 FR 49953, Nov. 4, 1982; 49 FR 33434, Aug. 23, 1984; 58 FR 69217, Dec. 30, 1993; 60 FR 40068, Aug. 7, 1995; 60 FR 50389, Sept. 29, 1995; 61 FR 53831, Oct. 16, 1996; 62 FR 10353, March 6, 1997; 62 FR 47751, Sept. 11, 1997; 63 FR 1334, Jan. 9, 1998; 64 FR 8494, Feb. 19, 1999; 64 FR 36561, July 7, 1999; 64 FR 68617, Dec. 8, 1999]

§ 235.2 Parole for deferred inspection.

(a) A district director may, in his or her discretion, defer the inspection of any vessel or aircraft, or of any alien, to another Service office or port-of-entry. Any alien coming to a United States port from a foreign port, from an outlying possession of the United States, from Guam, Puerto Rico, or the Virgin Islands of the United States, or from another port of the United States at which examination under this part was deferred, shall be regarded as an applicant for admission at that onward port.

(b) An examining immigration officer may defer further examination and refer the alien's case to the district director having jurisdiction over the place where the alien is seeking admission, or over the place of the alien's residence or destination in the United States, if the examining immigration officer has reason to believe that the alien can overcome a finding of inadmissibility by:

(1) Posting a bond under section 213 of the Act;

(2) Seeking and obtaining a waiver under section211 or 212(d)(3) or (4) of the Act; or

(3) Presenting additional evidence of admissibility not available at the time and place of the initial examination.

(c) Such deferral shall be accomplished pursuant to the provisions of section 212(d)(5) of the Act for the period of time necessary to complete the deferred inspection.

(d) Refusal of a district director to authorize admission under section 213 of the Act, or to grant an application for the benefits of section 211 or section 212(d) (3) or (4) of the Act, shall be without prejudice to the renewal of such application or the authorizing of such admission by the immigration judge without additional fee.

(e) Whenever an alien on arrival is found or believed to be suffering from a disability that renders it impractical to proceed with the examination under the Act, the examination of such alien, members of his or her family concerning whose admissibility it is necessary to have such alien testify, and any accompanying aliens whose protection or guardianship will be required should such alien be found inadmissible shall be deferred for such time and under such conditions as the district director in whose district the port is located imposes.

[22 FR 9791, Dec. 6, 1957; 62 FR 10355, March 6, 1997]

§ 235.3 Inadmissible aliens and expedited removal.

(a) Detention prior to inspection. All persons arriving at a port-of-entry in the United States by vessel or aircraft shall be detained aboard the vessel or at the airport of arrival by the owner, agent, master, commanding officer, person in charge, purser, or consignee of such vessel or aircraft until admitted or otherwise permitted to land by an officer of the Service. Notice or order to detain shall not be required. The owner, agent, master, commanding officer, person in charge, purser, or consignee of such vessel or aircraft shall deliver every alien requiring examination to an immigration officer for inspection or to a medical officer for examination. The Service will not be liable for any expenses related to such detention or presentation or for any expenses of a passenger who has not been presented for inspection and for whom a determination has not been made concerning admissibility by a Service officer.

(b) Expedited removal.

(1) Applicability. The expedited removal provisions shall apply to the following classes of aliens who are determined to be inadmissible under section 212(a)(6)(C) or (7) of the Act:

(i) Arriving aliens, as defined in § 1.1(q) of this chapter, except for citizens of Cuba arriving at a United States port-of-entry by aircraft;

(ii) As specifically designated by the Commissioner, aliens who arrive in, attempt to enter, or have entered the United States without having been admitted or paroled following inspection by an immigration officer at a designated port-of-entry, and who have not established to the satisfaction of the immigration officer that they have been physically present in the United States continuously for the 2–year period immediately prior to the date of determination of inadmissibility. The Commissioner shall have the sole discretion to apply the provisions of section 235(b)(1) of the Act, at any time, to any class of aliens described in this section. The Commissioner's designation shall become effective upon publication of a notice in the Federal Register. However, if the Commissioner determines, in the exercise of discretion, that the delay caused by publication would adversely affect the interests of the United States or the effective enforcement of the immigration laws, the Commissioner's designation shall become effective immediately upon issuance, and shall be published in the Federal Register as soon as practicable thereafter. When these provisions are in effect for aliens who enter without inspection, the burden of proof rests with the alien to affirmatively show that he or she has the required continuous physical presence in the United States. Any absence from the United States shall serve to break the period of continuous physical presence. An alien who was not inspected and admitted or paroled into the United States but who establishes that he or she has been continuously physically present in the United States for the 2–year period immediately prior to the date of determination of inadmissibility shall be detained in accordance with section 235(b)(2) of the Act for a proceeding under section 240 of the Act.

(2) Determination of inadmissibility.

(i) Record of proceeding. An alien who is arriving in the United States, or other alien as designated pursuant to paragraph (b)(1)(ii) of this section, who is determined to be inadmissible under section 212(a)(6)(C) or 212(a)(7) of the Act (except an alien for whom documentary requirements are waived under § 211.1(b)(3) or § 212.1 of this chapter), shall be ordered removed from the United States in accordance with section 235(b)(1) of the Act. In every case in which the expedited removal provisions will be applied and before removing an alien from the United States pursuant to this section, the examining immigration officer shall create a record of the facts of the case and statements made by the alien. This shall be accomplished by means of a sworn statement using Form I–867AB, Record of Sworn Statement in Proceedings under Section 235(b)(1) of the Act. The examining immigration officer shall read (or have read) to the alien all information contained on Form I–867A. Following questioning and recording of the alien's statement regarding identity, alienage, and inadmissibility, the examining immigration officer shall record the alien's response to the questions contained on Form I–867B, and have the alien read (or have read to him or her) the statement, and the alien shall sign and initial each page of the statement and each correction. The examining immigration officer shall advise the alien of the charges against him or her on Form I–860, Notice and Order of Expedited Removal, and the alien shall be given an opportunity to respond to those charges in the sworn statement. After obtaining supervisory concurrence in accordance with paragraph (b)(7) of this section, the examining immigration official shall serve the alien with Form I–860 and the alien shall sign the reverse of the form acknowledging receipt. Interpretative assistance shall be used if necessary to communicate with the alien.

(ii) No entitlement to hearings and appeals. Except as otherwise provided in this section, such alien is not entitled to a hearing before an immigration judge in proceedings conducted pursuant to section 240 of the Act, or to an appeal of the expedited removal order to the Board of Immigration Appeals.

(iii) Detention and parole of alien in expedited removal. An alien whose inadmissibility is being considered under this section or who has been ordered removed pursuant to this section shall be detained pending determination and removal, except that parole of such alien, in accordance with section 212(d)(5) of the Act, may be permitted only when the Attorney General determines, in the exercise of discretion, that parole is required to meet a medical emergency or is necessary for a legitimate law enforcement objective.

(3) Additional charges of inadmissibility. In the expedited removal process, the Service may not charge an alien with any additional grounds of inadmissibility other than section 212(a)(6)(C) or 212(a)(7) of the Act. If an alien appears to be inadmissible under other grounds contained in section 212(a) of the Act, and if the Service wishes to pursue such additional grounds of inadmissibility, the alien shall be detained and referred for a removal hearing before an immigration judge pursuant to sections 235(b)(2) and 240 of the Act for inquiry into all charges. Once the alien is in removal proceedings under section 240 of the Act, the Service is not precluded from lodging additional charges against the alien. Nothing in this paragraph shall preclude the Service from pursuing such additional grounds of inadmissibility against the alien in any subsequent attempt to reenter the United States, provided the additional grounds of inadmissibility still exist.

(4) Claim of asylum or fear of persecution or torture. If an alien subject to the expedited removal provisions indicates an intention to apply for asylum, or expresses a fear of persecution, a fear of torture, or a fear of return to his or her country, the inspecting officer shall not proceed further with removal of the alien until the alien has been referred for an interview by an asylum officer in accordance with § 208.30 of this chapter to determine if the alien has a credible fear of persecution or torture. The examining immigration officer shall record sufficient information in the sworn statement to establish and record that the alien has indicated such intention, fear, or concern, and to establish the alien's inadmissibility.

(i) Referral. The referring officer shall provide the alien with a written disclosure on Form M–444, Information About Credible Fear Interview, describing:

(A) The purpose of the referral and description of the credible fear interview process;

(B) The right to consult with other persons prior to the interview and any review thereof at no expense to the United States Government;

(C) The right to request a review by an immigration judge of the asylum officer's credible fear determination; and

(D) The consequences of failure to establish a credible fear of persecution or torture.

(ii) Detention pending credible fear interview. Pending the credible fear determination by an asylum officer and any review of that determination by an immigration judge, the alien shall be detained. Parole of such alien in accordance with section 212(d)(5) of the Act may be permitted only when the Attorney General determines, in the exercise of discretion, that parole is required to meet a medical emergency or is necessary for a legitimate law enforcement objective. Prior to the interview, the alien shall be given time to contact and consult with any person or persons of his or her choosing. Such consultation shall be made available in accordance with the policies and procedures of the detention facility where the alien is detained, shall be at no expense to the government, and shall not unreasonably delay the process.

(5) Claim to lawful permanent resident, refugee, or asylee status or U.S. citizenship.—

(i) Verification of status. If an applicant for admission who is subject to expedited removal pursuant to section 235(b)(1) of the Act claims to have been lawfully admitted for permanent residence, admitted as a refugee under section 207 of the Act, granted asylum under section 208 of the Act, or claims to be a U.S. citizen, the immigration officer shall attempt to verify the alien's claim. Such verification shall include a check of all available Service data systems and any other means available to the officer. An alien whose claim to lawful permanent resident, refugee, asylee status, or U.S. citizen status cannot be verified will be advised of the penalties for perjury, and will be placed under oath or allowed to make a declaration as permitted under 28 U.S.C. 1746, concerning his or her lawful admission for permanent residence, admission as a refugee under section 207 of the Act, grant of asylum status under section 208 of the Act, or claim to U.S. citizenship. A written statement shall be taken from the alien in the alien's own language and handwriting, stating that he or she declares, certifies, verifies, or states that the claim is true and correct. The immigration officer shall issue an expedited order of removal under section 235(b)(1)(A)(i) of the Act and refer the alien to the immigration judge for review of the order in accordance with paragraph (b)(5)(iv) of this section and § 235.6(a)(2)(ii). The person shall be detained pending review of the expedited removal order under this section. Parole of such person, in accordance with section 212(d)(5) of the Act, may be permitted only when the Attorney General determines, in the exercise of discretion, that parole is required to meet a medical emergency or is necessary for a legitimate law enforcement objective.

(ii) Verified lawful permanent residents. If the claim to lawful permanent resident status is verified, and such status has not been terminated in exclusion, deportation, or removal proceedings, the examining immigration officer shall not order the alien removed pursuant to section 235(b)(1) of the Act. The examining immigration officer will determine in accordance with section 101(a)(13)(C) of the Act whether the alien is considered to be making an application for admission. If the alien is determined to be seeking admission and the alien is otherwise admissible, except that he or she is not in possession of the required documentation, a discretionary waiver of documentary requirements may be considered in accordance with section 211(b) of the Act and § 211.1(b)(3) of this chapter or the alien's inspection may be deferred to an onward office for presentation of the required documents. If the alien appears to be inadmissible, the immigration officer may initiate removal proceedings against the alien under section 240 of the Act.

(iii) Verified refugees and asylees. If a check of Service records or other means indicates that the alien has been granted refugee status or asylee status, and such status has not been terminated in deportation, exclusion, or removal proceedings, the immigration officer shall not order the alien removed pursuant to section 235(b)(1) of the Act. If the alien is not in possession of a valid, unexpired refugee travel document, the examining immigration officer may accept an application for a refugee travel document in accordance with § 223.2(b)(2)(ii) of this chapter. If accepted, the immigration officer shall readmit the refugee or asylee in accordance with § 223.3(d)(2)(i) of this chapter. If the alien is determined not to be eligible to file an application for a refugee travel document the immigration officer may initiate removal proceedings against the alien under section 240 of the Act.

(iv) Review of order for claimed lawful permanent residents, refugees, asylees, or U.S. citizens. A person whose claim to U.S. citizenship has been verified may not be ordered removed. When an alien whose status has not been verified but who is claiming under oath or under penalty of perjury to be a lawful permanent resident, refugee, asylee, or U.S. citizen is ordered removed pursuant to section 235(b)(1) of the Act, the case will be referred to an immigration judge for review of the expedited removal order under section 235(b)(1)(C) of the Act and § 235.6(a)(2)(ii). If the immigration judge determines that the alien has never been admitted as a lawful permanent resident or as a refugee, granted asylum status, or is not a U.S. citizen, the order issued by the immigration officer will be affirmed and the Service will remove the alien. There is no appeal from the decision of the immigration judge. If the immigration judge determines that the alien was once so admitted as a lawful permanent resident or as a refugee, or was granted asylum status, or is a U.S. citizen, and such status has not been terminated by final administrative action, the immigration judge will terminate proceedings and vacate the expedited removal order. The Service may initiate removal proceedings against such an alien, but not against a person determined to be a U.S. citizen, in proceedings under section 240 of the Act. During removal proceedings, the immigration judge may consider any waivers, exceptions, or requests for relief for which the alien is eligible.

(6) Opportunity for alien to establish that he or she was admitted or paroled into the United States. If the Commissioner determines that the expedited removal provisions of section 235(b)(1) of the Act shall apply to any or all aliens described in paragraph (b)(2)(ii) of this section, such alien will be given a reasonable opportunity to establish to the satisfaction of the examining immigration officer that he or she was admitted or paroled into the United States following inspection at a port-of-entry. The alien will be allowed to present evidence or provide sufficient information to support the claim. Such evidence may consist of documentation in the possession of the alien, the Service, or a third party. The examining immigration officer will consider all such evidence and information, make further inquiry if necessary, and will attempt to verify the alien's status through a check of all available Service data systems. The burden rests with the alien to satisfy the examining immigration officer of the claim of lawful admission or parole. If the alien establishes that he or she was lawfully admitted or paroled, the case will be examined to determine if grounds of deportability under section 237(a) of the Act are applicable, or if paroled, whether such parole has been, or should be, terminated, and whether the alien is inadmissible under section 212(a) of the Act. An alien who cannot satisfy the examining officer that he or she was lawfully admitted or paroled will be ordered removed pursuant to section 235(b)(1) of the Act.

(7) Review of expedited removal orders. Any removal order entered by an examining immigration officer pursuant to section 235(b)(1) of the Act must be reviewed and approved by the appropriate supervisor before the order is considered final. Such supervisory review shall not be delegated below the level of the second line supervisor, or a person acting in that capacity. The supervisory review shall include a review of the sworn statement and any answers and statements made by the alien regarding a fear of removal or return. The supervisory review and approval of an expedited removal order for an alien described in section

235(b)(1)(A)(iii) of the Act must include a review of any claim of lawful admission or parole and any evidence or information presented to support such a claim, prior to approval of the order. In such cases, the supervisor may request additional information from any source and may require further interview of the alien.

(8) Removal procedures relating to expedited removal. An alien ordered removed pursuant to section 235(b)(1) of the Act shall be removed from the United States in accordance with section 241(c) of the Act and 8 CFR part 241.

(9) Waivers of documentary requirements. Nothing in this section limits the discretionary authority of the Attorney General, including authority under sections 211(b) or 212(d) of the Act, to waive the documentary requirements for arriving aliens.

(10) Applicant for admission under section 217 of the Act. The provisions of § 235.3(b) do not apply to an applicant for admission under section 217 of the Act.

(c) Arriving aliens placed in proceedings under section 240 of the Act. Except as otherwise provided in this chapter, any arriving alien who appears to the inspecting officer to be inadmissible, and who is placed in removal proceedings pursuant to section 240 of the Act shall be detained in accordance with section 235(b) of the Act. Parole of such alien shall only be considered in accordance with § 212.5(a) of this chapter. This paragraph shall also apply to any alien who arrived before April 1, 1997, and who was placed in exclusion proceedings.

(d) Service custody. The Service will assume custody of any alien subject to detention under paragraph (b) or (c) of this section. In its discretion, the Service may require any alien who appears inadmissible and who arrives at a land border port-of-entry from Canada or Mexico, to remain in that country while awaiting a removal hearing. Such alien shall be considered detained for a proceeding within the meaning of section 235(b) of the Act and may be ordered removed in absentia by an immigration judge if the alien fails to appear for the hearing.

(e) Detention in non-Service facility. Whenever an alien is taken into Service custody and detained at a facility other than at a Service Processing Center, the public or private entities contracted to perform such service shall have been approved for such use by the Service's Jail Inspection Program or shall be performing such service under contract in compliance with the Standard Statement of Work for Contract Detention Facilities. Both programs are administered by the Detention and Deportation section having jurisdiction over the alien's place of detention. Under no circumstances shall an alien be detained in facilities not meeting the four mandatory criteria for usage. These are:

(1) 24–Hour supervision,

(2) Conformance with safety and emergency codes,

(3) Food service, and

(4) Availability of emergency medical care.

(f) Privilege of communication. The mandatory notification requirements of consular and diplomatic officers pursuant to § 236.1(e) of this chapter apply when an inadmissible alien is detained for removal proceedings, including for purpose of conducting the credible fear determination.

[32 FR 9628, July 4, 1967, as amended at 34 FR 14727, Sept. 24, 1969; 47 FR 30046, July 9, 1982; 47 FR 46494, Oct. 19, 1982; 54 FR 101, Jan. 4, 1989; 54 FR 6365, Feb. 9, 1989; 60 FR 16043, March 29, 1995; 62 FR 10355, March 6, 1997; 64 FR 8494, Feb. 19, 1999]

§ 235.4 Withdrawal of application for admission.

The Attorney General may, in his or her discretion, permit any alien applicant for admission to withdraw his or her application for admission in lieu of removal proceedings under section 240 of the Act or expedited removal under section 235(b)(1) of the Act. The alien's decision to withdraw his or her application for admission must be made voluntarily, but nothing in this section shall be construed as to give an alien the right to withdraw his or her application for admission. Permission to withdraw an application for admission should not normally be granted unless the alien intends and is able to depart the United States immediately. An alien permitted to withdraw his or her application for admission shall normally remain in carrier or Service custody pending departure, unless the district director determines that parole of the alien is warranted in accordance with § 212.5(a) of this chapter.

[22 FR 9791, Dec. 6, 1957, as amended at 33 FR 4562, Mar. 15, 1968; 48 FR 35349, Aug. 4, 1983; 62 FR 10358, March 6, 1997; 62 FR 15363, April 1, 1997]

§ 235.5 Preinspection.

(a) In United States territories and possessions. In the case of any aircraft proceeding from Guam, Puerto Rico, or the United States Virgin Islands destined directly and without touching at a foreign port or place, to any other of such places, or to one of the States of the United States or the District of Columbia, the examination of the passengers and crew required by the Act may be made prior to the departure of the aircraft, and in such event, final determination of admissibility shall be made immediately prior to such departure. The examination shall be conducted in accordance with sections 232, 235, and 240 of the Act and 8 CFR parts 235 and 240. If it appears to the examining immigration officer that any person in the United States being examined under this section is prima facie removable from the United States, further action with respect to his or her examination shall be deferred and further proceedings regarding removability conducted as provided in section 240 of the Act and 8 CFR part 240. When the foregoing inspection procedure is applied to any aircraft, persons examined and found admissible shall be placed aboard the aircraft, or kept at the airport separate and apart from the general public until they are permitted to board the aircraft. No other person shall be permitted to depart on such aircraft until and unless he or she is found to be admissible as provided in this section.

(b) In foreign territory. In the case of any aircraft, vessel, or train proceeding directly, without stopping, from a port or place in foreign territory to a port-of-entry in the United States, the examination and inspection of passengers and crew required by the Act and final determination of admissibility may be made immediately prior to such departure at the port or place in the foreign territory and shall have the same effect under the Act as though made at the destined port-of-entry in the United States.

[23 FR 3997, June 7, 1958, as amended at 24 FR 2583, Apr. 3, 1959; 50 FR 11842, March 26, 1985; 54 FR 101, Jan. 4, 1989; 62 FR 10358, March 6, 1997]

§ 235.6 Referral to immigration judge.

(a) Notice.

(1) Referral by Form I–862, Notice to Appear. An immigration officer or asylum officer will sign and deliver a Form I–862 to an alien in the following cases:

(i) If, in accordance with the provisions of section 235(b)(2)(A) of the Act, the examining immigration officer detains an alien for a proceeding before an immigration judge under section 240 of the Act; or

(ii) If an asylum officer determines that an alien in expedited removal proceedings has a credible fear of persecution or torture and refers the case to the immigration judge for consideration of the application for asylum.

(iii) If the immigration judge determines that an alien in expedited removal proceedings has a credible fear of persecution or torture and vacates the expedited removal order issued by the asylum officer.

(iv) If an immigration officer verifies that an alien subject to expedited removal under section 235(b)(1) of the Act has been admitted as a lawful permanent resident refugee, or asylee, or upon review pursuant to § 235.3(b)(5)(iv) an immigration judge determines that the alien was once so admitted, provided that such status has not been terminated by final administrative action, and the Service initiates removal proceedings against the alien under section 240 of the Act.

(2) Referral by Form I–863, Notice of Referral to Immigration Judge. An immigration officer will sign and deliver a Form I–863 to an alien in the following cases:

(i) If an asylum officer determines that an alien does not have a credible fear of persecution or torture, and the alien requests a review of that determination by an immigration judge; or

(ii) If, in accordance with section 235(b)(1)(C) of the Act, an immigration officer refers an expedited removal order entered on an alien claiming to be a lawful permanent resident, refugee, asylee, or U.S. citizen for whom the officer could not verify such status to an immigration judge for review of the order.

(iii) If an immigration officer refers an applicant described in § 208.2(b)(1) of this chapter to an immigration judge for an asylum hearing under § 208.2(b)(2) of this chapter.

(b) Certification for mental condition; medical appeal. An alien certified under sections 212(a)(1) and 232(b) of the Act shall be advised by the examining immigration officer that he or she may appeal to a board of medical examiners of the United States Public Health Service pursuant to section 232 of the Act. If such appeal is taken, the district director shall arrange for the convening of the medical board.

[24 FR 6477, Aug. 12, 1959, as amended at 44 FR 4653, Jan. 23, 1979; 56 FR 50812, Oct. 9, 1991; 62 FR 9074, Feb. 28, 1997; 62 FR 10358, March 6, 1997; 64 FR 8494, Feb. 19, 1999]

PART 274A—CONTROL OF EMPLOYMENT OF ALIENS

Subpart A—Employer Requirements

§ 274a.1 Definitions.

For the purpose of this part—

(a) The term "unauthorized alien" means, with respect to employment of an alien at a particular time, that the alien is not at that time either: (1) Lawfully admitted for permanent residence, or (2) authorized to be so employed by this Act or by the Attorney General;

(b) The term "entity" means any legal entity, including but not limited to, a corporation, partnership, joint venture, governmental body, agency, proprietorship, or association;

(c) The term "hire" means the actual commencement of employment of an employee for wages or other remuneration. For purposes of section 274A(a)(4) of the Act and § 274a.5 of this part, a hire occurs when a person or entity uses a contract, subcontract or exchange entered into, renegotiated or extended after November 6, 1986, to obtain the labor of an alien in the United States, knowing that the alien is an unauthorized alien;

(d) The term "refer for a fee" means the act of sending or directing a person or transmitting documentation or information to another, directly or indirectly, with the intent of obtaining employment in the United States for such person, for remuneration whether on a retainer or contingency basis; however, this term does not include union hiring halls that refer union members or non-union individuals who pay union membership dues;

(e) The term "recruit for a fee" means the act of soliciting a person, directly or indirectly, and referring that person to another with the intent of obtaining employment for that person, for remuneration whether on a retainer or contingency basis; however, this term does not include union hiring halls that refer union members or non-union individuals who pay union membership dues;

(f) The term "employee" means an individual who provides services or labor for an employer for wages or other remuneration but does not mean independent contractors as defined in paragraph (j) of this section or those engaged in casual domestic employment as stated in paragraph (h) of this section;

(g) The term "employer" means a person or entity, including an agent or anyone acting directly or indirectly in the interest thereof, who engages the services or labor of an employee to be performed in the United States for wages or other remuneration. In the case of an independent contractor or contract labor or services, the term "employer" shall mean the independent contractor or contractor and not the person or entity using the contract labor;

(h) The term "employment" means any service or labor performed by an employee for an employer within the United States, including service or labor performed on a vessel or aircraft that has arrived in the United States and has been inspected, or otherwise included within the provisions of the Anti–Reflagging Act codified at 46 U.S.C. 8704, but not including duties performed by nonimmigrant crewmen defined in sections 101(a)(10) and (a)(15)(D) of the Act. However, employment does not include casual employment by individuals who provide domestic service in a private home that is sporadic, irregular or intermittent;

(i) The term "State employment agency" means any State government unit designated to cooperate with the United States Employment Service in the operation of the public employment service system;

(j) The term "independent contractor" includes individuals or entities who carry on independent business, contract to do a piece of work according to their own means and methods, and are subject to control only as to results. Whether an individual or entity is an independent contractor, regardless of what the individual or entity calls itself, will be determined on a case-by-case basis. Factors to be considered in that determination include, but are not limited to, whether the individual or entity: supplies the tools or materials; makes services available to the general public; works for a number of clients at the same time; has an opportunity for profit or loss as a result of labor or services provided; invests in the facilities for work; directs the order or sequence in which the work is to be done and determines the hours during which the work is to be done. The use of labor or services of an independent contractor are subject to the restrictions in section 274A(a)(4) of the Act and § 274a.5 of this part;

(k) The term "pattern or practice" means regular, repeated, and intentional activities, but does not include isolated, sporadic, or accidental acts;

(*l*)(1) The term "knowing" includes not only actual knowledge but also knowledge which may fairly be inferred through notice of certain facts and circumstances which would lead a person, through the exercise of reasonable care, to know about a certain condition. Constructive knowledge may include, but is not limited to, situations where an employer:

> **(i)** fails to complete or improperly completes the Employment Eligibility Verification Form, I–9;
>
> **(ii)** Has information available to it that would indicate that the alien is not authorized to work, such as Labor Certification and/or an Application for Prospective Employer; or
>
> **(iii)** Acts with reckless and wanton disregard for the legal consequences of permitting another individual to introduce an unauthorized alien into its work force or to act on its behalf.

(2) Knowledge that an employee is unauthorized may not be inferred from an employee's foreign appearance or accent. Nothing in this definition should be interpreted as permitting an employer to request more or different documents than are required under section 274(b) of the Act or to refuse to honor documents tendered that on their face reasonably appear to be genuine and to relate to the individual.

[52 FR 16221, May 1, 1987, as amended at 53 FR 8612, Mar. 16, 1988; 55 FR 25931, June 25, 1990; 56 FR 41783, Aug. 23, 1991]

§ 274a.2 Verification of employment eligibility.

(a) General. This section states the requirements and procedures persons or entities must comply with when hiring, or when recruiting or referring for a fee, or when continuing to employ individuals in the United States. For purposes of complying with section 274A(b) of the Act and this section, all references to recruiters and referrers for a fee are limited to a person or entity who is either an agricultural association, agricultural employer, or farm labor contractor (as defined in section 3 of the Migrant and Seasonal Agricultural Worker Protection Act, 29 U.S.C. 1802). The Form I–9, Employment Eligibility Verification Form, has been designated by the Service as the form to be used in complying with the requirements of this section. The Form I–9 may be obtained in limited quantities at INS District Offices, or ordered from the Superintendent of Documents, Washington, DC 20402. Employers may electronically generate blank Forms I–9, provided that: the resulting form is legible; there is no change to the name, content, or sequence of the data elements and instructions; no additional data elements or language are inserted; and the paper used meets the standards for retention and production for inspection specified under § 274a.2(b). When copying or printing the Form I–9, the text of the two-sided form may be reproduced by making either double-sided or single-sided copies. Employers need only complete the Form I–9 for individuals who are hired after November 6, 1986 and continue to be employed after May 31, 1987. Employers shall have until September 1, 1987 to complete the Form I–9 for individuals hired from November 7, 1986 through May 31, 1987. Recruiters and referrers for a fee need complete the Form I–9 only for those individuals who are recruited or referred and hired after May 31, 1987. In conjunction with completing the Form I–9, an employer or recruiter or referrer for a fee must examine documents that evidence the identity and employment eligibility of the individual. The employer or recruiter or referrer for a fee and the individual must each complete an attestation on the Form I–9 under penalty of perjury.

(b) Employment verification requirements—

(1) Examination of documents and completion of Form I–9.

(i) A person or entity that hires or recruits or refers for a fee an individual for employment must ensure that the individual properly:

(A) Complete section 1—"Employee Information and Verification"—on the Form I–9 at the time of hire; or if an individual is unable to complete the Form I–9 or needs it translated, someone may assist him or her. The preparer or translator must read the Form to the individual, assist him or her in completing Section 1—"Employee Information and Verification," and have the individual sign or mark the Form in the appropriate place. The preparer or translator must then complete the "Preparer/Translator Certification" portion of the Form I–9; and

(B) Present to the employer or the recruiter or referrer for a fee documentation as set forth in paragraph (b)(1)(v) of this section establishing his or her identity and employment eligibility within the time limits set forth in paragraphs (b)(1)(ii) through (b)(1)(v) of this section.

(ii) Except as provided in paragraph (b)(1)(viii) of this section, an employer, his or her agent, or anyone acting directly or indirectly in the interest thereof, must within three business days of the hire:

(A) Physically examine the documentation presented by the individual establishing identity and employment eligibility as set forth in paragraph (b)(1)(v) of this section and ensure that the documents presented appear to be genuine and to relate to the individual; and

(B) Complete section 2—"Employer Review and Verification"—of the Form I–9.

(iii) An employer who hires an individual for employment for a duration of less than three business days must comply with paragraphs (b)(1)(ii)(A) and (b)(1)(ii)(B) of this section at the time of the hire. An employer may not accept a receipt, as described in paragraph (b)(1)(vi) of this section, in lieu of the required document if the employment is for less than three business days.

(iv) A recruiter or referrer for a fee for employment must comply with paragraphs (b)(1)(ii)(A) and (b)(1)(ii)(B) of this section within three business days of the date the referred individual is hired by the employer. Recruiters and referrers may designate agents to complete the employment verification procedures on their behalf including but not limited to notaries, national associations, or employers. If a recruiter or referrer designates an employer to complete the employment verification procedures, the employer need only provide the recruiter or referrer with a photocopy of the Form I–9.

(v) The individual may present either an original document which establishes both employment authorization and identity, or an original document which establishes employment authorization and a separate original document which establishes identity. The identification number and expiration date (if any) of all documents must be noted in the appropriate space provided on the Form I–9.

(A) The following documents, so long as they appear to relate to the individual presenting the document, are acceptable to evidence both identity and employment eligibility:

(1) United States passport (unexpired or expired);

(2) Alien Registration Receipt Card or Permanent Resident Card, Form I–551;

(3) An unexpired foreign passport that contains a temporary I–551 stamp;

(4) An unexpired Employment Authorization Document issued by the Immigration And Naturalization Service which contains a photograph, Form I–766; Form I–688, Form I–688A, or Form I–688B;

(5) In the case of a nonimmigrant alien authorized to work for a specific employer incident to status, an unexpired foreign passport with an Arrival–Departure Record, Form I–94, bearing the same name as the passport and containing an endorsement of the alien's nonimmigrant status, so long as the period of endorsement has not yet expired and the proposed employment is not in conflict with any restrictions or limitations identified on the Form I–94.

(B) The following documents are acceptable to establish identity only:

(1) For individuals 16 years of age or older:

(i) A driver's license or identification card containing a photograph, issued by a state (as defined in section 101(a)(36) of the Act) or an outlying possession of the United States (as defined by section 101(a)(29) of the Act). If the driver's license or identification card does not contain a photograph, identifying information shall be included such as: name, date of birth, sex, height, color of eyes, and address;

(ii) School identification card with a photograph;

(iii) Voter's registration card;

(iv) U.S. military card or draft record;

(v) Identification card issued by federal, state, or local government agencies or entities. If the identification card does not contain a photograph, identifying information shall be included such as: name, date of birth, sex, height, color of eyes, and address;

(vi) Military dependent's identification card;

(vii) Native American tribal documents;

(viii) United States Coast Guard Merchant Mariner Card;

(ix) Driver's license issued by a Canadian government authority;

(2) For individuals under age 18 who are unable to produce a document listed in paragraph (b)(1)(v)(B)(1) of this section, the following documents are acceptable to establish identity only:

(i) School record or report card;

(ii) Clinic doctor or hospital record;

(iii) Daycare or nursery school record.

(3) Minors under the age of 18 who are unable to produce one of the identity documents listed in paragraph (b)(1)(v)(B) (1) or (2) of this section are exempt from producing one of the enumerated identity document if:

(i) The minor's parent or legal guardian completes on the Form I–9 Section 1—"Employee Information and Verification" and in the space for the minor's signature, the parent or legal guardian writes the words, "minor under age 18."

(ii) The minor's parent or legal guardian completes on the Form I–9 the "Preparer/Translator certification."

(iii) The employer or the recruiter or referrer for a fee writes in Section 2—"Employer Review and Verification" under List B in the space after the words "Document Identification #" the words, "minor under age 18."

(4) Individuals with handicaps, who are unable to produce one of the identity documents listed in paragraph (b)(1)(v)(B) (1) or (2) of this section, who are being placed into employment by a nonprofit organization, association or as part of a rehabilitation program, may follow the procedures for establishing identity provided in this section for minors under the age of 18, substituting where appropriate, the term "special placement" for "minor under age 18", and permitting, in addition to a parent or legal guardian, a representative from the nonprofit organization, association or rehabilitation program placing the individual into a position of employment, to fill out and sign in the appropriate section, the Form I–9. For purposes of this section the term "individual with handicaps" means any person who

(i) Has a physical or mental impairment which substantially limits one or more of such person's major life activities,

(ii) Has a record of such impairment, or

(iii) Is regarded as having such impairment.

(C) The following are acceptable documents to establish employment authorization only:

(1) A social security number card other than one which has printed on its face "not valid for employment purposes";

(2) A Certification of Birth Abroad issued by the Department of State, Form FS–545;

(3) A Certification of Birth Abroad issued by the Department of State, Form DS–1350;

(4) An original or certified copy of a birth certificate issued by a State, county, municipal authority or outlying possession of the United States bearing an official seal;

(5) Native American tribal document;

(6) United States Citizen Identification Card, INS Form I–197;

(7) Identification card for use of resident citizen in the United States, INS Form I–179;

(8) An unexpired employment authorization document issued by the Immigration and Naturalization Service.

(vi) Special rules for receipts. Except as provided in paragraph (b)(1)(iii) of this section, unless the individual indicates or the employer or recruiter or referrer for a fee has actual or constructive knowledge that the individual is not authorized to work, an employer or recruiter or referrer for a fee must accept a receipt for the application for a replacement document or a document described in paragraphs (b)(1)(vi)(B)(1) and (b)(1)(vi)(C)(1) of this section in lieu of the required document in order to comply with any requirement to examine documentation imposed by this section, in the following circumstances:

(A) Application for a replacement document. The individual:

(1) Is unable to provide the required document within the time specified in this section because the document was lost, stolen, or damaged;

(2) Presents a receipt for the application for the replacement document within the time specified in this section; and

(3) Presents the replacement document within 90 days of the hire or, in the case of reverification, the date employment authorization expires; or

(B) Form I–94 indicating temporary evidence of permanent resident status. The individual indicates in section 1 of the Form I–9 that he or she is a lawful permanent resident and the individual:

(1) Presents the arrival portion of Form I–94 containing an unexpired "Temporary I–551" stamp and photograph of the individual, which is designated for purposes of this section as a receipt for Form I–551; and

(2) Presents the Form I–551 by the expiration date of the "Temporary I–551" stamp or, if the stamp has no expiration date, within 1 year from the issuance date of the arrival portion of Form I–94; or

(C) Form I–94 indicating refugee status. The individual indicates in section 1 of the Form I–9 that he or she is an alien authorized to work and the individual:

(1) Presents the departure portion of Form I–94 containing an unexpired refugee admission stamp, which is designated for purposes of this section as a receipt for the Form I–766, Form I–688B, or a social security account number card that contains no employment restrictions; and

(2) Presents, within 90 days of the hire or, in the case of reverification, the date employment authorization expires, either an unexpired Form I–766 or Form I–688B, or a social security account number card that contains no employment restrictions, and a document described under paragraph (b)(1)(v)(B) of this section.

(vii) If an individual's employment authorization expires, the employer, recruiter or referrer for a fee must reverify on the Form I–9 to reflect that the individual is still authorized to work in the United States; otherwise the individual may no longer be employed, recruited, or referred. Reverification on the Form I–9 must occur not later than the date work authorization expires. In order to reverify on the Form I–9, the employee or referred individual must present a document that either shows continuing employment eligibility or is a new grant of work authorization. The employer or the recruiter or referrer for a fee must review this document, and if it appears to be genuine and to relate to the individual, reverify by noting the document's identification number and expiration date on the Form I–9.

(viii) An employer will not be deemed to have hired an individual for employment if the individual is continuing in his or her employment and has a reasonable expectation of employment at all times.

(A) An individual is continuing in his or her employment in one of the following situations:

(1) An individual takes approved paid or unpaid leave on account of study, illness or disability of a family member, illness or pregnancy, maternity or paternity leave, vacation, union business, or other temporary leave approved by the employer;

(2) An individual is promoted, demoted, or gets a pay raise;

(3) An individual is temporarily laid off for lack of work;

(4) An individual is on strike or in a labor dispute;

(5) An individual is reinstated after disciplinary suspension for wrongful termination, found unjustified by any court, arbitrator, or administrative body, or otherwise resolved through reinstatement or settlement;

(6) An individual transfers from one distinct unit of an employer to another distinct unit of the same employer; the employer may transfer the individual's Form I–9 to the receiving unit;

(7) An individual continues his or her employment with a related, successor, or reorganized employer, provided that the employer obtains and maintains from the previous employer records and Forms I–9 where applicable. For this purpose, a related, successor, or reorganized employer includes:

(i) The same employer at another location;

(ii) An employer who continues to employ some or all of a previous employer's workforce in cases involving a corporate reorganization, merger, or sale of stock or assets;

(iii) An employer who continues to employ any employee of another employer's workforce where both employers belong to the same multi-employer association and the employee continues to work in the same bargaining unit under the same collective bargaining agreement. For purposes of this subsection, any agent designated to complete and maintain the Form I–9 must record the employee's date of hire and/or termination each time the employee is hired and/or terminated by an employer of the multi-employer association; or

(8) An individual is engaged in seasonal employment.

(B) The employer who is claiming that an individual is continuing in his or her employment must also establish that the individual expected to resume employment at all times and that the individual's expectation is reasonable. Whether an individual's expectation is reasonable will be determined on a case-by-case basis taking into consideration several factors. Factors which would indicate that an individual has a reasonable expectation of employment include, but are not limited to, the following:

(1) The individual in question was employed by the employer on a regular and substantial basis. A determination of a regular and substantial basis is established by a comparison of other workers who are similarly employed by the employer;

(2) The individual in question complied with the employer's established and published policy regarding his or her absence;

(3) The employer's past history of recalling absent employees for employment indicates a likelihood that the individual in question will resume employment with the employer within a reasonable time in the future;

(4) The former position held by the individual in question has not been taken permanently by another worker;

(5) The individual in question has not sought or obtained benefits during his or her absence from employment with the employer that are inconsistent with an expectation of resuming employment with the employer within a reasonable time in the future. Such benefits include, but are not limited to, severance and retirement benefits;

(6) The financial condition of the employer indicates the ability of the employer to permit the individual in question to resume employment within a reasonable time in the future; or

(7) The oral and/or written communication between employer, the employer's supervisory employees and the individual in question indicates that it is reasonably likely that the individual in question will resume employment with the employer within a reasonable time in the future.

(2) Retention and Inspection of Form I–9.

(i) Form I–9 must be retained by an employer or a recruiter or referrer for a fee for the following time periods:

(A) In the case of an employer, three years after the date of the hire or one year after the date the individual's employment is terminated, whichever is later; or

(B) In the case of a recruiter or referrer for a fee, three years after the date of the hire.

(ii) Any person or entity required to retain Forms I–9 in accordance with this section shall be provided with at least three days notice prior to an inspection of the Forms I–9 by officers of the Service, the Special Counsel for Immigration–Related Unfair Employment Practices, or the Department of Labor. At the time of inspection, Forms I–9 must be made available in their original form or on microfilm or microfiche at the location where the request for production was made. If Forms I–9 are kept at another location, the person or entity must inform the officer of the Service, the Special Counsel for Immigration–Related Unfair Employment Practices, or the Department of Labor of the location where the forms are kept and make arrangements for the inspection. Inspections may be performed at an INS office. A recruiter or referrer for a fee who has designated an employer to complete the employment verification procedures may present a photocopy of the Form I–9 in lieu of presenting the Form I–9 in its original form or on microfilm or microfiche, as set forth in paragraph (b) (1) (iv) of this section. Any refusal or delay in presentation of the Forms I–9 for inspection is a violation of the retention requirements as set forth in section 274A(b) (3) of the Act. No Subpoena or warrant shall be required for such inspection, but the use of such enforcement tools is not precluded. In addition, if the person or entity has not complied with a request to present the Forms I–9, any Service officer listed in § 287.4 of this chapter may compel production of the Forms I–9 and any other relevant documents by issuing a subpoena. Nothing in this section is intended to limit the Service's subpoena power under section 235(a) of the Act.

(iii) The following standards shall apply to Forms I–9 presented on microfilm or microfiche submitted to an officer of the Service, the Special Counsel for Immigration–Related Unfair Employment Practices, or the Department of Labor: Microfilm, when displayed on a microfilm reader (viewer) or reproduced on paper must exhibit a high degree of legibility and readability. For this purpose, legibility is defined as the quality of a letter or numeral which enables the observer to positively and quickly identify it to the exclusion of all other letters or numerals. Readability is defined as the quality of a group of letters or numerals being recognizable as words or whole numbers. A detailed index of all microfilmed data shall be maintained and arranged in such a manner as to permit the immediate location of any particular record. It is the responsibility of the employer, recruiter or referrer for a fee:

(A) To provide for the processing, storage and maintenance of all microfilm, and

(B) To be able to make the contents thereof available as required by law. The person or entity presenting the microfilm will make available a reader-printer at the examination site for the ready reading, location and reproduction of any record or records being maintained on microfilm. Reader-printers made available to an officer of the Service, the Special Counsel for Immigration–Related Unfair Employment Practices, or the Department of Labor shall provide safety features and be in clean condition, properly maintained and in good working order. The reader-printers must have the capacity to display and print a complete page of information. A person or entity who is determined to have failed to comply with the criteria established by this regulation for the presentation of microfilm or microfiche to the Service, the Special Counsel for Immigration–Related Unfair Employment Practices, or the Department of Labor, and at the time of the inspection does not present a properly completed Form I–9 for the employee, is in violation of section 274A(a)(1)(B) of the Act and § 274a.2(b)(2).

(3) Copying of documentation. An employer, or a recruiter or referrer for a fee may, but is not required to, copy a document presented by an individual solely for the purpose of complying with the verification requirements of this section. If such a copy is made, it must be retained with the Form I–9. The retention requirements in paragraph (b)(2) of this section do not apply to the photocopies. The copying of any such document and retention of the copy does not relieve the employer from the requirement to fully complete section 2 of the Form I–9. An employer, recruiter or referrer for a fee should not, however, copy the documents only of individuals of certain national origins or citizenship statuses. To do so may violate section 274B of the Act.

(4) Limitation on use of Form I–9. Any information contained in or appended to the Form I–9, including copies of documents listed in paragraph (c) of this section used to verify an individual's identity or employment eligibility, may be used only for enforcement of the Act and Sections 1001, 1028, 1546, or 1621 of Title 18, United States Code.

(c) Employment verification requirements in the case of hiring an individual who was previously employed.

(1) When an employer hires an individual whom that person or entity has previously employed, if the employer has previously completed the Form I–9 and complied with the verification requirements set forth in paragraph (b) of this section with regard to the individual, the employer may (in lieu of completing a new Form I–9) inspect the previously completed Form I–9 and:

(i) If upon inspection of the Form I–9, the employer determines that the Form I–9 relates to the individual and that the individual is still eligible to work, that previously executed Form I–9 is sufficient for purposes of section 274A(b) of the Act if the individual is hired within three years of the date of the initial execution of the Form I–9 and the employer updates the Form I–9 to reflect the date of rehire; or

(ii) If upon inspection of the Form I–9, the employer determines that the individual's employment authorization has expired, the employer must reverify on the Form I–9 in accordance with paragraph (b)(1)(vii); otherwise the individual may no longer be employed.

(2) For purposes of retention of the Form I–9 by an employer for a previously employed individual hired pursuant to paragraph (c)(1) of this section, the employer shall retain the Form I–9 for a period of three years commencing from the date of the initial execution of the Form I–9 or one year after the individual's employment is terminated, whichever is later.

(d) Employment verification requirements in the case of recruiting or referring for a fee an individual who was previously recruited or referred.

(1) When a recruiter or referrer for a fee refers an individual for whom that recruiter or referrer for a fee has previously completed a Form I–9 and complied with the verification requirements set forth in paragraph (b) of this section with regard to the individual, the recruiter or referrer may (in lieu of completing a new Form I–9) inspect the previously completed Form I–9 and:

(i) If upon inspection of the Form I–9, the recruiter or referrer for a fee determines that the Form I–9 relates to the individual and that the individual is still eligible to work, that previously executed Form I–9 is sufficient for purposes of section 274A(b) of the Act if the individual is referred within three years of the date of the initial execution of the Form I–9 and the recruiter or referrer for a fee updates the Form I–9 to reflect the date of rehire; or

(ii) If upon inspection of the Form I–9, the recruiter or referrer determines that the individual's employment authorization has expired, the recruiter or referrer for a fee must reverify on the Form I–9 in accordance with paragraph (b)(1)(vii) of this section; otherwise the individual may no longer be recruited or referred.

(2) For purposes of retention of the Form I–9 by a recruiter or referrer for a previously recruited or referred individual pursuant to paragraph (d)(1) of this section, the recruiter or referrer shall retain the Form I–9 for a period of three years from the date of the rehire.

[53 FR 8612, March 16, 1988; 55 FR 25932 to 25934, June 25, 1990; 56 FR 41782, 41784–41786, Aug. 23, 1991; 58 FR 48780, Sept. 20, 1993; 59 FR 47063, Sept. 14, 1994; 60 FR 14353, March 17, 1995; 61 FR 46537, Sept. 4, 1996; 61 FR 52236, Oct. 7, 1996; 62 FR 51005, Sept. 30, 1997; 64 FR 6189, Feb. 9, 1999; 64 FR 11533, March 9, 1999]

§ 274a.3 Continuing employment of unauthorized aliens.

An employer who continues the employment of an employee hired after November 6, 1986, knowing that the employee is or has become an unauthorized alien with respect to that employment, is in violation of section 274A(a)(2) of the Act.

[52 FR 16224, May 1, 1987, as amended at 53 FR 8613, March 16, 1988]

§ 274a.4 Good faith defense.

An employer or a recruiter or referrer for a fee for employment who shows good faith compliance with the employment verification requirements of § 274a.2(b) of this part shall have established a rebuttable affirmative defense that the person or entity has not violated section 274A(a)(1)(A) of the Act with respect to such hiring, recruiting, or referral.

[52 FR 16224, May 1, 1987]

§ 274a.5 Use of labor through contract.

Any person or entity who uses a contract, subcontract, or exchange entered into, renegotiated, or extended after November 6, 1986, to obtain the labor or services of an alien in the United States knowing that the alien is an unauthorized alien with respect to performing such labor or services, shall be considered to have hired the alien for employment in the United States in violation of section 274A(a)(1)(A) of the Act.

[55 FR 25934, June 25, 1990; 56 FR 41782, Aug. 23, 1991]

§ 274a.6 State employment agencies.

(a) General. Pursuant to sections 274A(a)(5) and 274A(b) of the Act, a state employment agency as defined in § 274a.1 of this part may, but is not required to, verify identity and employment eligibility of individuals referred for employment by the agency. However, should a state employment agency choose to do so, it must:

(1) Complete the verification process in accordance with the requirements of § 274a.2(b) of this part *provided* that the individual may not present receipts in lieu of documents in order to complete the verification process as otherwise permitted by § 274a.2(b)(1)(vi) of this part; and

(2) Complete the verification process prior to referral for all individuals for whom a certification is required to be issued pursuant to paragraph (c) of this section.

(b) Compliance with the provisions of section 274A of the Act. A state employment agency which chooses to verify employment eligibility of individuals pursuant to § 274a.2(b) of this part shall comply with all provisions of section 274A of the Act and the regulations issued thereunder.

(c) State employment agency certification.

(1) A state employment agency which chooses to verify employment eligibility pursuant to paragraph (a) of this section shall issue to an employer who hires an individual referred for employment by the agency, a certification as set forth in paragraph (d) of this section. The certification shall be transmitted by the state employment agency directly to the employer, personally by an agency official, or by mail, so that it will be received by the employer within 21 business days of the date that the referred individual is hired. In no case shall the certification be transmitted to the employer from the state employment agency by the individual referred. During this period:

(i) The job order or other appropriate referral form issued by the state employment agency to the employer, on behalf of the individual who is referred and hired, shall serve as evidence, with respect to that individual, of the employer's compliance with the provisions of section 274A(a)(1)(B) of the Act and the regulations issued thereunder.

(ii) In the case of a telephonically authorized job referral by the state employment agency to the employer, an appropriate annotation by the employer shall be made and shall serve as evidence of the job order. The employer should retain the document containing the annotation where the employer retains Forms I–9.

(2) Job orders or other referrals, including telephonic authorizations, which are used as evidence of compliance pursuant to paragraph (c)(1)(i) of this section shall contain:

(i) The name of the referred individual;

(ii) The date of the referral;

(iii) The job order number or other applicable identifying number relating to the referral;

(iv) The name and title of the referring state employment agency official; and

(v) The telephone number and address of the state employment agency.

(3) A state employment agency shall not be required to verify employment eligibility or to issue a certification to an employer to whom the agency referred an individual if the individual is hired for a period of employment not to exceed 3 days in duration. Should a state agency choose to verify employment eligibility and to issue a certification to an employer relating to an individual who is hired for a period of employment not to exceed 3 days in duration, it must verify employment eligibility and issue certifications relating to *all* such individuals. Should a state employment agency choose not to verify employment eligibility or issue certifications to employers who hire, for a period not to exceed 3 days in duration, agency-referred individuals, the agency shall notify employers that, as a matter of policy, it does not perform verifications for individuals hired for that length of time, and that the employers must complete the identity and employment eligibility requirements pursuant to § 274a.2(b) of this part. Such notification may be incorporated into the job order or other referral form utilized by the state employment agency as appropriate.

(4) An employer to whom a state employment agency issues a certification relating to an individual referred by the agency and hired by the employer, shall be deemed to have complied with the verification requirements of § 274a.2(b) of this part provided that the employer:

(i) Reviews the identifying information contained in the certification to ensure that it pertains to the individual hired;

(ii) Observes the signing of the certification by the individual at the time of its receipt by the employer as provided for in paragraph (d)(13) of this section;

(iii) Complies with the provisions of § 274a.2(b)(1)(vii) of this part by either:

(A) Updating the state employment agency certification in lieu of Form I–9, upon expiration of the employment authorization date, if any, which was noted on the certification issued by the state employment agency pursuant to paragraph (d)(11) of this section; or

(B) By no longer employing an individual upon expiration of his or her employment authorization date noted on the certification;

(iv) Retains the certification in the same manner prescribed for Form I–9 in § 274a.2(b)(2) of this part, to wit, three years after the date of the hire or one year after the date the individual's employment is terminated, whichever is later; and

(v) Makes it available for inspection to officers of the Service or the Department of Labor, pursuant to the provisions of section 274A(b)(3) of the Act, and § 274a.2(b)(2) of this part.

(5) Failure by an employer to comply with the provisions of paragraph (c)(4)(iii) of this section shall constitute a violation of section 274A(a)(2) of the Act and shall subject the employer to the penalties contained in section 274A(e)(4) of the Act, and § 274a.10 of this part.

(d) Standards for state employment agency certifications. All certifications issued by a state employment agency pursuant to paragraph (c) of this section shall conform to the following standards. They must:

(1) Be issued on official agency letterhead;

(2) Be signed by an appropriately designated official of the agency;

(3) Bear a date of issuance;

(4) Contain the employer's name and address;

(5) State the name and date of birth of the individual referred;

(6) Identify the position or type of employment for which the individual is referred;

(7) Bear a job order number relating to the position or type of employment for which the individual is referred;

(8) Identify the document or documents presented by the individual to the state employment agency for the purposes of identity and employment eligibility verification;

(9) State the identifying number or numbers of the document or documents described in paragraph (d)(8) of this section;

(10) Certify that the agency has complied with the requirements of section 274A(b) of the Act concerning verification of the identity and employment eligibility of the individual referred, and has determined that, to the best of the agency's knowledge, the individual is authorized to work in the United States;

(11) Clearly state any restrictions, conditions, expiration dates or other limitations which relate to the individual's employment eligibility in the United States, or contain an affirmative statement that the employment authorization of the referred individual is not restricted;

(12) State that the employer is not required to verify the individual's identity or employment eligibility, but must retain the certification in lieu of Form I–9;

(13) Contain a space or a line for the signature of the referred individual, requiring the individual under penalty of perjury to sign his or her name before the employer at the time of receipt of the certification by the employer; and

(14) State that counterfeiting, falsification, unauthorized issuance or alteration of the certification constitutes a violation of federal law pursuant to Title 18, U.S.C. 1546.

(e) Retention of Form I–9 by state employment agencies. A Form I–9 utilized by a state employment agency in verifying the identity and employment eligibility of an individual pursuant to § 274a.2(b) of this part must be retained by a state employment agency for a period of three years from the date that the individual was last referred by the agency and hired by an employer. A state employment agency may retain a Form I–9 either in its original form, or on microfilm or microfiche.

(f) Retention of state employment agency certifications. A certification issued by a state employment agency pursuant to this section shall be retained:

(1) By a state employment agency, for a period of three years from the date that the individual was last referred by the agency and hired by an employer, and in a manner to be determined by the agency which will enable the prompt retrieval of the information contained on the original certification for comparison with the relating Form I–9;

(2) By the employer, in the original form, and in the same manner and location as the employer has designated for retention of Forms I–9, and for the period of time provided in paragraph (c)(4)(iv) of this section.

(g) State employment agency verification requirements in the case of an individual who was previously referred and certified. When a state employment agency refers an individual for whom the verification requirements have been previously complied with and a Form I–9 completed, the agency shall inspect the previously completed Form I–9:

(1) If, upon inspection of the Form, the agency determines that the Form I–9 pertains to the individual and that the individual remains authorized to be employed in the United States, no additional verification need be conducted and no new Form I–9 need be completed prior to issuance of a new certification *provided* that the individual is referred by the agency within 3 years of the execution of the initial Form I–9.

(2) If, upon inspection of the Form, the agency determines that the Form I–9 pertains to the individual but that the individual does not appear to be authorized to be employed in the United States based on restrictions, expiration dates or other conditions annotated on the Form I–9, the agency shall not issue a certification unless the agency follows the updating procedures pursuant to § 274a.2(b)(1)(vii) of this part; otherwise the individual may no longer be referred for employment by the state employment agency.

(3) For the purposes of retention of the Form I–9 by a state employment agency pursuant to paragraph (e) of this section, for an individual previously referred and certified, the state employment agency shall retain the Form for a period of 3 years from the date that the individual is last referred and hired.

(h) Employer verification requirements in the case of an individual who was previously referred and certified. When an employer rehires an individual for whom the verification and certification requirements have been previously complied with by a state employment agency, the employer shall inspect the previously issued certification.

(1) If, upon inspection of the certification, the employer determines that the certification pertains to the individual and that the individual remains authorized to be employed in the United States, no additional verification need be conducted and no new Form I–9 or certification need be completed *provided* that the individual is rehired by the employer within 3 years of the issuance of the initial certification, and that the employer follows the same procedures for the certification which pertain to Form I–9, as specified in § 274a.2(c)(1)(i) of this part.

(2) If, upon inspection of the certification, the employer determines that the certification pertains to the individual but that the certification reflects restrictions, expiration dates or other conditions which indicate that the individual no longer appears authorized to be employed in the United States, the employer shall verify that the individual remains authorized to be employed and shall follow the updating procedures for the certification which pertain to Form I–9, as specified in § 274a.2(c)(1)(ii) of this part; otherwise the individual may no longer be employed.

(3) For the purposes of retention of the certification by an employer pursuant to this paragraph for an individual previously referred and certified by a state employment agency and rehired by the employer, the employer shall retain the certification for a period of 3 years after the date that the individual is last hired, or one year after the date the individual's employment is terminated, whichever is later.

[52 FR 16224, May 1, 1987; as amended at 52 FR 43052, Nov. 9, 1987]

§ 274a.7 Pre-enactment provisions for employees hired prior to November 7, 1986.

(a) The penalty provisions set forth in section 274A(e) and (f) of the Act for violations of sections 274A(a)(1)(B) and 274A(a)(2) of the Act shall not apply to employees who were hired prior to November 7, 1986, and who are continuing in their employment and have a reasonable expectation of employment at all times (as set forth in § 274a.2(b)(1)(viii), except those individuals described in section 274a.2(b)(1)(viii)(A)(7)(iii) and (b)(1)(viii)(A)(8)).

(b) For purposes of this section, an employee who was hired prior to November 7, 1986 shall lose his or her pre-enactment status if the employee:

(1) Quits; or

(2) Is terminated by the employer; the term termination shall include, but is not limited to, situations in which an employee is subject to seasonal employment; or

(3) Is excluded or deported from the United States or departs the United States under a grant of voluntary departure; or

(4) Is no longer continuing his or her employment (or does not have a reasonable expectation of employment at all times) as set forth in § 274a.2(b)(1)(viii).

[52 FR 16224, May 1, 1987, as amended at 53 FR 8613, Mar. 16, 1988; 55 FR 25935, June 25, 1990; 56 FR 41786, Aug. 23, 1991]

§ 274a.8 Prohibition of indemnity bonds.

(a) General. It is unlawful for a person or other entity, in hiring or recruiting or referring for a fee for employment of an individual, to require the individual to post a bond or security, to pay or agree to pay an amount, or otherwise to provide a financial guarantee or indemnity, against any potential liability arising under this part relating to such hiring, recruiting, or referring of the individual. However, this prohibition does not apply to performance clauses which are stipulated by agreement between contracting parties.

(b) Penalty. Any person or other entity who requires any individual to post a bond or security as stated in this section shall, after notice and opportunity for an administrative hearing in accordance with section 274A(e)(3)(B) of the Act, be subject to a civil monetary penalty of $1,000 for each violation before September 29, 1999, and $1,100 for each violation occurring on or after September 29, 1999, and to an administrative order requiring the return to the individual of any amounts received in violation of this section or, if the individual cannot be located, to the general fund of the Treasury.

[52 FR 16224, May 1, 1987; as amended at 64 FR 47101, Aug. 30, 1999]

§ 274a.9 Enforcement procedures.

(a) Procedures for the filing of complaints. Any person or entity having knowledge of a violation or potential violation of section 274A of the Act may submit a signed, written complaint in person or by mail to the Service office having jurisdiction over the business or residence of the potential violator. The signed, written complaint must contain sufficient information to identify both the complainant and the potential violator, including their names and addresses. The complaint should also contain detailed factual allegations relating to the potential violation including the date, time and place of the alleged violation and the specific act or conduct alleged to constitute a violation of the Act. Written complaints may be delivered either by mail to the appropriate Service office or by personally appearing before any immigration officer at a Service office.

(b) Investigation. The Service may conduct investigations for violations on its own initiative and without having received a written complaint. When the Service receives a complaint from a third party, it shall investigate only those complaints that have a reasonable probability of validity. If it is determined after investigation that the person or entity has violated section 274A of the Act, the Service may issue and serve a Notice of Intent to Fine or a Warning Notice upon the alleged violator. Service officers shall have reasonable access to examine any relevant evidence of any person or entity being investigated.

(c) Warning notice. The Service and/or the Department of Labor may in their discretion issue a Warning Notice to a person or entity alleged to have violated section 274A of the Act. This Warning Notice will contain a statement of the basis for the violations and the statutory provisions alleged to have been violated.

(d) Notice of Intent to Fine. The proceeding to assess administrative penalties under section 274A of the Act is commenced when the Service issues a Notice of Intent to Fine on Form I–763. Service of this Notice shall be accomplished pursuant to Part 103 of this chapter. The person or entity identified in the Notice of Intent to Fine shall be known as the respondent. The Notice of Intent to Fine may be issued by an officer defined in § 242.1 of this chapter with concurrence of a Service attorney.

(1) Contents of the Notice of Intent to Fine.

(i) The Notice of Intent to Fine will contain the basis for the charge(s) against the respondent, the statutory provisions alleged to have been violated, and the penalty that will be imposed.

(ii) The Notice of Intent to Fine will provide the following advisals to the respondent:

(A) That the person or entity has the right to representation by counsel of his or her own choice at no expense to the government;

(B) That any statement given may be used against the person or entity;

(C) That the person or entity has the right to request a hearing before an Administrative Law Judge pursuant to 5 U.S.C. 554–557, and that such request must be made within 30 days from the service of the Notice of Intent to Fine;

(D) That the Service will issue a final order in 45 days if a written request for a hearing is not timely received and that there will be no appeal of the final order.

(e) Request for Hearing Before an Administrative Law Judge. If a respondent contests the issuance of a Notice of Intent to Fine, the respondent must file with the INS, within thirty days of the service of the Notice of Intent to Fine, a written request for a hearing before an Administrative Law Judge. Any written request for a hearing submitted in a foreign language must be accompanied by an English language translation. A request for a hearing is not deemed to be filed until received by the Service office designated in the Notice of Intent to Fine. In computing the thirty day period prescribed by this section, the day of service of the Notice of Intent to Fine shall not be included. If the Notice of Intent to Fine was served by ordinary mail, five days shall be added to the prescribed thirty day period. In the request for a hearing, the respondent may, but is not required to, respond to each allegation listed in the Notice of Intent to Fine.

(f) Failure to file a request for hearing. If the respondent does not file a request for a hearing in writing within thirty days of the day of service of the Notice of Intent to Fine (thirty-five days if served by ordinary mail), the INS shall issue a final order from which there is no appeal.

[53 FR 8613, March 16, 1988; 55 FR 25935, June 25, 1990; 56 FR 41782, 41786, Aug. 23, 1991; 61 FR 52236, Oct. 7, 1996]

§ 274a.10 Penalties.

(a) Criminal penalties. Any person or entity which engages in a pattern or practice of violations of subsection (a)(1)(A) or (a)(2) of the Act shall be fined not more than $3,000 for each unauthorized alien, imprisoned for not more than six months for the entire pattern or practice, or both, notwithstanding the provisions of any other Federal law relating to fine levels.

(b) Civil penalties. A person or entity may face civil penalties for a violation of section 274A of the Act. Civil penalties may be imposed by the Service or an administrative law judge for violations under section 274A of the Act. In determining the level of the penalties that will be imposed, a finding of more than one violation in the course of a single proceeding or determination will be counted as a single offense. However, a single offense will include penalties for each unauthorized alien who is determined to have been knowingly hired or recruited or referred for a fee.

(1) A respondent found by the Service or an administrative law judge to have knowingly hired, or to have knowingly recruited or referred for a fee, an unauthorized alien for employment in the United States or to have knowingly continued to employ an unauthorized alien in the United States, shall be subject to the following order:

(i) To cease and desist from such behavior;

(ii) To pay a civil fine according to the following schedule:

(A) First offense—not less than $250 and not more than $2,000 for each unauthorized alien with respect to whom the offense occurred before September 29, 1999, and not less than $275 and not exceeding $2,200, for each unauthorized alien with respect to whom the offense occurred occurring on or after September 29, 1999.

(B) Second offense—not less than $2,000 and not more than $5,000 for each unauthorized alien with respect to whom the second offense occurred before September 29, 1999, and not less than $2,200 and not exceeding $5,500, for each unauthorized alien with respect to whom the second offense occurred on or after September 29, 1999; or

(C) More than two offenses—not less than $3,000 and not more than $10,000 for each unauthorized alien with respect to whom the third or subsequent offense occurred before September 29, 1999, and not less than $3,300 and not exceeding $11,000, for each unauthorized alien with respect to whom the third or subsequent offense occurred on or after September 29, 1999; and

(iii) To comply with the requirements of section 274a.2(b) of this part, and to take such other remedial action as is appropriate.

(2) A respondent determined by the Service (if a respondent fails to request a hearing) or by an administrative law judge, to have failed to comply with the employment verification requirements as set forth in § 274a.2(b), shall be subject to a civil penalty in an amount of not less than $100 and not more than $1,000 for each individual with respect to whom such violation occurred before September 29, 1999, and not less than $110 and not more than $1,100 for each individual with respect to whom such violation occurred on or after September 29, 1999. In determining the amount of the penalty, consideration shall be given to:

(i) The size of the business of the employer being charged;

(ii) The good faith of the employer;

(iii) The seriousness of the violation;

(iv) Whether or not the individual was an unauthorized alien; and

(v) The history of previous violations of the employer.

(3) Where an order is issued with respect to a respondent composed of distinct, physically separate subdivisions which do their own hiring, or their own recruiting or referring for a fee for employment (without reference to the practices of, and under the control of, or common control with another subdivision) the subdivision shall be considered a separate person or entity.

(c) Enjoining pattern or practice violations. If the Attorney General has reasonable cause to believe that a person or entity is engaged in a pattern or practice of employment, recruitment or referral in violation of section 274A(a)(1)(A) or (2) of the Act, the Attorney General may bring civil action in the appropriate United States District Court requesting relief, including a permanent or temporary injunction, restraining order, or other order against the person or entity, as the Attorney General deems necessary.

[52 FR 16225, May 1, 1987, as amended at 55 FR 25935, June 25, 1990; 56 FR 41786, Aug. 23, 1991; 64 FR 47101, Aug. 30, 1999]

§ 274a.11 [Reserved].

Subpart B—Employment Authorization

§ 274a.12 Classes of aliens authorized to accept employment.

(a) Aliens authorized employment incident to status. Pursuant to the statutory or regulatory reference cited, the following classes of aliens are authorized to be employed in the United States without restrictions as to location or type of employment as a condition of their admission or subsequent change to one of the indicated classes. Any alien who is within a class of aliens described in paragraphs (a)(3) through (a)(8) or (a)(10) through (a)(13) of this section, and who seeks to be employed in the United States, must apply to the Service for a document evidencing such employment authorization.

(1) An alien who is a lawful permanent resident (with or without conditions pursuant to section 216 of the Act), as evidenced by Form I–551 issued by the Service. An expiration date on the Form I–551 reflects only that the card must be renewed, not that the bearer's work authorization has expired;

(2) An alien admitted to the United States as a lawful temporary resident pursuant to section 245A or 210 of the Act, as evidenced by an employment authorization document issued by the Service;

(3) An alien admitted to the United States as a refugee pursuant to section 207 of the Act for the period of time in that status, as evidenced by an employment authorization document issued by the Service;

(4) An alien paroled into the United States as a refugee for the period of time in that status, as evidenced by an employment authorization document issued by the Service;

(5) An alien granted asylum under section 208 of the Act for the period of time in that status, as evidenced by an employment authorization document issued by the Service;

(6) An alien admitted to the United States as a nonimmigrant fiance or fiancee pursuant to section 101(a)(15)(K) of the Act, or an alien admitted as the child of such alien, for the period of admission of the United States, as evidenced by an employment authorization document issued by the Service;

(7) An alien admitted as a parent (N–8) or dependent child (N–9) of an alien granted permanent residence under section 101(a)(27)(I) of the Act, as evidenced by an employment authorization document issued by the Service;

(8) An alien admitted to the United States as a citizen of the Federated States of Micronesia (CFA/FSM) or of the Marshall Islands (CFA/MIS) pursuant to agreements between the United States and the former trust territories, as evidenced by an employment authorization document issued by the Service;

(9) [Reserved]

(10) An alien granted withholding of deportation or removal for the period of time in that status, as evidenced by an employment authorization document issued by the Service;

(11) An alien who has been granted extended voluntary departure by the Attorney General as a member of a nationality group pursuant to a request by the Secretary of State. Employment is authorized for the period of time in that status as evidenced by an employment authorization document issued by the Service;

(12) An alien granted Temporary Protected Status under section 244 of the Act for the period of time in that status, as evidenced by an employment authorization document issued by the Service; or

(13) An alien granted voluntary departure by the Attorney General under the Family Unity Program established by section 301 of the Immigration Act of 1990, as evidenced by an employment authorization document issued by the Service.

(b) Aliens authorized for employment with a specific employer incident to status. The following classes of nonimmigrant aliens are authorized to be employed in the United States by the specific employer and subject to the restrictions described in the section(s) of this chapter indicated as a condition of their admission in, or subsequent change to, such classification. An alien in one of these classes is not issued an employment authorization document by the Service:

(1) A foreign government official (A–1 or A–2), pursuant to § 214.2(a) of this chapter. An alien in this status may be employed only by the foreign government entity;

(2) An employee of a foreign government official (A–3), pursuant to § 214.2(a) of this chapter. An alien in this status may be employed only by the foreign government official;

(3) A foreign government official in transit (C–2 or C–3), pursuant to § 214.2(c) of this chapter. An alien in this status may be employed only by the foreign government entity;

(4) [Reserved]

(5) A nonimmigrant treaty trader (E–1) or treaty investor (E–2), pursuant to § 214.2(e) of this chapter. An alien in this status may be employed only by the treaty-qualifying company through which the alien attained the status. Employment authorization does not extend to the dependents of the principal treaty trader or treaty investor (also designated "E–1" or "E–2"), other than those specified in paragraph (c)(2) of this section;

(6) A nonimmigrant (F–1) student who is in valid nonimmigrant student status and pursuant to 8 CFR 214.2(f) is seeking:

(i) On-campus employment for not more than twenty hours per week when school is in session or full-time employment when school is not in session if the student intends and is eligible to register for the next term or session. Part-time on-campus employment is authorized by the school and no specific endorsement by a school official or Service officer is necessary;

(ii) Part-time off-campus employment authorization based on an approved attestation from the employer pursuant to 8 CFR 214.2(f) and who presents an I–20 ID endorsed by the designated school official; or

(iii) Curricular practical training (internships, cooperative training programs, or work-study programs which are part of an established curriculum) after having been enrolled full-time in a Service-approved institution for at least nine months. Curricular practical training (part-time or full-time) is authorized by the Designated School Official on the student's I–20 ID; no Service endorsement is necessary.

(7) A representative of an international organization (G–1, G–2, G–3, or G–4), pursuant to § 214.2(g) of this chapter. An alien in this status may be employed only by the foreign government entity or the international organization;

(8) A personal employee of an official or representative of an international organization (G–5), pursuant to § 214.2(g) of this chapter. An alien in this status may be employed only by the official or representative of the international organization;

(9) A temporary worker or trainee (H–1, H–2A, H–2B, or H–3), pursuant to § 214.2(h) of this chapter. An alien in this status may be employed only by the petitioner through whom the status was obtained. In the case of a professional H–2B athlete who is traded from one organization to another organization, employment authorization for the player will automatically continue for a period of 30 days after acquisition by the new organization, within which time the new organization is expected to file a new Form I–129 to petition for H–2B classification. If a new Form I–129 is not filed within 30 days, employment authorization will cease. If a new Form I–129 is filed within 30 days, the professional athlete's employment authorization will continue until the petition is adjudicated. If the new petition is denied, employment authorization will cease;

(10) An information media representative (I), pursuant to § 214.2(i) of this chapter. An alien in this status may be employed only for the sponsoring foreign news agency or bureau. Employment authorization does not extend to the dependents of an information media representative (also designated "I");

(11) An exchange visitor (J–1), pursuant to § 214.2(j) of this chapter and 22 CFR 514.24. An alien in this status may be employed only by the exchange visitor program sponsor or appropriate designee and within the guidelines of the program approved by the United States Information Agency as set forth in the Certificate of Eligibility (Form IAP–66) issued by the program sponsor;

(12) An intra-company transferee (L–1), pursuant to § 214.2(1) of this chapter. An alien in this status may be employed only by the petitioner through whom the status was obtained;

(13) An alien having extraordinary ability in the sciences, arts, education, business, or athletics (O–1), and an accompanying alien (O–2), pursuant to § 214.2(*o*) of this chapter. An alien in this status may be employed only by the petitioner through whom the status was obtained. In the case of a professional O–1 athlete who is traded from one organization to another organization, employment authorization for the player will automatically continue for a period of 30 days after the acquisition by the new organization, within which time the new organization is expected to file a new Form I–129 petition for O nonimmigrant classification. If a new Form I–129 is not filed within 30 days, employment authorization will cease. If a new Form I–129 is filed within 30 days, the professional athlete's employment authorization will continue until the petition is adjudicated. If the new petition is denied, employment authorization will cease.

(14) An athlete, artist, or entertainer (P–1, P–2, or P–3), pursuant to § 214.2(p) of this chapter. An alien in this status may be employed only by the petitioner through whom the status was obtained. In the case of a professional P–1 athlete who is traded from one organization to another organization, employment authorization for the player will automatically continue for a period of 30 days after the acquisition by the new organization, within which time the new organization is expected to file a new Form I–129 for P–1 nonimmigrant classification. If a new Form I–129 is not filed within 30 days, employment authorization will cease. If a new Form I–129 is filed within 30 days, the professional athlete's employment authorization will continue until the petition is adjudicated. If the new petition is denied, employment authorization will cease;

(15) An international cultural exchange visitor (Q–1), according to § 214.2(q)(1) of this chapter. An alien may only be employed by the petitioner through whom the status was obtained;

(16) An alien having a religious occupation, pursuant to § 214.2(r) of this chapter. An alien in this status may be employed only by the religious organization through whom the status was obtained;

(17) Officers and personnel of the armed services of nations of the North Atlantic Treaty Organization, and representatives, officials, and staff employees of NATO (NATO–1, NATO–2, NATO–3, NATO–4, NATO–5 and NATO–6), pursuant to § 214.2(*o*) of this chapter. An alien in this status may be employed only by NATO;

(18) An attendant, servant or personal employee (NATO–7) of an alien admitted as a NATO–1, NATO–2, NATO–3, NATO–4, NATO–5, or NATO–6, pursuant to § 214.2(*o*) of this chapter. An alien admitted under this classification may be employed only by the NATO alien through whom the status was obtained;

(19) A nonimmigrant pursuant to section 214(e) of the Act. An alien in this status must be engaged in business activities at a professional level in accordance with the provisions of Chapter 16 of the North American Free Trade Agreement (NAFTA); or

(20) A nonimmigrant alien within the class of aliens described in paragraphs (b)(2), (b)(5), (b)(8), (b)(9), (b)(10), (b)(11), (b)(12), (b)(13), (b)(14), (b)(16), and (b)(19) of this section whose status has expired but who has filed a timely application for an extension of such stay pursuant to §§ 214.2 or 214.6 of this chapter. These aliens are authorized to continue employment with the same employer for a period not to exceed 240 days beginning on the date of the expiration of the authorized period of stay. Such authorization shall be subject to any conditions and limitations noted on the initial authorization. However, if the district director or service center director adjudicates the application prior to the expiration of this 240 day period and denies the application for extension of stay, the employment authorization under this paragraph shall automatically terminate upon notification of the denial decision.

(c) Aliens who must apply for employment authorization. An alien within a class of aliens described in this section must apply for work authorization. If authorized, such an alien may accept employment subject to any restrictions stated in the regulations or cited on the employment authorization document:

(1) An alien spouse or unmarried dependent child; son or daughter of a foreign government official (A–1 or A–2) pursuant to § 214.2(a)(2) of this chapter and who presents a fully executed Form I–566 bearing the endorsement of an authorized representative of the Department of State;

(2) An alien spouse or unmarried dependent son or daughter of an alien employee of the Coordination Council for North American Affairs (E–1) pursuant to § 214.2(e) of this chapter;

(3) A nonimmigrant (F–1) student who:

(i) Is seeking employment for purposes of optional practical training pursuant to 8 CFR 214.2(f), provided the alien will be employed only in an occupation which is directly related to his or her area of studies and that he or she presents an I–20 ID endorsed by the designated school official;

(ii) Has been offered employment under the sponsorship of an international organization within the meaning of the International Organization Immunities Act (59 Stat. 669) and who presents a written certification from the international organization that the proposed employment is within the scope of the organization's sponsorship. The F–1 student must also present an I–20 ID endorsed by the DSO in the last 30 days; or

(iii) Is seeking employment because of severe economic hardship pursuant to 8 CFR 214.2(f)(9)(ii)(C) and has filed the Form I–20, Form I–538 and any other supporting materials such as affidavits which further detail the unforeseen economic circumstances that require the student to seek employment authorization and evidence the fact that the student has attempted to find employment under 8 CFR 214.2(f)(9)(ii)(B);

(4) An alien spouse or unmarried dependent child; son or daughter of an officer of, representative to, or employee of an international organization (G–1, G–3 or G–4) pursuant to § 214.2(g) of this chapter who presents a fully executed Form I–566 bearing the endorsement of an authorized representative of the Department of State;

(5) An alien spouse or minor child of an exchange visitor (J–2) pursuant to § 214.2(j) of this chapter;

(6) A nonimmigrant (M–1) student seeking employment for practical training pursuant to 8 CFR 214.2(m) following completion of studies. The alien may be employed only in an occupation or vocation directly related to his or her course of study as recommended by the endorsement of the designated school official on the I–20 ID;

(7) A dependent of an alien classified as NATO–1 through NATO–7 pursuant to § 214.2(n) of this chapter;

(8) An alien who has filed a complete application for asylum or withholding of deportation or removal pursuant to 8 CFR part 208, whose application:

(i) Has not been decided, and who is eligible to apply for employment authorization under § 208.7 of this chapter because the 150–day period set forth in that section has expired. Employment authorization may be granted according to the provisions of § 208.7 of this chapter in increments to be determined by the Commissioner and shall expire on a specified date; or

(ii) Has been recommended for approval, but who has not yet received a grant of asylum or withholding or deportation or removal;

(9) An alien who has filed an application for adjustment of status to lawful permanent resident pursuant to part 245 of this chapter. Except as provided in §§ 245.13(j) and 245.15(n) of this chapter, employment authorization shall be granted in increments not exceeding one year during the period the application is pending (including any period when an administrative appeal or judicial review is pending) and shall expire on a specified date. For purposes of section 245(c)(8) of the Act, an alien will not be deemed to be an "unauthorized alien" as defined in section 274A(h)(3) of the Act while his or her properly filed Form I–485 application is pending final adjudication, if the alien has otherwise obtained permission from the Service pursuant to 8 CFR 274a.12 to engage in employment, or if the alien had been granted employment authorization prior to the filing of the adjustment application and such authorization does not expire during the pendency of the adjustment application. Upon meeting these conditions, the adjustment applicant need not file an application for employment authorization to continue employment during the period described in the preceding sentence;

(10) An alien who has filed an application for suspension of deportation under section 244 of the Act (as it existed prior to April 1, 1997), cancellation of removal pursuant to section 240A of the Act, or special rule cancellation of removal under section 309(f)(1) of the Illegal Immigration Reform and Immigrant Responsibility Act of 1996, enacted as Pub.L. 104–208 (110 Stat. 3009–625) (as amended by the Nicaraguan Adjustment and Central American Relief Act (NACARA)), title II of Pub.L. 105–100 (111 Stat. 2160, 2193) and whose properly filed application has been accepted by the Service or EOIR. Employment authorization shall be granted in increments not exceeding one year during the period the application is pending (including any period when an administrative appeal or judicial review is pending) and shall expire on a specified date;

(11) An alien paroled into the United States temporarily for emergency reasons or reasons deemed strictly in the public interest pursuant to § 212.5 of this chapter;

(12) An alien granted benefits under the Family Unity provisions of section 301 of IMMACT 90 and the provisions of part 236, Subpart B of this chapter.

(13) [Reserved]

(14) An alien who has been granted deferred action, an act of administrative convenience to the government which gives some cases lower priority, if the alien establishes an economic necessity for employment;

(15) [Reserved]

(16) Any alien who has filed an application for creation of record of lawful admission for permanent residence pursuant to part 249 of this chapter. Employment authorization shall be granted in increments not exceeding one year during the period the application is pending (including any period when an administrative appeal or judicial review is pending) and shall expire on a specific date;

(17) A nonimmigrant visitor for business (B–1) who:

(i) Is a personal or domestic servant who is accompanying or following to join an employer who seeks admission into, or is already in, the United States as a nonimmigrant defined under sections 101(a)(15)(B), (E), (F), (H), (I), (J), (L) or section 214(e) of the Act. The personal or domestic servant shall have a residence abroad which he or she has no intention of abandoning and shall demonstrate at least one year's experience as a personal or domestic servant. The nonimmigrant's employer shall demonstrate that the employer/employee relationship has existed for at least one year prior to the employer's admission to the United States; or, if the employer/employee relationship existed for less than one year, that the employer has regularly employed (either year-round or seasonally) personal or domestic servants over a period of several years preceding the employer's admission to the United States;

(ii) Is a domestic servant of a United States citizen accompanying or following to join his or her United States citizen employer who has a permanent home or is stationed in a foreign country, and who is visiting temporarily in the United States. The employer/employee relationship shall have existed prior to the commencement of the employer's visit to the United States; or

(iii) Is an employee of a foreign airline engaged in international transportation of passengers freight, whose position with the foreign airline would otherwise entitle the employee to classification under section 101(a)(15)(E)(i) of the Immigration and Nationality Act, and who is precluded from such classification solely because the employee is not a national of the country of the airline's nationality or because there is no treaty of commerce and navigation in effect between the United States and the country of the airline's nationality.

(18) An alien against whom a final order of deportation or removal exists and who is released on an order of supervision under the authority contained in section 241(a)(3) of the Act may be granted employment authorization in the discretion of the district director only if the alien cannot be removed due to the refusal of all countries designated by the alien or under section 241 of the Act to receive the alien, or because the removal of the alien is otherwise impracticable or contrary to the public interest. Additional factors which may be considered by the district director in adjudicating the application for employment authorization include, but are not limited to, the following:

(i) The existence of economic necessity to be employed;

(ii) The existence of a dependent spouse and/or children in the United States who rely on the alien for support; and

(iii) The anticipated length of time before the alien can be removed from the United States.

(19) An alien applying for Temporary Protected Status pursuant to section 244 of the Act shall apply for employment authorization only in accordance with the procedures set forth in part 244 of this chapter.

(20) Any alien who has filed a completed legalization application pursuant to section 210 of the Act (and part 210 of this chapter). Employment authorization shall be granted in increments not exceeding 1 year during the period the application is pending (including any period when an administrative appeal is pending) and shall expire on a specified date.

(21) A principal nonimmigrant witness or informant in S classification, and qualified dependent family members.

(22) Any alien who has filed a completed legalization application pursuant to section 245A of the Act (and part 245a of this chapter). Employment authorization shall be granted in increments not exceeding 1 year during the period the application is pending (including any period when an administrative appeal is pending) and shall expire on a specified date.

(23) An Irish peace process cultural and training program visitor (Q–2), pursuant to § 214.2(q)(15) of this chapter and 22 CFR 41.57 and 22 CFR part 139. An alien in this status may only accept employment with the employer listed on the Certification Letter issued by the DOS' Program Administrator.

(d) Basic criteria to establish economic necessity. Title 45—Public Welfare, Poverty Guidelines, 45 CFR 1060.2 should be used as the basic criteria to establish eligibility for employment authorization when the alien's economic necessity is identified as a factor. The alien shall submit an application for employee authorization listing his or her assets, income, and expenses as evidence of his or her economic need to work. Permission to work granted on the basis of the alien's application for employment authorization may be revoked under § 274a.14 of this chapter upon a showing that the information contained in the statement was not true and correct.

[53 FR 8614, March 16, 1988; 53 FR 46855, Nov. 21, 1988; 54 FR 16, Jan. 3, 1989; 54 FR 48577, Nov. 24, 1989; 55 FR 5576, Feb. 16, 1990; 55 FR 25935, 25936, June 25, 1990; 56 FR 624, Jan. 7, 1991; 56 FR 23496, 23499, May 22, 1991; 56 FR 41782, 41786, 41787, Aug. 23, 1991; 56 FR 55616, Oct. 29, 1991; 57 FR 6462, Feb. 25, 1992; 57 FR 31956, July 20, 1992; 57 FR 42884, Sept. 17, 1992; 58 FR 48780, Sept. 20, 1993; 58 FR 69217, Dec. 30, 1993; 59 FR 42487, Aug. 15, 1994; 59 FR 47063, Sept. 14, 1994; 59 FR 52894, Oct. 20, 1994; 59 FR 62302, Dec. 5, 1994; 60 FR 14353, March 17, 1995; 60 FR 21976, May 4, 1995; 60 FR 44271, Aug. 25, 1995; 60 FR 66067, 66069, Dec. 21, 1995; 61 FR 46537, Sept. 4, 1996; 62 FR 10389, March 6, 1997; 62 FR 18514, April 16, 1997; 62 FR 39425,

July 23, 1997; 62 FR 46553, Sept. 3, 1997; 63 FR 1334, Jan. 9, 1998; 63 FR 27833, May 21, 1998; 63 FR 63597, Nov. 16, 1998; 64 FR 25773, May 12, 1999; 64 FR 27881, May 21, 1999; 65 FR 14780, March 17, 2000; 65 FR 14774, March 24, 2000]

§ 274a.13 Application for employment authorization.

(a) General. Aliens authorized to be employed under § 274a.12(a)(3)–(8) and (10)–(13) must file an Application for Employment Authorization (Form I–765) in order to obtain documentation evidencing this fact.

(1) Aliens who may apply for employment authorization under § 274a.12(c) of this part, except for those who may apply under § 274a.12(c)(8), shall file a Form I–765 with the director having jurisdiction over applicant's residence, or the director having jurisdiction over the port of entry at which the alien applies, or with such other Service office as the Commissioner may designate. The approval of applications filed under § 274a.12(c) of this part, except for § 274a.12(c)(8), shall be within the discretion of the director or such other officer as the Commissioner may designate. Where economic necessity has been identified as a factor, the alien must provide information regarding his or her assets, income, and expenses in accordance with instructions on Form I–765.

(2) An initial Application for Employment Authorization (Form I–765) for asylum applicants under 274a.12(c)(8) of this part shall be filed in accordance with instructions on or attached to Form I–765 with the appropriate Service Center or with such other Service office as the Commissioner may designate. The applicant also must submit a copy of the underlying application for asylum or withholding of deportation, together with evidence that the application has been filed in accordance with §§ 208.3 and 208.4 of this chapter. An application for an initial employment authorization or for a renewal of employment authorization filed in relation to a pending claim for asylum shall be adjudicated in accordance with § 208.7 of this chapter. An application for renewal or replacement of employment authorization submitted in relation to a pending claim for asylum, as provided in § 208.7 of this chapter, shall be filed, with fee or application for waiver of such fee, in accordance with the instructions on or attached to Form I–765 with the appropriate Service Center or with such other Service office as the Commissioner may designate.

(b) Approval of application. If the application is granted, the alien shall be notified of the decision and issued an INS employment authorization document valid for a specific period and subject to any terms and conditions as noted.

(c) Denial of application. If the application is denied, the applicant shall be notified in writing of the decision and the reasons for the denial. There shall be no appeal from the denial of the application.

(d) Interim employment authorization. The director shall adjudicate the application within 90 days from the date of receipt of the application by the INS, except in the case of an initial application for employment authorization under § 274a.12(c)(8), which is governed by paragraph (a)(2) of this section, and § 274a.12(c)(9) insofar as it is governed by §§ 245.13(j) and 245.15(n) of this chapter. Failure to complete the adjudication within 90 days will result in the grant of an employment authorization document for a period not to exceed 240 days. Such authorization shall be subject to any conditions noted on the employment authorization document. However, if the director adjudicates the application prior to the expiration date of the interim employment authorization and denies the individual's employment authorization application, the interim employment authorization granted under this section shall automatically terminate as of the date of the director's adjudication and denial.

[53 FR 8614, March 16, 1988; 55 FR 25937, June 25, 1990; 56 FR 41782, 41787, Aug. 23, 1991; 57 FR 6462, Feb. 25, 1992; 57 FR 14627, April 21, 1992; 58 FR 12149, March 3, 1993; 58 FR 14145, March 16, 1993; 59 FR 33905, July 1, 1994; 59 FR 62303, Dec. 5, 1994; 60 FR 21976, May 4, 1995; 60 FR 66067, Dec. 21, 1995; 63 FR 27833, May 21, 1998; 63 FR 39121, July 21, 1998; 64 FR 25773, May 12, 1999; 65 FR 14774, March 24, 2000]

§ 274a.14 Termination of employment authorization.

(a) Automatic termination of employment authorization—

(1) Employment authorization granted under § 274a.12(c) of this chapter shall automatically terminate upon the occurrence of one of the following events:

(i) The expiration date specified by the Service on the employment authorization document is reached;

(ii) Exclusion or deportation proceedings are instituted (however, this shall not preclude the authorization of employment pursuant to § 274a.12(c) of this part where appropriate); or

(iii) The alien is granted voluntary departure.

(2) Termination of employment authorization pursuant to this paragraph does not require the service of a notice of intent to revoke; employment authorization terminates upon the occurrence of any event enumerated in paragraph (a)(1) of this section.

However, automatic revocation under this section does not preclude reapplication for employment authorization under § 274.12(c) of this part.

(b) Revocation of employment authorization—

(1) Basis for revocation of employment authorization. Employment authorization granted under § 274a.12(c) of this chapter may be revoked by the district director:

(i) Prior to the expiration date, when it appears that any condition upon which it was granted has not been met or no longer exists, or for good cause shown; or

(ii) Upon a showing that the information contained in the application is not true and correct.

(2) Notice of intent to revoke employment authorization. When a district director determines that employment authorization should be revoked prior to the expiration date specified by the Service, he or she shall serve written notice of intent to revoke the employment authorization. The notice will cite the reasons indicating that revocation is warranted. The alien will be granted a period of fifteen days from the date of service of the notice within which to submit countervailing evidence. The decision by the district director shall be final and no appeal shall lie from the decision to revoke the authorization.

(c) Automatic termination of temporary employment authorization granted prior to June 1, 1987—

(1) Temporary employment authorization granted prior to June 1, 1987, pursuant to 8 CFR 274a.12(c) (s 109.1(b) contained in the 8 CFR edition revised as of January 1, 1987), shall automatically terminate on the date specified by the Service on the document issued to the alien, or on December 31, 1996, whichever is earlier. Automatic termination of temporary employment authorization does not preclude a subsequent application for temporary employment authorization.

(2) A document issued by the Service prior to June 1, 1987, that authorized temporary employment authorization for any period beyond December 31, 1996, is null and void pursuant to paragraph (c)(1) of this section. The alien shall be issued a new employment authorization document upon application to the Service if the alien is eligible for temporary employment authorization pursuant to 274A.12(c).

(3) No notice of intent to revoke is necessary for the automatic termination of temporary employment authorization pursuant to this part.

[53 FR 8614, March 16, 1988; 53 FR 20087, June 1, 1988; 61 FR 46537, Sept. 4, 1996]

PART 292—REPRESENTATION AND APPEARANCES

§ 292.1 Representation of others.

(a) A person entitled to representation may be represented by any of the following:

(1) Attorneys in the United States. Any attorney as defined in § 1.1(f) of this chapter.

(2) Law students and law graduates not yet admitted to the bar. A law student who is enrolled in an accredited law school, or a law graduate who is not yet admitted to the bar, provided that:

(i) He or she is appearing at the request of the person entitled to representation;

(ii) In the case of a law student, he or she has filed a statement that he or she is participating, under the direct supervision of a faculty member, licensed attorney, or accredited representative, in a legal aid program or clinic conducted by a law school or non-profit organization, and that he or she is appearing without direct or indirect remuneration from the alien he or she represents;

(iii) In the case of a law graduate, he or she has filed a statement that he or she is appearing under the supervision of a licensed attorney or accredited representative and that he or she is appearing without direct or indirect remuneration from the alien he or she represents; and

(iv) The law student's or law graduate's appearance is permitted by the official before whom he or she wishes to appear (namely an immigration judge, district director, officer-in-charge, regional director, the Commissioner, or the Board). The official or officials may require that a law student be accompanied by the supervising faculty member, attorney, or accredited representative.

(3) Reputable individuals. Any reputable individual of good moral character, provided that:

(i) He is appearing on an individual case basis, at the request of the person entitled to representation;

(ii) He is appearing without direct or indirect remuneration and files a written declaration to that effect;

(iii) He has a pre-existing relationship or connection with the person entitled to representation (e.g., as a relative, neighbor, clergyman, business associate or personal friend), provided that such requirement may be waived, as a matter of administrative discretion, in cases where adequate representation would not otherwise be available; and

(iv) His appearance is permitted by the official before whom he wished to appear (namely, a special inquiry officer, district director, officer-in-charge, regional commissioner, the Commissioner, or the Board), provided that such permission shall not be granted with respect to any individual who regularly engages in immigration and naturalization practice or preparation, or holds himself out to the public as qualified to do so.

(4) Accredited representatives. A person representing an organization described in § 292.2 of this chapter who has been accredited by the Board.

(5) Accredited officials. An accredited official, in the United States, of the government to which an alien owes allegiance, if the official appears solely in his official capacity and with the alien's consent.

(6) Attorneys outside the United States. An attorney other than one described in § 1.1(f) of this chapter who is licensed to practice law and is in good standing in a court of general jurisdiction of the country in which he/she resides and who is engaged in such practice. Provided that he/she represents persons only in matters outside the geographical confines of the United States as defined in section 101(a)(38) of the Act, and that the Service official before whom he/she wishes to appear allows such representation as a matter of discretion.

(b) Persons formerly authorized to practice. A person, other than a representative of an organization described in § 292.2 of this chapter, who on December 23, 1952, was authorized to practice before the Board and the Service may continue to act as a representative, subject to the provisions of § 292.3 of this chapter.

(c) Former employees. No person previously employed by the Department of Justice shall be permitted to act as a representative in any case in violation of the provisions of 28 CFR 45.735–7.

(d) Amicus curiae. The Board may grant permission to appear, on a case-by-case basis, as amicus curiae, to an attorney or to an organization represented by an attorney, if the public interest will be served thereby.

(e) Except as set forth in this section, no other person or persons shall represent others in any case.

[40 FR 23271, May 29. 1975; 53 FR 7728, March 10, 1988; 55 FR 49251, Nov. 27, 1990; 61 FR 53610, Oct. 15, 1996; 62 FR 23634, May 1, 1997]

§ 292.2 Organizations qualified for recognition; requests for recognition; withdrawal of recognition; accreditation of representatives; roster.

(a) Qualifications of organizations. A non-profit religious, charitable, social service, or similar organization established in the United

States and recognized as such by the Board may designate a representative or representatives to practice before the Service alone or the Service and the Board (including practice before the Immigration Court). Such organization must establish to the satisfaction of the Board that:

(1) It makes only nominal charges and assesses no excessive membership dues for persons given assistance; and

(2) It has at its disposal adequate knowledge, information and experience.

(b) Requests for recognition. An organization having the qualifications prescribed in paragraph (a) of this section may file an application for recognition on a Form G–27 directly with the Board, along with proof of service of a copy of the application on the district director having jurisdiction over the area in which the organization is located. The district director, within 30 days from the date of service, shall forward to the Board a recommendation for approval or disapproval of the application and the reasons therefor, or request a specified period of time in which to conduct an investigation or otherwise obtain relevant information regarding the applicant. The district director shall include proof of service of a copy of such recommendation or request on the organization. The organization shall have 30 days in which to file a response with the Board to a recommendation by a district director that is other than favorable, along with proof of service of a copy of such response on the district director. If the Board approves a request for time to conduct an investigation, or in its discretion remands the application to the district director for further information, the organization shall be advised of the time granted for such purpose. The Service shall promptly forward the results of any investigation or inquiry to the Board, along with its recommendations for approval or disapproval and the reasons therefor, and proof of service of a copy of the submission on the organization. The organization shall have 30 days from the date of such service to file a response with the Board to any matters raised therein, with proof of service of a copy of the response on the district director. Requests for extensions of filing times must be submitted in writing with the reasons therefor and may be granted by the Board in its discretion. Oral argument may be heard before the Board in its discretion at such date and time as the Board may direct. The organization and Service shall be informed by the Board of the action taken regarding an application. Any recognized organization shall promptly notify the Board of any changes in its name, address, or public telephone number.

(c) Withdrawal of recognition. The Board may withdraw the recognition of any organization which has failed to maintain the qualifications required by § 292.2(a). Withdrawal of recognition may be accomplished in accordance with the following procedure:

(1) The Service, by the district director within whose jurisdiction the organization is located, may conduct an investigation into any organization it believes no longer meets the standards for recognition.

(2) If the investigation establishes to the satisfaction of the district director that withdrawal proceedings should be instituted, he shall cause a written statement of the grounds upon which withdrawal is sought to be served upon the organization, with notice to show cause why its recognition should not be withdrawn. The notice will call upon the organization to appear before a special inquiry officer for a hearing at a time and place stated, not less than 30 days after service of the notice.

(3) The special inquiry officer shall hold a hearing, receive evidence, make findings of fact, state his recommendations, and forward the complete record to the Board.

(4) The organization and the Service shall have the opportunity of appearing at oral argument before the Board at a time specified by the Board.

(5) The Board shall consider the entire record and render its decision. The order of the Board shall constitute the final disposition of the proceedings.

(d) Accreditation of representatives. An organization recognized by the Board under paragraph (b) of this section may apply for accreditation of persons of good moral character as its representatives. An organization may apply to have a representative accredited to practice before the Service alone or the Service and the Board (including practice before immigration judges). An application for accreditation shall fully set forth the nature and extent of the proposed representative's experience and knowledge of immigration and naturalization law and procedure and the category of accreditation sought. No individual may submit an application on his or her own behalf. An application shall be filed directly with the Board, along with proof of service of a copy of the application on the district director having jurisdiction over the area in which the requesting organization is located. The district director, within 30 days from the date of service, shall forward to the Board a recommendation for approval or disapproval of the application and the reasons therefor, or request a specified period of time in which to conduct an investigation or otherwise obtain relevant information regarding the applicant. The district director shall include proof of service of a copy of such recommendation or request on the organization. The organization shall have 30 days in which to file a response with the Board to a recommendation by a district director that is other than favorable, with proof of service of a copy of such response on the district director. If the Board approves a request for time to conduct an investigation, or in its discretion remands the application to the district director for further information, the organization shall be advised of the time granted for such purpose. The district director shall promptly forward the results of any investigation or inquiry to the Board, along with a recommendation for approval or disapproval and the reasons therefor, and proof of service of a copy of the submission on the organization. The organization shall have 30 days from the date of service to file a response with the Board to any matters raised therein, with proof or service of a copy of the response on the district director. Requests for extensions of filing times must be submitted in writing with the reasons therefor and may be granted by the Board in its discretion. Oral argument may be heard before the Board in its discretion at such date and time as the Board may direct. The Board may approve or disapprove an application in whole or in part and shall inform the organization and the district director of the action taken with regard to an application. The accreditation of a representative shall be valid for a period of three years only; however, the accreditation shall remain valid pending Board consideration of an application for renewal of accreditation if the application is filed at least 60 days before the third anniversary of the date of the Board's prior accreditation of the representative. Accreditation terminates when the Board's recognition of the organization ceases for any reason or when the representative's employment or other connection with the organization ceases. The organization shall promptly notify the Board of such changes.

(e) Roster. The Board shall maintain an alphabetical roster of recognized organizations and their accredited representatives. A copy of the roster shall be furnished to the Commissioner and he shall be advised from time to time of changes therein.

[40 FR 23272, May 29, 1975; 49 FR 44086, Nov. 2, 1984; 62 FR 9075, Feb. 28, 1997]

TITLE 20—EMPLOYEES' BENEFITS

Part 656—Labor Certification Process for Permanent Employment of Aliens in the United States

Sec.

656.3 Definitions, for purposes of this part, of terms used in this part.
656.10 Schedule A.
656.20 General filing instructions.
656.21 Basic labor certification process.
656.21a Applications for labor certifications for occupations designated for special handling.
656.22 Applications for labor certification for Schedule A occupations.
656.24 Labor certification determinations.
656.25 Procedures following a labor certification determination.
656.26 Board of Alien Labor Certification Appeals review of denials of labor certification.
656.27 Consideration by and decisions of the Board of Alien Labor Certification Appeals.
656.28 Document transmittal following the grant of a labor certification.
656.29 Filing of a new application after the denial of a labor certification.
656.30 Validity of and invalidation of labor certifications.
656.40 Determination of prevailing wage for labor certification purposes.

PART 656—LABOR CERTIFICATION PROCESS FOR PERMANENT EMPLOYMENT OF ALIENS IN THE UNITED STATES

§ 656.3 Definitions, for purposes of this part, of terms used in this part.

Act means the Immigration and Nationality Act, as amended, 8 U.S.C. 1101 et seq.

Administrative Law Judge means an official appointed pursuant to 5 U.S.C. 3105.

Agent means a person who is not an employee of an employer, and who has been designated in writing to act on behalf of an alien or employer in connection with an application for labor certification.

Application means an Application for Alien Employment Certification form and any other documents submitted by an alien and/or employer (or their agents) in applying for a labor certification under this part.

Area of intended employment means the area within normal commuting distance of the place (address) of intended employment. If the place of intended employment is within a Metropolitan Statistical Area (MSA), any place within the MSA is deemed to be within normal commuting distance of the place of intended employment.

Assistant Secretary means the Assistant Secretary of Labor for Employment and Training, the chief official of the Employment and Training Administration.

Attorney means any person who is a member in good standing of the bar of the highest court of any State, Possession, Territory, or Commonwealth of the United States, or the District of Columbia, and who is not under any order of any court or of the Board of Immigration Appeals suspending, enjoining, restraining, disbarring, or otherwise restricting him or her in the practice of law.

Attorney General means the chief official of the U.S. Department of Justice or the designee of the Attorney General.

Board of Alien Labor Certification Appeals means the permanent Board of Alien Labor Certification Appeals established by this Part, chaired by the Chief Administrative Law Judge, and consisting of Administrative Law Judges assigned to the Department of Labor and designated by the Chief Administrative Law Judge to be members of the Board of Alien Labor Certification Appeals. The Board of Alien Labor Certification Appeals is located in Washington, DC, and reviews and decides appeals in Washington, DC.

Certifying Officer means a Department of Labor official who makes determinations about whether or not to grant applications for labor certifications:

(1) A regional Certifying Officer designated by a Regional Administrator, Employment and Training Administration (RA) makes such determinations in a regional office of the Department;

(2) A national Certifying Officer makes such determinations in the national office of the USES.

(3) The addresses of the regional Certifying Officers are set forth in § 656.60 of this part.

Chief Administrative Law Judge means the chief official of the Office of Administrative Law Judges of the Department of Labor.

Consular Officer means an official of the U.S. Department of State who handles applications for labor certifications pursuant to this part.

Director means the chief official of the United States Employment Service or the Director's designee.

Employment means permanent full-time work by an employee for an employer other than oneself. For purposes of this definition an investor is not an employee.

Employment and Training Administration (ETA) means the agency within the Department of Labor (DOL) which includes the United States Employment Service (USES).

Employer means a person, association, firm, or a corporation which currently has a location within the United States to which U.S. workers may be referred for employment, and which proposes to employ a full-time worker at a place within the United States or the authorized representative of such a person association, firm, or corporation. For purposes of this definition an authorized representative means an employee of the employer whose position or legal status authorizes the employee to act for the employer in labor certification matters.

Federal research agency means a major organizational component of a Federal cabinet level agency or other agency operating with appropriated funds that has as its primary purpose the performance of scientific research. Federal research agencies are presumed to be doing nonproprietary research. To be considered a major organizational component of a cabinet level agency or other agency operating with appropriated funds for the purpose of this part the organizational component or other agency must be administered by a person who is no lower than Level V (or the equivalent) of the Executive Schedule (see 5 U.S.C. 5316).

Final Determination form means the form used by the Certifying Officer to notify employers (and aliens) for labor certification determinations (and was formerly known as the "Determination and Transmittal form").

Immigration and Naturalization Service (INS) means the agency within the U.S. Department of Justice which administers that Department's principal functions under the Act.

Immigration Officer means an official of the Immigration and Naturalization Service (INS) who handles applications for labor certifications pursuant to this part.

INS, see Immigration and Naturalization Service.

Job opportunity means a job opening for employment at a place in the United States to which U.S. workers can be referred.

Labor certification means the certification to the Secretary of State and to the Attorney General of the determination by the Secretary of Labor pursuant to section 212(a)(14) of the Immigration and Nationality Act (8 U.S.C. 1182(a)(14)):

(1) That there are not sufficient U.S. workers who are able, willing, qualified, and available at the time of an alien's application for a visa and admission to the United States and at the place where the alien is to perform the work; and

(2) That the employment of the alien will not adversely affect the wages and working conditions of similarly employed U.S. workers.

Local Employment Service office and local office mean a full-time office of a State Employment Service agency (also known as a State Employment Security Agency (SESA), also known as a State employment service), which is maintained for the purpose of providing placement and other services of the Employment Service System, and which serves a particular geographic area within a State. Unless specified otherwise in this part, the local office performing the functions required by this part shall be the local Employment Service office serving the area where the job opportunity is located.

Notice of Findings means a notice which sets for the bases upon which a Certifying Officer intends to deny a labor certification unless the bases are satisfactorily rebutted.

Occupation designated for special handling means an occupation, described at § 656.21a, for which DOL has determined that special labor market tests are appropriate.

Physicians (and/or surgeons) means persons who apply the art and science of medicine or surgery primarily in patient care to the diagnosis, prevention, and treatment of human diseases, disorders of the mind, and pregnancy. This definition includes persons practicing medicine, surgery, osteopathy, psychiatry, and ophthalmology. The physician or surgeon may specialize in treating a specific area of the body, or a particular disease, sex, or age group.

Professional nurses means persons who apply the art and science and nursing, which reflects comprehension of principles derived from the physical, biological, and behavioral sciences. Professional nursing generally includes the making of clinical judgments concerning the observation, care, and counsel of persons requiring nursing care; and administering of medicines and treatments prescribed by the physician or dentist; the participation in activities for the promotion of health and the prevention of illness in others. A program of study for professional nurses generally includes theory and practice in clinical areas such as: obstetrics, surgery, pediatrics, psychiatry, and medicine. This definition includes only those occupations within Occupational Group No. 075 of the Dictionary of Occupational Title (4th ed.)

Regional Administrator, Employment and Training Administration (RA) means the chief official of the Employment and Training Administration (ETA) in a Department of Labor (DOL) regional office.

Schedule A means the list of occupations set forth at § 656.10, with respect to which the Director has determined that there are not sufficient United States workers who are able, willing, qualified and available, and that the employment of aliens in such occupations will not adversely affect the wages and working conditions of United States workers similarly employed.

Schedule B means the list of occupations set forth in § 656.11, with respect to which the Director has determined that there are generally sufficient United States workers who are able, willing, qualified and available, and that the employment of aliens in such occupations will generally adversely affect the wages and working conditions of the United States workers similarly employed.

Secretary means the Secretary of Labor, the chief official of the U.S. Department of Labor, or the Secretary's designee.

Secretary of State means the chief official of the U.S. Department of State or the Secretary of State's designee.

United States, when used in a geographic sense, means the fifty States, the District of Columbia, Puerto Rico, the U.S. Virgin Islands, and Guam.

United States Employment Service (USES) means the agency of the U.S. Department of Labor, established under the Wagner–Peyser Act (29 U.S.C. 49 et seq.), which is charged with administering the national system of public employment offices (the Employment Service (ES) System) and with carrying out the functions of the Secretary under section 212(a)(14) of the Immigration and Nationality Act (8 U.S.C. 1182(a)(14)).

United States worker means any worker who is a U.S. citizen; is a U.S. national; is lawfully admitted for permanent residence; is granted the status of an alien lawfully admitted for permanent residence under 8 U.S.C. 1160(a), 1161(a), or 1255a(a)(1); is admitted as a refugee under 8 U.S.C. 1157; or is granted asylum under 8 U.S.C. 1158.

[45 FR 83933, Dec. 19, 1980; as amended at 52 FR 11219, April 8, 1987; 52 FR 20596, June 2, 1987; 56 FR 54930, Oct. 23, 1991; 63 FR 13756, March 20, 1998]

§ 656.10 Schedule A.

The Director, United States Employment Service (Director), has determined that there are not sufficient United States workers who are able, willing, qualified, and available for the occupations listed below on Schedule A and that the wages and working conditions of United States workers similarly employed will not be adversely affected by the employment of aliens in Schedule A occupations. An alien seeking a labor certification for an occupation listed on Schedule A may apply for that labor certification pursuant to § 656.22.

Schedule A

(a) Group I:

(1) Persons who will be employed as physical therapists, and who possess all the qualifications necessary to take the physical therapist licensing examination in the State in which they propose to practice physical therapy.

(2) Aliens who will be employed as professional nurses; and (i) who have passed the Commission on Graduates of Foreign Nursing Schools (CGFNS) Examination; or (ii) who hold a full and unrestricted license to practice professional nursing in the State of intended employment.

(3) Definitions of Group I occupations:

(i) "Physical therapist" means a person who applies the art and science of physical therapy to the treatment of patients with disabilities, disorders and injuries to relieve pain, develop or restore function, and maintain performance, using physical means, such as exercise, massage, heat, water, light, and electricity, as prescribed by a physician (or surgeon).

(ii) "Professional nurse" is defined in § 656.50.

(b) Group II:

Aliens (except for aliens in the performing arts) of exceptional ability in the sciences or arts including college and university teachers of exceptional ability who have been practicing their science or art during the year prior to application and who intend to practice the same science or art in the United States. For purposes of this group, the term "science or art" means any field of knowledge and/or skill with respect to which colleges and universities commonly offer specialized courses leading to a degree in the knowledge and/or skill. An alien, however, need not have studied at a college or university in order to qualify for the Group II occupation.

[45 FR 83933, Dec. 19, 1980; as amended at 52 FR 20596, June 2, 1987; 56 FR 54927, Oct. 23, 1991]

§ 656.20 General filing instructions.

(a) A request for a labor certification on behalf of any alien who is required by the Act to become a beneficiary of a labor certification in order to obtain permanent resident status in the United States may be filed as follows:

(1) Except as provided in paragraphs (a)(2) through (4) of this section, an application for a labor certification shall be filed pursuant to this section and § 656.21.

(2) An employer seeking a labor certification for an occupation designated for special handling shall apply for a labor certification pursuant to this section and § 656.21a.

(3) An alien seeking labor certification for an occupation listed on Schedule A may apply for a labor certification pursuant to this section and § 656.22.

(4) An employer seeking a labor certification for an occupation listed on Schedule B shall apply for a waiver and a labor certification pursuant to this section and §§ 656.21 and 656.23.

(b)(1) Aliens and employers may have agents represent them throughout the labor certification process. If an alien and/or an employer intends to be represented by an agent, the alien and/or the employer shall sign the statement set forth on the Application for Alien Employment Certification form: That the agent is representing the alien and/or employer and that the alien and/or employer takes full responsibility for the accuracy of any representations made by the agent.

(2) Aliens and employers may have attorneys represent them. Each attorney shall file a notice of appearance on Immigration and Naturalization Service (INS) Form G–28, naming the attorney's client or clients. Whenever, under this Part, any notice or other document is required to be sent to an employer or alien, the document shall be sent to their attorney or attorneys who have filed notices of appearance on INS Form G–28, if they have such an attorney or attorneys.

(3)(i) It is contrary to the best interests of U.S. workers to have the alien and/or agents or attorneys for the alien participate in interviewing or considering U.S. workers for the job offered the alien. As the beneficiary of a labor certification application, the alien cannot represent the best interests of U.S. workers in the job opportunity. The alien's agent and/or attorney cannot represent the alien effectively and at the same time truly be seeking U.S. workers for the job opportunity. Therefore, the alien and/or the alien's agent and/or attorney may not interview or consider U.S. workers for the job offered to the alien, unless the agent and/or attorney is the employer's representative as described in paragraph (b)(3)(ii) of this section.

(ii) The employer's representative who interviews or considers U.S. workers for the job offered to the alien shall be the person who normally interviews or considers, on behalf of the employer, applicants for job opportunities such as that offered the alien, but which do not involve labor certifications.

(4) No person under suspension or disbarment from practice before the United States Department of Justice's Board of Immigration Appeals pursuant to 8 CFR 292.3 shall be permitted to act as an agent, representative, or attorney for an employer and/or alien under this part.

(c) Job offers filed on behalf of aliens on the Application for Alien Employment Certification form must clearly show that:

(1) The employer has enough funds available to pay the wage or salary offered the alien;

(2) The wage offered equals or exceeds the prevailing wage determined pursuant to § 656.40, and the wage the employer will pay to the alien when the alien begins work will equal or exceed the prevailing wage which is applicable at the time the alien begins work;

(3) The wage offered is not based on commissions, bonuses or other incentives, unless the employer guarantees a wage paid on a weekly, bi-weekly, or monthly basis;

(4) The employer will be able to place the alien on the payroll on or before the date of the alien's proposed entrance into the United States;

(5) The job opportunity does not involve unlawful discrimination by race, creed, color, national origin, age, sex, religion, handicap, or citizenship;

(6) The employer's job opportunity is not:

(i) Vacant because the former occupant is on strike or is being locked out in the course of a labor dispute involving a work stoppage; or

(ii) At issue in a labor dispute involving a work stoppage;

(7) The employer's job opportunity's terms, conditions and occupational environment are not contrary to Federal, State or local law; and

(8) The job opportunity has been and is clearly open to any qualified U.S. worker.

(9) The conditions of employment listed in paragraphs (c)(1) through (8) of this section shall be sworn (or affirmed) to, under penalty of perjury pursuant to 28 U.S.C. 1746, on the Application for Alien Employment Certification form.

(d) If the application involves labor certification as a physician (or surgeon)(except a physician (or surgeon) of international renown), the labor certification application shall include the following documentation:

(1)(i) Documentation which shows clearly that the alien has passed Parts I and II of the National Board of Medical Examiners Examination (NBMEE), or the Foreign Medical Graduate Examination in the Medical Sciences (FMGEMS) offered by the Educational Commission for Foreign Medical Graduates (ECFMG); or

(ii) Documentation which shows clearly that:

(A) The alien was on January 9, 1978, a doctor of medicine fully and permanently licensed to practice medicine in a State within the United States;

(B) The alien was on January 9, 1978, practicing medicine in a State within the United States; or

(iii) The alien is a graduate of a school of medicine accredited by a body or bodies approved for the purpose by the Secretary of Education or that Secretary's designee (regardless of whether such school of medicine is in the United States).

(e) Whenever any document is submitted to a State or Federal agency pursuant to this part, the document either shall be in the English language or shall be accompanied by a written translation into the English language, certified by the translator as to the accuracy of the translation and his/her competency to translate.

(f) The forms required under this part for applications for labor certification are available at U.S. Consular offices abroad, at INS offices in the United States, and at local offices of the State; job service agencies. The forms will contain instructions on how to comply with the documentation requirements for applying for a labor certification under this part.

(g)(1) In applications filed under §§ 656.21 (Basic Process), 656.21a (Special Handling) and 656.22 (Schedule A), the employer shall document that notice of the filing of the Application for Alien Employment Certification was provided:

(i) To the bargaining representative(s) (if any) of the employer's employees in the occupational classification for which certification of the job opportunity is sought in the employer's location(s) in the area of intended employment.

(ii) If there is no such bargaining representative, by posted notice to the employer's employees at the facility or location of the employment. The notice shall be posted for at least 10 consecutive days. The notice shall be clearly visible and unobstructed while posted and shall be posted in conspicuous places, where the employer's U.S. workers can readily read the posted notice on their way to or from their place of employment. Appropriate locations for posting notices of the job opportunity include, but are not limited to, locations in the immediate vicinity of the wage and hour notices required by 20 CFR 516.4 or occupational safety and health notices required by 20 CFR 1903.2(a).

(2) In the case of a private household, notice is required under this paragraph (g) only if the household employs one or more U.S. workers at the time the application for labor certification is filed with a local Employment Service office.

(3) Any notice of the filing of an Application for Alien Employment Certification shall:

(i) State that applicants should report to the employer, not to the local Employment Service office;

(ii) State that the notice is being provided as a result of the filing of an application for permanent alien labor certification for the relevant job opportunity; and

(iii) State that any person may provide documentary evidence bearing on the application to the local Employment Service Office and/or the regional Certifying Officer of the Department of Labor.

(4) If an application is filed under § 656.21 and does not involve a request for reduction in recruitment, the notice shall be provided in conjunction with the recruitment required under § 656.21(f) of this part, shall contain the information required for advertisements by §§ 656.21 (g)(3) through (g)(8), and shall contain the information required by paragraph (g)(3) of this section.

(5) If an application is filed under the reduction in recruitment provisions at § 656.21(i) of this part, the notice does not have to be posted in conjunction with the recruitment required under § 656.21(f) of this part, but shall include the information required for advertisements by §§ 656.21 (g)(3) through (g)(8), and the requirements of paragraph (g)(3) of this section;

(6) If an application is filed on behalf of a college and university teacher pursuant to § 656.21a(a)(1)(iii) of this part, the notice shall include the information required for advertisements by § 656.21a(a)(1)(iii)(B), and the requirements of paragraph (g)(3) of this section.

(7) If an application is filed on behalf of an alien represented to be of exceptional ability in the performing arts, the notice required by this paragraph (g) shall include the information required for advertisements by §§ 656.21a(a)(iv)(B) (1) through (7) of this part, and the requirements of paragraph (g)(3) of this section.

(8) If an application is filed under the Schedule A procedures at § 656.22 of this part, the notice shall contain a description of the job and rate of pay, and the requirements of paragraphs (g)(3) (ii) and (iii) of this section.

(h)(1)(i) Any person may submit to the local Employment Service office or to the Certifying Officer documentary evidence bearing on an application for permanent alien labor certification filed under the basic labor certification process at § 656.21 of this part or under the special handling procedures at § 656.21a of this part.

(ii) Documentary evidence submitted pursuant to paragraph (h)(1)(i) of this section may include information on available workers, information on wages and working conditions, and information on the employer's failure to meet terms and conditions with respect to the employment of alien workers and co-workers. The Certifying Officer shall consider this information in making his or her determination.

(2)(ii) [sic] Any person may submit to the appropriate INS office documentary evidence of fraud or willful misrepresentation in a Schedule A application filed under § 656.22 of this part or a sheepherder application filed under § 656.21a(b) of this part.

(B) [sic] Documentary evidence submitted pursuant to paragraph (h)(2)(i) of this section shall be limited to information relating to possible fraud or willful misrepresentation. The INS may consider this information pursuant to § 656.31 of this part.

[45 FR 83933, Dec. 19, 1980; as amended at 49 FR 18295, April 30, 1984; 56 FR 54927, Oct. 23, 1991]

§ 656.21 Basic labor certification process.

(a) Except as otherwise provided by §§ 656.21a and 656.22, an employer who desires to apply for a labor certification on behalf of an alien shall file, signed by hand and in duplicate, a Department of Labor Application for Alien Employment Certification form and any attachments required by this part with the local Employment Service office serving the area where the alien proposes to be employed. The employer shall set forth on the Application for Alien Employment Certification form, as appropriate, or in attachments:

(1) A statement of the qualifications of the alien, signed by the alien;

(2) A description of the job offer for the alien employment, including the items required by paragraph (b) of this section; and

(3) If the application involves a job offer as a live-in household domestic service worker:

(i) A statement describing the household living accommodations;

(ii) Two copies of the employment contract, each signed and dated by both the employer and the alien (not by their agents). The contract shall clearly state:

(A) The wages to be paid on an hourly and weekly basis;

(B) Total hours of employment per week, and exact hours of daily employment;

(C) That the alien is free to leave the employer's premises during all non-work hours except that the alien may work overtime if paid for the overtime at no less than the legally required hourly rate;

(D) That the alien will reside on the employer's premises;

(E) Complete details of the duties to be performed by the alien;

(F) The total amount of any money to be advanced by the employer with details of specific items, and the terms of repayment by the alien of any such advance by the employer;

(G) That in no event shall the alien be required to give more than two weeks' notice of intent to leave the employment contracted for and that the employer must give the alien at least two weeks' notice before terminating employment;

(H) That a duplicate contract has been furnished to the alien;

(I) That a private room and board will be provided at no cost to the worker; and

(J) Any other agreement or conditions not specified on the Application for Alien Employment Certification form; and

(iii)(A) Documentation of the alien's paid experience in the form of statements from past or present employers setting forth the dates (month and year) employment started and ended, hours of work per day, number of days worked per week, place where the alien worked, detailed statement of duties performed on the job, equipment and appliances used, and the amount of wages paid per week or month. The total paid experience must be equal to one full year's employment on a full-time basis. For example, two year's experience working half-days is the equivalent of one year's full time experience. Time spent in a household domestic service training course cannot be included in the required one year of paid experience.

(B) Each statement must contain the name and address of the person who signed it and show the date on which the statement was signed. A statement not in the English language shall be accompanied by a written translation into the English language certified by the translator as to the accuracy of the translation, and as to the translator's competency to translate.

(b) Except for labor certification applications involving occupations designated for special handling (see § 656.21a) and Schedule A occupations (see §§ 656.10 and 656.22), the employer shall submit, as a part of every labor certification application, on the Application for Alien Employment Certification form or in attachments, as appropriate, the following clear documentation:

(1) If the employer has attempted to recruit U.S. workers prior to filing the application for certification, the employer shall document the employer's reasonable good faith efforts to recruit U.S.

workers without success through the Employment Service System and/or through other labor referral and recruitment sources normal to the occupation:

(i) This documentation shall include documentation of the employer's recruitment efforts for the job opportunity which shall:

(A) List the sources the employer may have used for recruitment, including, but not limited to, advertising; public and/or private employment agencies; colleges or universities; vocational, trade, or technical schools; labor unions; and/or development or promotion from within the employer's organization;

(B) Identify each recruitment source by name;

(C) Give the number of U.S. workers responding to the employer's recruitment;

(D) Give the number of interviews conducted with U.S. workers;

(E) Specify the lawful job-related reasons for not hiring each U.S. worker interviewed; and

(F) Specify the wages and working conditions offered to the U.S. workers; and

(ii) If the employer advertised the job opportunity prior to filing the application for certification, the employer shall include also a copy of at least one such advertisement.

(2) The employer shall document that the job opportunity has been and is being described without unduly restrictive job requirements:

(i) The job opportunity's requirements, unless adequately documented as arising from business necessity:

(A) Shall be those normally required for the job in the United States;

(B) Shall be those defined for the job in the Dictionary of Occupational Titles (D.O.T.) including those for subclasses of jobs;

(C) Shall not include requirements for a language other than English.

(ii) If the job opportunity involves a combination of duties, for example engineer-pilot, the employer must document that it has normally employed persons for that combination of duties and/or workers customarily perform the combination of duties in the area of intended employment, and or the combination job opportunity is based on a business necessity.

(iii) If the job opportunity involves a requirement that the worker live on the employer's premises, the employer shall document adequately that the requirement is a business necessity.

(iv) If the job opportunity has been or is being described with an employer preference, the employer preference shall be deemed to be a job requirement for purposes of this paragraph (b)(2).

(3) The employer shall document that its other efforts to locate and employ U.S. workers for the job opportunity, such as recruitment efforts by means of private employment agencies, labor unions, advertisements placed with radio or TV stations, recruitment at trade schools, colleges, and universities or attempts to fill the job opportunity by development or promotion from among its present employees, have been and continue to be unsuccessful. Such efforts may be required after the filing of an application if appropriate to the occupation.

(4) If unions are customarily used as a recruitment source in the area or industry, the employer shall document that they were unable to refer U.S. workers.

(5) The employer shall document that its requirements for the job opportunity, as described, represent the employer's actual minimum requirements for the job opportunity, and the employer has not hired workers with less training or experience for jobs similar to that involved in the job opportunity or that it is not feasible to hire workers with less training or experience than that required by the employer's job offer.

(6) If U.S. workers have applied for the job opportunity, the employer shall document that they were rejected solely for lawful job-related reasons.

(c) The local office shall determine if the application is for a labor certification involving Schedule A. If the application is for a Schedule A labor certification, the local office shall advise the employer that the forms must be filed with an INS or Consular Office pursuant to § 656.22, and shall explain that the Administrator has determined that U.S. workers in the occupation are unavailable throughout the United States (unless a geographic limitation is applicable) and that the employment of the alien in the occupation will not adversely affect U.S. workers similarly employed.

(d) The local office shall date stamp the application (see § 656.30 for the significance of this date), and shall make sure that the Application for Alien Employment Certification form is complete. If it is not complete the local office shall return it to the employer and shall advise the employer to refile it when it is completed.

(e) The local office shall calculate, to the extent of its expertise using wage information available to it, the prevailing wage for the job opportunity pursuant to § 656.40 and shall put its finding into writing. If the local office finds that the rate of wages offered is below the prevailing wage, it shall advise the employer in writing to increase the amount offered. If the employer refuses to do so, the local office shall advise the employer that the refusal is a ground for denial of the application by the Certifying Officer; and that if the denial becomes final, the application will have to be refiled at the local office as a new application.

(f) The local office, using the information on job offer portion of the Application for Alien Employment Certification form, shall prepare and process an Employment Service job order:

(1) If the job offer is acceptable, the local office, in cooperation with the employer, then shall attempt to recruit United States workers for the job opportunity for a period of thirty days, by placing the job order into the regular Employment Service recruitment system.

(2) If the employer's job offer is discriminatory or otherwise unacceptable as a job order under the Employment Service (ES) Regulations (§ Parts 651–658 of this chapter), the local office, as appropriate, either shall contact the employer to try to remedy the defect or shall return the Application for Alien Employment Certification form to the employer with instructions on how to remedy the defect. If the employer refuses to remedy the defect, the local office shall advise the employer that it is unable to recruit U.S. workers for the job opportunity and that the application will be transmitted to the Certifying Officer for determination.

(g) In conjunction with the recruitment efforts under paragraph (f) of this section, the employer shall place an advertisement for the job opportunity in a newspaper of general circulation or in a professional, trade, or ethnic publication, whichever is appropriate to the occupation and most likely to bring responses from able, willing, qualified, and available U.S. workers. The employer may request the local office's assistance in drafting the text. The advertisement shall:

(1) Direct applicants to report or send resumes, as appropriate for the occupation to the local office for referral to the employer;

(2) Include a local office identification number and the complete address or telephone number of the local office, but shall not identify the employer;

(3) Describe the job opportunity with particularity;

(4) State the rate of pay, which shall not be below the prevailing wage for the occupation, as calculated pursuant to § 656.40;

(5) Offer prevailing working conditions;

(6) State the employer's minimum job requirements;

(7) Offer training if the job opportunity is the type for which employers normally provide training;

(8) Offer wages, terms, and conditions of employment which are no less favorable than those offered to the alien; and

(9) If published in a newspaper of general circulation, be published for at least three consecutive days; or, if published in a professional, trade, or ethnic publication, be published in the next published edition.

(h) The employer shall supply the local office with required documentation or requested information in a timely manner. If documentation or requested information is not received within 45 calendar days of the date of the request the local office shall return the Application for Alien Employment Certification form, and any supporting documents submitted by the employer and/or the alien, to the employer to be filed as a new application.

(i) The Certifying Officer may reduce the employer's recruitment efforts required by §§ 656.21(f) and/or 656.21(g) of this part if the employer satisfactorily documents that the employer has adequately tested the labor market with no success at least at the prevailing wage and working conditions; but no such reduction may be granted for job offers involving occupations listed on Schedule B.

(1) To request a reduction of recruitment efforts pursuant to this paragraph (i), the employer shall file a written request along with the Application for Alien Employment Certification form at the appropriate local Job Service office. The request shall contain:

(i) Documentary evidence (which shall include, but is not limited to, a pre-application notice posted consistent with § 656.20(g) of this part) that within the immediately preceding six months the employer has made good faith efforts to recruit U.S. workers for the job opportunity, at least at the prevailing wage and working conditions, through sources normal to the occupation; and

(ii) Any other information which the employer believes will support the contention that further recruitment will be unsuccessful.

(2) Upon receipt of a written request for a reduction in recruitment efforts pursuant to this paragraph (i), the local office shall date stamp the request and the application form and shall review and process the application pursuant to this § 656.21, but without regard to §§ 656.21(f), 656.21(g), and 656.21(j)(1) of this part, advertisement, and job order; and the wait for results.

(3) After reviewing and processing the application pursuant to paragraph (i)(2) of this section, the local office (and the State Employment Service office) shall process the application pursuant to paragraphs (j)(2) and (k) of this section.

(4) The Certifying Officer shall review the documentation submitted by the employer and the comments of the local office. The Certifying Officer shall notify the employer and the local (or State)

Employment Service office of the Certifying Officer's decision on the request to reduce partially or completely the recruitment efforts required of the employer.

(5) Unless the Certifying Officer decides to reduce completely the recruitment efforts required of the employer, the Certifying Officer shall return the application to the local (or State) office so that the employer might recruit workers to the extent required in the Certifying Officer's decision, and in the manner required by §§ 656.20(g), 656.21(f), 656.21(g), and 656.21(j) of this part (i.e., by post-application internal notice, employment service job order, and advertising; and a wait for results). If the Certifying Officer decides to reduce completely the recruitment efforts required of the employer, the Certifying Officer then shall determine, pursuant to § 656.24 whether to grant or to deny the application.

(j)(1) The employer shall provide to the local office a written report of the results of all the employer's post-application recruitment efforts during the 30–day recruitment period; except that for job opportunities advertised in professional and trade, or ethnic publications, the written report shall be provided no less than 30 calendar days from the date of the publication of the employer's advertisement. The report of recruitment results shall:

(i) Identify each recruitment source by name;

(ii) State the number of U.S. workers responding to the employer's recruitment;

(iii) State the names, addresses, and provide resumes (if any) of the U.S. workers interviewed for the job opportunity and job title of the person who interviewed each worker; and

(iv) Explain, with specificity, the lawful job-related reasons for not hiring each U.S. worker interviewed.

(2) If, after the required recruitment period, the recruitment is not successful, the local office shall send the application, its prevailing wage finding, copies of all documents in the particular application file, and any additional appropriate information (such as local labor market data), to the Employment Service agency's State office or, if authorized, to the regional Certifying Officer.

(k) A Employment Service agency's State office which receives an application pursuant to paragraph (j)(2) of this section may add appropriate data or comments, and shall transmit the application promptly to the appropriate Certifying Officer.

[45 FR 83933, Dec. 19, 1980, as amended at 46 FR 3830, Jan. 16, 1981; 49 FR 18295, April 30, 1984; 56 FR 54928, Oct. 23, 1991]

§ 656.21a Applications for labor certifications for occupations designated for special handling.

(a) An employer shall apply for a labor certification to employ an alien as a college or university teacher or an alien represented to be of exceptional ability in the performing arts by filing, in duplicate, an Application for Alien Employment Certification form, and any attachments required by this Part, with the local Employment Service office serving the area where the alien proposes to be employed.

(1) The employer shall set forth the following on the Application for Alien Employment Certification form, as appropriate, or in attachments:

(i) A statement of the qualifications of the alien, signed by the alien.

(ii) A full description of the job offer for the alien employment.

(iii) If the application involves a job offer as a college or university teacher, the employer shall submit documentation to show clearly that the employer selected the alien for the job opportunity pursuant to a competitive recruitment and selection process, through which the alien was found to be more qualified than any of the United States workers who applied for the job. For purposes of this paragraph (a)(1)(iii), evidence of the "competitive recruitment and selection process" shall include:

(A) A statement, signed by an official who has actual hiring authority, from the employer outlining in detail the complete recruitment procedure undertaken; and which shall set forth:

(1) The total number of applicants for the job opportunity;

(2) The specific lawful job-related reasons why the alien is more qualified than each U.S. worker who applied for the job; and

(3) A final report of the faculty, student, and/or administrative body making the recommendation or selection of the alien, at the completion of the competitive recruitment and selection process;

(B) A copy of at least one advertisement for the job opportunity placed in a national professional journal, giving the name and the date(s) of publication; and which states the job title, duties, and requirements;

(C) Evidence of all other recruitment sources utilized; and

(D) A written statement attesting to the degree of the alien's educational or professional qualifications and academic achievements.

(E) Applications for permanent alien labor certification for job opportunities as college and university teachers shall be filed within 18 months after a selection is made pursuant to a competitive recruitment and selection process.

(iv) If the application is for an alien represented to have exceptional ability in the performing arts, the employer shall document that the alien's work experience during the past twelve months did require, and the alien's intended work in the United States will require, exceptional ability; and shall submit:

(A) Documentation to show this exceptional ability, such as:

(1) Documents attesting to the current widespread acclaim and international recognition accorded to the alien, and receipt of internationally recognized prizes or awards for excellence;

(2) Published material by or about the alien, such as critical reviews or articles in major newspapers, periodicals, and/or trade journals (the title, date, and author of such material shall be indicated);

(3) Documentary evidence of earnings commensurate with the claimed level of ability;

(4) Playbills and starbillings;

(5) Documents attesting to the outstanding reputation of theaters, concert halls, night clubs, and other establishments in which the alien has appeared, or is scheduled to appear; and/or

(6) Documents attesting to the outstanding reputation of repertory companies, ballet troupes, orchestras, or other organizations in which or with which the alien has performed during the past year in a leading or starring capacity; and

(B) A copy of at least one advertisement placed in a national publication appropriate to the occupation (and a statement of the results of that recruitment) which shall:

(1) Identify the employer's name, address, and the location of the employment, if other than the employer's location;

(2) Describe the job opportunity with particularity;

(3) State the rate of pay, which shall not be below the prevailing wage for the occupation, as calculated pursuant to § 656.40;

(4) Offer prevailing working conditions;

(5) State the employer's minimum job requirements;

(6) Offer training if the job opportunity is the type for which employers normally provide training; and

(7) Offer wages, terms, and conditions of employment which are no less favorable than those offered to the alien; and

(C) Documentation that unions, if customarily used as a recruitment source in the area or industry, were unable to refer equally qualified U.S. workers.

(2) The local Employment Service office, upon receipt of an application for a college or university teacher or an alien represented to have exceptional ability in the performing arts, shall follow the application processing and prevailing wage determination procedures set forth in §§ 656.21 (d) and (e), and shall transmit a file containing the application, the local office's prevailing wage findings, and any other information it determines is appropriate, to the State Employment Service agency office, or if authorized by the State office, to the appropriate Certifying Officer.

(3) If the local office transmits the file described in paragraph (a)(3) of this section to the State office, the State office shall follow the procedures set forth at § 656.21(k).

(b)(1) An employer shall apply for a labor certification to employ an alien (who has been employed legally as a nonimmigrant sheepherder in the United States for at least 33 of the preceding 36 months) as a sheepherder by filing an Application for Alien Employment Certification form, and any attachments required by this paragraph (b), directly with a Department of State Consular Officer or with a District Office of INS, not with a local or State office of a State Employment Service agency, and not with an office of DOL. The documentation for such an application shall include:

(i) A completed Application for Alien Employment Certification form, including the Job Offer for Alien Employment, and the Statement of Qualification of Alien; and

(ii) A signed letter or letters from all U.S. employers who have employed the alien as a sheepherder during the immediately preceding 36 months, attesting that the alien has been employed in the United States lawfully and continuously as a sheepherder, for at least 33 of the immediately preceding 36 months.

(2) An Immigration Officer, or a Consular Officer, shall review the application and the letters attesting to the alien's previous employment as a sheepherder in the United States, and shall determine whether or not the alien and the employer(s) have met the requirements of this paragraph (b).

(i) The determination of the Immigration or Consular Officer pursuant to this paragraph (b) shall be conclusive and final. The employer(s) and the alien, therefore, may not make use of the review procedures set forth at §§ 656.26 and 656.27.

(ii) If the alien and the employer(s) have met the requirements of this paragraph (b), the Immigration or Consular Officer shall indicate on the Application for Alien Employment Certification form the occupation, the immigration or consular office which made the determination pursuant to this paragraph (b), and the date of the determination (see § 656.30 of this part for the significance of this date). The Immigration or Consular Officer then shall forward promptly to the Director copies of the Application for Alien Employment Certification form, without the attachments.

(c) If an application for a college or university teacher, an alien represented to be of exceptional ability in the performing arts, or a sheepherder does not meet the requirements for an occupation designated for special handling under this section, the application may be filed pursuant to § 656.21.

[45 FR 83933, Dec. 19, 1980, as amended at 49 FR 18295, Apr. 30, 1984; 56 FR 54928, Oct. 23, 1991]

§ 656.22 Applications for labor certification for Schedule A occupations.

(a) An employer shall apply for a labor certification for a Schedule A occupation by filing an Application for Alien Employment Certification in duplicate with the appropriate Immigration and Naturalization Service office, not with the Department of Labor or a State Employment Service office.

(b) The Application for Alien Employment Certification form shall include:

(1) Evidence of prearranged employment for the alien beneficiary by having an employer complete and sign the job offer description portion of the application form. There is, however, no need for the employer to provide the other documentation required under § 656.21 of this part for non-Schedule A occupations.

(2) Evidence that notice of filing the application for Alien Employment Certification was provided to the bargaining representative or the employer's employees as prescribed in § 656.20(g)(3) of this part.

(c) An employer seeking labor certification under Group I of Schedule A shall file, as part of its labor certification application, documentary evidence of the following:

(1) An employer seeking Schedule A labor certification for an alien to be employed as a physical therapist (§ 656.10(a)(1) of this part) shall file as part of its labor certification application a letter or statement signed by an authorized State physical therapy licensing official in the State of intended employment, stating that the alien is qualified to take that State's written licensing examination for physical therapists. Application for certification of permanent employment as a physical therapist may be made only pursuant to this § 656.22 and not pursuant to §§ 656.21, 656.21a, or 656.23 of this part.

(2) An employer seeking a Schedule A labor certification as a professional nurse (§ 656.10(a)(2) of this part) shall file, as part of its labor certification application, documentation that the alien has passed the Commission on Graduates of Foreign Nursing Schools (CGFN) Examination; or that the alien holds a full and unrestricted (permanent) license to practice nursing in the State of intended employment. Application for certification of employment as a professional nurse may be made only pursuant to this § 656.22(c), and not pursuant to §§ 656.21, 656.21a, or 656.23 of this part.

(d) An employer seeking labor certification on behalf of an alien under Group II of Schedule A shall file, as part of its labor certification application, documentary evidence testifying to the widespread acclaim and international recognition accorded the alien by recognized experts in their field; and documentation showing that the alien's work in that field during the past year did, and the alien's intended work in the United States will, require exceptional ability. In addition, the employer shall file, as part of the labor certification application, documentation concerning the alien from at least two of the following seven groups:

(1) Documentation of the alien's receipt of internationally recognized prizes or awards for excellence in the field for which certification is sought.

(2) Documentation of the alien's membership in international associations, in the field for which certification is sought, which require outstanding achievement of their members, as judged by recognized international experts in their disciplines or fields.

(3) Published material in professional publications about the alien, relating to the alien's work in the field for which certification is sought, which shall include the title, date, and author of such published material.

(4) Evidence of the alien's participation on a panel, or individually, as a judge of the work of others in the same or in an allied field of specialization to that for which certification is sought.

(5) Evidence of the alien's original scientific or scholarly research contributions of major significance in the field for which certification is sought.

(6) Evidence of the alien's authorship of published scientific or scholarly articles in the field for which certification is sought, in international professional journals or professional journals with an international circulation.

(7) Evidence of the display of the alien's work, in the field for which certification is sought, at artistic exhibitions in more than one country.

(e) An Immigration Officer shall determine whether the employer and alien have met the applicable requirements of § 656.20 of this part, of this section, and of Schedule A (§ 656.10 of this part); shall review the application; and shall determine whether or not the alien is qualified for and intends to pursue the Schedule A occupation.

(1) The Immigration Officer may request an advisory opinion as to whether the alien is qualified for the Schedule A occupation from the Division of Foreign Labor Certifications, United States Employment Service, Washington, DC 20210.

(2) The Schedule A determination of INS shall be conclusive and final. The employer, therefore, may not make use of the review procedures at § 656.26 of this part.

(f) If the alien qualifies for the occupation, the Immigration Officer shall indicate the occupation on the Application for Alien Employment Certification form. The Immigration Officer then shall promptly forward a copy of the Application for Alien Employment Certification form, without attachments, to the Director, indicating thereon the occupation, the Immigration Officer who made the Schedule A determination, and the date of the determination (see § 656.30 of this part for the significance of this date).

[45 FR 83933, Dec. 19, 1980, as amended at 49 FR 18295, April 30, 1984; 52 FR 20596, June 2, 1987; 56 FR 54929, Oct. 23, 1991]

§ 656.24 Labor certification determinations.

(a) If the labor certification presents a special or unique problem, the regional Certifying Officer may refer the application to the national Certifying Officer for determination. If the Director has directed that certain types of applications or specific applications be handled in the USES national office, the regional Certifying Officer shall refer such applications to the national Certifying Officer.

(b) The regional or national Certifying Officer, as appropriate, shall make a determination either to grant the labor certification or to issue a Notice of Findings on the basis of whether or not:

(1) The employer has met the requirements of this part. However, where the Certifying Officer determines that the employer has committed harmless error, the Certifying Officer nevertheless may grant the labor certification, Provided, That the labor market has been tested sufficiently to warrant a finding of unavailability of and lack of adverse effect on U.S. workers. Where the Certifying Officer makes such a determination, the Certifying Officer shall document it in the application file.

(2) There is in the United States a worker who is able, willing, qualified and available for and at the place of the job opportunity according to the following standards:

(i) The Certifying Officer, in judging whether a U.S. worker is willing to take the job opportunity, shall look at the documented results of the employer's and the Local (and State) Employment Service office's recruitment efforts, and shall determine if there are other appropriate sources of workers where the employer should have recruited or might be able to recruit U.S. workers.

(ii) The Certifying Officer shall consider a U.S. worker able and qualified for the job opportunity if the worker, by education, training, experience, or a combination thereof, is able to perform in the normally accepted manner the duties involved in the occupation as customarily performed by other U.S. workers similarly employed, except that, if the application involves a job opportunity as a college or university teacher, or for an alien whom the Certifying Officer determines to be currently of exceptional ability in the performing arts, the U.S. worker must be at least as qualified as the alien.

(iii) In determining whether U.S. workers are available, the Certifying Officer shall consider as many sources as are appropriate and shall look to the nationwide system of public employment offices (the "Employment Service") as one source.

(iv) In determining whether a U.S. worker is available at the place of the job opportunity, the Certifying Officer shall consider U.S. workers living or working in the area of intended employment, and may also consider U.S. workers who are willing to move from elsewhere to take the job at their own expenses, or, if the prevailing practice among employers employing workers in the occupation in the area of intended employment is to pay such relocation expenses, at the employer's expense.

(3) The employment of the alien will have an adverse effect upon the wages and working conditions of U.S. workers similarly employed. In making this determination the Certifying Officer shall consider such things as labor market information, the special circumstances of the industry, organization, and/or occupation, the prevailing wage in the area of intended employment, and the prevailing working conditions, such as hours, in the occupation.

[45 FR 83933, Dec. 19, 1980, as amended at 56 FR 54930, Oct. 23, 1991]

§ 656.25 Procedures following a labor certification determination.

(a) After making a labor certification determination, the Certifying Officer shall notify the employer in writing of the determination and shall send a copy of the notice to the alien.

(b) If a labor certification is granted, the Certifying Officer shall follow the document transmittal procedures set forth at § 656.28.

(c) If a labor certification is not granted, the Certifying Officer shall issue to the employer, with a copy to the alien, a Notice of Findings, as defined in § 656.50. The Notice of Findings shall:

(1) Contain the date on which the Notice of Findings was issued;

(2) State the specific bases on which the decision to issue the Notice of Findings was made;

(3) Specify a date, 35 calendar days from the date of the Notice of Findings, by which documentary evidence and/or written argument may be submitted to cure the defects or to otherwise rebut the bases of the determination, and advise that if the rebuttal evidence and/or argument have not been mailed by certified mail by the date specified:

(i) The Notice of Findings shall automatically become the final decision of the Secretary denying the labor certification;

(ii) Failure to file a rebuttal in a timely manner shall constitute a refusal to exhaust available administrative remedies; and

(iii) The administrative-judicial review procedure provided in § 656.26 shall not be available; and

(4) Quote the rebuttal procedures set forth at paragraphs (d), (e), and (f) of this section.

(d) Written rebuttal arguments and evidence may be submitted;

(1) By the employer; and

(2) By the alien, but only if the employer also has submitted a rebuttal.

(e)(1) Documentary evidence and/or written arguments to rebut all of the bases of a Notice of Findings, which may include evidence that the defects noticed therein have been cured, shall be mailed by certified mail on or before the date specified in the Notice of Findings to the Certifying Officer who issued the Notice of Findings.

(2) Failure to file a rebuttal in a timely manner shall constitute a failure to exhaust available administrative appellate remedies.

(3) All findings in the Notice of Findings not rebutted shall be deemed admitted.

(f) If a rebuttal, as described above, is submitted on time, the Certifying Officer shall review that evidence in relation to the evidence in the file, and shall then either grant or deny the labor certification pursuant to the standards set forth in § 656.24(b).

(g) The Certifying Officer shall send a Final Determination form to the employer, and shall send a copy to the alien.

(1) If a labor certification is granted, the Certifying Officer shall follow the document transmittal procedures set forth at § 656.28.

(2) If the labor certification is denied, the Final Determination form shall:

(i) Contain the date of the determination;

(ii) State the reasons for the determination;

(iii) Quote the request for review procedures at § 656.26 (a) and (b); and

(iv) Advise that, if a request for review is not made within the specified time, the denial shall become the final determination of the Secretary.

[45 FR 83933, Dec. 19, 1980]

§ 656.26 Board of Alien Labor Certification Appeals review of denials of labor certification.

(a) If a labor certification is denied, a request for review of the denial made be made to the Board of Alien Labor Certification Appeals:

(1) By the employer; and

(2) By the alien, but only if the employer also requests such a review.

(b)(1) The request for review shall be in writing and shall be mailed by certified mail to the Certifying Officer who denied the application within 35 calendar days of the date of the determination, that is, by the date specified on the Final Determination form; shall clearly identify the particular labor certification determination from which review is sought; shall set forth the particular grounds for the request; and shall include all the documents which accompanied the Final Determination form.

(2) Failure to file a request for review in a timely manner shall constitute a failure to exhaust available administrative remedies.

(3) If the denial of labor certification involves an application for a job opportunity as a college or university teacher or an application on behalf of an alien represented to be of exceptional ability in the performing arts, the employer may designate the names and addresses of persons or organizations of specialized competence which the employer has asked to submit amicus briefs.

(4) The request for review, statements, briefs, and other submissions of the parties and amicus curiae shall contain only legal argument and only such evidence that was within the record upon which the denial of labor certification was based.

(c) Upon the receipt of a request for review, the Certifying Officer shall immediately assemble an indexed Appeal File:

(1) The Appeal File shall be in chronological order, shall have the index on top followed by the most recent document, and shall have numbered pages. The Appeal File shall contain the request for review, the complete application file, and copies of all the written material, such as pertinent parts and pages of surveys and/or reports upon which the denial was based.

(2) The Certifying Officer shall send the Appeal File to the Board of Alien Labor Certification Appeals, Office of Administrative Law Judges, 800 K Street, NW., Suite 400, Washington, DC 20001–8002.

(3) In denials involving college and university teachers and aliens represented to be of exceptional ability in the performing arts, two additional copies of the Appeal File shall be sent to the Board of Alien Labor Certification Appeals.

(4) The Certifying Officer shall send a copy of the Appeal File to the Solicitor of Labor, Attn: Associate Solicitor for Employment and Training Legal Services, Suite N2101—Frances Perkins Bldg., 200 Constitution Avenue NW., Washington, D.C. 20210.

(5) Unless the certification was denied by the national Certifying Officer, the Certifying Officer shall send a copy of the Appeal File to the Director.

(6) The Certifying Officer shall send copies of the index to the Appeal File to the employer and to the alien. The Certifying Officer shall afford the employer and the alien the opportunity to examine the complete Appeal File at the office of the Certifying Officer, for the purpose of satisfying the employer and the alien as to the contents. The employer and/or the alien may furnish or suggest directly to the Board of Alien Labor Certification Appeals the addition of any documentation which is not in the Appeal File, but which was submitted prior to the issuance of the Final Determination form. The employer and/or the alien shall submit such documentation in writing, and shall send a copy to the Associate Solicitor for Employment and Training Legal Services, Office of the Solicitor, U.S. Department of Labor, Washington, D.C. 20210.

(d) to (h) [Reserved]

(i) If a labor certification has been ordered granted, the Certifying Officer shall grant the certification and shall follow the document transmittal procedures set forth at § 656.28.

[45 FR 83933, Dec. 19, 1980, as amended at 52 FR 11218, April 8, 1987; 56 FR 54708, Oct. 22, 1991; 56 FR 54930, Oct. 23, 1991]

§ 656.27 Consideration by and decisions of the Board of Alien Labor Certification Appeals.

(a) Designations. In considering requests for review before it, the Board of Alien Labor Certification Appeals may sit in panels of three members. The Chief Administrative Law Judge may designate any Board of Alien Labor Certification Appeals member to submit proposed findings and recommendations to the Board of Alien Labor Certification Appeals or to any duly designated panel thereof to consider a particular case.

(b) Briefs and Statements of Position. In considering requests for review before it, the Board of Alien Labor Certification Appeals shall afford all parties 21 days to submit or decline to submit any appropriate Statement of Position or legal brief. The Department of Labor shall be represented solely by the Solicitor of Labor or the Solicitor's designated representative. In the cases involving college or university teachers and aliens represented to be of exceptional ability in the performing arts, if the employer has designated a person or organization to submit an amicus curiae brief, the Board of Alien Labor Certification Appeals shall afford amicus curiae 21 days to submit a brief. Briefs, statements, and amicus curiae briefs submitted pursuant to this paragraph (b) shall be deemed timely if either mailed or delivered to the Board of Alien Labor Certification Appeals on or before the end of the 21–day period set forth in this paragraph, and shall be consistent with the requirements of § 656.26(b)(4) of this Part.

(c) Review on the record. The Board of Alien Labor Certification Appeals shall review the denial of labor certification on the basis of the record upon which the denial of labor certification was made, the request for review, and any Statements of Position or legal briefs submitted and shall:

(1) Affirm the denial of the labor certification; or

(2) Direct the Certifying Officer to grant the certification; or

(3) Remand the matter to the Certifying Officer for further consideration or factfinding and determination; or

(4) Direct that a hearing on the case be held pursuant to paragraph (f) of this section.

(d) Notifications of decisions. The Board of Alien Labor Certification Appeals shall notify the employer, the alien, the Certifying Officer, and the Solicitor of Labor of the decision pursuant to paragraph (c) of this section, and shall return the record to the Certifying Officer unless the case has been set for hearing pursuant to paragraph (f) of this section.

(e) Remanded cases. If the case is remanded, the Certifying Officer shall do the additional factfinding or consideration in accordance with §§ 656.24 and 656.25 of this Part, but such factfinding and consideration shall be limited to the issues for which the case has been remanded.

(f) Hearings.

(1) Notification of hearing. If the case has been set for a hearing, the Board of Alien Labor Certification Appeals shall notify the employer, the alien, the Certifying Officer, and the Solicitor of

Labor of the date, time, and place of the hearing, and that the hearing may be rescheduled upon written request and for good cause shown.

(2) Hearing procedure.

(i) The "Rules of Practice and Procedure For Administrative Hearings Before the Office of Administrative Law Judges", set forth at 29 CFR Part 18, shall apply to hearings pursuant to this paragraph (f).

(ii) For the purposes of this paragraph (f)(2), references in 29 CFR Part 18 to: "administrative law judge" shall mean the Board of Alien Labor Certification Appeals member or the Board of Alien Labor Certification Appeals panel duly designated pursuant to § 656.27(a) of this Part; "Office of Administrative Law Judges" shall mean the Board of Alien Labor Certification Appeals; and "Chief Administrative Law Judge" shall mean the Chief Administrative Law Judge in that official's function of chairing the Board of Alien Labor Certification Appeals.

[52 FR 11218, April 8, 1987]

§ 656.28 Document transmittal following the grant of a labor certification.

If a labor certification is granted, except for labor certifications for occupations on Schedule A (§ 656.10) and for employment as a sheepherder pursuant to § 656.21a(b), the Certifying Officer shall send the certified application containing the official labor certification stamp, supporting documentation, and complete Final Determination form to the employer, or, if appropriate, to the employer's agent, indicating that the employer should file all the documents with the appropriate INS office.

[56 FR 54930, Oct. 23, 1991]

§ 656.29 Filing of a new application after the denial of a labor certification.

(a) A new application for labor certification by the same employer involving the same occupation may be filed at any time after the expiration of 6 months from the date of a denial of certification by the Certifying Officer, except that, if the certification was denied solely because the wage or salary offered was below the prevailing wage, the employer may reapply immediately pursuant to §§ 656.21, 656.21a, or 656.23, as appropriate.

(b) An alien who is denied a labor certification for a Schedule A occupation, except for employment as a physical therapist or as a professional nurse, may at any time have an employer file for a labor certification on the alien's behalf pursuant to § 656.21. Labor certifications for professional nurses and for physical therapists shall be considered only pursuant to §§ 656.10 and 656.22.

[45 FR 83933, Dec. 19, 1980]

§ 656.30 Validity of and invalidation of labor certifications.

(a) Except as provided in paragraph (d) of this section, a labor certification is valid indefinitely. Labor certifications for Household Domestic Service Workers and teachers which were granted under the previous regulations at 29 CFR Part 60 and which lapsed after one year, shall be deemed automatically revalidated on the effective date of this Part.

(b)(1) Labor certifications involving job offers shall be deemed validated as of the date of the local Employment Service office date-stamped the application; and

(2) Labor certifications for Schedule A occupations shall be deemed validated as of the date the applications were dated by the Immigration or Consular Officer.

(c)(1) A labor certification for a Schedule A occupation is valid only for the occupation set forth on the Application for Alien Employment Certification form, the alien for whom certification was granted, and throughout the United States unless the certification contains a geographic limitation.

(2) A labor certification involving a specific job offer is valid only for the particular job opportunity, the alien for whom certification was granted, and for the area of intended employment stated on the Application for Alien Employment Certification form.

(d) After issuance labor certifications are subject to invalidation by the INS or by a Consul of the Department of State upon a determination, made in accordance with those agencies, procedures or by a Court, of fraud or willful misrepresentation of a material fact involving the labor certification application. If evidence of such fraud or willful misrepresentation becomes known to a RA or to the Director, the RA or Director, as appropriate, shall notify in writing the INS or State Department, as appropriate. A copy of the notification shall be sent to the regional or national office, as appropriate, of the Department of Labor's Office of Inspector General.

(e) Certifying Officers shall issue duplicate labor certifications only upon the written request of a Consular or Immigration Officer. Certifying Officers shall issue such duplicate certifications only to the Consular or Immigration Officer who submitted the written request. An alien, employer, or an employer or alien's agent, therefore, may petition an Immigration or Consular Officer to request a duplicate from a Certifying Officer.

[45 FR 83933, Dec. 19, 1980, as amended at 56 FR 54930, Oct. 23, 1991]

§ 656.40 Determination of prevailing wage for labor certification purposes.

(a) Whether the wage or salary stated in a labor certification application involving a job offer equals the prevailing wage as required by § 656.21(b)(3), shall be determined as follows:

(1) If the job opportunity is in an occupation which is subject to a wage determination in the area under the Davis–Bacon Act, 40 U.S.C. 276a et seq., 29 CFR Part 1, or the McNamara–O'Hara Service Contract Act, 41 U.S.C. 351 et seq., 29 CFR Part 4, the prevailing wage shall be at the rate required under the statutory determination. Certifying Officers shall request the assistance of the DOL Employment Standards Administration wage specialists if they need assistance in making this determination.

(2) If the job opportunity is in an occupation which is not covered by a prevailing wage determined under the Davis–Bacon Act or the McNamara–O'Hara Service Contract Act, the prevailing wage for labor certification purposes shall be:

(i) The average rate of wages, that is, the rate of wages to be determined, to the extent feasible, by adding the wage paid to workers similarly employed in the area of intended employment and dividing the total by the number of such workers. Since it is not always feasible to determine such an average rate of wages with exact precision, the wage set forth in the application shall be considered as meeting the prevailing wage standard if it is within 5 percent of the average rate of wages; or

(ii) If the job opportunity is covered by a union contract which was negotiated at arms-length between a union and the employer, the wage rate set forth in the union contract shall be considered as not adversely affecting the wages of U.S. workers similarly employed, that is, it shall be considered the "prevailing wage" for labor certification purposes.

(b) For purposes of this section, except as provided in paragraph (c) of this section, "similarly employed" shall mean "having substantially comparable jobs in the occupational category in the area of intended employment," except that, if no such workers are employed by employers other than the employer applicant in the area of intended employment, "similarly employed" shall mean:

(1) "Having jobs requiring a substantially similar level of skills within the area of intended employment"; or

(2) If there are no substantially comparable jobs in the area of intended employment, "having substantially comparable jobs with employers outside of the area of intended employment."

(c) For purposes of this section, similarly employed in the case of researchers employed by colleges and universities, Federally Funded Research and Development Centers (FFRDC's) administered by colleges and universities or Federal research agencies, means researchers employed by colleges and universities, FFRDC's administered by colleges and universities, and Federal research agencies in the area of intended employment. If no researchers are employed by colleges and universities, FFRDC's administered by colleges and universities, and Federal research agencies other than the employer applicant, researchers employed by colleges and universities, FFRDC's administered by colleges and universities, and Federal research agencies outside the area of intended employment shall be considered "similarly employed."

(d) A prevailing wage determination for labor certification purposes made pursuant to this section shall not permit an employer to pay a wage lower than that required under any other Federal, State or local law.

[45 FR 83933, Dec. 19, 1980, as amended at 63 FR 13767, March 20, 1998]

*

IV. OTHER FEDERAL MATERIALS

Presidential Determination No. 99–45

64 Fed. Reg. 54505

Presidential Determination on FY 2000 Refugee Admissions Numbers and Authorizations of In–Country Refugee Status Pursuant to Sections 207 and 101(a)(42), Respectively, of the Immigration and Nationality Act, and Determination Pursuant to Section 2(b)(2) of the Migration and Refugee Assistance Act, as Amended

September 30, 1999

Memorandum for the Secretary of State

In accordance with section 207 of the Immigration and Nationality Act (the "Act") (8 U.S.C. 1157), as amended, and after appropriate consultation with the Congress, I hereby make the following determinations and authorize the following actions:

The admission of up to 90,000 refugees to the United States during FY 2000 is justified by humanitarian concerns or is otherwise in the national interest; provided, however, that this number shall be understood as including persons admitted to the United States during FY 2000 with Federal refugee resettlement assistance under the Amerasian immigrant admissions program, as provided below.

The 90,000 admissions numbers shall be allocated among refugees of special humanitarian concern to the United States in accordance with the following regional allocations; provided, however, that the number allocated to the East Asia region shall include persons admitted to the United States during FY 2000 with Federal refugee resettlement assistance under section 584 of the Foreign Operations, Export Financing, and Related Programs Appropriations Act of 1988, as contained in section 101(e) of Public Law 100–202 (Amerasian immigrants and their family members); provided further that the number allocated to the former Soviet Union shall include persons admitted who were nationals of the former Soviet Union, or in the case of persons having no nationality, who were habitual residents of the former Soviet Union, prior to September 2, 1991:

Africa	18,000
East Asia	8,000
Former Yugoslavia	17,000
Kosovo Crisis	10,000
NIS/Baltics	20,000
Latin America/Caribbean	3,000
Near East/South Asia	8,000

Unallocated	6,000

The 6,000 unallocated numbers shall be allocated as needed to regional ceilings where shortfalls develop. Unused admissions numbers allocated to a particular region may be transferred to one or more other regions if there is an overriding need for greater numbers for the region or regions to which the numbers are being transferred. You are hereby authorized and directed to consult with the Judiciary Committees of the Congress prior to any such use of the unallocated numbers or reallocation of numbers from one region to another.

Pursuant to section 2(b)(2) of the Migration and Refugee Assistance Act of 1962, as amended, 22 U.S.C. 2601(b)(2), I hereby determine that assistance to or on behalf of persons applying for admission to the United States as part of the overseas refugee admissions program will contribute to the foreign policy interests of the United States and designate such persons for this purpose.

An additional 10,000 refugee admissions numbers shall be made available during FY 2000 for the adjustment to permanent resident status under section 209(b) of the Immigration and Nationality Act (8 U.S.C. 1159(b)) of aliens who have been granted asylum in the United States under section 208 of the Act (8 U.S.C. 1158), as this is justified by humanitarian concerns or is otherwise in the national interest.

In accordance with section 101(a)(42) of the Act (8 U.S.C. 1101(a)(42)) and after appropriate consultation with the Congress, I also specify that, for FY 2000, the following persons may, if otherwise qualified, be considered refugees for the purpose of admission to the United States within their countries of nationality or habitual residence:

a. Persons in Vietnam

b. Persons in Cuba

c. Persons in the former Soviet Union

You are authorized and directed to report this determination to the Congress immediately and to publish it in the Federal Register.

WILLIAM J. CLINTON
THE WHITE HOUSE,
Washington, September 30, 1999.

V. STATE PROVISIONS

PROPOSITION 187 (CALIFORNIA)

November 8, 1994

Section 1. Findings and Declaration.

The People of California find and declare as follows:

That they have suffered and are suffering economic hardship caused by the presence of illegal aliens in this state.

That they have suffered and are suffering personal injury and damage by the criminal conduct of illegal aliens in this state.

That they have a right to the protection of their government from any person or persons entering this country unlawfully.

Therefore, the People of California declare their intention to provide for cooperation between their agencies of state and local government with the federal government, and to establish a system of required notification by and between such agencies to prevent illegal aliens in the United States from receiving benefits or public services in the State of California.

Section 2. Manufacture, Distribution or Sale of False Citizenship or Resident Alien Documents: Crime and Punishment.

Section 113 is added to the Penal Code, to read:

Section 113. Any person who manufactures, distributes or sells false documents to conceal the true citizenship or resident alien status of another person is guilty of a felony, and shall be punished by imprisonment in the state prison for five years or by a fine of seventy–five thousand dollars ($75,000).

Section 3. Use of False Citizenship or Resident Alien Documents: Crime and Punishment.

Section 114 is added to the Penal Code, to read:

Section 114. Any person who uses false documents to conceal his or her true citizenship or resident alien status is guilty of a felony, and shall be punished by imprisonment in the state prison for five years or by a fine of twenty–five thousand dollars ($25,000).

Section 4. Law Enforcement Cooperation with INS.

Section 834b is added to the Penal Code, to read:

Section 834b. (a) Every law enforcement agency in California shall fully cooperate with the United States Immigration and Naturalization Service regarding any person who is arrested if he or she is suspected of being present in the United States in violation of federal immigration laws.

(b) With respect to any such person who is arrested, and suspected of being present in the United States in violation of federal immigration laws, every law enforcement agency shall do the following:

(1) Attempt to verify the legal status of such person as a citizen of the United States, an alien lawfully admitted as a permanent resident, an alien lawfully admitted for a temporary period of time or as an alien who is present in the United States in violation of immigration laws. The verification process may include, but shall not be limited to, questioning the person regarding his or her date and place of birth and entry into the United States, and demanding documentation to indicate his or her legal status.

(2) Notify the person of his or her apparent status as an alien who is present in the United States in violation of federal immigration laws and inform him or her that, apart from any criminal justice precedings [sic], he or she must either obtain legal status or leave the United States.

(3) Notify the Attorney General of California and the United States Immigration and Naturalization Service of the apparent illegal status and provide any additional information that may be requested by any other public entity.

(c) Any legislative, administrative, or other action by a city, county, or other legally authorized local governmental entity with jurisdictional boundaries, or by a law enforcement agency, to prevent or limit the cooperation required by subdivision (a) is expressly prohibited.

Section 5. Exclusion of Illegal Aliens from Public Social Services.

Section 10001.5 is added to the Welfare and Institutions Code, to read:

Section 10001.5. (a) In order to carry out the intention of the People of California that only citizens of the United States and aliens lawfully admitted to the United States may receive the benefits of public social services and to ensure that all persons employed in the providing of those services shall diligently protect public funds from misuse, the provisions of this section are adopted.

(b) A person shall not receive any public social services to which he or she may be otherwise entitled until the legal status of that person has been verified as one of the following:

(1) A citizen of the United States.

(2) An alien lawfully admitted as a permanent resident.

(3) An alien lawfully admitted for a temporary period of time.

(c) If any public entity in this state to whom a person has applied for public social services determines or reasonably suspects, based upon the information provided to it, that the person is an alien in the United States in violation of federal law, the following procedures shall be followed by the public entity:

(1) The entity shall not provide the person with benefits or services.

(2) The entity shall, in writing, notify the person of his or her apparent illegal immigration status, and that the person must either obtain legal status or leave the United States.

(3) The entity shall also notify the State Director of Social Services, the Attorney General of California and the United States Immigration and Naturalization Service of the apparent illegal status, and shall provide any additional information that may be requested by any other public entity.

Section 6. Exclusion of Illegal Aliens from Publicly Funded Health Care.

Chapter 1.3 (commencing with Section 130) is added to Part 1 of Division 1 of the Health and Safety Code, to read:

Chapter 1.3. Publicly-funded Health-care Services

Section 130. (a) In order to carry out the intention of the People of California that, excepting emergency medical care as required by federal law, only citizens of the United States and aliens lawfully admitted to the United States may receive the benefits of publicly–funded health care, and to ensure that all persons employed in the providing of those services shall diligently protect public funds from misuse, the provisions of this section are adopted.

(b) A person shall not receive any health care services from a publicly–funded health care facility, to which he or she is otherwise entitled until the legal status of that person has been verified as one of the following:

(1) A citizen of the United States.

(2) An alien lawfully admitted as a permanent resident.

(3) An alien lawfully admitted for a temporary period of time.

(c) If any publicly–funded health care facility in this state from whom a person seeks health care services, other than emergency medical care as required by federal law, determines or reasonably suspects, based upon the information provided to it, that the person is an alien in the United States in violation of federal law, the following procedures shall be followed by the facility:

(1) The facility shall not provide the person with services.

(2) The facility shall, in writing, notify the person of his or her apparent illegal immigration status, and that the person must either obtain legal status or leave the United States.

(3) The facility shall also notify the State Director of Social Services, the Attorney General of California and the United States Immigration and Naturalization Service of the apparent illegal status, and shall provide any additional information that may be requested by any other public entity.

(d) For purposes of this section "publicly–funded health care facility" shall be defined as specified in Section 1200 and 1250 of the Health and Safety Code as of January 1, 1993.

Section 7. Exclusion of Illegal Aliens From Public Elementary and Secondary Schools.

Section 48215 is added to the Education Code to read:

Section 48215. (a) No public elementary or secondary school shall admit, or permit the attendance of, any child who is not a citizen of the United States, an alien lawfully admitted as a permanent resident, or a person who is otherwise authorized under federal law to be present in the United States.

(b) Commencing January 1, 1995, each school district shall verify the legal status of each child enrolling in the school district for the first time in order to ensure the enrollment or attendance only of citizens, aliens lawfully admitted as permanent residents, or persons who are otherwise authorized to be present in the United States.

(c) By January 1, 1996, each school district shall have verified the legal status of each child already enrolled and in attendance in the school district in order to ensure the enrollment or attendance only of citizens, aliens lawfully admitted as permanent residents, or persons who are otherwise authorized under federal law to be present in the United States.

(d) By January 1, 1996, each school district shall also have verified the legal status of each parent or guardian of each child referred to in subdivision (b) and (c) above, to determine whether such parent or guardian is one of the following:

(1) A citizen of the United States.

(2) An alien lawfully admitted as a permanent resident.

(3) An alien admitted lawfully for a temporary period of time.

(e) Each school district shall provide information to the State Superintendent of Public Instruction, the Attorney General of California and the United States Immigration and Naturalization Service regarding any enrollee or pupil, or parent or guardian, attending a public elementary or secondary school in the school district determined or reasonably suspected to be in violation of federal immigration laws within forty five days after becoming aware of an apparent violation. The notice shall also be provided to the parent or legal guardian of the enrollee or pupil, and shall state that an existing pupil may not continue to attend the school after ninety calendar days from the date of the notice, unless legal status is established.

(f) For each child who cannot establish legal status in the United States, each school district shall continue to provide education for a period of ninety days from the date of the notice. Such ninety day period shall be utilized to accomplish an orderly transition to a school in the child's country of origin. Each school district shall fully cooperate in this transition effort to ensure that the educational needs of the child are best served for that period of time.

Section 8. Exclusion of Illegal Aliens from Public Postsecondary Educational Institutions.

Section 66010.8. is added to the Education Code, to read:

Section 66010.8. (a) No public institution of postsecondary education shall admit, enroll, or permit the attendance of any person who is not a citizen of the United States, an alien lawfully admitted as a permanent resident, in the United States, or a person who is otherwise authorized under federal law to be present in the United States.

(b) Commencing with the first term or semester that begins after January 1, 1995, and at the commencement of each term or semester thereafter, each public postsecondary educational institution shall verify the status of each person enrolled or in attendance at that institution in order to ensure the enrollment or attendance only of United States citizens, aliens lawfully admitted as permanent residents in the United States, and persons who are otherwise authorized under federal law to be present in the United States.

(c) No later than 45 days after the admissions officer of a public postsecondary educational institution becomes aware of the application, enrollment, or attendance of a person determined to be, or who is under reasonable suspicion of being, in the United States in violation of federal immigration laws, that officer shall provide that information to the State Superintendent of Public Instruction, the Attorney General of California and the United States Immigration and Naturalization Service. The information shall also be provided to the applicant, enrollee, or person admitted.

Section 9. Attorney General cooperation with the INS.

Section 53069.65 is added to the Government Code, to read:

53069.65. Whenever the state or a city, or a county, or any other legally authorized local governmental entity with jurisdictional boundaries reports the presence of a person who is suspected of being present in the United States in violation of federal immigration laws to the Attorney General of California, that report shall be transmitted to the United States Immigration and Naturalization Service. The Attorney General shall be responsible for maintaining on–going and accurate records of such reports, and shall provide any additional information that may be requested by any other government entity.

Section 10. Amendment and Severability.

The statutory provisions contained in this measure may not be amended by the Legislature except to further its purposes by statute passed in each house by roll call vote entered in the journal, two–thirds of the membership concurring, or by a statute that becomes effective only when approved by the voters.

In the event that any portion of this act or the application thereof to any person or circumstance is held invalid, that invalidity shall not affect any other provision or application of the act, which can be given effect without the invalid provision or application, and to that end the provisions of this act are severable.

VI. INTERNATIONAL REFUGEE CONVENTIONS

CONVENTION RELATING TO THE STATUS OF REFUGEES

Done at Geneva, July 28, 1951

Entry into force, April 22, 1954

189 U.N.T.S. 137

PREAMBLE

THE HIGH CONTRACTING PARTIES

Considering that the Charter of the United Nations and the Universal Declaration of Human Rights approved on 10 December 1948 by the General Assembly have affirmed the principle that human beings shall enjoy fundamental rights and freedoms without discrimination,

Considering that the United Nations has, on various occasions, manifested its profound concern for refugees and endeavoured to assure refugees the widest possible exercise of these fundamental rights and freedoms,

Considering that it is desirable to revise and consolidate previous international agreements relating to the status of refugees and to extend the scope of and the protection accorded by such instruments by means of a new agreement,

Considering that the grant of asylum may place unduly heavy burdens on certain countries, and that a satisfactory solution of a problem of which the United Nations has recognized the international scope and nature cannot therefore be achieved without international co-operation,

Expressing the wish that all States, recognizing the social and humanitarian nature of the problem of refugees, will do everything within their power to prevent this problem from becoming a cause of tension between States,

Noting that the United Nations High Commissioner for Refugees is charged with the task of supervising international conventions providing for the protection of Refugees, and recognizing that the effective co-ordination of measures taken to deal with this problem will depend upon the co-operation of States with the High Commissioner,

Have agreed as follows.

CHAPTER I. GENERAL PROVISIONS

Article 1. Definition of the term "Refugee"

A. For the purposes of the present Convention, the term "refugee" shall apply to any person who:

(1) Has been considered a refugee under the Arrangements of 12 May 1926 and 30 June 1928 or under the Conventions of 28 October 1933 and 10 February 1938, the Protocol of 14 September 1939 or the Constitution of the International Refugee Organization;

Decisions of non-eligibility taken by the International Refugee Organization during the period of its activities shall not prevent the status of refugee being accorded to persons who fulfil the conditions of paragraph 2 of this section;

(2) As a result of events occurring before 1 January 1951 and owing to well-founded fear of being persecuted for reasons of race, religion, nationality, membership of a particular social group or political opinion, is outside the country of his nationality and is unable or, owing to such fear, is unwilling to avail himself of the protection of that country; or who, not having a nationality and being outside the country of his former habitual residence as a result of such events, is unable or, owing to such fear, is unwilling to return to it.

In the case of a person who has more than one nationality, the term "the country of his nationality" shall mean each of the countries of which he is a national, and a person shall not be deemed to be lacking the protection of the country of his nationality if, without any valid reason based on well-founded fear, he has not availed himself of the protection of one of the countries of which he is a national.

B. **(1)** For the purposes of this Convention, the words "events occurring before 1 January 1951" in Article 1, Section A, shall be understood to mean either:

(a) "events occurring in Europe before 1 January 1951" or

(b) "events occurring in Europe or elsewhere before 1 January 1951" and each Contracting State shall make a declaration at the time of signature, ratification or accession, specifying which of these meanings it applies for the purpose of its obligations under this Convention.

(2) Any Contracting State which has adopted alternative *(a)* may at any time extend its obligations by adopting alternative *(b)* by means of a notification addressed to the Secretary–General of the United Nations.

C. This Convention shall cease to apply to any person falling under the terms of Section A if:

(1) He has voluntarily re-availed himself of the protection of the country of his nationality; or

(2) Having lost his nationality, he has voluntarily re-acquired it; or

(3) He has acquired a new nationality, and enjoys the protection of the country of his new nationality; or

(4) He has voluntarily re-established himself in the country which he left or outside which he remained owing to fear of persecution; or

(5) He can no longer, because the circumstances in connexion with which he has been recognized as a refugee have ceased to exist, continue to refuse to avail himself of the protection of the country of his nationality;

Provided that this paragraph shall not apply to a refugee falling under section A(1) of this Article who is able to invoke compelling reasons arising out of previous persecution for refusing to avail himself of the protection of the country of nationality;

(6) Being a person who has no nationality he is, because the circumstances in connexion with which he has been recognized as a refugee have ceased to exist, able to return to the country of his former habitual residence;

Provided that this paragraph shall not apply to a refugee falling under section A(1) of this Article who is able to invoke compelling reasons arising out of previous persecution for refusing to return to the country of his former habitual residence.

D. This Convention shall not apply to persons who are at present receiving from organs or agencies of the United Nations other than the United Nations High Commissioner for Refugees protection or assistance.

When such protection or assistance has ceased for any reason, without the position of such persons being definitively settled in accordance with the relevant resolutions adopted by the General Assembly of the United Nations, these persons shall *ipso facto* be entitled to the benefits of this Convention.

E. This Convention shall not apply to a person who is recognized by the competent authorities of the country in which he has taken residence as having the rights and obligations which are attached to the possession of the nationality of that country.

F. The provisions of this Convention shall not apply to any person with respect to whom there are serious reasons for considering that:

(a) he has committed a crime against peace, a war crime, or a crime against humanity, as defined in the international instruments drawn up to make provision in respect of such crimes;

(b) he has committed a serious non-political crime outside the country of refuge prior to his admission to that country as a refugee;

(c) he has been guilty of acts contrary to the purposes and principles of the United Nations.

Article 2. General obligations

Every refugee has duties to the country in which he finds himself, which require in particular that he conform to its laws and regulations as well as to measures taken for the maintenance of public order.

Article 3. Non-discrimination

The Contracting States shall apply the provisions of this Convention to refugees without discrimination as to race, religion or country of origin.

Article 4. Religion

The Contracting States shall accord to refugees within their territories treatment at least as favourable as that accorded to their nationals with respect to freedom to practise their religion and freedom as regards the religious education of their children.

Article 5. Rights granted apart from this Convention

Nothing in this Convention shall be deemed to impair any rights and benefits granted by a Contracting State to refugees apart from this Convention.

Article 6. The term "in the same circumstances"

For the purpose of this Convention, the term "in the same circumstances" implies that any requirements (including requirements as to length and conditions of sojourn or residence) which the particular individual would have to fulfil for the enjoyment of the right in question, if he were not a refugee, must be fulfilled by him, with the exception of requirements which by their nature a refugee is incapable of fulfilling.

Article 7. Exemption from reciprocity

1. Except where this Convention contains more favourable provisions, a Contracting State shall accord to refugees the same treatment as is accorded to aliens generally.

2. After a period of three years' residence, all refugees shall enjoy exemption from legislative reciprocity in the territory of the Contracting States.

3. Each Contracting State shall continue to accord to refugees the rights and benefits to which they were already entitled, in the absence of reciprocity, at the date of entry into force of this Convention for that State.

4. The Contracting States shall consider favourably the possibility of according to refugees, in the absence of reciprocity, rights and benefits beyond those to which they are entitled according to paragraphs 2 and 3, and to extending exemption from reciprocity to refugees who do not fulfil the conditions provided for in paragraphs 2 and 3.

5. The provisions of paragraphs 2 and 3 apply both to the rights and benefits referred to in articles 13, 18, 19, 21 and 22 of this Convention and to rights and benefits for which this Convention does not provide.

Article 8. Exemption from exceptional measures

With regard to exceptional measures which may be taken against the person, property or interests of nationals of a foreign State, the Contracting States shall not apply such measures to a refugee who is formally a national of the said State solely on account of such nationality. Contracting States which, under their legislation, are prevented from applying the general principle expressed in this article, shall, in appropriate cases, grant exemptions in favour of such refugees.

Article 9. Provisional measures

Nothing in this Convention shall prevent a Contracting State, in time of war or other grave and exceptional circumstances, from taking provisionally measures which it considers to be essential to the national security in the case of a particular person, pending a determination by the Contracting State that that person is in fact a refugee and that the continuance of such measures is necessary in his case in the interests of national security.

Article 10. Continuity of residence

1. Where a refugee has been forcibly displaced during the Second World War and removed to the territory of a Contracting State, and is resident there, the period of such enforced sojourn shall be considered to have been lawful residence within that territory.

2. Where a refugee has been forcibly displaced during the Second World War from the territory of a Contracting State and has, prior to the date of entry into force of this Convention, returned there for the purpose of taking up residence, the period of residence before and after such enforced displacement shall be regarded as one uninterrupted period for any purposes for which uninterrupted residence is required.

Article 11. Refugee seamen

In the case of refugees regularly serving as crew members on board a ship flying the flag of a Contracting State, that State shall give sympathetic consideration to their establishment on its territory and the issue of travel documents to them on their temporary admission to its territory particularly with a view to facilitating their establishment in another country.

CHAPTER II. JURIDICAL STATUS

Article 12. Personal status

1. The personal status of a refugee shall be governed by the law of the country of his domicile or, if he has no domicile, by the law of the country of his residence.

2. Rights previously acquired by a refugee and dependent on personal status, more particularly rights attaching to marriage, shall be respected by a Contracting State, subject to compliance, if this be necessary, with the formalities required by the law of that State, provided that the right in question is one which would have been recognized by the law of that State had he not become a refugee.

Article 13. Movable and immovable property

The Contracting States shall accord to a refugee treatment as favourable as possible and, in any event, not less favourable than that accorded to aliens generally in the same circumstances as regards the acquisition of movable and immovable property and other rights pertaining thereto, and to leases and other contracts relating to movable and immovable property.

Article 14. Artistic rights and industrial property

In respect of the protection of industrial property, such as inventions, designs or models, trade marks, trade names, and of rights in literary, artistic and scientific works, a refugee shall be accorded in the country in which he has his habitual residence the same protection as is accorded to nationals of that country. In the territory of any other Contracting State, he shall be accorded the same protection as is accorded in that territory to nationals of the country in which he has habitual residence.

Article 15. Right of association

As regards non-political and non-profit-making associations and trade unions the Contracting States shall accord to refugees lawfully staying in their territory the most favourable treatment accorded to nationals of a foreign country, in the same circumstances.

Article 16. Access to courts

1. A refugee shall have free access to the courts of law on the territory of all Contracting States.

2. A refugee shall enjoy in the Contracting State in which he has his habitual residence the same treatment as a national in matters pertaining to access to the Courts, including legal assistance and exemption from *cautio judicatum solvi.*

3. A refugee shall be accorded in the matters referred to in paragraph 2 in countries other than that in which he has his habitual residence the treatment granted to a national of the country of his habitual residence.

CHAPTER III. GAINFUL EMPLOYMENT

Article 17. Wage-earning employment

1. The Contracting State shall accord to refugees lawfully staying in their territory the most favourable treatment accorded to nationals of a foreign country in the same circumstances, as regards the right to engage in wage-earning employment.

2. In any case, restrictive measures imposed on aliens or the employment of aliens for the protection of the national labour market shall not be applied to a refugee who was already exempt from them at the date of entry into force of this Convention for the Contracting States concerned, or who fulfils one of the following conditions:

(a) He has completed three years' residence in the country;

(b) He has a spouse possessing the nationality of the country of residence. A refugee may not invoke the benefits of this provision if he has abandoned his spouse;

(c) He has one or more children possessing the nationality of the country of residence.

3. The Contracting States shall give sympathetic consideration to assimilating the rights of all refugees with regard to wage-earning employment to those of nationals, and in particular of those refugees who have entered their territory pursuant to programmes of labour recruitment or under immigration schemes.

Article 18. Self-employment

The Contracting States shall accord to a refugee lawfully in their territory treatment as favourable as possible and, in any event, not less favourable than that accorded to aliens generally in the same circumstances, as regards the right to engage on his own account in agriculture, industry, handicrafts and commerce and to establish commercial and industrial companies.

Article 19. Liberal professions

1. Each Contracting State shall accord to refugees lawfully staying in their territory who hold diplomas recognized by the competent authorities of that State, and who are desirous of practising a liberal profession, treatment as favourable as possible and, in any event, not less favourable than that accorded to aliens generally in the same circumstances.

2. The Contracting States shall use their best endeavours consistently with their laws and constitutions to secure the settlement of such refugees in the territories, other than the metropolitan territory, for whose international relations they are responsible.

CHAPTER IV. WELFARE

Article 20. Rationing

Where a rationing system exists, which applies to the population at large and regulates the general distribution of products in short supply, refugees shall be accorded the same treatment as nationals.

Article 21. Housing

As regards housing, the Contracting States, in so far as the matter is regulated by laws or regulations or is subject to the control of public authorities, shall accord to refugees lawfully staying in their territory treatment as favourable as possible and, in any event, not less favourable than that accorded to aliens generally in the same circumstances.

Article 22. Public education

1. The Contracting States shall accord to refugees the same treatment as is accorded to nationals with respect to elementary education.

2. The Contracting States shall accord to refugees treatment as favourable as possible, and, in any event, not less favourable than that accorded to aliens generally in the same circumstances, with respect to education other than elementary education and, in particular, as regards access to studies, the recognition of foreign school certificates, diplomas and degrees, the remission of fees and charges and the award of scholarships.

Article 23. Public relief

The Contracting States shall accord to refugees lawfully staying in their territory the same treatment with respect to public relief and assistance as is accorded to their nationals.

Article 24. Labour legislation and social security

1. The Contracting States shall accord to refugees lawfully staying in their territory the same treatment as is accorded to nationals in respect of the following matters:

(a) In so far as such matters are governed by laws or regulations or are subject to the control of administrative authorities: remuneration, including family allowances where these form part of remuneration, hours of work, overtime arrangements, holidays with pay, restrictions on home work, minimum age of employment, apprenticeship and training, women's work and the work of young persons, and the enjoyment of the benefits of collective bargaining;

(b) Social security (legal provisions in respect of employment injury, occupational diseases, maternity, sickness, disability, old age, death, unemployment, family responsibilities and any other contingency which, according to national laws or regulations, is covered by a social security scheme), subject to the following limitations:

(i) There may be appropriate arrangements for the maintenance of acquired rights and rights in course of acquisition;

(ii) National laws or regulations of the country of residence may prescribe special arrangements concerning benefits or portions of benefits which are payable wholly out of public funds, and concerning allowances paid to persons who do not fulfil the contribution conditions prescribed for the award of a normal pension.

2. The right to compensation for the death of a refugee resulting from employment injury or from occupational disease shall not be affected by the fact that the residence of the beneficiary is outside the territory of the Contracting State.

3. The Contracting States shall extend to refugees the benefits of agreements concluded between them, or which may be concluded between them in the future, concerning the maintenance of acquired rights and rights in the process of acquisition in regard to social security, subject only to the conditions which apply to nationals of the States signatory to the agreements in question.

4. The Contracting States will give sympathetic consideration to extending to refugees so far as possible the benefits of similar agreements which may at any time be in force between such Contracting States and non-contracting States.

CHAPTER V. ADMINISTRATIVE MEASURES

Article 25. Administrative assistance

1. When the exercise of a right by a refugee would normally require the assistance of authorities of a foreign country to whom he cannot have recourse, the Contracting States in whose territory he is residing shall arrange that such assistance be afforded to him by their own authorities or by an international authority.

2. The authority or authorities mentioned in paragraph 1 shall deliver or cause to be delivered under their supervision to refugees such documents or certifications as would normally be delivered to aliens by or through their national authorities.

3. Documents or certifications so delivered shall stand in the stead of the official instruments delivered to aliens by or through their national authorities, and shall be given credence in the absence of proof to the contrary.

4. Subject to such exceptional treatment as may be granted to indigent persons, fees may be charged for the services mentioned herein, but such fees shall be moderate and commensurate with those charged to nationals for similar services.

5. The provisions of this article shall be without prejudice to articles 27 and 28.

Article 26. Freedom of movement

Each Contracting State shall accord to refugees lawfully in its territory the right to choose their place of residence and to move freely within its territory, subject to any regulations applicable to aliens generally in the same circumstances.

Article 27. Identity papers

The Contracting States shall issue identity papers to any refugee in their territory who does not possess a valid travel document.

Article 28. Travel documents

1. The Contracting States shall issue to refugees lawfully staying in their territory travel documents for the purpose of travel outside their territory unless compelling reasons of national security or public order otherwise require, and the provisions of the Schedule to this Convention shall apply with respect to such documents. The Contracting States may issue such a travel document to any other refugee in their territory; they shall in particular give sympathetic consideration to the issue of such a travel document to refugees in their territory who are unable to obtain a travel document from the country of their lawful residence.

2. Travel documents issued to refugees under previous international agreements by parties thereto shall be recognized and treated by the Contracting States in the same way as if they had been issued pursuant to this article.

Article 29. Fiscal charges

1. The Contracting States shall not impose upon refugees duties, charges or taxes, of any description whatsoever, other or higher than those which are or may be levied on their nationals in similar situations.

2. Nothing in the above paragraph shall prevent the application to refugees of the laws and regulations concerning charges in respect of the issue to aliens of administrative documents including identity papers.

Article 30. Transfer of assets

1. A Contracting State shall, in conformity with its laws and regulations permit refugees to transfer assets which they have brought into its territory, to another country where they have been admitted for the purposes of resettlement.

2. A Contracting State shall give sympathetic consideration to the application of refugees for permission to transfer assets wherever they may be and which are necessary for their resettlement in another country to which they have been admitted.

Article 31. Refugees unlawfully in the country of refuge

1. The Contracting States shall not impose penalties, on account of their illegal entry or presence, on refugees who, coming directly from a territory where their life or freedom was threatened in the sense of Article 1, enter or are present in their territory without authorization, provided they present themselves without delay to the authorities and show good cause for their illegal entry or presence.

2. The Contracting States shall not apply to the movements of such refugees restrictions other than those which are necessary and such restrictions shall only be applied until their status in the country is regularized or they obtain admission into another country. The Contracting States shall allow such refugees a reasonable period and all the necessary facilities to obtain admission into another country.

Article 32. Expulsion

1. The Contracting States shall not expel a refugee lawfully in their territory save on grounds of national security or public order.

2. The expulsion of such a refugee shall be only in pursuance of a decision reached in accordance with due process of law. Except where compelling reasons of national security otherwise require, the refugee shall be allowed to submit evidence to clear himself, and to appeal to and be represented for the purpose before competent authority or a person or persons specially designated by the competent authority.

3. The Contracting States shall allow such a refugee a reasonable period within which to seek legal admission into another country. The Contracting States reserve the right to apply during that period such internal measures as they may deem necessary.

Article 33. Prohibition of expulsion or return ("refoulement")

1. No Contracting State shall expel or return ("*refouler*") a refugee in any manner whatsoever to the frontiers of territories where his life or freedom would be threatened on account of his race, religion, nationality, membership of a particular social group or political opinion.

2. The benefit of the present provision may not, however, be claimed by a refugee whom there are reasonable grounds for regarding as a danger to the security of the country in which he is, or who, having been convicted by a final judgment of a particularly serious crime, constitutes a danger to the community of that country.

Article 34. Naturalization

The Contracting States shall as far as possible facilitate the assimilation and naturalization of refugees. They shall in particular make every effort to expedite naturalization proceedings and to reduce as far as possible the charges and costs of such proceedings.

CHAPTER VI. EXECUTORY AND TRANSITORY PROVISIONS

Article 35. Co-operation of the national authorities with the United Nations

1. The Contracting States undertake to co-operate with the Office of the United Nations High Commissioner for Refugees, or any other agency of the United Nations which may succeed it, in the exercise of its functions, and shall in particular facilitate its duty of supervising the application of the provisions of this Convention.

2. In order to enable the Office of the High Commissioner or any other agency of the United Nations which may succeed it, to make reports to the competent organs of the United Nations, the Contracting States undertake to provide them in the appropriate form with information and and statistical data requested concerning:

(a) the condition of refugees,

(b) the implementation of this Convention, and

(c) laws, regulations and decrees which are, or may hereafter be, in force relating to refugees.

Article 36. Information on national legislation

The Contracting States shall communicate to the Secretary–General of the United Nations the laws and regulations which they may adopt to ensure the application of this Convention.

Article 37. Relation to previous conventions

Without prejudice to article 28, paragraph 2, of this Convention, this Convention replaces, as between parties to it, the Arrangements of 5 July 1922, 31 May 1924, 12 May 1926, 30 June 1928 and 30 July 1935, the Conventions of 28 October 1933 and 10 February 1938, the Protocol of 14 September 1939 and the Agreement of 15 October 1946.

CHAPTER VII. FINAL CLAUSES

Article 38. Settlement of disputes

Any dispute between parties to this Convention relating to its interpretation or application, which cannot be settled by other means, shall be referred to the International Court of Justice at the request of any one of the parties to the dispute.

Article 39. Signature, ratification and accession

1. This Convention shall be opened for signature at Geneva on 28 July 1951 and shall thereafter be deposited with the Secretary–General of the United Nations. It shall be open for signature at the European Office of the United Nations from 28 July to 31 August 1951 and shall be reopened for signature at the Headquarters of the United Nations from 17 September 1951 to 31 December 1952.

2. This Convention shall be open for signature on behalf of all States Members of the United Nations, and also on behalf of any other State invited to attend the Conference of Plenipotentiaries on the Status of Refugees and Stateless Persons or to which an invitation to sign will have been addressed by the General Assembly. It shall be ratified and the instruments of ratification shall be deposited with the Secretary–General of the United Nations.

3. This Convention shall be open from 28 July 1951 for accession by the States referred to in paragraph 2 of this Article. Accession shall be effected by the deposit of an instrument of accession with the Secretary–General of the United Nations.

Article 40. Territorial application clause

1. Any State may, at the time of signature, ratification or accession, declare that this Convention shall extend to all or any of the territories for the international relations of which it is responsible. Such a declaration shall take effect when the Convention enters into force for the States concerned.

2. At any time thereafter any such extension shall be made by notification addressed to the Secretary–General of the United Nations and shall take effect as from the ninetieth day after the day of receipt by the Secretary–General of the United Nations of this notification, or as from the date of entry into force of the Convention for the State concerned, whichever is the later.

3. With respect to those territories to which this Convention is not extended at the time of signature, ratification or accession, each State concerned shall consider the possibility of taking the necessary steps in order to extend the application of this Convention to such territories, subject where necessary for constitutional reasons, to the consent of the governments of such territories.

Article 41. Federal clause

In the case of a Federal or non-unitary State, the following provisions shall apply:

(a) With respect to those articles of this Convention that come within the legislative jurisdiction of the federal legislative authority, the obligations of the Federal Government shall to this extent be the same as those of Parties which are not Federal States,

(b) With respect to those articles of this Convention that come within the legislative jurisdiction of constituent States, provinces or cantons which are not, under the constitutional system of the federation, bound to take legislative action, the Federal Government shall bring such articles with a favourable recommendation, to the notice of the appropriate authorities of States, provinces or cantons at the earliest possible moment.

(c) A Federal State Party to this Convention shall, at the request of any other Contracting State transmitted through the Secretary–General of the United Nations, supply a statement of the law and practice of the Federation and its constituent units in regard to any particular provision of the Convention showing the extent to which effect has been given to that provision by legislative or other action.

Article 42. Reservations

1. At the time of signature, ratification or accession, any State may make reservations to articles of the Convention other than to articles 1, 3, 4, 16(1), 33, 36 to 46 inclusive.

2. Any State making a reservation in accordance with paragraph 1 of this article may at any time withdraw the reservation by a communication to that effect addressed to the Secretary–General of the United Nations.

Article 43. Entry into force

1. This Convention shall come into force on the ninetieth day following the day of deposit of the sixth instrument of ratification or accession.

2. For each State ratifying or acceding to the Convention after the deposit of the sixth instrument of ratification or accession, the Convention shall enter into force on the ninetieth day following the day of deposit by such State of its instrument of ratification or accession.

Article 44. Denunciation

1. Any Contracting State may denounce this Convention at any time by a notification addressed to the Secretary–General of the United Nations.

2. Such denunciation shall take effect for the Contracting State concerned one year from the date upon which it is received by the Secretary–General of the United Nations.

3. Any State which has made a declaration or notification under article 40 may, at any time thereafter, by a notification to the Secretary–General of the United Nations, declare that the Convention shall cease to extend to such territory one year after the date of receipt of the notification by the Secretary–General.

Article 45. Revision

1. Any Contracting State may request revision of this Convention at any time by a notification addressed to the Secretary–General of the United Nations.

2. The General Assembly of the United Nations shall recommend the steps, if any, to be taken in respect of such request.

Article 46. Notifications by the Secretary–General of the United Nations

The Secretary–General of the United Nations shall inform all Members of the United Nations and non-member States referred to in article 39:

(a) of declarations and notifications in accordance with Section B of Article 1;

(b) of signatures, ratifications and accessions in accordance with article 39;

(c) of declarations and notifications in accordance with article 40;

(d) of reservations and withdrawals in accordance with article 42;

(e) of the date on which this Convention will come into force in accordance with article 43;

(f) of denunciations and notifications in accordance with article 44;

(g) of requests for revision in accordance with article 45.

In faith whereof the undersigned, duly authorized, have signed this Convention on behalf of their respective Governments,

Done at Geneva, this twenty-eighth day of July, one thousand nine hundred and fifty-one, in a single copy, of which the English and French texts are equally authentic and which shall remain deposited in the archives of the United Nations, and certified true copies of which shall be delivered to all Members of the United Nations and to the non-member States referred to in article 39.

Schedule

Paragraph 1

1. The travel document referred to in Article 28 of this Convention shall be similar to the specimen annexed hereto.

2. The document shall be made out in at least two languages, one of which shall be English or French.

Paragraph 2

Subject to the regulations obtaining in the country of issue, children may be included in the travel document of a parent or, in exceptional circumstances, of another adult refugee.

Paragraph 3

The fees charged for issue of the document shall not exceed the lowest scale of charges for national passports.

Paragraph 4

Save in special or exceptional cases, the document shall be made valid for the largest possible number of countries.

Paragraph 5

The document shall have a validity of either one or two years, at the discretion of the issuing authority.

Paragraph 6

1. The renewal or extension of the validity of the document is a matter for the authority which issued it, so long as the holder has not established lawful residence in another territory and resides lawfully in the territory of the said authority. The issue of a new document is, under the same conditions, a matter for the authority which issued the former document.

2. Diplomatic or consular authorities, specially authorized for the purpose, shall be empowered to extend, for a period not exceeding six months, the validity of travel documents issued by their Governments.

3. The Contracting States shall give sympathetic consideration to renewing or extending the validity of travel documents or issuing new documents to refugees no longer lawfully resident in their territory who are unable to obtain a travel document from the country of their lawful residence.

Paragraph 7

The Contracting States shall recognize the validity of the documents issued in accordance with the provisions of Article 28 of this Convention.

Paragraph 8

The competent authorities of the country to which the refugee desires to proceed shall, if they are prepared to admit him and if a visa is required, affix a visa on the document of which he is the holder.

Paragraph 9

1. The Contracting States undertake to issue transit visas to refugees who have obtained visas for a territory of Final destination.

2. The issue of such visas may be refused on grounds which would justify refusal of a visa to any alien.

Paragraph 10

The fees for the issue of exit, entry or transit visas shall not exceed the lowest scale of charges for visas on foreign passports.

Paragraph 11

When a refugee has lawfully taken up residence in the territory of another Contracting State, the responsibility for the issue of a new document, under the terms and conditions of Article 28, shall be that of the competent authority of that territory, to which the refugee shall be entitled to apply.

Paragraph 12

The authority issuing a new document shall withdraw the old document and shall return it to the country of issue, if it is stated in the document that it should be so returned; otherwise it shall withdraw and cancel the document.

Paragraph 13

1. Each Contracting State undertakes that the holder of a travel document issued by it in accordance with Article 28 of this Convention shall be re-admitted to its territory at any time during the period of its validity,

2. Subject to the provisions of the preceding sub-paragraph, a Contracting State may require the holder of the document to comply with such formalities as may be prescribed in regard to exit from or return to its territory.

3. The Contracting States reserve the right, in exceptional cases, or in cases where the refugee's stay is authorized for a specific period, when issuing the document, to limit the period during which the refugee may return to a period of not less than three months.

Paragraph 14

Subject only to the terms of paragraph 13, the provisions of this Schedule in no way affect the laws and regulations governing the conditions of admission to, transit through, residence and establishment in, and departure from, the territories of the Contracting States.

Paragraph 15

Neither the issue of the document nor the entries made thereon determine or affect the status of the holder, particularly as regards nationality.

Paragraph 16

The issue of the document does not in any way entitle the holder to the protection of the diplomatic or consular authorities of the country of issue, and does not confer on these authorities a right of protection.

ANNEX

Specimen Travel Document

The document will be in booklet form (approximately 15 x 10 centimetres).

It is recommended that it be so printed that any erasure or alteration by chemical or other means can be readily detected, and that the words "Convention of 28 July 1951" be printed in continuous repetition on each page, in the language of the issuing country.

(Cover of booklet)

TRAVEL DOCUMENT

(Convention of 28 July 1951)

No. ________________

(1)
TRAVEL DOCUMENT
(Convention of 28 July 1951)

This document expires on ....
unless its validity is extended or renewed.

Name ....

Forename(s) ....

Accompanied by ....child (children)

1. This document is issued solely with a view to providing the holder with a travel document which can serve in lieu of a national passport. It is without prejudice to and in no way affects the holder's nationality.

2. The holder is authorized to return to ....
....[state here the country whose authorities are issuing the document] on or before ....unless some later date is hereafter specified.
[The period during which the holder is allowed to return must not be less than three months]

3. Should the holder take up residence in a country other than that which issued the present document, he must, if he wishes to travel again, apply to the competent authorities of his country of residence for a new document. [The old travel document shall be withdrawn by the authority issuing the new document and returned to the authority which issued it.][1]

(This document contains .... pages, exclusive of cover.)

[1]The sentence in brackets to be inserted by Governments which so desire.

---

(2)

Place and date of birth ....
Occupation ....
Present residence..
*Maiden name and forename(s) of wife ....
....
*Name and forename(s) of husband..
....

Description

Height ____________________
Hair ____________________
Colour of eyes ____________________
Nose ____________________
Shape of face ____________________
Complexion ____________________
Special peculiarities ____________________

Children accompanying holder

Name	Forename(s)	Place and date of birth	Sex

*Strike out whichever does not apply.

(This document contains _____ pages, exclusive of cover.)

(3)

Photograph of holder and stamp of issuing authority
Finger-prints of holder (if required)

Signature of holder ____________________

(This document contains _____ pages, exclusive of cover.)

(4)

1. This document is valid for the following countries:

2. Document or documents on the basis of which the present document is issued:

Issued at ____________________
Date ____________________

Signature and stamp of authority issuing the document:

Fee paid: ____________________

(This document contains _____ pages, exclusive of cover.)

(5)

Extension or renewal of validity

Fee paid: From ____________________
To ____________________
Done at ____________________ Date____________________

Signature and stamp of authority extending or renewing the validity of the document:

Extension or renewal of validity

Fee paid: From ____________________
To ____________________
Done at ____________________ Date____________________

Signature and stamp of authority extending or renewing the validity of the document:

(This document contains _____ pages, exclusive of cover.)

(6)

Extension or renewal of validity

Fee paid: From ____________________
To ____________________
Done at ____________________ Date____________________

Signature and stamp of authority extending or renewing the validity of the document:

Extension or renewal of validity

Fee paid: From ____________________
To ____________________
Done at ____________________ Date____________________

Signature and stamp of authority extending or renewing the validity of the document:

(This document contains _____ pages, exclusive of cover.)

(7-32)

Visas

The name of the holder of the document must be repeated in each visa.

(This document contains _____ pages, exclusive of cover.

PROTOCOL RELATING TO THE STATUS OF REFUGEES

Done January 31, 1967

Entry into force, October 4, 1967

606 U.N.T.S. 267, 19 U.S.T. 6223, T.I.A.S. No. 6577

The States Parties to the present Protocol,

Considering that the Convention relating to the Status of Refugees done at Geneva on 28 July 1951 (hereinafter referred to as the Convention) covers only those persons who have become refugees as a result of events occurring before 1 January 1951,

Considering that new refugee situations have arisen since the Convention was adopted and that the refugees concerned may therefore not fall within the scope of the Convention,

Considering that it is desirable that equal status should be enjoyed by all refugees covered by the definition in the Convention irrespective of the dateline 1 January 1951,

Have agreed as follows:

Article I. General provision

1. The States Parties to the present Protocol undertake to apply articles 2 to 34 inclusive of the Convention to refugees as hereinafter defined.

2. For the purpose of the present Protocol, the term "refugee" shall, except as regards the application of paragraph 3 of this article, mean any person within the definition of article 1 of the Convention as if the words "As a result of events occurring before 1 January 1951 and ..." and the words "... as a result of such events", in article 1A(2) were omitted.

3. The present Protocol shall be applied by the States Parties hereto without any geographic limitation, save that existing declarations made by States already Parties to the Convention in accordance with article 1B(1)*(a)* of the Convention, shall, unless extended under article 1B(2) thereof, apply also under the present Protocol.

Article II. Co-operation of the national authorities with the United Nations

1. The States Parties to the present Protocol undertake to co-operate with the Office of the United Nations High Commissioner for Refugees, or any other agency of the United Nations which may succeed it, in the exercise of its functions, and shall in particular facilitate its duty of supervising the application of the provisions of the present Protocol.

2. In order to enable the Office of the High Commissioner, or any other agency of the United Nations which may succeed it, to make reports to the competent organs of the United Nations, the States Parties to the present Protocol undertake to provide them with the information and statistical data requested, in the appropriate form, concerning:

(a) The condition of refugees;

(b) The implementation of the present Protocol;

(c) Laws, regulations and decrees which are, or may hereafter be, in force relating to refugees.

Article III. Information on national legislation

The States Parties to the present Protocol shall communicate to the Secretary–General of the United Nations the laws and regulations which they may adopt to ensure the application of the present Protocol.

Article IV. Settlement of disputes

Any dispute between States Parties to the present Protocol which relates to its interpretation or application and which cannot be settled by other means shall be referred to the International Court of Justice at the request of any one of the parties to the dispute.

Article V. Accession

The present Protocol shall be open for accession on behalf of all States Parties to the Convention and of any other State Member of the United Nations or member of any of the specialized agencies or to which an invitation to accede may have been addressed by the General Assembly of the United Nations. Accession shall be effected by the deposit of an instrument of accession with the Secretary–General of the United Nations.

Article VI. Federal clause

In the case of a Federal or non-unitary State, the following provisions shall apply:

(a) With respect to those articles of the Convention to be applied in accordance with article I, paragraph 1, of the present Protocol that come within the legislative jurisdiction of the federal legislative authority, the obligations of the Federal Government shall to this extent be the same as those of States Parties which are not Federal States;

(b) With respect to those articles of the Convention to be applied in accordance with article I, paragraph 1, of the present Protocol that come within the legislative jurisdiction of constituent States, provinces or cantons which are not, under the constitutional system of the federation, bound to take legislative action, the Federal Government shall bring such articles with a favourable recommendation to

the notice of the appropriate authorities of States, provinces or cantons at the earliest possible moment;

(c) A Federal State Party to the present Protocol shall, at the request of any other State Party hereto transmitted through the Secretary-General of the United Nations, supply a statement of the law and practice of the Federation and its constituent units in regard to any particular provision of the Convention to be applied in accordance with article I, paragraph 1, of the present Protocol, showing the extent to which effect has been given to that provision by legislative or other action.

Article VII. Reservations and Declarations

1. At the time of accession, any State may make reservations in respect of article IV of the present Protocol and in respect of the application in accordance with article I of the present Protocol of any provisions of the Convention other than those contained in articles 1, 3, 4, 16(1) and 33 thereof, provided that in the case of a State Party to the Convention reservations made under this article shall not extend to refugees in respect of whom the Convention applies.

2. Reservations made by States Parties to the Convention in accordance with article 42 thereof shall, unless withdrawn, be applicable in relation to their obligations under the present Protocol.

3. Any State making a reservation in accordance with paragraph 1 of this article may at any time withdraw such reservation by a communication to that effect addressed to the Secretary-General of the United Nations.

4. Declarations made under article 40, paragraphs 1 and 2, of the Convention by a State Party thereto which accedes to the present Protocol shall be deemed to apply in respect of the present Protocol, unless upon accession a notification to the contrary is addressed by the State Party concerned to the Secretary-General of the United Nations. The provisions of article 40, paragraphs 2 and 3, and of article 44, paragraph 3, of the Convention shall be deemed to apply *mutatis mutandis* to the present Protocol.

Article VIII. Entry into force

1. The present Protocol shall come into force on the day of deposit of the sixth instrument of accession.

2. For each State acceding to the Protocol after the deposit of the sixth instrument of accession, the Protocol shall come into force on the date of deposit by such State of its instrument of accession.

Article IX. Denunciation

1. Any State Party hereto may denounce this Protocol at any time by a notification addressed to the Secretary-General of the United Nations.

2. Such denunciation shall take effect for the State Party concerned one year from the date on which it is received by the Secretary–General of the United Nations.

Article X. Notifications by the Secretary–General of the United Nations

The Secretary–General of the United Nations shall inform the States referred to in article V above of the date of entry into force, accessions, reservations and withdrawals of reservations to and denunciations of the present Protocol, and of declarations and notifications relating hereto.

Article XI. Deposit in the Archives of the Secretariat of the United Nations

A copy of the present Protocol, of which the Chinese, English, French, Russian and Spanish texts are equally authentic, signed by the President of the General Assembly and by the Secretary–General of the United Nations, shall be deposited in the archives of the Secretariat of the United Nations. The Secretary–General will transmit certified copies thereof to all States Members of the United Nations and to the other States referred to in article V above.

VII. THE CONSTITUTION OF THE UNITED STATES

Preamble

We the People of the United States, in Order to form a more perfect Union, establish Justice, insure domestic Tranquility, provide for the common defence, promote the general Welfare, and secure the Blessings of Liberty to ourselves and our Posterity, do ordain and establish this Constitution for the United States of America.

Article I

Section 1. All legislative Powers herein granted shall be vested in a Congress of the United States, which shall consist of a Senate and House of Representatives.

Section 2. [1] The House of Representatives shall be composed of Members chosen every second Year by the People of the several States, and the Electors in each State shall have the Qualifications requisite for Electors of the most numerous Branch of the State Legislature.

[2] No Person shall be a Representative who shall not have attained to the Age of twenty five Years, and been seven Years a Citizen of the United States, and who shall not, when elected, be an Inhabitant of that State in which he shall be chosen.

[3] Representatives and direct Taxes shall be apportioned among the several States which may be included within this Union, according to their respective Numbers, which shall be determined by adding to the whole Number of free Persons, including those bound to Service for a Term of Years, and excluding Indians not taxed, three fifths of all other Persons. The actual Enumeration shall be made within three Years after the first Meeting of the Congress of the United States, and within every subsequent Term of ten Years, in such Manner as they shall by Law direct. The Number of Representatives shall not exceed one for every thirty Thousand, but each State shall have at Least one Representative; and until such enumeration shall be made, the State of New Hampshire shall be entitled to chuse three, Massachusetts eight, Rhode Island and Providence Plantations one, Connecticut five, New York six, New Jersey four, Pennsylvania eight, Delaware one, Maryland six, Virginia ten, North Carolina five, South Carolina five, and Georgia three.

[4] When vacancies happen in the Representation from any State, the Executive Authority thereof shall issue Writs of Election to fill such Vacancies.

[5] The House of Representatives shall chuse their Speaker and other Officers; and shall have the sole Power of Impeachment.

Section 3. [1] The Senate of the United States shall be composed of two Senators from each State, chosen by the Legislature thereof, for six Years; and each Senator shall have one Vote.

[2] Immediately after they shall be assembled in Consequence of the first Election, they shall be divided as equally as may be into three Classes. The Seats of the Senators of the first Class shall be vacated at the Expiration of the Second Year, of the second Class at the Expiration of the fourth Year, and of the third Class at the Expiration of the sixth Year, so that one third may be chosen every second Year; and if Vacancies happen by Resignation, or otherwise, during the Recess of the Legislature of any State, the Executive thereof may make temporary Appointments until the next Meeting of the Legislature, which shall then fill such Vacancies.

[3] No Person shall be a Senator who shall not have attained to the Age of thirty Years, and been nine Years a Citizen of the United States, and who shall not, when elected, by an Inhabitant of that State for which he shall be chosen.

[4] The Vice President of the United States shall be President of the Senate, but shall have no Vote, unless they be equally divided.

[5] The Senate shall chuse their other Officers, and also a President pro tempore, in the Absence of the Vice President, or when he shall exercise the Office of President of the United States.

[6] The Senate shall have the sole Power to try all Impeachments. When sitting for that Purpose, they shall be on Oath or Affirmation. When the President of the United States is tried, the Chief Justice shall preside: And no Person shall be convicted without the Concurrence of two thirds of the Members present.

[7] Judgment in Cases of Impeachment shall not extend further than to removal from Office, and disqualification to hold and enjoy any Office of honor, Trust, or Profit under the United States: but the Party convicted shall nevertheless be liable and subject to Indictment, Trial, Judgment, and Punishment, according to Law.

Section 4. [1] The Times, Places and Manner of holding Elections for Senators and Representatives, shall be prescribed in each State by the Legislature thereof; but the Congress may at any time by Law make or alter such Regulations, except as to the Places of chusing Senators.

[2] The Congress shall assemble at least once in every Year, and such Meeting shall be on the first Monday in December, unless they shall by Law appoint a different Day.

Section 5. [1] Each House shall be the Judge of the Elections, Returns, and Qualifications of its own Members, and a Majority of each shall constitute a Quorum to do Business; but a smaller Number may adjourn from day to day, and may be authorized to compel the Attendance of absent Members, in such Manner, and under such Penalties as each House may provide.

[2] Each House may determine the Rules of its Proceedings, punish its Members for disorderly Behavior, and, with the Concurrence of two thirds, expel a Member.

[3] Each House shall keep a Journal of its Proceedings, and from time to time publish the same, excepting such Parts as may in their Judgment require Secrecy; and the Yeas and Nays of the Members of either House on any question shall, at the Desire of one fifth of those Present, be entered on the Journal.

[4] Neither House, during the Session of Congress, shall without the Consent of the other, adjourn for more than three days, nor to any other Place than that in which the two Houses shall be sitting.

Section 6. [1] The Senators and Representatives shall receive a Compensation for their Services, to be ascertained by Law, and paid out of the Treasury of the United States. They shall in all Cases, except Treason, Felony and Breach of the Peace, be privileged from Arrest during their Attendance at the Session of their respective Houses, and in going to and returning from the same; and for any Speech or Debate in either House, they shall not be questioned in any other Place.

[2] No Senator or Representative shall, during the Time for which he was elected, be appointed to any civil Office under the Authority of the United States, which shall have been created, or the Emoluments whereof shall have been increased during such time; and no Person holding any Office under the United States, shall be a Member of either House during his Continuance in Office.

Section 7. [1] All Bills for raising Revenue shall originate in the House of Representatives; but the Senate may propose or concur with Amendments as on other Bills.

[2] Every Bill which shall have passed the House of Representatives and the Senate, shall, before it become a Law, be presented to the President of the United States; If he approve he shall sign it, but if not he shall return it, with his Objections at large on their Journal, and proceed to reconsider it. If after such Reconsideration two thirds of that House shall agree to pass the Bill, it shall be sent together with the Objections, to the other House, by which it shall likewise be reconsidered, and if approved by two thirds of that House, it shall become a Law. But in all such Cases the Votes of both Houses shall be determined by yeas and Nays, and the Names of the Persons voting for and against the Bill shall be entered on the Journal of each House respectively. If any Bill shall not be returned by the President within ten Days (Sundays excepted) after it shall have been presented to him, the Same shall be a Law, in like Manner as if he had signed it, unless the Congress by their Adjournment prevent its Return in which Case it shall not be a Law.

[3] Every Order, Resolution, or Vote, to Which the Concurrence of the Senate and House of Representatives may be necessary (except on a question of Adjournment) shall be presented to the President of the United States; and before the Same shall take Effect, shall be approved

by him, or being disapproved by him, shall be repassed by two thirds of the Senate and House of Representatives, according to the Rules and Limitations prescribed in the Case of a Bill.

Section 8. [1] The Congress shall have Power To lay and collect Taxes, Duties, Imposts and Excises, to pay the Debts and provide for the common Defence and general Welfare of the United States; but all Duties, Imposts and Excises shall be uniform throughout the United States;

[2] To borrow money on the credit of the United States;

[3] To regulate Commerce with foreign Nations, and among the several States, and with the Indian Tribes;

[4] To establish an uniform Rule of Naturalization, and uniform Laws on the subject of Bankruptcies throughout the United States;

[5] To coin Money, regulate the Value thereof, and of foreign Coin, and fix the Standard of Weights and Measures;

[6] To provide for the Punishment of counterfeiting the Securities and current Coin of the United States;

[7] To Establish Post Offices and Post Roads;

[8] To promote the Progress of Science and useful Arts, by securing for limited Times to Authors and Inventors the exclusive Right to their respective Writings and Discoveries;

[9] To constitute Tribunals inferior to the supreme Court;

[10] To define and punish Piracies and Felonies committed on the high Seas, and Offenses against the Law of Nations;

[11] To declare War, grant Letters of Marque and Reprisal, and make Rules concerning Captures on Land and Water;

[12] To raise and support Armies, but no Appropriation of Money to that Use shall be for a longer Term than two Years;

[13] To provide and maintain a Navy;

[14] To make Rules for the Government and Regulation of the land and naval Forces;

[15] To provide for calling forth the Militia to execute the Laws of the Union, suppress Insurrections and repel Invasions;

[16] To provide for organizing, arming, and disciplining, the Militia, and for governing such Part of them as may be employed in the Service of the United States, reserving to the States respectively, the Appointment of the Officers, and the Authority of training the Militia according to the discipline prescribed by Congress;

[17] To exercise exclusive Legislation in all Cases whatsoever, over such District (not exceeding ten Miles square) as may, by Cession of particular States, and the Acceptance of Congress, become the Seat of the Government of the United States, and to exercise like Authority over all Places purchased by the Consent of the Legislature of the State in

which the Same shall be, for the Erection of Forts, Magazines, Arsenals, dock-Yards, and other needful Buildings;—And

[18] To make all Laws which shall be necessary and proper for carrying into Execution the foregoing Powers, and all other Powers vested by this Constitution in the Government of the United States, or in any Department or Officer thereof.

Section 9. [1] The Migration or Importation of Such Persons as any of the States now existing shall think proper to admit, shall not be prohibited by the Congress prior to the Year one thousand eight hundred and eight, but a Tax or duty may be imposed on such Importation, not exceeding ten dollars for each Person.

[2] The privilege of the Writ of Habeas Corpus shall not be suspended, unless when in Cases of Rebellion or Invasion the public Safety may require it.

[3] No Bill of Attainder or ex post facto Law shall be passed.

[4] No Capitation, or other direct, Tax shall be laid, unless in Proportion to the Census or Enumeration herein before directed to be taken.

[5] No Tax or Duty shall be laid on Articles exported from any State.

[6] No Preference shall be given by any Regulation of Commerce or Revenue to the Ports of one State over those of another: nor shall Vessels bound to, or from, one State be obliged to enter, clear, or pay Duties in another.

[7] No money shall be drawn from the Treasury, but in Consequence of Appropriations made by Law; and a regular Statement and Account of the Receipts and Expenditures of all public Money shall be published from time to time.

[8] No Title of Nobility shall be granted by the United States: And no Person holding any Office of Profit or Trust under them, shall, without the Consent of the Congress, accept of any present, Emolument, Office, or Title, of any kind whatever, from any King, Prince, or foreign State.

Section 10. [1] No State shall enter into any Treaty, Alliance, or Confederation; grant Letters of Marque and Reprisal; coin Money; emit Bills of Credit; make any Thing but gold and silver Coin a Tender in Payment of Debts; pass any Bill of Attainder, ex post facto Law, or Law impairing the Obligation of Contracts, or grant any Title of Nobility.

[2] No State shall, without the Consent of the Congress, lay any Imposts or Duties on Imports or Exports, except what may be absolutely necessary for executing it's inspection Laws: and the net Produce of all Duties and Imposts, laid by any State on Imports or Exports, shall be for the Use of the Treasury of the United States; and all such Laws shall be subject to the Revision and Controul of the Congress.

[3] No State shall, without the Consent of Congress, lay any Duty of Tonnage, keep Troops, or Ships of War in time of Peace, enter into any Agreement or Compact with another State, or with a foreign Power, or engage in War, unless actually invaded, or in such imminent Danger as will not admit of delay.

Article II

Section 1. [1] The executive Power shall be vested in a President of the United States of America. He shall hold his Office during the Term of four Years, and, together with the Vice President, chosen for the same Term, be elected, as follows:

[2] Each State shall appoint, in such Manner as the Legislature thereof may direct, a Number of Electors, equal to the whole Number of Senators and Representatives to which the State may be entitled in the Congress; but no Senator or Representative, or Person holding an Office of Trust or Profit under the United States, shall be appointed an Elector.

[3] The Electors shall meet in their respective States, and vote by Ballot for two Persons, of whom one at least shall not be an Inhabitant of the same State with themselves. And they shall make a List of all the Persons voted for, and of the Number of Votes for each; which List they shall sign and certify, and transmit sealed to the Seat of the Government of the United States, directed to the President of the Senate. The President of the Senate shall, in the Presence of the Senate and House of Representatives, open all the Certificates, and the Votes shall then be counted. The Person having the greatest Number of Votes shall be the President, if such Number be a Majority of the whole Number of Electors appointed; and if there be more than one who have such Majority, and have an equal Number of Votes, then the House of Representatives shall immediately chuse by Ballot one of them for President; and if no Person have a Majority, then from the five highest on the List the said House shall in like Manner chuse the President. But in chusing the President, the Votes shall be taken by States the Representation from each State having one Vote; A quorum for this Purpose shall consist of a Member or Members from two thirds of the States, and a Majority of all the States shall be necessary to a Choice. In every Case, after the Choice of the President, the Person having the greater Number of Votes of the Electors shall be the Vice President. But if there should remain two or more who have equal Votes, the Senate shall chuse from them by Ballot the Vice President.

[4] The Congress may determine the Time of chusing the Electors, and the Day on which they shall give their Votes; which Day shall be the same throughout the United States.

[5] No person except a natural born Citizen, or a Citizen of the United States, at the time of the Adoption of this Constitution, shall be eligible to the Office of President; neither shall any Person be eligible to that Office who shall not have attained to the Age of thirty five Years, and been fourteen Years a Resident within the United States.

[6] In case of the removal of the President from Office, or of his Death, Resignation or Inability to discharge the Powers and Duties of the said Office, the Same shall devolve on the Vice President, and the Congress may by Law provide for the Case of Removal, Death, Resignation or Inability, both of the President and Vice President, declaring what Officer shall then act as President, and such Officer shall act accordingly, until the Disability be removed, or a President shall be elected.

[7] The President shall, at stated Times, receive for his Services, a Compensation, which shall neither be increased nor diminished during the Period for which he shall have been elected, and he shall not receive within that Period any other Emolument from the United States, or any of them.

[8] Before he enter on the Execution of his Office, he shall take the following Oath or Affirmation: "I do solemnly swear (or affirm) that I will faithfully execute the Office of President of the United States, and will to the best of my Ability, preserve, protect and defend the Constitution of the United States."

Section 2. [1] The President shall be Commander in Chief of the Army and Navy of the United States, and of the militia of the several States, when called into the actual Service of the United States; he may require the Opinion, in writing, of the principal Officer in each of the Executive Departments, upon any Subject relating to the Duties of their respective Offices, and he shall have Power to grant Reprieves and Pardons for Offenses against the United States, except in Cases of Impeachment.

[2] He shall have Power, by and with the Advice and Consent of the Senate to make Treaties, provided two thirds of the Senators present concur; and he shall nominate, and by and with the Advice and Consent of the Senate, shall appoint Ambassadors, other public Ministers and Consuls, Judges of the supreme Court, and all other Officers of the United States, whose Appointments are not herein otherwise provided for, and which shall be established by Law; but the Congress may by Law vest the Appointment of such inferior Officers, as they think proper, in the President alone, in the Courts of Law, or in the Heads of Departments.

[3] The President shall have Power to fill up all Vacancies that may happen during the Recess of the Senate, by granting Commissions which shall expire at the End of their next Session.

Section 3. He shall from time to time give to the Congress Information of the State of the Union, and recommend to their Consideration such Measures as he shall judge necessary and expedient; he may, on extraordinary Occasions, convene both Houses, or either of them, and in Case of Disagreement between them, with Respect to the Time of Adjournment, he may adjourn them to such Time as he shall think proper; he shall receive Ambassadors and other public Ministers; he shall take Care that the Laws be faithfully executed, and shall Commission all the Officers of the United States.

Section 4. The President, Vice President and all civil Officers of the United States, shall be removed from Office on Impeachment for, and Conviction of, Treason, Bribery, or other high Crimes and Misdemeanors.

ARTICLE III

Section 1. The judicial Power of the United States, shall be vested in one supreme Court, and in such inferior Courts as the Congress may from time to time ordain and establish. The Judges, both of the supreme and inferior Courts, shall hold their Offices during good Behaviour, and shall, at stated Times, receive for their Services a Compensation, which shall not be diminished during their Continuance in Office.

Section 2. [1] The Judicial Power shall extend to all Cases, in Law and Equity, arising under this Constitution, the Laws of the United States, and Treaties made, or which shall be made, under their Authority;—to all Cases affecting Ambassadors, other public Ministers and Consuls;—to all Cases of admiralty and maritime Jurisdiction;—to Controversies to which the United States shall be a Party;—to Controversies between two or more States;—between a State and Citizens of another State;—between Citizens of different States;—between Citizens of the same State claiming Lands under the Grants of different States, and between a State, or the Citizens thereof, and foreign States, Citizens or Subjects.

[2] In all Cases affecting Ambassadors, other public Ministers and Consuls, and those in which a State shall be a Party, the supreme Court shall have original Jurisdiction. In all the other Cases before mentioned, the supreme Court shall have appellate Jurisdiction, both as to Law and Fact, with such Exceptions, and under such Regulations as the Congress shall make.

[3] The trial of all Crimes, except in Cases of Impeachment, shall be by Jury; and such Trial shall be held in the State where the said Crimes shall have been committed; but when not committed within any State, the Trial shall be at such Place or Places as the Congress may by Law have directed.

Section 3. [1] Treason against the United States, shall consist only in levying War against them, or, in adhering to their Enemies, giving them Aid and Comfort. No Person shall be convicted of Treason unless on the Testimony of two Witnesses to the same overt Act, or on Confession in open Court.

[2] The Congress shall have Power to declare the Punishment of Treason, but no Attainder of Treason shall work Corruption of Blood, or Forfeiture except during the Life of the Person attainted.

Article IV

Section 1. Full Faith and Credit shall be given in each State to the public Acts, Records, and judicial Proceedings of every other State. And the Congress may by general Laws prescribe the Manner in which such Acts, Records and Proceedings shall be proved, and the Effect thereof.

Section 2. [1] The Citizens of each State shall be entitled to all Privileges and Immunities of Citizens in the several States.

[2] A Person charged in any State with Treason, Felony, or other Crime, who shall flee from Justice, and be found in another State, shall on demand of the executive Authority of the State from which he fled, be delivered up, to be removed to the State having Jurisdiction of the Crime.

[3] No Person held to Service or Labour in one State, under the Laws thereof, escaping into another, shall, in Consequence of any Law or Regulation therein, be discharged from such Service or Labour, but shall be delivered up on Claim of the Party to whom such Service or Labour may be due.

Section 3. [1] New States may be admitted by the Congress into this Union; but no new State shall be formed or erected within the Jurisdiction of any other State; nor any State be formed by the Junction of two or more States, or Parts of States, without the Consent of the Legislatures of the States concerned as well as of the Congress.

[2] The Congress shall have Power to dispose of and make all needful Rules and Regulations respecting the Territory or other Property belonging to the United States; and nothing in this Constitution shall be so construed as to Prejudice any Claims of the United States, or of any particular State.

Section 4. The United States shall guarantee to every State in this Union a Republican Form of Government, and shall protect each of them against Invasion; and on Application of the Legislature, or of the Executive (when the Legislature cannot be convened) against domestic Violence.

Article V

The Congress, whenever two thirds of both Houses shall deem it necessary, shall propose Amendments to this Constitution, or, on the Application of the Legislatures of two thirds of the several States, shall call a Convention for proposing Amendments, which, in either Case, shall be valid to all Intents and Purposes, as part of this Constitution, when ratified by the Legislatures of three fourths of the several States, or by Conventions in three fourths thereof, as the one or the other Mode of Ratification may be proposed by the Congress; Provided that no Amendment which may be made prior to the Year One thousand eight hundred and eight shall in any Manner affect the first and fourth Clauses in the Ninth Section of the first Article; and that no State, without its Consent, shall be deprived of its equal Suffrage in the Senate.

ARTICLE VI

[1] All Debts contracted and Engagements entered into, before the Adoption of this Constitution shall be as valid against the United States under this Constitution, as under the Confederation.

[2] This Constitution, and the Laws of the United States which shall be made in Pursuance thereof; and all Treaties made, or which shall be made, under the Authority of the United States, shall be the supreme Law of the Land; and the Judges in every State shall be bound thereby, any Thing in the Constitution or Laws of any State to the Contrary notwithstanding.

[3] The Senators and Representatives before mentioned, and the Members of the several State Legislatures, and all executive and judicial Officers, both of the United States and of the several States, shall be bound by Oath or Affirmation, to support this Constitution; but no religious Test shall ever be required as a Qualification to any Office or public Trust under the United States.

ARTICLE VII

The Ratification of the Conventions of nine States shall be sufficient for the Establishment of this Constitution between the States so ratifying the Same.

ARTICLES IN ADDITION TO, AND AMENDMENT OF, THE CONSTITUTION OF THE UNITED STATES OF AMERICA, PROPOSED BY CONGRESS, AND RATIFIED BY THE LEGISLATURES OF THE SEVERAL STATES PURSUANT TO THE FIFTH ARTICLE OF THE ORIGINAL CONSTITUTION.

AMENDMENT I [1791]

Congress shall make no law respecting an establishment of religion, or prohibiting the free exercise thereof; or abridging the freedom of speech, or of the press; or the right of the people peaceably to assemble, and to petition the Government for a redress of grievances.

AMENDMENT II [1791]

A well regulated Militia, being necessary to the security of a free State, the right of the people to keep and bear Arms, shall not be infringed.

AMENDMENT III [1791]

No Soldier shall, in time of peace be quartered in any house, without the consent of the Owner, nor in time of war, but in a manner to be prescribed by law.

AMENDMENT IV [1791]

The right of the people to be secure in their persons, houses, papers, and effects, against unreasonable searches and seizures, shall not be violated, and no Warrants shall issue, but upon probable cause, supported by Oath or affirmation and particularly describing the place to be searched, and the persons or things to be seized.

Amendment V [1791]

No person shall be held to answer for a capital, or otherwise infamous crime, unless on a presentment or indictment of a Grand Jury, except in cases arising in the land or naval forces, or in the Militia, when in actual service in time of War or public danger; nor shall any person be subject for the same offence to be twice put in jeopardy of life or limb; nor shall be compelled in any criminal case to be a witness against himself, nor be deprived of life, liberty, or property, without due process of law; nor shall private property be taken for public use, without just compensation.

Amendment VI [1791]

In all criminal prosecutions, the accused shall enjoy the right to a speedy and public trial, by an impartial jury of the State and district wherein the crime shall have been committed, which district shall have been previously ascertained by law, and to be informed of the nature and cause of the accusation; to be confronted with the witnesses against him; to have compulsory process for obtaining witnesses in his favor, and to have the Assistance of Counsel for his defence.

Amendment VII [1791]

In Suits at common law, where the value in controversy shall exceed twenty dollars, the right of trial by jury shall be preserved, and no fact tried by jury, shall be otherwise re-examined in any Court of the United States, than according to the rules of the common law.

Amendment VIII [1791]

Excessive bail shall not be required, nor excessive fines imposed, nor cruel and unusual punishments inflicted.

Amendment IX [1791]

The enumeration in the Constitution, of certain rights, shall not be construed to deny or disparage others retained by the people.

Amendment X [1791]

The powers not delegated to the United States by the Constitution, nor prohibited by it to the States, are reserved to the States respectively, or to the people.

* * *

Amendment XIV [1868]

Section 1. All persons born or naturalized in the United States, and subject to the jurisdiction thereof, are citizens of the United States and of the State wherein they reside. No State shall make or enforce any law which shall abridge the privileges or immunities of citizens of the United States; nor shall any State deprive any person of life, liberty, or property, without due process of law; nor deny to any person within its jurisdiction the equal protection of the laws.

Section 2. Representatives shall be apportioned among the several States according to their respective numbers, counting the whole number of persons in each State, excluding Indians not taxed. But when the right to vote at any election for the choice of electors for President and Vice President of the United States, Representatives in Congress, the Executive and Judicial officers of a State, or the members of the Legislature thereof, is denied to any of the male inhabitants of such State, being twenty-one years of age, and citizens of the United States, or in any way abridged, except for participation in rebellion, or other crime, the basis of representation therein shall be reduced in the proportion which the number of such male citizens shall bear to the whole number of male citizens twenty-one years of age in such State.

Section 3. No person shall be a Senator or Representative in Congress, or elector of President and Vice President, or hold any office, civil or military, under the United States, or under any State, who having previously taken an oath, as a member of Congress, or as an officer of the United States, or as a member of any State legislature, or as an executive or judicial officer of any State, to support the Constitution of the United States, shall have engaged in insurrection or rebellion against the same, or given aid or comfort to the enemies thereof. But Congress may by a vote of two-thirds of each House, remove such disability.

Section 4. The validity of the public debt of the United States, authorized by law, including debts incurred for payment of pensions and bounties for services in suppressing insurrection or rebellion, shall not be questioned. But neither the United States nor any State shall assume or pay any debt or obligation incurred in aid of insurrection or rebellion against the United States, or any claim for the loss or emancipation of any slave; but all such debts, obligations and claims shall be held illegal and void.

Section 5. The Congress shall have power to enforce, by appropriate legislation, the provisions of this article.

AMENDMENT XV [1870]

Section 1. The right of citizens of the United States to vote shall not be denied or abridged by the United States or by any State on account of race, color, or previous condition of servitude.

Section 2. The Congress shall have power to enforce this article by appropriate legislation.

* * *

AMENDMENT XIX [1920]

[1] The right of citizens of the United States to vote shall not be denied or abridged by the United States or by any State on account of sex.

[2] Congress shall have power to enforce this article by appropriate legislation.

* * *

AMENDMENT XXIV [1964]

Section 1. The right of citizens of the United States to vote in any primary or other election for President or Vice President, for electors for President or Vice President, or for Senator or Representative in Congress, shall not be denied or abridged by the United States or any State by reason of failure to pay any poll tax or other tax.

Section 2. The Congress shall have power to enforce this article by appropriate legislation.

* * *

AMENDMENT XXVI [1971]

Section 1. The right of citizens of the United States, who are eighteen years of age or older, to vote shall not be denied or abridged by the United States or by any State on account of age.

Section 2. The Congress shall have power to enforce this article by appropriate legislation.

VIII. SELECTED IMMIGRATION FORMS

Form

Basic documents
- I–94, Arrival–Departure record
- Sample nonimmigrant visa
- I–551, Permanent resident card
- I–797B, Notice of action
- Border crossing card
- G–28, Notice of entry of appearance as attorney or representative

Petitions and applications
- I–129, Petition for nonimmigrant worker
- I–130, Petition for alien relative
- I–751, Petition to remove the conditions on residence
- I–140, Immigrant petition for alien worker
- ETA 750, Application for alien employment certification
- I–485, Application to register permanent residence or adjust status
- I–589, Application for asylum and withholding of removal

Visa application
- OF–156, Nonimmigrant visa application
- OF–230, Application for immigrant visa and alien registration

Affidavits of support
- I–864, Affidavit of support under section 213A of the Act
- I–864A, Contract between sponsor and household member

Employment
- I–9, Employment eligibility verification
- M–274, Handbook for employers, instructions for completing Form I–9
- I–765, Application for employment authorization

Administrative removal
- I–851, Notice of intent to issue final administrative removal order
- I–851A, Final administrative removal order

Expedited removal
- I–867AB, Record of sworn statement in proceedings under section 235(b)(1) of the Act
- M–444, Information about credible fear interview
- I–869 Record of negative credible fear finding and request for review by immigration judge
- I–863, Notice of referral to immigration judge
- I–860, Notice and order of expedited removal

Immigration court
- I–862, Notice to appear
- EOIR–42A, Application for cancellation of removal for certain permanent residents
- EOIR–42B, Application for cancellation of removal and adjustment of status for certain nonpermanent residents

Naturalization
- N–400, Application for naturalization

Form I–94 Arrival–Departure record

U.S. Department of Justice
Immigration and Naturalization Service

OMB 1115-0077

Admission Number

Welcome to the United States

927188900 03

I-94 Arrival/Departure Record - Instructions

This form must be completed by all persons except U.S. Citizens, returning resident aliens, aliens with immigrant visas, and Canadian Citizens visiting or in transit.

Type or print legibly with pen in ALL CAPITAL LETTERS. Use English. Do not write on the back of this form.

This form is in two parts. Please complete both the Arrival Record (Items 1 through 13) and the Departure Record (Items 14 through 17).

When all items are completed, present this form to the U.S. Immigration and Naturalization Service Inspector.

Item 7 - If you are entering the United States by land, enter **LAND** in this space. If you are entering the United States by ship, enter **SEA** in this space.

Form I-94 (04-15-86)1

Admission Number

927188900 03

Immigration and
Naturalization Service

I-94
Arrival Record

1. Family Name
2. First (Given) Name
3. Birth Date (Day Mo Yr)
4. Country of Citizenship
5. Sex (Male or Female)
6. Passport Number
7. Airline and Flight Number
8. Country Where You Live
9. City Where You Boarded
10. City Where Visa Was Issued
11. Date Issued (Day Mo Yr)
12. Address While in the United States (Number and Street)
13. City and State

Departure Number

927188900 03

Immigration and
Naturalization Service

I-94
Departure Record

14. Family Name
15. First (Given) Name
16. Birth Date (Day Mo Yr)
17. Country of Citizenship

SAMPLE

See Other Side

STAPLE HERE

This Side For Government Use Only

Primary Inspection

Applicant's Name ____________

Date Referred ________ Time ________ Insp. # ________

Reason Referred

☐ 212A ☐ PP ☐ Visa ☐ Parole ☐ SLB ☐ TWOV

☐ Other ____________

Secondary Inspection

End Secondary Time ________ Insp. # ________

Disposition ____________

18. Occupation	19. Waivers
20. INS File A -	21. INS FCO
22. Petition Number	23. Program Number
24. ☐ Bond	25. ☐ Prospective Student

26. Itinerary/Comments

27. TWOV Ticket Number

Warning - A nonimmigrant who accepts unauthorized employment is subject to deportation.

Important - Retain this permit in your possession; ***you must surrender it when you leave the U.S.*** Failure to do so may delay your entry into the U.S. in the future.

You are authorized to stay in the U.S. only until the date written on this form. To remain past this date, without permission from immigration authorities, is a violation of the law.

Surrender this permit when you leave the U.S.:
- By sea or air, to the transportation line;
- Across the Canadian border, to a Canadian Official;
- Across the Mexican border, to a U.S. Official.

Students planning to reenter the U.S. within 30 days to return to the same school, see "Arrival-Departure" on page 2 of Form I-20 **prior to surrendering this permit.**

Record of Changes

Port: **Departure Record**

Date:

Carrier:

Flight #/Ship Name:

For sale by the Superintendent of Documents, U.S. Government Printing Office
Washington, D.C. 20402 [G20,903]

Sample Nonimmigrant Visa

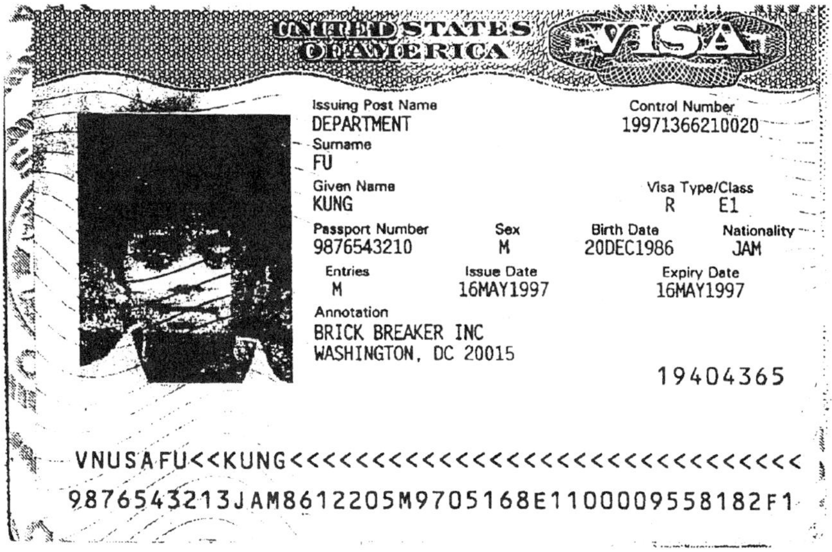

UNITED STATES OF AMERICA VISA

Issuing Post Name
DEPARTMENT

Control Number
19971366210020

Surname
FU

Given Name
KUNG

Visa Type/Class
R E1

Passport Number
9876543210

Sex
M

Birth Date
20DEC1986

Nationality
JAM

Entries
M

Issue Date
16MAY1997

Expiry Date
16MAY1997

Annotation
BRICK BREAKER INC
WASHINGTON, DC 20015

19404365

VNUSAFU<<KUNG<<<<<<<<<<<<<<<<<<<<<<<<<<<<<<<<<<<
9876543213JAM8612205M9705168E1100009558182F1

Form I–551 Permanent resident card

PERMANENT RESIDENT CARD

NAME CRITTENDEN, LEE W.

INS A# 022-345-679

Birthdate Category Sex

10/04/49 P26 M

Country of Birth

Canada

CARD EXPIRES 11/01/94

Resident Since 11/01/97

C1USA0223456791EAC9730050225<<

4910040M9411014CAN<<<<<<<<<<<<8

CRITTENDEN<<LEE<W<<<<<<<<<<<<<<

Form I–797B Notice of action

U.S. Department of Justice
Immigration and Naturalization Service

Notice of Action

THE UNITED STATES OF AMERICA

SPECIMEN

Form I 797B (Rev. 09/07/93)N

[G20,864]

- *Please save the upper portion of this notice for your records. Please enclose a copy if you have to write us or a U.S. Consulate about this case, or if you file another application based on this decision.*
- *You will be notified separately about any other applications or petitions you have filed.*

Additional Information

GENERAL.
The filing of an application or petition does not in itself allow a person to enter the United States and does not confer any other right or benefit.

INQUIRIES.
You should contact the office listed on the reverse of this notice if you have questions about the notice, or questions about the status of your application or petition. *We recommend you call.* However, if you write us, please enclose a copy of this notice with your letter.

APPROVAL OF NONIMMIGRANT PETITION.
Approval of a nonimmigrant petition means that the person for whom it was filed has been found eligible for the requested classification. If this notice indicated we are notifying a U. S. Consulate about the approval for the purpose of visa issuance, and you or the person you filed for have questions about visa issuance, please contact the appropriate U. S. Consulate directly.

APPROVAL OF AN IMMIGRANT PETITION.
Approval of an immigrant petition does not convey any right or status. The approved petition simply establishes a basis upon which the person you filed for can apply for an immigrant or fiance(e) visa or for adjustment of status.

A person is not guaranteed issuance of a visa or a grant of adjustment simply because this petition is approved. Those processes look at additional criteria.

If this notice indicates we have approved the immigrant petition you filed, and have forwarded it to the Department of State Immigrant Visa Processing Center, that office will contact the person you filed the petition for directly with information about visa issuance.

In addition to the information on the reverse of this notice, the instructions for the petition you filed provide additional information about processing after approval of the petition.

For more information about whether a person who is already in the U. S. can apply for adjustment of status, please see Form I-485, *Application to Register Permanent Residence or Adjust Status.*

ATTACHMENT FOR ALIEN WORKER
For your convenience this notice is prepared in two parts. You may retain the notice for your records. If the alien worker(s) needs to apply for a visa at an American Consulate, you may detach the lower portion and forward it to the alien worker(s). The alien worker(s) will then use the detached portion to apply for a visa at an American Consulate, or, if no visa is required, when applying for admission to the United States.

NOTICE TO ALIEN WORKER
This portion of the notice is provided for use when applying for a visa at an American Consulate, or, if no visa is required, when applying for admission to the United States.

[G20,985]

Border crossing card

USA B1/B2 VISA/BCC

NAME SAMPLE, KARLA BRIGITTE

Birthdate Sex

12/19/82 F

Nationality MEX

VISA/BCC EXPIRES 04/28/08

VISA/BCC ISSUED 04/29/98

U.S. Employment NOT Authorized

VBUSA9230002<<0<DPT000007869<<

8212199F0804286MEXDPT1998119<0

SAMPLE<<KARLA<BRIGITTE<<<<<<<<

Form G–28 Notice of entry of appearance as attorney or representative

NOTICE OF ENTRY OF APPEARANCE AS ATTORNEY OR REPRESENTATIVE

In re:	DATE
	FILE No.

I hereby enter my appearance as attorney for (or representative of), and at the request of, the following named person(s):

NAME — ☐ Petitioner ☐ Applicant ☐ Beneficiary ☐

ADDRESS (Apt. No.) (Number & Street) (City) (State) (ZIP Code)

NAME — ☐ Petitioner ☐ Applicant ☐ Beneficiary ☐

ADDRESS (Apt. No.) (Number & Street) (City) (State) (ZIP Code)

Check applicable Item(s) below:

☐ 1. I am an attorney and a member in good standing of the bar of the Supreme Court of the United States or of the highest court of the following State, territory, insular possession, or District of Columbia

_______________ _______________ and am not under a
(Name of Court)

court or administrative agency order suspending, enjoining, restraining, disbarring, or otherwise restricting me in practicing law.

☐ 2. I am an accredited representative of the following named religious, charitable, social service, or similar organization established in the United States and which is so recognized by the Board:

☐ 3. I am associated with _______________,
the attorney of record who previously filed a notice of appearance in this case and my appearance is at his request. (If you check this item, also check item 1 or 2 whichever is appropriate.)

☐ 4. Others (Explain fully.)

SIGNATURE	COMPLETE ADDRESS
NAME (Type or Print)	TELEPHONE NUMBER

PURSUANT TO THE PRIVACY ACT OF 1974, I HEREBY CONSENT TO THE DISCLOSURE TO THE FOLLOWING NAMED ATTORNEY OR REPRESENTATIVE OF ANY RECORD PERTAINING TO ME WHICH APPEARS IN ANY IMMIGRATION AND NATURALIZATION SERVICE SYSTEM OF RECORDS: _______________
(Name of Attorney or Representative)

THE ABOVE DISCLOSURE IS IN CONNECTION WITH THE FOLLOWING MATTER:

NAME OF PERSON CONSENTING	SIGNATURE OF PERSON CONSENTING	DATE

(NOTE: Execution of this box is required under the Privacy Act of 1974 where the person being represented is a citizen of the United States or an alien lawfully admitted for permanent residence.)

Form G-28
(Rev. 10-25-79)N

(OVER)

UNITED STATES DEPARTMENT OF JUSTICE
Immigration and Naturalization Service

APPEARANCES -An appearance shall be filed on Form G-28 by the attorney or representative appearing in each case. Thereafter, substitution may be permitted upon the written withdrawal of the attorney or representative of record or upon notification of the new attorney or representative. When an appearance is made by a person acting in a representative capacity, his personal appearance or signature shall constitute a representation that under the provisions of this chapter he is authorized and qualified to represent. Further proof of authority to act in a representative capacity may be required.

AVAILABILITY OF RECORDS -During the time a case is pending, and except as otherwise provided in 8 CFR 103.2(b), a party to a proceeding or his attorney or representative shall be permitted to examine the record of proceeding in a Service office. He may, in conformity with 8 CFR 103.10, obtain copies of Service records or information therefrom and copies of documents or transcripts of evidence furnished by him. Upon request, he may, in addition, be loaned a copy of the testimony and exhibits contained in the record of proceeding upon giving his receipt for such copies and pledging that it will be surrendered upon final disposition of the case or upon demand. If extra copies of exhibits do not exist, they shall not be furnished free on loan; however, they shall be made available for copying or purchase of copies as provided in 8 CFR 103.10.

" THIS FORM MAY NOT BE USED TO REQUEST RECORDS UNDER THE FREEDOM OF INFORMATION ACT OR THE PRIVACY ACT. THE MANNER OF REQUESTING SUCH RECORDS IS CONTAINED IN 8 CFR 103.10 AND 103.20 ET. SEQ."

Form I–129 Petition for a nonimmigrant worker

U.S. Department of Justice
Immigration and Naturalization Service

OMB NO. 1115-0168
Instructions for Form I-129

Purpose Of This Form.

This form is for an employer to petition for an alien to come to the U.S. temporarily to perform services or labor, or to receive training, as an H-1A, H-1B, H-2A, H-2B, H-3, L-1, O-1, P-2, or Q nonimmigrant worker.

This form is also for an employer to petition for an extension of stay or change of status for an alien as an E-1, E-2, R-1 or TC nonimmigrant. A petition is not required to apply for an E-1, E-2 or R-1 nonimmigrant visa or admission as a TC nonimmigrant. A petition is only required to apply for a change to such status or an extension of stay in such status.

This form consists of a basic petition, and different supplements that apply to each specific classification.

Who May File.

General. A U.S. employer may file to classify an alien in any nonimmigrant classification listed below. A foreign employer may file for certain classifications as indicated in the specific instructions.

Agents. A U.S. individual or company in business as an agent may file for types of workers who are traditionally self-employed or who traditionally use an agent to arrange short-term employment with numerous employers. A petition filed by an agent must include a complete itinerary of services or engagements, including dates, names and addresses of the actual employers, and the locations where the services will be performed. The agent must guarantee the wage offered and the other terms and conditions of employment by contract with the alien(s).

Including more than one alien in a petition. Aliens who will apply for their visas at the same consulate or, if they do not need visas, will enter at the same port of entry may be included in one petition filed by an employer or agent in the following classifications if the dates of employment are the same:

- H-1B if they are members of the same entertainment group or athletic team (accompanying aliens must be filed for on a separate petition);
- H-1B accompanying aliens if they will accompany the same H-1B or same H-1B group of artists, entertainers or athletes for the same period of time, in the same occupation, and in the same location(s);
- H2-A if they are included on the same labor certification and will perform the same duties;
- H-2B if they are included on the same labor certification and will perform the same duties;
- H-3 if they will receive the same training;
- P-2 if they are members of the same group (accompanying aliens must be filed for on a separate petition);
- P-2 accompanying aliens if they will accompany the same P-2 alien or group for the same period of time, in the same occupation, and in the same location(s);
- Q if they will be involved in the same international cultural exchange program.

Multiple locations. A petition for alien(s) to perform services or labor or receive training in more than one location must include an itinerary with the dates and locations where the services or training will take place.

Unnamed aliens. All aliens in a petition for an extension of stay or change of status must be named in the petition. All aliens included in any other petition must be named except:

- an H-2A petition for more than one worker may include unnamed aliens if they are unnamed on the labor certification;
- an H-2B petition for more than one worker may include unnamed aliens in emergent situations where you establish in the petition that you cannot yet provide names due to circumstances which you could not anticipate or control.

Where some or all of the aliens are not named, specify the total number of unnamed aliens and total number of aliens in the petition. Where the aliens must be named, petitions naming subsequent beneficiaries may be filed later with a copy of the same labor certification. Each petition must reference all previously filed petitions using that certification.

General Filing Instructions.
Complete the basic form and relating supplement. Indicate the specific classification you are requesting. Please answer all questions by typing or clearly printing in black ink. Indicate that an item is not applicable with "N/A". If the answer is "none," write "none". If you need extra space to answer any item, attach a sheet of paper with your name and your alien registration number (A#), if any, and indicate the number of the item to which the answer refers. You must file your petition with the required Initial Evidence. The petition must be properly signed and filed with the proper fee. Submit the petition in duplicate if you check block "a" or "b" in question 4 of Part 2 on the form.

Classification; Initial Evidence.
These instructions are divided into two parts. The first looks at classifications which require a petition for an initial visa or entry and for any extension or change of status. The second looks at those classifications which only require a petition for a change of status or extension of stay.

▸ **Petition always required:** The following classifications always require a petition. A petition for new or concurrent employment or for extension where there is a change in previously approved employment must be filed with the initial evidence listed below, and with the initial evidence required by the separate instructions for a change of status or extension of stay. However, a petition for an extension based on unchanged, previously approved employment need only be filed with the initial evidence required in the separate extension of stay instructions.

H-1A. An H-1A is an alien coming to perform services as a registered professional nurse. The petition must be filed by a U.S. employer that provides health care services (including nursing contractors), and must be filed with:

- evidence the alien has a full and unrestricted license to practice professional nursing in the country where he or she obtained nursing education, or that the nursing education was received in the U.S. or Canada;
- evidence the alien has either;
  - passed the test given by the Commission on Graduate of Foreign Nursing Schools (CGFNS),
  - a permanent license to practice professional nursing in the state of intended employment, or
  - a permanent license to practice professional nursing in any state or territory of the U.S. and has temporary authorization to practice professional nursing in the state of intended employment;
- evidence the alien is fully qualified and eligible under the laws of the state or territory of intended employment to work as a professional nurse immediately after entry;
- a statement indicating you intend to employ the alien solely as a registered professional nurse; and
- a copy of the Department of Labor's current notice of acceptance of the filing of your attestation on Form ETA 9029.

H-1B. An H-1B is an alien coming temporarily to perform services in a specialty occupation. A specialty occupation is one which requires the theoretical and practical application of a body of highly specialized knowledge to fully perform the occupation and requires completion of a specific course of education culminating in a baccalaureate degree in a specific occupational specialty. Write **H-1B1** in the classification requested block. The petition must be filed by the U.S. employer, and must be filed with:

- an approved labor condition application from the Department of Labor;
- evidence the proposed employment qualifies as within a specialty occupation;
- evidence the alien has the required degree by submitting either:
  - a copy of the person's U.S. baccalaureate or higher degree which is required by the specialty occupation,
  - a copy of a foreign degree and evidence it is equivalent to the U.S. degree, or
  - evidence of education and experience which is equivalent to the required U.S. degree;
- a copy of any required license or other official permission to practice the occupation in the state of intended employment; and
- a copy of any written contract between you and the alien or a summary of the terms of the oral agreement under which the alien will be employed.

H1-B. An H-1B is also an alien coming to perform services of an exceptional nature relating to a cooperative research and development project administered by the Department of Defense. A U.S. employer may file the petition. Write **H-1B2** in the classification requested block. It must be filed with:

- a description of the proposed employment and evidence the services and project meet the above conditions; and
- a statement listing the names of all aliens who are not permanent residents who are have been employed on the project within the past year, along with their dates of employment.

H-1B. An H-1B is also an artist, entertainer or fashion model who has national or international acclaim and recognition for achievements, individually or, in the case of entertainers, as part of a group, to be employed in a capacity requiring someone of distinguished merit and ability. (See the separate instructions for accompanying personnel.) A U.S. employer or foreign employer may file the petition. Write **H-1B3** in the classification requested block. It must be filed with:

- copies of evidence the alien or group is nationally or internationally recognized in the discipline by submitting at least 3 different types of documentation showing that the group:
  - has performed and will perform as a starring or leading entertainment group in productions or events which have a distinguished reputation as evidenced by critical reviews, advertisements, publicity releases, publications, or contracts,
  - has achieved national or international recognition and acclaim for outstanding achievement in their field as evidenced by reviews in major newspapers, trade journals, magazines, or other published material,
  - has received significant national or international awards or prizes for outstanding achievement in their field,
  - has performed and will perform services as a leading or starring group for organizations and establishments that have a distinguished reputation,
  - has a record of major commercial or critically acclaimed successes, as evidenced by such indicators as ratings, or standing in the field, box office receipts, record, cassette, or video sales, and other achievements in the field as reported in trade journals, major newspapers, or other publications,
  - has received significant recognition for achievements from organizations, critics, government agencies or other recognized experts in the field,
  - has received significant recognition for achievements from organizations, critics, government agencies or other recognized experts in the field,
  - commands a high salary or other substantial remuneration for services, evidenced by contracts or other reliable evidence;
- copies of evidence the services to be performed require a person of distinguished merit and ability and either:
  - involve an event, production or activity which has a distinguished reputation; or
  - the services are as a lead or starring participant in a distinguished activity for an organization or establishment that has a distinguished reputation or record of employing persons of distinguished merit and ability.

H-1B. An H-1B is also an alien coming temporarily to perform as an artist or entertainer, individually or as part of a group, in a unique or traditional art form. (See the separate instructions for accompanying personnel.) A U.S. employer or foreign employer may file the petiion. Write **H-1B4** in the classification requested block. It must be filed with:

- a description of the proposed activities and evidence they constitute a unique or traditional art form;
- affidavits, testimonials or letters from recognized experts attesting to the authenticity and excellence of the skills of the alien or group in presenting the unique or traditional art form and explaining the level of recognition accorded the alien or group in the native country and the U.S.;

- copies of evidence most of the performances or presentations will be culturally unique events sponsored by educational, cultural, or governmental agencies; and
- either:
  - an affidavit or testimonial from the ministry of culture, USIA Cultural Affairs Officer, the academy for the artistic discipline, a leading scholar, a cultural institution, or a major university in the alien's own country or from a third country,
  - a letter from a U.S. expert who has knowledge in the particular field, such as scholar, arts, administrator, critic, or representative of a cultural organization or government agency, or
  - a letter or certification from a U.S. government cultural or arts agency such as the Smithsonian Institution, the National Endowment for the Arts, the National Endowment for the Humanities, or the Library of Congress.

H-1B. An H-1B is also an alien coming temporarily to perform at a specific athletic competition as an athlete, individually or as part of a group or team, at a nationally or internationally recognized level of performance. (See the separate instructions for accompanying personnel.) A U.S. employer or foreign employer may file the petition. Write **H-1B5** in the classification requested block. The petition must be filed with:

- a copy of the contract with a major U.S. sports league or team or contract in an individual sport commensurate with national or international recognition in that sport.
- copies of evidence of at least 2 of the following:
  - participation to a substantial extent in a prior season with a major U.S. sports league,
  - participation in international competition with a national team,
  - participation to a substantial extent in a prior season for a U.S. college or university in intercollegiate competition,
  - a written statement from an official of a major U.S. sports league or an official of the governing body of the sport detailing how the alien or team is nationally orinternationally recognized,
  - a written statement from a member of the sports media or a recognized expert in the sport detailing how the alien or team is nationally or internationally recognized,
  - the individual or team is ranked if the sport has national or international rankings, or
  - the alien or team has received a significant honor or award in the sport.

H-1B Accompanying Support Personnel. Accompanying support personnel are highly skilled aliens coming temporarily as an essential and integral part of the competition or performance of a **H-1B** artist, entertainer or athlete because they perform support services which cannot be readily performed by a U.S. worker and which are essential to the successful performance or services by the H-1B. The aliens must each also have significant prior work experience with the H-1B alien. Write ***H-1BS*** in the classification requested block on the petition. The petition must be filed in conjunction with the employment of a H-1B alien. The petition must be filed with:

- a statement describing the alien's prior and current essentiality, critical skills and experience with the H-1B;
- statements or affidavits from persons with first hand knowledge that the alien has had substantial experience performing the critical skills and essential support services for the H-1B; and
- a copy of any written contract between you and the alien or a summary of the terms of the oral agreement under which the alien will be employed.

H-2A. An H-2A is an alien coming temporarily to engage in temporary or seasonal agricultural employment. The petition must be filed by a U.S. employer or an association of U.S. agricultural producers named as a joint employer on the certification. The petition must be filed with:

- a single valid temporary agricultural labor certification, or, if U.S. workers do not appear at the worksite, a copy of the Department of Labor's denial of a certification and appeal, and evidence that qualified domestic labor is unavailable; and
- copies of evidence that each named alien met the minimum job requirements stated in the certification when it was applied for.

H-2B. An H-2B is an alien coming temporarily to engage in non-agricultural employment which is seasonal, intermittent, to meet a peak load need, or for a one-time occurrence. The petition must be filed by a U.S. employer with:

- either:
  - a temporary labor certification from the Department of Labor, or the Governor of Guam if the proposed employment is solely in Guam, indicating that qualified U.S. workers are not available and that employment of the alien will not adversely affect the wages and working conditions of similarly employed U.S. workers, or
  - a notice from such authority that such certification cannot be made, along with evidence of the unavailability of U.S. workers and of the prevailing wage rate for the occupation in the U.S., and evidence overcoming each reason why the certification was not granted; and
- copies of evidence, such as employment letters and training certificates, that each named alien met the minimum job requirements stated in the certification when it was applied for.

H-3. An H-3 is an alien coming temporarily to participate in a special education training program in the education of children with physical, mental, or emotional disabilities. Custodial care of children must be incidental to the training program. The petition must be filed by the U.S. employer with:

- a description of the training, staff and facilities, evidence the program meets the above conditions, and details of the alien's participation in the program; and
- evidence the alien is nearing completion of a baccalaureate degree in special education, or already holds such a degree, or has extensive prior training and experience in teaching children with physical, mental, or emotional disabilities.

H-3. An H-3 is also an alien coming temporarily to receive other training from an employer in any field other than graduate education or training. The petition must be filed by the U.S. employer with:

- a detailed description of the structured training program, including the number of classroom hours per week and the number of hours of on-the-job training per week;
- a summary of the prior training and experience of each alien in the petition; and
- an explanation of why the training is required, whether similar training is available in the alien's country, how the training will benefit the alien in pursuing a career abroad, and why you will incur the cost of providing the training without significant productive labor.

L-1. An L-1 is an alien coming temporarily to perform services in a managerial or executive capacity, for the same corporation or firm, or for the branch, subsidiary or affiliate of the employer which employed him or her abroad for one continuous year within the three-year period immediately preceding the filing of the petition, in an executive, managerial or specialized knowledge capacity. Write **L-1A** in the classification requested block on the petition.

L-1. An L-1 is also an alien coming temporarily to perform services which entail specialized knowledge, for the same corporation or firm, or for the branch, subsidiary or affiliate of the employer which employed him or her abroad for one continuous year within the three year period immediately preceding the filing of the petition, in an executive, managerial or specialized knowledge capacity. Specialized knowledge is special knowledge of the employer's product or its application in international markets or an advanced level of the knowledge of the employer's processes and procedures. Write **L-1B** in the classification requested block on the petition.

L Petition Requirements. A U.S. employer or foreign employer may file the petition, but a foreign employer must have a legal business entity in the U.S. The petition must be filed with:

- evidence of the qualifying relationship between the U.S. and foreign employer based on ownership and control, such as an annual report, articles of incorporation, financial statements or copies of stock certificates;

- a letter from the alien's foreign qualifying employer detailing his/her dates of employment, job duties, qualifications and salary, demonstrating that the alien worked for the employer for at least one continuous year in the three-year period preceding the filing of the petition in an executive, managerial or specialized knowledge capacity; and
- a description of the proposed job duties and qualifications and evidence the proposed employment is in an executive, managerial or specialized knowledge capacity.

If the alien is coming to the U.S. to open a new office, also file the petition with copies of evidence the business entity in the U.S.:
- already has sufficient premises to house the new office;
- has or upon establishment will have the qualifying relationship to the foreign employer;
- has the financial ability to remunerate the alien and to begin doing business in the U.S., including evidence about the size of the U.S. investment, the organizational structure of both firms, the financial size and condition of the foreign employer, and, if the alien is coming as an L-1 manager or executive to open a new office, such evidence must establish that the intended U.S. operation will support the executive or managerial position within one year.

Blanket L petition. An L blanket petition simplifies the process of later filing for individual L-1A workers and L-1B workers who are specialized knowledge professionals, which are persons who possess specialized knowledge employed in positions which require the theoretical and practical application of a body of highly specialized knowledge to fully perform the occupation and require completion of a specific course of education culminating in a baccalaureate degree in a specific occupational specialty.

A blanket L petition must be filed by a U.S. employer who will be the single representative between INS and the qualifying organizations. Write LZ in the classification requested block. Do not name an individual employee. File the petition with copies of evidence that:

- you and your branches, subsidiaries and affiliates are engaged in commercial trade or services;
- you have an office in the U.S. that has been doing business for one year or more;
- you have 3 or more domestic and foreign branches, subsidiaries, or affiliates;
- you and your qualifying organizations have obtained approved petitions for at least 10 "L" managers, executives or specialized knowledge professionals during the previous 12 months, have U.S. subsidiaries or affiliates with combined annual sales of at least 25 million dollars, or have a U.S. work force of at least 1,000 employees.

After approval of a blanket petition, you may file for individual employees to enter as an L-1A alien or L-1B specialized knowledge professional under the blanket petition. If the alien is outside the U.S., file Form I-129S. If the alien is already in the U.S., file the I-129 to request a change of status based on this blanket petition. The petition must be filed with:
- a copy of the approval notice for the blanket petition;
- a letter from the alien's foreign qualifying employer detailing his/her dates of employment, job duties, qualifications, and salary for the 3 previous years; and
- if the alien is a specialized knowledge professional, a copy of a U.S. degree, a foreign degree equivalent to a U.S. degree, or evidence establishing the combination of the beneficiary's education and experience is the equivalent of a U.S. degree.

O-1. An O-1 is an alien coming temporarily who has extraordinary ability in the sciences,education or business. A U.S. employer or foreign employer may file the petition. The petition must be filed with:
- a written consultation with a peer group in the alien's area of ability (see GENERAL EVIDENCE);
- a copy of any written contract between you and the alien or a summary of the terms of the oral agreement under which the alien will be employed.
- copies of evidence the services to be performed either:

   - primarily involve a specific scientific or educational project, conference, convention, lecture, or exhibit sponsored by scientific or educational organizations or establishments, or
   - consist of a specific business project that requires an extraordinary executive, manager, or highly technical person due to the complexity of the project;
- evidence the alien has received a major, internationally-recognized award, such as a Nobel Prize, or copies of evidence of at least three of the following:
   - *receipt of nationally or internationally recognized prizes or awards for excellence in the field of endeavor,*
   - *membership in associations in the field* which require outstanding achievements as judged by recognized international experts,
   - published material in professional or major trade publications or newspapers about the alien and his work in the field,
   - participation on a panel or individually as a judge of the work of others in the field or an allied field,
   - original scientific or scholarly research contributions of major significance in the field,
   - authorship of scholarly articles in the field in professional journals or other major media, or
   - *evidence the alien commands a high* salary or other high remuneration for services.

P-2. A P-2 is an alien coming temporarily to perform as an artist or entertainer, individually or as part of a group, under a reciprocal exchange program between an organization in the U.S. and an organization in another country. (See the separate instructions for accompanying personnel.) The petition must be filed by the sponsoring organization or employer in the U.S. It must be filed with:

- written consultation with an appropriate labor organization (see GENERAL EVIDENCE);
- a copy of the formal reciprocal exchange agreement between the U.S. organization(s) sponsoring the aliens, and the organization(s) in a foreign country which will receive the U.S. artist or entertainers;
- a statement from the sponsoring organization describing the reciprocal exchange, including the name of the receiving organization abroad, names and occupations of U.S. artists or entertainers being sent abroad, length of their stay, activities in which they will be engaged and the terms and conditions of their employment; and
- *copies of evidence the aliens and the U.S.* artists or entertainers are experienced artists with comparable skills and that the terms and conditions of employment are similar.

P-2 Accompanying Support Personnel. Accompanying support personnel are highly skilled aliens coming temporarily as an essential and integral part of the competition or performance of a P-2, or because they perform support services which cannot be readily performed by a U.S. worker and which are essential to the successful performance or services by the P-2. The aliens must each also have significant prior work experience with the P-2 alien. Write *P-2S* in the classification requested block on the petition. The petition must be filed in conjunction with the employment of a P-2 alien. The petition must be filed with:

- *written consultation with a labor organization* in the skill in which the alien will be involved (see GENERAL EVIDENCE);
- *a statement describing the alien's prior and* current essentiality, critical skills and experience with the P-2;
- *statements or affidavits from persons with* first hand knowledge that the alien has had substantial experience performing the critical skills and essential support services for the P-2, and
- a copy of any written contract between you and the alien or a summary of the terms of the oral agreement under which the alien will be employed.

Q. A Q is an alien coming temporarily to participate in an international cultural exchange program approved by the Attorney General for the sharing of the attitude, customs, history, heritage, philosophy, and/or traditions of the alien's country of nationality. The culture sharing must take place in a school, museum, business, or other establishment where the public is exposed to aspects of a foreign culture as part of a structured program. The work component of the program may not be independent of the cultural component, but must serve as the vehicle to achieve the objectives of the cultural component. A U.S. employer or foreign employer may file the petition; however, a foreign employer's petition must be signed by a U.S. citizen or permanent resident employed by the qualified employer on a permanent basis in an executive, managerial, or supervisory capacity for the prior year. File the petition with:

- evidence you:
  - maintain an established international cultural exchange program;
  - have designated a qualified employee to administer the program and serve as liaison with INS;
  - have been doing business in the U.S. for the past two years;
  - will offer the alien wages and working conditions comparable to those accorded local domestic workers similarly employed;
  - employ at least 5 full)time U.S. citizen or permanent resident workers
  - have the financial ability to remunerate the participant(s), as shown by your most recent annual report, business income tax return, or other form of certified accountant's report;
- catalogs, brochures or other types of material which illustrate that:
  - the cultural component is designed to give a overview of the attitude, customs, history, heritage, philosophy, tradition, and/or other cultural attributes of the participant's home country;
  - the employment or training takes place in a public setting where the sharing of the culture of their country of nationality can be achieved through direct interaction with the American public; and
  - the American public will derive an obvious cultural benefit from the program.

However, if the proposed dates of employment are within 15 months of the approval of a prior "Q" petition filed by you for the same international cultural exchange program, and that earlier petition was filed with the above evidence of the program, you may submit a copy of the approval notice for that prior petition in lieu of the evidence about the program required above.

▸ **Petition only required for alien in the U.S. to change status or extend stay:** The following classifications do not require a petition for new employment if the alien is outside the U.S. The alien should instead contact a U.S. Consulate for information about a visa or admission. Use this form to petition for a change of status, concurrent employment, or an extension of stay.

A petition for change of status to one of the classifications described in this part must be filed with the initial evidence listed below and with the initial evidence required by the separate instructions for all petitions involving change of status. A petition for an extension of stay must be filed with the initial evidence listed below and with the initial evidence required by the separate instructions for all petitions for extension. However, a petition for an extension based on unchanged, previously approved employment need only be filed with the the initial evidence required by the separate extension of stay instructions.

E-1. An E-1 is a national of a country with which the U.S. has a treaty of friendship, commerce, and navigation who is coming to the U.S. to engage in substantial trade between the U.S. and the alien's country of nationality. Substantial trade means that your trading activities with the U.S. comprise more than 50% of your total volume of business transactions in the U.S. and that there is a continued course of international trade.

E-2. An E-2 is a national of a country with which the U.S. has a bilateral investment treaty or agreement, who is coming to the U.S. to direct and develop the operations of an enterprise in which he/she has invested or is in the process of investing substantially. A substantial investment is one in which personal funds or assets are put at risk in a real operating enterprise which generates services or goods. You must show that you are able to direct and develop the enterprise by having control over the business. You must also show that the investment is not your main source of income or that the proceeds from the investment are significantly greater than a subsistence income.

An **E-1 or E-2** may also be an employee of a qualified treaty alien or treaty company. If so, the alien must be an executive or manager, an individual with specialized qualifications that are essential to the efficient operation of the employer's business enterprise, a highly trained technician, or start-up personnel (E-2 only).

E Petition requirements. A principal treaty trader or investor or the qualified employer may file the petition. It must be filed with copies of evidence of:

- ownership and nationality, including lists of investors with current status and nationality, stock certificates, certificates of ownership issued by the commercial section of a foreign embassy, and reports from a certified professional accountant (CPA);
- substantial trade if filing for an E-1, including copies of three or more of the following: bills of lading, customs receipts, letters of credit, insurance papers documenting commodities imported, purchase orders, carrier inventories, trade brochures, sales contracts.
- substantial investment if filing for an E-2, including copies of partnership agreements (with a statement on proportionate ownership), articles of incorporation, payments for the rental of business premises or office equipment, business licenses, stock certificates, office inventories (goods and equipment purchased for the business), insurance appraisals, advertising invoices, annual reports, net worth statements from certified professional accountants, business bank accounts containing funds for routine operations, funds held in escrow;
- if filing for an employee, evidence he/she is a manager or executive, or evidence of special knowledge, skills, training, or education, such as certificates, diplomas or transcripts, letters from employers describing job titles, duties, and the level of education and knowledge required, operators' manuals, and for non-executive/managerial employees, evidence that qualified U.S. workers are not available.

R-1. An R-1 is an alien who, for at least 2 years, has been a member of a religious denomination having a bona fide nonprofit, religious organization in the U.S., coming temporarily to work solely:

- as a minister of that denomination,
- in a professional capacity in a religious vocation or occupation for that organization, or
- in a religious vocation or occupation for the organization or its nonprofit affiliate.

The petition must be filed by a U.S. employer with:

- a letter from the authorizing official of the religious organization establishing that the proposed services and alien qualify above;
- a letter or letters from the authorizing officials of the religious denomination or organization attesting to the alien's membership in the religious denomination explaining, in detail, the person's religious work and all employment during the past 2 years and the proposed employment; and
- a copy of the tax-exempt certificate showing the religious organization, and any affiliate which will employ the person, is a bona fide nonprofit, religious organization in the U.S. and is exempt from taxation in accordance with section 501(c)(3) of the Internal Revenue Code of 1986;

TC. A TC is a Canadian citizen coming to the U.S. temporarily under the provisions of the United States-Canada Free-Trade Agreement. A U.S. employer or a foreign employer may file the petition. File the petition with:

- a letter stating the activity to be engaged in, the purpose of entry, the anticipated length of stay, and the arrangements for remuneration; and
- evidence the alien meets the educational and/or licensing requirements for the profession or occupation.

Change of status.
In addition to the initial evidence for the classification you are requesting, a petition requesting a change of status for an alien in the U.S. must be filed with a copy of the Form I-94, Nonimmigrant Arrival/Departure Record, of the employee(s). [Family members should use Form I-539 to apply for a change of status.] A nonimmigrant who must have a passport to be admitted must keep that passport valid during his/her entire stay. If a required passport is not valid, file a full explanation with your petition.

The following are **not eligible** to change status:

- an alien admitted under a visa waiver program;
- an alien in transit (C) or in transit without a visa (TWOV);
- a crewman (D);
- a fiance(e) or his/her dependent (K);
- a J-1 exchange visitor whose status was for the purpose of receiving graduate medical training;
- a J-1 exchange visitor subject to the foreign residence requirement who has not received a waiver of that requirement;
- an M-1 student to an H classification if training received as an M-1 helped him/her qualify for H classification.

Extension of stay.
A petition requesting an extension of stay for an employee in the U.S. must be filed with a copy of the Form I-94, Nonimmigrant Arrival/Departure Record, of the employee(s), and a letter from the petitioner explaining the reasons for the extension. [Family members should use Form I-539 to file for an extension of stay.] A nonimmigrant who must have a passport to be admitted must keep that passport valid during his/her entire stay. If a required passport is not valid, file a full explanation with your petition. Where there has been a change in the circumstances of employment, also submit the evidence required for a new petition.

Where there has been no change in the circumstances of employment, file your petition with the appropriate supplement and with your letter describing the continuing employment, and:

- if for H-1A status, submit a current copy of the Department of Labor's notice of acceptance of the petitioner's attestation.
- if for H-1B status, submit an approved labor condition application for the specialty occupation valid for the period of time requested.
- if for H-2B status, submit a labor certification valid for the dates of the extension.
- if for H-2A status, submit a labor certification valid for the dates of the extension unless it is based on a continuation of employment authorized by the approval of a previous petition filed with a certification and the extension will last no longer than the previously authorized employment and no longer than 2 weeks.

General Evidence.
Written consultation. Noted classifications require a written consultation with a recognized peer group, union, and/or management organization regarding the nature of the work to be done and the alien's qualifications before the petition may be approved. To obtain timely adjudication of a petition, you should obtain a written advisory opinion from an appropriate peer group, union, and/or management organization and submit it with the petition.

If you file a petition without the advisory opinion, it is advisable for you to send a copy of the petition and all supporting documents to the appropriate organization when you file the petition with INS, and indicate in the petition which organization you sent it to. Explain to the organization that they will be contacted by INS for an advisory opinion. If an accepted organization does not issue an advisory opinion within a given time period, a decision will be made based upon the evidence of record. If you do not know the name of an appropriate organization with which to consult, please indicate so on the petition. However, it will require a substantially longer period to process a petition filed without the actual advisory opinion.

Translations. Any foreign language document must be accompanied by a full English translation which the translator has certified as complete and correct, and by the translator's certification that he or she is competent to translate from the foreign language into English.

Copies. If these instructions state that a copy of a document may be filed with this petition, and you choose to send us the original, we may keep that original for our records.

H-1B and H-2B Notice.
The Immigration and Nationality Act makes a petitioner liable for the reasonable cost of return transportation for an H-1B or H-2B alien who is dismissed before the end of the authorized employment.

When To File.
File your petition as soon as possible, but no more than 4 months before the proposed employment will begin or the extension of stay is required. If you do not submit your petition at least 45 days before the employment will begin, petition processing, and subsequent visa issuance, may not be completed before the alien's services are required or previous employment authorization ends.

Where to File.
Mail this petition to the appropriate INS Service Center, except that:

- if the person is applying for admission as an L-1 under the U.S.-Canada Free Trade Agreement, the petition may be filed at the port of entry when the person applies for entry;
- if the services or training will be solely in Guam or the Virgin Islands, file the petition at the local INS office there.

In any other instance, mail this petition to the Service Center indicated below. If the services or training will be in more than one place, mail the petition to the Service Center with jurisdiction over the first work or training site. A blanket L petition should be mailed to the Service center with jurisdiction over the petitioner's location.

If the work or training will be in:
Alabama, Connecticut, Delaware, District of Columbia, Florida, Georgia, Maine, Maryland, Massachusetts, New Hampshire, New Jersey, New York, North Carolina, Pennsylvania, Puerto Rico, Rhode Island, South Carolina, Vermont, Virginia, or West Virginia; mail your petition to USINS, Eastern Service Center, 75 Lower Welden Street, St. Albans, VT 05479-0001.

If the work or training will be in:
Arizona, California, Hawaii, or Nevada; mail your petition to USINS, Western Service Center, P.O. Box 30040, Laguna Niguel, CA 92607-0040.

If the work or training will be elsewhere in the United States; mail your petition to USINS Northern Service Center, 100 Centennial Mall North, Room, B-26, Lincoln, NE 68508.

Fee.
The fee for this petition is a base fee of $70.00 + either:

- $10 per worker if you are requesting consulate or POE notification for visa issuance or admission [block (a) in Part 2, Question 4]; or
- $80 per worker if requesting a change of status [block (b) in Part 2, Question 4]; or
- $50 per worker if requesting an extension of stay [block (c) in Part 2, Question 4].

The fee must be submitted in the exact amount. It cannot be refunded. DO NOT MAIL CASH. All checks and money orders must be drawn on a bank or other institution located in the United States and must be payable in United States currency. The check or money order should be made payable to the Immigration and Naturalization Service, except that:

- If you live in Guam, and are filing this application in Guam, make your check or money order payable to the "Treasurer, Guam."
- If you live in the Virgin Islands, and are filing this application in the Virgin Islands, make your check or money order payable to the "Commissioner of Finance of the Virgin Islands."

Checks are accepted subject to collection. An uncollected check will render the application and any document issued invalid. A charge of $5.00 will be imposed if a check in payment of a fee is not honored by the bank on which it is drawn.

[G20,915]

Processing Information.

Acceptance. Any petition that is not signed, or is not accompanied by the correct fee, will be rejected with a notice that the petition is deficient. You may correct the deficiency and resubmit the petition. A petition is not considered properly filed until accepted by the Service.

Initial processing. Once a petition has been accepted, it will be checked for completeness, including submission of the required initial evidence. If you do not completely fill out the form, or file it without required initial evidence, you will not establish a basis for eligibility, and we may deny your petition.

Requests for more information or interview. We may request more information or evidence, or we may request that you appear at an INS office for an interview. We may also request that you submit the originals of any copy. We will return these originals when they are no longer required.

Decision. The decision on a petition involves separate determinations of whether you have established that the alien is eligible for the requested classification based on the proposed employment, and whether he or she is eligible for any requested change of status or extension of stay. You will be notified of the decision in writing.

Penalties.

If you knowingly and willfully falsify or conceal a material fact or submit a false document with this request, we will deny the benefit you are filing for, and may deny any other immigration benefit. In addition, you will face severe penalties provided by law, and may be subject to criminal prosecution.

Privacy Act Notice.

We ask for the information on this form, and associated evidence, to determine if you have established eligibility for the immigration benefit you are filing for. Our legal right to ask for this information is in 8 USC 1154, 1184 and 1258. We may provide this information to other government agencies. Failure to provide this information, and any requested evidence, may delay a final decision or result in denial of your request.

Paperwork Reduction Act Notice.

We try to create forms and instructions that are accurate, can be easily understood, and which impose the least possible burden on you to provide us with information. Often this is difficult because some immigration laws are very complex. The estimated average time to complete and file this application is as follows: (1) 30 minutes to learn about the law and form; (2) 25 minutes to complete the form; and (3) 60 minutes to assemble and file the petition; for a total estimated average of 115 minutes per petition. If you have comments regarding the accuracy of this estimate, or suggestions for making this form simpler, you can write to both the Immigration and Naturalization Service, 425 I Street, N.W., Room 5304, Washington, D.C. 20536; and the Office of Management and Budget, Paperwork Reduction Project, OMB No. 1115-0168, Washington, D.C. 20503.

- 12 -

GPO : 1993 O – 151-725 QL 3
[G20,916]

U.S. Department of Justice
Immigration and Naturalization Service

OMB No. 1115-0168
Petition for a Nonimmigrant Worker

START HERE - Please Type or Print

Part 1. Information about the employer filing this petition.
If the employer is an individual, use the top name line. Organizations should use the second line.

Family Name	Given Name	Middle Initial

Company or Organization Name

Address - Attn:

Street Number and Name		Apt. #
City	State or Province	
Country		Zip/Postal Code

IRS Tax #

Part 2. Information about this Petition.
(See instructions to determine the fee)

1. **Requested Nonimmigrant classification:** (write classification symbol at right) ______
2. **Basis for Classification** (check one)
   a. ☐ New employment
   b. ☐ Continuation of previously approved employment without change
   c. ☐ Change in previously approved employment
   d. ☐ New concurrent employment
3. **Prior Petition.** If you checked other than "New Employment" in item 2 (above) give the most recent prior petition numbers for the worker(s): ______
4. **Requested Action:** (check one)
   a. ☐ Notify the office in Part 4 so the person(s) can obtain a visa or be admitted (NOTE: a petition is not required for an E-1, E-2, or R visa)
   b. ☐ Change the person(s) status and extend their stay since they are all now in the U.S. in another status (see instructions for limitations). This is available only where you check "New Employment" in item 2, above.
   c. ☐ Extend or amend the stay of the person(s) since they now hold this status.
5. **Total number of workers in petition:** ______
   (See instructions for where more than one worker can be included)

Part 3. Information about the person(s) you are filing for.
Complete the blocks below. Use the continuation sheet to name each person included in this petition.

If an entertainment group, give their group name.

Family Name	Given Name	Middle Initial
Date of Birth (Month/Day/Year)	Country of Birth	
Social Security #	A #	

If in the United States, complete the following:

Date of Arrival (Month/Day/Year)	I-94 #
Current Nonimmigrant Status	Expires (Month/Day/Year)

FOR INS USE ONLY

Returned	Receipt
Resubmitted	
Reloc Sent	
Reloc Rec'd	
Interviewed ☐ Petitioner ☐ Beneficiary	

Class: ______
# of Workers: ______
Priority Number: ______
Validity Dates: From ______ To ______

☐ **Classification Approved**
☐ Consulate/POE/PFI Notified
At: ______
☐ Extension Granted
☐ COS/Extension Granted

Partial Approval (explain)

Action Block

To be Completed by Attorney or Representative, if any
☐ Fill in box if G-28 is attached to represent the applicant
VOLAG#
ATTY State License #

Form I-129 (Rev. 12/11/91)N

Continued on back.

Part 4. Processing Information

a. If the person named in Part 3 is outside the U.S. or a requested extension of stay or change of status cannot be granted, give the U.S. consulate or inspection facility you want to be notified if this petition is approved.

Type of Office (check one): ☐ Consulate ☐ Pre-flight inspection ☐ Port of Entry

Office Address (City) U.S. State or Foreign Country

Person's Foreign Address

b. Does each person in this petition have a valid passport?
☐ Not required to have passport ☐ No - explain on separate paper ☐ Yes

c. Are you filing any other petitions with this one? ☐ No ☐ Yes - How many? ______

d. Are applications for replacement/Initial I-94's being filed with this petition? ☐ No ☐ Yes - How many? ______

e. Are applications by dependents being filed with this petition? ☐ No ☐ Yes - How many? ______

f. Is any person in this petition in exclusion or deportation proceedings? ☐ No ☐ Yes - explain on separate paper

g. Have you ever filed an immigrant petition for any person in this petition? ☐ No ☐ Yes - explain on separate paper

h. If you indicated you were filing a new petition in Part 2, within the past seven years has any person in this petition:

1) ever been given the classification you are now requesting? ☐ No ☐ Yes - explain on separate paper

2) ever been denied the classification you are now requesting? ☐ No ☐ Yes - explain on separate paper

i. If you are filing for an entertainment group, has any person in this petition not been with the group for at least 1 year?
☐ No ☐ Yes - explain on separate paper

Part 5. Basic Information about the proposed employment and employer.
Attach the supplement relating to the classification you are requesting.

Job Title | Nontechnical Description of Job

Address where the person(s) will work if different from the address in Part 1.

Is this a full-time position? ☐ No - Hours per week ☐ Yes | Wages per week or per year

Other Compensation (Explain) | Value per week or per year | Dates of intended employment From: To:

Type of petitioner - check one ☐ U.S. citizen or permanent resident ☐ Organization ☐ Other - explain on separate paper

Type of business | Year established

Current number of employees | Gross Annual Income | Net Annual Income

Part 6. Signature.
Read the information on penalties in the instructions before completing this section.

I certify, under penalty of perjury under the laws of the United States of America, that this petition, and the evidence submitted with it, is all true and correct. If filing this on behalf of an organization, I certify that I am empowered to do so by that organization. If this petition is to extend a prior petition, I certify that the proposed employment is under the same terms and conditions as in the prior approved petition. I authorize the release of any information from my records, or from petitioning organization's records, which the Immigration and Naturalization Service needs to determine eligibility for the benefit being sought.

Signature and title | Print Name | Date

Please note: If you do not completely fill out this form and the required supplement, or fail to submit required documents listed in the instructions, then the person(s) filed for may not be found eligible for the requested benefit, and this petition may be denied.

Part 7. Signature of person preparing form if other than above.

I declare that I prepared this application at the request of the above person and it is based on all information of which I have knowledge.

Signature | Print Name | Date

Firm Name and Address

OMB No. 1115-0168

U.S. Department of Justice
Immigration and Naturalization Service

E Classification
Supplement to Form I-129

Name of person or organization filing petition:

Name of person you are filing for:

Classification sought (check one):
☐ E-1 Treaty trader ☐ E-2 Treaty investor

Name of country signatory to treaty with U.S.

Section 1. Information about the Employer outside the U.S. (if any)

Name

Address

Alien's Position - Title, duties and number of years employed

Principal Product, merchandise or service

Total number of Employees

Section 2. Additional information about the U.S. Employer.

The U.S. company is, to the company outside the U.S. (check one):
☐ Parent ☐ Branch ☐ Subsidiary ☐ Affiliate ☐ Joint Venture

Date and Place of Incorporation or establishment in the U.S.

Nationality of Ownership (Individual or Corporate)

Name	Nationality	Immigration Status	% Ownership

Assets

Net Worth

Total Annual Income

Staff in the U.S.

Executive/Manager

Specialized Qualifications or Knowledge

Nationals of Treaty Country in E or L Status

Total number of employees in the U.S.

Total number of employees the alien would supervise; or describe the nature of specialized skills essential to the U.S. company.

Section 3. Complete if filing for an E-1 Treaty Trader

Total Annual Gross Trade/Business of the U.S. company
$

For Year Ending

Percent of total gross trade which is between the U.S. and the country of which the treaty trader organization is a national.

Section 4. Complete if filing for an E-2 Treaty Investor

Total Investment	Cash	Equipment	Other
	$	$	$
	Inventory	Premises	Total
	$	$	$

Form I-129 Supplement E/L (12/11/91)N

U.S. Department of Justice
Immigration and Naturalization Service

OMB No. 1115-0168
H Classification
Supplement to Form I-129

Name of person or organization filing petition: | Name of person or total number of workers you are filing for:

List the alien's and any dependent family members' prior periods of stay in H classification in the U.S. for the last six years. Be sure to list only those periods in which the alien and/or family members were actually in the U.S. in an H classification. If more space is needed, attach an additional sheet.

Classification sought (check one):

- ☐ H-1A Registered Professional nurse
- ☐ H-1B1 Specialty occupation
- ☐ H-1B2 Exceptional services relating to a cooperative research and development project administered by the U.S. Department of Defense
- ☐ H-1B3 Artist, entertainer or fashion model of national or international acclaim
- ☐ H-1B4 Artist or entertainer in unique or traditional art form
- ☐ H-1B5 Athlete
- ☐ H-1BS Essential support personnel for H-1B entertainer or athlete
- ☐ H-2A Agricultural worker
- ☐ H-2B Nonagricultural worker
- ☐ H-3 Trainee
- ☐ H-3 Special education exchange visitor program

Section 1. Complete this section if filing for H-1A or H1B classification.

Describe the proposed duties

Alien's present occupation and summary of prior work experience

Statement for H-1B specialty occupations only:

By filing this petition, I agree to the terms of the labor condition application for the duration of the alien's authorized period of stay for H1-B employment

Petitioner's Signature | Date

Statement for H-1B specialty occupations and DOD projects:

As an authorized official of the employer, I certify that the employer will be liable for the reasonable costs of the return transportation of the alien abroad if the alien is dismissed from employment by the employer before the end of the period of the authorized stay

Signature of authorized official of employer | Date

Statement for H1-B DOD projects only:

I certify that the alien will be working on a cooperative research and development project under a reciprocal Government-to-Government agreement administered by the Department of Defense.

DOD project manager's signature | Date

Section 2. Complete this section if filing for H-2A or H-2B classification.

Employment is: (check one)
- ☐ Seasonal
- ☐ Peakload
- ☐ Intermittent
- ☐ One-time occurrence

Temporary need is: (check one)
- ☐ Unpredictable
- ☐ Periodic
- ☐ Recurrent Annually

Explain your temporary need for alien's services (attach a separate paper if additional space is needed).

Form I-129 Supplement H (12/11/91) N

Continued on back.

Section 3. Complete this section if filing for H-2A classification.

The petitioner and each employer consent to allow government access to the site where the labor is being performed for the purpose of determining compliance with H-2A requirements. The petitioner further agrees to notify the Service in the manner and within the time frame specified if an H-2A worker absconds or if the authorized employment ends more than five days before the relating certification document expires, and pay liquidated damages of ten dollars for each instance where it cannot demonstrate compliance with this notification requirement. The petitioner also agrees to pay liquidated damages of two hundred dollars for each instance where it cannot be demonstrated that the H-2A worker either departed the United States or obtained authorized status during the period of admission or within five days of early termination, whichever comes first.

The petitioner must execute Part A. If the petitioner is the employer's agent the employer must execute Part B. If there are joint employers, they must each execute Part C.

Part A. Petitioner:

By filing this petition, I agree to the conditions of H-2A employment, and agree to the notice requirements and limited liabilities defined in 8 CFR 214.2 (h) (3) (vi).

Petitioner's signature Date

Part B. Employer who is not petitioner:

I certify that I have authorized the party filing this petition to act as my agent in this regard. I assume full responsibility for all representations made by this agent on my behalf, and agree to the conditions of H-2A eligibility.

Employer's signature Date

Part C. Joint Employers:

I agree to the conditions of H-2A eligibility.

Joint employer's signature(s) Date

Joint employer's signature(s) Date

Joint employer's signature(s) Date

Joint employer's signature(s) Date

Joint employer's signature(s) Date

Section 4. Complete this section if filing for H-3 classification.

If you answer "yes" to any of the following questions, attach a full explanation.

a. Is the training you intend to provide, or similar training available in the alien's country? ☐ No ☐ Yes
b. Will the training benefit the alien in pursuing a career abroad? ☐ No ☐ Yes
c. Does the training involve productive employment incidental to training? ☐ No ☐ Yes
d. Does the alien already have skills related to the training? ☐ No ☐ Yes
e. Is this training an effort to overcome a labor shortage? ☐ No ☐ Yes
f. Do you intend to employ the alien abroad at the end of the training? ☐ No ☐ Yes
If you do not intend to employ this person abroad at the end of this training, explain why you wish to incur the cost of providing this training, and your expected return from this training.

OMB No. 1115-0168

U.S. Department of Justice
Immigration and Naturalization Service

L Classification
Supplement to Form I-129

Name of person or organization filing petition: Name of person you are filing for:

This petition is (check one): ☐ An individual petition ☐ A blanket petition

Section 1. Complete this section if filing an individual petition

Classification (check one): ☐ L-1A manager or executive ☐ L-1B specialized knowledge

List the alien's, and any dependent family members' prior periods of stay in an L classification in the U.S. for the last seven years. Be sure to list only those periods in which the alien and/or family members were actually in the U.S. in an L classification.

Name and address of employer abroad

Dates of alien's employment with this employer. Explain any interruptions in employment.

Description of alien's duties for the past three years.

Description of alien's proposed duties in the U.S.

Summarize the alien's education and work experience.

The U.S. company is, to the company abroad: (check one)
☐ Parent ☐ Branch ☐ Subsidiary ☐ Affiliate ☐ Joint Venture

Describe the stock ownership and managerial control of each company.

Do the companies currently have the same qualifying relationship as they did during the one-year period of the alien's employment with the company abroad ☐ Yes ☐ No (attach explanation)

Is the alien coming to the U.S. to open a new office?
☐ Yes (explain in detail on separate paper) ☐ No

Section 2. Complete this section if filing a blanket petition.

List all U.S. and foreign parent, branches, subsidiaries and affiliates included in this petition.(Attach separate paper if additional space is needed)

Name and Address	Relationship

Explain in detail on separate paper.

Form I-129 Supplement E/L (12/11/91)N

OMB No. 1115-0168

U.S. Department of Justice
Immigration and Naturalization Service

O and P Classification
Supplement to Form I-129

Name of person or organization filing petition:

Name of person or group or total number of workers you are filing for:

Classification sought (check one):

☐ O-1 Alien of extraordinary ability in sciences, art, education, or business
☐ P-2 Artist or entertainer for reciprocal exchange program
☐ P-2S Essential Support Personnel for P-2

Explain the nature of the event

Describe the duties to be performed

If filing for O-2 or P support alien, dates of alien's prior experience with the O-1 or P alien.

Have you obtained the required written consultation(s)? ☐ Yes - attached ☐ No - Copy of request attached
If not, give the following information about the organization(s) to which you have sent a duplicate of this petition.

O-1 Extraordinary ability

Name of recognized peer group — Phone #

Address — Date sent

O-1 Extraordinary achievement in motion pictures or television

Name of labor organization — Phone #

Address — Date sent

Name of management organization — Phone #

Address — Date sent

O-2 or P alien

Name of labor organization — Phone #

Address — Date sent

Form I-129 Supplement O/P/Q/R (12/11/91) N

OMB No. 1115-0168

U.S. Department of Justice
Immigration and Naturalization Service

Q & R Classifications
Supplement to Form I-129

Name of person or organization filing petition: Name of person you are filing for:

Section 1. Complete this section if you are filing for a Q international exchange alien.

I hereby that the participant(s) in this international exchange program:

- is at least 18 years of age,
- has the ability to communicate effectively about the cultural attributes of his or her country of nationality to the American public, and
- has not previously been in the United States as a Q nonimmigrant unless he/she has resided and has been physically present outside the U.S. for the immediate prior year

I also certify that the same wages and working conditions are accorded the participants as are provided to similarly employed U.S. workers.

Petitioner's signature Date

Section 2. Complete this section if you are filing for an R religious worker.

List the alien's and any dependent family members, prior periods of stay in R classification in the U.S. for the last six years. Be sure to list only those periods in which the alien and/or family members were actually in the U.S. in an R classification.

Describe the alien's proposed duties in the U.S.

Describe the alien's qualifications for the vocation or occupation

Describe the relationship between the U.S. religious organization and the organization abroad of which the alien was a member.

Form I-129 Supplement O/P/Q/R (12/11/91) N

Form I–130 Petition for alien relative

U.S. Department of Justice
Immigration and Naturalization Service (INS)

Petition for Alien Relative

Instructions

Read the instructions carefully. If you do not follow the instructions, we may have to return your petition, which may delay final action. If more space is needed to complete an answer continue on separate sheet of paper.

1. Who can file?
A citizen or lawful permanent resident of the United States can file this form to establish the relationship of certain alien relatives who may wish to immigrate to the United States. You must file a separate form for each eligible relative.

2. For whom can you file?
A. If you are a citizen, you may file this form for:
1) your husband, wife, or unmarried child under 21 years old
2) your unmarried child over 21, or married child of any age
3) your brother or sister if you are at least 21 years old
4) your parent if you are at least 21 years

B. If you are a lawful permanent resident you may file this form for:
1) your husband or wife
2) your unmarried child

Note: If your relative qualifies under instruction A(2) or A(3) above, separate petitions are not required for his or her husband or wife or unmarried children under 21 years old. If your relative qualifies under instruction B(2) above, separate petitions are not required for his or her unmarried children under 21 years old. These persons will be able to apply for the same type of immigrant visa as your relative.

3. For whom can you not file?
You cannot file for people in the following categories:
A. An adoptive parent or adopted child, if the adoption took place after the child became 16 years old, or if the child has not been in the legal custody and living with the parent(s) for at least two years.
B. A natural parent if the United States citizen son or daughter gained permanent residence through adoption.
C. A stepparent or stepchild, if the marriage that created this relationship took place after the child became 18 years old.
D. A husband or wife, if your were not both physically present at the marriage ceremony, and the marriage was not consummated.
E. A husband or wife if you gained lawful permanent resident status by virtue of a prior marriage to a United States citizen or lawful permanent resident unless:
1) a period of five years has elapsed since you became a lawful permanent resident; OR
2) you can establish by clear and convincing evidence that the prior marriage (through which you gained your immigrant status) was not entered into for the purpose of evading any provision of the immigration laws; OR
3) your prior marriage (through which you gained your immigrant status) was terminated by the death of your former spouse.
F. A husband or wife if he or she was in exclusion, deportation, rescission, or judicial proceedings regarding his or her right to remain in the United States when the marriage took place, unless such spouse has resided outside the United States for a two-year period after the date of the marriage.
G. A husband or wife if the Attorney General has determined that such an alien has attempted or conspired to enter into a marriage for the purpose of evading the immigration laws.
H. A grandparent, grandchild, nephew, niece, uncle, aunt, cousin, or in-law.

4. What documents do you need?
You must give INS certain documents with this form to prove you are eligible to file. You must also give the INS certain documents to prove the family relations between you and your relative.
A. For each document needed, give INS the original and one copy. However, because it is against the law to copy a Certificate of Naturalization, a Certificate of Citizenship or an Alien Registration Receipt Card (Form I-151 or I-551) give INS the original only. **Originals will be returned to you.**
B. If you do not wish to give INS the original document, you may give INS a copy. The copy must be certified by:
1) an INS or U.S. consular officer, or
2) an attorney admitted to practice law in the United States, or
3) an INS accredited representative (INS may still require originals).
C. Documents in a foreign language must be accompanied by a complete English translation. The translator must certify that the translation is accurate and that he or she is competent to translate.

5. What documents do you need to show you are a United States citizen?
A. If you were born in the United States, give INS your birth certificate.
B. If you were naturalized, give INS your original Certificate of Naturalization.
C. If you were born outside the United States, and you are a U.S. citizen through your parents, give INS:
1) your original Certificate of Citizenship, or
2) your Form FS- 240 (Report of Birth Abroad of a United States Citizen).
D. In place of any of the above, you may give INS your valid unexpired U.S. passport that was initially issued for at least 5 years.
E. If you do not have any of the above and were born in the United States, see instruction under 8 below. *"What if a document is not available?"*

6. What documents do you need to show you are a permanent resident?
You must give INS your alien registration receipt card (Form I-151 or Form I-551). Do not give INS a photocopy of the card.

7. What documents do you need to prove family relationship?
You have to prove that there is a family relationship between your relative and yourself.

In any case where a marriage certificate is required, if either the husband or wife was married before, you must give INS documents to show that all previous marriages were legally ended. In cases where the names shown on the supporting documents have changed, give INS legal documents to show how the name change occurred (for example a marriage certificate, adoption decree, court order, etc.)

Find the paragraph in the following list that applies to the relative for whom you are filing.

Form I-130 (Rev. 10/13/98)N

If you are filing for your:

A. **husband or wife**, give INS
   1) your marriage certificate
   2) a color photo of you and one of your husband or wife, taken within 30 days of the date of this petition. These photos must have a white background. They must be glossy, unretouched, and not mounted. The dimension of the facial image should be about 1 inch from chin to top of hair in 3/4 frontal view, showing the right side of the face with the right ear visible. Using pencil or felt pen, lightly print name (and Alien Registration Number, if known) on the back of each photograph.
   3) a completed and signed G-325A (Biographic Information) for you and one for your husband or wife. Except for name and signature, you do not have to repeat on the G-325A the information given on your I-130 petition.

B. **child** and you are the **mother**, give the child's birth certificate showing your name and the name of your child.

C. **child** and you are the **father or stepparent**, give the child's birth certificate showing both parents' names and your marriage certificate. **Child** born out of wedlock and you are the **father**, give proof that a parent/child relationship exists or existed. For example, the child's birth certificate showing your name and evidence that you have financially supported the child. (A blood test may be necessary).

D. **brother or sister**, your birth certificate and the birth certificate of your brother or sister showing both parents' names. If you do not have the same mother, you must also give the marriage certificates of your father to both mothers.

E. **mother**, give your birth certificate showing your name and the name of your mother.

F. **father**, give your birth certificate showing the names of both parents and your parents' marriage certificate.

G. **stepparent**, give your birth certificate showing the names of both natural parents and the marriage certificate of your parent to your stepparent.

H. **adoptive parent or adopted child**, give a certified copy of the adoption decree, the legal custody decree if you obtained custody of the child before adoption, and a statement showing the dates and places you have lived together with the child.

8. What if a document is not available?

If the documents needed above are not available, you can give INS the following instead. (INS may require a statement from the appropriate civil authority certifying that the needed document is not available.)

A. Church record: A certificate under the seal of the church where the baptism, dedication, or comparable rite occurred within two months after birth, showing the date and place of child's birth, date of the religious ceremony, and the names of the child's parents.

B. School record: A letter from the authorities of the school attended (preferably the first school), showing the date of admission to the school, child's date and place of birth, and the names and places of birth parents, if shown in the school records.

C. Census record: State or federal census record showing the names, place of birth, and date of birth or the age of the person listed.

D. Affidavits: Written statements sworn to or affirmed by two persons who were living at the time and who have personal knowledge of the event you are trying to prove; for example, the date and place of birth, marriage, or death. The persons making the affidavits need not be citizens of the United States. Each affidavit should contain the following information regarding the person making the affidavit his or her full name, address, date and place of birth, and his or her relationship to you, if any; full information concerning the event; and complete details concerning how the person acquired knowledge of the event.

9. How should you prepare this form?

A. Type or print legibly in ink.

B. If you need extra space to complete any item, attach a continuation sheet, indicate the item number, and date and sign each sheet.

C. Answer all questions fully and accurately. If any item does not apply, please write "N/A".

10. Where should you file this form?

A. If you live in the United States, send or take the form to the INS office that has jurisdiction over where you live.

B. If you live outside the United States, contact the nearest American Consulate to find out where to send or take the completed form.

11. What is the fee?

You must pay one hundred ten dollars ($110.00) to file this form. **The fee will not be refunded, whether the petition is approved or not.** DO NOT MAIL CASH. All checks or money orders, whether U.S. or foreign, must be payable in U.S. currency at a financial institution in the United States. When a check is drawn on the account of a person other than yourself, write your name on the face of the check. If the check is not honored, INS will charge you $30.00.

Pay by check or money order in the exact amount. Make the check Or money order payable to "Immigration and Naturalization Service". However,

A. if you live in Guam: Make the check or money order payable to Treasurer, Guam", or

B. if you live in the U.S. Virgin Islands: Make the check or money order payable to "Commissioner of Finance of the Virgin Islands".

12. When will a visa become available?

When a petition is approved for the husband, wife, parent, or unmarried minor child of a United States citizen, these relatives do not have to wait for a visa number, as they are not subject to the immigrant visa limit. However, for a child to qualify for this category, all processing must be completed and the child must enter the United States before his or her 21st birthday.

For all other alien relatives there are only a limited number of immigrant visas each year. The visas are given out in the order in which INS receives properly filed petitions. To be considered properly filed, a petition must be completed accurately and signed, the required documents must be attached, and the fee must be paid.

For a monthly update on the dates for which immigrant visas are available, you may call (202) 647-0508.

13. What are the penalties for committing marriage fraud or submitting false information or both?

Title 8, United States Code, Section 1325 states that any individual who knowingly enters into a marriage contract for the purpose of evading any provision of the immigration laws shall be imprisoned for not more than five years, or fined not more than $250,000.00 or both.

Title 18, United States Code, Section 1001 states that whoever willfully and knowingly falsifies a material fact, makes a false statement, or makes use of a false document will be fined up to $10,000 or imprisoned up to five years, or both.

14. What is our authority for collecting this information?

We request the information on the form to carry out the immigration laws contained in Title 8, United States Code, Section 1154(a). We need this information to determine whether a person is eligible for immigration benefits. The information you provide may also be disclosed to other federal, state, local, and foreign law enforcement and regulatory agencies during the course of the investigation required by this Service. You do not have to give this information. However, if you refuse to give some or all of it, your petition may be denied.

15. Reporting Burden.

A person is not required to respond to a collection of information unless it displays a currently valid OMB control number. Public reporting burden for this collection of information is estimated to average 30 minutes per response, including the time for reviewing instructions, searching existing data sources, gathering and maintaining the data needed, and completing and reviewing the collection of information. Send comments regarding this burden estimate or any other aspect of this collection of information, including suggestions for reducing this burden, to: U.S. Department of Justice, Immigration and Naturalization Service (Room 5307),Washington, D.C. 20536; OMB No.1115-0054. **DO NOT MAIL YOUR COMPLETED APPLICATION TO THIS ADDRESS.**

It is not possible to cover all the conditions for eligibility or to give instructions for every situation. If you have carefully read all the instructions and still have questions, please contact your nearest INS office.

U.S. Department of Justice
Immigration and Naturalization Service (INS)

OMB #1115-0054

Petition for Alien Relative

DO NOT WRITE IN THIS BLOCK - FOR EXAMINING OFFICE ONLY

Case ID#	Action Stamp	Fee Stamp
A#		
G-28 or Volag #		
Section of Law: ☐ 201 (b) spouse ☐ 201 (b) child ☐ 201 (b) parent ☐ 203 (a)(1) ☐ 203 (a)(2) ☐ 203 (a)(4) ☐ 203 (a)(5) AM CON: ______		Petition was filed on: ______ (priority date) ☐ Personal Interview ☐ Previously Forwarded ☐ Pet. ☐ Ben. "A" File Reviewed ☐ Stateside Criteria ☐ Field Investigations ☐ I-485 Simultaneously ☐ 204 (a)(2)(A) Resolved ☐ 204 (h) Resolved

Remarks:

A. Relationship

1. The alien relative is my ☐ Husband/Wife ☐ Parent ☐ Brother/Sister ☐ Child

2. Are you related by adoption? ☐ Yes ☐ No

3. Did you gain permanent residence through adoption? ☐ Yes ☐ No

B. Information about you

1. **Name** (Family name in CAPS) (First) (Middle)

2. **Address** (Number and Street) (Apartment Number)
   (Town or City) (State/Country) (ZIP/Postal Code)

3. **Place of Birth** (Town or City) (State/Country)

4. **Date of Birth** (Mo/Day/Yr)

5. **Sex** ☐ Male ☐ Female

6. **Marital Status** ☐ Married ☐ Single ☐ Widowed ☐ Divorced

7. **Other Names Used** (including maiden name)

8. **Date and Place of Present Marriage** (if married)

9. **Social Security Number**

10. **Alien Registration Number** (if any)

11. **Names of Prior Husbands/Wives**

12. **Date(s) Marriages(s) Ended**

13. **If you are a U.S. citizen, complete the following:**
    My citizenship was acquired through (check one)
    ☐ Birth in the U.S.
    ☐ Naturalization (Give number of certificate, date and place it was issued)
    ☐ Parents
    Have you obtained a certificate of citizenship in your own name?
    ☐ Yes ☐ No
    If "Yes", give number of certificate, date and place it was issued

14a. **If you are a lawful permanent resident alien, complete the following:**
    Date and place of admission for, or adjustment to, lawful permanent residence, and class of admission:

14b. **Did you gain permanent resident status through marriage to a United States citizen or lawful permanent resident?** ☐ Yes ☐ No

C. Information about your alien relative

1. **Name** (Family name in CAPS) (First) (Middle)

2. **Address** (Number and Street) (Apartment Number)
   (Town or City) (State/Country) (ZIP/Postal Code)

3. **Place of Birth** (Town or City) (State/Country)

4. **Date of Birth** (Mo/Day/Yr)

5. **Sex** ☐ Male ☐ Female

6. **Marital Status** ☐ Married ☐ Single ☐ Widowed ☐ Divorced

7. **Other Names Used** (including maiden name)

8. **Date and Place of Present Marriage** (if married)

9. **Social Security Number**

10. **Alien Registration Number** (if any)

11. **Names of Prior Husbands/Wives**

12. **Date(s) Marriages(s) Ended**

13. **Has your relative ever been in the U.S.?**
    ☐ Yes ☐ No

14. **If your relative is currently in the U.S., complete the following: He or she last arrived as a** (visitor, student, stowaway, without inspection, etc.)

Arrival/Departure Record (I-94) Number **Date arrived** (Month/Day/Year)

Date authorized stay expired, or will expire, as shown on Form I-94 or I-95

15. **Name and address of present employer** (if any)

Date this employment began (Month/Day/Year)

16. **Has your relative ever been under immigration proceedings?**
    ☐ Yes ☐ No Where ______ When ______
    ☐ Exclusion ☐ Deportation ☐ Recission ☐ Judicial Proceedings

INITIAL RECEIPT	RESUBMITTED	RELOCATED		COMPLETED		
		Rec'd	Sent	Approved	Denied	Returned

Form I-130 (Rev. 10/13/98)N

C. (continued) Information about your alien relative

16. **List husband/wife and all children of your relative** (if your relative is your husband/wife, list only his or her children).

(Name)	(Relationship)	(Date of Birth)	(Country of Birth)

17. **Address in the United States where your relative intends to live**
(Number and Street) (Town or City) (State)

18. **Your relative's address abroad**
(Number and Street) (Town or City) (Province) (Country) (Phone Number)

19. **If your relative's native alphabet is other than Roman letters, write his or her name and address abroad in the native alphabet:**
(Name) (Number and Street) Town or City) (Province) (Country)

20. **If filing for your husband/wife, give last address at which you both lived together:** **From** (Month) (Year) **To** (Month) (Year)
(Name) (Number and Street) (Town or City) (Province) (Country)

21. **Check the appropriate box below and give the information required for the box you checked:**

☐ Your relative will apply for a visa abroad at the American Consulate in ______________
(City) (Country)

☐ Your relative is in the United States and will apply for adjustment of status to that of a lawful permanent resident in the office of the Immigration and Naturalization Service at ______________. If your relative is not eligible for adjustment of status, he or she will
(City) (State)
apply for a visa abroad at the American Consulate in ______________,
(City) (Country)

(Designation of a consulate outside the country of your relative's last residence does not guarantee acceptance for processing by that consulate. Acceptance is at the discretion of the designated consulate.)

D. Other Information

1. **If separate petitions are also being submitted for other relatives, give names of each and relationship.**

2. **Have you ever filed a petition for this or any other alien before?** ☐ Yes ☐ No
If "Yes," give name, place and date of filing, and result.

Warning: The INS investigates claimed relationships and verifies the validity of documents. The INS seeks criminal prosecutions when family relationships are falsified to obtain visas.

Penalties: You may, by law be imprisoned for not more than five years, or fined $250,000, or both, for entering into a marriage contract for the purpose of evading any provision of the immigration laws and you may be fined up to $10,000 or imprisoned up to five years or both, for knowingly and willfully falsifying or concealing a material fact or using any false document in submitting this petition.

Your Certification: I certify, under penalty of perjury under the laws of the United States of America, that the foregoing is true and correct. Furthermore, I authorize the release of any information from my records which the Immigration and Naturalization Service needs to determine eligibility for the benefit that I am seeking.

Signature ______________ Date ______________ Phone Number ______________

Signature of Person Preparing Form if Other than Above

I declare that I prepared this document at the request of the person above and that it is based on all information of which I have any knowledge.

Print Name ______________ (Address) ______________ (Signature) ______________ (Date) ______________

G-28 ID Number ______________

Volag Number ______________

Form I-130 (Rev. 10/13/98)N

NOTICE TO PERSONS FILING FOR SPOUSES IF MARRIED LESS THAN TWO YEARS

Pursuant to section 216 of the Immigration and Nationality Act, your alien spouse may be granted conditional permanent resident status in the United States as of the date he or she is admitted or adjusted to conditional status by an officer of the Immigration and Naturalization Service. Both you and your conditional permanent resident spouse are required to file a petition, Form I-751, Joint Petition to Remove Conditional Basis of Alien's Permanent Resident Status, during the ninety day period immediately before the second anniversary of the date your alien spouse was granted conditional permanent residence.

Otherwise, the rights, privileges, responsibilities and duties which apply to all other permanent residents apply equally to a conditional permanent resident. A conditional permanent resident is not limited to the right to apply for naturalization, to file petitions in behalf of qualifying relatives, or to reside permanently in the United States as an immigrant in accordance with the immigration laws.

Failure to file Form I-751, Joint Petition to Remove the Conditional Basis of Alien's Permanent Resident Status, will result in termination of permanent residence status and initiation of deportation proceedings.

NOTE: You must complete Items 1 through 6 to assure that petition approval is recorded. Do not write in the section below item 6.

1. **Name of relative** (Family name in CAPS) (First) (Middle)

2. **Other names used by relative** (Including maiden name)

3. **Country of relative's birth**

4. **Date of relative's birth** (Month/Day/Year)

5. **Your name** (Last name in CAPS) (First) (Middle)

6. **Your phone number**

Action Stamp

SECTION
- ☐ 201 (b)(spouse)
- ☐ 201 (b)(child)
- ☐ 201 (b)(parent)
- ☐ 203 (a)(1)
- ☐ 203 (a)(2)
- ☐ 203 (a)(4)
- ☐ 203 (a)(5)

DATE PETITION FILED

☐ **STATESIDE CRITERIA GRANTED**

SENT TO CONSUL AT:

CHECKLIST

Have you answered each question?

Have you signed the petition?

Have you enclosed:

- ☐ The filing fee for each petition?
- ☐ Proof of your citizenship or lawful permanent residence?
- ☐ All required supporting documents for each petition?

If you are filing for your husband or wife have you included:

- ☐ Your picture?
- ☐ His or her picture?
- ☐ Your G-325A?
- ☐ His or her G-325A?

Relative Petition Card
Form I-130 (Rev. 10/13/98)N

Form I–751 Petition to remove the conditions on residence

U.S. Department of Justice
Immigration and Naturalization Service

OMB No. 1115-0145

Petition to Remove the Conditions on Residence

Purpose Of This Form.
This form is for a conditional resident who obtained such status through marriage to apply to remove the conditions on his or her residence.

Who May File.
If you were granted conditional resident status through marriage to a U.S. citizen or permanent resident, use this form to petition for the removal of those conditions. Your petition should be filed jointly by you and the spouse through whom you obtained conditional status if you are still married. However, you can apply for a waiver of this joint filing requirement on this form if:

- you entered into the marriage in good faith, but your spouse subsequently died;
- you entered into the marriage in good faith, but the marriage was later terminated due to divorce or annulment;
- you entered nto the marriage in good faith, and remain married, but have been battered or subjected to extreme mental cruelty by your U.S. citizen or permanent resident spouse; or
- the termination of your status, and deportation, would result in extreme hardship.

You may include your conditional resident children in your petition, or they can file separately.

General Filing Instructions.
Please answer all questions by typing or clearly printing in black ink. Indicate that an item is not applicable with "N/A". If an answer is "none," write "none". If you need extra space to answer any item, attach a sheet of paper with your name and your alien registration number (A#), and indicate the number of the item to which the answer refers. You must file your petition with the required Initial Evidence. Your petition must be properly signed and accompanied by the correct fee. If you are under 14 years of age, your parent or guardian may sign the petition in your behalf.

Translations. Any foreign language document must be accompanied by a full English translation which the translator has certified as complete and correct, and by the translator's certification that he or she is competent to translate from the foreign language into English.

Copies. If these instructions state that a copy of a document may be filed with this petition, and you choose to send us the original, we may keep that original for our records.

Initial Evidence.
Alien Registration Card. You must file your petition with a copy of your alien registration card, and with a copy of the alien registration card of any of your conditional resident children you are including in your petition.

Evidence of the relationship. Submit copies of documents indicating that the marriage upon which you were granted conditional status was entered into in "good faith", and was not for the purpose of circumventing immigration laws. You should submit copies of as many documents as you wish to establish this fact and to demonstrate the circumstances of the relationship from the date of the marriage to date, and to demonstrate any circumstances surrounding the end of the relationship, if it has ended. The documents should cover as much of the period since your marriage as possible. Examples of such documents are:

- Birth certificate(s) of child(ren) born to the marriage.
- Lease or mortgage contracts showing joint occupancy and/ or ownership of your communal residence.
- Financial records showing joint ownership of assets and joint responsibility for liabilities, such as joint savings and checking accounts, joint federal and state tax returns, insurance policies which show the other as the beneficiary, joint utility bills, joint installment or other loans.
- Other documents you consider relevant to establish that your marriage was not entered into in order to evade the immigration laws of the United States.
- Affidavits sworn to or affirmed by at least 2 people who have known both of you since your conditional residence was granted and have personal knowledge of your marriage and relationship. (Such persons may be required to testify before an immigration officer as to the information contained in the affidavit.) The original affidavit must be submitted, and it must also contain the following information regarding the person making the affidavit: his or her full name and address; date and place of birth; relationship to you or your spouse, if any; and full information and complete details explaining how the person acquired his or her knowledge. Affidavits must be supported by other types of evidence listed above.

If you are filing to waive the joint filing requirement due to the death of your spouse, also submit a copy of the death certificate with your petition.

If you are filing to waive the joint filing requirement because your marriage has been terminated, also submit a copy of the divorce decree or other document terminating or annulling the marriage with your petition.

If you are filing to waive the joint filing requirement because you and/or your conditional resident child were battered or subjected to extreme mental cruelty, also file your petition with the following.

- Evidence of the physical abuse, such as copies of reports or official records issued by police, judges, medical personnel, school officials, and representatives of social service agencies, and original affidavits as described under *Evidence of the Relationship*; or
- Evidence of the extreme mental cruelty, and an original evaluation by a professional recognized by the Service as an expert in the field. These experts include clinical social workers, psychologists and psychiatrists. A clinical social worker who is not licensed only because the State in which he or she practices does not provide for licensing is considered a licensed professional recognized by the Service if he or she is included by the National Association of Social Workers or is certified by the American Board of Examiners in Clinical Social Work. Each evaluation must contain the professional's full name, professional address and license number. It must also identify the licensing, certifying or registering authority.
- A copy of your divorce decree if your marriage was terminated by divorce on grounds of physical abuse or mental cruelty.

If you are filing for a waiver of the joint filing requirement because the termination of your status, and deportation would result in "extreme hardship", you must also file your petition with evidence your deportation would result in hardship significantly greater than the hardship encountered by other aliens who are deported from this country after extended stays. The evidence must relate only to those factors which arose since you became a conditional resident.

If you are a child filing separately from your parent, also file your petition with a full explanation as to why you are filing separately, along with copies of any supporting documentation.

When To File.
Filing jointly. If you are filing this petition jointly with your spouse, you must file it during the 90 days immediately before the second anniversary of the date you were accorded conditional resident status. This is the date your conditional residence expires. However, if you and your spouse are outside the United States on orders of the U.S. Government during the period in which the petition must be filed, you may file it within 90 days of your return to the U.S.

Form I-751 (Rev. 10/13/98)N

Filing with a request that the joint filing requirement be waived. You may file this petition at any time after you are granted conditional resident status and before you are deported.

Effect Of Not Filing. If this petition is not filed, you will automatically lose your permanent resident status as of the second anniversary of the date on which you were granted this status. You will then become deportable from the United States. If your failure to file was through no fault of your own, you may file your petition late with a written explanation and request that INS excuse the late filing. Failure to file before the expiration date may be excused if you demonstrate when you file the application that the delay was due to extraordinary circumstances beyond your control and that the length of the delay was reasonable.

Effect of Filing.
Filing this petition extends your conditional residence for six months. You will receive a filing receipt which you should carry with your alien registration card (Form I-551). If you travel outside the U.S. during this period, you may present your card and the filing receipt to be readmitted.

Where To File.
If you live in Connecticut, Delaware, District of Columbia, Maine, Maryland, Massachusetts, New Hampshire, New Jersey, New York, Pennsylvania, Puerto Rico, Rhode Island, Vermont, Virgin Islands, Virginia, or West Virginia, mail your petition to: USINS Eastern Service Center, 75 Lower Welden Street, St. Albans, VT 05479-0001.

If you live in Alabama, Arkansas, Florida, Georgia, Kentucky, Louisiana, Mississippi, New Mexico, North Carolina, Oklahoma, South Carolina, Tennessee, or Texas, mail your petition to: USINS Southern Service Center, P.O. Box 152122, Dept. A, Irving, TX 75015-2122.

If you live in Arizona, California, Guam, Hawaii, or Nevada, mail your petition to: USINS Western Service Center, P.O. Box 30111, Laguna Niguel, CA 92607-0111.

If you live in elsewhere in the U.S., mail your petition to: USINS Northern Service Center, 100 Centennial Mall North, Room B-26, Lincoln, NE 68508.

Fee.
The fee for this petition is $125.00. The fee must be submitted in the exact amount. It cannot be refunded. **DO NOT MAIL CASH.**

All checks and money orders must be drawn on a bank or other institution located in the United States and must be payable in United States currency. The check or money order should be made payable to the Immigration and Naturalization Service, except that:

- If you live in Guam, and are filing this petition in Guam, make your check or money order payable to the "Treasurer, Guam".
- If you are living in the Virgin Islands, and are filing this application in the Virgin Islands, make your check or money order payable to the "Commissioner of Finance of the Virgin Islands".

Checks are accepted subject to collection. An uncollected check will render the application and any document issued invalid. A charge of $30.00 will be imposed if a check in payment of a fee is not honored by the bank on which it is drawn.

Processing Information.
Acceptance. Any petition that is not signed, or is not accompanied by the correct fee, will be rejected with a notice that the petition is deficient. You may correct the deficiency and resubmit the petition. A petition is not considered properly filed until accepted by the Service.

Initial processing. Once a petition has been accepted, it will be checked for completeness, including submission of the required initial evidence. If you do not completely fill out the form, or file it without required initial evidence, you will not establish a basis for eligibility, and we may deny your petition.

Requests for more information or interview. We may request more information or evidence, or we may request that you appear at an INS office for an interview. We may also request that you submit the originals of any copy. We will return these originals when they are no longer required.

Decision. You will be advised in writing of the decision on your petition.

Penalties.
If you knowingly and willfully falsify or conceal a material fact or submit a false document with this request, we will deny the benefit you are filing for, and may deny any other immigration benefit. In addition, you will face severe penalties provided by law, and may be subject to criminal prosecution.

Privacy Act Notice.
We ask for the information on this form, and associated evidence, to determine if you have established eligibility for the immigration benefit you are filing for. Our legal right to ask for this information is in 8 USC 1184, 1255 and 1258. Failure to provide this information, and any requested evidence, may delay a final decision or result in denial of your request.

All the information provided on this form, including addresses, are protected by the Privacy Act and the Freedom of Information Act. This information will not be released in any form whatsoever to a third party, other than another government agency, who requests it without a court order, or without your written consent, or, in the case of a child, the written consent of the parent or legal guardian who filed the form on the child's behalf.

Paperwork Reduction Act Notice.
A person is not required to respond to a collection of information unless it displays a currently valid OMB control number. We try to create forms and instructions that are accurate, can be easily understood, and which impose the least possible burden on you to provide us with information. Often this is difficult because some immigration laws are very complex. The estimated average time to complete and file this application is as follows: (1) 15 minutes to learn about the law and form; (2) 15 minutes to complete the form; and (3) 50 minutes to assemble and file the petition; for a total estimated average of 1 hour and 20 minutes per petition. If you have comments regarding the accuracy of this estimate, or suggestions for making this form simpler, you can write to the Immigration and Naturalization Service, 425 I Street, N.W., Room 5307, Washington, D.C. 20536; OMB No. 1115-0145. **DO NOT MAIL YOUR COMPLETED APPLICATION TO THIS ADDRESS.**

U.S. Department of Justice
Immigration and Naturalization Service

OMB No. 1115-0145

Petition to Remove the Conditions on Residence

START HERE - Please Type or Print

Part 1. Information about you.

Family Name	Given Name	Middle Initial

Address - C/O:

Street Number and Name		Apt. #
City	State or Province	
Country		ZIP/Postal Code

Date of Birth (month/day/year)	Country of Birth
Social Security #	A #
Conditional residence expires on (month/day/year)	

Mailing address if different from residence in C/O:

Street Number and Name		Apt #
City	State or Province	
Country		ZIP/Postal Code

Part 2. Basis for petition *(check one)*.

a. ☐ My conditional residence is based on my marriage to a U.S. citizen or permanent resident, and we are filing this petition together.

b. ☐ I am a child who entered as a conditional permanent resident and I am unable to be included in a Joint Petition to Remove the Conditional Basis of Alien's Permanent Residence (Form I-751) filed by my parent(s).

My conditional residence is based on my marriage to a U.S. citizen or permanent resident, but I am unable to file a joint petition and I request a waiver because: (check one)

c. ☐ My spouse is deceased.

d. ☐ I entered into the marriage in good faith, but the marriage was terminated though divorce/annulment.

e. ☐ I am a conditional resident spouse who entered in to the marriage in good faith, or I am a conditional resident child, who has been battered or subjected to extreme mental cruelty by my citizen or permanent resident spouse or parent.

f. ☐ The termination of my status and deportation from the United States would result in an extreme hardship.

Part 3. Additional information about you.

Other names used *(including maiden name)*:	Telephone #
Date of Marriage	Place of Marriage

If your spouse is deceased, give the date of death (month/day/year)

Are you in deportation or exclusion proceedings? ☐ Yes ☐ No

Was a fee paid to anyone other than an attorney in connection with this petition? ☐ Yes ☐ No

Continued on back.

FOR INS USE ONLY

Returned	Receipt
Resubmitted	
Reloc Sent	
Reloc Rec'd	
☐ Applicant Interviewed	

Remarks

Action

To Be Completed by Attorney or Representative, if any
☐ Fill in box if G-28 is attached to represent the applicant

VOLAG#

ATTY State License #

Form I-751 (Rev. 10/13/98)N

Part 3. Additional Information about you. (con't)

Since becoming a conditional resident, have you ever been arrested, cited, charged, indicted, convicted, fined or imprisoned for breaking or violating any law or ordinace (excluding traffic regulations), or committed any crime for which you were not arrested?	☐ Yes ☐ No
If you are married, is this a different marriage than the one through which conditional residence status was obtained?	☐ Yes ☐ No
Have you resided at any other address since you became a permanent resident?	☐ Yes ☐ No *(If yes, attach a list of all addresses and dates.)*
Is your spouse currently serving employed by the U. S. government and serving outside the U.S.?	☐ Yes ☐ No

Part 4. Information about the spouse or parent through whom you gained your conditional residence.

Family Name	Given Name	Middle Initial	Phone Number ( )
Address			
Date of Birth *(month/day/year)*	Social Security #	A#	

Part 5. Information about your children. *List all your children. Attach another sheet if necessary*

Name	Date of Birth *(month/day/year)*	If in U.S., give A#, current immigration status and U.S. Address	Living with you?
1			☐ Yes ☐ No
2			☐ Yes ☐ No
3			☐ Yes ☐ No
4			☐ Yes ☐ No

Part 6. Complete if you are requesting a waiver of the joint filing petition requirement based on extreme mental cruelty.

Evaluator's ID Number: State: ☐☐ Number: ☐☐☐☐☐☐☐☐☐	Expires on *(month/day/year)*	Occupation
Last Name	First Name	Address

Part 7. Signature. *Read the information on penalties in the instructions before completing this section. If you checked block "a" in Part 2 your spouse must also sign below.*

I certify, under penalty of perjury under the laws of the United States of America, that this petition, and the evidence submitted with it, is all true and correct. If conditional residence was based on a marriage, I further certify that the marriage was entered into in accordance with the laws of the place where the marriage took place, and was not for the purpose of procuring an immigration benefit. I also authorize the release of any information from my records which the Immigration and Naturalization Service needs to determine eligibility for the benefit being sought.

Signature	Print Name	Date
Signature of Spouse	Print Name	Date

Please note: If you do not completely fill out this form, or fail to submit any required documents listed in the instructions, then you cannot be found eligible for the requested benefit, and this petition may be denied.

Part 8. Signature of person preparing form if other than above.

I declare that I prepared this petition at the request of the above person and it is based on all information of which I have knowledge.

Signature	Print Name	Date
Firm Name and Address		

Page 2 Form I-751 (Rev. 10/13/98)N

Form I–140 Immigrant petition for alien worker

U.S. Department of Justice
Immigration and Naturalization Service

OMB No. 1115-0061

Immigrant Petition for Alien Worker

Purpose Of This Form.

This form is used to petition for an immigrant based on employment.

Who May File.

Any person may file this petition on behalf of an alien who:

- has extraordinary ability in the sciences, arts, education, business, or athletics, demonstrated by sustained national or international acclaim, whose achievements have been recognized in the field; or
- is a member of the profession holding an advanced degree or is claiming exceptional ability in the sciences, arts, or business, and is seeking an exemption of the requirement of a job offer in the national interest.

A U.S. employer may file this petition who wishes to employ:

- an outstanding professor or researcher, with at least 3 years of experience in teaching or research in the academic area, who is recognized internationally as outstanding,
  - in a tenured or tenure-track position at a university or institution of higher education to teach in the academic area,
  - in a comparable position at a university or institution of higher education to conduct research in the area, or
  - in a comparable position to conduct research for a private employer who employs at least 3 persons in full-time research activities and has achieved documented accomplishments in an academic field;
- an alien who, in the 3 years preceding the filing of this petition, has been employed for at least 1 year by a firm or corporation or other legal entity and who seeks to enter the U.S. to continue to render services to the same employer or to a subsidiary or affiliate in a capacity that is managerial or executive;
- a member of the professions holding an advanced degree or an alien with exceptional ability in the sciences, arts, or business who will substantially benefit the national economy, cultural or educational interests, or welfare of the U.S.;
- a skilled worker (requiring at least 2 years of specialized training or experience in the skill)- to perform labor for which qualified workers are not available in the U.S.;
- a member of the professions with a baccalaureate degree; or
- an unskilled worker to perform labor for which qualified workers are not available in the U.S.

General Filing Instructions.

Please answer all questions by typing or clearly printing in black ink. Indicate that an item is not applicable with "N/A." If an answer to a question is "none," write "none." If you need extra space to answer any item, attach a sheet of paper with your name and your A#, if any, and indicate the number of the item to which the answer refers. You must file your petition with the required Initial Evidence. Your petition must be properly signed and filed with the correct fee.

Initial Evidence.

If you are filing for an alien of extraordinary ability in the sciences, arts, education, business, or athletics, you must file your petition with:

- evidence of a one-time achievement (i.e., a major, internationally-recognized award), or
- at least three of the following:
  - receipt of lesser nationally or internationally recognized prizes or awards for excellence in the field of endeavor,
  - membership in associations in the field which require outstanding achievements as judged by recognized national or international experts,
  - published material about the alien in professional or major trade publications or other major media,
  - participation on a panel or individually as a judge of the work of others in the field or an allied field,
  - original scientific, scholarly, artistic, athletic, or business-related contributions of major significance in the field,
  - authorship of scholarly articles in the field, in professional or major trade publications or other major media,
  - display of the alien's work at artistic exhibitions or showcases,
  - evidence that the alien has performed in a leading or critical role for organizations or establishments that have a distinguished reputation,
  - evidence that the alien has commanded a high salary or other high remuneration for services, or
  - evidence of commercial successes in the performing arts, as shown by box office receipts or record, casette, compact disk, or video sales.
  - If the above standards do not readily apply to the alien's occupation, you may submit comparable evidence to establish the alien's eligibility; and
- evidence that the alien is coming to the U.S. to continue work in the area of expertise. Such evidence may include letter(s) from prospective employer(s), evidence of prearranged commitments such as contracts, or a statement from the alien detailing plans on how he or she intends to continue his or her work in the U.S.

Form I-140 (Rev. 10/13/98)N

A U.S. employer filing for an outstanding professor or researcher must file the petition with:

- evidence of at least 2 of the following:
  - receipt of major prizes or awards for outstanding achievement in the academic field,
  - membership in associations in the academic field, which require outstanding achievements of their members,
  - published material in professional publications written by others about the alien's work in the academic field,
  - participation on a panel, or individually, as the judge of the work of others in the same or an allied academic field,
  - original scientific or scholarly research contributions to the academic field, or
  - authorship of scholarly books or articles, in scholarly journals with international circulation, in the academic field;
- evidence the beneficiary has at least 3 years of experience in teaching and/or research in the academic field; and
- if you are a university or other institution of higher education, a letter indicating that you intend to employ the beneficiary in a tenured or tenure-track position as a teacher or in a permanent position as a researcher in the academic field, or
- if you are a private employer, a letter indicating that you intend to employ the beneficiary in a permanent research position in the academic field, and evidence that you employ at least 3 full-time researchers and have achieved documented accomplishments in the field.

A U.S. employer filing for a multinational executive or manager must file the petition with a statement which demonstrates that:

- If the worker is now employed outside the U.S., that he or she has been employed outside the U.S. for at least 1 year in the past 3 years in an executive or managerial capacity by the petitioner or by its parent, branch, subsidiary or affiliate, or, if the worker is already employed in the U.S., that he or she was employed outside the U.S. for at least 1 year in the 3 years preceding admission as a nonimmigrant in an executive or managerial capacity by the petitioner or by its parent, branch, subsidiary or affiliate;
- the prospective employer in the U.S. is the same employer or a subsidiary or affiliate of the firm or corporation or other legal entity by which the alien was employed abroad;
- the prospective U.S. employer has been doing business for at least one year; and
- the alien is to be employed in the U.S. in a managerial or executive capacity. A description of the duties to be performed should be included.

A U.S. employer filing for a member of the professions with an advanced degree or a person with exceptional ability in the sciences, arts, or business must file the petition with:

- a labor certification (see GENERAL EVIDENCE) and either:
- an official academic record showing that the alien has a U.S. advanced degree or an equivalent foreign degree, or an official academic record showing that the alien has a U.S. baccalaureate degree or an equivalent foreign degree and letters from current or former employers showing that the alien has at least 5 years of progressive post-baccalaureate experience in the specialty; or
- at least 3 of the following:
- an official academic record showing that the alien has a degree, diploma, certificate, or similar award from an institution of learning relating to the area of exceptional ability;
- letters from current or former employers showing that the alien has at least 10 years of full-time experience in the occupation for which he/she is being sought;
- a license to practice the profession or certification for a particular profession or occupation;
- evidence that the alien has commanded a salary, or other remuneration for services, which demonstrates exceptional ability;
- evidence of membership in professional associations; or
- evidence of recognition for achievements and significant contributions to the industry or field by peers, governmental entities, or professional or business organizations.
- If the above standards do not readily apply to the alien's occupation, you may submit comparable evidence to establish the alien's eligibility.

A U.S. employer filing for a skilled worker must file the petition with:

- a labor certification (see GENERAL EVIDENCE);
- evidence that the alien meets the educational, training, or experience and any other requirements of the labor certification (the minimum requirement is 2 years of training or experience).

A U.S. employer filing for a professional must file the petition with:

- a labor certification (see GENERAL EVIDENCE);
- evidence that the alien holds a U.S. baccalaureate degree or equivalent foreign degree; and
- evidence that a baccalaureate degree is required for entry into the occupation.

A U.S. employer filing for its employee in Hong Kong must file its petition (on or before September 30 1993) with a statement that demonstrates that:

- the company is owned and organized in the United States;
- the employee is a resident of Hong Kong;
- the company, or its subsidiary or affiliate, is employing the person in Hong Kong and has been employing him or her there for the past 12 months, or the company, or its subsidiary or affiliate, is employing him or her outside of Hong Kong during a temporary absence (i.e., of limited duration), and he or she had been employed in Hong Kong for 12 consecutive months prior to such absence(s), and that such employment is, and for that period has been, as an officer or supervisor, or in a capacity that is executive, managerial or involves specialized knowledge;
- the company employs at least 100 employees in the U.S. and at least 50 employees outside the U.S. and has a gross annual income of at least $50,000,000; and
- the company intends to employ the person in the United States as an officer or supervisor, or in a capacity that is executive or managerial or involves specialized knowledge, with salary and benefits comparable to others with similar responsibilities and experience within the company. A specific job description is required for immediate immigration; a commitment to a qualifying job is required for deferred immigration.

A U.S. employer filing for an unskilled worker must file the petition with:

- a labor certification (see GENERAL EVIDENCE); and
- evidence that the beneficiary meets any education, training, or experience requirements required in the labor certification.

General Evidence.

Labor certification. Petitions for certain classifications must be filed with a certification from the Department of Labor or with documentation to establish that the alien qualifies for one of the shortage occupations in the Department of Labor's Labor Market Information Pilot Program or for an occupation in Group I or II of the Department of Labor's Schedule A. A certification establishes that there are not sufficient workers who are able, willing, qualified, and available at the time and place where the alien is to be employed and that employment of the alien, if qualified, will not adversely affect the wages and working conditions of similarly employed U.S. workers. Application for certification is made on Form ETA-750 and is filed at the local office of the State Employment Service. If the alien is in a shortage occupation, or for a Schedule A/Group I or II occupation, you may file a fully completed, uncertified Form ETA-750 in duplicate with your petition for determination by INS that the alien belongs to the shortage occupation.

Ability to pay wage. Petitions which require job offers must be accompanied by evidence that the prospective U.S. employer has the ability to pay the proffered wage. Such evidence shall be in the form of copies of annual reports, federal tax returns, or audited financial statements.

Page 3

In a case where the prospective U.S. employer employs 100 or more workers, a statement from a financial officer of the organization which establishes ability to pay the wage may be submitted. In appropriate cases, additional evidence, such as profit/loss statements, bank account records, or personnel records, may be submitted.

Translations. Any foreign language document must be accompanied by a full English translation, which the translator has certified as complete and correct, and by the translator's certification that he or she is competent to translate from the foreign language into English.

Copies. If these instructions state that a copy of a document may be filed with this petition and you choose to send us the original, we may keep that original for our records.

Where To File.

File this petition at the INS Service Center with jurisdiction over the place where the alien will be employed. If the employment will be in Alabama, Connecticut, Delaware, District of Columbia, Florida, Georgia, Maine, Maryland,
Massachusetts, New Hampshire, New Jersey, New York, North Carolina, Pennsylvania, Puerto Rico, Rhode Island, South Carolina, Vermont, the Virgin Islands, Virginia, or West Virginia, mail your petition to: USINS Eastern Service Center, 75 Lower Welden Street, St. Albans, VT 05479-0140.

If the employment will be in Arizona, California, Guam, Hawaii, or Nevada, mail your petition to: USINS Western Service Center, P.O. Box 10140, Laguna Niguel, CA 92607-0140.

If the employment will be elsewhere in the U.S., mail your petition to: USINS Northern Service Center, P. O. Box 82521, Lincoln, NE 68501-2521.

Fee.

The fee for this petition is $115.00. The fee must be submitted in the exact amount. It cannot be refunded. **DO NOT MAIL CASH.** All checks and money orders must be drawn on a bank or other institution located in the United States and must be payable in United States currency. The check or money order should be made payable to the Immigration and Naturalization Service, except:

- If you live in Guam, and are filing this application in Guam, make your check or money order payable to the "Treasurer, Guam."
- If you live in the Virgin Islands, and are filing this application in the Virgin Islands, make your check or money order payable to the "Commissioner of Finance of the Virgin Islands."

Checks are accepted subject to collection. An uncollected check will render the application and any document issued invalid. A charge of $30.00 will be imposed if a check in payment of a fee is not honored by the bank on which it is drawn.

Form I-140 (Rev. 10/13/98)N

Processing Information.

Acceptance. Any petition that is not signed or is not accompanied by the correct fee will be rejected with a notice that it is deficient. You may correct the deficiency and resubmit the petition. However, a petition is not considered properly filed until accepted by the Service. A priority date will not be assigned until the petition is properly filed.

Initial processing. Once the petition has been accepted, it will be checked for completeness, including submission of the required initial evidence. If you do not completely fill out the form, or file it without required initial evidence, you will not establish a basis for eligibility, and we may deny your petition.

Requests for more information or interview. We may request more information or evidence, or we may request that you appear at an INS office for an interview. We may also request that you submit the originals of any copy. We will return these originals when they are no longer required.

Decision. If you have established eligibility for the benefit requested, your petition will be approved. If you have not established eligibility, your petition will be denied. You will be notified in writing of the decision on your petition.

Meaning of petition approval.
Approval of a petition means you have established that the person you are filing for is eligible for the requested classification. This is the first step towards permanent residence. However, this does not in itself grant permanent residence or employment authorization. You will be given information about the requirements for the person to receive an immigrant visa or to adjust status after your petition is approved.

Penalties.

If you knowingly and willfully falsify or conceal a material fact or submit a false document with this request, we will deny the benefit you are filing for and may deny any other immigration benefit. In addition, you will face severe penalties provided by law and may be subject to criminal prosecution.

Privacy Act Notice.

We ask for the information on this form, and associated evidence, to determine if you have established eligibility for the immigration benefit you are filing for. Our legal right to ask for this information is in 8 USC 11854. We may provide this information to other government agencies. Failure to provide this information, and any requested evidence, may delay a final decision or result in denial of your request.

Paperwork Reduction Act Notice.

A person is not required to respond to a collection of information unless it displays a currently valid OMB control number. We try to create forms and instructions that are accurate, can be easily understood, and which impose the least possible burden on you to provide us with information. Oftenthis is difficult because some immigration laws are very complex. The estimated average time to complete and file this application is as follows: (1) 20 minutes to learn about the law and form; (2) 15 minutes to complete the form; and (3) 45 minutes to assemble and file the petition; for a total estimated average of 1 hour and 20 minutes per petition. If you have comments regarding the accuracy of this estimate, or suggestions for making this form simpler, you can write to the Immigration and Naturalization Service, 425 I Street, N.W., Room 5307, Washington, D.C. 20536; OMB No. 1115-0061. **DO NOT MAIL YOUR COMPLETED APPLICATION TO THIS ADDRESS**

U.S. Department of Justice
Immigration and Naturalization Service

OMB No. 1115-0061

Immigrant Petition for Alien Worker

START HERE - Please Type or Print

Part 1. Information about the person or organization filing this petition. If you are filing for yourself and do not want to use an alternate mailing address, skip this part and go to part 2.

If an individual is filing, use the top name line. Organizations should use the second line.

Family Name	Given Name	Middle Initial
Company or Organization		
Address - Attn:		
Street Number and Name		Room #
City	State or Province	
Country	ZIP/Postal Code	
IRS Tax #	Social Security #	

Part 2. Petition Type.

1. This petiton is being filed for: *(check one)*

- a. ☐ An alien of extraordinary ability
- b. ☐ An outstanding professor or researcher
- c. ☐ A multinational executive or manager
- d. ☐ A member of the professions holding an advanced degree or an alien of exceptional ability
- e. ☐ A skilled worker (requiring at least two years of specialized training or experience) or professional
- f. ☐ Any other worker (requiring less than two years training or experience)
- g. ☐ An employee of a U.S. business operating in Hong Kong
- h. ☐ Soviet Scientist

Part 3. Information about the person you are filing for.

Family Name	Given Name	Middle Initial
Address - C/O		
Street # and Name		Apt. #
City	State or Province	
Country	Zip or Postal Code	
Date of Birth (Month/Day/Year)	Country of Birth	
Social Security # (if any)	A # (if any)	
If in the U.S. — Date of Arrival (Month/Day/Year)	I-94#	
If in the U.S. — Current Nonimmigrant Status	Expires on (Month/Day/Year)	

Continued on back.

FOR INS USE ONLY

Returned	Receipt
Resubmitted	
Reloc Sent	
Reloc Rec'd	
☐ Petitioner Interviewed	
☐ Beneficiary Interviewed	

Classification
- ☐ 203(b)(1)(A) Alien Of Extraordinary Ability
- ☐ 203(b)(1)(B) Outstanding Professor or Researcher
- ☐ 203(b)(1)(C) Multi-national executive or manager
- ☐ 203(b)(2) Member of professions w/adv. degree or of exceptional ability
- ☐ 203(b)(3) (A) (i) Skilled worker
- ☐ 203(b)(3) (A) (ii) Professional
- ☐ 203(b)(3) (A) (iii) Other worker
- ☐ Sec. 124 IMMACT-Employee of U.S. business in Hong Kong

Certification:
Blanket Labor Certification
Schedule A, Group I
Schedule A, Group II

Priority Date	**Consulate**

Remarks

Action Block

To Be Completed by
Attorney or Representative, if any
☐ Fill in box if G-28 is attached to represent the petitioner

VOLAG#

ATTY State License #

Form I-140 (Rev. 10/13/98)N

Part 4. Processing Information.

A. Check one:

☐ The person named in Part 3 is now in the U.S. and an application to adjust status to permanent resident is attached or will be filed in this petition is approved.

☐ If the Petition is approved, but the adjustment of status cannot be approved, send the petition to an American Consulate abroad, which the Department of State will identify based on the following information:

Country of Nationality of person named in Part 3:________________

Country of current residence or, if no in the U.S., last permanent residence abroad, of person named in part 3:___________

If you gave a U.S. address in Part 3, print the person's print the person's foreign address below.

Name:______________________Address:____________________

If your employee's native alphabet is other than Roman Letter, write the foreign address in the native alphabet:

Are you filing any other petitions or applications with this one?	☐ No	☐ Yes-attach an explanation
Is the person you are filing for in exclusion or deportation proceedings?	☐ No	☐ Yes-attach an explanation
Has an immigrant visa petition ever been filed by or on behalf of this person?	☐ No	☐ Yes-attach an explanation

Part 5. Additional information about the employer.

Type of petitioner *(check one)*	☐ Self	☐ Individual U.S. Citizen	☐ Company or organization
	☐ Permanent Resident	☐ Other - explain_______________	

If a company, give the following: Type of business			
Date Established	Current # of employees	Gross Annual Income	Net Annual Income
If an individual, give the following: Occupation		Annual Income	

Part 6. Basic information about the proposed employment.

Job Title		Nontechnical description of job	
Address where the person will work if different from address in Part 1.			
Is this a full-time position?	☐ Yes	No (hours per week ________)	Wages per week
Is this a permanent position?:	☐ Yes ☐ No	Is this a new position? ☐ Yes ☐ No	

Part 7. Information on spouse and all children of the person you are filing for.

Provide an attachment listing the family members of the person you are filing for. Be sure to include their full name, relationship, date and country of birth, and present address.

Part 8. Signature.

Read the information on penalties in the instructions before completing this section. If someone helped you prepare this petition, he or she must complete Part 9.

I certify under penalty of perjury under the laws of the United States of America that this petition and the evidence submitted with it are all true and correct. I authorize the release of any information from my records which the Immigration and Naturalization Service needs to determine eligibility for the benefit I am seeking.

Petitioner's Signature	Print Name	Date	Daytime Telephone No. ( )

Please Note: *If you do not completely fill out this form or fail to submit required documents listed in the instructions, you cannot be found eligible for the requested document and this application may be denied.*

Part 9. Signature of person preparing form if other than above. *(Sign below)*

I declare that I prepared this application at the request of the above person and it is based on all information of which I have knowledge.

Signature	Print Name	Date	Daytime Telephone No. ( )

Firm Name and Address

Page 2 Form I-140 (Rev. 10/13/98)N

Form ETA 750 Application for alien employment certification

OMB Approval No. 44-R1301

U.S. DEPARTMENT OF LABOR
Employment and Training Administration

APPLICATION
FOR
ALIEN EMPLOYMENT CERTIFICATION

IMPORTANT: READ CAREFULLY BEFORE COMPLETING THIS FORM

PRINT legibly in ink or use a typewriter. If you need more space to answer questions in this form, use a separate sheet. Identify each answer with the number of the corresponding question. SIGN AND DATE each sheet in original signature.

To knowingly furnish any false information in the preparation of this form and any supplement thereto or to aid, abet, or counsel another to do so is a felony punishable by $10,000 fine or 5 years in the penitentiary, or both (18 U.S.C. 1001)

PART A. OFFER OF EMPLOYMENT

1. Name of Alien (Family name in capital letter, First, Middle, Maiden)

2. Present Address of Alien (Number, Street, City and Town, State ZIP code or Province, Country)

3. Type of Visa (If in U.S.)

The following information is submitted as an offer of employment.

4. Name of Employer (Full name of Organization)

5. Telephone

6. Address (Number, Street, City and Town, State ZIP code)

7. Address Where Alien Will Work (if different from item 6)

8. Nature of Employer's Business Activity	9. Name of Job Title	10. Total Hours Per Week		11. Work Schedule (Hourly)	12. Rate of Pay	
		a. Basic	b. Overtime	a.m. p.m.	a. Basic $ per ____	b. Overtime $ per hour

13. Describe Fully the job to be Performed (Duties)

14. State in detail the MINIMUM education, training, and experience for a worker to perform satisfactorily the job duties described in item 13 above.

EDU-CATION (Enter number of years)	Grade School	High School	College	College Degree Required (specify) / Major Field of Study
TRAIN-ING	No. Yrs.		No. Mos.	Type of Training
EXPERI-ENCE	Job Offered (Number: Yrs. Mos.)		Related Occupation (Number: Yrs. Mos.)	Related Occupation (specify)

15. Other Special Requirements

16. Occupational Title of Person Who Will Be Alien's Immediate Supervisor

17. Number of Employees Alien Will Supervise

ENDORSEMENTS (Make no entry in section - for Government use only)

Date Forms Received	
L.O.	S.O.
R.O.	N.O.
Ind. Code	Occ. Code
Occ. Title	

Replaces MA 7-50A, B and C (Apr. 1970 edition) which is obsolete.

ETA 750 (Oct. 1979)

18. COMPLETE ITEMS ONLY IF JOB IS TEMPORARY			19. IF JOB IS UNIONIZED (Complete)	
a. No. of Openings To Be Filled By Aliens Under Job Offer	b. Exact Dates You Expect To Employ Alien		a. Number of Local	b. Name of Local
	From	To		c. City and State

20. STATEMENT FOR LIVE-AT-WORK JOB OFFERS (Complete for Private Household ONLY)						
a. Description of Residence		b. No. Persons residing at Place of Employment				c. Will free board and private room not shared with any-one be provided? ("X" one)
("X" one)	Number of Rooms	Adults		Children	Ages	
☐ House			BOYS			☐ YES ☐ NO
☐ Apartment			GIRLS			

21. DESCRIBE EFFORTS TO RECRUIT U.S. WORKERS AND THE RESULTS. (Specify Sources of Recruitment by Name)

22. Applications require various types of documentation. Please read Part II of the instructions to assure that appropriate supporting documentation is included with your application.

23. EMPLOYER CERTIFICATIONS

By virtue of my signature below, I HEREBY CERTIFY the following conditions of employment.

a. I have enough funds available to pay the wage or salary offered the alien.

b. The wage offered equals or exceeds the prevailing wage and I guarantee that, if a labor certification is granted, the wage paid to the alien when the alien begins work will equal or exceed the prevailing wage which is applicable at the time the alien begins work.

c. The wage offered is not based on commissions, bonuses, or other incentives, unless I guarantee a wage paid on a weekly, bi-weekly, or monthly basis.

d. I will be able to place the alien on the payroll on or before the date of the alien's proposed entrance into the United States.

e. The job opportunity does not involve unlawful discrimination by race, creed, color, national origin, age, sex, religion, handicap, or citizenship.

f. The job opportunity is not:

(1) Vacant because the former occupant is on strike or is being locked out in the course of a labor dispute involving a work stoppage.

(2) At issue in a labor dispute involving a work stoppage.

g. The job opportunity's terms, conditions and occupational environment are not contrary to Federal, State or local law.

h. The job opportunity has been and is clearly open to any qualified U.S. worker.

24. DECLARATIONS

DECLARATION OF EMPLOYER ➤ Pursuant to 28 U.S.C. 1746, I declare under penalty of perjury the foregoing is true and correct.

SIGNATURE	DATE
NAME (Type or Print)	TITLE

AUTHORIZATION OF AGENT OF EMPLOYER ➤ I HEREBY DESIGNATE the agent below to represent me for the purposes of labor certification and I TAKE FULL RESPONSIBILITY for accuracy of any representations made by my agent.

SIGNATURE OF EMPLOYER	DATE
NAME OF AGENT (Type or Print)	ADDRESS OF AGENT (Number, Street, City, State, ZIP code)

PART B. STATEMENT OF QUALIFICATIONS OF ALIEN

FOR ADVICE CONCERNING REQUIREMENTS FOR ALIEN EMPLOYMENT CERTIFICATION: If alien is in the U.S., contact nearest office of Immigration and Naturalization Service. If alien is outside U.S., contact nearest U.S. Consulate.

IMPORTANT: READ ATTACHED INSTRUCTIONS BEFORE COMPLETING THIS FORM.

Print legibly in ink or use a typewriter. If you need more space to fully answer any questions on this form, use a separate sheet. Identify each answer with the number of the corresponding question. Sign and date each sheet.

1. Name of Alien (Family name in capital letters) | First name | Middle name | Maiden name

2. Present Address (No., Street, City or Town, State or Province and ZIP code) | Country | 3. Type of Visa (If in U.S.)

4. Alien's Birthdate (Month, Day, Year) | 5. Birthplace (City or Town, State or Province) | Country | 6. Present Nationality or Citizenship (Country)

7. Address in United States Where Alien Will Reside

8. Name and Address of Prospective Employer if Alien has job offer in U.S. | 9. Occupation in which Alien is Seeking Work

10. "X" the appropriate box below and furnish the information required for the box marked

a. ☐ Alien will apply for a visa abroad at the American Consulate in → | City in Foreign Country | Foreign Country

b. ☐ Alien is in the United States and will apply for adjustment of status to that of a lawful permanent resident in the office of the Immigration and Naturalization Service at → | City | State

11. Names and Addresses of Schools, Colleges and Universities Attended (Include trade or vocational training facilities)	Field of Study	FROM Month	FROM Year	TO Month	TO Year	Degrees or Certificates Received

SPECIAL QUALIFICATIONS AND SKILLS

12. Additional Qualifications and Skills Alien Possesses and Proficiency in the use of Tools, Machines or Equipment Which Would Help Establish if Alien Meets Requirements for Occupation in Item 9.

13. List Licenses (Professional, journeyman, etc.)

14. List Documents Attached Which are Submitted as Evidence that Alien Possesses the Education, Training, Experience, and Abilities Represented

Endorsements | DATE REC. DOL | O.T. & C.

(Make no entry in this section - FOR Government Agency USE ONLY)

(Items continued on next page)

15. WORK EXPERIENCE. List all jobs held during the last three (3) years. Also, list any other jobs related to the occupation for which the alien is seeking certification as indicated in item 9.

a. NAME AND ADDRESS OF EMPLOYER			
NAME OF JOB	DATE STARTED Month Year	DATE LEFT Month Year	KIND OF BUSINESS
DESCRIBE IN DETAIL THE DUTIES PERFORMED, INCLUDING THE USE OF TOOLS, MACHINES OR EQUIPMENT			NO. OF HOURS PER WEEK

b. NAME AND ADDRESS OF EMPLOYER			
NAME OF JOB	DATE STARTED Month Year	DATE LEFT Month Year	KIND OF BUSINESS
DESCRIBE IN DETAIL THE DUTIES PERFORMED, INCLUDING THE USE OF TOOLS, MACHINES OR EQUIPMENT			NO. OF HOURS PER WEEK

c. NAME AND ADDRESS OF EMPLOYER			
NAME OF JOB	DATE STARTED Month Year	DATE LEFT Month Year	KIND OF BUSINESS
DESCRIBE IN DETAIL THE DUTIES PERFORMED, INCLUDING THE USE OF TOOLS, MACHINES OR EQUIPMENT			NO. OF HOURS PER WEEK

16. DECLARATIONS

DECLARATION OF ALIEN ➤ ➤	Pursuant to 28 U.S.C. 1746, I declare under penalty of perjury the foregoing is true and correct.
SIGNATURE OF ALIEN	DATE
AUTHORIZATION OF AGENT OF ALIEN ➤ ➤	I hereby designate the agent below to represent me for the purposes of labor certification and I take full responsibility for accuracy of any representations made by my agent.
SIGNATURE OF ALIEN	DATE
NAME OF AGENT (Type or print)	ADDRESS OF AGENT (No., Street, City, State, ZIP code)

Form I–485 Application to register permanent residence or adjust status

OMB No. 1115-0053

U.S. Department of Justice
Immigration and Naturalization Service

Form I-485, Application to Register Permanent Residence or Adjust Status

Purpose of This Form.
This form is used by a person who is in the United States to apply to the Immigration and Naturalization Service (INS) to adjust to permanent resident status or register for permanent residence. It may also be used by certain Cuban nationals to request a change in the date their permanent residence began.

Who May File.
Based on an immigrant petition. You may apply to adjust your status if:

- an immigrant visa number is immediately available to you based on an approved immigrant petition; or
- you are filing this application with a complete relative, special immigrant juvenile or special immigrant military petition, which if approved, would make an immigrant visa number immediately available to you.

Based on being the spouse or child (derivative) at the time another adjustment applicant (principal) files to adjust status or at the time a person is granted permanent resident status in an immigrant category that allows derivative status for spouses and children.

- **If the spouse or child is in the United States**, the individual derivatives may file their Form I-485 adjustment of status applications concurrently with the Form I-485 for the principal beneficiary, or file the Form I-485 at anytime after the principal is approved, if a visa number is available.
- **If the spouse or child is residing abroad**, the person adjusting status in the United States should file the **Form I-824, Application for Action on an Approved Application or Petition, concurrently** with the principal's adjustment of status application to allow the derivates to immigrate to the United States without delay, if the principal's adjustment of status application is approved. **No I-824 fee will be refunded if the principal's adjustment is not granted.**

Based on admission as the fiance(e) of a U. S. citizen and subsequent marriage to that citizen. You may apply to adjust status if you were admitted to the U. S. as the K-1 fiance(e) of a U. S. citizen and you married that citizen within 90 days of your entry. If you were admitted as the K-2 child of such a fiance(e), you may apply based on your parent's adjustment application.

Based on asylum status. You may apply to adjust status if you have been granted asylum in the U. S. after being physically present in the U. S. for one year after the grant of asylum, if you still qualify as an asylee or as the spouse or child of a refugee.

Based on Cuban citizenship or nationality. You may apply to adjust status if:

- you are a native or citizen of Cuba, were admitted or paroled into the U.S. after January 1, 1959, and thereafter have been physically present in the U.S. for at least one year; or
- you are the spouse or unmarried child of a Cuban described above, and regardless of your nationality, you were admitted or paroled after January 1, 1959, and thereafter have been physically present in the U.S. for at least one year.

Based on continuous residence since before January 1, 1972. You may apply for permanent residence if you have continuously resided in the U.S. since before January 1, 1972.

Applying to change the date your permanent residence began. If you were granted permanent residence in the U. S. prior to November 6, 1966, and are a native or citizen of Cuba, his or her spouse or unmarried minor child, you may ask to change the date your lawful permanent residence began to your date of arrival in the U. S. or May 2, 1964, whichever is later.

Other basis of eligibility. If you are not included in the above categories, but believe you may be eligible for adjustment or creation of record of permanent residence, contact your local INS office.

Persons Who Are Ineligible.
Unless you are applying for creation of record based on continuous residence since before January 1, 1972, or adjustment of status under a category in which special rules apply (such as asylum adjustment, Cuban adjustment, special immigrant juvenile adjustment or special immigrant military personnel adjustment), **you are not eligible for adjustment of status if <u>any</u> of the following apply to you:**

- you entered the U.S. in transit without a visa;
- you entered the U.S. as a nonimmigrant crewman;
- you were not admitted or paroled following inspection by an immigration officer;
- your authorized stay expired before you filed this application; you were employed in the U.S. prior to filing this application, without INS authorization; or you otherwise failed to maintain your nonimmigrant status, other than through no fault of your own or for technical reasons, unless you are applying because you are an immediate relative of a U.S. citizen (parent, spouse, widow, widower or unmarried child under 21 years old), a K-1 fiance(e) or K-2 fiance(e) dependent who married the U.S. petitioner within 90 days of admission or an "H" or "I" or special immigrant (foreign medical graduates, international organization employees or their derivative family members);
- you are or were a J-1 or J-2 exchange visitor, are subject to the two-year foreign residence requirement and have not complied with or been granted a waiver of the requirement;
- you have an A, E or G nonimmigrant status, or have an occupation which would allow you to have this status, unless you complete Form I-508 (I-508F for French nationals) to wave diplomatic rights, privileges and immunities, and if you are an A or G nonimmigrant, unless you submit a complete Form I-566;
- you were admitted to Guam as a visitor under the Guam visa waiver program;
- you were admitted to the U.S. as a visitor under the Visa Waiver Pilot Program, unless you are applying because you are an immediate relative of a U.S. citizen (parent, spouse, widow, widower or unmarried child under 21 years old);
- you are already a conditional permanent resident;
- you were admitted as a K-1 fiance(e) but did not marry the U.S. citizen who filed the petition for you, or were admitted as the K-2 child of a fiance(e) and your parent did not marry the U.S. citizen who filed the petition.

General Filing Instructions.
Please answer all questions by typing or clearly printing in black ink. Indicate that an item is not applicable with **"N/A."** If the answer is **"none,"** write **"none."** If you need extra space to answer any item, attach a sheet of paper with your name and your alien registration number (A#), if any, and indicate the number of the item to which the answer refers. You must file your application with the required **Initial Evidence** described below, beginning on this page. Your application must be properly signed and filed with the correct fee. If you are under 14 years of age, your parent or guardian may sign your application.

Translations. Any foreign language document must be accompanied by a full English translation which the translator has certified as complete and correct, and by the translator's certification that he or she is competent to translate the foreign language into English.

Copies. If these instructions state that a copy of a document may be filed with this application, and you choose to send us the original, we may keep the original for our records.

Initial Evidence.
You must file your application with the following evidence:

- **Birth certificate.** Submit a copy of your foreign birth certificate or other record of your birth that meets the provisions of secondary evidence found in 8 CFR 103.2(b)(2).
- **Copy of passport page with nonimmigrant visa.** If you have obtained a nonimmigrant visa(s) from an American consulate abroad within the last year, submit a photocopy(ies) of the page(s) of your passport with the visa(s).
- **Photos.** Submit two (2) identical natural color photographs of yourself, taken within 30 days of the application. Photos must have a white background, be unmounted, printed on thin paper and be glossy and unretouched. They must show a three-quarter frontal profile showing the right side of your face, with your right ear visible and with your head bare. You may wear a headdress if required by a religious order of which you are a member. The photos must be no larger than 2 X 2 inches, with the distance from the top of the head to just below the chin about 1 and 1/4 inches. Lightly print your A# (or your name if you have no A#) on the back of each photo, using a pencil.
- **Fingerprints.** If you are between the ages of 14 and 75, you must be fingerprinted. After filing this application, INS will notify you in writing of the time and location where you must go to be fingerprinted. Failure to appear to be fingerprinted may result in denial of your application.
- **Police clearances.** If you are filing for adjustment of status as a member of a special class described in an I-485 supplement form, please read the instructions on the supplement form to see if you need to obtain and submit police clearances, in addition to the required fingerprints, with your application.
- **Medical examination (Section 232 of the Act).** When required, submit a medical examination report on the form you have obtained from INS.

Form I-485 (Rev. 02/07/00)N

-- **A. Individuals applying for adjustment of status through the INS Service Center: 1) General:** If you are filing your adjustment of status application with the INS Service Center, include your medical exam report with the application, unless you are a refugee or asylee. **2) Refugees:** If you are applying for adjustment of status one year after you were admitted as a refugee, you only need to submit a vaccination supplement with your adjustment of status application, not the entire medical report, **unless** there were medical grounds of inadmissibility that arose during the initial exam you had overseas.

-- **B. Individuals applying for adjustment of status through the local INS office and asylees applying for adjustment of status through the Service Center:** If you are filing your adjustment of status application with the local INS office, or if you are an asylee filing an adjustment of status application with the Service Center, one year after you were granted asylum, do not submit a medical report with your adjustment of status application. Wait for further instructions from INS about how and where to take the medical exam and submit the medical exam report.

-- **Fiance(e)s:** If you are a K-1 fiance(e) or K-2 dependent who had a medical exam within the past year as required for the nonimmigrant fiance (e) visa, you only need to submit a vaccination supplement, not the entire medical report. You may include the vaccination supplement with your adjustment of status application.

-- **Individuals not required to have a medical exam:** The medical report is not required if you are applying for creation of a record for admission as a lawful permanent resident under section 249 of the Act as someone who has continuously resided in the United States since January 1, 1972 (registry applicant).

- **Form G-325A, Biographic Information Sheet.** You must submit a completed G-325A if you are between 14 and 79 years of age.
- **Evidence of status.** Submit a copy of your Form I-94, Nonimmigrant Arrival/Departure Record, showing your admission to the U.S. and current status, or other evidence of your status.
- **Affidavit of Support/Employment Letter.**

-- **Affidavit of Support.** Submit the Affidavit of Support (Form I-864) if your adjustment of status application is based on your entry as a fiance(e), or a relative visa petition (Form I-130) filed by your relative or on an employment based visa petition (Form I-140) based on a business that is five percent or more owned by your family.

-- **Employment Letter.** If your adjustment of status application is based on an employment based visa petition (Form I-140), you must submit a letter on the letterhead of the petitioning employer which confirms that the job on which the visa petition is based is still available to you. The letter must also state the salary that will be paid.

(Note: The affidavit of support and/or employment letter are not required if you applying for creation of record based on continuous residence since before January 1, 1972, asylum adjustment, or a Cuban or a spouse or unmarried child of a Cuban who was admitted after January 1, 1959.)

- **Evidence of eligibility.**

-- **Based on an immigrant petition.** Attach a copy of the approval notice for an immigrant petition which makes a visa number immediately available to you, or submit a complete relative, special immigrant juvenile or special immigrant military petition which, if approved, will make a visa number immediately available to you.

-- **Based on admission as the K-1 fiance(e) of a U.S. citizen and subsequent marriage to that citizen.** Attach a copy of the fiance(e) petition approval notice, a copy of your marriage certificate and your Form I-94.

-- **Based on asylum status.** Attach a copy of the letter or Form I-94 which shows the date you were granted asylum.

-- **Based on continuous residence in the U.S. since before January 1, 1972.** Attach copies of evidence that shows continuous residence since before January 1, 1972.

-- **Based on Cuban citizenship or nationality.** Attach evidence of your citizenship or nationality, such as a copy of your passport, birth certificate or travel document.

-- **Based on derivative status as the spouse or child of another adjustment applicant or person granted permanent residence based on issuance of an immigrant visa.** File your application with the application of that other applicant, or with evidence that it is pending with the Service or has been approved, or evidence that your spouse or parent has been granted permanent residence based on an immigrant visa and:

- If you are applying as the spouse of that person, also attach a copy of your marriage certificate and copies of documents showing the legal termination of all other marriages by you and your spouse;
- If you are applying as the child of that person, also attach a copy of your birth certificate, and if the other person is not your natural mother, copies of evidence (such as a marriage certificate and documents showing the legal termination of all other marriages and an adoption decree) to demonstrate that you qualify as his or her child.

- **Other basis for eligibility.** Attach copies of documents proving that you are eligible for the classification.

Where to File.

File this application at the INS office having jurisdiction over your place of residence.

Fee. The fee for this application is **$220,** except that it is **$160** if you are less than 14 years old. There is no application fee if you are filing as a refugee under section 209(a) of the Act. If you are between the ages of 14 and 75, there is a $25 fingerprinting fee in addition to the application fee. For example, if your application fee is $220 and you are between the ages of 14 and 75, the total fee you must pay is $245. You may submit one check or money order for both the application and fingerprinting fees. Fees must be submitted in the exact amount. **DO NOT MAIL CASH.** Fees cannot be refunded. All checks and money orders must be drawn on a bank or other institution located in the United States and must be payable in United States currency. The check or money order should be made payable to the Immigration and Naturalization Service, except that:

-- if you live in Guam and are filing this application in Guam, make your check or money order payable to the "Treasurer, Guam."

-- if you live in the U.S. Virgin Islands and are filing this application in the U.S. Virgin Islands, make your check or money order payable to the "Commissioner of Finance of the Virgin Islands."

Checks are accepted subject to collection. An uncollected check in payment of an application fee will render the application and any document issued invalid. A charge of $30 will be imposed if a check in payment of a fee is not honored by the bank on which it is drawn.

Processing Information.

Acceptance. Any application that is not signed, or is not accompanied by the correct application fee, will be rejected with a notice that the application is deficient. You may correct the deficiency and resubmit the application. An application is not considered properly filed until accepted by the INS.

Initial Processing. Once an application has been accepted, it will be checked for completeness, including submission of the required initial evidence. If you do not completely fill out the form, or file it without required initial evidence, you will not establish a basis for eligibility, and we may deny your application.

Requests for More Information. We may request more information or evidence. We may also request that you submit the originals of any copy. We may return these originals when they are no longer required.

Interview. After you file your application you will be notified to appear at an INS office to answer questions about the application. You will be required to answer these questions under oath or affirmation. You must bring your Arrival-Departure Record (Form I-94) and any passport to the interview.

Decision. You will be notified in writing of the decision on your application.

Selective Service Registration. If you are a male at least 18 years old, but not yet 26 years old, and required according to the Military Selective Service Act to register with the Selective Service System, the INS will help you register. When your signed application is filed and accepted by the INS, we will transmit your name, current address, Social Security number, date of birth and the date you filed the application to the Selective Service to record your registration as of the filing date. If the INS does not accept your application, and if still so required, you are responsible to register with the Selective Service by other means, provided you are under 26 years of age. If you have already registered, the Selective Service will check its records to avoid any duplication. **(Note: men 18 through 25 years old, who are applying for student financial aid, government employment or job training benefits should register directly with the Selective Service or such benefits may be denied. Men can register at a local post office or on the Internet at http://www.sss.gov).**

Form I-485 (Rev. 02/07/00)N Page 2

Travel Outside the U.S. for Adjustment of Status Applicants Under Sections 209 and 245 of the Act and Registry Applicants Under Section 249 of the Act. Your departure from the U.S. (including brief visits to Canada or Mexico) constitutes an abandonment of your adjustment of status application, unless you are granted permission to depart and you are inspected upon your return to the U.S. Such permission to travel is called "advance parole." To request advance parole, you must file Form I-131, with fee, with the INS office where you applied for adjustment of status.

-- **Exceptions: 1) H and L nonimmigrants:** If you are an H or L nonimmigrant who continues to maintain his or her status, you may travel on a valid H or L visa without obtaining advance parole. **2) Refugees and Asylees:** If you are applying for adjustment of status one year after you were admitted as a refugee or one year after you were granted asylum, you may travel outside the United States on your valid refugee travel document, if you have one, without the need to obtain advance parole.

-- **WARNING:** Travel outside of the U.S. may trigger the 3-and 10-year bars to admission under section 212(a)(9)(B)(i) of the Act for adjustment applicants, but not registry applicants. This ground of inadmissibility is triggered if you were unlawfully present in the U.S. (i.e., you remained in the United States beyond the period of stay authorized by the Attorney General) for more than 180 days before you applied for adjustment of status, and you travel outside of the U.S. while your adjustment of status application is pending. **(Note:** Only unlawful presence that accrued on or after April 1, 1997, counts towards the 3-and 10-year bars under section 212 (a)(9)(B)(i) of the Act.)

-- If you become inadmissible under section 212(a)(9)(B)(i) of the Act while your adjustment of status application is pending, you will need a waiver of inadmissibility under section 212(a)(9)(B)(v) of the Act before your adjustment of status application can be approved. This waiver, however, is granted on a case-by-case basis and in the exercise of discretion. It requires a showing of extreme hardship to your U.S. citizen or lawful permanent resident spouse or parent, unless you are a refugee or asylee. For refugees and asylees, the waiver may be granted for humanitarian reasons, to assure family unity or if it is otherwise in the public interest.

Penalties. If you knowingly and willfully falsify or conceal a material fact or submit a false document with this request, we will deny the benefit you are filing for and may deny any other immigration benefit. In addition, you will face severe penalties provided by law and may be subject to criminal prosecution.

Privacy Act Notice. We ask for the information on this form and associated evidence to determine if you have established eligibility for the immigration benefit you are seeking. Our legal right to ask for this information is in 8 USC 1255 and 1259. We may provide this information to other government agencies, including the Selective Service System. Your failure to provide this information on this form and any requested evidence may delay a final decision or result in denial of your application.

Paperwork Reduction Act Notice. A person is not required to respond to a collection of information unless it displays a current valid OMB number. We try to create forms and instructions that are accurate, can be easily understood and which impose the least possible burden on you to provide us with information. Often this is difficult because some immigration laws are very complex. The estimated average time to complete and file this application is computed as follows: (1) 20 minutes to learn about the law and form; (2) 25 minutes to complete the form and (3) 270 minutes to assemble and file the application, including the required interview and travel time -- for a total estimated average of 5 hours and 15 minutes per application. If you have comments regarding the accuracy of this estimate or suggestions to make this form simpler, you should write to the Immigration and Naturalization Service, 425 I Street, N.W., Room 5307, Washington, D.C. 20536; OMB No. 1115-0053. **DO NOT MAIL YOUR COMPLETED APPLICATION TO THIS ADDRESS.**

OMB No. 1115-0053

U.S. Department of Justice
Immigration and Naturalization Service

Form I-485, Application to Register Permanent Resident or Adjust Status

START HERE - Please Type or Print

Part 1. Information About You.

Family Name	Given Name	Middle Initial
Address - C/O		
Street Number and Name		Apt. #
City		
State	Zip Code	
Date of Birth (month/day/year)	Country of Birth	
Social Security #	A # (if any)	
Date of Last Arrival (month/day/year)	I-94 #	
Current INS Status	Expires on (month/day/year)	

Part 2. Application Type. *(check one)*

I am applying for an adjustment to permanent resident status because:

a. ☐ an immigrant petition giving me an immediately available immigrant visa number has been approved. (Atttach a copy of the approval notice-- or a relative, special immigrant juvenile or special immigrant military visa petition filed with this application that will give you an immediately available visa number, if approved.)

b. ☐ my spouse or parent applied for adjustment of status or was granted lawful permanent residence in an immigrant visa category that allows derivative status for spouses and children.

c. ☐ I entered as a K-1 fiance(e) of a U.S. citizen whom I married within 90 days of entry, or I am the K-2 child of such a fiance(e). [Attach a copy of the fiance(e) petition approval notice and the marriage certificate.]

d. ☐ I was granted asylum or derivative asylum status as the spouse or child of a person granted asylum and am eligible for adjustment.

e. ☐ I am a native or citizen of Cuba admitted or paroled into the U.S. after January 1, 1959, and thereafter have been physically present in the U.S. for at least one year.

f. ☐ I am the husband, wife or minor unmarried child of a Cuban described in (e) and am residing with that person, and was admitted or paroled into the U.S. after January 1, 1959, and thereafter have been physically present in the U.S. for at least one year.

g. ☐ I have continuously resided in the U.S. since before January 1, 1972.

h. ☐ Other basis of eligibility. Explain. (If additional space is needed, use a separate piece of paper.)

____

I am already a permanent resident and am applying to have the date I was granted permanent residence adjusted to the date I originally arrived in the U.S. as a nonimmigrant or parolee, or as of May 2, 1964, whichever date is later, and: *(Check one)*

i. ☐ I am a native or citizen of Cuba and meet the description in (e), above.

j. ☐ I am the husband, wife or minor unmarried child of a Cuban, and meet the description in (f), above.

FOR INS USE ONLY

Returned	Receipt
Resubmitted	
Reloc Sent	
Reloc Rec'd	
Applicant Interviewed	

Section of Law
☐ Sec. 209(b), INA
☐ Sec. 13, Act of 9/11/57
☐ Sec. 245, INA
☐ Sec. 249, INA
☐ Sec. 2 Act of 11/2/66
☐ Sec. 2 Act of 11/2/66
☐ Other ____________

Country Chargeable

Eligibility Under Sec. 245
Approved Visa Petition
Dependent of Principal Alien
Special Immigrant
Other ____________

Preference

Action Block

To be Completed by
***Attorney or Representative,* if any**
☐ Fill in box if G-28 is attached to represent the applicant.
VOLAG #

ATTY State License #

Continued on back

Form I-485 (Rev. 02/07/00)N Page 1

Part 3. Processing Information.

A. City/Town/Village of Birth	Current Occupation
Your Mother's First Name	Your Father's First Name

Give your name exactly how it appears on your Arrival /Departure Record (Form I-94)

Place of Last Entry Into the U.S. (City/State)	In what status did you last enter? *(Visitor, student, exchange alien, crewman, temporary worker, without inspection, etc.)*
Were you inspected by a U.S. Immigration Officer? ☐ Yes ☐ No	
Nonimmigrant Visa Number	Consulate Where Visa Was Issued
Date Visa Was Issued (month/day/year) Sex: ☐ Male ☐ Female	Marital Status ☐ Married ☐ Single ☐ Divorced ☐ Widowed

Have you ever before applied for permanent resident status in the U.S.? ☐ No ☐ Yes If you checked "Yes," give date and place of filing and final disposition.

B. List your present husband/wife and all your sons and daughters. (If you have none, write "none." If additional space is needed, use a separate piece of paper.)

Family Name	Given Name	Middle Initial	Date of Birth (month/day/year)
Country of Birth	Relationship	A #	Applying with You? ☐ Yes ☐ No
Family Name	Given Name	Middle Initial	Date of Birth (month/day/year)
Country of Birth	Relationship	A #	Applying with You? ☐ Yes ☐ No
Family Name	Given Name	Middle Initial	Date of Birth (month/day/year)
Country of Birth	Relationship	A #	Applying with You? ☐ Yes ☐ No
Family Name	Given Name	Middle Initial	Date of Birth (month/day/year)
Country of Birth	Relationship	A #	Applying with You? ☐ Yes ☐ No
Family Name	Given Name	Middle Initial	Date of Birth (month/day/year)
Country of Birth	Relationship	A #	Applying with You? ☐ Yes ☐ No

C. List your present and past membership in or affiliation with every political organization, association, fund, foundation, party, club, society or similar group in the United States or in other places since your 16th birthday. Include any foreign military service in this part. If none, write "none." Include the name(s) of the organization(s), location(s), dates of membership from and to, and the nature of the organization (s). If additional space is needed, use a separate piece of paper.

Form I-485 (Rev. 02/07/00)N Page 2

Part 3. Processing Information. *(Continued)*

Please answer the following questions. (If your answer is **"Yes"** to any one of these questions, explain on a separate piece of paper. Answering **"Yes"** does not necessarily mean that you are not entitled to adjust your status or register for permanent residence.)

1. Have you ever, in or outside the U. S.:
   a. knowingly committed any crime of moral turpitude or a drug-related offense for which you have not been arrested? ☐ Yes ☐ No
   b. been arrested, cited, charged, indicted, fined or imprisoned for breaking or violating any law or ordinance, excluding traffic violations? ☐ Yes ☐ No
   c. been the beneficiary of a pardon, amnesty, rehabilitation decree, other act of clemency or similar action? ☐ Yes ☐ No
   d. exercised diplomatic immunity to avoid prosecution for a criminal offense in the U. S.? ☐ Yes ☐ No

2. Have you received public assistance in the U.S. from any source, including the U.S. government or any state, county, city or municipality (other than emergency medical treatment), or are you likely to receive public assistance in the future? ☐ Yes ☐ No

3. Have you ever:
   a. within the past ten years been a prostitute or procured anyone for prostitution, or intend to engage in such activities in the future? ☐ Yes ☐ No
   b. engaged in any unlawful commercialized vice, including, but not limited to, illegal gambling? ☐ Yes ☐ No
   c. knowingly encouraged, induced, assisted, abetted or aided any alien to try to enter the U.S. illegally? ☐ Yes ☐ No
   d. illicitly trafficked in any controlled substance, or knowingly assisted, abetted or colluded in the illicit trafficking of any controlled substance? ☐ Yes ☐ No

4. Have you ever engaged in, conspired to engage in, or do you intend to engage in, or have you ever solicited membership or funds for, or have you through any means ever assisted or provided any type of material support to, any person or organization that has ever engaged or conspired to engage, in sabotage, kidnapping, political assassination, hijacking or any other form of terrorist activity? ☐ Yes ☐ No

5. Do you intend to engage in the U.S. in:
   a. espionage? ☐ Yes ☐ No
   b. any activity a purpose of which is opposition to, or the control or overthrow of, the government of the United States, by force, violence or other unlawful means? ☐ Yes ☐ No
   c. any activity to violate or evade any law prohibiting the export from the United States of goods, technology or sensitive information? ☐ Yes ☐ No

6. Have you ever been a member of, or in any way affiliated with, the Communist Party or any other totalitarian party? ☐ Yes ☐ No

7. Did you, during the period from March 23, 1933 to May 8, 1945, in association with either the Nazi Government of Germany or any organization or government associated or allied with the Nazi Government of Germany, ever order, incite, assist or otherwise participate in the persecution of any person because of race, religion, national origin or political opinion? ☐ Yes ☐ No

8. Have you ever engaged in genocide, or otherwise ordered, incited, assisted or otherwise participated in the killing of any person because of race, religion, nationality, ethnic origin or political opinion? ☐ Yes ☐ No

9. Have you ever been deported from the U.S., or removed from the U.S. at government expense, excluded within the past year, or are you now in exclusion or deportation proceedings? ☐ Yes ☐ No

10. Are you under a final order of civil penalty for violating section 274C of the Immigration and Nationality Act for use of fradulent documents or have you, by fraud or willful misrepresentation of a material fact, ever sought to procure, or procured, a visa, other documentation, entry into the U.S. or any immigration benefit? ☐ Yes ☐ No

11. Have you ever left the U.S. to avoid being drafted into the U.S. Armed Forces? ☐ Yes ☐ No

12. Have you ever been a J nonimmigrant exchange visitor who was subject to the two-year foreign residence requirement and not yet complied with that requirement or obtained a waiver? ☐ Yes ☐ No

13. Are you now withholding custody of a U.S. citizen child outside the U.S. from a person granted custody of the child? ☐ Yes ☐ No

14. Do you plan to practice polygamy in the U.S.? ☐ Yes ☐ No

Continued on back

Form I-485 (Rev. 02/07/00)N Page 3

Part 4. Signature. *(Read the information on penalties in the instructions before completing this section. You must file this application while in the United States.)*

I certify, under penalty of perjury under the laws of the United States of America, that this application and the evidence submitted with it is all true and correct. I authorize the release of any information from my records which the INS needs to determine eligibility for the benefit I am seeking.

Selective Service Registration. The following applies to you if you are a man at least 18 years old, but not yet 26 years old, who is required to register with the Selective Service System: I understand that my filing this adjustment of status application with the Immigration and Naturalization Service authorizes the INS to provide certain registration information to the Selective Service System in accordance with the Military Selective Service Act. Upon INS acceptance of my application, I authorize INS to transmit to the Selective Service System my name, current address, Social Security number, date of birth and the date I filed the application for the purpose of recording my Selective Service registration as of the filing date. If, however, the INS does not accept my application, I further understand that, if so required, I am responsible for registering with the Selective Service by other means, provided I have not yet reached age 26.

Signature	*Print Your Name*	*Date*	*Daytime Phone Number*

Please Note: *If you do not completely fill out this form or fail to submit required documents listed in the instructions, you may not be found eligible for the requested benefit and this application may be denied.*

Part 5. Signature of Person Preparing Form, If Other Than Above. *(Sign Below)*

I declare that I prepared this application at the request of the above person and it is based on all information of which I have knowledge.

Signature	*Print Your Name*	*Date*	*Daytime Phone Number*

Firm Name and Address

Form I-485 (Rev. 02/07/00)N Page 4

Form I–589 Application for asylum and withholding of removal

U.S. Department of Justice
Immigration and Naturalization Service

OMB No. 1115-0086

Instructions for Form I-589
Application for Asylum and for Withholding of Removal

Purpose of This Form.

This form is used to apply for asylum in the United States (U.S.), and for withholding of removal (formerly called "withholding of deportation"). You may file for asylum and for withholding of removal if you are physically present in the United States and you are not a United States citizen.

NOTE: You **must** submit an application for asylum within one (1) year of arriving in the United States, unless there are changed circumstances that materially affect your eligibility for asylum or extraordinary circumstances relating to a delay in filing for asylum. (See Part 1: Filing Instructions, Section V, "Completing the Form," Part D, for further explanation.)

You may include in your application your spouse and your unmarried children who are under 21 years of age and physically present in the United States. Married children and children 21 years of age or older must file a separate Form I-589 application. If your spouse and/or unmarried children under the age of 21 are outside the United States, you may file a petition for them to gain similar benefits, if you are granted asylum.

This instruction pamphlet is divided into two (2) sections. The first section has filing instructions. It discusses eligibility and will guide you through filling out and filing the application. The second section describes how your application will be processed. This section also describes potential interim benefits while your application is pending. You will not be authorized to work based on filing this application.

Please read these instructions carefully. The instructions will help you complete your application and understand how it will be processed.

WARNING: **Applicants who are in the United States illegally are subject to removal if their asylum or withholding claims are not granted by an asylum officer or an Immigration Judge. Any information provided in completing this application may be used as a basis for the institution of, or as evidence in, removal proceedings, even if the application is later withdrawn. Applicants determined to have knowingly made a frivolous application for asylum will be permanently ineligible for any benefits under the Immigration and Nationality Act. See INA Section 208(d)(6) and 8 CFR 208.18.**

Form I-589 (Rev. 5-01-98) N

INDEX

PART 1. FILING INSTRUCTIONS 2

I. Who May Apply and Filing Deadlines 2
II. Basis of Eligibility 2
A. Asylum 2
B. Withholding of Removal 3
C. Legal Sources Relating to Eligibility . 3
III. Confidentiality 3
IV. Right to Counsel 3
V. Completing the Form 4
Part A. Information About You 4
Part B. Spouse and Children 4
Part C. Information About Your Claim for Asylum 5
Part D. Additional Information About Your Application for Asylum ... 5
Part E. Your Signature 6
Part F. Signature of Person Preparing Form if Other than You 6
Part G. To Be Completed at Interview ... 6
VI. Required Documents and Required Number of Copies 6
VII. Additional Documents that You May Submit 7
VIII. Fee 7
IX. Fingerprints 7
X. Organizing Your Application 8
XI. Incomplete Asylum Applications 8
XII. Where to File 8

PART 2. INFORMATION REGARDING POST- FILING REQUIREMENTS 9

I. Notification Requirements when Address Changes 9
II. Asylum Interview Process 10
III. Status While Your Claim is Pending 10
IV. Travel Outside the United States 10
V. Employment Authorization While Your Application is Pending 10
VI. Privacy Act Notice 11
VII. Paperwork Reduction Act Notice 11

SUPPLEMENTS TO THE I-589 FORM

I-589 Form, Supplement A Form 10
(For use in completing Part B)
I-589 Form, Supplement B Form 11
(For use in completing Parts C and D)

PART 1: FILING INSTRUCTIONS

I. Who May Apply and Filing Deadlines

You may apply for asylum irrespective of your immigration status, and even if you are in the United States unlawfully.

You MUST file this application within one (1) year after you arrived in the United States, unless you can show that there are changed circumstances that affect your eligibility for asylum or extraordinary circumstances that prevented you from filing within one (1) year. (See Part 1: Filing Instructions, Section V, "Completing the Form," Part D, for further explanations of this requirement.)

If you have previously been denied asylum by an Immigration Judge or the Board of Immigration Appeals, you must show that there are changed circumstances that affect your eligibility for asylum.

The determination of whether you are permitted to apply for asylum will be made once you have had an asylum interview with an asylum officer or a hearing before an Immigration Judge. Even if you are not eligible to apply for asylum because of the reasons stated above, you may still be eligible to apply for withholding of removal.

II. Basis of Eligibility

A. Asylum

In order to qualify for asylum, you must establish that you are a refugee. A refugee is a person who is unable or unwilling to return to his or her country of nationality or last habitual residence because of persecution or a well-founded fear of persecution on account of race, religion, nationality, membership in a particular social group, or political opinion.

If you are granted asylum, you and any eligible dependents included in your application will be permitted to remain and work in the United States and may eventually adjust to lawful permanent resident status. **If you are not granted asylum, the Immigration and Naturalization Service (INS) may use the information you provide in this application to establish that you are removable from the United States.**

Page 2

B. Withholding of Removal

Your asylum application is also considered to be an application for withholding of removal under section 241(b)(3) of the Immigration and Nationality Act (INA), as amended. If asylum is not granted, you may still be eligible for withholding of removal.

In order to qualify for withholding of removal, you must establish that it is more likely than not that you would be persecuted on account of race, religion, nationality, membership in a particular social group, or political opinion, in the proposed country of removal pursuant to section 241(b)(3) of the INA, as amended.

If you obtain an order withholding your removal, you cannot be returned to the country in which your life or freedom would be threatened. Withholding of removal does not apply to any spouse or child included in the application. They would have to apply for such protection on their own. If you are granted withholding of removal, this would not give you the right to bring dependents to the United States. It also would not give you the right to become a lawful permanent resident of the United States.

C. Legal Sources Relating to Eligibility

The documents listed below are some of the legal sources relating to asylum eligibility. These sources are provided for reference only. You do not need to refer to them in order to complete your application.

- Section 101(a)(42) of the Immigration and Nationality Act, 8 U.S.C. 1101(a)(42) (defining "refugee");
- Section 208 of the Immigration and Nationality Act, 8 U.S.C. 1158 (regarding eligibility for asylum);
- Section 241(b)(3) of the Immigration and Nationality Act, 8 U.S.C. 1251(b)(3) (regarding eligibility for withholding of removal);
- Title 8 of the Code of Federal Regulations, section 208, et. seq.;
- The 1967 United Nations Protocol Relating to the Status of Refugees;
- The 1951 Convention Relating to the Status of Refugees;
- Office of the United Nations High Commissioner for Refugees, Handbook on Procedures and Criteria for Determining Refugee Status (Geneva, 1992).

III. Confidentiality

The information collected will be used to make a determination on your application. It may also be provided to other government agencies (federal, state, local and/or foreign) for purposes of investigation or legal action on criminal and/or civil matters and for issues arising from the adjudication of benefits. However, no information indicating that you have applied for asylum will be provided to any government or country from which you claim a fear of persecution. Regulations protect the confidentiality of asylum claims.

IV. Right to Counsel

Although we have tried to make this form easy to use, immigration law concerning asylum is complex. You have a right to provide your own legal representation at an asylum interview and during removal proceedings before the Immigration Court, at no cost to the United States Government. If you need, or would like, help in completing this form and preparing your written statements, assistance from pro bono attorneys and/or voluntary agencies may be available. Voluntary agencies may help you for no fee or for a reduced fee and attorneys on the list may take your case for no fee. If you have not already received from INS or the Immigration Court a list of attorneys and accredited representatives, you may obtain a list by calling 1-800-870-FORM (3676).

Representatives of the United Nations High Commissioner for Refugees (UNHCR) may be able to assist you in identifying persons to help you complete the application. You may, if you wish, forward a **copy** of your application and other supporting documents to the UNHCR. (For instructions on where to file the original, please see Part 1: Filing Instructions, Section XII. "Where to File." The current address of the UNHCR is:

United Nations High Commissioner for Refugees
1775 K Street, NW, Third Floor
Washington, DC 20006
Telephone: (202) 296-5191

V. Completing the Form

Type or print all of your answers in **black** ink on the Form I-589. Your answers must be completed in English. Forms completed in a language other than English will be returned to you.

Provide the specific information requested about you and your family. **Answer ALL of the questions asked.** If any question does not apply to you or you do not know the information requested by the question, answer "none," "not applicable," or "unknown." Provide detailed information and answer the questions as completely as possible. If you need more space, attach the Supplement A or B Forms (included in the application package) and/or an additional sheet(s) indicating the question number(s) you are answering. You are strongly urged to attach additional written statements and documents that support your claim. Your written statements should include events, dates, and details of your experiences that relate to your claim for asylum.

NOTE: Please put your Alien Registration Number (A#), (if any), name (exactly as it appears in Part A of the form), signature, and date on each supplemental sheet and on the cover page of any supporting documents.

You will be permitted to amend or supplement your application at the time of your asylum interview before an asylum officer and at your hearing in Immigration Court by providing additional information and explanations about your asylum claim.

Part A. Information About You

This part asks for basic information about you. Alien Registration Number (A#) refers to your INS file number. If you do not already have an A#, the INS will assign one to you. You must provide your residential street address in the United States in Part A, Question 7, of the asylum application. You may also provide a mailing address, if different from the address where you reside, in Question 8.

In Question 12, use the current name of the country. Do not use historical, ethnic, provincial, or other local names.

The I-94#, referred to in Question 18e, is the number on Form I-94, Departure Record, given to you when you entered the United States. In Question 18f, enter the date as it appears on the Form I-94. If you did not receive a Form I-94, write "None". If you entered without being inspected by an immigration officer, write "No Inspection" in Question 18d.

Part B. Spouse and Children

You should list your spouse and all your children in this application regardless of whether they are in the United States when you file your asylum application.

You may ask to have included in your asylum application your spouse and/or any children who are unmarried, if they are in the United States. Children who are married and/or children who are 21 years of age or older must file separately for asylum by submitting their own asylum application (Form I-589).

If you apply for asylum while in proceedings before the Immigration Court, the Immigration Judge may not have authority to grant asylum to any spouse or child included in your application who is not also in proceedings.

When including family members in your asylum application, you MUST submit one additional copy of your completed asylum application and the documentary evidence establishing your family relationship, for each family member, as described below.

- If you are including your spouse in your application, submit three (3) copies of your marriage certificate.
- If you are including any unmarried children under 21 years of age in your application, submit three (3) copies of each child's birth certificate.

If you do not have, and are unable to obtain these documents, you may submit an affidavit from at least one (1) person for each event you are trying to prove. Affidavits may be provided by relatives or others. Persons providing affidavits need not be United States citizens or lawful permanent residents. **Affidavits must:**

- fully describe the circumstances or event in question and fully explain how the person acquired knowledge of the event(s);
- be sworn to, or affirmed by, persons who were alive at the time of the event(s) and have personal knowledge of the event(s) (date and place of birth, marriage, etc.) that you are trying to prove; and
- show the full name, address, date, and place of birth of each person giving the affidavit, and indicate any relationship between you and the person giving the affidavit.

If you have more than two (2) children, complete the Supplement A Form for each additional child, or attach additional pages and documentation providing the same information asked in Part B of the Form I-589.

Part C. Information about Your Claim for Asylum

This part asks specific questions relevant to eligibility for asylum and for withholding of removal. Check "yes" or "no" in the box provided for each question. If you answer "yes" to any question, explain in detail using the Supplement B Form continuation sheets as needed. You should clearly describe any of your experiences, or those of family members or others who have had similar experiences, that may show that you are a refugee.

If you have experienced harm that is difficult for you to write down and express, you should be aware that these experiences may be very important to the decision-making process regarding your request to remain in the United States. At your interview with an asylum officer or hearing with an Immigration Judge, you will need to be prepared to discuss the harm you have suffered. If you are having trouble remembering or talking about past events, it is suggested that you talk to a lawyer, an accredited representative, or a health professional who may be able to help you explain your experiences and current situation.

Part D. Additional Information about Your Application for Asylum

Check "yes" or "no" in the box provided for each question. If you answer "yes" to any question, explain in detail using the Supplement B Form continuation sheets as needed.

If you answer "yes" to question 6, you must explain why you did not apply for asylum within the first year after you arrived in the United States. The government will accept as an explanation certain changes in the conditions in your country, certain changes in your own circumstances, and certain other events that may have prevented you from applying earlier. For example, some of the events the government might consider as valid explanations include, but are not limited to, the following:

- You have learned that human rights conditions in your country have worsened since you left;
- Because of your health, you were not able to submit this application within a year after you arrived;
- You submitted an application, but it was returned to you because it was not complete, and you submitted a complete application within a reasonable amount of time.

Federal regulations specify some of the other types of events that may also qualify as valid explanations for why you filed late. These regulations are found at Title 8, Section 208.4 of the Code of Federal Regulations. The list in the Code of Federal Regulations is not all-inclusive, and the government recognizes that there are many other circumstances that might be acceptable reasons for filing more than one year after arrival.

If you are unable to explain why you did not apply for asylum within the first year after you arrived in the United States, or your explanation is not accepted by the government, you may not be eligible to apply for asylum, but you could still be eligible for withholding of removal.

Part E. Your Signature

You must sign your application in Part E and provide the information requested. Sign after you have completed and reviewed the application.

If it is determined that you have knowingly made a frivolous application for asylum you can be permanently ineligible for any benefits under the Immigration and Nationality Act. According to Title 8, Section 208.18 of the Code of Federal Regulations, an application is frivolous if any of its material elements is deliberately fabricated. (See Part 1: Filing Instructions, Section IV, "Right to Counsel," in the event that you have any questions.)

Part F. Signature of Person Preparing Form if Other than You

Any person, other than an immediate family member (your spouse, parent(s), or children) who helped prepare your application must sign the application and provide the information requested.

Penalty for Perjury. All statements contained in response to questions contained in this application are declared to be true and correct under penalty of perjury. You and anyone, other than an immediate family member, who assists you in preparing the application must sign the application under penalty of perjury. Your signature is evidence that you are aware of the contents of this application. Any person assisting you in preparing this form, other than an immediate family member, must include his or her name and address and sign the application where indicated in Part F. Failure of the preparer to sign will result in the application being returned to you as an incomplete application. If the INS later learns that you received assistance from someone other than an immediate family member, and the person who assisted you failed to sign the application, this may result in an adverse ruling against you.

Title 18, United States Code, Section 1546, provides in part:

> Whoever knowingly makes under oath, or as permitted under penalty of perjury under Section 1746 of Title 28, United States Code, knowingly subscribes as true, any false statement with respect to a material fact in any application, affidavit, or other document required by the immigration laws or regulations prescribed thereunder, or knowingly presents any such application, affidavit, or other document containing any such false statement shall be fined in accordance with this title or imprisoned not more than five years, or both.

If you knowingly provide false information on this application, you or the preparer of this application may be subject to criminal penalties under Title 18 of the United States Code and to civil penalties under Section 274C of the Immigration and Nationality Act, 8 U.S.C. 1324c.

Part G. To Be Completed at Interview

Do not sign your application in Part G before filing this form. You will be asked to sign your application in this space at the conclusion of the interview regarding your claim.

NOTE: You must, however, sign Part E of the application.

VI. Required Documents and Required Number of Copies that You Must Submit with Your Application

You must submit the following documents to apply for asylum and withholding of removal:

- **The completed, signed original and two (2) copies of your completed application, Form I-589,** and the original and two (2) copies of any supplementary sheets and supplementary statements. If you choose to submit additional supporting material (See Part 1: Filing Instructions, Section VII, "Additional Documents that You May Submit," page 7), you MUST include three (3) copies of each document. You should make and keep one (1) additional copy of the completed application for your own records.

- **An additional copy of your completed application, Form I-589,** with supplementary sheets and supplementary statements, for each family member listed in Part B who you want to have included in your application.
- **Three (3) copies of any documentary evidence of relationship,** such as birth records of your children, marriage certificate, or proof of termination of marriage, for each family member listed in Part B who you want to have included in your application. NOTE: If you do not have, and are unable to obtain, these forms of documentary evidence, you must submit an original and two (2) copies of an affidavit from a third person who knows of the relationship. (For affidavit requirements, see Part 1: Filing Instructions, Section V, "Completing the Form," Part B.)
- **One (1) passport-style photograph** of you and each family member listed in Part B who is included in your application. The photos must have been taken no more than 30 days before you file your application. Print the person's complete name and A# (if any) on the back of his or her photo with a pencil.
- **A copy of all passports or other travel documents** (cover to cover) in your possession, and a copy of any U.S. Immigration documents, such as an I-94 Departure Record, for you and each family member who you want included in your application, if you have such documents.
- If you have **other identification documents** (for example, birth certificate, military or national identification card, drivers license, etc.), it is recommended that you submit a copy with your application and bring the original(s) with you to the interview.

Original documents may be retained if submitted. If these instructions state that a copy of a document may be filed with this application and you choose to send the original, the INS or Immigration Court may keep that original for its records.

Translation of documents not in English is required. Any document in a language other than English must be accompanied by an adequate English translation that the translator has certified as complete and correct, and by the translator's certification that he or she is competent to translate into English the language used in the document.

VII. Additional Documents that You May Submit

You may also submit any supporting documents, such as newspaper articles, affidavits of witnesses or experts, medical and/or psychological records, doctors' statements, periodicals, journals, books, photographs, official documents, or personal statements. If you have difficulty discussing harm you have suffered in the past, you may wish to submit a health professional's report explaining this difficulty.

VIII. Fee

There is no fee for filing this application.

IX. Fingerprints

Applicants for asylum are subject to a check of all appropriate records and other information databases maintained by the Attorney General and by the Secretary of State. You and all of your dependents over the age of fourteen (14) listed on your asylum application must be fingerprinted and photographed. You and your dependents will be given instructions on how to complete this requirement. You will be notified in writing of the time and location of the Application Support Center or the designated Law Enforcement Agency where you must go to be fingerprinted and photographed. Failure to appear for a scheduled fingerprinting may delay eligibility for work authorization and/or result in an asylum officer dismissing your asylum application or referring it to an Immigration Judge. For applicants before an Immigration Judge, such failure will make the applicant ineligible for asylum and may delay eligibility for work authorization.

You are required to submit photographs as specified in Part 1: Filing Instructions, Section VI, "Required Documents and Required Number of Copies" of the I-589 instructions at the time you file your I-589 Application for Asylum and Withholding of Removal.

X. Organizing Your Application

Put your application together in the following order (if possible, secure with binder clips and rubber bands so that material may be easily separated):

- Your original Form I-589, with all questions completed, and the application signed by you, in Part E, and signed by any preparer, in Part F; and
- One (1) passport-style photo of you stapled to the form at Part E.

Behind your original Form I-589, attach in the following order:

- One (1) Form G-28, if represented by an attorney or other representative, signed by you and the attorney/ representative;
- The original of all supplemental sheets and supplementary statements submitted with your application;
- One (1) copy of the evidence of your relationship to your spouse and unmarried children under 21 years of age who you want included in your application, if any;
- Two (2) copies of the items listed above in your original package, except photograph.

If you are including family members in your application, attach one (1) additional package for each family member. Arrange each family member's package as follows:

- One (1) copy of your completed, signed Form I-589 and supplemental sheets submitted with the original application. In Part B, staple in the upper right hand corner one (1) passport-style photo of the family member to be included; and
- One (1) copy of Form G-28, if any.

For example, if you include your spouse and two (2) children, you should submit your original package, plus two (2) duplicates for you, plus one (1) package for your spouse, plus one (1) package for each child, for a total of six (6) packages. Be sure each has the appropriate documentation.

NOTE: Any additional pages submitted should include the applicant's printed name (exactly as it appears in Part A of the form), A# (if any), signature and date.

XI. Incomplete Asylum Applications

An asylum application that is incomplete shall be returned to you by mail within thirty (30) days of receipt of the application by the INS. An application that has not been returned to you within thirty (30) days of having been received by the INS shall be considered complete.

The filing of a complete application starts the 150-day period you must wait before you may apply for employment authorization. If your application is not complete and is returned to you, the 150-day period will not begin until you complete the application and resubmit it. (See Part 2: Information Regarding Post-Filing Requirements, Section V, "Employment Authorization," for further information regarding eligibility for employment authorization.)

An application will be considered incomplete in each of the following cases:

- The application does not include a response to each of the questions contained in the Form I-589;
- The application is unsigned;
- The application is submitted without the required photograph;
- The application is sent without the appropriate number of copies for any supporting materials submitted;
- You indicated in Part E that the application was prepared by someone other than yourself or an immediate family member and the preparer failed to complete Part F of the asylum application.

XII. Where to File

Although the INS will confirm in writing its receipt of your application, you may wish to send the completed forms by registered mail (return receipt requested).

If you are in proceedings in Immigration Court:

If you are currently in proceedings in Immigration Court (that is, if you have been served with Form I-221, Order to Show Cause; Form I-122, Notice to Applicant for Admission Detained for Hearing; Form I-862, Notice to Appear; or Form I-863, Notice of Referral to Immigration Judge), you are required to file your application, Form I-589, with the Immigration Court having jurisdiction over your case.

If you are NOT in proceedings in Immigration Court:

You are to mail your completed application for asylum and withholding of removal, Form I-589, and any other additional information, to the INS Service Center as indicated below.

If you live in Alabama, Arkansas, Colorado, Commonwealth of Puerto Rico, District of Columbia, Florida, Georgia, Louisiana, Maryland, Mississippi, New Mexico, North Carolina, Oklahoma, western Pennsylvania, South Carolina, Tennessee, Texas, United States Virgin Islands, Utah, Virginia, West Virginia, or Wyoming, mail your application to:

USINS Texas Service Center
Attn: Asylum
P.O. Box 851892
Mesquite, TX 75185-1892

If you live in Alaska, northern California, Hawaii, Idaho, Illinois, Indiana, Iowa, Kansas, Kentucky, Michigan, Minnesota, Missouri, Montana, Nebraska, northern Nevada, North Dakota, Ohio, Oregon, South Dakota, Territory of Guam, Washington, or Wisconsin, mail your application to:

USINS Nebraska Service Center
P.O. Box 87589
Lincoln, NE 68501-7589

If you live in Arizona, southern California, or southern Nevada, mail your application to:

USINS California Service Center
P.O. Box 10589
Laguna Niguel, CA 92607-0589

If you live in Connecticut, Delaware, Maine, Massachusetts, New Hampshire, New Jersey, New York, eastern Pennsylvania, Rhode Island, or Vermont, mail your application to:

USINS Vermont Service Center
Attn: Asylum
75 Lower Welden Street
St. Albans, VT 05479-0589

PART 2: INFORMATION REGARDING POST-FILING REQUIREMENTS

I. Notification Requirements when Address Changes

If you change your address you **must** inform the INS in writing within ten (10) days of moving.

While your asylum application is pending before the asylum office, you must notify the asylum office on Form AR-11 (Change of Address Form) or by a signed and dated letter of any changes of address within ten (10) days after you change your address. The address that you provide on the application, or the last change of address notification you submitted, will be used by the INS for mailing. Any notices mailed to that address shall constitute adequate service of all notices. These notices include an interview notice, or other documents, except a Notice to Alien Detained for Hearing by an Immigration Judge (Form I-122), and an Order to Show Cause (Form I-221), and a Notice and Order of Expedited Removal (Form I-860), in which personal service may be required.

If you are already in proceedings in Immigration Court, you MUST notify the Immigration Court on Form EOIR 33 (Change of Address Form) or by a signed and dated letter of any changes of address within five (5) days of the change in address. You must send the notification to the Immigration Court having jurisdiction over your case.

II. Asylum Interview Process

If you are not in proceedings in Immigration Court, you will be notified by the INS asylum office of the date, time and place (address) of a scheduled interview. The INS suggests that you bring a copy of your application with you when you have your asylum interview. An asylum officer will interview you under oath and make a determination concerning your claim. In most cases, you will not be notified of the decision in your case until a date after your interview. You have the right to legal representation at your interview, at no cost to the United States Government. (See Part 1: Filing Instructions, Section IV, "Right to Counsel.") You also may bring witnesses to testify on your behalf.

If you are unable to proceed with the asylum interview in fluent English, you must provide at no expense to the INS, a competent interpreter fluent in both English and a language that you speak fluently. Your interpreter must be at least 18 years of age. The following persons cannot serve as your interpreter: your attorney or representative of record, a witness testifying on your behalf at the interview or a representative or employee of your country. Quality interpretation may be crucial to your claim. Such assistance must be obtained, at your expense, prior to the interview.

Failure without good cause to bring a competent interpreter to your interview may be considered an unexcused failure to appear for the interview. Any unexcused failure to appear for an interview may prevent you from receiving work authorization, and your asylum application may be dismissed or referred directly to the Immigration Court.

If available, you must bring some form of identification to your interview, including any passport(s), other travel or identification documents, or Form I-94 Departure Record. You may bring to the interview any additional available items documenting your claim that you have not already submitted with your application.

If **members of your family** are included in your application for asylum, they must also appear for the interview and bring any identity or travel documents they have in their possession.

III. Status While Your Claim is Pending

While your case is pending, you will be permitted to remain in the United States. After your asylum interview, if you have not been granted asylum and appear to be deportable under Section 237 of the INA, 8 U.S.C. 1227, or inadmissible under Section 212 of the INA, 8 U.S.C. 1182, your application will be filed with the Immigration Court upon referral by the asylum office.

IV. Travel Outside the United States

If you leave the United States without first obtaining advance parole from the INS, it will be presumed that you have abandoned your application. If you obtain advance parole and return to the country of claimed persecution, it will be presumed that you abandoned your application, unless you can show that there were compelling reasons for your return.

V. Employment Authorization while Your Application is Pending

You will be granted permission to work if your asylum application is granted.

You may request permission to work if your asylum application is pending and 150 days have lapsed since your application was accepted by the INS. See 8 CFR 208.7(a)(1). If your asylum application has not been denied within 180 days from the date of filing a complete asylum application, you may be granted employment authorization. You may request permission to work by filing an Application for Employment Authorization, Form I-765. Follow the instructions on that application and submit it with a copy of evidence that you have a pending asylum application. Each family member you have asked to have included in your application who also wants permission to work must submit a separate Form I-765. You may obtain a Form I-765 by calling 1-800-870-FORM (3676).

You may NOT apply for employment authorization until your application for asylum or withholding of removal has been pending for at least 150 days since acceptance by the INS or the Immigration Court. If you file an application for employment authorization before 150 days have expired, that application will be denied. Any delay in the processing of your asylum application that you request or cause shall not be counted as part of the 150-day time period.

VI. Privacy Act Notice.

The authority to collect this information is contained in Title 8 of the United States Code. Furnishing the information on this form is voluntary; however, failure to provide all of the requested information may result in the delay of a final decision or denial of your request.

VII. Paperwork Reduction Act Notice.

Under the Paperwork Reduction Act, a person is not required to respond to a collection of information unless it displays a currently valid OMB control number. We try to create forms and instructions that are accurate, can be easily understood, and which impose the least possible burden on you to provide us with information. Often this is difficult because some immigration laws are very complex. The estimated average time to complete and file this application is as follows: (1) 2 hours to learn about the form; (2) 5 hours to complete the form; and (3) 5 hours to assemble and file the application; for a total estimated average burden hours of 12 hours per application. The estimated time to complete the form will vary dependent on the complexity of your individual circumstances. If you have comments regarding the accuracy of this estimate or suggestions for making this form simpler, you can write to the Immigration and Naturalization Service, Policy Directives and Instructions Branch, 425 I Street, NW., Room 5307, Washington, DC 20536, OMB No. 1115-0086. **Do not mail your completed application to this address.**

Page 11

U.S. Department of Justice
Immigration and Naturalization Service

OMB No. 1115-0086

Application for Asylum and for Withholding of Removal

Start Here - Please Type or Print. USE BLACK INK. SEE THE SEPARATE INSTRUCTION PAMPHLET FOR INFORMATION ABOUT ELIGIBILITY AND HOW TO COMPLETE AND FILE THIS APPLICATION.

PART A. INFORMATION ABOUT YOU.

1. Alien Registration Number(s), if any (A#'s)
2. Social Security Number
3. Complete Last Name
4. First Name
5. Middle Name
6. What Other Names Have You Used? *(Include maiden name and aliases)*
7. Residence in the U.S. C/O — Telephone Number
   Street Number and Name — Apt. No.
   City — State — ZIP Code
8. Mailing Address in the U.S. if Other than Above C/O — Telephone Number
   Street Number and Name — Apt. No.
   City — State — ZIP Code
9. Sex Male Female
10. Marital Status: ☐ Single ☐ Married ☐ Divorced ☐ Widowed
11. Date of Birth *(Mo/Day/Yr)*
12. City and Country of Birth
13. Present Nationality *(Citizenship)*
14. Nationality at Birth
15. Race, Ethnic or Tribal Group
16. Religion
17. *Check each box that applies.*
   I am **not** now in removal, deportation or exclusion proceedings.
   I am now in removal, deportation or exclusion proceedings.
   I was previously in removal, deportation or exclusion proceedings.
   I have never been in removal, deportation or exclusion proceedings.
18. *Complete 18a through 18g.*
   a. When did you last leave your country? *(Mo/Day/Yr)*
   b. When did you last enter the U.S.? *(Mo/Day/Yr)*
   c. Where did you last enter the U.S.?
   d. What was your status when you last entered the U.S.? *(What type of visa did you have, if any)?*
   e. What is your I-94 Number?
   f. What is the expiration date of your authorized stay, if any?
   g. Have you previsously entered the U.S.? No Yes. If YES, list place, date, and your status for each entry. *(Attach additional sheets as needed.)*
   Date ________ Place ________ Status ________
   Date ________ Place ________ Status ________
   Date ________ Place ________ Status ________

FOR INS USE ONLY

Returned	Receipt
Resubmitted	
Reloc Sent	
Reloc Rec'd	
Action: Interview Date:	

Asylum:
Granted
Denied
Referred
Recommended Approval Date ________

Date A.O. final decision or referral issued ________

Total number of persons granted asylum ________

For EOIR Use Only

To Be Completed by Attorney or Representative, if any

Check if G-28/EOIR-28 is attached showing you represent the applicant.

INS VOLAG or PIN #

ATTY State License # ________

Form I-589 (Rev. 05-01-98) N

OMB No. 1115-0086

Information About You - Continued.

19. What is your native language?	20. Are you fluent in English? Yes No	21. What other languages do you speak fluently?

22. Have you ever applied to the United States Government or to any other Government(s) for refugee status, asylum, withholding of deportation, or withholding of removal?
- ☐ No.
- ☐ I was included in a pending application of my parent(s). However, I am now 21 years old or married so I am filing my own application.
- ☐ I was included in my spouse's application, but now I wish to file my own application.
- ☐ Yes. (*In what country and what was the decision? Also specify the date of the decision.*) *Country* ______________ *Date* ________
  Decision ______________

23. What country issued your last passport or travel document?	24. Passport # Travel Document #	25. Expiration Date

26. Prior address in last country of residence or country in which you fear persecution. *(List Address, City/Town, Province, State, Department, and Country)*

27. Provide the following information about your education, beginning with the most recent.

Name of School	Type of School	Location	Attended From *(Mo/Yr)*	To *(Mo/Yr)*

28. Provide the following information about your residences during the last five years. List your present address first. *(Use additional sheets of paper if necessary.)*

Number and Street	City	Province or State	Country	Dates From *(Mo/Yr)*	To *(Mo/Yr)*

29. Provide the following information about your employment during the last five years. List your present employment first. *(Use additional sheets of paper if necessary.)*

Name and Address of Employer	Your Occupation	Dates From *(Mo/Yr)*	To *(Mo/Yr)*

30. Provide the following information about your parents.

Name	Country and City of Birth	Location

Page 2 (Rev. 05-01-98) N

OMB No. 1115-0086

PART B. INFORMATION ABOUT YOUR SPOUSE AND CHILDREN.

Your Spouse. ☐ I am not married. *(Skip to Part B, Your Children.)*

1. Alien Registration Number (A#)		2. Passport/ID Card, etc.#	
3. Complete Last Name	4. First Name	5. Middle Name	6. Date of Birth *(Mo/Day/Yr)*
7. Date of Marriage *(Mo/Day/Yr)*	8. Place of Marriage	9. City and Country of Birth	
10. Nationality *(Citizenship)*	11. Race, Ethnic or Tribal Group		12. Sex ☐ Male ☐ Female
13. Is this person in the U.S.? ☐ Yes. *(Complete blocks 13 to 24.)* ☐ No. *(Specify Location)*			14. Social Security #
15. Place of Last Entry in the U.S.?	16. Date of Last Entry in the U.S.? *(Mo/Day/Yr)*	17. I-94#	18. Status when Last Admitted *(Visa type, if any)*
19. Expiration of Status *(Mo/Day/Yr)*	20. Is your spouse in removal, deportation or exclusion proceedings? ☐ Yes ☐ No	21. If previously in the U.S., Date of Previous Arrival *(Mo/Day/Yr)*	
22. Place of Previous Arrival		23. Status at Time of Previous Arrival	

24. If in the U.S., is this person to be included in this application? *(Check the appropriate box.)*

☐ Yes. *(Attach one (1) photograph of your spouse in the upper right hand corner of Page 3 on the extra copy of the application submitted for this person.)*
☐ No, because my spouse is/has:
- ☐ Filing separately.
- ☐ Separate application pending.
- ☐ Other reasons.

All of Your Children, Regardless of Age or Marital Status.
(Use Supplement A Form or attach additional pages and documentation if you have more than two (2) children.)

1. Alien Registration Number (A#)		2. Passport/ID Card, etc.#	
3. Complete Last Name	4. First Name	5. Middle Name	6. Date of Birth *(Mo/Day/Yr)*
7. City and Country of Birth	8. Nationality *(Citizenship)*	9. Race, Ethnic or Tribal Group	10. Sex ☐ Male ☐ Female
11. Is this child in the U.S.? ☐ Yes. *(Complete blocks 12 to 22.)* ☐ No. *(Specify Location)*			12. Social Security #
13. Place of Last Entry in the U.S.?	14. Date of Last Entry in the U.S.? *(Mo/Day/Yr)*	15. I-94#	16. Status when Last Admitted *(Visa type, if any)*
17. Expiration of Status *(Mo/Day/Yr)*	18. Is this child in removal, deportation or exclusion proceedings? ☐ Yes ☐ No	19. If previously in the U.S., Date of Previous Arrival *(Mo/Day/Yr)*	
20. Place of Previous Arrival		21. Status at Time of Previous Arrival	

22. If in the U.S., is this person to be included in this application? *(Check the appropriate box.)*

☐ Yes. *(Attach one (1) photograph of your child in the upper right hand corner of Page 3 on the extra copy of the application submitted for this person.)*
☐ No, because child is/has:
- ☐ Filing separately.
- ☐ Separate application pending.
- ☐ Over 21 years of age.
- ☐ Married.
- ☐ Other reasons.

Page 3 (Rev. 05-01-98) N

OMB No. 1115-0086

Information About Your Spouse and Children - Continued *(Use Supplement A Form or attach additional sheets of paper to list additional children.)*

All of Your Children, Regardless of Age or Marital Status.

1. Alien Registration Number (A#):		2. Passport/ID Card, etc. #	
3. Complete Last Name	4. First Name	5. Middle Name	6. Date of Birth *(Mo/Day/Yr)*
7. City and Country of Birth	8. Nationality *(Citizenship)*	9. Race, Ethnic or Tribal Group	10. Sex ☐ Male ☐ Female
11. Is this person in the U.S.? ☐ Yes. *(Complete blocks 11 to 22.)* ☐ No. *(Specify Location)*			12. Social Security #
13. Place of Last Entry in the U.S.?	14. Date of Last Entry in the U.S.? *(Mo/Day/Yr)*	15. I-94#	16. Status when Last Admitted *(Visa type, if any)*
17. Expiration of Status *(Mo/Day/Yr)*	18. Is this child in removal, deportation or exclusion proceedings? ☐ Yes ☐ No		19. If previously in the U.S., Date of Previous Arrival *(Mo/Day/Yr)*
20. Place of Previous Arrival			21. Status at Time of Previous Arrival

22. If in the U.S., is this person to be included in this application? *(Check the appropriate box.)*

☐ Yes. *(Attach one (1) photograph of your child in the upper right hand corner of Page 3 on the extra copy of the application submitted for this person.)*
☐ No, because child is/has:
- ☐ Filing separately.
- ☐ Separate application pending.
- ☐ Over 21 years of age.
- ☐ Married.
- ☐ Other reasons.

PART C. INFORMATION ABOUT YOUR CLAIM TO ASYLUM.
(Use Supplement B Form or attach additional sheets of paper as needed to complete your responses to the questions contained in Part C.)

1. Why are you seeking asylum? Explain in detail what the basis is for your claim. *(Attach additional sheets of paper as needed.)*

Page 4 (Rev. 05-01-98) N

OMB No. 1115-0086

Information About Your Claim to Asylum - Continued.

2. Have you or any member of your family ever belonged to or been associated with any organizations or groups in your home country, such as, but not limited to, a political party, student group, labor union, religious organization, military or paramilitary group, civil patrol, guerrilla organization, ethnic group, human rights group, or the press or media?

No. ☐ Yes. If yes, provide a detailed explanation of your or your relatives' involvement with each group and include the name of each organization or group; the dates of membership or affiliation; the purpose of the organization; your duties or your relatives' duties or responsibilities in the group or organization; and whether you or your relatives are still active in the group(s). *(Attach additional sheets of paper as needed.)*

3. Have you or any member of your family ever been mistreated or threatened by the authorities of your home country or any other country or by a group or groups that are controlled by the government, or that the government of the country is unable or unwilling to control?

☐ No. ☐ Yes. If YES, was it because of any of the following reasons? *(Check each of the following boxes that apply.)*

☐ Race ☐ Religion ☐ Nationality ☐ Membership in a particular social group ☐ Political Opinion

On a separate sheet of paper, specify for each instance, what occurred and the circumstances; the relationship to you of the person involved; the date; the exact location; who it was who took such action against you or your family member(s); his/her position in the government or group; the reason why the incident occurred. Attach documents referring to these incidents, if they are available. *(Attach additional sheets of paper as needed.)*

4. Have you or any member of your family ever been accused, charged, arrested, detained, interrogated, convicted and sentenced, or imprisoned in your country or any other country, including the United States?

☐ No. ☐ Yes. If YES, for each instance, specify what occurred and the circumstances; dates; location; the duration of the detention or imprisonment; the reason(s) for the detention or conviction; the treatment received during the detention or imprisonment; any formal charges that were lodged against you or your relatives; the reason for release; treatment after release. Attach documents referring to these incidents if they are available. *(Attach additional sheets of paper as needed.)*

Page 5 (Rev. 05-01-98) N

OMB No. 1115-0086

Information About Your Claim to Asylum - Continued.

5. Do you fear being subjected to torture (severe physical or mental pain or suffering, including rape or other sexual abuse) in your home country or any other country if you return?

☐ No. ☐ Yes. If YES, explain why. *(Attach additional sheets of paper as needed.)*

6. What do you think would happen to you if you returned to the country from which you claim you would be subjected to persecution? Explain in detail and provide information or documentation to support your statement, if available. *(Attach additional sheets of paper as needed.)*

7. Describe in detail your trip to the United States from your home country. After leaving the country from which you are claiming asylum, did you or your spouse or child(ren), who are now in the United States, travel through or reside in any other country before entering the United States?

☐ No. ☐ Yes. If YES, for each person, identify each country and indicate the length of stay; the person's status while there; the reasons for leaving; whether the person is entitled to return for residence purposes; and if the person applied for refugee status or for asylum while there; or why he or she did not do so. *(Attach additional sheets of paper as needed.)*

Page 6 (Rev. 05-01-98) N

OMB No. 1115-0086

PART D. ADDITIONAL INFORMATION ABOUT YOUR APPLICATION FOR ASYLUM.

(Use Supplement B Form or attach additional sheets of paper as needed to complete your responses to the questions contained in Part D.)

1. Do you, your spouse, or your child(ren) now hold, or have you ever held, permanent residence, other permanent status, or citizenship, in any country other than the one from which you are now claiming asylum?

☐ No. ☐ Yes. If YES, explain. *(Attach additional sheets of paper as needed).*

2. Have you, your spouse, your child(ren), your parents ever filed for, been processed for, or been granted or denied refugee status or asylum by the United States Government?

☐ No. ☐ Yes. If YES, explain the decision and what happened to any status you received as a result of that decision. If you have been denied asylum by an Immigration Judge or the Board of Immigration Appeals, please describe any change in country conditions or your own circumstances since the date of the denial that may affect your eligibility for asylum. *(Attach additional sheets of paper as needed.)*

3. Have you, your spouse, your child(ren), or your parents ever filed for, been processed for, or been granted or denied refugee status or asylum by any other country?

☐ No. ☐ Yes. If YES, explain the decision and what happened to any status you received as a result of that decision. *(Attach additional sheets of paper as needed.)*

4. Have you, your spouse, or child(ren) ever caused harm or suffering to any person because of his or her race, religion, nationality, membership in a particular social group or belief in a particular political opinion, or ever ordered, assisted, or otherwise participated in such acts?

☐ No. ☐ Yes. If YES, describe, in detail, each such incident and your own or your spouse's or child(ren)'s involvement. *(Attach additional sheets of paper as needed.)*

5. After you left your country of claimed persecution for the reasons you have described, did you return to that country?

☐ No. ☐ Yes. If YES, describe, in detail, the circumstances of your visit, for example, the date(s) of the trip(s), the purpose(s) of the trip(s), and the length of time you remained in that country for the visit(s). *(Attach additional sheets of paper as needed.)*

6. Are you filing the application more than one year after your last arrival in the United States?

☐ No. ☐ Yes. If YES, explain why you did not file within the first year after you arrived. You should be prepared to explain at your interview or hearing why you did not file your asylum application within the first year after you arrived. For guidance in answering this question see Part 1: Filing Instructions, Section V. "Completing the Form," Part D. *(Attach additional sheets of paper as needed.)*

Page 7 (Rev. 05-01-98) N

OMB No. 1115-0086

PART E. SIGNATURE.

After reading the information on penalties in the instructions, complete and sign below. If someone helped you prepare this application, he or she must complete Part F.

I certify, under penalty of perjury under the laws of the United States of America, that this application and the evidence submitted with it is all true and correct. Title 18, United States Code, Section 1546, provides in part: "Whoever knowingly makes under oath, or as permitted under penalty of perjury under Section 1746 of Title 28, United States Code, knowingly subscribes as true, any false statement with respect to a material fact in any application, affidavit, or other document required by the immigration laws or regulations prescribed thereunder, or knowingly presents any such application, affidavit, or other document containing any such false statement or which fails to contain any reasonable basis in law or fact -- shall be fined in accordance with this title or imprisoned not more than five years, or both". I authorize the release of any information from my record which the Immigration and Naturalization Service needs to determine eligibility for the benefit I am seeking.

Staple your photograph here.

WARNING: **Applicants who are in the United States illegally are subject to removal if their asylum or withholding claims are not granted by an asylum officer or an Immigration Judge. Any information provided in completing this application may be used as a basis for the institution of, or as evidence in, removal proceedings even if the application is later withdrawn. Applicants determined to have knowingly made a frivolous application for asylum will be permanently ineligible for any benefits under the Immigration and Nationality Act. See INA 208(d)(6) and 8 CFR 208.18.**

Signature of Applicant *(The person named in Part A)*

[______________________________] ____________________

Sign your name so it all appears within the brackets. Date *(Mo/Day/Yr)*

Print Name	Write your name in your native alphabet

Did your spouse, parent or child(ren) assist you in completing this application? No Yes *(If YES, list their name(s) and relationship.)*

(Name) ______________ *(Relationship)* ______________ *(Name)* ______________ *(Relationship)* ______________

Did someone other than you or your spouse, parent or child(ren) prepare this application? No Yes *(Complete Part F)*

Asylum applicants may be represented by counsel. Have you been provided with a list of persons who may be available to assist you, at little or no cost, with your asylum claim? No Yes

PART F. SIGNATURE OF PERSON PREPARING FORM IF OTHER THAN ABOVE. *Sign below.*

I declare that I have prepared this application at the request of the person named in Part E, that the responses provided are based on all information of which I have knowledge, or which was provided to me by the applicant and that the completed application was read to the applicant in his or her native language for verification before he or she signed the application in my presence. I am aware that the knowing placement of false information on the Form I-589 may also subject me to civil penalties under 8 U.S.C. Section 1324(c).

Signature of Preparer	Print Name	Date *(Mo/Day/Yr)*

Daytime Telephone Number ( )	Address of Preparer: Street Number and Name

Apt. No.	City	State	ZIP Code

PART G. TO BE COMPLETED AT INTERVIEW.

You will be asked to complete this Part when you appear before an asylum officer of the Immigration and Naturalization Service (INS), or an Immigration Judge of the Executive Office for Immigration Review (EOIR) for examination.

I swear (affirm) that I know the contents of this application that I am signing, including the attached documents and supplements, that they are all true or not all true to the best of my knowledge and that corrections numbered ________ to ________ were made by me or at my request.

Signed and sworn to before me by the above-name applicant on:

____________________ Signature of Applicant

____________________ Date *(Mo/Day/Yr)*

____________________ Write your Name in your Native Alphabet

____________________ Signature of Asylum Officer or Immigration Judge

Page 8 (Rev. 05-01-98) N

OMB No. 1115-0086
SUPPLEMENT A FORM I-589

A# *(If available)*	Date
Applicant's Name	Applicant's Signature

ALL OF YOUR CHILDREN, REGARDLESS OF AGE OR MARITAL STATUS.

(Attach additional pages and documentation if you have more than two (2) children.)

1. Alien Registration Number (A#):
2. Passport/ID Card, etc.#
3. Complete Last Name
4. First Name
5. Middle Name
6. Date of Birth *(Mo/Day/Yr)*
7. City and Country of Birth
8. Nationality *(Citizenship)*
9. Race, Ethnic or Tribal Group
10. Sex ☐ Male ☐ Female
11. Is this child in the U.S.? ☐ Yes. *(Complete blocks 12 to 22.)* ☐ No. *(Specify Location)*
12. Social Security #
13. Place of Last Entry in the U.S.?
14. Date of Last Entry in the U.S.? *(Mo/Day/Yr)*
15. I-94#
16. Status when Last Admitted *(Visa type, if any)*
17. Expiration of Status *(Mo/Day/Yr)*
18. Is this child in removal, deportation or exclusion proceedings? ☐ Yes ☐ No
19. If previously in the U.S., Date of Previous Arrival *(Mo/Day/Yr)*
20. Place of Previous Arrival
21. Status at Time of Previous Arrival
22. If in the U.S., is this person to be included in this application? *(Check the appropriate box.)*

☐ Yes. *(Attach one (1) photograph of your child in the upper right hand corner of Page 3 on the extra copy of the application submitted for this person.)*
☐ No, because child is/has:
- ☐ Filing separately.
- ☐ Separate application pending.
- ☐ Over 21 years of age.
- ☐ Married.
- ☐ Other reasons.

1. Alien Registration Number (A#):
2. Passport/ID Card, etc.#
3. Complete Last Name
4. First Name
5. Middle Name
6. Date of Birth *(Mo/Day/Yr)*
7. City and Country of Birth
8. Nationality *(Citizenship)*
9. Race, Ethnic or Tribal Group
10. Sex ☐ Male ☐ Female
11. Is this child in the U.S.? ☐ Yes. *(Complete blocks 12 to 22.)* ☐ No. *(Specify Location)*
12. Social Security #
13. Place of Last Entry in the U.S.?
14. Date of Last Entry in the U.S.? *(Mo/Day/Yr)*
15. I-94#
16. Status when Last Admitted *(Visa type, if any)*
17. Expiration of Status *(Mo/Day/Yr)*
18. Is this child in removal, deportation or exclusion proceedings? ☐ Yes ☐ No
19. If previously in the U.S., Date of Previous Arrival *(Mo/Day/Yr)*
20. Place of Previous Arrival
21. Status at Time of Previous Arrival
22. If in the U.S., is this person to be included in this application? *(Check the appropriate box.)*

☐ Yes. *(Attach one (1) photograph of your child in the upper right hand corner of Page 3 on the extra copy of the application submitted for this person.)*
☐ No, because child is/has:
- ☐ Filing separately.
- ☐ Separate application pending.
- ☐ Over 21 years of age.
- ☐ Married.
- ☐ Other reasons.

Page 9 (Rev. 05-01-98) N

OMB No. 1115-0086
SUPPLEMENT B FORM I-589

ADDITIONAL INFORMATION ABOUT YOUR CLAIM TO ASYLUM.

A# *(If available)*	Date
Applicant's Name	Applicant's Signature

Use attached blank response sheet to supplement any information requested. Please copy and complete as needed.

PART ___

QUESTION ___

Page 10 (Rev. 05-01-98) N

OMB No. 1115-0086
SUPPLEMENT B FORM I-589

ADDITIONAL INFORMATION ABOUT YOUR CLAIM TO ASYLUM.

A# *(If available)*	Date
Applicant's Name	Applicant's Signature

Use attached blank response sheet to supplement any information requested. Please copy and complete as needed.

PART ____

QUESTION ____

Page 11 (Rev. 05-01-98) N

U. S. Department of Justice
Immigration and Naturalization Service

OMB No. 1115-0086

SUPPLEMENTAL INSTRUCTIONS TO FORM I-589
APPLICATION FOR ASYLUM AND WITHOLDING OF REMOVAL

I. Application for withholding of removal under Article 3 of the Convention against Torture and other Cruel, Inhuman or Degrading Treatment or Punishment ("Convention against Torture")

Form I-589 application for asylum and withholding of removal will be considered an application for withholding of removal under the Convention against Torture if you tell the Immigration Judge that you would like to be considered for withholding of removal under the Convention against Torture or if it is determined that the evidence you present indicates you may be tortured in the country of removal. To apply for withholding of removal under the Convention against Torture, you must fully complete the I-589. You should include a detailed explanation of why you fear torture in response to Question 5, Part C of the application. In response to Question 3, Part C you should write about any mistreatment you experienced or any threats made against you by a government or somebody connected to a government.

Only Immigration Judges and the Board of Immigration Appeals may grant withholding of removal or deferral of removal under the Convention against Torture. The Immigration Judge will first determine whether you are eligible for asylum under the Immigration and Nationality Act (INA) section 208 or for withholding of removal under INA section 241(b)(3). If you are not eligible for either form of relief from removal, the Immigration Judge will determine whether the Convention against Torture prohibits your removal to a country in which you fear torture.

II. What is withholding of removal under Article 3 of the Convention against Torture?

Article 3 of the Convention against Torture, prohibits the United States from removing you to a country in which it is more likely than not that you would be subject to torture. The Convention against Torture does not prohibit the United States from returning you to any other country where you would not be tortured. This means that you may be removed to a third country even if you are protected from removal to the country in which you would be tortured. Although you are protected from removal to a country where it is more likely than not that you will be tortured, withholding of removal does not allow you to adjust to lawful permanent resident status or to petition to bring family members to come to, or remain in, the United States.

III. Who is eligible for withholding of removal under the Convention against Torture?

To be granted withholding of removal to a country under the Convention against Torture, you must show that it is more likely than not that you would be tortured in that country. "Torture" is defined in Article 1 of the Convention against Torture and at 8 CFR 208.18(a). For an act to be considered torture, it must be an extreme form of cruel and inhuman treatment; it must cause severe physical or mental pain and suffering; and it must be intended to cause severe pain and suffering. Torture is an act inflicted for such purposes as obtaining from the victim or a third person information or a confession, punishing the victim for an act he or she or a third person has committed or is suspected of having committed, or intimidating or coercing the victim or a third person, or for any reason based on discrimination of any kind. Torture must be inflicted by or at the instigation of a public official or someone acting in official capacity, or it must be inflicted with the consent or acquiescence of a public official or person acting in official capacity. The victim must be in the custody or physical control of the torturer. Torture does not include pain or suffering that arises from or is incidental to lawful sanctions.

IV. Who is barred from being granted withholding of removal and what happens to someone who is barred?

You may not be granted withholding of removal pursuant to 8 CFR 208.16 if you are barred from withholding of removal under INA section 241(b)(3)(B). If you 1) assisted in Nazi persecution or engaged in genocide, 2) have persecuted another person, 3) have been convicted of a particularly serious crime and therefore represent a danger to the community of the United States, 4) are considered for serious reasons to have committed a serious non-political crime outside the United States, or 5) represent a danger to the security of the United States, you may not be granted withholding of removal. If it is more likely than not that you will be tortured in a country but are ineligible for withholding of removal, your removal will be deferred under 8 CFR 208.17(a). Deferral of removal does not confer any lawful or permanent immigration status in the United States and does not necessarily result in release from detention. Deferral of removal is effective only until it is terminated. Deferral of removal is subject to review and termination if it is determined that it is no longer more likely than not that you would be tortured in the country to which your removal is deferred or if you request that your deferral be terminated.

Form I-589S (3/22/99)

Form OF–156 Nonimmigrant visa application

Approved OMB 1405–0018
Expires 10–31–95
Estimated Burden 1 hour *

THIS FORM IS SUPPLIED GRATIS

NONIMMIGRANT VISA INFORMATION

IMPORTANT – READ CAREFULLY

A valid VISA is necessary for most aliens who wish to apply for entry into the United States. Under U.S. law, all aliens seeking admission are presumed to require an immigrant visa unless they establish that they are entitled to receive a visa in one of the nonimmigrant visa categories. The most widely known nonimmigrant visa category is the visitor visa, which is used by aliens who wish to enter the United States temporarily for business purposes (B–1) or for tourism, visit to relatives and friends, or similar reasons (B–2). Other categories of nonimmigrant visas are required for persons who wish to enter as representatives of foreign governments (A & G), in transit (C), as crewmen (D), treaty traders and investors (E), students in academic or language programs (F), temporary workers and trainees (H), journalists (I), exchange visitors (J), fiance(e)s of U.S. citizens (K), intracompany transferees (L), and students in vocational or other nonacademic programs (M), the parents of certain special immigrants (N), temporary workers of extraordinary ability (O), athletes and entertainers (P), cultural exchange visitors (Q), and religious workers (R).

A nonimmigrant visa for a particular category is valid for entry only for the purpose for which it was originally issued. For example, a student visa cannot be used for entry as a visitor, nor can the possessor of a visitor visa enter to study.

A visa is not a guarantee of entry into the United States. The bearer of a visa is subject to inspection at the port of entry by U.S. Immigration officials who have authority to deny admission. Therefore, the recipient of a visa should carry with him/her, for possible presentation to immigration inspectors, the evidence submitted to the consular officer when the visa was obtained.

The validity period shown in a nonimmigrant visa relates only to the period during which it may be used in making application for admission into the United States; it does not indicate the length of time the alien may spend in the United States. The period for which the bearer of a nonimmigrant visa is authorized to remain in the United States is determined by the U.S. Immigration authorities at the port of entry. A nonimmigrant who remains in the United States beyond the period for which he/she has been granted permission to stay may become subject to deportation.

Certain categories of nonimmigrant visas require special documentation which can be furnished only by an authority in the United States. These categories include students, who must have a valid Form I–20 A–B or I–20 M–N issued by the prospective school; exchange visitors, who must have a Form IAP–66 issued by the sponsoring organization; and temporary workers and trainees, intracompany transferees, fiance(e)s of U.S citizens, athletes and entertainers, and cultural exchange visitors, all of whom must have a specific petition filed on their behalf and approved by the U.S. Immigration and Naturalization Service.

There may be a fee charged for your visa. If there is a fee it is approximately the same as that which is charged by your government to a United States citizen for a similar type visa.

TO APPLY FOR A NONIMMIGRANT VISA

1. Complete this application form by PRINTING all of the answers.

2. Submit your passport with the completed application form. Your passport should be valid for at least 6 months longer than your intended period of stay in the United States.

3. A separate application is required for each traveler, regardless of age, and whether or not more than one person is included in the same passport.

4. Present a recent photograph 1–1/2 inches square (37 x 37 mm) with your usual signature written on the REVERSE side. Children under the age of 16 are not required to submit a photograph.

5. Evidence substantiating the purpose of your trip and your intention to depart from the United States after a temporary visit may be required. Such evidence might include: a letter from your employer, documents outlining your plans while in the United States, and other evidence showing why you would return abroad after a short stay, such as family ties, employment, or similar binding obligations in your home country. Students are required to present a completed Form I–20 A–B or I–20 M–N; exchange visitors must present a Form IAP–66; and temporary workers and intracompany transferees, fiance(e)s, athletes and entertainers, and cultural exchange visitors must show evidence of a petition approved by the Immigration Service. Supplementary information will also be required of treaty traders and investors, fiance(e)s, and religious workers. Evidence should also be submitted regarding the arrangements you have made to cover your expenses while in the United States and to provide for your departure from the United States.

The above requirements are not inclusive, in that all applicants will not be required to submit all documents, and some applicants will be required by the consular officer to submit additional documents. In order to avoid delay, it is to your advantage to submit as complete documentation as possible when you first submit your visa application.

*Public reporting burden for this collection of information is estimated to average 1 hour per response, including time required for searching existing data sources, gathering the necessary data, providing the information required, and reviewing the final collection. Send comments on the accuracy of this estimate of the burden and recommendations for reducing it to: Department of State (OIS/RA/DR) Washington, D.C. 20520–0264, and to the Office of Information and Regulatory Affairs, Office of Management and Budget, Paperwork Reduction Project (1405–0018), Washington, D. C. 20503.

OPTIONAL FORM 156 (Rev. 6–93)
Department of State

IMPORTANT – Turn over page for details

VISAS BY MAIL

If you wish to apply for a nonimmigrant visa without making a personal appearance at a United States Consular Office, complete this form after having carefully read all of the information contained there. Sign and date the form. Enclose all of the documentation requested. In some localities and under certain circumstances the consular officer may require an applicant to appear in person to apply for a visa. You will be informed if this is considered necessary in your case.

SUPPLY A SELF-ADDRESSED ENVELOPE - LARGE ENOUGH TO RETURN YOUR PASSPORT TO YOU. AFFIX SUFFICIENT POSTAGE TO THE ENVELOPE TO EXPEDITE THE RETURN OF YOUR PASSPORT.

NOTE: As soon as we receive your application, and if your eligibility for a visa can be determined on the basis of the application form and the documents submitted therewith, a NON-IMMIGRANT VISA will be stamped in your passport which will be returned to you promptly. If there is a question concerning your documentation or eligibility, you will be invited by mail or telephone to visit the Consular Office for a discussion of your plans to visit the U.S.A.

APPLY FOR YOUR VISA EARLY AND BEFORE YOU MAKE FINAL TRAVEL ARRANGEMENTS

HOLIDAY NOTICE

Consular Offices are closed on all legal holidays of this country and of the United States of America.

Holidays of the U.S.A.

January 1	New Year's Day
Third Monday in January	Martin Luther King, Jr.'s Birthday
Third Monday in February	President's Day
Last Monday in May	Memorial Day
July 4	Independence Day
First Monday in September	Labor Day
Second Monday in October	Columbus Day
November 11	Veterans' Day
Fourth Thursday in November	Thanksgiving Day
December 25	Christmas Day

For sale by the U.S. Government Printing Office
Superintendent of Documents, Mail Stop: SSOP, Washington, D.C. 20402–9328

*U.S. Government Printing Office: 1997 — 418-149/40113

PLEASE TYPE OR PRINT YOUR ANSWERS IN THE SPACE PROVIDED BELOW EACH ITEM.

1. SURNAMES OR FAMILY NAMES *(Exactly as in Passport)*

2. FIRST NAME AND MIDDLE NAME *(Exactly as in Passport)*

3. OTHER NAMES *(Maiden, Religious, Professional, Aliases)*

4. DATE OF BIRTH *(Day, Month, Year)*

8. PASSPORT NUMBER

5. PLACE OF BIRTH
City, Province | Country

DATE PASSPORT ISSUED *(Day, Month, Year)*

6. NATIONALITY

7. SEX
☐ Male
☐ Female

DATE PASSPORT EXPIRES *(Day, Month, Year)*

9. HOME ADDRESS *(Include apartment no., street, city, province, and postal zone)*

10. NAME AND STREET ADDRESS OF PRESENT EMPLOYER OR SCHOOL *(Postal box number unacceptable)*

11. HOME TELEPHONE NO.

12. BUSINESS TELEPHONE NO.

13. COLOR OF HAIR

14. COLOR OF EYES

15. COMPLEXION

16. HEIGHT

17. MARKS OF IDENTIFICATION

18. MARITAL STATUS
☐ Married ☐ Single ☐ Widowed ☐ Divorced ☐ Separated
If married, give name and nationality of spouse.

19. NAMES AND RELATIONSHIPS OF PERSONS TRAVELING WITH YOU(NOTE: *A separate application must be made for a visa for each traveler, regardless of age.)*

20. HAVE YOU EVER APPLIED FOR A U.S. VISA BEFORE, WHETHER IMMIGRANT OR NONIMMIGRANT?
☐ No
☐ Yes Where? ____________
When? ____________ Type of visa? ____________
☐ Visa was issued ☐ Visa was refused

21. HAS YOUR U.S. VISA EVER BEEN CANCELED?
☐ No
☐ Yes Where? ____________
When? ____________ By whom? ____________

22. Bearers of visitors visas may generally not work or study in the U.S.
DO YOU INTEND TO WORK IN THE U.S.? ☐ No ☐ Yes
If YES, explain.

23. DO YOU INTEND TO STUDY IN THE U.S.? ☐ No ☐ Yes
If YES, write name and address of school as it appears on form I-20.

DO NOT WRITE IN THIS SPACE

B-1/B-2 MAX B-1 MAX B-2 MAX

OTHER ____________ MAX
Visa Classification

MULT OR ____________
Number Applications

MONTHS ____________
Validity

L.O. CHECKED ____________

ISSUED /REFUSED

ON ____________ BY ____________

UNDER SEC ____________ INA

REFUSAL REVIEWED BY ____________

MRV#

24. PRESENT OCCUPATION *(If retired, state past occupation)*

25. WHO WILL FURNISH FINANCIAL SUPPORT INCLUDING TICKETS?

26. AT WHAT ADDRESS WILL YOU STAY IN THE U.S.A.? *(City and State)*

27. WHAT IS THE PURPOSE OF YOUR TRIP?

28. WHEN DO YOU INTEND TO ARRIVE IN THE U.S.A.?

29. HOW LONG DO YOU PLAN TO STAY IN THE U.S.A.?

30. HAVE YOU EVER BEEN IN THE U.S.A.?
☐ No
☐ Yes When? ____________
For how long? ____________

NONIMMIGRANT VISA APPLICATION

COMPLETE ALL QUESTIONS ON REVERSE OF FORM

OPTIONAL FORM 156 (REV. 6/96) PAGE 1 50156-106
Department of State

31. (a) HAVE YOU OR ANYONE ACTING FOR YOU EVER INDICATED TO A U.S. CONSULAR OR IMMIGRATION EMPLOYEE A DESIRE TO IMMIGRATE TO THE U.S.? (b)HAS ANYONE EVER FILED AN IMMIGRANT VISA PETITION ON YOUR BEHALF?(c) HAS LABOR CERTIFICATION FOR EMPLOYMENT IN THE U.S. EVER BEEN REQUESTED BY YOU OR ON YOUR BEHALF?

(a) ☐ No ☐ Yes (b) ☐ No ☐ Yes (c) ☐ No ☐ Yes

32. ARE ANY OF THE FOLLOWING IN THE U.S.? ( ) NO ( ) YES (If YES, circle appropriate relationship and indicate that person's status in the U.S., i.e., studying, working, U.S. permanent resident, U.S. citizen, etc.)

HUSBAND/WIFE__________ FIANCE/FIANCEE __________ BROTHER/SISTER __________

FATHER/MOTHER__________ SON/DAUGHTER __________

33. PLEASE LIST THE COUNTRIES WHERE YOU HAVE LIVED FOR MORE THAN 6 MONTHS DURING THE PAST 5 YEARS BEGIN WITH YOUR PRESENT RESIDENCE.

Countries	Cities	Approximate Dates

34. IMPORTANT: ALL APPLICANTS MUST READ AND CHECK THE APPROPRIATE BOX FOR EACH ITEM.

A visa may not be issued to persons who are within specific categories defined by law as inadmissible to the United States (except when a waiver is obtained in advance). Are any of the following applicable to you?

- Have you ever been afflicted with a communicable disease of public health significance, a dangerous physical or mental disorder, or been a drug abuser or addict? ☐ Yes ☐ No
- Have you ever been arrested or convicted for any offense or crime, even though subject of a pardon, amnesty, or other such legal action? ☐ Yes ☐ No
- Have You ever been a controlled substance (drug) trafficker, or a prostitute or procurer? ☐ Yes ☐ No
- Have you ever sought to obtain or assist others to obtain a visa, entry into the U.S., or any U.S. immigration benefit by fraud or willful misrepresentation? ☐ Yes ☐ No
- Were you deported from the U.S.A. within the last 5 years? ☐ Yes ☐ No
- Do you seek to enter the United States to engage in export control violations, subversive or terrorist activities, or any unlawful purpose? ☐ Yes ☐ No
- Have you ever ordered, incited, assisted, or otherwise participated in the persecution of any person because of race, religion, national origin, or political opinion under the control, direct or indirect, of the Nazi Government of Germany, or of the government of any area occupied by, or allied with, the Nazi Government of Germany, or have you ever participated in genocide? ☐ Yes ☐ No
- Have you ever voted in the U.S.A. in violation of law? ☐ Yes ☐ No
- Are you a former U.S. Citizen who renounced citizenship after 09/30/1996 to avoid taxation? ☐ Yes ☐ No
- Are you a member or representative of a terrorist organization? ☐ Yes ☐ No

A YES answer does not automatically signify ineligibility for a visa, but if you answered YES to any of the above, or if you have any question in this regard, personal appearance at this office is recommended. If appearance is not possible at this time, attach a statement of facts in your case to this application.

35. I certify that I have read and understood all the questions set forth in this application and the answers I have furnished on this form are true and correct to the best of my knowledge and belief. I understand that any false or misleading statement may result in the permanent refusal of a visa or denial of entry into the United States. I understand that possession of a visa does not entitle the bearer to enter the United States of America upon arrival at port of entry if he or she is found inadmissible.

DATE OF APPLICATION ____________________

APPLICANT'S SIGNATURE____________________

If this application has been prepared by a travel agency or another person on your behalf, the agent should indicate name and address of agency or person with appropriate signature of individual preparing form.

SIGNATURE OF PERSON PREPARING FORM
(if other than applicant) ____________________

DO NOT WRITE IN THIS SPACE

37 mm x 37 mm

PHOTO

Glue photo here

Form OF–230 Application for immigrant visa and alien registration

In accordance with 5 CFR 1320 5 (b), persons are not required to respond to the collection of this information unless this form displays a currently valid OMB control number

Approved OMB 1405-0015
Expires 3-31-2001
Estimated Burden 1 hour*

APPLICATION FOR IMMIGRANT VISA AND ALIEN REGISTRATION

PART 1 - BIOGRAPHIC DATA

INSTRUCTIONS: Complete one copy of this form for yourself and each member of your family, regardless of age, who will immigrate with you. Please print or type your answer to all questions. Questions that are **Not Applicable** should be so marked. If there is insufficient room on the form, answer on a separate sheet using the same numbers as appear on the form. Attach the sheet to this form.

WARNING: Any false statement or concealment of a material fact may result in your permanent expulsion from the United States.

This form (OF-230 PART I) is Part I of two parts which, together with Optional Form OF-230 PART II, constitute the complete Application for Immigrant Visa and Alien Registration.

1. FAMILY NAME FIRST NAME MIDDLE NAME

2. OTHER NAMES USED OR BY WHICH KNOWN *(If married woman, give maiden name)*

3. FULL NAME IN NATIVE ALPHABET *(If Roman letters not used)*

4. DATE OF BIRTH *(Day) (Month) (Year)*

5. AGE

6. PLACE OF BIRTH *(City or town) (Province) (Country)*

7. NATIONALITY *(If dual national, give both)*

8. GENDER ☐ MALE ☐ FEMALE

9. MARITAL STATUS ☐ Single *(Never married)* ☐ Married ☐ Widowed ☐ Divorced ☐ Separated

Including my present marriage, I have been married ________ times.

10. MARKS OF IDENTIFICATION

11. PRESENT ADDRESS *(City or Town) (Province) (Country)*

Telephone number: Home Office

12. NAME OF SPOUSE *(Maiden or family name) (First name) (Middle name)*

Date and place of birth of spouse:

Address of spouse *(If different from your own)*:

Spouse's occupation:

13. LIST NAME, DATE AND PLACE OF BIRTH, AND ADDRESSES OF ALL CHILDREN

NAME	DATE AND PLACE OF BIRTH	ADDRESS *(If different from your own)*

14A. PERSON(S) NAMED IN 12 AND 13 WHO WILL ACCOMPANY ME TO THE UNITED STATES NOW.

14B. PERSON(S) NAMED IN 12 AND 13 WHO WILL FOLLOW ME TO THE UNITED STATES AT A LATER DATE.

OF 230 Part I (ENGLISH) **THIS FORM MAY BE OBTAINED GRATIS AT CONSULAR OFFICES OF THE UNITED STATES OF AMERICA**
(Rev. 03-1998)
DEPT. OF STATE
50230(1) 101

PAGE 2

15. NAME OF FATHER, DATE AND PLACE OF BIRTH, AND ADDRESS *(If deceased, so state and give year of death)*

16. MAIDEN NAME OF MOTHER, DATE AND PLACE OF BIRTH, AND ADDRESS *(If deceased, so state and give year of death)*

17. LIST BELOW ALL EMPLOYMENT FOR THE LAST TEN YEARS

EMPLOYER	LOCATION	JOB TITLE	FROM/TO

In what occupation do you intend to work in the United States? __________

18. LIST BELOW ALL EDUCATIONAL INSTITUTIONS ATTENDED

SCHOOL AND LOCATION	FROM/TO	COURSE OF STUDY	DEGREE OR DIPLOMA

Languages spoken or read: __________

Professional associations of which you are a member: __________

19. MILITARY SERVICE: ☐ Yes ☐ No

Branch: __________ Dates of Service: __________

Rank/Position: __________ Military Speciality/Occupation: __________

20. LIST BELOW ALL PLACES YOU HAVE LIVED FOR AT LEAST SIX MONTHS SINCE REACHING THE AGE OF 16. BEGIN WITH YOUR PRESENT RESIDENCE.

CITY OR TOWN	PROVINCE	COUNTRY	FROM/TO

21. LIST DATES OF ALL PREVIOUS VISITS TO OR RESIDENCE IN THE UNITED STATES. *(If never, so state)* GIVE TYPE OF VISA STATUS, IF KNOWN. GIVE "A" NUMBER, IF ANY.

FROM/TO	LOCATION	VISA	TYPE OR "A" NO. *(If known)*

SIGNATURE OF APPLICANT	DATE

NOTE: Return this completed form immediately to the consular office address on the covering letter. This form will become part of your immigrant visa and your visa application cannot be processed until this form is complete.

* Public reporting burden for this collection of information is estimated to average 1 hour per response, including time required for searching existing data sources, gathering the necessary data, providing the information required, and reviewing the final collection. Send comments on the accuracy of this estimate of the burden an recommendations for reducing it to: Department of State (OIS/RA/DR) Washington, D.C. 20520 0264, and to the Office of information and Regulatory Affairs, Office of Management and Budget, Paperwork Reduction Project (1405-0015), Washington, D.C. 20503.

In accordance with 5 CFR 1320 5(b), persons are not required to respond to the collection of this information unless this form displays a currently valid OMB control number.

Approved OMB 1405-0015
Expires 3-31-2001
Estimated Burden 23 Hours *

APPLICATION FOR IMMIGRANT VISA AND ALIEN REGISTRATION

PART II - SWORN STATEMENT

INSTRUCTIONS: Complete one copy of this form for yourself and each member of your family, regardless of age, who will immigrate with you. Please print or type your answer to all questions. Questions that are **Not Applicable** should be so marked. If there is insufficient room on the form, answer on a separate sheet using the same numbers as appear on the form. Attach the sheet to this form. DO NOT SIGN this form until instructed to do so by the consular officer. The fee for filing this application is listed under tariff item No. 20. The fee should be paid in United States dollars or local currency equivalent, or by bank draft, when you appear before the consular officer.

WARNING: Any false statement or concealment of a material fact may result in your permanent expulsion from the United States. Even though you should be admitted to the United States, a fraudulent entry could be grounds for your prosecution and/or deportation.

This form (OF-230 PART II) is a continuation of Form OF-230 PART I, which together, constitute the complete Application for Immigrant Visa and Alien Registration.

22. FAMILY NAME FIRST NAME MIDDLE NAME

23. OTHER NAMES USED OR BY WHICH KNOWN *(If married woman, give maiden name)*

24. FULL NAME IN NATIVE ALPHABET *(If Roman letter not used)*

25. PERMANENT ADDRESS IN THE UNITED STATES *(Street address including zip code)*

Telephone number:

26. PERSON YOU INTEND TO JOIN AT YOUR PERMANENT ADDRESS IN THE UNITED STATES *(Name, address, and relationship)*

Telephone number:

27. NAME AND ADDRESS OF SPONSORING PERSON OR EMPLOYER

Telephone number:

28. **United States laws governing the issuance of visas require each applicant to state whether or not he or she is a member of any class of individuals excluded from admission into the United States. The excludable classes are described below in general terms. You should read carefully the following list and answer YES or NO to each category. The answers you give will assist the consular officer to reach a decision on your eligibility to receive a visa.**

EXCEPT AS OTHERWISE PROVIDED BY LAW, ALIENS WITHIN THE FOLLOWING CLASSIFICATIONS ARE INELIGIBLE TO RECIEVE A VISA. DO ANY OF THE FOLLOWING CLASSES APPLY TO YOU?

a. An alien who has a communicable disease of public health significance; who has failed to present documentation of having received vaccinations in accordance with U.S. law; who has or has had a physical or mental disorder that poses or is likely to pose a threat to the safety or welfare of the alien or others; or who is a drug abuser or addict. [212(a)(1)] ☐ Yes ☐ No

b. An alien convicted of, or who admits having committed a crime involving moral turpitude or violation of any law relating to a controlled substance; who has been convicted of 2 of more offenses for which the aggregate sentences were 5 years or more; who is coming to the United States to engage in prostitution or commercialized vice or who has engaged in prostitution or procuring within the past 10 years; who is or has been an illicit trafficker in any controlled substance; or who has committed a serious criminal offense in the United States and who has asserted immunity from prosecution. [212(a)(2)] ☐ Yes ☐ No

c. An alien who seeks to enter the United States to engage in espionage, sabotage, export control violations, terrorist activities, overthrow of the Government of the United States or other unlawful activity; who is a member of or affiliated with the Communist or other totalitarian party; who participated in Nazi persecutions or genocide; or who has engaged in genocide. Are you a member or representative of a terrorist organization as currently designated by the U.S. Secretary of State? [212(a)(3)] ☐ Yes ☐ No

d. An alien who is likely to become a public charge [212 (a)(4)] ☐ Yes ☐ No

e. An alien who seeks to enter for the purpose of performing skilled or unskilled labor who has not been certified by the Secretary of Labor; who is a graduate of a foreign medical school seeking to perform medical services who has not passed the NBME exam or its equivalent; or a health care worker seeking to perform such work without a certificate from the CGFNS or from an equivalent approved independent credentialing organization. [212(a)(5)] ☐ Yes ☐ No ☐ Not Applicable

f. An alien who failed to attend a hearing on deportation or inadmissibility within the last 5 years; who seeks or has sought a visa, entry into the United States, or any immigration benefit by fraud or misrepresentation; who knowingly assisted any other alien to enter or try to enter the United States in violation of law; who, after November 30, 1996, attended on student (F) visa status a U.S. public elementary school or who attended a U.S. public secondary school without reimbursing the school; or who is subject to a civil penalty under INA 274C [212(a)(6)] ☐ Yes ☐ No

g. An alien who is permenently ineligible to U.S. citizenship; or who departed the United States to evade military service in time of war. [212(a)(8)] ☐ Yes ☐ No

Previous editions obsolate
OF 230 Part II (ENGLISH)
(REV. 03-1998)
DEPT. OF STATE
NSN 7540-00-149-0919
50230(1) 101

*Public reporting burden for this collection of information is estimated to average 24 hours per response, including time required for searching existing data sources, gathering the necessary data, providing the information required, and reviewing the final collection. Send comments on the accuracy of this estimate of the burden and recommendations for reducing it to. Department of State (OIS/RA/DR) Washington D.C. 20520 0264, and to the Office of Information and Regulatory Affairs, Office of Management and Budget, Paperwork Reduction Project (1405-0015), Washington D.C. 20503.

h. An alien previously ordered removed within 5 years or ordered removed a second time within 20 years; who was previously unlawfully present and ordered removed within 10 years or ordered removed a second time within 20 years; who was convicted of an aggravated felony and ordered removed; who was previously unlawfully present in the United States for more than 180 days but less than one year who voluntarily departed within the last 3 years; or who was unlawfully present for more than one year or an aggregate of one year within the last 10 years. [212(a)(9)] ☐ Yes ☐ No

i. An alien who is coming to the United States to practice polygamy; who withholds custody of a U.S. citizen child outside the United States from a person granted legal custody by a U.S. court; who has voted in the United States in violation of any law or regulation; or who renounced U.S. citizenship to avoid taxation. [212(a))10)] ☐ Yes ☐ No

j. An alien who is a former exchange visitor who has not fulfilled the 2-year foreign residence requirement. [212(e)] ☐ Yes ☐ No

k. An alien physically present in the United States within 90 days who was not maintaining lawful nonimmigrant status at the time of depature. [212(o)] ☐ Yes ☐ No

l. An alien determined by the Attorney General to have knowingly made a frivolous application for asylum. [208(d)(6)] ☐ Yes ☐ No

29. HAVE YOU EVER BEEN CHARGED, ARRESTED OR CONVICTED OF ANY OFFENSE OR CRIME? ☐ Yes ☐ No
(If answer is Yes, please explain)

30. HAVE YOU EVER BEEN REFUSED ADMISSION TO THE UNITED STATES AT A PORT-OF-ENTRY? ☐ Yes ☐ No
(If answer is Yes, please explain)

31. HAVE YOU EVER APPLIED FOR A SOCIAL SECURITY NUMBER?
☐ Yes. Give Number: ________________ ☐ No

Do you want a Social Security Card issued to you? ☐ Yes ☐ No

32. WERE YOU ASSISTED IN COMPLETING THIS APPLICATION? ☐ Yes ☐ No
(If answer is Yes, give name and address of person assisting you, indicating whether relative, friend, travel agent, attorney, or other)

33. THE FOLLOWING DOCUMENTS ARE SUBMITTED IN SUPPORT OF THIS APPLICATION:

☐ Passport	☐ Military record	☐ Evidence of own assets
☐ Birth Certificate	☐ Police Certificate	☐ Affidavit of support
☐ Marriage Certificate	☐ Medical records	☐ Offer of employment
☐ Death Certificate	☐ Photographs	☐ Educational records
☐ Divorce decree	☐ Birth Certificate of all children who will not be immigrating at this time. (List those for whom birth certificates are not available.)	☐ Other *(describe)*

DO NOT WRITE BELOW THE FOLLOWING LINE
The consular officer will assist you in ansewering items 34 and 35.

34. I claim to be exempt from ineligibility to receive a visa and exclusion under item ____________ in Part 28 for the following reasons:

212(a)(5)	Beneficiary of a Waiver under:		
☐ Not Applicable	☐ 212(a)(3)(D)(ii)	☐ 212(e)	☐ 212(h)
☐ Not Required	☐ 212(a)(3)(D)(iii)	☐ 212(g)(1)	☐ 212(i)
☐ Attached	☐ 212(a)(3)(D)(iv)	☐ 212(g)(2)	

35. I claim to be:

☐ A Family-Sponsored Immigrant
☐ An Employment Based-Immigrant
☐ A Diversity Immigrant
☐ A Special Category ______________________
(Returning resident, Hong Kong, Tibetan, Private Legislation, etc.)

☐ I derive foreign state chargeability under Sec. 202(b) through my ____________

☐ Preference: ________________

☐ Numerical limitation: ____________ *(foreign state)*

I understand that I am required to surrender my visa to the United States Immigration Officer at the place where I apply to enter the United States, and that the possession of a visa does not entitle me to enter the United States if at that time I am found to be inadmissible under the Immigration laws.

I understand that any willfully false or misleading statement or willful concealment of a material fact made by me herein may subject me to permanent exclusion from the United States and, if I am admitted to the United States, may subject me to criminal prosecution and/or deportation.

I, the undersigned applicant for a United States Immigrant visa, do solemnly swear *(or affirm)* that all statements which appear in this application, consisting of Optional Forms 230 PART I and 230 PART II combined, have been made by me, including the answers to items 1 through 35 inclusive, and that they are true and complete to the best of my knowledge and belief. I do further swear *(or affirm)* that, if admitted into the United States, I will not engage in activities which would be prejudicial to the public interest, or endanger the welfare, safety, or security of the United States; in activities which would be prohibited by the laws of the United States relating to espionage, sabotage, public disorder, or in other activities subversive to the national security; in any activity a purpose of which is the opposition to or the control, or overthrow of, the Government of the United States, by force, violence, or other unconstitutional means.

I understand that completion of this form by persons required by law to register with the Selective Service System *(males 18 through 25 years of age)* constitutes such registration in accordance with the Military Selective Service Act.

I understand all the foregoing statements, having asked for and obtained an explanation on every point which was not clear to me.

The relationship claimed in items 12 and 13 verified by documentation submitted to consular officer except as noted:

____
(Signature of Applicant)

Subscribed and sworn to before me this ________ day of ________________ , 19 _____ at: ______________________

TARIFF ITEM NO. 20.

____
(Consular Officer)

THIS FORM MAY BE OBTAINED GRATIS AT CONSULAR OFFICES OF THE UNITED STATES OF AMERICA

Form I–864 Affidavit of support under section 213A of the Act

U.S. Department of Justice
Immigration and Naturalization Service

OMB NO. 1115-0214
Affidavit of Support Under Section 213A of the Act

INSTRUCTIONS

Purpose of this Form
This form is required to show that an intending immigrant has adequate means of financial support and is not likely to become a public charge.

Sponsor's Obligation
The person completing this affidavit is the sponsor. A sponsor's obligation continues until the sponsored immigrant becomes a U.S. citizen, can be credited with 40 qualifying quarters of work, departs the United States permanently, or dies. Divorce does not terminate the obligation. By executing this form, you, the sponsor, agree to support the intending immigrant and any spouse and/or children immigrating with him or her and to reimburse any government agency or private entity that provides these sponsored immigrants with Federal, State, or local means-tested public benefits.

General Filing Instructions
Please answer all questions by typing or clearly printing in black ink only. Indicate that an item is not applicable with "N/A". If an answer is "none," please so state. If you need extra space to answer any item, attach a sheet of paper with your name and Social Security number, and indicate the number of the item to which the answer refers.

You must submit an affidavit of support for each applicant for immigrant status. You may submit photocopies of this affidavit and all supporting documentation for any spouse or children immigrating with an immigrant you are sponsoring, but the signature on each photocopied affidavit must be original. For purposes of this form, a spouse or child is immigrating with an immigrant you are sponsoring if he or she is: 1) listed in Part 3 of this affidavit of support; and 2) applies for an immigrant visa or adjustment of status within 6 months of the date this affidavit of support is originally completed and signed. The signature on the affidavit, including the signature on photocopies, must be notarized by a notary public or signed before an Immigration or a Consular Officer.

You should give the completed affidavit of support with all required documentation to the sponsored immigrant for submission to either a Consular Officer with Form OF-230, Application for Immigrant Visa and Alien Registration, or an Immigration Officer with Form I-485, Application to Register Permanent Residence or Adjust Status. You may enclose the affidavit of support and accompanying documents in a sealed envelope to be opened only by the designated Government official. The sponsored immigrant must submit the affidavit of support to the Government within 6 months of its signature.

Who Needs an Affidavit of Support under Section 213A?
This affidavit must be filed at the time an intending immigrant is applying for an immigrant visa or adjustment of status. It is required for:

- All immediate relatives, including orphans, and family-based immigrants. (Self-petitioning widow/ers and battered spouses and children are exempt from this requirement); and
- Employment-based immigrants where a relative filed the immigrant visa petition or has a significant ownership interest (5 percent or more) in the entity that filed the petition.

Who Completes an Affidavit of Support under Section 213A?

- For immediate relatives and family-based immigrants, the family member petitioning for the intending immigrant must be the sponsor.
- For employment-based immigrants, the petitioning relative or a relative with a significant ownership interest (5 percent or more) in the petitioning entity must be the sponsor. The term "relative," for these purposes, is defined as husband, wife, father, mother, child, adult son or daughter, brother, or sister.
- If the petitioner cannot meet the income requirements, a joint sponsor may submit an additional affidavit of support.

A sponsor, or joint sponsor, must also be:

- A citizen or national of the United States or an alien lawfully admitted to the United States for permanent residence;
- At least 18 years of age; and
- Domiciled in the United States or its territories and possessions.

Sponsor's Income Requirement
As a sponsor, your household income must equal or exceed 125 percent of the Federal poverty line for your household size. For the purpose of the affidavit of support, household size includes yourself, all persons related to you by birth, marriage, or adoption living in your residence, your dependents, any immigrants you have previously sponsored using INS Form I-864 if that obligation has not terminated, and the intending immigrant(s) in Part 3 of this affidavit of support. The poverty guidelines are calculated and published annually by the Department of Health and Human Services. Sponsors who are on active duty in the U.S. Armed Forces other than for training need only demonstrate income at 100 percent of the poverty line *if* they are submitting this affidavit for the purpose of sponsoring their spouse or child.

If you are currently employed and have an *individual* income which meets or exceeds 125 percent of the Federal poverty line or (100 percent, if applicable) for your household size, you do not need to list the income of any other person. When determining your income, you may include the income generated by individuals related to you by birth, marriage, or

Form I-864 (1/21/98)Y

adoption who are living in your residence, if they have lived in your residence for the previous 6 months, or who are listed as dependents on your most recent Federal income tax return whether or not they live in your residence. For their income to be considered, these household members or dependents must be willing to make their income available for the support of the sponsored immigrant(s) if necessary, and to complete and sign Form I-864A, Contract Between Sponsor and Household Member. However, a household member who is the immigrant you are sponsoring only need complete Form I-864A if his or her income will be used to determine your ability to support a spouse and/or children immigrating with him or her.

If in any of the most recent 3 tax years, you and your spouse each reported income on a joint income tax return, but you want to use only your own income to qualify (and your spouse is not submitting a Form I-864A), you may provide a separate breakout of your individual income for these years. Your individual income will be based on the earnings from your W-2 forms, Wage and Tax Statement, submitted to IRS for any such years. If necessary to meet the income requirement, you may also submit evidence of other income listed on your tax returns which can be attributed to you. You must provide documentation of such reported income, including Forms 1099 sent by the payer, which show your name and Social Security number.

You must calculate your household size and total household income as indicated in Parts 4.C. and 4.D. of this form. You must compare your total household income with the minimum income requirement for your household size using the poverty guidelines. For the purposes of the affidavit of support, determination of your ability to meet the income requirements will be based on the most recent income-poverty guidelines published in the Federal Register at the time the Consular or Immigration Officer makes a decision on the intending immigrant's application for an immigrant visa or adjustment of status. Immigration and Consular Officers will begin to use updated poverty guidelines on the first day of the second month after the date the guidelines are published in the Federal Register.

If your total household income is equal to or higher than the minimum income requirement for your household size, you do not need to provide information on your assets, and you may *not* have a joint sponsor unless you are requested to do so by a Consular or Immigration Officer. If your total household income does not meet the minimum income requirement, the intending immigrant will be ineligible for an immigrant visa or adjustment of status, unless:

- You provide evidence of assets that meet the requirements outlined under "Evidence of Assets" below; and/or
- The immigrant you are sponsoring provides evidence of assets that meet the requirements under "Evidence of Assets" below; or
- A joint sponsor assumes the liability of the intending immigrant with you. A joint sponsor must execute a separate affidavit of support on behalf of the intending immigrant and any accompanying family members. A joint sponsor must individually meet the minimum requirement of 125 percent of the poverty line based on his or her household size and income and/or assets, including any assets of the sponsored immigrant.

The Government may pursue verification of any information provided on or in support of this form, including employment, income, or assets with the employer, financial or other institutions, the Internal Revenue Service, or the Social Security Administration.

Evidence of Income

In order to complete this form you must submit the following evidence of income:

- A copy of your complete Federal income tax return, as filed with the Internal Revenue Service, for each of the most recent 3 tax years. If you were not required to file a tax return in any of the most recent 3 tax years, you must provide an explanation. If you filed a joint income tax return and are using only your own income to qualify, you must also submit copies of your W-2s for each of the most recent 3 tax years, and *if* necessary to meet the income requirement, evidence of other income reported on your tax returns, such as Forms 1099.
- If you rely on income of any members of your household or dependents in order to reach the minimum income requirement, copies of their Federal income tax returns for the most recent 3 tax years. These persons must each complete and sign a Form I-864A, Contract Between Sponsor and Household Member.
- Evidence of current employment or self-employment, such as a recent pay statement, *or* a statement from your employer on business stationery, showing beginning date of employment, type of work performed, and salary or wages paid. You must also provide evidence of current employment for any person whose income is used to qualify.

Evidence of Assets

If you want to use your assets, the assets of your household members or dependents, and/or the assets of the immigrant you are sponsoring to meet the minimum income requirement, you must provide evidence of assets with a cash value that equals at least five times the difference between your total household income and the minimum income requirement. For the assets of a household member, other than the immigrant(s) you are sponsoring, to be considered, the household member must complete and sign Form I-864A, Contract Between Sponsor and Household Member.

All assets must be supported with evidence to verify location, ownership, and value of each asset. Any liens and liabilities relating to the assets must be documented. List only assets that can be readily converted into cash within 1 year. Evidence of assets includes, but is not limited to the following:

Form I-864 (1/21/98)Y **Page 2**

- Bank statements covering the last 12 months, *or* a statement from an officer of the bank or other financial institution in which you have deposits, including deposit/withdrawal history for the last 12 months, and current balance;
- Evidence of ownership and value of stocks, bonds, and certificates of deposit, and date(s) acquired;
- Evidence of ownership and value of other personal property, and date(s) acquired; and
- Evidence of ownership and value of any real estate, and date(s) acquired.

Change of Sponsor's Address

You are required by 8 U.S.C. 1183a(d) and 8 CFR 213a.3 to report every change of address to the Immigration and Naturalization Service and the State(s) in which the sponsored immigrant(s) reside(s). You must report changes of address to INS on Form I-865, Sponsor's Notice of Change of Address, within 30 days of any change of address. You must also report any change in your address to the State(s) in which the sponsored immigrant(s) live.

Penalties

If you include in this affidavit of support any material information that you know to be false, you may be liable for criminal prosecution under the laws of the United States.

If you fail to give notice of your change of address, as required by 8 U.S.C. 1183a(d) and 8 CFR 213a.3, you may be liable for the civil penalty established by 8 U.S.C. 1183a(d)(2). The amount of the civil penalty will depend on whether you failed to give this notice because you were aware that the immigrant(s) you sponsored had received Federal, State, or local means-tested public benefits.

Privacy Act Notice

Authority for the collection of the information requested on this form is contained in 8 U.S.C. 1182(a)(4), 1183a, 1184(a), and 1258. The information will be used principally by the INS or by any Consular Officer to whom it is furnished, to support an alien's application for benefits under the Immigration and Nationality Act and specifically the assertion that he or she has adequate means of financial support and will not become a public charge. Submission of the information is voluntary. Failure to provide the information will result in denial of the application for an immigrant visa or adjustment of status.

The information may also, as a matter of routine use, be disclosed to other Federal, State, and local agencies or private entities providing means-tested public benefits for use in civil action against the sponsor for breach of contract. It may also be disclosed as a matter of routine use to other Federal, State, local, and foreign law enforcement and regulatory agencies to enable these entities to carry out their law enforcement responsibilites.

Reporting Burden

A person is not required to respond to a collection of information unless it displays a currently valid OMB control number. We try to create forms and instructions that are accurate, can be easily understood, and which impose the least possible burden on you to provide us with information. Often this is difficult because some immigration laws are very complex. The reporting burden for this collection of information on Form I-864 is computed as follows: 1) learning about the form, 17 minutes; 2) completing the form, 22 minutes; and 3) assembling and filing the form, 30 minutes, for an estimated average of 69 minutes per response. The reporting burden for collection of information on Form I-864A is computed as: 1) learning about the form, 5 minutes; 2) completing the form, 8 minutes; 3) assembling and filing the form, 2 minutes, for an estimated average of 15 minutes per response. If you have comments regarding the accuracy of this estimates, or suggestions for making this form simpler, you can write to the Immigration and Naturalization Service, 425 I Street, N.W., Room 5307, Washington, D.C. 20536. **DO NOT MAIL YOUR COMPLETED AFFIDAVIT OF SUPPORT TO THIS ADDRESS.**

CHECK LIST

The following items must be submitted with Form I-864, Affidavit of Support Under Section 213A:

For *ALL* sponsors:

This form, the **I-864, completed and signed** before a notary public or a Consular or Immigration Officer.

Proof of **current employment** or self employment.

Your individual Federal **income tax returns for the most recent 3 tax years,** or an explanation if fewer are submitted. Your **W-2s** for any of the most recent 3 tax years for which you filed a joint tax return but are using only your own income to qualify. Forms 1099 or evidence of other reported income *if* necessary to qualify.

For *SOME* sponsors:

If the immigrant you are sponsoring is bringing a spouse or children, **photocopies of the immigrant's affidavit of support and all supporting documentation with original notarized signatures** on each photocopy, of the affidavit for each spouse and/or child immigrating with the immigrant you are sponsoring.

If you are on active duty in the Armed Forces and are sponsoring a spouse or child using the 100 percent of poverty level exception, **proof of your active military status.**

If you are using the income of ***persons in your household or dependents*** *to qualify,*

A separate **Form I-864A** for each person whose income you will use other than a sponsored immigrant/household member who is not immigrating with a spouse and/or child.

Proof of their **residency** and **relationship** to you if they are not listed as dependents on your income tax return for the most recent tax year.

Proof of their **current employment** or self-employment.

☐ Copies of their individual Federal **income tax returns for the 3 most recent tax years**, or an explanation if fewer are submitted.

If you use your assets or the assets of the sponsored immigrant to qualify,

☐ **Documentation of assets** establishing location, ownership, date of acquisition, and value. Evidence of any liens or liabilities against these assets.

☐ A separate **Form I-864A** for each household member other than the sponsored immigrant/household member.

If you or a household member or dependent has used any type of means-tested public benefits in the last 3 years,

☐ **A list of the programs and dates.**

If you are a joint sponsor or the relative of an employment-based immigrant requiring an affidavit of support, **proof of your citizenship status.**

☐ For U.S. citizens or nationals, a copy of your birth certificate, passport, or certificate of naturalization or citizenship.

☐ For lawful permanent residents, a copy of both sides of your I-551, Alien Registration Receipt Card.

U.S. Department of Justice
Immigration and Naturalization Service

OMB #1115-0214

Affidavit of Support Under Section 213A of the Act

START HERE - Please Type or Print

Part 1. Information on Sponsor (You)

Last Name	First Name	Middle Name	
Mailing Address *(Street Number and Name)*		Apt/Suite Number	
City		State or Province	
Country		ZIP/Postal Code	Telephone Number ( )

Place of Residence if different from above *(Street Number and Name)*		Apt/Suite Number
City		State or Province
Country	ZIP/Postal Code	Telephone Number ( )
Date of Birth *(Month, Day, Year)*	Place of Birth *(City, State, Country)*	Are you a U.S. Citizen? ☐ Yes ☐ No
Social Security Number	A-Number *(If any)*	

FOR AGENCY USE ONLY

This Affidavit	Receipt
[ ] Meets [ ] Does not meet Requirements of Section 213A Officer's Signature Location Date	

Part 2. Basis for Filing Affidavit of Support

I am filing this affidavit of support because *(check one)*:

a. ☐ I filed/am filing the alien relative petition.

b. ☐ I filed/am filing an alien worker petition on behalf of the intending immigrant, who is related to me as my ________________ *(relationship)*.

c. ☐ I have ownership interest of at least 5% of ________________ *(name of entity which filed visa petition)* which filed an alien worker petition on behalf of the intending immigrant, who is related to me as my ________________ *(relationship)*.

d. ☐ I am a joint sponsor willing to accept the legal obligations with any other sponsor(s).

Part 3. Information on the Immigrant(s) You Are Sponsoring

Last Name	First Name	Middle Name
Date of Birth *(Month,Day,Year)*	Sex: ☐ Male ☐ Female	Social Security Number *(If any)*
Country of Citizenship	A-Number *(If any)*	
Current Address *(Street Number and Name)*	Apt/Suite Number	City
State/Province	Country	ZIP/Postal Code	Telephone Number ( )

List any spouse and/or children immigrating with the immigrant named above in this Part: *(Use additional sheet of paper if necessary.)*

Name	Relationship to Sponsored Immigrant			Date of Birth			A-Number *(If any)*	Social Security Number *(If any)*
	Spouse	Son	Daughter	Mo.	Day	Yr.		

Form I-864 (1/21/98)Y

Part 4. Eligibility to Sponsor

To be a sponsor you must be a U.S. citizen or national or a lawful permanent resident. If you are not the petitioning relative, you must provide proof of status. To prove status, U.S. citizens or nationals must attach a copy of a document proving status, such as a U.S. passport, birth certificate, or certificate of naturalization, and lawful permanent residents must attach a copy of both sides of their Alien Registration Card (Form I-551).

The determination of your eligibility to sponsor an immigrant will be based on an evaluation of your demonstrated ability to maintain an annual income at or above 125 percent of the Federal poverty line (100 percent if you are a petitioner sponsoring your spouse or child and you are on active duty in the U.S. Armed Forces). The assessment of your ability to maintain an adequate income will include your current employment, household size, and household income as shown on the Federal income tax returns for the 3 most recent tax years. Assets that are readily converted to cash and that can be made available for the support of sponsored immigrants if necessary, including any such assets of the immigrant(s) you are sponsoring, may also be considered.

The greatest weight in determining eligibility will be placed on current employment and household income. If a petitioner is unable to demonstrate ability to meet the stated income and asset requirements, a joint sponsor who *can* meet the income and asset requirements is needed. Failure to provide adequate evidence of income and/or assets or an affidavit of support completed by a joint sponsor will result in denial of the immigrant's application for an immigrant visa or adjustment to permanent resident status.

A. Sponsor's Employment

I am: 1. ☐ Employed by ______________________ *(Provide evidence of employment)*
Annual salary $ __________ *or* hourly wage $ __________ *(for* ______ *hours per week)*
2. ☐ Self employed ______________________ *(Name of business)*
Nature of employment or business ______________________
3. ☐ Unemployed or retired since ______________________

B. Use of Benefits

Have you or anyone related to you by birth, marriage, or adoption living in your household or listed as a dependent on your most recent income tax return received any type of means-tested public benefit in the past 3 years?
☐Yes ☐ No *(If yes, provide details, including programs and dates, on a separate sheet of paper)*

C. Sponsor's Household Size — Number

1. Number of persons (related to you by birth, marriage, or adoption) living in your residence, including yourself. *(Do NOT include persons being sponsored in this affidavit.)* ______
2. Number of immigrants being sponsored in this affidavit *(Include all persons in Part 3.)* ______
3. Number of immigrants **NOT** living in your household whom you are still obligated to support under a previously signed affidavit of support using Form I-864. ______
4. Number of persons who are otherwise dependent on you, as claimed in your tax return for the most recent tax year. ______
5. Total household size. ***(Add lines 1 through 4.)*** **Total** ______

List persons below who are included in lines 1 or 3 for whom you previously have submitted INS Form I-864, *if your support obligation has not terminated.*
(If additional space is needed, use additional paper)

Name	A-Number	Date Affidavit of Support Signed	Relationship

Form I-864 (1/21/98)Y **Page 2**

Part 4. Eligibility to Sponsor *(Continued)*

D. Sponsor's Annual Household Income

Enter total unadjusted income from your Federal income tax return for the most recent tax year below. If you last filed a joint income tax return but are using only your *own* income to qualify, list total earnings from your W-2 Forms, or, *if* necessary to reach the required income for your household size, include income from other sources listed on your tax return. If your *individual* income does not meet the income requirement for your household size, you may also list total income for anyone related to you by birth, marriage, or adoption currently living with you in your residence if they have lived in your residence for the previous 6 months, or any person shown as a dependent on your Federal income tax return for the most recent tax year, even if not living in the household. For their income to be considered, household members or dependents must be willing to make their income available for support of the sponsored immigrant(s) and to complete and sign Form I-864A, Contract Between Sponsor and Household Member. A sponsored immigrant/household member only need complete Form I-864A if his or her income will be used to determine your ability to support a spouse and/or children immigrating with him or her.

You must attach evidence of current employment and copies of income tax returns as filed with the IRS for the most recent 3 tax years for yourself and all persons whose income is listed below. See "Required Evidence" in Instructions. Income from all 3 years will be considered in determining your ability to support the immigrant(s) you are sponsoring.

- ☐ I filed a single/separate tax return for the most recent tax year.
- ☐ I filed a joint return for the most recent tax year which includes only my own income.
- ☐ I filed a joint return for the most recent tax year which includes income for my spouse and myself.
  - ☐ I am submitting documentation of my individual income (Forms W-2 and 1099).
  - ☐ I am qualifying using my spouse's income; my spouse is submitting a Form I-864A.

Indicate most recent tax year	________ *(tax year)*
Sponsor's individual income	$________
or	
Sponsor and spouse's combined income *(If joint tax return filed; spouse must submit Form I-864A.)*	$________
Income of other qualifying persons. *(List names; include spouse if applicable. Each person must complete Form I-864A.)*	
________	$________
________	$________
________	$________
Total Household Income	$________

Explain on separate sheet of paper if you or any of the above listed individuals are submitting Federal income tax returns for fewer than 3 years, or if other explanation of income, employment, or evidence is necessary.

E. Determination of Eligibility Based on Income

1. ☐ I am subject to the 125 percent of poverty line requirement for sponsors.
   ☐ I am subject to the 100 percent of poverty line requirement for sponsors on active duty in the U.S. Armed Forces sponsoring their spouse or child.
2. Sponsor's total household size, from Part 4.C., line 5 ________.
3. Minimum income requirement from the Poverty Guidelines chart for the year of ________ *(year)* is $ ________ for this household size.

If you are currently employed and your household income for your household size is equal to or greater than the applicable poverty line requirement (from line E.3.), you do not need to list assets (Parts 4.F. and 5) or have a joint sponsor (Part 6) unless you are requested to do so by a Consular or Immigration Officer. You may skip to Part 7, Use of the Affidavit of Support to Overcome Public Charge Ground of Admissibility. **Otherwise, you should continue with Part 4.F.**

Form I-864 (1/21/98) **Page 3**

Part 4. Eligibility to Sponsor *(Continued)*

F. Sponsor's Assets and Liabilities

Your assets and those of your qualifying household members and dependents may be used to demonstrate ability to maintain an income at or above 125 percent (or 100 percent, if applicable) of the poverty line *if* they are available for the support of the sponsored immigrant(s) and can readily be converted into cash within 1 year. The household member, other than the immigrant(s) you are sponsoring, must complete and sign Form I-864A, Contract Between Sponsor and Household Member. List the cash value of each asset *after* any debts or liens are subtracted. Supporting evidence must be attached to establish location, ownership, date of acquisition, and value of each asset listed, including any liens and liabilities related to each asset listed. See "Evidence of Assets" in Instructions.

Type of Asset	Cash Value of Assets *(Subtract any debts)*
Savings deposits	$
Stocks, bonds, certificates of deposit	$
Life insurance cash value	$
Real estate	$
Other *(specify)*	$
Total Cash Value of Assets	$

Part 5. Immigrant's Assets and Offsetting Liabilities

The sponsored immigrant's assets may also be used in support of your ability to maintain income at or above 125 percent of the poverty line *if* the assets are or will be available in the United States for the support of the sponsored immigrant(s) and can readily be converted into cash within 1 year.

The sponsored immigrant should provide information on his or her assets in a format similar to part 4.F. above. Supporting evidence must be attached to establish location, ownership, and value of each asset listed, including any liens and liabilities for each asset listed. See "Evidence of Assets" in Instructions.

Part 6. Joint Sponsors

If household income and assets do not meet the appropriate poverty line for your household size, a joint sponsor is required. There may be more than one joint sponsor, but each joint sponsor must individually meet the 125 percent of poverty line requirement based on his or her household income and/or assets, including any assets of the sponsored immigrant. By submitting a separate Affidavit of Support under Section 213A of the Act (Form I-864), a joint sponsor accepts joint responsibility with the petitioner for the sponsored immigrant(s) until they become U.S. citizens, can be credited with 40 quarters of work, leave the United States permanently, or die.

Part 7. Use of the Affidavit of Support to Overcome Public Charge Ground of Inadmissibility

Section 212(a)(4)(C) of the Immigration and Nationality Act provides that an alien seeking permanent residence as an immediate relative (including an orphan), as a family-sponsored immigrant, or as an alien who will accompany or follow to join another alien is considered to be likely to become a public charge and is inadmissible to the United States unless a sponsor submits a legally enforceable affidavit of support on behalf of the alien. Section 212(a)(4)(D) imposes the same requirement on an employment-based immigrant, and those aliens who accompany or follow to join the employment-based immigrant, if the employment-based immigrant will be employed by a relative, or by a firm in which a relative owns a significant interest. Separate affidavits of support are required for family members at the time they immigrate if they are not included on this affidavit of support or do not apply for an immigrant visa or adjustment of status within 6 months of the date this affidavit of support is originally signed. The sponsor must provide the sponsored immigrant(s) whatever support is necessary to maintain them at an income that is at least 125 percent of the Federal poverty guidelines.

I submit this affidavit of support in consideration of the sponsored immigrant(s) not being found inadmissible to the United States under section 212(a)(4)(C) (or 212(a)(4)(D) for an employment-based immigrant) and to enable the sponsored immigrant(s) to overcome this ground of inadmissibility. I agree to provide the sponsored immigrant(s) whatever support is necessary to maintain the sponsored immigrant(s) at an income that is at least 125 percent of the Federal poverty guidelines. I understand that my obligation will continue until my death or the sponsored immigrant(s) have become U.S. citizens, can be credited with 40 quarters of work, depart the United States permanently, or die.

Form I-864 (1/21/98) **Page 4**

Part 7. Use of the Affidavit of Support to Overcome Public Charge Grounds *(Continued)*

Notice of Change of Address.

Sponsors are required to provide written notice of any change of address within 30 days of the change in address until the sponsored immigrant(s) have become U.S. citizens, can be credited with 40 quarters of work, depart the United States permanently, or die. To comply with this requirement, the sponsor must complete INS Form I-865. Failure to give this notice may subject the sponsor to the civil penalty established under section 213A(d)(2) which ranges from $250 to $2,000, unless the failure to report occurred with the knowledge that the sponsored immigrant(s) had received means-tested public benefits, in which case the penalty ranges from $2,000 to $5,000.

If my address changes for any reason before my obligations under this affidavit of support terminate, I will complete and file INS Form I-865, Sponsor's Notice of Change of Address, within 30 days of the change of address. I understand that failure to give this notice may subject me to civil penalties.

Means-tested Public Benefit Prohibitions and Exceptions.

Under section 403(a) of Public Law 104-193 (Welfare Reform Act), aliens lawfully admitted for permanent residence in the United States, with certain exceptions, are ineligible for most Federally-funded means-tested public benefits during their first 5 years in the United States. This provision does not apply to public benefits specified in section 403(c) of the Welfare Reform Act or to State public benefits, including emergency Medicaid; short-term, non-cash emergency relief; services provided under the National School Lunch and Child Nutrition Acts; immunizations and testing and treatment for communicable diseases; student assistance under the Higher Education Act and the Public Health Service Act; certain forms of foster-care or adoption assistance under the Social Security Act; Head Start programs; means-tested programs under the Elementary and Secondary Education Act; and Job Training Partnership Act programs.

Consideration of Sponsor's Income in Determining Eligibility for Benefits.

If a permanent resident alien is no longer statutorily barred from a Federally-funded means-tested public benefit program and applies for such a benefit, the income and resources of the sponsor and the sponsor's spouse will be considered (or deemed) to be the income and resources of the sponsored immigrant in determining the immigrant's eligibility for Federal means-tested public benefits. Any State or local government may also choose to consider (or deem) the income and resources of the sponsor and the sponsor's spouse to be the income and resources of the immigrant for the purposes of determining eligibility for their means-tested public benefits. The attribution of the income and resources of the sponsor and the sponsor's spouse to the immigrant will continue until the immigrant becomes a U.S. citizen or has worked or can be credited with 40 qualifying quarters of work, provided that the immigrant or the worker crediting the quarters to the immigrant has not received any Federal means-tested public benefit during any creditable quarter for any period after December 31, 1996.

I understand that, under section 213A of the Immigration and Nationality Act (the Act), as amended, this affidavit of support constitutes a contract between me and the U.S. Government. This contract is designed to protect the United States Government, and State and local government agencies or private entities that provide means-tested public benefits, from having to pay benefits to or on behalf of the sponsored immigrant(s), for as long as I am obligated to support them under this affidavit of support. I understand that the sponsored immigrants, or any Federal, State, local, or private entity that pays any means-tested benefit to or on behalf of the sponsored immigrant(s), are entitled to sue me if I fail to meet my obligations under this affidavit of support, as defined by section 213A and INS regulations.

Civil Action to Enforce.

If the immigrant on whose behalf this affidavit of support is executed receives any Federal, State, or local means-tested public benefit before this obligation terminates, the Federal, State, or local agency or private entity may request reimbursement from the sponsor who signed this affidavit. If the sponsor fails to honor the request for reimbursement, the agency may sue the sponsor in any U.S. District Court or any State court with jurisdiction of civil actions for breach of contract. INS will provide names, addresses, and Social Security account numbers of sponsors to benefit-providing agencies for this purpose. Sponsors may also be liable for paying the costs of collection, including legal fees.

Part 7. Use of the Affidavit of Support to Overcome Public Charge Grounds ***(Continued)***

I acknowledge that section 213A(a)(1)(B) of the Act grants the sponsored immigrant(s) and any Federal, State, local, or private agency that pays any means-tested public benefit to or on behalf of the sponsored immigrant(s) standing to sue me for failing to meet my obligations under this affidavit of support. I agree to submit to the personal jurisdiction of any court of the United States or of any State, territory, or possession of the United States if the court has subject matter jurisdiction of a civil lawsuit to enforce this affidavit of support. I agree that no lawsuit to enforce this affidavit of support shall be barred by any statute of limitations that might otherwise apply, so long as the plaintiff initiates the civil lawsuit no later than ten (10) years after the date on which a sponsored immigrant last received any means-tested public benefits.

Collection of Judgment.

I acknowledge that a plaintiff may seek specific performance of my support obligation. Furthermore, any money judgment against me based on this affidavit of support may be collected through the use of a judgment lien under 28 U.S.C. 3201, a writ of execution under 28 U.S.C. 3203, a judicial installment payment order under 28 U.S.C. 3204, garnishment under 28 U.S.C. 3205, or through the use of any corresponding remedy under State law. I may also be held liable for costs of collection, including attorney fees.

Concluding Provisions.

I, ______________________________, certify under penalty of perjury under the laws of the United States that:

(a) I know the contents of this affidavit of support signed by me;
(b) All the statements in this affidavit of support are true and correct;
(c) I make this affidavit of support for the consideration stated in Part 7, freely, and without any mental reservation or purpose of evasion;
(d) Income tax returns submitted in support of this affidavit are true copies of the returns filed with the Internal Revenue Service; and
(e) Any other evidence submitted is true and correct.

______________________________ ______________________________
(Sponsor's Signature) *(Date)*

Subscribed and sworn to *(or affirmed)* before me this

__________day of ________________, ____________
(Month) *(Year)*

at ______________________________.

My commission expires on ____________________.

____
(Signature of Notary Public or Officer Administering Oath)

____
(Title)

Part 8. If someone other than the sponsor prepared this affidavit of support, that person must complete the following:

I certify under penalty of perjury under the laws of the United States that I prepared this affidavit of support at the sponsor's request, and that this affidavit of support is based on all information of which I have knowledge.

Signature	Print Your Name	Date	Daytime Telephone Number
			( )

Firm Name and Address

Form I-864 (1/21/98)Y **Page 6**

U. S. Department of Justice
Immigration and Naturalization Service

OMB# 1115-0214
Poverty Guidelines

2000 Poverty Guidelines*
Minimum Income Requirement For Use in Completing Form I-864

For the 48 Contiguous States, the District of Columbia, Puerto Rico, the U.S. Virgin Islands, and Guam:

Sponsor's Household Size	100% of Poverty Line For sponsors on active duty in the U.S. Armed Forces who are petitioning for their spouse or child.	125% of Poverty Line **For all other sponsors**
2	$11.250	**$14,062**
3	14,150	**17,687**
4	17,050	**21,312**
5	19,950	**24,937**
6	22,850	**28,562**
7	25,750	**32,187**
8	28,650	**35,812**
	Add $2,900 for each additional person.	**Add $3,625 for each additional person.**

	For Alaska		For Hawaii	
Sponsor's Household Size	100% of Poverty Line For sponsors on active duty in the U.S. Armed Forces who are petitioning for their spouse or child	125% of Poverty Line **For all other sponsors**	100% of Poverty Line For sponsors on active duty in the U.S. Armed Forces who are petitioning for their spouse or child	125% of Poverty Line **For all other sponsors**
2	$14,060	**$17,575**	$12,930	**$16,162**
3	17,690	**22,112**	16,270	**20,337**
4	21,320	**26,650**	19,610	**24,512**
5	24,950	**31,187**	22,950	**28,687**
6	28,580	**35,725**	26,290	**32,862**
7	32,210	**40,262**	29,630	**37,037**
8	35,840	**44,800**	32,970	**41,212**
	Add $3,630 for each additional person.	**Add $4,537 for each additional person.**	Add $3,340 for each additional person.	**Add $4,175 for each additional person.**

Means-tested Public Benefits

Federal Means-tested Public Benefits. To date, Federal agencies administering benefit programs have determined that Federal means-tested public benefits include Food Stamps, Medicaid, Supplemental Security Income (SSI), Temporary Assistance for Needy Families (TANF), and the State Child Health Insurance Program (CHIP).

State Means-tested Public Benefits. Each State will determine which, if any, of its public benefits are means-tested. If a State determines that it has programs which meet this definition, it is encouraged to provide notice to the public on which programs are included. Check with the State public assistance office to determine which, if any, State assistance programs have been determined to be State means-tested public benefits.

Programs Not Included: The following Federal and State programs are ***not*** included as means-tested benefits: emergency Medicaid; short-term, non-cash emergency relief; services provided under the National School Lunch and Child Nutrition Acts; immunizations and testing and treatment for communicable diseases; student assistance under the Higher Education Act and the Public Health Service Act; certain forms of foster-care or adoption assistance under the Social Security Act; Head Start Programs; means-tested programs under the Elementary and Secondary Education Act; and Job Training Partnership Act programs.

*** These poverty guidelines remain in effect for use with the Form I-864 Affidavit of Support from April 1, 2000 until new poverty guidelines go into effect in the Spring of 2001.**

Form I-864P (Rev. 3/14/00)N

Form I–864A Contract between sponsor and household member

U.S. Department of Justice
Immigration and Naturalization Service

OMB #1115-0214

Contract Between Sponsor and Household Member

Sponsor's Name *(Last, First, Middle)*	Social Security Number	A-Number (If any)

General Filing Instructions:

Form I-864A, Contract Between Sponsor and Household Member, is an attachment to Form I-864, Affidavit of Support Under Section 213A of the Immigration and Nationality Act (the Act). The sponsor enters the information above, completes Part 2 of this form, and signs in Part 5. The household member completes Parts 1 and 3 of this form and signs in Part 6. A household member who is also the sponsored immigrant completes Parts 1 and 4 (Instead of Part 3) of this form and signs in Part 6. The Privacy Act Notice and information on penalties for misrepresentation or fraud are included on the instructions to Form I-864.

The signatures on the I-864A must be notarized by a notary public or signed before an Immigration or Consular Officer. A separate form must be used for each household member whose income and/or assets are being used to qualify. This blank form may be photocopied for that purpose. A sponsored immigrant who qualifies as a household member is only required to complete this form if he or she has one or more family members immigrating with him or her and is making his or her *income* available for their support. Sponsored immigrants who are using their *assets* to qualify are not required to complete this form. This completed form is submitted with Form I-864 by the sponsored immigrant with an application for an immigrant visa or adjustment of status.

Purpose:

This contract is intended to benefit the sponsored immigrant(s) and any agency of the Federal Government, any agency of a State or local government, or any private entity to which the sponsor has an obligation under the affidavit of support to reimburse for benefits granted to the sponsored immigrant, and these parties will have the right to enforce this contract in any court with appropriate jurisdiction. This contract must be completed and signed by the sponsor and any household member, including the sponsor's spouse, whose income is included as household income by a person sponsoring one or more immigrants under Section 213A of Act. The contract must also be completed if a sponsor is relying on the assets of a household member who is not the sponsored immigrant to meet the income requirements. If the sponsored immigrant is a household member immigrating with a spouse or children, and is using his or her income to assist the sponsor in meeting the income requirement, he or she must complete and sign this contract as a "sponsored immigrant/household member."

By signing this form, a household member, who is not a sponsored immigrant, agrees to make his or her income and/or assets available to the sponsor to help support the immigrant(s) for whom the sponsor has filed an affidavit of support and to be responsible, along with the sponsor, to pay any debt incurred by the sponsor under the affidavit of support. A sponsored immigrant/household member who signs this contract agrees to make his or her income available to the sponsor to help support any spouse or children immigrating with him or her and to be responsible, along with the sponsor, to pay any debt incurred by the sponsor under the affidavit of support. The obligations of the household member and the sponsored immigrant/household member under this contract terminate when the obligations of the sponsor under the affidavit of support terminate. For additional information see section 213A of the Act, part 213a of title 8 of the Code of Federal Regulations, and Form I-864, Affidavit of Support Under Section 213A of the Act.

Definitions:

1) An "affidavit of support" refers to INS Form I-864, Affidavit of Support Under Section 213A of the Act, which is completed and filed by the sponsor;
2) A "sponsor" is a person, either the petitioning relative, the relative with a significant ownership interest in the petitioning entity, or another person accepting joint and several liability with the sponsor, who completes and files the Affidavit of Support under Section 213A of the Act on behalf of a sponsored immigrant;
3) A "household member" is any person (a) sharing a residence with the sponsor for at least the last 6 months who is related to the sponsor by birth, marriage, or adoption, *or* (b) whom the sponsor has lawfully claimed as a dependent on the sponsor's most recent Federal income tax return even if that person does not live at the same residence as the sponsor, *and* whose income and/or assets will be used to demonstrate the sponsor's ability to maintain the sponsored immigrant(s) at an annual income at the level specified in section 213A(f)(1)(E) or 213A(f)(3) of the Act;
4) A "sponsored immigrant" is a person listed on this form on whose behalf an affidavit of support will be completed and filed; and
5) A "sponsored immigrant/household member" is a sponsored immigrant who is also a household member.

Form I-864A (1/21/98)Y

Part 1. Information on Sponsor's Household Member or Sponsored Immigrant/Household Member

Last Name	First Name	Middle Name
Date of Birth *(Month,Day,Year)*	Social Security Number *(Mandatory for non-citizens; voluntary for U.S. citizens)*	A-Number *(If any)*

Address *(Street Number and Name)* Apt Number	City	State/Province	ZIP/Postal Code

Telephone Number ( )	Relationship to Sponsor:________ I am: ☐ The sponsor's household member. *(Complete Part 3.)* ☐ The sponsored immigrant/household member. *(Complete Part 4.)*	Length of residence with sponsor (____ years, ____months)

Part 2. Sponsor's Promise

I, THE SPONSOR, ________________ *(Print name of sponsor)*, in consideration of the household member's promise to support the sponsored immigrant(s) and to be jointly and severally liable for any obligations I incur under the affidavit of support, promise to complete and file an affidavit of support on behalf of the following__________ *(Indicate number)* sponsored immigrant(s):

Name of Sponsored Immigrant *(First, Middle, Last)*	Date of Birth *(Month, Day, Year)*	Social Security Number *(If any)*	A-Number *(If any)*

Part 3. Household Member's Promise

I, THE HOUSEHOLD MEMBER, ________________ *(Print name of household member)*, in consideration of the sponsor's promise to complete and file the affidavit of support on behalf of the sponsored immigrant(s):

1) Promise to provide any and all financial support necessary to assist the sponsor in maintaining the sponsored immigrant(s) at or above the minimum income provided for in section 213A(a)(1)(A) of the Act (not less than 125 percent of the Federal poverty line) during the period in which the affidavit of support is enforceable;

2) Agree to be jointly and severally liable for payment of any and all obligations owed by the sponsor under the affidavit of support to the sponsored immigrant(s), to any agency of the Federal Government, to any agency of a State or local government, or to any private entity;

3) Agree to submit to the personal jurisdiction of any court of the United States or of any State, territory, or possession of the United States if the court has subject matter jurisdiction of a civil lawsuit to enforce this contract or the affidavit of support; and

4) Certify under penalty of perjury under the laws of the United States that all the information provided on this form is true and correct to the best of my knowledge and belief and that the income tax returns I submitted in support of the sponsor's affidavit are true copies of the returns filed with the Internal Revenue Service.

Form I-864A (1/21/98)Y **Page 2**

Part 4. Sponsored Immigrant/Household Member's Promise

I, THE SPONSORED IMMIGRANT/HOUSEHOLD MEMBER, ______________________________
(Print name of sponsored immigrant)

in consideration of the sponsor's promise to complete and file the affidavit of support on behalf of the sponsored immigrant(s) accompanying me:

1) Promise to provide any and all financial support necessary to assist the sponsor in maintaining any sponsored immigrant(s) immigrating with me at or above the minimum income provided for in section 213A(a)(1)(A) of the Act (not less than 125 percent of the Federal poverty line) during the period in which the affidavit of support is enforceable;

2) Agree to be jointly and severally liable for payment of any and all obligations owed by the sponsor under the affidavit of support to any sponsored immigrant(s) immigrating with me, to any agency of the Federal Government, to any agency of a State or local government, or to any private entity;

3) Agree to submit to the personal jurisdiction of any court of the United States or of any State, territory, or possession of the United States if the court has subject matter jurisdiction of a civil lawsuit to enforce this contract or the affidavit of support; and

4) Certify under penalty of perjury under the laws of the United States that all the information provided on this form is true and correct to the best of my knowledge and belief and that the income tax returns I submitted in support of the sponsor's affidavit of support are true copies of the returns filed with the Internal Revenue Service.

Part 5. Sponsor's Signature

______________________________ Date: ______________________________
Sponsor's Signature

Subscribed and sworn to *(or affirmed)* before me this __________ day of ______________, __________
(Month) *(Year)*

at ______________________________. My commission expires on ______________.

______________________________ ______________________________
Signature of Notary Public or Officer Administering Oath *Title*

Part 6. Household Member's or Sponsored Immigrant/Household Member's Signature

______________________________ Date: ______________________________
Household Member's or Sponsored Immigrant/Household Member's Signature

Subscribed and sworn to *(or affirmed)* before me this __________ day of ______________, __________
(Month) *(Year)*

at ______________________________. My commission expires on ______________.

______________________________ ______________________________
Signature of Notary Public or Officer Administering Oath *Title*

Form I-864A (1/21/98)Y **Page 3**

Form I–9 Employment eligibility verification

U.S. Department of Justice
Immigration and Naturalization Service

OMB No. 1115-0136
Employment Eligibility Verification

INSTRUCTIONS

PLEASE READ ALL INSTRUCTIONS CAREFULLY BEFORE COMPLETING THIS FORM.

Anti-Discrimination Notice. It is illegal to discriminate against any individual (other than an alien not authorized to work in the U.S.) in hiring, discharging, or recruiting or referring for a fee because of that individual's national origin or citizenship status. It is illegal to discriminate against work eligible individuals. Employers **CANNOT** specify which document(s) they will accept from an employee. The refusal to hire an individual because of a future expiration date may also constitute illegal discrimination.

Section 1 - Employee. All employees, citizens noncitizens, hired after November 6, 1986, must complete Section 1 of this form at the time of hire, which is the actual beginning of employment. **The employer is responsible for ensuring that Section 1 is timely and properly completed.**

Preparer/Translator Certification. The Preparer/Translator Certification must be completed if Section 1 is prepared by a person other than the employee. A preparer/translator may be used only when the employee is unable to complete Section 1 on his/her own. However, the employee must still sign Section 1 personally.

Section 2 - Employer. For the purpose of completing this form, the term "employer" includes those recruiters and referrers for a fee who are agricultural associations, agricultural employers, or farm labor contractors.

Employers must complete Section 2 by examining evidence of identity and employment eligibility within three (3) business days of the date employment begins. If employees are authorized to work, but are unable to present the required document(s) within three business days, they must present a receipt for the application of the document(s) within three business days and the actual document(s) within ninety (90) days. However, if employers hire individuals for a duration of less than three business days, Section 2 must be completed at the time employment begins. **Employers must record: 1)** document title; **2)** issuing authority; **3)** document number, **4)** expiration date, if any; and **5)** the date employment begins. Employers must sign and date the certification. Employees must present original documents. Employers may, but are not required to, photocopy the document(s) presented. These photocopies may only be used for the verification process and must be retained with the I-9. **However, employers are still responsible for completing the I-9.**

Section 3 - Updating and Reverification. Employers must complete Section 3 when updating and/or reverifying the I-9. Employers must reverify employment eligibility of their employees on or before the expiration date recorded in Section 1. Employers **CANNOT** specify which document(s) they will accept from an employee.

- If an employee's name has changed at the time this form is being updated/ reverified, complete Block A.
- If an employee is rehired within three (3) years of the date this form was originally completed and the employee is still eligible to be employed on the same basis as previously indicated on this form (updating), complete Block B and the signature block.
- If an employee is rehired within three (3) years of the date this form was originally completed and the employee's work authorization has expired **or** if a current employee's work authorization is about to expire (reverification), complete Block B and:
  - examine any document that reflects that the employee is authorized to work in the U.S. (see List A **or** C),
  - record the document title, document number and expiration date (if any) in Block C, and
  - complete the signature block.

Photocopying and Retaining Form I-9. A blank I-9 may be reproduced provided both sides are copied. The Instructions must be available to all employees completing this form. Employers must retain completed I-9s for three (3) years after the date of hire **or** one (1) year after the date employment ends, whichever is later.

For more detailed information, you may refer to the INS Handbook for Employers, (Form M-274). You may obtain the handbook at your local INS office.

Privacy Act Notice. The authority for collecting this information is the Immigration Reform and Control Act of 1986, Pub. L. 99-603 (8 U.S.C. 1324a).

This information is for employers to verify the eligibility of individuals for employment to preclude the unlawful hiring, or recruiting or referring for a fee, of aliens who are not authorized to work in the United States.

This information will be used by employers as a record of their basis for determining eligibility of an employee to work in the United States. The form will be kept by the employer and made available for inspection by officials of the U.S. Immigration and Naturalization Service, the Department of Labor, and the Office of Special Counsel for Immigration Related Unfair Employment Practices.

Submission of the information required in this form is voluntary. However, an individual may not begin employment unless this form is completed since employers are subject to civil or criminal penalties if they do not comply with the Immigration Reform and Control Act of 1986.

Reporting Burden. We try to create forms and instructions that are accurate, can be easily understood, and which impose the least possible burden on you to provide us with information. Often this is difficult because some immigration laws are very complex. Accordingly, the reporting burden for this collection of information is computed as follows: **1)** learning about this form, 5 minutes; **2)** completing the form, 5 minutes; and **3)** assembling and filing (recordkeeping) the form, 5 minutes, for an average of 15 minutes per response. If you have comments regarding the accuracy of this burden estimate, or suggestions for making this form simpler, you can write to both the Immigration and Naturalization Service, 425 I Street, N.W., Room 5304, Washington, D. C. 20536; and the Office of Management and Budget, Paperwork Reduction Project, OMB No. 1115-0136, Washington, D.C. 20503.

Form I-9 (Rev. 11-21-91) N

EMPLOYERS MUST RETAIN COMPLETED I-9
PLEASE DO NOT MAIL COMPLETED I-9 TO INS

U.S. Department of Justice
Immigration and Naturalization Service

OMB No. 1115-0136
Employment Eligibility Verification

Please read instructions carefully before completing this form. The instructions must be available during completion of this form. ANTI-DISCRIMINATION NOTICE. It is illegal to discriminate against work eligible individuals. Employers CANNOT specify which document(s) they will accept from an employee. The refusal to hire an individual because of a future expiration date may also constitute illegal discrimination.

Section 1. Employee Information and Verification. To be completed and signed by employee at the time employment begins

Print Name: Last First Middle Initial | Maiden Name

Address *(Street Name and Number)* Apt. # | Date of Birth *(month/day/year)*

City State Zip Code | Social Security #

I am aware that federal law provides for imprisonment and/or fines for false statements or use of false documents in connection with the completion of this form.

I attest, under penalty of perjury, that I am (check one of the following):
A citizen or national of the United States
A Lawful Permanent Resident (Alien # A__________
An alien authorized to work until__/__/__
(Alien # or Admission #______________

Employee's Signature | Date *(month/day/year)*

Preparer and/or Translator Certification. *(To be completed and signed if Section 1 is prepared by a person other than the employee.) I attest, under penalty of perjury, that I have assisted in the completion of this form and that to the best of my knowledge the information is true and correct.*

Preparer's/Translator's Signature | Print Name

Address *(Street Name and Number, City, State, Zip Code)* | Date *(month/day/year)*

Section 2. Employer Review and Verification. To be completed and signed by employer. **Examine one document from List A OR examine one document from List B and one from List C** as listed on the reverse of this form and record the title, number and expiration date, if any, of the document(s)

List A	OR	List B	AND	List C
Document title: ________		________		________
Issuing authority: ________		________		________
Document #: ________		________		________
Expiration Date *(if any)*: __/__/__		__/__/__		__/__/__
Document #: ________				
Expiration Date *(if any)*: __/__/__				

CERTIFICATION - I attest, under penalty of perjury, that I have examined the document(s) presented by the above-named employee, that the above-listed document(s) appear to be genuine and to relate to the employee named, that the employee began employment on *(month/day/year)* **__/__/__ and that to the best of my knowledge the employee is eligible to work in the United States. (State employment agencies may omit the date the employee began employment).**

Signature of Employer or Authorized Representative | Print Name | Title

Business or Organization Name | Address *(Street Name and Number, City, State, Zip Code)* | Date *(month/day/year)*

Section 3. Updating and Reverification. To be completed and signed by employer

A. New Name *(if applicable)* | B. Date of rehire *(month/day/year) (if applicable)*

C. If employee's previous grant of work authorization has expired, provide the information below for the document that establishes current employment eligibility.
Document Title:__________Document #:__________Expiration Date (if any):__/__/__

I attest, under penalty of perjury, that to the best of my knowledge, this employee is eligible to work in the United States, and if the employee presented document(s), the document(s) I have examined appear to be genuine and to relate to the individual.

Signature of Employer or Authorized Representative | Date *(month/day/year)*

Form I-9 (Rev. 11-21-91) N

LISTS OF ACCEPTABLE DOCUMENTS

LIST A

Documents that Establish Both Identity and Employment Eligibility

1. U.S. Passport (unexpired or expired)
2. Certificate of U.S. Citizenship *(INS Form N-560 or N-561)*
3. Certificate of Naturalization *(INS Form N-550 or N-570)*
4. Unexpired foreign passport, with *I-551 stamp or* attached *INS Form I-94* indicating unexpired employment authorization
5. Alien Registration Receipt Card with photograph *(INS Form I-151 or I-551)*
6. Unexpired Temporary Resident Card *(INS Form I-688)*
7. Unexpired Employment Authorization Card *(INS Form I-688A)*
8. Unexpired Reentry Permit *(INS Form I-327)*
9. Unexpired Refugee Travel Document *(INS Form I-571)*
10. Unexpired Employment Authorization Document issued by the INS which contains a photograph *(INS Form I-688B)*

OR

LIST B

Documents that Establish Identity

1. Driver's license or ID card issued by a state or outlying possession of the United States provided it contains a photograph or information such as name, date of birth, sex, height, eye color, and address
2. ID card issued by federal, state, or local government agencies or entities provided it contains a photograph or information such as name, date of birth, sex, height, eye color, and address
3. School ID card with a photograph
4. Voter's registration card
5. U.S. Military card or draft record
6. Military dependent's ID card
7. U.S. Coast Guard Merchant Mariner Card
8. Native American tribal document
9. Driver's license issued by a Canadian government authority

For persons under age 18 who are unable to present a document listed above:

10. School record or report card
11. Clinic, doctor, or hospital record
12. Day-care or nursery school record

AND

LIST C

Documents that Establish Employment Eligibility

1. U.S. social security card issued by the Social Security Administration *(other than a card stating it is not valid for employment)*
2. Certification of Birth Abroad issued by the Department of State *(Form FS-545 or Form DS-1350)*
3. Original or certified copy of a birth certificate issued by a state, county, municipal authority or outlying possession of the United States bearing an official seal
4. Native American tribal document
5. U.S. Citizen ID Card *(INS Form I-197)*
6. ID Card for use of Resident Citizen in the United States *(INS Form I-179)*
7. Unexpired employment authorization document issued by the INS *(other than those listed under List A)*

Illustrations of many of these documents appear in Part 8 of the Handbook for Employers (M-274)

Form I-9 (Rev. 11-21-91) N

Form M–274 Handbook for employers, instructions for completing Form I–9

Acceptable Documents for Verifying Employment Eligibility

Immigration and Naturalization Service

(Rev. 11/21/91)

Document List A

Documents That Establish Both Identity and Employment Eligibility

The following illustrations in this handbook do not necessarily reflect the actual size of the documents.

United States Passport

Issued by the Department of State to United States citizens and nationals.

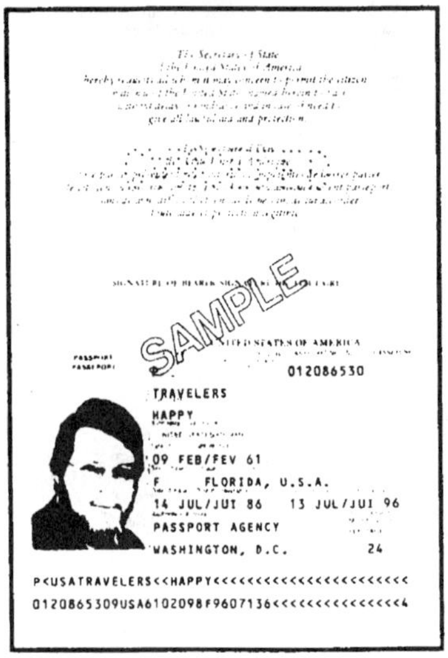

Certificate of United States Citizenship N-560 or N-561

Issued by INS to individuals who: 1) derived citizenship through parental naturalization; 2) acquired citizenship at birth abroad through a United States parent or parents; or 3) acquired citizenship through application by United States citizen adoptive parent(s); and who, pursuant to section 341 of the Act, have applied for a certificate of citizenship.

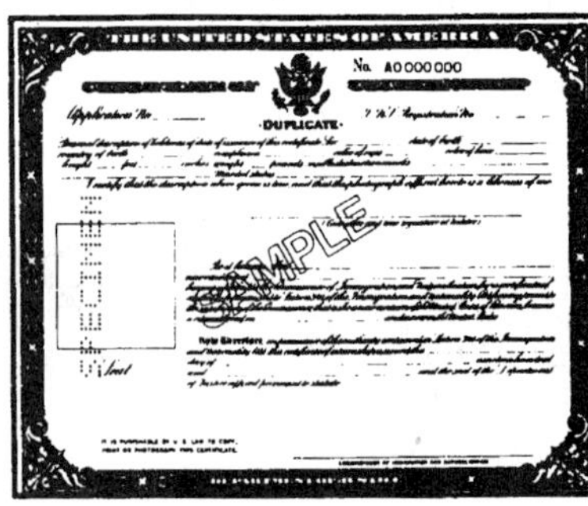

Certificate of Naturalization N-550 or N-570

Issued by INS to naturalized United States citizens.

Certificate of Naturalization N-550

Issued by INS to naturalized United States citizens who file for naturalization after October 1, 1991.

[G11011]

Unexpired Foreign Passport with I-551 Stamp

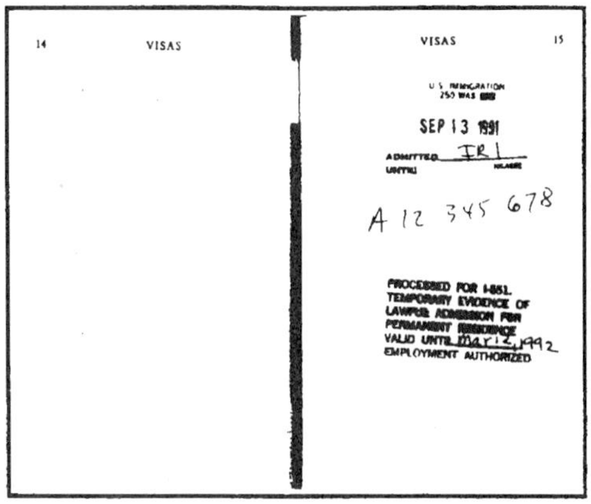

I-94 Arrival/Departure Record

Arrival-departure record issued by INS to nonimmigrant aliens. An individual in possession of the departure portion of this document may only be employed if the document bears an "employment authorization" stamp or employment incident to the nonimmigrant classification is authorized with a specific employer (i.e. A-1, A-2, A-3, C-2, C-3, E-1, E-2, G-1, G-2, G-3, G-4, G-5, H-1A, H-1B, H-2A, H-2B, H-3, I, L-1, O-1, O-2, P-1, P-2, P-3, Q, NATO 1-7 and TC). The expiration date is noted on the Form I-94.

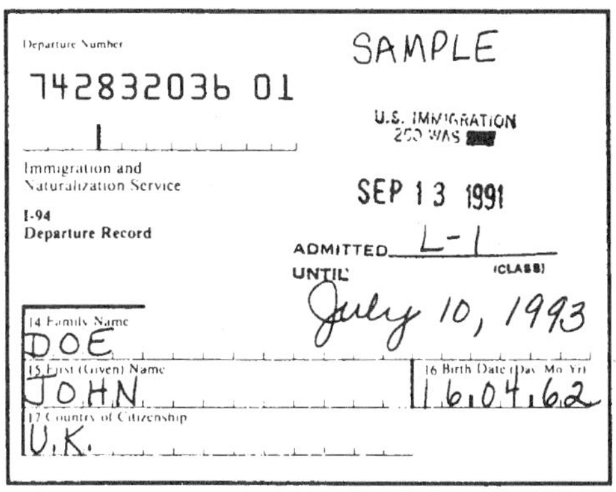

Departure Number
742832036 01

SAMPLE

U.S. IMMIGRATION
250 WAS [redacted]

Immigration and
Naturalization Service

I-94
Departure Record

SEP 13 1991

ADMITTED L-1 (CLASS)
UNTIL July 10, 1993

14 Family Name
DOE

15 First (Given) Name
JOHN

16 Birth Date (Day Mo Yr)
16 04 62

17 Country of Citizenship
U.K.

[G11012]

Alien Registration Receipt Card I-151

Issued by INS prior to June 1978, to lawful permanent resident aliens. There are numerous versions of this card because it was periodically revised. Although this card is no longer issued, it is valid indefinitely. This card is also commonly referred to as a "green card" although most versions were blue.

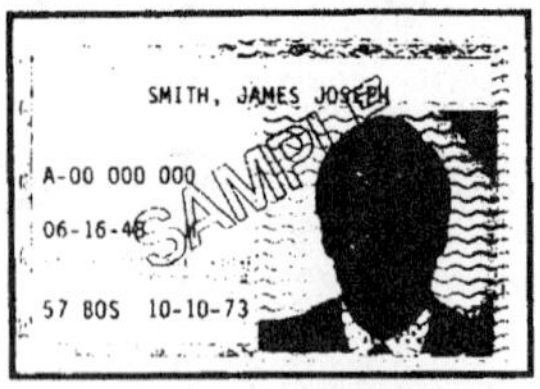

Alien Registration Receipt Card (Resident Alien Card) I-551

Issued by INS after March 1977, to lawful permanent resident aliens. Although this card is no longer issued, it is valid indefinitely. This card is commonly referred to as a "green card" and is the replacement for the Form I-151. This version is white with a blue logo.

Alien Registration Receipt Card (Conditional Resident Alien Card) I-551

Issued by INS after January 1987, to conditional permanent resident aliens such as alien spouses of United States citizens or lawful permanent resident aliens. It is similar to the I-551 issued to permanent resident aliens. Although this card is no longer issued, it is valid for 2 years from the date of admission or adjustment. The expiration date is stated on the back of the card. This version is white with a blue logo.

Alien Registration Receipt Card (Resident Alien Card) I-551

Currently issued by INS since 1989 to both conditional and lawful permanent resident aliens. Although it is similar to the previously issued I-551s, this card is valid only for a limited period of time -- 2 years from the date of admission or adjustment for conditional permanent resident aliens and 10 years from issuance for lawful permanent resident aliens. The expiration date is stated on the front of the card. This version is rose-colored with a blue logo.

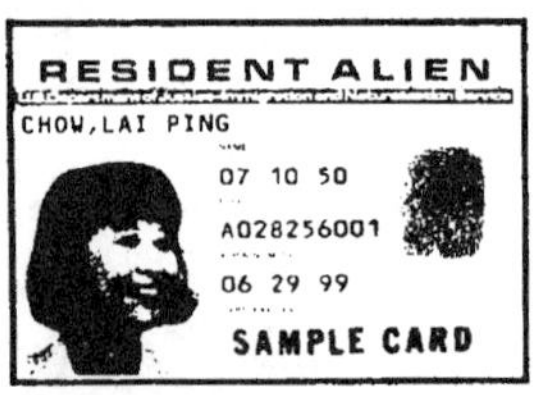

[G11013]

Temporary Resident Card I-688

Issued by INS to aliens granted temporary resident status under the Legalization or Special Agricultural Worker program. It is valid until the expiration date stated on the face of the card or on the sticker(s) placed on the back of the card.

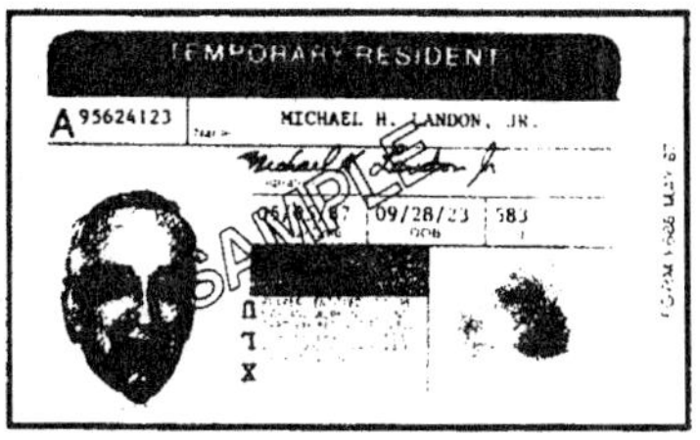

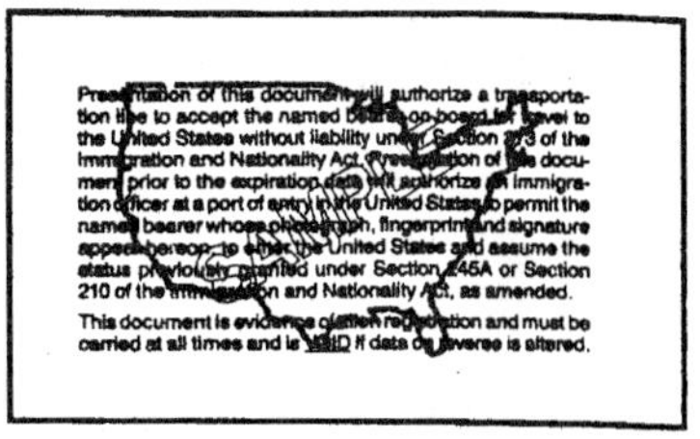

Employment Authorization Card I-688A

Issued by INS to applicants for temporary resident status after their interview for Legalization or Special Agricultural Worker status. It is valid until the expiration date stated on the face of the card or on the sticker(s) placed on the back of the card.

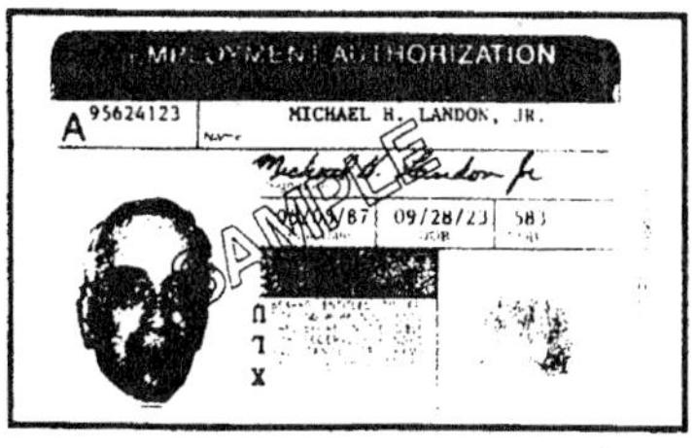

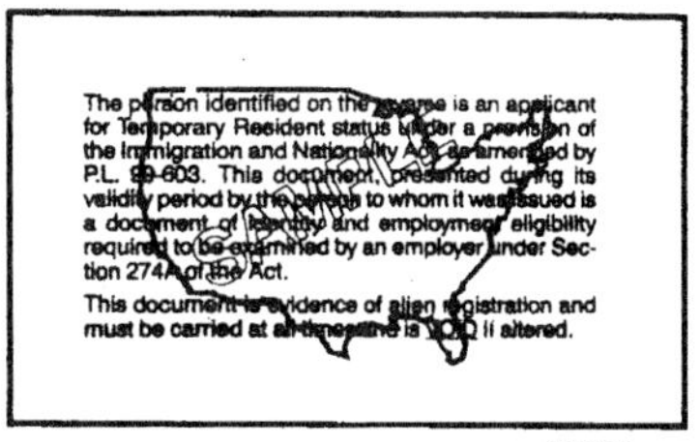

[G11014]

Employment Authorization Card I-688B

Issued by INS to aliens granted temporary employment authorization in the U.S. The expiration date is noted on the face of the card.

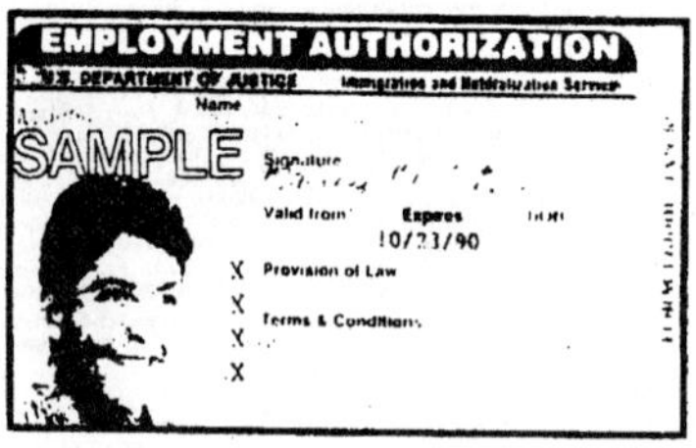

Unexpired Re-Entry Permit I-327

Issued by INS to lawful permanent resident aliens before they leave the United States for a 1-2 year period.

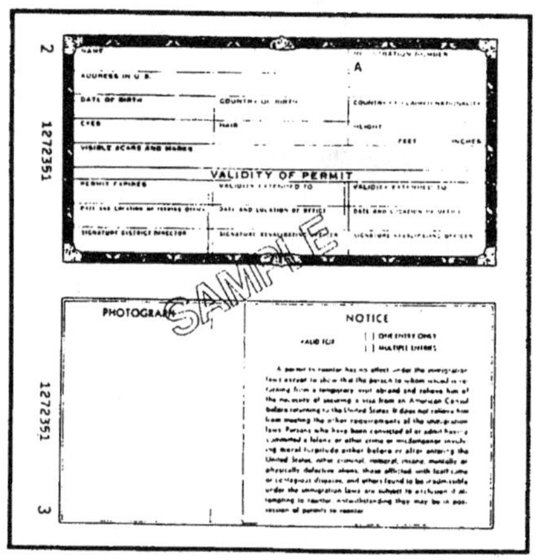

(G11015)

Unexpired Refugee Travel Document I-571

Issued by INS to aliens who have been granted refugee status. The expiration date is stated on page four (4).

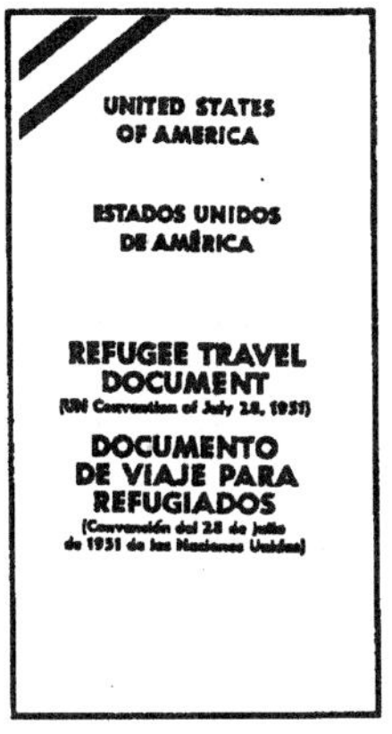

UNITED STATES OF AMERICA

ESTADOS UNIDOS DE AMÉRICA

REFUGEE TRAVEL DOCUMENT

(UN Convention of July 28, 1951)

DOCUMENTO DE VIAJE PARA REFUGIADOS

(Convención del 28 de julio de 1951 de las Naciones Unidas)

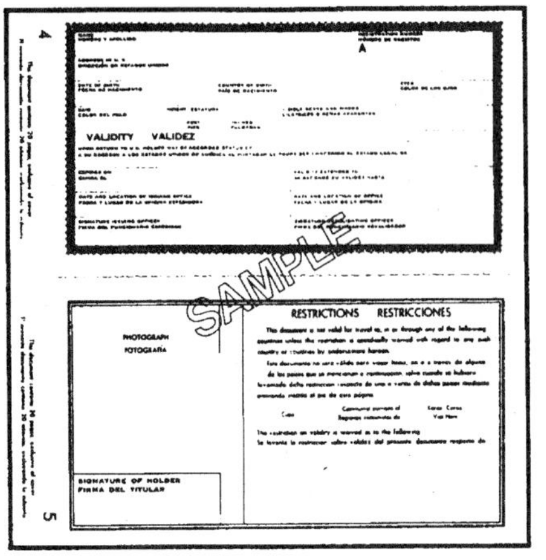

[G11016]

Document List B

Documents That Establish Identity Only

The following illustrations in this handbook do not necessarily reflect the actual size of the documents.

Sample Driver's License

A driver's license issued by any state or outlying possession of the United States (including the District of Columbia, Puerto Rico, the Virgin Islands, Guam, the Northern Mariana Islands, and American Samoa) or by a Canadian government authority is acceptable if it contains a photograph or other identifying information such as name, date of birth, sex, height, color of eyes, and address.

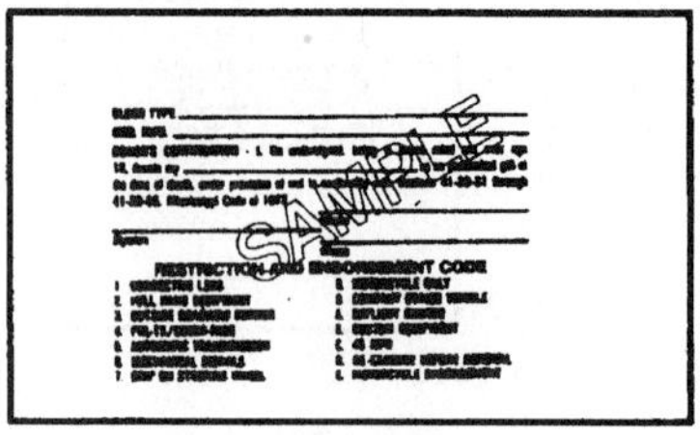

Sample State Identification Card

An identification card issued by any state (including the District of Columbia, Puerto Rico, the Virgin Islands, Guam, and the Northern Mariana Islands) or by a local government is acceptable if it contains a photograph or other identifying information such as name, date of birth, sex, height, color of eyes, and address.

See List C for ID cards issued by INS.

[G11017]

Document List C

Documents That Establish Employment Eligibility Only

The following illustrations in this handbook do not necessarily reflect the actual size of the documents.

Social Security Card (other than one stating "NOT VALID FOR EMPLOYMENT," metal or plastic reproductions, or certain laminated cards.) There are many versions of this card.

Certifications of Birth Issued by the Department of State

FS-545
Issued by U.S. embassies and consulates overseas to United States citizens born abroad.

DS-1350
Issued by the U.S. Department of State to United States citizens born abroad.

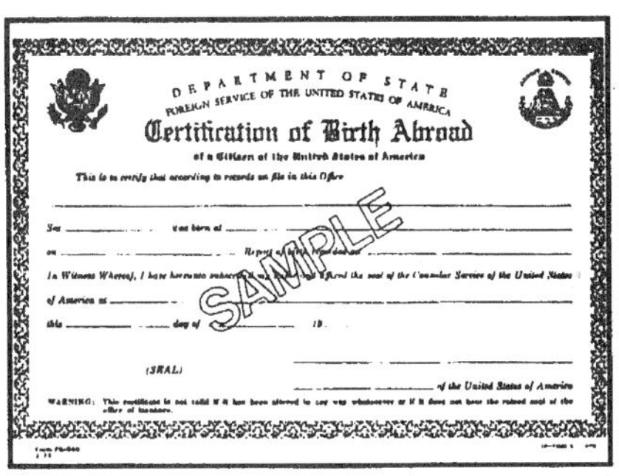

(G11018)

Sample Birth Certificates

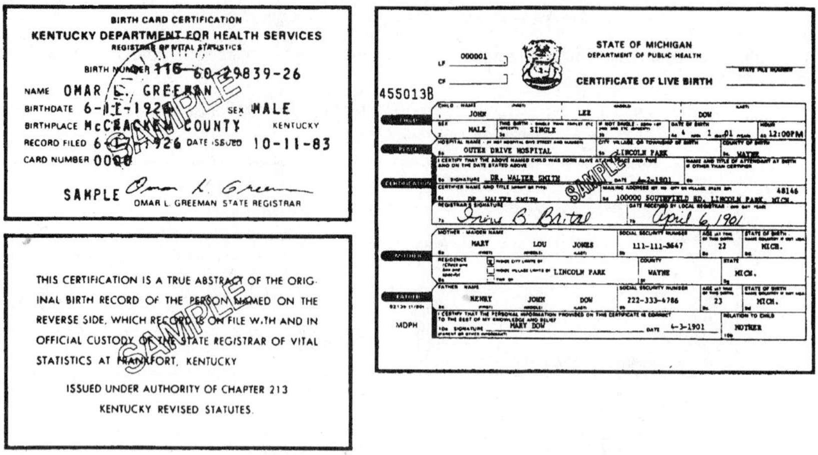

BIRTH CARD CERTIFICATION
KENTUCKY DEPARTMENT FOR HEALTH SERVICES
REGISTRAR OF VITAL STATISTICS
BIRTH NUMBER 116-60-29839-26
NAME OMAR L. GREEMAN
BIRTHDATE 6-11-1926 SEX MALE
BIRTHPLACE McCRACKEN COUNTY KENTUCKY
RECORD FILED 6-17-1926 DATE ISSUED 10-11-83
CARD NUMBER 0000
SAMPLE OMAR L. GREEMAN STATE REGISTRAR

THIS CERTIFICATION IS A TRUE ABSTRACT OF THE ORIGINAL BIRTH RECORD OF THE PERSON NAMED ON THE REVERSE SIDE, WHICH RECORD IS ON FILE WITH AND IN OFFICIAL CUSTODY OF THE STATE REGISTRAR OF VITAL STATISTICS AT FRANKFORT, KENTUCKY

ISSUED UNDER AUTHORITY OF CHAPTER 213
KENTUCKY REVISED STATUTES

STATE OF MICHIGAN
DEPARTMENT OF PUBLIC HEALTH
CERTIFICATE OF LIVE BIRTH
LF 000001
455013B
CHILD NAME: JOHN LEE DOW
SEX: MALE — THIS BIRTH: SINGLE — DATE OF BIRTH: 4 1 01 — HOUR: 12:00PM
HOSPITAL NAME: OUTER DRIVE HOSPITAL — CITY, VILLAGE OR TOWNSHIP OF BIRTH: LINCOLN PARK — COUNTY OF BIRTH: WAYNE
I CERTIFY THAT THE ABOVE NAMED CHILD WAS BORN ALIVE AT THE PLACE AND TIME AND ON THE DATE STATED ABOVE
SIGNATURE: DR. WALTER SMITH — DATE: 4-2-1901
CERTIFIER NAME AND TITLE: DR. WALTER SMITH — MAILING ADDRESS: 100000 SOUTHFIELD RD. LINCOLN PARK, MICH. 48146
REGISTRAR'S SIGNATURE: Irvine B. Brital — DATE RECEIVED BY LOCAL REGISTRAR: April 6, 1901
MOTHER MAIDEN NAME: MARY LOU JONES — SOCIAL SECURITY NUMBER: 111-111-3647 — AGE: 22 — STATE OF BIRTH: MICH.
RESIDENCE: LINCOLN PARK — COUNTY: WAYNE — STATE: MICH.
FATHER NAME: HENRY JOHN DOW — SOCIAL SECURITY NUMBER: 222-333-4786 — AGE: 23 — STATE OF BIRTH: MICH.
I CERTIFY THAT THE PERSONAL INFORMATION PROVIDED ON THIS CERTIFICATE IS CORRECT TO THE BEST OF MY KNOWLEDGE AND BELIEF
SIGNATURE: MARY DOW — DATE: 4-3-1901 — RELATION TO CHILD: MOTHER
MDPH
SAMPLE

United States Citizen Identification Card I-197
Issued by INS to United States citizens. Although INS no longer issues this card, it is valid indefinitely.

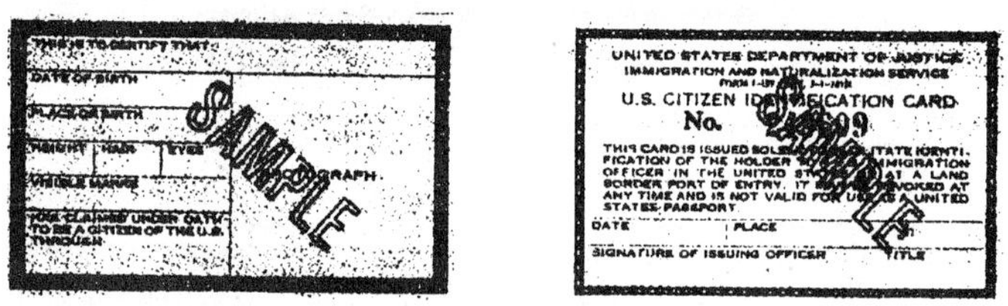

THIS IS TO CERTIFY THAT:
DATE OF BIRTH
PLACE OF BIRTH
HEIGHT — HAIR — EYES
VISIBLE MARKS
PHOTOGRAPH
WHO CLAIMED UNDER OATH TO BE A CITIZEN OF THE U.S. THROUGH
SAMPLE

UNITED STATES DEPARTMENT OF JUSTICE
IMMIGRATION AND NATURALIZATION SERVICE
U.S. CITIZEN IDENTIFICATION CARD
No. [illegible]
THIS CARD IS ISSUED SOLELY AS A STATE IDENTIFICATION OF THE HOLDER TO IMMIGRATION OFFICER IN THE UNITED STATES AT A LAND BORDER PORT OF ENTRY. IT MAY BE REVOKED AT ANY TIME AND IS NOT VALID FOR USE AS A UNITED STATES PASSPORT
DATE — PLACE
SIGNATURE OF ISSUING OFFICER — TITLE
SAMPLE

Identification Card for Use of Resident Citizen in the United States I-179
Issued by INS to United States citizens who are residents of the United States. Although INS no longer issues this card, it is valid indefinitely.

THIS IS TO CERTIFY THAT
SAMPLE

[G11019]

I-20 ID Card Accompanied by a Form I-94

The Form I-94 for F-1 nonimmigrant students must be accompanied by an I-20 Student ID endorsed with employment authorization by the Designated School Official for off-campus employment or curriculum practical training. INS will issue Form I-688B (Employment Authorization Document) to all students (F-1 and M-1) authorized for a post-completion practical training period.

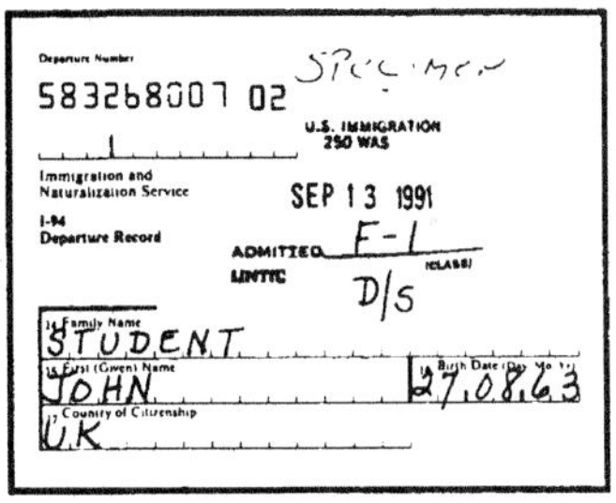

Departure Number
583268007 02
SPECIMEN
U.S. IMMIGRATION
250 WAS
Immigration and Naturalization Service
SEP 13 1991
I-94
Departure Record
ADMITTED F-1
(CLASS)
UNTIL D/S
Family Name
STUDENT
First (Given) Name
JOHN
Birth Date (Day/Mo/Yr)
27.08.63
Country of Citizenship
U.K.

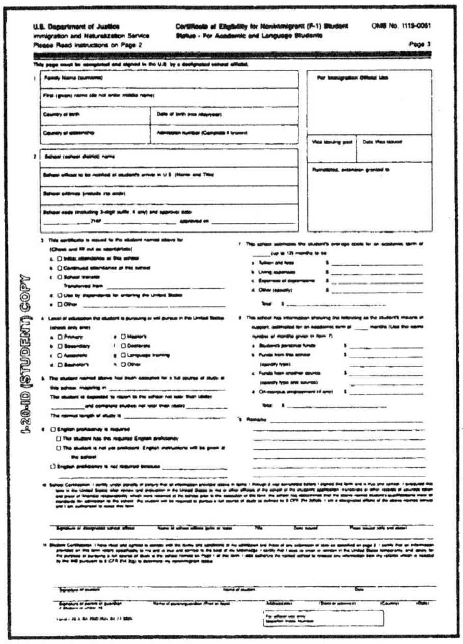

U.S. Department of Justice
Immigration and Naturalization Service
Please Read Instructions on Page 2
Certificate of Eligibility for Nonimmigrant (F-1) Student Status - For Academic and Language Students
OMB No. 1115-0051
Page 3
I-20 ID (STUDENT) COPY

Form I-20 Student ID (Reverse)
Endorsement by Designated School Official for Employment Authorization.

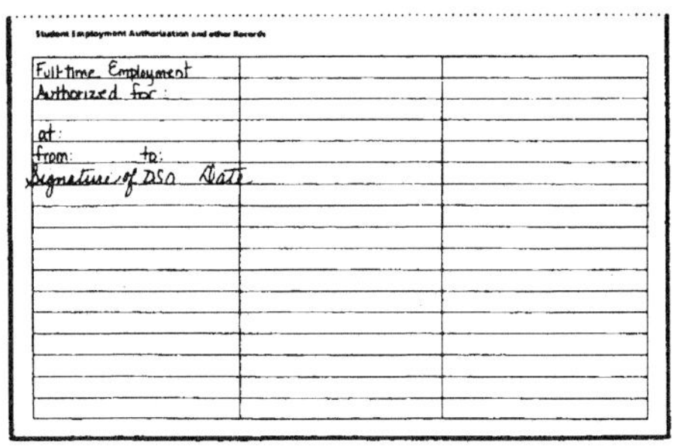

Student Employment Authorization and other Records
Full-time Employment
Authorized for:
at:
from: to:
Signature of DSO Date

[G11020]

IAP-66 Accompanied by a Form I-94

Nonimmigrant exchange visitors (J-1) must have an I-94 accompanied by an unexpired IAP-66, specifying the sponsor and issued by the United States Information Agency (USIA). (J-1 students working outside the program indicated on the IAP-66 also need a letter from their responsible school officer.)

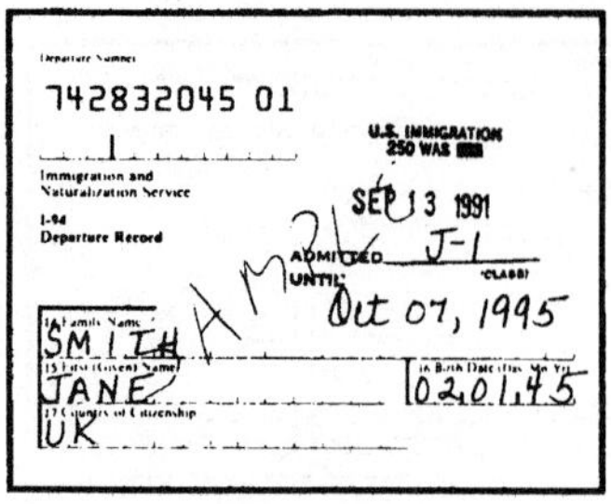
Departure Number
742832045 01
Immigration and Naturalization Service
I-94
Departure Record
U.S. IMMIGRATION
250 WAS
SEP 13 1991
ADMITTED J-1
UNTIL (CLASS)
Oct 07, 1995
14 Family Name
SMITH
15 First (Given) Name
JANE
16 Birth Date (Day Mo Yr)
020145
17 Country of Citizenship
UK

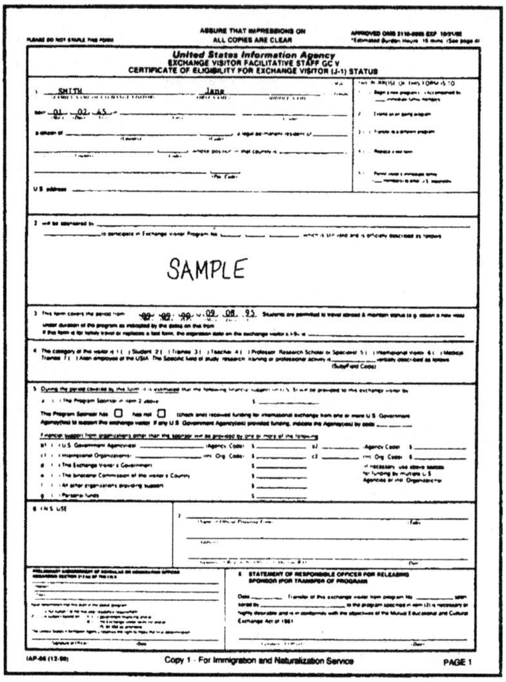
ASSURE THAT IMPRESSIONS ON ALL COPIES ARE CLEAR
United States Information Agency
EXCHANGE VISITOR FACILITATIVE STAFF GC V
CERTIFICATE OF ELIGIBILITY FOR EXCHANGE VISITOR (J-1) STATUS
SMITH
Jane
SAMPLE
Copy 1 - For Immigration and Naturalization Service
PAGE 1

[G11021]

Form I–765 Application for employment authorization

U.S.Department of Justice
Immigration and Naturalization Service

OMB No. 1115-0163

Application for Employment Authorization

INSTRUCTIONS FOR APPLICATION FOR EMPLOYMENT AUTHORIZATION Form I-765

The Immigration and Naturalization Service (INS) recommends that you retain a copy of your completed application for your records.

INDEX

Parts	Page No.
1. General	01
2. Eligibility Categories	01
3. Required Documentation With Each Application	04
4. Fee	04
5. Where To File	05
6. Processing Information	05
7. Other Information	06

PART 1. GENERAL.

Purpose of the Application. Certain aliens who are temporarily in the United States may file a Form I-765, Application for Employment Authorization, to request an Employment Authorization Document (EAD). Other aliens who are authorized to work in the United States without restrictions should also use this form to apply to the INS for a document evidencing such authorization. Please review Part 2 ELIGIBILITY CATEGORIES to determine whether you should use this form.

If you are a Lawful Permanent Resident, a Conditional Resident, or a nonimmigrant authorized to be employed with a specific employer under 8 CFR 274a.12(b), please do NOT use this form.

DEFINITIONS.

Employment Authorization Document (EAD): Form I-688; Form I-688A; Form I-688B; or any successor document issued by the INS as evidence that the holder is authorized to work in the United States.

Renewal EAD: an EAD issued to an eligible applicant at or after the expiration of a previous EAD issued under the same category.

Replacement EAD: an EAD issued to an eligible applicant when the previously issued EAD has been lost, stolen, mutilated, or the previously issued card contains erroneous information, such as a misspelled name.

Interim EAD: an EAD issued to an eligible applicant when the INS has failed to adjudicate an application within 90 days of receipt of a properly filed EAD application or within 30 days of a properly filed initial EAD application based on an asylum application filed on or after January 4, 1995. The interim EAD will be granted for a period not to exceed 240 days and is subject to the conditions noted on the document.

PART 2. ELIGIBILITY CATEGORIES.

The INS adjudicates a request for employment authorization by determining whether an applicant has submitted the required information and documentation, and whether the applicant is eligible. In order to determine your eligibility, you must identify the category in which you are eligible and fill in that category in question 16 on the Form I-765. Enter only one of the following category numbers on the application form.

NOTE: **Category (c)(13) is no longer available.** You may not renew or replace your EAD based on (c)(13). If you have an EAD based on that category, please review the categories below to determine if you are eligible under another category.

APPLICATIONS TO BE FILED AT SERVICE CENTERS.

Asylee, (granted asylum)–(a)(5). File your EAD application with a copy of the INS letter granting you asylum. It is not necessary to apply for an EAD as an asylee until 90 days before the expiration of your current EAD.

Refugee–(a)(3). File your EAD application with either a copy of your Form I-590, Registration for Classification as Refugee, approval letter or a copy of a Form I-730, Refugee/Asylee Relative Petition, approval notice.

Paroled as a Refugee–(a)(4). File your EAD application with a copy of your Form I-94, Departure Record.

Asylum Applicant (with a pending asylum application) who Filed for Asylum on or after January 4, 1995–(c)(8). If you filed a Form I-589, Request for Asylum and for Withholding of Deportation, on or after January 4, 1995, you must wait at least 150 days before you are eligible to apply for an EAD. If you file your EAD application early, it will be denied and you will have to file a new application. File your EAD application with:

- A copy of the INS acknowledgement mailer which was mailed to you; or
- Other evidence that your Form I-589 was filed with the INS; or
- Evidence that your Form I-589 was filed with an Immigration Judge at the Executive Office for Immigration Review (EOIR); or
- Evidence that your asylum application remains under administrative or judicial review.

Form I-765 (Rev. 10/13/98)N Page 1

Asylum Applicant (with a pending asylum application) who Filed for Asylum and Withholding of Deportation Prior to January 4, 1995 and is *NOT* in Exclusion or Deportation Proceedings--(c)(8). You may file your EAD application at any time; however, it will only be granted if the INS finds that your asylum application is not frivolous. File your EAD application with:

- A complete copy of your previously filed Form I-589; and
- A copy of your INS receipt notice; or
- A copy of the INS acknowledgement mailer; or
- Evidence that your Form I-589 was filed with EOIR; or
- Evidence that your asylum application remains under administrative or judicial review; or
- Other evidence that you filed an asylum application.

Asylum Applicant (with a pending asylum application) who Filed an Initial Request for Asylum Prior to January 4, 1995, and *IS IN* Exclusion or Deportation Proceedings--(c)(8). If you filed your Request for Asylum and Withholding of Deportation (Form I-589) prior to January 4, 1995 and you ARE IN exclusion or deportation proceedings, file your EAD application with:

- A date-stamped copy of your previously filed Form I-589; or
- A copy of Form I-221, Order to Show Cause and Notice of Hearing, or Form I-122, Notice to Applicant for Admission Detained for Hearing Before Immigration Judge; or
- A copy of EOIR-26, Notice of Appeal, date stamped by the Office of the Immigration Judge; or
- A date-stamped copy of a petition for judicial review or for *habeas corpus* issued to the asylum applicant; or
- Other evidence that you filed an asylum application with EOIR.

Asylum Applicant under the ABC Settlement Agreement--(c)(8). If you are an El Salvadoran or Guatemalan national eligible for benefits under the ABC settlement agreement, American Baptist Churches v. Thornburgh, 760 F. Supp. 796 (N.D. Cal. 1991), there are special instructions applicable to filing your Form I-765 which supplement these instructions. These instructions and the application can be obtained by asking for an "ABC packet" at your local INS office or by calling 1-800-755-0777.

Deferred Enforced Departure (DED)/Extended Voluntary Departure--(a)(11). File your EAD application with evidence of your identity and nationality.

F-1 Student Seeking Optional Practical Training in an Occupation Directly Related to Studies--(c)(3)(i). File your EAD application with a Certificate of Eligibility of Nonimmigrant (F-1) Student Status (Form I-20 A-B/I-20 ID) endorsed by a designated school official within the past 30 days.

F-1 Student Offered Off-Campus Employment under the Sponsorship of a Qualifying International Organization--(c)(3)(ii). File your EAD application with the international organization's letter of certification that the proposed employment is within the scope of its sponsorship and a Certificate of Eligibility of Nonimmigrant (F-1) Student Status--For Academic and Language Students (Form I-20 A-B/I-20 ID) endorsed by the designated school official within the past 30 days.

F-1 Student Seeking Off-Campus Employment Due to Severe Economic Hardship--(c)(3)(iii). File your EAD application with Form I-20 A-B/I-20 ID, Certificate of Eligibility of Nonimmigrant (F-1) Student Status--For Academic and Language Students; Form I-538, Certification by Designated School Official, and any evidence you wish to submit, such as affidavits, which detail the unforeseen economic circumstances that cause your request, and evidence you have tried to find off-campus employment with an employer who has filed a labor and wage attestation.

J-2 Spouse or Minor Child of an Exchange Visitor--(c)(5). File your EAD application with a copy of your J-1's (principal alien's) Certificate of Eligibility for Exchange Visitor (J-1) Status (Form IAP-66). You must submit a written statement, with any supporting evidence showing, that your employment is not necessary to support the J-1 but is for other purposes.

M-1 Student Seeking Practical Training after Completing Studies--(c)(6). File your EAD application with a completed Form I-538, Application by Nonimmigrant Student for Extension of Stay, School Transfer, or Permission to Accept or Continue Employment, Form I-20 M-N, Certificate of Eligibility for Nonimmigrant (M-1) Student Status--For Vocational Students endorsed by the designated school official within the past 30 days.

Dependent of CCNAA E-1 Nonimmigrant--(c)(2). File your EAD application with the required certification from the American Institute in Taiwan if you are the spouse, or unmarried child, of an E-1 employee of the Coordination Council for North American Affairs.

Dependent of NATO Personnel--(c)(7). File your EAD application with a letter from the Department of Defense or NATO/SACLANT verifying your principal alien's status, your status, and your relationship to your principal alien.

N-8 or N-9 Nonimmigrant--(a)(7). File your EAD application with the required evidence listed in Part 3.

Family Unity Program–(a)(13). File your EAD application with a copy of the approval notice, if you have been granted status under this program. You may choose to file your EAD application concurrently with your Form I-817, Application for Voluntary Departure under the Family Unity Program. The INS may take up to 90 days from the date upon which you are granted status under the Family Unity Program to adjudicate your EAD application. If you were denied Family Unity status solely because your legalized spouse or parent first applied under the Legalization/SAW programs after May 5, 1988, file your EAD application with a new Form I-817 application and a copy of the original denial. However, if your EAD application is based on continuing eligibility under (c)(12), please refer to **Deportable Alien Granted Voluntary Departure**.

K-1 Nonimmigrant Fiance(e) of U.S. Citizen or K-2 Dependent–(a)(6). File your EAD application if you are filing within 90 days from the date of entry. This EAD cannot be renewed. Any EAD application other than for a replacement must be based on your pending application for adjustment under (c)(9).

Citizen of Micronesia or the Marshall Islands or Palau–(a)(8). File your EAD application if you were admitted to the United States as a citizen of the Federated States of Micronesia (CFA/FSM) or of the Marshall Islands (CFA/MIS) pursuant to agreements between the United States and the former trust territories.

B-1 Nonimmigrant who is the personal or domestic servant of a nonimmigrant employer–(c)(17)(i). File your EAD application with:

- Evidence from your employer that he or she is a B, E, F, H, I, J, L, M, O, P, R or TN nonimmigrant and you were employed for at least one year by the employer before the employer entered the United States or your employer regularly employs personal and domestic servants and has done so for a period of years before coming to the United States; <u>and</u>
- Evidence that you have either worked for this employer as a personal or domestic servant for at least one year or, evidence that you have at least one year's experience as a personal or domestic servant; <u>and</u>
- Evidence establishing that you have a residence abroad which you have no intention of abandoning.

B-1 Nonimmigrant Domestic Servant of a U.S. Citizen–(c)(17)(ii). File your EAD application with:

- Evidence from your employer that he or she is a U.S. Citizen; <u>and</u>
- Evidence that your employer has a permanent home abroad or is stationed outside the United States and is temporarily visiting the United States or the citizen's current assignment in the United States will not be longer than four (4) years; and
- Evidence that he or she has employed you as a domestic servant abroad for at least six (6) months prior to your admission to the United States.

B-1 Nonimmigrant Employed by a Foreign Airline–(c)(17)(iii). File your EAD application with a letter, from the airline, fully describing your duties and indicating that your position would entitle you to E nonimmigrant status except for the fact that you are not a national of the same country as the airline or because there is no treaty of commerce and navigation in effect between the United States and that country.

APPLICATIONS TO BE FILED AT LOCAL INS OFFICES.

Temporary Protected Status (TPS)--(a)(12). File your EAD application with Form I-821, Application for Temporary Protected Status.

- <u>Initial</u> TPS-based application only, include evidence of identity and nationality as required by the Form I-821 instructions.
- <u>Extension</u> of TPS status, include a copy (front and back) of your last available TPS document: EAD, Form I-94 or approval notice.
- <u>Registration</u> for TPS only without employment authorization, file the Form I-765, Form I-821, and a letter indicating that this form is for registration purposes only. No fee is required for the Form I-765 filed as part of TPS registration. (Form I-821 has separate fee requirements.)

Applying for Temporary Protected Status (TPS)/Temporary Treatment Benefits–(c)(19). ***<u>File your EAD application with your TPS application, Form I-821.</u>*** If you are using this application to register for TPS and do not want to work in the United States, you must submit a letter indicating this application is for registration purposes only. No fee is required to register.

Granted Withholding of Deportation–(a)(10). File your EAD application with a copy of the Immigration Judge's order. It is not necessary to apply for a new EAD until 90 days before the expiration of your current EAD.

Dependent of A-1 or A-2 Foreign Government Officials–(c)(1). File your EAD application with a Form I-566, Application for Employment by Spouse or Unmarried Dependent Son or Daughter of A-1 or A-2 Official or Employee of Diplomatic or Consular Establishment or G-4 Officer or Employee of International Organization, with the Department of State endorsement.

Dependent of G-1, G-3 or G-4 Nonimmigrant–(c)(4). File your EAD application with a Form I-566, Application for Employment by Spouse or Unmarried Dependent Son or Daughter of A-1 or A-2 Official or Employee of Diplomatic or Consular Establishment or G-4 Officer or Employee of International Organization, with the Department of State endorsement if you are the dependent of a qualifying G-1, G-3 or G-4 officer of, representative to, or employee of an international organization and you hold a valid nonimmigrant status.

Adjustment Applicant–(c)(9). File your EAD application with a copy of the receipt notice or other evidence that your Form I-485, Application for Permanent Residence, is pending. You may file Form I-765 together with your Form I-485.

Applicant for Suspension of Deportation–(c)(10). File your EAD application with evidence that your Form I-256A, Application for Suspension of Deportation, is pending.

Paroled in the Public Interest–(c)(11). File your EAD application if you were paroled into the United States for emergent reasons or reasons strictly in the public interest.

Deportable Alien Granted Voluntary Departure–(c)(12). File your EAD application with a copy of the order or notice granting voluntary departure, and evidence establishing your economic need to work.

Deferred Action–(c)(14). File your EAD application with a copy of the order, notice or document placing you in deferred action and evidence establishing economic necessity for an EAD.

Adjustment Applicant Based on Continuous Residence Since January 1, 1972–(c)(16). File your EAD application with your Form I-485, Application for Permanent Residence; a copy of your receipt notice; or other evidence that the Form I-485 is pending.

Final Order of Deportation–(c)(18). File your EAD application with a copy of the order of supervision and a request for employment authorization which may be based on, but not limited to the following:

- Existence of economic necessity to be employed;
- Existence of a dependent spouse and/or children in the United States who rely on you for support; and
- Anticipated length of time before you can be removed from the United States.

PART 3. REQUIRED DOCUMENTATION WITH EACH APPLICATION.

All applications must be filed with the documents required below, in addition to the evidence required for the category listed in Part 2 ELIGIBILITY CATEGORIES, with fee, if required.

If you are required to show economic necessity for your category (See Part 2), submit a list of your assets, income and expenses.

Please assemble the documents in the following order:

Your application with the filing fee. See Part 4 FEE for details.

If you are mailing your application to the INS, you must also submit:

- Form I-765 Signature Card. If one is not enclosed with your application, ask your local INS office for one. Sign the card in the blue box marked "signature". Your signature must fit within the blue box. DO NOT fold this card when you mail your application.
- A copy of Form I-94 Departure Record (front and back), if available.
- A copy of your last EAD (front and back).
- 2 photos with a white background taken no earlier than 30 days before submission to the INS. They should be unmounted; printed on thin paper; glossy; and unretouched. The photos should show a three-quarter front profile of the right side of your face, with your right ear visible. Your head should be bare unless you are wearing a headdress as required by a religious order to which you belong. The photo should not be larger than 1 ½ X 1 ½ inches, with the distance from the top of the head to just below the chin about 1¼ inches. Lightly print your name and your A#, if known, on the back of each photo with a pencil.

PART 4. FEE.

Applicants must pay a fee of $100 to file this form unless noted below. If a fee is required, it will not be refunded. Pay in the exact amount. Checks and money orders must be payable in U.S. currency. Make check or money order payable to "Immigration and Naturalization Service." If you live in Guam make your check or money order payable to "Treasurer, Guam." If you live in the U.S. Virgin Islands make your check or money order payable to "Commissioner of Finance of the Virgin Islands." A charge of $30.00 will be imposed if a check in payment of a fee is not honored by the bank on which it is drawn

Please do not send cash in the mail.

Initial EAD: If this is your initial application and you are applying under one of the following categories, a filing fee is not required:

- (a)(3) Refugee;
- (a)(4) Paroled as Refugee;
- (a)(5) Asylee;
- (a)(7) N-8 or N-9 nonimmigrant;
- (a)(8) Citizen of Micronesia, Marshall Islands or Palau.
- (a)(10) Granted Withholding of Deportation;
- (a)(11) Deferred Enforced Departure;
- (c)(1) or (c)(4) Dependent of certain foreign government or international organization personnel; or
- (c)(8) Applicant for asylum [an applicant filing under the special ABC procedures must pay the fee].

Renewal EAD: If this is a renewal application and you are applying under one of the following categories, a filing fee is not required:

Form I-765 (Rev. 10/13/98)N Page 4

- (a)(8) Citizen of Micronesia, Marshall Islands, or Palau.
- (a)(10) Granted Withholding of Deportation;
- (a)(11) Deferred Enforced Departure; or
- (c)(1) or (c)(4) Dependent of certain foreign government or international organization personnel.

Replacement EAD: If this is your replacement application and you are applying under one of the following categories, a filing fee is not required:

- (c)(1) or (c)(4) Dependent of certain foreign government or international organization personnel.

You may be eligible for a fee waiver under 8 CFR 103.7(c).

The INS will use The Community Service Administration Income Poverty Guidelines ("Poverty Guidelines") found at 45 CFR 1060.2 as the basic criteria in determining the applicant's eligibility when economic necessity is identified as a factor.

The Poverty Guidelines will be used as a guide, but not as a conclusive standard, in adjudicating fee waiver requests for employment authorization applications requiring a fee.

PART 5. WHERE TO FILE.

If your response to question 16 is:

(a)(3), (a)(4), (a)(5), (a)(7), or (a)(8)

mail your application to:

INS Service Center
P.O. Box 87765
Lincoln, NE 68501-7765

If your response to question 16 is:

(a)(6), (a)(11), (a)(13),
(c)(2), (c)(3)(i), (c)(3)(ii), (c)(3)(iii), (c)(5), (c)(6), (c)(7), (c)(8), (c)(17)(i), (c)(17)(ii), or (c)(17)(iii)

mail your application based on your address to the appropriate Service Center:

If you live in: Connecticut, Delaware, the District of Columbia, Maine, Maryland, Massachusetts, New Hampshire, New Jersey, New York, Pennsylvania, Puerto Rico, Rhode Island, Vermont, Virginia, West Virginia or the U.S. Virgin Islands, mail your application to:

INS Service Center
P.O. Box 9765
St. Albans, VT 05479-9765

If you live in: Arizona, California, Guam, Hawaii or Nevada, mail your application to:

INS Service Center
P.O. Box 10765
Laguna Niguel, CA 92607-0765

If you live in: Alabama, Arkansas, Florida, Georgia, Kentucky, Louisiana, Mississippi, New Mexico, N. Carolina, Oklahoma, S. Carolina, Tennessee or Texas, mail your application to:

INS Service Center
P.O. Box 152122, Department A
Irving, TX 75015-2122

If you live elsewhere in the U.S., mail your application to:

INS Service Center
P.O. Box 87765
Lincoln, NE 68501-7765

If your response to question 16 is:

(a)(10), (a)(12),
(c)(1), (c)(4), (c)(10), (c)(11), (c)(12), (c)(14), (c)(16), (c)(18), or (c)(19)

apply at the local INS office having jurisdiction over your place of residence.

If your response to question 16 is **(c)(9)**, file your application at the same local INS office or Service Center where you submitted your adjustment application.

If your response to question 16 is **(c)(8)** under the special ABC filing instructions and you are filing your asylum and EAD applications together, mail your application to the office where you are filing your asylum application.

PART 6. PROCESSING INFORMATION.

Acceptance. An application filed without the required fee, evidence, signature or photographs (if required) will be returned to you as incomplete. You may correct the deficiency and resubmit the application; however, an application is not considered properly filed until the INS accepts it. If your application is complete and filed at an INS Service Center, you will be mailed a Form I-797 receipt notice.

Decision on your application.

- **Approval.** If approved, your EAD will either be mailed to you or you may be required to appear at your local INS office to pick it up.
- **Request for evidence.** If additional information or documentation is required, a written request will be sent to you specifying the information or advising you of an interview.
- **Denial.** If your application cannot be granted, you will receive a written notice explaining the basis of your denial.

Form I-765 (Rev. 10/13/98)N Page 5

No decision

- **Interim EAD.** If you have not received a decision within 90 days of receipt by the INS of a properly filed EAD application or within 30 days of a properly filed initial EAD application based on an asylum application filed on or after January 4, 1995, you may obtain interim work authorization by appearing in person at your local INS district office. You must bring proof of identity and any notices that you have received from the INS in connection with your application for employment authorization.

PART 7. OTHER INFORMATION.

Penalties for Perjury. All statements contained in response to questions in this application are declared to be true and correct under penalty of perjury. Title 18, United States Code, Section 1546, provides in part:

> . . . Whoever knowingly makes under oath, or as permitted under penalty of perjury under 1746 of Title 28, United States Code, knowingly subscribes as true, any false statement with respect to a material fact in any application, affidavit, or other document required by the immigration laws or regulations prescribed thereunder, or knowingly presents any such application, affidavit, or other document containing any such false statement - shall be fined in accordance with this title or imprisoned not more than five years, or both.

The knowing placement of false information on this application may subject you and/or the preparer of this application to criminal penalties under Title 18 of the United States Code. The knowing placement of false information on this application may also subject you and/or the preparer to civil penalties under Section 274C of the Immigration and Nationality Act (INA), 8 U.S.C. 1324c. Under 8 U.S.C. 1324c, a person subject to a final order for civil document fraud is deportable from the United States and may be subject to fines.

Authority for Collecting this Information. The authority to require you to file Form I-765, Application for Employment Authorization, when applying for employment authorization is found at 8 U.S.C. 274A(b)(1)(C)(iii). Information you provide on your Form I-765 is used to determine whether you are eligible for employment authorization and for the preparation of your Employment Authorization Document if you are found eligible. Failure to provide all information as requested may result in the denial or rejection of this application. The information you provide may also be disclosed to other federal, state, local and foreign law enforcement and regulatory agencies during the course of the INS investigations.

Paperwork Reduction Act. A person is not required to respond to a collection of information unless it displays a currently valid OMB control number. The Immigration and Naturalization Service (INS) tries to create forms and instructions which are accurate and easily understood. Often this is difficult because immigration law can be very complex. The public reporting burden for this form is estimated to average three (3) hours and twenty-five (25) minutes per response, including the time for reviewing instructions, gathering and maintaining the data needed, and completing and reviewing the collection of information. The INS welcomes your comments regarding this burden estimate or any other aspect of this form, including suggestions for reducing this burden, to: U.S. Department of Justice, Immigration and Naturalization Service 425 I Street, N.W. Room 5307, Washington, D.C. 20536; OMB No. 1115-0163. **DO NOT MAIL YOUR COMPLETED APPLICATION TO THIS ADDRESS.**

Form I-765 (Rev. 10/13/98)N Page 6

U. S. Department of Justice
Immigration and Naturalization Service

OMB # 1115-0163

Application for Employment Authorization

Do Not Write in This Block

Remarks	Action Stamp	Fee Stamp
A#		
Applicant is filing under 274a.12 ______		

☐ Application Approved. Employment Authorized / Extended (Circle One) ______________ (Date).
until ______________ (Date).

Subject to the following conditions: ______________

☐ Application Denied.

☐ Failed to establish eligibility under 8 CFR 274a.12 (a) or (c).

☐ Failed to establish economic necessity as required in 8 CFR 274a.12(c) (14), (18) and 8 CFR 214.2(f)

I am applying for: ☐ Permission to accept employment
☐ Replacement (of lost employment authorization document).
☐ Renewal of my permission to accept employment (attach previous employment authorization document).

1. Name (Family Name in CAPS) (First) (Middle)

2. Other Names Used (Include Maiden Name)

3. Address in the United States (Number and Street) (Apt. Number)
(Town or City) (State/Country) (ZIP Code)

4. Country of Citizenship/Nationality

5. Place of Birth (Town or City) (State/Province) (Country)

6. Date of Birth (Month/Day/Year)

7. Sex ☐ Male ☐ Female

8. Marital Status ☐ Married ☐ Single ☐ Widowed ☐ Divorced

9. Social Security Number (Include all Numbers you have ever used)

10. Alien Registration Number (A-Number) or I-94 Number (if any)

11. Have you ever before applied for employment authorization from INS?
☐ Yes (If yes, complete below) ☐ No
Which INS Office? Date(s)
Results (Granted or Denied - attach all documentation)

12. Date of Last Entry into the U.S. (Month/Day/Year)

13. Place of Last Entry into the U.S.

14. Manner of Last Entry (Visitor, Student, etc.)

15. Current Immigration Status (Visitor, Student, etc.)

16. Go to Part 2 of the instructions, Eligibility Categories. In the space below, place the letter and number of the category you selected from the instructions (For example, (a)(8), (c)(17)(iii), etc.).
Eligibility under 8 CFR 274a.12
( ) ( ) ( )

Certification

Your Certification: I certify, under penalty of perjury under the laws of the United States of America, that the foregoing is true and correct. Furthermore, I authorize the release of any information which the Immigration and Naturalization Service needs to determine eligibility for the benefit I am seeking. I have read the Instructions in Part 2 and have identified the appropriate eligibility category in Block 16.

Signature Telephone Number Date

Signature of Person Preparing Form if Other Than Above: I declare that this document was prepared by me at the request of the applicant and is based on all information of which I have any knowledge.

Print Name Address *Signature* Date

Initial Receipt	Resubmitted	Relocated		Completed		
		Rec'd	Sent	Approved	Denied	Returned

Form I-765 (Rev. 10/13/98)N Page 7

Form I–851 Notice of intent to issue a final administrative removal order

U.S. Department of Justice
Immigration and Naturalization Service **Notice of Intent to Issue a Final Administrative Removal Order**

In removal proceedings under section 238(b) of the Immigration and Nationality Act

File No: ____________________

To: ____________________

Address: ____________________
(Number, street, city state and ZIP code)

Telephone: ____________________
(Area code and phone number)

Pursuant to section 238(b) of the Immigration and Nationality Act (Act), 8 USC 1228(b), the Immigration and Naturalization Service (Service) has determined that you are amenable to expedited administrative removal proceedings. The determination is based on the following allegations:

1. You are not a citizen or national of the United States.
2. You are a native of ____________________ and a citizen of ____________________.
3. You entered the United States (at)(near) ____________________ on or about ____________________.
4. At that time you entered ____________________.
5. You are not lawfully admitted for permanent residence.
6. You were, on ____________________, convicted in the ____________________ Court ____ ____________________ for the offense of ____________________ in violation of ____________________ for which the term of imprisonment imposed was ____________________.

__Charge:__
You are deportable under section 237(a)(2)(A)(iii) of the Act, 8 USC 1227(a)(2)(A)(iii), as amended, because you have been convicted of an aggravated felony as defined in section 101(a)(43) of the Act, 8 USC 1101(a)(43).

Based upon section 238(b) of the Act, the Service is serving upon you this NOTICE OF INTENT TO ISSUE A FINAL ADMINISTRATIVE REMOVAL ORDER ("Notice of Intent") without a hearing before an Immigration Judge.

__Your Rights and Responsibilities__
You may choose to be represented (at no expense to the United States government) by counsel, authorized to practice in this proceeding. If you wish legal advice and cannot afford it, contact legal counsel from the list of available free legal services provided to you.

You must respond to the above charges in writing to the Service address provided below within 10 calendar days of service of this notice (or 13 calendar days if service is by mail). In your response you may: request, for good cause, an extension of time; rebut the charges stated above (with supporting evidence); request an opportunity to review the government's evidence; admit deportability; and/or designate the country to which you choose to be removed in the event that a final order of removal is issued (which designation the Service will honor only to the extent permitted under section 241 of the Act).

You may seek judicial review of any final administrative order by filing a petition for review within 14 calendar days after the date such final administrative order is issued, or you may waive such appeal by stating, in writing, your desire not to appeal.

____________________ (Signature and title of issuing officer) ____________________ (City and state of issuance) ____________________ (Date and time)

__Certificate of Service__

I served this Notice of Intent. I have determined that the person served with this document is the above named individual.

____________________ (Signature and title of officer) ____________________ (Date and manner of service)

☐ I explained and/or served this Notice of intent to the alien in the ____________________ language.
Name of Interpreter ____________________
Location/Employer ____________________

Form I-851 (Rev. 4-1-97)N

I ACKNOWLEDGE THAT I HAVE RECEIVED THIS NOTICE OF INTENT TO ISSUE A FINAL ADMINISTRATIVE REMOVAL ORDER

____________________ (Signature of respondent) ________________ (Date and Time)

☐ Alien refused to acknowledge receipt of this document.

____________________ (Signature and Title of Officer) ________________ (Date and Time)

I WISH TO CONTEST

I contest my deportability because: (*Attach any supporting documentation*):

☐ I am a citizen or national of the United States.
☐ I am a lawful permanent resident of the United States.
☐ I was not convicted of the criminal offense described in allegation number 6 above.
☐ I am attaching documents in support of my rebuttal and request for further review.

____________________ (Signature of Respondent) ____________________ (Printed Name of Respondent) ________________ (Date and Time)

I DO NOT WISH TO CONTEST

☐ I admit the allegations and charge in this Notice of Intent. I admit that I am deportable and acknowledge that I am not eligible for any form of relief from removal. I waive my right to rebut and contest the above charges and my right to file a petition for review of the Final Removal Order. I wish to be deported to ____________________.
☐ I also waive the 14 day period of execution of the Final Removal Order.

____________________ (Signaturee of Respondent) ____________________ (Printed Name of Respondent) ________________ (Date and Time)

____________________ (Signature of Witness) ____________________ (Printed Name of Witness) ________________ (Date and Time)

RETURN THIS FORM TO:

United States Department of Justice
Immigration and Naturalization Service

____
____
____

ATTENTION:

Form I-851 (Rev. 4-1-97)N

Form I–851A Final administrative removal order

U.S. Department of Justice
Immigration and Naturalization Service

Final Administrative Removal Order

FINAL ADMINISTRATIVE REMOVAL ORDER
UNDER SECTION 238(b) OF THE
IMMIGRATION AND NATIONALITY ACT

File No: ____________________

Date: ____________________

To:____

Address: ____:
(Number, street, city state and ZIP code)

Telephone: ____________________
(Area code and phone number)

ORDER

Based upon the allegations set forth in the Notice of Intent to Issue a Final Administrative Removal Order and evidence contained in the administrative record, I, the undersigned Deciding Service Officer of the Immigration and Naturalization Service, make the following findings of fact and conclusions of law. I find that you are not a citizen or national of the United States and that you were not lawfully admitted for permanent residence. I further find that you have a final conviction of an aggravated felony as defined in section 101(a)(43) of the Act, 8 U.S.C. 1101(a)(43), and are ineligible for any relief from removal that the Attorney General may grant in an exercise of discretion. I further find that the administrative record established by clear, convincing, and unequivocal evidence that you are deportable as an alien convicted of an aggravated felony pursuant to section 237(a)(2)(A)(iii) of the Act, 8 U.S.C. 1227(a)(2)(A)(iii). By the power and authority vested in the Attorney General and in me as the Attorney General's delegate under the laws of the United States, I find you deportable as charged and order that you be removed from the United States to ____________________ or to any alternate country prescribed in section 241 of the Act.

____
(Signature of Authorized INS Official)

____
(Title of official)

____
(Date and office location)

Petition for review: ☐ Waived by respondent.
☐ Reserved by respondent.

Certificate of Service

I served this FINAL ADMINISTRATIVE REMOVAL ORDER upon the above named individual.

____
(Date, time, place and manner of service)

____
(Signature and title of officer)

Form I-851A (Rev. 4/1/97)N

Form I-867AB Record of sworn statement in proceedings under section 235(b)(1) of the Act

U.S. Department of Justice
Immigration and Naturalization Service

Record of Sworn Statement in Proceedings under Section 235(b)(1) of the Act

Office: ______________________ File No: ______________________

Statement by: ____

In the case of: ____

Date of Birth: ______________________ Gender (circle one): Male Female

At: ______________________ Date: ______________________

Before: ____
(Name and Title)

In the ____________ language. Interpreter ______________ Employed by ______________

I am an officer of the United States Immigration and Naturalization Service. I am authorized to administer the immigration laws and to take sworn statements. I want to take your sworn statement regarding your application for admission to the United States. Before I take your statement, I also want to explain your rights, and the purpose and consequences of this interview.

You do not appear to be admissible or to have the required legal papers authorizing your admission to the United States. This may result in your being denied admission and immediately returned to your home country without a hearing. If a decision is made to refuse your admission into the United States, you may be immediately removed from this country, and if so, you may be barred from reentry for a period of 5 years or longer.

This may be your only opportunity to present information to me and the Immigration and Naturalization Service to make a decision. It is very important that you tell me the truth. If you lie or give misinformation, you may be subject to criminal or civil penalties, or barred from receiving immigration benefits or relief now or in the future.

Except as I will explain to you, you are not entitled to a hearing or review.

> U.S. law provides protection to certain persons who face persecution, harm or torture upon return to their home country. If you fear or have a concern about being removed from the United States or about being sent home, you should tell me so during this interview because you may not have another chance. You will have the opportunity to speak privately and confidentially to another officer about your fear or concern. That officer will determine if you should remain in the United States and not be removed because of that fear.

Until a decision is reached in your case, you will remain in the custody of the Immigration and Naturalization Service.

Any statement you make may be used against you in this or any subsequent administrative proceeding.

Q: Do you understand what I've said to you?

A.

Q. Do you have any questions?

A.

Q. Are you willing to answer my questions at this time?

A.

Q. Do you swear or affirm that all the statements you are about to make are true and complete?

A.

Page 1 of ____ I-867A (4-1-97)

U.S. Department of Justice
Immigration and Naturalization Service

Jurat for Record of Sworn Statement in Proceedings under Section 235(b)(1) of the Act

Q: Why did you leave your home country or country of last residence?

A.

Q. Do you have any fear or concern about being returned to your home country or being removed from the United States?

A.

Q. Would you be harmed if you are returned to your home country or country of last residence?

A.

Q. Do you have any questions or is there anything else you would like to add?

A.

I have read (or have had read to me) this statement, consisting of ______ pages (including this page). I state that my answers are true and correct to the best of my knowledge and that this statement is a full, true and correct record of my interrogation on the date indicated by the above-named officer of the Immigration and Naturalization Service. I have initialed each page of this statement (and the corrections noted on page(s) __________).

Signature: ______________________________

Sworn and subscribed to before me at ____
on ________________.

____
Officer, United States Immigration and Naturalization Service

Witnessed by: ____

Page _____ of _____

I-867B (4-1-97)

Form M–444 Information about credible fear interview

U.S. Department of Justice

Immigration and Naturalization Service

Information about Credible Fear Interview

Purpose of this notice

The purpose of this notice is to explain what will happen while you are in detention, what rights you have, and what may happen to you as a result of statements you make. It is important that you understand your rights and what will happen. **PLEASE READ THIS NOTICE CAREFULLY.**

You have been detained because the U.S. Immigration and Naturalization Service (INS) believes that you may not have the right to stay in the United States. You have indicated an intention to apply for asylum or a fear of persecution or return to your country. You will be interviewed by a specially-trained asylum officer to determine if you have a "credible fear of persecution." You will be detained until that interview takes place. If the INS finds that you have a credible fear of persecution, you may or may not be released.

Right to consult with other persons

Normally, the interview will not take place sooner than 48 hours after you arrive at the detention facility. You may use this time to rest and consult with family members, friends, or other representatives. In unusual circumstances, you may be given additional time to contact someone. If you need this additional time, you should inform an INS officer. You may request that the interview take place sooner if you are prepared to discuss your fears or claim immediately.

You may consult with a person or persons of your choosing, provided that such consultation is at no expense to the government and does not delay the process. A person of your choice can be present with you at your interview. A list of representatives who may be able to speak to you free of charge is attached to this notice. You may use the telephone while you are in detention to call a representative, friend or family member in the United States, collect or at your own expense. If you wish to call someone, you should inform an INS officer for assistance. You also may contact the United States Office of the United Nations High Commissioner for Refugees, at (202) 296-5191 from 9:00 a.m - 5:00 p.m. (eastern standard time), Monday thru Friday.

Description of credible fear interview

The purpose of the credible fear interview is to determine whether you might be eligible to apply for asylum before an immigration judge. This interview is not your formal asylum hearing. It is only to help us determine whether there is a significant possibility that you may qualify as a refugee.

At your interview, you will have the opportunity to explain to the asylum officer why you think you should not be returned to your home country. If you want to apply for asylum in the United States, or think you will be harmed, persecuted or tortured if you return to your home country, you must show an asylum officer that you have a credible fear of being harmed or persecuted because of your race, religion, nationality, membership in a particular social group or political opinion, or that it is likely that you will be tortured.

If the officer determines that you have a credible fear or persecution or that you might face torture if you are returned to your home country, you may be eligible to remain in the United States.

It is very important that you tell the officer all the reasons why you have concerns about returning to your home country or are afraid to return to your home country. There are regulations protecting the confidentiality of asylum claims.

It is also very important that you tell the truth during your interview. Although the purpose of this interview is not to gather evidence against you, failure to tell the truth could be used against you in this or any future immigration proceeding.

Form M-444(Rev. 4-1-97)

Need for interpreter or special consideration

If you do not speak English well or if you prefer to be interviewed in your own language, INS will provide an interpreter for the interview. The interpreter has been told to keep the information you discuss confidential. If the interpreter is not translating correctly or you don't feel comfortable with the interpreter, you may request another interpreter. The officer will take written notes.

If you will need to tell the asylum officer information that is very personal and very difficult to talk about, you may request a female officer and female interpreter, or a male officer and male interpreter. The INS will provide them if they are available. You will also have the opportunity to speak with the asylum officer separately from your family if you so desire.

Consequences of failure to establish credible fear and review of determination

If the asylum officer determines that you do not have a credible fear of persecution, you may request to have that decision reviewed by an immigration judge. The immigration judge's review will be in person or by telephone or video connection. The review will happen as soon as possible, to the maximum extent practicable within 24 hours, but in no case later than 7 days from the date of the asylum officer's decision. You may consult with a person or person of your choosing before the review by the immigration judge, provided it does not cause unreasonable delay. You will be given a copy of the asylum officer's record of determination to examine prior to the review by the immigration judge. If any of the information is incorrect, you should notify the immigration judge. The immigration judge may decide that you do have a credible fear and that you are eligible for a full asylum hearing before an immigration judge. If you are ordered removed, you may be barred from reentry to the United States for a period of 5 years or longer.

Interpreter Certification

I ______________________________(name of interpreter) certify that I am fluent in both the ________________ and English languages, that I interpreted the above information from English to ______________________ completely and accurately, and that the recipient understood my interpretation.

____
Signature of interpreter

____
Date

Alien Acknowledgment of Receipt

I acknowledge that I have been given notice concerning my credible fear interview. I understand that I may consult with a person or persons of my choosing prior to the interview as long as it does not unreasonably delay the process and is at no expense to the Government.

____
Alien's signature

____
Date

Form M-444(Rev. 4-1-97)

Form I–869 Record of negative credible fear finding and request for review by immigration judge

U.S. Department of Justice
Immigration and Naturalization Service

Record of Negative Credible Fear Finding and Request for Review by Immigration Judge

File No: ______________

1. To be explained to the alien by the asylum officer:

The INS has determined that you do not have a credible fear of persecution for the following reasons:

- ☐ You were not found credible because:
  - ☐ Your testimony was internally inconsistent on material issues.
  - ☐ Your testimony was not consistent with country conditions on material issues.
  - ☐ Your testimony was not consistent with documentation on material issues.
  - ☐ Your testimony was vague and lacked detail on material issues.
- ☐ Your have not established a credible fear because:
  - ☐ You have not expressed a credible fear.
  - ☐ There is no significant possibility that any harm you suffered in the past or fear in the future constitutes persecution.
  - ☐ There is no significant possibility that the harm you fear in the future is well-founded.
  - ☐ There is no significant possibility that any harm or fear you expressed is on account of one or more of the five grounds for asylum.
- ☐ You are subject to the following mandatory bar(s) to being granted asylum:
  - ☐ You have been convicted of an aggravated felony.
  - ☐ (Other mandatory bar): ______________
- ☐ Other reason: ______________

Therefore, I will order you removed from the United States. You may request that an immigration judge review this decision.

If you request that an immigration judge review this decision, you will remain in detention until an immigration judge reviews your case. That review could occur in as long as 7 days after you receive this decision.

If you do not request that an immigration judge review this decision, you may be removed from the United States immediately.

2. To be completed by the alien:

☐ **Yes, I request immigration judge review** of the officer's decision that I do not have a credible fear of persecution.

☐ **No, I do not request immigration judge review** of the officer's decision that I do not have a credible fear of persecution.

______________ Last Name/Surname (Print) ______________ First Name, Middle Name

______________ Signature ______________ Date

Form I-869 (4-1-97)

Form I-863 Notice of referral to immigration judge

U.S. Department of Justice
Immigration and Naturalization Service

Notice of Referral to Immigration Judge

Date	
File	

Name (Family Name in CAPS, First, Middle)	
Place and Manner of Arrival	Date of Arrival

To immigration judge:

☐ 1. The above-named alien has been found inadmissible to the United States and ordered removed pursuant to section 235(b)(1) of the Immigration and Nationality Act (Act). A copy of the removal order is attached. The alien has requested asylum and the matter has been reviewed by an asylum officer who has concluded the alien does not have a credible fear of persecution. The alien has requested a review of that determination in accordance with section 235(b)(1)(B)(iii)(III) of the Act.

☐ 2. The above-named alien arrived in the United States as a stowaway and has been ordered removed pursuant to section 235(a)(2) of the Act. The alien has requested asylum and the matter has been reviewed by an asylum officer who has concluded the alien does not have a credible fear of persecution. The alien has requested a review of that determination in accordance with section 235(b)(1)(B)(iii)(III) of the Act.

☐ 3. The above-named alien arrived in the United States in the manner described below and has requested asylum. The matter is referred for a determination in accordance with 8 CFR 208.2(b). Arrival category (check one):

☐ Crewmember/applicant ☐ Crewmember/refused ☐ Crewmember/landed
☐ Crewmember/overstay ☐ VWPP/applicant ☐ VWPP/overstay
☐ 235(c) order ☐ S-visa nonimmigrant ☐ Stowaway: credible fear determination attached

☐ 4. The above-named alien has been ordered removed by an immigration officer pursuant to section 235(b)(1) of the Act. A copy of the removal order is attached. In accordance with section 235(b)(1)(C) of the Act, the matter is referred for review of that order. The above-named alien claims to be (check one):

☐ a United States citizen ☐ a lawful permanent resident alien
☐ an alien granted refugee status under section 207 of the Act ☐ an alien granted asylum under section 208 of the Act.

NOTICE TO APPLICANT

You are ordered to report for a hearing before an immigration judge for the reasons stated above. Your hearing is scheduled on

______________ at ______________. You are to appear at ____________________
(Date) (Time)

____
(Complete office address)

☐ You may be represented in this proceeding, at no expense to the government, by an attorney or other individual authorized and qualified to represent persons before an Immigration Court. If you wish to be so represented, your attorney or representative should appear with you at this hearing. In the event of your release from custody, you must immediately report any change of your address to the Immigration Court on Form EOIR-33, which is provided with this notice. If you fail to appear for a scheduled hearing, a decision may be rendered in your absence.

☐ You may consult with a person or persons of your own choosing prior to your appearance in Immigration Court. Such consultation is at no expense to the government and may not unreasonably delay the process.

☐ Attached is a list of recognized organizations and attorneys which provide free legal services.

____
(Signature and title of immigration officer)

(Certificate of Service is included on the reverse of this notice)

Form I-863 (4-1-97)

CERTIFICATE OF SERVICE

The contents of this notice were read and explained to the applicant in the ______________________ language.

The original of this notice was delivered to the above-named applicant by the undersigned on ______________ and the alien has been advised of communication privileges pursuant to 8 CFR 236.1(e).

____
(Signature and title of immigration officer)

Attachments to copy presented to immigration judge:

- ☐ Passport
- ☐ Visa
- ☐ Form I-94
- ☐ Forensic document analysis
- ☐ Fingerprints and photographs
- ☐ EOIR-33
- ☐ Form I-860
- ☐ Asylum officer's credible fear determination worksheet
- ☐ Other (specify): ______________________________

Form I-863 (4-1-97)

Form I–860 Notice and order of expedited removal

U.S. Department of Justice
Immigration and Naturalization Service

Notice and Order of Expedited Removal

DETERMINATION OF INADMISSIBILITY

File No: ________________

Date: ________________

In the Matter of: ____

Pursuant to section 235(b)(1) of the Immigration and Nationality Act (Act), (8 U.S.C. 1225(b)(1)), the Immigration and Naturalization Service has determined that you are inadmissible to the United States under section(s) 212(a) ☐ (6)(C)(i); ☐ (6)(C)(ii); ☐ (7)(A)(i)(I); ☐ (7)(A)(i)(II); ☐ (7)(B)(i)(I); and/or ☐ (7)(B)(i)(II) of the Act, as amended, and therefore are subject to removal, in that:

____
____
____
____
____
____
____

Name and title of immigration officer (Print)	Signature of immigration officer

ORDER OF REMOVAL UNDER SECTION 235(b)(1) OF THE ACT

Based upon the determination set forth above and evidence presented during inspection or examination pursuant to section 235 of the Act, and by the authority contained in section 235(b)(1) of the Act, you are found to be inadmissible as charged and ordered removed from the United States.

Name and title of immigration officer (Print)	Signature of immigration officer
Name and title of supervisor (Print)	Signature of supervisor, if available

☐ Check here if supervisory concurrence was obtained by telephone or other means (no supervisor on duty).

CERTIFICATE OF SERVICE

I personally served the original of this notice upon the above-named person on ________________
(Date)

____
Signature of immigration officer

Form I-860 (Rev. 4-1-97)

Form I–862 Notice to appear

U.S. Department of Justice
Immigration and Naturalization Service

Notice to Appear

In removal proceedings under section 240 of the Immigration and Nationality Act

File No: ____________________

In the Matter of:

Respondent: ______________________________ currently residing at:

______________________________ ____________
(Number, street, city, state and ZIP code) (Area code and phone number)

☐ 1. You are an arriving alien.
☐ 2. You are an alien present in the United States who has not been admitted or paroled.
☐ 3. You have been admitted to the United States, but are deportable for the reasons stated below.

The Service alleges that you:

On the basis of the foregoing, it is charged that you are subject to removal from the United States pursuant to the following provision(s) of law:

☐ This notice is being issued after an asylum officer has found that the respondent has demonstrated a credible fear of persecution.

☐ Section 235(b)(1) order was vacated pursuant to: ☐ 8 CFR 208.30(f)(2) ☐ 8 CFR 235.3(b)(5)(iv)

YOU ARE ORDERED to appear before an immigration judge of the United States Department of Justice at:

____
(Complete Address of Immigration Court, Including Room Number, if any)

on ____________ at ____________ to show why you should not be removed from the United States based on the
(Date) (Time)
charge(s) set forth above.

____
(Signature and Title of Issuing Officer)

Date: ____________ ______________________________
(City and State)

See reverse for important information

Form I-862 (Rev. 4-1-97)

Notice to Respondent

Warning: Any statement you make may be used against you in removal proceedings.

Alien Registration: This copy of the Notice to Appear served upon you is evidence of your alien registration while you are under removal proceedings. You are required to carry it with you at all times.

Representation: If you so choose, you may be represented in this proceeding, at no expense to the Government, by an attorney or other individual authorized and qualified to represent persons before the Executive Office for Immigration Review, pursuant to 8 CFR 3.16. Unless you so request, no hearing will be scheduled earlier than ten days from the date of this notice, to allow you sufficient time to secure counsel. A list of qualified attorneys and organizations who may be available to represent you at no cost will be provided with this Notice.

Conduct of the hearing: At the time of your hearing, you should bring with you any affidavits or other documents which you desire to have considered in connection with your case. If any document is in a foreign language, you must bring the original and a certified English translation of the document. If you wish to have the testimony of any witnesses considered, you should arrange to have such witnesses present at the hearing.

At your hearing you will be given the opportunity to admit or deny any or all of the allegations in the Notice to Appear and that you are inadmissible or deportable on the charges contained in the Notice to Appear. You will have an opportunity to present evidence on your own behalf, to examine any evidence presented by the Government, to object, on proper legal grounds, to the receipt of evidence and to cross examine any witnesses presented by the Government. At the conclusion of your hearing, you have a right to appeal an adverse decision by the immigration judge.

You will be advised by the immigration judge before whom you appear, of any relief from removal for which you may appear eligible including the privilege of departing voluntarily. You will be given a reasonable opportunity to make any such application to the immigration judge.

Failure to appear: You are required to provide the INS, in writing, with your full mailing address and telephone number. You must notify the Immigration Court immediately by using Form EOIR-33 whenever you change your address or telephone number during the course of this proceeding. You will be provided with a copy of this form. Notices of hearing will be mailed to this address. If you do not submit Form EOIR-33 and do not otherwise provide an address at which you may be reached during proceedings, then the Government shall not be required to provide you with written notice of your hearing. If you fail to attend the hearing at the time and place designated on this notice, or any date and time later directed by the Immigration Court, a removal order may be made by the immigration judge in your absence, and you may be arrested and detained by the INS.

Request for Prompt Hearing

To expedite a determination in my case, I request an immediate hearing. I waive my right to have a 10-day period prior to appearing before an immigration judge.

____
(Signature of Respondent)

Before: ____________________________ Date: ____________________________
(Signature and Title of INS Officer)

Certificate of Service

This Notice to Appear was served on the respondent by me on __________________ (Date), in the following manner and in compliance with section 239(a)(1)(F) of the Act:

☐ in person ☐ by certified mail, return receipt requested ☐ by regular mail

☐ Attached is a list of organizations and attorneys which provide free legal services.

☐ The alien was provided oral notice in the __________________ language of the time and place of his or her hearing and of the consequences of failure to appear as provided in section 240(b)(7) of the Act.

____________________________ ____________________________
(Signature of Respondent if Personally Served) (Signature and Title of Officer)

Form I-862 (Rev. 4-1-97)

Form EOIR-42A Application for cancellation of removal for certain permanent residents

U.S. Department of Justice
Executive Office for Immigration Review

OMB#1125-0001
Application for Cancellation of Removal For Certain Permanent Residents

ADVICE TO APPLICANT

PLEASE READ CAREFULLY. FEE WILL NOT BE RETURNED.

I. Certain Permanent Resident Aliens Eligible for Cancellation of Removal: You may be eligible to have your removal cancelled under section 240A(a) of the Immigration and Nationality Act (INA) if:

A. You have been a permanent resident for at least 5 years;

B. Prior to service of the Notice to Appear; or prior to committing a criminal or related offense referred to in sections 212(a)(2) and 237(a)(2) of the INA; or prior to committing a security or related offense referred to in section 237(a)(4) of INA;

- you have at least 7 years continuous residence in the United States after having been lawfully admitted in any status; and

NOTE: If you have served on active duty in the Armed Forces of the United States for at least 24 months, you do not have to meet the requirements of continuous residence in the United States. You must, however, have been in the United States when you entered the Armed Forces. If you are no longer in the Armed Forces, you must have been separated under honorable conditions.

C. You have not been convicted of an aggravated felony.

II. Certain Permanent Resident Aliens NOT Eligible for Cancellation of Removal: You are not eligible to have your removal cancelled under section 240A(a) of the INA if you:

A. Entered the United States as a crewman after June 30, 1964;

B. Were admitted to the United States as, or later became, a nonimmigrant exchange alien as defined in section 101(a)(15)(J) of the INA in order to receive graduate medical education or training, regardless of whether you are subject to or have fulfilled the 2 year foreign residence requirement of section 212(e) of the INA;

C. Were admitted to the United States, as or later became, a nonimmigrant exchange alien as defined in section 101(a)(15)(J) of the INA, other than to receive graduate medical education or training, and are subject to the 2 year foreign residence requirement of section 212(e) of the INA but have neither fulfilled nor obtained a waiver of that requirement;

D. Are an alien who is either inadmissible under section 212(a)(3) of the INA or deportable under section 237(a)(4) of the INA;

E. Are an alien who ordered, incited, assisted, or otherwise participated in the persecution of an individual because of the individual's race, religion, nationality, membership in a particular social group, or political opinion; or

F. Are an alien who was previously granted relief under section 212(c) of the INA, or section 244(a) of the INA as such sections were in effect prior to the enactment of the Illegal Immigration Reform and Immigrant Responsibility Act of 1996, or whose removal has previously been cancelled under section 240A of the INA.

U.S. Department of Justice
Executive Office for Immigration Review

OMB#1125-0001
Application for Cancellation of Removal For Certain Permanent Residents

III. How Certain Permanent Resident Aliens Can Apply for Cancellation of Removal

In order for certain permanent resident aliens to apply for cancellation of removal, you must answer all the questions on the attached Form EOIR-42A fully and accurately. An instruction sheet is attached to guide you in completing your application, paying the filing fee, serving your application on the Immigration and Naturalization Service, and filing your application with the appropriate Immigration Court. Please read the instruction sheet carefully before completing your application.

U.S. Department of Justice
Executive Office for Immigration Review

OMB#1125-0001
Application for Cancellation of Removal For Certain Permanent Residents

INSTRUCTIONS

1. PREPARATION OF APPLICATION.

To apply for cancellation of removal as a permanent resident alien under section 240A(a) of the Immigration and Nationality Act (INA), you must fully and accurately answer all questions on the attached Form EOIR-42A. A separate application must be prepared and executed for each person applying for cancellation of removal. An application on behalf of an alien who is mentally incompetent or is a child under 14 years of age shall be executed by a parent or guardian.

Your responses must be typed or printed legibly in ink. Do not leave any questions unanswered or blank. If any questions do not apply to you, write "none" or "not applicable" in the appropriate space.

To the extent possible, answer all questions directly on the form. If there is insufficient room to fully respond to a question, please continue your response on an additional sheet. Please indicate the number of the question being answered next to your resonse on the additional sheet and sign, date, and securely attach the additional to the Form EOIR-42A.

2. BURDEN OF PROOF.

The burden is on you to prove that you meet all of the statutory requirements for cancellation of removal for certain permanent resident aliens under section 240A(a) of the Immigration and Nationality Act and that you are entitled to such relief as a matter of discretion. To meet this burden, your responses to the questions on the application should be as detailed and complete as possible. You should also attach to your application any documents that demonstrate your eligibility for relief ("supporting documents").

3. SUPPORTING DOCUMENTS.

You should submit documentary evidence to show both that you have been a permanent resident alien for at least five years and that you have 7 years of continuous residence in the United States after being lawfully admitted in any status. This evidence may include, but is not limited to, Immigration stamps in passports, INS Form I-94, leases, deeds, licenses, receipts, letters, church records, school records, employment records, and tax payment records.

The original of all supporting documents must be available for inspection at the hearing. If you wish to have the original documents returned to you, you should also present reproductions.

4. REQUIRED DOCUMENTS.

Each applicant 14 years of age or older must also complete a Biographic Information Form G-325A and a Fingerprint Card, FD-258. Applicants may be fingerprinted by law enforcement officers, outreach centers, charitable and voluntary agencies, or other reputable persons or organizations. The fingerprint card on which the prints are submitted, the ink used, and the quality of the prints must meet the standards prescribed by the Federal Bureau of Investigation. The card must be signed by you in the presence of the person taking your fingerprints and that person must then sign his/her name and enter the date in the spaces provided. It is important to furnish all the information on the card.

5. TRANSLATIONS.

Any document in a foreign language must be accompanied by an English language translation and a certificate signed by the translator stating that he/she is competent to translate the document and that the translation is true and accurate to the best of the translator's abilities. Such certification must be printed legibly or typed.

OMB#1125-0001

U.S. Department of Justice
Executive Office for Immigration Review

Application for Cancellation of Removal For Certain Permanent Residents

6. FEES.

Before you file your Form EOIR-42A with the Immigration Court, you must pay the required $100 fee to the Immigration and Naturalization Service. Evidence of payment of this fee in the form of a fee stamp or a receipt must accompany your Form EOIR-42A. This fee will not be refunded, regardless of the action taken on your application. Therefore, it is important that you read the advice, instructions, and application carefully before responding. **If you are unable to pay the fee, you may ask the Immigration Judge to permit you to file your Form EOIR-42A without fee.**

DO NOT SEND CASH. All fees must be submitted in the exact amount. Remittance may be made by cash, personal check, cashier's check, certified bank check, bank international money order, or foreign draft drawn on a financial institution in the United States and payable to the "Immigration and Naturalization Service" in United States currency. If the applicant resides in the Virgin Islands, the check or money order must be payable to the "Commissioner of Finance of the Virgin Islands." If the applicant resides in Guam, the check or money order must be payable to the "Treasurer, Guam." Personal checks are accepted subject to collectibility. An uncollectible check will render the application and any documents issued pursuant thereto invalid. A charge of $5.00 will be imposed if a check in payment of a fee is not honored by the bank on which it is drawn. When the check is drawn on an account of a person other than the applicant, the name and alien registration number of the applicant must be entered on the face of the check. All checks must be drawn on a bank located in the United States.

7. SERVING & FILING YOUR APPLICATION.

You must serve the following documents on the INS District Counsel:

- a copy of your Form EOIR-42A, Application for Cancellation of Removal, with all supporting documents and additional sheets,
- evidence of payment of the filing fee or a request for a waiver of the fee by an Immigration Judge,
- the original Biographical Information Form G-325A, and
- the original Fingerprint Card, FD-258.

You must file the following documents with the appropriate Immigration Court:

- the original Form EOIR-42A with all supporting documents and additional sheets,
- evidence of payment of the filing fee or a request for a wavier of the fee by an Immigration Judge,
- a copy of Biographical Information Form G-325A,
- a copy of Fingerprint Card, FD-258, and
- a certificate showing service of these documents on the INS District Counsel, unless service is made on the record at the hearing.

8. PENALTIES.

You must answer all questions on Form EOIR-42A truthfully and submit only genuine documents in support of your application. **You will be required to swear or affirm that the contents of your application and the supporting documents are true to the best of your knowledge.** Your answer to the questions on this form and the supporting documents you present will be used to determine whether your removal should be cancelled and whether you should be permitted to retain your permanent resident status. Any answer you give and any supporting document you present may also be used as evidence in any proceeding to determine your right to be admitted or readmitted, re-enter, pass through, or reside in the United States. Your application may be denied if any of your answers or supporting documents are found to be false.

OMB#1125-0001

U.S. Department of Justice
Executive Office for Immigration Review

Application for Cancellation of Removal
For Certain Permanent Residents

Presenting false answers or false documents may also subject you to criminal prosecution under 18 U.S.C. 1546 and/or subject you to civil penalties under 8 U.S.C. 1324c if you submit your application knowing that the application or any supporting document contains any false statement with respect to a material fact, or if you swear or affirm that the contents of your application and the supporting documents are true, knowing that the application or any supporting document contains any false statement with respect to a material fact. If convicted, you could be fined up to $250,000.00, imprisoned for up to 5 years, or both. 18 U.S.C. 1546(a), 3559(a)(4), 357(b)(3). If it is determined you have violated the prohibition against document fraud and a final order is entered against you, you could be subject to a civil penalty up to $2,000.00 for each document used or created for the first offense and up to $5,000.00 for any second, or subsequent offense. In addition, if you are the subject of a final order for violating 8 U.S.C. 1324c, relating to civil penalties for document fraud, you will be removable from the United States.

9. PAPERWORK REDUCTION ACT.

We try to create forms and instructions that are accurate, can easily be understood, and which impose the least possible burden on you to provide us with information. Often this is difficult because some immigration laws are very complex. The reporting burden for this collection of information is computed as follows: (1) learning about the form, 45 minutes, (2) completing the form, 2 hours, and (3) assembling and filing the form, 3 hours, for an estimated average of 5 hours, 45 minutes per response. If you have comments regarding the accuracy of this burden estimate or any other aspect of this collection of information, including suggestions for reducing this burden, you may write to the U.S. Department of Justice, Executive Office for Immigration Review, Office of the General Counsel, 5107 Leesburg Pike, Suite 2400, Falls Church, Virginia 22041.

10. REPORTING BURDEN.

A person is not required to respond to a collection of information unless it displays a currently valid OMB control number.

U.S. Department of Justice
Executive Office for Immigration Review

OMB #1125-0001
Application for Cancellation of Removal For Certain Permanent Residents
(Under Section 240A of the Immigration and Nationality Act)

PLEASE READ ADVICE AND INSTRUCTIONS BEFORE FILLING IN FORM

PLEASE TYPE OR PRINT

Fee Stamp

PART 1 - INFORMATION ABOUT YOURSELF

1) My present true name is: *(Last, First, Middle)*	2) Alien Registration Number:
3) My name given at birth was: *(Last, First, Middle)*	4) Birth Place: *(City, Country)*

5) Date of Birth: *(Month, Day, Year)*	6) Gender: ☐ Male ☐ Female	7) Height:	8) Hair Color:	9) Eye Color:
10) Current Nationality & Citizenship:	11) Social Security Number:	12) Home Phone Number:	13) Work Phone Number:	

14) I currently reside at:

Apt. number and/or in care of
Number and Street
City or Town *State* *ZIP Code*

15) I have been known by these additional name(s):

16) I have resided in the following locations in the United States: (List PRESENT ADDRESS FIRST, and work back in time for at least 7 years.)

Street and Number - Apt. or Room# - City or Town - State - ZIP Code	Resided From: *(Month, Day, Year)*	Resided To: *(Month, Day, Year)*
		PRESENT

PART 2 - INFORMATION ABOUT THIS APPLICATION

17) I, the undersigned, hereby request that my removal be cancelled under the provisions of section 240A(a) of the Immigration and Nationality Act (INA). I believe that I am eligible for this relief because I have been a lawful permanent resident alien for 5 or more years, have 7 years of continuous residence in the United States, and have not been convicted of an aggravated felony. I was admitted as or adjusted to the status of an alien lawfully admitted for permanent residence on ______________ *(date)*

at ______________________________ *(place)* .

Please use a separate sheet for additional entries
(1)

Form EOIR-42A
4/97

PART 3 - INFORMATION ABOUT YOUR PRESENCE IN THE UNITED STATES

18) My first arrival into the United States was under the name of: *(Last, First, Middle)*

19) My first arrival to the United States was on: *(Month, Day, Year)*

20) Place or port of first Arrival: *(Place or Port, City, and State)*

21) I : ☐ was admitted as a lawful permanent resident.
☐ was admitted as a nonimmigrant. Specify visa type: ____________
☐ entered without inspection.
☐ other - specify ____________

22) If admitted as a nonimmigrant, period for which admitted: *(Month, Day, Year)* to

23) My last extension of stay in the United States expired on: *(Month, Day, Year)*

24) Since the date of my first arrival, I departed from and returned to the United States at the following places and on the following dates: *(Please list all departures regardless of how briefly you were absent from the United States)*
If you have never departed from the United States since your original date of arrival, please mark an X in the box: ☐

Port of Departure *(Place or Port, City and State)*	Departure Date *(Month, Day, Year)*	Purpose of Travel	Destination
Port of Return *(Place or Port, City and State)*	Return Date *(Month, Day, Year)*	Manner of Return	Inspected & Admitted? ☐ Yes ☐ No
Port of Departure *(Place or Port, City and State)*	Departure Date *(Month, Day, Year)*	Purpose of Travel	Destination
Port of Return *(Place or Port, City and State)*	Return Date *(Month, Day, Year)*	Manner of Return	Inspected & Admitted? ☐ Yes ☐ No

25) Have you ever departed the United States:
a) under an order of deportation, exclusion or removal? ------- ☐ Yes ☐ No
b) pursuant to a grant of voluntary departure? ----------------- ☐ Yes ☐ No

PART 4 - INFORMATION ABOUT YOUR MARITAL STATUS AND SPOUSE *(Continued on page 3)*

26) I am not married: ☐
I am married: ☐

27) If married, the name of my spouse is: *(Last, First, Middle)*

28) Date of marriage: *(Month, Day, Year)*

29) The marriage took place in: *(City and Country)*

30) Birth place of spouse: *(City and Country)*

31) My spouse currently resides at:

Apt. number and/or in care of

Number and Street

City or Town *State/Country* *ZIP Code*

32) Birth date of spouse: *(Month, Day, Year)*

33) My spouse is a citizen of: *(Country)*

34) If your spouse is other than a native born United States citizen, answer the following:
He/she arrived in the United States at: *(City and State)* ____________
He/she arrived in the United States on: *(Month, Day, Year)* ____________
His/her alien registration number is: A# ____________
He/she was naturalized on: *(Month, Day, Year)* ____________ at ____________ *(City and State)*

35) My spouse ☐ - is ☐ - is not employed. If employed, please give salary and the name and address of the place(s) of employment:

Full Name and Address of Employer:	Earnings Per Week *(Approximate)*
	$
	$
	$

Please use a separate sheet for additional entries.
(2)

Form EOIR-42A
4/97

PART 4 - INFORMATION ABOUT YOUR MARITAL STATUS AND SPOUSE *(Continued)*

36) I ☐ -have ☐ -have not been previously married: *(If previously married, list the name of each prior spouse, the dates on which each marriage began and ended, the place where the marriage terminated, and describe how each marriage ended.)*

Name of prior spouse: *(Last, First, Middle)*	Date marriage began: Date marriage ended:	Place marriage ended: *(City and Country)*	Description or manner of how marriage was terminated or ended:

Name of prior spouse: *(Last, First, Middle)*	Date marriage began: Date marriage ended:	Place marriage ended: *(City and Country)*	Description or manner of how marriage was termanated or ended:

37) Have you been ordered by any court, or are otherwise under any legal obligation, to provide child support and/or spousal maintenance as a result of a separation and/or divorce? ☐ -Yes ☐ -No

PART 5 - INFORMATION ABOUT YOUR EMPLOYMENT AND FINANCIAL STATUS

38) Since my arrival into the United States, I have been employed by the following - named persons or firms: *(Please begin with present employment and work back in time. Any periods of unemployment or school attendance should be specified.)*

Full Name and Address of Employer	Earnings Per Week *(Approximate)*	Type of Work Performed	Employed From: *(Month, Day, Year)*	Employed To: *(Month, Day, Year)*
	$			PRESENT
	$			
	$			

39) If self-employed, describe the nature of the business, the name of the business, its address, and net income derived therefrom:

40) My assets (and if married, my spouse's assets) in the United States and other countries, not including clothing and household necessities, are:

Self

Cash, Stocks, and Bonds ----------- $

Real Estate ----------------------- $

Automobile (value minus amount owed)- $

Other (describe on line below) ------- $

TOTAL $

Jointly Owned with Spouse

Cash, Stocks, and Bonds ----------- $

Real Estate ----------------------- $

Automobile (value minus amount owed)- $

Other (describe on line below) --------- $

TOTAL $

41) I ☐ -have ☐-have not received public or private relief or assistance(e.g. Welfare, Unemployment Benefits, Medicaid, ADC, etc.). If you have, please give full details including the type of relief or assistance received, date for which relief or assistance was received, place, and amount received during this time:

42) Please list each of the years in which you have filed an income tax return with the Internal Revenue Service:

Please use a separate sheet for additional entries.
(3)

Form EOIR-42A
4/97

PART 6 - INFORMATION ABOUT YOUR FAMILY *(Continued on page 5)*

43) I have____________ *(Number of)* children. Please list information for each child below, include assets and earnings information for children over the age of sixteen who have separate incomes:

Name of Child: *(Last, First, Middle)* Child's Alien Registration Number:	Citizen of What Country: Birth Date: *(Month, Day, Year)*	Now Residing At: *(City and Country)* Birth Place: *(City and Country)*	Immigration Status of Child?
A#:			
Estimated Total of Assets: $________	Estimated Average Weekly Earnings: $________		
A#:			
Estimated Total of Assets: $________	Estimated Average Weekly Earnings: $________		
A#:			
Estimated Total of Assets: $________	Estimated Average Weekly Earnings: $________		

44) If your application is denied, would your spouse and all of your children accompany you to your:

Country of Birth - ☐ Yes ☐ No

Country of Nationality - ☐ Yes ☐ No

Country of Last Residence - ☐ Yes ☐ No

If you answered "NO" to any of the responses, please explain: ____________

45) Members of my family, including my spouse and/or child(ren) ☐- have ☐- have not received public or private relief or assistance (e.g., Unemployment Benefits, Welfare, Medicaid, ADC, etc.). If any member of your immediate family has received such relief or assistance, please give full details including identity of person(s) receiving relief or assistance, dates for which relief or assistance was received, place, and amount received during this time: ____________

46) Please give the requested information about your parents, brothers, sisters, aunts, uncles, and grandparents. As to residence, show street address, city, and state, if in the United States; otherwise show only country:

Name: *(Last, First, Middle)* Alien Registration Number:	Citizen of What Country: Birth Date: *(Month, Day, Year)*	Relationship to Me: Birth Place: *(Place and Country)*	Immigration Status of Listed Relative
A#:			
Complete Address of Current Residence:			
A#:			
Complete Address of Current Residence:			

Please use a separate sheet for additional entries.
(4)

Form EOIR-42A
4/97

PART 7 - MISCELLANEOUS INFORMATION *(Continued on page 6)*

47) I ☐ - have ☐ - have not entered the United States as a crewman after June 30, 1964.

48) I ☐ - have ☐ - have not been admitted as, or after arrival in the United States acquired the status of, an exchange alien.

49) I ☐- have ☐ - have not submitted address reports as required by section 265 of the Immigration and Nationality Act.

50) I ☐-have ☐ -have never(either in the United Stated or in any foreign country)been arrested, summoned into court as a defendant, convicted, fined, imprisoned, placed on probation, or forfeited collateral for an act involving a felony, misdemeanor, or breach of any public law or ordinance(including, but not limited to, traffic violations or driving incidents involving alcohol). *(If answer is in the affirmative, please give a brief description of each offense including the name and location of the offense, date of conviction, any penalty imposed,any sentence imposed, and the time actually served).* ______

51) Have you ever served in the Armed Forces of the United States? ☐- Yes ☐ - No. If "Yes" please state branch *(Army, Navy, etc.)* and service number. ______
Place of entry on duty: *(City, and State)* ______
Date of entry on duty: *(Month, Day, Year)* ______ Date of discharge: *(Month, Day, Year)* ______
Type of discharge *(Honorable, Dishonorable, etc.)*: ______
I served in active duty status from: *(Month, Day, Year)* ______ to *(Month, Day, Year)* ______

52) Have you ever left the United States or the jurisdiction of the district where you registered for the draft to avoid being drafted into the military or naval forces of the United States? ☐ Yes ☐ No

53) Have you ever deserted from the military or naval forces of the United Stated while the United Stated was at war? ☐Yes ☐ No

54) If male, did you register under the Selective Service (Draft) Law of 1917, 1918, 1948, 1951, or later Draft Laws? ☐Yes ☐ No
If "Yes," please give date, Selective Service number, local draft board number, and your last draft classification: ______

55) Were you ever exempted from service because of conscientious objection, alienage, or any other reason? ☐Yes ☐ No

56) Please list your present or past membership in or affiliation with every political organization, association, fund, foundation, party, club, society, or similar group in the United States or any other place since your 16th birthday. Include any foreign military service in this part. If none, write "NONE". Include the name of the organization, location, nature of the organization, and the dates of membership.

Name of Organization	Location of Organization	Nature of Organization	Member From: *(Month, Day, Year)*	Member To: *(Month, Day, Year)*

Please a separate sheet for additional entries.

(5)

Form EOIR-42A
4/97

PART 7 - MISCELLANEOUS INFORMATION *(Continued)*

57) Have you ever:

☐ Yes ☐ No been ordered deported or removed?

☐ Yes ☐ No overstayed a grant of voluntary departure from an Immigration Judge or the Immigration and Naturalization Service (INS)?

☐ Yes ☐ No failed to appear for deportation or removal?

58) Have you ever been:

☐ Yes ☐ No a habitual drinker?

☐ Yes ☐ No one whose income is derived principally from illegal gambling?

☐ Yes ☐ No one who has given false testimony for the purpose of obtaining immigration benefits?

☐ Yes ☐ No engaged in prostitution or unlawful commercialized vice?

☐ Yes ☐ No involved in a serious criminal offense and asserted immunity from prosecution?

☐ Yes ☐ No a polygamist?

☐ Yes ☐ No one who aided and/or abetted another to enter the United States Illegally?

☐ Yes ☐ No a trafficker of a controlled substance, or a knowing assister, abettor, conspirator, or colluder with others in any such controlled substance offense (not including a single offense of simple possession of 30 grams or less of marijuana)?

☐ Yes ☐ No inadmissible or deportable on security-related grounds under sections 212(a)(3) or 237(a)(4) of the INA?

☐ Yes ☐ No one who has ordered, incited, assisted, or otherwise participated in the persection of an individual on account of his or her race, religion, nationality, membership in a particular social group,or political opinion?

☐ Yes ☐ No a person previously granted relief under sections 212(c) or 244(a) of the INA or whose removal has perviously been cancelled under section 240A of the INA?

59) The following certificates or other supporting documents are attached hereto as a part of this application; *(Refer to the Instruction Sheet for documents which* ***should be Attached).***

Please use a separate sheet for additional entries.
(6)

Form EOIR-42A
4/97

PART 7 - MISCELLANEOUS INFORMATION *(Continued)*

APPLICATION NOT TO BE SIGNED BELOW UNTIL APPLICANT APPEARS BEFORE AN IMMIGRATION JUDGE

I do swear (affirm) that the contents of the above application, including the documents attached hereto, are true to the best of my knowledge and that this application is now signed by me with my full, true name.

____
(Complete and true signature of applicant or parent or guardian)

Subscribed and sworn to before me by the above-named applicant at ______________________________

____
Immigration Judge

____
Date: (Month, Day, Year)

CERTIFICATE OF SERVICE

I hereby certify that a copy of the foregoing was: ☐ - delivered in person, ☐ - mailed first class, postage prepaid on ____________ *(Month, Day, Year)* to ______________________________

____

____

____
Signature of Applicant (or attorney or representative)

Please use a separate sheet for additional entries.
(7)

Form EOIR-42A
4/97

Form EOIR–42B Application for cancellation of removal and adjustment of status for certain nonpermanent residents

U.S. Department of Justice
Executive Office for Immigration Review

OMB#1125-0001
Application for Cancellation of Removal and Adjustment of Status for Certain Nonpermanent Residents

ADVICE TO APPLICANT

PLEASE READ CAREFULLY. FEE WILL NOT BE RETURNED.

I. Aliens Eligible for Cancellation of Removal - You may be eligible to have your removal cancelled under section 240A(b) of the Immigration and Nationality Act (INA). To qualify for this benefit, you must establish in a hearing before an Immigration Judge that:

A. 1. Prior to the service of the Notice to Appear, you have maintained a continuous physical presence in the United States for 10 years or more and you have been a person of good moral character as defined in section 101(f) of the INA during such period.

2. You have not been convicted of an offense covered under sections 212(a)(2), 237(a)(2), or 237(a)(3) of the INA.

3. Your removal would result in exceptional and extremely unusual hardship to your United States citizen or lawful permanent resident spouse, parent or child, and you are deserving of a favorable exercise of discretion on your application.

OR

B. 1. You have been battered or subjected to extreme cruelty in the United States by your United States citizen or lawful permanent resident spouse or parent, or you are the parent of a child of a United States citizen or lawful permanent resident and the child has been battered or subjected to extreme cruelty in the United States by such citizen or permanent resident parent.

2. Prior to the service of the Notice to Appear, you have maintained a continuous physical presence in the United States for 3 years or more and you have been a person of good moral character as defined in section 101(f) of the INA during such period.

3. You are not inadmissible under sections 212(a)(2) or 212(a)(3) of the INA, you are not deportable under section 237(a)(1)(G) or sections 237(a)(2)-(4) of the INA, and you have not been convicted of an aggravated felony as defined under the INA.

4. a. Your removal would result in extreme hardship to you or your child who is the child of a United States citizen or lawful permanent resident; or

b. You are a child whose removal would result in extreme hardship to yourself or your parent.

5. You are deserving of a favorable exercise of discretion on your application.

NOTE: If you have served on active duty in the Armed Forces of the United States for at least 24 months, you do not have to meet the requirements of continuous physical presence in the United States. You must, however, have been in the United States when you entered the Armed Forces. If you are no longer in the Armed Forces, you must have been separated under honorable conditions.

II. Aliens NOT Eligible for Cancellation of Removal - You are not eligible for cancellation of removal under section 240A(b)(1) of the INA if you:

A. Entered the United States as a crewman after June 30, 1964;

OMB#1125-0001

U.S. Department of Justice
Executive Office for Immigration Review

Application for Cancellation of Removal an
Adjustment of Status for Certain Nonpermanent Resident

B. Were admitted to the United States as, or later became, a nonimmigrant exchange alien as defined in section 101(a)(15)(J) of the INA in order to receive graduate medical education or training, regardless of whether you are subject to or have fulfilled the 2-year foreign residence requirement of section 212(e) of the INA

C. Were admitted to the United States as, or later became, a nonimmigrant exchange alien as defined in section 101(a)(15)(J) of the INA, other than to receive graduate medical education or training, and you are subject to the 2-year foreign residence requirement of section 212(e) of the INA but have neither fulfilled nor obtained a waiver of that requirement;

D. Are an alien who is either inadmissible under section 212(a)(3) of the INA or deportable under section 237(a)(4) of the INA;

E. Are an alien who ordered, incited, assisted, or otherwise participated in the persecution of an individual because of the individual's race, religion, nationality, membership in a particular social group or political opinion; or

F. Are an alien who was previously granted relief under sections 212(c) or 244(a) of the INA as such sections were in effect prior to the enactment of the Illegal Immigration Reform and Immigrant Responsibility Act of 1996 (IIRIRA), or whose removal has previously been cancelled under section 240A or the INA.

III. How to Apply for Cancellation of Removal

In order to apply for cancellation of removal, you must answer all the questions on the attached Form EOIR-42B fully and accurately. You must pay the filing fee, serve a copy of your application on the Immigration and Naturalization Service, and file your application with the appropriate Immigration Court. An instruction sheet is attached to guide you in completing and filing your application. Please read the instruction sheet carefully before completing your application.

U.S. Department of Justice
Executive Office for Immigration Review

OMB#1125-0001
Application for Cancellation of Removal and Adjustment of Status for Certain Nonpermanent Residents

INSTRUCTIONS

1. PREPARATION OF APPLICATION.

To apply for cancellation of removal under section 240A(b) of the Immigration and Nationality Act (INA), you must fully and accurately answer all questions on the attached Form EOIR-42B. A separate application must be prepared and executed for each person applying for cancellation of removal. An application on behalf of an alien who is mentally incompetent or is a child under 14 years of age shall be executed by a parent or guardian.

Your responses must be typed or printed legibly in ink. Do not leave any questions unanswered or blank. If any questions do not apply to you, write "none" or "not applicable" in the appropriate space.

To the extent possible, answer all questions directly on the form. If there is insufficient room to fully respond to a question, please continue your response on an additional sheet. Please indicate the number of the question being answered next to your response on the additional sheet and sign, date, and securely attach the additional sheet to the Form EOIR-42B.

2. BURDEN OF PROOF.

The burden is on you to prove that you meet all of the statutory requirements for cancellation of removal for certain nonpermanent resident aliens under section 240A(b) of the Immigration and Nationality Act and that you are entitled to such relief as a matter of discretion. To meet this burden, your responses to the questions on the application should be as detailed and complete as possible. You should also attach to your application any documents that demonstrate your eligibility for cancellation of removal ("supporting documents").

3. SUPPORTING DOCUMENTS.

You should submit documentary evidence to show that you have maintained continuous physical presence in the United States for the required period. Documents which may evidence your physical presence in the United States include, but are not limited to, bankbooks, leases, deeds, licenses, receipts, letters, birth records, church records, school records, employment records, and evidence of tax payments.

You should submit documents which help to show that you are and have been a person of good moral character during the entire period of continuous physical presence in the United States required for eligibility for cancellation of removal. You should submit police records from each jurisdiction in which you resided during such period. To show good moral character, it is recommended that you submit the affidavits of witnesses, preferably citizens of the United States, and if you are employed, of your employer. The affidavit from your employer should include information regarding the nature and duration of your employment and your earnings.

You should submit official certification to establish your relationship to those you claim would suffer hardship by your removal, and if such persons are citizens of the United States or lawful permanent residents, evidence of their citizenship or lawful permanent resident status. Documentary evidence of such relationships may include, but are not limited to, birth records, marriage certificates, proof of divorce or termination of a marriage, and death certificates.

You should also submit with your application copies of any documents which you were issued by the Immigration and Naturalization Service. The Immigration Judge may require you to submit additional records relating to your request for cancellation of removal. These documents may include, but are not limited to, documents which reflect payment of taxes, court convictions, or payment of child support during your physical presence in the United States.

The original of all supporting documents must be available for inspection at the hearing. If you wish to have the original documents returned to you, you should also present reproductions.

4. REQUIRED DOCUMENTS.

Each applicant 14 years of age or older must also complete a Biographic Information Form G-325A and a Fingerprint Card, FD-258. Applicants may be fingerprinted by law enforcement officers, outreach centers, charitable and voluntary agencies, or other reputable persons or organizations. The fingerprint card on which the prints are submitted, the ink used, and the quality of the prints must meet the standards prescribed by the Federal Bureau of Investigation. The card must be signed by you in the presence of the person taking your fingerprints and that person must then sign his/her name and enter the date in the spaces provided. It is important to furnish all the information on the card.

U.S. Department of Justice
Executive Office for Immigration Review

OMB#1125-0001
Application for Cancellation of Removal and Adjustment of Status for Certain Nonpermanent Residents

5. TRANSLATIONS.

Any document in a foreign language must be accompanied by an English language translation and a certificate signed by the translator stating that he/she is competent to translate the document and that the translation is true and accurate to the best of the translator's abilities. Such certification must be printed legibly or typed.

6. PHOTOGRAPHS.

Unless you are incarcerated or detained in a facility which prevents your compliance with the following, you must submit two glossy, unretouched, color photographs of yourself taken within 30 days of the date of this application. These photos must have a white background and must not be mounted. The dimension of your facial image in the photograph should be about 1 inch from chin to top of hair and you should be shown in 3/4 frontal view showing the right side of your face with your right ear visible. Using a pencil or felt pen you should lightly print your name and alien registration number on the back of each photograph.

7. FEES.

Before you file your Form EOIR-42B with the Immigration Court, you must pay the required $100 fee to the Immigration and Naturalization Service. Evidence of payment of this fee in the form of a fee stamp or a receipt must accompany your Form EOIR-42B. This fee will not be refunded, regardless of the action taken on your application. Therefore, it is important that you read the advice, instructions, and application carefully before responding. **If you are unable to pay the fee, you may ask the Immigration Judge to permit you to file your Form EOIR-42B without fee.**

DO NOT SEND CASH. All fees must be submitted in the exact amount. Remittance may be made by cash, personal check, cashier's check, certified bank check, bank international money order, or foreign draft drawn on a financial institution in the United States and payable to the "Immigration and Naturalization Service" in United States currency. If the applicant resides in the Virgin Islands, the check or money order must be payable to the "Commissioner of Finance of the Virgin Islands." If the applicant resides in Guam, the check or money order must be payable to the "Treasurer, Guam." Personal checks are accepted subject to collectibility. An uncollectible check will render the application and any documents issued pursuant thereto invalid. A charge of $5.00 will be imposed if a check in payment of a fee is not honored by the bank on which it is drawn. When the check is drawn on an account of a person other than the applicant, the name and alien registration number of the applicant must be entered on the face of the check. All checks must be drawn on a bank located in the United States.

8. SERVING & FILING YOUR APPLICATION.

You must serve the following documents on the INS District Counsel:

- a copy of your Form EOIR-42B, Application for Cancellation of Removal, with all supporting documents and additional sheets,
- evidence of payment of the filing fee or a request for a waiver of the fee by an Immigration Judge,
- the original Biographical Information Form G-325A,
- the original Fingerprint Card, FD-258, and
- a photograph of you which meets the requirements of #6 above.

You must file the following documents with the appropriate Immigration Court:

- the original Form EOIR-42B with all supporting documents and additional sheets,
- evidence of payment of the filing fee or a request for a wavier of the fee by an Immigration Judge,
- a copy of Biographical Information Form G-325A,
- a copy of Fingerprint Card, FD-258,
- a photograph of you which meets the requirements of #6 above, and
- a certificate showing service of these documents on the INS District Counsel, unless service is made on the record at the hearing.

OMB#1125-0001

U.S. Department of Justice
Executive Office for Immigration Review

Application for Cancellation of Removal and Adjustment of Status for Certain Nonpermanent Residents

9. PENALTIES.

You must answer all questions on Form EOIR-42B truthfully and submit only genuine documents in support of your application. **You will be required to swear or affirm that the contents of your application and the supporting documents are true to the best of your knowledge.** Your answer to the questions on this form and the supporting documents you present will be used to determine whether your removal should be cancelled. Any answer you give and any supporting document you present may also be used as evidence in any proceeding to determine your right to be admitted, be readmitted, pass through, or reside in the United States. Your application may be denied if any of your answers or supporting documents are found to be false.

Presenting false answers or false documents may also subject you to criminal prosecution under 18 U.S.C. 1546 and/or subject you to civil penalties under 8 U.S.C. 1324c if you submit your application knowing that the application or any supporting document contains any false statement with respect to a material fact, or if you swear or affirm that the contents of your application and the supporting documents are true, knowing that the application or any supporting document contains any false statement with respect to a material fact. If convicted, you could be fined up to $250,000.00, imprisoned for up to 5 years, or both. 18 U.S.C. 1546(a), 3559(a)(4), 357(b)(3). If it is determined you have violated the prohibition against document fraud and a final order is entered against you, you could be subject to a civil penalty up to $2,000.00 for each document used or created for the first offense and up to $5,000.00 for any second or subsequent offense. In addition, if you are the subject of a final order for violating 8 U.S.C. 1324c, relating to civil penalties for document fraud, you will be removable from the United States.

10. PAPERWORK REDUCTION ACT.

We try to create forms and instructions that are accurate, can easily be understood, and which impose the least possible burden on you to provide us with information. Often this is difficult because some immigration laws are very complex. The reporting burden for this collection of information is computed as follows: (1) learning about the form, 45 minutes, (2) completing the form, 2 hours, and (3) assembling and filing the form, 3 hours, for an estimated average of 5 hours, 45 minutes per response. If you have comments regarding the accuracy of this burden estimate or any other aspect of this collection of information, including suggestions for reducing this burden, you may write to the U.S. Department of Justice, Executive Office for Immigration Review, Office of the General Counsel, 5107 Leesburg Pike, Suite 2400, Falls Church, Virginia 22041.

11. REPORTING BURDEN.

A person is not required to respond to a collection of information unless it displays a currently valid OMB control number.

U.S. Department of Justice
Executive Office for Immigration Review

OMB #1125-0001
Application for Cancellation of Removal and Adjustment of Status Certain Nonpermanent Residents

PLEASE READ ADVICE AND INSTRUCTIONS BEFORE FILLING IN FORM

PLEASE TYPE OR PRINT

Fee Stamp

PART 1 - INFORMATION ABOUT YOURSELF

1) My present true name is: *(Last, First, Middle)*	2) Alien Registration Number:
3) My name given at birth was: *(Last, First, Middle)*	4) Birth Place: *(City, Country)*

5) Date of Birth: *(Month, Day, Year)*	6) Gender: ☐ Male ☐ Female	7) Height:	8) Hair Color:	9) Eye Color:
10) Current Nationality & Citizenship:	11) Social Security Number:	12) Home Phone Number:	13) Work Phone Number:	

14) I currently reside at: *Apt. number and/or in care of* *Number and Street* *City or Town* *State* *ZIP Code*	15) I have been known by the additional name(s):

16) During the last 10 years, I resided in the following locations in the United States: (If less than 10 years, set forth the information for the period you have been in the United States) List PRESENT ADDRESS FIRST and work back in time

Street and Number - Apt. or Room# - City or Town - State - ZIP Code	Resided From: *(Month, Day, Year)*	Resided To: *(Month, Day, Year)*
		PRESENT

PART 2 - INFORMATION ABOUT THIS APPLICATION

17) I, the undersigned, hereby request that my removal be cancelled under the provisions of section 244A(b) of the Immigration and Nationality Act (INA). I believe that I am eligible for cancellation of removal because: (check all apply)

☐ My removal would result in exceptional and extremely unusual hardship to my: *(Place a* **USC** *in the space if the family member is a citizen of the United States, an* **L** *if the family member is a lawful permanent resident of the United States, an* **X** *if the family member is neither and leave* **BLANK** *if not applicable.)*

_____ **Husband** _____ **Wife** _____ **Father** _____ **Mother** _____ **Child or Children**

With the exception of absences described in question #25, I have resided in the United States since:
(Month, Day, Year) ________________________________

☐ I, or my child, have been battered or subjected to extreme cruelty by a United States citizen or lawful permanent resident spouse or parent.

With the exception of the absences described in question #25, I have been physically present in the United States since:
(Month, Day, Year) ________________________________

Please use a separate sheet for additional entries.
(1)

Form EOIR-42B
4/97

PART 3 - INFORMATION ABOUT YOUR PRESENCE IN THE UNITED STATES

18) I first entered the United States under the name of: *(Last, First, Middle)*

19) I first entered the United States on: *(Month, Day, Year)*

20) Place or port of first arrival: *(Place or Port, City, and State)*

21) I arrived: ☐ as a lawful permanent resident, ☐ as a Visitor, ☐ as a Student, ☐ without inspection, or ☐ Other *(Place an X in the correct box, if Other is selected please explain)*:

22) If admitted as a nonimmigrant, period for which admitted: *(Month, Day, Year)* to

23) My last extension of stay in the United States expired on: *(Month, Day, Year)*

24) If not inspected or if arrival occurred at other than a regular port, describe the circumstances as accurately as possible:

25) Since the date of my first arrival I departed from and returned to the United States at the following places and on the following dates:
(Please list all departures regardless of how briefly you were absent from the United States)
If you have never departed from the United States since your original date of arrival, please mark an X in the box: ☐

Port of Departure *(Place or Port, City and State)*	Departure Date *(Month, Day, Year)*	Purpose of Travel	Destination
Port of Return *(Place or Port, City and State)*	Return Date *(Month, Day, Year)*	Manner of Return	Inspected & Admitted? ☐ Yes ☐ No
Port of Departure *(Place or Port, City and State)*	Departure Date *(Month, Day, Year)*	Purpose of Travel	Destination
Port of Return *(Place or Port, City and State)*	Return Date *(Month, Day, Year)*	Manner of Return	Inspected & Admitted? ☐ Yes ☐ No

26) Have you ever departed the United States:
a) under an order of deportation, exclusion or removal? ------- ☐ Yes ☐ No
b) pursuant to a grant of voluntary departure? ----------------- ☐ Yes ☐ No

PART 4 - INFORMATION ABOUT YOUR MARITAL STATUS AND SPOUSE *(Continued on page 3)*

27) I am not married: ☐
I am married: ☐

28) If married, the name of my spouse is: *(Last, First, Middle)*

29) Date of marriage: *(Month, Day, Year)*

30) The marriage took place in: *(City and Country)*

31) Birth place of spouse: *(City and Country)*

32) My spouse currently resides at:

Apt. number and/or in care of

Number and Street

City or Town *State/Country* *ZIP Code*

33) Birth date of spouse: *(Month, Day, Year)*

34) My spouse is a citizen of: *(Country)*

35) If your spouse is other than a native born United States citizen, answer the following:
He/she arrived in the United States at: *(City and State)* __________
He/she arrived in the United States on: *(Month, Day, Year)* __________
His/her alien registration number is: A# __________
He/she was naturalized on: *(Month, Day, Year)* __________ at __________ *(City and State)*

36) My spouse ☐ - is ☐ - is not employed. If employed, please give salary and the name and address of the place(s) of employment:

Full Name and Address of Employer:	Earnings Per Week *(Approximate)*
	$
	$
	$

Please use a separate sheet for additional entries.
(2)

Form EOIR-42B
4/97

PART 4 - INFORMATION ABOUT YOUR MARITAL STATUS AND SPOUSE *(CONTINUED)*

37) I ☐ -have ☐ -have not been previously married: *(If previously married, list the name of each prior spouse, the dates on which each marriage began and ended, the place where the marriage terminated, and describe how each marriage ended.)*

Name of prior spouse: *(Last, First, Middle)*	Date marriage began: Date marriage ended:	Place marriage ended: *(City and Country)*	Description or manner of how marriage was terminated or ended:

38) My present spouse ☐-has ☐ -has not been previously married: *(If previously married, list the name of each prior spouse, the dates on which the marriage began and ended, the place where the marriage terminated, and describe how each marriage ended.)*

Name of prior spouse: *(Last, First, Middle)*	Date marriage began: Date marriage ended:	Place marriage ended: *(City and Country)*	Description or manner of how marriage was termanated or ended:

39) Have you been ordered by any court, or are otherwise under any legal obligation, to provide child support and/or spousal maintenance as a result of a separation and/or divorce? ☐ -Yes ☐ -No

PART 5 - INFORMATION ABOUT YOUR EMPLOYMENT AND FINANCIAL STATUS

40) Since my arrival into the United States, I have been employed by the following - named persons or firms: *(Please begin with present employment and work back in time. Any periods of unemployment or school attendance should be specified.)*

Full Name and Address of Employer	Earnings Per Week *(Approximate)*	Type of Work Performed	Employed From: *(Month, Day, Year)*	Employed To: *(Month, Day, Year)*
	$			PRESENT
	$			
	$			

41) If self-employed, describe the nature of the business, the name of the business, its address, and net income derived therefrom:

42) My assets (and if married, my spouse's assets) in the United States and other countries, not including clothing and household necessities, are:

Self		**Jointly Owned with Spouse**	
Cash, Stocks, and Bonds	$	Cash, Stocks, and Bonds	$
Real Estate	$	Real Estate	$
Automobile (dollar value-amount owed)-	$	Automobile (dollar value-amount owed)-	$
Other (describe on line below)	$	Other (describe on line below)	$
TOTAL	**$**	**TOTAL**	**$**

43) I ☐ -have ☐-have not received public or private relief or assistance(e.g. Welfare, Unemployment Benefits, Medicaid, ADC, etc.). If you have, please give full details including the type of relief or assistance received, date for which relief or assistance was received, place, and amount received during this time:

44) Please list each of the years in which you have filed an income tax return with the Internal Revenue Service:

Please use a separate sheet for additional entries.

(3)

Form EOIR-42B
4/97

PART 6 - INFORMATION ABOUT YOUR FAMILY *(Continued on page 5)*

45) I have_____________ *(Number of)* children. Please list information for each child below, include assets and earnings information for children over the age of sixteen who have separate incomes:

Name of Child: *(Last, First, Middle)* Child's Alien Registration Number:	Citizen of What Country: Birth Date: *(Month, Day, Year)*	Now Residing At: *(City and Country)* Birth Place: *(City and Country)*	Immigration Status of Child?
A#:			
Estimated Total of Assets: $_______	Estimated Average Weekly Earnings: $_______		
A#:			
Estimated Total of Assets: $_______	Estimated Average Weekly Earnings: $_______		
A#:			
Estimated Total of Assets: $_______	Estimated Average Weekly Earnings: $_______		

46) If your application is denied, would your spouse and all of your children accompany you to your:

Country of Birth - ☐ Yes ☐ No

Country of Nationality - ☐ Yes ☐ No

Country of Last Residence - ☐ Yes ☐ No

If you answered "NO" to any of the responses, please explain: _______________

47) Members of my family, including my spouse and/or child(ren) ☐- have ☐- have not received public or private relief or assistance (e.g., Unemployment Benefits, Welfare, Medicaid, ADC, etc.). If any member of your immediate family has received such relief or assistance, please give full details including identity of person(s) receiving relief or assistance, dates for which relief or assistance was received, place, and amount received during this time: _______________

48) Please give the requested information about your parents, brothers, sisters, aunts, uncles. and grandparents. As to residence, show street address, city, and state, if in the United States; otherwise show only country:

Name: *(Last, First, Middle)* Alien Registration Number:	Citizen of What Country: Birth Date: *(Month, Day, Year)*	Relationship to Me: Birth Place: *(Place and Country)*	Immigration Status of Listed Relative
A#:			
Complete Address of Current Residence:			
A#:			
Complete Address of Current Residence:			

Please use a separate sheet for additional entries.

(4)

Form EOIR-42B
4/97

PART 6 - INFORMATION ABOUT YOUR FAMILY *(Continued)*

IF THIS APPICATION IS BASED ON HARDSHIP TO A PARENT OR PARENTS, QUESTIONS 49 TO 52 MUST BE ANSWERED.

49) As such parent who is not a citizen of the United States, give the date and place of arrival in the United States including full details as to the manner and terms of admission into the United States: ____________________

____

____

50) My father ☐ - is ☐ -is not employed. If employed, please give salary and the name and address of the place(s) of employment.

Full Name and Address of Employer	Earnings Per Week *(Approximate)*
	$

51) My mother ☐ - is ☐ - is not employed. If employed, please give salary and the name and address of the place(s) of employment.

Full Name and Address of Employer	Earnings Per Week *(Approximate)*
	$

52) My parent's assets in the United States and other countries not including clothing and household necessities are:

Assets of Father consist of the following:		**Assets of mother consist of the following:**	
Cash, Stocks, and Bonds	$	Cash, Stocks, and Bonds	$
Real Estate	$	Real Estate	$
Automobile (dollar value - amount owed) -	$	Automobile (dollar value - amount owed) -	$
Other (describe on line below)	$	Other (describe on line below)	$
________ **TOTAL**	$	________ **TOTAL**	$

PART 7 - MISCELLANEOUS INFORMATION *(Continued on page 6)*

53) I ☐ - have ☐ - have not entred the United States as a crewman after June 30, 1964.

54) I ☐ - have ☐ - have not been admitted as, or after arrival in the United States acquired the status of, an exchange alien.

55) I ☐ - have ☐ - have not submitted address reports as required by section 265 of the Immigration and Nationality Act.

56)I ☐ -have ☐ -have never(either in the United Stated or in any foreign country)been arrested, summoned into court as a defendant convicted, fined, imprisoned, placed on probation, or forfeited collateral for an act involving a felony, misdemeanor, or breach of any public law or ordinance(including, but not limited to, traffic violations or driving incidents involving alcohol). *(If answer is in the affirmative, please give a brief description of each offense including the name and location of the offense, any penalty imposed, any sentence imposed, and the time actually served).* ____________________

____

____

____

57) Have you ever served in the Armed Forces of the United States? ☐ - Yes ☐ - No. If "Yes" please state branch *(Army, Navy, etc.)* and service number. ____________________

Place of entry on duty: *(Place, City, and State)* ____________________

Date of entry on duty: *(Month, Day, Year)* __________ Date of discharge: *(Month, Day, Year)* __________

Type of discharge *(Honorable, Dishonorable, etc.)*: ____________________

I served in active duty status from: *(Month, Day, Year)* __________ to *(Month, Day, Year)* __________

58) Have you ever left the United States or the jurisdiction of the district where you registered for the draft to avoid being drafted into the military or naval forces of the United States? ☐ Yes ☐ No

Please a separate sheet for additional entries.

PART 7 - MISCELLANEOUS INFORMATION *(Continued)*

59) Have you ever deserted from the military or naval forces of the United Stated while the United Stated was at war? ☐ Yes ☐ No

60) If male, did you register under the Selective Service (Draft) Law of 1917, 1918, 1948, 1951, or later Draft Laws? ☐ Yes ☐ No
If "Yes," please give date, Selective Service number, local draft board number, and your last draft classification: ________

61) Were you ever exempted from service because of conscientious objection, alienage, or any other reason? ☐ Yes ☐ No

62) Please list your present or past membership in or affiliation with every political organization, association, fund, foundation, party, club, society, or similar group in the United States or any other place since your 16th birthday. Include any foreign military service in this part. If none, write "NONE". Include the name of the organization, location, nature of the organization, and the dates of membership.

Name of Organization	Location of Organization	Nature of Organization	Member From: *(Month, Day, Year)*	Member To: *(Month, Day, Year)*

63) Have you ever:
☐ Yes ☐ No been ordered deported or removed?
☐ Yes ☐ No overstayed a grant of voluntary departure from an Immigration Judge or the Immigration and Naturalization Service (INS)?
☐ Yes ☐ No failed to appear for removal or deportation?

64) Have you ever been:
☐ Yes ☐ No a habitual drinker?
☐ Yes ☐ No one whose income is derived principally from illegal gambling?
☐ Yes ☐ No one who has given false testimony for the purpose of obtaining immigration benefits?
☐ Yes ☐ No engaged in prostitution or unlawful commercialized vice?
☐ Yes ☐ No involved in a serious criminal offense and asserted immunity from prosecution?
☐ yes ☐ No a polygamist?
☐ Yes ☐ No one who aided and/or abetted another to enter the United States Illegally?
☐ Yes ☐ No a trafficker of a controlled substance, or a knowing assister, abettor, conspirator, or colluder with others in any such controlled substance offense (not including a single offense of simple possession of 30 grams or less of marijuana)?
☐ Yes ☐ No inadmissible or deportable on security-related grounds under sections 212(a)(3) or 237(a)(4) of the INA?
☐ Yes ☐ No one who has ordered, incited, assisted, or otherwise participated in the persection of an individual on account of his or her race, religion, nationality, membership in a particular social group,or political opinion?
☐ Yes ☐ No a person previously granted relief under sections 212(c) or 244(a) of the INA or whose removal has perviously been cancelled under section 240A of the INA?

64)Are you: ☐ Yes ☐ No the beneficiary of an approved visa petition?
If yes, can you: ☐ Yes ☐ No arrange a trip outside the United States to obtain an immigrant visa. If no, please explain:

____
____
____
____

Please use a separate sheet for additional entries
(6)

Form EOIR-42B
4/97

PART 7 - MISCELLANEOUS INFORMATION *(Continued)*

65) The following certificates or other supporting documents are attached hereto as a part of this application: *(Refer to the Instruction Sheet for documents which should be attached).*

APPLICATION NOT TO BE SIGNED BELOW UNTIL APPLICANT APPEARS BEFORE AN IMMIGRATION JUDGE

I do swear (affirm) that the contents of the above application, including the documents attached hereto, are true to the best of my knowledge, and that this application is now signed by me with my full, true name.

(Complete and true signature of applicant or parent or guardian)

Subscribed and sworn to before me by the above-named applicant at

Immigration Judge

Date: (Month, Day, Year)

CERTIFICATE OF SERVICE

I hereby certify that a copy of the foregoing was: ☐ - delivered in person, ☐ - mailed first class, postage prepaid on *(Month, Day, Year)* to *(INS District Counsel and Address)*

Signature of Applicant (or attorney or representative)

Please use a separate sheet for additional entries.
(7)

Form EOIR-42B
4/97

Form N–400 Application for naturalization

U.S. Department of Justice
Immigration and Naturalization Service

OMB No. 1115-0009
Application for Naturalization

INSTRUCTIONS

Purpose of This Form.
This form is for use to apply to become a naturalized citizen of the United States.

Who May File.
You may apply for naturalization if:

- you have been a lawful permanent resident for five years;
- you have been a lawful permanent resident for three years, have been married to a United States citizen for those three years, and continue to be married to that U.S. citizen;
- you are the lawful permanent resident child of United States citizen parents; or
- you have qualifying military service.

Children under 18 may automatically become citizens when their parents naturalize. You may inquire at your local Service office for further information. If you do not meet the qualifications listed above but believe that you are eligible for naturalization, you may inquire at your local Service office for additional information.

General Instructions.
Please answer all questions by typing or clearly printing in black ink. Indicate that an item is not applicable with "N/A". If an answer is "none," write "none". If you need extra space to answer any item, attach a sheet of paper with your name and your alien registration number (A#), if any, and indicate the number of the item.

Every application must be properly signed and filed with the correct fee. If you are under 18 years of age, your parent or guardian must sign the application.

If you wish to be called for your examination at the same time as another person who is also applying for naturalization, make your request on a separate cover sheet. Be sure to give the name and alien registration number of that person.

Initial Evidence Requirements.
You must file your application with the following evidence:

A copy of your alien registration card.

Photographs. You must submit two color photographs of yourself taken within 30 days of this application. These photos must be glossy, unretouched and unmounted, and have a white background. Dimension of the face should be about 1 inch from chin to top of hair. Face should be 3/4 frontal view of right side with right ear visible. Using pencil or felt pen, lightly print name and A#, if any, on the back of each photo. This requirement may be waived by the Service if you can establish that you are confined because of age or physical infirmity.

Fingerprints. If you are between the ages of 14 and 75years of age, you must be fingerprinted in connection with this application. *Applications residing in the United States.* After filing the application, INS will notify you in writing of the time and location where you must go to be fingerprinted. Failure to appear to be fingerprinted may result in denial of the application. *Applicants residing Abroad.* A completed fingerprint card (Form FD-258) must be submitted with the application. Do not bend, fold, or crease the fingerprint card. Fingerprint cards must be prepared by a United States consular office or United States military installation.

U.S. Military Service. If you have ever served in the Armed Forces of the United States at any time, you must submit a completed Form G-325B. If your application is based on your military service you must also submit Form N-426, "Request for Certification of Military or Naval Service."

Application for Child. If this application is for a permanent resident child of U.S. citizen parents, you must also submit copies of the child's birth certificate, the parents' marriage certificate, and evidence of the parents' U.S. citizenship. If the parents are divorced, you must also submit the divorce decree and evidence that the citizen parent has legal custody of the child.

Where to File.
File this application at the local Service office having jurisdiction over your place of residence.

Fee.
The fee for this application is $225. If you are between the ages of 14 and 75 and residing in the United States, there is a $25 fingerprinting fee in addition to the application fee, for a total fee of $250. You may submit one check or money order for both the application and fingerprinting fees. Fees must be submitted in the exact amount. Fees cannot be refunded. **DO NOT MAIL CASH.**

All checks and money orders must be drawn on a bank or other institution located in the United States and must be payable in United States currency. The check or money order should be made payable to the Immigration and Naturalization Service, except that:

- If you live in Guam, and are filing this application in Guam, make your check or money order payable to the "Treasurer, Guam."
- If you live in the Virgin Islands, and are filing this application in the Virgin Islands, make your check or money order payable to the "Commissioner of Finance of the Virgin Islands."

Checks are accepted subject to collection. An uncollected check will render the application and any document issued invalid. A charge of $30.00 will be imposed if a check in payment of a fee is not honored by the bank on which it is drawn.

Form N-400 (Rev. 01/15/99)N

Processing Information.

Rejection. Any application that is not signed or is not accompanied by the proper fee will be rejected with a notice that the application is deficient. You may correct the deficiency and resubmit the application. However, an application is not considered properly filed until it is accepted by the Service.

Requests for more information. We may request more information or evidence. We may also request that you submit the originals of any copy. We will return these originals when they are no longer required.

Interview. After you file your application, you will be notified to appear at a Service office to be examined under oath or affirmation. This interview may not be waived. If you are an adult, you must show that you have a knowledge and understanding of the history, principles, and form of government of the United States. There is no exemption from this requirement.

You will also be examined on your ability to read, write, and speak English. If on the date of your examination you are more than 50 years of age and have been a lawful permanent resident for 20 years or more, or you are 55 years of age and have been a lawful permanent resident for at least 15 years, you will be exempt from the English language requirements of the law. If you are exempt, you may take the examination in any language you wish.

Oath of Allegiance. If your application is approved, you will be required to take the following oath of allegiance to the United States in order to become a citizen:

"I hereby declare, on oath, that I absolutely and entirely renounce and abjure all allegiance and fidelity to any foreign prince, potentate, state or sovereignty, of whom or which I have heretofore been a subject or citizen; that I will support and defend the Constitution and laws of the United States of America against all enemies, foreign and domestic; that I will bear true faith and allegiance to the same; that I will bear arms on behalf of the United States when required by the law; that I will perform noncombatant service in the armed forces of the United States when required by the law; that I will perform work of national importance under civilian direction when required by the law; and that I take this obligation freely without any mental reservation or purpose of evasion; so help me God."

If you cannot promise to bear arms or perform noncombatant service because of religious training and belief, you may omit those statements when taking the oath. "Religious training and belief" means a person's belief in relation to a Supreme Being involving duties superior to those arising from any human relation, but does not include essentially political, sociological, or philosophical views or merely a personal moral code.

Oath ceremony. You may choose to have the oath of allegiance administered in a ceremony conducted by the Service or request to be scheduled for an oath ceremony in a court that has jurisdiction over the applicant's place of residence. At the time of your examination you will be asked to elect either form of ceremony. You will become a citizen on the date of the oath ceremony and the Attorney General will issue a Certificate of Naturalization as evidence of United States citizenship.

If you wish to change your name as part of the naturalization process, you will have to take the oath in court.

Penalties.

If you knowingly and willfully falsify or conceal a material fact or submit a false document with this request, we will deny the benefit you are filing for, and may deny any other immigration benefit. In addition, you will face severe penalties provided by law, and may be subject to criminal prosecution.

Privacy Act Notice.

We ask for the information on this form, and associated evidence, to determine if you have established eligibility for the immigration benefit you are filing for. Our legal right to ask for this information is in 8 USC 1439, 1440, 1443, 1445, 1446, and 1452. We may provide this information to other government agencies. Failure to provide this information, and any requested evidence, may delay a final decision or result in denial of your request.

Paperwork Reduction Act Notice.

A person is not required to respond to a collection of information unless it displays a currently valid OMB control number. We try to create forms and instructions that are accurate, can be easily understood, and which impose the least possible burden on you to provide us with information. Often this is difficult because some immigration laws are very complex. Accordingly, the reporting burden for this collection of information is computed as follows: (1) learning about the law and form, 20 minutes; (2) completing the form, 25 minutes; and (3) assembling and filing the application (includes statutory required interview and travel time, after filing of application), 3 hours and 35 minutes, for an estimated average of 4 hours and 20 minutes per response. If you have comments regarding the accuracy of this estimate, or suggestions for making this form simpler, you can write to the Immigration and Naturalization Service, 425 I Street, N.W., Room 5307, Washington, D.C. 20536; OMB No. 1115-0009, **DO NOT MAIL YOUR COMPLETED APPLICATION TO THIS ADDRESS.**

U.S. Department of Justice
Immigration and Naturalization Service

OMB #1115-0009

Application for Naturalization

START HERE - Please Type or Print

Part 1. Information about you.

Family Name	Given Name	Middle Initial

U.S. Mailing Address - Care of

Street Number and Name	Apt. #

City	County

State	ZIP Code

Date of Birth (month/day/year)	Country of Birth

Social Security #	A #

Part 2. Basis for Eligibility *(check one)*.

a. ☐ I have been a permanent resident for at least five (5) years .

b. ☐ I have been a permanent resident for at least three (3) years and have been married to a United States Citizen for those three years.

c. ☐ I am a permanent resident child of United States citizen parent(s) .

d. ☐ I am applying on the basis of qualifying military service in the Armed Forces of the U.S. and have attached completed Forms N-426 and G-325B

e. ☐ Other. (Please specify section of law)________________

Part 3. Additional information about you.

Date you became a permanent resident (month/day/year)	Port admitted with an immmigrant visa or INS Office where granted adjustment of status.

Citizenship

Name on alien registration card (if different than in Part 1)

Other names used since you became a permanent resident (including maiden name)

Sex	Height	Marital Status:
☐ Male ☐ Female		☐ Single ☐ Married ☐ Divorced ☐ Widowed

Can you speak, read and write English ? ☐No ☐Yes.

Absences from the U.S.:

Have you been absent from the U.S. since becoming a permanent resident? ☐ No ☐Yes.

If you answered **"Yes"** , complete the following, Begin with your most recent absence. If you need more room to explain the reason for an absence or to list more trips, continue on separate paper.

Date left U.S.	Date returned	Did absence last 6 months or more?	Destination	Reason for trip
		☐ Yes ☐ No		
		☐ Yes ☐ No		
		☐ Yes ☐ No		
		☐ Yes ☐ No		
		☐ Yes ☐ No		
		☐ Yes ☐ No		

Continued on back.

FOR INS USE ONLY

Returned	Receipt
Resubmitted	
Reloc Sent	
Reloc Rec'd	
☐ Applicant Interviewed	

At interview

☐ request naturalization ceremony at court

Remarks

Action

To Be Completed by *Attorney or Representative*, if any

☐ Fill in box if G-28 is attached to represent the applicant

VOLAG#

ATTY State License #

Form N-400 (Rev. 01/15/99)N

Part 4. Information about your residences and employment.

A. List your addresses during the last five (5) years or since you became a permanent resident, whichever is less. Begin with your current address. If you need more space, continue on separate paper:

Street Number and Name, City, State, Country, and Zip Code	Dates (month/day/year)	
	From	To

B. List your employers during the last five (5) years. List your present or most recent employer first. If none, write "None". If you need more space, continue on separate paper.

Employer's Name	Employer's Address	Dates Employed (month/day/year)		Occupation/position
	Street Name and Number - City, State and ZIP Code	From	To	

Part 5. Information about your marital history.

A. Total number of times you have been married _______ . If you are now married, complete the following regarding your husband or wife.

Family name	Given name	Middle initial

Address

Date of birth (month/day/year)	Country of birth	Citizenship
Social Security#	A# *(if applicable)*	Immigration status (If not a U.S. citizen)

Naturalization (If applicable)
(month/day/year) Place (City, State)

If you have ever previously been married or if your current spouse has been previously married, please provide the following on separate paper: Name of prior spouse, date of marriage, date marriage ended, how marriage ended and immigration status of prior spouse.

Part 6. Information about your children.

B. Total Number of Children _________ . Complete the following information for each of your children. If the child lives with you, state "with me" in the address column; otherwise give city/state/country of child's current residence. If deceased, write "deceased" in the address column. If you need more space, continue on separate paper.

Full name of child	Date of birth	Country of birth	Citizenship	A - Number	Address

Page 2 *Continued on next page* Form N-400 (Rev. 01/15/99) N

Continued on back

Part 7. Additional eligibility factors.

Please answer each of the following questions. If your answer is "**Yes**", explain on a separate paper.

1. Are you now, or have you ever been a member of, or in any way connected or associated with the Communist Party, or ever knowingly aided or supported the Communist Party directly, or indirectly through another organization, group or person, or ever advocated, taught, believed in, or knowingly supported or furthered the interests of communism? ☐ Yes ☐ No
2. During the period March 23, 1933 to May 8, 1945, did you serve in, or were you in any way affiliated with, either directly or indirectly, any military unit, paramilitary unit, police unit, self-defense unit, vigilante unit, citizen unit of the Nazi party or SS, government agency or office, extermination camp, concentration camp, prisoner of war camp, prison, labor camp, detention camp or transit camp, under the control or affiliated with:
   a. The Nazi Government of Germany? ☐ Yes ☐ No
   b. Any government in any area occupied by, allied with, or established with the assistance or cooperation of, the Nazi Government of Germany? ☐ Yes ☐ No
3. Have you at any time, anywhere, ever ordered, incited, assisted, or otherwise participated in the persecution of any person because of race, religion, national origin, or political opinion? ☐ Yes ☐ No
4. Have you ever left the United States to avoid being drafted into the U.S. Armed Forces? ☐ Yes ☐ No
5. Have you ever failed to comply with Selective Service laws? ☐ Yes ☐ No
   If you have registered under the Selective Service laws, complete the following information:
   Selective Service Number:____________________ Date Registered:______________
   If you registered before 1978, also provide the following:
   Local Board Number:____________________ Classification:______________
6. Did you ever apply for exemption from military service because of alienage, conscientious objections or other reasons? ☐ Yes ☐ No
7. Have you ever deserted from the military, air or naval forces of the United States? ☐ Yes ☐ No
8. Since becoming a permanent resident , have you ever failed to file a federal income tax return ? ☐ Yes ☐ No
9. Since becoming a permanent resident , have you filed a federal income tax return as a nonresident or failed to file a federal return because you considered yourself to be a nonresident? ☐ Yes ☐ No
10. Are deportation proceedings pending against you, or have you ever been deported, or ordered deported, or have you ever applied for suspension of deportation? ☐ Yes ☐ No
11. Have you ever claimed in writing, or in any way, to be a United States citizen? ☐ Yes ☐ No
12. Have you ever:
    a. been a habitual drunkard? ☐ Yes ☐ No
    b. advocated or practiced polygamy? ☐ Yes ☐ No
    c. been a prostitute or procured anyone for prostitution? ☐ Yes ☐ No
    d. knowingly and for gain helped any alien to enter the U.S. illegally? ☐ Yes ☐ No
    e. been an illicit trafficker in narcotic drugs or marijuana? ☐ Yes ☐ No
    f. received income from illegal gambling? ☐ Yes ☐ No
    g. given false testimony for the purpose of obtaining any immigration benefit? ☐ Yes ☐ No
13. Have you ever been declared legally incompetent or have you ever been confined as a patient in a mental institution? ☐ Yes ☐ No
14. Were you born with, or have you acquired in same way, any title or order of nobility in any foreign State? ☐ Yes ☐ No
15. Have you ever:
    a. knowingly committed any crime for which you have not been arrested? ☐ Yes ☐ No
    b. been arrested, cited, charged, indicted, convicted, fined or imprisoned for breaking or violating any law or ordinance excluding traffic regulations? ☐ Yes ☐ No

(If you answer yes to 15 , in your explanation give the following information for each incident or occurrence the **city, state,** and **country,** where the offense took place, the **date** and **nature** of the offense, and the **outcome** or **disposition** of the case).

Part 8. Allegiance to the U.S.

If your answer to any of the following questions is "**NO**", attach a full explanation:

1. Do you believe in the Constitution and form of government of the U.S.? ☐ Yes ☐ No
2. Are you willing to take the full Oath of Allegiance to the U.S.? (see instructions) ☐ Yes ☐ No
3. If the law requires it, are you willing to bear arms on behalf of the U.S.? ☐ Yes ☐ No
4. If the law requires it, are you willing to perform noncombatant services in the Armed Forces of the U.S.? ☐ Yes ☐ No
5. If the law requires it, are you willing to perform work of national importance under civilian direction? ☐ Yes ☐ No

 Continued on back

Part 9. Memberships and organizations.

A. List your present and past membership in or affiliation with every organization, association, fund, foundation, party, club, society, or similar group in the United States or in any other place. Include any military service in this part. If none, write "none". Include the name of organization, location, dates of membership and the nature of the organization. If additional space is needed, use separate paper.

Part 10. Complete only if you checked block " C " in Part 2.

How many of your parents are U.S. citizens? ☐ One ☐ Both (Give the following about one U.S. citizen parent:)

Family Name | Given Name | Middle Name

Address

Basis for citizenship:
☐ Birth
☐ Naturalization Cert. No.

Relationship to you (check one): ☐ natural parent ☐ adoptive parent
☐ parent of child legitimated after birth

If adopted or legitimated after birth, give date of adoption or, legitimation: *(month/day/year)*_______________.

Does this parent have legal custody of you? ☐ Yes ☐ No

(Attach a copy of relating evidence to establish that you are the child of this U.S. citizen and evidence of this parent's citizenship.)

Part 11. Signature. *(Read the information on penalties in the instructions before completing this section).*

I certify or, if outside the United States, I swear or affirm, under penalty of perjury under the laws of the United States of America that this application, and the evidence submitted with it, is all true and correct. I authorize the release of any information from my records which the Immigration and Naturalization Service needs to determine eligibility for the benefit I am seeking.

Signature | **Date**

Please Note: *If you do not completely fill out this form, or fail to submit required documents listed in the instructions, you may not be found eligible for naturalization and this application may be denied.*

Part 12. Signature of person preparing form if other than above. *(Sign below)*

I declare that I prepared this application at the request of the above person and it is based on all information of which I have knowledge.

Signature | **Print Your Name** | **Date**

Firm Name and Address

DO NOT COMPLETE THE FOLLOWING UNTIL INSTRUCTED TO DO SO AT THE INTERVIEW

I swear that I know the contents of this application, and supplemental pages 1 through_______, that the corrections , numbered 1 through_______, were made at my request, and that this amended application, is true to the best of my knowledge and belief.

(Complete and true signature of applicant)

Subscribed and sworn to before me by the applicant.

(Examiner's Signature) *Date*

Form N-400 (Rev. 01/15/99) N

Page 4

TOPICAL INDEX

CITATIONS

INA § ....Section number of the Immigration and Nationality Act
—— USCA § ——........................Title and section number of the U.S. Code
—— CFR § —— ....Title and section number of the Code of Federal Regulations
Ap F ....Appended forms

ACTIONS AND PROCEEDINGS
Removal
  Aliens, INA §§ 239, 240, 241
  Failure to appear, hearings, discretionary relief, INA § 240
  Right to counsel, INA §§ 240, 292
Unlawful employment, unfair immigration-related practices, aliens. Rules and Regulations, generally, this index

ADJUSTMENT
Status, generally, this index

ADMINISTRATIVE LAW JUDGES
Hearings, document fraud, conduct of procedures, etc., INA § 274C

ADMISSION
Immigration,
  Aliens, this index

AGGRAVATED FELONY
Ineligible for visas or admission,
Removal of, expedited proceedings, INA § 238

AGRICULTURAL WORKERS
  See also, Labor and Employment, generally, this index
Special agricultural workers, INA § 210

ALASKA
Nationality, birth on or after certain date, INA § 304

ALIENS
Adjustment, status,
  Resident aliens to nonimmigrant status, exceptions, INA § 247
Admission,
  Qualifications, H–2A temporary workers, INA § 218
Application, employment certification, ApF ETA–750
Crewmen, this index
Removal, this index
Diplomatic and semidiplomatic immunities, INA § 102
Inadmissibility. Immigration, generally, post, this heading
Immigration,
  Admission,
    Affidavit of support, INA § 213A, ApF I–864, I–864A
    Permanent residence, entry in U.S. prior to certain date, record, INA § 249
    Qualifications,

ALIENS—Continued
Immigration—Continued
Admission—Continued
Qualifications—Continued
Generally, INA § 211 et seq.
Bond or undertaking, giving of, INA § 213
Conditional permanent resident status, certain alien spouses and sons and daughters, INA § 216
Inadmissible aliens, INA § 212
Guam, generally, this index
Nonimmigrants, INA § 214
Return, bond or undertaking, permanent departure, INA § 213
Inspection and exclusion,
Generally, INA § 231 et seq.
Adjacent islands, entry through or from, INA § 233
Aircraft, arrival by, designation, ports of entry, INA § 234
Designation, ports of entry, arrival by aircraft, INA § 234
Detention for observation and examination upon arrival, INA § 232
Detention, generally, INA §§ 236, 241
Foreign contiguous territory, entry through or from, INA § 233
Inspection by Immigration officers, INA § 235
Lists, passengers arriving and departing, INA § 231
Passengers arriving and departing, lists of, INA § 231
Preinspection at foreign airports, INA § 235A
Physical and mental examinations, INA § 232
Proceedings, INA §§ 235, 240
Records of admission, INA § 240C
Exclusion. Inspection and exclusion, generally, post, this subheading
Fines, penalties and forfeitures. Penalties, generally, post, this subheading
General provisions, employment, unlawful, INA § 274A
Penalties, general provisions, INA § 271
Aiding or assisting subversive alien to enter, INA § 277
Bringing in certain aliens, INA § 274
Clearance papers, INA § 272
Collection, penalties and expenses, INA § 280
Complaints, immigration-related employment practices, time for filing, INA § 274B
Deported alien, reentry, INA § 276
Disability, bringing in aliens subject to, INA § 272
Disease, bringing in aliens with, INA § 272
District courts, jurisdiction, INA § 279
Document fraud, INA § 274C
Employment,
Unfair immigration-related practices, INA § 274B
Entry, improper, INA § 275
Exceptions, bringing in aliens subject to disability, etc., INA § 272
Expenses, collection, INA § 280
Failure to report unauthorized landing, INA § 271
Harboring certain aliens, INA § 274
Immoral purpose, importation for, INA § 278
Importation, immoral purpose, INA § 278
Improper entry, INA § 275
Jurisdiction, district courts, INA §§ 242, 279
Liability,
Bringing in persons, subject to disability, etc., INA § 272
Owners and operators of international bridges and toll roads, INA § 271
Prevention, unauthorized landing, INA § 271
Prima facie evidence, INA § 271
Reentry, removed alien, INA § 276
Related to removal, INA § 243
Subversive aliens, aiding or assisting entry, INA § 277
Unauthorized landing, prevention, INA § 271
Unfair immigration-related practices, INA § 274B
Unlawful bringing of aliens into U.S., INA § 273
Unlawful employment, INA § 274A
Qualifications. Admission, ante, this subheading

ALIENS—Continued
Record, admission for permanent residence, entry into U.S. prior to certain date, INA § 249
Registered nurses, special classification, INA § 212
Registration, INA § 262
  Address, INA § 265
  Contents, INA § 261
  Entry, alien seeking, INA § 261
  Fingerprinting,
    Forms for, INA § 264
  Forms, INA § 264
  Penalties, violations, INA § 266
  Special groups, INA § 263
Removal, falling into distress, INA § 250
Travel control, INA § 215
Nationality, generally, this index
Nonimmigrant aliens, nurses, registered, "immigrant" as excluding, INA § 101

AMERICAN INDIANS
Canada, birth in,
  Applicability of immigration provisions to, INA § 289

APPEALS AND REVIEW
Aliens,
  Aggravated felony convictions, expedited proceedings, INA § 238
  Removal proceedings, INA § 240
Document fraud proceedings, decisions of Administrative Law Judge, INA § 274C
Removal orders, judicial review, INA § 242

APPLICATIONS
Forms, generally, this index

ARMED FORCES
Foreign Countries, generally, this index
Immigration provisions, applicability to members of, INA § 284
Naturalization,
  Active duty service during World War I, World War II, hostilities, etc., INA § 329
  Deserters ineligible, INA § 314
  Nationality,
    Alien relieved of service due to alienage, denial of citizenship, etc., INA § 315
  Records, conclusiveness, citizenship denied alien relieved of service in Armed Forces, etc., INA § 315
  Service in, requirements, INA § 328

ASYLUM
Immigration,
  Procedures, regulations, INA § 208; 8 CFR § 208

ATTORNEY GENERAL
Detention, criminal, aliens, INA § 236
Powers, duties, functions, etc.,
  Fraud prevention, control of illegal immigration, INA § 210
  Immigration and nationality, INA § 101 et seq.
  Nationality through naturalization, INA § 310
  Temporary protected status, INA § 244
  Treatment of frivolous behavior, deportation proceedings, INA § 240
Registration and fingerprinting, alien children, powers and duties, etc., INA § 262

ATTORNEYS AND COUNSELORS
Proceedings for exclusion or deportation, right to counsel, INA § 292
Representation and appearances, 8 CFR § 292, ApF G–28
Sanctions, frivolous conduct, deportation proceedings, INA § 240

BIRTH
Nationality, this index

BONDS
Deportation and detention proceedings, INA § 236

CANADA
American Indians, this index
Nonimmigrants. Immigration, generally, this index

CANAL ZONE
Nationality, birth on or after certain date, INA § 303

CENTRAL INTELLIGENCE AGENCY
Liaison with Commissioner, etc., INA § 105

CERTIFICATES AND CERTIFICATION
Nationality, this index

CHILDREN
See Parent and Child, generally, this index

CITIZENS AND CITIZENSHIP
Nationality, generally, this index

COMMISSIONER
See Immigration and Naturalization Service, this index

CONGRESS
Reports,
  Immigration User Fee Account, by AG, INA § 286
  Temporary protected status, by AG, INA § 244

CONTROLLED SUBSTANCES
Aliens, convictions, grounds for inadmissibility, removal, INA §§ 212, 237

COSTS
See Fees and Costs, generally, this index

COUNSELORS
See Attorneys and Counselors, generally, this index

CREWMEN
Aliens,
  Special provisions relating to,
      Generally, INA § 251 et seq.
    Bringing crewmen into U.S. with intent to evade immigration laws, INA § 257
    Conditional permits to land temporarily, INA § 252
    Control, INA § 254
    Discharge of, INA § 256
    Employment on passenger vessels, affliction with certain disabilities, INA § 255
    Hospital treatment, affliction with certain diseases, INA § 253
    Penalties,
      Bringing crewmen into U.S. with intent to evade immigration laws, INA § 257
      Discharge in violation of provisions, INA § 256

CRIMES AND OFFENSES
Aliens, convictions,
  Grounds for removal, INA § 237
  Grounds for inadmissibility, INA § 212
Detention, criminal aliens, INA § 236
Penalties for failure to depart, INA § 243

CUSTODY
Pending removal proceedings, INA § 236

DAUGHTERS
See Parent and Child, generally, this index

DEATH
Officers and employees of INS, immigration officers and Border Patrol agents, death outside U.S., expense of transporting remains, INA § 283

DEFINITIONS
Adjacent islands, immigration and nationality, INA § 101
Administrator, immigration and nationality, INA § 101

DEFINITIONS—Continued
Advocates, immigration and nationality, INA § 101
Aggravated felony, immigration and nationality, INA § 101
Alien, immigration and nationality, INA § 101
Alien son or daughter, immigration, admission qualifications, conditional permanent resident status, etc., INA § 216
Alien spouse, immigration, admission qualifications, conditional permanent resident status, etc., INA § 216
Alien terrorist, INA § 501
Application for admission, immigration and nationality, INA § 101
Application period, unlawful employment, enforcement deferral with respect to seasonal agricultural services, INA § 274A
Appropriate consultation, immigration, selection system, annual admission of refugees, etc., INA § 207
Attorney General, immigration and nationality, INA § 101
Border crossing identification card, immigration and nationality, INA § 101
Child, immigration and nationality, INA § 101
Clerk of court, immigration and nationality, INA § 101
Commissioner,
Immigration and nationality, INA § 101
Consular officer, immigration and nationality, INA § 101
Conviction, INA § 101
Crewman, immigration and nationality, INA § 101
Deputy Commissioner, immigration and nationality, INA § 101
Diplomatic visa, immigration and nationality, INA § 101
Doctrine, immigration and nationality, INA § 101
Eligible individual, immigration, admission qualifications, temporary H-2A workers, INA § 218
Engage in terrorist activity, excludable aliens, INA § 212
Entry, immigration and nationality, INA § 101
Exceptional circumstances, removal proceedings, INA § 240
Executive capacity, INA § 101
Extraordinary ability, INA § 101
Facility, registered nurses, special nonimmigrant classification, INA § 212
Father, immigration and nationality, INA § 101
Foreign state, immigration and nationality, INA § 101
Foreign terrorist organization, INA § 219
Graduates of a medical school, immigration and nationality, INA § 101
H-2A worker, immigration, admission qualifications, INA § 218
Husband, immigration and nationality, INA § 101
Immediate relatives, immigration, selection system, INA § 201
Immigrant, immigration and nationality, INA § 101
Immigrant visa, immigration and nationality, INA § 101
Immigration laws, immigration and nationality, INA § 101
Immigration officer, immigration and nationality, INA § 101
Ineligible to citizenship, immigration and nationality, INA § 101
Initial period, immigration, visa waiver pilot program for certain visitors, INA § 217
Lawfully admitted for permanent residence, immigration and nationality, INA § 101
Major change, unlawful employment of aliens, Congressional review, INA § 274A
Managerial capacity, INA § 101
Medical assistance, adjustment, status of certain entrants, etc., temporary disqualification, certain public welfare assistance, INA § 245A
Mother, immigration and nationality, INA § 101
National, immigration and nationality, INA § 101
National of the United States, immigration and nationality, INA § 101
Naturalization, immigration and nationality, INA § 101
Naturalization court, immigration and nationality, INA § 101
Noncombatant service, immigration and nationality, INA § 101
Nonimmigrant visa, immigration and nationality, INA § 101
Organization, immigration and nationality, INA § 101
Outlying possessions of the United States, immigration and nationality, INA § 101
Parent, immigration and nationality, INA § 101
Passport, immigration and nationality, INA § 101
Permanent, immigration and nationality, INA § 101
Person,

DEFINITIONS—Continued
Person—Continued
Bringing in aliens subject to disability or afflicted with disease, etc., INA § 272
Immigration, travel control of aliens, INA § 215
Immigration and nationality, INA § 101
Petitioning spouse, immigration, admission qualifications, conditional permanent resident status, etc., INA § 216
Profession, immigration and nationality, INA § 101
Qualifying marriage, immigration, admission qualifications, conditional permanent resident status for certain alien spouses, etc., INA § 216
Refugee,
Assistance, INA § 412
Immigration and nationality, INA § 101
Residence, immigration and nationality, INA § 101
Seasonal agricultural services,
Special agricultural workers, INA § 210
Unlawful employment, enforcement deferral, INA § 274A
Service,
Immigration and nationality, INA § 101
Spanish-American War, immigration and nationality, INA § 101
Special agricultural worker (SAW), INA § 210
Special immigrant, immigration and nationality, INA § 101
Special inquiry officer, immigration and nationality, INA § 101
Spousal second preference petition, immigration, Selection System, procedure for granting immigrant status, INA § 204
Spouse, immigration and nationality, INA § 101
State,
Immigration and nationality, INA § 101
Stowaway, INA § 101
Terrorist activity, inadmissible alien, INA § 212
Totalitarian dictatorship, immigration and nationality, INA § 101
Totalitarian party, immigration and nationality, INA § 101
Totalitarianism, immigration and nationality, INA § 101
Transportation company, immigration, entry to or from foreign contiguous territory, etc., INA § 233
Transportation line, immigration, entry through or from foreign contiguous territory, etc., INA § 233
United States,
Immigration, travel control of aliens, INA § 215
Immigration and nationality, INA § 101
Unmarried, immigration and nationality, INA § 101
Veteran, immigration and nationality, INA § 101
Wife, immigration and nationality, INA § 101
World communism, immigration and nationality, INA § 101

DETENTION
Criminal aliens, by Attorney General, INA § 236

DIPLOMATS
Diplomatic and semidiplomatic immunities, INA § 102

DOCUMENTS
Immigration,
Fraud, enforcement hearings, etc., INA § 274C

EMPLOYEES
See Officers and Employees, generally, this index

EMPLOYMENT
See Labor and Employment, generally, this index

EVIDENCE
Burden of proof. Nationality, generally, this index
Nationality, generally, this index

EXEMPTIONS
Numerical limitations, Selection System. Immigration, generally, this index

EXPENSES
Officers and employees of Service dying outside U.S., transportation of remains, INA § 283

FEDERAL AGENCIES
Information from, availability to INS, INA § 290

FEDERAL BUREAU OF INVESTIGATION
Liaison with Commissioner, etc., INA § 105

FEDERAL DEPARTMENTS
Information from, availability to INS, INA § 290

FEDERAL GENITAL MUTILATION
Information regarding, 8 USC § 1374

FILING
See specific index headings

FINES, PENALTIES AND FORFEITURES
Aliens, generally, this index
Civil money penalties,
  Anti-discrimination violations, INA § 274B
  Document fraud, INA § 274C
  Employer sanctions, INA § 274A
  Failure to deport, INA § 274D
  Related to removal, INA § 243
Crewmen, generally, this index
Immigration,
  Aliens, this index

FINGERPRINTS AND FINGERPRINTING
Aliens in removal proceedings, INA § 287
Registration, etc., alien children, waiver, INA § 262

FIREARMS
INS officers, authority to carry, INA § 287

FOREIGN COUNTRIES
Removal, generally, this index
Immigration, selection system, numerical limitations, individual foreign states, INA § 202
Naturalization,
  Certificate of nationality, issuance for person not naturalized citizen for use in proceedings of, INA § 359

FOREIGN RELATIONS
Rules and Regulations, generally, this index

FORFEITURES
See Fines, Penalties and Forfeitures, generally, this index

FORMS
Alien registration card, I–551
Applications,
  Alien employment certification, ETA–750
  Cancellation of removal, EOIR–42A, EOIR–42B
  Employment authorization, I–765
  Immigrant visa, OF–230
  Naturalization, N–400
  Nonimmigrant visa, OF–156
  Permanent residence, I–485
Arrival, departure, non-immigrants, I–94
  Final administrative removal order, I–851A
Employment,
  Eligibility verification, I–9
Immigration,
  Blank forms, printing of, INA § 282
Notice,
  Action, I–797B
  Entry of appearance, G–28

FORMS—Continued
Notice—Continued
Expedited removal, M–444, I–860, I–867AB, I–869
Intent to issue final administrative removal order, I–851
To appear, I–862
Petitions and petitioners,
Affidavit of support, I–864
Contract between sponsor and household member, I–864A
Alien relative, I–130
Nonimmigrant worker, I–129
Prospective immigrant employee, I–140
Removal of conditional status for spouses, I–751
Sponsorship, I–864A

GUAM
Nationality, persons living and born in, INA § 307

H–2A WORKERS
Labor and Employment, generally, this index

HAWAII
Nationality, birth, on or after certain date, INA § 304

HEARINGS
Anti-discrimination, INA § 274B
Document fraud, orders, INA § 274C
Employer sanctions, INA § 274A
Naturalization, denial of, INA § 336

HUSBAND AND WIFE
See, also, Marriage, generally, this index
Immigration, admission, qualifications, alien spouses, conditional permanent resident status for, INA § 216
Naturalization, INA § 319
Regulations,
Conditional basis of lawful permanent residence status, 8 CFR § 216

IMMIGRATION
Generally, INA § 201
Adjustment, status,
Change, non-immigrant classification, INA § 248
Entrants before certain date, to that of person admitted for lawful residence, INA § 245A
Naturalized citizen, rescission of adjustment, effect, INA § 246
Nonimmigrants, INA §§ 245, 248
Report, Congress, rescission, effect upon naturalized citizen, INA § 246
Rescission, effect upon naturalized citizen, INA § 246
Resident aliens to nonimmigrant status, exceptions, INA § 247
Admission, this index
Agricultural Workers, this index
Armed Forces members, applicability of provisions, INA § 284
Asylum, this index
Attorney General, powers, duties, functions, etc., INA § 101 et seq.
Collection, moneys, disposition, INA § 286
Control of illegal immigration,
Fraud prevention, SAW program, duties of Attorney General, INA § 210
Qualified designated entities, INA § 245A
Definitions, generally, this index
Removal, generally, this index
Deposit, cash received to secure immigration bonds, INA § 293
Diplomatic and semidiplomatic immunities, INA § 102
Inspection and exclusion,
Aliens, this index
Appeal, findings, physical and mental examinations, etc., INA § 232
Forms, this index
General provisions, INA § 101 et seq.
Guam, generally, this index

IMMIGRATION—Continued
Immigrant visas. Visas, generally, this index
Immigration and Naturalization Service, generally, this index
Immigration Examinations Fee Account, provisions, INA § 286
Interest, cash received to secure immigration bonds, INA § 293
Issuance, entry documents. Visas, generally, this index
Labor and Employment, this index
Licenses and Permits, this index
Local jurisdiction over immigrant stations, INA § 288
Moneys collected, disposition, INA § 286
Nonimmigrant inspected and admitted or paroled into U.S., adjustment of status, INA § 245
Nonimmigrant visas. Visas, generally, this index
Nonimmigrants,
  Admission into U.S. as, INA §214
  Professionals from Canada or Mexico, INA § 214
  Registered nurses, as nonimmigrant aliens, INA § 101
Officers and Employees, this index
Parents, "immigrant" as excluding, abandoning parents, etc., INA § 101
Penalties. Aliens, this index
President of the United States, this index
Privileges at immigrant stations, disposal of, INA § 285
Receipts, disposal of privileges, etc., at immigrant stations, disposition, INA § 285
Refugees, this index
Registered nurses, special classification, nonimmigrant status, INA § 212
Rentals, immigrant stations, INA § 285
Secretary of State, powers, duties, etc., INA § 101 et seq.
Selection System,
  Admission. Refugees, this index
  Agricultural Workers, this index
  Asylum procedure, INA § 208
  Immigrant status,
    Procedure for granting, INA § 204
    Revocation, approval of petitions for, notice, etc., INA § 205
  Numerical limitations,
    Admissions, INA § 201
    Individual foreign states, INA § 202
    Lawful admissions, total, INA § 201
  Procedure,
    Asylum, INA § 208
    Granting immigrant status, INA § 204
  Refugees, this index
  Revocation, approval of petitions for immigrant status, notice, etc., INA § 205
Service. Immigration and Naturalization Service, generally, this index
Stations,
  Disposal of privileges at, INA § 285
  Local jurisdiction, INA § 288
Visas, generally, this index

IMMIGRATION AND NATURALIZATION SERVICE
Commissioner,
  Central file, establishment, INA § 290
  Liaison with internal security officers, INA § 105
  Powers, duties, functions, etc., immigration and nationality, INA § 101 et seq.
Employees. Officers and Employees, generally, this index

INADMISSIBILITY
Aliens, generally, this index
Diplomatic and semidiplomatic immunities, INA § 102
Expedited removal, INA § 235
Removal orders, judicial review, INA § 242
Proceedings for, right to counsel, INA § 292

INDIANS
American Indians, generally, this index

INTELLIGENCE
Central Intelligence Agency, generally, this index

INVESTIGATION
Federal Bureau of Investigation, generally, this index
Document fraud, immigration proceedings, INA § 274C
Undercover activity, INA § 294

JURISDICTION
Local jurisdiction, immigrant stations, INA § 288
Naturalization, INA § 310

LABOR AND EMPLOYMENT
Agricultural Workers, generally, this index
Applications,
  Employment authorization, ApF I–765
  Labor certification, ApF ETA–750
Eligibility verification, ApF, I–9
Employer sanctions, INA § 274A, 8 CFR § 274a
Forms, generally, this index
Immigration,
  H–2A temporary workers, admission, INA § 218
Labor certification, 20 CFR § 656
Unfair immigration-related employment practices of aliens, INA § 274B

LICENSES AND PERMITS
Immigration,
  Documents, issuance, re-entry permit, INA § 223
  Reentry permits,
    Printing of, INA § 282

LOSS OF NATIONALITY
Nationality, this index

MARRIAGE
  See, also, Husband and Wife, generally, this index
Nationality, children born out-of-wedlock, INA § 309

MIGRATION AND REFUGEE ASSISTANCE
See Refugee Assistance, generally, this index

NATIONALITY
  Generally, INA § 301 et seq.
Birth,
  Alaska, on or after certain date, INA § 304
  Canal Zone, on or after certain date, INA § 303
  Guam, persons living and born in, INA § 307
  Hawaii, on or after certain date, INA § 305
  Nationals and citizens of U.S. at, INA § 301
  Nationals but not U.S. citizens at, INA § 308
  Panama, Republic of, on or after certain date, INA § 303
  Puerto Rico, on or after certain date, INA § 302
  Virgin Islands, persons living and born in, INA § 306
Cancellation of passports and consular reports of birth, INA § 361
Certificate of,
  Diplomatic or consular officer as to loss of American nationality, INA § 358
  Nationality, issuance for person not naturalized citizen for use in proceedings of foreign state, INA § 359
  Naturalization. Naturalization, generally, post, this heading
Definitions, generally, this index
Denial, rights and privileges as national, INA § 360
English language, history, etc. requirements respecting, waivers, INA § 312
Fingerprinting, registration, alien children, waiver, INA § 262
Foreign citizens losing citizenship by entering foreign country's Armed Forces during World War II, requirements, etc., INA § 327
General provisions, INA § 101 et seq.
Immigration and Naturalization Service, generally, this index
Loss,

NATIONALITY—Continued
Loss—Continued
Acts, performance of, INA § 356
Burden of proof, INA § 349
Certificate of diplomatic or consular officer, INA § 358
Conditions, fulfillment of, INA § 356
Exceptions, application of treaties, INA § 357
Expatriation, restrictions, INA § 351
Native-born or naturalized citizen, INA § 349
Presumptions, INA § 349
Restrictions, expatriation, INA § 351
Treaties, application of, INA § 357
Voluntary action, INA § 349
Naturalization,
Administration, INA § 332
Aliens,
Enemies, specified conditions, INA § 331
Armed Forces of foreign countries, former citizens losing citizenship by entering during World War II, requirements, INA § 327
Armed Forces of U.S. Armed Forces, this index
Attorney General, powers, duties, etc., INA § 310 et seq.
Automatic citizenship, conditions, children born outside of U.S. of one alien and one citizen parent, INA § 320
Birth outside U.S., one alien and one citizen parent, conditions for automatic citizenship, INA § 320
Burden of proof, lawful entry, INA § 318
Cancellation, certificates issued by Attorney General, Commissioner, etc., effect, INA § 342
Certificates,
Citizenship or U.S. non-citizen national status, INA § 341
Contents, etc., INA § 338
Issued by Attorney General, Commissioner, etc., cancellation, effect, INA § 342
Children. Parent and Child, generally, this index
Citizenship,
Former citizens losing citizenship by entering Armed Forces of foreign countries during World War II, requirements, etc., INA § 327
Former citizens regaining, requirements, INA § 324
Text books, publication and distribution, INA § 346
Clerk of court, failure to do duty, INA § 348
Compilation, statistics and payment for equipment, INA § 347
Contents, certificate of naturalization, INA § 338
Copies issued by Attorney General, INA § 343
Declaration of intention, INA § 334
Documents issued by Attorney General, INA § 343
Eligibility, INA § 311
Employees, certain nonprofit organizations, INA § 319
English language, history, etc., requirements respecting, INA § 312
Evidence,
Admissibility, statements voluntarily made to officers or employees, etc., INA § 348
Burden of proof, lawful entry, INA § 318
Fees and Costs, INA § 346
Final hearing, INA § 336
Fiscal provisions, INA § 344
Functions and duties, clerks of naturalization courts, INA § 339
Hearings, final hearing, INA § 336
Immigration and Naturalization Service, generally, this index
Investigation, petitioners, INA § 335
Jurisdiction to naturalize, INA § 310
Married persons, INA § 319
Nationals but not citizens, INA § 325
Number, photographs, INA § 333
Oath of renunciation and allegiance, INA § 337
Opposing to government or law, prohibition on naturalization, INA § 313
Petitioners, investigation, INA § 335
Petitions, INA § 334

NATIONALITY—Continued
Naturalization—Continued
Philippine citizens, residents, exception from certain requirements, INA § 326
Photographs, number, INA § 333
Prerequisite to, INA § 318
Prohibition, opposition to government, law, etc., INA § 313
Religious duties, temporary absence of persons performing, INA § 317
Requirements, INA § 316
English language, history, etc., INA § 312
Residence within outlying possessions, national but not citizens, INA § 325
Resident Philippine citizens exception from certain requirements, INA § 326
Revocation, INA § 340
Statements voluntarily made to officers or employees, etc., admissibility in evidence, INA § 348
Totalitarian forms of government, prohibition on naturalization, persons favoring, INA § 313
United States vessels, constructive residence through service on, INA § 330
Rules and Regulations, this index
Secretary of State, powers, duties, etc., INA § 101 et seq., INA § 301 et seq.

NATURALIZATION
See Nationality, this index

NONIMMIGRANTS
See Immigration, this index

NURSES
Registered, nonimmigrant classification, establishment, etc., INA § 101

OATHS AND AFFIRMATIONS
Naturalization, renunciation and allegiance, INA § 337

OFFICE OF REFUGEE RESETTLEMENT
Establishment, appointment of Director, functions, etc., INA § 411 et seq.

OFFICERS AND EMPLOYEES
Immigration and Naturalization Service,
Arrest power, INA § 287
Expenses, travel, transportation of remains, etc., INA § 283
Powers and duties, INA § 287

PANAMA, REPUBLIC OF
Nationality, birth on or after certain date, INA § 303

PARENT AND CHILD
Immigration, admission, qualifications, alien spouses, conditional permanent residence, status for, INA § 216
Naturalization,
Birth outside U.S., INA § 322
Alien parents, conditions, automatic citizenship, INA § 321
One alien and one citizen parent, conditions, automatic citizenship, INA § 320
Registration and fingerprinting, alien children, waiver, INA § 262

PAROLE
Power of Attorney General to grant, INA § 212

PASSENGERS
Immigration, entry and exclusion, lists of passengers arriving and departing, INA § 231

PENALTIES
See Fines, Penalties and Forfeitures, generally, this index

PERMITS
See Licenses and Permits, generally, this index

PETITIONS AND PETITIONERS
Forms, generally, this index
Naturalization. Nationality, this index

PHILIPPINES, REPUBLIC OF
Naturalization, resident Philippine citizens exception from certain requirements, INA § 326

PHOTOGRAPHS AND PHOTOGRAPHY
Naturalization, number, INA § 333

PILOT PROGRAMS
Visa waiver, certain visitors, INA § 217

PRESUMPTIONS
Deportability, aliens convicted of aggravated felonies, INA § 238

PRINTING
Immigration, reentry permits and blank forms of manifest and crew lists, INA § 282

PROCEEDINGS
See Actions and Proceedings, generally, this index

PUBLIC BENEFITS
Attribution of sponsor's income, 8 USCA § 1631
Definitions, 8 USCA § 1641
Eligibility, 8 USCA §§ 1601, 1611, 1612, 1613, 1615, 1645

PUERTO RICO
Nationality, birth on or after certain date, INA § 302

REFUGEE ASSISTANCE
Domestic resettlement and assistance to refugees, authorization for programs, INA § 412
Office of Refugee Resettlement, establishment, appointment of Director, functions, etc., INA § 411 et seq.
Programs, domestic resettlement and assistance to refugees, authorization, INA § 412
Reports, Congressional committees, INA § 413
Secretary of State, powers, duties, etc., INA § 101 et seq., INA § 412 et seq.

REFUGEES
Assistance. Refugee Assistance, generally, this index
Designation and Adjustment of Soviet and Indochinese Refugees, 8 USCA § 1157 nt
Haitian Refugee Immigration Fairness Act of 1998, 8 USCA § 1255, nts
Immigration,
- Admission,
  - Selection system, generally, post, this subheading
- Asylum, INA § 208, 8 CFR § 208, ApF I–589
- Selection system, admission, INA § 207
  - Annual admission, INA § 207
  - Emergency situation refugees, INA § 207
  - Refugees and emergency situation refugees, INA § 207
  - Status, adjustment, INA § 209

Involuntary return, 22 USC 2601, nt

REMOVAL
Actions and Proceedings, this index
- Expedited, INA § 235, 8 CFR § 235
- Expedited, of aggravated felons, INA § 238

Aliens,
- Generally, INA § 237 et seq.
- Aggravated felony, deportation for commission of, INA § 237
- Apprehension, INA § 236
- Countries to which deported, INA § 241
- Cancellation of removal, INA § 240A
- Weapons violations, INA § 241

Diplomatic and semidiplomatic immunities, INA § 102
Initiation of proceedings, INA § 239
Orders of, judicial review, INA § 242
Proceedings, INA § 240

REPUBLIC OF PANAMA
Nationality, birth on or after certain date, INA § 303

REPUBLIC OF PHILIPPINES
See Philippines, Republic of, generally, this index

REVIEW
See Appeals and Review, generally, this index

REVOCATION
Naturalization, INA § 340

RULES AND REGULATIONS
Employer sanctions, 8 CFR § 274a
Immigration,
  Aliens,
    Conditional basis of lawful permanent residence, certain spouses, sons and daughters, 8 CFR § 216
    Immigrant petitions, 8 CFR § 204.5
  Asylum procedures, 8 CFR § 208
Labor certification, 20 CFR § 656
Representation and appearances, 8 CFR §§ 292.1, 292.2, ApF G–28

SALES
Immigration,
  Blank forms of manifests and crew lists, etc., INA § 282

SECRETARY OF LABOR
Immigration, registered nurses, duties and requirements, special nonimmigrant status, INA § 212

SECRETARY OF STATE
Powers, duties, functions, etc., immigration and nationality, INA § 104

SONS AND DAUGHTERS
See Parent and Child, generally, this index

SPOUSE
See Husband and Wife, generally, this index

STATES AND LOCALITIES
Authority to limit public benefits, 8 USCA §§ 1612, 1622
Authority to provide for attribution, 8 USCA § 1632
Communication with INS, 8 USCA § 1644

TEMPORARY PROTECTED STATUS
General authority, AG, INA § 244

TERRORIST REMOVAL PROCEDURES
Appeals, INA § 505
Custody and release, §§ 506, 507
Definitions, § 501
Hearing, § 504
Removal court, § 502
Removal court procedure, § 503

TORTURE CONVENTION
Procedures, regulations, 8 CFR § 208
Involuntary return, 8 USC 1231, nt

TRAVEL
Immigration, aliens, control, INA § 215

TRAVELING EXPENSES AND ALLOWANCES
Officers and employees of Service, INA § 283

UNFAIR IMMIGRATION–RELATED EMPLOYMENT PRACTICES
Generally, INA § 274B

VESSELS
Naturalization, constructive residence through service on, INA § 330

VIRGIN ISLANDS
Nationality, persons living and born in, INA § 306

VISAS
Aliens, immigration, burden of proof, application for visa, INA § 291
Diplomatic and semidiplomatic immunities, INA § 102
Immigrant visas,
  Allocation, INA § 203
  Unused, INA § 206
Immigration,
  Fees,
    Nonimmigrant visas, INA § 281
  Issuance,
      Generally, INA § 221 et seq.
    Application for, INA § 222
    Immediate relative visas, INA § 224
    Re-entry permit, INA § 223
    Special immigrant visas, INA § 224
  Waiver pilot program, certain visitors, etc., INA § 217
Nonimmigrant visas,
  Fees, INA § 281
Unused immigrant visas, INA § 206

VOLUNTARY DEPARTURE
Generally, INA § 240B

WAIVER
See specific index headings

WARRANTS
INS officers, powers to execute, INA § 287

WIFE
See Husband and Wife, generally, this index

†